Planning and Control of Land Development

CASES AND MATERIALS

DANIEL R. MANDELKER

Stamper Professor of Law
Washington University

ROGER A. CUNNINGHAM

Professor of Law
University of Michigan

THE BOBBS-MERRILL COMPANY, INC.
PUBLISHERS
INDIANAPOLIS • NEW YORK • CHARLOTTESVILLE, VIRGINIA

PLANNING AND CONTROL OF LAND DEVELOPMENT

CONTEMPORARY LEGAL EDUCATION SERIES

To Jana

and

To Beth

Preface

New developments in the field of land use planning and development control have expanded the range of problems that must be addressed in a casebook devoted to the planning and control of land development. At one time the casebook editor could be satisfied with a heavy dose of nuisance law, the progenitor of modern land use regulation, and a thorough but often restricted tour of zoning problems. Pressures for environmental protection, growth management and the provision of housing for lower income groups have now forced a new perspective on course materials devoted to this subject. Concurrently, the intervention of higher levels of government in the land management process has directed attention to governmental programs at more than just the municipal level.

This casebook has been fashioned with these modern developments in mind. It holds its focus almost entirely on land use regulation through the police power — the noncompensatory control of development through municipal ordinances and state and federal statutes. Problems dealing with the private control of land development are better left to courses dealing exclusively with these problems. Eminent domain and land acquisition issues are touched upon as background for police power regulation, but no extensive analysis of eminent domain doctrine is attempted. Throughout, the emphasis is on the preparation of the practitioner for service to public agency or private clients. Theory is not entirely shut out, and serves as an important backdrop for the examination of fundamental problems concerning the permissible range of police power regulation.

We open with a review of planning principles and practice, a decision reflecting the growing awareness, late though it may be, that a sound plan and planning policy must form the basis of any meaningful land use regulation program. Basic concepts underlying land use regulation are considered next, arising as they do out of early nuisance doctrine and fundamental assumptions that underlie the judicial perception of the "taking" issue. A thorough exploration of zoning follows, moving in historical fashion from an examination of the initial focus on the pre-ordainment of land use distributions through land use districts to the evolution of zoning as an ongoing process for the allocation of land resources. Innovative techniques for the extension of the zoning function are noted along the way, and exclusionary zoning issues are comprehensively explored.

Attention is directed next to subdivision control as a method for regulating residential development, and this chapter forms the basis for later consideration of even more sophisticated land development controls such as planned unit development. The teacher wedded to the more traditional system may want to concentrate on these early chapters, with perhaps a look at some of the more innovative techniques reviewed in Chapter 6. This chapter covers aesthetic and design controls, transfer of development rights, the recapture of land value, and similar innovations.

Subsequent chapters deal more particularly with recent developments in planning and land use regulation. Each stands alone and the teacher may pick and chose as he or she pleases. Growth management, environmentally related land development controls, and regional and state planning and land development control are examined in turn. Much of the material in these later chapters is textual. As yet there are not many court cases on these legal frontiers, but we hope that the perceptive instructor will find that the varied statutory and regulatory programs have been presented in a manner that will excite class attention and participation. A final chapter considers an important but often neglected problem, the role of real estate property taxation as a determinant of land use.

We hope that this casebook will find a place in planning schools and related university departments as well as in law schools. Instructors in these areas might well avoid the more esoteric legal issues and concentrate on the leading cases; they are all there. Later chapters, with their textual emphasis, need less in the way of a preliminary legal background.

Diagrams and maps appearing in this casebook for the first time were prepared by Moustafa Baghdadi and William Taylor. Maps of the cases have been specially prepared for these materials and are based on facts of each case as reported in the official reports.

Our appreciation is due to our student research assistants. Linda Reiman and Felice Taub at Washington University School of Law and to Patricia M. Aldrich, Reference Librarian, Washington University Law Library, who responded along with other members of the library staff to our many requests for documents and information. Thanks are also due to Mrs. Jamie Graham, Urban and Regional Studies Librarian at Olin Library, Washington University, whose careful attention to the ongoing literature helped make this book possible.

Daniel R. Mandelker
Roger A. Cunningham

April 1, 1978

Notes on a Bibliography

What follows are notes on literature and bibliograhic sources that will assist the interested student who wants to extend a knowledge of land use and zoning law. This area of the law, which has not been well served, has seen the inauguration of new journals and the publication of new treatises in recent years that substantially expand the available literature. For those who take the time to look, however, there is much from which to choose.

Treatises. Several excellent treatises on land use and zoning law are now available. Perhaps the most notable is Professor Norman Williams' four-volume work, *American Law of Zoning,* first published in 1974 with annual supplements. Another new entry in this field is the three-volume set published in 1978 by Professor Patrick Rohan, *Zoning and Land Use Controls.* Professor Robert Anderson's *American Law of Zoning* was published in a second edition in 1976, and Rathkopf's *Law of Zoning* is undergoing revision as is *Yokley on Zoning.* A fine one-volume treatment is Professor Donald Hagman's *Urban Planning and Land Development Control Law,* published in 1971 with a 1975 supplement.

Periodicals. Several periodicals, both legal and non-legal, carry articles on planning and land use control topics and some concentrate exclusively on these subject areas. Three law school journals are devoted to the urban law field and usually contain leading articles and student work on planning and land use controls. These are the *Urban Law Annual,* now published twice a year in book form at Washington University School of Law (St. Louis), the *Journal of Urban Law,* published by the University of Detroit College of Law, and the *Fordham Urban Law Journal.* Another important urban law periodical is the *Urban Lawyer,* the publication of the Section on Local Government Law of the American Bar Association.

Digests of recent cases and of recent legislation are provided in the *Land Use Controls and Zoning Digest* published by the American Society of Planning Officials (ASPO). The *Digest* also contains Reporter's Notes on leading land use cases as well as articles of general interest. ASPO also publishes a monthly *Planning* magazine containing articles of interest to lawyers. The professional organization of planners, the American Institute of Planners (AIP) publishes two periodicals. One is the *Journal of the American Institute of Planners,* which in addition to leading articles on planning topics also has an extensive book review section and regularly lists important articles in legal and non-legal periodicals on planning and related subjects. *Practicing Planner* is the second periodical published by AIP. It contains articles on planning and land use control practice problems that are often of interest to lawyers.

Land Economics is another non-legal journal which occasionally contains articles on land use planning topics.

There are several journals devoted to environmental law. Of these, the *Ecology Law Quarterly, Environmental Law,* and *Environmental Affairs* are most likely to carry articles on land use and zoning topics. An annual bound volume of selected articles on environmental law is published each year and is entitled *Environmental Law Review* (Sherrod ed.). Two additional environmentally oriented legal periodicals that should be watched for articles on land use law are the *Natural Resources Journal* and the *Land and Water Law Review.* The *Coastal Zone Management Journal* is entirely devoted to coastal zone topics and carries articles on legal aspects of coastal zone programs.

The Urban Land Institute in Washington, D.C., publishes two periodicals of interest. *Environmental Comment* is issued monthly and often contains articles on land use problems related to environmental controls. Another monthly publication, *Urban Land,* contains articles on residential development problems and often features articles on land use topics. The *Harvard Journal on Legislation* will occasionally publish articles on legislation dealing with land use and related problems. Articles reporting research funded by the American Bar Association, which occasionally includes land use topics, are published in the *American Bar Foundation Research Journal.*

Services. A commercial service containing case digests and articles of interest on zoning problems is *Zoning and Planning Law Report* (Clark Boardman Company, Ltd.), which began publication in late 1977. The Bureau of National Affairs (BNA) publishes two services that are of interest. One, the *Housing and Development Reporter,* presently contains a land use and growth controls section that reports on recent developments in these fields. The BNA *Environment Reporter* will also occasionally report on land use developments. A weekly commercial service, the *Land Use Planning Report,* is devoted to new developments in land use and environmental law programs.

Bibliographic services. A variety of bibliographic services are available that cover the land use field. One of the best is published by the Council of Planning Librarians, P.O. Box 229, Monticello, Illinois, which issues periodic surveys of the literature in a variety of fields relating to planning. Often these bibliographies will contain legal references and occasionally a legal bibliography is published. Perhaps the most extensive bibliographic service in this field, which covers housing as well as land use topics, is *Recent Publications on Governmental Problems,* published bimonthly by the Joint Reference Library of the governmental service organizations housed at 1313 East 60th Street, Chicago, Illinois. This library serves the American Society of Planning Officials. A similar bibliography, *Housing and Planning References,* is published monthly by the U.S. Department of Housing and Urban Development.

Government Publications. Many valuable publications on land use planning and land use control topics are issued by government agencies or are funded by federal or state research grants. Governmental publications of interest are listed in *Planning* magazine and in *Recent Publications* on *Governmental Problems.* For federal agency and congressional publications the *Monthly Catalog* of the U.S. Government Printing Office should be consulted. All federally funded research reports are deposited in the National Technical Information Service, Warrenton, Virginia 22161. Copies of these reports may be obtained from the Service either in mimeographed form or on microfiche. The Service also publishes a valuable periodic and annotated list of publications received, including bibliographies on topics of interest in the land use planning and environmental fields.

N.B. In late 1978, the American Society of Planning Officials and the American Institute of Planners merged into a new organization, the American Planning Association.

Acknowledgments

We acknowledge with thanks permission to reprint the following materials:

American Institute of Planners for permission to reprint from Sedway and Loyd, Building Block Zoning Provides Flexibility, Practicing Planning (1977). Reprinted from Practicing Planner (Vol. 7, #3, September, 1977), a magazine of the American Institute of Planners, Washington, D.C.

The American Law Institute for permission to reprint from A Model Development Code. Copyright 1976 by The American Law Institute.

American Society of Planning Officials for permission to reprint from Catanese, Plan? or Process? in Planning, the magazine of the American Society of Planning Officials, June 1974, 14-16.

The American Society of Planning Officials for permission to reprint from Commentary on James v. Valtierra, by Fred P. Bosselman (1971). Reprinted with permission from Vol. 23, Zoning Digest, American Society of Planning Officials, 1313 E. 60th Street, Chicago, Illinois 60637.

The American Society of Planning Officials for permission to reprint from Control of Competition as a Proper Purpose in Zoning, by Daniel R. Mandelker (1962). Reprinted with permission from Vol. 14, Zoning Digest, American Society of Planning Officials, 1313 E. 60th Street, Chicago, Illinois 60637.

American Society of Planning Officials for permission to reprint from D. Mandelker, Controlling Planned Residential Developments 3-8 (1966).

The American Society of Planning Officials for permission to reprint from PAS Report 318, by Michael Meshenberg (1976). Reprinted with permission from PAS Report 318, The Administration of Flexible Zoning Techniques, American Society of Planning Officials, 1313 E. 60th Street, Chicago, Illinois 60637.

American Society of Planning Officials for permission to reprint from Regulations for Flood Plains, Figure 17, p. 45, PAS Report No. 277. Copyright 1972 by American Society of Planning Officials, Chicago.

Association of American Geographers for permission to reprint P. Muller, The Outer City 18-20 (1976). Reproduced by permission from the Association of American Geographers' Resource Paper Series, 1975, #2, P. Muller, The Outer City: Geographical Consequences of the Urbanization of the Suburbs.

Behavioral Science for permission to reprint from Economic Development, Research and Development, Policy Making: Some Converging Views. Reprinted from Behavioral Science, Volume 7, No. 2, 1962, by permission of James G. Miller, M.D., Ph.D., Editor.

Mr. David Brower for permission to reprint from D. Godschalk et al., Constitutional Issues of Growth Management 149-154 (1977).

Council of State Governments for permission to reprint from State Community Development Policy: The Case of New Communities, The Council of State Governments, July 1976.

Professor Gilbert L. Finnell, Jr., School of Law, University of Houston, Houston, Texas for permission to reprint from Finnell, Saving Paradise: The Florida Environmental Land and Water Management Act of 1972, 1973 Urban L. Ann. 103.

Harvard Journal on Legislation for permission to reprint from Note, Site Value Taxation: Economic Incentives and Land Use Planning. Reprinted from 9 Harvard Journal on Legislation 115 (1971).

Harvard Law Review for permission to reprint from Michelman, Property, Utility, and Fairness: Comments on the Ethical Foundations of Just Compensation Law, 80 Harv. L. Rev. 1165, 1172-77, 1181-83 (1967). Copyright 1967 by the Harvard Law Review Association.

Harvard Law Review for permission to reprint from The Supreme Court, 1975 Term, 90 Harv. L. Rev. 1, 196-204 (1976). Copyright 1976 by the Harvard Law Review Association.

International City Managers Association for permission to reprint from W. Goodman and E. Freund, Eds., Principles and Practice of Urban Planning 342-43, 449-54 (1968).

Iowa Law Review for permission to reprint from Hines, A Decade of Nondegradation Policy in Congress and the Courts: The Erratic Pursuit of Clean Air and Clean Water, 62 Iowa L. Rev. 643, 651 (1977).

The Johns Hopkins University Press for permission to reprint from R. Healy, Land Use and the States, pp. 6-12, published for Resources for the Future by The Johns Hopkins University Press, 1976.

The Journal of the American Institute of Planners for permission to reprint from Book Review, Altshuler, The Costs of Sprawl. Reprinted from 43 Journal of the American Institute of Planners 207-09 (1977).

Law and Contemporary Problems for permission to reprint from Dukeminier, Zoning for Aesthetic Objectives: A Reappraisal, 20 Law & Contemp. Prob. 218 (1955). Reprinted with permission from a symposium on Land Planning in a Democracy appearing in Law and Contemporary Problems, Volume 20, Number 2, Spring, 1955, published by the Duke University School of Law, Durham, North Carolina. Copyright 1955 by Duke University.

The League of Minnesota Cities for permission to reprint from G. Isberg, Local and Regional Planning in Minnesota, 21-22, 29-30, 32 (1975).

National League of Cities for permission to reprint from Penne, Boulder: A Case Study in the Management of Urban Growth, Nation's Cities, September 1976. Reprinted from Nation's Cities, the magazine of the National League of Cities copyright 1976.

The New York Times for permission to reprint from Oakwood at Madison by Alan S. Oser, January 27, 1978. Copyright 1978 by The New York Times Company.

The Potomac Institute, Inc. for permission to reprint from H. Franklin, Controlling Urban Growth — But for Whom? 4-6, 13-15 (1973).

The Potomac Institute, Inc. for permission to reprint from H. Franklin, D. Falk & A. Levin, In-Zoning: A Guide for Policy-Makers on Inclusionary Land Use Programs (1974).

Texas Law Review for permission to reprint from Comment, Areawide Planning Under the Federal Water Pollution Control Act Amendments of 1972: Intergovernmental and Land Use Implications, 54 Texas L. Rev. 1047 (1976).

Texas Law Review for permission to reprint from Mandelker, Racial Discrimination and Exclusionary Zoning: A Perspective on Arlington Heights, 55 Texas L. Rev. 1217, 1245-49, 1250-52 (1977).

Texas Law Review for permission to reprint from Plater, The Takings Issue in a Natural Setting: Flood-lines and the Police Power, 52 Texas L. Rev. 201 (1974).

The Urban Institute for permission to reprint from Fiscal Woes Multiply for Large Cities, in Search: A Report from the Urban Institute, Vol. 5, Nos. 506, at 304 (Winter 1975).

The Urban Institute for permission to reprint from Nelson M. Rosenbaum, Citizen Involvement in Land Use Governance (Washington, D.C.: The Urban Institute, 1976).

The Urban Land Institute for permission to reprint from Agelasto, No-Growth and the Poor: Equity Considerations in Controlled Growth Policies in I Management and Control of Growth 426.

The Urban Land Institute for permission to reprint from Miner, Coordination of Development Regulation: Untangling the Maze, Environmental Comment, May 1976.

The Urban Land Institute for permission to reprint from Rivkin, Growth Control Via Sewer Moratoria, 33 Urban Land 10, 11, 15 (1974). Reprinted with permission from Urban Land, March 1974, published by ULI-The Urban Land Institute, 1200 18th Street, N.W., Washington, D.C. 20036.

The Urban Land Institute for permission to reprint from Roberts, Energy and Land Use: Analysis of Alternative Development Patterns, Environmental Comment, September 1975.

Urban Law Annual for permission to reprint from Tarlock, Consistency with Adopted Land Use Plans as a Standard of Review: The Case Against, 9 Urban L. Ann. 69, 75-80 (1975).

Washington Law Review and Fred B. Rothman & Co. for permission to reprint from Mary Miles Teachout, State Taxation — Use of Taxing Power to Achieve Environmental Goals: Vermont Taxes Gains Realized from the Sale or Exchange of Land Held Less Than Six Years, 49 Wash. L. Rev. 1159 (1974).

Washington University Law Quarterly for permission to reprint from Mandelker, Delegation of Power and Function in Zoning Administration, 1963 Wash. U.L.Q. 60, 61, 63. Copyright 1963.

The Yale Law Journal Company and Fred B. Rothman and Company for permission to reprint from Note, Sewers, Clean Water, and Planned Growth: Restructuring the Federal Pollution Abatement Effort, 86 Yale L.J. 733 (1977).

A Note

Only selected footnotes from the cases and other reprinted materials have been reproduced and these have been renumbered. Insertions within reprinted material have been placed in brackets.

Summary Table of Contents

Table of Contents

Page

Chapter 1

ISSUES AND PROBLEMS IN LAND USE PLANNING AND REGULATION

Land use planning and regulation is not solely a response to abstract ideas and concepts. It also reflects economic and social pressures created by the ever changing face of the nation, and which force public attention to the control of growth and development. To provide a perspective on the issues that growth and development controls raise, this chapter reviews trends and problems in national and regional development that land use planning and regulation must face as America moves into the last quarter of the Twentieth Century. The chapter opens with a review of growth and development trends at national and regional levels. It concludes with a brief review of three major issues — housing, the environment and growth control — which are increasingly dominant in public debate over the proper reach of public power and authority over land use and development.

A. NATIONAL AND REGIONAL GROWTH AND DEVELOPMENT TRENDS

ADVISORY COMMISSION ON INTERGOVERNMENTAL RELATIONS, IMPROVING URBAN AMERICA: A CHALLENGE TO FEDERALISM 201-21 (1976)

The most dramatic population movement in American history is not the great westward flow of population but the more recent concentration of population in a few metropolitan areas. This concentration has been duly noted over the years in Census reports and in a burgeoning literature on metropolitanization. Those notations need not be repeated here. It is only necessary to observe that, in 1790, 95 percent of the American people were rural residents and 85 percent lived on farms. Of the 5 percent classified as urban, only half lived in communities of over 10,000. During the 19th century, a steady shift toward more concentrated settlement occurred, and the balance tipped in the second decade of the 20th century — the 1920 Census was the first to show an urban majority. By 1970, 74 percent of the nation's citizenry lived in urban places (defined as a community of over 2,500 people), and 58 percent lived in urbanized areas of 50,000 or more.

Quite clearly the metropolis is now the dominant pattern of urban growth, and nearly every projection as to future growth shows that the vast majority of it will take place in the urbanized areas. By 1985, it is reckoned that approximately seven out of every ten Americans will live in an urbanized area. By the year 2000, this is slated to be even greater.

As in the past, most future growth is expected to occur in expanding suburban areas around major cities. Within metropolitan areas, reflecting the American preference for the detached single family home on its own plot of ground, urban population growth has always been concentrated on the fringe of urbanized areas. That is where most of the vacant land suitable for industrial development and for building new houses is located. . . .

In many parts of the nation, metropolitan areas are growing together as their suburbs expand. Most major development is occurring along the transportation corridors that connect the larger cities. Megalopolitan areas, gigantic urban regions stretching over hundreds of miles, already are well formed. Three such complexes stand out now: one stretching up the Atlantic Coast from Northern Virginia to Boston, another centering around Chicago and the Great Lakes, and a third on the West Coast connecting San Francisco and San Diego. By the year 2000, projections are that the first two regions will have merged into "one vast rectangular or T-shaped urban region, with its corners at Waterville, Me., in the Northeast; Norfolk, Va., in the South; and Chicago and Indianapolis in the West," and that the third will cover "most of California from Sacramento to the Mexican border." In addition, there may be as many as 25 more such regions, each with a population of more than a million, including "one Florida city that [will extend] from Jacksonville to Miami and across the peninsula to Tampa." Those urban regions "will be the flourishing one-sixth of the country; the other five-sixths, embracing 15 percent of the population, will be stagnant or in decline."

. . . .

SOME DYNAMICS OF URBAN DEVELOPMENT

Migration from the Farms

Metropolitan development began with rural migration into central cities. In 1920 (the earliest year for which there is reliable data), the farm population of the United States stood at 32-million persons, 59 percent of the total rural population and 30 percent of the total national population. By 1950, rural farm population had declined to 23-million. For the first time, there were more rural residents living off farms than on them.

The years since 1950 have seen a continuation of the movement off the farm. In 1970, less than 10-million people lived on farms. This left farm residents accounting for only 18 percent of the rural population and only 5 percent of the total population.

. . . .

[Recent statistics on migration from the farms indicate that this migration has now levelled off as farm population has stabilized. Environmental Quality — 1976: The Seventh Annual Report of the Council on Environmental Quality 303 (1976). — Eds.]

Suburban Development

By the time really heavy in-migration from rural areas began to swell metropolitan areas, widespread automobile ownership had become common, permitting workers to live some distance from their jobs. As a result, suburbia began to grow faster than central cities. The percentage of population increase in central cities versus suburbia between 1900 and 1960 was 11.6 percent inside central cities and 45.9 percent outside central cities. . . .

Between 1960 and 1970, the aggregate population of central cities increased by 6.4 percent; the aggregate population of those cities' suburban areas increased by 26.7 percent. Put differently, between 1960 and 1970 over 80 percent of the total population increase in American metropolitan areas occurred in suburban locations, and less than 20 percent occurred in central cities. . . .

The Census Bureau reported early in 1972 that there had been about a 33-1/3 percent increase in land considered suburban during the 1960s; that about two-thirds of the population of the United States then lived on less than 2 percent of the land, concentrated in urban areas; and that the dual trend of more people living in metropolitan areas but spreading out more within them had become well established.

. . . .

The 1974 *Report on National Growth and Development* reported a slackening of metropolitan growth generally, and a slower pace of suburbanization in the large metropolitan areas between 1970 and 1974. Those areas exceeding 2-million in population experienced net out-migration in that period of time. Many medium-sized and smaller metropolitan areas, on the other hand, continued to gain population through net in-migration. By 1974, about 37 percent of the national population lived in metropolitan rings, while the remainder was divided about evenly between central cities and non-metropolitan areas. . . .

[Additional discussion of non-metropolitan growth trends can be found in Environmental Quality—1976, *supra* at 286-308.—Eds.]

Since 1970, Census Bureau surveys show a shift in population patterns toward non-metropolitan areas, perhaps for the first time in American history. Survey data show that non-metropolitan counties — those with no population center of 50,000 or more — gained 4.2 percent in population between April 1970 and July 1973, while metropolitan areas gained by 2.9 percent during the same period. Some of the shift is merely the extension of the movement to suburbia that has been going on for years, only further into the countryside, but some of it is occurring in small towns and rural areas away from metropolitan centers. Whether this trend will be confirmed in the rest of the 1970s and beyond remains to be demonstrated. If the spread of industry to remoter areas and a consequent improvement of the rural economy and the migration of retired people out of the great metropolitan complexes continue, it may well be confirmed.

Diminishing Density

The basic pattern of SMSA development — higher density at the center, lower densities around the edges — has remained virtually the same for almost a century. However, for some time, urban areas have spread out, due to the drift to suburbia of central city populations and heavy in-migration into suburban areas from outside individual SMSAs. This spread has been faster than population growth alone would justify. As a result, population density has tended to decline in both central cities and in urban areas as a whole.

Comprehensive data on density are not available prior to 1950. . . .

The density data available since 1950 show that in 1950, the average population density in all "urbanized areas" in the nation was 5,408 per square mile; by 1960, it had declined to 3,752 per square mile; and by 1970, to 3,376 per square mile. For central cities alone, density fell from 7,786 per square mile in 1950 to 4,463 in 1970. During these same years, population densities in the suburban portions of urbanized areas fell from 3,167 per square mile to 2,627 per square mile.

. . . .

Mobility, Migration, and Immobility

Population changes, it should be noted, are due to two forces — mobility and migration. Both mobility and migration are reflected in metropolitan growth. Mobility represents short-range moves within city or county boundaries, and migration refers to a move across an SMSA boundary, across intrastate county lines, or from one state to another. Each year recently, one American in five has moved, but about two-thirds of these moves are made within the same county, and less than one-sixth are across a state line. Long distance moves between SMSAs are not proportionally much greater than they were over a century ago.

. . . .

Economic and Racial Divisions

Another significant trend in metropolitan area population growth relates to the changing composition of the metropolitan population itself. Economics has been a basic factor prompting migration out from the center. As central city residents have been able to afford houses of their own, they have left the central city for the suburbs, leaving the older housing stock there for newcomers, who have most often been poorer families and individuals. With the boundaries of most central cities becoming virtually fixed, this movement has led to the concentration of the poor within central city boundaries. By 1970, 13.4 percent of the central city population was composed of people with incomes below what was then defined as the poverty level, whereas only 7.2 percent of the suburban population was composed of such individuals.

Accompanying the economic division of metropolitan areas has been a trend toward racial separation. As blacks have migrated into the metropolitan areas, most went to the central cities, and within those cities, to segregated neighborhoods. Both economic and social forces have operated to limit the availability of housing for blacks and other minorities outside the central city area. During the 1960s, the black population of the nation's central cities grew by 3.2-million, while the white population there declined by 600,000. In contrast, only 800,000 blacks were added to suburban populations, while the white population showed a 15.5-million increase. Most of the increase in black population outside of central cities took place in only a few SMSAs; in 1970, two out of every three new black suburbanites were in one of the 12 largest metropolitan areas, and more than one in three of them were in the New York, Los Angeles, and Washington metropolitan areas. . . .

The 1974 *National Growth Report* noted that the loss of white population in the central cities has accelerated since 1970. Whereas between 1960 and 1970 the white population in central cities had decreased by little more than 1 percent, between 1970 and 1974 the decrease in white population was over 8 percent. And whereas between 1960 and 1970 only a fifth of the 4-million increase of blacks in metropolitan areas took place in the suburbs, between 1970 and 1973 the black population increased more rapidly in the suburbs (1.8%) than in the central cities (0.3%). Blacks, however, continued to represent an increasing proportion of the central city population and a decreasing proportion of the suburban population. . . .

Problems Associated with Growth

Shifts in population and changes in the location of economic activity have had a substantial impact on the physical, social, and economic vitality of many central cities. . . . The influx of low-income families and individuals has placed a heavy burden on municipal services and facilities, a burden not likely to decline rapidly in the future. At the same time, the revenue sources available to pay for them have shrunk, as higher income families and industry have moved to the suburbs. The stagnant, or declining, tax bases of many central cities, together with the growing costs of police, fire, welfare, and sanitation services there, have often led to a reduction in the quality of service provided. This falls especially hard on poor families, since they suffer the consequences of crime, vandalism, drug addiction and neighborhood deterioration more than other Americans.

Increasing population in large metropolitan areas has intensified problems of air, water, and noise pollution as well as other forms of environmental degradation. Forest, streams, swamps, shorelines, wetlands, open space, and service areas have been consumed by metropolitan development. Few cities have found ways to control traffic congestion. Many urban dwellers spend substantial portions of their time contending with problems of clogged streets and highways, and trying to find parking places at their destination. At the same time, declining densities within metropolitan areas have made it difficult to provide efficient, self-supporting public transportation systems.

In most areas of the country, rapid increases in land costs have accompanied urban growth. Census Bureau surveys of the prices of new homes indicate that land values increased about 6 percent annually between 1963 and 1969. The National Association of Homebuilders reports that the proportion of a new home's value accounted for by site costs rose from 11 percent in 1949 to 24 percent in 1969. Similarly, site costs of houses financed with FHA-insured loans rose from 17 percent of total value in 1960 to 20 percent in 1970. And inflation in land prices contributed to the 75 percent increase in housing costs during the 1965-1976 period. These costs have continued to rise since then.

. . . .

THE BLEAK SIDE OF BURGEONING URBANIZATION

With the growth of urban areas, a way of life has emerged that is economically productive, in many ways stimulating, and, for many who live it, thoroughly satisfactory. Yet, there is a darker side, characterized by physical disorder, wastefulness, and human distress.

The Lust for Land

The shape of settlement in metropolitan areas reflects the great growth in suburban population, the impact of the automobile, the effect of the FHA mortgage insurance program, the desire of some to escape the city, and the obsolescence of areas in the central city. Each year hundreds of thousands of acres, mostly in the outskirts of metropolitan areas, are converted to urban use. A majority of Americans apparently want, as Daniel Elazar notes, to become urbanized but not citified, for "they have clearly sought the suburban conditions of lawns and automobiles." All too commonly, however, the resulting outward growth involves unsightly patterns of settlement in many metropolitan fringe areas.

By and large, those patterns of settlement have been directed — if direction indeed there was — by private economic interests which have acquired land from earlier land owners in the metropolitan fringe, or by the land owners themselves who have decided to parcel out their holdings to individual buyers or to subdivision developers. Though some control has been exerted over such land development in metropolitan fringe areas through extraterritorial zoning and subdivision regulation by metropolitan cities and/or counties, the major decision-making force has been private. Of course, government influences fringe development by its decisions as to location of water and sewer lines (local), highways (state), and airports (national), and by grants-in-aid and loan guarantee programs (national), but the fact remains that metropolitan growth has so far been chiefly a factor of private decisions to put land to urban uses.

One type of growth, sometimes referred to as "scatteration," consists of low density development with single-family homes built on lots of two to five acres or more. This low density settlement consumes large amounts of land that might be better used in the future at higher density ratios. Because it is uneconomic to service the homes with sewer and water lines, development tends to depend upon wells and septic tanks. But this is what millions of Americans prefer and will continue to prefer, regardless of how much professional planners, economists, and other "experts" inveigh against urban sprawl.

A second form consists of more intensive, asterisk-shaped growth out along major highway routes from built-up areas. Although the wedges of space between the strips are underdeveloped, utilities can be installed along the corridors.

Finally, suburban settlement is also characterized by "leapfrog" development, where relatively compact urbanization takes place in nodes, with substantial tracts of raw land left between them. The relatively compact areas usually require the greatest initial capital expenditures for urban services. Here is where small independent water and sewer systems are often found. As development begins to fill in the spaces, these local systems compete usually in an uneconomical fashion until they are absorbed by a larger system.

Unplanned development, scattered or leapfrogging over the countryside, can destroy natural open space needed for recreation and other purposes. It can set off a spiraling of public service costs for sewer and water lines, highways, and school bus transportation;

also, it can frequently destroy any possibility of an efficient and economic mass transit system.

Many a suburbanite and city dweller is familiar with the garish ribbon along major streets and highways composed of drive-in restaurants, gas stations, car lots, motels, bypassed vacant lots, and an occasional shopping center. A large number of recent court decisions on land use matters has involved zoning along these roads. Pressure for such development and the notion that lots fronting heavily traveled streets are not ideal for any other use sometimes cause even the most high minded of communities to buckle. A related factor is the tendency of some localities to "overzone" for business — to put long strips of vacant highway frontage in business zones.

In older settled areas, on the other hand, another kind of development problem emerges. The "gray areas" in large cities and in adjacent suburbs are not yet slums, but neighborhoods where signs of deterioration are beginning to appear. Here, pressures develop to allow commercial and residential uses that often cause blight; rooming houses, garages, filling stations, bars, lunch counters, and second-hand stores.

"Gray areas" frequently have highly mobile populations and lack the community cohesion necessary to resist these commercial encroachments. Where rapid transition is taking place in the population — where, for example, middle income and especially white residents are moving out — political influence and involvement often wane. New residents may lack the means and the sophistication to insist on enforcement of housing regulations and to oppose requests for rezoning. Persons anxious to sell and move out may, in fact, encourage a change in zoning to widen their potential market. Once these new uses are permitted and appear, the floodgates usually open wide.

. . . .

The Rural Remainder — and Its Plant

The shift from rural to metropolitan America has depopulated farms and drawn young people out of the small towns and the cutover, strip-mined, automated-farming, and mechanized-mining areas of our country.

Many scattered small towns, with underoccupied housing, abandoned or half-used schools, empty streamside factories, and underused utility facilities, present a bleak picture of wasted "fixed plant." The idea is sometimes expressed that some of these towns carry the seeds of expansion and, with assistance, could absorb some of the development that otherwise would occur in larger metropolitan centers.

The 1974 *Report on National Growth and Development* demonstrates, indeed, that since 1970, the decline in rural farm population is being more than offset by an increase in rural non-farm population in those very villages and small towns — especially those in the rural parts of metropolitan areas. Since 1970, out-migration from many non-metropolitan areas has halted. From 1970 to 1973, non-metropolitan areas averaged a greater increase in job growth than metropolitan areas (2.5% as compared to 1.2%), and a greater increase in population growth as well (4.2% compared to 2.9%). "A growth pattern of this type is unprecedented in the modern history of the United States, with the exception of a brief period during the worst of the Depression years."

Over all, the decade 1960-1970 saw manufacturing jobs in non-metropolitan areas increase about 36 percent, from 3.6- to 4.9-million, whereas metropolitan area jobs in manufacturing increased only about 13 percent, from 13.2- to 14.9-million. Non-metropolitan manufacturing jobs continued to grow between 1970 and 1973, to 5.3-million, but those same jobs in metropolitan areas declined to 14.2-million. . . .

In the latter part of the 1960s, other factors stimulated non-metropolitan growth: the environmental and youth movements, reactions to problems encountered in big cities, and of course the urban riots in the late 1960s. These factors combined to make major metropolitan areas seem less desirable places to reside or do business relative to smaller-scale cities and towns.

Yet, in many cases, the governmental institutions of rural areas and small town, originally designed to handle the less difficult challenges of an earlier age of greater self-sufficiency, are unable to provide the kind of public services needed today. Local government expenditures per person in many rural jurisdictions are disproportionately high for the frequently inadequate levels of service they provide. To complicate matters, the limited administrative machinery and scarcity of leadership often combine to hinder the planning and development necessary to overcome their handicaps. A further decline in the capacity of many towns and hamlets to support basic public services will hasten the erosion of significant sectors of rural America. With the contradictory trends of a declining farm sector and a generally less favorable position (as compared to metropolitan areas) regarding its educational and health facilities, and its housing, poverty and income levels, and of the recent growth of non-farm population and of jobs, rural America at this point in time faces a highly uncertain future — a future which in various major respects is closely linked to that of her urban brethren.

Within metropolitan areas, the expansion of industry and commerce — especially those of the labor intensive type — along the suburban fringe seems likely to continue, thereby widening the gap between the declining economy of the central city and the dynamic one of many of its suburban neighbors. What growth there has been in central cities has tended to offer employment opportunities in the professional, managerial, technical, and highly skilled sectors — in short, jobs for suburbanites.

With the relative drop in central city job opportunities, the migrating poor, less educated, and non-white logically should shift to the suburbs. But the scarcity of older low-cost suburban housing and the barrier of discrimination in the case of minorities tend to sustain the white noose around the central cities. For some migrating poor whites, small settlements along the metropolitan periphery sometimes prove attractive.

Comments: The Advisory Commission Report highlights a series of developments in American growth patterns that have intensified what some have called "spread city" — the gradual breaking up of inner city core areas and the dispersal of population throughout metropolitan areas, accompanied now by a buildup of population in nonmetropolitan areas of the country. Table 1 presents in composite form a summary of past and projected growth trends in the United States. The next group of readings examines in more detail the social and economic trends that have occurred in metropolitan areas, focusing on problems affecting declining cities, suburban and inner city social and economic disparities, and the problems of suburban growth.

Table 1. Growth Trends in the United States

Past and Projected Residence of U.S. Population, 1950-1990

	1950	1970	1974	1990	Implicit Growth Rate 1950-70	1970-90
		(millions)			(percent per year)	
Major Metropolitan	55.6	115.0	118.2	130.0	3.7	0.6
Over 2,000,000	36.3	75.2	76.2	79.6	3.7	0.3
500,000 to 1,999,999	19.3	39.8	42.0	50.4	3.7	1.3
Minor Metropolitan (50,000 to 499,000)	23.0	34.8	36.7	42.0	2.1	0.8
Nonmetropolitan (under 50,000)	56.9	53.5	56.4	62.	−0.3	0.7
Total U.S.	135.6	203.3	211.4	234.6	2.0	0.7
		(percent of total)				
Major Metropolitan	41.0	56.6	55.9	55.4		
Over 2,000,000	26.8	37.0	36.0	33.9		
500,000 to 1,999,999	14.2	19.6	19.9	21.5		
Minor Metropolitan	17.0	17.1	17.4	17.9		
Nonmetropolitan	42.0	26.3	26.7	26.7		
Total U.S.	100.0	100.0	100.0	100.0		

Current Shifts in Population, 1970-1974

| | Population | | Natural | Net | Annual Rate of Change | |
	April 1, 1970	July 1, 1974	Increase, 1970-74	Migration, 1970-74	Natural Increase	Net Migration
	(thousands)					
Major Metropolitan (61 areas)	115,033	118,216	3,346	−163	0.7	0.0
Over 2,000,000 (16 areas)	75,195	76,206	2,030	−1,019	0.6	−0.3
500,000−1,999,999 (45 areas)	39,838	42,010	1,316	856	0.8	0.5
Minor Metropolitan (198 areas)	34,783	36,746	1,281	682	0.9	0.5
Nonmetropolitan	53,484	56,426	1,396	1,547	0.6	0.7
Total United States	203,300	211,388	6,023	2,066	0.7	0.4

Source: Adapted from St. Louis Post-Dispatch, May 17, 1976, § C, p. 4.

FISCAL WOES MULTIPLY FOR LARGE CENTRAL CITIES, IN SEARCH: A REPORT FROM THE URBAN INSTITUTE, Vol. 5, Nos. 5-6, at 3-4 (Winter 1975)

[This article is a summary of the findings contained in T. Muller, Growing and Declining Urban Areas: A Fiscal Comparison (1975). — Eds.]

. . . .

Where Are the Declining and Expanding Cities?

During the first half of the 1970s there has been a considerable net outmigration of households from the large urban areas of the East North Central states and the Middle Atlantic states. And there has been substantial net inmigration into the South Atlantic, South Central, West, and Mountain states. . . . These shifts appear to occur for various reasons.

Areas losing population tend to have *high energy costs* compared to growing areas. Consumers in the New York region paid 170 percent more than Houston area consumers for the same amount of electricity in 1974. Manufacturing in declining areas tends to be characterized by a high proportion of *aging capital stock* and *high labor costs.* The relatively newer industrial plants and lower wages in the expanding areas attract further industrialization, resulting in more job opportunities. *Federal government expenditures* for both military and civilian programs are concentrated in the states that are attracting inmigrants. For example, during 1969, total federal payrolls accounted for 12 percent of all personal income in the ten most rapidly growing states, but for only 3 percent in the five states with the largest absolute outmigration. *Military contracts* were also allocated in ways that favor growing over declining areas — $134 per capita in the Northeastern and North Central states as against $196 in the rest of the nation in 1972.

Contrary to the common notion that *public transfer payments —*

welfare, social security, and so forth — are concentrated in the declining areas, such payments constituted a higher percentage of total personal income in the growing states in 1969. Also, their rate of increase between 1969 and 1973 was substantially more rapid in these same states. For example, transfer payments increased by 68 percent in New York State and 71 percent in Massachusetts in the four-year period; they more than doubled in Arizona, Florida, Nevada and Hawaii.

Another factor is the *cost of living,* especially housing costs and local-state taxes. Also, the *warmer, sunnier regions* are attracting many older people at or near retirement and many young people, too.

Why Are Population Changes Important?

Migrants are not representative of the population generally. Interregional migrants tend to have higher family incomes, more job skills, lower age levels, and higher educational attainment than nonmigrants. These attributes benefit the areas which attract them; the cities and regions they leave behind are disadvantaged. . . .

The largest metropolitan areas still enjoy the highest levels of personal income, but their *rate of income growth* has been below average. The two largest urban areas, New York City and Los Angeles, had annual income increases of 5.8 percent and 6.5 percent, respectively, between 1969 and 1973. At the same time, all other SMSAs enjoyed a per capita income growth rate of 8.7 percent.

Wealth is also shifting to southern and western states. In 1961, taxable assessed property in SMSAs of the Northeast and North Central states averaged about $2,330 per capita as compared to $1,700 in the South and West. By 1971 that gap had narrowed substantially: per capita property wealth in the Northeast and North Central states had increased by 56 percent to $3,640, while the other states doubled their property value to $3,400.

Private job growth also accompanies population growth, and the SMSAs losing population register a drop in private jobs, in part because of the migrants' characteristics which were cited earlier. . . . *Public employment* has been expanding in both growing and declining areas. However, these gains in declining areas did not offset private job losses.

[The Report then examines municipal government costs, and finds them to be substantially higher in declining cities. For example, declining cities spent 71 percent more for personnel costs, and also spent more for capital outlays and debt service. At the same time, declining cities did not have the same fiscal ability to pay for these services, and levied higher taxes in order to meet their service demands. In other words, they had a higher tax effort. — Eds.]

1976 REPORT ON NATIONAL GROWTH AND DEVELOPMENT: THE CHANGING ISSUES FOR NATIONAL GROWTH 31-34 (1976)

[The following excerpt from the national growth report highlights in more detail the intra-metropolitan changes in economic base that are occurring in metropolitan areas, and indicates what consequences these changes might have for the older, inner cities. — Eds.]

Continued Erosion of Older Central City Economic and Population Base

Central cities, considered collectively, have evidenced a slight population decline since 1970, with [some] decrease from 1970 to 1974 versus a six percent increase during the 1960's. The suburban rings kept adding people at twice the national rate, although their population growth is slower than in the past. And 39 percent of the nation's civilian noninstitutional population lived in the suburbs in 1974, while central cities claimed 30 percent.

The growth of the suburbs is a continuation of trends established in the 1950's and 1960's. Especially during the 1960's, there was a significant shift of manufacturing and office employment within metropolitan labor markets from central cities to suburbs. This movement included business enterprises exporting goods and services to the rest of the nation and not simply those producing for local consumption. . . . The pattern continued in most metropolitan areas from 1970 to 1975.

The movement of manufacturing concerns from the central cities is a particular concern, given the large concentration of minority workers and individuals with limited skills and education who reside in town and lack transportation to suburban job locations. Between 1951 and 1970, significant decreases occurred in manufacturing employment within 12 of the 30 largest cities in the nation, primarily in the older and more industrialized centers of the Northeast and North Central regions. The declines in Boston and Philadelphia exceeded ten percent of the industrial labor force. The few central cities that attracted new manufacturing employment in this period were located for the most part in the South and Southwestern regions, with the largest gains in Phoenix 144 percent, Dallas with 73 percent, Houston 60 percent, and San Antonio with 56 percent. To various degrees in different areas, however, the expansion of other jobs, particularly in the service sectors, has replaced manufacturing jobs.

Concurrently, an acceleration in the growth of suburban employment occurred around the 30 largest cities, with the exception of San Antonio, and suburban jobs at least doubled in nine of the metropolitan areas involved. In metropolitan areas nationally, employment grew in the suburbs by 3.2 percent between 1973 and 1975, while declining in the central cities by 3.7 percent. Increased participation of women in the labor force has been a major factor in the suburban gain with their employment in the suburbs up 9.3 percent. The central city decline, by contrast, was the result primarily of decreased employment of adult white males.

Central city employment problems will continue to involve changes in the labor forces due to immigration, increased numbers of women and young workers entering the labor force, loss of skilled and professional workers to the suburbs, and the need for two wage earners per household in high cost of living areas. And competition for fewer jobs could aggravate labor problems for firms located in central cities and encourage movement to areas relatively free of such problems. High unemployment rates among blacks, Mexican Americans, Puerto Ricans and among youth, the elderly and women in central cities may persist if job competition intensifies as the result of immigration, including illegal aliens.

. . . .

Diversity of Central Cities Suggests New Trends

Not all central cities are in decline. Age and the size of the SMSA which contains the central city have an effect. From 1960 to 1970 at least, an inverse relationship existed between the population of the SMSA and the rate of population growth in the central city. In addition, older large cities tended to lose population while younger large cities gained.

Some central cities in fact enjoy better conditions than their suburbs. The Brookings Institution recently compared the conditions of core cities and their suburbs in all metropolitan areas of over .5 million population. The comparison used a hardship index measuring six factors: unemployment, dependency rates, extent of education, income level, overcrowded housing, and poverty. The most significant findings relate to the regional grouping of results. With the exception of Atlanta, the ten most troubled cities are grouped in the North East and North Central regions with Newark, New Jersey leading the list and New York City tenth. By contrast, of the 12 central cities revealed as enjoying measurably better conditions than their suburbs, all but one were in the South or West.

These discrepancies can be attributed in part to historic patterns of inter-regional migration and to the problems endemic to the more mature economies of the Northeastern and North Central states. The findings also result to some extent from differing degrees of jurisdictional fragmentation from one SMSA to another. For example, because of liberal annexation laws, the central cities of Houston, and Phoenix house more than 50 percent of the population within their metropolitan areas. Finally, in some regions, the older suburbs are undergoing a process of economic and physical decline more commonly associated with central cities.

Comments: 1. Additional information and discussion on employment patterns in metropolitan areas is contained in Post-Industrial America: Metropolitan Decline and Inter-Regional Job Shifts (G. Sternlieb & J. Hughes eds. 1975). For a valuable study on industrial relocation that finds land values to be the critical factor in suburban relocation, see A. Hamer, Industrial Exodus from the Central City: Public Policy and the Comparative Costs of Location (1973).

Major national studies have looked at two prime examples of inner city decline and suburban expansion, contrasting the declining fortunes of the city of St. Louis with the burgeoning urban sprawl of San Jose, California. *See, e.g.,* Morrison, Urban Growth and Decline: San Jose and St. Louis in the 1960's, Sci., Aug. 30, 1974, at 757; Stanford Environmental Law Soc'y, San Jose: Sprawling City (1971). The major analytic effort on St. Louis is contained in a Rand Corporation report, B. William, St. Louis: A City and Its Suburbs (1973). The Rand Report attracted much attention for its prediction that St. Louis faced inevitable decline and decay without substantial federal financial assistance.

2. As the national growth report suggests, the shift of employment opportunities to the suburbs is one of the major trends affecting the character and structure of metropolitan areas. Nevertheless, some observers have questioned data showing massive job shifts to the suburbs, claiming that growth in service and office jobs in the inner city have counterbalanced this trend. *See, e.g.,* Berry & Cohen, Decentralization of Commerce and Industry: The Restructuring of Urban America in The Urbanization of the Suburbs 431 (L. Masotti & J. Hadden eds. 1973). Berry and Cohen nevertheless maintain that the suburban job shift has led to major changes in the structural characteristics of metropolitan areas:

> What all of this means, for example, is that the black resident of the metropolis finds himself in a central-city ghetto abandoned by both whites and, increasingly, employment. The flight of white city dwellers into the expanding peripheries of metropolitan regions is an accelerating phenomenon as minorities move toward majority status in the city center. The exurban fringes of many of the nation's urban regions have now pushed one hundred miles and more from the traditional city centers. More important, the core orientation implied in use of the term "central city" and "central business district" is fast on the wane. No longer is it necessary to have a single, viable, growing heart. Today's urban systems appear to be multinodal, multiconnected social systems in action, in which the traditional centralization of the population into metropolitan areas has been counterbalanced by a multifaceted reverse thrust of decentralization. The situation is very different from the period at the end of the nineteenth century from which we derive the concept of urbanization. Decentralization and an outward urge have replaced centralization and core orientation; differentiation and segregation substitute for the integrative role of the melting pot.

Id. at 453. The volume in which this article appears contains valuable essays on recent governmental, social and economic changes in suburbia. For an article by a noted urban expert suggesting that the energy crisis and increases in gasoline and thus commuter costs will reduce the trend to suburbanization see Downs, Squeezing Spread City, New York Times Magazine, Mar. 17, 1974, at 38.

3. The next selection highlights growth and development problems that occur in rapidly growing metropolitan fringe areas, focusing on the Minneapolis-St. Paul metropolitan area, in which a comprehensive set of regional planning and land use controls has been developed. In evaluating this excerpt the reader should ask whether the author has adopted an implicit model of how metropolitan growth ought to occur, which he then uses as the basis for criticizing existing trends and patterns. Does the persistence of the trends and patterns discussed in the excerpt indicate that American preferences for suburban living are perhaps at odds with the planner's concepts of how Americans ought to live? If so, what are the implications for planning programs that attempt to reverse if not eliminate the typical American preference for low density living which is described?

G. ISBERG, DEVELOPMENT PROBLEMS IN THE URBAN-RURAL FRINGE: NEED FOR UNIFIED PLANS AND PROGRAMS (1972) *

TYPICAL GROWTH PATTERN IN THE URBAN-RURAL FRINGE

The Twin Cities of St. Paul and Minneapolis are located at the confluence of the Minnesota and Mississippi Rivers with the two downtowns being located approximately 14 miles apart. The Twin Cities Metropolitan Area has a total area of slightly under 3,000 square miles and a 1970 population of 1,865,000.

... [T]he Twin Cities Metropolitan Area is very governmentally fragmented, being made up of a total of 297 units of governments — 7 counties, 75 school districts, 194 municipalities (27 cities, 108 villages, 56 townships), and 21 special districts. The size of the communities vary from 58 acres for Landfall to 34,432 acres for Minneapolis and in population from 82 for Lakeland Shores to 435,712 for Minneapolis.

The growth pattern in the Twin Cities Area has followed the national trend of rapid population growth in suburbs. Indeed, the latest population figures indicate that for the first time in modern history, the population in the suburbs now outnumber the population in the central cities.

This population growth has resulted in much land being converted from agriculture to urban land uses in the urban-rural fringe. For example, the amount of agricultural land in Dakota County, one of the most rapid[ly] growing counties in the metropolitan area, de-

---

* On file with the editors.

creased from 288,403 acres (73.9% of the total area) to 256,576 acres (67.4%) between 1964 and 1969. During the same period, the number of farms decreased from 1,286 to 1,021. Furthermore, most of this farmland is being acquired by developers, land investors, and speculators rather than farm expansion buyers. For example, the majority of purchasers of the farmland during 1969-70 in Dakota County came from outside the communities in which the land is situated, paid from $100 to $300 more per acre than farm expansion buyers and accounted for almost all of the increase in land prices for this area.

Urban growth in the urban-rural fringe usually starts with scattered single-family housing on relatively large lots (minimum lot sizes vary from 1 to 5 acres) strung out along township and county roads. Occasionally, small subdivisions of 5-10 houses will be constructed in various parts of the townships. Larger clusters of housing and subdivisions then follow and usually locate in or near the most scenic areas, such as near attractive lakes or in wooded, gently rolling areas. The large tract developments usually locate where the land is expansive and relatively flat and low in cost. After sufficient residential development has taken place to create a sufficient market and labor force, commercial and industrial growth takes place in or near areas of good accessibility. The trend has been for industrial developments to take place in planned industrial parks where the accessibility is good and the services and utilities are available. The trend has also been for commercial development in the suburbs to take place in medium sized and even large "diversified" centers.

This growth pattern seldom follows an orderly, "steady wave" pattern of expansion, but rather skips around, often taking place at some distance from the existing urban development. . . . There are several reasons for this so-called "leap-frog" development. For one, the most scenic and attractive areas for residential development (and therefore the most saleable) are often located at some distance from existing urban development. Second, land which is located at some distance from existing development is usually lower in cost and therefore will often be acquired by land investors and speculators. Once the speculators own the land, they usually put pressure on local governments to re-zone the areas for industrial or commercial development to inflate the land values. Obviously, the faster the land values can be inflated through re-zoning or construction of such community facilities as sanitary sewers and highways, the better it is for the land investor or speculator. All too often, the town boards or village councils "cave-in" to these pressures for a number of reasons, such as a lack of a development plan or development ordinances or inadequate knowledge of development problems which result from leap-frog developments. In many cases, the town boards consist of conservative farmers who never have had a high regard for zoning or other forms of development controls.

Finally, this scattered or leap-frog pattern of urban development is often reinforced by mayors, city managers, and other public officials in smaller towns located in the rural-urban fringe areas. Many of these local officials have adopted an "aggressive" growth policy for their communities, due to the fact that their primary yardstick for measuring the success of their administration is by how much urban growth they were able to bring to the community. Many officials are beginning to realize that all forms of urban growth are not necessarily a blessing, especially if not accompanied by commercial or industrial growth to increase the property tax base of the community. Thus, while the attitudes of some towards urban growth may be changing from simple "quantity" to "quality and balance", many still retain an aggressive growth policy.

PROBLEMS RESULTING FROM PRESENT PATTERN OF GROWTH IN THE URBAN-RURAL FRINGE

The "broad-band" pattern of "leap-frog" development, has resulted in a number of problems for the residents, communities, and school districts in the fringe areas. One of the most pressing problems facing the local communities is how to provide such urban services as fire and police protection at a time when the property tax base is usually low. Even if a community is able to contract with an adjacent, more established community for these services, as is often the practice, the cost is usually high.

Developments that attract young couples with children place a heavy burden on the local school district which must provide added school facilities. The result is relatively high property taxes, especially in those school districts which are in the early stages of urban development and have not yet attracted substantial industrial or commercial developments.

The local communities are also in many cases under pressure by developers, speculators, and homeowners to extend sanitary sewer or water facilities to serve "leap-frog" developments. Since the cost of financing these services is usually based on special assessment against the benefited property (most often on a front-footage basis), a heavy financial burden is placed on the owner of agricultural or open land through which the sewer or water pipes must be extended. Often this results in "forced" sales and added pressure for "premature" development of this land. Once the land is sold to the speculator or developer, there will be added pressure on the local communities to re-zone these areas to residential, commercial or industrial land uses. More often than not this re-zoning is granted. In addition to the special assessments, there is often a general rise in taxes on agricultural land due to increased property appraisals brought about from sales of adjacent land to speculators. As was indicated previously, land investors in Dakota County pay $100 to $300 more per acre for land than farm expansion buyers. Since appraisers use recent sales or "comparables" as a major factor in determining land values, the result is higher taxes for the farmer located adjacent to the property acquired by the speculator. Part of this problem is due to the difficulty in accurately determining land values in the urban-rural fringe because of speculative activity. In any event, this general rise in property taxes places pressure on the farmer to sell his land, which he often will do if he is near retirement age and no one is left on the farm to "take over".

In many cases, valuable land for parks or "protection" open space (natural resources) is permanently lost to urban development because the value of the land has increased to such a degree that it becomes prohibitively expensive and beyond the ability of the governmental agencies to acquire even with substantial federal and state aid. . . .

The result of the present pattern of development is low density "sprawl" and the loss of open space, and unique and valuable natural resources. It also usually results in relatively high cost for services to these developments. A by-product of this pattern of development is the relatively large amount of vacant land which results from land speculation and from "over-zoning" for industrial and commercial development. Many communities will zone large areas for industrial use due to pressures from speculators and also due to "over-optimism" by the community in its ability to attract industries. For example, it has been estimated that there presently is enough land in the Twin Cities Metropolitan Area zoned for industrial uses to meet the projected needs way into the 21st century. This land has a tendency to remain permanently vacant, since it is almost unheard of to re-zone an area from industrial to residential uses.

In summary, the present "broad-band" and low density pattern of development tends to be a reinforcing system due to speculative activity, the present property tax system and lack of strong development standards and ordinances by the local communities in the urban-rural fringe. However, in defense of the local communities it may be that the present land use controls such as zoning or subdivision regulations, if used by themselves, are not sufficient to withstand the strong pressures from speculative activity due to the potential high gain from land speculation. Furthermore, there seems to be little consensus or incentive to date in most metropolitan areas towards controlling urban sprawl. Land speculators, realtors, financial institutions, such as banks and insurance industries, builders, planning and engineering consultants, attorneys, and local suburban officials, all either favor expansion or stand to gain from it. It is only lately that the central cities, becoming alarmed at the exodus of population, industry, and commercial enterprise have expressed concern over urban sprawl. Many county planning agencies have been concerned over this problem and have spear-headed studies related to urban sprawl and how to control it.

B. MAJOR POLICY PROBLEMS

Planning and land use controls have historically addressed themselves to a wide variety of issues, ranging from capital facilities planning to land use allocation to urban design and aesthetics. Currently, three major policy problems are stimulating a major rethinking of the scope of planning and control techniques — the need to provide for lower income housing, the need to protect the environment and the need to control growth. Each of these problems is the subject of detailed treatment in later chapters. At this point, however, brief attention will be given to background issues affecting the treatment of each of these problems as they arise in the land planning and control process.

1. Housing

Housing as a land use control issue has surfaced largely in the context of suburban planning and zoning programs. The excerpt from the Advisory Commission report, *supra* p. 1, briefly noted contemporary trends in racial segregation in metropolitan areas. Using the suburb as its focus, the excerpt from the study that follows portrays in more detail the present pattern of segregation in suburban areas, and provides a racial context in which the planning and zoning policies of the suburbs may be evaluated.

P. MULLER, THE OUTER CITY: GEOGRAPHICAL CONSEQUENCES OF THE URBANIZATION OF THE SUBURBS 18-20 (1976)*

The Segregation of Suburban Social Groups

The segregation of subcultural communities in contemporary social space appears to be intensifying. The social districts are carefully delimited with a pervasive spirit of every-group-for-itself, and they defend their territory against outside challengers or those

---

* Association of American Geographers, Resource Paper No. 75-2. References cited throughout the text have been omitted.

who might threaten their social and economic status. The social barricades are unsubtle — palisade fences, guarded gates, and other "keep out" landscape symbols — as the groups consciously wall themselves off from each other. . . .

Affluent residents of comfortable neighborhoods may express satisfaction with the present conditions of suburban social segregation. This is not the case with many disadvantaged groups who constitute increasingly important elements in urban social geography. One major disadvantaged group, suburban blacks, have encountered social barriers in the outer city to such an extent that their resulting social isolation and spatial segregation is perhaps the most pronounced pattern on suburbia's residential map.

There is a deeply imbedded and pervasive racial segregation within the fragmented social geography of the outer city. Whereas blacks comprise 11 percent of the total U.S. population and 12 percent of its metropolitan residents, they account for less than five percent of the nation's suburbanites. . . .

Black Suburbanization Trends

Twentieth-century black trends . . . reveal that such popular suburban epithets as "lily white" and "white noose" have some factual basis. It would certainly not be an overstatement to claim that blacks largely have been denied entrance to the suburbs. Prewar patterns are insignificant since comparatively few blacks lived in the North, but postwar trends clearly show a rapidly widening divergence of whites and blacks in the suburbs. . . . [There has been] a stable black suburban population over recent decades. A large proportion of this population still inhabits tiny, widely dispersed, and highly segregated traditionally black areas with settlement histories of five decades or more. In some instances, large enclaves of similar age are present in satellite towns adjacent to large central cities, i.e., Evanston, Illinois; Pasadena, California; and Mount Vernon, New York. Together, these black suburbs have accounted for a stable three percent of the total population in the outer rings of non-Southern SMSAs since the 1920s. The modest postwar growth of black suburbs has intensified residential densities within these older pockets. Very recently, however, black population increases have also resulted from selective expansion of central city ghettos into contiguous inner suburbs — a potentially significant trend for future suburban social geography.

An overview of the latest census data indicates that America's suburbs remain all but closed to blacks. During the 1960s the percentage of blacks in the suburban population of SMSAs (as defined in 1970) increased imperceptibly from 4.78 to 4.82. Although 800,000 blacks did enter suburbia in the sixties, their gains were all but obliterated by the more than 15.5 million whites who constituted 95 percent of the decade's new suburban migrants.

Viewed from the slightly different perspective of the total black population itself, census findings are similar. From 1960 to 1970 the percentage of this group residing in the suburbs increased only from 15.1 to 16.2 percent, compared to the 35.4 to 40.4 percent rise for whites; in terms of percentage increases whites (+ 14 percent) again led blacks (+ 7.2 percent) by a wide margin. By region, the West (25.6 to 29.5 percent), North Central (11.6 to 12.8 percent), and South (14.2 to 14.8 percent) gained in black suburban population, whereas the Northeast held a constant 18.7 percent. On the other hand, black concentration in central cities during the sixties increased notably (52.8 to 58.0 percent) at a time when the corresponding white population declined (from 31.5 to 27.8 percent).

Because of the much smaller absolute number of suburban blacks in the 1960 base data — 2.8 million to 56.3 million whites — suburbanization rates during the 1960s are deceptive (29 percent growth for blacks, 28 percent for whites). Nevertheless every region recorded modest black gains except the South, where overall black suburban population declined from 12.6 to 10.3 percent. This trend must be balanced against the conclusive findings of a study undertaken by the Federal Reserve Bank of Boston indicating that black suburbanization in the sixties did not result in any meaningful progress toward racial integration. Specifically, this study concluded that: (1) there was very little change in the distribution of blacks both between and within central cities and suburbs during the 1960s; (2) new suburban black migrants were moving overwhelmingly into widely scattered already-black neighborhoods with almost no penetration of white residential areas; and (3) despite small absolute and proportionate nonwhite suburban SMSA increases from 1960 to 1970, intermunicipal segregation in the decade actually increased by an average of 15 percent in 14 large SMSAs surveyed.

. . . .

Black Suburban Settlement Types

Spatial patterns of black suburban settlement are intricately tied to the urban ghettoization process which concentrates blacks in a limited number of residential areas (to the extent that they dominate neighborhoods in excess of fifty percent of the total population). These are sealed off, surrounded by powerful social barriers maintained through constant external pressures. Rose . . . has classified these outlying racial concentrations into two distinct spatial forms: *colonized* and *ghettoized* black suburban enclaves. . . .

Colonized black communities tend to be small stable pockets which have persisted for several decades originating as "shacktowns" on the then rural-urban fringe. In the Northeast these congregations are commonly attached to old rail corridors, such as suburban Philadelphia's Main Line, and are direct descendants of the nineteenth-century servants' quarters, usually relegated to undesirable trackside locations, which housed the domestic employees of wealthy landowners of the period. Always segregated, these low income black colonies have become completely isolated by the social barriers erected as modern suburban development engulfed them.

Although most colonized black suburbs are characterized by aged, dilapidated housing, stagnant or declining low income populations, and a deteriorating quality of life, there are a few exceptions. One is Glenarden in Prince Georges County, Maryland, just northeast of the District of Columbia. Here local black political control enabled annexation of nearby unbuilt land for development in detached and garden apartment dwellings which have attracted hundreds of middle income families. Another is Hollydale, Ohio, northwest of Cincinnati, which has had similar success as a new outlier of the older adjacent Woodlawn-Lincoln Heights colony. A third exception is Lawnside, New Jersey, southeast of Philadelphia, which has maintained a staunchly independent middle-class black population for over a century and has recently added new housing by developing previously bypassed residentially-zoned properties.

Since World War Two *ghettoized* black suburbanization commonly has been of the spillover type. This results from a sectoral expansion of the central city ghetto across city lines into adjacent suburban territory. . . . As poorest blacks are forced to abandon unlivable dwellings at the inner edge of the ghetto, they move outward to the nearest available housing. This housing in turn has been abandoned by less poor blacks seeking better housing in outer ghetto neighborhoods. The more favorable residential environment of the inner suburban margins of the advancing black community has attracted a middle-class population of better-educated, young black families. This spillover process is well-advanced in many cities, such as Cleveland, St. Louis, Washington, D.C., Chicago, Atlanta, Miami, Los Angeles, and parts of the New York Metropolis. . . .

The other form of ghettoized suburb is the *leapfrog* type, most often an exclave located beyond the spillover ghetto. . . . This is a newly emerging phenomenon, and Rose has identified three such clusters in central Long Island, as well as a fourth in East Palo Alto, California. These black pockets are relatively undesirable residential areas and almost always consist of deteriorating, cheaply constructed early postwar tract housing which whites have abandoned.

Comments: For an excellent discussion of black suburbanization trends see H. Rose, Black Suburbanization (1976). For an article tracing the nature of black movement into suburbs having the highest gain nationally see Connolly, Black Movement into the Suburbs, 9 Urb. Aff. Q. 91 (1973).

2. The Environment

> There is a new mood in America. Increasingly, citizens are asking what urban growth will add to the quality of their lives. They are questioning the way relatively unconstrained, piecemeal urbanization is changing their communities and are rebelling against the traditional processes of government and the marketplace which, they believe, have inadequately guided development in the past. They are measuring new development proposals by the extent to which environmental criteria are satisfied — by what new housing or business will generate in terms of additional traffic, pollution of air and water, erosion, and scenic disturbance.

The Use of Land: A Citizens' Policy Guide to Urban Growth 33 (W. Reilly ed. 1973).

This statement, which is from a major Task Force Report sponsored by the Rockefeller Brothers Fund, suggests the new mood in America, which is increasingly concerned with the enhancement and maintenance of environmental quality. The environmental movement, in turn, and the environmental controls which it has spawned, have had major impacts on land use planning and land use controls. Historically, land planning and control has not noticeably been environmentally oriented. As one major survey indicated, land planning has had "an inclination toward searching for a balance among multiple objectives, only some of which are environmental. . . ." E. Kaiser et al., Promoting Environmental Quality Through Urban Planning and Control 64 (1973).

Links between environmental quality and land use and development are nevertheless clear. On a limited scale, for example, unthinking land development can disturb critical wetland resources and indirectly affect water quality. An even more fundamental question to ask is whether changes in the form and pattern of urban development can have an impact on major environmental problems, such as air and water pollution. This question was addressed in a recent study:

> A fundamental environmental issue . . . is whether a growth management strategy to achieve an optimum spatial pattern for air and water quality is more effective than the application of site specific management devices or other control methods that are applied with little regard to questions of spatial form. [Generally, site specific devices include techniques such as providing retention ponds in residential development to hold back stormwater during and after a storm. — Eds.] The question on the effectiveness

of planning to achieve an optimum land use pattern raises another series of questions as to which of the characteristics of spatial pattern are instrumental in bringing about the desired levels of air and water quality. Are such factors as population size, geographic location or density the key determinants of the optimal pattern? Which of the characteristics are most necessary in supporting specific work/residence/shopping spatial relationships for maximizing public transit use?

Association of Bay Area Governments, Integrated Land Use/Air Quality/Water Quality Control Study for Sonoma County, California at III-3 (1977). The Sonoma study reached the following conclusions:

> The basic conclusions reached in this study are: 1) the assimilative capacity of air and water basins are key determinants of future levels of population and employment activities that can ... be supported within basins without violating environmental standards; 2) the population and employment size and density are the most critical factors affecting both air and water quality as compared to other variables such as location, land use type or meteorological conditions (excluding reactive air pollutants); and 3) other pollution control approaches such as site specific land management techniques generally have greater influence on air and water quality than variations in spatial configurations or intensity of land use.

Id. at VII-1.

Studies of the impact of urban form and regional patterns on air and water quality have led to conflicting conclusions. The conclusions of the Sonoma study should be tempered by the fact that it was limited to a sub-area in the San Francisco region and did not consider the impact of regional development on air and water quality. A cross-national study of metropolitan areas which relied extensively on census data has found that urban form does have a significant impact on air and water quality levels:

> What we have added to the previous literature is firm evidence that urban form plays a significant role in translating these basic city characteristics (size, density and the economic base) into land use, and that the land use pattern, as shaped by urban form, is directly related to the nature and intensity of environmental pollution. Most importantly, *holding the effects of city size and manufacturing concentration constant,* and controlling for an inverse relationship between income levels and pollution (probably an effect of pollution rather than a cause, via migration of people and activities to the least polluted

amenity-rich environments in the past two decades), we have found that:

   1) The core-oriented urban region with a radial transportation network and a steep density gradient
     a) displays greater intensity of land use, a lower percentage of land developed and used for residential and commercial purposes, and more open space, and
     b) as a consequence of this land use mix and pattern, has superior air and water quality to:
   2) The dispersed urban region, which has a less focussed transport network and lower, more uniform population densities. This urban form
     a) displays urban sprawl, with a higher percentage of residential and commercial land use and less open space than in the core-oriented case, and
     b) as a consequence of this land use mix, has inferior air and water quality.

B. Berry et al., Land Use, Urban Form and Environmental Quality 411, 413 (1974).

Links between environmental quality and urban form suggest the importance of growth strategies in controlling environmental impacts. The review of regional development trends in this chapter also sets the stage for a review of the growth control movement, which interestingly enough has surfaced at the local and suburban and not at the regional level in most metropolitan areas. The selection that follows examines growth control programs in land planning and land use control settings.

3. Growth Controls

H. FRANKLIN, CONTROLLING URBAN GROWTH — BUT FOR WHOM? 4-6 (Potomac Institute, 1973)

   . . . The genesis of controlled growth policies may be found in the adverse reaction in many communities to rapid residential expansion. This growth has produced three sources of concern: (1) housing has been developed that is not supported by adequate community facilities, such as roads and schools, which have become overcrowded as a result; (2) the public financing of these facilities has occasioned a rapid increase in real property taxation, particularly for earlier arrivals to the community; and (3) the failure to provide some facilities, such as sewers and waste treatment plants, has contributed to deterioration of the quality of ground water or nearby streams, lakes or other bodies of water.

"Slow growth" or "no growth" policies are therefore being adopted or considered with increasing frequency to reduce the volume of housing and public facilities in many localities that have experienced or fear rapid population growth. These policies take various forms. "Moratoriums" on residential building permits, sewer hookups, or new sewer construction are commonly employed. Other policies sometimes purport to place specific numerical limits on the ultimate population in a locality without any plan for more efficient use of resources. More conventional policies, such as underzoning of land for residential use generally or apartments in particular, or limiting the number of bedrooms in an apartment — so-called fiscal zoning — have of course been common for many years. In addition, the transfer of costs for sewage, drainage, roads, or recreation from municipalities to residential developers can provide a means to assure that more expensive housing, or less housing altogether, will result.

Although there often is a valid temporary health and safety basis for some local policies — avoiding pollution of the ground water, for example — many localities may use newly popular ecological reasons for "slow growth" or "no growth" policies that in reality are intended to serve fiscal purposes. Increases in local real estate taxes can be forestalled in the short run by limiting the entry into the community of new residents, particularly low- or moderate-income residents with school-age children, or limiting the entry of any new residents who may use community facilities.

The existing system of land conversion to urban uses in metropolitan areas can produce serious environmental "overloads." An inefficient and regressive method of financing public facilities for urban growth, and the failure of public planning to control both the timing and nature of private residential development, often leads to this result. The private developer thus becomes the visible political target of an aroused populace that is only dimly aware of how to reform public processes to avoid the exploitation of land for private profit.

Consequently, certain measures aimed at ecological problems appear to be attractive even though their remedial effect on the environment will be minimal compared to their potential economic and social effects. For example, the existing sewage effluent in a sanitary district or locality may fall well below acceptable water quality standards, and the affected surface water may be badly polluted. A common official reaction to this situation is to "temporarily" ban the connection of more housing units to sewers. Such a ban, however, may do little to improve water quality, because the increased pollution resulting from incremental urbanization is trivial in relation to the total problem facing the inadequate sewage treatment capacity. A ban in such circumstances may therefore have a depressant effect on the availability of housing out of reasonable proportion to its remedial effect on environmental quality. Once water quality has badly deteriorated, the most reasonable solution may unfortunately be the most costly one: rapid and substantial upgrading of treatment facilities. It may be more expedient, however, to declare a moratorium on urbanization than to confront the difficult question of paying for such facilities.

If the existing processes of land development produce environmental problems, they also contribute to a serious social problem: the increasing separation of people by income and race in metropolitan areas. Quite apart from covert or overt racial discrimination, the increase in the cost of newly constructed houses is building in a pattern of economic separation that will persist for many years. . . .

A pervasive anti-growth mood in urbanizing areas may reinforce the built-in, long-term economic segregation implied by these cost trends. Nevertheless, this mood, and the potential for reform in the political force behind it, cannot be dismissed by those primarily concerned with a more equitable urban growth policy. The existing system is inequitable as well as ecologically irresponsible; preservation of the status quo will not produce socially more desirable outcomes. "Unchecked growth," in the words of one observer, "will not guarantee integration, social justice, or economic uplifting of the disadvantaged in the future any more than it has in the past." For example, local policies that call for houses on large lots whose waste is "disposed of" through septic tanks are frequently ecologically damaging and exclusionary at the same time. . . .

Comments: Franklin makes passing reference to moratoria, which are often used in many municipalities as an interim control on growth pending the development of more permanent, long-term policies. Like other growth controls, moratoria can have a significant impact on land prices, and in this way influence indirectly the shape and direction of new development in the region. The regional growth patterns examined earlier in this chapter may thus be altered significantly by growth control programs, often with counterproductive effects, as the following excerpt indicates:

In areas where a moratorium is in effect, the amount of available land for development necessarily decreases. The result is one of decreasing land supply while demand continues unabated at the same rate prior to the moratorium. This can have a major effect on residential development. First, development is channeled to other nearby areas where land costs may be lower — outside the moratorium areas, but within sewer service areas — on the fringe of current development. Thus, the burden of growth may be shifted outward to jurisdictions even less capable, administratively and fiscally, of accommodating rapid urban growth. Because land for residential development is further limited, costs (and prices) begin to rise, thereby resulting in more expensive housing. The small developer, unable to shift location or scale of operations, is likely to be forced out of the market, further reducing the supply of housing or the range of prices and styles. . . . High-density residential developments are discriminated against since single-family units can, in the case of the common sewer moratorium, usually still be built on large lots with septic tanks. At the same time, small scattered sites fully serviced by public facilities may remain undeveloped by the departure of the small builder. Thus, undesirable development patterns (i.e., low-density sprawl) may in fact be exacerbated by the use of moratoria.

By increasing risk and uncertainty about the location and potential size of tracts to be removed from the moratorium sometime in the future, moratoria create inefficiencies in the development industry in the form of erratic and unbalanced housing production schedules. However, a few developers can mitigate the intent of moratoria in the short run by stockpiling development approvals, i.e., by obtaining a backlog of building permits, sewer and water tap-in permits, etc. Such developers are then in a monopoly position with all the implications for supply price which monopolists enjoy. Although widely used at present, moratoria are ineffective land-use controls for the following reasons: their impact may be easily circumvented, they are restricted to a short-range focus, and they lack enduring solutions to basic underlying problems. . . .

E. Bergman, External Validity of Policy Related Research on Development Controls and Housing Costs 33-34 (1974).

Subsequent chapters will explore in more detail the legal problems associated with land use controls for lower income housing, environmental quality, and growth management programs. An initial step is to secure a firm grip on the mechanics and fundamentals of the municipal land use planning and control system, and how it operates. The problems and issues raised in these early pages will be relevant, however, even to an examination of these municipal land use control and planning systems. The place at which to begin this examination is with the major guidance document that is intended to provide a framework for the exercise of land use controls at the local level — the comprehensive land use plan. This topic will be examined in the next chapter.

Chapter 2

THE PLANNING PROCESS AND THE COMPREHENSIVE PLAN

A. THE THEORY OF THE PLANNING PROCESS

Comprehensive planning for land use regulation would be a comparatively simple process if there were widespread agreement on the goals and objectives to be furthered by that process. Unfortunately, getting agreement on these goals and objectives often proves an elusive task. As the review of housing, growth management and environmental problems in the last chapter has indicated, it is often difficult to pursue one objective in land use management without adopting policies that conflict with the pursuit of another, equally desirable, goal.

An evaluation of the role of comprehensive planning in land use control can begin on a different level, however, which does not (or does not appear) to implicate the land use planner in goal conflict problems. This beginning point finds its place in the market, for land use planning and development control have important impacts on the operation of the land market that must be considered in any review of the planning and land development control system. In a market economy, a basis must be found for public intervention that will overcome the widely held preference that land use decisions be left to the autonomous bargaining that is characteristic of marketplace behavior. Planning and land development controls interfere with that bargaining process. For what reasons do we tolerate this intervention?

The Efficiency and Externality Problem

In order to determine whether, and under what conditions, public intervention in the market is justified we must begin with a criterion or standard under which we can decide whether market performance is satisfactory. Economists usually apply an efficiency criterion in order to make this judgment. One acceptable definition of efficiency is the following:

> ... [R]esources are efficiently allocated to the production of a commodity when there is the greatest difference between the total benefits received from consuming the commodity produced and the total costs of producing the commodity. (Emphasis deleted.)

A. Schreiber, P. Gatons, & R. Clemmer, Economics of Urban Problems 16 (1971). If for "production of a commodity" we

31

substitute "allocation of land resources" we have a definition of efficiency which can be useful in determining whether or not the market for land uses is operating in a satisfactory manner.

Externalities impede the operation of an efficient market:

> Externalities cause problems in achieving the efficient allocation of resources because the private market system takes into account only private benefits and private costs; thus, net social benefits are not maximized because indirect costs or benefits are excluded in making resource allocation choices. . . . Thus, demand in a market system reflects the consumer's net private benefits and ignores the indirect benefits or costs of consumption. The same is true of production decisions, so that the supply in a market system does not reflect the indirect cost of production.

Id. at 25.

What are externalities? These can be divided into both positive and negative externalities. A positive externality is an indirect benefit conferred by the market process. An example in the land use context would be the development of a major shopping center. The shopping center makes the surrounding land more valuable for residential development. A negative externality is an indirect cost that is generated by the market process. An example in the land use context would be the noise, congestion, and other undesirable features of a new industry which locates in a residential neighborhood. *See id.* at 26-28.

Most analyses of planning and land development control have focused on the role of the system in controlling negative externalities. There has not been as much concentration on the role of the system in controlling positive externalities, although both problems equally demand attention.

The inability of the market to account for externalities leads to a phenomenon known as market failure. The following simple example makes the point:

> A more interesting case analytically is visual intrusion. If market forces were allowed to operate freely, one would expect a tendency for buildings to be crammed together at high densities. The first comer would buy his plot of land and build on it. The second would buy the adjacent land and would give much less weight to the interests of his neighbour; he would find it in his own interests to build his house at a density that is most likely to blanket his neighbour's view and even affect his ventilation. He is not likely to be deterred from a high plot-ratio by the thought that the next comer will perform the same trick on him, since there is no guarantee, if he is a good neighbour and considers the interest of those who arrived before him, that

this will have any influence on those who arrive after him. His only effective policy is to buy a larger site than he would otherwise require in order to keep his neighbour at a distance. Thus, in such a world of market freedom, one would expect people to buy larger plots (and economize on something else). Then if the land were being developed in sequence, they would locate as near the boundary of existing neighbours as possible, leaving as much room as they can between them and the plots which the next comers will buy to develop on. At least this seems a plausible scenario. Another possibility is that such a situation makes it possible for those who come later to hold up to ransom those who came before. Rationally someone who built a house with a vacant plot next door would be prepared to pay up to his valuation of the disutility he would receive from having his vision obscured or to the point where he would rather move, whichever was the less. This is capable of being analysed as a divergence between private and social costs, but it is an example of a special case of such a divergence which seems to be of central importance for the evaluation of planning.

Foster, Planning and the Market in The Future of Urban Planning 132, 148-49 (P. Cowan ed. 1973). *See also* Oxley, Economic Theory and Urban Planning, 7 Env. and Plan. 497 (1975).

The Equity Problem

Efficiency is not the only criterion to consider in the making of resource allocations, however. Equity is another. "Equity implies a 'fair' distribution of income [and resources — Eds.] which depends in part on a 'fair' distribution of the costs and benefits of government programs among individuals." Economics of Urban Problems, *supra* at 35. These authors provide two general standards that further define equity:

> *Horizontal equity* requires that individuals in the same position or circumstances pay the same costs or receive the same benefits (equal treatment of equals). *Vertical equity* refers to how much of the total costs or benefits should be received by individuals in different positions or circumstances (unequal treatment of unequals).

Id.

The Rationale for Collective Action

Market failures in the control of externalties provide the justification for collective action to intervene in the market in order to adjust and correct these externalities. This market intervention, in turn, raises equity problems as governmental intervention in the allocation of resources usually redistributes these resources from one group of persons to another, with redistributive effects raising equity issues. In the following discussion of the rationale for collective action note that Professor Michelman treats both the efficiency and the equity issue. His analysis relates to the problem of when compensation should be paid for government intervention that has a redistributive effect on the allocation of land resources, a question that will be addressed in a later chapter. *See infra* Chapter 3.

MICHELMAN, PROPERTY, UTILITY, AND FAIRNESS: COMMENTS ON THE ETHICAL FOUNDATIONS OF "JUST COMPENSATION" LAW, 80 Harvard Law Review 1165, 1172-77, 1181-83 (1967)

I. The Purposes of Collective Action

The problem of defining the social purposes which justify governmental action arises both when government imposes a tax to finance public development and when government exercises its eminent domain or regulatory powers to override the market-expressed preferences of owners about the use of resources and thereby (through retrospective impact on investments already made and expectations already formed) gives rise to claims for compensation. . . .

What social purposes, then, are we looking for?

A prominent one, certainly, is "efficiency": augmentation of the gross social product where it has been determined that a change in the use of certain resources will increase the net pay-off of goods (however defined or perceived) to society "as a whole." . . .

[Professor Michelman then elaborates on the efficiency concept. — Eds.]

Note, please, that nothing has yet been asserted about the ethical rightness of social measures which are thus "efficient." Before proceeding to the ethical question it will be useful to dwell briefly on the reasons why collective action should ever be necessary to the attainment of efficiency as above defined. For if an efficient change in the use of resources benefits gainers more than it costs losers, it might seem that gainers could be relied upon to make offers (directly to losers or indirectly through third-party enterprisers) which would suffice to induce losers to quit their objections to the change and, if they are in the way, to step aside. Conversely, if an inefficient change is one which costs losers more than it benefits gainers, it might seem that losers could be relied upon to make offers to induce gainers to abandon their proposal even if the losers could not directly block it.

This reasoning overlooks the extreme difficulty of arranging human affairs in such a way that each person is both enabled and required to take account of all the costs, or all the missed opportunities for mutual benefit, entailed by his proposed course of action before he decides whether he will embark on it. In addition, it overlooks the extreme difficulty of concluding voluntary arrangements to take account of such costs, or to exploit such opportunities, even after they become evident — a difficulty which stems from inertia, the expense (in time and effort) of bargaining, and strategic concealment. . . .

. . .[A] government's regulatory activity may claim an efficiency justification. Consider an enactment requiring A to desist from operating a brickyard on land surrounded by other people's homes. The proposition implicit in the law (if we take efficiency to be its goal) is that A's neighbors stand to gain more from A's moving or altering his technology so as to reduce the nuisance than A or his customers would lose. It might, then, be argued that the measure is unnecessary because, if its premises are sound, we should expect the neighbors to offer A an acceptable sum in return for his agreement to cooperate. Conversely, the very fact that no such transaction has spontaneously evolved may be said to prove that A's operation, granting that the neighbors are sustaining some of its costs, is efficient. Apparently, it is worth more to A to continue than it would be worth to the neighbors collectively to have him stop. The argument, however, is imperfect. A sufficient criticism, for present purposes, is that the failure of the neighbors to make an offer may indicate, not that it would not be worthwhile for each of them to contribute some sum to a fund whose total would be acceptable to A in exchange for his moving, but only that they are unable to arrive (except by the expenditure of more time and effort than it would be worth) at a settlement with A, and among themselves, about what the total price should be and how the burden should be distributed. The situation will be complicated by the impulse of each neighbor to be secretive about his true preferences because he hopes that others will take up the whole burden, thereby yielding him a free benefit. And A, dealing with a group instead of with an individual, may turn more than usually cagey himself. There will, in addition, be side costs of drafting agreements, checking on their legality, and so forth.

Now, even if we are agreed that efficiency is an intelligible goal and one which may necessitate some governmental allocating, it remains to establish that efficiency is a "good thing." The possible objections to efficiency as a goal for government are not only that one cannot intelligibly compare the levels of satisfaction of different persons, but that even if one could, there is no ethical justification for enriching A at B's expense, no matter if A does (we think) gain more than B loses.

. . . Implicit in the notion of efficiency is an ethical premise which few would care to dispute: that a change in resource use which can improve the situations of some people without damaging the situations of any is desirable. This outcome — improvement for some accompanied by no damage to others — describes the effect after actual payment of those compensations which beneficiaries must be willing to pay, the losers must be willing to accept, if the measure is efficient under our definition. But the definition requires only hypothetical willingness to pay and accept; it does not require actual payment. Thus the result of an "efficient" change may be benefit to some at the expense of others, a result not so obviously appealing to ethical sensibilities. If, indeed, this result is ethically unacceptable, then the compensation issue is settled with respect to any measure claiming efficiency as its sole justification. Improvement is unambiguously present only when gross benefits are shared to the point where no net losses have been sustained; and compensation must, therefore, be paid.

It may well be asked, therefore, why a measure not actually accompanied by compensation should ever be deemed justified by a purely hypothetical capacity to produce benefits to some without damage to any. True, we might choose to view majoritarian collective action not as a succession of unrelated particular measures, each having an independently calculable distributional impact, but — more faithfully to the facts of political life — as an ongoing process of accommodation leaving in its wake a deposit of varied distributional impacts which significantly offset each other. On this view the benefit-sharing requirement would be converted into an insistence that collective activity be conducted in such a way that it can reasonably be expected that, when the effects of all measures are summed from time to time, no one will have been hurt while some will have benefited through the overall collective enterprise. . . .

[Professor Michelman's article should be consulted at this point for the qualifications he places on the previous statement. — Eds.]

But we cannot stand on the assumption that efficiency is the only goal. Few people any longer doubt that governments are properly engaged in controlling the distribution of wealth and income among members of society, as well as in controlling resource use so as to maximize the aggregate social product. It is, no doubt, intellectually most satisfying and productive to isolate the government's distribution function from its allocation function. One can then analyze public budgetary problems as if distributional decisions were always embodied in a "pure" form, such as a payment of "welfare" benefits, which both makes clear their distributional purposes and impacts and prevents distributional considerations from impairing the efficiency judgments which alone ought to govern decisions about resource use. But no one contends that such rigid compartmentalization is followed in practice or that most people would prefer to see it instituted. It is widely felt that redistribution "in kind," through a government program ostensibly concerned with decisions about what to produce rather than with how products should be distributed, is sometimes preferable because redistribution in this form puts less strain on the sensibilities of the parties affected and also, perhaps, because in this form redistribution can be combined with a little disguised paternalism. A public housing program, for example, surely makes its main appeal to the electorate through its redistributive and protective effects rather than through the idea that conversion of resources to this use is efficient.

. . . .

For the purposes of this essay I propose to rely on a proposition which will, I believe, command general and intuitive agreement. The proposition is that a designed redistribution by government action will surely be regarded as arbitrary unless it has a general and apparent "equalizing" tendency — unless its evident purpose is to redistribute from the better off to the worse off. Progressive income taxes and social welfare programs are, of course, excellent examples of such measures.

. . . .

. . . [M]easures such as the restriction on foundry operations in residential areas and the conversion of a neighborhood street into an arterial highway may be accompanied by accidental losses which, while not justified by any recognized distributional precept, are universally admitted to be noncompensable. It appears, then, that a redistribution which would have been unacceptable if undertaken for its own sake may be tolerated if it is the accidental consequence of a measure claiming the independent justification of efficiency. . . .

Comments: 1. Professor Michelman's article draws heavily on concepts of distributive justice formulated by Professor Rawls and subsequently published in book form, J. Rawls, A Theory of Justice (1971). For commentary see Flynn & Ruffingeo, Distributive Justice: Some Institutional Implications of Rawls' *A Theory of Justice,* 1975 Utah L. Rev. 123.

For additional analysis of the concepts discussed in Professor Michelman's article see D. Erwin & H. Stoevener, Land Use Controls: Evaluating Economic and Political Effects (1977); Comment, the General Welfare, Welfare Economics, and Zoning Variances, 38 S. Cal. L. Rev. 548 (1965). For a set of readings dealing with these problems see Economic Foundations of Property Law (B. Ackerman ed. 1975).

2. Not all commentators are universally enthusiastic about the ability of planning to deal in a satisfactory manner with market imperfections. *See, e.g.,* H. Van Gunsteren, The Quest for Control, ch. 1 (1976). In the following selection, Professor Tarlock places the generalized analysis offered by Professor Michelman in a planning context and offers a dissenting view on the planning process.

TARLOCK, CONSISTENCY WITH ADOPTED LAND USE PLANS AS A STANDARD OF REVIEW: THE CASE AGAINST, 9 Urban Law Annual 69, 75-80 (1975)

The legitimacy of a planning choice rests on the assertion that collective intervention produces a net gain in society's aggregate welfare. The planner's claim is that his or her proposal will promote the most efficient allocation of available resources. A planning choice would be readily perceived as legitimate if, by curing market imperfections, it achieved an allocation equivalent to that produced by a perfectly competitive market. Too often, however, the aggregate gains of a planning choice cannot be demonstrated. The planning choice is not designed to force internalization of external costs, which are difficult enough to quantify, but is based upon the assumption that the planner's re-distributive values are superior to those of the market and will result in a net gain to the aggregate welfare.

Planners assert that land use allocation is amenable to rational evaluation, that collective goals can be evaluated and welded into a single hierarchy of community objectives, and that planners can expertly resolve goal conflicts. The planner's choices derived from their overall perspective, however, risk being arbitrary since planners bear little responsibility for distribution of the costs or benefits of their activity. Furthermore, the choices are unlikely to rest upon a widespread consensus that would silence those adversely affected by short-term losses with the assurance of long-term efficiency gains. Thus the choices may be unacceptable to many members of the community because they appear unfair. The failure to consider the opportunity costs of the decision will make the planner's efficiency claims vulnerable to disproof.

. . . .

The planner's claimed ability to comprehensively analyze a city and make more accurate land use projections than those of the free market stems from the reform tradition of planning, which asserted the superiority of decision-making by neutral experts.

The basic concepts of master planning are that a city is a complex, dynamic system and that, if the welfare of all groups is to be advanced, the city's development must be coordinated in space and over time. The Standard State Zoning Enabling Act (SZEA) in large measure adopted the central idea of master planning, but the lawyers who developed the present structure for land use controls opted for a narrow theory of market intervention and hence a narrow theory of planning as well. Unfortunately, little systematic thought had been given to the relationship between planning and market intervention at the time land use controls became operational. By and large planners attempted only to achieve the objectives of free circulation, provision of adequate land for uses the community desired to encourage, and preservation of stable neighborhoods.

While the idea that planning was more than preservation of the status quo never truly died, it simply never became operational. During the 1930's, as planners became increasingly alienated from the market, the static theory of master planning as a fixed-end state objective was replaced by theories that emphasized planning as a "continuous process" that would shape and guide the physical growth and arrangement of towns in harmony with their social and economic needs.

. . . .

While goal formulation through the political process is assumed as a given, public officials too often refuse to set goals, thereby shifting the task to planners. Planners, as do all reformers, tend to minimize the importance of conflict, and they assume that consensus is possible without recognizing the deep value cleavages involved in many land use conflicts. Their biases, therefore, often lead to the selection of goals unacceptable to their client groups. And in addition to the problem of goal formulation, the high cost of obtaining information makes accurate projections either unavailable or available only at prohibitive cost.

Comments: The two selections that follow provide a perspective on planning which is more directly related to the comprehensive land use planning process as it is practiced at the local level. The first of these spells out in more detail the way in which the rational model of comprehensive planning is made operational in the planning process. The second continues Professor Tarlock's critique of planning but applies it to problems that arise in the planning process at the local level and also discusses several proposals for changing the nature of that process.

WHAT IS THIS THING CALLED PLANNING? BUREAU OF COMMUNITY PLANNING, UNIVERSITY OF ILLINOIS, Newsletter, Vol. 7, Nos. 1, 2, Fall-Winter 1966-67, at 5, 6

THE PLANNING PROCESS

The types of planning that are carried out in various organizations may be looked upon as falling into three categories. First, *functional planning,* which concerns itself with planning a small segment of a larger operation; next, *project planning,* which concerns itself with the formal direction of a team effort toward the execution of a particular project, which might be the building of a new school, a new highway, or a new type of air-craft; and *comprehensive planning.*

This latter includes the lower orders of planning, but exceeds them in scope, complexity, and significance. It represents a maximum attempt by man such as that needed to control all aspects of his environment, or to alter the future course of events over a significant area. It is characterized by an attempt to include not only the production of a physical entity, but also the formulation of goals and objectives, together with appropriate laws and regulations to implement the selected policy. In this type of planning, many considerations arise which are either not found, or are of less significance, in the lower orders of planning. These considerations include basic objectives, value judgments, and the general desires of those affected by the planning.

The three different forms of planning which have been mentioned, share a common methodology for their accomplishment, and parallels may be seen to the simple forms of planning which we carry out as private citizens. We usually refer to this as "the planning process," from which arises the cliché that you will hear very often if you talk to planners, namely that "planning is a process." In saying this, the planner wishes to emphasize the fact that planning is not undertaken as a single operation to produce a plan; but that this process of planning continues, thus automatically taking into consideration changing conditions and policies, leading to adjustments in the plan, which is thus always kept contemporary.

In order to plan for a community certain steps must be taken. Typically these will include:

(1) *A Survey and Analysis,* or a collection and review of basic data relating to the physical, economic, and social conditions in the area of jurisdiction. This is really a kind of stocking to ascertain the community's assets, and it may be augmented by a brief historical review to see how things came to be the way they are now.

(2) *A Projection* which indicates, based on present trends, the way in which the community is now moving. This will involve an estimate of the future population, the future economy, possible changes in land use, and other similar items. Basically, it involves an estimation of the aggregate effect on development which is likely as the result both of private decision making and the guidance imposed by public controls and policies on private and public development.

(3) *Development of Policies and Objectives* that the community wishes to achieve. These should form the rationale for the subsequent standards and proposals embodied in the plan. They should relate to such items as land use of all types, the economy, all aspects of transportation, and community facilities such as parks, playgrounds, schools, libraries, and utilities.

(4) *Plan Formulation.* This should involve an identification of alternative patterns and schemes for development and an examination of possible standards on which such development should be based.

(5) *Testing Alternative Plans and Policies* for physical, financial, and political feasibility, also for general desirability and effectiveness.

(6) *The Selection of the Plan* which seems to maximize the chosen goals, standards, and policies in regard to such items as future land

use, public facilities and buildings, streets and other transportation facilities, community facilities and utilities, and the reservation of strategic development sites.

(7) *Implementation of the Plan,* including a schedule for financial programming and execution, through a series of legal, financial, and administrative actions. . . .

REGIONAL AND LOCAL PLANNING

You will notice that in explaining the planning process the word "community" has been used several times in connection with the area for which the plan is being prepared. This term is often used to denote an area in which there is a recognizable common interest, and it may apply to a village, a city, a county, a region, or even a state, under certain given circumstances. . . .

Planning may be carried out for any of these areas, the process employed by the responsible agency in preparing the plan being basically similar in all cases and in accordance with the list which has been given. However, several aspects of the plan will vary according to the area for which the plan is being formulated.

––––––––––

R. J. BURBY, III, PLANNING AND POLITICS: TOWARD A MODEL OF PLANNING-RELATED POLICY OUTPUTS IN AMERICAN LOCAL GOVERNMENT 2-15, 1968 (University of North Carolina Environmental Policies and Urban Development Thesis Series No. 12)

[The author provides extensive textual citations to the existing literature. These have been edited, but for ease of reading the omissions have not been indicated. For a similar but less comprehensive discussion, using some of the same material, see American Law Institute, A Model Land Development Code 109-20 (1976). — Eds.]

Planning and Public Policy

Planning, most generally, can be defined as "deciding in advance what to do." Thus, planning involves choice and the allocation of values. In this broad sense, planning and political decision-making are highly interrelated — political decisions involve planning and governmental planning by its very nature is political. However, planning is generally endowed with an important characteristic which may or may not accompany political decisions. Because values are scarce as compared to wants, planning carries the further assumption that decisions must not only allocate values, but that they must be allocated rationally.

The rational model

Planning   seeks   to   achieve   rationality   by   developing   data concerning the consequences of political decisions. This focus implies a concern for events which may occur in the future, and thus, prediction. In planning three forms of prediction are generally utilized: forecasting, prediction, and conditional prediction. Most forecasts are based on the generalized, and often implied, predictor, "if past trends continue, then Y." Prediction is based on a more rigorous specification of predictor variables, while conditional prediction includes not only the rigorous specification of variables, but also the determination of which of these can be controlled by the decision maker.

In recent years a formal model of planning and public policy has developed based on the utilization of conditional prediction. Kaysen describes this model (which we will term the Rational planning model) as follows,

> The variables . . . are divided into two classes: (1) controlled variables or "instruments," the value of which the policymaker can determine directly within some constraints, and (2) uncontrolled variables, which can be influenced only indirectly through the policy-maker's choice of instrument variables. Some subset of all the variables are "the targets," whose values the policy-maker seeks to influence. It is assumed that he has the capacity to specify the relative desirability of alternate combinations of the target variables — i.e., that he has a "utility function" which can be inserted in the appropriate equations. The policy-maker's problem then becomes the choice of instrument variables that will result in the maximization of the utility function, subject to the constraints imposed by the system. . . . After he does so, the rest of the job belongs to the economists and econometricians, and in theory is a politically neutral one.

Although originally developed as a tool for the determination of economic policy, the Rational model has been diffused throughout the policy-oriented professions, including city planning.

In its most familiar form the Rational model sets forth a planning-policy process consisting of five interrelated steps. These are: (1) identifying and evaluating objectives, (2) translating objectives into design criteria, (3) utilizing design criteria to devise plans for the optimal development of specified systems or achievement of objectives, (4) evaluating the consequences of alternative planned courses of action, and (5) implementing the plan through appropriate public policies. . . .

Currents of change: critiques of the rational model

The Rational model of planning, though currently in vogue, has been subject to searching criticisms. The most pervasive of these has been that Rational planning is irrelevant to a pluralist political system and as a consequence is ineffective. Factors which contribute to this apparent ineffectiveness have been attributed to almost every aspect of the Rational model.

First, the Rational model requires that goals be clearly and unambiguously specified by policy-makers. This is the major task of the political system, but there is mounting evidence that participants in the political process are not likely to either specify social goals or limit their policy involvement to this level of abstraction. . . .

The second step in the Rational model specifies that goals be translated into design criteria (objectives). This aspect of the model has been subject to three related criticisms: (1) lack of attention to social as opposed to physical objectives; (2) lack of attention to substantive as opposed to functional rationality; and (3) lack of attention to policy coordination. The Rational planning submodel requires that goals be translated into quantitative objectives. Since physical objects and processes are infinitely easier to measure than social objects and processes, it is sometimes claimed that the Rational planner ignores the social aspects of program design. As Perloff suggests, objectives originally defined in physical terms have proven "difficult to 'translate' into meaningful social and human resource terms." This problem is reinforced by the tendency of planners to be "method" rather than "goal" oriented. Gans writes,

> . . . the planner concerns himself largely with improvement in methods. In this process, however, he loses sight of goals which his methods are intended to achieve, or problems they are to solve. Thus, he does not ask whether these methods achieve these goals, or whether they achieve any goals.

Thus, by focusing on proximate objectives which can be measured, the planner may well achieve functional rationality, but be substantively irrational since there is no way of knowing whether a course of action is consistent or inconsistent with "higher order" goals. Further, since the Rational planning method is most effective when objectives are clearly and narrowly defined, the Rational model may lead to partial planning of the kind where normative choices can be reduced to a minimum and "expert" solutions to problems can be determined. This, in turn, can be seen to strengthen planners who are responsible for various disparate governmental functions to the detriment of coordinated public policy.

The problems inherent in devising a plan to maximize objectives, the third step in the Rational model, have been widely discussed. For instance, Braybrooke and Lindblom claim that limited intellectual capacity, limited knowledge, limited funds for analysis, limited ability to construct complete rational deductive systems, interdependence between fact and value, the openness of analytic systems, and the diversity of forms in which problems actually arise all conspire against "synoptic" rationality. Lindblom has stated,

> One of the fundamental characteristic difficulties, which only recently the literature on policy making has begun to respect, lies in the contrast between the extraordinary complexity of a public policy decision and the capacity of any one man's mind. Even with electric computation at its disposal, the mind cannot cope with the size, the complexity, the intricacy, the subtlety of large problems of public policy. Problems simply run beyond our capacity . . . . It is only slowly coming to be recognized that one has to adapt any procedure for making decisions to this disproportion between capacity and problem complexity.

In recognition of these limitations, planning technicians tend to simplify the problem of devising courses of action to achieve even narrowly defined proximate objectives. Hitch and McKean write,

> . . . analyses must be piecemeal, since it is impossible for a single analysis to cover all problems of choice simultaneously in a large organization. Thus, comparisons of alternative courses of action always pertain to a part of the government's (or corporation's) problem. Other parts of the over-all problem are temporarily put aside, possible decisions about some matters being ignored, specific decisions about others being taken for granted. The resulting analyses are intended to provide assistance in finding optimal, or at least good, solutions to sub-problems: in the jargon of systems and operations research, they are sub-optimizations.
>
> . . . .

Concurrent with the development of a plan or alternative plans in the plan-making phase of the Rational model, the plan(s) must be evaluated as to their correspondence with design criteria (objectives). This involves conditional prediction. The alternatives which comprise the choice situation (controlled variables) become the "ifs" of predictive equations, and the probability of various consequences are determined. The problem of conditional prediction in planning, however, is more complex. Prediction is based on the observation (or assumption) that one object or event varies with another. Yet if planning is to predict the consequences of alternative political choices, it must further assume that the predicted relation is a causal one, that a given choice will produce (with a given probability of occurrence) certain consequences. This assumption requires that conditional prediction be accompanied by explanation. If it is safe to assume that any consequence has multiple causes rather than a single cause, then the problem of effecting conditional predictions is greatly exacerbated. The planner must not only be concerned with the effects of controlled variables (alternative choices or plans), but also uncontrolled variables which may also affect variations in decision consequences, either directly or through interaction with the controlled variable(s). As Lowry notes, "explicit predictions must still be made for other exogenous events, since these may reinforce or counteract the effects of the hypothetical change in X" (the alternative decision choices). The great number of exogenous factors which may impinge on the consequences of policy choices combined with our low level of understanding of social, economic, and political systems with which policy choices interact impose a serious constraint on the operation of this aspect of the Rational model.

The final phase of the Rational model consists of implementation of the plan or course of action which best achieves the stated objectives. However, deviation from any of the plan's specifications for public action will tend to upset the plan's internal consistency such that the extent that objectives will be obtained becomes indeterminate. Most empirical studies of public decision-making suggest that deviation from planned courses of action tends to be the rule rather than the exception. . . .

[Burby next discusses several attempts to adapt the rational model to complex environmental problems. — Eds.]

Coordinative planning, including variants generally known as the "informal coordinator catalyst" strategy, "policy planning" strategy, and "probabilistic programming" strategy, drops the assumption of political neutrality from the Rational model. Rather than designing a course of action to maximize objectives, the role of the planner is redefined to focus on achieving rational present as opposed to future behavior. In the case of the "coordinator catalyst" strategy, this is to be achieved through active participation in the policy-making process. The "policy planning" strategy seeks to institutionalize this role by elevating the planning function to a coordinate level with the chief executive, and instituting a policy planning process which, as described by Fagin, would,

> . . . express in one place the social, economic, physical and political policies intended to guide the evolution of the particular area of governmental jurisdiction. It would contain physical plans coordinating spatial relationships; schedules coordinating time relationships; and narrative texts and tables describing and coordinating proposed activity programs.

The "probabilistic programming" strategy is based on the assumption that increased knowledge will lead to increased rationality in both public and private decision-making. Thus, rather than devising an optimal course of action or actually participating in policy coordination, the planner would restrict himself to predicting the consequences of various alternative choices available to decision-makers.

Ameliorative planning, including "disjointed incrementalism" and "contingency planning," shares many of the characteristics of Coordinative approaches, but further limits the scope of planning. Attention is restricted to current problems (crises) and remedies which, though partial, promise to be immediately effective. In this respect the planner is viewed as a general "trouble shooter" attempting to mitigate problems as they arise rather than guiding the system to achieve specified ends.

A third emerging planning paradigm is Normative planning, including both "advocacy" planning and "innovative" planning. . . .

Comments: 1. Burby makes reference to "models." What is a "model," in the sense that it is used by Burby? "A model is an abstraction of realty. The purpose of a model is usually to predict the consequences of a real-world action, and its success in this regard depends upon the relevance of the abstraction."[1] Planners are most interested in urban development models, and especially in predictive models. They select several key variables, express mathematically and in quantitative terms a relationship among these variables, and are then able to predict future urban development patterns on the basis of information which is fed into the model, and whose analysis is handled by complicated computer programs. There are obvious weaknesses in the technique. One is that not all the important relationships can be quantified. Another is that the model can only test policy; it cannot generate policy.

2. Professor Lindblom's point of view, which is mentioned in the Burby selection, was first expressed in Lindblom, The Science of "Muddling Through," 19 Pub. Ad. Rev. 79 (1959). The Lindblom view is summarized in Hirschman & Lindblom, Economic Development, Research and Development, Policy Making: Some Converging Views, 7 Behavioral Sci. 211 (1962), from which the following excerpt is taken (pp. 215-16):

> A third converging line is represented in Lindblom's papers on policy-making processes. . . . These papers aspire to fairly large-scale generalizations or to what, in some usages, would be called theory construction. . . .
>
> Lindblom's point of departure is a denial of the general validity of two assumptions implicit in most of the literature on policy making. The first is that public policy problems can best be solved by attempting to understand them; the second is that there exists sufficient agreement to provide adequate criteria for choosing among possible alternative policies. Although the first is widely accepted — in many circles almost treated as a self-evident truth — it is often false. The second is more often questioned in contemporary social science; yet many of the most common

---

[1] D.B. Lee, Models and Techniques for Urban Planning 1-4 (1968) (AD 843 620). Lee's report is an excellent summary of the state-of-the-art. *See also* Lee, Requiem for Large-Scale Models, 30 J. Am. Inst. Planners 163 (1973).

prescriptions for rational problem solving follow only if it is true. ". . . [R]ational decision making . . . is not possible to the degree that clarification of objectives founders on social conflict, that required information is either not available or available only at prohibitive cost, or that the problem is simply too complex for man's finite intellectual capacities. Its complexity may stem from an impossibly large number of alternative policies and their possible repercussions from imponderables in the delineation of objectives even in the absence of social disagreement on them, from a supply of information too large to process in the mind, or from still other causes.

It does not logically follow, Lindblom argues, that when synoptic decision making is extremely difficult it should nevertheless be pursued as far as possible. And he consequently suggests that in many circumstances substantial departures from comprehensive understanding are both inevitable and on specific grounds desirable. For the most part, these departures are familiar; and his exposition of them serves therefore to formalize our perceptions of certain useful problem-solving strategies often mistakenly dismissed as aberrations in rational problem solving.

These strategies, which we shall call "disjointed incrementalism," are the following:

A. Attempt at understanding is limited to policies that differ only incrementally from existing policy.

B. Instead of simply adjusting means to ends, ends are chosen that are appropriate to available or nearly available means.

C. A relatively small number of means (alternative possible policies) is considered, as follows from A.

D. Instead of comparing alternative means or policies in the light of postulated ends or objectives, alternative ends or objectives are also compared in the light of postulated means or policies and their consequences.

E. Ends and means are chosen simultaneously; the choice of means does not follow the choice of ends.

F. Ends are indefinitely explored, reconsidered, discovered, rather than relatively fixed.

G. At any given analytical point ("point" refers to any one individual, group, agency, or institution), analysis and policy making are serial or successive; that is, problems are not "solved" but are repeatedly attacked.

H. Analysis and policy making are remedial; they move away from ills rather than toward known objectives.

I. At any one analytical point, the analysis of consequences is quite incomplete.

J. Analysis and policy making are socially fragmented; they go on at a very large number of separate points simultaneously.

The most striking characteristic of disjointed incrementalism is (as indicated in I) that no attempt at comprehensiveness is made; on the contrary, unquestionably important consequences of alternative policies are simply ignored at any given analytical or policy-making point. But Lindblom goes on to argue that through various specific types of partisan mutual adjustment among the large number of individuals and groups among which analysis and policy-making is fragmented (see J), what is ignored at one point in policy-making becomes central at another point. Hence, it will often be possible to find a tolerable level of rationality in decision making when the process is viewed as a whole in its social or political context, even if at each individual policy-making point or center analysis remains incomplete. Similarly, errors that would attend overly ambitious attempts at comprehensive understanding are often avoided by the remedial and incremental character of problem solving. And those not avoided can be mopped up or attended to as they appear, because analysis and policy-making are serial or successive (as in G).

While we cannot here review the entire argument, Lindblom tries to show how the specific characteristics of disjointed incrementalism, taken in conjunction with mechanisms for partisan mutual adjustment, meet each of the characteristic difficulties that beset synoptic policy-making: value conflicts, information inadequacies, and general complexity beyond man's intellectual capacities. His line of argument shows the influence of pluralist thinkers on political theory, but he departs from their interest in the control of power and rather focuses on the level of rationality required or appropriate for decision making.[2]

3. The specification of goals and objectives — what Burby calls a "utility function" — presents extremely difficult conceptual problems. The problem has been well stated by Professor Dyckman:

> [T]he traditional ideas of the physical planner are found, like those of an earlier economics, to be based on a culturally narrow definition of "efficiency." The segregation of traffic streams, the arrangement of residences to minimize journeys to work and to school, the hierarchical ordering of uses, and a dozen other favored city planning "principles" can be shown to have derived from a comparatively naive view of conventional least-cost efficiency. As notions of more sophisticated objectives — such as the elusive "welfare" criteria — diffuse through the planning profession, the need for richer, higher quality information becomes apparent to urban planners. Dyckman, The Scientific World of the City Planners, Am. Behavioral Scientist, No. 6, p. 46, at 47, Feb. 1963.

Frank Beal has put the problem another way:

> But, as soon as they assume the role of normative planners, that is, planners concerned about ends rather than means — then the stage is set for conflict. Thus, in the very area where planning could make a major contribution, that is, the normative, it is very likely to be politically unacceptable or else ineffectual. Planners must, therefore, make their peace with the public decision making process or forever remain as outsiders. In other words, planners must always keep in mind that the public interest has two distinct components which, only through their fusion, may achieve the greatest good for the greatest number. One of these components grows out of diversity and reflects the fact that we live in a pluralistic, complex democratic society: it is partial, it is short-range, it is opportunistic, and it expresses itself through the political process. The other component of the public interest

---

[2] *See also* C.E. Lindblom, The Intelligence of Democracy (1965).

grows out of an organic conception of communal interests: it takes the long-range view, it is systematic, and it brings to bear on present decisions a realistic assessment of the future. It is the component contributed by planners. The final decision that results from the combination of these two components is not likely to be satisfactory to anyone. It will always be a somewhat uneasy compromise between the forces of diversity and communality. Yet, in any particular instance, it may be said to represent the most concrete version of the public interest that is attainable. Seen in this light, subsequent programs will not be rational in a pure sense, but they may well be optimal in a loose way with respect to all the important interests at stake.

Beal, Defining the Public Interest in Metropolitan Areas, at 9, in Division of Planning of the Indiana Dep't of Commerce, Metropolitan Organization for Planning (1968).

An excellent review of these problems, with emphasis on the contribution to be made by economic analysis and welfare economics doctrine, may be found in Steiner, The Public Sector and the Public Interest, in U. S. Congress, Joint Economic Committee, 91st Cong., 1st Sess., The Analysis and Evaluation of Public Expenditures: The PPB System, at 13 (1969).

4. The classic analysis of the urban planning process, with special emphasis on its political implications, is contained in A. A. Altshuler, The City Planning Process (1965) (paperback edition available). Altshuler's analysis is based on several careful studies of the planning process in the Minneapolis-St. Paul metropolitan area. Altshuler deals explicitly with the problem of values and choice in the planning process. As he points out, "One might say that the planner needs coordinative power only because some specialists stupidly or obstinately refuse to cooperate with others in the interests of 'simple efficiency,' even though no significant values are threatened. The answer is that . . . cooperation and isolation in themselves have important effects on organizations.

> If an agency head claims that a measure advanced in the name of efficiency actually threatens important values . . . no outsider can refute him until he examines the bases of his arguments in detail. . . . In the end, no act of coordination is without its effect on other values than efficiency." [3]

Altshuler is also concerned with the ways in which urban planners and related planners define their expertise.[4] He notes that these professionals gains credibility by claiming a competence to make judgments on issues that are defined by a limited number of variables. Professionals are very careful in selecting the variables which limit their expertise, and the most successful tend to limit narrowly the variables over which they claim a concern. He gives as an example the highway engineer, who confines himself to decisions limited to optimizing traffic flows. In the process, other important variables, such as the impact of the highway on its environment, are slighted or ignored. Altshuler then suggests that the selection of the variables which are considered critical to judgment carries with it the selection of the values

---

[3] A.A. Altshuler, The City Planning Process 331-32 (1965).

[4] *Id.* ch. 6.

we are trying to implement. "In practical affairs, however, men easily slip into treating familiar variables as ultimate values." [5]

Altshuler also points out that the law contemplates a judicial decision-making process which does not claim legitimacy through selection of a limited number of variables and so is carried out under conditions in which goals are highly uncertain. The judicial process avoids the problems of goal selection by slipping around them, claiming its credibility on the basis of collective decision-making through a process of incremental change. Question: To what extent does the process of judicial decision-making fit Lindblom's model? Nevertheless, the statutory framework for urban planning, land use control, and related functions legitimizes several selected values as appropriate for consideration in public decision-making processes.

5. Burby, in his paper, makes reference to advocacy planning as one of the newer planning forms. Advocacy planning had its origins in the social programs of the late 1960's, and with the demise of these programs has somewhat gone into eclipse. For a good discussion see N. Fainstein & S. Fainstein, Urban Political Movements (1974). Nevertheless, advocacy planning has a role to play in the land use planning process as well. In its motivation to provide a power base for lower income and disadvantaged groups it has reflected the pluralist approach to planning, which is captured to some extent in Professor Tarlock's article.

More recently, the citizen participation movement in planning has gained a wider focus, as concern about citizen involvement in the planning process has moved beyond the earlier concentration on the needs and interests of lower income groups. In the next selection, Nelson Rosenbaum discusses the pressures that have led to increased citizen participation in planning, and then examines one of the more important issues to be faced in structuring citizen participation — the representative nature of that participation and the need to find some acceptable structure for articulating citizen interests.

N. ROSENBAUM, CITIZEN INVOLVEMENT IN LAND USE GOVERNANCE 2-4, 34-41 (1976)

THE SENSITIVITY OF LAND USE GOVERNANCE

Since the beginning of the postwar movement to bring governmental decision making under greater popular control, land use planning and regulation have been high on the agenda of reform. Indeed, the first federal program to incorporate a specific mandate for citizen involvement — the urban renewal program — dealt with land use planning. The reason is that land use decisions are extraordinarily sensitive, both in the scope and immediacy of their impact.

Perhaps of foremost importance, land use decisions directly affect the enjoyment of private property rights. The drafting of a comprehensive plan, approval of a zoning variance, or review of a

---

[5] *Id.* at 337.

subdivision plat usually involves thousands and often millions of dollars in increased or decreased property values. The sensitivity of these private economic effects is, of course, explicitly recognized in the American legal tradition, which requires compensation for extreme diminution of value under the "takings clause" of the federal and state constitutions.

. . . .

Second, land use decisions are sensitive because they influence many other aspects of a community's lifestyle — e.g., population composition, environmental quality, recreational opportunity, and fiscal stability. In the past ten to fifteen years, these community impacts have begun to receive as much attention as private economic impacts. This attention reflects two developments. First, there has been a marked upsurge in community commitment and organization in inner-city neighborhoods, stemming largely from federal programs of the 1950's and 1960's. Second, there has been a more recent shift in the mood of suburban communities — away from accepting unfettered entrepreneurialism and rapid development, toward concern about the costs of growth and the need to preserve open space as a vital community resource. As a result, land use decisions now generate wider controversy than would derive from private economic impacts alone.

The extreme sensitivity of land use governance has resulted in numerous instances of conflict and confrontation between citizens and government. Abetted by dramatic increases in the education and income levels of the American population and by extensive political experience gained in previous social movements, citizens display extraordinary levels of mobilization and organization on land use issues. Citizen groups have demonstrated again and again that, if not satisfied with decisions, they can impede, obstruct, and delay the execution of policy for extended periods of time.

This is not to justify or defend the tactics of all citizen groups. Governmental decision makers should not be intimidated by the prospect of citizen opposition and cannot attempt to appease all groups that have the potential to obstruct and delay. However, in an area involving both great sensitivity and a strong potential for public mobilization, it is pragmatic as well as theoretically desirable to maximize popular access and involvement, in the hope that delay and obstruction can be kept to a minimum.

Over the last five years, as the extent of governmental control over land use has dramatically expanded, the sensitivity of policy making has been increasingly recognized. Thus, citizen involvement mandates figure prominently in many legislative enactments.

At the federal level, the Coastal Zone Management Act of 1972 declares that it is national policy "to encourage the participation of the public" in the planning and execution of coastal land use management. Among recent state statutes, Oregon's well-known land use law (S.B. 100, 1973) calls for "widespread citizen involvement in all phases of the planning process." Florida's Growth Management Act (S.B. 53, 1975) requires that each city and county preparing a comprehensive plan "shall establish procedures for providing effective public participation in the comprehensive planning process."

On the county level, the official resolution establishing a new Planning and Land Use System (PLUS) in Fairfax County, Virginia, declares that officials must "assure citizen imput into every phase throughout the program." The resolution also requires that citizen imput "be highly integrated with the decision-making processes of the County Board."

. . . .

SELECTING ORGANIZATIONAL UNITS

How can citizen involvement programs be organized systematically over large areas, substantial populations, and long time spans? This question has challenged large cities for some time and is increasing in importance as counties, regions, and states assume expanded land use responsibilities. The core issue is whether affected citizens should be approached and involved directly as a collection of individuals or whether a citizen involvement program should be organized around representational units, such as subordinate governmental jurisdictions or voluntary interest organizations.

In terms of both efficiency and comprehensiveness, the latter strategy has much appeal. On the other hand, the quality of information transmitted through intervening units may be less complete and representative of citizen preferences than a program based upon direct contact. In addition, there is always the danger of encouraging and subsidizing the local parochialism so often found in land use conflicts. In short, this is another set of difficult issues requiring explicit resolution by elected officials rather than by administrative or planning staff. The following discussion will consider two aspects of the issue separately; first, governmental units and second, private organizations.

Subordinate Jurisdictions

Should citizen involvement in land use governance be screened and mediated by units of government smaller than the decision-making jurisdiction itself? The "default" response to this question is usually negative. Most planners and administrators assume that a citizen involvement program should be built around individual participation rights and direct contact with citizens. However, in the past few years there has been increased advocacy of such an intermediary and coordinating role for subordinate governmental units, particularly in the context of newly expanded regional and state land use programs.

In Massachusetts, for example, a 1975 statute established a state-wide growth policy planning process based explicitly on citizen involvement conducted through local governments. Local jurisdictions are encouraged to organize growth policy committees consisting of citizen representatives and public officials, through which the concerns and needs of local residents can be voiced to state planning officials. State growth policy will then be established by aggregating and synthesizing the contributions of the local organizing units.

This approach contracts sharply, for example, with the approach to citizen involvement in the development of State Planning Goals and Guidelines in Oregon. In that state, the Land Conservation and Development Commission relied exclusively on direct contact with thousands of individual Oregonians through public workshops held across the state.

On the municipal level, most jurisdictions continue to rely on direct contact between citizens and decision makers, but the use of subordinate organizational units has recently increased in large cities. . . .

[Rosenbaum then states three arguments for the use of subordinate jurisdictions in citizen participation: many observers believe that the neighborhood is the effective focus of the average citizen's emotional and intellectual concern; use of neighborhood governments or other jurisdictions assures a comprehensive participation program if all units within an area can be induced to participate; and the use of subordinate jurisdictions is efficient because these jurisdictions may already be engaging in some type of planning on their own. Efficiency is also achieved through this method because subordinate jurisdictions can extend their interests to planning without creating another organization that will drain off citizen time and effort. — Eds.]

Reliance on subordinate governmental jurisdictions as the organizational units of a citizen involvement program thus promises a number of advantages and benefits, both to the citizen participant and the superior jurisdiction. However, before authorizing such an approach to this vital element of program design, legislators and elected executives should carefully consider several serious pitfalls.

Perhaps the foremost problem is that reliance on subordinate jurisdictions may help to foster and perpetuate geographical and social parochialism. Official recognition of geographical distinctions as the basis of representation helps to legitimize a narrow focus on local impacts, to the exclusion of broader concerns and perspectives. Of course, there is no assurance that individual citizens will adopt a nonparochial view of land use issues either. Indeed, the experience of most citizen involvement programs indicates that educating the public to see the broader implications of land use decisions is one of the most difficult challenges of program implementation, no matter how the program is organized. However, since reliance on subordinate governmental units is likely to increase the challenge, there are grounds for serious concern about adopting this organizational approach.

A second problem with this approach is that it tends to perpetuate the sense of distance and distrust between citizens and decision makers of higher level jurisdictions. Unfamiliarity and the distrust it breeds are major difficulties, for example, in many new state land use programs. Through extensive direct contact with citizens, officials of large-scale jurisdictions can attempt to bridge the sense of distance. Relying on subordinate units to organize and transmit the results of citizen involvement does nothing to dissolve the "we-them" attitude and may indeed reinforce it.

A final caution relates to the quality of the information about citizen preferences transmitted through subordinate governmental units. The typical posture of subordinate units is to report only the compromise or consensus position of citizen participants. Thus, the richness of input provided by contact with individual citizens is often lost. The dissenting view, the expert opinion, the personal experience may be subordinated within the overall preference pattern reported by subordinate units.

. . . .

Private, Voluntary Associations

Should a citizen involvement program be organized around and accord special standing to private interest groups? Whatever the design decisions reached on jurisdictional residence, on outreach to inactive citizens, and on the use of subordinate jurisdictions, legislators and elected executives must eventually face the independent issue of exactly what role private associations will play.

A focus on established private groups is perhaps the predictable design choice. These organizations are ubiquitous and politically powerful. They typically make extravagant representational claims and loudly demand special recognition and status. However, there are also numerous reasons for caution in organizing an involvement program around such groups.

In the area of land use planning and regulation, two types of groups have been the most insistent and aggressive in demanding special organizational standing and prerogatives: first, associations of businesspeople, developers, farmers, and other large landowners who have a direct economic stake in the general pattern of land use in a community; and second, associations of residential property owners, usually organized in neighborhood civic groups or betterment organizations, who have a direct economic stake in the specific pattern of land use in their immediate vicinity.

These groups are often joined in demands for special recognition by narrower special-interest groups such as conservation and environmental associations, sportsmen's clubs, and good government organizations, based on their members' ideological, social, or recreational interests.

Jurisdictions have conferred special prerogatives and organizational standing on such private, voluntary associations in a variety of ways. One of the simplest, most common approaches is reserving a special place on advisory committees for representatives of particular groups. Another approach is providing private groups with privileged intervenor status in land use regulatory proceedings. For example, the Model Land Development Code of the American Law Institute (A.L.I.) automatically provides interested-party status in administrative hearings to neighborhood civic organizations meeting certain standards of size and representation. [*See* Code § 2-304. — Eds.] All individual citizens, on the other hand, must convince the hearing officer that they have a "significant interest" in the subject matter before being granted official standing in the proceedings.

Some jurisdictions have gone beyond these simple procedural arrangements to accord a more systematic organizational role to private associations. In Portland, Oregon, for example, the entire land use planning and regulatory process is based on a network of private neighborhood civic organizations coordinated by the city's Office of Neighborhood Associations. These organizations have primary responsibility for soliciting and transmitting citizen input on a wide variety of planning and regulatory matters. In San Diego, the city government delegates official land use planning responsibility to selected neighborhood organizations that fulfill certain criteria of open membership and structure. Similarly, some jurisdictions help subsidize the production of "alternative plans" by private voluntary associations. These plans serve as principal background documents in the development of official plans and policies.

The attractions of organizing a citizen involvement program around the private, voluntary associations are clear and straightforward. First, the leaders and active members of such associations are typically highly knowledgeable and sophisticated about land use planning and regulation. Even in opposition, they are easier and more comfortable to deal with than the less articulate and interested citizens. These individuals speak the same jargon as decision makers, read the same publications and research studies, and can be relied upon to be "responsible" in presenting and defending a position.

Second, if one accepts the typical broad claims of representation at face value, reliance on such organizations provides an efficient and convenient means of consulting with large groups of concerned citizens at relatively low cost.

Third, since these groups have the greatest potential for effective obstruction and delay of decision making, there is a natural inclination to take the views of their leaders most seriously and to try to accommodate them whenever possible.

Finally, of course, the essence of the matter is that these groups exist as tangible manifestations of interest and concern about land use matters. It is easier to accept and recognize this voluntary activity as deserving special recognition than to challenge and deny it. Without such organizations, planners and administrators would be thrown back completely on their own conceptions in identifying and consulting with the affected public. Certainly, special recognition of such voluntary organizations does not eliminate the need to consider the interests of inactive and unorganized citizens who may be affected by a decision. However, that recognition does provide a firm base from which to explore unfamiliar territory.

Despite the manifest attractions of reliance on private associations as organizational units, there has been growing skepticism and criticism recently about the dominance of such groups in citizen involvement programs. Perhaps the foremost criticism concerns the representational claims of such groups. Private, voluntary organizations are notoriously hazy about the size of their membership, attendance at meetings, percentage of active compared to passive participants, and similar matters. In addition, numerous critics and observers have questioned the extent of internal democracy within such organizations. Leadership tends to be perpetuated by a small group of activists who dominate association operations. Thus, there is often a valid question about whom the leadership of these association[s] represents.

A second problem with reliance on private, voluntary associations is that they tend to operate by consensus. Of course, the presentation of a united front is understandable since this is the way to maximize political influence. However, the presentation of consensual positions does raise serious questions about the quality of information reaching decision makers. The heart of a citizen involvement program is a free, open, and lively debate about options and alternatives. To the extent that voluntary organizations fail to report significant dissenting opinions and personal views, the richness of the debate is lost.

If a citizen involvement program is to be organized around private, voluntary associations, some effort should be made to address these problems. Perhaps the most common approach is requiring private organizations that are granted special status to conform to certain standards of open membership and procedural fairness, as in

Portland, Oregon, and San Diego, California. These efforts, however, have aroused considerable opposition from the citizen organizations, particularly the neighborhood groups, which resent intrusion upon what they consider to be their own organizational prerogatives. Despite such opposition, legislators and elected executives must insist upon establishing and enforcing appropriate standards. Special prerogatives and organizational status are privileges, not rights. The alternative of consulting directly with active and interested citizens is always available.

Comments: 1. Rosenbaum makes reference to the citizen participation requirement in the planning program in Fairfax County, Virginia, a fast growing suburb in the Washington, D.C., metropolitan area. This planning program, which in the mid-1970's attempted an extensive growth management system, relied heavily on citizen input to help formulate planning goals. The story of this planning effort, including the citizen participation element, has now been brilliantly told in G. Dawson, No Little Plans (1977).

To assist in the development of the plan, the county planners set up a series of citizen groups for each of the areas of the county for which detailed area plans were drawn as a complement to the more generalized county plan. This method of organization appears to fit Rosenbaum's first citizen participation mode, although the citizen groups were organized specially for purposes of providing input into the planning program. They did not represent either a previously organized neighborhood constituency or a previously organized private group.

Chapter 6 of Dawson's book details the frustrations and difficulties of citizen participation in the Fairfax County planning process, and her conclusions on the impact of citizen participation on the Fairfax County plan provide an interesting footnote to Rosenbaum's more generalized observations:

> Ironically, the considerable citizen involvement was the major factor in the county's failure to channel growth. Where the individual supervisors took strong mediating roles with the planning staff on behalf of active citizens, citizen preferences had a major impact on the program and in particular upon the specific content of the Area Plans. This impact ranged from large-scale considerations, such as the desire of residents near proposed fixed-rail transit stations to prohibit high-intensity land uses in their neighborhoods, to parcel-specific requests that certain pieces of land be zoned for single-family development on one-acre rather than half-acre lots. When the demands of the active citizen groups were backed up by the individual supervisors or planning commissioners, the planners most often acquiesced to these demands. In areas where either citizen preferences were not so strongly expressed or the individual supervisor or planning commissioner chose to take a broader view of the county's problems, the impact of the organized citizenry was less obvious. On balance, however, cases in which citizens played a major role in modifying many of the staff recommendations were the rule rather than the exception.

As Ken Doggett, one of the area planners, aptly put it, "We began by sketching basically status quo plans — plans that did not call for idealistic or radical changes in the existing land-use patterns in the county — because we were aware of the strong desire of the citizens for the status quo. These initial plans further reinforced the status quo as a result of detailed citizen revisions. We didn't lose on every issue — there were some fairly innovative ideas, at least from a planning perspective, that survived the citizen review process — but by and large, the plans that were finally adopted very closely reflected the desires of the bulk of the citizenry who took part in the program."

Id. at 110-11. For an extensive bibliography on citizen participation in planning see J. Hulchanski, Citizen Participation in Urban and Regional Planning (Council of Planning Librarians Exchange Bibliography No. 1297, 1977).

2. Before we turn to a more detailed analysis of the comprehensive plan, consider the following judicial definitions of the planning process. What theory of planning do they adopt?

Municipal planning is designed to promote, with the greatest efficiency and economy, the coordinated development of the municipality and the general welfare and prosperity of its people.... Its aim is to secure the uniform and harmonious growth of villages, towns and cities.... Zoning is concerned primarily with the use of property.

Kiska v. Skrensky, 138 A.2d 523, 525 (Conn. 1958).

By its very nature and purpose, realistic municipal "planning" is and must be comprehensive, flexible, and prospective, for it attempts to anticipate the future destiny as well as project protection for the existing social, civic, physical, and economic values of the particular municipal area involved. Logically, it must be susceptible of timely and continuing re-evaluation and potential alteration if it is to keep in step with unforeseen or changing municipal circumstances, conditions and mores.

Shelton v. City of Bellevue, 435 P.2d 949, 953 (Wash. 1968).

The almost universal statutory requirement [is] that zoning conform to a "well-considered plan" or "comprehensive plan." ... The thought behind the requirement is that consideration must be given to the needs of the community as a whole. In exercising their zoning powers, the local authorities must act for the benefit of the community as a whole following a calm and deliberate consideration of the alternatives, and not because of the whims of either an articulate minority or even majority of the community.

Udell v. Haas, 235 N.E.2d 897, 900 (N.Y. 1968).

A FOOTNOTE ON THE HISTORY OF THE PLANNING MOVEMENT IN AMERICA

Of interest to an understanding of the planning process is the history of the planning movement in America. What is now known as comprehensive land-use planning finds its origins in three rather disparate developments which occurred about the turn of the twentieth century:

(1) The city beautiful movement, spurred in part by the Columbian Exposition in Chicago in 1893, and which concentrated on the aesthetic side of the urban environment.

(2) The city functional movement, which attracted the city engineer, and which concentrated on the provision of the basic transportation and utility facilities which were demanded by the ever-growing urban centers.

(3) The social reform movement, which concentrated primarily on poverty and housing slums, and which sought explicitly to remedy the deficiencies of bad housing conditions.

The history of American planning is the history of the failure to articulate and coordinate these movements in any systematic way; this historic failure is reflected in the writings that have appeared in this chapter. What is apparent is that the city functionalists won an early victory, helped in part by the lack of success of the aesthetes and by the disinterest in reform programs which was characteristic of America after the First World War. City planning in America has been dominated by the functionalist school, especially as the nurturing of the housing reform movement was left to the social work profession into and through the 1930's. These diverse origins of American land-use planning make themselves evident in the materials that follow. For discussion see Johnston, *A Preface to the Institute,* 31 J. Am. Inst. of Planners 198 (1965).

B. THE COMPREHENSIVE PLAN

The end result of the planning process, and the document that provides a guide to the exercise of land use controls in local communities, is known variously as the general, master, or comprehensive plan. The following excerpt describes what goes into the comprehensive plan. It should be read again after reviewing the statutory requirements for a comprehensive plan that are reproduced *infra* p. 72.

G. ISBERG, LOCAL AND REGIONAL PLANNING IN MINNESOTA 21-22, 29-30, 32 (1975)

[The following excerpts describe the comprehensive planning process in Minnesota, which is typical of most states. — Eds.]

ELEMENTS OF A STANDARD COMPREHENSIVE PLAN

. . . .

1. Survey and analysis

Since local communities differ substantially in population characteristics, size, natural features, degree of urbanization, etc., it is necessary to gather background data about the community in order to determine the major development problems as well as opportunities for improvements in the community. This information in turn will assist the community in developing goals, policies, and programs for the future development of the community. Usually, the survey and analysis will deal with the following elements:

Population. Analysis of past and future projected population growth, population characteristics, such as age, sex, etc.

Economy. Analysis of past and future projected economic growth, including the types of industry and commercial enterprises, income, and employment.

Physical and natural resources. Analysis and inventory of soils, topography, geology, woodland and other vegetation, lakes, rivers, and wetlands.

Land use. Analysis and location of the various types of land uses such as residential, commercial, industrial, institutional (fire halls, village halls, police stations), and parks and playgrounds.

Existing public utilities. Analysis and inventory of existing public utilities such as sanitary sewer systems, water systems, gas and oil pipelines, electric transmission lines.

Circulation system. Analysis and inventory of existing highways and public transportation systems.

The survey and analysis stage deals not only with gathering of various background data about the community, but also with an analysis of any problems or deficiencies in the existing system which need to be corrected or assets and opportunities which the community should build upon.

2. Goals and policy formulation

Perhaps the most important, yet most difficult, stage of the comprehensive planning process is to establish the goals and policies for future development or redevelopment of a community or region. This will be determined in part by the findings in the survey and analysis stage which should point out the major problems and/or opportunities for future development or redevelopment in the community.

Basically, the goals should consist of relatively broad objectives for future development of the community and should reflect the aims and desires of its citizens. It is imperative that imaginative approaches be established for stimulating citizen input at this stage, if the final plan is to have any legitimacy. This can be done in a variety of ways such as through questionnaires, interviews, and public hearings. The goals, however, should not merely consist of "motherhood" or "apple pie" statements, but rather should be sufficiently specific so as to lead to future policies and action programs.

Perhaps one of the most basic goals to be established at the outset relates to the community's over-all future growth and development. A number of different approaches are possible. For example, a community may adopt an open growth policy whereby growth is actively encouraged in all parts of the community. On the other hand, a community might adopt a zero growth policy and attempt to discourage all development. A middle ground which is becoming more popular is to adopt a "staged growth" policy whereby public utilities such as highways and sanitary sewers are staged according to a capital improvements program; in this way, growth in the community is also staged.

Once the basic determination is made, goals are usually developed for the different land use categories such as housing goals, industrial goals, commercial goals, open space goals, transportation goals. In addition, goals may be formulated for reaching various social objectives such as low income housing goals, for example.

3. Comprehensive plan development

After the major goals and objectives have been established for the community, the policies and programs are developed. In the past, the comprehensive plan usually consisted of a rather rigid and inflexible master plan which indicated specific land uses throughout the community in an "end-use" plan with the community fully developed. In most cases, this end-use plan would not be realized until some distant time in the future. . . . [T]his is increasingly giving way to policy planning and staged growth planning which are much more flexible. Under the policy planning approach, policies are developed for various functional areas such as housing policies, open space policies, etc., with various alternative methods available for implementing the policies. Under the staged growth approach to planning, growth is usually encouraged in certain portions of a community and discouraged in other areas, staging the growth to coincide with utility extensions (sewers and highways). This method leaves a maximum amount of flexibility for the location of future growth. Another approach used in some communities is to develop a comprehensive plan from a series of neighborhood sub-area plans. These neighborhood plans usually involve the clustering of housing around such neighborhood facilities as parks, schools or commercial shopping facilities.

The following are the major components of a comprehensive plan for a community:

> **.A land use plan** which designates the existing and proposed location and intensity of urbanization (residential, commercial, industrial and institutional uses), agriculture, conservation (woodlands, wetlands, slopes, flood plains, shorelands) and mineral extraction.
>
> **.A public facilities plan** which indicates the location, timing

and capacity of existing and future public facilities. This element of the plan usually includes:

   a. **A sewer system** plan including the location of such facilities as sanitary sewer treatment plants, sewer interceptors, storm sewer system including natural drainage ways and wetlands.

   b. **A water supply system** plan including such facilities as water holding tanks, water supply lines, and others.

.A thoroughfare plan which indicates the location, timing and capacity of existing and proposed future streets and highways, public transit facilities and pedestrian ways.

.A parks and open space plan which indicates the location, timing and capacity of existing and proposed recreation parks, protection open space area (natural resource areas), recreational trail systems, and other related features.

. . . .

4. Adopting the comprehensive plan

. . . .

Public hearing. Before the plan is adopted, the planning agency must hold at least one public hearing on the proposed plan. A notice of the time, place and purpose of the public hearing must be published in the legal newspaper at least 10 days prior to holding of the hearing. The proposed plan must be submitted to the governing body prior to the time the notice of hearing is published. . . .

The main purposes of the public hearing are to discuss the proposed plan with the public and to give the citizens an opportunity to comment on the plan before it is adopted. The public hearing should be conducted by the planning commission or planning department, and care should be used to explain the history and background of the planning program and a summary of what is being proposed in the comprehensive plan.

. . . .

Adoption by planning commission. After the public hearing and regional review, the planning commission, after making appropriate changes as a result of the public hearing, should adopt the comprehensive plan by resolution and submit it to the governing body.

Adoption by the governing body. After adoption by the planning commission, the plan should be submitted to the governing body. The plan has no effect and is purely advisory until the governing body adopts the plan.

The governing body may amend any parts of the plan prior to adoption. The governing body should then by resolution adopt the comprehensive plan.

5. Plan implementation

The plan implementation stage is one of the most important parts of the planning process; even so, it has been the most neglected in the past. For example, most comprehensive planning reports will devote but a few pages in the back of a report to a discussion of implementation devices and strategies and usually in a very perfunctory manner, even though without a proper implementation program, the comprehensive plan will be for nought.

The plan implementation section of the comprehensive plan should discuss the various devices available, such as zoning ordinances, subdivision regulations, the official map, tax devices, utility extension policies and programs, land acquisition of full or partial rights (easements) and the strengths and legal limitations of these tools. It should set forth an implementation strategy and program that has been carefully thought out. In some communities only a few of the various tools are appropriate, whereas in other communities the full range of tools may be necessary to guide development.

6. Updating the comprehensive plan

The initial development and adoption of a comprehensive plan is only the beginning of the total planning process. Due to the rapid changes in today's society, planning should be considered as an on-going process rather than as a "one-shot" affair. This means that the comprehensive plan needs to be re-evaluated and updated on a periodic basis.

. . . .

7. Capital improvements program

The final outcome of a properly conducted planning program should be a capital improvements program.

Capital improvements are those projects which require the expenditure of public funds for the acquisition, construction or replacement of the various types of public buildings such as police and fire halls, schools, and city halls; roads and highways; water and sewer facilities, parks and open space, and public trails.

A capital improvements program is a listing of proposed public projects according to some schedule of priorities over the next few years, which usually amounts to a five- or six-year period. Perhaps the most difficult part of this program is to establish the priorities among the many competing programs. The method used by many communities is to establish the priorities on the basis of serving public safety and health; that is, to give priority to those items that deal directly with public safety and health such as police and fire protection or sanitary sewer facilities. A lower priority is given to those projects which either are expendable or can be delayed for a year or more. . . .

The Capital Improvements Budget is a list of the projects and expenditures by priorities for the capital improvements for the next fiscal year, which is the first year of the six-year capital improvements program. Again, this budget should be established by some system of priorities, which in turn will determine the expenditure for each item.

A capital improvements program is one of the natural outgrowths of a comprehensive planning program. Goals, policies and programs established in the comprehensive plan should serve as the basis for a capital improvements program, and such a program should be used along with the other implementation devices (zoning, subdivision regulations, etc.) as a means to implement the comprehensive plan. This tie-in of scheduled capital improvements with the plan is the very reason that some elected officials are opposed to comprehensive planning. By establishing a system of priorities or scheduling of public projects, it removes their prerogatives of obtaining a public project in their district for political reasons prior to election time.

Capital improvements program as a method of staging growth and development. Capital improvements such as highways, parks, and sewer and water facilities can have a substantial effect on land values and urban growth and development. In the past, these capital improvements programs were usually provided in response to a need resulting from development taking place in an area. Recently, planners and other urban specialists have advocated that the capital improvements be constructed and phased in such a way as to purposely influence the location and timing of development. . . .

Comments: As Mr. Isberg briefly noted, planning that results in a fixed "end-use" or "end-state" plan is giving away in some areas to a more open and flexible policies plan which does not always contain mapped land use designations. This shift has tremendous consequences for the plan implementation process, as policy plan guidelines are less specific and provide less guidance for implementing the plan through zoning ordinances and the like.

Professor Gans has indicated how the policy planning process might work:

> The . . . task is the development, literally of national [or state or local — Eds.] *policy catalogs,* describing in detail the effective policies for a large number of specific goals — of various political shadings — in all the substantive areas, together with their costs and other consequences. . . . [E]ach policy catalog would deal with one substantive area, listing the activities and resources needed to achieve every conceivable goal, innovative and conventional, radical and conservative, and the like, for that area. Once developed, these catalogs will constitute the basic technical contribution to the planning process, . . . and the individual professional will plan by adapting these policies to the distinctive situation in which he is operating.

Gans, From Urbanism to Policy-Planning, 36 J. Am. Inst. Planners 223, 224 (1970).

Gans was talking about policies for a wide variety of social and economic as well as physical problems, but the technique can be adapted to land use planning. Consider the following summary of a policies plan for King County (Seattle), Washington.

BEAL, DEFINING DEVELOPMENT OBJECTIVES IN PRINCIPLES AND PRACTICE OF URBAN PLANNING 327, 342-43 (W. Goodman & E. Freund Eds. 1968)

. . . .

King County, Washington. The Comprehensive Plan for King County, Washington, published in 1964, consists of two parts: "Plan Policies" and "Plan Map." The general philosophy of the plan is described below:

> Because King County is now more than three-quarters undeveloped, and is rapidly converting its vacant land to urban uses, it is impossible to determine in advance the locations of all land uses. Therefore, the conventional method of attempting to show everything in detailed map form has been replaced by a 'development policy' approach to the Comprehensive Plan. These development policies have been carefully determined and interrelated in order to translate the Regional Goals and the Urban Center Development Concept into generalized mapped proposals. They, furthermore, provide a guide for short-range decisions, specific recommendations, and detailed regulations.
>
> The use of policy statements will encourage consistency in administrative actions and development control. Their use will promote efficiency in handling frequently encountered problems in that the groundwork for making the decisions will already have been laid. Each time the same or similar situation arises, the agency will not be required to start at the very beginning in its deliberations. Moreover, the policy statements provide a framework for the Comprehensive Plan [map], clarify the objectives of various implementing measures, and provide a source for public reference. The development policy statements contained in this Comprehensive Plan are not to be considered as legal controls in themselves, but as a guide to be applied to local conditions.

The plan contains five general development goals and a "development concept." The development concept is presented diagrammatically as an area with a strong central core, outlying sub-centers, moderate densities, and intervening open spaces. The bulk of the plan is a series of literally hundreds of physical development policies which have been divided into several major categories: transportation, business, industrial, residential, open spaces, public buildings, and utilities. The policies are inserted throughout the text of the report which provides background information and the rationale behind each of the policies.

To illustrate the range and character of these policy statements, six of the 39 residential area policies are reproduced below:

Residential areas should be encouraged to develop primarily in the plateau and gentle slope areas rather than in river valleys.

Residential areas shall have varying densities dependent upon the type of development, location, and degree of improvements.

A maximum density of three housing units per gross acre shall be employed in rural tracts adjoining stream, lake, or saltwater frontage.

Areas where the allowed average residential density is three housing units per gross acre or greater should include the following minimum improvements:

a. paved streets, curbs, and sidewalks;

b. street lighting;

c. underground drainage lines except where surface storm drainage facilities are deemed adequate;

d. publicly approved water supply (normally publicly owned); and

e. sanitary sewers or suitable alternatives on temporary basis only.

The street system should be laid out with a minimum number of connections with major arterials. In general, intersections on the major arterials should not be closer than 1,000 feet.

Multi-family residential areas shall always be located functionally convenient to a major or secondary arterial highway. Adequate arterial and collector streets should exist prior to or be developed concurrently with the establishment of such uses.

Comments: 1. For an evaluation of how the King County plan was implemented through the use of the zoning amendment process to provide for apartment uses see D. Mandelker, The Zoning Dilemma, ch. IV (1971).

2. At this point it is well to balance Beal's description of the King County policy plan with an account of political and professional reaction to policy planning at the state level in Hawaii. While focused on the state planning process, the reaction to policy planning in Hawaii could also apply to similar planning at the local level. Hawaii eventually adopted a revised state planning act that calls for the more conventional type of planning at the state level. Hawaii Rev. Stat. § 221-21 (1977).

CATANESE, PLAN? OR PROCESS?, in Planning, June 1974 at 14

Almost nothing in the recent planning literature advocates the master plan as the most important tool in planning. Most current literature focuses on planning as a continuing process of providing recommendations to decision makers. But the old conflict of plan vs. process has reemerged. . . . The primary advocates of restoration of the master plan concept in more binding form are a loose coalition of environmentalists, conservationists, some planners who seem to be involved primarily in design and physical planning, and some politicians who sense a good issue to use against incumbent administrations and their planners. Those in opposition to mandatory master plans and binding legislative directives tend to be politicians (usually those in office and in the majority party) and some planners and administrators involved primarily in policy and management aspects of the planning process.

All of this controversy could be found encapsulated in recent legislative hearings in Hawaii. Three House committees have been holding joint hearings this session on a state planning bill. The bill proposes that the 1957 legislation establishing the Department of Planning and Economic Development be amended to permit the DPED to undertake an eight-part planning process. The bill would provide for: (1) authority for the DPED to establish a framework for planning that goes beyond the historical master plan concept; (2) coordination of functional planning in the Department of Planning and Economic Development; (3) review of capital expenditures by the DPED; (4) administration of federal funds and programs by the DPED; (5) technical assistance by the DPED to other state and county agencies and citizen groups; (6) the establishment of a data and information function as a permanent part of the DPED program; (7) an applied research program; and (8) various educational programs in support of planning.

This bill can hardly be called radical. . . .

But the bill encountered considerable opposition at the joint committee hearings. While some of the opposition was undoubtedly political and directed toward specific personalities, the more substantive criticisms were launched against the very section of the bill that gave flexibility in determining the general plan requirement. The opposition argued that a general plan was absolutely necessary so as to bind the government to a fixed set of policies with built-in rules, making diversions very difficult. The opposition argued not only for a definitive master plan concept, but for legal structures to force adherence to the plan. In fact, one coalition of opponents submitted its own version of a state planning bill which essentially would reorganize the state planning function and make the formulation of a statewide comprehensive policy plan the basic function of the reorganized state planning office. This plan would serve as a pinnacle of a "hierarchy of plans" and would be binding on lower-level plans through adoption by the legislature. In other words, this bill would create a super master plan to serve as binding policy for all state departmental plans as well as all local plans. The plans of state agencies and local governments would be evaluated annually to insure compliance with the super master plan, and the legislative auditor would have review powers over these evaluative factors.

The opposition bill was drafted by a coalition of environmentalists, conservationists, community groups, architects, and some planners assembled through the efforts of the Hawaii Republican party, although great pains were taken to insure that the bill had a bipartisan outlook. The coalition was generally unsympathetic toward recent planning theory which holds that planning should be a part of the decision-making process through advisory roles and conflict resolution. Instead, the coalition believed that planning should "have teeth," to repeat an overused phrase, including mandatory master planning and legislative institutionalization of the plan. . . .

More Than a Shouting Match

The issues that emerged during the testimony involved more than the usual, predictable, shouting matches between the environmental crazies and the intellectual planners. The testimony was more reminiscent of a journal debate. Many of the witnesses showed surprising familiarity with professional planning theory and practice. Several witnesses expressed grave concern and discouragement at the inability of planners to implement proposals. The most significant issue, however, was the master plan (backed by legislation) vs. the process-oriented approach.

The witnesses backing the administration bill discussed the emergence of planning as a process and its role in decision making. They carefully traced the political, technical, and participatory aspects of this evolution. . . .

The public interest groups, notably the League of Women Voters, expressed opposition to the administration bill because it did not specifically require the DPED to produce a document. The League's witness argued that citizens have a right to know exactly what a public agency is doing and who is doing what in that agency. The proof, she reasoned, must take the form of a documentlike plan. She then argued that the DPED should have a detailed and specific list of tasks to perform under law and should be held accountable if those tasks are not performed. The paramount task would be the formulation of a statewide plan for growth control and development policy. The League also wanted the law to require the legislature to adopt the plan so as to make it "official public policy." . . .

As the testimony of civic and environmental groups continued through the hearings, the pattern was clearly established. These groups did not believe that a process of planning at the state level would be adequate to insure that their interests would receive proper attention. They certainly did not trust professional planners. One group argued, for example, that population control would be ignored unless it was a mandatory provision of the master plan. Another group argued that limits on tourism could be invoked only if the legislature made them a required element of the master plan. Clearly these groups were arguing that the legislature must insist upon a document with a specific list of essential components because the professional planners would not tackle the controversial issues unless they were forced into it.

The most damaging testimony against the administration's process-oriented bill in favor of the master plan concept was made by other professional planners. The county planning directors all expressed cautious support for a statewide master plan on the ground that such a document "would let us know what the state is going to do in our county" and thereby allow for better planning. They expressed mild disapproval of the administration bill on the ground that a process approach would not necessarily assure state cooperation with local planning agencies. The local chapter of the American Institute of Planners did not take an official position; but its legislative committee chairman spoke in favor of the master plan approach, arguing that only this would enable a specific set of policies to be established at the state level. Thus professional planners were debating one another about whether or not the master plan was the paramount tool of planning, and they offered contradictory interpretations of the evolution of planning thought and practice. This was very damaging, because it showed that planners themselves tend to be of different minds regarding the value of a master plan. Yet those in favor of the master plan made laudatory claims for its potency that politicians knew from experience to be dubious. The process-oriented planners had difficulty convincing the legislators that contemporary planning theory and thought could be translated into action.

Will Super Plans Dominate?

. . . .

The issue is whether professional planners are going to be given a broad and flexible mandate to develop a process for guiding decisions or whether they are to use the master plan concept as the key tool for effecting decisions. In reading the literature on the subject, one would be misled into thinking that the process approach is universally accepted. This is not the case. Activist community and environmental groups have shown that they are suspicious of planners and the planning process and that they want their legislatures to give planners more restrictive and specific mandates. Much depends upon the trust and confidence these groups have, or do not have, in planners.

. . . .

Comments: For additional discussion see American Law Institute, A Model Land Development Code 109-21 (1976); J. Bollens & H. Schmandt, The Metropolis: Its People, Politics, and Economic Life, ch. 9 (3d ed. 1975); M. Branch, Planning Urban Environment, ch. 7 (1974).

C. THE STATUTORY BASIS FOR THE COMPREHENSIVE PLAN

Having completed a review of planning theory and the form and function of the comprehensive planning process, we can now turn to an examination of the statutory basis for planning and the comprehensive plan. All states now have statutes authorizing a comprehensive planning process. These statutes still generally derive from one of two twin model acts proposed by the United States Department of Commerce in the 1920's, U.S. Dep't of Commerce, A Standard City Planning Enabling Act (1928). Excerpts from that Act follow. They are from Title I, the planning title.

STANDARD CITY PLANNING ENABLING ACT

SEC. 2. GRANT OF POWER TO MUNICIPALITY. — Any municipality is hereby authorized and empowered to make, adopt, amend, extend, add to, or carry out a municipal plan as provided in this act and create by ordinance a planning commission with the powers and duties herein set forth. . . .

SEC. 3. PERSONNEL OF THE COMMISSION. — The commission shall consist of nine members, namely, the mayor, one of the administrative officials of the municipality selected by the mayor, and a member of council to be selected by it as members ex officio, and six persons who shall be appointed by the mayor, if the mayor be an elective officer, otherwise by such officer as council may in the ordinance creating the commission designate as the appointing power. . . .

[The remainder of this section contains provisions governing length of term, removal for cause, and like matters. Note the lack of statutory qualifications for commission members. This omission was explicit, reflecting the intent of the draftsmen that the commission provide lay leadership for the municipal planning function. In footnote 16 to the Act they state: "Similarly, it seems a mistake to prescribe any professional qualifications of the members, since capacity for leadership in city planning, rather than any particular type of technical or professional training, constitutes the best qualification." Section 4 and 5 provide for the organization and rules of the commission and for commission staff and finances. — Eds.]

SEC. 6. GENERAL POWERS AND DUTIES. — It shall be the function and duty of the commission to make and adopt a master plan for the physical development of the municipality, including any areas outside of its boundaries which, in the commission's judgment, bear relation to the planning of such municipality. Such plan, with the accompanying maps, plats, charts, and descriptive matter shall show the commission's recommendations for the development of said territory, including, among other things, the general location, character, and extent of streets, viaducts, subways, bridges, waterways, water fronts, boulevards, parkways, playgrounds, squares, parks, aviation fields, and other public ways, grounds and open spaces, the general location of public buildings and other public property, and the general location and extent of public utilities and terminals, whether publicly or privately owned or operated, for water, light, sanitation, transportation, communications, power, and other purposes; also the removal, relocation, widening, narrowing, vacating, abandonment, change of use or extension of any of the foregoing ways, grounds, open spaces, buildings, property, utilities, or terminals; as well as a zoning plan for the control of the height, area, bulk, location, and use of buildings and premises. As the work of making the whole master plan progresses, the commission may from time to time adopt and publish a part or parts thereof, any such part to cover one or more major sections or divisions of the municipality or one or more of the aforesaid or other functional matters to be included in the plan. The commission may from time to time amend, extend, or add to the plan.

SEC. 7. PURPOSES IN VIEW. — In the preparation of such plan the commission shall make careful and comprehensive surveys and studies of present conditions and future growth of the municipality and with due regard to its relation to neighboring territory. The plan shall be made with the general purpose of guiding and accomplishing a coordinated, adjusted, and harmonious development of the municipality and its environs which will, in accordance with present and future needs, best promote health, safety, morals, order, convenience, prosperity, and general welfare, as well as efficiency and economy in the process of development; including, among other things, adequate provision for traffic, the promotion of safety from fire and other dangers, adequate provision for light and air, the promotion of the healthful and convenient distribution of population, the promotion of good civic design and arrangement, wise and efficient expenditure of public funds, and the adequate provision of public utilities and other public requirements.

SEC. 8. PROCEDURE OF COMMISSION. — The commission may adopt the plan as a whole by a single resolution or may by successive resolutions adopt successive parts of the plan, said parts corresponding with major geographical sections or divisions of the municipality or with functional subdivisions of the subject matter of the plan, and may adopt any amendment or extension thereof or addition thereto. . . . [The commission is to hold at least one hearing on the plan. — Eds.] The adoption of the plan or of any such part or amendment or extension or addition shall be by resolution of the commission carried by the affirmative votes of not less than six members of the commission. . . . [The rest of the section provides for the form of the adopting resolution and for its certification to the council. — Eds.]

[Note that the Standard Act provides for the adoption of the general plan by the commission. In footnote 44 the draftsmen indicate why adoption by the legislature was not required. They point out that the plan should cover a period of years longer than the term of any council; that the council deals with "pressing and immediate needs" and not with long-term policy; that the plan in any event will presumptively be binding on the council when it determines public expenditures (*see* Sec. 9); and that a hostile council may overturn a plan adopted by an earlier council.

[The American Law Institute's Model Land Development Code § 3-106(2) (1976) requires adoption by the council. Its draftsmen note:

> But in view of the scheme of this Code — to focus legislative attention on the problems of physical development and location of activities that use land and on concrete programs aimed at their solution — legislative consideration and adoption are necessary to achieve consideration and implementation by a representative body.

Id. at 135. The controversy continues; some planning enabling acts require adoption by the council and some do not. For a strong endorsement of council adoption of the plan see T. Kent, The Urban General Plan ch. 3 (1964). — Eds.]

SEC. 9. LEGAL STATUS OF OFFICIAL PLAN. — Whenever the commission shall have adopted the master plan of the municipality or of one or more major sections or districts thereof no street, square, park, or other public way, ground, or open space, or public building or structure, or public utility, whether publicly or privately owned, shall be constructed or authorized in the municipality or in such planned section or district until the location, character, and extent thereof shall have been submitted to and approved by the commission: *Provided,* that in case of disapproval the commission shall communicate its reasons to council, which shall have the power to overrule such disapproval by a recorded vote of not less than two-thirds of its entire membership. . . .

Modern State Planning Enabling Legislation

No state has retained the Standard Planning Enabling Act in the form in which it was proposed, and from the outset it did not achieve the popularity of its sister model act, the Standard Zoning Enabling Act. Indeed, the quaint language of Section 6 sounds strange in modern ears. (Aviation fields?) Nevertheless, the structure of the model planning act has shaped the character and content of the planning function to the present day, so that comment on the assumptions that lay behind the Standard Planning Enabling Act is in order.

Perhaps the most important of these assumptions was that the planning function should be optional at the local level, not mandatory. Note that planning is only "authorized." There was no guarantee that a municipality would plan, nor that all of the municipalities in a metropolitan area would be covered by adopted plans. Indeed, the model act was directed to municipalities. County planning enabling acts came much later; in almost all states county planning has now been authorized by statute.

Another important characteristic of the model act was its shopping list of plan elements in Section 6. These elements were made mandatory — "Such plan . . . shall show" — but no substantive policies were stated in the statute and the linkages among the elements were left to the planning process to determine. Consequently, the statute failed to provide a structure for the planning process or to suggest how the plan elements might be linked and grouped to comprise an integrated planning product.

Next, the plan was to be applied to both public and private development, with little recognition that the role of the planning process and the problems of legal implementation are very different in these two situations. While the plan's proposals that affect private development are to be directly implemented through legal techniques such as zoning, the model act provides only a weak veto over public development in the planning commission. It can be overriden by a two-thirds vote of the council. Title II of the model act does provide a link between the plan and the approval of subdivisions, however. Actually, most planning for major public facility projects, such as highways and wastewater treatment plants, has now been elevated to the regional level under the impetus of federal legislation.

Another unfortunate confusion arose from the requirement that municipalities prepare a "zoning plan" as well as the public facilities plan that generally was required by the first part of Section 6. This zoning plan requirement introduced a major confusion in the planning process. The plan is intended to be long-range and general and has no legal effect on property, while the zoning ordinance is short-range and precise and does have a legal effect on property use. The inclusion of a zoning plan requirement in the comprehensive planning enabling act muddled these two concepts and has encouraged municipalities to prepare zoning regulations without having first considered the long-range policies on which these ordinances should be based.

These and other problems in the Standard Planning Enabling Act are noted in Black, The Comprehensive Plan in Principles and Practice of Urban Planning, *supra* at 349, 353-55. He notes that the Standard Act encouraged the adoption of the plan piecemeal instead of comprehensively; that it failed to define the essential technical elements of the plan; and that it separated the planning process from the council, the political body, by placing the responsibility to prepare the plan on the planning commission. All of these characteristics have persisted to some extent in modern planning practice.

For additional background on the adoption of the Standard Planning Enabling Act see T. Kent, The Urban General Plan 28-38 (1964).

Recent planning enabling legislation has departed in major concept from the original planning model projected by the Standard Act. These innovations have taken the form of more sophisticated expressions of the required planning elements, an emphasis on dynamic planning opportunities rather than static proposals, and a requirement for mandatory planning. The state and model legislation that follows illustrate these trends. These statutes nonetheless are atypical. The planning enabling acts in many states still follow the general outlines of the Standard Act, and some contain a comparable recital of public facilities and the like for which plans are to be prepared. However, the Pennsylvania municipalities planning enabling act which follows has recast the elements of the comprehensive plan in a manner which captures more of the dynamics of the planning process:

PENNSYLVANIA STATUTES ANNOTATED tit. 53 (Supp. 1972)

§ 10301. . . . The comprehensive plan consisting of maps, charts and textual matter, shall indicate the recommendations of the planning agency for the continuing development of the municipality. The comprehensive plan shall include, but need not be limited to, the following related basic elements:

(1) A statement of objectives of the municipality concerning its future development;

(2) A plan for land use, which may include the amount, intensity, and character of land use proposed for residence, industry, business, agriculture, major traffic and transit facilities, public grounds, flood plans and other areas of special hazards and other similar uses;

(3) A plan for movement of people and goods, which may include expressways, highways, local street systems, parking facilities, mass transit routes, terminals, airfields, port facilities, railroad facilities and other similar facilities or uses;

(4) A plan for community facilities and utilities, which may include public and private education, recreation, municipal buildings, libraries, water supply, sewage disposal, refuse disposal, storm drainage, hospitals, and other similar uses; and

(5) A map or statement indicating the relationship of the municipality and its proposed development to adjacent municipalities and areas.

In preparing the comprehensive plan the planning agency shall make careful surveys and studies of existing conditions and prospects for future growth in the municipality.

Perhaps the most comprehensive planning enabling legislation has been enacted by the state of California, a state in which planning is mandatory at the local level. Over the years, the legislature has included a series of mandatory and optional planning elements in its planning statute which substantially extend the scope of planning as contemplated by the Standard Act. These statutory provisions follow. Some are more detailed than others, apparently reflecting legislative interest in the element at hand. Only the essential statutory material is reproduced, and some statutory detail is omitted.

CALIFORNIA GOVERNMENT CODE (Deering 1974, Supp. 1977)

§ 65300.5. Legislative intent

In construing the provisions of this article, the Legislature intends that the general plan and elements and parts thereof comprise an integrated, internally consistent and compatible statement of policies for the adopting agency.

[This section, added in 1975, apparently is an attempt to overcome the shopping list character of most planning enabling acts, which simply list planning elements without providing a framework through which these elements are to be ordered into an integrated planning product. Is this language enough to overcome this deficiency? What else would you add? — Eds.]

§ 65302. Statement of development policies: Inclusion of diagram and text setting forth objectives, etc.: Elements to be included

The general plan shall consist of a statement of development policies and shall include a diagram or diagrams and text setting forth objectives, principles, standards, and plan proposals. The plan shall include the following elements:

(a) A land use element which designates the proposed general distribution and general location and extent of the uses of the land for housing, business, industry, open space, including agriculture, natural resources, recreation, and enjoyment of scenic beauty, education, public buildings and grounds, solid and liquid waste disposal facilities, and other categories of public and private uses of land. The land use element shall include a statement of the standards of population density and building intensity recommended for the various districts and other territory covered by the plan. The land use element shall also identify areas covered by the plan which are subject to flooding and shall be reviewed annually with respect to such areas.

(b) A circulation element consisting of the general location and extent of existing and proposed major thoroughfares, transportation routes, terminals, and other local public utilities and facilities, all correlated with the land use element of the plan.

(c) A housing element, to be developed pursuant to regulations established under Section 41134 of the Health and Safety Code, consisting of standards and plans for the improvement of housing and for provision of adequate sites for housing. This element of the plan shall make adequate provision for the housing needs of all economic segments of the community.

[The reference to the Health and Safety Code is a reference to guidelines for the housing element to be prepared by the state housing agency, and which are to follow federal guidelines as nearly as possible. What judicial disposition should be made of a zoning ordinance which does not contain provisions implementing the housing element of the plan to the extent that it requires the provision of sites for lower income housing? For discussion of the California housing element see Knight, California Planning Law:

Requirements for Low and Moderate Income Housing, 2 Pepperdine L. Rev. S159 (1975). — Eds.]

(d) A conservation element for the conservation, development, and utilization of natural resources including water and its hydraulic force, forests, soils, rivers and other waters, harbors, fisheries, wildlife, minerals, and other natural resources. That portion of the conservation element including waters shall be developed in coordination with any countywide water agency and with all district and city agencies which have developed, served, controlled or conserved water for any purpose for the county or city for which the plan is prepared. The conservation element may also cover:

(1) The reclamation of land and waters.

(2) Flood control.

(3) Prevention and control of the pollution of streams and other waters.

(4) Regulation of the use of land in stream channels and other areas required for the accomplishment of the conservation plan.

(5) Prevention, control, and correction of the erosion of soils, beaches, and shores.

(6) Protection of watersheds.

(7) The location, quantity and quality of the rock, sand and gravel resources.

. . . .

(e) An open-space element as provided in Article 10.5 (commencing with Section 65560) of this chapter. [*See* § 65563, *infra.* — Eds.]

(f) A seismic safety element consisting of an identification and appraisal of seismic hazards such as susceptibility to surface ruptures from faulting, to ground shaking, to ground failures, or to effects of seismically induced waves such as tsunamis and seiches.

The seismic safety element shall also include an appraisal of mudslides, landslides, and slope stability as necessary geologic hazards that must be considered simultaneously with other hazards such as possible surface ruptures from faulting, ground shaking, ground failure and seismically induced waves.

(g) A noise element, which shall recognize guidelines adopted by the Office of Noise Control ... and which quantifies the community noise environment in terms of noise exposure contours for both near and long-term levels of growth and traffic activity. Such noise exposure information shall become a guideline for use in development of the land use element to achieve noise compatible land use and also to provide baseline levels and noise source identification for local noise ordinance enforcement.

. . . .

[Additional details concerning the preparation of the noise element have been omitted. — Eds.]

(h) A scenic highway element for the development, establishment, and protection of scenic highways. . . .

(i) A safety element for the protection of the community from fires and geologic hazards including features necessary for such protection as evacuation routes, peak load water supply requirements, minimum road widths, clearances around structures, and geologic hazard mapping in areas of known geologic hazards.

The requirements of this section shall apply to charter cities.

§ 65302.1. Inclusion of Safety Element for Protection from Fires and Geologic Hazards

The general plan shall also include, in addition to the elements specified in Section 65302, a safety element for the protection of the community from fires and geologic hazards including features necessary for such protection as evacuation routes, peak load water supply requirements, minimum road widths, clearances around structures, and geologic hazard mapping in areas of known geologic hazards.

§ 65303. Additional Includible Elements

The general plan may include the following elements or any part or phase thereof:

(a) A recreation element showing a comprehensive system of areas and public sites for recreation, including the following, and, when practicable, their locations and proposed development:

(1) Natural reservations.
(2) Parks.
(3) Parkways.
(4) Beaches.
(5) Playgrounds.
(6) Other recreation areas.

(b) The circulation element provided for in Section 65302(b) may also include recommendations concerning parking facilities and building setback lines and the delineations of such systems on the land; a system of street naming, house and building numbering; and such other matters as may be related to the improvement of circulation of traffic.

(c) A transportation element showing a comprehensive transportation system, including locations of rights-of-way, terminals, viaducts, and grade separations. This element of the plan may also include port, harbor, aviation, and related facilities.

(d) A transit element showing a proposed system of transit lines, including rapid transit, streetcar, motor coach and trolley coach lines, and related facilities.

(e) A public services and facilities element showing general plans for sewerage, refuse disposal, drainage, and local utilities, and rights-of-way, easements, and facilities for them.

(f) A public building element showing locations and arrangements of civic and community centers, public schools, libraries, police and fire stations, and other public buildings, including their architecture and the landscape treatment of their grounds.

(g) A community design element consisting of standards and principles governing the subdivision of land, and showing recommended designs for community and neighborhood development and redevelopment, including sites for schools, parks, playgrounds and other uses.

(h) A housing element consisting of standards and plans for the elimination of substandard dwelling conditions.

(i) A redevelopment element consisting of plans and programs for the elimination of slums and blighted areas and for community redevelopment, including housing sites, business and industrial sites, public building sites, and for other purposes authorized by law.

(j) A historical preservation element for the identification, establishment, and protection of sites and structures of architectural, historical, archaeological or cultural significance, including significant trees, hedgerows and other plant materials. The historical preservation element shall include a program which develops actions to be taken in accomplishing the policies set forth in this element.

. . . .

(k) Such additional elements dealing with other subjects which in the judgment of the planning agency relate to the physical development of the county or city.

§ 65563. Local open-space plans: Preparation, adoption, and submission

On or before December 31, 1973, every city and county shall prepare, adopt and submit to the Secretary of the Resources Agency a local open-space plan for the comprehensive and long-range preservation and conservation of open-space land within its jurisdiction. Every city and county shall by August 31, 1972, prepare, adopt and submit to the Secretary of the Resources Agency, an interim open-space plan, which shall be in effect until December 31, 1973, containing, but not limited to, the following:

(a) The officially adopted goals and policies which will guide the preparation and implementation of the open-space plan; and

(b) A program for orderly completion and adoption of the open-space plan by December 31, 1973, including a description of the methods by which open-space resources will be inventoried and conservation measures determined.

Comments: 1. In 1975 the Florida legislature enacted a mandatory local comprehensive planning act with a series of mandatory planning elements in general form and content similar to those contained in the California legislation. Fla. Stat. Ann. § 163.3177 (Supp. 1978). Some of the requirements for planning in the Florida law depart from the traditional land use focus of comprehensive planning, or at least extend the basis for land use planning. Note the following language in the statute:

(3) The economic assumptions on which the plan is based and any amendments thereto shall be analyzed and set out as a part of the plan. . . .

. . . .

(6) . . . [T]he comprehensive plan shall include . . . :

. . . .

(h) An intergovernmental coordination element showing relationships and stating principles and guidelines to be used in the accomplishment of coordination of the adopted comprehensive plan with the plans of school boards and other units of local government providing services but not having regulatory authority over the use of land, with the comprehensive plans of adjacent municipalities, of the county or adjacent counties, or the region and to the state comprehensive plan, as the case may require and as such adopted plans or plans in preparation may exist. . . .

. . . .

(k) An economic element setting forth principles and guidelines for the commercial and industrial development, if any, and the employment and manpower utilization within the area. The element may detail the type of commercial and industrial development sought, correlated to the present and projected employment needs of the area and to other elements of the plans and may set forth methods by which a balanced and stable economic base will be pursued.

In paragraph (f) the Florida law also contains a requirement for a mandatory housing element which is to make provision for low and moderate income housing as well as "housing for existing residents and the anticipated population growth of the area." Does this provision guarantee that housing will be available for workers employed in a municipality by new industry attracted under the incentives for new industrial and commercial development apparently contemplated by paragraph (k), *supra* ? Both the California and the Florida legislation contain requirements that zoning be consistent with the adopted comprehensive plan. *See infra* p. 757. For discussion of the planning elements which should be required by planning enabling legislation see Mandelker, The Role of the Local Comprehensive Plan in Land Use Regulation, 74 Mich. L. Rev. 799, 951-56 (1976).

2. In 1975, the American Law Institute adopted a Model Land Development Code intended to provide guidance to state legislatures in modernizing their enabling legislation for planning and for land development control. The Code does not mandate planning at the local level, but provides for an optional local planning process that seeks to meet some of the objections to conventional planning which have been described above, particularly in the Burby article, *supra* p. 41. This legislation contemplates what the Code draftsmen call a continuous planning process, and incorporates suggestions made by Richard Bolan in his article, Emerging Views of Planning, 33 J. Am. Inst. Planners 233 (1967). What is intended by the Code is indicated in commentary:

. . . First, the [planning] Article does not jettison long-term goal setting, but encourages the assembly of a wide variety of information, the making of trend predictions, and the statement of long-run objectives. The planners are asked to estimate probable economic and social consequences of both governmental inaction and governmental intervention to realize the stated objectives. These efforts, however, are designed to provide a framework for a systematized program of government action over a relatively short period of time, after which readjustment of the framework is expected.

Second, the Article, by emphasizing the short-term program of intervention and requiring identification of and focus on problems, recognizes the limitations of comprehensive planning. It invites the use of new techniques such as program planning in the fashioning of the short-term program, and it explicitly requires evaluation of the success of each such program.

American Law Institute, A Model Land Development Code 119 (1976). One consequence of this approach is that the Code drops the listing of planning elements which has been typical of planning enabling legislation. The following excerpt from the Code, stating the purposes of preparing a local comprehensive plan, captures the essence of the Code's approach:

AMERICAN LAW INSTITUTE, A MODEL LAND DEVELOPMENT CODE (1976)

Section 3-102. Purposes of Preparing a Local Land Development Plan

The purposes of preparing a Local Land Development Plan are:

(1) to initiate comprehensive studies of factors relevant to development;

(2) to recognize and state major problems and opportunities concerning development and the environmental, social and economic effects of development;

(3) to set forth the desired sequence, patterns, and characteristics of future development and its probable environmental, economic and social consequences;

(4) to provide a statement of programs to obtain the desired sequence, patterns, and characteristics of development; and

(5) to determine the probable environmental, economic and social consequences of the desired development and the proposed programs.

Note that this provision of the code reflects the draftsmen's intention that "the plan should have a physical development nucleus but should require that specified economic and social data be taken into consideration in its preparation and consideration." Model Land Development Code, *supra* at 112-13. The code commentary, *id.* at 110-14 reviews the long-standing controversy over whether the comprehensive plan should cover physical development problems only. The code's definition of a local plan does not require that the plan contain a map. *Id.* § 3-101(1).

3. The early standard planning act provided for an independent planning commission, which was to prepare the comprehensive plan. The planning commission mode of organization was recommended on the ground that civic-minded leaders could be appointed to the commission and could provide leadership for the planning process, and that isolation of the planning commission from politics and from the ongoing administration of local government would improve the possibilities for the success of the planning effort. These assumptions about governmental organization were typical of reformist movements of the time, and helped spawn the independent board and commission in state and local government structures.

The independent local planning commission has long been under attack; one of the first comprehensive criticisms was contained in R. Walker, The Planning Function in Urban Government (1941). Suggestions have long been made for alternative organizational forms for local planning. For example, the American Law Institute's Model Land Development Code does not require a planning commission to be appointed and leaves it to the local government to determine the organizational structure for carrying out the planning process.

How the planning process is presently organized is surveyed in a recent report, Internat'l City Manag. Ass'n, Administration of Local Planning: Analysis of Structures and Functions (Urban Data Service Rep. Vol. 3, no. 12, 1971). Data compiled in this report indicate a shift away from the independent planning commission in recent years, with the planning function increasingly assigned to a planning department directly responsible to the local executive.

A NOTE ON THE FEDERAL PROGRAM OF PLANNING ASSISTANCE

Since the 1950's, the federal Department of Housing and Urban Development has had a grant-in-aid program of financial assistance for planning by state, regional and local planning agencies. This program, though modest at first, has increasingly provided major support for planning activities in this country. Since it was necessary to define the kinds of activities eligible for assistance the federal statute authorizing this program, known as the "701" program for the section of the National Housing Act in which it first appeared, has always had a definition of the planning that is eligible for aid.

This definition has been amended several times and in its most recent form, as amended in 1974, introduced a major innovation by requiring planning agencies receiving federal funds to produce a housing and land use element as a part of their plan. These elements are defined as follows:

> Each recipient of assistance under this section shall carry out an ongoing comprehensive planning process which . . . shall include, as a minimum, each of the following elements:
>
> (1) A housing element which shall take into account all available evidence of the assumptions and statistical bases upon which the projection of zoning, community facilities, and population growth is based, so that the housing needs of both the region and the local communities studied in the planning will be adequately covered in terms of existing and prospective population growth. The development and formulation of State and local goals pursuant to . . . [the national housing goal] shall be a part of such a housing element.
>
> (2) A land-use element which shall include (A) studies, criteria, standards, and implementing procedures necessary for effectively guiding and controlling major decisions as to where growth shall take place within the recipient's boundaries, and (B) as a guide for governmental policies and activities, general plans with respect to the pattern and intensity of land use for residential, commercial, industrial, and other activities.
>
> Each of the elements set forth above shall specify (i) broad goals and annual objectives (in measurable terms wherever possible), (ii) programs designed to accomplish these

objectives, and (iii) procedures, including criteria set forth in advance, for evaluating programs and activities to determine whether they are meeting objectives. Such elements shall be consistent with each other and consistent with stated national growth policy.

40 U.S.C. § 461(c) (1976).

The federal planning assistance statute also contains a definition of the comprehensive planning process:

(4) The term "comprehensive planning" includes the following:

(A) preparation, as a guide for governmental policies and action, of general plans with respect to (i) the pattern and intensity of land use, (ii) the provision of public facilities (including transportation facilities) and other government services, and (iii) the effective development and utilization of human and natural resources;

(B) identification and evaluation of area needs (including housing, employment, education, and health) and formulation of specific programs for meeting the needs so identified;

(C) surveys of structures and sites which are determined by the appropriate authorities to be of historic or architectural value;

(D) long-range physical and fiscal plans for such action;

(E) programing of capital improvements and other major expenditures, based on a determination of relative urgency, together with definite financing plans for such expenditures in the earlier years of the program;

(F) coordination of all related plans and activities of the State and local governments and agencies concerned; and

(G) preparation of regulatory and administrative measures in support of the foregoing.

Id., § 461(m)(4).

Planning agencies receiving federal planning assistance under this statute must of course meet the federal planning requirements in order to establish eligibility for the program. The question that next arises is whether state planning legislation authorizes all of the planning activities required under the federal law, especially the land use and housing elements. Reread the state planning enabling legislation reproduced above to determine whether it fully authorizes all of the work elements required by the federal statute. (Is the definition of "comprehensive planning" quoted above from the federal statute a requirement or merely an indication of possible planning activities which may be federally funded?) Since the availability of federal assistance is often the determining factor in whether or not planning will be carried out by the governmental unit, the importance of the federal planning requirements is obvious. Nevertheless, state legislatures have not generally revised their planning enabling legislation to conform to what the federal statute demands.

D. THE LEGAL EFFECT OF THE COMPREHENSIVE PLAN

Under much planning legislation the comprehensive plan is adopted by ordinance or resolution of the local governing body, and to this extent it does have legal effect. Moreover, as will be noted later, see *infra* Chapter 4, the plan is given legal effect in many states through statutory and judicial requirements that local zoning and land use regulation be consistent with the plan. At this point, however, the question to be raised is whether the adoption of the plan has legal effect independent of any implementing local regulation. First to be considered is whether the adoption of the plan can, under any circumstances, be considered a taking of property. Next to be considered is the local official map, a regulatory control which is directly dependent on the comprehensive plan and which does have a regulatory impact on land use.

1. The Plan as a "Taking" of Property

Mapped plans, and even policy plans, generally show future land use locations and so can be expected to have an impact on the expectations of property owners whose land is covered by the plan. The question to ask next is whether the plan has a legal effect on property and property values such that its policies are subject to legal challenge in a case that might allege, for example, that the policies of the plan are so restrictive that they constitute a taking without due process of law.

Some perspective on this problem is provided by a case which held that the resolution of a city council adopting a comprehensive plan was subject to referendum. The court commented in part:

> It is apparent that the plan is, in short, a constitution for all future development within the city. No mechanical reading of the plan itself is sufficient. To argue that property rights are not affected by the general plan (as the city so asserts) as adopted ignores that which is obvious. Any zoning ordinance adopted in the future would surely be interpreted in part by its fidelity to the general plan as well as by the standards of due process. Frequently it has occurred that where a general plan was adopted, and later a zoning change was made which appeared to be in accord with the plan, that fact in and of itself was some evidentiary

weight in the determination as to whether the zoning ordinance was proper or otherwise. If the general plan is anything at all, it is a meaningful enactment and definitely affects the community and, among other things, changes land market values. The general plan is legislatively adopted by the council. True, it is couched in part in general terms, but there are many specifics, and once adopted it becomes very effective. Many facets of activities between other public agencies and the city are effectively determined by the plan. Any subdivision or other development would necessarily be considered in its relation to the general plan, and such consideration practically by itself would be a sufficient legislative guide to the exercise of such discretions.

O'Loane v. O'Rourke, 42 Cal. Rptr. 283, 288 (Cal. App. 1965).

Nevertheless, property owners adversely affected by a plan may seek to challenge it directly in court if they believe that the effect of the plan is adverse to their interests. Of course, a generalized policy plan which does not show specific land use locations will not likely trigger this kind of challenge. When the plan is quite specific, however, as in the next case, property owners may complain.

COCHRAN v. PLANNING BOARD OF SUMMIT

Superior Court of New Jersey, Law Division
87 N.J. Super. 526, 210 A.2d 99 (1965)

Feller, J. S. C.

This is an action in lieu of prerogative writs challenging the adoption of a master plan by the Planning Board of the City of Summit and seeking to enjoin the city and its agencies, boards, and officials from implementing the master plan in any way. In particular, plaintiffs object to that part of the plan which would permit an expansion of the Ciba Corporation's parking area and research and office space into the residential area which adjoins the rear of plaintiffs' property.

Plaintiffs are citizens, taxpayers and owners of lands located at 249 Kent Place Boulevard in Summit. Their property is adjacent and contiguous to property owned by the Ciba Corporation (hereinafter Ciba). Plaintiffs' premises and that portion of the Ciba tract in question are presently in the A-15 zoning district, which is limited to one-family residences with a minimum lot area of 15,000 square feet. Prior to 1958 the Ciba tract was in an A-10 zone, which was limited to one-family residences with a minimum lot area of 10,000 square feet. The tract is bordered on three sides by one-family residences and is presently subject to enforceable deed restrictions which limit the use of the tract to the erection of one-family residences until 1975.

On December 9, 1963 defendant planning board adopted a master plan for the city, which provided in part that the Ciba tract, namely, 63½ acres in the A-15 zone, should be rezoned for parking areas and research and office building use. This rezoning is for the purpose of providing for the eventual expansion therein of Ciba's existing operations. The plan requires a 125-foot buffer zone, which would separate the rear line of plaintiffs' property from the proposed Ciba construction. This zone would contain trees, shrubs and a screen, all of them calculated to preserve the existing residential atmosphere of the area. . . .

Plaintiffs also contend that the master plan is confiscatory in that it destroys existing property values to the special damage of plaintiffs, in violation of N.J.S.A. 40:55-1.12, which requires that a master plan preserve property values previously established. . . . Plaintiffs claim that their personal and property rights have been violated in contravention of the New Jersey and Federal Constitutions. . . .

II

The second question is whether plaintiffs' property has been harmed or damaged by the adoption of the master plan and whether their suit is premature. If the action is premature, they have sustained no damage or harm to their property, and a determination of the procedural inadequacies and conflicts of interest alleged by plaintiffs would be unnecessary.

Plaintiffs request the court to declare the master plan null and void because it represents a taking of private property for public use without just compensation. On the basis of this allegation, together with the allegation of their ownership of land in Summit, plaintiffs ask that the master plan be set aside because it violates their constitutional rights, is arbitrary, illegal and unreasonable, and constitutes spot-zoning.

Defendants contend that plaintiffs' failure to allege and prove injury to their property rights results in the presentation of legal questions which are premature and which do not present justiciable controversies. This court agrees that such allegations and proof of injury to private property rights are necessary before the requested relief may be considered and granted by this court. Plaintiffs have not demonstrated that degree of injury which would entitle them to relief.

The evidence and testimony of Agle, the expert planning consultant, reveal that if the proposed master plan were adopted as an ordinance by the city council, the resulting zoning ordinance would provide for a 125-foot buffer zone between plaintiffs' land and the Ciba property. The Ciba property would be devoted to a parking area and office and research buildings. The buildings would be limited to a maximum height of 68 feet. A seven-foot high screen on Ciba's property line would also be required. The result would make the buildings no more than one-third as high as the distance from them to the Ciba property line. This fact, together with the new trees in the 125-foot buffer zone, would adequately screen the visibility of the six-story-high buildings which Ciba would erect. Theoretically, then, plaintiffs' view would not be disturbed aesthetically.

If plaintiffs cannot demonstrate injury, then they may not obtain relief; if their claims are based upon assumed potential invasions of rights, then these are not enough to warrant judicial intervention. . . .

The crux of this problem is clear when it is remembered that a master plan is of no force and effect until it is adopted by the governing body of the municipality. Thus, the master plan under consideration in the City of Summit is of no effect until it is adopted by the municipal governing body.

The master plan represents at a given time the best judgment of the planning agency as to the proper course of action to be followed. In this stage the plan for community development remains flexible and is not binding, either on government or individual. . . . A master plan is not a straitjacket delimiting the discretion of the legislative body, but only a guide for the city, . . . furthermore, a master plan is nothing more than the easily changed instrumentality which will show a commission from day to day the progress it has made. . . .

The mere adoption and recording of a master plan has no legal consequence. The plan is merely a declaration of policy and a disclosure of an intention which must thereafter be implemented by the adoption of various ordinances. . . .

In New Jersey the fact that a master plan adopted by a planning board has no legal consequences is substantiated, not only by the absence of statutory language to that effect, but also by the necessity of a municipality's adoption of the master plan by the governing body before the plan takes effect. See N.J.S.A. 40:55-1.13; *Wollen v. Fort Lee,* 27 N.J. 408, 424, 142 A.2d 881, 890 (1958), where the court said that "the master plan is not conclusive on the governing body." Moreover, it is not mandatory for a township to create a planning board, and a governing body could assume directly the duties of a planning board. . . .

Professor Cunningham, in his "Controls of Land Use in New Jersey" 15 Rutg.L. Rev. 1, 19 (1960), said:

". . . The statute does not require that the governing body shall accept the recommendation of the planning board nor does it require a vote of more than a majority of the governing body to adopt an official map . . . which is inconsistent with the planning board's recommendation. *It would thus appear that even after the planning board has adopted a master plan, the governing body is free to ignore*

*the recommendation of the planning board based on the master plan
when the governing body adopts or amends an official map."*
(Emphasis added)

It is clear that a master plan is only a plan, and that it requires
legislative implementation before its proposals have binding effect
and legal consequences. If the necessary legislative implementation
is taken — and, of course, such implementation must be taken
according to the applicable statutes — then a zoning ordinance and
not a master plan would be before the court. Until appropriate
municipal legislative action is taken, however, the municipality has
only a dormant plan which differs from proposals that may be under
consideration by any municipal board or citizen of the municipality
in that it is comprehensive and has been reduced to printed form.
Indeed, a master plan is not even a statutory prerequisite to zoning
action. *Kozesnik v. Montgomery Township,* 24 N.J. 154, 165, 131
A.2d 1 (1957).

The issue here is whether a plan for municipal development, not
yet implemented by the necessary legislative action, may be legally
considered to deprive one of the enjoyment of his property, contrary
to the United States and New Jersey Constitutions. The statutes
providing for the adoption of a master plan were upheld as
constitutional in *Mansfield & Swett, Inc. v. West Orange,* 120 N.J.L.
145, 198 A. 225 (Sup.Ct.1938). The court, in the course of its
opinion, said that the State possesses the inherent authority to resort,
in the building and expansion of its community life, to such measures
as may be necessary to secure the essential common material and
moral needs. The public welfare is of prime importance, and the
correlative restrictions upon individual rights, either of person or of
property, are considered a negligible loss compared with the
resultant advantages to the community as a whole. Municipal
planning confined to the common need is inherent in the authority
to create the municipality itself. It is as old as government itself; it
is of the very essence of civilized society. A comprehensive scheme
of physical development is requisite to community efficiency and
progress.

The court further said that the police power of the State may be
delegated to its municipal subdivisions created for the administration
of local self-government, to be exerted whenever necessary for the
general good and welfare; and the right of property yields to the
exercise of this reserve element of sovereignty. The principle is
firmly established in our federal jurisprudence that injury to private
property ensuing from governmental action in a proper sphere,
reasonably taken for the public good, and for no other purpose, is
not necessarily classable as a "taking" of such property within the
intendment of the constitutional guaranties against the deprivation

of property without due process of law, or the taking of private property for public use without compensation.

In *Erie Railroad Co. v. Passaic,* 79 N.J.L. 19, 74 A. 338 (Sup.Ct.1909), the court said:

". . . It would be absurd to say that the location of sewers upon a map made actual sewers. It is equally inadmissible to contend that the location of streets on the same map, under the same statutory authority, makes actual streets. Nor can it be said that the making of the map was a dedication which the city might afterwards accept. The map is made by the city authorities themselves, and they are without right to dedicate land that belongs to others." (at p. 21, 74 A. at p. 339)

. . . .

Comments: 1. The *Cochran* case is not quite the case we would like to have to test the legal effect of the comprehensive plan. First, the plan was apparently quite detailed. By calling for a rezoning of the property in question it departed from the generalized type of policy statement which we have associated with the comprehensive plan. Next, the plan had not been adopted by the council, so that the court could consider the case as premature. Does the court nevertheless consider what the legal effect of the plan would be had it been adopted by the council? Does the court pass on the constitutionality of the plan as applied? Are they led in this direction by the zoning proposal contained in the plan?

2. Toward the end of the opinion the *Cochran* court confused a comprehensive plan regulating land use with a comprehensive plan reserving land for future acquisition by public agencies. This function of the plan was specifically contemplated by the Standard Planning Act, but must be distinguished from the role of the plan in allocating private developmental opportunities. One important distinction is that land reserved by the plan for public acquisition will eventually be acquired by the public agency. In this situation the plan designation acts primarily as a land reservation or holding technique pending public acquisition.

A somewhat different problem thus arises when courts consider the legal effect of the plan in this context. Since the effect of the planning designation is to foreclose any private development of the property, the owner of the land may allege that there has been a taking of his land to the extent that development is prevented during the interim period prior to the governmental taking. Consider the following two cases:

Selby Realty Co. v. City of San Buenaventura, 514 P.2d 111 (Cal. 1973): The city and county jointly adopted an area general plan. This plan contained a circulation element generally indicating the location of existing and proposed streets, and indicating several proposed streets and a street extension over plaintiff's property. Plaintiff filed application with the city for a building permit for multifamily dwellings on a portion of its property which the plan showed for the street extension. Because the plaintiff refused to dedicate the required land for the extension, the city denied the building permit. Plaintiff brought an action seeking declaratory relief, damages, and a writ of mandate against the city, the county, and several of its officials, and argued as well that the adoption of the plan constituted a taking of its property.

The legal issues arising out of the denial of the building permit raise complicated questions which need not detain us at this time, but the court's handling of the plan is of interest. Recall that it was the city, not the county, which denied plantiff's building permit. When it turned to the effect of the county plan the court thus was able to hold:

> We cannot discern in the foregoing allegations any concrete dispute between plaintiff and the county which admits of definitive and conclusive judicial relief. The county has taken no action with respect to plaintiff's land except to enact a general plan describing proposed streets, as required by state law. . . . The plan is by its very nature merely tentative and subject to change. Whether eventually any part of plaintiff's land will be taken for a street depends upon unpredictable future events. If the plan is implemented by the county in the future in such manner as actually to affect plaintiff's free use of his property, the validity of the county's action may be challenged at that time. . . .
>
> . . .[No decision of this court] of which we are aware holds that the enactment of a general plan for the future development of an area, indicating potential public uses of privately owned land, amounts to inverse condemnation [*i.e.,* a "taking." — Eds.] of that land. . . .
>
> If a governmental entity and its responsible officials were held subject to a claim for inverse condemnation merely because a parcel of land was designated for potential public use on one of these several authorized plans, the process of community planning would either grind to a halt, or deteriorate to publication of vacuous generalizations regarding the future use of land. . . .

Id. at 115-17. *See* Hagman, No Good Fortune for Selby in San Buenaventura, 25 Zoning Dig. 208 (1973).

Conroy-Prugh Glass Co. v. Commonwealth, 321 A.2d 598 (Pa. 1974). The Commonwealth had proposed an extension of a boulevard which covered both sides of the company's property and included an interchange. Several alternative plans for the extension and interchange had been proposed though none had been formally approved. Each of the proposals would require the complete taking of the company's property. This boulevard extension had received wide publicity, following which the company began to lose tenants in its property and ultimately was forced to list it for sale. The court found a taking. It noted that the taking of the company's property was "inevitable," and that the "property owner alleges that the publicity about the inevitable condemnation caused a loss of tenants, making the property useless for its highest and best use — commercial property. It is the presence of this fact which serves to distinguish. . . the instant case from *Commonwealth Appeal,* 221 A.2d 289 (Pa. 1966). In that case, we held that the recording of a plan designating the future location of a proposed highway which recording precluded a property owner from making any improvements within the designated route did not constitute a 'taking.'" *Id.* at 600. What distinguishes this case from *Selby*? Is it important that in *Selby* the property owner's land was vacant and undeveloped? *Cf. Sayre v. City of Cleveland,* 493 F.2d 64 (6th Cir. 1974). *See also Helms v. Chester Redev. Auth.,* 379 A.2d 660 (Pa. Commw. Ct. 1977) (no de facto taking; condemnation not inevitable).

3. In a variant of the *Conroy-Prugh* fact situation the court may not be able to characterize the acquisition as inevitable but may yet give relief to the property owner. For example, a local authority may embark on a long-term urban renewal project. As acquisitions proceed, the area may decline, and as property owners find it increasingly difficult to find tenants for their properties they may turn to the courts for relief. In these situations, often characterized as "planning" or "condemnation" blight, the courts will often find a taking or, when the public agency moves to acquire the property, adjust the condemnation award so that the property owner can recoup his losses. *See generally* Kanner, Condemnation Blight: Just How Just is Just Compensation? 48 Notre Dame Law. 765 (1973); Comment, Condemnation Blight, De Facto Taking and Abandonment in Reliance — Compensation of Losses in Urban Development, 1973 Urb. L. Ann. 343.

4. In *Selby* the street proposals were shown on a general comprehensive plan. Many states also have statutory provisions calling for what is known as an Official Map, and which shows quite precisely the area of land reservations for future streets and sometimes for future parks and other publicly owned areas as well. These official maps may or may not be based on the comprehensive plan. Official maps raise constitutional and taking questions quite similar to those raised in the cases discussed in these comments; these questions are examined in the next section.

2. The Official Map as a "Taking" of Property

Official mapping of streets is an old American practice, dating to the beginning of the nineteenth century, at which time the proprietor of a town simply laid out the lots and blocks and reserved the land that was needed. With the end of the days of proprietorship, crude legislation was passed in New York and other eastern states at the close of the nineteenth century which reserved future street lines but which contained no escape provisions for affected landowners who suffered hardship.

Many states presently have some form of statute which authorizes the official mapping of streets and sometimes of parks and other community facilities. These statutes are based on models, prepared at the time of the original zoning enabling legislation, and which have been widely copied. Advance protection of streets was one of the genuine hopes of the early leaders of the planning movement, and they viewed the official map as a critical device. The municipality was authorized to prepare a detailed and precise map of the location of future streets, and once the map was filed no one could build in the bed of the street without permission, usually obtainable only on a showing of hardship. The model legislation, either explicitly or implicitly, called for the preparation of a comprehensive plan as the basis for adoption of the official map.

The key to the use of the official map is the hardship variance. Since the official map relies on the police power, and since the statutes do not provide for the payment of compensation, some method must be provided to take care of the hard cases in which the landowner challenges the constitutionality of the regulation. Unlike the zoning ordinance, the official map prohibits any development at all in the bed of the street, and may be said to have taken a temporary easement precluding development until the frontage for the street improvement can be acquired. In earlier versions of the official map law, antedating modern planning, no variance provision had been required, and most courts accordingly held these laws unconstitutional. Addition of the variance requirement blunts the constitutional attack by affording relief in cases in which no reasonable return can be realized on the property — a case in which the restriction would be held unconstitutional otherwise. The hardship variance, in turn, became a device through which the municipality could regulate development in the bed of the street during the interim period prior to acquisition.

In point of fact, the official map has been little used, a recent survey finding official map ordinances in only 170 communities in ten states. Where the device has been used, however, it has been quite successful, and planning agencies have been very reluctant to grant variances. Signs of renewed interest in the official map have begun to appear, however. Enabling legislation is increasingly extended to counties, and several states have now authorized the counterpart of the official map for the protection of highways in the state highway system. This power has been lodged with the state highway agency. The following materials raise some of the statutory, constitutional, and administrative problems surrounding the use of the official map device.[6]

STATUTORY AUTHORITY FOR OFFICIAL MAPS

Most statutes authorizing official maps at the county or municipal level are based on three early statutory models. One of these was based on provisions contained in the Standard City Enabling Act. These provisions required compensation to be paid to landowners affected by an official map reservation, and for this reason have not

---

[6] The classic treatment of official map laws is Kucirek & Beuscher, Wisconsin's Official Map Law: Its Current Popularity and Implications for Conveyancing and Platting, 1957 Wis. L. Rev. 176. *See also* L. Walton & W. Savage, An Investigation of Methods of Protecting and/or Reducing Cost of Future Rights of Way (Virginia Hwy. Research Council, 1967).

been widely adopted. The second model was drafted by Edward Bassett and Frank Williams, and was derived from a similar statute they had drafted and which had been adopted in New York State in 1926. The third model was drafted by Alfred Bettman, a leading planning lawyer in the period before the second World War. Both the Bassett-Williams and Bettman model rely on the police power for the official map reservation, do not require the payment of compensation, and contain hardship variance clauses. There are drafting differences in these two models, however. All three of the models are summarized in the chart which follows:

Model Legislation for Local Official Map Acts

Model	Authority Given To:	Master Plan Required	Rights-of-way Protected	Time Limit	Permission Required for Improvements In Right-of-way	Compensation Denied to Structure Illegally In Right-of-way	Compensation Payable for Restriction
Standard Act	Municipalities	Major Street Plan	Plats showing "exact location of the lines of a street"	Council shall fix	No provision	Yes	Required
Bassett-Williams	Municipalities	Not explicit; planning board to report on proposed rights-of-way	New or widened streets, highways and freeways	No	"[B]uilding in the bed of any street, highway or freeway," as variance	No	No
Bettman	Municipalities	Major Street Plan as part of master plan	New, extended, widened or narrowed streets	No	"[A]ny building or structure or part thereof . . . between the mapped lines of any street," as variance	No	No

Model	Standard for Variance	Conditions Imposed	Comments
Standard Act	No provision		
Bassett-Williams	(a) land within mapped street is not yielding fair return; (b) building shall as little as practicable increase cost of street or change map; (c) permit refused if applicant not substantially damaged	Reasonable requirements to promote health, safety and welfare of community	Similar statute proposed for counties.
Bettman	(a) property of which mapped street is part does not yield reasonable return or (b) balancing interests of municipality against interests of owner, permit required by considerations of justice and equity	Location, ground area, height, duration and other details of extent and character of building or structure	Similar statute proposed for county and regional plan commissions

[Based on D. Mandelker & G. Waite, A Study of Future Acquisition and Reservation of Highway Rights-of-Way 112, 116 (U.S. Bureau of Public Roads, 1963).]

The following official map act from the 1975 revision of New Jersey's planning and zoning enabling legislation is typical of statutes of this type. Which of the above models does it follow?

NEW JERSEY STATUTES ANNOTATED (WEST SUPP. 1977)

ARTICLE 5. THE OFFICIAL MAP

SECTION 40:55D-32. Establish an official map

The governing body may by ordinance adopt or amend an official map of the municipality, which shall reflect the appropriate provisions of any municipal master plan; provided that the governing body may adopt an official map or an amendment or revision thereto which, in whole or in part, is inconsistent with the appropriate designations in the subplan elements of the master plan, but only by the affirmative vote of a majority of its full authorized membership with the reasons for so acting recorded in the minutes when adopting the official map. Prior to the hearing on the adoption of any official map or any amendment thereto, the governing body shall refer the proposed official map or amendment to the planning board. . . .

The official map shall be deemed conclusive with respect to the location and width of streets and public drainage ways and the location and extent of flood control basins and public areas, whether or not such streets, ways, basins or areas are improved or unimproved or are in actual physical existence. Upon receiving an application for development, the municipality may reserve for future public use, the aforesaid streets, ways, basins, and areas. . . [in subdivision approval. — Eds.] [7]

. . . .

SECTION 40:55D-34. Issuance of permits for buildings or structures

For purpose of perserving the integrity of the official map of a municipality no permit shall be issued for any building or structure in the bed on any street or public drainage way, flood control basin or public area reserved pursuant to . . . [this article] as shown on the official map, or shown on a plat filed pursuant to this act before adoption of the official map, except as herein provided. Whenever one or more parcels of land, upon which is located the bed of such

---

[7] Section 41 provides that if the official map or master plan provides for the reservation or designation of the streets and facilities listed in Section 32 the planning board may further require that they be shown on the subdivision plat and reserved for one year.

a mapped street or public drainage way, flood control basin or public area . . . cannot yield a reasonable return to the owner unless a building permit is granted, the board of adjustment, in any municipality which has established such a board, may, in a specific case, by an affirmative vote of a majority of the full authorized membership of the board, direct the issuance of a permit for a building or structure in the bed of such mapped street or public drainage way or flood control basin or public area . . ., which will as little as practicable increase the cost of opening such street, or tend to cause a minimum change of the official map and the board shall impose reasonable requirements as a condition of granting the permit so as to promote the health, morals, safety and general welfare of the public. . . . In any municipality in which there is no board of adjustment, the planning board shall have the same powers and be subject to the same restrictions as provided in this section.

SECTION 40:55D-35. Building lot to abut street

No permit for the erection of any building or structure shall be issued unless the lot abuts a street giving access to such proposed building or structure. Such street shall have been duly placed on the official map or shall be (1) an existing State, county or municipal street or highway, or (2) a street shown upon a plat approved by the planning board, or (3) a street on a plat duly filed in the office of the county recording officer prior to the passage of an ordinance under this act or any prior law which required prior approval of plats by the governing body or other authorized body. Before any such permit shall be issued, such street shall have been certified to be suitably improved to the satisfaction of the governing body, or such suitable improvement shall have been assured by means of a performance guarantee, in accordance with standards and specifications for road improvements approved by the governing body, as adequate in respect to the public health, safety and general welfare of the special circumstance of the particular street.

SECTION 40:55D-36. Appeals

Where the enforcement of [the previous] section . . . would entail practical difficulty or unnecessary hardship, or where the circumstances of the case do not require the building or structure to be related to a street, the board of adjustment may upon application or appeal, vary . . . [its] application. . . and direct the issuance of a permit subject to conditions that will provide adequate access for firefighting equipment, ambulances and other emergency vehicles necessary for the protection of health and safety and that will protect any future street layout shown on the official map or on a general circulation plan element of the municipal master plan. . . .

Comments: 1. The American Law Institute's Model Land Development

Code § 3-201 proposes a much abbreviated statutory authorization for official maps. It provides, § 3-201(1): "The development ordinance of a local government may designate land as reserved for future acquisition by governmental agencies. The ordinance may specify the general development, if any, permitted in the designated areas prior to acquisition, or may authorize the Land Development Agency to permit as special development any development that will not be substantially inconsistent with the purposes of the reservation." Section 302(2) lists the kinds of facilities for which land may be reserved, including roads, schools, parks and "areas to be acquired for any other public purposes." Section 303(2) limits the reservation to a period of time no longer than the short-term program adopted for the municipality, see *supra* p. 79, but land may again be designated for reservation after the initial reservation has expired.

Note that the ALI model dispenses with the variance procedure authorized by the New Jersey law. What does the ALI model substitute in its place? You should consider the constitutionality of the ALI model in light of the decisions interpreting the constitutionality of the more conventional models, which are reproduced and discussed below.

2. Several states have official map statutes which do not contain a variance provision. *See,* for example, Wash. Rev. Code Ann. §§ 47.28.025-026 (1970). This statute authorizes any "authority in behalf of the state" to establish and record a plan showing new highway locations. No buildings may be constructed or improvements to buildings made within any highway location lines shown on the plan, and no compensation is payable for any buildings constructed or improvements made within these lines. No permits for any improvements are to be issued within these highway location lines by any authority. Unless an action to condemn or acquire land located within the highway location lines is commenced within one year of the filing of the plan the reservation lapses. Again, what about the constitutionality of this statute?

D. MANDELKER & G. WAITE, A STUDY OF FUTURE ACQUISITION AND RESERVATION OF HIGHWAY RIGHTS-OF-WAY, 36, 37 (U.S. Bureau of Public Roads, 1963)

[The early cases on official maps were inconclusive, as the following excerpt indicates. Note, indeed, how the New York and Wisconsin courts avoided a direct holding on constitutionality by adopting exhaustion of remedies and prematurity approaches in their decisions. — Eds.]

A good example is the history of map legislation in New York State. After a very early decision upholding the nineteenth-century map law, the upper court held that law unconstitutional in *Forster v. Scott* [32 N.E. 976 (N.Y. 1893)]. Here the official map covered all of the lot. This fact heavily influenced the court's decision, which noted that the owner was virtually deprived of his right to build. Furthermore, at that time the law denied compensation for any building placed in the bed of an unopened street, and contained no variance provision. This combination of restrictions led the court to hold the law invalid, on the ground that it deprived the owner of any beneficial use of his property without compensation.

Following the *Forster* case, the [model] Bassett-Williams version of the official map law was adopted, and several changes were made. The provision denying compensation was deleted. The variance provision was inserted. In *Headley v. City of Rochester* [5 N.E.2d 198 (N.Y. 1936)] the new version of the act was sustained by the upper court. It found that the official map was necessary to protect the integrity of the street. Any questions about the taking of land without payment of compensation were solved by the variance provision, which could take care of hardship cases. In this case, no application for a permit was made, and as compared with the *Forster* case, the lot owner was left the major portion of his lot on which to build. Finally, the provision denying compensation had been removed.

While the *Headley* case may be read on the narrow procedural point that the person challenging the statute had not first applied for a permit, the significance of this holding is deeper than might at first be realized. The issues are sharpened considerably in the Wisconsin case upholding an official map law, *State ex rel. Miller v. Manders* [86 N.W.2d 469 (Wis. 1957)]. In this case, practically ninety percent of the available lot frontage had been placed in the bed of the proposed street. The Wisconsin court first approved the planning objective of the statute, noting that "the constitution will accommodate a wide range of community planning devices to meet the pressing problems of community growth, deterioration, and change." Thus the official map was sustained as a planning technique and *ad hoc* approaches to a similar problem were distinguished. [*I.e.,* the court distinguished cases in which zoning ordinances had restricted the use of property in order to depress its value for condemnation purposes. — Eds.]

The Wisconsin court then held that the lot owner's proper remedy in a case like this was to seek a variance and then, if it was denied, to seek court review of the denial by means of certiorari. In other words, what the *Headley* and *Manders* cases mean is that the official map act will be insulated from constitutional attack if the court follows the exhaustion doctrine. As in the case of zoning laws, the court approves the map act in principle, and relegates any allegations of substantial damage to administrative relief by way of the variance procedure. This approach was taken in the *Manders* case even though the court hinted that the substantial restriction placed on the lot would have presented an appropriate case for administrative relief.

A final subsidiary point is left undecided by these opinions. Under the Bassett-Williams model of the official map act, adopted both in New York and in Wisconsin, the statute does not deny compensation to buildings placed in the bed of an unopened street. A provision to this effect has been inserted in that part of the Wisconsin law which is applicable to extraterritorial extensions of the map, but was not involved in the *Manders* decision. The problem is not a difficult one as a matter of statutory construction, since a building erected without a permit would appear to be an illegal structure and removable as such. However, the *Headley* case relied on the absence of such a clause in dismissing the challenge to the New York act, and only in Pennsylvania has a denial-of-compensation clause been litigated and sustained. (The Pennsylvania statute did not contain a hardship variance provision.)

Even so, the removal-by-injunction analogy ought to be helpful here. Injunctive relief would clearly be available to remove an offending structure that was erected without a permit, and denial of compensation would appear equally as reasonable as a penalty. [For a published version of the police power section of the report, see Mandelker, Planning the Freeway: Interim Controls in Highway Programs, 1964 Duke L.J. 439. — Eds.]

Comments: Recent doctrinal developments have placed conflicting pressures on official map legislation. This legislation is supported by a tendency to uphold regulatory programs based on comprehensive planning, and by increasing judicial receptiveness to interim regulatory controls, of which the official map is one example. On the other hand, see *infra* p. 236, the courts have become increasingly sensitized to regulatory programs that impose unreasonable delays, and will strive in these cases to find an unconstitutional taking. In addition, the courts are hostile to over-restrictive regulation which amounts to a confiscation of the landowner's property. The following case from New York State illustrates these tendencies:

ROCHESTER BUSINESS INSTITUTE v. CITY OF ROCHESTER

Supreme Court of New York, Appellate Division
(Intermediate Appellate Court)
25 App. Div. 2d 97, 267 N.Y.S.2d 274 (1966)

Before WILLIAMS, P. J., and GOLDMAN, HENRY, DEL VECCHIO and MARSH, JJ.

PER CURIAM:

Defendant City of Rochester appeals from a judgment which declared that Section 35 of the General City Law, the Official Map or Plan of the City of Rochester and the ordinances establishing it are unconstitutional and void to the extent that their application prevents the plaintiffs Rochester Business Institute, Inc. (hereinafter referred to as R.B.I.) and Franklin-Andrews Corporation (hereinafter referred to as Franklin-Andrews) from constructing a building within the area of the proposed Court Street widening. The judgment further directed the City upon presentation of plans for the building described in the complaint, which otherwise comply with the ordinances and regulations, to issue to the plaintiffs the necessary permits for construction.

Plaintiff R.B.I. in 1962 leased from plaintiff Franklin-Andrews property located on the south side of Court Street extending from Chestnut to Cortland Streets in the City of Rochester, which property adjoined a parcel owned by R.B.I. to the south, the combined plot having an area of approximately 40,000 square feet. The lease provided for a term of fifty years, annual net rental of $15,000 and included a five year option to purchase for $300,000.

In 1930, pursuant to Article 3 of the General City Law (Cons. Laws, ch. 21), the Rochester City Council adopted an ordinance (No. 2174), commonly known as the Bartholomew Major Street Plan, which provided for the widening of certain streets and the future construction of proposed streets. The Official Map then adopted provided for a 30-foot widening of the south side of Court Street, and particularly covered the Franklin-Andrews property leased to R.B.I. and other properties in the vicinity. Notwithstanding this ordinance, R.B.I. on July 10, 1963 filed plans with the City Building Bureau for the proposed construction of a ten-story building fronting on Court Street. These plans disregarded the 30-foot setback requirement and a permit was refused. Plaintiffs appealed to the Zoning Board of Appeals, which on September 26th approved the application on the specific condition that the building should be set back 14 feet from the line of Court Street. This reduction of the 30-foot setback was the recognition by the Zoning Board of an ordinance which had been introduced in the City Council on September 10th, upon the recommendation of the Planning Commission, which amended the 1930 ordinance to make it more comprehensive and current. The adoption of this ordinance on October 8th amended the 1930 "official map or plan, by striking therefrom certain proposed changes and substituting therefor proposals known as central business district official street map". This ordinance updated the original plan to make it more appropriate and responsive to contemporary conditions of traffic due to changes which had occurred in the thirty-three years since its adoption. It specifically provided for a 14-foot widening of Court Street from Clinton Avenue South to Broadway, which area included the Franklin-Andrews property leased to R.B.I. It should be noted here that Court Street west of Clinton Avenue South is and has been 64 feet wide and that commencing at Clinton Avenue South and proceeding east to Broadway the width of Court Street is reduced to 50 feet. Plaintiffs contend that the City's denial of their right to construct the R.B.I. building on the 14 feet of the proposed bed of Court Street violates the Constitutions of the United States and the State of New York for it constitutes a taking of their property without due process and without just compensation.

Section 35 of the General City Law provides that no permit shall be issued to build in the mapped bed of a proposed street as laid out on the official map or plan of a city, such as provided for in the Bartholomew Major Street Plan. This legislation recognized that there may be instances where an exception should be made for it provided:

> that if the land within such mapped street or highway is not yielding a fair return on its value to the owner, the board of appeals or other similar board in any city which has established such a board having power to make variances or exception in zoning regulations shall have power in a specific case. . . to grant a permit for a building in such street or highway which will as little as practicable increase the cost of opening such street or highway, or tend to cause a change of such official map or plan, and such board may impose reasonable requirements as a condition of granting such permit, which requirements shall inure to the benefit of the city.

The question is whether this statute can be sustained on the facts in this record as a valid exercise of the police power on the ground that it promotes the general welfare, or whether it has been so applied as to render it unconstitutional. The essence of the testimony produced by the parties was directed toward the all important question of whether or not R.B.I. would suffer substantial damage if it were compelled to set back its proposed building 14 feet. Two sets of plans were introduced into evidence — the so-called original plan in which was incorporated the use of roller rink structure owned by R.B.I. and destroyed by fire before trial and a new plan made after the fire, which included the setback and a redesigned building where the roller rink formerly stood. R.B.I. planned to construct a ten-story building with a school for its own use and offices which it would rent, the complex to cost approximately $2,500,000. The inability to use the 14-foot strip resulted in a 7.1 per cent land loss to the combined parcels owned by both plaintiffs. R.B.I.'s architect testified that in order to have the same amount of floor space without the use of the 14-foot strip it would require "about one or two more stories on the tower" and would increase the cost "around five or six per cent more." The Trial Court found that the setback requirement would add substantially more to the construction and maintenance cost of the building and would afford substantially less rental income. Applying the plaintiffs' estimate of six per cent, the construction costs would increase $150,000, but there would be no diminution in rental income for the change in plans would result in the same amount of office space as originally planned. It should be noted that plaintiffs' plans provided for a 10-foot setback from the property line with a four foot overhang starting with the second floor. Thus, if the building were moved back but four more feet, the building line would comply with the 14-foot setback and there would be a resulting loss of only four feet. This would, as the Trial Court found, produce some changes in the plans, such as the elimination of a thirty foot courtyard between the buildings and others, but would not substantially change the appearance or utility of the structure.

Assuming, however, that the setback requirement would cause some injury to the plaintiffs, we are confronted with the question of whether this injury is of such substantial character as to constitute a taking of plaintiffs' property without just compensation. This very same question, involving an attack on the constitutionality of General City Law § 35 and the Bartholomew Plan, was presented for adjudication thirty years ago in *Headley v. City of Rochester,* 272 N.Y. 197, 5 N.E.2d 198. In discussing the background and reasons for Section 35 of the General City Law the court established guidelines at page 201, 5 N.E.2d at page 199:

> The mere adoption of a general plan or map showing streets and parks to be laid out or widened in the future, without acquisition by the city of title to the land in the bed of the street, can be of little benefit to the public if the development of the land abutting upon and in the bed of the proposed streets proceeds in a haphazard way, without taking into account the general plan adopted and, especially, if permanent buildings are erected on the land in the bed of the proposed street which would hamper its acquisition or use for its intended purpose. So long as the owners of parcels of land which lie partly in the bed of streets shown on such a map are free to place permanent buildings in the bed of a proposed street and to provide private ways and approaches which have no relation to the proposed system of public streets, the integrity of the plan may be destroyed by the haphazard or even malicious development of one parcel or tract to the injury of other owners who may have developed their own tracts in a manner which conforms to the general map or plan.

The court noted that the basic conflict is this: if the City were compelled to acquire title now and pay for lands within the mapped streets, its ability to plan now for the future would become illusory. Alternatively, if the land were encumbered and left in private ownership without just compensation and the encumbrance restricted its use and substantially diminished its value, this might be beyond the power of the state or municipality. To resolve this conflict Section 35 was enacted.

It is clear that "the issue as to whether a particular governmental restriction amounted to a constitutional taking... [is] a question properly turning upon the particular circumstances of each case" (*United States v. Central Eureka Mining Co.,* 357 U.S. 155, 168, 78) and requires balancing the interests between the general public welfare and the extent of the diminution of the property value. Thus, constitutionality of the statute depends upon the substantiality of damage as compared with the effect upon public purpose and the advancement of the general welfare. . . . If the impact of the planning map produces such substantial damage as to render the property useless for any reasonable purpose, there is an unconstitutional taking. . . . On the other hand, if the restriction placed upon the property is necessary to promote the general welfare and does not deprive the owner of use for a reasonable purpose, then the attack upon Section 35 must fail. There is little doubt that an objective which seeks to achieve better city planning falls fully within the concept of promoting the general welfare. . . . The Trial Court found that "the proposed widening of Court Street is presently desirable and may eventually become necessary". This was based upon the physical fact of the narrowing of Court Street from 64 feet to 50 feet at one of the busiest and most heavily travelled intersections in the business district and immediately at the point of the present construction of a thirty story office building, the tallest structure in the State outside of Metropolitan New York City. The record fully supports not only the desirability but the vital need for street widening at this juncture.

The plaintiffs' "Compensation for such interference with and restriction in the use of [their] property is [not only] found in the share that the owner enjoys in the common benefit secured to all" (*People ex rel. Wineburgh Adv. Co. v. Murphy,* 195 N.Y. 126, 131, 88 N.E. 17, 19,) but also in the case at bar in the fact that reasonable and profitable use of their property, in the form of the proposed building, can be made. The increase of six per cent in the construction cost, which will give plaintiff R.B.I. the full use it intends to make of the property, with little or no loss in rental income, is truly trivial damage when compared to the great injury to the general welfare which will result if the City is prevented from planning for this essential improvement of traffic conditions. If the minimal damage to plaintiffs involved here by enforcement of the setback restriction renders the specific application of the Rochester Plan unconstitutional, then the public is in grave danger of being deprived of the very valuable tool of city planning for the future. Furthermore, the negotiations of plaintiffs' attorney with the City Manager in an effort to sell the 14 feet to the City negates any reasonable claim that plaintiffs cannot make profitable use of the parcel without building in the reserved portion.

The City's position is supported by the test asserted by Judge Van

Voorhis in *Vangellow v. City of Rochester,* 190 Misc. 128, 134, 71 N.Y.S.2d 672, 678, in this significant statement:

> Nevertheless, provided that it can be accomplished without materially diminishing the value or usefulness of the premises, constitutional law does not prevent the City, in the exercise of the police power pursuant to the enabling act, from requiring that the new building be erected in such manner as to minimize the damage thereto which will result when and if, in the future, the City shall decide to widen West Main Street.

We recognize that the ordinance and statute cannot be used as a substitute for condemnation proceedings to defeat payment of just compensation by depressing values and thus reducing the amount to be paid for the 14 feet when actually taken. It requires no clairvoyance or great real property expertise to deduce from this record that the delay of the City in appropriating this property will result in a greater cost to it of the land. The erection of the Xerox complex almost directly across the street from the subject property should greatly enhance land values in the vicinity.

As in all matters dealing with ordinances and statutes, the court must so construe the official map law as to sustain its constitutionality in a given situation if it is possible to do so. . . . In our judgment, plaintiffs' evidence fails to rebut the presumption of constitutionality as applied to the land in question and the City's requirement of a 14-foot setback is a valid exercise of the police power and consonant with sound city planning.

The judgment should be reversed upon the law and the facts and defendant City is entitled to judgment declaring that Section 35 of the General City Law, the Official Map and Plan of the City of Rochester and the ordinances establishing it are valid and constitutional; all of which shall be without prejudice to plaintiffs, if so advised, to make a new application to the Zoning Board of Appeals for a permit to construct a building which complies with the ordinances of the City of Rochester.

Judgment unanimously reversed on the law and facts without costs of this appeal to either party and declaratory judgment directed in favor of defendant in accordance with the judgment.

Comments: 1. *See also Grisor, S.A. v. City of New York,* 374 N.Y.S.2d 549 (N.Y. Sup. Ct. 1975) (trial court), *rev'd on other grounds,* 387 N.Y.S.2d 271 (N.Y. App. Div. 1976). The city had embarked on an expansion of a waste water treatment plant and as part of that expansion planned to develop a peripheral street system around the plant. As part of this system the city filed an official map indicating a new street, which was to run through plaintiff's property. A hardship permit for a building on the property was denied, in part because the building could be placed on another part of the property, outside the bed of the mapped street.

In its action the plaintiff claimed that the application of the official map law and the denial of the permit were unconstitutional. Since the proposed building could be placed outside the bed of the mapped street the court found that the plaintiff had not been deprived of the use of his property. Expansion of the treatment plant was under way, and so the court could not find that the official map would deprive the plaintiff of the use of its property for an indefinite period. Therefore, the official map could be sustained as a valid interim regulation of the plaintiff's property. However, the court added that "prolonged and continued procrastination and unreasonable delay on the part of the municipality. . . might well ripen into an unconscionable and unconstitutional taking of plaintiff's property." *Id.* at 553.

In its opinion the court distinguished *Roer Constr. Corp. v. City of New Rochelle,* 136 N.Y.S.2d 414 (N.Y. Sup. Ct. 1954) (trial court). In this case the court had held the official map act unconstitutional as applied to plaintiff's property because all of its land had been placed within the official map, with the result that the map would deprive it of the use of its property for an indefinite time. *Accord, Jensen v. City of New York,* 369 N.E.2d 1179 (N.Y. 1977).

2. Not all of the decisions have been hospitable to the official map, and some of the recent decisions have been adverse on the constitutionality issue. Consider the following:

Miller v. City of Beaver Falls, 82 A.2d 34 (Pa. 1957). This case considered the constitutionality of an official map act authorizing a three-year reservation for parks and playgrounds. While admitting that the use of the official map to reserve future locations for streets had long been held constitutional in Pennsylvania, the court refused to extend this protection to the park reservation. "Shall this principle relating to streets, which are narrow, well defined and absolutely necessary, be extended to parks and playgrounds which may be very large and very desirable but not necessary? . . . [P]lotting this ground for a park or playground and freezing it for three years is, in reality, a taking of property by possibility, contingency, blockade and subterfuge. . . ." *Id.* at 36.

Lomarch Corp. v. Mayor & Common Council, 237 A.2d 881 (N.J. 1968). This case considered the constitutionality of a New Jersey law that authorized the municipality, upon application for approval of a subdivision plat, to reserve for public future use any land shown on the official map for park or playground use. The reservation was effective for one year. The court held that the reservation amounted to a unilateral option to reserve the land, and was constitutional only if the municipality paid fair compensation for the reservation of the option. It noted that the landowner should receive the value of an option to purchase the land for one year, a requirement which has now been codified, N.J. Stat. Ann. § 40:55D-44 (West Supp. 1977).

Compare the treatment of the *Lomarch* case in the following New Jersey decisions: *Far-Gold Constr. Co. v. Borough of Chatham,* 357 A.2d 765 (N.J.

Super. 1976): adoption of resolution expressing desire to acquire tract of land does not fall within *Lomarch* rule; this was merely planning in anticipation of a public improvement; *Kingston East Realty Co. v. State,* 336 A.2d 40 (N.J. Super. 1975): state official map act authorizing no more than 120-day reservation of land for highways does not fall within *Lomarch* rule; period of restriction was substantially less and was designed to reduce costs of public acquisition; *Meadowland Regional Dev. Agency v. Hackensack Meadowlands Dev. Comm'n,* 293 A.2d 192 (N.J. Super.), *cert. denied,* 299 A.2d 69 (N.J. 1972): interim ordinance freezing construction in Meadowlands area pending preparation of comprehensive plan does not fall within *Lomarch* rule. Can these cases be reconciled?

Lackman v. Hall, 364 A.2d 1244 (Del. Ch. 1976): This case considered the constitutionality of an official map act authorizing the reservation of land for future acquisition for state highways. There was no variance provision, but the act did contain a provision (found in some official map acts) that if the affected landowner filed application for a building permit the permit had to be granted unless the state proceeded within a stated period of time to acquire the land.

It was this feature of the law which the court found objectionable: "Plaintiffs with considerable logic say that this places them on the horns of a dilemma. The price they pay for seeking a building permit to improve their property may not only be denial of the permit but also the immediate loss of the property through condemnation." *Id.* at 1251. Moreover, should the state move to acquire their land for future highway use they would transgress the holding of an earlier Delaware case prohibiting the acquisition of land for highways in advance of need. See the discussion in the Note, *infra* p. 108. Can you draft an official map act which would meet the objections of all of these cases?

3. There has been some judicial interpretation of the variance provisions found in some official map statutes. Similar variance provisions in zoning ordinances have been interpreted to include a uniqueness requirement; the hardship to the property must be unique before the variance can be granted. However, since all of the property affected by an official map will be equally affected it can be argued that the uniqueness test of the zoning cases should not be applied. *Phillips v. Westfield Bd. of Adjustment,* 130 A.2d 866 (N.J. Super.), *appeal dismissed,* 132 A.2d 558 (N.J. 1957), indicates that a "uniqueness" requirement may not be applicable to hardship variances granted under official map laws. This case construed a provision of the New Jersey planning act which provided that no building permit may be issued unless the structure fronts on a "suitably improved" street. The statute authorized a hardship variance.

In this case, twenty lots had been laid out along an accepted but unimproved street. Applicant's lot was one of these, and adjoined a corner lot which fronted on an improved street. The applicant was granted a variance which allowed him to install an access road which did not meet standard paving specifications. In upholding the variance, the court held that a uniqueness requirement could not be imported into the planning law. The choice in implementing the plan, said the court, is not whether individual lots require special consideration. Instead, the problem is whether the plan calls for a street in that location, and if so, whether a temporary roadway will be sufficient for present purposes. Although other owners of property on the street might also be entitled to a variance, this consideration is not determinative. Besides, as the street is built up the municipality may pave it, and the grounds for hardship may disappear.

Compare *59 Front St. Realty Corp. v. Klaess,* 160 N.Y.S.2d 265 (N.Y. Sup. Ct. 1957) (trial court), where virtually one half of the property was covered by a street widening line shown on an official map. The board of appeals had refused a variance, but the court reversed. It may have been influenced by the fact that the village had adopted an amendment widening the official map line after the property owner's building had burned, and after he had applied for a reconstruction permit.

4. Some ticklish compensation problems arise in the use of official maps. For example, if the theory of the *Lomarch* case is adopted and compensation is required for the interim period of the restriction, what compensation should be provided? The New Jersey statute cited *supra* adopted suggestions made by the *Lomarch* opinion and provides:

> . . .[J]ust compensation shall be deemed to be the fair market value of an option to purchase the land reserved for the period of reservation;. . . [and] shall include, but not be limited to, consideration of the real property taxes apportioned to the land reserved and prorated for the period of reservation. The developers shall be compensated for the reasonable increased cost of legal, engineering, or other professional services incurred in connection with obtaining subdivision approval or site plan approval, as the case may be, caused by the reservation.

Note that this provision, which is in part of the statute authorizing subdivision control, was enacted prior to some of the post-*Lomarch* decisions discussed in Comment 2.

The *Lomarch* decision had indicated that the expenses listed in the last sentence should be compensated only if the municipality took title to the land. Why this distinction?

If the land placed in the reserved area is undeveloped at the time of acquisition what value should be placed on it when the agency moves to acquire it? What if the local zoning authority rezones land around the proposed right-of-way for industrial use, but omits the land within the right-of-way, restricting it to residential uses? If substantial development occurs in the vicinity of the restricted land after it is placed on the official map but before it is taken, can the landowner argue enhanced value? For a situation that arose when different levels of government were involved in the planning and highway building process see *County of Santa Clara v. Curtner,* 54 Cal. Rptr. 257 (Cal. App. 1966).

State Nat'l Bank v. Planning & Zoning Comm'n, 239 A.2d 528 (Conn. 1968). The tract in question was zoned residential and was also shown on the town's comprehensive plan as a proposed civic center site. Rezoning to commercial uses was denied, and the zoning was upheld. Finding the residential zoning reasonable under the circumstances, the court did not find the ordinance unconstitutional simply because the town plan showed the civic center reservation. If the property owner had been denied the use of the land for the zoned use because of the planning designation, that would have been a different matter. Besides, a town plan is merely advisory.

If this land is later acquired for a civic center what compensation will be paid?

5. Setback restrictions are common in local zoning ordinances. They usually authorize a setback of buildings and improvements on the property at designated distances from the street. These ordinances, which present constitutional problems similar to the official map, have usually been held constitutional. *Gorieb v. Fox,* 274 U.S. 603 (1927) (upholding setback as density control preventing encroachment and light and air). Problems have nevertheless arisen when the setback has been used to preserve the right-of-way for a proposed street. In *Mayer v. Dade County,* 82 So.2d 513 (Fla. 1955), the property owner intended to build a hospital on its tract. To protect a right-of-way for a proposed street the county imposed an additional 15-foot setback. This requirement was successfully challenged, the court holding that the property owner had been singled out for an "unusual" application of the setback ordinance. *See also Gordon v. City of Warren Planning & Urban Renewal Comm'n,* 199 N.W.2d 65 (Mich. 1972) (zoning statute authorizing setbacks does not authorize reservation for street right-of-way). For discussion see 1964 Duke L.J., *supra* at 440-46.

PROBLEM

Controls related to official maps can be used as interim protection devices in large-scale projects, such as new towns and urban renewal projects. Consider the following:

(1) In an urban renewal project, the urban renewal agency wishes to prevent any new development from occurring until its plan has been completed and project implementation has started. To put this control into effect, the agency secures from the city council an ordinance prohibiting any new development or substantial changes in existing structures during the interim period between the designation of the project and the adoption of the urban renewal plan. Judicial reaction to this kind of ordinance has varied. *See State ex rel. Mumma v. Stansberry,* 214 N.E.2d 684 (Ohio App. 1964) (held invalid). *Contra, Hunter v. Adams,* 4 Cal. Rptr. 776 (Cal. App. 1960). Note that several years may elapse between the designation of the project and the adoption of the urban renewal plan.

(2) What if the same approach is used in an area planned to be built as a new town? Since the developer is not able to acquire all the land needed for the new town at one time, he has the county council designate the area of the new town as a new town planning area, and then secures passage of an ordinance similar to that described in the urban renewal example given above.

A NOTE ON THE ADVANCE ACQUISITION OF LAND FOR PUBLIC IMPROVEMENTS AND FACILITIES

As an alternative to the reservation of land for highways and other public facilities under official map acts, state and local agencies often embark on advance land acquisition programs to obtain land needed for future public uses. Indeed, the federal-aid highway law now authorizes a program of federal loans to the states for the advance acquisition of land for highways. 23 U.S.C. § 108 (1976). Actual construction must begin no later than ten years following the end of the fiscal year in which the funds are advanced. *Id.* § 108(c)(3).

Two problems in the use of advance acquisition programs arise at the state and local level. One is the question of statutory authority. In the highway programs, for example, most states have impliedly or expressly authorized the advance acquisition of land for highway purposes. A second question is whether the advance acquisition is needed. If the proposed improvement is too conjectural or uncertain some courts will hold that there is no "necessity" for the advance acquisition. Most courts have reacted favorably on this question, aided by the usual judicial presumption accorded determinations of necessity by the courts.

State Road Dep't v. Southland, Inc., 117 So.2d 512 (Fla. 1960), is a typical case. This was an advance acquisition for an interstate highway, carried out to forestall residential development. No construction on this segment of the highway had been started, no public use of the land acquired was planned for at least two years, no funds for construction of the planned segment had been budgeted, and no engineering plans for construction had been drawn. However, the department clearly intended to use the land acquired for the highway, and rights-of-way had been acquired for other portions of the highway.

The court upheld the advance acquisition, noting the usual rule that a determination of the need for an acquisition will not be upset in the absence of fraud, bad faith, or a gross abuse of discretion. None of these was found in this case. The court appeared to rely on the fact that construction of the interstate system, including this segment, was part of a national program in which the Florida department had cooperated with the national agency in the selection of the highway routes. It added that "[l]ong-range planning of a coordinated system of interstate highways has been recognized as an economic necessity by the legislature. . . ." *Id.* at 516. Moreover, advance acquisition could not injure but in most cases would benefit the landowner. *Contra, State v. 14.69 Acres of Land,* 226 A.2d 828 (Del. 1967), and *see Lackman v. Hall, supra* p. 106.

Is the court's optimism in *Southland* about the effect of the advance acquisition on the landowner always justified? In that case the highway would sever a subdivision owned by Southland which was in the course of development. Southland therefore argued that damages to the subdivision from a possible change of grade resulting from the highway construction could not be assessed at the time of advance acquisition, reasoning that construction plans for the highway were not known. To this the court answered that, because the new highway would be a limited access facility, no access to the highway would be permitted from the subdivision. Therefore, no possible damages from a change of grade would be compensable. The advance acquisition was to take all rights, including rights of access, air, view and light appurtenant to the land taken, so that the jury could award any compensation resulting from the taking of the land and the loss of these rights. Is this a sufficient answer? Of course, if the construction of the highway visited any physical damage on the Southland development, through possible flooding due to the highway construction or otherwise, an action for damages would lie by way of inverse condemnation, so-called "reverse" eminent domain. *See generally* Note,

Problems of Advance Land Acquisition, 52 Minn. L. Rev. 1175 (1968). For discussion of advance acquisition in the highway context see Vance, Advance Acquisition of Highway Rights-of-Way, in 2 Selected Studies in Highway Law 903 (J. Vance ed. 1976).

If just compensation is paid and can properly be assessed, why should a court disfavor advance acquisition as an alternative to reservation through the official map technique? Does the payment of compensation completely foreclose consideration of the "taking" problems considered in the official map cases? Are courts perhaps worried that the advance acquisition of land not needed by the public agency would allow it at some future time to speculate in the later sale of the land at a profit? Note the inconvenience to the developer in the *Southland* case that will occur if the highway is not built. Recall in that case that the proposed highway severed the development.

Chapter 3

THE LEGAL BASES FOR LAND USE CONTROLS
A. NUISANCE LAW AND THE POLICE POWER

BOVE v. DONNER-HANNA COKE CORPORATION

Supreme Court of New York, Appellate Division
236 App.Div. 37, 258 N.Y.S. 229 (1932)

EDGCOMB, J. The question involved upon this appeal is whether the use to which the defendant has recently put its property constitutes a private nuisance, which a court of equity should abate.

In 1910 plaintiff purchased two vacant lots at the corner of Abby and Baraga streets in the city of Buffalo, and two years later built a house thereon. The front of the building was converted into a grocery store, and plaintiff occupied the rear as a dwelling. She rented the two apartments on the second floor.

Defendant operates a large coke oven on the opposite side of Abby street. The plant runs twenty-four hours in the day, and three hundred and sixty-five days in the year. Of necessity, the operation has to be continuous, because the ovens would be ruined if they were allowed to cool off. The coke is heated to a temperature of around 2,000 degrees F., and is taken out of the ovens and run under a "quencher," where 500 or 600 gallons of water are poured onto it at one time. This is a necessary operation in the manufacture of coke. The result is a tremendous cloud of steam, which rises in a shaft and escapes into the air, carrying with it minute portions of coke, and more or less gas. This steam and the accompanying particles of dirt, as well as the dust which comes from a huge coal pile necessarily kept on the premises, and the gases and odors which emanate from the plant, are carried by the wind in various directions, and frequently find their way onto the plaintiff's premises and into her house and store. According to the plaintiff this results in an unusual amount of dirt and soot accumulating in her house, and prevents her opening the windows on the street side; she also claims that she suffers severe headaches by breathing the impure air occasioned by this dust and these offensive odors, and that her health and that of her family has been impaired, all to her very great discomfort and annoyance; she also asserts that this condition has lessened the rental value of her property, and has made it impossible at times to rent her apartments.

Claiming that such use of its plant by the defendant deprives her of the full enjoyment of her home, invades her property rights, and constitutes a private nuisance, plaintiff brings this action in equity

111

to enjoin the defendant from the further maintenance of said nuisance, and to recover the damages which she asserts she has already sustained.

As a general rule, an owner is at liberty to use his property as he sees fit, without objection or interference from his neighbor, provided such use does not violate an ordinance or statute. There is, however, a limitation to this rule; one made necessary by the intricate, complex and changing life of to-day. The old and familiar maxim that one must so use his property as not to injure that of another (*sic utere tuo ut alienum non laedas*) is deeply imbedded in our law. An owner will not be permitted to make an unreasonable use of his premises to the material annoyance of his neighbor if the latter's enjoyment of life or property is materially lessened thereby. This principle is aptly stated by Andrews, Ch. J., in *Booth v. R., W. & O. T. R. R. Co.* (140 N.Y. 267, 274, 35 N.E. 592, 594) as follows: "The general rule that no one has absolute freedom in the use of his property, but is restrained by the co-existence of equal rights in his neighbor to the use of his property, so that each in exercising his right must do no act which causes injury to his neighbor, is so well understood, is so universally recognized, and stands so impregnably in the necessities of the social state, that its vindication by argument would be superfluous. The maxim which embodies it is sometimes loosely interpreted as forbidding all use by one of his own property, which annoys or disturbs his neighbor in the enjoyment of his property. The real meaning of the rule is that one may not use his own property to the injury of any legal right of another."

Such a rule is imperative, or life to-day in our congested centers would be intolerable and unbearable. If a citizen was given no protection against unjust harassment arising from the use to which the property of his neighbor was put, the comfort and value of his home could easily be destroyed by any one who chose to erect an annoyance nearby, and no one would be safe, unless he was rich enough to buy sufficient land about his home to render such disturbance impossible. When conflicting rights arise, a general rule must be worked out which, so far as possible, will preserve to each party that to which he has a just claim.

While the law will not permit a person to be driven from his home, or to be compelled to live in it in positive distress or discomfort because of the use to which other property nearby has been put, it is not every annoyance connected with business which will be enjoined. Many a loss arises from acts or conditions which do not create a ground for legal redress. *Damnum absque injuria* is a familiar maxim. Factories, stores and mercantile establishments are essential to the prosperity of the nation. They necessarily invade our cities, and interfere more or less with the peace and tranquility of the neighborhood in which they are located.

One who chooses to live in the large centers of population cannot expect the quiet of the country. Congested centers are seldom free from smoke, odors and other pollution from houses, shops and factories, and one who moves into such a region cannot hope to find the pure air of the village or outlying district. A person who prefers the advantages of community life must expect to experience some of the resulting inconveniences. Residents of industrial centers must endure without redress a certain amount of annoyance and discomfiture which is incident to life in such a locality. Such inconvenience is of minor importance compared with the general good of the community.

. . .

Whether the particular use to which one puts his property constitutes a nuisance or not is generally a question of fact, and depends upon whether such use is reasonable under all the surrounding circumstances. What would distress and annoy one person would have little or no effect upon another; what would be deemed a disturbance and a torment in one locality would be unnoticed in some other place; a condition which would cause little or no vexation in a business, manufacturing or industrial district might be extremely tantalizing to those living in a restricted and beautiful residential zone; what would be unreasonable under one set of circumstances would be deemed fair and just under another. Each case is unique. No hard and fast rule can be laid down which will apply in all instances. . . .

The inconvenience, if such it be, must not be fanciful, slight or theoretical, but certain and substantial, and must interfere with the physical comfort of the ordinarily reasonable person. . . .

Applying these general rules to the facts before us, it is apparent that defendant's plant is not a nuisance *per se,* and that the court was amply justified in holding that it had not become one by reason of the manner in which it had been conducted. Any annoyance to plaintiff is due to the nature of the business which the defendant conducts, and not to any defect in the mill, machinery or apparatus. The plant is modern and up to date in every particular. It was built under a contract with the Federal government, the details of which are not important here. The plans were drawn by the Kopperas Construction Company, one of the largest and best known manufacturers of coke plants in the world, and the work was done under the supervision of the War Department. No reasonable change or improvement in the property can be made which will eliminate any of the things complained of. If coke is made, coal must be used. Gas always follows the burning of coal, and steam is occasioned by throwing cold water on red hot coals.

The cases are legion in this and other States where a defendant has been held guilty of maintaining a nuisance because of the annoyance which he has caused his neighbor by reason of noise, smoke, dust, noxious gases and disagreeable smells which have emanated from his property. But smoke and noisome odors do not always constitute a nuisance. I find none of these cases controlling here; they all differ in some particular from the facts in the case at bar.

It is true that the appellant was a resident of this locality for several years before the defendant came on the scene of action, and that, when the plaintiff built her house, the land on which these coke ovens now stand was a hickory grove. But in a growing community changes are inevitable. This region was never fitted for a residential district; for years it has been peculiarly adapted for factory sites. This was apparent when plaintiff bought her lots and when she built her house. The land is low and lies adjacent to the Buffalo river, a navigable stream connecting with Lake Erie. Seven different railroads run through this area. Freight tracks and yards can be seen in every direction. Railroads naturally follow the low levels in passing through a city. Cheap transportation is an attraction which always draws factories and industrial plants to a locality. It is common knowledge that a combination of rail and water terminal facilities will stamp a section as a site suitable for industries of the heavier type, rather than for residential purposes. In 1910 there were at least eight industrial plants, with a total assessed valuation of over a million dollars, within a radius of a mile from plaintiff's house.

With all the dirt, smoke and gas which necessarily come from factory chimneys, trains and boats, and with full knowledge that this region was especially adapted for industrial rather than residential purposes, and that factories would increase in the future, plaintiff selected this locality as the site of her future home. She voluntarily moved into this district, fully aware of the fact that the atmosphere would constantly be contaminated by dirt, gas and foul odors; and that she could not hope to find in this locality the pure air of a strictly residential zone. She evidently saw certain advantages in living in this congested center. This is not the case of an industry, with its attendant noise and dirt, invading a quiet, residential district. It is just the opposite. Here a residence is built in an area naturally adapted for industrial purposes and already dedicated to that use. Plaintiff can hardly be heard to complain at this late date that her peace and comfort have been disturbed by a situation which existed, to some extent at least, at the very time she bought her property, and which condition she must have known would grow worse rather than better as the years went by.

To-day there are twenty industrial plants within a radius of less than a mile and three-quarters from appellant's house, with more than sixty-five smokestacks rising in the air, and belching forth clouds of smoke; every day there are 148 passenger trains, and 225 freight trains, to say nothing of switch engines, passing over these various railroad tracks near to the plaintiff's property; over 10,000 boats, a large portion of which burn soft coal, pass up and down the Buffalo river every season. Across the street, and within 300 feet from plaintiff's house, is a large tank of the Iroquois Gas Company which is used for the storage of gas.

The utter abandonment of this locality for residential purposes, and its universal use as an industrial center, becomes manifest when one considers that in 1929 the assessed valuation of the twenty industrial plants above referred to aggregated over $20,000,000, and that the city in 1925 passed a zoning ordinance putting this area in the third industrial district, a zone in which stockyards, glue factories, coke ovens, steel furnaces, rolling mills and other similar enterprises were permitted to be located.

One has only to mention these facts to visualize the condition of the atmosphere in this locality. It is quite easy to imagine that many of the things of which the plaintiff complains are due to causes over which the defendant has no control. At any rate, if appellant is immune from the annoyance occasioned by the smoke and odor which must necessarily come from these various sources, it would hardly seem that she could consistently claim that her health has been impaired, and that the use and enjoyment of her home have been seriously interfered with solely because of the dirt, gas and stench which have reached her from defendant's plant.

It is very true that the law is no respecter of persons, and that the most humble citizen in the land is entitled to identically the same protection accorded to the master of the most gorgeous palace. However, the fact that the plaintiff has voluntarily chosen to live in the smoke and turmoil of this industrial zone is some evidence, at least, that any annoyance which she has suffered from the dirt, gas and odor which have emanated from defendant's plant is more imaginary and theoretical than it is real and substantial.

I think that the trial court was amply justified in refusing to interfere with the operation of the defendant's coke ovens. No consideration of public policy or private rights demands any such sacrifice of this industry.

Plaintiff is not entitled to the relief which she seeks for another reason.

Subdivision 25 of section 20 of the General City Law (added by Laws of 1917, chap. 483) gives to the cities of this State authority to regulate the location of industries and to district the city for that purpose. Pursuant to such authority the common council of the city of Buffalo adopted an ordinance setting aside the particular area in which defendant's plant is situated as a zone in which coke ovens might lawfully be located.

After years of study and agitation it has been found that development in conformity with some well-considered and comprehensive plan is necessary to the welfare of any growing municipality. The larger the community the greater becomes the need of such plan. Haphazard city building is ruinous to any city. Certain areas must be given over to industry, without which the country cannot long exist. Other sections must be kept free from the intrusion of trade and the distraction of business, and be set aside for homes, where one may live in a wholesome environment. Property owners, as well as the public, have come to recognize the absolute necessity of reasonable regulations of this character in the interest of public health, safety and general welfare, as well as for the conservation of property values. Such is the purpose of our zoning laws.

After due consideration the common council of Buffalo decreed that an enterprise similar to that carried on by the defendant might properly be located at the site of this particular coke oven. It is not for the court to step in and override such decision, and condemn as a nuisance a business which is being conducted in an approved and expert manner, at the very spot where the council said that it might be located. A court of equity will not ordinarily assume to set itself above officials to whom the law commits a decision, and reverse their discretion and judgment, unless bad faith is involved. No such charge is made here. . . .

I see no good reason why the decision of the Special Term should be disturbed. I think that the judgment appealed from should be affirmed.

All concur.

Judgment affirmed, with costs.

SCHLOTFELT v. VINTON FARMER'S SUPPLY COMPANY

Supreme Court of Iowa
252 Iowa 1102, 109 N.W.2d 695 (1961)

THOMPSON, Justice. Plaintiff's action was originally brought at law, but by stipulation of the parties was tried in equity. It alleged the creation and maintenance of a nuisance by the defendant in the operation of its feed grinding, feed mixing and fertilizer sales business in the City of Vinton, asked injunctive relief and further prayed for damages. The trial court entered its judgment and decree awarding plaintiff damages in the sum of $3,605 for depreciation in the rental value of plaintiff's property adjoining defendant's plant, and granting an injunction against the use of a public alley running along the south side of plaintiff's residence and of the plant for defendant's business purposes; ordering defendant to arrange its entrances and exits so that defendant and its customers would not use the alley in going to and from its plant; restraining defendant from operating its machinery so as to cause vibration, noise and annoyance to the occupants of plaintiff's property; and from so using its plant as to cause oat hulls, dust, or noxious odors to be emitted into the air either by normal or accidental means. The decree was entered on June 25, 1959, and the defendant was given until September 1 next to comply with the injunctive part of the decree; after that date the court decreed that a further hearing should be had to determine whether the defendant had corrected its procedures in conformity to the court's judgment. The defendant apparently did not elect to make the ordered changes, but on July 23, 1959, filed its notice of appeal to this court. We shall therefore consider the decree and judgment as final.

On May 6, 1939, the plaintiff acquired title to Lot 1 in Block 3, South Vinton, an addition to the City of Vinton, and has owned it at all times since. The property was then and still is improved by a substantial, modern, two-story residence. At the time plaintiff acquired his title Lots 2 and 3, lying immediately west, were unimproved. In 1942 the defendant purchased these two lots, and soon thereafter erected on Lot 3, the westerly one, a building 60 feet east and west and 120 feet north and south. It then began the business of grinding and mixing stock feeds, and selling fertilizer, and has since at all times continued handling feeds and fertilizer and livestock equipment, both at wholesale and retail. It grinds feed for farmer customers, and sells fertilizer and other equipment. The average employed force is about eight persons.

At the time of the erection of the first building, known in the record as No. 1, Vinton had no zoning ordinance affecting this block. About March 14, 1946, the city adopted a zoning ordinance which classified the properties of plaintiff and defendant as being in a restricted residence district. In March, 1958, that part of Block 3, which includes these properties, was rezoned as a restricted industry area. The plaintiff contends that there is no proper proof of this last-referred-to ordinance; but we think, although the matter is not of great importance, there was a sufficient showing that since 1958 the properties have been in a restricted industry zone. There is a good deal of discussion in the briefs of the effect of the zoning ordinances or absence of same, and whether the defendant did or did not secure permits for some of its buildings, if they were required. But as we view the case none of these questions is of controlling weight and we give them little consideration.

In March, 1946, the defendant built an addition to the No. 1 building. This structure was on Lot 2, immediately adjoining plaintiff's lot. Defendant's two lots have a combined area about 133 feet square. The 1946 building was 40 feet east and west and 120 feet north and south. It is a cement block fireproof structure, and its easterly wall is about one foot from the west line of plaintiff's property, and about eight feet from the rear porch of his house. Apparently the east wall of the No. 2 building was 20 feet in height. In 1951 the defendant built a silo at the southeast corner of its property. The east edge of this structure is within a few feet — from 2 to 6 feet, as shown by the evidence — of the west side of plaintiff's garage, which is attached to his house. In 1954 or 1955, the silo was enlarged by an addition on the top, which brought its total height to 36 feet. This was augmented by dust collectors 13 feet high, so that the silo with the additions is now 49 feet above the ground. It is within 10 to 12 feet of the southwest corner of plaintiff's house.

It is evident that the No. 2 building, with the silo at the south end, must seriously interfere with plaintiff's enjoyment of light and air. However, the trial court did not grant any injunctive relief against this condition, and plaintiff has not appealed. It is discussed, however, in connection with the question of damages allowed because of the decreased rental value of plaintiff's property. Other facts will be referred to in the divisions following.

I. Certain principles of law applicable to nuisances of the sort claimed to exist here are well settled. Some definitions are found in our statutes. Section 657.1, Code of 1958, I.C.A., provides: "Whatever is . . . offensive to the senses, or an obstruction to the free use of property, so as essentially to interfere with the comfortable enjoyment of life or property, is a nuisance, and a civil action by ordinary proceedings may be brought to enjoin and abate the same and to recover damages sustained on account thereof." Following this is a definition of nuisances which includes this language found in Section 657.2: "The following are nuisances: 1. . . . using any building or other place for the exercise of any trade, . . . which, by occasioning noxious exhalations, offensive smells, or other annoyances, becomes injurious and dangerous to the health, comfort, or property of individuals. . . ." These statutory definitions and enumerations do not modify the common-law rule applicable to nuisances. . . .

Another well established rule is that one must use his own property so that his neighbor's comfortable and reasonable use and enjoyment of his estate will not be unreasonably interfered with or disturbed. . . . We have also held: "A fair test as to whether the operation of such industry constitutes a nuisance has been said to be the reasonableness of conducting it in the manner, at the place and under the circumstances in question." *Riter v. Keokuk Electro-Metals Company*, supra, 248 Iowa 710, 722, 82 N.W.2d 151, 158. And to justify the abatement of a claimed nuisance the annoyance must be such as would cause physical discomfort or injury to a person of ordinary sensibilities. . . .

II. The record shows that the location of plaintiff's property and of defendant's plant is in what is generally a residential district of Vinton. There are two neighborhood groceries within a few blocks; there is a woodworking shop conducted in a small way in a garage; and there is some evidence of a filling station and a beauty salon not far away. The Rock Island railroad tracks are just north of the location. But the area is chiefly devoted to substantial residences, and has been so at all times material here. The city of Vinton had a population as shown by the federal census, in 1940, of 4,163; in 1950, of 4,307; and in 1960, of 4,781. It is a beautiful and prosperous small city; but it is evident it is not a great industrial center.

We have said that we do not regard the question of the zoning of the tract in which the properties are located as of importance. Nor do we consider the issuance of permits, or their refusal, as in any way controlling. The city could not, by zoning as an industrial district, or issuing permits for construction, authorize the creation or maintenance of a nuisance. . . . In *Pauly v. Montgomery,* 209 Iowa 699, 705, 706, 228 N.W. 648, 651, we said: "The city could not, by its action in issuing a permit *or otherwise,* authorize appellees to so conduct their business as to create a nuisance." (Italics supplied.) This rule is somewhat modified in *Dawson v. Laufersweiler,* supra, at page 856 of 241 Iowa, at page 730 of 43 N.W.2d, by the statement that granting a permit is an expression of municipal opinion which it is proper to consider on the matter of nuisance, but is not conclusive. In fact, it seems it should be given little attention in the case at bar. A building permit, or a commercial or industrial zoning, cannot be claimed to be an approval by the city of the conduct of a business so that a nuisance is caused to adjoining property owners.

III. We come next to a fact which we think is of much importance in the case at bar. It is uncontradicted that the plaintiff "was there first." When his house was built and first occupied is not shown; but certainly it was there in 1939 when plaintiff purchased it. Defendant's lots were then vacant; it was not until 1942 that its first building was erected. This brings into application another rule also well settled both by authority and by reason. In *Mahlstadt v. City of Indianola,* 251 Iowa 222, 231, 100 N.W.2d 189, 194, we quoted with approval from 66 C.J.S. Nuisances, § 8e, page 746, with reference to the distinction between a long-established business and a new business erected or threatened in the same vicinity. We pointed out, through this quotation and our own language, that it requires a much clearer case to justify a court of equity in interfering with a business long present than with a new business. We also said that the right of a person to pure air may be surrendered in part by his election to live in a location that is already occupied by business or industry which fouls the air with smoke, gas, soot or other impurities. The converse of this is, of course, that one has a considerably greater right to protest against the conduct of a business in a residence area where the objector has established his home with no knowledge that such an invasion is contemplated or may be attempted in the future. Priority of occupation is a circumstance of considerable weight, and it militates strongly in favor of the plaintiff here. The district, including plaintiff's home, was residential before defendant's plant was built; and in fact, at least up to the time of the trial, there was no other industry in any way comparable to that operated by defendant within an area of many blocks.

IV. The trial court ordered the defendant to cease operation of its machinery unless it could be done without annoyance to the occupants of the plaintiff's dwelling; by which we understand is meant that the machinery must be operated, if at all, so as not to cause undue noises and vibrations which would cause annoyance and discomfort to persons of ordinary sensibilities. The court also restrained the defendant from so operating its plant as to cause dust, oat hulls, or other particles of material, or noxious odors to be emitted into the air by normal or accidental means. . . .

The defendant says that these provisions of the decree, if enforced, will prevent the operation of its business; will, in fact, necessarily result in its closing. We can only hope this view is unduly pessimistic; for, as between the plaintiff, who found his clean and quiet residential neighborhood invaded by a business enterprise which causes loud and unusual noises and pollutes the air with dust and other matters, and the defendant, which erected its plant in such a neighborhood with full knowledge, the equities are altogether with the plaintiff. The defendant must have known of the character of the area and of its duty not to create or maintain a nuisance there when it built its plant; and the record shows that there were numerous complaints from time to time from householders in the vicinity both before and after the erection of the additions in later years. It must abate the nuisance it has created, even if unfortunately it means it can no longer operate its plant. . . .

V. The court enjoined the defendant from using the alley which runs along the south side of both properties except as "a usual and normal use of said public alley, applicable generally to residence districts in the City of Vinton, and (the injunction) shall not require the defendant to prevent its customers from making use of said public alley when said customers are not involved in the act of entering defendant's premises, or leaving defendant's premises, involving business transactions with the defendant." The defendant was further ordered to so arrange the entrances to and exits from its place of business that its customers will in the normal course of business not use the alley in coming to and leaving the plant. It was further enjoined from making any use of the alley, "by itself or through its customers," which creates noises or disturbances of peace and quiet in excess of noises normally prevailing in connection with the use of public alleys in residence districts.

In this we think the court went too far. The question can be decided on the fact that the decision on this point goes entirely beyond anything in the pleadings. . . .

Nor do we think, apart from the matter of pleading, this part of the court's decree can be upheld. The alley is, as the court states, a public thoroughfare. Customers of a commercial business must approach it over some public way; and generally, immediately or remotely, they will traverse some residential district in so doing. Here, the effect of the injunction would be to compel the defendant to so arrange its entrances and exits that some other street, also in a residential district, since the proof is that the area for several blocks around is residential, would necessarily be used; perhaps to the detriment of persons living thereon. It may be argued that it would be better to use a street, presumably somewhat wider than the alley in question; but we do not think this consideration justifies the prohibition of the use of the alley altogether. Again, it is urged by the defendant that it should not be compelled to control its customers and in any event could not do so. There is merit in this contention. Of course those who have business with the defendant may not create a nuisance in the alley nor may they block it with standing vehicles. But this is something over which the defendant may not exercise control. It is conducting a lawful business; and the fact that it attracts many customers does not in itself make it a nuisance. . . . But we find nothing in the record in the case at bar which shows that the plaintiff has suffered special damage because of the travel through the alley, other than the possible annoyance occasioned in any residence district because of heavy traffic made necessary in order to reach the premises of a legitimate enterprise. It is true the operation of an amusement place, such as a baseball park, which necessarily attracts large crowds, may be enjoined if accompanied by annoying noise, trespasses, or danger. . . . But there must be a substantial showing of nuisance, and we think no such showing appears here. An injunction will not issue against a defendant unless he is in control of the action restrained. Under the injunction granted by the trial court the defendant would be in contempt if its customers, or one of them, drove through the alley to reach its place of business; and we know of no way, short of abandoning the business, by which it could prevent this. . . . Since we have held that in any event this part of the injunctive relief granted is beyond the scope of the pleadings, we shall not further analyze the issue. The decree must be modified by striking out all that part which forbids use of the alley in reaching defendant's plant and requires it to change its place of entrance and exit.

VI. The defendant urges that this is not a proper case for

injunction, but at most any relief granted should be confined to damages. It cites *Riter v. Keokuk Electro-Metals Company,* supra, where we so held. But the circumstances here are different. Plaintiff was in present occupation of his premises when the defendant's plant was built and its operation commenced. The plant is located in what has been at all times and still is substantially a residential district. As between the plaintiff, whose property and rights have been seriously injured by the operation, and the defendant, which must be held to have known of the existing circumstances, we must agree the plaintiff is entitled to injunctive relief. . . .

BOOMER v. ATLANTIC CEMENT COMPANY

Court of Appeals of New York
26 N.Y.2d 219, 309 N.Y.S.2d 312, 257 N.E.2d 870 (1970)

BERGAN, Judge. Defendant operates a large cement plant near Albany. These are actions for injunction and damages by neighboring land owners alleging injury to property from dirt, smoke and vibration emanating from the plant. A nuisance has been found after trial, temporary damages have been allowed; but an injunction has been denied.

The public concern with air pollution arising from many sources in industry and in transportation is currently accorded ever wider recognition accompanied by a growing sense of responsibility in State and Federal Governments to control it. Cement plants are obvious sources of air pollution in the neighborhoods where they operate.

But there is now before the court private litigation in which individual property owners have sought specific relief from a single plant operation. The threshold question raised by the division of view on this appeal is whether the court should resolve the litigation between the parties now before it as equitably as seems possible; or whether, seeking promotion of the general public welfare, it should channel private litigation into broad public objectives.

A court performs its essential function when it decides the rights of parties before it. Its decision of private controversies may sometimes greatly affect public issues. Large questions of law are often resolved by the manner in which private litigation is decided. But this is normally an incident to the court's main function to settle controversy. It is a rare exercise of judicial power to use a decision in private litigation as a purposeful mechanism to achieve direct public objectives greatly beyond the rights and interests before the court.

Effective control of air pollution is a problem presently far from solution even with the full public and financial powers of government. In large measure adequate technical procedures are yet to be developed and some that appear possible may be economically impracticable.

It seems apparent that the amelioration of air pollution will depend on technical research in great depth; on a carefully balanced consideration of the economic impact of close regulation; and of the actual effect on public health. It is likely to require massive public expenditure and to demand more than any local community can accomplish and to depend on regional and interstate controls.

A court should not try to do this on its own as a by-product of private litigation and it seems manifest that the judicial establishment is neither equipped in the limited nature of any judgment it can pronounce nor prepared to lay down and implement an effective policy for the elimination of air pollution. This is an area beyond the circumference of one private lawsuit. It is a direct responsibility for government and should not thus be undertaken as an incident to solving a dispute between property owners and a single cement plant — one of many — in the Hudson River valley.

The cement making operations of defendant have been found by the court at Special Term to have damaged the nearby properties of plaintiffs in these two actions. That court, as it has been noted, accordingly found defendant maintained a nuisance and this has been affirmed at the Appellate Division. The total damage to plaintiffs' properties is, however, relatively small in comparison with the value of defendant's operation and with the consequences of the injunction which plaintiffs seek.

The ground for the denial of injunction, notwithstanding the finding both that there is a nuisance and that plaintiffs have been damaged substantially, is the large disparity in economic consequences of the nuisance and of the injunction. This theory cannot, however, be sustained without overruling a doctrine which has been consistently reaffirmed in several leading cases in this court and which has never been disavowed here, namely that where a nuisance has been found and where there has been any substantial damage shown by the party complaining an injunction will be granted.

The rule in New York has been that such a nuisance will be enjoined although marked disparity be shown in economic consequence between the effect of the injunction and the effect of the nuisance.

The problem of disparity in economic consequence was sharply in focus in *Whalen v. Union Bag & Paper Co.,* 208 N.Y. 1, 101 N.E. 805. A pulp mill entailing an investment of more than a million dollars polluted a stream in which plaintiff, who owned a farm, was "a lower riparian owner." The economic loss to plaintiff from this pollution was small. This court, reversing the Appellate Division, reinstated the injunction granted by the Special Term against the argument of the mill owner that in view of "the slight advantage to plaintiff and the great loss that will be inflicted on defendant" an injunction should not be granted (p. 2, 101 N.E. p. 805). "Such a balancing of injuries cannot be justified by the circumstances of this case," Judge Werner noted (p. 4, 101 N.E. p. 805). He continued: "Although the damage to the plaintiff may be slight as compared with the defendant's expense of abating the condition, that is not a good reason for refusing an injunction" (p. 5, 101 N.E. p. 806).

Thus the unconditional injunction granted at Special Term was reinstated. The rule laid down in that case, then, is that whenever the damage resulting from a nuisance is found not "unsubstantial," viz., $100 a year, injunction would follow. This states a rule that had been followed in this court with marked consistency (*McCarty v. Natural Carbonic Gas Co.,* 189 N.Y. 40, 81 N.E. 549; *Strobel v. Kerr Salt Co.,* 164 N.Y. 303, 58 N.E. 142; *Campbell v. Seaman,* 63 N.Y. 568).

There are cases where injunction has been denied. *McCann v. Chasm Power Co.,* 211 N.Y. 301, 105 N.E. 416 is one of them. There, however, the damage shown by plaintiffs was not only unsubstantial, it was non-existent. Plaintiffs owned a rocky bank of the stream in which defendant had raised the level of the water. This had no economic or other adverse consequence to plaintiffs, and thus injunctive relief was denied. Similar is the basis for denial of injunction in *Forstmann v. Joray Holding Co.,* 244 N.Y. 22, 154 N.E. 652 where no benefit to plaintiffs could be seen from the injunction sought (p. 32, 154 N.E. 655). Thus if, within *Whalen v. Union Bag & Paper Co.,* supra which authoritatively states the rule in New York, the damage to plaintiffs in these present cases from defendant's cement plant is "not unsubstantial," an injunction should follow.

Although the court at Special Term and the Appellate Division held that injunction should be denied, it was found that plaintiffs had been damaged in various specific amounts up to the time of the trial and damages to the respective plaintiffs were awarded for those amounts. The effect of this was, injunction having been denied, plaintiffs could maintain successive actions at law for damages thereafter as further damage was incurred.

The court at Special Term also found the amount of permanent damage attributable to each plaintiff, for the guidance of the parties in the event both sides stipulated to the payment and acceptance of such permanent damage as a settlement of all the controversies among the parties. The total of permanent damages to all plaintiffs thus found was $185,000. This basis of adjustment has not resulted in any stipulation by the parties.

This result at Special Term and at the Appellate Division is a departure from a rule that has become settled; but to follow the rule literally in these cases would be to close down the plant at once. This court is fully agreed to avoid that immediately drastic remedy; the difference in view is how best to avoid it.*

One alternative is to grant the injunction but postpone its effect to a specified future date to give opportunity for technical advances to permit defendant to eliminate the nuisance; another is to grant the injunction conditioned on the payment of permanent damages to plaintiffs which would compensate them for the total economic loss to their property present and future caused by defendant's operations. For reasons which will be developed the court chooses the latter alternative.

If the injunction were to be granted unless within a short period — e. g., 18 months — the nuisance be abated by improved methods, there would be no assurance that any significant technical improvement would occur.

The parties could settle this private litigation at any time if defendant paid enough money and the imminent threat of closing the plant would build up the pressure on defendant. If there were no improved techniques found, there would inevitably be applications to the court at Special Term for extensions of time to perform on showing of good faith efforts to find such techniques.

Moreover, techniques to eliminate dust and other annoying by-products of cement making are unlikely to be developed by any research the defendant can undertake within any short period, but will depend on the total resources of the cement industry nationwide and throughout the world. The problem is universal wherever cement is made.

For obvious reasons the rate of the research is beyond control of defendant. If at the end of 18 months the whole industry has not found a technical solution a court would be hard put to close down this one cement plant if due regard be given to equitable principles.

On the other hand, to grant the injunction unless defendant pays plaintiffs such permanent damages as may be fixed by the court seems to do justice between the contending parties. All of the attributions of economic loss to the properties on which plaintiffs' complaints are based will have been redressed.

The nuisance complained of by these plaintiffs may have other public or private consequences, but these particular parties are the only ones who have sought remedies and the judgment proposed will fully redress them. The limitation of relief granted is a limitation only within the four corners of these actions and does not foreclose public health or other public agencies from seeking proper relief in a proper court.

---

* Respondent's investment in the plant is in excess of $45,000,000. There are over 300 people employed there.

It seems reasonable to think that the risk of being required to pay permanent damages to injured property owners by cement plant owners would itself be a reasonable effective spur to research for improved techniques to minimize nuisance.

The power of the court to condition on equitable grounds the continuance of an injunction on the payment of permanent damages seems undoubted. (See, e. g., the alternatives considered in *McCarty v. Natural Carbonic Gas Co.,* supra, as well as *Strobel v. Kerr Salt Co.,* supra.)

The damage base here suggested is consistent with the general rule in those nuisance cases where damages are allowed. "Where a nuisance is of such a permanent and unabatable character that a single recovery can be had, including the whole damage past and future resulting therefrom, there can be but one recovery" (66 C.J.S. Nuisances § 140, p. 947). It has been said that permanent damages are allowed where the loss recoverable would obviously be small as compared with the cost of removal of the nuisance *(Kentucky-Ohio Gas Co. v. Bowling,* 264 Ky. 470, 477, 95 S.W.2d 1).

The present cases and the remedy here proposed are in a number of other respects rather similar to *Northern Indiana Public Service Co. v. W. J. & M. S. Vesey,* 210 Ind. 338, 200 N.E. 620 decided by the Supreme Court of Indiana. The gases, odors, ammonia and smoke from the Northern Indiana company's gas plant damaged the nearby Vesey greenhouse operation. An injunction and damages were sought, but an injunction was denied and the relief granted was limited to permanent damages "present, past, and future" (p. 371, 200 N.E. 620).

Denial of injunction was grounded on a public interest in the operation of the gas plant and on the court's conclusion "that less injury would be occasioned by requiring the appellant [Public Service] to pay the appellee [Vesey] all damages suffered by it . . . than by enjoining the operation of the gas plant; and that the maintenance and operation of the gas plant should not be enjoined" (p. 349, 200 N.E. p. 625).

The Indiana Supreme Court opinion continued: "When the trial court refused injunctive relief to the appellee upon the ground of public interest in the continuance of the gas plant, it properly retained jurisdiction of the case and awarded full compensation to the appellee. This is upon the general equitable principle that equity will give full relief in one action and prevent a multiplicity of suits" (pp. 353-354, 200 N.E. p. 627).

It was held that in this type of continuing and recurrent nuisance permanent damages were appropriate. See, also, *City of Amarillo v. Ware,* 120 Tex. 456, 40 S.W.2d 57 where recurring overflows from a system of storm sewers were treated as the kind of nuisance for which permanent depreciation of value of affected property would be recoverable.

There is some parallel to the conditioning of an injunction on the payment of permanent damages in the noted "elevated railway cases" *(Pappenheim v. Metropolitan El. Ry. Co.,* 128 N.Y. 436, 28 N.E. 518 and others which followed). Decisions in these cases were based on the finding that the railways created a nuisance as to adjacent property owners, but in lieu of enjoining their operation, the court allowed permanent damages.

Judge Finch, reviewing these cases in *Ferguson v. Village of Hamburg,* 272 N.Y. 234, 239-240, 5 N.E.2d 801, 803, said: "The courts decided that the plaintiffs had a valuable right which was being impaired, but did not grant an absolute injunction or require the railway companies to resort to separate condemnation proceedings. Instead they held that a court of equity could ascertain the damages and grant an injunction which was not to be effective unless the defendant failed to pay the amount fixed as damages for the past and permanent injury inflicted." . . .

Thus it seems fair to both sides to grant permanent damages to plaintiffs which will terminate this private litigation. The theory of damage is the "servitude on land" of plaintiffs imposed by defendant's nuisance. (See *United States v. Causby,* 328 U.S. 256, 261, 262, 267, 66 S.Ct. 1062, 90 L.Ed. 1206, where the term "servitude" addressed to the land was used by Justice Douglas relating to the effect of airplane noise on property near an airport.)

The judgment, by allowance of permanent damages imposing a servitude on land, which is the basis of the actions, would preclude future recovery by plaintiffs or their grantees. . . .

This should be placed beyond debate by a provision of the judgment that the payment by defendant and the acceptance by plaintiffs of permanent damages found by the court shall be in compensation for a servitude on the land.

Although the Trial Term has found permanent damages as a possible basis of settlement of the litigation, on remission the court should be entirely free to re-examine this subject. It may again find the permanent damage already found; or make new findings.

The orders should be reversed, without costs, and the cases remitted to Supreme Court, Albany County to grant an injunction which shall be vacated upon payment by defendant of such amounts of permanent damage to the respective plaintiffs as shall for this purpose be determined by the court.

JASEN, Judge (dissenting).

I agree with the majority that a reversal is required here, but I do not subscribe to the newly enunciated doctrine of assessment of permanent damages, in lieu of an injunction, where substantial property rights have been impaired by the creation of a nuisance.

It has long been the rule in this State, as the majority acknowledges, that a nuisance which results in substantial continuing damage to neighbors must be enjoined. . . . To now change the rule to permit the cement company to continue polluting the air indefinitely upon the payment of permanent damages is, in my opinion, compounding the magnitude of a very serious problem in our State and Nation today.

In recognition of this problem, the Legislature of this State has enacted the Air Pollution Control Act (Public Health Law, Consol. Laws, c. 45, §§ 1264 to 1299-m) declaring that it is the State policy to require the use of all available and reasonable methods to prevent and control air pollution (Public Health Law § 1265).

The harmful nature and widespread occurrence of air pollution have been extensively documented. Congressional hearings have revealed that air pollution causes substantial property damage, as well as being a contributing factor to a rising incidence of lung cancer, emphysema, bronchitis and asthma.

The specific problem faced here is known as particulate contamination because of the fine dust particles emanating from defendant's cement plant. The particular type of nuisance is not new, having appeared in many cases for at least the past 60 years. It is interesting to note that cement production has recently been identified as a significant source of particulate contamination in the Hudson Valley. This type of pollution, wherein very small particles escape and stay in the atmosphere, has been denominated as the type of air pollution which produces the greatest hazard to human health. We have thus a nuisance which not only is damaging to the plaintiffs, but also is decidedly harmful to the general public.

I see grave dangers in overruling our long-established rule of granting an injunction where a nuisance results in substantial continuing damage. In permitting the injunction to become inoperative upon the payment of permanent damages, the majority is, in effect, licensing a continuing wrong. It is the same as saying to the cement company, you may continue to do harm to your neighbors so long as you pay a fee for it. Furthermore, once such permanent damages are assessed and paid, the incentive to alleviate the wrong would be eliminated, thereby continuing air pollution of an area without abatement.

It is true that some courts have sanctioned the remedy here proposed by the majority in a number of cases, but none of the authorities relied upon by the majority are analogous to the situation before us. In those cases, the courts, in denying an injunction and awarding money damages, grounded their decision on a showing that the use to which the property was intended to be put was primarily for the public benefit. Here, on the other hand, it is clearly established that the cement company is creating a continuing air pollution nuisance primarily for its own private interest with no public benefit.

This kind of inverse condemnation . . . may not be invoked by a private person or corporation for private gain or advantage. Inverse condemnation should only be permitted when the public is primarily served in the taking or impairment of property. . . . The promotion of the interests of the polluting cement company has, in my opinion, no public use or benefit.

Nor is it constitutionally permissible to impose servitude on land, without consent of the owner, by payment of permanent damages where the continuing impairment of the land is for a private use. . . . This is made clear by the State Constitution (art. I, § 7, subd. [a]) which provides that "[p]rivate property shall not be taken for *public use* without just compensation" (emphasis added). It is, of course, significant that the section makes no mention of taking for a *private* use.

In sum, then, by constitutional mandate as well as by judicial pronouncement, the permanent impairment of private property for private purposes is not authorized in the absence of clearly demonstrated public benefit and use.

I would enjoin the defendant cement company from continuing the discharge of dust particles upon its neighbors' properties unless, within 18 months, the cement company abated this nuisance.

It is not my intention to cause the removal of the cement plant from the Albany area, but to recognize the urgency of the problem stemming from this stationary source of air pollution, and to allow the company a specified period of time to develop a means to alleviate this nuisance.

I am aware that the trial court found that the most modern dust control devices available have been installed in defendant's plant, but, I submit, this does not mean that *better* and more effective dust control devices could not be developed within the time allowed to abate the pollution.

Moreover, I believe it is incumbent upon the defendant to develop such devices, since the cement company, at the time the plant commenced production (1962), was well aware of the plaintiffs' presence in the area, as well as the probable consequences of its contemplated operation. Yet, it still chose to build and operate the plant at this site.

In a day when there is a growing concern for clean air, highly developed industry should not expect acquiescence by the courts, but should, instead, plan its operations to eliminate contamination of our air and damage to its neighbors.

Accordingly, the orders of the Appellate Division, insofar as they denied the injunction, should be reversed, and the actions remitted to Supreme Court, Albany County to grant an injunction to take effect 18 months hence, unless the nuisance is abated by improved techniques prior to said date.

FULD, C. J., and BURKE and SCILEPPI, JJ., concur with BERGAN, J. JASEN, J., dissents in part and votes to reverse in a separate opinion. BREITEL and GIBSON, JJ., taking no part.

In each action: Order reversed, without costs, and the case remitted to Supreme Court, Albany County, for further proceedings in accordance with the opinion herein.

Comments: 1. Most nuisance litigation has focused on the reasonableness of the defendant's conduct. Since all landholders are equally entitled to the reasonable use and enjoyment of their lands, some balance must be struck between the conflicting interests of different landholders in different, and often discordant, uses of their lands. As Prosser has pointed out,

> The plaintiff must be expected to endure some inconvenience rather than curtail the defendant's freedom of action, and the defendant must so use his own property that he causes no unreasonable harm to the plaintiff. The law of private nuisance is very largely a series of adjustments to limit the reciprocal rights and privileges of both. In every case the court must make a comparative evaluation of the conflicting interests according to objective legal standards, and the gravity of the harm to the plaintiff must be weighed against the utility of the defendant's conduct.

Prosser, Torts 596 (4th ed. 1971).

The gravity of the harm to the plaintiff depends upon both the extent and the duration of the interference and the character of the harm. The plaintiff's interest in the use and enjoyment of his land may be interfered with in various ways — *e.g.,* nontrespassory interference with the physical condition of the land itself, through blasting, vibrations caused by industrial operations, flooding, raising the water table, polluting a stream, or causing destruction of crops by the emission of dust, soot, or fumes; or interference with the health, comfort, or convenience of the plaintiffs by the emission of unpleasant odors, dust, soot, fumes, loud noises, excessive light or heat, and the like. If there is an interference with the physical condition of the land itself, there will often, though not always, be an interference with the health, comfort, or convenience of the occupant. If there is no interference with the physical condition of the land, the interference with the health, comfort, or convenience of the occupant must normally affect his "physical" senses, not merely his mental state. But this rule has been relaxed in a few instances — *e.g.,* maintenance of a bawdy house, an undertaking establishment or a tuberculosis hospital near the plaintiffs' residences. And a threat of future interference with the physical condition of the plaintiffs' land, or with their health, comfort, or convenience, may be such a substantial and unreasonable interference with their present use or enjoyment of the land as to constitute a nuisance.

Absent an interference with the physical condition of the land, an activity which reduces the value of the plaintiff's land is generally not a nuisance unless it "physically" affects the plaintiffs' health, comfort, or convenience.

Of course, the value of the plaintiffs' land is not likely to be reduced unless there is some "physical" interference with the condition of the land or with the plaintiffs' health, comfort, or safety. But the maintenance of a structure or the carrying on of an activity which offends the plaintiffs' aesthetic sense may, in fact reduce the value of their property as well as cause "mental" discomfort. In such cases, most courts have refused to find a nuisance because of the difficulty of establishing generally acceptable aesthetic standards.

Most nuisance cases involve recurrent activity rather than an isolated wrongful act. This has led some courts and writers to say that a nuisance necessarily involves continuance or recurrence over an appreciable period of time. In many cases, of course, continuance or recurrence is required in order to meet the substantial interference test. In other cases, it is necessary before injunctive relief can be obtained by the plaintiff. And if the harm was neither foreseeable in the first instance or a result of ultra-hazardous activity, some continuance of the defendant's activity is necessary to establish his fault and consequent liability. Moreover, the duration or frequency of the invasion of the plaintiff's interest certainly has a bearing on the reasonableness of his conduct.

The utility of the defendant's conduct depends, of course, upon the social value which the courts attach to its ultimate purpose. Modern society requires factories, smelters, oil refineries, chemical plants, power stations, and use of explosives for blasting. Such activities may not be nuisances even though they cause substantial discomfort or inconvenience to neighboring landholders, if they are carried on in suitable localities and the adverse impact upon neighboring landholders is avoidable only at prohibitive expense. But if the defendant's conduct has little or no social value, or is a result of pure malice or spite, the defendant may be liable for causing a nuisance although the harm to the plaintiff is relatively slight.

2. The judicially developed doctrine that some activities are *per se* unreasonable in certain localities emphasizes the fact that the decisive considerations in many nuisance cases are the nature of the locality and the suitability of the uses to which the plaintiff and the defendant have put their land. Courts have come to recognize that certain localities, because of their physical character or the pattern of community development (or both) are properly and primarily devoted to certain activities and that the introduction of incompatible activities must be deemed unreasonable. In short, to the extent that adjudication on a case-by-case basis permits, courts have engaged in "judicial zoning." *See* Beuscher and Morrison, Judicial Zoning Through Recent Nuisance Cases, 1955 Wis. L. Rev. 440. But nuisance theory is of limited use in the areas in which it could be most useful — slum and mixed fringe areas in which the patterns of land use are less than desirable and do not provide an acceptable measure against which an intruding and offensive use may be judged. Moreover, even where the nuisance *per se* approach allows a court to concentrate on the character of the neighborhood involved, the result of a litigated case is difficult to predict. In part this is because there is no universally accepted standard of "social value" or "suitability"; hence different courts will necessarily vary in their appraisal of the "reasonableness" of particular land uses in particular localities. And in part the difficulty of prediction results from uncertainty as to the availability of injunctive relief. This uncertainty exists both in cases where the plaintiff seeks to enjoin a proposed new land use on the ground that it will be a nuisance and in cases where the court finds that an established land use is a nuisance.

3. The plaintiff in a nuisance case usually seeks injunctive relief. As Ellickson has recently pointed out,

> Commentators have traditionally offered four primary rationales for injunctions. First, since market values do not reflect the subjective losses a plaintiff suffers and since those losses are hard to monetize by any other means, the remedy of damages is said to be inadequate. . . . A second justification for . . . [the injunctive remedy] is the moral assertion that a landowner should not be able in effect to exercise a private power of eminent domain and force others to exchange basic property rights for damages. . . . The third rationale used for injunctions is that damages are inadequate when the defendant is judgment-proof. . . . A fourth justification for . . . injunctions is that administrative factors can make granting an injunction more efficient than awarding damages.

Ellickson, Alternatives to Zoning: Covenants, Nuisance Rules, and Fines as Land Use Controls, 40 U. Chi. L. Rev. 681, 739-42 (1973).

Most courts will not enjoin a proposed land use in advance of its establishment unless it can be shown that it will constitute a nuisance *per se* at the *locus in quo*. If the plaintiff waits to sue until an offensive land use is established nearby, however, the court may deny injunctive relief on the basis of estoppel. More important, even if the court determines that the defendant is causing a nuisance, most courts will try to "balance the hardships," and will refuse to grant an injunction if there is a great disparity between the economic consequences of the nuisance and the injunction — *i.e.,* if the plaintiff's economic loss is small in comparison to the economic loss that the injunction would visit upon the defendant and upon the community at large. *See, e.g., City of Harrisonville v. W.S. Dickey Clay Mfg. Co.,* 289 U.S. 334 (1933); *Koseris v. J.R. Simplot Co.,* 352 P.2d 235 (Idaho 1960) (over 1,000 employees); *Dundalk Holding Co. v. Easter,* 137 A.2d 667 (Md.), *cert. denied,* 358 U.S. 821, *rehearing denied,* 358 U.S. 901 (1958); *Antonik v. Chamberlain,* 78 N.E.2d 752 (Ohio App. 1947) ("life and death of a legitimate and necessary business"); *Storey v. Central Hide & Rendering Co.,* 225 S.W.2d 615 (Tex. 1950) (only plant in county); *Akers v. Mathieson Alkali Works,* 144 S.E. 492 (Va. 1928).

From a very early date, some American courts have held that whenever the damage resulting from a nuisance is substantial, the plaintiff is entitled to injunctive relief as a matter of right. As indicated in the *Boomer* opinions, this was formerly the rule in New York. It is also the rule in California and Pennsylvania. *See, e.g., Hulbert v. California Portland Cement Co.,* 118 P. 928 (Cal. 1911); *Sullivan v. Jones,* 57 A. 1065 (Pa. 1904). As Judge Jasen makes clear in his dissent in *Boomer,* the rule that injunctive relief is a matter of right in nuisance cases is based largely on the idea that allowing only damages and refusing an injunction really has the effect of imposing a servitude on the plaintiff's land, and that this amounts to a "taking" of private property for a private (rather than a public) use in violation of constitutional guarantees. What do you think of this idea? Would there be an unconstitutional "taking" of private property for a private use if a court should refuse to order specific performance of a contract for the sale of land and limit the purchaser to damages for breach of contract?

4. We might now try to develop an economic model of nuisance-based land use conflicts along the following lines: Land use conflicts adjudicated in a nuisance setting present a classic case of legal intervention to modify externalities. Let us assume a developing residential area; a factory now seeks to locate in that area. If that location is the best location possible for that industry, then we can consider the location optimal if the gains to society from that location are greater than the costs which that location imposes on existing uses. Unfortunately, the private market has no way to force the intruding user to compensate those already in the neighborhood for negative externalities which its location imposes.

Nuisance law provides a method for imposing a duty to compensate on the intruding use. It does this either by awarding damages, or by granting equitable relief which will force the intruder to make improvements minimizing the effect on surrounding properties. In the extreme case, the intruder will be compelled to relocate. This remedy seems unwise in some cases: (1) it ignores the fact that a land-use conflict is two-sided, and arises as much from the fact that existing uses may be harm-sensitive as from the fact that the intruder may be harm-productive; (2) the judicial context of the nuisance lawsuit is not conducive to a full consideration of aggregate social and economic costs and benefits; (3) to assume that existing uses are entitled to preempt any given spatial location improperly ratifies private land use decisions; (4) relocation of the existing use may be less costly and impose less economic dislocation than relocation of the intruding use; (5) the intruder may bring positive as well as negative externalities. Thus, a new factory may attract other related and economically desirable uses to the area. In view of these considerations, what alternative decision model would you construct for nuisance litigation? *See* D. Mandelker, The Zoning Dilemma, ch. 2 (1971); Note, An Economic Analysis of Land Use Conflicts, 21 Stan. L. Rev. 293 (1969).

See also Ellickson, Alternatives to Zoning: Covenants, Nuisance Rules, and Fines as Land Use Controls, 40 U. Chi. L. Rev. 681, 738-48 (1973), arguing that "[n]uisance law would function better if, in general, a plaintiff in a nuisance case were limited to choosing between the remedies of . . . damages and . . . compensated injunction," which would permit the plaintiff

> to enjoin the defendant's conduct, but only if he compensates the defendant for the defendant's losses caused by the injunction. . . . A rebuttable presumption against . . . injunctions [without compensation] should exist in nuisance cases, and be overcome only when the plaintiff can show that his personal safety or fundamental freedoms are vitally threatened by the defendant's activity.

5. To fill out our economic model of the nuisance adjudication of land use conflicts we might also add a spatial component. *Patton v. Westwood Country Club Co.,* 247 N.E.2d 761 (Ohio App. 1969). Here an adjacent homeowner brought an action in nuisance to enjoin the operation of a golf and country club. The court dismissed the action, relying in part on the fact that when plaintiff constructed her residence the golf club was already there.

But, it pointed out, the golf club had taken steps to protect the plaintiff. It changed the sprinkling system on the nearest fairway, moved the fairway further away from plaintiff's residence, and planted twenty pine trees adjacent to plaintiff's lot. The cost of these changes was approximately $2,000.

Can we generalize from the *Patton* case by suggesting that intruders may foreclose the possibility of nuisance litigation simply by purchasing enough excess land to "buffer" their intruding use against existing and possibly future uses with which it will conflict? Notice that buffering is impossible in an established residential neighborhood. But if courts are willing to intervene on nuisance grounds only in established areas, the intruder may have no opportunity to buffer. In these situations, the court will have to accept existing patterns of landownership as their legal reference point, and in established residential neighborhoods the ownership pattern will be fragmented and small. Nevertheless, the externality problem will have to be judged from this perspective. Here lies a critical key to an understanding of the entire land use control and land development process.

There are also objections to the buffering approach in undeveloped areas. For example, if we require an industrial use in an undeveloped area to "buffer" by acquiring excess land, don't we assume that the "destiny" of the area will lie in the other direction, and that the area will come to be developed for conflicting residential uses? On what basis do we make this assumption? *See* Michelman, Property, Utility, and Fairness: Comments on the Ethical Foundations of "Just Compensation" Law, 80 Harv. L. Rev. 1165, 1242-44 (1967).

Does the answer lie in comprehensive planning? Consider the following:

> Thus, in order to distinguish between external and internal values it is necessary to pinpoint the exact locus of decision-making power. . . . If the planning horizon is limited, if the locus of responsibility is set low, then few values will be internal and many values will be external. As the analytical horizon widens . . . an increasing portion of costs and gains moves into the internal sphere. Once his terms of reference are determined, the decision maker tends to be guided by internal effects only. This really follows definitionally.

T. E. Kuhn, Public Enterprise Economics and Transport Problems 8 (1962).

HADACHECK v. SEBASTIAN

Supreme Court of the United States
239 U.S. 394, 60 L. Ed. 348, 36 S. Ct. 143 Ann. Cas. 1917B 927 (1915)

Mr. Justice MCKENNA delivered the opinion of the court.

Habeas corpus prosecuted in the Supreme Court of the State of California for the discharge of plaintiff in error from the custody of defendant in error, Chief of Police of the City of Los Angeles.

Plaintiff in error, to whom we shall refer as petitioner, was convicted of a misdemeanor for the violation of an ordinance of the City of Los Angeles which makes it unlawful for any person to establish or operate a brick yard or brick kiln, or any establishment, factory or place for the manufacture or burning of brick within described limits in the city. Sentence was pronounced against him and he was committed to the custody of defendant in error as Chief of Police of the City of Los Angeles.

Being so in custody he filed a petition in the Supreme Court of the State for a writ of *habeas corpus.* The writ was issued. Subsequently defendant in error made a return thereto supported by affidavits, to which petitioner made sworn reply. The court rendered judgment discharging the writ and remanding petitioner to custody. The Chief Justice of the court then granted this writ of error. . . . [Petitioner alleged that he was the owner of land within the limits described in the ordinance on which land there was a very valuable bed of clay worth about $800,000 for brick-making purposes, but worth only about $60,000 for any purpose other than the manufacture of brick; that he had made excavations of considerable depth and extent on his land, so that the land could not be used for residential purposes or any purpose other than extraction of the clay and manufacture of brick; that he purchased the land because of the bed of clay located thereon, at a time when the land was outside the limits of the city and distant from any dwellings; that he had erected expensive machinery for the manufacture of bricks on the land; that if the ordinance should be declared valid he would be compelled entirely to abandon his business and would be deprived of the use of his property because the manufacture of brick must necessarily be carried on where suitable clay is found and the clay cannot be transported to some other location; that there was no reason for the prohibition of the brick making business because it was so conducted as not to be a nuisance; that the district described in the ordinance included only about three square miles, was sparsely settled and contained large tracts of unsubdivided and unoccupied land; that there were at the time of the adoption of the ordinance in other districts of the city thickly built up with residences brick yards maintained more detrimental to the inhabitants of the city, but permitted to be maintained without prohibition or regulation; that no ordinance had been passed at any time regulating or attempting to regulate brick yards or inquiry made whether they could be maintained without being a nuisance or detrimental to health; and that the ordinance in question was enacted for the sole and specific purpose of prohibiting and suppressing the business of petitioner and that of the other brick yard within the district described in the ordinance.

The City of Los Angeles denied the charge that the ordinance was arbitrarily directed against the business of petitioner and alleged that there was another district in which brick yards were prohibited. There was a denial of the allegations that the brick yard was or could be conducted sanitarily and so as not to be offensive to health, with supporting affidavits alleging that the fumes, gases, smoke, soot, steam and dust arising from petitioner's brick factory had from time to time caused sickness and serious discomfort to those living in the vicinity. There was no specific denial of petitioner's allegations as to the value of his property and his inability to move the brick factory elsewhere, but there was a general denial that enforcement of the ordinance would "entirely deprive petitioner of his property and the use thereof."

The Supreme Court of California considered the petitioner's business one which could be regulated and that regulation was not precluded by the fact "that the value of investments made in the business prior to any legislative action will be greatly diminished" or that petitioner had been engaged in brick making in that locality for a long period. The court said the evidence tended to show that the district had become primarily a residential section and that the residents were seriously incommoded by petitioner's operation of his factory; and that such evidence, "when taken in connection with the presumptions in favor of the propriety of the legislative determination, overcame the contention that the ordinance was a mere arbitrary invasion of private right, not supported by any tenable belief that the continuance of the business was so detrimental to the interests of others as to require suppression." The court thus rejected the contention that the ordinance was not in good faith enacted as police measure and that it was intended to discriminate against petitioner. With respect to the charge of discrimination between localities, the court said that the determination where brick making should be prohibited was for the local legislative body.]

We think the conclusion of the court is justified by the evidence and makes it unnecessary to review the many cases cited by petitioner in which it is decided that the police power of a state cannot be arbitrarily exercised. The principle is familiar, but in any given case it must plainly appear to apply. It is to be remembered that we are dealing with one of the most essential powers of government, one that is the least limitable. It may, indeed, seem harsh in its exercise, usually is on some individual, but the imperative necessity for its existence precludes any limitation upon it when not exerted arbitrarily. A vested interest cannot be asserted against it because of conditions once obtaining. . . . To so hold would preclude development and fix a city forever in its primitive conditions. There must be progress, and if in its march private interests are in the way they must yield to the good of the community. The logical result of petitioner's contention would seem to be that a city could not be formed or enlarged against the resistance of an occupant of the ground and that if it grows at all it can only grow as the environment of the occupations that are usually banished to the purlieus.

The police power and to what extent it may be exerted we have recently illustrated in *Reinman v. Little Rock,* 237 U.S. 171. The circumstances of the case were very much like those of the case at bar and give reply to the contentions of petitioner, especially that which asserts that a necessary and lawful occupation that is not a nuisance *per se* cannot be made so by legislative declaration. There was a like investment in property, encouraged by the then conditions; a like reduction of value and deprivation of property was asserted against the validity of the ordinance there considered; a like assertion of an arbitrary exercise of the power of prohibition. Against all of these contentions, and causing the rejection of them all, was adduced the police power. There was a prohibition of a business, lawful in itself, there as here. It was a livery stable there; a brick yard here. They differ in particulars, but they are alike in that which cause and justify prohibition in defined localities — that is, the effect upon the health and comfort of the community.

The ordinance passed upon prohibited the conduct of the business within a certain defined area in Little Rock, Arkansas. This court said of it: granting that the business was not a nuisance *per se,* it was clearly within the police power of the State to regulate it, "and to that end to declare that in particular circumstances and in particular localities a livery stable shall be deemed a nuisance in fact and in law." And the only limitation upon the power was stated to be that the power could not be exerted arbitrarily or with unjust discrimination. There was a citation of cases. We think the present case is within the ruling thus declared.

There is a distinction between *Reinman v. Little Rock* and the case at bar. There a particular business was prohibited which was not affixed to or dependent upon its locality; it could be conducted elsewhere. Here, it is contended, the latter condition does not exist, and it is alleged that the manufacture of brick must necessarily be carried on where suitable clay is found and that the clay on petitioner's property cannot be transported to some other locality. This is not urged as a physical impossibility but only, counsel say, that such transportation and the transportation of the bricks to places where they could be used in construction work would be prohibitive "from a financial standpoint." But upon the evidence the Supreme Court considered the case, as we understand its opinion, from the standpoint of the offensive effects of the operation of a brick yard and not from the deprivation of the deposits of clay, and distinguished *Ex parte Kelso,* 147 Cal. 609, 82 P. 241, wherein the court declared invalid an ordinance absolutely prohibiting the maintenance or operation of a rock or stone quarry within a certain portion of the city and county of San Francisco. The court there said that the effect of the ordinance was "to absolutely deprive the owners of real property within such limits of a valuable right incident to their ownership, — viz., the right to extract therefrom such rock and stone as they might find it to their advantage to dispose of." The court expressed the view that the removal could be regulated but that "an absolute prohibition of such removal under the circumstances," could not be upheld.

In the present case there is no prohibition of the removal of the brick clay; only a prohibition within the designated locality of its manufacture into bricks. And to this feature of the ordinance our opinion is addressed. Whether other questions would arise if the ordinance were broader, and opinion on such questions, we reserve.

Petitioner invokes the equal protection clause of the Constitution and charges that it is violated in that the ordinance (1) "prohibits him from manufacturing brick upon his property while his competitors are permitted, without regulation of any kind, to manufacture brick upon property situated in all respects similarly to that of plaintiff in error"; and (2) that it "prohibits the conduct of his business while it permits the maintenance within the same district of any other kind of business, no matter how objectionable the same may be, either in its nature or in the manner in which it is conducted."

If we should grant that the first specification shows a violation of classification, that is, a distinction between businesses which was not within the legislative power, petitioner's contention encounters the objection that it depends upon an inquiry of fact which the record does not enable us to determine. It is alleged in the return to the petition that brickmaking is prohibited in one other district and an ordinance is referred to regulating business in other districts. To this plaintiff in error replied that the ordinance attempts to prohibit the operation of certain businesses having mechanical power and does not prohibit the maintenance of any business or the operation of any machine that is operated by animal power. In other words, petitioner makes his contention depend upon disputable considerations of classification and upon a comparison of conditions of which there is no means of judicial determination and upon which nevertheless we are expected to reverse legislative action exercised upon matters of which the city has control.

To a certain extent the latter comment may be applied to other contentions, and, besides, there is no allegation or proof of other objectionable businesses being permitted within the district, and a speculation of their establishment or conduct at some future time is too remote.

In his petition and argument something is made of the ordinance as fostering a monopoly and suppressing his competition with other brickmakers. The charge and argument are too illusive. It is part of the charge that the ordinance was directed against him. The charge, we have seen, was rejected by the Supreme Court, and we find nothing to justify it.

It may be that brick yards in other localities within the city where the same conditions exist are not regulated or prohibited, but it does not follow that they will not be. That petitioner's business was first in time to be prohibited does not make its prohibition unlawful. And it may be, as said by the Supreme Court of the State, that the conditions justify a distinction. However, the inquiries thus suggested are outside of our province.

There are other and subsidiary contentions which, we think, do not require discussion. They are disposed of by what we have said. It may be that something else than prohibition would have satisfied the conditions. Of this, however, we have no means of determining, and besides we cannot declare invalid the exertion of a power which the city undoubtedly has because of a charge that it does not exactly accommodate the conditions or that some other exercise would have been better or less harsh. We must accord good faith to the city in the absence of a clear showing to the contrary and an honest exercise of judgment upon the circumstances which induced its action.

We do not notice the contention that the ordinance is not within the city's charter powers nor that it is in violation of the state constitution, such contentions raising only local questions which must be deemed to have been decided adversely to petitioner by the Supreme Court of the State.

Judgment affirmed.

Comments: 1. The term "nuisance" has been applied from an early date to conduct which invades two different types of legally protected interests: (1) the interest of a landowner, tenant, or other possessor of land in freedom from any unreasonable, nontrespassory interference with his use and enjoyment of the land — the interest asserted by plaintiffs in the *Bove, Schlotfelt,* and *Boomer* cases, *supra* — and (2) the public interest in freedom from activity which endangers the health or safety or property of a considerable number of persons, offends public morals, or interferes with the comfort or convenience of a considerable number of persons. Invasion of the former is said to constitute a "private" nuisance; invasion of the latter, a "public" nuisance. Beuscher and Morrison have concluded, however, that the private-public dichotomy has little significance when nuisance cases are approached in terms of the extent to which courts are meeting demands for protection against discordant land uses in unzoned areas. This is mainly because the same activity may invade both private and public interests of the types protected by the law of nuisance, and many nuisances are "public" merely because they have adverse effects on the use and enjoyment of a large number of privately owned parcels of land. In the latter case the "public" nuisance is "merely a composite of numerous private nuisances." *See* Beuscher and Morrison, Judicial Zoning Through Recent Nuisance Cases, 1955 Wis. L. Rev. 440.

2. It is clear that the *Hadacheck* court thought that the Los Angeles ordinance was designed to protect the "public" health and comfort by eliminating the nuisance-like effects of the operation of a brick factory in an area which had become primarily residential as the city developed, although the area was sparsely populated when the brick factory was established. Do you think the neighboring residential landowners could have persuaded a court that the brick factory was a common law "public" nuisance in light of the fact that they "came to the nuisance"? In most "private" nuisance cases where plaintiffs have succeeded, they were "there first," as in the *Schlotfelt* case, *supra*.

3. The Supreme Court held in *Hadacheck* that the Los Angeles ordinance prohibiting continuance of the petitioner's brick-making business was a proper exercise of the "police power." But the court's opinion does not very clearly indicate what the "police power" is, nor why the controversy in the principal case raises a federal constitutional issue.

The "police power" in its broadest sense includes all the inherent powers of sovereign governments. These powers were divided between the Federal government and the states by the United States Constitution. Exercise of the powers delegated to the Federal government is limited by the Fifth Amendment: "No person shall be deprived of life, liberty, or property, without due process of law; nor shall private property be taken for public use without just compensation." The exercise of the powers reserved to the states is limited by state constitutional provisions and by the Fourteenth Amendment to the United States Constitution, which provides (*inter alia*): "No state shall . . . deprive any person of life, liberty, or property, without due process of law; nor deny to any person within its jurisdiction the equal protection of the laws." The constitutions of all but three states expressly prohibit the taking of private property for public use without compensation, and in these three states the constitutions have been judicially interpreted to require compensation. Moreover, the United States Supreme Court has held that the "due process" clause of the Fourteenth Amendment makes the "compensation" clause of the Fifth Amendment applicable to the states. *Chicago, B. & Q. R. R. Co. v. Chicago,* 166 U.S. 226 (1897).

In view of the universal requirement of compensation when the federal or state governments exercise the power of eminent domain to "take" private property for public use, it is not surprising that the term "police power" is today rarely used in its broadest sense. Instead, the "police power" is generally considered to be the power to "regulate" human conduct — without any compensable "taking" of property — in order to protect the public health, safety, morals, or general welfare. State or local regulatory legislation that is not a proper exercise of the "police power" has been held to result in a deprivation of liberty or property, or both, without "due process of law" in violation of the Fourteenth Amendment. Thus, the constitutional issue in the principal case arises under the Fourteenth Amendment's "due process" clause, and also — insofar as the petitioner alleged that the ordinance operated in a discriminatory manner against him — its "equal protection" clause.

4. Did the Supreme Court in the *Hadacheck* case hold that the Los Angeles legislative body, in exercising its delegated (from the state) police power, "reasonably" determine that a brick factory is a nuisance *per se* in a developed residential area? How did the court decide whether such a legislative determination was "reasonable" and not "arbitrary"? Did the court independently weigh the reasonableness and social utility of the petitioner's use of his land for brick manufacture against the gravity of the harm to, and the social utility of, the residential land uses in the neighborhood? If not, why not?

5. In *Hadacheck,* did the Supreme Court give serious consideration to the petitioner's allegations that the ordinance and reduced the value of his clay deposits from about $800,000 to about $60,000? Why was this not reduction in value, if proved, a "taking" of the petitioner's property that went beyond the police power and deprived the petitioner of property without due process of law, in violation of the Fourteenth Amendment? Are you satisfied with the court's statement that, "[i]n the present case there is no prohibition of the removal of the brick clay; only a prohibition within the designated locality of its manufacture into bricks," and its conclusion that it was legally irrelevant that transportation of the clay to "some other locality" for manufacture and transportation of the bricks to "places where they could be used in construction work" would be prohibitive "from a financial standpoint"? Is the court justified in its conclusion by the traditional rule that "just compensation" in eminent domain for the "taking" of real property does not include "consequential" business losses even if the business is completely destroyed? For a discussion of the *Hadacheck* factual situation from the viewpoint of economic efficiency goals see Michelman, *supra* p. 34.

B. THE BORDERLAND OF POLICE POWER AND EMINENT DOMAIN

PENNSYLVANIA COAL CO. v. MAHON

Supreme Court of the United States
260 U.S. 393, 67 L. Ed. 322, 43 S. Ct. 158 (1922)

MR. JUSTICE HOLMES delivered the opinion of the Court.

This is a bill in equity brought by the defendants in error to prevent the Pennsylvania Coal Company from mining under their property in such way as to remove the supports and cause a subsidence of the surface and of their house. The bill sets out a deed executed by the Coal Company in 1878, under which the plaintiffs claim. The deed conveys the surface, but in express terms reserves the right to remove all the coal under the same, and the grantee takes the premises with the risk, and waives all claim for damages that may arise from mining out the coal. But the plaintiffs say that whatever may have been the Coal Company's rights, they were taken away by an Act of Pennsylvania, approved May 27, 1921, P. L. 1198, commonly known there as the Kohler Act. The Court of Common Pleas found that if not restrained the defendant would cause the damage to prevent which the bill was brought, but denied an injunction, holding that the statute if applied to this case would be unconstitutional. On appeal the Supreme Court of the State agreed that the defendant had contract and property rights protected by the Constitution of the United States, but held that the statute was a legitimate exercise of the police power and directed a decree for the plaintiffs. A writ of error was granted bringing the case to this Court.

The statute forbids the mining of anthracite coal in such way as to cause the subsidence of, among other things, any structure used as a human habitation, with certain exceptions, including among them land where the surface is owned by the owner of the underlying coal and is distant more than one hundred and fifty feet from any improved property belonging to any other person. As applied to this case the statute is admitted to destroy previously existing rights of property and contract. The question is whether the police power can be stretched so far.

Government hardly could go on if to some extent values incident to property could not be diminished without paying for every such change in the general law. As long recognized, some values are enjoyed under an implied limitation and must yield to the police power. But obviously the implied limitation must have its limits, or the contract and due process clauses are gone. One fact for consideration in determining such limits is the extent of the diminution. When it reaches a certain magnitude, in most if not in all cases there must be an exercise of eminent domain and compensation to sustain the act. So the question depends upon the particular facts. The greatest weight is given to the judgment of the legislature, but it always is open to interested parties to contend that the legislature has gone beyond its constitutional power.

This is the case of a single private house. No doubt there is a public interest even in this, as there is in every purchase and sale and in all that happens within the commonwealth. Some existing rights may be modified even in such a case. . . . But usually in ordinary private affairs the public interest does not warrant much of this kind of interference. A source of damage to such a house is not a public nuisance even if similar damage is inflicted on others in different places. The damage is not common or public. . . . The extent of the public interest is shown by the statute to be limited, since the statute ordinarily does not apply to land when the surface is owned by the owner of the coal. Furthermore, it is not justified as a protection of personal safety. That could be provided for by notice. Indeed the very foundation of this bill is that the defendant gave timely notice of its intent to mine under the house. On the other hand the extent of the taking is great. It purports to abolish what is recognized in Pennsylvania as an estate in land — a very valuable estate — and what is declared by the Court below to be a contract hitherto binding the plaintiffs. If we were called upon to deal with the plaintiffs' position alone, we should think it clear that the statute does not disclose a public interest sufficient to warrant so extensive a destruction of the defendant's constitutionally protected rights.

But the case has been treated as one in which the general validity of the act should be discussed. The Attorney General of the State, the City of Scranton, and the representatives of other extensive interests were allowed to take part in the argument below and have submitted their contentions here. It seems, therefore, to be our duty to go farther in the statement of our opinion, in order that it may be known at once, and that further suits should not be brought in vain.

It is our opinion that the act cannot be sustained as an exercise of the police power, so far as it affects the mining of coal under streets or cities in places where the right to mine such coal has been reserved. As said in a Pennsylvania case, "For practical purposes, the right to coal consists in the right to mine it." *Commonwealth v. Clearview Coal Co.,* 256 Pa. St. 328, 331. What makes the right to mine coal valuable is that it can be exercised with profit. To make it commercially impracticable to mine certain coal has very nearly the same effect for constitutional purposes as appropriating or destroying it. This we think that we are warranted in assuming that the statute does.

It is true that in *Plymouth Coal Co. v. Pennsylvania,* 232 U.S. 531, it was held competent for the legislature to require a pillar of coal to be left along the line of adjoining property, that, with the pillar on the other side of the line, would be a barrier sufficient for the safety of the employees of either mine in case the other should be abandoned and allowed to fill with water. But that was a requirement for the safety of employees invited into the mine, and secured an average reciprocity of advantage that has been recognized as a justification of various laws.

The rights of the public in a street purchased or laid out by eminent domain are those that it has paid for. If in any case its representatives have been so short sighted as to acquire only surface rights without the right of support, we see no more authority for supplying the latter without compensation than there was for taking the right of way in the first place and refusing to pay for it because the public wanted it very much. The protection of private property in the Fifth Amendment presupposes that it is wanted for public use, but provides that it shall not be taken for such use without compensation. A similar assumption is made in the decisions upon the Fourteenth Amendment. . . . When this seemingly absolute protection is found to be qualified by the police power, the natural tendency of human nature is to extend the qualification more and more until at last private property disappears. But that cannot be accomplished in this way under the Constitution of the United States.

The general rule at least is, that while property may be regulated to a certain extent, if regulation goes too far it will be recognized as a taking. It may be doubted how far exceptional cases, like the blowing up of a house to stop a conflagration, go — and if they go beyond the general rule, whether they do not stand as much upon tradition as upon principle. . . . In general it is not plain that a man's misfortunes or necessities will justify his shifting the damages to his neighbor's shoulders. . . . We are in danger of forgetting that a strong public desire to improve the public condition is not enough to warrant achieving the desire by a shorter cut than the constitutional way of paying for the change. As we already have said, this is a question of degree — and therefore cannot be disposed of by general propositions. But we regard this as going beyond any of the cases decided by this Court. The late decisions upon laws dealing with the congestion of Washington and New York, caused by the war, dealt with laws intended to meet a temporary emergency and providing for compensation determined to be reasonable by an impartial board. They went to the verge of the law but fell far short of the present act. *Block v. Hirsh,* 256 U. S. 135. *Marcus Brown Holding Co. v. Feldman,* 256 U. S. 170. *Levy Leasing Co. v. Siegel,* 258 U. S. 242.

We assume, of course, that the statute was passed upon the conviction that an exigency existed that would warrant it, and we assume that an exigency exists that would warrant the exercise of eminent domain. But the question at bottom is upon whom the loss of the changes desired should fall. So far as private persons or communities have seen fit to take the risk of acquiring only surface rights, we cannot see that the fact that their risk has become a danger warrants the giving to them greater rights than they bought.

Decree reversed.

MR. JUSTICE BRANDEIS, dissenting.

The Kohler Act prohibits, under certain conditions, the mining of anthracite coal within the limits of a city in such a manner or to such an extent "as to cause the . . . subsidence of any dwelling or other structure used as a human habitation, or any factory, store, or other industrial or mercantile establishment in which human labor is employed." Coal in place is land; and the right of the owner to use his land is not absolute. He may not so use it as to create a public nuisance; and uses, once harmless, may, owing to changed conditions, seriously threaten the public welfare. Whenever they do, the legislature has power to prohibit such uses without paying compensation; and the power to prohibit extends alike to the manner, the character and the purpose of the use. Are we justified in declaring that the Legislature of Pennsylvania has, in restricting the right to mine anthracite, exercised this power so arbitrarily as to violate the Fourteenth Amendment?

Every restriction upon the use of property imposed in the exercise of the police power deprives the owner of some right theretofore enjoyed, and is, in that sense, an abridgment by the State of rights in property without making compensation. But restriction imposed to protect the public health, safety or morals from dangers threatened is not a taking. The restriction here in question is merely the prohibition of a noxious use. The property so restricted remains in the possession of its owner. The State does not appropriate it or make any use of it. The State merely prevents the owner from making a use which interferes with paramount rights of the public. Whenever the use prohibited ceases to be noxious, — as it may because of further change in local or social conditions, — the restriction will have to be removed and the owner will again be free to enjoy his property as heretofore.

The restriction upon the use of this property can not, of course, be lawfully imposed, unless its purpose is to protect the public. But the purpose of a restriction does not cease to be public, because incidentally some private persons may thereby receive gratuitously valuable special benefits. Thus, owners of low buildings may obtain, through statutory restrictions upon the height of neighboring structures, benefits equivalent to an easement of light and air. *Welch v. Swasey,* 214 U. S. 91. Compare *Lindsley v. Natural Carbonic Gas Co.,* 220 U. S. 61; *Walls v. Midland Carbon Co.,* 254 U. S. 300. Furthermore, a restriction, though imposed for a public purpose will not be lawful, unless the restriction is an appropriate means to the public end. But to keep coal in place is surely an appropriate means of preventing subsidence of the surface; and ordinarily it is the only available means. Restriction upon use does not become inappropriate as a means, merely because it deprives the owner of the only use to which the property can then be profitably put. The liquor and the oleomargarine cases settled that. *Mugler v. Kansas,* 123 U. S. 623, 668, 669; *Powell v. Pennsylvania,* 127 U. S. 678, 682. See also *Hadacheck v. Los Angeles,* 239 U. S. 394; *Pierce Oil Corporation v. City of Hope,* 248 U. S. 498. Nor is a restriction imposed through exercise of the police power inappropriate as a means, merely because the same end might be effected through exercise of the power of eminent domain, or otherwise at public expense. Every restriction upon the height of buildings might be secured through acquiring by eminent domain the right of each owner to build above the limiting height; but it is settled that the State need not resort to that power. Compare *Laurel Hill Cemetery v. San Francisco,* 216 U. S. 358; *Missouri Pacific Ry. Co. v. Omaha,* 235 U. S. 121. If by mining anthracite coal the owner would necessarily unloose poisonous gasses, I suppose no one would doubt the power of the State to prevent the mining, without buying his coal fields. And why may not the State, likewise, without paying compensation, prohibit one from digging so deep or excavating so near the surface, as to expose the community to like dangers? In the latter case, as in the former, carrying on the business would be a public nuisance.

It is said that one fact for consideration in determining whether the limits of the police power have been exceeded is the extent of the resulting diminution in value; and that here the restriction destroys existing rights of property and contract. But values are relative. If we are to consider the value of the coal kept in place by the restriction, we should compare it with the value of all other parts of the land. That is, with the value not of the coal alone, but with the value of the whole property. The rights of an owner as against the public are not increased by dividing the interests in his property into surface and subsoil. The sum of the rights in the parts can not be greater than the rights in the whole. The estate of an owner in land is grandiloquently described as extending *ab orco usque ad coelum.* But I suppose no one would contend that by selling his interest above one hundred feet from the surface he could prevent the State from limiting, by the police power, the height of structures in a city. And why should a sale of underground rights bar the State's power? For aught that appears the value of the coal kept in place by the restriction may be negligible as compared with the value of the whole property, or even as compared with that part of it which is represented by the coal remaining in place and which may be extracted despite the statute. Ordinarily a police regulation, general in operation, will not be held void as to a particular property, although proof is offered that owing to conditions peculiar to it the restriction could not reasonably be applied. . . . But even if the particular facts are to govern, the statute should, in my opinion, be upheld in this case. For the defendant has failed to adduce any evidence from which it appears that to restrict its mining operations was an unreasonable exercise of the police power. Compare *Reinman v. Little Rock,* 237 U. S. 171, 177, 180; *Pierce Oil Corporation v. City of Hope,* 248 U. S. 498, 500. Where the surface and the coal belong to the same person, self-interest would ordinarily prevent mining to such an extent as to cause a subsidence. It was, doubtless, for this reason that the legislature, estimating the degrees of danger, deemed statutory restriction unnecessary for the public safety under such conditions.

It is said that this is a case of a single dwelling house; that the restriction upon mining abolishes a valuable estate hitherto secured by a contract with the plaintiffs; and that the restriction upon mining cannot be justified as a protection of personal safety, since that could be provided for by notice. The propriety of deferring a good deal to tribunals on the spot has been repeatedly recognized. . . . May we say that notice would afford adequate protection of the public safety where the legislature and the highest court of the State, with greater knowledge of local conditions, have declared, in effect, that it would not? If public safety is imperiled, surely neither grant, nor contract, can prevail against the exercise of the police power. . . . The rule that the State's power to take appropriate measures to guard the safety of all who may be within its jurisdiction may not be bargained away was applied to compel carriers to establish grade crossings at their own expense, despite contracts to the contrary; *Chicago, Burlington & Quincy R. R. Co. v. Nebraska,* 170 U. S. 57; and, likewise, to supersede, by an employers' liability act, the provision of a charter exempting a railroad from liability for death of employees, since the civil liability was deemed a matter of public concern, and not a mere private right. *Texas & New Orleans R. R. Co. v. Miller,* 221 U. S. 408. . . . Nor can existing contracts between private individuals preclude exercise of the police power. "One whose rights, such as they are, are subject to state restriction, cannot remove them from the power of the State by making a contract about them." *Hudson County Water Co. v. McCarter,* 209 U. S. 349, 357; *Knoxville Water Co. v. Knoxville,* 189 U. S. 434, 438; *Rast v. Van Deman & Lewis Co.,* 240 U. S. 342. The fact that this suit is brought by a private person is, of course, immaterial to protect the community through invoking the aid, as litigant, of interested private citizens is not a novelty in our law. That it may be done in Pennsylvania was decided by its Supreme Court in this case. And it is for a State to say how its public policy shall be enforced.

This case involves only mining which causes subsidence of a dwelling house. But the Kohler Act contains provisions in addition to that quoted above; and as to these, also, an opinion is expressed. These provisions deal with mining under cities to such an extent as to cause subsidence of —

(a) Any public building or any structure customarily used by the public as a place of resort, assemblage, or amusement, including, but not being limited to, churches, schools, hospitals, theatres, hotels, and railroad stations.

(b) Any street, road, bridge, or other public passageway, dedicated to public use or habitually used by the public.

(c) Any track, roadbed, right of way, pipe, conduit, wire, or other facility, used in the service of the public by any municipal corporation or public service company as defined by the Public Service Company Law.

A prohibition of mining which causes subsidence of such structures and facilities is obviously enacted for a public purpose; and it seems, likewise, clear that mere notice of intention to mine would not in this connection secure the public safety. Yet it is said that these provisions of the act cannot be sustained as an exercise of the police power where the right to mine such coal has been reserved. The conclusion seems to rest upon the assumption that in order to justify such exercise of the police power there must be "an average reciprocity of advantage" as between the owner of the property restricted and the rest of the community; and that here such reciprocity is absent. Reciprocity of advantage is an important consideration, and may even be an essential, where the State's power is exercised for the purpose of conferring benefits upon the property of a neighborhood, as in drainage projects, *Wurts v. Hoagland,* 114 U. S. 606; *Fallbrook Irrigation District v. Bradley,* 164 U. S. 112; or upon adjoining owners, as by party wall provisions, *Jackman v. Rosenbaum Co., ante,* 22. But where the police power is exercised, not to confer benefits upon property owners, but to protect the public from detriment and danger, there is, in my opinion, no room for considering reciprocity of advantage. There was no reciprocal advantage to the owner prohibited from using his oil tanks in 248 U. S. 498; his brickyard, in 239 U. S. 394; his livery stable, in 237 U. S. 171; his billiard hall, in 225 U. S. 623; his oleomargarine factory, in 127 U. S. 678; his brewery, in 123 U. S. 623; unless it be the advantage of living and doing business in a civilized community. That reciprocal advantage is given by the act to the coal operators.

Comments: 1. It was quite clear, under Pennsylvania law, that the coal company's reserved "right to remove all the coal" without liability for injury caused by subsidence of the surface was a "property" right, not a mere "contract" right. As counsel for the coal company, John W. Davis, pointed out in the oral argument in *Mahon,* "the courts of Pennsylvania have recognized three distinct estates in mining property: (1) The right to use the surface; (2) the ownership of the subjacent minerals; (3) the right to have the surface supported by the subjacent strata." (260 U.S. at 395.) The coal company's reserved right would appear to be an easement burdening the surface estate. Thus, Holmes might simply have said that, to the extent the Kohler Act destroyed or transferred to the surface estate owner the coal company's easement, it was a "taking" or "deprivation" of the coal company's property without compensation, and therefore "without due process of law." Why do you think Holmes rejected this approach in favor of a holding that, where the severity of the consequences of shifting the economic loss involved in improving "the public condition" from the public to the landowner becomes too great, the governmental objective cannot constitutionally be achieved unless just compensation is paid to the landowner? Was Holmes right in finding a duty to compensate where the exercise of the coal company's property right would clearly cause serious injury to occupied land and might well cause physical harm to its inhabitants? Would not the removal of supporting coal "pillars" constitute a "noxious" use of the coal company's property, tantamount to a nuisance, as Brandeis argued in his dissent? In light of *Reinman v. Little Rock* and *Hadacheck v. Sebastian,* was it not clear that the Kohler Act was a legitimate exercise of Pennsylvania's police power for the purpose of protecting the public safety and welfare, rather than a "taking" or "deprivation" of the coal company's property? Surely there is no "property right" in a "nuisance."

2. It has sometimes been said that Holmes' opinion in *Mahon* supports the use by the courts of "a balancing test — a weighing of the public benefits of the regulation against the extent of the loss of property values." Bosselman, Callies, and Banta, The Taking Issue 321 (Council on Environmental Quality, 1973). Do you think this is an accurate statement? How can one "balance" a very great danger to public health, safety, or general welfare against a governmental restriction that leaves a landowner with no "reasonable" use of his land and thus reduces its value almost to zero? Does either the Holmes or the Brandeis approach help you with this problem?

3. Even if we accept the Holmes thesis that, "while property may be regulated to a certain extent, if regulation goes too far it will be recognized as a taking," on what basis did Holmes find that the regulation went "too far" in *Mahon?* Was Brandeis not right in arguing that, "[i]f we are to consider the value of the coal kept in place by the restriction, we should compare it with the value of all other parts of the [coal company's] land"? In ignoring this point, did Holmes implicitly hold that requiring "pillars" of coal to be kept in place to support the surface was *ipso facto* a "taking," without regard to the relative value of the "pillars" and "all other parts of the land"?

4. In *Mahon,* Holmes said that "[t]o make it commercially impracticable to mine certain coal [*i.e.,* the "pillars" required for surface support] has very nearly the same effect for constitutional purposes as appropriating or destroying it." This statement was based on the fact the cost of providing artifical support in lieu of the "pillars" of coal would exceed the value of the "pillars." (See the coal company's argument, 260 U.S. at 395.) Is Holmes' statement consistent with the court's conclusion in *Hadacheck v. Sebastian* that there was no "taking" despite the fact that transportation of Hadacheck's brick clay to some other locality for manufacturing would be impractical "from a financial standpoint," since the Los Angeles ordinance only prohibited the manufacture of bricks and not the removal of the clay?

PENN CENTRAL TRANSPORTATION COMPANY v. CITY OF NEW YORK

Supreme Court of the United States
98 S. Ct. 2646 (1978)

[The following statement of facts is taken from the official Syllabus. Under New York City's Landmarks Preservation Law (Landmarks Law), which was enacted to protect historic landmarks and neighborhoods from precipitate decisions to destroy or fundamentally alter their character, the Landmarks Preservation Commission (Commission) may designate a building to be a "landmark" on a particular "landmark site" or may designate an area to be a "historic district." The Board of Estimate may thereafter modify or disapprove the designation, and the owner may seek judicial review of the final designation decision. The owner of the designated landmark must keep the building's exterior "in good repair" and before exterior alterations are made must secure Commission approval. Under two ordinances owners of landmark sites may transfer development rights from a landmark parcel to proximate lots. Under the Landmarks Law, the Grand Central Terminal (Terminal), which is owned by the Penn Central Transportation Co. and its affiliates (Penn Central), was designated a "landmark" and the block it occupies a "landmark site." Appellant Penn Central, though opposing the designation before the Commission, did not seek judicial review of the final designation decision. Thereafter appellant Penn Central entered into a lease with appellant UGP, whereby UGP was to construct a multistory office building over the Terminal. After the Commission had rejected appellants' plans for the building as destructive of the Terminal's historic and aesthetic features, with no judicial review thereafter being sought, appellants brought suit in state court claiming that the application of the Landmarks Law had "taken" their property without just compensation in violation of the Fifth and Fourteenth Amendments and arbitrarily deprived them of their property without due process of law in violation of the Fourteenth Amendment. The trial court's grant of relief was reversed on appeal, the New York Court of Appeals ultimately concluding that there was no "taking" since the Preservation Law had not transferred control of the property to the City, but only restricted appellants' exploitation of it; and that there was no denial of due process because (1) the same use of the Terminal was permitted as before; (2) the appellants had not shown that they could not earn a reasonable return on their investment in the Terminal itself; (3) even if the Terminal proper could never operate at a reasonable profit, some of the income from Penn Central's extensive real estate holdings in the area must realistically be imputed to the Terminal; and (4) the development rights above the Terminal, which were made transferable to numerous sites in the vicinity provided significant compensation for lose of rights above the Terminal itself.]

MR. JUSTICE BRENNAN delivered the opinion of the Court.

. . . .

II

The issues presented by appellants are (1) whether the restrictions imposed by New York City's law upon appellants' exploitation of the Terminal site effect a "taking" of appellants' property for a public use within the meaning of the Fifth Amendment, which of course is made applicable to the States through the Fourteenth Amendment, see *Chicago B. & Q. R. Co.* v. *Chicago,* 166 U. S. 226, 239 (1897) and, (2) if so, whether the transferable development rights afforded appellants constitute "just compensation" within the meaning of the Fifth Amendment. We need only address the question whether a "taking" has occurred.[1]

A

Before considering appellants' specific contentions, it will be useful to review the factors that have shaped the jurisprudence of the Fifth Amendment injunction "nor shall private property be taken for public use, without just compensation." The question of what constitutes a "taking" for purposes of the Fifth Amendment has proved to be a problem of considerable difficulty. While this Court has recognized that the "Fifth Amendment's guarantee [is] designed to bar Government from forcing some people alone to bear public burdens which, in all fairness and justice, should be borne by the public as a whole," *Armstrong* v. *United States,* 364 U. S. 40, 49 (1960), this Court, quite simply, has been unable to develop any "set formula" for determining when "justice and fairness" require that economic injuries caused by public action be compensated by the Government, rather than remain disproportionately concentrated on a few persons. See *Goldblatt* v. *Hempstead,* 369 U. S. 590, 594 (1962). Indeed, we have frequently observed that whether a particular restriction will be rendered invalid by the Government's failure to pay for any losses proximately caused by it depends largely "upon the particular circumstances [in that] case." *United States* v. *Central Eureka Mining Co.,* 357 U. S. 155, 168 (1958); see *United States* v. *Caltex, Inc.,* 344 U. S. 149, 156 (1952).

In engaging in these essentially ad hoc, factual inquiries, the Court's decisions have identified several factors that have particular significance. The economic impact of the regulation on the claimant and, particularly, the extent to which the regulation has interfered with distinct investment backed expectations are of course relevant considerations. See *Goldblatt* v. *Hempstead, supra,* at 594. So too is the character of the governmental action. A "taking" may more readily be found when the interference with property can be characterized as a physical invasion by Government, see, *e. g., Causby* v. *United States,* 328 U. S. 256 (1946), than when interference arises from some public program adjusting the benefits and burdens of economic life to promote the common good.

---

[1] As is implicit in our opinion, we do not embrace the proposition that a "taking" can never occur unless Government has transferred physical control over a portion of a parcel.

"Government could hardly go on if to some extent values incident to property could not be diminished without paying for every such change in the general law." *Pennsylvania Coal Co.* v. *Mahon,* 260 U. S. 393, 413 (1922), and this Court has accordingly recognized, in a wide variety of contexts, that Government may execute laws or programs that adversely affect recognized economic values. Exercises of the taxing power are one obvious example. A second are the decisions in which this Court has dismissed "taking" challenges on the ground that, while the challenged Government action caused economic harm, it did not interfere with interests that were sufficiently bound up with the reasonable expectations of the claimant to constitute "property" for Fifth Amendment purposes. See, *e. g., United States* v. *Willow River Power Co.,* 324 U. S. 499 (1945) (interest in high water level of river for run off for tail waters to maintain power head is not property); *United States* v. *Chandler-Dunbar Water Power Co.,* 229 U. S. 53 (1913) (no property interest can exist in navigable waters); see also . . . Sax, Takings and the Police Power, 74 Yale L. J. 36, 61-62 (1963).

More importantly for the present case, in instances in which a state tribunal reasonably concluded that "the health, safety, morals or general welfare" would be promoted by prohibiting particular contemplated uses of land, this Court has upheld land use regulations that destroyed or adversely affected recognized real property interests. . . . Zoning laws are of course the classic example, see *Euclid* v. *Ambler Realty Co.,* 272 U. S. 365 (1926) (prohibition of industrial use); *Gorieb* v. *Fox,* 274 U. S. 603, 608 (1927) (requirement that portions of parcels be left unbuilt); *Welch* v. *Swasey,* 214 U. S. 91 (1909) (height restriction), which have been viewed as permissible governmental action even when prohibiting the most beneficial use of the property. . . .

Zoning laws generally do not affect existing uses of real property, but taking challenges have also been held to be without merit in a wide variety of situations when the challenged governmental actions prohibited a beneficial use to which individual parcels had previously been devoted and thus caused substantial individualized harm. *Miller* v. *Schoene,* 276 U. S. 272 (1928), is illustrative. In that case, a state entomologist, acting pursuant to a state statute, ordered the claimants to cut down a large number of ornamental red cedar trees because they produced cedar rust fatal to apple trees cultivated nearby. Although the statute provided for recovery of any expense incurred in removing the cedars, and permitted claimants to use the felled trees, it did not provide compensation for the value of the standing trees or for the resulting decrease in market value of the properties as a whole. A unanimous Court held that this latter omission did not render the statute invalid. The Court held that the State might properly make "a choice between the preservation of one class of property and that of the other" and since the apple industry was important in the State involved, concluded that the State had not exceeded "its constitutional powers by deciding upon the destruction of one class of property [without compensation] in order to save another, which, in the judgment of the legislature, is of greater value to the public." *Id., at 279.*

Again, *Hadacheck* v. *Sebastian,* 239 U. S. 394 (1915), upheld a law prohibiting the claimant from continuing his otherwise lawful business of operating a brickyard in a particular physical community on the ground that the legislature had reasonably concluded that the presence of the brickyard was inconsistent with neighboring uses. See also *United States* v. *Central Eureka Mining Co., supra* (government order closing gold mines so that skilled miners would be available for other mining work held not a taking); *Atchison, T. & S. F. R. Co.* v. *Public Utilities Comm.,* 346 U. S. 346 (1953) (railroad may be required to pay cost of constructing railroad grade crossing); *Walls* v. *Midland Carbon Co.,* 254 U. S. 300 (1920) (law prohibiting manufacture of carbon black upheld), *Reinman* v. *Little Rock,* 237 U. S. 171 (1915) (law prohibiting livery stable upheld); *Mugler* v. *Kansas,* 123 U. S. 623 (1887) (law prohibiting liquor business upheld).

Goldblatt v. *Hempstead, supra,* is a recent example. There, a 1958 city safety ordinance banned any excavations below the water table and effectively prohibited the claimant from continuing a sand and gravel mining business that had been operated on the particular parcel since 1927. The Court upheld the ordinance against a "taking" challenge, although the ordinance prohibited the present and presumably most beneficial use of the property and had, like the regulations in *Miller* and *Hadacheck,* impacted severely on a particular owner. The Court assumed that the ordinance did not prevent the owner's reasonable use of the property since the owner made no showing for an adverse effect on the value of the land. Because the restriction served a substantial public purpose, the Court thus held no taking had occurred. It is of course implicit in *Goldblatt* that a use restriction on real property may constitute a "taking" if not reasonably necessary to the effectuation of a substantial public purpose, see *Nectow* v. *Cambridge,* . . . [277 U. S. 183 (1928)]; cf. *Moore* v. *City of East Cleveland,* 431 U. S. 494, 513-514 (1977) (STEVENS, J., concurring), or perhaps if it has an unduly harsh impact upon the owner's use of the property.

Pennsylvania Coal Co. v. *Mahon,* 260 U. S. 393 (1922), is the leading case for the proposition that a state statute that substantially furthers important public policies may so frustrate distinct investment-backed expectations as to amount to a "taking." There the claimant had sold the surface rights to particular parcels of property, but expressly reserved the right to remove the coal thereunder. A Pennsylvania statute, enacted after the transactions, forbade any mining of coal that caused the subsidence of any house, unless the house was the property of the owner of the underlying coal and was more than 150 feet from the improved property of another. Because the statute made it commercially impracticable to mine the coal, *id.,* at 414, and thus had nearly the same effect as the complete destruction of rights claimant had purchased from the owners of the surface land, see *id.,* at 414-415, the Court held that the statute was invalid as effecting a "taking" without just compensation. See also *Armstrong* v. *United States, supra.* (Government's complete destruction of a materialman's lien in certain property held a "taking"); *Hudson Water Co.* v. *McCarter,* 209 U. S. 349, 355 (1908) (if height restriction makes property wholly useless "the right of property prevails over the public interest" and compensation is required). See generally Michelman, Property, Utility, and Fairness: Comments on the Ethical Foundations of "Just Compensation" Law, 80 Harv. L. Rev. 1165, 1229-1234 (1967).

Finally, Government actions that may be characterized as acquisitions of resources to permit or facilitate uniquely public functions have often been held to constitute "takings." *Causby* v. *United States, supra,* is illustrative. In holding that direct overflights above the claimant's land, that destroyed the present use of the land as a chicken farm, constituted a "taking." *Causby* emphasized that Government had not "merely destroyed property [but was] using a part of it for the flight of its planes." *Id.,* at 262-263, n. 7. See also *Griggs* v. *Allegheny County,* 369 U. S. 84 (1962) (overflights held a taking); *Portsmouth Co.* v. *United States,* 260 U. S. 327 (1922) (United States' military installations repeated firing of guns over claimant's land is a taking); *United States* v. *Cress,* 243 U. S. 316 (1917) (repeated floodings of land caused by water project is taking); but see *YMCA* v. *United States,* 395 U. S. 85 (1969) (damage caused to building when federal officers who were seeking to protect building were attacked by rioters held not a taking). See generally Michelman, 80 Harv. L. Rev. 1165, 1226-1229 (1967); Sax, 74 Yale L. J. 36 (1963).

B

In contending that the New York City law has "taken" their property in violation of the Fifth and Fourteenth Amendments, appellants make a series of arguments, which, while tailored to the facts of this case, essentially urge that any substantial restriction imposed pursuant to a landmark law must be accompanied by just compensation if it is to be constitutional. Before considering these, we emphasize what is not in dispute. Because this Court has recognized, in a number of settings, that States and cities may enact land use restrictions or controls to enhance the quality of life by preserving the character and desirable aesthetic features of a city, see *City of New Orleans* v. *Dukes,* 427 U. S. 297 (1976); *Young* v. *American Mini Theatres, Inc.,* 427 U. S. 50 (1976); *Village of Belle Terre* v. *Boraas,* 416 U. S. 1, 9-10 (1974); *Berman* v. *Parker,* 348 U. S. 26, 33 (1954); *Welch* v. *Swasey, supra,* at 108, appellants do not contest that New York City's objective of preserving structures and areas with special historic, architectural, or cultural significance is an entirely permissible governmental goal. They also do not dispute that the restrictions imposed on its parcel are appropriate means of securing the purposes of the New York City law. Finally, appellants do not challenge any of the specific factual premises of the decision below. They accept for present purposes both that the parcel of land occupied by Grand Central Terminal must, in its present state, be regarded as capable of earning a reasonable return, and that the transferable development rights afforded appellants by virtue of the Terminal's designation as a landmark are valuable, even if not as valuable as the rights to construct above the Terminal. In appellants' view none of these factors derogate from their claim that New York City's law has effected a "taking."

They first observe that the air space above the Terminal is a valuable property interest, citing *United States* v. *Causby, supra.* They urge that the Landmark Law has deprived them of any gainful use of their "air rights" above the Terminal and that, irrespective of the value of the remainder of their parcel, the city has "taken" their right to this superadjacent air space, thus entitling them to "just compensation" measured by the fair market value of these air rights.

Apart from our own disagreement with appellants' characterization of the effect of the New York law, see *infra,* the submission that appellants may establish a "taking" simply by showing that they have been denied the ability to exploit a property interest that they heretofore had believed was available for development is quite simply untenable. Were this the rule, this Court would have erred not only in upholding laws restricting the development of air rights, see *Welch* v. *Swasey, supra,* but also in approving those prohibiting both the subjacent, see *Goldblatt* v. *Hempstead, supra,* and the lateral development, see *Gorieb* v. *Fox, supra,* of particular parcels.[2] "Taking" jurisprudence does not divide

---

[2] These cases dispose of any contention that might be based on *Pennsylvania Coal Co.* v. *Mahon, supra,* that full use of air rights is so bound up with the investment backed expectations of appellants that Governmental deprivation of these rights invariably — *i. e.,* irrespective of the impact of the restriction on the value of the parcel as a whole — constitutes a "taking." Similarly, *Welch, Goldblatt,* and *Gorieb* illustrate the fallacy of appellants' related contention that a "taking" must be found to have occurred whenever the land use restriction may be characterized as imposing a "servitude" on the claimant's parcel.

a single parcel into discrete segments and attempt to determine whether rights in a particular segment have been entirely abrogated. In deciding whether a particular governmental action has effected a taking, this Court focuses rather both on the character of the action and on the nature and extent of the interference with rights in the parcel as a whole, here, the city tax block designated as the "landmark site."

Secondly, appellants, focusing on the character and impact of the New York City law, argue that it effects a "taking" because its operation has significantly diminished the value of the Terminal site. Appellants concede that the decisions sustaining other land use regulations, which, like the New York law, are reasonably related to the promotion of the general welfare, uniformly reject the proposition that diminution in property value, standing alone, can establish a taking, see *Euclid* v. *Ambler Realty Co., supra* (75% diminution in value caused by zoing law); *Hadacheck* v. *Sebastian, supra* (87½% diminution in value) . . ., and that the taking issue in these contexts is resolved by focusing on the uses the regulations permit. See also *Goldblatt* v. *Hempstead, supra.* Appellants, moreover, also do not dispute that a showing of diminution in property value would not establish a taking if the restriction had been imposed as a result of historic district legislation, see generally *Maher* v. *City of New Orleans,* 516 F.2d 1051 (CA5 1975), but appellants argue that New York City's regulation of individual landmarks is fundamentally different from zoning or from historic district legislation because the controls imposed by New York City's law apply only to individuals who own selected properties.

Stated baldly, appellants' position appears to be that the only means of ensuring that selected owners are not singled out to endure financial hardship for no reason is to hold that any restriction imposed on individual landmarks pursuant to the New York scheme is a "taking" requiring the payment of "just compensation." Agreement with this argument would of course invalidate not just New York City's law, but all comparable landmark legislation in the Nation. We find no merit in it.

It is true, as appellants emphasize, that both historic district legislation and zoning laws regulate all properties within given physical communities whereas landmark laws apply only to selected parcels. But, contrary to appellants' suggestions, landmark laws are not like discriminatory, or "reverse spot," zoning: that is, a land use decision which arbitrarily singles out a particular parcel for different, less favorable treatment than the neighboring ones. . . . In contrast to discriminatory zoning, which is the antithesis of land use control as part of some comprehensive plan, the New York City law embodies a comprehensive plan to preserve structures of historic or aesthetic interest wherever they might be found in the city,[3] and as noted, over 400 landmarks and 31 historic districts have been designated pursuant to this plan.

Equally without merit is the related argument that the decision to designate a structure as a landmark "is inevitably arbitrary or at least subjective because it basically is a matter of taste." Reply Brief of Appellant 22, thus unavoidably singling out individual landowners for disparate and unfair treatment. The argument has a particularly hollow ring in this case. For appellants not only did not seek judicial review of either the designation or of the denials of the certificates of appropriateness and of no exterior effect, but do not even now suggest that the Commission's decisions concerning the Terminal were in any sense arbitrary or unprincipled. But, in any event, a landmark owner has a right to judicial review of any Commission decision, and, quite simply, there is no basis whatsoever for a conclusion that courts will have any greater difficulty identifying arbitrary or discriminatory action in the context of landmark regulation than in the context of classic zoning or indeed in any other context.[4]

Next, appellants observe that New York City's law differs from zoning laws and historic district ordinances in that the Landmark Law does not impose identical or similar restrictions on all structures located in particular physical communities. It follows, they argue, that New York City's law is inherently incapable of producing the fair and equitable distribution of benefits and burdens of governmental action which is characteristic of zoning laws and historic district legislation and which they maintain is a constitutional requirement if "just compensation" is not to be afforded. It is of course true that

---

[3] Although the New York Court of Appeals contrasted the New York City Landmark Law with both zoning and historic district legislation and stated at one point that landmark laws do not "further a general community plan," 42 N. Y. 2d, at 330, it also emphasized that the implementation of the objectives of the landmark law constitutes an "acceptable reason to single out one particular parcel for different and less favorable treatment." *Ibid.* Therefore, we do not understand the New York Court of Appeals to disagree with our characterization of the Act.

[4] When a property owner challenges the application of a zoning ordinance to his property, the judicial inquiry focuses upon whether the challenged restriction can reasonably be deemed to promote the objectives of the community land use plan, and will include consideration of the treatment of similar parcels. See generally *Nectow* v. *Cambridge, supra.* When a property owner challenges a landmark designation or restriction as arbitrary or discriminatory, a similar inquiry presumably will occur.

the Landmark Law has a more severe impact on some landowners than on others, but that in itself does not mean that the law effects a "taking." Legislation designed to promote the general welfare commonly burdens some more than others. The owners of the brickyard in *Hadacheck,* of the cedar trees in *Miller* v. *Schoene,* and of the gravel and sand mine in *Goldblatt* v. *Hempstead,* were uniquely burdened by the legislation sustained in those cases.[5] Similarly, zoning laws often impact more severely on some property owners than others but have not been held to be invalid on that account. For example, the property owner in *Euclid* who wished to use his property for industrial purposes was affected far more severely by the ordinance than his neighbors who wished to use their land for residences.

In any event, appellants' repeated suggestions that they are solely burdened and unbenefited is factually inaccurate. This contention overlooks the fact that the New York City law applies to vast numbers of structures in the city in addition to the Terminal — all the structures contained in the 31 historic districts and over 400 individual landmarks, many of which are close to the Terminal.[6] Unless we are to reject the judgment of the New York City Council that the preservation of landmarks benefits all New York citizens and all structures, both economically and by improving the quality of life

---

[5] Appellants attempt to distinguish these cases on the ground that, in each, Government was prohibiting a "noxious" use of land and that in the present case, in contrast, appellants' proposed construction above the Terminal would be beneficial. We observe that the uses in issue in *Hadacheck, Miller,* and *Goldblatt* were perfectly lawful in themselves. They involved no "blameworthiness, . . . moral wrongdoing, or conscious act of dangerous risk-taking which induce[d society] to shift the cost to a particular individual." Sax, 74 Yale L. J. 36, 50 (1964). These cases are better understood as resting not on any supposed "noxious" quality of the prohibited uses but rather on the ground that the restrictions were reasonably related to the implementation of a policy — not unlike historic preservation — expected to produce a widespread public benefit and applicable to all similarly situated property.

Nor, correlatively, can it be asserted that the destruction or fundamental alteration of a historic landmark is not harmful. The suggestion that the beneficial quality of appellants' proposed construction is established by the fact the construction would have been consistent with applicable zoning laws ignores the development in sensibilities and ideals reflected in landmark legislation like New York City's. Cf. *West Brother Brick Co.* v. *Alexandria,* 169 Va. 271, 282-283, *appeal dismissed for want of a substantial federal question,* 302 U.S. 658 (1937).

[6] There are some 53 designated landmarks and three historic districts or scenic landmarks in Manhattan between 14th and 59th Streets. See Landmarks Preservation Commission, Landmarks and Historic Districts (1977).

in the city as a whole — which we are unwilling to do — we cannot conclude that the owners of the Terminal have in no sense been benefited by the Landmark Law. Doubtless appellants believe they are more burdened than benefited by the law, but that must have been true too of the property owners in *Miller, Hadacheck, Euclid,* and *Goldblatt.*[7]

Appellants' final broad-based attack would have us treat the law as an instance, like that in *United States* v. *Causby, supra,* in which Government, acting in an enterprise capacity, has appropriated part of their property for some strictly governmental purpose. Apart from the fact that *Causby* was a case of invasion of airspace that destroyed the use of the farm beneath and this New York City law has in no wise impaired the present use of the Terminal, the Landmark Law neither exploits appellants' parcel for city purposes nor facilitates nor arises from any entrepreneurial operations of the city. The situation is not remotely like that in *Causby* when the airspace above the Terminal was in the flight pattern for military aircraft. The Landmarks Law's effect is simply to prohibit appellants or anyone else from occupying portions of the airspace above the Terminal, while permitting appellants to use the remainder of the parcel in a gainful fashion. This is no more an appropriation of property by Government for its own uses than is a zoning law prohibiting, for "aesthetic" reasons, two or more adult theatres within a specified area, see *Young* v. *American Mini Theatres, Inc., supra,* or a safety regulation prohibiting excavations below a certain level. See *Goldblatt* v. *City of Hempstead, supra.*

C

Rejection of appellants' broad arguments is not however the end of our inquiry, for all we thus far have established is that the New York law is not rendered invalid by its failure to provide "just compensation" whenever a landmark owner is restricted in the exploitation of property interests, such as air rights, to a greater extent than provided for under applicable zoning laws. We now must consider whether the interference with appellants' property is of such a magnitude that "there must be an exercise of eminent domain and compensation to sustain [it]." *Pennsylvania Coal Co.* v. *Mahon,* 260 U. S., at 413. That inquiry may be narrowed to the question of the severity of the impact of the law on appellants' parcel, and its

---

[7] It is of course true that the fact the duties imposed by zoning and historic district legislation apply throughout particular physical communities provides assurances against arbitrariness, but the applicablity of the landmarks law to large numbers of parcels in the city, in our view, provides comparable, if not identical, assurances.

resolution in turn requires a careful assessment of the impact of the regulation on the Terminal site.

Unlike the governmental acts in *Goldblatt, Miller, Causby, Griggs,* and *Hadacheck,* the New York City law does not interfere in any way with the present uses of the Terminal. Its designation as a landmark not only permits but contemplates that appellants may continue to use the property precisely as it has for the past 65 years: as a railroad terminal containing office space and concessions. So the law does not interfere with what must be regarded as Penn Central's primary expectation concerning the use of the parcel. More importantly, on this record, we must regard the New York City law as permitting Penn Central not only to profit from the Terminal but to obtain a "reasonable return" on its investment.

Appellants, moreover, exaggerate the effect of the Act on its ability to make use of the air rights above the Terminal in two respects.[8] First, it simply cannot be maintained, on this record, that appellants have been prohibited from occupying *any* portion of the airspace above the Terminal. While the Commission's actions in denying applications to construct an office building in excess of 50 stories above the Terminal may indicate that it will refuse to issue a certificate of appropriateness for any comparably sized structure, nothing the Commission has said or done suggests an intention to prohibit *any* construction above the Terminal. The Commission's report emphasized that whether any construction would be allowed depended upon whether the proposed addition "would harmonize in scale, material, and character with [the Terminal]." Record 2251. Since appellants have not sought approval for the construction of a smaller structure, we do not know that appellants will be denied any use of any portion of the airspace above the Terminal.[9]

Second, to the extent appellants have been denied the right to build above the Terminal, it is not literally accurate to say that they have been denied *all* use of even those pre-existing air rights. Their ability to use these rights has not been abrogated; they are made transferable to at least eight parcels in the vicinity of the Terminal, one or two of which have been found suitable for the construction of new office buildings. Although appellants and others have argued that New York City's transferable development rights program is far from ideal, the New York courts here supportably found that, at least

---

[8] Appellants of course argue at length that the transferable development rights, while valuable, do not constitute "just compensation." Brief for Appellants 36—43.

[9] Counsel for appellants admitted at oral argument that the Commission has not suggested that it would not, for example, approve a 20-story office tower along the lines of that which was part of the original plan for the Terminal. See Tr. of Oral Arg. 19.

in the case of the Terminal, the rights afforded are valuable. While these rights may well not have constituted "just compensation" if a "taking" had occurred, the rights nevertheless undoubtedly mitigate whatever financial burdens the law has imposed on appellants and, for that reason, are to be taken into account in considering the impact of regulation. Cf. *Goldblatt* v. *Hempstead, supra,* at 594 n. 3.

On this record we conclude that the application of New York City's Landmark Preservation Law has not effected a "taking" of appellants' property. The restrictions imposed are substantially related to the promotion of the general welfare and not only permit reasonable beneficial use of the landmark site but afford appellants opportunities further to enhance not only the Terminal site proper but also other properties.[10]

Affirmed.

MR. JUSTICE REHNQUIST, with whom THE CHIEF JUSTICE and MR. JUSTICE STEVENS join, dissenting.

. . . .

Appellees have . . . destroyed — in a literal sense, "taken" — substantial property rights of Penn Central. While the term "taken" might have been narrowly interpreted to include only physical seizures of property rights, "the construction of the phrase has not been so narrow. The courts have held that the deprivation of the former owner rather than the accretion of a right or interest to the sovereign constitutes a taking." *United States* v. *General Motors,* 323 U.S., at 378. . . . Because "not every destruction or injury to property by governmental action has been held to be a 'taking' in the constitutional sense," *Armstrong* v. *United States,* 364 U.S. 40, 48 (1960), however, this does not end our inquiry. But an examination of the two exceptions where the destruction of property does *not* constitute a taking demonstrates that a compensable taking has occurred here.

1

As early as 1887, the Court recognized that the government can prevent a property owner from using his property to injure others without having to compensate the owner for the value of the forbidden use. . . . [Citing and quoting from *Mugler* v. *Kansas,* 123 U.S. 623, 668-69 (1887). — Eds.]

---

[10] We emphasize that our holding today is on the present record which in turn is based on Penn Central's present ability to use the Terminal for its intended purposes and in a gainful fashion. The city conceded at oral argument that if appellants can demonstrate at some point in the future that circumstances have changed such that the Terminal ceases to be, in the city's counsel's words, "economically viable," appellants may obtain relief. See Tr. of Oral Arg. 42—43.

. . . .

Appellees are not prohibiting a nuisance. The record is clear that the proposed addition to the Grand Central Terminal would be in full compliance with zoning, height limitations, and other health and safety requirements. Instead, appellees are seeking to preserve what they believe to be an outstanding example of Beaux Arts architecture. Penn Central is prevented from further developing its property basically because it did *too good* of a job in designing and building it. The city of New York, because of its unadorned admiration for the design, has decided that the owners of the building must preserve it unchanged for the benefit of sightseeing New Yorkers and tourists.

Unlike in the case of land use regulations, appellees are not prohibiting Penn Central from using its property in a narrow sense. Instead, appellees have placed an affirmative duty on Penn Central to maintain the Terminal in its present state of "good repair." Appellants are not free to use their property as they see fit within broad outer boundaries but must strictly adhere to their past use except where appellees conclude that alternative uses would not detract from the Landmark. While Penn Central may continue to use the Terminal as it is presently designed, appellees otherwise "exercise complete dominion and control over the surface of the land," *United States v. Causby,* 328 U.S. 256, 262 (1946), and must compensate the owner for his loss. . . .

2

Even where the government prohibits a noninjurious use, the Court has ruled that a taking does not take place if the prohibition applies over a broad cross section of land and thereby "secure[s] an average reciprocity of advantage." *Pennsylvania Coal Co. v. Mahon,* 260 U.S. 393, 415 (1922). While zoning at times reduces *individual* property values, the burden is shared relatively evenly and it is reasonable to conclude that on the whole an individual who is harmed by one aspect of the zoning will be benefited by another.

Here, however, a mutimillion dollar loss has been imposed on appellants; it is uniquely felt and is not offset by any benefits flowing from the preservation of some 500 other "Landmarks" in New York. Appellees have imposed a substantial cost on less than one-tenth of one percent of the buildings in New York for the general benefit of all its people. It is exactly this imposition of general costs on a few individuals at which the "taking" protection is directed. . . .

. . . .

Appellees in response would argue that a taking only occurs where a property owner is denied *all* reasonable value of his property. The

Court has frequently held that, even where a destruction of property rights would not *otherwise* constitute a taking, the inability of the owner to make a reasonable return on his property requires compensation under the Fifth Amendment. . . . But the converse is not true. A taking does not become a noncompensable exercise of police power simply because the government in its grace allows the owner to make some "reasonable" use of his property. "[I]t is the character of the invasion, not the amount of damage resulting from it, so long as the damage is substantial, that determines the question whether it is a taking." *United States v. Cress,* 243 U.S. 316, 328 (1917); *United States v. Causby,* 328 U.S. 256, 266 (1946); see also *Goldblatt v. Hempstead,* 369 U.S. 590, 594 (1962).

Comments: 1. What guidance does the majority opinion in the principal case give to state courts seeking to determine when regulations based on the "police power" are to be deemed to result in a "taking" in violation of the Fourteenth Amendment? Is it accurate to say that the majority opinion adopts the views stated by Justice Brandeis in *Pennsylvania Coal Co.* v. *Mahon* and that the dissenting opinion adopts the views stated by Justice Holmes in *Pennsylvania Coal Co.?* Is the majority's statement that " '[t]aking' jurisprudence does not divide a single parcel into discrete segments and attempt to determine whether rights in a particular segment have been entirely abrogated" consistent with the Court's decision in *Pennsylvania Coal Co.?*

2. As the majority points out, the "safety ordinance" sustained by the Court in *Goldblatt v. Hempstead,* 369 U.S. 590 (1962), "banned any excavations below the water table and effectively prohibited the claimant from continuing a sand and gravel mining business that had been operated on the particular parcel since 1927." The court's "assumption" in *Goldblatt* "that the ordinance did not prevent the owner's reasonable use of the property since the owner made no showing of an adverse effect on the value of the land" appears to be justified if we consider the land as a whole. Although it was quite clear than no use except sand and gravel mining was possible as to the 20 acres of Goldblatt's land occupied by a lake 25 feet in average depth, there was no evidence at all as to possible uses, other than sand and gravel mining, that might be appropriate for the other 18 acres of the tract. The absence of any evidence on this point made it unnecessary for the court to resolve the tension between the Holmes and Brandeis positions in *Pennsylvania Coal Co.,* although the *Goldblatt* opinion recognized that " governmental action in the form of regulation" may "be so onerous as to constitute a taking which constitutionally requires compensation." The *Goldblatt* opinion also observed that,

> . . . There is no set formula to determine where regulation ends and taking begins. Although a comparison of values before and after is revelant, see *Pennsylvania Coal Co. v. Mahon,* . . . it is by no means conclusive, see *Hadacheck* v. *Sebastian,* . . . where a diminution in value from $800,000 to $60,000 was upheld.

3. The dissenting opinion in the New York high court in *Goldblatt* contains the following observation:

> [T]he record here indicates a systematic attempt to force the defendants out of business. The decision below has that practical effect. . . . [A]n examination of the clauses in the 1958 amendments. . . supports the contention that it was directed at this single operation and designed to accomplish what the 1956 lawsuit failed to do, viz., to destroy a lawful pre-existing use under the Town Zoning Ordinance.

Town of Hempstead v. Goldblatt, 172 N.E.2d 562, 565-66 (N.Y. 1961). Is this observation relevant to the "taking" issue?

4. A detailed treatment of "zoning" as a technique for control of land use and development will be found *infra* in Chapter 4. A fairly detailed treatment of "historic preservation" and "transfer of development rights" will be found *infra* in Chapter 6.

5. There has been a good deal of writing about the "taking" problem in recent years. Among the major monographs and articles exploring the conceptual basis for distinguishing "regulation" from "taking," the following are especially noteworthy: Bosselman, Callies, & Banta, The Taking Issue (Council on Environmental Quality, 1973); Sax, Taking, Private Property and Public Rights, 81 Yale L.J. 149 (1971); Michelman, Property, Utility, and Fairness: Comments on the Ethical Foundations of "Just Compensation" Law, 80 Harv. L. Rev. 1165 (1967); Sax, Takings and the Police Power, 74 Yale L.J. 36 (1964); Dunham, A Legal and Economic Basis for City Planning, 58 Colum. L. Rev. 650 (1958). *See also* Waite, Governmental Power and Private Property, 16 Cath. U.L. Rev. 283 (1967).

SNEED v. COUNTY OF RIVERSIDE

District Court of Appeal of California
218 Cal.App.2d 205, 32 Cal.Rptr. 318 (1963)

BROWN, Justice.

Plaintiff has appealed from a judgment of dismissal entered after demurrers were sustained to the first amended supplemental complaint without leave to amend.

The first amended supplemental complaint (hereinafter called complaint) seeks to establish a cause of action in inverse condemnation against defendant County of Riverside, with the proceeds of such action belonging to plaintiff and not to defendants James Minor and Jessie F. Minor (hereinafter called Minor).

The only question is whether the court erred in sustaining a demurrer to the complaint. For that purpose the allegations of the complaint must be accepted as true. . . . We have concluded the complaint sets forth a cause of action.

In substance the complaint states that plaintiff owned 234½ acres of improved real property adjacent to Ryan Airport which is owned, operated and maintained by Riverside County; pursuant to the authority given counties by Government Code sections

50485-50485.14, on February 10, 1958 the Riverside County Board of Supervisors adopted Ordinance No. 448, which was an "Ordinance of the County of Riverside establishing airport operating areas and regulating height standards and limits therein."

Plaintiff claims that by reason of the Ordinance the County took from him an air navigation easement over approximately 60 acres of his property, the easement ranging from 4 feet in height at that part of the property closest to the airport to a height of 75 feet farthest away, all within the "Glide Angle of the Clear Zone and Approach Zone." In his closing brief plaintiff asserts the 4 feet mentioned above is wrong and instead the minimum distance above his property at the beginning of the easement is 3 inches. Whether the minimum figure is 3 inches, 4 feet, or 24 feet as claimed by respondent County, is a question of fact to be determined in trial.

The property over which the Ordinance is effective has a railroad on one side, a highway on the other, a road on the third side, and the fourth side is 10 feet from the airport runway. It is alleged that large numbers of aircraft have used the airport since the Ordinance was adopted; the intent and purpose of the Ordinance was to obtain for the County and for all parties using the airport a flight easement at all levels above the "Glide Angle of the Clear Zone and Approach Zone" ranging from 4 feet to 75 feet above plaintiff's land.

Plaintiff's property was a thoroughbred race horse breeding and training farm, certain improvement structures of which exceed the height permitted by the Ordinance.

It is claimed the fair market value of the property was reduced from $550,000 before the Ordinance was passed to $225,000 afterwards. Plaintiff filed his claim and it was rejected by the Board of Supervisors of Riverside County.

After suit was begun plaintiff sold the property to defendants Minor who knew of the lawsuit and orally agreed the proceeds should be plaintiff's property. Defendants do not question or argue this subject matter in their briefs.

The basic controversy is whether the Riverside County Ordinance is in reality a height limit ordinance authorized under the police power or whether it takes an air easement over plaintiff's property without payment of compensation therefor.

Article I, section 14 of the California Constitution provides:

"Private property shall not be taken or damaged for public use without just compensation having first been made to, or paid into court for, the owner. . . ."

The Code of Civil Procedure, sections 1239.2 and 1239.4 authorize counties to acquire airspace or air easements through eminent domain proceedings, in airspace above property if the taking of such is necessary to protect the approaches to airports.

The Airport Approaches Zoning Law, Government Code sections 50485-50485.14 defines and authorizes the elimination of airport hazards, to "be accomplished, *to the extent legally possible,* by exercise of the police power. . . ." (Government Code section 50485.2.) (Italics ours.)

Section 50485.13 provides:

"In any case in which: . . . (b) the approach protection necessary cannot, *because of constitutional limitations,* be provided by airport zoning regulations under this article . . . the . . . county within which the property . . . is located or the . . . county owning the airport or served by it may acquire, by purchase, grant, or condemnation in the manner provided by the law under which a . . . county is authorized to acquire real property for public purposes, such air right, air navigation easement, or other estate or interest in the property or nonconforming structure or use in question as may be necessary to effectuate the purposes of this article." (Italics ours.)

Ordinance No. 448 of Riverside County, which is attached to the complaint as an exhibit, describes itself as the "Airport Approaches Zoning Ordinance," and states that it is adopted pursuant to the Airport Approaches Zoning Law recited in the Government Code, supra.

Section 8 of Ordinance No. 448 provides in part:

"Nothing in this ordinance shall be construed as depriving any person who shall suffer damages by reason of the use of airspace adjacent to or over his property by aircraft of bringing an appropriate notice for such damages."

In summary, the zoning law and the zoning ordinance permit elimination of airport hazards in approaches to airports through the exercise of the police power "to the extent legally possible" (Gov. Code, sec. 50485.2); where "constitutional limitations" prevent the necessary approach protection under the police power, the necessary property right may be acquired by purchase, grant, or condemnation in the manner provided by law.

While height restriction zoning has long been recognized as a valid exercise of the police power, there has been a reluctance to extend this method to the protection of approaches to airports; instead, air easements with payment of compensation appear to be the more acceptable, although not undisputed, method of protecting approach zones. (See 13 Hastings Law Journal 397, Airport Zoning and Height Restriction.)

We believe there is a distinction between the commonly accepted and traditional height restriction zoning regulations of buildings and zoning of airport approaches in that the latter contemplates actual use of the airspace zoned, by aircraft, whereas in the building cases there is no invasion or trespass to the area above the restricted zone.

In his complaint plaintiff seeks to set forth two bases upon which he is entitled to compensation, (1) upon an easement obtained through the Ordinance, and (2) on the ground that large numbers of aircraft take off and land, fly at low altitudes over plaintiff's property pursuant to instructions from the employees of defendant County. We believe that a cause of action has been stated on each ground.

In *Griggs v. Allegheny County,* 369 U.S. 84, 82 S.Ct. 531, 7 L.Ed.2d 585, the court held the operator of an airport was liable, under certain circumstances, for the taking of an easement of flight over property necessary for the use of airplanes in landing and taking off from the airport. The circumstances of that case involved actual interference with the livability of residential quarters near the end of the runway.

Johnson v. Airport Authority of City of Omaha, 173 Neb. 801, 115 N.W.2d 426, was an action brought by the Airport Authority to condemn airspaces over lands in the vicinity of an airport and to condemn obstructions within the designated airspaces. The action was brought pursuant to statutory provisions relating to the taking and damaging of private property for public use. The lowest portion of the easement was 26 feet over plaintiff's property; two trees were taken which extended above the 26 foot limit, and in another phase of the case was the "incorporeal taking above that height of the right of use and occupancy in the landing and taking off of aircraft." (Page 429)

The right to condemn and take was not questioned in the case; the Airport Authority conceded damages for the taking of the trees, but contended damages sustained by the incorporeal taking were not compensable. The court stated at page 431, "The legal authorities are in substantial accord in the view that a taking of real property in the establishment of an avigation easement which reduces the value of that to which the easement attaches entitles the owner to damages in the amount of the difference in value before and after the taking. See, *United States v. Causby,* 328 U.S. 256, 66 S.Ct. 1062, 90 L.Ed. 1206; *Griggs v. County of Allegheny,* 369 U.S. 84, 82 S.Ct. 531, 7 L.Ed.2d 585; . . . .

. . . .

". . . [A]ll of the decisions previously cited herein from the United States courts clearly declare that damage to the value of land caused by navigation within an avigation easement amounts to a taking within the meaning of the Fifth Amendment."

A temporary invasion of airspace by aircraft over land of another is privileged so long as it does not unreasonably interfere with persons or property on the land. . . .

See also *Thornburg v. Port of Portland,* 376 P.2d 100 (Or.) and *Ackerman v. Port of Seattle,* 55 Wash.2d 400, 348 P.2d 664, 77 A.L.R.2d 1344. In the *Ackerman* case the court stated:

One of the fundamental principles involved in this action is the ownership of private property and the right to the free use and enjoyment thereof. Another basic principle is the authority of the government (always subject to constitutional safeguards) to regulate the use and utilization of private property for the promotion of the public welfare. At times, as in the instant litigation, these principles are in conflict, and the courts are called upon to resolve the resulting problem in human and legal relationships. In doing so, the courts constantly emphasize the concepts of (1) 'regulation' under the police power, and (2) 'constitutional taking or damaging' under the eminent domain power. When restrictions upon the ownership of private property fall into the category of 'proper exercise of the police power,' they, validly, may be imposed without payment of compensation. The difficulty arises in deciding whether a restriction is an exercise of the police power or an exercise of the eminent domain power. When private property rights are actually destroyed through the governmental action, then police power rules are *usually* applicable. . . . But, when private property rights are taken from the individual and are conferred upon the public for public use, eminent domain principles are applicable. . . . In this connection it is well to recall the words of Justice Holmes in *Pennsylvania Coal Co. v. Mahon,* 1922, 260 U.S. 393, 415, 416, 43 S.Ct. 158, 160, 67 L.Ed. 322:

". . . The protection of private property in the Fifth Amendment presupposes that it is wanted for public use, but provides that it shall not be taken for such use without compensation. A similar assumption is made in the decisions upon the Fourteenth Amendment. (Citing case.) When this seemingly absolute protection is found to be qualified by the police power, the natural tendency of human nature is to extend the qualification more and more until at last private property disappears. But that cannot be accomplished in this way under the Constitution of the United States.

". . . *We are in danger of forgetting that a strong public desire to improve the public condition is not enough to warrant achieving the desire by a shorter cut than the constitutional way of paying for the change.* . . ." (Emphasis supplied.) (pp. 668–669.)

The court held in *Ackerman,* supra, that the "alleged continuing and frequent low flights over the appellants' land amount to a taking of an air easement for the purpose of flying airplanes over the land" and that the port, which did not operate the planes, but operated the airport, was liable for the alleged taking.

In *Jensen v. United States,* 305 F.2d 444 (Ct.Cl.) plaintiffs sued in four related cases for just compensation for the taking of avigation easements over their properties. The government did not deny a taking occurred and conceded if the claims were not barred by limitations it was proper for the court to allow compensation for the taking. The facts indicated it was clear the flights directly and immediately interfered with the use and enjoyment of plaintiffs' properties; there was noise intensity as well as frequent low level flights by large airplanes. (See also *Aaron v. United States,* Ct.Cl., 311 F. 2d 798.)

The minority view in United States is expressed in the case of *Harrell's Candy Kitchen, Inc. v. Sarasota-Manatee Airport Authority,* 111 So.2d 439 (Fla.).

Defendants contend plaintiff failed to exhaust his administrative remedies as a prerequisite to judicial relief; that he should have sought a permit from the Planning Commission with respect to nonconforming uses or variances under Section 7 of Ordinance No. 448; and cite *Dunham v. City of Westminister,* 202 Cal. App.2d 245, 20 Cal.Rptr. 772, as authority for the point that administrative remedies must be exhausted. In the *Dunham* case a city building department refused to file an application for a building permit unless plaintiffs dedicated and agreed to improve a portion of their property for street purposes, or were relieved from same by obtaining a variance; plaintiffs asserted the ordinance was unconstitutional; this court held plaintiffs had not exhausted their administrative remedies. In the instant case, however, the situation is different in that it is not the plaintiff who has sought or obtained a change from what existed before, but the County which has invaded the alleged property rights of plaintiff, and in response thereto plaintiff does not challenge the constitutionality of the Ordinance but merely seeks damages in inverse condemnation as provided in Section 8 of the Ordinance.

Judgment reversed.

GRIFFIN, P. J., and COUGHLIN, J., concur.

Comments: 1. The *Sneed* case involves an "inverse" or "reverse" condemnation action. Inverse condemnation actions are brought in two kinds of cases. In one type of case, part of the landowner's property has been taken and the action is brought to recover remainder damages which the property owner alleges have not been compensated in the original and formal eminent domain proceeding. Inverse condemnation may also be used to assert a claim for consequential damages, when no property has formally and physically been taken by the condemnee, but the property owner alleges that he has suffered compensable damage. The principal case is in the second category, and we will concentrate on these cases here.

The theory of inverse condemnation is impossibly muddled. *See generally* Mandelker, Inverse Condemnation: The Constitutional Limits of Public Responsibility, 1966 Wis. L. Rev. 3 (based on monograph, PB 170 880). The difficulty stems from the language of state constitutions which provide that compensation must be paid for "property" that has been "taken," or that has been "taken or damaged" by public agencies. Courts attempting to explain a recovery under these provisions may concentrate on an analysis of the property interest that is alleged to have been taken, or may explore instead the question of whether a taking, or a taking or damaging, has in fact occurred. Outcomes differ according to the nature of the judicial rationale, and the addition of the "damaged" clause to the constitutional language does not necessarily guarantee a more favorable result for the property owner.

Problems also arise between cases in which there has been an actual physical invasion of property, and cases in which there has not, and many inverse condemnation cases deal with claimed liability for unintended physical damage inflicted by the condemnor. The facts in *Commonwealth, Dep't of Highways v. Cochrane*, 397 S.W.2d 155 (Ky. 1965), are typical: "Plaintiffs had a lake on their land an acre and a half in size. Some 1,000 feet from the property, along the watershed line, the Department of Highways constructed a new highway which required cuts, and a fill approximately 35 feet at its highest point. The excavation and fill work left an unseeded and unsodded area exposed to the weather for about a year. Shortly after the work commenced one of the plaintiffs noticed mud and fill entering the lake." *Id.* at 155-56. Inverse liability was found.

For a good recent treatment of inverse condemnation, see B. Hering and M. Ordover, Theory and Practice in Inverse Condemnation for Five Representative States, in 2 Selected Studies in Highway Law 797 (J. Vance ed. 1976).

When the damage cannot be classified as physical, the issues grow murkier. The following notes will help to put the principal case in perspective.

2. The use and enjoyment of privately owned land is frequently interfered with by airplane flights to and from a nearby publicly-owned airport. When the airplane flights are directly over the claimant's land, the right to recover in an inverse condemnation proceeding on one theory or another is now recognized. The is some reasoning in the cases that continuing overflights amount to the taking of an easement. When, however, the overflights are near to but not over the claimant's property the courts have more difficulty. Some find no liability on the conventional theory that the damages are consequential and not compensable. The cases and the literature are summarized in *Ferguson v. City of Keene*, 238 A.2d 1 (N.H. 1968) (denying compensation). *Contra, Thornburg v. Port of Portland*, 376 P.2d 100 (Ore. 1962). Cases which deny liability in the absence of direct overflights are hard to square with the well-established judicial view which finds liability for the establishment and conduct of a nuisance on the ground, although they are consistent with the cases that deny liability for adjacent highway noise. The highway and airplane noise cases are contrasted and distinguished in *Northcutt v. State Road Dep't*, 209 So.2d 710 (Fla. 1968).

In *Thornburg v. Port of Portland, supra,* the court held, in effect, that the Port of Portland might be found to have "taken" an easement to inflict a "nuisance" upon the plaintiff landowners by means of repeated flights near but not directly over their land. The court referred to Restatement,

Torts §§ 826-831 for "principles for balancing gravity [of the harm] against utility [of defendant's activity] which can be adapted to jury instruction so that the question of reasonableness need not be any more mysterious to the jury in this type of case than it is in an automobile accident case." On remand, a further trial resulted in a jury verdict for the defendant. On a second appeal, the court reversed and remanded (for the second time) on the following grounds:

> . . . If the jury finds an interference with the plaintiff's use and enjoyment of his land, substantial enough to result in a loss of market value, there is a taking. If the jury determines that there has been a taking, its only concern is to fix the monetary compensation therefor. . . . The error below was in telling the jury in effect to consider the utility of the airport in deciding whether the plaintiff's property had been depreciated in value by the defendant's activities. This notion is wholly inconsistent with the law of eminent domain, and had no place in the jury's consideration of a decrease in fair market value.

Thornburg v. Port of Portland, 415 P.2d 750, 752, 753 (Ore. 1966).

In the *Thornburg* case (first appeal), the court said, "Inverse condemnation . . . provides the remedy where an injunction would not be in the public interest, and where the continued interference amounts to a taking for which the constitution demands a remedy." Why would an injunction "not be in the public interest" in *Thornburg?* Would it have been "in the public interest" in *Sneed ?*

3. What about vehicular pollution — the noise, smoke, vibration, and lights that traffic on the highway brings? When there has been a severance caused by a partial taking, highway noise may also be compensable. *United States v. Certain Parcels of Land,* 252 F. Supp. 319 (W.D. Mich. 1966). But when there has been no physical severance, highway noise and related damage has usually been held to be "consequential" and thus noncompensable. The rule is consistent with special benefit offset rules when it is remembered that benefits may be offset only when there has been a partial taking.

But see Thomsen v. State, 170 N.W.2d 575 (Minn. 1969). The state highway department narrowed a roadway in front of plaintiff's house in order to avoid physically taking any of his property. He then brought an action in mandamus to compel the state to commence condemnation proceedings to assess the noise and related damage attributable to the highway. Mandamus was awarded and the state appealed. Affirmed. Whether "plaintiff's property has been so unfairly, directly, substantially, and peculiarly injured that it has been damaged in the constitutional sense" is a question of law to be determined by the court in the condemnation proceedings. *See generally* Netherton, Implementation of Land Use Policy: Police Power vs. Eminent Domain, 3 (Univ. Wyo.) Land & Water L. Rev. 33 (1968).

The "nuisance" rationale has been employed in other types of "inverse condemnation" cases. *See Glace v. Town of Pilot Mountain,* 143 S.E.2d 78 (N.C. 1965), awarding damages for impairment of the property value of a residence caused by the proximity of a municipal sewage lagoon. This approach to liability comes from the well-accepted conceptual view of property, which defines it to include the right to "use" the property. Thus, it is possible that liability may be found whenever there is an impairment of value resulting from interference with use. But when there is no physical harm and conventional nuisance principles do not apply, courts hesitate to impose liability. In *Gervasi v. Board of Comm'rs,* 256 N.Y.S.2d 910 (N.Y. Sup. Ct. 1965) (trial court) in which owners of residences sought compensation for the reduced value of their homes caused by the construction of a water tower, the court noted that aesthetic "considerations" are not compensable. *But cf. Edwards v. Bridgeport Hydraulic Co.,* 211 A.2d 679 (Conn. 1965) (similar; liability based on statute).

4. . . . [T]he relevant litigation ordinarily appears in the subtle disguise of a controversy as to whether the limits of governmental "police power" have been exceeded, in the misleading cloak of an issue as to whether the seeker after compensation ever possessed a legally cognizable "property" right, or as a feigned dispute as to whether the governmental defendant was acting . . . in the exercise of its "eminent domain" or "regulatory" power. Yet, in each instance, the basic clash of interests involves the same fundamental problem: the extent to which governmentally compelled indirect contributions to the general public welfare must be compensated.

Van Alstyne, Just Compensation of Intangible Detriment: Criteria for Legislative Modifications in California, 16 U.C.L.A.L. Rev. 491, 492 (1969).

5. PROBLEM: As part of a city program of slum cleanup the building department proceeds to raze and demolish over 100 buildings which it finds to be unsafe. It acts under a state statute authorizing the city to demolish, without compensation, any "unsafe" building which the city finds to be a "nuisance." A property owner whose building was demolished brings suit in inverse condemnation, alleging that his building was not, in fact, unsafe, and that it had a market value of $10,000. Liability was denied in this situation in *MacLeod v. City of Tacoma Park*, 263 A.2d 581 (Md. 1970), but the overwhelming weight of authority has always allowed a recovery in these cases if the court finds that grounds justifying an uncompensated demolition were not present. Which view is correct?

COLBERG, INC. v. STATE DEPARTMENT OF PUBLIC WORKS

Supreme Court of California
67 Cal.2d 408, 62 Cal. Rptr. 401, 432 P.2d 3 (1967)

SULLIVAN, Justice.

These consolidated actions for declaratory relief present the common issue whether plaintiff shipyard owners will have any causes of action for damages under the law of eminent domain arising out of the impairment of their access to the Stockton Deep Water Ship Channel as a result of the construction of two proposed fixed low level parallel bridges spanning a connecting navigable waterway to which their properties are riparian. Separate judgments on the pleadings in favor of defendant State of California were entered below and all plaintiffs have appealed.

. . . .

The Stockton Deep Water Ship Channel is a navigable tidal waterway extending from the mouth of the San Joaquin River to the Port of Stockton. From the turning basin adjoining the port, the channel continues easterly for about 5,000 feet and comes to a dead end within the confines of the city. This portion of the waterway is known as the Upper Stockton Channel. Plaintiffs Colberg and Stephens Marine, Inc. (Stephens), own real property in the City of Stockton riparian to the Upper Stockton Channel upon which for more than sixty years they have conducted shipyards for the construction and repair of yachts and ocean-going vessels. Both yards are improved with marineways, buildings, docks and allied facilities. Colberg's property consists of approximately eight acres; Stephens' of approximately six. Ships and other craft now using the Upper Stockton Channel can proceed to the turning basin and the Stockton Deep Water Ship Channel and thereupon navigate to the open sea by way of the Carquinez Straits and San Francisco Bay.

The state proposes to construct twin stationary freeway bridges across the Upper Stockton Channel between plaintiffs' properties and the turning basin. The vertical clearance of these bridges is to be, generally speaking, 45 feet above the water line. Pursuant to federal law the state applied to the Secretary of the Army and the Chief of Engineers for a permit to build such bridges. (See 33 U.S.C.A. § 525, subd. (b)). After a public hearing, consideration of the views of various interested persons including these plaintiffs, and an extensive economic survey, approval of the location and plans of the bridges was granted by federal authorities in February 1964, subject to conditions not here necessary to be detailed.

Colberg alleges that 81 percent of its current business involves ships standing more than 45 feet above the water line. Plaintiff Stephens alleges that 35 percent of its current business involves such ships. The present minimum clearance between plaintiffs' yards and the Pacific Ocean is 135 feet, established by the Antioch Bridge. Plaintiffs allege in substance that after the construction of the proposed bridges, no vessel with fixed structure in excess of 45 feet above the water line will be able to enter their respective shipyards; that there is no other access by water to the yards from the San Joaquin River, San Francisco Bay and the oceans of the world; and that plaintiffs, their properties and their businesses will suffer loss and damages because of the impairment of access resulting from the construction of the bridges.[11] Plaintiffs in both actions allege that an

---

[11] Colberg alleges that its property "will be totally lost and destroyed"; and that it is "the only shipyard facility which lies on the Upper Stockton Channel that relies principally upon the repair and construction of large vessels for its income."

actual controversy exists . . . between each of them and the state as to whether the alleged impairment of access to "the main channel of the San Joaquin River" is compensable.

Counsel for the state pointed out to us at oral argument that a bridge of vertical clearance sufficient to accommodate plaintiffs' shipyard traffic would involve greatly increased construction costs because it would entail extended approaches; [12] that the added height of such approaches would have an adverse effect upon intangible community values; and that a draw or swing bridge would be unsuitable for freeway purposes.

The trial court granted the state's motion for judgment on the pleadings in both cases and entered judgments accordingly. In its memorandum opinion it held that diminution of the scope of plaintiffs' access from their respective properties to the Stockton Deep Water Ship Channel as a result of the state's proposed action relative to its navigable waters would not constitute a taking or damaging of private property for which just compensation would be required.

It is not disputed that an actual controversy exists between the parties on this question; that if plaintiffs were required to await construction of the bridge before commencing an action at law, they would suffer irreparable damage because of interference with their businesses during construction; that a declaratory judgment resolving the question of compensability in their favor prior to completion of the bridge project will permit relocation of their respective operations with a minimum of inconvenience; and that plaintiffs will be unable to plan their businesses or enter into necessary long-term business contracts, until such question is settled. We are satified that

---

Stephens alleges that as a result of the construction of the bridges, its shipyard "can only be operated at substantial loss to the plaintiff and the value of plaintiff's property will be substantially diminished."

[12] Colberg alleges on information and belief that the state "has determined the comparative costs of the bridges at different levels, including structure, roadway, and right of way acquisitions to be as follows:

"50 foot vertical clearance above mean sea level: $27,448,000.00

"63 foot vertical clearance above mean sea level: $38,724,000.00

"100 foot vertical clearance above mean sea level: $46,398,000.00

"No estimate of cost has been made by the defendant for a bridge 135 feet above mean sea level"; further alleges that "the determination of the defendant to construct said bridges with a vertical clearance of 50 feet above mean sea level, and to construct them without facilities for a lift type or draw-bridge type bridge, has been made solely upon considerations of economy and the advantages to motor vehicle traffic safety and utility, and not upon any consideration to improve navigation. Plaintiffs further allege that said bridges are an obstruction to navigation and do not improve navigation in any manner whatsoever."

under the above circumstances plaintiffs were entitled to invoke declaratory relief.

The sole question in this case is whether the alleged impairment of plaintiffs' access to the Stockton Deep Water Ship Channel constitutes a taking or damaging of private property within the meaning of article I, section 14 of the California Constitution. In order to answer this question we are led to an examination of the interest of the state in its navigable waters; in the course of this examination we explain the relationship between the state's power to deal with its navigable waters and the extent of its constitutional duty to make compensation for damage caused by the exercise of that power.

In order to put the controversy into proper focus, we must first make some preliminary observations concerning plaintiffs' position and the nature and extent of their claim. First, it is clear that plaintiffs must assert the taking or damaging of a *private* right in order to bring themselves within the protective embrace of article I, section 14. Thus, they cannot ground their claim in the right of navigation, for this is a public right from the abridgment of which plaintiffs will suffer no damage different in character from that to be suffered by the general public.[13] . . . Instead, they must have recourse to the private right of an owner riparian to a navigable waterway to have access to the channel. . . . However, it appears that the access from plaintiffs' property to the navigable portion of the waterway to which they are riparian, to wit, the Upper Stockton Channel, will not be impaired by the proposed project, so that their private right of access, if limited to its traditional scope, will not be "taken or damaged" and no claim for compensation can arise. It is therefore plaintiffs' position that the private right of access must be expanded. They assert that the construction of the bridge in question will render their private right of access useless insofar as it pertains to vessels with a fixed structure more than 45 feet above the waterline; that after such construction they "can launch ships, but they can go nowhere." Action which renders a right valueless, they urge, effectively "takes or damages" that right.

---

[13] Indeed, plaintiffs, while scrupulously eschewing all claims based on a public right, have been forced into the position of extending a private right in a meandering continuum from their properties to the Pacific Ocean and, as counsel for the state observed at oral argument, now claim a property right in "a column of air 135 feet high extending from their properties to the sea." We cannot refrain from observing that were the bridge here involved proposed for the Carquinez Straits instead of the Upper Stockton Channel, plaintiffs, consistently with the theory of their pleadings, would advance the same basic claim for compensation. If such claim could be considered valid for plaintiffs, it would also be assertible by the countless riparian owners in the intervening section of the watercourse.

We deem it unnecessary to decide this question, for we have determined that, whatever the scope of plaintiffs' right of riparian access *as against other private persons,* that right must yield without compensation to a proper exercise of the power *of the state* over its navigable waters. It is to a discussion of this latter power that we now turn.

The State of California holds all of its navigable waterways and the lands lying beneath them "as trustee of a public trust for the benefit of the people." . . . Its power to control, regulate and utilize such waters within the terms of the trust is absolute except as limited by the paramount supervisory power of the federal government over navigable waters. . . . The nature and extent of the trust under which the state holds its navigable waterways has never been defined with precision, but it has been stated generally that acts of the state with regard to its navigable waters are within trust purposes when they are done "for purposes of commerce, navigation, and fisheries for the benefit of all the people of the state." . . . *Mallon v. City of Long Beach,* (1955) 44 Cal.2d 199, 205, 282 P.2d 481, 484; . . .

The courts have construed the purposes of the trust with liberality to the end of benefiting all the people of the state. In the early case of *People v. Potretro & B.V.R.R. Co.,* 7 P. 445 (Cal. 1855) defendant, under authority of a franchise granted by the Legislature, constructed a railroad bridge across Islais Creek, a navigable waterway. The bridge was an obstruction to navigation, and the Board of State Harbor Commissioners sought to have it abated as a nuisance. It was contended that the legislative act granting the right to build the bridge was in conflict with the act of Congress admitting California into the Union, which act provided that " 'all the navigable waters within the state shall be common highways, and forever free, as well to the inhabitants of said state as to the citizens of the United States, without any tax, impost, or duty therefor.' " This court rejected this contention, holding *inter alia* that "while the power of the state with respect to the construction, regulation, and control of bridges . . . is subordinate to that of congress, still until congress acts on the subject, the power of the state is plenary." (7 P. at p. 447.) Though we there made no explicit reference to the extent of the trust relating to navigable waters, we impliedly held that the spanning of navigable waters by a railroad bridge was an act within the trust purposes of "commerce, navigation, and fisheries."

In *Boone v. Kingsbury,* 273 P. 797 the state surveyor-general had refused to issue to plaintiffs permits to prospect for oil and gas upon tidal lands covered by navigable sea waters upon the ground, *inter alia,* that the granting of such permits would constitute an act without the scope of the trust because such prospecting would not be "in aid and furtherance of commerce and navigation." We rejected that contention, holding that the relationship of gasoline to commerce was manifest. "Gasoline is the power that largely moves the commerce of nations over lands and sea; . . . Gasoline is so closely allied with state and national welfare as to make its production a matter of state and national concern. If it can be said of any industry that its output is 'in aid and furtherance of commerce and navigation,' and its production 'a public benefit,' the production of gasoline, by reason of the motive elements that inhere in it and its universal use and adaptability to varied uses and the convenient and portable form in which it may be confined, would entitle it to a high classification in the scale of useful, natural products. It is a mover of commerce and fills the office of 'a public benefit.' " (273 P. at p. 812.)

Finally, in the case of *Gray v. Reclamation District No. 1500,* . . . 174 Cal. 622, 163 P. 1024 [1917], plaintiffs sought to enjoin the operations of defendant district, which was engaged in efforts to reclaim land and prevent flooding, with incidental benefits to navigation, near the confluence of the Sacramento and Feather Rivers. We there rejected plaintiffs' contention that the state had no power to deal with its navigable waters unless its dominant purpose was to improve navigation. "The supreme control of the state over its navigable waters was early declared in *Eldridge v. Cowell,* 4 Cal. 80, approved in *United States v. Mission Rock Co.,* 189 U.S. 391, 23 S.Ct. 606, 47 L.Ed. 865. This right of control embraces within it not alone the power to destroy the navigability of certain waters for the benefit of others, but extends in the case of streams to the power to regulate and control the navigable or nonnavigable tributaries, as in the debris cases, *to the erection of structures along or across the stream,* to deepening or changing the channel, to diverting or arresting tributaries; *in short, to do anything subserving the great purpose, ...*" (Emphasis added.) (174 Cal. at p. 636, 163 P. at p. 1030.)

We deem it too clear to warrant the citation of further authority that the state, as trustee for the benefit of the people, has power to deal with its navigable waters in any manner consistent with the improvement of commercial intercourse, whether navigational or otherwise. It is equally clear, however, that the question of governmental *power* is quite different from that of *compensation* for damage caused by the exercise of such power. It is to the latter question that we now turn.

We have referred above to the paramount supervisory power of the federal government over navigable waters. This power, though superior to that of the state, is not grounded in ownership of the navigable waterways upon which it operates, but rather derives from the commerce clause of the Untied States Constitution, and it has been stated that it may properly be exercised *only* in order to aid navigation. . . . The Fifth Amendment to the United States

Constitution is of course applicable to the exercise of the federal navigational power within its proper scope, just as article I, section 14 of the state Constitution is applicable to the exercise of state power over navigable waters, but in many cases compensation for "damage" caused by exercise of the federal power is denied because the rights and values affected are deemed to be burdened with the so-called federal "navigation servitude."[14] Among the rights so burdened is that of the access from riparian land to the affected navigable waterway. . . . The limits of the servitude are reached, however, and just compensation must be paid in spite of the fact that the power has been exercised within its scope, when permanent physical encroachment upon or invasion of land riparian to the navigable waterway but above the ordinary high-water mark results. . . .

As we have shown above, the power of the State of California to deal with its navigable waters, though subject to the superior federal power, is considerably wider in scope than that paramount power. The state, as owner of its navigable waterways subject to a trust for the benefit of the people, may act relative to those waterways in any manner consistent with the improvement of commercial traffic and intercourse. We are of the further view that the law of California burdens property riparian or littoral to navigable waters with a servitude commensurate with the power of the state over such navigable waters, and that "when the act [of the state] is done, if it does not embrace the actual taking of property, but results merely in some injurious effect upon the property, the property owner must, for the sake of the general welfare, yield uncompensated obedience." (*Gray v. Reclamation District No. 1500,* supra, 174 Cal. 622, 636, 163 P. 1024, 1030.)

We have arrived at this conclusion after an examination of cases from other jurisdictions. It appears that in some states the servitude operates only when the state acts upon its navigable waters for the purpose of improving navigation, and that private rights "damaged" by acts not in aid of navigation are therefore compensable. . . . This appears to be the law of the State of New York. . . . Other jurisdictions hold as we do in the instant case, that the state's servitude operates upon certain private rights, including those of access, whenever the state deals with its navigable waters in a manner consistent with the public trust under which they are held. . . . We

---

[14] There is some doubt as to the origin and basis of the dominant navigational servitude in favor of the federal government. Perhaps the most satisfactory explanation is that derived from the common law concept of *jus publicum,* that interest of the Crown in its navigable waterways whereby the subjects were assured that such waterways would be utilized for public benefit, and that private interference with such utilization would be prevented. (See Morreale, *op. cit.,* at pp. 19-31.)

are of the opinion that this view is supported not only by the present law of California, but also by considerations of sound public policy.

The limitation of the servitude to cases involving a strict navigational purpose stems from a time when the sole use of navigable waterways for purposes of commerce was that of surface water transport. (See Morreale, op. cit., at p. 26.) That time is no longer with us. The demands of modern commerce, the concentration of population in urban centers fronting on navigable waterways, the achievements of science in devising new methods of commercial intercourse — all of these factors require that the state, in determining the means by which the general welfare is best to be served through the utilization of navigable waters held in trust for the public, should not be burdened with an outmoded classification favoring one mode of utilization over another.

It is clear that the conclusions above expressed dispose of plaintiffs' contention that their right of access to the navigable waters fronting on their respective properties must, in order to be of utility, include the right to navigate freely to the sea.[15] Whatever the scope and character of their right to have access to those navigable waters, we hold that such right is burdened with a servitude in favor of the state which comes into operation when the state properly exercises its power to control, regulate, and utilize such waters.

In *City of Newport Beach v. Fager,* supra, 39 Cal.App.2d 23, 102 P.2d 438, defendants' access to navigable waters over their littoral land was *wholly* cut off when the city, a political subdivision of the state, filled and reclaimed the tidelands in front of their land. When the city sought to quiet title to the lands thus filled, defendants contended that they had at least a right of access over such lands to navigable water. The court rejected this contention. "We are satisfied that the correct rule is that the littoral owner of uplands upon a navigable bay has no right of access to the waters of the bay over intervening tidelands, whether filled or unfilled, which have been granted by the state to a city in trust for the purpose of improving such navigable bay in furtherance of commerce and navigation. [Citations.] Although it is true that as against a stranger a littoral owner of upland bordering upon navigable waters may not be deprived of his right of access to such waters, no such right exists in favor of such littoral owner as against the state or its grantee in the exercise of a lawful use or purpose." (39 Cal.App.2d at p. 28,

---

[15] It should be noted that the "private property" right upon which plaintiffs base their claims is of even larger scope than a simple right to navigate freely to the sea, for that right is not here curtailed except insofar as it concerns ships with fixed structures more than 45 feet above the waterline. Thus, the "right of access" claimed by plaintiffs would seem to include a right to navigate to the sea in vessels of any size. (See fn. [13], infra.)

102 P.2d at p. 441. . . . We are neither advised of, nor can conceive of, any reason why rules relating to one kind of navigable waters, to wit, tidewaters, should not be applied with equal reason to similar situations involving other kinds of navigable waters. In any event, we take judicial notice of the fact that tidal influence extends some distance up the San Joaquin River past the Port of Stockton. . . .

We also reject plaintiffs' contention that our highway access cases . . . require that compensation be paid for any substantial impairment of plaintiffs' right of access. We are not persuaded that the analogy between highway access and navigational access will bear close scrutiny. The right of access to a land highway derives from the "land service road" concept, whereby roads are conceived of as arteries constructed through condemnation of private land for the purpose of serving other land abutting on them, rather than for the purpose of serving public traffic passing over them. (See Note (1965) 38 So.Cal.L.Rev. 689, 690, and authorities cited in fn. 9 thereof.) Principles applicable to such a right cannot reasonably be extended to the case of navigable waterways, which constitute a natural resource retained within the public domain for the purpose of serving public traffic in accordance with the greatest common benefit.

Finally, we emphasize that the state servitude upon lands riparian or littoral to navigable waters, like the federal servitude burdening such lands, does not extend to cases wherein the proper exercise of state power results in actual physical invasion of or encroachment upon fast lands. In the case of *Miramar Co. v. City of Santa Barbara,* supra, 23 Cal.2d 170, 143 P.2d 1, plaintiff was the owner of lands littoral to a navigable bay and defendant, a political subdivision of the state, constructed a permanent breakwater in the bay about three miles to the west of plaintiff's property. The effect of this breakwater upon natural drifts and currents operated in the course of time to denude plaintiff's property of sandy beach, rendering the property valueless as a beach resort. It was alleged that defendant, before it built its breakwater, knew that the effect complained of would occur. Plaintiff sued in inverse condemnation, and the trial court entered a judgment of dismissal after sustaining defendants' demurrer without leave to amend. Upon affirmance of the judgment by this court it was said: "Plaintiff's littoral right to sandy water [which provided the accretion necessary to offset tidal washing], like its littoral right to access to the ocean, was derived entirely from the proximity of plaintiff's land to the ocean. It gave to plaintiff's land the advantage of sandy accretions. Nevertheless, the enjoyment of that advantage did not constitute a right to its perpetuation, for plaintiff's littoral rights were always subordinate to the state's right to improve navigation.[16] The duration of the sandy accretions depended entirely upon the continuation of the littoral right, which from the beginning was subject to termination by the state. The withdrawal of the sandy accretions, constituting the damage to plaintiff's land, was an incidental consequence of the state's use of the public domain for a public interest that was at all times superior to private littoral rights. There has therefore been no taking or damaging of private property for public use within the meaning of article I, section 14, of the California Constitution." (23 Cal.2d at p. 176, 143 P.2d at p. 4.) In a separate concurring opinion, it was said that direct physical encroachment or invasion upon plaintiff's lands was required in order that there be "a taking within the meaning of the constitutional provision." (23 Cal.2d at p. 178, 143 P.2d at p. 5.) After reference to certain cases of the United States Supreme Court to which we have adverted above (e. g., *Pumpelly v. Green Bay Company,* supra, 80 U.S. (13 Wall.) 166, 20 L.Ed. 557) the concurring opinion concluded that "The doctrine of taking under the Fifth Amendment has never been extended beyond the rule stated, and certainly there is no necessity for doing so under a constitutional provision which provides compensation for both taking and damaging." (143 P.2d at p. 5.) Three justices of the court dissented upon the basis that under the facts a physical taking of the plaintiff's land *was* involved.

It therefore appears that this court in the *Miramar* case, though divided as to the proper result under the facts there at issue, reached fundamental agreement on the extent to which the state, through the proper exercise of its trust power to deal with navigable waters, may impair without compensation rights appurtenant to property riparian or littoral to such waters. The servitude with which such property is burdened precludes compensation for impairment or curtailment of all rights not damaged by permanent physical invasion of or encroachment upon fast lands; when the exercise of the power does cause such physical invasion or encroachment, the servitude is inapplicable and rights damaged as a result are compensable in accordance with article I, section 14, of the state Constitution.

We hold that plaintiffs' right of access from their respective riparian properties to the waters of the channel, whatever its scope as against private parties, is burdened with a servitude in favor of the state and that, since there is here no direct physical invasion of, or encroachment upon, said properties by the state, plaintiffs are not entitled to compensation for the abridgment or diminution, if any, of such right of access as a result of the lawful exercise of the state's power to regulate, control and deal with its navigable waters.

---

[16] The improvement involved in *Miramar* was in aid of navigation. However, as we have explained supra, the state's power to regulate and control its navigable waters is not limited to purposes of navigation, and the servitude in its favor is of commensurate scope.

The judgments are, and each of them is, affirmed.

TRAYNOR, C. J., and MᴄCOMB, TOBRINER, and BURKE, JJ., concur.

DISSENTING OPINION

PETERS, Justice.

I dissent.

I cannot agree that because the state wants to build two low level highway bridges across the mouth of an inlet where plaintiffs' shipyards are located, plaintiffs must suffer the complete loss caused by the impairment of their right of one-way water access to deep water. Principles of fairness, logic and public policy suggest that this loss is a part of the cost of the freeway that should not be borne by plaintiffs but should be borne by the public. Compensation should therefore be allowed.

The access impaired here is one-way access to the oceans of the world. Such access is indispensable to the operation of plaintiffs' businesses.[17] So, the impairment is not technical. It is substantial and different in nature and degree from the impairment suffered by the general public. There is not involved the mere hypothetical damage to vacant land, nor are we dealing with speculators, nor with newly created businesses. Both plaintiffs have been operating bona fide shipyards in the inlet for over 60 years. Thus, we are not involved with a mere incidental impairment of the right of access but are dealing with a very substantial impairment. The impairment is not caused by a construction strictly in aid of navigation but the bridges are part of a state freeway. If the freeway impaired land access to the same degree such impairment would be compensable. These facts are indisputable.

The majority hold that, under these facts, case law and public policy dictate the conclusion that compensation should not be allowed. So far as case law is concerned the majority have done a commendable job in collecting the cases discussing the nature of the rights involved. But all that this exhaustive analysis proves is that there are no definitive cases in California, and that the decisions of other states reach conflicting results. A decision either way is permissible under the cases. Thus, the decision in this case is really a public policy one, and the majority, recognizing this, claim that public policy supports their conclusion. How can there be a public policy to cut off plaintiffs' only access to deep water and so put well

---

[17] Colberg alleges that 81 percent of its current business is derived from ships unable to reach its shipyard under a bridge but 45 feet in height. Stephens alleges it will lose 35 percent of their business if the bridges are built. The Carquinez bridges, it should be mentioned, are 135 feet above the water.

established businesses out of operation without compensation? The answer is obvious. There can be and is no such public policy. The question is not an open one. It has been decided that, as a matter of public policy, impairment of land access under such circumstances requires compensation. The majority fly in the face of that determination.

Today government is big and complex and constantly growing bigger. The legitimate need of government for property is constantly expanding. Thus, more and more frequently, the rights of individuals and the government come into conflict. When this occurs then this court must referee the conflict and try to protect the rights of the state and the rights of the individual. In doing so we must keep in mind the admonition of our Constituion that property "shall not be taken or damaged for public use without just compensation."

Nowhere is this conflict between the state and the individual made more apparent than by the state's need to build new highways and freeways which frequently include, as here, the building of bridges. The problem became very apparent in the construction of the freeways and the approaches leading to the San Francisco Bay Bridge. Rights of access were obviously impaired. In the case of *Bacich v. Board of Control,* 23 Cal.2d 343, 144 P.2d 818, where the construction of the approaches to the Bay Bridge placed plaintiff's land and property in a cul-de-sac, the problem was directly presented. Plaintiff had still one-way access to the general system of streets but his access in the other direction was substantially cut off. There was no controlling case in California. Cases elsewhere were in conflict. The court recognized that it was a problem of first impression, and that it was required to determine the public policy of this state. It then showed no hesitancy, as it does now, to declare such policy. It held that when the right of access was impaired, as distinguished from a physical taking or damaging, there must be a weighing of the conflicting rights. Thus, where the impairment is substantial and peculiar to the plaintiff, and can be compensated for without prohibitive cost, it is compensable. But where the impairment is incidental and where the cost of compensation is prohibitive it is not compensable. Thus, impairment of access to one in a cul-de-sac was held compensable, but property owners beyond the next intersecting street were not to be compensated. Nor were property owners to be compensated where their access street was made into a one-way street or into a divided highway, or left turns were prohibited. (See *Bacich v. Board of Control,* supra, 23 Cal.2d 343, pp. 356, 358 et seq., 144 P.2d 818, pp. 826, 827 et seq., particularly the concurring opinion of Edmonds, J.; . . . .) The court showed no reluctance in *Bacich* and the other cases in declaring that a material impairment of the right of access should be compensable as a matter of public policy. But the majority in the instant case repudiate that public policy and purport to hold that public policy now compels a contrary result. The two lines of authority are inconsistent and incompatible. If we were right in the land access cases the majority are wrong in this case.

The major error in the majority opinion is its holding that all the state's uses of its navigable waters must be treated in the same identical fashion. It may be that when the state acts strictly in aid of navigation that the right of the state is absolute and the property owner is entitled to no compensation . . . for impairment of his rights. But where the use by the state is not strictly for navigation purposes, but, as here, is for freeway purposes, principles of equity, justice, fairness, and certainly of public policy, dictate that the same public policy declared in the land access cases should apply.

When this case was before the Court of Appeal of the Third Appellate District, Justice Friedman prepared a scholarly and exhaustive opinion for the court that discusses these positions in depth. The following portions of that opinion are adopted as part of this dissent. (*Colberg, Inc. v. State of California,* (Cal.App.) 55 Cal.Rptr. 159.)

"The amendment of state constitutions, including California's, to provide compensation when private property is 'damaged' as well as 'taken' for public use, indicates an intent to expand the area of compensability, requiring the courts to fix its limits by placing the economic interests of the public in balance against the sacrifices imposed on the landowner. . . . The case-by-case balancing of these competing interests results in judicial expansion or contraction of a group of intangible rights recognized as compensable 'private property.' Compensable property, it is now recognized, includes not only the physical land and improvements but certain intangible rights of access between the land and the outside world. Thus, although the owner uses the streets in common with the rest of the public, he owns a private easement of access which consists of the right to get into the street abutting his property and thence to the general system of public streets and highways. . . . Not every impairment of access to the general system of public streets is compensable in eminent domain. Compensability, rather, requires an individualized finding of substantial impairment, a finding of fact delegated to the trial court and not the jury. . . .

"The central problem is to locate a line between compensable damage to private property and disadvantages of the kind called 'consequential.' Of the latter sort are such elements as loss of business and diminution of traffic caused by diversion of traffic and circuity of travel. (*People ex rel. Department of Public Works v. Symons,* 54 Cal.2d 855, 860, 9 Cal.Rptr. 363, 357 P.2d 451.) Applying the economic balancing test, the Supreme Court points out that awards of the latter sort would severely burden the public treasury and produce 'an embargo upon the creation of new and desirable roads.' (Ibid., p. 862, 9 Cal.Rptr. p. 367, 357 P.2d p. 455.)

"The street access doctrine represents an expanded notion of the constitutional concept of private property whose invasion or damage is compensable in eminent domain. It means that 'property' in an eminent domain sense includes not only a piece of the earth's surface but an intangible right of movement between it and the outside world; that, although the channels of movement are shared with the public, they are 'private' and compensable when a public improvement devalues a particular piece of land by substantially impairing these channels. Navigable waterways are channels of movement no less than streets and highways. . . . There is no difference in principle or policy between land and sea access which affirms an easement of access by land and denies it by water. If a public project obstructs the owner's access to the outside world, he is equally hurt whether the barrier blocks him by land or by sea. A littoral property owner's easement of access includes both media of movement.

"Claims for loss of street access often arise because the public improvement places private property on a cul-de-sac, restricting accessability to one direction only. . . . The Colberg and Stephens shipyards are situated on a natural cul-de-sac. Without the intervention of the public improvement, they have marine access to the outside world in one direction only. According to the complaints, construction of the public project will obstruct much of the single marine route between their property and the outside world. Their private right of access to the navigable water in front of their property has little value if that is as far as they can go. Location on a partially blocked, marine cul-de-sac is one element in the group of circumstances indicating the occurrence or absence of a substantial impairment of the easement of access.

"Doubtless these shipyards have street access on the landward side. Shoreline properties have obvious economic attributes resulting from their accessibility by water. Residual access by land may supply scant economic solace when marine access beyond the immediate waterfront is obstructed or destroyed. The substantial impairment rule supplies a criterion for determining whether the retention of land access and the destruction or obstruction of marine access result in compensable damage.

"The state contends that the street access doctrine is only an analogy. It suggests that the public policy of the street access cases, where economic balancing is possible, does not apply to loss of marine access; that the public can supply economical alternative routes to compensate for closed streets but not for closed waterways; further, that a bridge of limited clearance across a busy waterway may elicit damage claims so heavy and widespread as to prevent the project. These factors evoke no policy considerations excluding access by water from general easement of access recognized in eminent domain. The balancing approach is much broader than the street access cases. It is employed to measure the reach of the policy underlying the eminent domain provision of the State Constitution, laying down a line which separates compensable injuries from noncompensable disadvantages. In *Albers v. County of Los Angeles,* . . . [398 P.2d 129 (Cal. 1965)] it is used in the context of a landslide damage claim; in *Clement v. State Reclamation Board,* 35 Cal.2d 628, 642, 220 P.2d 897, to determine compensability of flood damage. In the course of the latter decision the court states: 'The decisive consideration is whether the owner of the damaged property if uncompensated would contribute more than his proper share to the public undertaking.' (*Clement v. State Reclamation Board,* supra, 35 Cal.2d at p. 642, 220 P.2d at p. 905.)

"Viewed in the light of the economic balancing criterion, the present injuries are sharply focused on two properties. They arouse no concern for the public purse beyond that involved in any eminent domain proceeding. While shared with the general public, marine passage along Upper Stockton Channel without a height restriction is a unique economic attribute of two commercial shipyards located on a marine cul-de-sac. The prospect of damage claims from the two owners is not so monumental as to discourage the freeway project of which the bridges are a part. The taxpayers can absorb the cost with far less hardship than the owners. . . .

"The selection between a low level bridge and reasonable alternatives is essentially a budgetary and planning choice by the administrator. Potential damage to the littoral owners may approach the cost of raising the bridge level. At that point the administrator starts thinking of an acceptable alternative, for example, a higher bridge. Intangible community values imperiled by the extended ramps of a high bridge may impel his return to the low level design. Whatever motivates the administrator to choose a low level bridge, dollars or intangible community values, the individual property owner 'if uncompensated would contribute more than his proper share to the public undertaking.' (*Clement v. State Reclamation Board,* supra, 35 Cal.2d at p. 642, 220 P.2d at p. 905.)

"The spector of widespread damage claims caused by a bridge athwart a busy artery of marine commerce arouses no policy tremors. Potential economic injuries from obstructions to navigation are limited by federal statutes investing the Chief of Engineers and the Secretary of the Army with discretionary permit powers in the interest of protecting navigation. . . . Unless the federal officials abdicate their responsibilities, a low level, drawless bridge across the Carquinez Straits or the mouth of the Mississippi is a theoretical but not practical possibility. It is reasonable to suggest that the present bridge project merited a federal permit only because the 45-foot limitation on navigation had narrow economic impact on two shipyards located on a marine cul-de-sac; that at some point potential injury to additional maritime interests would provoke denial of a federal permit. Injury claims remaining after the federal screening must then pass a second screening, that imposed by the economic balancing test, which measures the limit of compensability under the California Constitution. Finally, the claim must pass the substantial impairment test. These successive filters prevent compensable injuries to navigation so widely diffused that they are more public than private.

"We resist the invitation to follow the nuisance and equity decisions which deny upstream owners relief against downstream bridges which obstruct navigation. . . . Such decisions turn largely on the 'public' character of the right of navigation and the private plaintiff's lack of standing to seek relief against a public nuisance not peculiar to himself. In the search for an eminent domain concept of 'private property,' equity and nuisance decisions are not a trustworthy guide . . . . Preferable to analogies drawn from other branches of the law is the self-contained 'easement of access' doctrine developed as part of the California law of eminent domain.

"Eminent domain decisions in other states on compensability of obstructions to navigation vary. The variation is often prompted by the language of the particular state's constitutional provision. . . . None of these decisions considered the easement of access doctrine evolved as part of the California law of eminent domain. None of them considered the balancing of policies implicit in the easement of access doctrine.

"Both sides seek support in *City of Los Angeles v. Aitken,* 10 Cal.App.2d 460, 52 P.2d 585. The action was one to condemn littoral rights on a navigable lake whose level would be lowered by the condemning agency's diversion of tributary streams. The defendant owned shoreline resort property. According to the opinion, the marginal owner's privilege of boating was not itself compensable, but constituted an element in the valuation of his shoreline property. The case supplies no precedent here, since it involves a destruction of the littoral owner's private right of access to navigable water directly fronting on his property.

"The second major question is posed by the doctrine denying compensation when a littoral owner's interests in navigable water are damaged through the exercise of the 'navigation servitude,' that is, through the public's paramount power to control navigable waters in the interest of navigation and commerce. . . . The state relies upon cases which seemingly extend the doctrine to public improvements which aid commerce as well as those aiding navigation. . . . It points out that the proposed bridges are part of an interstate freeway project which will improve access to Stockton harbor and benefit land and water transportation.

"Broad dicta in some of the decisions permit identification of the navigation servitude with the promotion of 'commerce' without express restriction to waterborne commerce. Such statements should not be taken out of context. Decisional law rejects the notion that any project facilitating commerce is *ipso facto* within the sovereign power over waterways. Nor do the parallel powers of the federal and state governments over navigation include every public project affecting the navigable capacity of water. Although most generalizations entail some peril, the general tenor of the decisions is that the navigation servitude is limited to public works designed to aid or control navigation, excluding projects for other purposes. A leading case refers to the navigation servitude as one embracing 'such use of the submerged lands and of the waters flowing over them as may be consistent with or demanded by the public right of navigation.' (*Scranton v. Wheeler,* 179 U.S. 141, 163, 21 S.Ct. 48, 57, 46 L.Ed. 126.) Freeways and streets along the waterfront are outside the scope of the navigation servitude . . . although there is contrary authority. . . . Deepening the channel of a stream to prevent overflows harmful to roads and bridges is not an exercise of the navigation power. . . . The proposed freeway bridges across the Upper Stockton Channel will not aid its development as a medium of commerce. Rather they will obstruct its navigability, albeit the obstruction will be sanctioned by federal law. . . .

"The state seeks to extend the navigation servitude on the strength of decisions permitting improvements on publicly owned tidelands without compensation for the upland owner's loss of access . . . [citing cases — Eds.]. In those cases the public's immunity is said to extend not only to tideland projects promoting navigation but to any 'lawful use or purpose.' . . . The tideland cases turn upon the principle that the littoral rights of an owner whose land adjoins publicly owned tidelands may be terminated by whatever disposition of the tidelands the public chooses to make. . . . Although public tidelands are held in trust for commerce, navigation and fishery, projects on tidelands may have nothing to do with navigation. Subject to the restrictions in statutory grants, public tidelands may be devoted to any use which does not prejudice the public rights of navigation and fishing. . . . Thus the public's power to improve its tidelands without compensating littoral owners is not a measure of the navigation servitude when tideland use is not involved.

"Finally, the state urges that the federal permit to construct the low level bridge project across Upper Stockton Channel is 'conclusive.' Perhaps it is, in the limited sense that a court may not restrain an obstruction to navigation permitted by federal law. . . . The permit is only a declaration of federal assent, not a delegation of power. Federal assent to the project does not shield the state from the eminent domain provision of [its] own constitution. 'It must be remembered . . . that damage may be inflicted within the meaning of such a constitutional provision by the mere exercise of unquestioned public rights.'" (2 Nichols, op. cit., p. 265.)

"We conclude that the bridge project is not an exercise of the state's navigation servitude; that the project will cause compensable damage to plaintiffs' private properties if, in an appropriate proceeding, a court finds substantial impairment of their respective easements of access."

For these reasons I believe the judgments should be reversed.

Mosk, J., concurs.

Rehearing denied; Peters and Mosk, JJ., dissenting.

Comments: 1. With respect to the "paramount supervisory power of the federal government over navigable waters," consider the following excerpt from *United States v. Willow River Power Co.,* 324 U.S. 499, 510-11 (1945):

> Rights, property or otherwise, which are absolute against all the world are certainly rare, and water rights are not among them. Whatever rights may be as between equals such as riparian owners, they are not the measure of riparian rights on a navigable stream relative to the function of the Government in improving navigation. Where these interests conflict they are not to be reconciled as between equals, but the private interest must give way to the superior right, or perhaps it would be more accurate to say that as against the Government such private interest is not a right at all.
>
> Operations of the Government in aid of navigation ofttimes inflict serious damage or inconvenience or interfere with advantages formerly enjoyed by riparian owners, but damage alone gives courts no power to require compensation where there is not an actual taking of property.... Such losses may be compensated by legislative authority, not by force of the Constitution alone.
>
> The uncompensated damages sustained by this riparian owner on a public waterway are not different from those often suffered without indemnification by owners abutting on public highways by land. It has been held in nearly every state in the Union that "there can be no recovery for damages to abutting property resulting from a mere change in grade in the street in front of it, there being no physical injury to the property itself, and the change being authorized by law." This appears to be the law of Wisconsin. . . . It would be strange if the State of Wisconsin is free to raise an adjacent land highway without compensation but the United States may not exercise an analogous power to raise a highway by water without making compensation where neither takes claimant's lands, but each cuts off access to and use of a natural level.
>
> We hold that claimant's interest or advantage in the high-water level of the St. Croix River as a run-off for tail waters to maintain its power head is not a right protected by law [as against the power of the Government to raise the level of the St. Croix by construction of a dam to improve navigation — Eds.] and that the award below based exclusively on the loss in value thereof must be reversed.

2. Under the [federal navigation] servitude doctrine, the Supreme Court has permitted the divestment of existing uses [of water based upon prior appropriation doctrine — Eds.], lawful when initiated, to accomodate subsequently arising needs of navigation. See generally Morreale, Federal Power in Western Waters: The Navigation Power and the Rule of No Compensation, 3 Nat. Res. J. 1 (1963). While one is tempted to assert that the navigation power is merely the product of historical rules, the fact is that the Court today is rather more assertive, and more confident of itself in divesting existing uses than it was seventy years ago when the first American cases arose. . . . At the same time, the Court has been somewhat cautious in dealing with the scope of the servitude, and has hesitated to go as far as the logic of the servitude might carry it. . . . The Court in the servitude cases has sometimes rested on the notion that one undertook his use with notice of possible later defeasance . . . , which is true in a sense, although equally true in a good many other cases where the courts have refused to divest existing uses. It has also sometimes expounded upon the inconceivability that private proprietary rights may be acquired in navigable waters. Why this is less conceivable than that one should acquire property rights in other 'public' resources, such as land, oil, or timber is not clear except upon historical grounds. The fact seems to be that the navigation servitude is something of a sport in American law, and is a precedent which is not readily transferable to other situations."

J. Sax, Water Law, Planning and Policy 278 (1968).

3. Where landowners claim that highway construction results in impairment of access to their property, the question of compensability is determined by whether reasonable access remains available to the landowner notwithstanding the effects of the highway construction.

In applying this principle, courts have dismissed some claims by finding that the claimant-landowner had no right of access at the time the highway construction occurred. Cases involving construction of controlled-access highways entirely on a new location furnish many examples of this view held by the great majority of the States.

A similar result generally has prevailed where a landowner's existing access to an adjacent street or highway is restricted by installation of median barriers or other devices for traffic channelization designed to reduce lateral friction from vehicles entering and leaving the main traffic lanes. In such cases it is said that the circuity of travel resulting from these barriers is an inconvenience shared by all of the public, and therefore the abutting landowner's injury is not specific to his property.

Most instances in which new highway construction results in diversion of traffic from an old highway have been held to involve noncompensable injuries, justified by the same reasoning that the inconvenience is to the public as a whole.

Where access to abutting land is restricted by construction of barriers at the outer margins of an existing highway, or by widening an existing highway and converting it into a controlled-access facility, State court decisions have shown a pattern of diversity. No single rationale has been successful in distinguishing between the types of situations that are compensable and those that are not. Nor has the substitution of access to a frontage road always been acceptable as providing reasonable access for the landowner.

Compensability of damages due to changes of street or highway grade generally is a simpler concept than where damages are due to interference with access in the ways described in the preceding paragraph. The reasonableness of the interference with the landowner's property does not appear to be the decisive factor, and damages due to change of grade are either compensable or noncompensable in a particular State. Where State constitutions guarantee compensation for property "taken or damaged" provable injuries due to change of grade are compensable. In States where constitutional guarantees run only to property that is "taken," compensation is denied unless a right to payment has been established by statute.

R. Netherton, Damnum Absque Injuria and the Concept of Just Compensation in Eminent Domain, in 1 Selected Studies in Highway Law 25, at 64 (J. Vance ed. 1976).

4. What about this situation: a property owner owns a warehouse which previously faced and had access to a city street. The state highway department constructed a multi-laned expressway on a viaduct placed on concrete piers over the street. The piers are entirely in the street right-of-way, but they are spaced in such a way that access to the warehouse is somewhat diminished. Access to the property may now be had either from the city street system or from the expressway on the viaduct, but the exit ramps from the viaduct (in each direction) are several blocks away. Has there been a compensable loss of access? The Texas court thought so. *City of Waco v. Texland Corp.*, 446 S.W.2d 1 (Tex. 1969). It held that loss of access is compensable when it is "materially or substantially" impaired, and emphasized that because of the piers, trucks would have difficulty entering the warehouse property. The Colorado court thought not. *Troiano v. Colorado Dep't of Highways*, 463 P.2d 448 (Colo. 1969). It emphasized that access to the city street system was not impaired. In this case there was a motel on the property, but the court found no loss of access from the diversion of traffic or circuity of travel that the construction of the viaduct imposed. Nor was the construction of the viaduct a change of grade. What about an argument that motor vehicle access to the motel was impaired by the piers? Or does it make a difference that cars are smaller than trucks?

5. PROBLEM: What should a state highway commission do if it wishes to restrict access, but does not believe that the particular restriction is compensable? One possibility may be a situation in which the commission simply decides to construct curbing along a property line, or erect a fence. If it moves to condemn access rights, it may be forced to pay compensation. *Commonwealth v. Carlisle,* 363 S.W.2d 104 (Ky. 1962): "We conceive that it would be practically impossible, procedurally, in a condemnation case, to attempt to value an access right in relation to the extent it possibly could be restricted under the police power, if exercised." On the other hand, if the commission stands by and does nothing the legal status of the restriction may be in doubt. In that event, what remedies does the property owner have?

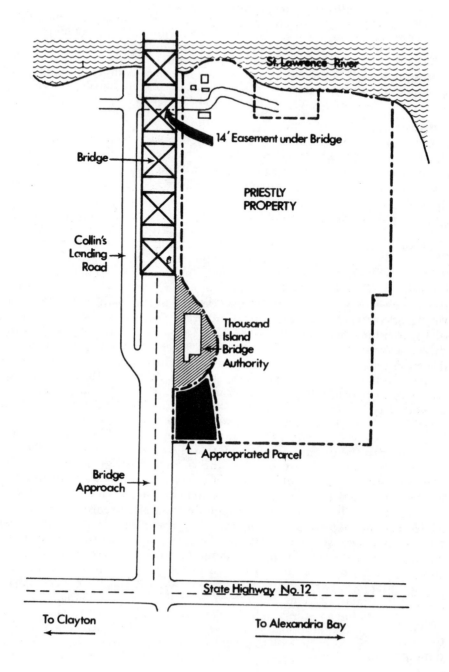

St. Lawrence River

14' Easement under Bridge

Bridge

PRIESTLY
PROPERTY

Collin's
Landing
Road

Thousand
Island
Bridge
Authority

Appropriated Parcel

Bridge
Approach

State Highway No. 12

To Clayton

To Alexandria Bay

Priestly v. State, New York, 1968

PRIESTLY v. STATE

Court of Appeals of New York
23 N.Y.2d 152, 242 N.E.2d 827 (1968)

BURKE, Judge. Three parcels of land, the subject of the two claims herein, were located on the approach to the Thousand Island Bridge and were taken by the State for highway and bridge approach purposes. Before the taking, the entire property, of which these parcels were a part, covered some 80 acres in a roughly rectangular shape running on a north-south axis, with its western boundary parallel to the bridge approach and the bridge itself. The parcels taken, totaling some 2.8 acres in the extreme southwestern corner of the property, included as frontage of some 200 feet on the east side of the bridge approach and were appropriated without right of access to the bridge approach. There were structural improvements on the northwestern portion of the property and its northern boundary fronted on the St. Lawrence River. The remaining acreage, including the land immediately to the east of the appropriated parcels, was unimproved. Both prior to and after the taking, there was access to the remaining property by means of a road to the west of the bridge approach and parallel to it which ran in a northerly direction and intersected with another road which ran easterly under the bridge and continued part of the way onto claimants' property in the vicinity of a residence and barn. At the trial, the parties stipulated that there was legal and physical access to the subject property both before and after the taking by means of the road described above.

The claimants' expert appraiser testified that the highest and best use of the subject property was that of commercial and residential development and that, because the remaining access was inadequate for such development, the remaining property had suffered consequential damages. He testified to a before-taking value of $132,500, an after-taking value of $79,900 and total damages of $52,600, equally divided between direct and consequential damages. The State's expert testified that the highest and best use of the subject property was residential with limited developmental potential. He testified that the loss of direct access damaged the developmental potential of the remaining land east of the appropriated parcels and, therefore, also found consequential damages. He found a before-taking value of $57,300 and total damages of $33,300, of which $16,300 was direct and $17,000 was consequential.

The Court of Claims in its decision found a before-taking value of $80,000 and an after-taking value of $40,000, with the total damages of $40,000 being equally divided between direct and consequential. The consequential damages were allocated $16,000 to one claim, and $4,000 to the second claim. In the Appellate

Division, direct damages were not disputed, but the State contended that, on the law and on the facts, the award of consequential damages was improper. The Appellate Division held that there was no basis in the record to support the award of consequential damages. Citing our decision in *Selig v. State of New York,* 10 N.Y.2d 34, 217 N.Y.S.2d 33, 176 N.E.2d 59 and Appellate Division cases, it held that, since access was not destroyed or rendered unsuitable and insufficient, the resulting circuity of access was noncompensable and, therefore, struck from the judgment the awards for consequential damages.

Claimants' appeal from that determination revolves upon the rather murky distinction between access which is merely "circuitous" and, therefore, insufficient as a basis for consequential damages and that which is "unsuitable" and, therefore, compensable. It is beyond dispute that mere circuity of access does not constitute a basis for an award of consequential damages. . . . But, this legal proposition is controlling in a particular case only if, as a question of fact, the access involved is shown to be *merely* circuitous. . . . If the facts established at the trial of a claim show that the access involved is more than merely circuitous so that it can be characterized as "unsuitable," compensability follows. The trial court in this case, by necessary implication from its award of consequential damages and by its reference to the damage caused by the loss of access to the bridge approach, found the access remaining to be unsuitable, while the Appellate Division disagreed and found it to be merely circuitous and not unsuitable and insufficient. In this posture, the issue then is whether the record as a whole supports the determination of the trial court or that of the Appellate Division. . . .

Before attempting to evaluate the evidence as to the nature and character of the remaining access with a view toward the ultimate characterization of it either as merely circuitous or as unsuitable, it is first necessary that those concepts be given content and substance. Case law has indicated that mere inconvenience of access is insufficient to constitute unsuitability . . . and that "Suitable access now is any access by which entrance may be had to a property without difficulty" . . . and, further, that the question of suitability is a factual one directly related to the highest and best use of the property. . . . Such formulations, however, do not provide any definite or certain guides to the decision of particular cases. In light of this, the very definition of the concepts involved can provide a basis upon which to approach such determinations. "Circuitous," in its commonly accepted understanding, indicates that which is roundabout and indirect but which nevertheless leads to the same destination. "Suitable," in its commonly accepted understanding, describes that which is adequate to the requirements of or answers the needs of a particular object. The concepts are not mutually exclusive and, therefore, a finding that a means of access is indeed circuitous does not eliminate the possibility that that same means of access might also be unsuitable in that it is inadequate to the access needs inherent in the highest and best use of the property involved.

The access remaining after the appropriation of the property involved in this appeal illustrates the proposition that unsuitability may well be superimposed upon what is undoubtedly circuitous access. The property remaining here consisted of some 77 acres in a rectangular shape to which access could be had only by means of a roadway which led onto the property at its northwestern border beneath a bridge. The expert testimony established a highest and best use of the property which was that of residential development, differing only as to the *degree* to which that developmental potential had been damaged by the character of the remaining access. On this evidence, together with its view of the premises, the trial court clearly had abundant justification for its finding of unsuitability. Even the State's expert on the State's direct case found that there were substantial ($17,000) consequential damages flowing from the character of the only remaining access. On this record, the evidence clearly supports the finding of the trial court. Indeed, there is virtually no evidence to support the Appellate Division's finding that it was merely circuitous, though its circuity was acutely apparent from the fact that the remaining access requires vehicles to cross an opposing stream of traffic on a heavily travelled bridge approach in order to reach a road paralleling the bridge approach and the bridge itself on the side opposite the claimants' property, and that that road intersects with a road which then leads under a bridge to the extreme northern portion of claimants' property, whereas the property taken would have allowed direct access from the bridge approach to the southern portion of the property. The evidence fairly compels the conclusion that the remaining access, concededly circuitous, was also clearly unsuitable to the established highest and best use of residential development. Since the evidence so clearly supports the finding and judgments of the Court of Claims, its judgments should be reinstated and the orders of the Appellate Division should be reversed.

The orders of the Appellate Division should be reversed, with costs to the appellant, and the judgments of the Court of Claims reinstated.

FULD, C. J., and SCILEPPI, BERGAN, KEATING, BREITEL and JASEN, JJ., concur.

Orders reversed, with costs in this court and in the Appellate Division, and judgments of the Court of Claims reinstated.

Comments: 1. In *Priestly,* the state had clearly "taken" a fee simple estate in part of the claimant's land. Should this make a difference on the issue of compensation for loss of access? Could not the claimant have simply invoked the well-settled "partial taking" rule:

> When the property taken is physically (and not merely functionally) an integral part of a larger plot and what is left is

substantially deteriorated by reason of the significant relationship in value of that taken to the entire property, the obvious resulting consequential damages to the remaining part are allowed as part of the sum awarded . . . for the value of the property taken; or . . . an award is made first for the value of the part taken and then damages to the remainder, which may either be stated separately or in a lump sum, or even by an award for the difference between the fair market value of the property before and after the taking in which just compensation is measured by the difference of the whole before that taking and the value of the remainder after the taking.

4A Nichols, Eminent Domain § 14.2 (3d rev. ed. 1976).

2. How much of the "market value" of the claimant's land prior to the "taking" in *Priestly* was attributable to the fact that it abutted a state highway? What factors should be taken into account on the "market value" issue? *See State v. Wilson,* 420 P.2d 992 (Ariz. App. 1966), *vacated on appeal from remand,* 438 P.2d 760 (Ariz. 1968). Land was taken from a guest ranch to be used in the construction of an interchange on a limited-access highway. Before the taking the ranch had direct access to an unlimited access highway. After the taking access could only be had by means of the interchange, which was designed for low speed, low density traffic. The damages awarded included loss of access, and the state appealed:

> Generally, the state contends that a property owner's right of access in an abutting public highway is a private easement which does not extend to patrons, clients and customers, nor to the traveling public upon the through highway, and that any damage caused to the property owner by interference with access pertaining to such persons is damnum absque injuria because resulting from an exercise of police power.
>
> It is, of course, well-established law that damages resulting from an exercise of the police power of the state are noncompensable. . . .
>
> We believe it also to be well-established law that the property owner has no property right in the traffic flowing by his property, as such, and that a diversion of such traffic by the state authorities is noncompensable. . . .
>
> [W]e believe that the state fundamentally misconceives the nature of an abutting property owner's rights of access as established by prior Supreme Court decisions in our state and that much of its argument pertaining to the police power therefore misses the mark. . . .
>
> In *Thelberg,* damages were allowed on the basis that by placing the Thelberg property upon a new frontage road and depriving it of its access to the old roadway, the highest and best use of the remaining portion had been changed from that of commercial to residential. (87 Ariz. at 326, 350 P.2d 988.) It is most apparent in *Thelberg* that damages were being allowed for the deprivation of access to the through traffic. The result reached is completely inconsistent with appellant's thesis here that the abutting owner's access rights do not include prospective customers who may be a portion of this through traffic. . . .

The rationale of these decisions must lie in the essence of the right of access, as recognized by our Supreme Court. The decisions are only reconcilable if the right of access in question is regarded as an easement appurtenant to the abutting, privately owned land attaching to the specific land occupied by the abutting highway as the servient estate. . . .

The equities inherent in the origins of this right of access urge that it be dignified as a right-in-land and our court has so considered it. When this right is considered as a real property right, it no longer appears "absurd" that there are remarkable differences in the value of rights of access depending upon the particular location of the interstate non-access highway. All real estate has relative value by reason of its location. This is an economic axiom affecting the value of access rights as well as all other real property. When public authority through its power of eminent domain severs from the dominant tenement of the landowner the appurtenant easement over the servient real estate (in this case, the highway), and if the servient estate by reason of its particular location is used and is going to be used in the foreseeable future as an interstate highway, it seems clear that the property owner has been damaged by such extinguishment substantially more than if the servient estate was an untraveled dirt road. The additional damage caused by reason of the fact that the servient estate is a well-traveled highway cannot be relegated to the classification of damnum absque injuria merely because such traffic is subject to being diverted to another location at some speculative future time. The important thing in cases such as this is that the traffic has *not* been diverted; rather the land over which the abutting property owner has an easement carries heavy traffic and will continue to do so into the foreseeable future.

Id. at 997-99.

3. Does the fact that the landowner was suing the state in *Priestly* indicate that the suit was one for inverse condemnation? Consider the following:

Under the NEW YORK HIGHWAY LAW, land is acquired by the State for the construction and reconstruction of highways via an administrative procedure which involves the filing of a description and map of the property sought, followed by the automatic vesting of title. The Superintendent of Public Works is authorized, by Section 30(13) of the HIGHWAY LAW, to settle claims for the value of the property so appropriated, but the only condemnation procedure available is that brought under Section 30(14), authorizing any owner of property so appropriated to present his claim for its value to the Court of Claims.

B. Hering and M. Ordover, Theory and Practice in Inverse Condemnation for Five Representative States, in 2 Selected Studies in Highway Law 797, at 832 (J. Vance ed. 1976). In most states, where the state is the plaintiff in a formal condemnation proceeding, the issue of "severance damages" for a "partial taking" would be litigated in that proceeding.

4. Professor Van Alstyne suggests that compensation in access cases should be legislatively defined to depend on a variety of factors. Among them are:

> The extent to which the property retains direct access capabilities reasonably adequate for its highest and best use in light of (i) the nature and requirements of that use; (ii) the number, physical dimensions, and usefulness of access facilities; and (iii) any other circumstances relevant to effective utilization of the property, including reasonably available alternatives.

Van Alstyne, Just Compensation of Intangible Detriment: Criteria for Legislative Modifications in California, 16 U.C.L.A. L. Rev. 491, 512-13 (1969). *See also* Comment, Traffic Oriented Business and Highway Vacations: A Diversion, 30 U. Pitt. L. Rev. 671 (1969).

Chapter 4

CONTROL OF LAND USE BY "ZONING"

A. THE EARLY HISTORY OF ZONING

For the past sixty years, the most important form of governmental control of land use in urban areas has been "zoning," defined as "the division of land into districts having different regulations" by Edward M. Bassett, the "father of zoning." [1] Early examples of "zoning" may be found in Boston and Los Angeles.[2] But New York City was the first American municipality to adopt a comprehensive "zoning" ordinance of the modern type. The New York City Building Zone Resolution of 1916, authorized by a 1914 special act of the New York legislature, was based on three years of painstaking research and investigation by a committee of which Bassett was a member. The Building Zone Resolution of 1916 embodied a complete and comprehensive system of building and land use control for all the five boroughs of New York City. It established three separate classes of districts to regulate, respectively, the use of land and buildings, the height of buildings, and the percentage of a lot that could be occupied by buildings, with a separate set of maps for each class. There were three "use" districts: residential, business, and unrestricted. In the residence districts, business and industry of all types were prohibited. In business districts, specified businesses and industries — mainly nuisance-creating manufacturing businesses such as boiler making, ammonia manufacturing, and paint manufacturing — were prohibited, and all other uses were permitted. In unrestricted districts, all kinds of residential, business, and industrial uses were permitted.

---

[1] E. Bassett, Zoning 9 (1940).

[2] The Massachusetts legislature enacted height regulations for the entire city of Boston in 1904-05. These restrictions embodied the "zoning" principle, since there were different maximum heights in different districts. The Boston height restrictions were sustained against constitutional attack in *Welch v. Swasey,* 214 U.S. 91 (1909). In 1909, Los Angeles adopted an ordinance dividing the city into industrial and residential districts. The exclusion of laundries from a residential district was upheld by the California court in *Ex parte Quong Wo,* 118 P. 714 (Cal. 1911). In 1910, Los Angeles adopted an ordinance exluding brick factories from one or two of the industrial districts. The 1910 ordinance was sustained against constitutional attack in *Hadacheck v. Sebastian, supra* p. 134.

It should be noted that the New York Building Zone Resolution of 1916 did not apply retroactively to existing lawfully established uses of land or buildings. As one early commentator said, "[i]t did not attempt to cure past and existing evils by ordering the demolition of particular types of buildings or removal of certain types of businesses to other areas. But it did prescribe a rational plan for future building in the city." [3]

"Zoning" spread rapidly after the New York Building Zone Resolution was sustained against constitutional attack by the New York court in 1920.[4] In 1922, it was reported that some 20 state zoning enabling acts and 50 municipal zoning ordinances were in force or in process of formulation. Some municipalities proceeded to adopt zoning ordinances without waiting for enactment of enabling legislation, but it was generally believed, and occasionally held, that the broad grant of police power by state legislatures to local units of government, even under Home Rule constitutional provisions, was insufficient to empower local governments to regulate land use by means of "zoning." Hence, in the states where interest in "zoning" was greatest, new enabling legislation was generally enacted.

By 1926, all but five of the then 48 states had adopted zoning enabling acts; some 420 municipalities with a total population of more than 27,000,000 had adopted zoning ordinances; and hundreds of other municipalities were engaged in preparing zoning ordinances. But judicial acceptance of zoning was far from unanimous in 1926. Decisions favorable to the constitutionality of zoning had been rendered by the highest courts of California, Illinois, Kansas, Louisiana, Massachusetts, Minnesota, New York, Ohio, Oregon, and Wisconsin. Adverse decisions had been rendered by the highest courts of Delaware, Georgia, Maryland, Missouri, and New Jersey. The United States Supreme Court had not yet passed on the constitutionality of zoning; but the Court was to rehear, at the 1926 October Term, an appeal from a United States District Court decision holding the comprehensive zoning ordinance of the Village of Euclid, Ohio, unconstitutional.

---

[3] J. McGoldrick, S. Graubard, and R. Horowitz, Building Regulation in New York City 93 (1944). For a more detailed discussion of the background and drafting of the New York City Building Zone Resolution of 1916, see S. Toll, Zoned American 78-187 (1969).

[4] *Lincoln Trust Co. v. Williams, Bldg. Corp.*, 128 N.E. 209 (N.Y. 1920).

VILLAGE OF EUCLID v. AMBLER REALTY COMPANY

Supreme Court of the United States
272 U.S. 365, 71 L.Ed. 303, 47 S.Ct. 114 (1926)

Mr. Justice SUTHERLAND delivered the opinion of the Court.

The Village of Euclid is an Ohio municipal corporation. It adjoins and practically is a suburb of the City of Cleveland. Its estimated population is between 5,000 and 10,000, and its area from twelve to fourteen square miles, the greater part of which is farm lands or unimproved acreage. It lies, roughly, in the form of a parallelogram measuring approximately three and one-half miles each way. East and west it is traversed by three principal highways: Euclid Avenue, through the southerly border, St. Clair Avenue, through the central portion, and Lake Shore Boulevard, through the northerly border in close proximity to the shore of Lake Erie. The Nickel Plate railroad lies from 1,500 to 1,800 feet north of Euclid Avenue, and the Lake Shore railroad 1,600 feet farther to the north. The three highways and the two railroads are substantially parallel.

Appellee is the owner of a tract of land containing 68 acres, situated in the westerly end of the village, abutting on Euclid Avenue to the south and the Nickel Plate railroad to the north. Adjoining this tract, both on the east and on the west, there have been laid out restricted residential plats upon which residences have been erected.

On November 13, 1922, an ordinance was adopted by the Village Council, establishing a comprehensive zoning plan for regulating and restricting the location of trades, industries, apartment houses, two-family houses, single family houses, etc., the lot area to be built upon, the size and height of buildings, etc.

The entire area of the village is divided by the ordinance into six classes of use districts, denominated U-1 to U-6, inclusive; three classes of height districts, denominated H-1 to H-3, inclusive; and four classes of area districts, denominated A-1 to A-4, inclusive. The use districts are classified in respect of the buildings which may be erected within their respective limits, as follows: U-1 is restricted to single family dwellings, public parks, water towers and reservoirs, suburban and interurban electric railway passenger stations and rights of way, and farming, non-commercial greenhouse nurseries and truck gardening; U-2 is extended to include two-family dwellings; U-3 is further extended to include apartment houses, hotels, churches, schools, public libraries, museums, private clubs, community center buildings, hospitals, sanitariums, public playgrounds and recreation buildings, and a city hall and courthouse; U-4 is further extended to include banks, offices, studios, telephone exchanges, fire and police stations, restaurants, theatres and moving picture shows, retail stores and shops, sales offices, sample rooms, wholesale stores for hardware, drugs and groceries, stations for gasoline and oil (not exceeding 1,000 gallons storage) and for ice delivery, skating rinks and dance halls, electric substations, job and newspaper printing, public garages for motor vehicles, stables and wagon sheds (not exceeding five horses, wagons or motor trucks) and distributing stations for central store and commercial enterprises; U-5 is further extended to include billboards and advertising signs (if permitted), warehouses, ice and ice cream manufacturing and cold storage plants, bottling works, milk bottling and central distribution stations, laundries, carpet cleaning, dry cleaning and dyeing establishments, blacksmith, horseshoeing, wagon and motor vehicle repair shops, freight stations, street car barns, stables and wagon sheds (for more than five horses, wagons or motor trucks), and wholesale produce markets and salesrooms; U-6 is further extended to include plants for sewage disposal and for producing gas, garbage and refuse incineration, scrap iron, junk, scrap paper and rag storage, aviation fields, cemeteries, crematories, penal and correctional institutions, insane and feeble minded institutions, storage of oil and gasoline (not to exceed 25,000 gallons), and manufacturing and industrial operations of any kind other than, and any public utility not included in, a class U-1, U-2, U-3, U-4 or U-5 use. There is a seventh class of uses which is prohibited altogether.

Class U-1 is the only district in which buildings are restricted to those enumerated. In the other classes the uses are cumulative; that is to say, uses in class U-2 include those enumerated in the preceding class, U-1; class U-3 includes uses enumerated in the preceding classes, U-2 and U-1; and so on. In addition to the enumerated uses, the ordinance provides for accessory uses, that is, for uses customarily incident to the principal use, such as private garages. Many regulations are provided in respect of such accessory uses.

The height districts are classified as follows: In class H-1, buildings are limited to a height of two and one-half stories or thirty-five feet; in class H-2, to four stories or fifty feet; in class H-3, to eighty feet. To all of these, certain exceptions are made, as in the case of church spires, water tanks, etc.

The classification of area districts is: In A-1 districts, dwellings or apartment houses to accommodate more than one family must have at least 5,000 square feet for interior lots and at least 4,000 square feet for corner lots; in A-2 districts, the area must be at least 2,500 square feet for interior lots, and 2,000 square feet for corner lots; in A-3 districts, the limits are 1,250 and 1,000 square feet, respectively; in A-4 districts, the limits are 900 and 700 square feet, respectively. The ordinance contains, in great variety and detail, provisions in respect of width of lots, front, side and rear yards, and other matters, including restrictions and regulations as to the use of bill boards, sign boards and advertising signs.

A single family dwelling consists of a basement and not less than three rooms and a bathroom. A two-family dwelling consists of a basement and not less than four living rooms and a bathroom for each family; and is further described as a detached dwelling for the occupation of two families, one having its principal living rooms on the first floor and the other on the second floor.

Appellee's tract of land comes under U-2, U-3 and U-6. The first strip of 620 feet immediately north of Euclid Avenue falls in class U-2, the next 130 feet to the north, in U-3, and the remainder in U-6. The uses of the first 620 feet, therefore, do not include apartment houses, hotels, churches, schools, or other public and semi-public buildings, or other uses enumerated in respect of U-3 to U-6, inclusive. The uses of the next 130 feet include all of these, but exclude industries, theatres, banks, shops, and the various other uses set forth in respect of U-4 to U-6, inclusive.*

Annexed to the ordinance, and made a part of it, is a zone map, showing the location and limits of the various use, height and area districts, from which it appears that the three classes overlap one another; that is to say, for example, both U-5 and U-6 use districts are in A-4 area districts, but the former is in H-2 and the latter in H-3 height districts. The plan is a complicated one and can be better understood by an inspection of the map, though it does not seem necessary to reproduce it for present purposes.

The lands lying between the two railroads for the entire length of the village area and extending some distance on either side to the north and south, having an average width of about 1,600 feet, are left open, with slight exceptions, for industrial and all other uses. This includes the larger part of appellee's tract. Approximately one-sixth of the area of the entire village is included in U-5 and U-6 use districts. That part of the village lying south of Euclid Avenue is principally in U-1 districts. The lands lying north of Euclid Avenue

---

* The court below seemed to think that the frontage of this property on Euclid Avenue to a depth of 150 feet came under U-1 district and was available only for single family dwellings. An examination of the ordinance and subsequent amendments, and a comparison of their terms with the maps, shows very clearly, however, that this view was incorrect. Appellee's brief correctly interpreted the ordinance: "The northerly 500 feet thereof immediately adjacent to the right of way of the New York, Chicago & St. Louis Railroad Company under the original ordinance was classed as U-6 territory and the rest thereof as U-2 territory. By amendments to the ordinance a strip 630 [620] feet wide north of Euclid Avenue is classed as U-2 territory, a strip 130 feet wide next north as U-3 territory and the rest of the parcel to the Nickel Plate right of way as U-6 territory."

and bordering on the long strip just described are included in U-1, U-2, U-3 and U-4 districts, principally in U-2.

The enforcement of the ordinance is entrusted to the inspector of buildings, under rules and regulations of the board of zoning appeals. Meetings of the board are public, and minutes of its proceedings are kept. It is authorized to adopt rules and regulations to carry into effect provisions of the ordinance. Decisions of the inspector of buildings may be appealed to the board by any person claiming to be adversely affected by any such decision. The board is given power in specific cases of practical difficulty or unnecessary hardship to interpret the ordinance in harmony with its general purpose and intent, so that the public health, safety and general welfare may be secure and substantial justice done. Penalties are prescribed for violations, and it is provided that the various provisions are to be regarded as independent and the holding of any provision to be unconstitutional, void or ineffective shall not affect any of the others.

The ordinance is assailed on the grounds that it is in derogation of § 1 of the Fourteenth Amendment to the Federal Constitution in that it deprives appellee of liberty and property without due process of law and denies it the equal protection of the law, and that it offends against certain provisions of the Constitution of the State of Ohio. The prayer of the bill is for an injunction restraining the enforcement of the ordinance and all attempts to impose or maintain as to appellee's property any of the restrictions, limitations or conditions. The court below held the ordinance to be unconstitutional and void, and enjoined its enforcement. 297 F. 307.

Before proceeding to a consideration of the case, it is necessary to determine the scope of the inquiry. The bill alleges that the tract of land in question is vacant and has been held for years for the purpose of selling and developing it for industrial uses, for which it is especially adapted, being immediately in the path of progressive industrial development; that for such uses it has a market value of about $10,000 per acre, but if the use be limited to residential purposes the market value is not in excess of $2,500 per acre; that the first 200 feet of the parcel back from Euclid Avenue, if unrestricted in respect of use, has a value of $150 per front foot, but if limited to residential uses, and ordinary mercantile business be excluded therefrom, its value is not in excess of $50 per front foot.

It is specifically averred that the ordinance attempts to restrict and control the lawful uses of appellee's land so as to confiscate and destroy a great part of its value; that it is being enforced in accordance with its terms; that prospective buyers of land for industrial, commercial and residential uses in the metropolitan district of Cleveland are deterred from buying any part of this land because of the existence of the ordinance and the necessity thereby entailed of conducting burdensome and expensive litigation in order to vindicate the right to use the land for lawful and legitimate purposes; that the ordinance constitutes a cloud upon the land, reduces and destroys its value, and has the effect of diverting the normal industrial, commercial and residential development thereof to other and less favorable locations.

The record goes no farther than to show, as the lower court found, that the normal, and reasonably to be expected, use and development of that part of appellee's land adjoining Euclid Avenue is for general trade and commercial purposes, particularly retail stores and like establishments, and that the normal, and reasonably to be expected, use and development of the residue of the land is for industrial and trade purposes. Whatever injury is inflicted by the mere existence and threatened enforcement of the ordinance is due to restrictions in respect of these and similar uses; to which perhaps should be added — if not included in the foregoing — restrictions in respect of apartment houses. Specifically, there is nothing in the record to suggest that any damage results from the presence in the ordinance of those restrictions relating to churches, schools, libraries and other public and semi-public buildings. It is neither alleged nor proved that there is, or may be, a demand for any part of appellee's land for any of the last named uses; and we cannot assume the existence of facts which would justify an injunction upon this record in respect of this class of restrictions. For present purposes the provisions of the ordinance in respect of these uses may, therefore, be put aside as unnecessary to be considered. It is also unnecessary to consider the effect of the restrictions in respect of U-1 districts, since none of appellee's land falls within that class.

We proceed, then, to a consideration of those provisions of the ordinance to which the case as it is made relates, first disposing of a preliminary matter.

A motion was made in the court below to dismiss the bill on the ground that, because complainant [appellee] had made no effort to obtain a building permit or apply to the zoning board of appeals for relief as it might have done under the terms of the ordinance, the suit was premature. The motion was properly overruled. The effect of the allegations of the bill is that the ordinance of its own force operates greatly to reduce the value of appellee's lands and destroy their marketability for industrial, commercial and residential uses; and the attack is directed, not against any specific provision or provisions, but against the ordinance as an entirety. Assuming the premises, the existence and maintenance of the ordinance, in effect, constitutes a present invasion of appellee's property rights and a threat to continue it. Under these circumstances, the equitable jurisdiction is clear. . . .

It is not necessary to set forth the provisions of the Ohio Constitution which are thought to be infringed. The question is the same under both Constitutions, namely, as stated by appellee: Is the ordinance invalid in that it violates the constitutional protection "to the right of property in the appellee by attempted regulations under the guise of the police power, which are unreasonable and confiscatory?"

Building zone laws are of modern origin. They began in this country about twenty-five years ago. Until recent years, urban life was comparatively simple; but with the great increase and concentration of population, problems have developed, and constantly are developing, which require, and will continue to require, additional restrictions in respect of the use and occupation of private lands in urban communities. Regulations, the wisdom, necessity and validity of which, as applied to existing conditions, are so apparent that they are now uniformly sustained, a century ago, or even half a century ago, probably would have been rejected as arbitrary and oppressive. Such regulations are sustained, under the complex conditions of our day, for reasons analogous to those which justify traffic regulations, which, before the advent of automobiles and rapid transit street railways, would have been condemned as fatally arbitrary and unreasonable. And in this there is no inconsistency, for while the meaning of constitutional guaranties never varies, the scope of their application must expand or contract to meet the new and different conditions which are constantly coming within the field of their operation. In a changing world, it is impossible that it should be otherwise. But although a degree of elasticity is thus imparted, not to the *meaning,* but to the *application* of constitutional principles, statutes and ordinances, which, after giving due weight to the new conditions, are found clearly not to conform to the Constitution, of course, must fall.

The ordinance now under review, and all similar laws and regulations, must find their justification in some aspect of the police power, asserted for the public welfare. The line which in this field separates the legitimate from the illegitimate assumption of power is not capable of precise delimitation. It varies with circumstances and conditions. A regulatory zoning ordinance, which would be clearly valid as applied to the great cities, might be clearly invalid as applied to rural communities. In solving doubts, the maxim *sic utere tuo ut alienum non laedas,* which lies at the foundation of so much of the common law of nuisances, ordinarily will furnish a fairly helpful clew. And the law of nuisances, likewise, may be consulted, not for the purpose of controlling, but for the helpful aid of its analogies in the process of ascertaining the scope of, the power. Thus the question whether the power exists to forbid the erection of a building of a particular kind or for a particular use, like the question whether a particular thing is a nuisance, is to be determined, not by an abstract consideration of the building or of the thing considered apart, but by considering it in connection with the circumstances and the locality. . . . A nuisance may be merely a right thing in the wrong place, — like a pig in the parlor instead of the barnyard. If the validity of the legislative classification for zoning purposes be fairly debatable, the legislative judgment must be allowed to control. . . .

There is no serious difference of opinion in respect of the validity of laws and regulations fixing the height of buildings within reasonable limits, the character of materials and methods of construction, and the adjoining area which must be left open, in order to minimize the danger of fire or collapse, the evils of over-crowding, and the like, and excluding from residential sections offensive trades, industries and structures likely to create nuisances. . . .

Here, however, the exclusion is in general terms of all industrial establishments, and it may thereby happen that not only offensive or dangerous industries will be excluded, but those which are neither offensive nor dangerous will share the same fate. But this is no more than happens in respect of many practice-forbidding laws which this Court has upheld although drawn in general terms so as to include individual cases that may turn out to be innocuous in themselves. . . . The inclusion of a reasonable margin to insure effective enforcement, will not put upon a law, otherwise valid, the stamp of invalidity. Such laws may also find their justification in the fact that, in some fields, the bad fades into the good by such insensible degrees that the two are not capable of being readily distinguished and separated in terms of legislation. In the light of these considerations, we are not prepared to say that the end in view was not sufficient to justify the general rule of the ordinance, although some industries of an innocent character might fall within the proscribed class. It can not be said that the ordinance in this respect "passes the bounds of reason and assumes the character of a merely arbitrary fiat." *Purity Extract Co. v. Lynch,* 226 U.S. 192. Moreover, the restrictive provisions of the ordinance in this particular may be sustained upon the principles applicable to the broader exclusion from residential districts of all business and trade structures, presently to be discussed.

It is said that the Village of Euclid is a mere suburb of the City of Cleveland; that the industrial development of that city has now reached and in some degree extended into the village and, in the obvious course of things, will soon absorb the entire area for industrial enterprises; that the effect of the ordinance is to divert this natural development elsewhere with the consequent loss of increased values to the owners of the lands within the village borders. But the village, though physically a suburb of Cleveland, is politically a separate municipality, with powers of its own and authority to govern itself as it sees fit within the limits of the organic law of its creation and the State and Federal Constitutions. Its governing authorities, presumably representing a majority of its inhabitants and voicing their will, have determined, not that industrial development shall cease at its boundaries, but that the course of such development shall proceed within definitely fixed lines. If it be a proper exercise of the police power to relegate industrial establishments to localities separated from residential sections, it is not easy to find a sufficient reason for denying the power because the effect of its exercise is to divert an industrial flow from the course which it would follow, to the injury of the residential public if left alone, to another course where such injury will be obviated. It is not meant by this, however, to exclude the possibility of cases where the general public interest would so far outweigh the interest of the municipality that the municipality would not be allowed to stand in the way.

We find no difficulty in sustaining restrictions of the kind thus far reviewed. The serious question in the case arises over the provisions of the ordinance excluding from residential districts, apartment houses, business houses, retail stores and shops, and other like establishments. This question involves the validity of what is really the crux of the more recent zoning legislation, namely, the creation and maintenance of residential districts, from which business and trade of every sort, including hotels and apartment houses, are excluded. Upon that question this Court has not thus far spoken. The decisions of the state courts are numerous and conflicting; but those which broadly sustain the power greatly outnumber those which deny altogether or narrowly limit it; and it is very apparent that there is a constantly increasing tendency in the direction of the broader view. . . .

As evidence of the decided trend toward the broader view, it is significant that in some instances the state courts in later decisions have reversed their former decisions holding the other way. . . .

The decisions enumerated in the first group cited above agree that the exclusion of buildings devoted to business, trade, etc., from residential districts, bears a rational relation to the health and safety of the community. Some of the grounds for this conclusion are — promotion of the health and security from injury of children and others by separating dwelling houses from territory devoted to trade and industry; suppression and prevention of disorder; facilitating the extinguishment of fires, and the enforcement of street traffic regulations and other general welfare ordinances; aiding the health and safety of the community by excluding from residential areas the confusion and danger of fire, contagion and disorder which in greater or less degree attach to the location of stores, shops and factories. Another ground is that the construction and repair of streets may be rendered easier and less expensive by confining the greater part of the heavy traffic to the streets where business is carried on. . . .

The matter of zoning has received much attention at the hands of commissions and experts, and the results of their investigations have been set forth in comprehensive reports. These reports, which bear every evidence of painstaking consideration, concur in the view that the segregation of residential, business, and industrial buildings will make it easier to provide fire apparatus suitable for the character and intensity of the development in each section; that it will increase the safety and security of home life; greatly tend to prevent street accidents, especially to children, by reducing the traffic and resulting confusion in residential sections; decrease noise and other conditions which produce or intensify nervous disorders; preserve a more favorable environment in which to rear children, etc. With particular reference to apartment houses, it is pointed out that the development of detached house sections is greatly retarded by the coming of apartment houses, which has sometimes resulted in destroying the entire section for private house purposes; that in such sections very often the apartment house is a mere parasite, constructed in order to take advantage of the open spaces and attractive surroundings created by the residential character of the district. Moreover, the coming of one apartment house is followed by others, interfering by their height and bulk with the free circulation of air and monopolizing the rays of the sun which otherwise would fall upon the smaller homes, and bringing, as their necessary accompaniments, the disturbing noises incident to increased traffic and business, and the occupation, by means of moving and parked automobiles, of larger portions of the streets, thus detracting from their safety and depriving children of the privilege of quiet and open spaces for play, enjoyed by those in more favored localities, — until, finally, the residential character of the neighborhood and its desirability as a place of detached residences are utterly destroyed. Under these circumstances, apartment houses, which in a different environment would be not only entirely unobjectionable but highly desirable, come very near to being nuisances.

If these reasons, thus summarized, do not demonstrate the wisdom or sound policy in all respects of those restrictions which we have indicated as pertinent to the inquiry, at least, the reasons are sufficiently cogent to preclude us from saying, as it must be said before the ordinance can be declared unconstitutional, that such provisions are clearly arbitrary and unreasonable, having no substantial relation to the public health, safety, morals, or general welfare. . . .

It is true that when, if ever, the provisions set forth in the ordinance in tedious and minute detail, come to be concretely applied to particular premises, including those of the appellee, or to particular conditions, or to be considered in connection with specific complaints, some of them, or even many of them, may be found to be clearly arbitrary and unreasonable. But where the equitable remedy of injunction is sought, as it is here, not upon the ground of a present infringement or denial of a specific right, or of a particular injury in process of actual execution, but upon the broad ground that the mere existence and threatened enforcement of the ordinance, by materially and adversely affecting values and curtailing the opportunities of the market, constitute a present and irreparable injury, the court will not scrutinize its provisions, sentence by sentence, to ascertain by a process of piecemeal dissection whether there may be, here and there, provisions of a minor character, or relating to matters of administration, or not shown to contribute to the injury complained of, which, if attacked separately, might not withstand the test of constitutionality. In respect of such provisions, of which specific complaint is not made, it cannot be said that the land owner has suffered or is threatened with an injury which entitles him to challenge their constitutionality. . . .

. . . What would be the effect of a restraint imposed by one or more of the innumerable provisions of the ordinance, considered apart, upon the value or marketability of the lands is neither disclosed by the bill nor by the evidence, and we are afforded no basis, apart from mere speculation, upon which to rest a conclusion that it or they would have any appreciable effect upon those matters. Under these circumstances, therefore, it is enough for us to determine, as we do, that the ordinance in its general scope and dominant features, so far as its provisions are here involved, is a valid exercise of authority, leaving other provisions to be dealt with as cases arise directly involving them.

And this is in accordance with the traditional policy of this Court. In the realm of constitutional law, especially, this Court has perceived the embarrassment which is likely to result from an attempt to formulate rules or decide questions beyond the necessities of the immediate issue. It has preferred to follow the method of a gradual approach to the general by a systematically guarded application and extension of constitutional principles to particular cases as they arise, rather than by out of hand attempts to establish general rules to which future cases must be fitted. This process applies with peculiar force to the solution of questions arising under the due process clause of the Constitution as applied to the exercise of the flexible powers of police, with which we are here concerned.

Decree reversed.

Mr. Justice VAN DEVANTER, Mr. Justice McREYNOLDS and Mr. Justice BUTLER, dissent.

Comments: 1. In holding the Euclid zoning ordinance unconstitutional the District Judge said:

The argument supporting this ordinance proceeds . . . both on a mistaken view of what is property and of what is police power. Property, generally speaking, defendant's counsel concede, is protected against a taking without compensation, by the guaranties of the Ohio and United States Constitutions. But their view seems to be that so long as the owner remains clothed with the legal title thereto and is not ousted from the physical possession thereof, his property is not taken, no matter to what extent his right to use is invaded or destroyed or its present or prospective value is depreciated. This is an erroneous view. The right to property, as used in the Constitution, has no such limited meaning. As has often been said in substance by the Supreme Court: "There can be no conception of property aside from its control and use, and upon its use depends its value." . . . In defendants' view, the only difference between the police power and eminent domain is that the taking under the former may be done without compensation and under the latter a taking must be paid for. It seems to be the further view that whether one power or the other is exercised depends wholly on what the legislative department may see fit to recite on that subject. Such, however, is not the law. If police power meant what is claimed, all private property is now held subject to temporary and passing phases of public opinion, dominant for a day, in legislative or municipal assemblies. . . . Obviously, police power is not susceptible of exact definition. . . . And yet there is a wide difference between the power of eminent domain and the police power; and it is not true that the public welfare is a justification for the taking of private property for the general good. . . . Nor can the ordinances here be sustained by invoking the average reciprocity of advantage rule. . . . It is a futile suggestion that plaintiff's present and obvious loss from being deprived of the normal and legitimate use of its property would be compensated indirectly by benefits accruing to that land from the restrictions imposed by the ordinance on other land. It is equally futile to suppose that other property in the village will reap the benefit of the damage to plaintiff's property and that of others similarly situated. The only reasonable probability is that the property values taken from plaintiff and other owners similarly situated will simply disappear, or at best be transferred to other unrestricted sections of the Cleveland industrial area, or at the worst, to some other and far distant industrial area. So far as plaintiff is concerned, it is a pure loss. In the average reciprocity of advantage there is a measureless difference between adjoining property owners as regards a party wall or a boundary pillar, and the owners of property restricted as in this case. In the former there may be some reciprocity of advantage, even though unequal in individual cases. In the present case, the property values are either dissipated or transferred to unknown and more or less distant owners.

The plain truth is that the true object of the ordinance is to place all of the property in an undeveloped area of 16 square miles in a straitjacket. The purpose to be accomplished is really to regulate the mode of living of persons who may hereafter inhabit it. In the last analysis, the result to be accomplished is to classify the population and segregate them according to their income or situation in life. . . .

Aside from contributing to these results and furthering such class tendencies, the ordinance also has an aesthetic purpose; that is to say, to make this village develop into a city along lines now conceived by the village council to be attractive and beautiful. The assertion that this ordinance may tend to prevent congestion, and thereby contribute to the health and safety, would be more substantial if provision had been or could be made for adequate east and west and north and south street highways. Whether these purposes and objects would justify the taking of plaintiff's property as and for a public use need not be considered. It is sufficient to say that . . . as applied to plaintiff's property, it may not be done without compensation under the guise of exercising the police power.

Ambler Realty Co. v. Village of Euclid, 297 F. 307, 313-16 (N.D. Ohio 1924).

2. After the *Euclid* case was argued for the first time in the Supreme Court, a majority of the justices were apparently in favor of holding the Euclid zoning ordinance unconstitutional. See McCormack, A Law Clerk's Recollections, 46 Colum. L. Rev. 710, 712 (1946): "Justice Sutherland . . . was writing an opinion for the majority in *Village of Euclid v. Ambler Realty Co.,* holding the zoning ordinance unconstitutional, when talks with his dissenting brethren (principally Stone, I believe) shook his convictions and led him to request a reargument, after which he changed his mind and the ordinance was upheld." In view of the District Court's opinion and the powerful argument of Newton D. Baker on behalf of the Ambler Realty Company, the decision in favor of the Euclid ordinance after the rehearing, and the Court's opinion by the conservative Justice Sutherland, are rather surprising. One of the factors strongly influencing the Court toward a favorable decision on the broad issue of constitutionality of zoning as a legal technique for land use control was undoubtedly the brief filed by Alfred Bettman as counsel for several *Amici Curiae,* including the National Conference on City Planning, the Ohio State Conference on City Planning, the National Housing Association, and the Massachusetts Federation of Town Planning Boards. In the opening paragraph of his brief, Bettman said:

This brief is designed to discuss solely the question of the constitutionality of comprehensive zoning. We do not intend to argue any issues of either fact or law which may have been raised by the parties to the case, except as they relate themselves to this matter of the constitutionality of zoning. . . . In so far as the contentions of the parties relate to the reasonableness or arbitrariness of the Euclid Village ordinance itself in its districting of the particular property of the appellee, that is, in so far as the issues of this case relate themselves specially to this ordinance and its provisions for this piece of property, we do not feel it within our province to present any statement whatever. The attorneys for the appellee, however, have not chosen to restrict themselves to an attack upon a particular provision of this particular ordinance or the special nature of its effect upon the particular piece of property of the appellee, but have attacked the constitutionality of zoning of the general type of the ordinance in this case. As they have sought to support that attack by what we deem to be fallacious arguments on constitutional law, as well as entirely mistaken citation of authorities, and as many general expressions in the opinion of the District Judge may be and are being interpreted as adverse to the validity of zoning, and as we deem zoning to be a vital necessity to the welfare of that increasing majority of the inhabitants of the United States who live in urban communities, we have availed ourselves of the leave granted by the Court to file this brief.[5]

It is quite clear that Justice Sutherland decided only "the constitutionality of comprehensive zoning" and not "the reasonableness or arbitrariness of that detail of the ordinance which . . . placed appellee's land in a residential rather than an industrial zone," as Bettman urged in the part of his brief quoted above. Thus the Court was able to avoid any serious consideration of the appellee's contention that the Euclid zoning ordinance reduced the value of its land so greatly as to result in a "taking" without compensation, in violation of the Fourteenth Amendment's "due process" clause.

3. Much confusion in land use planning has resulted from an insensitive reading of the *Euclid* case. In appraising the impact of this decision, consider the following factors: (1) the case arose in a middle-class suburban community, and the court did not review the policy basis for that community's zoning ordinance; (2) while much of Euclid was not built up at the time of this decision, the case projects an image of the community which assumes a closely-developed suburb at fairly high densities; (3) judicial notice was taken of techniques of apartment building, now outmoded, which provided an important factual backdrop for the opinion; (4) what worried the court most was the separation of incompatible uses; (5) an implied hierarchy of land use categories was erected which placed single-family residential at the top of the pyramid. But the court completely failed to notice that if, *e.g.,* single-family dwellings were built at the same density as apartments, the parking problems would be the same; and that, if apartments were built at the same height as single-family dwellings the light and air problems would disappear. By ignoring the possibilities for accommodation between "uses" which more sophisticated site and density controls might have provided, the Supreme Court in the *Euclid* case ratified a control technique based on the separation of mutually incompatible land uses, and thus the exclusion of the less desirable "intruding" uses from what might be called "harm-sensitive" land.

---

[5] A. Bettman, City and Regional Planning Papers 157 (1946). The Bettman brief is especially interesting in light of the following opinion expressed by Bettman in 1924:

> Regarding the Euclid Village zoning decision, the case was unfortunate. . . . The City made no scientific survey, and in an effort to keep the village entirely residential, the local authorities zoned all as residential and business, except a very narrow piece along the railroads, too narrow for a practical industrial development. It was a piece of arbitrary zoning and on the facts not justifiable. . . . Everybody advised against an appeal [from the District Court decision], because on appeal the decision is sure to be affirmed, even though the upper court disagrees with the opinion.

Letter from A. Bettman to D. J. Underwood, City Attorney, Tulsa, Oklahoma, Sept. 29, 1924.

4. What do you think of the District Court's conclusion, in *Euclid,* that "the result [of the zoning ordinance] . . . is to classify the population and segregate them according to their income or situation in life"? On this point, consider Hagman, Urban Land Development and Land Development Law 473-75 (1971):

> [U]nder most zoning ordinances, there are several residential districts varying from large lot single family zones to multiple family high-rise building zones. What is the basic reason for such a system? . . . [H]ow is it that the single family zone became known as the 'highest use' zone, rather than the multiple [family] residential zones, which had greater densities of people? If zoning is in the interest of the poor, why is it that apartment buildings are the buffer zone between industrial-commercial zones and single-family residential zones, rather than the single-family zones, with fewer people, being the neighbor of the undesirable commercial and industrial uses? If safety of pedestrian children is a major concern, how is it that the apartments housing the poor are on the major traffic arteries rather than the single family homes? If adequate light and air is provided for residents in multiple family high-rise buildings in the interests of their health, safety and welfare, how is the police power justified in providing more light and air by imposing regulations limiting land use to single family development? The several residential districts exist because most people want economic segregation.

5. In *Nectow v. City of Cambridge,* 277 U.S. 183 (1928), the court had before it a comprehensive zoning ordinance which, in its general scope, was conceded to be constitutional within the decision in *Euclid v. Ambler Realty Co., supra.* Plaintiff landowner attacked the ordinance, however, on the ground that, as specifically applied to him, it deprived him of his property without due process of law in contravention of the Fourteenth Amendment. The Supreme Court held the residential use classification of plaintiff's property to be invalid. In his opinion for the court, Justice Sutherland said:

> Here, the express finding of the master, already quoted, confirmed by the court below, is that the health, safety, convenience and general welfare of the inhabitants of the part of the city affected will not be promoted by the disposition made by the ordinance of the locus in question. This finding of the master, after a hearing and an inspection of the entire area affected, supported, as we think it is, by other findings of fact, is determinative of the case. That the invasion of the property of plaintiff in error was serious and highly injurious is clearly established; and, since a necessary basis for the support of that invasion is wanting, the action of the zoning authorities comes within the ban of the Fourteenth Amendment and cannot be sustained.

Id. at 188-89.

6. The *Euclid* case, in its analogy to nuisance law as a basis for zoning, appears to give judicial sanction to the use of the zoning power as a method for controlling negative externalities in land use. See the discussion *supra* p. 31. This point of view is expressed in a well-known article by Professor

Allison Dunham, who would appear to limit the zoning power to negative externality control. Dunham, A Legal and Economic Basis for City Planning, 58 Colum. L. Rev. 650 (1958).

Dunham states his argument in terms of costs and benefits. He points out that some land use regulation restricts private use in order to confer benefits on the public. He gives as an example an ordinance which requires the landowner to maintain his property as open space. On the other hand, other types of land use regulation merely attempt to keep the landowner from casting unjustifiable external costs on others. An example would be an ordinance excluding industry from residential areas. It is only the second kind of regulation which Dunham finds justifiable:

> Thus, while a city planner may control location decisions concerning public works and other land use in order either to prevent a harm or to induce an external benefit, he may control decisions as to location and kinds of private land use only in order to allocate or control a cost which the private activity imposes on others. While the state has as much interest in promoting welfare by securing beneficial use and development as by preventing harmful development, a distinction is drawn in political and ethical judgments between compelling an owner without compensation to furnish the beneficial development and compelling him to bear the cost of his activity.

Id. at 669, 670.

Consider the following comments on Dunham's argument:

> Two queries come immediately to mind. First, are the impacts of uses on each other regularly more important in site decisions than the intended purposes of each use? Second, can locational problems be separated meaningfully from all other problems? For illustrative purposes, . . . how should the health benefits of a . . . medical center be balanced against the traffic congestion it would produce? . . . Another objection to this definition of planner competence is that it provides only the haziest indication of the legitimate jurisdiction of planners and of the government. Just what is a locational decision?

A. Altshuler, The City Planning Process 326, 327 (1965).

> Professor Dunham's test suffers from the circumstances that every restriction on land use both reduces costs for adjacent owners and confers benefits on the public. The problem is definitional. If cost is viewed only in terms of the separation of incompatible uses, then the point is clear. The test then ratifies the function of zoning as it was first conceived, and so has an historical basis. Is there any other reason for excluding other costs from the accounting?

Mandelker, Notes from the English: Compensation in Town and Country Planning, 49 Calif. L. Rev. 699, 703 (1961).

How does all of this analysis square with the usual judicial attitude which justifies noncompensatory economic regulation in terms of the conventional police power nouns, especially the "general welfare"? *See* Williams, Planning Law and the Supreme Courts I, 13 Zoning Dig. 57

(1961). Williams points out that we need more specific constitutional criteria to guide and justify the planning and plan implementation function.

A NOTE ON A NATIONAL JURISPRUDENCE IN PLANNING AND ZONING

In *Nectow v. City of Cambridge, supra,* the United States Supreme Court seemed to have embarked on a course foreshadowed in *Euclid:* close supervision of the exercise of the zoning power "concretely applied to particular premises." The Court went on later to strike down an amendment to the Seattle zoning ordinance which would have permitted a philanthropic home for children or old people to be established in a residential district upon approval by the owners of two thirds of the land within 400 feet of the proposed philanthropic use. *Washington ex rel. Seattle Trust Co. v. Roberge,* 278 U.S. 116 (1928). But after 1928, the Supreme Court consistently refused to review any cases raising legal issues in the planning and zoning field until it decided *Village of Belle Terre v. Boraas,* 416 U.S. 1 (1974). Having established the basic constitutionality of zoning, the Supreme Court left it to the state courts to apply the constitutional principle of reasonableness to individual cases. The refusal of the Supreme Court to review zoning cases seems justified insofar as the underlying issues in zoning litigation are more often factual than legal. But one effect of the Supreme Court's unwillingness to provide leadership in a field in which constitutional problems are pervasive has been the development of decided differences in doctrine and emphasis from one jurisdiction to the next. Appellate courts in Illinois, Michigan, and Pennsylvania, for example, have become known for their "conservative" (*i.e.,* property-protective) attitudes, while appellate courts in California and New Jersey, for example, have become known their "liberal" attitudes.

Recently, the highest appellate courts in a few states have limited their jurisdiction in zoning litigation. The problem has arisen in states in which there is an intermediate appellate court, and in which appeals to the highest appellate court as a matter of right are limited. For example, in New Jersey an appeal may be taken to the highest court as a matter of right in cases "arising" under the constitution of the state. The validity of a zoning ordinance which prohibited the plaintiff from erecting petroleum storage facilities in a heavy industrial zone was challenged in *Tidewater Oil Co. v. Mayor and Council of Carteret,* 209 A.2d 105 (N.J. 1965). Holding that there was no absolute right of appeal, the court commented as follows:

> The plaintiff's conclusional contention that the ordinance prohibition of the proposed use by Tidewater is unconstitutionally capricious and discriminatory is broadly cast in the familiar due process and equal protection concepts of the Fourteenth Amendment. But the

supporting argument boils down, as in most cases of this kind, to a claim that, in this particular factual setting, the ordinance treatment is unreasonable because not within the purposes and essential considerations or the requirement of uniform regulations specified by the zoning enabling act as necessary to undergird valid local legislation. . . . While these statutory prerequisites have loose constitutional connotations, the fundamental question here resolves itself into a matter of application of statutory standards to a particular factual situation under long established principles. At this relatively advanced stage of the law of land use regulation, it will be the rare case concerned with the validity of use classification which will present an issue of sufficient constitutional involvement for purposes of [an appeal as of right] . . . .

Id. at 108.

A similar position has been taken by the Supreme Court of Illinois. *First Nat'l Bank & Trust Co. v. City of Evanston,* 197 N.E.2d 705 (Ill. 1964). In addition, as states continue to create intermediate appellate courts, there is less likelihood that zoning litigation will reach the highest state court appellate level.

B. ENABLING LEGISLATION AND THE ZONING ORDINANCE

At the present time, all of the 50 states have zoning enabling legislation for municipalities, and many states also have zoning enabling legislation for counties. Most of the zoning enabling legislation originally adopted prior to 1924 was based on the New York general city enabling act of 1917. Most of the zoning enabling acts adopted after 1924, however, were modelled on the Standard State Zoning Enabling Act, which was prepared under the aegis of the United States Department of Commerce and first published in mimeographed form in 1923. The Standard Act, revised and printed for the first time in 1924, and reprinted in 1926, was itself based on the New York general city enabling act, but departed substantially in some respects from the New York model. Although many current zoning enabling acts embody even more substantial changes from the Standard Act, the majority of the current statutes still retains the substance of the Standard Act.

We reprint here the Standard State Zoning Enabling Act and the zoning enabling legislation currently in force in California.

A STANDARD STATE ZONING ENABLING ACT [b]

Section 1. Grant of Power. For the purpose of promoting health, safety, morals, or the general welfare of the community, the

---

[b] The draftsmen's footnotes have been omitted. The Standard State Zoning Enabling Act is no longer in print in its original form as a publication of the U. S. Department of Commerce, but it is reprinted in full, with the draftsmen's footnotes

legislative body of cities and incorporated villages is hereby empowered to regulate and restrict the height, number of stories, and size of buildings and other structures, the percentage of lot that may be occupied, the size of yards, courts, and other open spaces, the density of population, and the location and use of buildings, structures, and land for trade, industry, residence, or other purposes.

Sec. 2. Districts. For any or all of said purposes the local legislative body may divide the municipality into districts of such number, shape, and area as may be deemed best suited to carry out the purposes of this act; and within such districts it may regulate and restrict the erection, construction, reconstruction, alteration, repair, or use of buildings, structures, or land. All such regulations shall be uniform for each class or kind of building throughout each district, but the regulations in one district may differ from those in other districts.

Sec. 3. Purposes in View. Such regulations shall be made in accordance with a comprehensive plan and designed to lessen congestion in the streets; to secure safety from fire, panic, and other dangers; to promote health and the general welfare; to provide adequate light and air; to prevent the overcrowding of land; to avoid undue concentration of population; to facilitate the adequate provision of transportation, water, sewerage, schools, parks, and other public requirements. Such regulations shall be made with reasonable consideration, among other things, to the character of the district and its peculiar suitability for particular uses, and with a view to conserving the value of buildings and encouraging the most appropriate use of land throughout such municipality.

Sec. 4. Method of Procedure. The legislative body of such municipality shall provide for the manner in which such regulations and restrictions and the boundaries of such districts shall be determined, established, and enforced, and from time to time amended, supplemented, or changed. However, no such regulation, restriction, or boundary shall become effective until after a public hearing in relation thereto, at which parties in interest and citizens shall have an opportunity to be heard. At least 15 days' notice of the time and place of such hearing shall be published in an official paper, or a paper of general circulation, in such municipality.

Sec. 5. Changes. Such regulations, restrictions, and boundaries may from time to time be amended, supplemented, changed, modified, or repealed. In case, however, of a protest against such change, signed by the owners of 20 per cent or more either of the

as Appendix A, in American Law Institute, A Model Land Development Code, Tentative Draft No. 1, at p. 210 (1968).

area of the lots included in such proposed change, or of those immediately adjacent in the rear thereof extending _____ feet therefrom, or of those directly opposite thereto extending_____ feet from the street frontage of such opposite lots, such amendment shall not become effective except by the favorable vote of three-fourths of all the members of the legislative body of such municipality. The provisions of the previous section relative to public hearings and official notice shall apply equally to all changes or amendments.

Sec. 6. Zoning Commission. In order to avail itself of the powers conferred by this act, such legislative body shall appoint a commission, to be known as the zoning commission, to recommend the boundaries of the various original districts and appropriate regulations to be enforced therein. Such commission shall make a preliminary report and hold public hearings thereon before submitting its final report, and such legislative body shall not hold its public hearings or take action until it has received the final report of such commission. Where a city plan commission already exists, it may be appointed as the zoning commission.

Sec. 7. Board of Adjustment. Such local legislative body may provide for the appointment of a board of adjustment, and in the regulations and restrictions adopted pursuant to the authority of this act may provide that the said board of adjustment may, in appropriate cases and subject to appropriate conditions and safeguards, make special exceptions to the terms of the ordinance in harmony with its general purpose and intent and in accordance with general or specific rules therein contained.

The board of adjustment shall consist of five members, each to be appointed for a term of three years and removable for cause by the appointing authority upon written charges and after public hearing. Vacancies shall be filled for the unexpired term of any member whose term becomes vacant.

The board shall adopt rules in accordance with the provisions of any ordinance adopted pursuant to this act. Meetings of the board shall be held at the call of the chairman and at such other times as the board may determine. Such chairman, or in his absence the acting chairman, may administer oaths and compel the attendance of witnesses. All meetings of the board shall be open to the public. The board shall keep minutes of its proceedings, showing the vote of each member upon each question, or, if absent or failing to vote, indicating such fact, and shall keep records of its examinations and other official actions, all of which shall be immediately filed in the office of the board and shall be a public record.

Appeals to the board of adjustment may be taken by any person aggrieved or by any officer, department, board, or bureau of the municipality affected by any decision of the administrative officer.

Such appeal shall be taken within a reasonable time, as provided by the rules of the board, by filing with the officer from whom the appeal is taken and with the board of adjustment a notice of appeal specifying the grounds thereof. The officer from whom the appeal is taken shall forthwith transmit to the board all the papers constituting the record upon which the action appealed from was taken.

An appeal stays all proceedings in furtherance of the action appealed from, unless the officer from whom the appeal is taken certifies to the board of adjustment after the notice of appeal shall have been filed with him that by reason of facts stated in the certificate a stay would, in his opinion, cause imminent peril to life or property. In such case proceedings shall not be stayed otherwise than by a restraining order which may be granted by the board of adjustment or by a court of record on application on notice to the officer from whom the appeal is taken and on due cause shown.

The board of adjustment shall fix a reasonable time for the hearing of the appeal, give public notice thereof, as well as due notice to the parties in interest, and decide the same within a reasonable time. Upon the hearing any party may appear in person or by agent or by attorney.

The board of adjustment shall have the following powers:

1. To hear and decide appeals where it is alleged there is error in any order, requirement, decision, or determination made by an administrative official in the enforcement of this act or of any ordinance adopted pursuant thereto.

2. To hear and decide special exceptions to the terms of the ordinance upon which such board is required to pass under such ordinance.

3. To authorize upon appeal in specific cases such variance from the terms of the ordinance as will not be contrary to the public interest, where, owing to special conditions, a literal enforcement of the provisions of the ordinance will result in unnecessary hardship, and so that the spirit of the ordinance shall be observed and substantial justice done.

In exercising the above-mentioned powers such board may, in conformity with the provisions of this act, reverse or affirm, wholly or partly, or may modify the order, requirement, decision, or determination appealed from and may make such order, requirement, decision, or determination as ought to be made, and to that end shall have all the powers of the officer from whom the appeal is taken.

The concurring vote of four members of the board shall be necessary to reverse any order, requirement, decision, or determination of any such administrative official, or to decide in favor of the applicant on any matter upon which it is required to pass under any such ordinance, or to effect any variation in such ordinance.

Any person or persons, jointly or severally, aggrieved by any decision of the board of adjustment, or any taxpayer, or any officer, department, board, or bureau of the municipality, may present to a court of record a petition, duly verified, setting forth that such decision is illegal, in whole or in part, specifying the grounds of the illegality. Such petition shall be presented to the court within 30 days after the filing of the decision in the office of the board.

Upon the presentation of such petition the court may allow a writ of certiorari directed to the board of adjustment to review such decision of the board of adjustment and shall prescribe therein the time within which a return thereto must be made and served upon the relator's attorney, which shall not be less than 10 days and may be extended by the court. The allowance of the writ shall not stay proceedings upon the decision appealed from, but the court may, on application, on notice to the board and on due cause shown, grant a restraining order.

The board of adjustment shall not be required to return the original papers acted upon by it, but it shall be sufficient to return certified or sworn copies thereof or of such portions thereof as may be called for by such writ. The return shall concisely set forth such other facts as may be pertinent and material to show the grounds of the decision appealed from and shall be verified.

If, upon the hearing, it shall appear to the court that testimony is necessary for the proper disposition of the matter, it may take evidence or appoint a referee to take such evidence as it may direct and report the same to the court with his findings of fact and conclusions of law, which shall constitute a part of the proceedings upon which the determination of the court shall be made. The court may reverse or affirm, wholly or partly, or may modify the decision brought up for review.

Costs shall not be allowed against the board unless it shall appear to the court that it acted with gross negligence, or in bad faith, or with malice in making the decision appealed from.

All issues in any proceeding under this section shall have preference over all other civil actions and proceedings.

Sec. 8. Enforcement and Remedies. The local legislative body may provide by ordinance for the enforcement of this act and of any ordinance or regulation made thereunder. A violation of this act or of such ordinance or regulation is hereby declared to be a misdemeanor, and such local legislative body may provide for the punishment thereof by fine or imprisonment or both. It is also empowered to provide civil penalties for such violation.

In case any building or structure is erected, constructed, reconstructed, altered, repaired, converted, or maintained, or any building, structure, or land is used in violation of this act or of any ordinance or other regulation made under authority conferred hereby, the proper local authorities of the municipality, in addition to other remedies, may institute any appropriate action or proceedings to prevent such unlawful erection, construction, reconstruction, alteration, repair, conversion, maintenance, or use, to restrain, correct, or abate such violation, to prevent the occupancy of said building, structure, or land, or to prevent any illegal act, conduct, business, or use in or about such premises.

Sec. 9. Conflict with other Laws. Wherever the regulations made under authority of this act require a greater width or size of yards, courts, or other open spaces, or require a lower height of building or less number of stories, or require a greater percentage of lot to be left unoccupied, or impose other higher standards than are required in any other statute or local ordinance or regulation, the provisions of the regulations made under authority of this act shall govern. Wherever the provisions of any other statute or local ordinance or regulation require a greater width or size of yards, courts, or other open spaces, or require a lower height of building or a less number of stories, or require a greater percentage of lot to be left unoccupied, or impose other higher standards than are required by the regulations made under authority of this act, the provisions of such statute or local ordinance or regulation shall govern.

CALIFORNIA GOVERNMENT CODE (Deering 1974, Supp. 1977)

§ 65800. Legislative purpose and intention

It is the purpose of this chapter to provide for the adoption and administration of zoning laws, ordinances, rules and regulations by counties and cities, as well as to implement such general plan as may be in effect in any such county or city. . . . [T]he Legislature declares that in enacting this chapter it is its intention to provide only a minimum of limitation in order that counties and cities may exercise the maximum degree of control over local zoning matters.
. . . .

§ 65850. General powers

Pursuant to the provisions of this chapter, the legislative body of any county or city by ordinance may:
(a) Regulate the use of buildings, structures and land as between industry, business, residents, open space, including agriculture, recreation, enjoyment of scenic beauty and use of natural resources, and other purposes.
(b) Regulate signs and billboards.
(c) Regulate location, height, bulk, number of stories and size of

buildings and structures; the size and use of lots, yards, courts and other open spaces; the percentage of a lot which may be occupied by a building or structure; the intensity of land use.

(d) Establish requirements for off-street parking and loading.

(e) Establish and maintain building setback lines.

(f) Create civic districts around civic centers, public parks, public buildings or public grounds and establish regulations therefor.

§ 65851. Division of city, county, or portions thereof into zones.

For such purposes the legislative body may divide a county, a city, or portions thereof, into zones of the number, shape and area it deems best suited to carry out the purpose of this chapter.

§ 65852. Uniformity of regulations

All such regulations shall be uniform for each class or kind of building or use of land throughout each zone, but the regulation in one type of zone may differ from those in other types of zones.

. . . .

[The statute then provides for detailed notice and hearing procedures, which are to apply to a zoning ordinance amendment which "changes any property from one zone to another." § 65853. This kind of change is known as a zoning map amendment, because it is a change in the zoning map. It should be distinguished from an amendment to the text of the zoning ordinance. See the model zoning ordinance, *infra* p. 227. These procedures also apply to the adoption of a zoning ordinance. In these two instances, the planning commission is to make a recommendation to the legislative body. § 65855. The legislative body's function is spelled out as follows: — Eds.]

§ 65856. Legislative body's hearing, and notice thereof

Upon receipt of the recommendation of the planning commission, the legislative body shall hold a public hearing; provided, however, that if the matter under consideration is an amendment to a zoning ordinance to change property from one zone to another, and the planning commission has recommended against the adoption of such amendment, the legislative body shall not be required to take any further action thereon unless otherwise provided by ordinance or unless an interested party shall request such a hearing by filing a written request with the clerk of the legislative body within five days after the planning commission files its recommendations with the legislative body. . . .

§ 65857. Approval, modification, or disapproval of recommendation

The legislative body may approve, modify or disapprove the recommendation of the planning commission; provided that any modification of the proposed ordinance or amendment by the legislative body not previously considered by the planning commission during its hearing, shall first be referred to the planning commission for report and recommendation, but the planning commission shall not be required to hold a public hearing thereon. Failure of the planning commission to report within forty (40) days after the reference, or such longer period as may be designated by the legislative body, shall be deemed to be approval of the proposed modification.

§ 65858. Interim ordinance as urgency measure

Without following the procedures otherwise required preliminary to the adoption of a zoning ordinance, the legislative body, to protect the public safety, health and welfare, may adopt as an urgency measure an interim ordinance prohibiting any uses which may be in conflict with a contemplated zoning proposal which the legislative body, planning commission or the planning department is considering or studying or intends to study within a reasonable time. Such urgency measure shall require a four-fifths vote of the legislative body for adoption. . . . [This section provides that interim ordinances may not be in effect for a period of more than two years. — Eds.]

§ 65859. Prezoning unincorporated territory adjoining city

A city may prezone unincorporated territory adjoining the city for the purpose of determining the zoning that will apply to such property in the event of subsequent annexation to the city. The method of accomplishing such prezoning shall be as provided by this chapter for zoning within the city. Such zoning shall become effective at the same time that the annexation becomes effective.

If a city has not prezoned territory which is annexed, it may adopt an interim ordinance in accordance with the provisions of Section 65858.

§ 65860. Conformity to general plan: Action to enforce compliance

[This provision is reproduced *infra,* Chapter 4, Section E (3). — Eds.]

§ 65861. Functioning of legislative body in absence of city planning commission

When there is no city planning commission, the legislative body of such city shall do all things required or authorized by this chapter of the city planning commission.

. . . .

§ 65900. Creation of boards, etc.: Members' compensation and expenses

The legislative body of a city or county may, by ordinance, create and establish either a board of zoning adjustment, or the office of zoning administrator or both. It may also, by ordinance, create and establish a board of appeals. Members of a board of zoning adjustment and members of a board of appeals may receive compensation for their attendance at each meeting of their respective boards in a sum to be fixed by the legislative body by which they are appointed. In addition, they may also receive reasonable traveling expenses to and from the usual place of business of such board to any place of meeting of the board within the county or city.

§ 65901. Powers and duties of board or administrator: Hearing and deciding applications for permits and variances

The board of zoning adjustment or zoning administrator shall hear and decide applications for conditional uses or other permits when the zoning ordinance provides therefor and establishes criteria for determining such matters, and applications for variances from the terms of the zoning ordinance. Said board or said zoning administrator may also exercise such other powers as may be granted by local ordinance, and adopt all rules and procedures necessary or convenient for the conduct of its or his business.

§ 65902. Planning commission's exercise of functions and duties

In the event that neither a board of zoning adjustment nor the office of a zoning administrator has been created and established, the planning commission shall exercise all of the functions and duties of said board or said administrator.

The legislative body of a county may provide that an area planning commission shall exercise all of the functions and duties of a board of zoning adjustment or a zoning administrator in a prescribed portion of the county.

§ 65903. Board of appeals' functions and proceedings

A board of appeals, if one has been created and established by local ordinance, shall hear and determine appeals from the decisions of the board of zoning adjustment or the zoning administrator, as the case may be. Procedures for such appeals shall be as provided by local ordinance. Such board may reverse or affirm, wholly or partly, or may modify the order, requirement, decision or determination appealed from, and may make such order, requirement, decision, or determination as should be made, and such action shall be final.

§ 65904. Legislative body's exercise of functions and duties

If a board of appeals has not been created and established the local legislative body shall exercise all of the functions and duties of the board of appeals in the same manner and to the same effect as provided in Section 65903.

. . . .

§ 65906. Granting variances

Variances from the terms of the zoning ordinances shall be granted only when, because of special circumstances applicable to the property, including size, shape, topography, location or surroundings, the strict application of the zoning ordinance deprives such property of privileges enjoyed by other property in the vicinity and under identical zoning classification.

Any variance granted shall be subject to such conditions as will assure that the adjustment thereby authorized shall not constitute a grant of special privileges inconsistent with the limitations upon other properties in the vicinity and zone in which such property is situated.

A variance shall not be granted for a parcel of property which authorizes a use or activity which is not otherwise expressly authorized by the zone regulation governing the parcel of property. The provisions of this section shall not apply to conditional use permits.

. . . .

§ 65909. Prohibited conditions for issuance of permit or variance

No local governmental body, or any agency thereof, may condition the issuance of any building or use permit or zone variance on any or all of the following:
(1) The dedication of land for any purpose not reasonably related to the use of the property for which the variance, building, or use permit is requested.
(2) The posting of a bond to guarantee installation of public improvements not reasonably related to the use of the property for which the variance, building, or use permit is requested.

§ 65910. Preparation and adoption of ordinance

Every city and county by December 31, 1973, shall prepare and adopt an open-space zoning ordinance consistent with the local open-space plan. . . .

§ 65911. Variances from ordinance

Variances from the terms of an open-space zoning ordinance shall be granted only when, because of special circumstances applicable to the property, including size, shape, topography, location or surroundings, the strict application of the zoning ordinance deprives such property of privileges enjoyed by other property in the vicinity and under identical zoning classification.

Any variance granted shall be subject to such conditions as will assure that the adjustment thereby authorized shall not constitute a grant of special privileges inconsistent with the limitations upon other properties in the vicinity and zone in which such property is situated.

This section shall be literally and strictly interpreted and enforced so as to protect the interest of the public in the orderly growth and development of cities and counties and in the preservation and conservation of open-space lands.

§ 65912. Legislative intent as to compensation for taking or damaging property

The Legislature hereby finds and declares that this article is not intended, and shall not be construed, as authorizing the city or the county to exercise its power to adopt, amend or repeal an open-space zoning ordinance in a matter which will take or damage private property for public use without the payment of just compensation therefor. This section is not intended to increase or decrease the rights of any owner of property under the Constitution of the State of California or of the United States.

THE ZONING ORDINANCE

All states have followed the practice of delegating to units of local government the power to enact and enforce zoning regulations. These regulations are almost invariably embodied in a "zoning ordinance." Local zoning ordinances of the type adopted in New York City in 1916, with different classes of regulations for "use," "height," and "land coverage," are no longer common. There are, of course, vast differences between the zoning ordinances adopted in different municipalities and counties. It is obviously impossible to draft a "standard" or "model" set of substantive zoning regulations, since the needs of different municipalities and counties are almost infinitely variable. It is possible, however, to draft a "standard" or "model" set of administrative provisions for use in zoning ordinances. The following illustrative ordinance contains administrative provisions based on American Society of Planning Officials, The Text of a Model Zoning Ordinance (3d ed. 1966).

ARTICLE I. PURPOSES.

[Some zoning authorities recommend including a statement of purpose as a method of helping to insure a favorable judicial reception. — Eds.]

ARTICLE II. DEFINITIONS.

Except as otherwise defined by this ordinance, terms or words used herein shall be interpreted as follows:

The present tense includes the future tense, the singular number includes the plural, and the plural number includes the singular. The word *shall* is mandatory and the word *may* is permissive. The word *used* or *occupied* includes the words, *intended, designed* or *arranged to be used or occupied.*

Building — Any structure, whether stationary or movable, enclosed by extensive walls, and constructed or used for residence, business or public or private uses, or uses accessory thereto, other than a fence or boundary wall.

Dwelling — A house or other building designed for occupancy by one family.

Family — One or more persons occupying a single dwelling and using common cooking facilities, provided that no family shall contain more than five adult persons.

Lot — A piece, or parcel of land in one undivided ownership, of at least sufficient size to meet minimum zoning requirements for use, coverage and area, and having such yards and other open space areas as provided by this ordinance.

Non-conforming Use — A legally existing use which fails to comply with the uses permitted by this ordinance.

Sign — Any device or free-standing structure used for purposes of advertising or display.

Structure — Anything constructed or erected, the use of which requires location on the ground, or attachment to something having location on the ground. Structures include buildings but exclude fences and boundary walls.

Yard — A space on the same lot with a principal building, open, unoccupied and unobstructed by buildings or structures from 30 inches above the ground level upwards.

   A. *Yard, Front* — A yard extending between side lot lines across the front of a lot. Depth of required front yards shall be measured at right angles to a straight line joining the foremost points on the side lot lines. In the case of rounded property lines, the foremost points of the side lot lines shall be assumed to be the point at which the side and front lot lines would have met without such rounding.

   B. *Yard, Side* — A yard extending from the rear line of the required front yard to the rear lot line.

[Are there too many definitions? Too few? What other words might be defined? — Eds.]

ARTICLE III. ESTABLISHMENT OF DISTRICTS.

Section 1. Types of Districts. The Town of Outer Metro is divided into the following three districts:

A. A Residential District

B. A Multi-Family District

C. A Neighborhood Retail District

[Sections 2 and 3 provide for a zoning map and state rules for determining district boundaries at street and lot lines. — Eds.]

ARTICLE IV. DISTRICT REGULATIONS.

Section 1. Application of Regulations.

A. No building, structure, or land shall hereafter be used or occupied, and no building or structure or part thereof shall hereafter be erected, constructed, moved, or altered unless in conformity with all of the regulations applicable to the district in which it is located. All other uses, buildings, and structures are prohibited.

B. No building or other structure shall hereafter be erected or altered:

1. to exceed the height;

2. to accommodate or house a greater number of families;

3. to occupy a greater percentage of lot area;

4. to have narrower or smaller rear yards, front yards or side yards than required by the provisions of this ordinance.

C. No part of a yard, open space, or off-street parking space required about or in connection with any building for the purpose of complying with this ordinance, shall be included as part of a yard, open space, or off-street parking space similarly required for any other building.

Section 2. Residential District.

A. *Permitted Principal Uses.*

1. Single-family dwelling.

2. Parks, playgrounds and parking areas, if publicly owned.

B. *Permitted Accessory Uses,* located in the same lot with the permitted principal use.

1. Private garage with capacity for not more than two (2) motor vehicles.

2. Home occupations, as regulated by Paragraph J.

3. Other customary accessory uses and buildings, provided such uses are incidental to the principal use and do not include any activity commonly conducted as a business, except as expressly permitted by Paragraph J. Any accessory building or use shall be located on the same lot with the principal building.

C. *Advertising Signs.*

One sign advertising the sale or rent of the land or buildings upon which it is located shall be permitted, provided that such signs shall not exceed three (3) square feet in area and shall be distant from the street line not less than one-half of the front yard depth.

D. *Conditional Uses,* permitted upon the issuance of a Special Permit as provided in Section 6, Article IV.

1. Churches or similar places of worship; rectories and parish houses.
2. Community meeting halls; lodges and private clubs not conducted primarily for profit.
3. Nurseries and day care centers for pre-school children, if not conducted in an existing dwelling.

E. *Required Lot Area.*

Residential lots shall be not less than 7500 square feet in area and not less than 75 feet in width.

F. *Percentage of Lot Coverage.*

All buildings including accessory buildings, porches, breezeways and roof projections shall cover not more than 30 per cent of the area of the lot.

G. *Building Height.*

1. Two and one-half stories, but not exceeding 35 feet, for single-family dwellings.
2. The maximum height permitted for accessory buildings shall be 18 feet.

H. *Ground Floor Area Per Dwelling,* exclusive of porches and breezeways.

1. One story dwellings — not less than 1200 square feet.
2. Dwellings having more than one story — 800 square feet.

I. *Yards — Single Family Dwellings.*

Each lot shall have front and side yards with depths and widths of not less than the following:

1. Front yard depth — 35 feet; but if 50 per cent or more of the frontage on a block has been developed, then the depth of the front yard shall be the average of the depths of the front yards previously established.
2. Side yard width — 5 feet, except that no building located on a corner lot shall be less than 20 feet from the side lot line fronting on the adjacent street.

J. [This paragraph regulates home occupations. — Eds.]

Section 3. Multi-Family District.

[If a separate district for apartment development is provided, the regulations may look very much like the regulations for single family residential development except that the numbers may be changed. Just how they will be changed is another matter. For example, the minimum lot area required for the apartment site may be raised, while an area requirement for each dwelling unit in the apartment complex may be added but will probably be lower than the area requirement for dwelling units in the single family districts. Side and other perimeter requirements for apartment developments may be increased.

This approach is what might be called the conventional treatment. It implies a separation of single family and apartment developments into separate "use" districts. We cannot explore all of the complexities here, but several problems come to mind. Why treat apartments and single family dwellings as separate uses? Since, as we have suggested, the real problem is density and site control, why not write the ordinance in these terms? Is the zoning envelope treatment for single family dwellings, which contemplates one dwelling unit for each lot, really applicable to apartment developments? — Eds.]

Section 4. Neighborhood Business District.

A. *Permitted Principal Uses.*

    1. Convenience establishments.

    2. Bakeries, florists, gift shops, stationery stores, and liquor establishments.

    3. Restaurants, other than drive-in establishments.

B. *Permitted Accessory Uses.* Uses and structures which are customarily incidental and accessory to principal uses and structures.

C. *Conditional Uses,* permitted upon the issuance of a Special Permit as provided in Section 5, Article IV.

    1. Gasoline filling stations; car wash facilities.

D. *Advertising Signs.*

    1. One non-illuminated wall sign, not to exceed one square foot of sign area for each lineal front foot of building frontage, but not in excess of 100 square feet of sign area.

    2. One non-illuminated ground sign, not to exceed 12 square feet in sign area, and to be set back a minimum of 50 feet from the property line.

[Also, a minimum lot area of 5000 square feet, a minimum lot width of 50 feet, but no yard requirements except that a minimum yard of ten feet must be provided adjacent to any street. — Eds.]

Section 5. Off-street Parking.

A. *Requirements.*

Off-street parking shall be provided and maintained for each residence or other building permitted by these regulations which is erected, enlarged, or altered after the date on which this ordinance becomes effective. The space provided shall be as follows:

    1. Dwelling — (Residential) — A minimum of one parking space for each dwelling unit.

2. Restaurant — A minimum of one parking space for each five seats in accordance with designed capacity.

3. Retail stores — At least one parking space for each sixty square feet of floor area.

B. To meet the requirements of this ordinance, a parking space shall conform to the following standards:

1. All parking spaces shall be surfaced with an all-weather, dustfree material, and shall be located on the same lot with the building or in a dedicated but unaccepted roadway.

2. An off-street parking space shall comprise an area of not less than nine by twenty square feet.

C. *Prohibited Parking.* No parking space shall be provided or maintained for mobile homes or for commercial vehicles of over one-ton carrying capacity.

Section 6. Conditional Use Permits.

A. *Procedure Required.*

1. An application for a conditional use permit shall be submitted to the Plan Commission.

2. The application shall be accompanied by a plan for the proposed use. Such plan shall indicate the location and specifications of all buildings, parking areas, traffic access and circulation drives, open spaces, landscaping, storm and sewage drainage facilities. The plan shall also contain any other information that the Plan Commission, in its discretion, may require in order to determine if the proposed conditional use meets the provisions of this ordinance.

3. Upon receiving an application for a conditional use permit, the Plan Commission shall review the application in conjunction with the standards set forth in Paragraph B of this section. After due investigation and review, if the application is tentatively approved, a public hearing shall be authorized and conducted in the following manner:

   a. The Plan Commission shall hold a public hearing on the application within 60 days after its receipt.

   b. Written notice of the hearing shall be given to the applicant and to all persons who own property within 1000 feet of the proposed conditional use. A notice of the hearing shall be published at least 10 days prior to the hearing in a newspaper of general circulation in the town. All notices shall be at the applicant's expense.

   c. Within 30 days after the public hearing, the conditional use permit shall be granted or denied. In granting the conditional permit, the Plan Commission shall be authorized to permit the use applied for subject to such reasonable conditions as it may impose. These conditions may contain such requirements for improving, maintaining, operating, and screening the conditional use as will protect the character of the surrounding property.

B. *Standards Applicable to Conditional Uses.*
 1. The location and size of the use, the nature and intensity of the operations involved and the size of the site in relation to it shall be in harmony with the orderly development of the district. The location, nature, and height of buildings, walls and fences shall be such as will not discourage the permitted use of adjacent land and buildings.
 2. No conditional use shall be more objectionable to nearby properties by reason of noise, fumes, vibrations, or lights than any other use allowable without permit under the provisions of this ordinance.
 3. The principal and accessory buildings shall cover no more than 35 per cent of the area of the lot.
 4. No building shall be located within 50 feet of the lot line of a contiguous lot. However, an existing dwelling in which a home occupation is to be conducted shall be subject to the yard requirements of Section 2 (I), Article IV.
 5. No building shall be erected to a height in excess of two stories, or 35 feet. This requirement shall not apply to churches or similar places of worship.
 6. Off-street parking shall be provided as required by Section 5, Article IV. However, nurseries and day-care centers for pre-school children shall provide one off-street parking space for each employee.
C. *Expiration.* A conditional permit shall be deemed to authorize only one particular use and shall expire if the conditional use shall cease for more than six months for any reason.
D. *Existing Violations.* No conditional permit shall be issued for a conditional use for an existing building which is in violation of any provision of this ordinance.

[How do you feel about the standards contained in this section? Does the externality basis of land use control make the drafting of standards a difficult and complex exercise? *See* Mandelker, Delegation of Power and Function in Zoning Administration, 1963 Wash. U.L.Q. 60. — Eds.]

Section 7. Planned Development Unit. [Omitted. The planned development unit is an innovation in zoning controls, and consideration may be deferred till later. The planned development provision in this ordinance is uniquely drafted to take care of special local conditions. — Eds.]

Section 8. Non-conforming Uses.

A. *Intent* — Within the districts established by this ordinance there exist lots, structures, and uses of land and structures which were lawful before this ordinance was passed or amended, but which would be prohibited, regulated, or restricted under the terms of the ordinance. It is the intent of this ordinance to permit these non-conformities to continue until they are removed, but not to encourage their survival. As used in this section, the term "structures" also includes buildings. (See definitions.)

B. *Non-conforming Structures* — If on the effective date of this ordinance, a structure exists that could not be built under the terms of this ordinance by reason of restrictions on area, lot coverage, height, yards, or other characteristics of the structure or its location on the lot, such structure may be continued subject to the following provisions:

1. No such structure may be enlarged or altered in any way which increases its non-conformity, except with the permission of the Board of Zoning Appeals. Upon application to the Board of Zoning Appeals, the Board may permit an enlargement or extension of a non-conforming structure, or it may permit a new non-conforming structure on the same lot with the existing non-conforming structure. The Board shall first determine that the enlarged, extended or new structure is necessary to the conduct of the non-conforming use, and is not detrimental to the neighborhood in which it is located. The provisions of Section 2, Article V, shall apply to the decisions of the Board of Zoning Appeals, under this subsection.

2. If, by any means, a non-conforming structure is destroyed in an amount in excess of 50 percent of twice its assessed value at the time of destruction, it shall not be reconstructed except in conformity with the provisions of this ordinance.

3. Any non-conforming sign shall become a prohibited and unlawful use at the expiration of two years from the date of this ordinance and shall be discontinued.

C. *Non-conforming Uses of Structures.* If on the effective date of this ordinance, a use of a structure or of a structure and premises in combination, exists that would not be allowed in the district under the terms of this ordinance, the use may be continued, subject to the following provisions:

1. No non-conforming use of an existing structure shall be changed except to a use permitted in the district in which it is located, nor may the non-conforming use thereafter be resumed.

2. When a non-conforming use of a structure, or of a structure and premises in combination, is discontinued or abandoned

for six consecutive months or for 18 months during any three year period, the structure, or structure and premises in combination, shall not thereafter be used except in conformance with the regulations of the district in which it is located.

D. *Repairs and Maintenance.* On any building devoted in whole or in part to any non-conforming use, work may be done in any period of 12 consecutive months on ordinary repairs, or repairs or replacement of non-bearing walls, fixtures, wiring or plumbing, to an extent not exceeding 20 percent of twice the assessed value of the building. However, the cubic content of the building as it existed at the effective date of this ordinance shall not be increased.

Nothing in this ordinance shall be deemed to prevent the strengthening or restoring to a safe condition of any building or part thereof declared to be unsafe by any official charged with protecting the public safety.

E. *Conditional Permits.* An authorized conditional use or Planned Development Unit shall not be deemed a non-conforming use, but shall be deemed a conforming use in the district in which it is located. [ASPO's Model also contains related provisions governing the non-conforming use of land. How important are these provisions? — Eds.]

ARTICLE V. ADMINISTRATION AND ENFORCEMENT.

Section 1. Administration.

A. *Building Commissioner.* This ordinance shall be enforced by the Building Commissioner, who shall be appointed by the Town Board. No building permit or certificate of occupancy shall be issued by the Building Commissioner unless all the provisions of this ordinance have been met.

B. *Improvement Location Permit.* No building or structure shall be erected, added to, or structurally altered until a permit therefor has been issued by the Building Commissioner. The permit shall state that the building or structure or proposed use thereof complies with the provisions of this ordinance.

C. *Certificate of Occupancy.* No land shall be used or occupied and no building or structure hereafter erected, altered or extended, used or changed in use until a certificate of occupancy shall have been issued by the Building Commissioner. The permit shall state that the building or structure or proposed use thereof complies with the provisions of this ordinance.

D. *Forms.* [Omitted. — Eds.]

Section 2. Board of Zoning Appeals.

A. *Creation.* A Board of Zoning Appeals is hereby established, which shall consist of five (5) members to be appointed by the Town Board as prescribed by statute.

B. *Procedure.* Reference is hereby made to the applicable sections of the Planning Act for the provisions governing procedures before the Board of Zoning Appeals. The Board shall adopt any additional rules necessary to the conduct of its affairs, and in keeping with the provisions of the Planning Act and this ordinance.

C. *Interpretation.* On an appeal by the Building Commissioner, by the Plan Commission, by the Town Board, or by any other person aggrieved, the Board of Zoning Appeals shall decide any question involving the interpretation or administration of this ordinance.

D. *Variances.* The Board of Zoning Appeals may vary or adapt any provisions of this ordinance. Except as authorized by Section 8(c)(1) of Article IV, the Board shall not grant a variance to allow a use not permitted by the terms of this ordinance. No variance shall be granted unless the Board first makes positive findings on all of the following points:

1. That the lot is exceptionally irregular, narrow, shallow, or steep, or that the land, or building, or structure is subject to other exceptional physical conditions peculiar to it;

2. That the application of the provisions of this ordinance to the land, building, or structure would result in practical difficulty or unnecessary hardship that would deprive the owner of the reasonable use of the land, building, or structure;

3. That the granting of the variance will be in harmony with the general purposes and intent of this ordinance, and will not be injurious to the neighborhood or otherwise detrimental to the public welfare.

E. *Conditions.* When allowing any appeal, or when granting any variance, the Board of Zoning Appeals may prescribe any conditions that it considers necessary or desirable.

Section 3. Enforcement. [Omitted. —Eds.]

C. SOME BASIC ZONING PROBLEMS

1. "Regulation" or "Taking"

ARVERNE BAY CONSTRUCTION CO. v. THATCHER

Court of Appeals of New York
287 N.Y. 222, 15 N.E.2d 587 (1938)

Appeal from a judgment, entered February 28, 1938, upon an order of the Appellate Division of the Supreme Court in the second judicial department reversing, on the law, a judgment in favor of plaintiff entered upon a decision of the court on trial at Special Term and directing a dismissal of the complaint.

LEHMAN, J. The plaintiff is the owner of a plot of vacant land on the northerly side of Linden boulevard in the borough of Brooklyn. Until 1928 the district in which the property is situated was classified as an "unrestricted" zone, under the Building Zone Resolution of the city of New York (New York Code of Ordinances, Appendix B). Then, by amendment of the ordinance and the "Use District Map," the district was placed in a residence zone. The plaintiff, claiming that its property could not be used properly or profitably for any purpose permitted in a residence zone and that, in consequence, the zoning ordinance imposed unnecessary hardship upon it, applied to the Board of Standards and Appeals, under section 21 of the Building Zone Resolution, for a variance which would permit the use of the premises for a gasoline service station. The application was denied, and, upon review in certiorari proceedings, the courts sustained the determination of the board. . . .

Defeated in its attempt to obtain permission to put its property to a profitable use, the plaintiff has brought this action to secure an adjudication that the restrictions placed upon the use of its property by the zoning ordinance result in deprivation of its property without due process of law and that, in so far as the ordinance affects its property, the ordinance violates the provisions of the Constitution of the United States and the Constitution of the State of New York. In this action it demands as a right what has been refused to it as a favor. The defendant challenges the right of the plaintiff to urge the invalidity of the zoning ordinance after denial of an application for a variance made under its provisions. At the outset, and before considering the merits of the plaintiff's cause of action, we must dispose of this challenge to the plaintiff's right to maintain this action.

The application for the favor of a variance is an appeal primarily to the discretion of the board, conferred upon it by the ordinance. It necessarily assumes the validity of the ordinance. A successful attack upon the validity of the ordinance destroys the foundation of any discretion conferred by the statute. To invoke the discretion of the board, an owner of property must show "unnecessary hardship." When that has been shown the board may grant "a special privilege" denied to others differently situated. (*People ex rel. Fordham M. R. Church v. Walsh,* 244 N.Y. 280, 155 N.E. 575.) Without such "special privilege," strict enforcement of a general rule restricting the use of all property within a district might work such hardship upon a particular owner that in effect it would deprive the owner of his property without compensation. The power to grant a variation might give such flexibility to the rule or its application that a property owner can, without violation of its terms, make reasonable use of his property. . . .

The rule established by that case is this: To sustain an attack upon the validity of the ordinance an aggrieved property owner must show that if the ordinance is enforced the consequent restrictions upon his property preclude its use for any purpose to which it is reasonably adapted. Thus it must appear either that the ordinance does not authorize a variation of the general rule which would admit of such use or that such variation has been refused by the administrative board in the exercise of a discretion which the ordinance confers upon it. Only two possible questions can be presented for decision upon an application for a variation: First, does the ordinance confer upon the administrative board power to grant the variation which is asked; second, if the board has power to grant it, does the exercise of a wise discretion call for the use of the power in the particular case? The issue whether without such variation the strict enforcement of the general rule would work such hardship as to constitute the taking of property without due process of law is not directly presented upon an application for a variation, and it follows that the denial of the application cannot be a binding adjudication that, without such variation, enforcement of the general rule will not deprive the applicant of his property without due process of law. True, where the board in the exercise of its discretion denies an application for a variation which it has power to grant, argument may be made that a refusal to exercise such discretion can, logically, be based only upon a finding that even without such variation there is no unnecessary hardship, and that the enforcement of the general rule would not deprive the owner of his property or preclude a reasonable use of the property. Then the same considerations which induced the board to deny the application might constrain the court to decide that the statute is valid. None the less, the questions presented would not be identical and the denial of the application for a variance would not be a conclusive adjudication of the validity of the statute; and that would be true even though the courts had, upon review by certiorari, sustained the determination of the board. We proceed, then, to a consideration of the merits of the plaintiff's claim, and in our discussion it will appear that in this case the denial of the application for a variation may have been based upon considerations which cannot affect the judgment of the court in passing upon the validity of the ordinance in so far as it applies to the plaintiff's property.

The amendment to the zoning ordinance, about which complaint is made, changed from an unrestricted zone to a residential district the property abutting on Linden boulevard for a distance of four miles, with the exception of a small section at a railroad crossing. The district is almost undeveloped. There had been no building construction in that area for many years prior to the amendment. The chairman of the building zone commission which drafted the zoning ordinance, testifying as an expert witness for the defendant, described the district as in a "transition state from the farms as I knew them thirty and forty years ago south of this location." There are some old buildings used for non-conforming purposes, left from the days when the district was used for farming. There are only three buildings on Linden boulevard in a distance of about a mile. One of these buildings is a cow stable and a second building is used as an office in connection with a dairy business conducted there. A gasoline station erected on that boulevard would, it is plain, not adversely affect the health, morals, safety or general welfare of the people who now live in that neighborhood. Justification, if any, for the ordinance restricting the use of the property on Linden boulevard to residential purposes must be found in the control over future development which will result from such restrictions.

Without zoning restrictions, the self-interest of the individual property owners will almost inevitably dictate the form of the development of the district. The plaintiff claims, and has conclusively shown at the trial, that at no time since the amendment of the zoning resolution could its property be profitably used for residential purposes. The expert witness for the city, to whose testimony we have already referred and whose qualifications are universally recognized, admits that such a residential improvement would, even now after the lapse of ten years, be "premature." The property, then, must for the present remain unimproved and unproductive, a source of expense to the owner, or must be put to some non-conforming use. In a district otherwise well adapted for residences a gasoline station or other non-conforming use of property may render neighboring property less desirable for use as a private residence. The development of a district for residential purposes might best serve the interests of the city as a whole and, in the end, might perhaps prove the most profitable use of the property within such district. A majority of the property owners might conceivably be content to bear the burden of taxes and other carrying charges upon unimproved land in order to reap profit in the future from the development of the land for residential purposes. They could not safely do so without reasonable assurance that the district will remain adapted for residence use and will not be spoilt for such purpose by the intrusion of structures used for less desirable purposes. The zoning ordinance is calculated to provide such assurance to property owners in the district and to constrain the property owners to develop their land in a manner which in the future will prove of benefit to the city. Such considerations have induced the Appellate Division to hold that the ordinance is valid.

There is little room for disagreement with the general rules and tests set forth in the opinion of the Appellate Division. The difficulty arises in the application of such rules and tests to the particular facts in this case. We are not disposed to define the police power of the State so narrowly that it would exclude reasonable restrictions placed upon the use of property in order to aid the development of new districts in accordance with plans calculated to advance the public welfare of the city in the future. We have said that "the need for vision of the future in the governance of cities has not lessened with the years. The dweller within the gates, even more than the stranger from afar, will pay the price of blindness." (*Hesse v. Rath,* 249 N.Y. 436, 438, 164 N.E. 342.) We have, indeed, recognized that long-time planning for zoning purposes may be a valid exercise of the police power, but at the same time we have pointed out that the power is not unlimited. "We are not required to say that a merely temporary restraint of beneficial enjoyment is unlawful where the interference is necessary to promote the ultimate good either of the municipality as a whole or of the immediate neighborhood. Such problems will have to be solved when they arise. If we assume that the restraint may be permitted, the interference must be not unreasonable, but on the contrary must be kept within the limits of necessity." (*People ex rel. St. Albans-Springfield Corp. v. Connell,* 257 N.Y. 73, 83, 177 N.E. 313, 316.) The problem presented upon this appeal is whether or not the zoning ordinance as applied to the plaintiff's property is unreasonable.

Findings of the trial judge, sustained by evidence presented by the plaintiff, establish that, in the vicinity of the plaintiff's premises, the city operates an incinerator which "gives off offensive fumes and odors which permeate plantiff's premises." About 1,200 or 1,500 feet from the plaintiff's land, "a trunk sewer carrying both storm and sanitary sewage empties into an open creek . . . . The said creek runs to the south of plaintiff's premises and gives off nauseating odors which permeate the said property." The trial judge further found that other conditions exist which, it is plain, render the property entirely unfit, at present, for any conforming use. Though the defendant urges that the conditions are not as bad as the plaintiff's witnesses have pictured, yet as the Appellate Division has said: "It must be conceded, upon the undisputed facts in this case, that this property cannot, presently or in the immediate future, be profitably used for residential purposes." (253 App.Div. 285, 286, 2 N.Y.S.2d 112, 114.)

We may assume that the zoning ordinance is the product of farsighted planning calculated to promote the general welfare of the city at some future time. If the State or the city, acting by delegation from the State, had plenary power to pass laws calculated to promote the general welfare, then the validity of the ordinance might be sustained; for "we have nothing to do with the question of the wisdom or good policy of municipal ordinances." (*Village of Euclid v. Ambler Realty Co.,* 272 U.S. 365, 393, 47 S.Ct. 114, 120, 71 L.Ed. 303, 54 A.L.R. 1016.) The legislative power of the State is, however, not plenary, but is limited by the Constitution of the United States and by the Constitution of the State. It may not take private property without compensation even for a public purpose and to advance the general welfare. . . . "The protection of private property in the fifth amendment presupposes that it is wanted for public use, but provides that it shall not be taken for such use without compensation. A similar assumption is made in the decisions upon the fourteenth amendment. . . . When this seemingly absolute protection is found to be qualified by the police power, the natural tendency of human nature is to extend the qualification more and more until at last private property disappears. But that cannot be accomplished in this way under the constitution of the United States." (*Pennsylvania Coal Co. v. Mahon,* 260 U.S. 393, 415, 43 S.Ct. 158, 160, 67 L.Ed. 322, 28 A.L.R. 1321.)

In the prevailing opinion in that case, Mr. Justice Holmes pointed out that "the general rule at least is, that while property may be regulated to a certain extent, if regulation goes too far it will be recognized as a taking" (p. 415, 43 S.Ct. page 160). Whether a regulation does go too far is "a question of degree — and therefore cannot be disposed of by general propositions," and here Mr. Justice Holmes gave warning that "we are in danger of forgetting that a strong public desire to improve the public condition is not enough to warrant achieving the desire by a shorter cut than the constitutional way of paying for the change" (p. 416, 43 S.Ct. page 160). The dissent of Mr. Justice Brandeis in that case is not based upon difference of opinion in regard to general principles, but upon different evaluation of the degree of the restrictions there challenged.

The warning of Mr. Justice Holmes should perhaps be directed rather to Legislatures than to courts; for the courts have not hesitated to declare statutes invalid wherever regulation has gone so far that it is clearly unreasonable and must be "recognized as taking;" and unless regulation does clearly go so far the courts may not deny force to the regulation. We have already pointed out that in the case which we are reviewing, the plaintiff's land cannot at present or in the immediate future be profitably or reasonably used without violation of the restriction. An ordinance which *permanently* so restricts the use of property that it cannot be used for any reasonable purpose goes, it is plain, beyond regulation, and must be recognized as a taking of the property. The only substantial difference, in such case, between restriction and actual taking, is that the restriction leaves the owner subject to the burden of payment of taxation, while outright confiscation would relieve him of that burden.

The situation, of course, might be quite different where it appears that within a reasonable time the property can be put to a profitable use. The temporary inconvenience or even hardship of holding unproductive property might then be compensated by ultimate benefit to the owner or, perhaps, even without such compensation, the individual owners might be compelled to bear a temporary burden in order to promote the public good. We do not pass upon such problems now, for here no inference is permissible that within a reasonable time the property can be put to a profitable use or that the present inconvenience or hardship imposed upon the plaintiff is temporary. True, there is evidence that the neighborhood is improving and that some or all of the conditions which now render the district entirely unsuitable for residence purposes will in time be removed. Even so, it is conceded that prognostication that the district will in time become suited for residences rests upon hope and not upon certainty and no estimate can be made of the time which must elapse before the hope becomes fact.

During the nine years from 1928 to 1936, when concededly the property was unsuitable for any conforming use, the property was assessed at $18,000, and taxes amounting to $4,566 were levied upon it, in addition to assessments of several thousand dollars; yet, so far as appears, the district was no better suited for residence purposes at the time of the trial in 1936 than it was when the zoning ordinance was amended in 1928. In such case the ordinance is clearly more than a temporary and reasonable restriction placed upon the land to promote the general welfare. It is in substance a taking of the land prohibited by the Constitution of the United States and by the Constitution of the State.

We repeat here what under similar circumstances the court said in *People ex rel. St. Albans-Springfield Corp. v. Connell* (supra, p. 83, 177 N.E. page 316): "we are not required to say that a merely temporary restraint of beneficial enjoyment is unlawful where the interference is necessary to promote the ultimate good, either of the municipality as a whole or of the immediate neighborhood." There the court held that the "ultimate good" could be attained and a "productive use" allowed by a variation of the zoning ordinance that "will be temporary and provisional and readily terminable." Here the application of the plaintiff for any variation was properly refused, for the conditions which render the plaintiff's property unsuitable for residential use are general and not confined to plaintiff's property. In such case, we have held that the general hardship should be remedied by revision of the general regulation, not by granting the special privilege of a variation to single owners. . . . Perhaps a new ordinance might be evolved by which the "ultimate good" may be attained without depriving owners of the productive use of their property. That is a problem for the legislative authority, not for the courts. Now we hold only that the present regulation *as applied to plaintiff's property* is not valid.

The judgment of the Appellate Division should be reversed and that of the Special Term affirmed, with costs in this court and in the Appellate Division.

Judgment accordingly.

Comments: 1. In the earlier proceeding to obtain a variance to permit construction of a gasoline service station on the property involved in the principal case, the Court of Appeals affirmed (without opinion) the Appellate Division's holding "that the unfavorable conditions to which the referee referred were not peculiar to the site in question but affected a wide area; that under these circumstances there was no showing of unnecessary hardship or practical difficulty applicable peculiarly to this site, and that relief, if any, should be achieved through appeal to the legislative authority which created the zone." (3 N.E.2d 457, 458 (N.Y. 1936).) Since it must have been obvious to the plaintiff that "the unfavorable conditions . . . were not peculiar to the site in question but affected a wide area," why do you suppose he sought a variance? It is not clear just when the plaintiff filed his application for a variance, but it must have been in 1934 or 1935. The rule that a variance cannot be properly granted "upon proof and finding of hardship due to general conditions existing in the neighborhood" was established by *In re Levy v. Board of Standards & Appeals,* 196 N.E. 284 (1935) (cited in the principal case).

2. Did the decision of the Court of Appeals in the principal case assure that plaintiff would be able to construct a gasoline service station on its property? Clearly it did not, since New York follows the prevailing rule that, even though the court finds a zoning regulation to be invalid, it will not order a change in the zoning ordinance to permit the land use desired by the landowner. The rule is based on the concept that amendment of the zoning ordinance is a "legislative" act, and that the courts should not engage in "legislative" action. Thus, in the principal case, the governing body could rezone the plaintiff's land in any way it wished, so long as nonresidential uses were permitted, without necessarily authorizing use of the land for a gasoline service station. The unwillingness of courts to order a zoning ordinance amendment that will permit the landowner to utilize his land as he desires, after the court has held the existing zoning invalid, obviously makes it possible for the local governing body, in many cases, to rezone the land to a slightly different classification that is equally frustrating to the landowner.

A few courts do not follow this rule, and find some way of giving the property owner affirmative relief when a suit challenging the constitutionality of a zoning ordinance is successful. For a discussion see Note, Beyond Invalidation: The Judicial Power to Zone, 9 Urb. L. Ann. 159 (1975).

3. Since the Court of Appeals in the principal case considered that "the unfavorable conditions . . . were not peculiar to the site in question but affected a wide area," so that it would have been improper to grant the plaintiff a variance, does it follow that the court's holding that the residential zoning was invalid is applicable to the entire "wide area"? Can other landowners in that "wide area" claim the benefit of the decision when they apply for building permits to construct nonresidential structures within the "wide area"? If the governing body wishes to preserve the existing residential zoning in the area as long as possible, may it simply rezone the Arverne Bay Construction Company's land and force other landowners in the area to bring their own actions challenging the residential zoning classification? Could the other landowners bring a class action for this purpose? If so, how should the composition of the class be determined?

4. If the New York City governing body had wished to preserve the area involved in the principal case for future residential development, what could it have done to avoid having the restriction to residential use held invalid? Would an abatement of all property taxes until residential development became feasible have been sufficient? Could the city have purchased an "easement against commercial and industrial development" from the owners of the property in the area? Or should the city have sought to eliminate the "nuisance" conditions that made the area unattractive for residential development?

5. In the principal case the court said "[t]he situation . . . might be quite different where it appears that within a reasonable time the property can be put to profitable use." What do you think the court would have done if the record had contained proof that the conditions complained of by the plaintiff would be eliminated within a year or two and that residential development would then be feasible? That this in fact is what occurred is indicated by a report of the New York City Board of Standards and Appeals, No. 740-38-BZ (Feb. 11, 1939), from which the following excerpt is drawn:

> The applicant in this present application, two blocks away to the east on the same side of Linden boulevard claims that his hardship consists of the same nuisance conditions which persuaded the Court of Appeals in their decision on the question of constitutionality [in *Arverne Bay Constr. Co. v. Thatcher* — Eds.]. He mentions the incinerator and garbage disposal plant, the trunk and open sewer, the dumping ground for depositing and burning garbage, the cow shed, as among the nuisances still existing. That he is incorrect in these statements is evident from the testimony of nearby owners at the hearing and from the exhaustive inspection made by the Committee of the Board of the extensive area between Linden boulevard and Jamaica Bay and from reports requested by the Board from the Borough President of Brooklyn, the Department of Public Works, the Department of Parks, and the Department of Sanitation. By these reports, confirming the inspection by a Committee of the Board, it is shown that the main nuisances referred to have been entirely abated by the construction and extension of a large sewer for 2500 feet southerly and the filling in and grading by a W.P.A. project of vacant plots formerly used for dumping and burning garbage, by chlorination, and by discontinuance of the incinerator formerly used by the Sanitation department. . . . The Committee found no non-conforming uses existing in the area of notification, other than the gasoline station on the northerly side of Linden boulevard diagonally opposite and the pocket book factory at 818 Pennsylvania avenue. . . . While the immediate area adjacent to the plot under appeal and to the south of Linden boulevard is not

greatly developed, west thereof and across Linden boulevard [it] is largely developed. . . . Pennsylvania avenue southerly from Linden boulevard is a wide paved avenue to Fairfield avenue, which is an extension of Flatlands avenue and is used largely as a short cut for traffic from South Brooklyn. When the Circumferential Highway is completed, the entire area between it and Linden boulevard should be immediately available for development.

In view of the holding on the variance issue in the principal case, why would another property owner in the same general area apply for a variance in late 1938 or early 1939?

CONSOLIDATED ROCK PRODUCTS CO. v. CITY OF LOS ANGELES

Supreme Court of California
57 Cal.2d 515, 370 P.2d 342, *appeal dismissed,* 371 U.S. 36 (1962)

DOOLING, Justice. This is an appeal from a judgment for defendant in an action seeking declaratory relief and to enjoin defendant from enforcing a zoning restriction alleged to be unconstitutional insofar as it applies to prevent rock and gravel operations on plaintiffs' property.

Plaintiff Valley Real Estate Company is the owner and Consolidated Rock Products Company is the lessee of 348 acres of land situated in the watercourse known as the Tujunga Wash, and lying northeasterly (upstream) of Hansen Dam in the San Fernando Valley. This property — about two miles long and one-quarter mile wide — runs in a generally east-west direction and is divided approximately in the center by Foothill Boulevard, a north-south roadway at that point. The property forms substantially the apex of the Tujunga Cone, the second largest alluvial cone of rock, sand and gravel in Los Angeles County. The Tujunga Wash from the eastern to the western termini of the subject property is bordered on the north by the base of the mountains and on the south by bluffs of low hills except for relatively narrow plateaus on either side above the level of the land. The property is composed of rock, sand and gravel to a depth of about 40 feet. It is isolated from land presently being used for other purposes and is situated in a natural amphitheater surrounded by the rugged terrain of the Angeles National Forest on the north, by Tujunga Canyon on the east, by Hansen Dam and its debris basin on the west, and by high hills and cliffs on the south.

Except for the Livingston Rock and Gravel Plant on 125 acres contiguous to the westerly portion of plaintiffs' property — an operation conducted since 1931, now substantially depleted in the course of some 30 years' activity, and with but a doubtful number of remaining years left for economic extraction — rock and gravel operations in the Tujunga Wash have been confined to the area *downstream* from Hansen Dam. Since 1946 defendant City of Los Angeles has not created any new rock and gravel districts *upstream* from Hansen Dam but has specifically denied applications for such designated districts upon premises immediately adjacent to plaintiffs' property.

The twin residential communities of Sunland and Tujunga adjoin plaintiffs' property, with their mainly developed portions lying east and southeast thereof. In recent years the trend of development in these communities has been in a westerly direction toward plaintiffs' property and along and upon the bluffs north and south thereof.

Plaintiffs' property — 348 acres — is zoned for agricultural and residential use; and rock, sand and gravel operations are prohibited thereon. During the trial, the trial judge pursuant to stipulation of counsel made an extensive tour of plaintiffs' property and the surrounding area.

The trial court found that the subject property has great value if used for rock, sand and gravel excavation but "no appreciable economic value" for any other purpose, and in view of the "continuing flood hazard and the nature of the soil," any suggestion that the property has economic value for any other use, including those uses for which it was zoned, "is preposterous." With respect to the effect that rock and gravel excavating operations would have on nearby residential communities, the trial court found that the "creation of dust for air-borne convection" could be "reduced to a point of pollution below an acceptable standard," that the "inevitable" noise could be controlled to the point where it would be "minimal," that there would be no extraordinary danger to children; and in summation, that the "business of excavating . . . rock, sand and gravel and activities incidental and related thereto can be conducted on the plaintiffs' said property with compatibility to adjacent properties and with minimal detriment to the living amenities of health conditions of the inhabitants of adjacent properties or in the general area and without probable depreciation in property values to the adjacent properties."

While expressing these views on vital matters affecting the "public health" of the adjacent communities, the trial court further found that they "are all factors which, in their totality, the legislative body [the Los Angeles City Council] may properly consider and act upon" and that "reasonable minds might differ and have differed upon these" factors.[7]

The trial court also found that "the Sunland-Tujunga area . . . has a national reputation as a haven for sufferers from respiratory

---

[7] The Planning Commission approved with certain recommended conditions plaintiffs' application for designation of their property as a "Rock and Gravel District"; the City Council ultimately denied such application.

ailments and is inhabited by many such sufferers and that a considerable portion of its economy is based upon such reputation"; that "the possible advent of a substantial rock, sand and gravel extraction and processing operation upon the subject property has caused considerable apprehension to the residents and the communities of Sunland and Tujunga of air pollution, traffic and other dangers and annoyances as a result thereof"; and that "a rock and gravel operation upon the subject property could adversely affect the reputation of the Sunland-Tujunga area as a haven for sufferers from respiratory ailments."

There was substantial evidence that even though operated with all possible safeguards, the extraction of sand and gravel from the subject property would still create appreciable quantities of dust, which would be carried by the prevailing winds to the residences and sanitariums of Sunland and Tujunga; that this dust would have a damaging effect upon the sufferers from respiratory ailments; and also that such operations would adversely affect property values in those communities. The trial court concluded that plaintiffs' property was "not arbitrarily, capriciously or unreasonably zoned" under the ordinances prohibiting rock and gravel operations thereon; and that such zoning was "not discriminatory" nor did it offend constitutional guarantees protecting plaintiffs' property rights. (U.S. Const., 5th and 14th Amends; Cal. Const., art. I, §§ 1, 13 and 14.) Accordingly, judgment was entered for defendant.

Plaintiffs argue that the zoning restriction in its application to their property is unconstitutional and void as being: (a) a denial of due process; (b) a denial of equal protection of the laws; (c) a taking of private property for public use without compensation; and (d) discriminatory in operation. They claim that the record clearly shows that their property is so-called "one use property," having economic value only for the excavation of rock, sand and gravel; and that under the guise of enforcing police regulations, defendant is guilty of "an unwarranted and arbitrary interference with" their constitutional right "to carry on a lawful business" so as to render their property valueless.

The trial judge in his findings and conclusions of law which he drew therefrom showed a clear recognition of the respective functions of the legislative body in enacting a comprehensive zoning ordinance and of the courts in passing upon the constitutionality of such legislation. . . .

It was in clear recognition of this principle of the division of functions between the legislative and judicial branches that the trial judge in effect concluded that although his own determination, if the questions presented had been his to decide, would have been to the contrary, since under the evidence presented to the legislative body and to the court reasonable minds could differ, he must bow to the legislative conclusion. Plaintiffs do not question the correctness of this rule as a general guide to be followed in determining the constitutionality of zoning ordinances, but they make the narrower contention that where property is primarily or preponderantly valuable for the extraction therefrom of a natural resource, here the valuable sand and gravel deposits in their land, the legislative authorities may not constitutionally prohibit it altogether, although they admit that they may otherwise regulate the extraction and recovery of such natural resources. In support of this position plaintiffs primarily rely upon five California cases and one case from the Supreme Court of the United States: *In re Kelso* (1905), 147 Cal. 609, 82 P. 241, 2 L.R.A., N.S., 796; *In re Throop* (1915), 169 Cal. 93, 145 P. 1029; *People v. Hawley* (1929), 207 Cal. 395, 279 P. 136; *Wheeler v. Gregg* (1949), 90 Cal. App.2d 348, 203 P.2d 37; *Morton v. Superior Court* (1954), 124 Cal.App.2d 577, 269 P.2d 81, 47 A.L.R.2d 478; *Pennsylvania Coal Company v. Mahon* (1922), 260 U.S. 393, 43 S.Ct. 158, 67 L.Ed. 322.

We must admit that there is language in these cases, which pressed to its ultimate conclusion, and divorced from the facts of each particular case in which it was used, lends color to plaintiffs' position. Typical is the statement in the earliest of them, *Kelso,* 147 Cal. at page 612, 82 P. at page 242: "It [the ordinance under attack] is in no sense a mere regulation as to the manner in which rock or stone may be removed from the land by the owner thereof, but is an absolute prohibition of any such removal. However valuable the rock or stone may be if removed, and however valueless if not removed, the owner must allow it to remain in its place of deposit. Such a prohibition might be justified, if the removal could not be effected without improperly invading the rights of others, but it cannot be doubted that rock and stone may, under some circumstances, be so severed from the land and removed as not in the slightest degree to inflict any injury which the law will recognize. So far as such use of one's property may be had without injury to others it is lawful use, which cannot be absolutely prohibited by the legislative department under the guise of the exercise of the police power."

Of this case and *Throop,* supra, 169 Cal. 93, 145 P. 1029, it is to be noted that both were decided long before the principle of comprehensive zoning had been enacted into legislation anywhere in the United States; and hence long before the precise constitutional theories upon which such legislation was later sustained had been anywhere formulated. The primary purpose of comprehensive zoning is to protect others, and the general public, from uses of property which will, if permitted, prove injurious to them. Thus in saying in *Kelso:* "So far as such use of one's property may be had *without injury to others,* it is a lawful use, which cannot be absolutely prohibited," (emphasis added) this court, somewhat prophetically, left open the very question with which we are here concerned, because the legislative body in our case has determined that the prohibited use cannot be had without injury to others and the trial court has found that that is a question upon which reasonable minds may differ, and for that reason is concluded by the legislative determination. . . .

Too many cases have been decided upholding the constitutionality of comprehensive zoning ordinances prohibiting the removal of natural products from lands in certain zones for us now to accept at full value the suggestion that there is such an inherent difference in natural products of the property that in a case where reasonable minds may differ as to the necessity of such prohibition the same power to prohibit the extraction of natural products does not inhere in the legislative body as it has to prohibit uses of other sorts.

. . . .

[The court here cited cases upholding zoning ordinances which prohibited extraction of oil and gas, gravel, sand, brick clay, and topsoil. — Eds.]

Plaintiffs rely heavily upon the finding of the trial court "that the subject property has no appreciable economic value for any of the uses permitted in the A1, A2 or RA zones, or for any other use except for the purpose of excavating, crushing and processing rock, sand and gravel and activities related or incidental thereto, and if such use is prohibited, it will destroy the economic value thereof." There was testimony before the legislative body that the property could be successfully devoted to certain other uses, i.e., for stabling horses, cattle feeding and grazing, chicken raising, dog kennels, fish hatcheries, golf courses, certain types of horticulture, and recreation. It must be conceded that in relation to its value for the extraction of rock, sand and gravel the value of the property for any of the described uses is relatively small if not minimal, and that as to a considerable part of its seasonal flooding might prevent its continuous use for any purpose. "However, the very essence of the police power as differentiated from the power of eminent domain is that the deprivation of individual rights and property cannot prevent its operation, once it is shown that its exercise is proper and that the method of its exercise is reasonably within the meaning of due process of law. . . . And it is recognized that oil production is a business which must operate, if at all, where the resources are found. Nevertheless city zoning ordinances prohibiting the production of oil in designated areas have been held valid." (*Beverly Oil Co. v. City of Los Angeles,* supra, 40 Cal.2d 552, 557-558, 254 P.2d 865, 867.)

In *Beverly* at page 557, 254 P.2d at page 867 this court quoted from *Hadacheck v. Sebastian,* 239 U.S. 394, 410, 36 S. Ct. 143, 60 L.Ed. 348: "It is to be remembered that we are dealing with one of the most essential powers of the government, — one that is the least limitable. It may, indeed, seem harsh in its exercise, usually is on some individual but the imperative necessity for its existence precludes any limitation upon it when not exerted arbitrarily. A vested interest cannot be asserted against it because of conditions once obtaining. [Citation.] To so hold would preclude development and fix a city forever in its primitive conditions. There must be progress, and if in its march private interests are in the way, they must yield to the good of the community." . . .

Finally on this point we quote from the *West Bros. Brick Co.* case, . . . [*West Bros. Brick Co. v. City of Alexandria,* 192 S.E. 881, 890 (Va. 1937)]: "The enactment of zoning ordinances and cases which test them are all within the recollection of most of us. General rules applicable thereto are now well settled. They must not be wholly unreasonable, but they are presumed to be valid and to have been promulgated by those familiar with local conditions. Vested interests will not defeat them, and of course constitutional rights are not to be measured in terms of money. That, however, is a consideration to be remembered. Great financial losses should not be inflicted where benefits to others are negligible, but public welfare and public convenience do control and are in themselves terms constantly adjusted to meet new conditions. Upon those who would set aside such ordinances rests a heavy burden of proof. They stand when their validity is debatable."

It is our conclusion that, having found on substantial evidence that the necessity and propriety of the legislative action in this case is one upon which reasonable minds may differ, the trial court properly found in favor of the ordinance's constitutionality.

Plaintiffs also contend that the challenged zoning law discriminates against their property in that Livingston Rock and Gravel Company conducts operations on some 125 acres contiguous to plaintiffs' property. The Livingston property adjoins plaintiffs' property west of Foothill Boulevard. About half of plaintiffs' property lies east of Foothill Boulevard and it has developed differently from the property west of the boulevard. The original permit for the Livingston rock and gravel operations was issued in 1931; the property having been worked some thirty years, is substantially depleted and its number of remaining years of economic operation is doubtful. The Livingston property, 125 acres, is considerably smaller than plaintiffs' property, 348 acres; it is not in the center of Tujunga Wash but in a side pocket formed by the hills; and according to expert evidence, its dust was less subject to being stirred and carried by the winds in the Tujunga Wash. As heretofore stated, the trial judge pursuant to stipulation of counsel made an extensive tour of inspection of plaintiffs' property and the surrounding area, which observations became evidence in the case in support of the findings. . . . Appropriate here for consideration is the extensive memorandum opinion filed by the trial judge and included in the record . . . , wherein the comment is made that upon "viewing the Livingston parcel and the subject property, each in its entirety, reasonable minds can differ on the question of whether authority granted to operate one for the extraction of rock, sand and gravel and to deny the same operation to the other is arbitrary and discriminatory." In concluding that it could not "find a discriminatory application" of the zoning law to plaintiffs' property, the trial court noted that there were "substantial differences in the terrain and degree of development of the land south of and adjacent to the subject property east of Foothill Boulevard than west thereof. Viewing as we must the character of the property of the objecting parties, the nature of the surrounding terrain, the use to which each has been put, recent trends of development, . . . we cannot fail to observe but that the differences between the plaintiffs' entire parcel and the Livingston property are 'fairly debatable', . . . and when comparability is debatable we may not substitute our judgment for that of the legislative body." As was stated in *Miller v. Board of Public Works*, . . . [234 P. 381, 388 (Cal. 1925)]: "Somewhere the line of demarcation must be drawn, and it is primarily the province of the municipal body to which the zoning function is committed to draw that line of demarcation, and it is neither the province nor the duty of courts to interfere with the discretion with which such bodies are invested in the absence of a clear showing of an abuse of that discretion."

We are satisfied that the zoning law is consistent with the obvious legislative policy in municipal planning and development of this area in furtherance of the best interests and general welare of the community as a whole: To confine rock and gravel operations in the Tujunga Wash to the area *downstream* from the Hansen Dam, and to encourage and protect the welfare and growth of the residential communities of Sunland and Tujunga by preventing the extension of rock and gravel operations upstream from the dam, meanwhile letting the already existing but substantially depleted Livingston operation gradually work itself into oblivion. . . .

The judgment is affirmed.

GIBSON, C. J., and TRAYNOR, PETERS and WHITE, JJ., concur.

McCOMB, Justice.

I dissent. I would reverse the judgment for the reasons expressed by Mr. Presiding Justice Fox in the opinion prepared by him for the District Court of Appeal in *Consolidated Rock Products Co. v. City of Los Angeles,* 195 A.C.A. 114, 15 Cal.Rptr. 775.

SCHAUER, J., concurs.

Rehearing denied; SCHAUER and McCOMB, JJ., dissenting.

Comments: 1. Do you think the decision and the stated rationale of the principal case are consistent with the *Mahon* and the *Arverne Bay* cases, *supra?* What is the significance of the United States Supreme Court's dismissal of the appeal in the *Consolidated Rock Prods. Co.* case "for want of a substantial federal question"? (*See* 371 U.S. 36 (1962).) Does this mean that a majority of the Court believes there is no "deprivation of property without due process of law" even though a zoning ordinance completely destroys the economic value of land, provided "reasonable minds might differ" as to the necessity for the zoning restrictions in order to protect public health, safety, or general welfare? Or did the Court simply view the principal case as a "rerun" of *Hadacheck,* where the prohibited land use was in substance declared by the local legislative body to be "a nuisance in fact and in law"? Is it significant that in *Hadacheck* the extraction of valuable clay from the land was not prohibited, while in the principal case the extraction of rock and gravel was prohibited?

2. In *West Bros. Brick Co. v. City of Alexandria,* 192 S.E. 881 (Va. 1937), *appeal dismissed,* 302 U.S. 658 (1937), the court sustained a zoning ordinance classifying practically all of plaintiff's land as "residential," thus precluding any use of the bed of clay located thereon, which was from eight to fourteen feet deep and suitable for use in plaintiff's brick and tile business. The land in controversy was an undeveloped eighteen-acre tract nine blocks from the business section of the city. Several years before the enactment of the zoning ordinance, plaintiff purchased this tract to provide a reserve supply of clay for use in its business. The zoning ordinance was based upon a "comprehensive zoning plan" prepared by the city planner for the Maryland-National Capitol Park & Planning Commission in conjunction with the Alexandria Zoning Commission. All the land between plaintiff's tract and the business section was zoned "residential." There was conflicting testimony as to whether. plaintiff's land was better suited to residential or industrial use.

ELDRIDGE v. CITY OF PALO ALTO

California Court of Appeal
57 Cal. App. 3d 613, 129 Cal. Rptr. 575 (1976)

Elkington, Associate Justice.

These appeals, with similar subject matter and issues, have been consolidated for the purpose of our consideration and disposition of them.

Plaintiffs Eldridge and Beyer were the owners, respectively, of 750 acres and 22.27 acres of generally unimproved land in the foothills of the City of Palo Alto (hereafter the "City"). The City had enacted zoning ordinances which, among other things, classified their property as "permanent open space and conservation lands."

[Until 1959 the City lay entirely upon a flat alluvial plain in northern Santa Clara County. It was then almost fully developed, with nearly 14,000 residence untis occupying 2,483 acres. During that year about 6,000 acres of privately owned and virtually undeveloped foothills to the west were annexed by the City. The foothills which included plaintiffs' land, among other permitted uses, were promptly zoned for single-family residential use on minimum *1-acre* sites.

During the year 1969 the City commenced land-use studies of its foothills. Two years later it "adopted an amendment to its General Plan re-classifying over 90% of the undeveloped foothills" (over 5,900 acres, including plaintiffs' land) to "Open Space and/or Conservation and Park" uses. Thereafter by successive ordinances plaintiffs' land was rezoned to "O-S (Open Space)."

Thereafter a "Staff Report On Regulation To Preserve Foothills Open Space" was prepared by the City's Director of Planning and Community Development. Among other things, it recited:

"[T]he City Council directed the staff to pursue all available means toward achieving the open space objective in the Foothills including the exploration of methods and resources available for acquisition. This was followed by the amendment to the Palo Alto General Plan designating uses for the Foothills as open space, conservation, and/or parks which formally established the City's policy in this respect. Subsequently, the Planning Commission requested the staff to pursue ways to achieve the open space objective other than by acquisition."

"There have been various studies and lengthy deliberations by the Planning Commission and City Council focused on the Foothills during the last few years. These studies and deliberations resulted in the amendment to the General Plan to designate the Foothills for Open Space, Conservation and/or Park uses, and in the recent adoption of the Open Space Element. In consideration of the newly recognized crisis of constantly diminishing open space, implementation of the adopted policies is in order. Zoning controls to protect and preserve natural resources (including protecting against hazards), agricultural resources, recreation areas, scenic areas, watershed lands, and wildlife areas, and, particularly when situated close-in or near urbanized concentrations, are not only desirable but also necessary."

Three alternative methods for achieving the City's "open space, conservation and/or parks" goal for the foothills were submitted by the "Staff Report."

"Alternative 3" follows in substantial part:

"3. *Adopt a new zoning ordinance regulation (and apply it to the Foothills) . . . but recognizing open space as a land use of a stature equal to all other categories. Such an ordinance would be significantly more restrictive in respect to parcel size and the amount of building coverage permitted [by an alternative plan]. An additional regulation would put a limit [of 3.5%] on the total permitted impervious area. . . .''* (Emphasis in original.)

"Alternative 3 is innovative in that it goes beyond the traditional large lot zoning concept and recognizes open space as a valuable resource worthy of preservation for not only the present but also future generations. It allows a reasonable use of the land consistent with the open space goal in the Foothills at a 10 acre minimum lot size. Since the development controls and site and design review would prescribe how and where the impervious areas (those areas covered by buildings, terraces, pools, roads, etc., which will not absorb rainwater) shall be placed; how the roads, structures, and other improvements shall harmonize with the existing natural landscape, and to what extent the natural landscape shall be altered by exotic landscape materials as well as the buildings and roads, therefore, the essence of the natural state of the open space will be retained. A paths and trails system will be planned which will allow public access through the Foothills lands.''

"One important consideration that cannot be overlooked in any zoning proposal is the effect on the property owner. It is most important that he be allowed a reasonable use of his land. The long established 1-acre (R-E) and 5-acre (A-C) zones appear to meet this criteria without any question. At 10, 20, or 40 acres the restriction on the property owner increases. In respect to the value of the property, we can reasonably [expect] that large acreage mountain homes would have a definite market, particularly when located 'close-in' to the metropolitan area. In this respect, we have existing examples in the Los Altos Hills, Portola Valley, and Woodside areas.

"Considering the various environmental, ecological, aesthetic, and legal factors involved, Alternative 3 with a minimum parcel size of 10 acres is recommended as a reasonable balance between achieving the open space objectives on the one hand and allowing a reasonable (although more restricted) use of property on the other hand. It is suggested that the resultant ordinance be designated O-S, Open Space. . . .''

The recommended "Alternative 3" was approved and adopted by the City. The ensuing ordinances were designated, as suggested, "O-S, Open Space."

We need not set forth in full the lengthy and involved zoning ordinances of the City here under consideration. It is sufficient to say that they follow and implement the above-described plans and other activities and decisions of the City and its agencies and employees. We think it proper however to point out a few of their highlights.

The open-space land of the ordinances is the City's foothill land (including that of plaintiffs), which is "essentially unimproved or in its natural state," and which is designated for an "open space use."

The ordinances' purpose, among other things, is to "protect and preserve [such] open space land" and to "carry out federal, state, regional, county, and city open space plans." The "open space use" of the ordinances, among other things, "means the use of land for (1) Public recreation." Among the state's "open space plans," carried out by the ordinances, is the use of such land for "outdoor recreation" and "park and recreation purposes." (See Gov.Code, §§ 65560, 65561.)] [8]

Plaintiff Beyer thereafter commenced an action against the City and its council and council members. The complaint alleged, *inter alia*, that the effect of the ordinances was to arbitrarily, unreasonably, and by means of excess regulation and in contravention of the state Constitution (art. I, former § 14) and federal Constitution (5th and 14th Amends.), take and damage his property for public use without compensating him therefor. He prayed for damages in inverse condemnation or, in the alternative, that the ordinances be declared "illegal, unconstitutional and void as applied to [his] property."

Plaintiff Eldridge also filed a complaint with similar allegations, against the City alone. The only relief sought by him, however, was for damages in inverse condemnation; he conceded the ordinances' validity.

The superior court sustained the City's general demurrers in each of the actions and, over objection, denied leave to amend the complaints. Each of the plaintiffs has appealed from a judgment which was thereafter entered dismissing his action.

. . . .

A preliminary question is presented. May a zoning ordinance operate so oppressively upon affected property owners as to require payment of compensation in an action for inverse condemnation? Or, in such a case, is the landowner's sole remedy an action to invalidate the ordinance, at least as to himself, on constitutional or other grounds? It will be seen that if the latter is the exclusive remedy, plaintiff Eldridge's complaint stated no cause of action, as did plaintiff Beyer's insofar as it sought damages in inverse condemnation.

The United States Supreme Court tersely discussed this subject in *Penna. Coal Co. v. Mahon* (1922) 260 U.S. 393. It said: *"The general rule at least is, that while property may be regulated to a certain extent, if regulation goes too far it will be recognized as a taking."* (Emphasis added.)

More recently the same court in *Goldblatt v. Hempstead* (1962) 369 U.S. 590, citing *Penna. Coal Co. v. Mahon,* supra, held that "the

---

[8] The bracketed statement of facts is from the majority opinion, but has been moved from near the middle to near the beginning of the opinion. — Eds.

form of regulation [can] be so onerous as to constitute a taking *which constitutionally requires compensation."* (Emphasis added.)

No express holding of this state's Supreme Court on the subject is to be found. But nevertheless the following decisions of that court bear upon the problem.

Klopping v. City of Whittier (1972) 8 Cal.3d 39, 104 Cal.Rptr. 1, 500 P.2d 1345. Discussing "de facto taking cases," the court declared (p. 46, 104 Cal.Rptr. p. 7, 500 P.2d p. 1351) that before such a "taking results there must be a 'physical invasion or direct legal restraint.' . . . One example of a 'legal restraint' discussed in several California cases has been a particularly harsh zoning regulation, . . ." This recital reasonably must mean that a valid, but particularly harsh, zoning regulation may give rise to damages in inverse condemnation, for if the regulation were invalid it could have no effect giving rise to such damages.

HFH, Ltd. v. Superior Court (1975) 15 Cal.3d 508, 125 Cal.Rptr. 365, 542 P.2d 237. The petitioners of that case sought inverse condemnation damages resulting from a down-zoning ordinance which drastically reduced their property's market value, but nevertheless allowed a substantial and reasonable beneficial use. They urged (p. 516, fn. 13, 125 Cal.Rptr. p. 371, 542 P.2d p. 243) "that the injury constituting the taking was the reduction in market value of the land." The high court found the dismissal of their action, upon the sustaining of a demurrer to their complaint, to have been proper. It was made clear by the court (p. 514, 125 Cal.Rptr. p. 369, 542 P.2d p. 241) that the ruling was predicated on pleadings where the zoning ordinance's "only alleged effect was a diminution in the market value of the property in question." In such a case there would be no injury or at least no legal or compensable injury. But the court held (p. 516, fn. 13, 125 Cal.Rptr. p. 371, 542 P.2d p. 243): "If such a reduction constituted an injury, *it would occur regardless of the legality of the zoning action occasioning it; . . ."* (Emphasis ours.)

California's Legislature has also recognized that an unreasonably drastic open-space zoning ordinance, although otherwise valid, may result in a taking requiring "just compensation therefor." (Gov.Code, § 65912.)

And the state's Court of Appeal has frequently reached similar conclusions.

. . . .

Lower federal courts have also held that an action in inverse condemnation will lie when a valid zoning ordinance is "exceptionally restrictive," or "arbitrary and capricious," or "allows no reasonable use of plaintiff's property."

Brown v. Tahoe Regional Planning Agency (D.C., 1973) 385 F.Supp. 1128, 1132. "[P]ublic welfare and necessity may reasonably require exceptionally restrictive land use classification . . . but . . .

such valid regulations may nevertheless constitute a taking of private property for public use entitling the owner to just compensation."

Dahl v. City of Palo Alto (D.C., 1974) 372 F.Supp. 647. This case dealt with precisely the zoning ordinances and issues concerned in the appeals at hand. Rejecting the city's motion to dismiss, the court held that the complaint stated a cause of action for damages in inverse condemnation.

Arastra Limited Partnership v. City of Palo Alto (N.D.Cal., 1975) 401 F.Supp. 962. This case also concerned the zoning ordinances and foothills here at issue. Following a trial on the merits the court held that the plaintiff had established a right to damages on the theory of inverse condemnation.

We opine, from a consideration of the foregoing authority, that a valid zoning ordinance may nevertheless operate so oppressively as to amount to a taking, thus giving an aggrieved landowner a right to damages in inverse condemnation.

We are brought to the question whether the zoning ordinances here at issue may reasonably be found to be of that class.

. . . .

We advert now to the principal issue before us. It concerns the proper accommodation of the rapidly developing public policy of environmental protection, to the constitutionally guaranteed right (U.S. Const., 5th and 14th Amends.; Cal.Const., art. I, former § 14) that one's "private property shall not be taken or damaged for public use without just compensation." Respected authority admonishes that: "In this conflict between the ecological and the constitutional, it is plain that neither is to be consumed by the other." (Supreme Judicial Court of Massachusetts, in *Commissioner of Natural Resources v. S. Volpe & Co.* (1965) 349 Mass. 104, 206 N.E.2d 666, 671.)

At the outset it should be pointed out that it is now the settled law of this state that:

"[A] zoning action which merely decreases the market value of property does not violate the constitutional provisions forbidding uncompensated taking or damaging, . . ."

The rule was reiterated in such a manner by the previously discussed decision, *HFH, Ltd. v. Superior Court,* 15 Cal.3d 508, 518, 125 Cal.Rptr. 365, 542 P.2d 237, of the state's Supreme Court. But the court made it clear that where the zoning action goes beyond the mere diminution of market value, and instead has the substantial effect of depriving the landowner of any reasonable or beneficial use of his property, the rule will not necessarily apply.

Reviewing earlier authority the same court in *Holtz v. Superior Court* (1970) 3 Cal.3d 296, 303, 90 Cal.Rptr. 345, 349, 475 P.2d 441, 445, discussed the underlying rationale of the constitutional principles here at issue. It said:

"The relevant 'policy' basis of article I, section 14, was succinctly defined in *Clement v. State Reclamation Board* (1950) 35 Cal.2d 628, 642, 220 P.2d 897: 'The decisive consideration is whether the owner of the damaged property if uncompensated would contribute more than his proper share to the public undertaking.' *In other words, the underlying purpose of our constitutional provision in inverse — as well as ordinary — condemnation is 'to distribute throughout the community the loss inflicted upon the individual by the making of public improvements'* (*Bacich v. Board of Control* (1943) 23 Cal.2d 343, 350, 144 P.2d 818): . . . ." (Emphasis added.)

. . . .

Summarizing broad authority, 1 Nichols on Eminent Domain (3d rev. ed. 1975) Nature and Origin of Power, section 1.42[1], pages 116-121, states: "Not only is an actual physical appropriation, under an attempted exercise of the police power, in practical effect an exercise of the power of eminent domain, but if regulative legislation is so unreasonable or arbitrary as virtually to deprive a person of the complete use of enjoyment of his property, it comes within the purview of the law of eminent domain."

Finally, on the instant issue, we note that the state's recently enacted "open-space" legislation (see Gov.Code, §§ 16140 — 16153, 51070 — 51097, 65910 — 65912) does not purport to enlarge the power of zoning authorities to take land for such purposes without compensation. Instead, as previously indicated, Government Code section 65912 (enacted 1970) provides:

"The Legislature hereby finds and declares that this article [entitled "Open-Space Zoning"] is not intended, and shall not be construed, as authorizing the city or the county to exercise its power to adopt, amend or repeal an open-space zoning ordinance in a manner which will take or damage private property for public use *without the payment of just compensation therefor.* This section is not intended to increase or decrease the rights of any owner of property under the Constitution of the State of California or of the United States." (Emphasis added.)

As pointed out, the gist of plaintiffs' complaints is that the City's open-space ordinances denied them any reasonable or beneficial use of their land.

[This legislation authorizes the adoption of an open space zoning ordinance and is reproduced *supra* p. 222. — Eds.]

Whether a zoning restriction is so "arbitrary," or "unreasonable," or "burdensome," as to transcend "proper bounds in its invasion of property rights," is ordinarily *a question of fact to be determined by trial of the issue, and not by demurrer.*

. . . .

Among the many factual issues to be resolved in the cases before us is whether the 10-acre homesites of plaintiffs' land are salable at all. This question would seem to be of particular significance, since the same homesites are designated by the ordinances for "open space use," including public park and recreation purposes and "wildlife habitat." Other factual inquiries would concern: the extent, and impact, of the intrusion upon plaintiffs' property by the "paths and trails system" planned to allow "public access through the Foothill lands"; whether there is any reasonable basis for the ordinances' declared aims of encouraging agricultural usage, preserving natural resources and creating wildlife sanctuaries on the land; and generally, the reasonableness of the ordinances' concept that although the foothills may be subdivided into 10-acre homesites, they must nevertheless without compensation therefor remain "open space" according to the definitions and usages of Government Code section 65560. The resolution of these and other such issues will determine whether plaintiffs have in fact been denied any reasonable or beneficial use of their land.

The City's demurrers, of course, raised an issue of law whether plaintiffs' complaints stated causes of action for damages in inverse condemnation. . . .

In the light of the above-related authority on the subject we are unable to say, *as a matter of law,* the plaintiffs' complaints have not stated a cause of action for damages in inverse condemnation against the City.

We are aided in this conclusion by the previously mentioned decisions, in what might be called companion cases to those before us, of *Arastra Limited Partnership v. City of Palo Alto,* 401 F.Supp. 962, and *Dahl v. City of Palo Alto,* 372 F.Supp. 647. Those cases, as noted, involved the same foothills, ordinances and actions of the City, and apparently the same factual and legal contentions as are presented here; it was concluded that the plaintiffs therein had pleaded causes of action for damages in inverse condemnation.

There remains, however, the question whether plaintiff Beyer's complaint also stated a cause of action for a judicial declaration that the ordinances were "illegal, unconstitutional and void" as applied to his property. The issue may be stated as whether the open-space and other public purposes of the City's zoning ordinances were constitutionally permissible objectives.

There appear to be no federal constitutional restraints on such objectives, according to the following authority.

. . . .

Berman v. Parker (1954) 348 U.S. 26, 33, 75 S.Ct. 98, 103, 99 L.Ed. 27. "It is within the power of the legislature to determine that the community should be beautiful as well as healthy, spacious as well as clean, well-balanced as well as carefully patrolled."

Sierra Club v. Morton (1972) 405 U.S. 727, 734, 92 S.Ct. 1361, 1366, 31 L.Ed.2d 636. "Aesthetic and environmental well-being, like economic well-being, are important ingredients of the quality of life in our society, and the fact that particular environmental interests are shared by the many rather than the few does not make them less deserving of legal protection through the judicial process."

The public policy of the state in reference to the subject here under consideration has been expressed by the Legislature in this manner:

Government Code section 6953 (enacted 1959): "The Legislature further declares that the acquisition of interest or rights in real property for the preservation of open spaces and areas constitutes a public purpose: . . ."

Government Code section 51072 (enacted 1974): "The Legislature hereby declares that open-space lands, if preserved and maintained, would constitute important physical, social, economic or aesthetic assets to existing or pending urban development."

. . . .

It was in pursuit of the public policy expressed by the above authority that the City's zoning ordinances were enacted. We hold that they were valid exercises of the state's police power and beyond constitutional or other attack except, as indicated, in proceedings for damages in inverse condemnation. Insofar as plaintiff Beyer sought a declaration that they were constitutionally invalid, his complaint stated no cause of action.

We see no merit in the City's contention that a "comprehensive [land use] zoning ordinance" or regulation (see *Consolidated Rock Products Co. v. City of Los Angeles* (1962) 57 Cal.2d 515, 520-521, 20 Cal.Rptr. 638, 370 P.2d 342) is in some way immune from the application of the rule of *Penna. Coal Co. v. Mahon,* supra, 260 U.S. 393, 415, 43 S.Ct. 158, 160, and its kindred cases, that where the "regulation goes too far it will be recognized as a taking." No authority is offered or found so holding.

. . . .

Another reason stated by the superior court for its ruling, and relied upon by the City, was that plaintiff's "administrative remedies have not been exhausted."

The same argument was made, and found invalid, in *Dahl v. City of Palo Alto,* supra, 372 F.Supp. 647, 649, which it will be recalled dealt with the same foothills and ordinances and regulations here confronting us. The court said: "As to the lack of subject matter jurisdiction in this Court, defendant makes two arguments. First, it urges the Court to refuse to exercise jurisdiction because of plaintiff's failure to exhaust available administrative remedies. Plaintiff has, however, made a claim for inverse condemnation in accordance with California Government Code § 905. The only other remedy referred to by defendant is plaintiff's failure to apply for a variance. It is highly improbable that a variance would, or legally could, be granted where as much land as here is involved (291 acres) and where development would be completed contrary to the goal of preserving the land in its natural or near natural state. The Court will not require such a useless course."

The court in *Sneed v. County of Riverside,* supra, 218 Cal.App.2d 205, 212, 32 Cal.Rptr. 318, 322, made a similar determination, stating: "Defendants contend plaintiff failed to exhaust his administrative remedies as a prerequisite to judicial relief; that he should have sought a permit from the Planning Commission with respect to nonconforming uses or variances. . . . In the instant case . . . it is not the plaintiff who has sought or obtained a change from what existed before, but the county which has invaded the alleged property rights of plaintiff, and in response thereto plaintiff does not challenge the constitutionality of the ordinance but merely seeks damages in inverse condemnation . . . ."

Dooley v. Town Plan & Zon. Com'n of Town of Fairfield, supra, 197 A.2d 770, 774, passed upon a like contention, saying: "Under the circumstances in the present case, it is not only unlikely but highly improbable that the zoning board of appeals would or legally could, by acting on an application for a variance, grant to the plaintiffs the relief which they seek. [Citations.] To grant a variance which would afford the plaintiffs any appreciable relief would seriously undermine the legislative purpose of the defendant in creating a flood plain district. An application for a variance would be doomed to almost certain failure. Such a useless course is unnecessary."

We have reached the same conclusion here.

From the foregoing considerations we conclude, and hold, that each of the plaintiffs' complaints stated a cause of action for damages in inverse condemnation against the City. It follows that the judgment of dismissal in each of the actions must be set aside.

. . . .

The judgments of dismissal are reversed. The superior court will set aside its orders sustaining the City of Palo Alto's demurrers without leave to amend. It will grant plaintiffs leave to amend their complaints if they shall be so advised, and will otherwise take further proceedings not inconsistent with the views we have expressed. Plaintiffs Beyer and Eldridge will recover their costs of appeal from the City of Palo Alto.

MOLINARI, P. J., concurs.

SIMS, Associate Justice (dissenting).

I respectfully dissent.

In the first place I question whether the two cases of *Beyer v. City of Palo Alto et al.* (1 Civ. 34134) and *Eldridge v. City of Palo Alto* (1 Civ. 33517) should have been consolidated for appeal. It is true that each involves a claim that damages must be paid on the theory of inverse condemnation because of actions taken by the governing board of the city over a period of years prior to the filing of the complaint in each action, and that each of such claims is predicated on the same course of conduct by the city. On the one hand, however, Eldridge claims that the action of the city was proper under its police power, but nevertheless gave rise to a cause of action for damages. Beyer on the other hand claims that the action of the city exceeded the bounds of its authorized police power, and seeks, as alternative relief, a declaration that the regulatory ordinance of the city is illegal, unconstitutional and void. The latter claim raises many issues not raised by Eldridge. Moreover, the city has moved to dismiss Beyer's appeal because he has disposed of the land which is the subject of the city's regulatory ordinance.

In disposing of the *Beyer* case, the majority opinion reaches the paradoxical, illogical and unwarranted conclusion that since Beyer's property was taken by the city's exercise of its regulatory powers, he was entitled to compensation, but he was not entitled to secure an adjudication that the ordinance was invalid. That decision flies in the face of *Penna. Coal Co. v. Mahon* (1922) 260 U.S. 393 on which the majority relies, and all of the cases which have recognized that a property owner is entitled to be relieved of the burden of a regulatory law or ordinance which so restricts the use of his property as to constitute a taking. (See fns. 2, 3 and 4 below.)

For the foregoing reasons I would treat the cases separately.

Eldridge v. City of Palo Alto

It is no secret that this case was heretofore the subject of a split decision of this court (Cal.App., 124 Cal.Rptr. 547) which was vacated by a grant of hearing by the Supreme Court. That court further ordered, "The cause is transferred to this court and retransferred to the Court of Appeal, First District, Division One, for reconsideration in the light of *HFH, Ltd. v. Superior Court* (1975) 15 Cal.3d 508, 125 Cal.Rptr. 365, 542 P.2d 237." (Supreme Court Minutes, Jan. 21, 1976. Official Advance Sheets of the Supreme Court No. 5, February 17, 1976, p. (1).)

In my opinion *HFH, Ltd.* does support the action of the lower court which sustained the demurrer in *Eldridge,* and my view that the judgment in favor of the city should be affirmed. I reluctantly must concede, however, that the decision leaves loopholes through which the plaintiff, as manifested from the present majority opinion, can pursue his claim for the cause of action in inverse condemnation.

It is clear that *HFH, Ltd.* holds (1) that inverse condemnation does not lie in zoning actions in which the complaint alleges mere reduction in market value (15 Cal.3d at pp. 513-518, 125 Cal.Rptr. 365, 542 P.2d 237); (2) that plaintiffs may not seek damages in a mandate action for *interim* damages in the event they successfully secure an adjudication that the rezoning is invalid *(id.,* at pp. 518-520, 125 Cal.Rptr. 365, 542 P.2d 237); and (3) that constitutional values of "fairness" do not require a ruling that inverse condemnation lies for any zoning action which reduces the market value of any tract of land, but that considerations of policy and the limitations of judicial instructions lead to a contrary conclusion (*id.,* at pp. 520-523, 125 Cal.Rptr. 365, 542 P.2d 237). Nevertheless, the court in footnotes recognized that there were situations not covered by the facts as alleged in the cause of action in *HFH, Ltd.,* which was before the court.

The court stated, "Neither *Selby* [*Selby Realty Co. v. City of San Buenaventura* (1973) 10 Cal.3d 110, 109 Cal.Rptr. 799, 514 P.2d 111] nor this case presents the distinct problems arising from inequitable zoning actions undertaken by a public agency as a prelude to public *acquisition* (*Klopping v. City of Whittier* (1972) 8 Cal.3d 39, 104 Cal.Rptr. 1, 500 P.2d 1345; *Peacock v. County of Sacramento* (1969) 271 Cal.App.2d 845, 77 Cal.Rptr. 391); or from zoning classifications invoked in order to evade the requirement that land *used* by the public must be acquired in eminent domain proceedings (*Sneed v. County of Riverside* (1963) 218 Cal.App.2d 205, 32 Cal.Rptr. 318). Thus in *Klopping* the city in question made public announcements that it intended to acquire the plaintiff's land, then unreasonably delayed commencement of eminent domain proceedings, with the predicable result that the property became commercially useless and suffered a decline in market value. We held only that the plaintiff should be able to include in his eminent domain damages the decline in value attributable to this unreasonable precondemnation action by the city. The case thus in no way resembles the instant one, in which plaintiffs make no allegations that the city intends to condemn the tract in question.

"Similarly in *Peacock* the county had refused to permit any development of the land in question (barring even the growth of most vegetation), while assuring the owner that the restrictions were of no consequence because the county intended to acquire the land for an airport. When, after denying the owner any use of his property for five years, the county renounced its intent to acquire the land, the Court of Appeal affirmed a trial court finding that ' "[t]he exceptional and extraordinary circumstances heretofore enumerated ... constituted a take [sic] of the subject property by inverse condemnation." ' (271 Cal.App.2d at p. 854, 77 Cal.Rptr. at p. 298.) Again one sees that the down-zoning rises to a taking only in connection with inequitable precondemnation actions by the public agency.

"Finally, the cases hold that a public agency may not use a zoning ordinance to evade the requirement that the state acquire property which it uses for public purposes. Thus in *Sneed,* the county, rather than acquiring land for an air navigation easement, simply enacted a zoning ordinance forbidding any structure or vegetation more than three inches high and proceeded to operate flights over the area thus restricted. The Court of Appeal held that the plaintiff had stated a cause of action in inverse condemnation. Unlike the instant case, *Sneed* involved a zoning ordinance creating an actual public use of the property." (15 Cal.3d at p. 517, fn. 14, 125 Cal.Rptr. at p. 371, 542 P.2d at p. 243.) It also noted, "This case does not present, and we therefore do not decide, the question of entitlement to compensation in the event a zoning regulation forbade substantially *all* use of the land in question. We leave the question for another day." (*Id.*, p. 518, fn. 16, 125 Cal.Rptr. p. 372, 542 P.2d p. 244.)

In *Eldridge,* and in *Beyer* as well, the plaintiff relied upon a course of conduct by the city which he claims brought his case within the exceptions noted above. In my judgment neither plaintiff has done so, but I do not believe either case may be summarily disposed of by reference to *HFH, Ltd. v. Superior Court.* I have accordingly reiterated what I said before in connection with *Eldridge v. City of Palo Alto,* with slight editorial changes, and added my views with respect to *Beyer v. City of Palo Alto, et al.*

A review of the record reflects that the plaintiff-landowner has stipulated himself out of court.[9] He contends that a valid exercise

---

[9] The complaint alleges that the plaintiff's real property had a fair market value of $4,000,000 prior to the alleged taking. His prayer is for "compensation in the sum of $4,000,000.00; his costs, disbursements and expenses, including reasonable attorney, appraisal, and engineering fees actually incurred herein; legal interest thereon from the date of taking or damaging; and for such further relief as the Court deems proper."

In support of the complaint, plaintiff's attorney advised the trial court, "The validity and public purpose of defendant's transactions in implementing its Open-Space project is unquestioned." In his closing brief he states, ". . . appellant believes, as respondent does, that the States 1970-72 open-space legislation and respondents thereby enabled open-space activities pursued during the same period legally constitute a valid exercise of the police power."

At the hearing on the demurrer plaintiff's counsel requested that in the event the demurrer should be sustained he be granted leave to amend to put in "a tremendous amount of evidentiary factual material surrounding" the transactions involved. The order sustaining the demurrer without leave to amend was signed and filed on March 16, 1973, and judgment of dismissal was filed and entered March 26. On the same day plaintiff prepared, and on the following day filed, a notice of motion for reconsideration of ruling on demurrer. No date was noted for hearing but a request was made for setting a time and place convenient for the court. The notice states, "Said motion is made in the furtherance of justice and on the grounds that the Court should reconsider its ruling upon consideration of plaintiff's proposed amended complaint." It refers to a proposed amended complaint. No such complaint is attached to the notice of motion in the record, nor does plaintiff's request for a clerk's transcript designate any such proposed amended complaint as a part of the record. The city filed a memorandum in opposition, but so far as appeared from the record, no amended complaint was ever prepared, nor was the notice motion, or any other motion seeking review of the order and/or judgment, ever brought on for hearing. There is no suggestion that plaintiff ever sought relief other than that set forth in his original prayer.

of the police power may give rise to an action for damages and that the plans, ordinances and actions of the city as alleged fall within that category. Nevertheless, with exceptions noted below, he relies upon authorities which, in reference to governmental action in the fields of planning and rezoning, hold that regulations which are confiscatory are invalid and not a proper exercise of the police power. By his refusal to seek declaratory relief, mandate or other recognized remedies for relief against governmental restrictions on the use of his property, he has left himself without a remedy. He seeks to retain his property, which has not been subjected to any physical appropriation, or invasion, and to be compensated for it too.

I

The keystone of plaintiff's attack is found in *Penna. Coal Co. v. Mahon,* supra, 260 U.S. 393, where Justice Holmes in ringing words pronounced, "We are in danger of forgetting that a strong public desire to improve the public condition is not enough to warrant achieving the desire by a shorter cut than the constitutional way of paying for the change. . . . [¶] We assume, of course, that the statute was passed upon the conviction that an exigency existed that would warrant it, and we assume that an exigency exists that would warrant the exercise of eminent domain. But the question at bottom is upon whom the loss of the changes desired should fall. So far as private persons or communities have seen fit to take the risk of acquiring only surface rights, we cannot see that the fact that their risk has become a danger warrants the giving to them greater rights than they bought." (260 U.S. at p. 416.) The court, however, did not award the coal company compensation for the inroads which the state had made into the company's mining rights by legislation which purported to require that the company support the surface of land which it had granted subject to mineral rights, including the right to mine without liability for subsidence.[10] It merely declared the

---

[10] The lone voice of Justice Brandeis appears more attuned to modern concepts. He stated in dissent, ". . . . where the police power is exercised, not to confer benefits upon property owners, but to protect the public from detriment and danger, there is, in my opinion, no room for considering reciprocity of advantage. There was no reciprocal advantage to the owner prohibited from using his oil tanks [citation]; his brickyard [citation]; his livery stable [citation]; his billard hall [citation]; his oleomargarine factory [citation]; his brewery [citation]; unless it be the advantage of living and doing business in a civilized community. That reciprocal advantage is given by the act to the coal operators." (260 U.S. at p. 422, 43 S.Ct. at p. 163.) Concepts of what constitutes a civilized community are ever changing. Justice Lennon over 50 years ago recognized, "Thus it is apparent that the police power is not a circumscribed prerogative, but is elastic and, in keeping with the growth of knowledge and the belief in the popular mind of the need for its application, capable of expansion to meet existing conditions of modern life, and

legislation unconstitutional and reversed a decision of the Supreme Court of Pennsylvania which had directed that an injunction be issued against the coal company's violation of the regulation. It is clear from the decision that the confiscatory nature of the regulation is not grounds for a cause of action for damages, but the measure of the constitutional power to regulate.[11]

In *Beverly Oil Co. v. City of Los Angeles* (1953) 40 Cal.2d 552, 254 P.2d 865, the court recognized the essential distinction as follows: ". . . the very essence of the police power as differentiated from the power of eminent domain is that the deprivation of individual rights and property cannot prevent its operation, once it is shown that its exercise is proper and that the method of its exercise is reasonably within the meaning of due process of law." (40 Cal.2d at p. 557, 254 P.2d at p. 867. See also *Consolidated Rock Products Co. v. City of Los Angeles* (1962) 57 Cal.2d 515, 530, 20 Cal.Rptr. 638, 370 P.2d 342.) In the case last cited the court referred with approval to decisions which indicated that the *Pennsylvania Coal Co.* case was inapplicable to comprehensive zoning (57 Cal.2d at p. 529, 20 Cal.Rptr. 638, 370 P.2d 342).

II

Plaintiff alleges that he has not been able to find a single decided case passing on the compensability of a claimed taking by a particular local government application of a state mandated open-space conservation planning and zoning project. By stating the problem in such limited form he seeks to escape the general rules, reviewed below, that planning itself can give rise to no right of action, and that zoning, if not confiscatory, is not actionable merely because it precludes the most profitable use of property. He also disavows finding a case passing on the compensability of government-compelled contribution of all development rights as a condition of

---

thereby keep pace with the social, economic, moral, and intellectual evolution of the human race." (*Miller v. Board of Public Works* (1925) 195 Cal. 477, 485, 234 P. 381, 383. See also *Consolidated Rock Products Co. v. City of Los Angeles* (1962) 57 Cal.2d 515, 522, 20 Cal.Rptr. 638, 370 P.2d 342.)

[11] Holmes stated, "Government hardly could go on if to some extent values incident to property could not be diminished without paying for every such change in the general law. As long recognized, some values are enjoyed under an implied limitation and must yield to the police power. But obviously the implied limitation must have its limits, or the contract and due process clauses are gone. One fact for consideration in determining such limits is the extent of the diminution. When it reaches a certain magnitude, in most if not in all cases there must be an exercise of eminent domain and compensation to sustain the act. So the question depends upon the particular facts. The greatest weight is given to the judgment of the legislature, but it always is open to interested parties to contend that the legislature has gone beyond its constitutional power." . . .

owning undeveloped but developable land in the compelling jurisdiction. The absence of such authority is indicative that such action, if arbitrary and confiscatory, is to be attacked directly as unconstitutional and, since it cannot bind the property, no compensation is in order unless the public body elects to proceed to condemn the interests which are so protected.

The problems posed by this case are not as ephemeral as plaintiff would have us believe. They may be resolved by examination of his contention that a continued series of cumulative regulatory activities prohibiting or "freezing" all private and beneficial use of private property, in the implementation of a local public project, gives rise to a right of action in inverse condemnation. Plaintiff seeks support for this position in a series of cases beginning with *Kissinger v. City of Los Angeles* (1958) 161 Cal.App.2d 454, 327 P.2d 10.

Kissinger was not a claim for damages, but an action for declaratory relief. The court recognized, "... it is the duty of the courts to set aside an ordinance which under the facts is clearly unreasonable and oppressive or discriminatory. [Citations.]" (161 Cal.App.2d at p. 460, 327 P.2d at p. 15.) ... Insofar as this case is concerned, the court, in declaring the ordinance invalid, observed, "A zoning ordinance may not be used as a device to take property for public use without the payment of compensation. [Citations.]" (*Id.,* p. 462, 327 P.2d p. 16.) This would assist plaintiff if he was seeking a similar declaration and could show that the city was discriminating against his property to lower its value with the intent to condemn it for a park or other uses.[12] It in no way creates an election to sue the offending public body for damages.[13]

---

[12] Whether distinguished or applied *Kissinger* is generally limited to that principle. In *Selby Realty Co. v. City of San Buenaventura,* supra, 10 Cal.3d 110, 109 Cal.Rptr. 799, 514 P.2d 111, the court distinguished *Kissinger,* referring to it as a case which "involved an unconstitutional attempt to rezone the plaintiff's property so that it could be acquired for a public use upon payment of a lower price." (10 Cal.3d at p. 120, 109 Cal.Rptr. at p. 805, 514 P.2d at p. 117....

[13] It is established that the provisions of sections 818.4 and 821.2 of the Government Code immunize the public entity and the public employee from liability caused by the erroneous refusal to issue a permit where the issuance of such permit is discretionary. The person injured is limited to his action to require the issuance of the permit if discretion was abused.... Analogous provisions protect the public entity and the public employee from liability for an injury caused by the adoption or failure to adopt an enactment. (Gov.Code, § 818.2 and § 821.... Nor can a public employee be held liable for damages resulting from acts in good faith under an enactment which is unconstitutional, invalid or inapplicable. (Gov.Code, § 820.6....

It is unnecessary to determine the applicability of the foregoing provisions to the facts upon which plaintiff Eldridge seeks to recover. They have not been referred to by either party, and for reasons set forth below it is otherwise clear that plaintiff has no action for damages. They were raised by the city in the *Beyer* case.

Plaintiff's next pillar is *Sneed v. County of Riverside* (1963) 218 Cal.App.2d 205, 32 Cal.Rptr. 318, in which the court found that the plaintiff had stated a cause of action for inverse condemnation. . . .

. . . It stated, "We believe there is a distinction between the commonly accepted and traditional height restriction zoning regulations of buildings and zoning of airport approaches in that the latter contemplates actual use of the airspace zoned, by aircraft, whereas in the building cases *there is no invasion or trespass to the area above the restricted zone.*" (*Id.,* at p. 209, 32 Cal.Rptr. at p. 320, emphasis added.) It concluded: "In his complaint plaintiff seeks to set forth two bases upon which he is entitled to compensation, (1) upon an easement obtained through the ordinance, and (2) on the ground that large numbers of aircraft take off and land, fly at low altitudes over plaintiff's property pursuant to instructions from the employees of defendant county. We believe that a cause of action has been stated on each ground." *(Id.)* This is a far step from saying that a plan or rezoning which affects the value of a landowner's property is a taking when it is not accompanied by an invasion of his property. *Sneed* is generally limited to its factual situation.

We approach a step closer to plaintiff's claim with *Peacock v. County of Sacramento* (1969) 271 Cal.App.2d 845, 77 Cal.Rptr. 391. Here a judgment for the landowner in inverse condemnation was sustained. . . . In *Peacock* there was, as in *Sneed,* an attempt to take the airspace without compensation. Moreover, there was an express purpose (later revoked) to take the particular property involved and to affect the value of that property by the restrictions. (See 271 Cal.App.2d at pp. 859-863, 77 Cal.Rptr. 391.)

As a result, *Peacock* has been referred to by the Supreme Court as a case which "upheld a claim of inverse condemnation because the county had announced its intention to condemn plaintiff's land for an airport, rezoned and restricted the use of that property so that its value would be depressed in the event of future public acquisition, refused permission to subdivide, and finally abandoned the airport project altogether." (*Selby Realty Co. v. City of San Buenaventura* (1973) 10 Cal.3d 110, 120, 109 Cal.Rptr. 799, 805, 514 P.2d 111, 117. . . .)

Klopping v. City of Whittier, supra, 8 Cal.3d 39, 104 Cal.Rptr. 1, 500 P.2d 1345, is a case of similar tenor. . . .

In *Dahl v. City of Palo Alto* (N.D.Cal. 1974) 372 F.Supp. 647, the plaintiff sought damages by reason of same actions of the city as are the subject of the complaint in this case. The court held that allegations that the regulation imposed by the city "is arbitrary and capricious and that it allows no reasonable use of plaintiff's property" were sufficient to raise a factual issue as to whether the zoning regulations were a proper exercise of the police power. (372 F.Supp. at pp. 648-649.) With this I can agree, and it would be applicable here if the plaintiff had not stipulated to the contrary.

The District Court also found that there were sufficient allegations to establish that the moratorium on the use of her land constituted a taking under principles enunciated in *Peacock v. City of Sacramento,* supra. For reasons set forth herein, I cannot reach a similar conclusion in this case. That court also found that there were facts alleged which created an equitable estoppel against the city sustaining the plaintiff's claim of breach of contract and misrepresentation (*id.,* p. 649). . . .

The opinion fails to confront the issue of whether the plaintiff's recourse is limited to having the regulation invalidated and her property restored to its former status. It assumes that there was a taking despite the alleged improper exercise of the regulatory power. I, therefore, find the opinion unpersuasive and inconsistent with the opinions of the Supreme Court of this state which have denied a right to inverse condemnation under similar circumstances.

In *Arastra Limited Partnership v. City of Palo Alto* (N.D.Cal.1975) 401 F.Supp. 962, the federal court again upheld a landowner's right to recover damages for inverse condemnation on the basis of the actions of the City of Palo Alto, many of which have a common effect on the lands of Eldridge and of Beyer. In my opinion the complaint in this action fails to fall within the framework of that case because plaintiff has failed to allege that he ever had initiated or secured approval of any development plan which was foreclosed by the series of actions taken by the city, or that the city ever designated his particular parcel for acquisition to the extent shown in the cited case. Moreover, in my opinion the District Court erred in not relegating the landowner to his right to develop the property under the prior zoning if, as it found, the new zoning was confiscatory. I express no opinion as to whether under the circumstances related in the cited case, the landowner would be entitled to some compensation under *Klopping* for the period commencing with the determination to take its property and terminating with the abandonment of that type of action.

Other cases which recognize an action for inverse condemnation where the plaintiff's property has been physically invaded, or has been diminished in value because of actual use of the airspace,[14] are not controlling or persuasive on the issues raised by the plaintiff's complaint.

---

[14] . . . Allegations that the city, without the permission of plaintiff, constructed certain access improvements on plaintiff's property, are admittedly without foundation, and are not themselves relied upon by plaintiff as giving him right to a cause of action for inverse condemnation, because no claim was filed for any specific damage so occasioned.

III

According to the complaint, plaintiff's property consists of an undeveloped parcel of approximately 750 contiguous acres on Skyline Boulevard and Page Mill Road in the San Francisco peninsula foothills overlooking San Francisco Bay. He acquired the property March 15, 1968, for the sum of $2,050,000, plus assumption of an assessment balance of $406,662.38 for municipal sewer and water utilities which had been financed by an assessment district in 1963,[15] four years after the city in 1959 had annexed an area of approximately 6,000 acres of which the property subsequently purchased by plaintiff was a part. At the time of the annexation of the property, the improvements on the property were limited to some old ranch buildings, electric and telephone utility service and public road on two sides. There is no mention that any improvements other than those mentioned above were constructed before or after the acquisition by plaintiff. At the time of acquisition the property was zoned R-E:A (Residential Estate — Agricultural) for low density single-family residential development on minimum one-acre lots with one primary dwelling unit per lot. The plaintiff purchased the property for the purposes of long term investment and planned development, intending to make use of its many rolling hills, wooded glens and spectacular panoramic views of the entire San Francisco Bay area.

The gravamen of plaintiff's complaint is found in allegations that a series of public acts and transactions commencing in 1969, and "in particular those of defendant CITY occurring between February 28, 1972, and August 14, 1972, constitute a taking of plaintiff's private property for public use as permanent open space without prior payment of just compensation as required by Article I, section 14, of the Constitution of the State of California." A second cause of action seeks recovery under the Fifth and Fourteenth Amendments to the Constitution of the United States, and alleges, "Said series of acts and transactions of defendant CITY have devalued plaintiff's land by more than three-fourths of its fair market value and to substantially below its actual cost, which is a wholly unreasonable degree in that it is thus impossible to reasonably develop the said property with a fair return or otherwise." A third cause of action

---

[15] The complaint alleges that on October 10, 1972, following rezoning of the property (see text below), the amount of the assessment was reduced to one-third of the original amount, $451,734.29, by the city.

alleges, "Said series of acts and transactions of the defendant CITY amount to a damaging according to proof of plaintiff's private property for public use without just compensation having first been paid, in violation of Article I, Section 14, of the Constitution of the State of California." Plaintiff seeks $4,000,000 which he alleges was the fair market value of his property prior to the alleged taking. Claim for damages was made to the city as required by law on September 14, 1972, and the action was filed December 18, 1972, after the city failed to act on the claim.

The kernel of plaintiff's complaint must be the rezoning which on June 5, 1972, added open space regulations to the zoning code, and on August 14, 1972, classified plaintiff's property in that category. This changed the classification of the property from "R-E:A (Residential Estate — Agricultural), for low-density single-family residential development on minimum one-acre lots with one primary dwelling unit per lot" to "O-S (Open Space)." Under the new zoning "construction of one-family dwellings on the property ... is expressly limited to 10-acre minimum lots with a maximum of impervious area and building coverage of 3.5 per cent. . . ." Uses are limited to "(1) Public recreation (2) Enjoyment of scenic beauty (3) Conservation of use of natural resources (4) Production of food or fiber (5) Protection of man and his artifacts (buildings, property, etc.) (6) Containment and structuring of urban development."

There may well be a justiciable issue as to whether this zoning meets the test of the regulatory power as limited in *Pennsylvania Coal Co. v. Mahon,* supra. Plaintiff has alleged, "The aforesaid acts and transactions of defendant CITY have deprived plaintiff of all private uses of his said property and appropriated his private property rights therein" and "The aforesaid acts and transactions of defendant CITY have deprived plaintiff of any reasonable or economically feasible use of his said property." These statements are legal conclusions and not allegations of ultimate fact. . . . Nevertheless they contain the germ of facts which might render the new ordinance invalid if it can be shown to be confiscatory. . . .

The combination of the moratorium, plan and rezoning does not establish an illegal whole which entitles the plaintiff to relief despite the legality of its parts. Nor is he aided by the allegation that more than two months after he filed his claim the city publicly announced "that the open space rezoning enacted on said August 14, 1972, 'signified that one of Palo Alto's greatest assets — its green and golden foothills — would be conserved as backdrop to the city for generations to come' ", and declared " 'the 1,400 acres which the City owns in Foothills Park and a public *trails* and path system, which is being designed for the foothills, will allow Palo Altans to enjoy the open space.' " If the plaintiff's property is condemned for parks, trails or paths, or if the city attempts to use it for such purposes without condemnation he has his legal remedies, and in an action for condemnation, direct or indirect, he may assert his contention that the property is illegally zoned and seek compensation on a value free from the zoning. He also had the right to seek a declaration that the actual restrictions placed on his property were illegal, or, in the alternative, a right to seek to force the city to permit him to develop his property in a manner consistent with the prior zoning. He has elected not to pursue those remedies. . . . He is not entitled to compensation on the facts alleged in his complaint. . . .

The trial court properly sustained the demurrer to the complaint on the ground that no cause of action was stated for inverse condemnation. Plaintiff's failure to attack the zoning ordinance directly renders it unnecessary to determine whether he has alleged facts sufficient to show that it was not a valid exercise of the police power, and I express no opinion on that ground, or on the issue of whether plaintiff should have applied for a variance before so attacking the ordinance. Because plaintiff so restricted his prayer and failed to produce, on rehearing, any amended complaint, there was no error in denying his request to amend. I would affirm the judgment in *Eldridge v. City of Palo Alto.*

Beyer v. City of Palo Alto et al.

For the reasons set forth above I am of the opinion that the plaintiff in this action failed to set forth facts sufficient to constitute a cause of action to recover damages for inverse condemnation. He did, however, unlike Eldridge, seek a declaration that the open space ordinance was illegal, unconstitutional and void. Those allegations suggested many interesting issues which have been thoroughly briefed by the litigants and two *amici curiae.*[16] Because of intervening developments brought to the attention of the court by the city's motion to dismiss the appeal as moot, it is, in my opinion, unnecessary to reach those issues.

---

[16] Among the arguments raised by Beyer, in support of his contention that the open space zoning ordinance is illegal, unconstitutional and void, are the following: It will not and cannot achieve its legislative objective of preserving open space; it forces the 17 persons who owned the land so restricted to furnish benefits of open space to the public without compensation; it conflicts with the State of California's Open Space Zoning Laws; it is inconsistent with the City of Palo Alto General Plan; it was improperly enacted to reduce the price of land to be acquired by the city or by a regional park district; it benefits the wealthy and excludes housing for low and moderate income people; and because of exceptional circumstances the city is estopped to adopt such restrictive zoning. One *amicus curiae* has supported the theory that the ordinance is invalid because it excludes low and moderate cost housing in an area of need, and unconstitutionally discriminates against persons with low incomes and unconstitutionally impinges on the right to travel. . . .

The judgment of dismissal was entered July 12, 1973, and Beyer appealed on July 25, 1973. The city has asked us to, and I do, take judicial notice of certain public records which indicate that by deed dated April 3, 1974, and recorded May 8, 1974, the Beyer property was conveyed to one Harrington. Prior thereto on March 11, 1974, Harrington had secured approval of the city council for his application to divide the property into two lots. Thereafter on May 13, 1974, the council, upon recommendation of the planning commission approved Harrington's application for site and design approval of a single family residence on one of the lots. On August 12, 1974, a building permit was issued to him and thereafter various inspections of the work were made and supplementary permits issued. Meanwhile, by deed dated June 24, 1974, and recorded January 20, 1975, Harrington conveyed away a portion of the property. Neither Harrington nor his grantees have intervened or been substituted in the Beyer's action, and for all that appears they are satisfied to have acquired and developed the property under the open space zoning.

Beyer does not contest the foregoing facts, but he claims he is still entitled to a declaration that the ordinance is invalid. He relies upon *Millbrae Assn. for Residential Survival v. City of Millbrae* (1968) 262 Cal.App.2d 222, 69 Cal.Rptr. 251, wherein this court observed, in connection with a similar motion, "[W]hen one acts under compulsion or coercion in compliance with a judgment, he does not lose his right of appeal from that judgment." (262 Cal. App.2d at pp. 232-233, 69 Cal.Rptr. at p. 259.) There is nothing in the record except a bare statement in plaintiff's reply brief to show that he was under compulsion to sell his land to realize cash in order to meet his debts and remain solvent. In the case cited it also appeared that there was a continuity of interest between the vendor and vendee, and that the former had undertaken to continue the litigation for the benefit of the latter (*id.*, at p. 232, 69 Cal.Rptr. 251). No such showing was made here. It would appear that the plaintiff no longer has a pecuniary or other interest in having the open space zoning declared unconstitutional, illegal and void. . . .

Plaintiff also seeks to equate his position with plaintiff Sarff in *Klopping v. City of Whittier,* supra, 8 Cal.3d 39, 104 Cal.Rptr. 1, 500 P.2d 1345. Sarff filed his suit in inverse condemnation on March 26, 1968, and lost his property through foreclosure the following May 16. The court stated, "Certainly this fortuity does not preclude him from recovering for any damages caused by the city in making the two announcements in question. Sarff complains that he was unable to rent the property in the period following the precondemnation announcements. Under the rules discussed above rental loss is a proper element of recovery. In the petition for hearing filed herein, it also appears that he seeks recovery for damages occasioned by the fact that his property was ultimately foreclosed because the condemnation resolution prevented him from deriving income from his land in order to make mortgage payments. The availability of this element of damage can be more fully explored on remand." (8 Cal.3d at p. 58, 104 Cal.Rptr. at p. 16, 500 P.2d at p. 1360.) As we have seen, *Klopping* involves the depressive effect of improper steps toward condemnation. Beyer has failed to show that the city was attempting to condemn his property. He claims damages from the moratoria and the ultimate open space zoning. No damages may be recovered on either ground. . . .

I would, therefore, dismiss the *Beyer* appeal because events occurring after the judgment have rendered the appeal moot. . . .

Hearing denied; WRIGHT, C. J., and TOBRINER and MOSK, JJ., dissenting.

Comments: 1. On the appeal from the Superior Court to the District Court of Appeal, both Elkington, J., and Sims, J., filed opinions substantially identical with those they filed after remand of the case by the California Supreme Court "for reconsideration in the light of *HFH, Ltd. v. Superior Court.*" For a thorough discussion of the problems involved in the *HFH, Ltd.* case, discussed in both the *Eldridge* opinions, see Comment, Limiting the Availability of Inverse Compensation as a Landowner's Remedy for Down Zoning, 13 Urb. L. Ann. 263 (1977). *See generally* Note, Inverse Condemnation: The Case for Diminution in Property Value as Compensable Damage, 28 Stan. L. Rev. 779 (1976).

What is the present California rule as to the availability of "inverse condemnation" as a remedy for the landowner when a zoning ordinance operates "so oppressively as to amount to a taking"? What conclusion should be drawn from the refusal of the California Supreme Court to hear the *Eldridge* case after the District Court of Appeal filed the opinions reprinted above? If "inverse condemnation" is to be available as an alternative to obtaining an adjudication that the zoning regulations are invalid as applied to the land in question, should the landowner have the option to sue for whichever form of relief is most advantageous to him? Or should the local governing body simply have the option, to avoid a holding that the zoning regulations are invalid, to pay compensation to the landowner for the "taking" of his property?

2. In *Arastra Ltd. Partnership v. City of Palo Alto,* discussed in both opinions in *Eldridge, supra,* the developer (Arastra) had acquired a 515-acre tract in the same "Foothills" area involved in *Eldridge* after the tract was rezoned from REA (residential, 1-acre lots) to P-C (Planned Community District) and after a development plan for the tract was approved by the city council. Sometime in early 1968, Arastra began formulating a new and different development plan, and on August 1, 1969, it filed an application for approval of the new plan, which contemplated 1,776 housing units, a 150,000 square foot commercial site, a 200,000 square foot office-professional complex, an elementary school and other related public facilities on a 24-acre site, and approximately 250 acres of open space. (This was the so-called "1776 Plan.") On October 29, 1969, the city's planning consultant delivered the first in a series of reports with respect to the manner and extent to which the Foothills area should be developed. On March 16, 1970, the City Council passed a resolution deferring action on Arastra's 1776 Plan pending receipt of a final report from its planning consultant.

This report was submitted to the City Council in June, 1970; in part, it recommended: (a) that the "lower Foothills" below Foothills Park, including the Arastra tract, be purchased by the City; (b) that the City deny approval to all development proposals for the "lower Foothills"; (c) that the City be prepared to purchase land in the "lower Foothills," when necessary to prevent development; (d) that all "lower Foothills" land be rezoned so as to prohibit more than one dwelling unit per five acres, in order to prevent development prior to acquisition of the land by the City; and (e) that there be further study of alternative means of acquiring such land. On November 9, 1970, the City Council voted to accept the consultant's recommendations, and its action was publicized in local news media as a decision to purchase "the lower Foothills" area, including the Arastra tract. On November 16, 1970, the City Council unanimously voted to deny approval of Arastra's 1776 Plan, and this action was also publicized in local news media as being in furtherance of the decision of the City to purchase "the lower Foothills" area. Arastra in fact believed that Palo Alto had decided to purchase its property and made no further plans to develop its tract, although it made repeated efforts to induce the City to reverse its decision to prohibit development of the tract.

Between January 13 and July 19, 1971, Palo Alto officials proceeded with planning for acquisition of the entire "lower Foothills" area, and on July 19 the City Council adopted an ordinance establishing a six-month moratorium on development in that area. On August 6, 1971, the City Manager rendered a report to the City Council entitled "Foothills Financing Plan" wherein three alternative financing plans were suggested. On August 23, 1971, the City Council passed an ordinance increasing its budget appropriations for "Foothills Land Acquisition" by $665,900 (from $3,334,100 to $4,000,000). On August 30, however, the Palo Alto City Planning Staff reported to the City Council that the receipt of federal funds to aid in the purchase of "the lower Foothills" area was unlikely. On October 4, the City Council in a closed session decided to make no further effort to obtain federal funds for land acquisition in the "lower Foothills" area. On February 28, 1972, the development moratorium was extended for another six-month period. Shortly thereafter, the Council apparently decided that acquisition of the "lower Foothills" with City funds alone would be too expensive.

As indicated in *Eldridge,* the Council on June 5, 1972, added "O-S Open Space District Regulations" to the Palo Alto Municipal Code, and on August 14, 1972, adopted an ordinance reclassifying the "lower Foothills," including both the Eldridge and Arastra tracts, as "O-S Open Space." On December 20, 1972, Arastra brought an inverse condemnation action against the City of Palo Alto. The court held as follows:

> When the open space ordinance is examined in . . . context, it compels the conclusion that the City had the purpose, by way of zoning regulation, to accomplish without expense to the taxpayers

all of the benefits it could have received from the acquisition [of Arastra's tract]. . . .

It is somewhat ironic for the defendant to contend that there is an absolute bar to inverse condemnation because there has been no physical invasion of plaintiff's property. Of course, physical invasion of the property is precisely what the City is attempting to prevent. Their whole objective is to have the property remain unused, undisturbed, and in natural state so that the open space and scenic qualities may be preserved. . . . There has clearly been the appropriation of a valuable property right of the plaintiff . . . whether the taking be deemed a scenic easement, an open space easement, or something different.
. . . .

Considered narrowly, the damages here might be computed solely upon the basis of the easements constructively acquired by the City and the losses resulting. This, however, would leave the parties in intolerable positions. The City would have paid out amounts which well could approach the full value of fee title but would have no title. The plaintiff, on the other hand, would have title but little more.

Relief in such a matter should be framed as equitably as possible, considering the position of both parties. The original plan of the City was to acquire the fee; it has never abandoned its purpose to do so. Requiring it to carry out that purpose would serve the interest of both parties. The City with fee title could deal with the entire property in any fashion that public purposes required, including its original concept of land banking some portion of the land for future controlled development. Plaintiff on the other hand would be fully compensated for its property without being left with a naked fee that could well be a liability rather than an asset. Accordingly, . . . the measure of plaintiff's damages shall be the fair market value of the fee title on the effective date of the Open Space Ordinance, and it will be further ordered that, concurrently with payment therefor, plaintiff shall convey such fee title to the City.

The sole remaining question is whether, at the trial to determine fair market value, the Court may decide as a matter of law the density to which the property might probably have been permitted to be developed, had not the taking intervened, or whether that is a question of fact to be decided by the jury. It would appear that this determination, just as all other facts affecting compensation, must be left to the jury. . . . The Court has, however, already heard what may well be all of the evidence which will bear upon this issue. On the present record, the Court would be constrained to find that there is no evidence which would support a jury finding that development would probably have been permitted to an intensity in excess of 1,250 residential units, plus office and commercial structures, all subject to the then requirements of the P-C (Planned Community) zoning regulations.

401 F. Supp. at 980, 981-82.

3. Do you agree with the result reached in the *Arastra* case? Or would you instead agree with Sims, J., who said in his dissent in *Eldridge* that "the District Court [in *Arastra*] erred in not relegating the landowner to his right to develop the property under the prior zoning if, as it found, the new zoning was confiscatory"? If you agree with Sims, J., would you also agree that in *Arastra* "the landowner would be entitled to some compensation . . .

for the period commencing with the determination to take its property and terminating with the abandonment of that type of action"?

Several recent California intermediate appellate cases since *Eldridge* have considered the "inverse condemnation" problem. In *Pan Pac. Properties, Inc. v. County of Santa Cruz,* 146 Cal. Rptr. 428 (Cal. App. 1978), and *Friedman v. City of Fairfax,* 146 Cal. Rptr. 687 (Cal. App. 1978), it was held that the landowners had no inverse condemnation cause of action because of mere "downzoning" designed to preserve open space, there being no evidence in either case of any attempt by the municipality to obtain the land for public use through "downzoning" or of inequitable pre-condemnation activities. In neither case did the court find that the landowner was deprived of all reasonable and beneficial use of its land, although the diminution in land value was about 80 percent in *Friedman.* In *San Diego Gas & Elec. Co. v. City of San Diego,* 146 Cal. Rptr. 103 (Cal. App. 1978), and *Furey v. City of Sacramento,* 146 Cal. Rptr. 485 (Cal. App. 1978), however, landowners were held entitled to inverse condemnation damages.

In the *San Diego* case a "taking" was found to have resulted from a combination of factors: the city's adoption of an open space element as part of its general plan; the "downzoning" of part of the land in question to an agricultural use classification, with an "open space overlay" for the rest of the land, which retained its industrial use classification; and overtures by the city for a purchase of the land for open space preservation. The court found that because of the location and peculiar characteristics of the land it was suitable only for industrial development, and that, although part of the land retained its industrial zoning, the city's policy was not to permit any development inconsistent with its general plan and that the city would deny any application for industrial development on this parcel because of its open space designation in the general plan. "In addition, there was expert testimony that after the open space element was adopted, the land had no economic use and no one would buy it. This was substantial evidence to support the court's conclusion there was inverse condemnation." *Id.* at 113.

In *Furey* the court held that agricultural—open space zoning pursuant to adoption of an open space element as part of the city's general plan was *not* a "taking" because agriculture was the historic and current use of the property and there was no allegation that its value for such use had diminished. The court said that "[t]he fact that plaintiffs' dollar investment may be so great that they cannot return a profit from agriculture is simply one of the risks of the marketplace, as pointed out in *HFH.*" But the court also found that there was a "taking" of the moneys paid by the plaintiffs on a sewer assessment previously placed on their land at a time when the city constructed sewer trunk lines and a sewage treatment plant in anticipation of commercial and residential development in the area later designated as open space. The court said:

> The problem is not merely that plaintiffs have been deprived of the use of the sewer and treatment plant [by continuation of the agricultural — open space zoning]; it is that they have been required *to pay for* such a facility for the use of others and not themselves. From and after the effective date of the Open Space Ordinance, as each bond installment has accrued and been paid, plaintiffs' dollars (property) have been taken for public use (to

amortize the sewer bonds) without just compensation (the substantial availability for use of the sewer facility).

Id. at 493.

4. Compare the *Eldridge* and *Arastra* cases with *City of Plainfield v. Borough of Middlesex,* 173 A.2d 785 (N.J.L. 1961), where the court invalidated a zoning ordinance amendment which created a new zone "limited as to use to parks, playgrounds and schools" and including all the land owned by the plaintiff landowners, as well as certain land previously sold by the plaintiffs to the Middlesex Borough Board of Education on which was located a new high school. One month after adoption of the amendment, the defendant municipality's borough council passed a resolution declaring that acquisition of all the lands in this area except that owned by the board of education was "necessary for public use for the purposes of public parks, playgrounds, athletic fields and similar public recreational purposes," and authorizing its attorney to commence condemnation proceedings to obtain title thereto. No further steps toward condemnation were taken, and the plaintiffs filed their action asking that the zoning amendment be set aside and that defendant borough be directed to proceed with its condemnation proceeding if it desired to acquire the plaintiffs' property, or, in the alternative, that defendant borough be restrained from publicly claiming or threatening to take the property in question by eminent domain. In holding the zoning ordinance, as amended, invalid, the court said:

> [T]he plaintiffs are limited by the ordinance to using the property for a school or for public parks and playgrounds. They are barred from developing the land for residential or business purposes. It naturally follows that plaintiffs' potential buyers are equally limited as to use. Plaintiffs, under the ordinance, in order to realize the economic value of the property, must therefore find some purchaser who will either build a school or use the property for public parks or playgrounds. While it is conceivable that they could find a private school willing to build on the property, as a practical matter the effect of the zoning ordinance is to limit the purchaser to defendant borough or to the Board of Education of the Borough of Middlesex. While the separate legal entities of the two are recognized, nevertheless, together they represent in fact a single buyer, that is, the people of the Borough of Middlesex. The net result of the ordinance is to destroy for all practical purposes the full value of plaintiffs' property and to leave plaintiffs at the mercy of the defendant as to the price that the latter may be willing to pay. However desirable the property may be for defendant for parks and playgrounds, defendant cannot use its power to zone as a method of depreciating the value of the property for the purposes of purchase.
>
> . . . .
>
> It is the opinion of the court that the exercise by defendant municipality of its power to zone has here been used to unconstitutionally deprive plaintiffs of the full value of their property, notwithstanding that the desire of the municipality to acquire the lands and premises for parks, playgrounds and schools is otherwise in all respects legitimate.
>
> Defendant has cited cases in which a zoning ordinance does not contravene constitutional limitations merely because the restrictive use is not the most profitable one to the owner. . . . This

is undoubtedly true. On the other hand, it has been held that if a zoning ordinance leaves property useless to the owner, it is confiscatory and therefore unconstitutional. . . . We think that ordinance No. 323 as applied in the present situation comes within the orbit of the latter holding and that its enactment is beyond the power of the defendant municipality.

Id. at 787, 789-90.

Do you understand the court to mean, in the *Borough of Middlesex* case, that "if a zoning ordinance leaves property useless to the owner, it is confiscatory and therefore unconstitutional" regardless of the legislative purpose in enacting the ordinance? Would the New Jersey court have decided the *Consolidated Rock Prods. Co.* case, *supra,* differently? If, in fact, the purpose of the borough council in the *Borough of Middlesex* case was not relevent, why did the court say that "defendant cannot use its power to zone as a method of depreciating the value of the property *for the purposes of purchase*"? (Emphasis added.)

5. In *State ex rel. Tingley v. Gurda,* 243 N.W. 317, 320 (Wis. 1932), the court said:

The zoning power is one which may be used to the great benefit and advantage of a city, but, as this case indicates, it is a power which may be greatly abused if it is to be used as a means to depress the values of property which the city may upon some future occasion desire to take under the power of eminent domain. Such a use of the power is utterly unreasonable, and cannot be sanctioned. It is entirely beyond the purpose of the zoning law to condemn a block in the heart of an industrial section to residential purposes only, for which purposes it is largely valueless because of the reason that it is in the heart of an industrial area. We have little hesitation in pronouncing this ordinance, in so far as it places relator's property in a residential district, utterly unreasonable and void, for which reason the judgment of the lower court must be affirmed.

Id. at 320.

This quotation was cited with approval in *Grand Trunk Western R. Co. v. City of Detroit,* 40 N.W.2d 195 (Mich. 1949), and again in *Long v. City of Highland Park,* 45 N.W.2d 10 (Mich. 1950).

In the *Borough of Middlesex* case, *supra,* the court cited the *Gurda, Grand Trunk,* and *Long* cases, and then went on to say:

It must be admitted that in the latter three cases the zoning limitation was as to a use not reasonable for the lands in question, whereas in the case at bar we have no evidence that the use of the lands for schools, parks or playgrounds is unreasonable insofar as the quality and nature of the property are concerned. What we do have, however, is a use limitation so restrictive that plaintiffs themselves cannot use the property and can sell it only to the very party imposing the restrictions. In effect, plaintiffs are deprived of their full property rights without full compensation.

Id. at 788.

Consider the following problem: A zoning ordinance zones an owner's land in a commercial area solely for parking lot purposes. It then provides that the owner, on notice from the city, shall attempt to sell the property to an adjacent private owner for a parking lot. Failing that, and failing negotiations to sell the property to the city, the city may condemn the property by eminent domain. In this instance, the zoning restriction to parking lots is not to be taken into account, and the property is to be valued as if it were zoned for purposes "available" to the immediately surrounding property owners. Held unconstitutional in *Sanderson v. City of Willmar,* 162 N.W.2d 494 (Minn. 1968). The court noted that the "power to regulate by zoning may not be applied to appease the city's desire to restrain the natural operation of the laws of economics." *Id.* at 497. *But see Brandau v. City of Grosse Pointe Park,* 175 N.W.2d 755 (Mich. 1970).

6. Other interesting cases involving extremely restrictive zoning regulations somewhat like those in *Eldridge, Arastra,* and *Borough of Middlesex* include *Vernon Park Realty, Inc. v. City of Mt. Vernon,* 121 N.E.2d 517 (N.Y. 1954), and *McCarthy v. City of Manhattan Beach,* 264 P.2d 932 (Cal. 1953), *cert. denied,* 348 U.S. 817 (1954).

In *Vernon Park Realty,* the subject premises, owned by the New York, New Haven & Hartford Railroad, were adjacent to the railroad station, in the middle of a developed business district, and had "always been used by the patrons of the railroad and others for the parking of private automobiles." When the city first enacted a zoning ordinance in 1922, the existing central business district, including the subject premises, was placed in a Business "B" district. In 1927, without any objection from the railroad, the subject premises were changed to a Residence "B" classification. Automobile parking on the premises continued thereafter as a lawful nonconforming use. The railroad and its then tenant obtained a variance to permit installation of a gasoline filling station in 1932. In 1951 the railroad sold the subject premises and the purchaser, after an unsuccessful application for a variance to permit construction of a shopping center, brought an action to invalidate the Residence "B" regulations as applied to the subject premises. In 1952, after joinder of issue, the city rezoned the subject premises into a newly created Designed Parking District, and the plaintiff amended its complaint to include the new classification in its attack. The court held that both the Residence "B" and the Designed Parking District regulations were unconstitutional on due process grounds. The court said:

> However compelling and acute the community traffic problem may be, its solution does not lie in placing an undue and uncompensated burden on the individual owner of a single parcel of land in the guise of regulation, even for a public purpose. True it is that for a long time the land has been devoted to parking, a nonconforming use, but it does not follow that an ordinance prohibiting any other use is a reasonable exercise of the police power. . . .
>
> On this record, the plaintiff . . . has met the burden of proof by establishing that the property is so situated that it has no possibilities for residential use and that the use added by the 1952 amendment does not improve the situation but, in fact, will operate to destroy the greater part of the value of the property since, in authorizing its use for parking and incidental services, it necessarily permanently precludes the use for which it is most readily adapted, i.e., a business use such as permitted and actually carried on by the owners of all the surrounding property. . . .

In *McCarthy,* the California court upheld a "beach recreational district" classification permitting development and use of the subject land as a beach with various accessory facilities for which a fee could be charged—but not for residential development—in a high-density coastal resort suburb of Los Angeles. In the adjoining municipality (Hermosa Beach), the existing residential development extended one block further onto the beach than in Manhattan Beach. The Manhattan Beach governing body clearly wanted to acquire its beach land for public use, and had long been seeking state or county funds to purchase or lease the beach land. The beach land was rezoned into a "beach recreational district" when such funds were not forthcoming. The court applied the usual presumption of validity and sustained the beach zoning as a "legitimate exercise of the city's police power in the interests of public health, safety, morals and general welfare." The reference to "morals" resulted from the trial court's finding that "the construction of houses on pilings [for protection against floods] might create problems by reason of the possible use of the areas under the residences for immoral purposes"! *Id.* at 938.

7. Extremely restrictive zoning regulations may be imposed on land for a great variety of purposes. In many cases in recent years—as in *Eldridge, Arastra,* and *McCarthy, supra*—the purpose, broadly speaking, is environmental protection. Cases dealing with the use of zoning regulations to protect wetlands, shorelands, flood plains, and coastal areas against development will be found *infra* in the chapter on Environmental Land Use Controls.

Should the courts distinguish between zoning regulations which (1) substantially decrease or destroy land values in furtherance of recognized zoning objectives such as the separation of incompatible land uses, (2) substantially decrease or destroy land values in furtherance of environmental protection objectives that could also be achieved by public land acquisition, (3) substantially decrease or destroy land values as an incidental result of prohibiting private land development pending ultimate public acquisition, and (4) are intended to substantially decrease or destroy land values as a prelude to public acquisition?

8. Many courts have held that landowners must "exhaust their administrative remedies" by seeking a variance before directly challenging the validity of zoning regulations as applied to a particular tract of land. In this situation, the "exhaustion" requirement has been defended on separation of power principles. Application of the "exhaustion" rule is ordinarily tempered by judicial recognition that resort to the administrative process should not be required when such resort would be futile. This was recognized by the majority in the *Eldridge* case, *supra,* and by the majority in the *Girsh* case, *infra* p. 347. *Accord, Sinclair Pipe Line Co. v. Village of Richton Park,* 167 N.E.2d 406 (Ill. 1960) (no need to apply for a variance because a variance may not be employed to change the permitted use of land). But there is a good deal of uncertainty as to when the "exhaustion" rule will be applied. In *Arverne Bay Constr. Co. v. Thatcher, supra* p. 236, the plaintiff landowner in fact had sought a variance before he directly attacked the constitutionality of the zoning regulations, but the variance was denied on the ground that "the unfavorable conditions [which were the basis of the application for a variance — Eds.] . . . were not peculiar to the site in question." If the landowner had first sued to invalidate the zoning regulations, without first seeking a variance, *quaere* whether the court would have applied the "exhaustion" requirement.

When judicial review of the adverse administrative decision is available, the landowner may be required to seek that relief before seeking an independent judicial remedy to invalidate the zoning regulations. In other words, he may be required to seek direct judicial review of the administrative decision to deny him a variance. As in *Poe v. City of Baltimore,* 216 A.2d 707 (Md. 1966), the court may decide to review the "validity" of the ordinance when an appeal is taken from the administrative decision to deny a variance. Review of "validity" will be hampered, however, if the landowner has not been allowed to make a record on the "validity" issue before the zoning board of adjustment. He will not be allowed to make such a record if the board decides that it does not have jurisdiction to hear the constitutional issue, as is likely in most jurisdictions. Even if the landowner is allowed to make a record on the "validity" issue, he will be hampered by the fact that the variance hearing is not an adversary proceeding. For discussion, see Note, Exhaustion of Remedies in Zoning Cases, 1964 Wash. U.L.Q. 368.

In jurisdictions where "use" variances may not be granted by the zoning board of adjustment, a landowner may be required to seek legislative relief—*i.e.,* a rezoning amendment—before he brings an action to challenge the validity of the "use" regulations applicable to his land, unless it would be futile to do so. What constitutes "futility" remains a mystery. See *National Brick Co. v. City of Chicago,* 235 N.E.2d 301 (Ill. App. 1968), refusing to apply the futility rule in a case in which the property owner failed to seek a zoning amendment, and argued that the city's failure to observe an earlier adverse court decision on the same property indicated that it would not rezone. But see *Fiore v. City of Highland Park,* 221 N.E.2d 323 (Ill. App. 1966), applying the futility rule in a case in which the property owner's application was pending before the plan commission at the time he filed suit but it appeared that the commission would not respond favorably.

Does the exhaustion doctrine apply when a challenge to a zoning action is brought by third parties? This issue was considered in *Environmental Law Fund, Inc. v. Town of Corte Madera,* 122 Cal. Rptr. 282 (Cal. App. 1975). The Fund and two other individual plaintiffs brought an action challenging the validity of a development approval given to a developer. Neither the Fund nor other third parties were parties in the administrative proceedings in which a development permit was issued to the developer, and they did not have notice of these proceedings. The town argued that the third party challengers were barred from seeking judicial relief against the development approval because they had not appealed to the town board, as authorized by the town ordinance.

The court refused to apply the exhaustion doctrine in this case. It noted that when the exhaustion doctrine is applied to parties to an administrative proceeding only their private rights are at issue. "Application of the [exhaustion] doctrine against them is therefore consonant with such familiar principles as waiver and *res judicata,* and the interests of justice are not disserved." *Id.* at 286 (emphasis by the court).

The court continued:

> Application of the [exhaustion] doctrine against . . . [the Fund and other third parties] would involve substantially more. . . . [These third parties] are thus pursuing more than privately-held rights, and are asserting more than privately-held grievances; they are acting as members of the public and in the public interest. Application of the exhaustion doctrine against them, by reason of

their "default" in the administrative proceeding to which they were not "parties" at all, would mean in effect the imputation of their "default" to the public in the absence of any factual basis for such imputation.

Id. at 287. Should the court have held the other way if the Fund had been a party to the proceeding? If it had had notice of the proceeding but had chosen not be become a party?

2. The "Districting" Requirement

ROCKHILL v. CHESTERFIELD TOWNSHIP

Supreme Court of New Jersey
23 N.J. 117, 128 A.2d 473 (1956)

The opinion of the court was delivered by
HEHER, J.

The issue here concerns the legal sufficiency of an ordinance of the defendant Township of Chesterfield adopted October 1, 1955, entitled "An ordinance regulating and restricting the location, the size and use of buildings and structures and the use of land in the Township of Chesterfield in the County of Burlington, providing for [its] administration and enforcement . . . , fixing penalties for the violation thereof and establishing a zoning board of adjustment."

The regulation is denominated a "zoning ordinance"; and its "purpose" is declared to be: ". . . lessening congestion in the streets; securing safety from fire, panic and other dangers; promoting health, morals or the general welfare; providing adequate light, air and sanitation, preventing the overcrowding of land or buildings; and avoiding undue concentration of population, . . .," the statutorily-enumerated considerations of policy involved in use zoning. R.S. 40:55-32, N.J.S.A.

But the zoning scheme laid down in the ordinance is not in the conventional pattern; and the inquiry is whether it conforms to the constitutional and statutory principle and policy.

Land and building uses, Article III, shall be "in conformance with the provisions" of the ordinance and the attached "schedule of regulations" entitled "Schedule of Permitted Uses and General Regulations"; and "In addition, certain uses may be permitted and certain modification of requirements may be made in accordance with the special provisions" of the ordinance. "Normal agricultural uses shall be permitted in accordance with the general standards set forth in the schedule," Article IV, including "Accessory uses on the same lot with and customarily incidental to the principal use," in particular, "a roadside stand for sale of farm products conducted solely by the farm operator," and "Migrant housing facilities to be used only on a seasonal basis for migratory farm workers . . . when the buildings are on the farm property and migrant workers perform

their labor for occupants of the farm," conditioned as to location in
relation to the highway and the observance of statutes and state
health regulations pertaining to "migrant housing."

"Residential uses shall be permitted in accordance with the general
standards set forth in the schedule," Article V, including certain
"Accessory uses on the same lot and customarily incidental to the
permitted dwelling unit," provided that (a) "No dwelling unit shall
be located within 250 feet of, or between buildings of an existing or
permitted light industrial activity"; (b) where a dwelling unit is
located on a corner lot, there shall be a side yard as therein
prescribed; and (c) there shall be "off-street parking for all
residences," as set down in the schedule.

Provision is then made, Article VI, for "Special Uses"; and this is
the declared "Purpose": "In view of the rural characteristics of the
Township, it is deemed desirable to permit certain structures and
uses but only after investigation has shown that such structures and
uses will be beneficial to the general development"; and "In order
to assure that such structures and uses meet all requirements and
standards, all applications for zoning permits shall be referred to the
Planning Board for review in accordance with Revised Statutes
40:55-1.13 [N.J.S.A.]" The planning board is directed to "investigate
the matter in accordance with the standards herein provided and
submit its recommendations in writing to the Governing Body within
45 days after the filing of the application with the Zoning Officer."
But the board shall, before the recommendation is made, conduct
a public hearing in accordance with the procedure provided by R.S.
40:55-1.7, N.J.S.A., on the notice "required for subdivision plat
approval." And the governing body "shall, no later than the second
regularly scheduled meeting after the receipt" of the board's report,
"either approve or disapprove the application by resolution based
on the standards as set forth" in the ordinance; and "if approved,
the necessary zoning permit shall then be issued."

These are the stated "special structures and uses which may be
permitted only in keeping with the special standards herein listed,"
Article VI: (a) an "existing one-family dwelling may be converted into
multi-family dwelling units," subject to certain conditions and
specifications and the submission of the plans to the planning board
"prior to approval or disapproval"; (b) "Neighborhood business"
may be permitted subject to prescribed physical conditions,
including these particular uses: groceries and foodstuffs; package
liquors; drugs and pharmaceuticals; confectionery; dry goods and
notions; feed and grain; stationery; hardware and paints; radio and
television services; books and tobacco; periodicals and newspapers;
antiques; barber and beauty shops; tailoring and dress-making; dry
cleaning and laundry collection but not processing facilities; shoe
repairing; banks and professional offices; and service or repair

establishments not employing more than three persons, all "neighborhood businesses" to provide "off-street loading and unloading facilities . . . located on the same lot" but not "in the required front yard area," and to conform to regulations as to signs indicating the business use; (c) "Designed shopping center units may be permitted" subject to specified conditions, and "Any business use that is not specifically prohibited within the Township and not included in Section 3, paragraph b, of Article VI may be considered to be a permitted business use if the Planning Board deems such business use to be desirable and to the best interests of the Township," provided that "An area at least five feet in width and following the lot lines of the business property if adjacent to residential properties shall be properly landscaped to form a buffer screen between residential and business uses," and the required illumination during evening business periods "shall be shielded from adjacent residential properties and public roads or streets"; (d) "Gasoline and Filling stations may be permitted" if certain requirements are met, provided that the "use shall be located on a lot whose lot lines are located not less than 300 feet from any existing dwelling and not less than 1000 feet from any public school or church," and at least 25 feet from the street line and rear and side property lines, and "any gasoline station shall not be located at the corner of any dangerous street or road intersection which is so termed by the Township Committee"; (e) "Restaurants and roadside refreshment uses may be permitted," at the same distances from other land uses prescribed in (d) *supra,* and provided, *inter alia,* that parking space "shall be available to adequately meet maximum capacity conditions," and parking areas shall be illuminated during evening business operations and "shielded from adjacent residential properties and public roads or streets"; (f) "Light industrial uses and other similar facilities having no adverse effect on surrounding property and deemed desirable to the general economic well-being of the Township may be permitted," and "Included among such uses may be administrative offices, laboratories, research offices and light manufacturing or processing," provided that the "industrial activity shall not by its own inherent characteristics or industrial processes be noxious or injurious to the adjacent properties by reason of the production or emission of dust, smoke, refuse matter, odor, gas, fumes, noise, vibration, unsightly conditions, or other similar conditions," also that certain sanitation requirements shall be met, and that no "building or structure" shall be located within 1,000 feet of an "existing or proposed school or public facility" or 250 feet from the "adjoining lot line of any existing dwelling unit" or 200 feet from the "adjoining lot line of any business use"; and (g) "Public utility uses such as distribution lines, towers, substations and telephone exchanges but no service or storage yards may be permitted," provided the planning board finds that the "design of any structure in connection with facility conforms to the general character of the surrounding area and will in no way adversely affect the safe and comfortable enjoyment of property rights of the Township," and there is provision for "adequate and attractive fences and other safety devices" and "sufficient landscaping . . . periodically maintained."

"Non-conforming uses" are continued, Article VII; and there are "general regulations," Article VIII, pertaining to "open space" and "visibility at intersections" which need not be set out here.

Certain uses are prohibited altogether, Article IX . . . these among others: "Commercial or periodic auction sales"; "Used car lots or used car sales"; "Tourist cabins, motels and trailer camps"; "Manufacture or sale of pottery and cast stone decorations"; "Drive-in theatres"; "Slaughter houses and *abbatoirs*"; "Junk yards and scrap reclamation"; "Garbage-fed piggeries"; "Billboards and advertising of products not for sale on the premises"; "Salvage and wrecking activities"; and "Multi-family dwelling units, other than permitted conversions; and similar types of uses of land, structures and buildings so adjudged by the Zoning Board of Adjustment."

Provision is made for the "enforcement" of the ordinance by a "zoning officer" to be appointed by the governing body, and for zoning permits and certificates of occupancy where the terms of the ordinance have been met.

   . . . .

The Law Division of the Superior Court set aside Article VI, section 3(c) iv, of the ordinance providing that "any business use . . . not specifically prohibited" within the township, and not included in section 3, paragraph B of that Article, "may be considered to be a permitted business use," if the planning board deems such use "to be desirable and to the best interest of the township," as a regulation wanting in "proper constitutional standards to guide the administrative action" of the board and the township committee, but sustained the ordinance otherwise; and we certified here plaintiff's appeal from so much of the judgment as affirms the ordinance in part. There was no cross-appeal. . . .

The constitutional and statutory zoning principle is territorial division according to the character of the lands and structures and their peculiar suitability for particular uses, and uniformity of use within the division. And the legislative grant of authority has the selfsame delineation. R.S. 40:55-30, as amended by L. 1948, c. 305, p. 1221, N.J.S.A.

The local governing body is empowered, R.S. 40:55-31, as amended by L. 1948, c. 305, N.J.S.A., to divide the municipality into districts of such number, shape, and area as may be deemed best suited to carry out the statutory policy, and to regulate and restrict the construction and use of buildings and other structures and the use of land within such districts, provided that "All such regulations shall be uniform for each class or kind of buildings or other structures or uses of land throughout each district, but the regulations in one district may be different from those in other districts." And such regulations shall be, R.S. 40:55-32, N.J.S.A., in accordance with a "comprehensive plan and designed" to subserve the public welfare in one or more of the enumerated particulars involving the public health, safety, morals, or the general welfare, and "shall be made with reasonable consideration among other things, to the character of the district and its peculiar suitability for particular uses, and with a view of conserving the value of property and encouraging the most appropriate use of land throughout such municipality." And thus it is basic to the local exercise of the power that the use restrictions be general and uniform in the particular district, delimited in keeping with the constitutional and statutory considerations; otherwise, there would be the arbitrary discrimination at war with the substance of due process and the equal protection of the laws.

Classification to this end must be reasonably based in the public interest to be served. It is fundamental in our zoning policy that all property in like circumstances be treated alike. There cannot be invidious distinctions. And so it is that the use-district restraints are required to be general and uniform. All this, in virtue of the legislative grant itself, quite apart from constitutional zoning concept and the precepts for the fulfillment of basic civil liberties. *Raskin v. Town of Morristown,* 21 N.J. 180, 121 A.2d 378 (1956); *Beirn v. Morris,* 14 N.J. 529, 103 A.2d 361 (1954). Constitutional uniformity and equality demands that classification be founded in real and not feigned differences related to the purposes for which the classes are formed, *i. e.,* zoning by districts according to the "nature and extent" of the use of land and buildings, to serve the statutory police considerations, some or all, the regulations to have reasonable regard to the "character of the district and its peculiar suitability for particular uses." *Katobimar Realty Company v. Webster,* 20 N.J. 114, 118 A.2d 824 (1955). "Spot zoning" would contravene the constitutional and statutory principle of zoning by districts in consonance with the character of the lands and structures and use suitability, and uniformity of use within the division. *Moriarty v. Pozner,* 21 N.J. 199, 121 A.2d 527 (1956). Such is the case here.

The scheme of the ordinance is the negation of zoning. It overrides the basic concept of use zoning by districts, that is to say, territorial division according to the character of the lands and structures and their peculiar use suitability and a comprehensive regulatory plan to advance the general good within the prescribed range of the police power. The local design is "normal agricultural" and residence uses and the specified "special uses" by the authority of the planning board and the local governing body, generally where "investigation has shown that such structures and uses will be beneficial to the general development," and "light industrial uses and other similar facilities having no adverse effect on surrounding property and deemed desirable to the general economic well-being of the Township," terms hardly adequate to channel local administrative discretion but, at all events, making for the "piecemeal" and "spot" zoning alien to the constitutional and statutory principle of land use zoning by districts and comprehensive planning for the fulfillment of the declared policy. The fault is elementary and vital; the rule of the ordinance is *ultra vires* and void. See *Raskin v. Town of Morristown,* supra.

Reserving the use of the whole of the municipal area for "normal agricultural" and residence uses, and then providing for all manner of "special uses," "neighborhood" and other businesses, even "light industrial" uses and "other similar facilities," placed according to local discretion without regard to districts, ruled by vague and illusive criteria, is indeed the antithesis of zoning. It makes for arbitrary and discriminatory interference with the basic right of private property, in no real sense concerned with the essential common welfare. The statute, N.J.S.A. 40:55-39, provides for regulation by districts and for exceptions and variances from the prescribed land uses under given conditions. The course taken here would flout this essential concept of district zoning according to a comprehensive plan designed to fulfull the declared statutory policy. Comprehensive zoning means an orderly and coordinate system of community development according to socio-economic needs. See Professor Haar's exposition of the relation between planning principles and the exercise of the zoning power, "In Accordance With a Comprehensive Plan," 68 Harv.L.Rev. 1154, and the comment, p. 1170, that the phrase "in accordance with a comprehensive plan" apparently had its origin in section 3 of the Standard State Zoning Enabling Act, accompanied by this explanatory note: "This will prevent haphazard or piecemeal zoning."

. . . .

Zoning and planning are not identical in concept. *Mansfield & Swett, Inc., v. Town of West Orange,* 120 N.J.L. 145, 198 A. 225 (Sup.Ct.1938). Zoning is a separation of the municipality into districts for the most appropriate use of the land, by general rules according to a comprehensive plan for the common good in matters within the domain of the police power. And, though the landowner does not have a vested right to a particular zone classification, one of the essential purposes of zoning regulation is the stabilization of property uses. Investments are made in lands and structures on the faith of district use control having some degree of permanency, a well considered plan that will stand until changing conditions dictate otherwise. Such is the nature of use zoning by districts according to a comprehensive plan. . . . The regulations here are in contravention of the principle.

The ordinance is vacated as *ultra vires* the enabling statute; and the cause is remanded for judicial action accordingly.

For reversal: Chief Justice VANDERBILT and Justices HEHER, OLIPHANT, WACHENFELD, BURLING and JACOBS—6.

For affirmance: None.

———

Comments: 1. At the time of the principal case, the New Jersey zoning enabling act was practically identical to the Standard State Zoning Enabling Act, *supra* p. 217. The basic grant of power in both statutes was "to regulate and restrict the height, number of stories, and size of buildings and other structures, the percentage of lot that may be occupied, the size of yards, courts, and other open spaces, the density of population, and the location and use of buildings, structures, and land for trade, industry, residence, or other purposes." Was this basic grant of power limited by the further provision, included in both statutes, that "[f]or any or all of said purposes [*i.e.*, promoting health, safety, morals or the general welfare of the community] the local legislative body *may* divide the municipality into districts of such number, shape, and area as may be deemed best suited to carry out the purposes of this act"? (Emphasis supplied.) Does the latter provision *require* that the municipality be divided into "districts" in order that buildings and land uses may be regulated? Should the latter provision be construed as prohibiting the local governing body from treating the entire municipality as a single district in which residential and "normal" agricultural uses are permitted as a matter of right, and other land uses are "permitted only in keeping with the special standards . . . listed"? Why may the local governing body not regulate the designated "special structures and uses" by setting up "performance standards" instead of segregating them in different districts?

2. Does the fact that the ultimate location of the "special structures and uses" listed in the township's ordinance cannot be predicted in advance mean that the zoning regulations of Chesterfield Township are not "in accordance with a comprehensive plan"? Will the granting of permits for the listed "special structures and uses" result in the sort of "haphazard or piecemeal zoning" which the draftsmen of the Standard Act sought to prevent by requiring the zoning regulations to be "in accordance with a comprehensive plan"?

3. Even if it were assumed, *arguendo,* that the New Jersey zoning enabling act did not preclude the regulation of the "special structures and uses" listed in the township's ordinance by means of a permit system, should the ordinance be held invalid on constitutional "equal protection" grounds — *i.e.,* because the designated "special structures and uses" could be "placed according to local discretion . . . ruled by vague and illusive criteria," with resulting "arbitrary and discriminatory interference with the basic right of private property"? Were the "performance standards" set out with respect to the designated "special structures and uses" in fact too

"vague and illusive" to provide assurance that the local planning board and governing body would act in a nondiscriminatory manner in granting or denying permits?

4. It can be argued that a zoning ordinance of the kind held invalid in the principal case is, in fact, well fitted to the needs of a largely rural community which expects urban development to overtake it within a relatively short time. Perhaps the best analysis of this type of zoning — called "reserve-special use zoning" by the author — is to be found in Note, 30 U. Cin. L. Rev. 297 (1961), which also discusses other zoning techniques for dealing with urban development in previously undeveloped communities. Other courts have also ruled against zoning techniques comparable to those considered in *Rockhill. See Town of Hobart v. Collier,* 87 N.W.2d 868 (Wis. 1958).

5. As an alternative or usually in addition to land use zones, some communities have experimented with the adoption of performance standards. These standards are usually applicable to industrial uses, and regulate these uses by imposing specifications relating to such factors as noise and smell. For example, in a given zone the noise level may be regulated by imposing a maximum decibel limit beyond which the industry is not allowed to go. In theory, performance standards can provide an alternative to zoning by districts because they afford a method for controlling the harmful effects that are supposed to result from discordant land uses. In practice they present problems of application, especially because their administration is difficult and requires constant monitoring. *See* Gillespie, Industrial Zoning and Beyond: Compatibility Through Performance Standards, 46 J. Urb. L. 723 (1969). *See also* G. Hagevik, D. Mandelker & R. Brail, Air Quality Management and Land Use Planning 166-81 (1974).

3. The Fall-Out from "Districting": Nonconforming Uses

One of the most troublesome problems which faces the planners and administrators of zoning ordinances is where to draw the boundary lines of use districts. The haphazard growth of our cities and villages has resulted in an interlarding of strips of residential areas with stores, gas stations, and even heavy industrial properties. To super-impose a use map upon an established urban area must inevitably result in creating large numbers of nonconforming uses and, in may cases, in establishing dividing lines between use districts which will offend those who own property on or near the border line.

R. Babcock, The Illinois Supreme Court and Zoning: A Study in Uncertainty, 15 U. Chi. L. Rev. 87, 94 (1947).

Whether a zoning ordinance will create nonconforming uses often becomes a strategic question which affects the drawing of district boundaries. This point is often overlooked in discussions of the nonconforming use problem, which typically start with the assumption that land use mixtures are evil and should be eliminated.

The draftsmen of the Standard State Zoning Enabling Act omitted any reference to nonconforming uses, and most of the early zoning legislation (including the pioneering New York legislation) was as silent as the Standard Act on this point. The omission of any reference to the problem of nonconforming uses was apparently based largely on political considerations; the draftsmen of the early enabling statutes feared that state legislatures would not enact them if they expressly authorized the elimination of nonconforming uses without payment of compensation. Thus, Bassett states that,

> During the preparatory work for the zoning of Greater New York fears were constantly expressed by property owners that existing nonconforming buildings would be ousted. The demand was general that this should not be done. The Zoning Commission went as far as it could to explain that existing nonconforming uses could continue, that zoning looked to the future, and that if orderliness could be brought about in the future the nonconforming buildings would to a considerable extent be changed by natural causes as time went on. It was also stated by the Commission that the purpose of zoning was to stabilize and protect lawful investments and not to injure assessed valuations or existing uses. This has always been the view in New York. No steps have been taken to oust existing nonconforming uses. Consideration for investments made in accordance with the earlier laws has been one of the strong supports of zoning in that city.

E. Bassett, Zoning 113 (rev. ed. 1940).

Whether the United States Supreme Court, in the 1920's, would have upheld zoning regulations requiring termination of lawfully established nonconforming uses without compensation is far from clear. *Hadacheck* and *Reinman* would certainly have supported termination requirements applicable to "nuisance" types of land use, but would not necessarily have supported termination requirements where the nonconforming use, though "incompatible" with surrounding land uses, was not close to being a "nuisance." Moreover, the *Pennsylvania Coal Co.* case could have been adduced against any termination requirement in cases where the capital value of the nonconforming use was substantial. In any case, many state courts could have been expected to take a stricter view of the limits of the police power and to hold that elimination of nonconforming uses without compensation was an unconstitutional "taking" of private property.

A few of the early zoning enabling acts expressly provided that nonconforming uses could not be eliminated without payment of compensation. *See, e.g.,* Michigan's City and Village Zoning Act § 3a, as amended in 1947, Mich. Stat. Ann. § 5.2933(1) (1976):

The lawful use of land or a structure exactly as such existed at the time of the enactment of the ordinance affecting them, may be continued, except as hereinafter provided, although such use or structure does not conform with the provisions of such ordinance. The legislative body [of the municipality] may in its discretion provide by ordinance for the resumption, restoration, reconstruction, extension or substitution of non-conforming uses or structures upon such terms and conditions as may be provided in the ordinance. In addition to the power granted in this section, cities and villages may acquire by purchase, condemnation or otherwise private property for the removal of non-conforming uses and structures: Provided, The property shall not be used for public housing. The legislative body may in its discretion provide that the cost and expense of acquiring such private property be paid from general funds, or the cost and expense or any portion thereof be assessed to a special district. The elimination of such non-conforming uses and structures in a zoned district as herein provided is hereby declared to be for a public purpose and for a public use. The legislative body shall have authority to institute and prosecute proceedings for the condemnation of non-conforming uses and structures under the power of eminent domain in accordance with the laws of the state or provisions of any city or village charter relative to condemnation.

When the state's zoning enabling act was silent on the subject of nonconforming uses, the early zoning ordinances almost invariably provided expressly that lawfully established nonconforming uses might continue, although many ordinances contained a wide variety of restrictive regulations which were meant to hasten their disappearance. Such provisions are still a feature of almost all local zoning ordinances. Typically, they prohibit or severely restrict the physical extention of nonconforming uses, impose limitations on the repair, alteration, or reconstruction of nonconforming structures, and prohibit the resumption of nonconforming uses after "abandonment" or "discontinuance."

Physical extension of nonconforming use. The usual position on this question is strict, as is evidenced by *Martin v. Cestone,* 110 A.2d 54 (N.J. Super. 1954). The nonconforming parcel consisted of four lots, only one of which was used for the outdoor storage of heavy equipment on the date the zoning ordinance was effective. The owner of the lot was not allowed to extend the storage of equipment to the other three parcels. Exemption from the ordinance was held to be based on preexisting use and not intention, and in this case there was no action taken which evidenced a preexisting use of the remaining three lots prior to the effective date of the ordinance. Sand

and gravel and other extractive nonconforming uses may be considered as distinguished, as these may not be continued without extending them. "The policy of the law in this State . . . is to restrict rather than to extend a nonconforming use." *Id.* at 56. *See also Kelley-Williamson Co. v. City of Rockford,* 209 N.E.2d 681 (Ill. App. 1965).

For a contrary case see *Conway v. City of Greenville,* 173 S.E.2d 648 (S.C. 1970). Part of a large tract had been used for commercial purposes — the operation of a construction business — and the court held that this prior nonconforming use justified the use of the entire property for construction of a shopping center. It quoted a statement in a zoning annotation to the effect that the question is whether the character and adaptability of the incipient use to the entire parcel implies an appropriation of the entire parcel. The court so found here, primarily on the ground that the tract fronted on a heavily traveled highway, and that the area around it had been developed commercially.

Repairs, alterations, and reconstructions. The relationship between the zoning code, governing land-use, and building codes, governing safety, can be difficult. In *Application of O'Neal,* 92 S.E.2d 189 (N.C. 1956), the nonconforming use was a small nursing home. Its owners were notified that the building must be torn down because it was not fireproof and because it violated the institutional provisions of the building code. The owners wished to reconstruct a fireproof nursing home on their premises.

The court noted that the new home could not exceed the capacity of the old, but held that the applicants were entitled to rebuild their building. The protection of preexisting "lawful" uses referred to the zoning code and not the building code, and protected any use that was lawful under the zoning regulations. A reasonable construction of the zoning regulations required that a balance be struck between the impairment of neighborhood character and the restriction of an existing use of land by means of new regulations. This ordinance did not contain a prohibition on "structural alterations" and, in addition, the new construction was imposed involuntarily under the building code.

But compare *Granger v. Board of Adjustment,* 44 N.W.2d 399 (Iowa 1950), in which a manufacturer of burial vaults was allowed to replace the brick and frame walls and roof of his nonconforming building with concrete and steel. The court held that the work could be categorized as a reasonable repair rather than as a structural alteration. *Contra, Selligman v. Von Allmen Bros.,* 179 S.W.2d 207 (Ky. 1944). What is the effect on this kind of case of the provision, sometimes found in zoning ordinances, which permits structural alterations "required by law"? *See A. L. Carrithers & Son v. City of*

Louisville, 63 S.W.2d 493 (Ky. 1933) (construed to permit alteration).

Abandonment and discontinuance. Zoning ordinance provisions often provide that a nonconforming use that has been discontinued may not be resumed, and have usually been interpreted to require an abandonment of the nonconforming use before the right to continue will be terminated. The effectiveness of these provisions has been limited by the requirement that an actual intent to abandon must be shown. *See* Annot., 56 A.L.R.3d 14, 43-46 (1974). The intent rule can be nullified by an ordinance provision specifying a time limit on the failure to exercise a nonconforming use; under these provisions, mere nonuse for the stated period of time is sufficient to terminate the nonconforming use. *See, e.g., State ex rel. Peterson v. Burt,* 166 N.W.2d 207 (Wis. 1969). Nevertheless, court decisions generally have been overwhelmingly favorable to landowners wishing to resume a nonconforming use that has been discontinued over a period of time. *See* 56 A.L.R.3d at 27-30, *supra.*

PROBLEM: Following local civil rights disturbances, the owner of a store in a ghetto neighborhood closed up the premises. It took him almost a year to find a new tenant. His use was nonconforming, and the local ordinance provided that a nonconforming use abandoned for more than six months could not be resumed. The ordinance defined "abandonment" as the "cessation" of a nonconforming use for the six-month period. Has the nonconforming use been abandoned? The court thought so in *Canada's Tavern, Inc. v. Town of Glen Echo,* 271 A.2d 664 (Md. 1970), construing an identical ordinance. A dissenting opinion found "grave" constitutional questions in this holding. What are they? The dissent suggested, in part, that an amortization period of six months would have been unconstitutional as well.

Some commentators have deplored the backward-looking character of zoning regulation which is implicit in the nonconforming use concept and have suggested that enabling legislation be written simply to authorize the regulation of any "development." This approach is basically the English method of land use control. "Development," as in the American Law Institute's Model Land Development Code, § 1-202 (2) (1976), would then be defined to include the following:

"(b) a reconstruction, alteration of the size, or material change in the external appearance, of a structure or land;

"(c) a change in the intensity of use of land, such as an increase in the number of businesses, manufacturing establishments, offices or dwelling units in a structure or on land."

Do you consider this approach to land use regulation an improvement over the present system?

Quite early in the history of zoning, it was occasionally argued that there was no justification for treating established nonconforming uses differently — and more favorably — than merely planned or potential future uses, and that permitting nonconforming uses to continue was arbitrary and discriminatory. Most of the early cases sustained such differential treatment. *See, e.g., State ex rel. Manhein v. Harrison,* 114 So. 159 (La. 1927) (reasonable measure to avoid unduly harsh treatment of nonconforming uses).

The term "nonconforming use" is imprecise. It may include any of the following: (a) various types of open land use such as junkyards, lumber yards, and storage yards for heavy machinery; (b) small structures of a nonconforming type such as a shed or a billboard; (c) buildings designed for a conforming use, or at least capable of such use, which have in fact been devoted to some nonconforming use — *e.g.,* an office or store on the ground floor of a residential building; (d) buildings designed, and really only usable, for nonconforming purposes — *e.g.,* a factory building; (e) the use of a building of a generally conforming type for a conforming use, but with some nonconformity as to lot size, lot frontage, setbacks, height, or bulk.

It is not always easy to determine when a nonconforming use has been lawfully established. Where the "use" itself — whether of open land or of a structure — rather than the structure (if any) with which it is associated is nonconforming, most courts seem to require a qualitatively substantial devotion of the property to that use prior to the date when the zoning regulation prohibiting the use becomes effective. *See, e.g., Township of Fruitport v. Baxter,* 148 N.W.2d 888 (Mich. App. 1967), holding that it was not sufficient that several truckloads of junked cars were moved onto the tract just before the effective date of the zoning regulation. *But see Kubby v. Hammond,* 198 P.2d 134 (Ariz. 1948) (nonconforming junkyard was established by a show of intent to establish such a use — building a fence and placing a few junked cars on the tract); *County of DuPage v. Gary-Wheaton Bank,* 192 N.E.2d 311 (Ill. App. 1963) (nonconforming gravel pit was established by one day's work therein).

Where a developer undertakes a building project which becomes nonconforming under new lot area, frontage, setback, height, bulk, density or building type regulations before construction is completed, a more difficult problem is presented. Up to and through the stage where the developer obtains a building permit, very few courts have found that the developer acquires a vested right to a nonconforming use. Subsequent to the building permit stage, however, the developer normally signs contracts for the construction of the project, does clearance work on the site, and makes other expenditures in reliance on the building permit. Some courts find a vested right to a nonconforming use at this stage, and a vested right is even more often found to have accrued when the developer has started to install the foundations on the site. Most courts would probably find a vested right to a nonconforming use when the foundation work is completed and substantial work has been done above ground level. *See also infra* p. 679.

Although the most important factor in the court's determination as to accrual of a vested right to a nonconforming use is the stage which the project reached before the zoning ordinance prohibited it, other factors may also be significant. Thus, if the developer rushed to beat the deadline on a proposed zoning regulation which he knew was under consideration, courts tend to be unsympathetic to him, viewing his situation, in effect, as one of self-inflicted hardship. On the other hand, if the local governing body rushes to change the zoning regulations in order to block a particular development, or the local officials have obviously been stalling on the issuance of a building permit while trying to get a zoning amendment passed to stop the project, this tends to favor the developer. And courts are likely to be sympathetic to the developer if the local officials have encouraged the developer to go ahead, although courts are reluctant to find that a municipality is estopped by the acts of its officials.

For thorough and detailed consideration of problems arising in connection with nonconforming uses, see 1 R. Anderson, American Law of Zoning, ch. 6 (2d ed. 1976); 4 N. Williams, American Land Planning Law, ch. 109 (1975).

HARBISON v. CITY OF BUFFALO

Court of Appeals of New York
4 N.Y.2d 553, 152 N.E.2d 42 (1958)

FROESSEL, J. Petitioner Andrew Harbison, Sr., purchased certain real property located at 35 Cumberland Avenue in the city of Buffalo on January 5, 1924. Shortly thereafter he erected a 30-by 40-foot-frame building thereon, and commenced operating a cooperage business, which, with his son, he has continued to date. The building has not been enlarged, and the volume of petitioners' business is stated to be the same now as then. The only difference is that, whereas petitioners formerly dealt mainly with wooden barrels, they now recondition, clean and paint "used" steel drums or barrels. No issue of that difference is made here. These drums, or barrels, are stacked to a height of about 10 feet in the yard, and on an average day about 600 or 700 barrels are stored there.

When petitioner Andrew Harbison, Sr., established his business in 1924, the street upon which it was located was an unpaved extension of an existing street, the city operated a dump in the area, and there was a glue factory in the vicinity. At the present time, the glue factory has gone, and there are residences adjoining both sides of petitioners' property and across the street. The change in the surrounding area is reflected by the fact that in 1924 the land was unzoned, but since 1926 (except for the period between 1949 and

1953, when it was zoned for business), the land has been zoned for residential use; and it is presently in an "R3" dwelling district.

Thus it is clear that at the time of the enactment of the first zoning ordinance affecting the premises, petitioners had an existing nonconforming use, that is, the conduct of a cooperage business in a residential zone. In 1936, under an ordinance which included the operations of petitioners in a definition of "junk dealers", petitioners applied for and received a license to carry on their business. Licenses were obtained by petitioners every year from 1936 through the fiscal year of 1956.

However, the ordinances of the City of Buffalo were amended, effective as of July 30, 1953, so as to state in chapter LXX (§ 18): "1. Continuing existing uses: Except as provided in this section, any nonconforming use of any building, structure, land or premises may be continued. Provided, however, that on premises situate in any 'R' district each use which is not a conforming use in the 'R5' district and which falls into one of the categories hereinafter enumerated shall cease or shall be changed to a conforming use within 3 years from the effective date of this amended chapter. The requirements of this subdivision for the termination of non-conforming uses shall apply in each of the following cases: . . . . (d) Any junk yard". (Defined in § 23, subd. 24.)

On November 27, 1956 the director of licenses of the City of Buffalo sent a letter to petitioners stating: "At a meeting of the Common Council under date of November 13, 1956 . . . [it] evinced its intention not to amend or modify the provisions of Chapter 18, Subdivision I of Chapter LXX of the Ordinances relating to non-conforming uses by junk yards . . . in 'R' districts. . . . You are hereby notified to discontinue the operation of your junk yard . . . at once". A subsequent application by petitioners for a wholesale junk license and one for a "drum reconditioning license" were refused on the ground that "said premises lie within an area zoned as 'R3' Dwelling District . . . and the operation of a junk yard and the outside storage of used materials is prohibited therein". Petitioners then brought this article 78 proceeding in the nature of mandamus in which they sought an order directing the city to issue a wholesale junk license to them, and the lower courts sustained them.

. . . .

In the major point involved on this appeal, the city argues that the ordinance requiring the termination of petitioners' nonconforming use of the premises as a junk yard within three years of the date of said ordinance is a valid exercise of its police power. Its claim is not based on the theory of nuisance . . . , and indeed this record contains little evidence as to the manner of operation of petitioners' business and the nature of the surrounding neighborhood. Rather, in this case, the city bases its claim largely on out-of-State decisions which have sustained ordinances requiring the termination of nonconforming uses or structures after a period of permitted continuance, where such "amortization" period was held reasonable.

When zoning ordinances are initially adopted to limit permissible uses of property, or when property is rezoned so as to prevent uses of property previously allowed, a degree of protection is constitutionally required to be given owners of property then using their premises in a manner forbidden by the ordinance. Thus we have held that, where substantial expenditures were made in the commencement of the erection of a building, a zoning ordinance may not deprive the owner of the "vested right" to complete the structure. . . . So, where the owner already has structures on the premises, he cannot be directed to cease using them . . ., just as he has the right to continue a prior business carried on there.

However, where the benefit to the public has been deemed of greater moment than the detriment to the property owner, we have sustained the prohibition of continuation of prior nonconforming uses. These cases involved the prior use of property for parking lots. . . . We have also upheld the restriction of projected uses of the property where, at the time of passage of the ordinance, there had been no substantial investment in the nonconforming use. . . . In these cases, there is no doubt that the property owners incurred a loss in the value of their property and otherwise as a result of the fact that they were unable to carry out their prospective uses; but we held that such a deprivation was not violative of the owners' constitutional rights. In *People v. Miller* [304 N.Y. 105, 108, 106 N.E.2d 34, 35], we explained these cases by stating that they involved situations in which the property owners would sustain only a "relatively slight and insubstantial" loss.

It should be noted that even where the zoning authorities may not prohibit a prior nonconforming use, they may adopt regulations which restrict the right of the property owner to enlarge or extend the use or to rebuild or make alterations to the structures on the property. . . .

As these cases indicate, our approach to the problem of permissible restrictions on nonconforming uses has recognized that, while the benefit accruing to the public in terms of more complete and effective zoning does not justify the immediate destruction of substantial businesses or structures developed or built prior to the ordinance (*People v. Miller,* supra, 304 N.Y. at p. 108, 106 N.E.2d at p. 35), the policy of zoning embraces the concept of the ultimate elimination of nonconforming uses, and thus the courts favor reasonable restriction of them. But, where the zoning ordinance could have required the cessation of a sand and gravel business on one year's notice, we have held it unconstitutional (*Town of Somers v. Camarco,* 308 N.Y. 537, 127 N.E.2d 327. . .).

The development of the policy that nonconforming uses should be protected and their existence preserved at the stage of development existing at the time of passage of the ordinance seems to have been based upon the assumption that the ultimate ends of zoning would be accomplished as the nonconforming use terminated with time. But this has not proven to be the case, as commentators have noted that the tendency of many of these uses is to flourish, capitalizing on the fact that no new use of that nature could be begun in the area. . . . Because of this situation, communities have sought new forms of ordinances restricting nonconforming uses, and in particular have turned to provisions which require termination after a given period of time.

With the exception of a decision of the Ohio Supreme Court (which may be explained on the basis of the particular language and application of the ordinance) in *City of Akron v. Chapman* (160 Ohio St. 382, 116 N.E.2d 697, 42 A.L.R.2d 1140 [criticized in 67 Harv.L.Rev. 1283]), the decisions have sustained ordinances where the time provided was held reasonable (*Livingston Rock & Gravel Co. v. County of Los Angeles,* 43 Cal.2d 121, 123-127, 272 P.2d 4; *City of Los Angeles v. Gage,* 127 Cal.App.2d 442, 453-458, 274 P:2d 34; *Standard Oil Co. v. City of Tallahassee,* 183 F.2d 410, cert. denied 340 U.S. 892, 71 S.Ct. 208, 95 L.Ed. 647; *Spurgeon v. Board of Comrs. of Shawnee County,* 181 Kan. 1008, 317 P.2d 798; *Grant v. Mayor & City Council of Baltimore,* 212 Md. 301, 129 A.2d 363; *State ex rel. Dema Realty Co. v. Jacoby,* 168 La. 752, 123 So. 314; *State ex rel. Dema Realty Co. v. McDonald,* 168 La. 172, cert. denied 280 U.S. 556, 50 S.Ct. 16, 74 L.Ed. 612; see *Robinson Brick Co. v. Luthi,* 115 Colo. 106, 111-112, 116 P.2d 171, 166 A.L.R. 655; *City of Corpus Christi v. Allen,* 152 Tex. 137, 142, 254 S.W.2d 759; *Stoner McCray System v. City of Des Moines,* 247 Iowa 1313, 1320, 78 N.W.2d 843; *United Adv. Co. v. Borough of Raritan,* 11 N.J. 144, 152, 93 A.2d 362).

A number of States and municipal bodies have adopted statutes authorizing this approach to the problem (as, e.g., Ill.Ann.Stat., ch. 24, & 73-1; 3 Va.Code [1950], § 15-843; see also list in n. 1 in *Grant v. Mayor & City Council of Baltimore,* supra); and the textwriters generally express the opinion that they would be constitutional if reasonable (1 Antieau on Municipal Corporation Law, § 7.03[3]; Bassett on Zoning, pp. 115-116; 8 McQuillin on Municipal Corporations [3d ed.], § 25.190; see, also, Law Reviews cited supra). . . .

Leaving aside eminent domain and nuisance, we have often stated in our decisions that the owner of land devoted to a prior nonconforming use, or on which a prior nonconforming structure exists (or has been substantially commenced), has the right to continue such use, but we have never held that this right may continue virtually in perpetuity. Now that we are for the first time squarely faced with the problem as to whether or not this right may be terminated after a reasonable period, during which the owner may have a fair opportunity to amortize his investment and to make future plans, we conclude that it may be, in accordance with the overwhelming weight of authority found in the courts of our sister States, as well as with the textwriters and commentators who have expressed themselves upon the subject.

With regard to prior nonconforming *structures,* reasonable termination periods based upon the amortized life of the structure are not, in our opinion, unconstitutional. They do not compel the immediate destruction of the improvements, but envision and allow for their normal life without extensive alterations or repairs. Such a regulation is akin to those we have sustained relating to restrictions upon the extension or substantial repair or replacement of prior nonconforming structures.

As to prior nonconforming *uses,* the closest case we have had is *Town of Somers v. Camarco* (308 N.Y. 537, 127 N.E.2d 327, supra; see discussion thereof in this connection in 7 Syracuse L.Rev. 158-161). In that case we held that, in view of defendant's investment and the business which had been built up and carried on over the years, the provisions of the ordinance which required defendant to apply for a permit to continue its business every year, and provided further that on the termination of any approval period any structure or improvement on the premises could be ordered removed and the premises restored to their original condition as nearly as practicable, were unreasonable. There the land involved had unusual resources which made it especially suitable for the nonconforming use carried on; the improvements were necessary for the operation of the business, and the period of termination was unreasonably short. Under these circumstances the ordinance would have deprived the property owner of his "vested rights". As was pointed out in the opinion (307 N.Y. at pp. 540-541, 127 N.E.2d at p. 328), "The courts, in order to afford stability to property owners who do have existing nonconforming uses, have imposed the test of reasonableness upon such exercise of the police powers. Therefore broad general rules and tests, such as expressed in *People v. Miller* (304 N.Y. 105, 106 N.E.2d 34), must always be considered in this context."

If, therefore, a zoning ordinance provides a sufficient period of permitted nonconformity, it may further provide that at the end of such period the use must cease. This rule is analogous to that with respect to nonconforming structures. In ascertaining the reasonable period during which an owner of property must be allowed to continue a nonconforming use, a balance must be found between social harm and private injury. We cannot say that a legislative body may not in any case, after consideration of the factors involved, conclude that the termination of a use after a period of time sufficient to allow a property owner an opportunity to amortize his investment and make other plans is a valid method of solving the problem.

To enunciate a contrary rule would mean that the use of land for such purposes as a tennis court, an open air skating rink, a junk yard or a parking lot — readily transferable to another site — at the date of the enactment of a zoning ordinance vests the owner thereof with the right to utilize the land in that manner in perpetuity, regardless of the changes in the neighborhood over the course of time. In the light of our ever expanding urban communities, such a rule appears to us to constitute an unwarranted restriction upon the Legislature in dealing with what has been described as "One of the major problems in effective administration of modern zoning ordinances" (1951 Wis.L.Rev. 685). When the termination provisions are reasonable in the light of the nature of the business of the property owner, the improvements erected on the land, the character of the neighborhood, and the detriment caused the property owner, we may not hold them constitutionally invalid.

. . . .

Here, petitioners are engaged in the business of reconditioning barrels or used steel drums. We are told that the value of the property together with the improvements is $20,000; but there is no indication of the relative value of the land and improvements separately. It was further alleged that the improvement consists of a 30- by 40-foot-frame building erected in 1924, and, in addition thereto, petitioners claim that at the insistence of the City of Buffalo, three years before the ordinance went into effect, they were obliged to install a special sewage system at a cost of $2,000 and a boiler at a cost of $700.

Material triable issues of fact thus remain, and a further hearing should adduce evidence relating to the nature of the surrounding neighborhood, the value and condition of the improvements on the premises, the nearest area to which petitioners might relocate, the cost of such relocation, as well as any other reasonable costs which bear upon the kind and amount of damages which petitioner might sustain, and whether petitioners might be able to continue operation of their business if not allowed to continue storage of barrels or steel drums outside their frame building. It is only upon such evidence that it may be ascertained whether the resultant injury to petitioners would be so substantial that the ordinance would be unconstitutional as applied to the particular facts of this case.

The order of the Appellate Division should be reversed, without costs, and the matter remanded to Special Term for a trial of the material issues and further proceedings as outlined in this opinion.

Van Voorhis, Judge (dissenting). The decision which is about to be rendered marks, in my view, the beginning of the end of the constitutional protection of property rights in this State in preexisting nonconforming uses under zoning ordinances. . . .

The plaintiffs' business is being confiscated, as has been mentioned, not on the basis that the improvements are assessed within $500, but regardless of how much the improvements may be worth. It is being terminated under the language of this ordinance for the sole reason that it is classified as a junk yard. I agree with what was said by the Appellate Division that "Whatever the law may be in California or Florida or other jurisdictions, in this State, the rule is as stated in *People v. Miller* (304 N.Y. 105, 107, 109, 106 N.E.2d 34, 35), to wit: 'It is the law of this state that nonconforming uses or structures, in existence when a zoning ordinance is enacted, are, as a general rule, constitutionally protected and will be permitted to continue, notwithstanding the contrary provision of the ordinance.' " Not less than nine cases are cited in our opinion in *People v. Miller* (304 N.Y. 105, 106 N.E.2d 34), as authority for this statement (304 N.Y. at p. 107, 106 N.E. at p. 34). Plaintiffs' business is not a nuisance. It is not injurious to life or health or morals. The neighbors whose sensibilities are offended would have found difficulty in abating it (even if it were a nuisance), for the reason that they "came to the nuisance," in the time honored phrase, by purchasing and moving into the neighborhood while petitioners' business was in operation. Neither, in my mind, can the city abolish this business under this ordinance. Even if this case came under the clause abrogating nonconforming uses where the buildings or structures on the lot do not exceed $500 in assessed value, the ordinance would still be unconstitutional. Zoning relates to the future development of municipalities. Areas in cities that have already been developed cannot be zoned retroactively. That is the function of municipal redevelopment, which is constitutionally authorized by statutes directing payment of just compensation for property that is appropriated. It is arbitrary, in my view, to draw the line at buildings or structures valued at $500 or less. That sum is negligible in the case of large stores or factories, whereas it may represent the savings of years to small proprietors. If the line can be drawn at $500, it will soon be extended to $5,000 or perhaps to $50,000. If, in principle, the city is allowed to confiscate property without payment of just compensation, it is no answer to say that it is taking only $500. It would be a novel proposition that a municipality can take private property for a public use without compensation provided that it does not take too much. Retroactive zoning, as this clearly is, resembles slum clearance more than zoning, which is for the future. If $500 is so small an amount, then why should not the city be obliged to pay it before confiscating this use, by the same token whereby it would be required to pay just compensation in cases of slum clearance? That there is no existing statutory authority to make such a payment in this case is not justification for confiscating the prior use which is a vested right. It would be no answer to argue that the small businessman does not need to be compensated provided that he is small enough. No such rule as that can be applied in zoning administration. If any distinction of that kind were relevant, it would be more appropriate to be guided by what proportion of the businessman's assets have been invested in improvements to his property. Observing the vagaries of modern zoning, many a businessman (large or small) might properly hesitate to invest his life savings in a store or other commercial or industrial property knowing that his investment is liable to be expropriated after the enterprise has been successfully launched, if some pressure group succeeds in obtaining favorable action from a municipal legislature. That is not in the public interest. Constitutional security against such developments is infinitely more important to the public at large than the occasional presence of a nonconforming use, or the possibility that a nonconforming use may acquire some advantage by way of monopoly in the use district. The comment by Chief Judge Hutcheson, of the United States Court of Appeals in the Fifth Circuit, is relevant in his dissenting opinion in *Standard Oil Co. v. City of Tallahassee* (183 F.2d 410, 413-414): "recognizing that even in this age of enlightenment the Constitution still protects the citizen against arbitrary and unreasonable action, I am in no doubt that in sustaining this admittedly confiscatory ordinance, a good general principle, the public interest in zoning, has been run into the ground, the tail of legislative confiscation by caprice has been permitted to wag the dog of judicial constitutional protection." This accords with the statement in *Incorporated Vil. of North Hornell v. Rauber* (181 Misc. 546, 552, 40 N.Y.S.2d 938, 944): "Rather is it argued that what used to be called confiscation is justifiable in an enlightened age, if enough people desire it and the amount to be taken away from the owner is not too great." . . .

In this instance, as has been said, the limitation to $500 assessed valuation in this zoning ordinance does not apply. Petitioners come under a different subdivision which outlaws after three years "Any junk yard, auto wrecking or dismantling establishment." This subdivision has no relation to the amount of money invested in physical improvements. In the case of petitioners' business, it stands admitted by the pleadings that petitioners have recently invested a substantial sum in the improvement of their property at the instance of the city, much more than $500. Junk yards or cooperage businesses are not operated without buildings and other improvements upon the land. Auto dismantling establishments, it is well known, are frequently conducted by unit auto parts companies which require sizable structures in which to dismantle the discarded automobiles and to store and merchandise the variety of used automobile parts and equipment. The reason on account of which these nonconforming uses are interdicted does not relate to the quantity of capital invested in buildings or improvements, but is that they are of a kind which is frequently disliked by the neighbors.

The circumstance that this is a cooperage establishment or junk yard ought not to obscure that the principle of the decision applies to any kind of business which, due to lapse of time, has been overtaken by changes in the neighborhood. . . .

Zoning, as originally conceived, related to the future development of municipalities. It was not an attempt to reconstruct the past. Cases such as *Village of Euclid v. Ambler Realty Co.* (272 U.S. 365, 47 S.Ct. 114, 71 L.Ed. 303) and *Lincoln Trust Co. v. Williams Bldg. Corp.* (229 N.Y. 313, 128 N.E. 209) were decided in this frame of reference. Pre-existing nonconforming uses were uniformly excepted from the operation of zoning ordinances, and the proprietors thereof were held to have the constitutional right to continue such uses . . . . We are now told that the protection of nonconforming uses in the beginning was a stratagem of city planners, "prompted by a fear that the courts would hold unconstitutional any zoning ordinance which attempted to eliminate existing nonconforming uses." 1951 Wis.L.Rev. 685; 35 Va.L.R. 352, citing Bassett on Zoning, p. 108, n. 1; also Noel, Retroactive Zoning and Nuisances, 41 Col.L.Rev. 457, 473.) The Virginia Law Review note, citing these authorities, states: "Those who led the zoning movement in its early stages adopted a lenient attitude towards nonconforming buildings. They did so because they did not wish to arouse the animosity of a large segment of property owners at a time when opposition might have jeopardized the whole success of zoning." The reasoning of these and other commentators, and of some decisions in other States, is that all zoning interferes with property rights to some degree, even in case of unused vacant land, and that now another step should be taken by eliminating pre-existing uses which were formerly held to constitute vested property rights. . . . In the Louisiana cases it was held that a grocery store and a drugstore could be eliminated in one year by passing a zoning ordinance; in the California cases, a plumbing establishment and a cement batching plant were required to be removed respectively in five years and one year after the enactment or amendment of such an ordinance; in the Federal case in Florida, an automobile service station was required to be eliminated on the amendment of such an ordinance in ten years; in the Kansas case an automobile wrecking business was required to be removed within two years; and in the Maryland case billboards, which may be in a different category, were required to be removed from residential areas after a tolerance period of five years. Most of these cases were decided over vigorous dissents. There are decisions to the opposite effect in other states (*O'Connor v. City of Moscow,* 69 Idaho 37, 202 P.2d 401, Ann., 9 A.L.R.2d 1039; *City of Akron v. Chapman,* 160 Ohio St. 382, 116 N.E.2d 697, Ann., 42 A.L.R.2d 1146; *James v. City of Greenville,* 227 S.C. 565, 88 S.E.2d 661; *City of Corpus Christi v. Allen,* 152 Tex. 137, 254 S.W.2d 729, aff'g 247 S.W.2d 130). Our *Town of Somers v. Camarco* (308 N.Y. 537, 127 N.E.2d 327) has been cited in the same context (see *Grant v. Mayor & City Council of Baltimore,* supra). The Texas case held unconstitutional an ordinance compelling the removal of an automobile salvage and wrecking yard, which is included in the same category as a junk yard under the ordinance of the City of Buffalo under adjudication herein. . . .

This citation of authority is enough to display the confusion into which this subject is becoming involved in some jurisdictions in consequence of departing from the established rule. The courts find themselves obliged, without any guiding principle, to pick and choose between instances where a prior nonconforming use will or will not be protected in the courts. It is generally implied in discussions of the subject that the sponsors of the zoning movement were merely temporizing with the courts by leading them in the beginning to hold that a prior use constituted a vested right. The facts in the cases cited, where there has been a departure from that rule, illustrate how impossible it would be to confine a ruling like the one in this case to a junk yard, or to determine judicially what would be a reasonable period of time for removal in a specific case within the meaning of the Constitution. In some of them stores were removed, in another a gasoline service station, in one a plumbing shop and in another a cement batching plant. The grace periods allowed bear no discoverable relation to the kinds of property or businesses involved. An auto wrecking establishment was given five years, and a gasoline service station ten years, whereas a grocery store, drugstore and cement batching establishment were allowed but one year. Different periods purport to be allowed by ordinances elsewhere. Thus it is stated (9 U.Chi.L.Rev. 481-482): "The proposals vary greatly. Some pertain only to particular uses such as billboards, garages, gasoline stations, and junk yards. Still others attempt to eliminate many more nonconforming uses. Nor are the lengths of the amortization periods uniform. Under some proposals a two-year period is allowed, others allow ten or twenty years. Although most of the provisions are silent as to the administrative techniques by which the amortization provisions are to be applied, the boards of zoning appeals will probably be given varying degrees of discretion by which individual hardships may be mitigated within the larger, less flexible framework of the definite elimination period.". . .

The lack of any principle in applying the novel theory of "amortization" betrays a fundamental weakness in the theory. Zoning, like other public programs, is not always best administered at the hands of its enthusiasts. The existence of nonconforming uses has spoiled the symmetry in the minds of zoning experts. It has bulked so large in this context that, desirable as the elimination of nonconforming uses may be, it has sometimes been presented as though it were more important than ordinary property rights. "Many means of eliminating and controlling nonconforming uses have been proposed and tried. Among these means are retroactive zoning, amortization of nonconforming uses, abatement of nonconforming uses as nuisances, public purchase and eminent domain, prohibition of the resumption of a nonconforming use after a period of discontinuance, and refusal to provide governmental services to nonconforming users" (1951 Wis.L.Rev. 687). This Wisconsin Law Review article points out how most of these different proposals have been tried and found wanting, particularly the method by exercising the power of eminent domain which is said to have been discarded mainly for the reason that it is too expensive. The same is said at page 93 of Volume 102 of the Pennsylvania Law Review. The fault found with eminent domain is that it failed to achieve the object of destroying the owner's right in his property without paying for it. Consequently the most promising legal theory at the moment is known as "amortization". This theory is discussed in some of the cases and in most of the law review articles which have been cited as upholding constitutionality of these measures. "Amortization" is explained as follows: [17]

" 'The only positive method of getting rid of nonconforming uses yet devised is to amortize a nonconforming building. That is, to determine the normal useful remaining life of the building and prohibit the owner from maintaining it after the expiration of that time.' " The opinion in *City of Los Angeles v. Gage* (127 Cal.App.2d at p. 455, 274 P.2d at p. 41) adds: "The length of time given the owner to eliminate his nonconforming use or building varies with the city and with the type of structure."

This theory to justify extinguishing nonconforming uses means less the more one thinks about it. It offers little more promise of ultimate success than the other theories which have been tried and abandoned. In the first place, the periods of time vary so widely in the cases which have been cited from different States where it has been tried, and have so little relation to the useful lives of the

---

[17] Crolly and Norton, Termination of Nonconforming Uses, 62 Zoning Bulletin 1, Regional Plan Assn., June, 1952, quoted in *City of Los Angeles v. Gage,* supra, pp. 454-455.

structures, that this theory cannot be used to reconcile these discordant decisions. Moreover the term "amortization", as thus employed, has not the same meaning which it carries in law or accounting. It is not even used by analogy. It is just a catch phrase, and the reasoning is reduced to argument by metaphor. Not only has no effort been made in the reported cases where this theory has been applied to determine what is the useful life of the structure, but almost all were decided under ordinances or statutes which prescribe the same time limit for many different kinds of improvements. This demonstrates that it is not attempted to measure the life of the particular building or type of building, and that the word "amortization" is used as an empty shibboleth. This comment applies to the ordinance at issue on this appeal. There could be no presumption that all junk yards, all auto wrecking or dismantling establishments, and all improvements assessed for tax purposes at not more than $500 will or have any tendency to depreciate to zero in three years. This shows that the ordinance in suit could not possibly have been based on the amortization theory.

Moreover this theory, if it were seriously advanced, would imply that the owner should not keep up his property by making necessary replacements to restore against the ravages of time. Such replacements would be money thrown away. The amortization theory would thus encourage owners of nonconforming uses to allow them to decay and become slums.

Although the courts of other States are divided on this question, the better reason seems to me to be on the side of the rule heretofore established in this State, wherefore I vote to affirm.

Judge BURKE concurs with Judge FROESSEL; Judges DESMOND and FULD concur in result upon the principles stated in *People v. Miller* (304 N.Y. 105, 108, 109, 106 N.E.2d 34, 35, 36); Judge VAN VOORHIS dissents in an opinion in which Chief Judge CONWAY and Judge DYE concur.

Order reversed, etc.

Comments: 1. On the rehearing of the principal case in the lower court, the court concluded that if the petitioners were required to move their business it would cost them approximately $20,000 and that the "amortization" ordinance was "unconstitutional as applied to the particular facts of this case." Note, 44 Cornell L.Q. 450, 451 (1959).

In the principal case, only Judge Burke concurred in Judge Foessel's opinion, while Judges Desmond and Fuld concurred in the result and three judges dissented. Thus the acceptance of the "amortization" principle in New York was left somewhat uncertain. That uncertainty has now been eliminated by the decision in *Modjeska Sign Studios, Inc. v. Berle,* 373 N.E.2d 255 (N.Y. 1977). In the *Modjeska* case the Court of Appeals considered the constitutionality of a statute requiring removal after a six-and-one-half-year amortization period, without compensation, of certain advertising signs located in New York state parks. The court said (per Jasen, J.):

> Although we do not believe that plaintiff is entitled to monetary compensation for the removal of nonconforming billboards, we are of the opinion that a regulation requiring the immediate removal of billboards without compensation in some instances might be an unconstitutional deprivation of property. . . . [A] regulation enacted to enhance the aesthetics of a community generally does not provide a compelling reason for immediate implementation with respect to existing structures or uses. . . .
>
> Fortunately, rather than requiring immediate removal, the state has chosen to provide an amortization period as a means of ameliorating the burden cast upon affected billboard owners. This court has previously sustained the constitutionality of the concept of amortization, as long as the amortization period is reasonable. Whether an amortization period is reasonable is a question that must be answered in the light of the facts of each particular case. Certainly, a critical factor is the length of the amortization period in relation to the investment. Similarly, another factor considered significant by some courts is the nature of the nonconforming activity prohibited; generally a shorter period may be provided for a nonconforming use as opposed to a nonconforming structure. The critical question, however, that must be asked is whether the public gain achieved by the exercise of the police power outweighs the private loss suffered by the owners of nonconforming uses. While an owner need not be given that period of time necessary to recoup his investment entirely, the amortization period should not be so short as to result in a substantial loss. In determining what constitutes a substantial loss, the court should look to, for example, such factors as: initial capital investment, investment realization to date, life expectancy of the investment, and the existence or nonexistence of a lease obligation as well as a contingency clause permitting termination of the lease. Generally, most regulations requiring the removal of nonconforming billboards and providing a reasonable amortization period should pass constitutional muster. In this case, the reasonableness of the amortization period, as a question of fact, was never addressed. Thus, a remand is required.

Id. at 260-61.

See also *Suffolk Outdoor Advertising Co. v. Town Bd. of Southampton,* 373 N.E.2d 263 (N.Y. 1977), where the court made the following observations in regard to a three-year amortization period for nonconforming advertising signs:

> . . . While the purpose of an amortization period is to provide a billboard owner with an opportunity to recoup his investment, an owner need not be given that period of time necessary to permit him to recoup his investment entirely. Nor, however, should the amortization period be so short as to result in a substantial loss of his investment. In this respect, the plaintiffs should be entitled

to show that the three-year amortization period provided in the Southampton ordinance is unreasonable as applied. . . .

However, . . . the ordinance in this case affords plaintiffs an opportunity to obtain an extension of the amortization period if it can be established that, "as to a particular sign," the amortization period of three years is unreasonable. . . . This the plaintiffs concededly did not do. We believe that the plaintiffs were required to exhaust the administrative remedy available under the ordinance before instituting this action. Until plaintiffs make application to the Town Board for an extension of the amortization period and the Town Board renders a determination thereon, he can only speculate as to the total amortization period which plaintiffs may have been granted under the ordinance. Hence, it would be premature for a court to pass upon the reasonableness of the amortization period, as applied.

2. The Maryland and other courts have added yet another perspective: ". . . [T]here is no difference in kind, merely of degree, between a use which has been nonconforming since zoning began and one that is made nonconforming by a reclassifying ordinance, and . . . one in existence when zoning began may be required to stop. Because every zoning regulation affects property owned by someone at the time of its enactment, it brings about some curtailment of property rights either by restricting prospective uses or prohibiting existing ones." *Eutaw Enterprises, Inc. v. City of Baltimore,* 217 A.2d 348, 354 (Md. 1966). Here the nonconforming use was a check-cashing agency for recipients of unemployment compensation checks.

3. For a detailed tabulation of the types of nonconforming uses and structures eliminated by the amortization technique in cases where the technique was held valid and the amortization periods reasonable, see American Law Institute, Model Land Development Code 147-48 (1976), listing 28 cases. Nine of these involved advertising signs; five involved junkyards or auto wrecking yards; and three involved gasoline service stations. This suggests that the courts are more receptive to the amortization of "open land" uses and billboards as compared with structures in which there is a substantial investment.

In *Art Neon Co. v. City and County of Denver,* 488 F.2d 118 (10th Cir. 1974), it was held that an ordinance requiring the removal of existing outdoor advertising signs over a period of five years in accordance with an amortization schedule depending on the replacement value of particular signs was invalid as written, because the replacement costs were "not related to any of the relevant factors in the reasonableness tests"; but that, with the differing amortization periods stricken out and with the flat five-year time limit applicable to all signs, the ordinance was valid. However, in *Combined Communications Corp. v. City and County of Denver,* 542 P.2d 79 (Colo. 1975), the state supreme court struck down the same Denver ordinance on the ground that the city did not have the power completely to exclude the advertising industry; and since the prohibition of new advertising signs was invalid, the amortization provisions applicable to existing nonconforming signs was also held invalid.

Regulation of outdoor advertising is treated in more detail *infra* in Chapter 6.

4. If long "amortization" periods are permitted, as in *Livingston Rock & Gravel Co. v. Los Angeles County,* 272 P.2d 4 (Cal. 1954) (20 years), and in *Swain v. Board of Adjustment,* 433 S.W.2d 727 (Tex. Civ. App. 1968), *appeal dismissed,* and *cert. denied,* 396 U.S. 277, *rehearing denied,* 397 U.S. 977 (1970) (25 years), the municipality is faced with a formidable task of record-keeping in order to assure that the use is, in fact, eliminated at the end of the "amortization" period. *See* Comment, Elimination of Nonconforming Uses: Alternatives and Adjuncts to Amortization, 14 U.C.L.A.L. Rev. 354 (1966).

5. The following reflections on the amortization problem may be helpful:

(1) If the courts really mean that the retroactive elimination problem is no different from the prospective prohibition problem then the same principles ought to apply in both situations. There seems to be some sense of this in judicial comments that the reasonableness of amortization periods depends on circumstances and environment. *See Shifflett v. Baltimore County,* 230 A.2d 310 (Md. 1967).

(2) If the idea is that a vested property right is being amortized, then it is not clear just what the property right is. When there is a building, the emphasis appears to be on the building's physical life. *La Mesa v. Tweed & Gambrell Planing Mill,* 304 P.2d 803 (Cal. App. 1957) (five-year amortization invalid as applied to 20-year-old building with remaining life of 20 years). See also *National Advertising Co. v. Monterey County,* 464 P.2d 33 (Cal. 1970), accepting Internal Revenue Service amortization regulations as evidence of amortization of advertising structures under a zoning ordinance. When advertising structures are erected on leased premises, the emphasis may be placed on the compensable interest in the leases. *Naegele Outdoor Advertising Co. v. Village of Minnetonka,* 162 N.W.2d 206 (Minn. 1968). Billboard leases are usually for short terms but are also usually renewed, although no renewal is promised. The courts generally hold in condemnation cases that just compensation must include a premium for the likelihood of a leasehold renewal. What bearing should this rule have on a court's attitude toward the amortization of a billboard that is on a short-term lease? The issue was considered in *Art Neon Co. v. City and County of Denver, supra* at 121. The property right analysis appears even more confused when the use to be amortized is an "open land" use, such as a junkyard or auto salvage yard.

(3) As some courts continue to emphasize the monopoly position of the nonconforming use, they appear to justify the amortization provision on the basis of the monopoly profits which the user may obtain during the amortization period. This approach appears faulty. First, a glance at any zoning map will belie the monopoly analysis. Next, the analysis assumes that the nonconforming user's trading area is the immediate neighborhood. The junkyard example contradicts this point. Finally, the knowledge that the business must move will inhibit investment in the business, and business volume and profits may actually decline during the amortization period.

(4) We have grown very concerned about urban renewal relocation, but we seem very heartless about zoning relocation. If the urban renewal experience is any guide, many relocated amortized businesses will not survive the move. Many would have failed in any event. Even so, the

hardships of business relocation seem deserving of attention in zoning administration.

6. In 1971, the American Society of Planning Officials polled its membership to determine the extent to which "amortization" was being used to eliminate nonconforming uses. Out of 489 cities and counties responding, 159 reported that they had zoning ordinances providing for "amortization," but only 27 municipalities reported use of the "amortization" technique against buildings. The report indicated that "amortization" has most frequently been used against billboards and other uses involving a small capital investment. Most of the zoning administrators who responded expressed dissatisfaction with the "amortization" technique. R. Scott, The Effect of Nonconforming Land-Use Amortization (American Soc'y of Planning Officials, Planning Advisory Service Rep. No. 280, May 1972).

7. The A.L.I. Model Land Development Code Art. 4 Commentary contains the following observations on "amortization" and, more generally, the handling of nonconforming uses by local governing bodies and administrative agencies and by the courts:

> In part the failure to utilize amortization reflects the limitations placed on the technique by the courts, which while upholding the principle, have often expressed skepticism about its applicability to particular cases. . . . But even in states where the courts have been particularly favorable to amortization, such as California, the actual use of the technique is much more limited than the court decisions might suggest. Perhaps this reflects a general disillusionment with some of the principles that underlie the whole concept of "nonconformity."
>
> The reluctance of local governments to exert strong pressure on nonconforming uses probably reflects a general public disbelief in the original underlying principle of comprehensive zoning — that cities should be divided into districts of homogeneous uses.
>
> . . . .
>
> Where the local government has no strong desire to preserve a neighborhood of homogeneous uses, it frequently grants permission for new development that is not in compliance with the zoning regulations. Thus many urban neighborhoods are dotted with variances, spot zones and special exceptions. If the local government frequently grants permits for new land uses that break the pattern of the regulations, how can it penalize existing uses that break the pattern? . . . In a neighborhood where numerous deviations from the existing regulations have been permitted, an attempt to eliminate preexisting deviations is likely to smack of injustice and be struck down by a reviewing court.
>
> Where an area is substantially undeveloped the elimination of nonconforming uses becomes even more tenuous. In such areas communities are increasingly using a process that the National Commission on Urban Problems characterized as "wait and see" zoning. They place the area in a highly restrictive zoning classification, typically allowing only single-family houses on large lots, with the understanding that it will be rezoned if the local authorities like the developer's proposal. National Commission on Urban Problems, Building the American City 206 (1968). . . .
>
> Whatever the other merits and demerits of wait-and-see zoning,

it is apparent that it makes the traditional concept of nonconforming use obsolete. The whole concept of nonconforming use depends on self-executing regulations which have long-term stability. The wait-and-see approach to zoning undercuts the very basis of the idea of nonconforming use — the idea that there are meaningful regulations to which a use can "conform." Conformity makes sense only if the regulations embody a policy that favors the maintenance of a specially-defined neighborhood character over a substantial period of time. Where the regulations serve merely a temporary holding function, and it is the process of deviating from them that is important, the concept of nonconforming use becomes impossible to apply." . . .

In summary, the existing law of nonconforming uses consists of ineffective or unenforced regulations that seek to promote a poorly-defined concept — conformity — the value of which seems increasingly questionable. Considerable confusion has resulted. . . . The difference between a nonconforming building and a building constructed in violation of law becomes increasingly fuzzy, and boards of adjustment regularly grant variances from any attempt by the zoning officials to limit the expansion of nonconforming uses. . . .

Nuisance-type ordinances are likely to be more effective means of eliminating noxious uses than any regulations artifically based on the desire to promote homogeneous land uses. . . .

American Law Institute, A Model Land Development Code 150-58 (1976).

8. In addition to the secondary sources cited in the principal case and in the preceding comments, a sampling of the enormous literature on nonconforming uses might include the following: Anderson, Nonconforming Uses — A Product of Euclidean Zoning, 10 Syracuse L. Rev. 214 (1959); Katarincic, Elimination of Nonconforming Uses, Buildings, and Structures by Amortization — Concept v. Law, 2 Duq. L. Rev. 1 (1962); Norton, Elimination of Incompatible Uses and Structures, 20 Law & Contemp. Prob. 305 (1955); Wood, Zoning Ordinances Requiring the Termination of a Nonconforming Use in 1973 S.W. Legal Foundation Inst. on Planning, Zoning & Eminent Domain 65; Comment, 102 U. Pa. L. Rev. 91 (1953); Comment, 30 Ind. L. J. 521 (1955); Comment, 26 U. Chi. L. Rev. 442 (1962); Comment, 57 Nw. U.L. Rev. 323 (1962); Note, 50 Cal. L. Rev. 101 (1962).

4. Residential "Use" Classifications: Segregation by Building Type and by Life-Style

The 1916 New York City Zoning Resolution drew no distinctions between different residential building types. But, as the zoning movement gained momentum, other municipalities soon began to create one-and-two family districts from which all other building types were excluded. A number of state court decisions sustained the exclusion of apartments from one-and-two family districts even before the Supreme Court decision in the *Euclid* case. Although the Village of Euclid's zoning ordinance provided for both an exclusive single-family district and for a one-and-two family district, the *Euclid* opinion did not expressly deal with the validity of the former; and the court's "nuisance" rationale for approving the exclusion of apartment houses from a one-and-two family district would not necessarily justify exclusion of two-family houses as well as apartments from the single-family district. But *Brett v. Building Comm'r,* 145 N.E. 269 (Mass. 1924), had already sustained an exclusive single-family residence classification some two years before *Euclid* was decided. The rationale of the *Brett* case was as follows:

> Restriction of the use of land to buildings each to be occupied as a residence for a single family may be viewed at least in two aspects. It may be regarded as preventive of fire. It seems to us manifest that, other circumstances being the same, there is less danger of a building becoming ignited if occupied by one family than if occupied by two or more families. Any increase in the number of persons or of stoves or lights under a single roof increases the risk of fire. A regulation designed to decrease the number of families in one house may reasonably be thought to diminish that risk. The space between buildings likely to arise from the separation of people into a single family under one roof may rationally be thought also to diminish the hazard of conflagration in a neighborhood. Statutes designed to minimize this hazard by regulations as to mechanical construction, air spaces and similar contrivances are familiar and have been upheld. . . . We cannot say that it may not be a rational means to the same end to require that no more than one family inhabit one house, where conditions as to population permit.
>
> It may be a reasonable view that the health and general physical and mental welfare of society would be promoted by each family dwelling in a house by itself. Increase in fresh air, freedom for the play of children and of movement for adults, the opportunity to cultivate a bit of land, and the reduction in the spread of contagious diseases may be thought to be advanced by a general custom that each family live in a house standing by itself with its own curtilage. These features of family life are equally essential or equally advantageous for all inhabitants, whatever may be their social standing or material prosperity. There is nothing on the face of this by-law to indicate that it will not operate indifferently for the general benefit. It is matter of common knowledge that there are in numerous districts plans for real estate development involving modest single-family dwellings within the reach as to price of the thrifty and economical of moderate wage earning capacity.
>
> This provision of the by-law does not extend to the entire territory of the town. That is not such inequality as denies equal protection of the laws to those within the restricted area. Reasonable classification as to the designation of areas as well as in other respects must be permitted to the law-making power. . . . That is a necessary corollary of a zoning law of any kind.

The question to be decided is not whether we approve such a by-law. It is whether we can pronounce it an unreasonable exercise of power having no rational relation to the public safety, public health or public morals. We do not see our way clear to do that. In reaching this conclusion we are not unmindful of decisions either reaching the opposite conclusion or having a contrary appearance. . . . We think the sounder reasoning and the weight of authority supports the conclusion we have reached.

Id. at 271.

In the *Brett* case, the plaintiff's brief included the following arguments against exclusive single-family zoning:

The most evident object aimed at by the creation of a one-family zone is social. As single houses are in general unprofitable as investments, the occupants will usually be people either well-to-do or rich, and able to afford the luxury of such a house. Therefore a district of single houses is likely to be inhabited by people of a higher level of wealth and general culture than any other. It is human nature to desire the most congenial neighbors. . . .

A second purpose readily discernible is purely aesthetic. It cannot be gainsaid that a district of single residences with broad lawns and well-kept gardens is pleasing to the eye. . . . However, it cannot be said that a district of two-family houses is distressing except to some very fastidious person.

A third purpose is served — that of preserving the values of existing single homes. Naturally a person in the market for a single house will, of two similar houses, prefer the one in the more "high class" neighborhood. We can see nothing laudable in this purpose, for it preserves the values of the single houses directly at the expense of owners of unimproved land in the district. Especially with present costs of building, it needs no argument to show that land restricted to single houses has trifling value compared with land less drastically restricted.

If it be said that, though obnoxious in other ways, this by-law tends to promote public convenience or welfare, we would ask, in what respect? Some definite convenience must be shown, and the objects just described, much as they may benefit those owning single houses, do not promote the convenience of welfare of the public in general. We can see no way in which it can be said that the mere fact that some people are willing to build and others live in two-family houses has any tendency to inconvenience the public or injure its welfare. The contrary seems plain. The erection of more houses in which people can live comfortably and at reasonable rentals, in which they can have sufficient light and fresh air, would seem to be a distinct benefit to the public. Particularly is this so at the present time, when we have not by any means made up the shortage in housing that has been such a distressing feature of life in the last few years. Setting off whole areas in which only the fortunate few can possibly live constitutes a positive detriment to the public. If there were no other reason against this by-law, this should be enough to invalidate it.

Brief for Petitioners, pp. 12-13, reprinted in 2 N. Williams, American Land Planning Law 263-64 (1974).

Since the 1920's, it seems generally to have been assumed that exclusive one-family residential districts are constitutionally permissible. However, two early Illinois cases pointedly criticized one-family zoning classifications as an ineffective means of density control. See Merrill v. City of Wheaton, 190 N.E. 918 (Ill. 1934) (unreasonable to allow boarding and rooming houses with up to 16 boarders and 12 roomers, but not two-family houses, in a one-family district); Harmon v. City of Peoria, 27 N.E.2d 525 ·(Ill. 1940) (unreasonable to allow four roomers in a one-family house, but to exclude two-family houses). Later Illinois cases expressly approved exclusive one-family districts on the ground that they are more desirable for residential purposes than districts where two-family uses are permitted. Anderson v. County of Cook, 138 N.E.2d 485 (Ill. 1956); Wesemann v. Village of LaGrange Park, 94 N.E.2d 904 (Ill. 1950). See also Cosmopolitan Nat'l Bank v. Village of Mt. Prospect, 177 N.E.2d 365 (Ill. 1961), where the court expressly sustained the validity of a one-and-two-family district, overturning the trial master's holding that there was no justification for any intermediate districts between an exclusive one-family and a general multiple-family district.

Both Euclid and Brett purport to furnish a rationale for segregating residential buildings by building type. A more complete summary of the reasons advanced by courts to justify such segregation would include the following:

(a) More restrictive building-type districts tend to have a lower density; i.e., a single-family district usually has a lower density than a two-family or a multiple-family district. This results in the following benefits: (i) limitation on the resulting traffic in the area; (ii) protection of peace and quiet, and reduction in the amount of noise in the area; (iii) protection of access to light, air, and sunlight; (iv) protection of public health, by wider spacing between dwelling units, with correspondingly greater protection against contagious diseases; (v) increased safety from fire, primarily also as a result of increased space between dwelling units; (vi) limitation of the burden on public services such as sewerage, water supply, police and fire protection, and consequent limitation of the burden of property taxes.

(b) Multiple-family dwellings are incompatible with the residential character of the area for aesthetic reasons, and also because their occupancy is more transient than that of single-family dwellings.

(c) Because of the factors listed in (a) and (b), above, multiple-family dwellings lower the value of single-family homes in the same area and start a trend toward blight and the development of slums.

(d) Segregation of residential structures by building type provides for a more "orderly" and "balanced" pattern of development.

The arguments based upon "density" clearly are no longer always valid. As Norman Williams, Jr. has pointed out:

> In much recent construction, particularly in the larger cities, a substantial number of apartment projects have approximated the density of certain building-types which are traditionally considered to have a lower density, including row houses and some examples of two-family areas. There are several reasons for this. The amount of open space around residential buildings has been increasing rapidly in most recent construction, so much so as to become a significant factor affecting density; and the opportunities for providing significant open space are obviously greater in a larger apartment project — by pooling open space, by minimizing the area in streets, etc. Moreover, the number of families living in a given building is obviously one factor affecting the density of an area, but it is not necessarily the most important factor, even as to occupancy. Density also depends upon various other factors, including family size — which varies widely according to the size of dwelling units, the age structure of the residents and their ethnic and religious backgrounds, etc. — and also the number of boarders, lodgers, etc. As a result building type is less and less reliable as an index of relative density. . . .

N. Williams, 2 American Land Planning Law 320 (1974).

KRAUSE v. CITY OF ROYAL OAK

Court of Appeals of Michigan
11 Mich. App. 183, 160 N.W.2d 769 (1968)

Before LEVIN, P. J., and BURNS and McGREGOR, JJ.

BURNS, Judge. The city of Royal Oak appeals from a judgment restraining it from enforcing a zoning ordinance which places plaintiffs' property in a one-family residential use classification. The judgment permits plaintiffs to use their land for multiple-family residential purposes.

Plaintiffs' property is located in the city of Royal Oak and consists of approximately 3.5 acres of land, which, for purposes of this opinion, can be described in terms of a geometrically imperfect right triangle. The Grand Trunk Western railroad, which is elevated and runs in a northwesterly and southeasterly direction, forms the hypotenuse of this triangle. Starr road, which runs roughly east and west, provides a southern base for the triangle. The remaining part of the triangle, the western border of plaintiffs' property, is composed of one lot which fronts on the north side of Starr road and other lots which front on the east side of Benjamin avenue, a north-south thoroughfare. Within this area are 14 subdivided lots surrounding a 350 foot, undeveloped cul-de-sac.

The territory bounded by the railroad, Starr road and Benjamin avenue has been zoned for one-family residential use since 1957. Other than one nonconforming 3-family multiple dwelling, which was erected prior to 1957 when multiple dwellings were permissible, the east side of Benjamin avenue and the first 2 lots on the north side of Starr avenue, east of Benjamin, are developed with single-family residences. Located upon the subject property itself are 2 comparatively old one-family homes which, all parties agree, will be removed for purposes of replatting, regardless of the course of future development.

The neighborhood surrounding the area bounded by Starr road, Benjamin avenue and the railroad is of a mixed character.

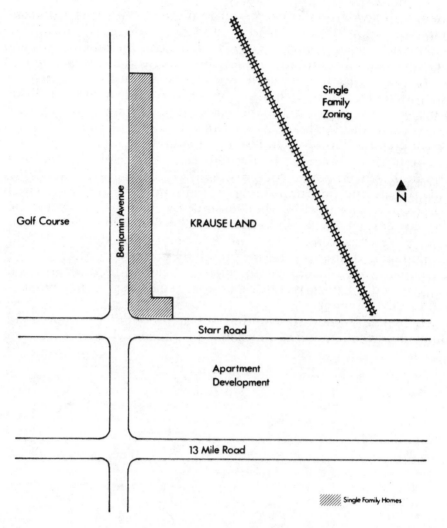

Krause v. City of Royal Oak, Michigan, 1968

The Royal Oak municipal golf course is on the west side of Benjamin (across the street from the lots which back up to the subject property). The area north and east of the railroad is zoned for one-family residences, and improvements exist on a number of those lots. The property south of Starr road is zoned for and has been developed with multiple-family dwellings. This property also fronts upon heavily travelled 13 Mile road which is exclusively bounded by multiple-family complexes from the Grand Trunk Western railroad tracks west to one of the main arteries of the Detroit metropolitan area, Woodward avenue (US-10), where nonresidential uses are permitted.

Since 1961 owners of part of the subject property have made

unsuccessful applications for a zoning change, but it was not until 1966 that plaintiffs commenced this action to enjoin the defendant from enforcing the zoning ordinance as it affects their land. The trial judge listened to the proofs, viewed the premises, and held that the one-family zoning classification was void because it constituted an unreasonable and arbitrary exercise of the police power of the city of Royal Oak and was confiscatory in that it deprived plaintiffs of their property without due process of law.

Our review of this judgment is guided by certain elementary principles. . . .

The propositions that an "ordinance is presumed valid" and that it is plaintiff's burden to overcome that presumption "by clear and satisfactory proof" are of critical importance in this case. . . .

To place this case in its proper perspective, we should note that plaintiff did not claim that any depreciation in property value resulted from the adoption of the zoning ordinance imposing the restriction to which the property was not previously subject. Rather, it appears that the essence of plaintiffs' objection is that their land should be freed of the restriction imposed by the ordinance of 1957 to the end that they might have the benefit of appreciated value. Although one witness, a home builder testifying on behalf of plaintiffs, stated the land was unsuited for single-residential use, another one of the plaintiffs' witnesses, an appraiser who was more familiar with property values, testified that the land was not without value as zoned but that it would be more valuable for multiple-family use. Defendant conceded that such was the case but disputed the ratio of difference in valuations as computed by plaintiffs' witnesses.

According to the plaintiffs' witnesses, the marketability of the property for one-family residences was impaired by the presence of the railroad. The proximity of the tracks to the lots made it impossible to obtain Federal Housing Administration financing, thereby eliminating a good percentage of prospective buyers who could not secure Veterans Administration or conventional loans. In addition, plaintiffs' witnesses pointed out the undesirability of constructing one-family residences next to a railroad because of the vibration, noise, possible danger to children, and the smell. Yet, by plaintiffs' proposal to build multiple dwellings (40 one-bed units and 40 two-bed units) they would invite many more persons (than the 14 one-family houses would accommodate) to share in this feigned misery. The alleged adverse effect the railroad may have on marketability of single-family homes is at best dubious because of plaintiffs' own appraiser's acknowledgment upon cross-examination that a number of single-family homes in Royal Oak lie adjacent to the railroad although these areas located next to the tracks have been the last to develop for residential purposes. The proximity of a railroad does not render zoning for one-family residential purposes arbitrary and unreasonable. See *City of Hillsdale v. Hillsdale Iron & Metal Company, Inc.* (1960), 358 Mich. 377, 100 N.W.2d 467.

This is not to say, however, that the value of the property and the effect, if any, a railroad has on that value, plays no role in our deliberations. The Supreme Court of Michigan has repeatedly recognized that "the mere fact that land may have a greater selling value for a possible use of different character than that for which it is zoned is not a sufficient basis for holding the ordinance invalid, as applied to such property, although, of course, it is a matter to be considered with other elements affecting the situation." *Paka Corp. v. City of Jackson* (1961), 364 Mich. 122, 127, 110 N.W.2d 620, 623; *Smith v. Village of Wood Creek Farms* (1963), 371 Mich. 127, 123 N.W.2d 210.

The disparity of valuations in the cases cited by the plaintiffs wherein zoning ordinances have been held for naught are invariably accompanied by other factors which clearly affect the public health, safety or general welfare of the people. For instance, in *Smith v. Village of Wood Creek Farms,* supra, the disparity of value of 3 lots and the presence of 2 busy highways and nearby commercial locations were sufficient to invalidate an ordinance restricting those lots to residential purposes, whereas the disparity of value of a fourth lot, which was bordered on but one side by a highway, was insufficient to negate the zoning ordinance.

In the present case the difference in value is accompanied by no convincing evidence bearing on the improper use of the police power. The most positive evidence tendered by plaintiffs was the testimony of the city's planning director who said that no question of public health is involved. Other than this, plaintiffs' proofs fail to adequately cope with most of the public interest considerations which we must assume prompted the adoption of the zoning ordinance.

In this respect, however, there was some testimony introduced regarding the impact that a multiple dwelling development would have upon the people whose backyards abut the subject property. During plaintiffs' case in chief, plaintiffs' appraiser testified that the presence of multiple dwellings would have no adverse effect on the immediate neighborhood, but the adverse effect to which he referred was in terms of price not people. Plaintiffs' home building witness also testified as to this problem, but his concept of adverse effect was his personal opinion of whether or not he would purchase a house completely surrounded with multiple dwellings. Both of plaintiffs' witnesses who spoke on this issue approached the problem as one of basic economics. Contrary to this dollars and cents approach, we have the defendant's planning director's testimony which probably explains a portion of the rationale for having the subject property zoned as it is.

"*Q. [Counsel for defendant]* In your professional opinion, as a person who works in the field of zoning and community planning, does the existing one-family zoning of the subject property tend to promote the public peace, safety and general welfare?

"*A. [City planning director]* In my opinion it does, yes.

"*Q.* Will you tell us why?

"*A.* Well, I might preface my comments to the fact that in this specific area the public involved would be the public that would be in the triangle for the immediate vicinity of the lots in question. This would be from 13 Mile road on the south, Benjamin on the west, and essentially the Grand Trunk on the easterly boundary. They would be the immediate public involved. The area is predominantly single-family north of Starr road and these people would be forced to experience the increased confusion and congestion, noise, *et cetera* that would accompany a development other than single-family, a development that would allow a drastic increase in the total number of people that would live in the three acres more or less in question. The single-family zoning in the area would promote a 13-family development, at least 13 families, would generate at best 26 cars so there would not be a traffic problem coming into or off of Benjamin from Starr road. Also the nature of the residential amenities that accrue to other residential properties from single-family developments would tend to go along with the type of development that is already north of Starr road. Also, we feel that this type of zoning does allow for the natural growth of single-family development with the schools and the other residential amenities [which] are in the area. . . .

"*Q.* Mr. Bowman, as a professional in the field of planning and zoning, what is your opinion as to the comparative desirability of having multiple-family residences back up to single-family residences, compared to facing multiple-family to single-family with a street in between, sir?

"*A.* Well, it's my opinion, based upon the experiences we have had in the recent past, over the past 2 or 3 years, with the rapid development of apartments in Royal Oak and in our surrounding communities, that due to the general demand of the occupants of apartments for parking, for the use of a swimming pool, other recreational facilities, the high density of people living in these developments, that it is far better to face the apartment development across a street which is 50 or 60 feet in width to the single-family development rather than having it abut to the rear yards where all of the service parking and all of the congestion takes place; that we have found that we have more and more of our abutting property owners object where it is a rear yard situation rather than a face to face situation."

We think it is fair to conclude, therefore, that the municipal authority enacting this ordinance was trying to avoid the situation described in *Euclid v. Ambler Realty Company* (1926), 272 U.S. 365 . . . where Justice Sutherland said:

. . . .

[Here the court quoted that paragraph in the *Euclid* case which held, in effect, that apartment development was parasitical in single family residential areas. — Eds.]

Not to be overlooked is plaintiffs' evidence which, we surmise, was directed to the claim that the city's zoning practice in this instance was arbitrary and capricious. In 1964 a triangular-shaped parcel of property, which is also situated next to the Grand Trunk Western railroad and directly northwest of the subject property, was rezoned from one-family to multiple-family residential. We gather from the city planning director's testimony, however, that there were no existing one-family houses on the rezoned land and there are on the subject property. Furthermore, it is important to note that the area catercorner from this parcel is zoned for heavy industry purposes and that it bordered predominantly with multiple-family or non-residential zoning classifications. The 1964 rezoning was completely reasonable in our opinion and bears no relation to the alleged unreasonable characterization of plaintiffs' property.

Plaintiffs' case, amounting to substantially nothing more than a partial deprivation of the best economic use of their property, does not persuade us to subvert the interests of the public as expressed by the legislative body which enacted the zoning ordinance in question. The evidence introduced by plaintiffs is alarmingly insufficient to rebut the ordinance's presumption of validity. At best, plaintiffs' evidence presents nothing more than a debatable question.

Judgment vacated. No costs, a public question being involved.

LEVIN, Presiding Judge (dissenting).

The plaintiffs challenged their property's present zoning both on the ground that it bears no substantial relationship to public health, morals, safety, or general welfare and on the ground that it deprives the property of any reasonable use. Holding for the plaintiffs on both grounds, the trial judge found the zoning both irrational and confiscatory.

Concluding that at best plaintiffs' evidence presented nothing more than a "debatable question" on the rationality of present zoning, the majority reverses the trial judge. However, even if zoning is entirely reasonable in the sense it bears a substantial relationship to public health, morals, safety, or general welfare, it may nonetheless be unreasonable in its application to particular property if that property cannot reasonably be used as zoned. Zoning which prevents any reasonable use of property is confiscatory and, for that reason, invalid.

While the trial judge and we must find for the municipality if we find there is a debatable question concerning the rationality of the zoning, i.e., zoning is not irrational if, on the evidence presented, its rationality remains debatable, a "debatable question" rule has not been established where the question presented is whether the zoning is unreasonable because it is confiscatory. Whether zoning is confiscatory is more a question of fact than of judgment. That fact may be proved like any other fact. It is not necessary for one claiming confiscation to prove it beyond dispute.

The evidence presented here concerning the confiscation issue was in conflict. The trial judge correctly went about resolving that factual dispute in the same manner he would approach decision of any disputed factual issue in a case tried to him. Merely because all reasonable men would not necessarily have reached the same decision did not oblige the trial judge to decide the issue of confiscation for the municipality. . . .

On the entire evidence I am not left with the *definite and firm conviction* that a mistake was committed by the trial judge. The trial judge stated that the plaintiffs' house builder witness "made the greatest impression on the court. A home builder with considerable experience in Royal Oak, he testified that plaintiff's land was totally unsuited to single residence development and that at least to him the land had no value for that purpose. Based on his own experience he said that lots adjacent to the unsightly and noisy railroad tracks were not readily salable for single residence purposes. He has owned 2 comparable lots for some time and has been unable to dispose of them. Furthermore, again based on his own experience, he said that adequate home financing could not be obtained on land adjacent to railroad tracks."

The trial judge thereby indicated he chose to adopt the testimony offered in behalf of the plaintiffs in preference to testimony offered in behalf of the defendant.

There is no reason to reject the trial judge's evaluation of the conflicting testimony. The testimony of plaintiffs' house builder witness so adopted by the trial judge was not incredible. It was supported by the testimony of plaintiffs' appraisal witness who, while he valued the property at $11,500, stated that a prudent developer would not buy it. I interpret that to mean a speculator could be found to buy the property, but not a developer. The question before the trial judge and us, on the issue of confiscation, is whether the property can reasonably be *used* as zoned, not whether it has an exchange value. That a buyer could be found for it, that it has a buying and selling value, does not establish that anyone could be found who would develop and use the property.

Passage of time and accompanying changes in controlling facts, a change in zoning itself, might make the property more valuable and justify a speculator's investment. And then again the property might become worth less. This judicial inquiry is not concerned with the speculative possibilities of the property, but rather seeks to determine whether it can now be reasonably *used* as now zoned.

That the 12 home owners between plaintiffs' property and Benjamin avenue foresee damage to their property from further multiple development, bears out plaintiffs' expert testimony that it would be difficult to find home buyers willing to make an investment in single-family residences constructed on plaintiffs' property located, as it is, alongside extensive multiple development to the south. It is entirely believable that, with the location disadvantages of both adjoining multiple dwellings to the south and adjoining railroad tracks to the east, plaintiffs' property could not prudently be developed consistent with present zoning.

The defendant acknowledges that the property could not be developed for single family use until the existing structures are removed, the property platted and utilities and other land improvements installed. On the record before him, the trial judge was entirely justified in concluding it would be so difficult to find a land developer or house builder willing to speculate in the improvement of this land in preference to land which does not have the location disadvantages which this land has, that this land was not suitable for *development* with single-family residences, and that, accordingly, present zoning was confiscatory. Such finding not being clearly erroneous, I would affirm on that issue.

Comments: 1. Several points about the principal case are of interest. First, the geographic area which provided the basis for the court's assessment of the zoning ordinance appeared to be the immediate neighborhood, and not the entire community. Is this planning? In addition, the court seemed to assume an incompatibility. In a case in which a challenge was brought to a rezoning for apartments, the North Carolina court rejected the *Euclid* analysis of an apartment's detrimental impact. *Allred v. City of Raleigh,* 173 S.E.2d 533 (N.C. App. 1970), *rev'd on other grounds,* 178 S.E.2d 432 (N.C. 1971). It pointed out that "Many modern and luxurious apartment buildings tend to compliment the area where they are located." *Id.* at 538.

Neither opinion in *Krause* was very explicit about when "confiscation" does occur. Note, incidentally, that when it is the developer who attacks the ordinance, the focus is on the extent of his probable financial loss. Compare *Bartlett v. City of Chicago,* 204 N.E.2d 780 (Ill. App. 1965), in which the court held invalid the application of single family residential zoning to a tract of land virtually surrounded by high-rise apartments.

Another successful attack by an apartment developer on single-family zoning is *Socha v. Smith,* 306 N.Y.S.2d 551 (N.Y. App. Div. 1969), *aff'd,* 259 N.E.2d 738 (N.Y. 1970). Here the tract was surrounded by single-family residences. However, the developer's tract was swampy and so there was evidence that to make a profit for single-family uses he would have to develop it for expensive homes, for which there was no market.

2. Sometimes the attack on single-family zoning comes from a developer who wants to build a commercial project. For a successful attack by such a developer, see *Tomasek v. City of Des Plaines,* 325 N.E.2d 345 (Ill. App. 1975), holding that the unsuitability of the subject property for single-family development was established by evidence that the property would be worth $150,000 more if zoned for commerical use; that the property was bounded by railroad tracks in the rear and a four-lane arterial street in the front; that a city garage and a general manufacturing district were located nearby; and that the property had remained undeveloped for a long time despite a strong demand for single-family houses in Des Plaines. In similar situations, some courts may simply find the zoning invalid as "confiscatory." *Summers v. City of Glen Cove,* 217 N.E.2d 663 (N.Y. 1966) (corner lot was zoned residential, in an area generally zoned for business and apartment uses). *See also Mary Chess, Inc. v. City of Glen Cove,* 219 N.E.2d 406 (N.Y. 1966).

3. One way of handling the problem of incompatible uses in close proximity is to provide for a buffer zone. A general residential district in which apartments are permitted is often used as a buffer between single-family districts and commercial districts. *See, e.g., Evanston Best & Co. v. Goodman,* 16 N.E.2d 131, 132 (Ill. 1938), approving the use of this technique "to prevent an impact between the intensity of the use to which commercial areas are put with the quiet and cleanliness which are essential to property devoted to higher type residential uses." *Accord, Carlson v. City of Bellevue,* 435 P.2d 957 (Wash. 1968) (district allowing multifamily housing and nonretail business may be used as buffer between "prime residential" and industrial areas). But *cf.* Hagman's criticism: "[i]f zoning is in the interest of the poor, why is it that apartment buildings are the buffer zone between industrial-commercial zones and single-family residential zones, rather than the single-family zones, with fewer people, being the neighbor of the undesirable commercial and industrial uses?" D. Hagman, Urban Planning and Land Development Control Law 474 (1971).

Sometimes a landscaped strip must be provided as a buffer between residential and nonresidential use districts. *See, e.g., State v. Gallop Building,* 247 A.2d 350 (N.J. Super. 1968), where a 20-foot screen belt of trees was required for every business use adjacent to a residential district. An objection was made that requiring a strip this wide was unconstitutional. The court appeared to think not, and approved the buffer concept implicit in the ordinance. Why would the business property owner object to this requirement? On buffer zones generally, see 1 R. Anderson, American Law of Zoning §§ 8.08, 8.11 (2d ed. 1976).

VILLAGE OF BELLE TERRE v. BORAAS

Supreme Court of the United States
416 U.S. 1, 39 L.Ed.2d 797, 94 S.Ct. 1536 (1974)

MR. JUSTICE DOUGLAS delivered the opinion of the Court.

Belle Terre is a village on Long Island's north shore of about 220 homes inhabited by 700 people. Its total land area is less than one square mile. It has restricted land use to one-family dwellings excluding lodging houses, boarding houses, fraternity houses, or multiple dwelling houses. The word "Family" as used in the ordinance means, "One or more persons related by blood, adoption, or marriage, living and cooking together as a single housekeeping unit, exclusive of household servants. A number of persons but not exceeding two (2) living and cooking together as a single housekeeping unit though not related by blood, adoption, or marriage shall be deemed to constitute a family."

Appellees (Dickmans) are owners of a house in the village and leased it in December, 1971 for a term of 18 months to Michael Truman. Later Bruce Boraas became a colessee. Then Anne Parish moved into the house along with three others. These six are students at nearby State University at Stony Brook and none is related to the other by blood, adoption, or marriage. When the village served the Dickmans with an "Order to Remedy Violations" of the ordinance, the owners plus three tenants thereupon brought this action under 42 U.S.C. § 1983 for an injunction declaring the ordinance unconstitutional. The District Court held the ordinance constitutional and the Court of Appeals reversed, one judge dissenting. 2 Cir., 476 F.2d 806. The case is here by appeal, 28 U.S.C. § 1254(2); and we noted probable jurisdiction, 414 U.S. 907.

This case brings to this Court a different phase of local zoning regulations than we have previously reviewed. *Village of Euclid v. Ambler Realty Co.,* 272 U.S. 365, involved a zoning ordinance classifying land use in a given area into six categories. Appellee's tracts fell under three classifications: U-2 that included two-family dwellings; U-3 that included apartments, hotels, churches, schools, private clubs, hospitals, city hall and the like; and U-6 that included sewage disposal plants, incinerators, scrap storage, cemeteries, oil and gas storage and so on. Heights of buildings were prescribed for each zone; also the size of land areas required for each kind of use was specified. The land in litigation was vacant and being held for industrial development; and evidence was introduced showing that under the restricted use ordinance the land would be greatly reduced in value. The claim was that the land owner was being deprived of liberty and property without due process within the meaning of the Fourteenth Amendment.

The Court sustained the zoning ordinance under the police power of the State, saying that the line "which in this field separates the legitimate from the illegitimate assumption of power is not capable of precise delimitation. It varies with circumstances and conditions." 272 U.S., at 387. And the Court added "A nuisance may be merely a right thing in the wrong place, like a pig in the parlor instead of the barnyard. If the validity of the legislative classification for zoning purposes be fairly debatable, the legislative judgment must be allowed to control." *Id.,* at 388. The Court listed as considerations bearing on the constitutionality of zoning ordinances the danger of fire or collapse of buildings, the evils of overcrowding people, and the possibility that "offensive trades, industries, and structures" might "create nuisance" to residential sections. *Ibid.* But even those historic police power problems need not loom large or actually be existent in a given case. For the exclusion of "all industrial establishments" does not mean that "only offensive or dangerous industries will be excluded." *Ibid.* That fact does not invalidate the ordinance; the Court held:

> "The inclusion of a reasonable margin to insure effective enforcement, will not put upon a law, otherwise valid, the stamp of invalidity. Such laws may also find their justification in the fact that, in some fields, the bad fades into the good by such insensible degrees that the two are not capable of being readily distinguished and separated in terms of legislation." *Id.,* 388-389.

The main thrust of the case in the mind of the Court was in the exclusion of industries and apartments and as respects that it commented on the desire to keep residential areas free of "disturbing noises"; "increased traffic"; the hazard of "moving and parked automobiles"; the "depriving children of the privilege of quiet and open spaces for play, enjoyed by those in more favored localities." *Id.,* at 394. The ordinance was sanctioned because the validity of the legislative classification was "fairly debatable" and therefore could not be said to be wholly arbitrary. *Id.,* at 388.

Our decision in *Berman v. Parker,* 348 U.S. 26, sustained a land use project in the District of Columbia against a land owner's claim that the taking violated the Due Process Clause and the Just Compensation Clause of the Fifth Amendment. The essence of the argument against the law was, while taking property for ridding an area of slums was permissible, taking it "merely to develop a better balanced, more attractive community" was not, 348 U.S., at 31. We refused to limit the concept of public welfare that may be enhanced by zoning regulations. We said:

> "Miserable and disreputable housing conditions may do more than spread disease and crime and immorality. They may also suffocate the spirit by reducing the people who live there to the status of cattle. They may indeed make living an almost unsufferable burden. They may also be an ugly sore, a blight on the community which robs it of charm, which makes it a place from which men turn. The misery of housing may despoil a community as an open sewer may ruin a river.
>
> "We do not sit to determine whether a particular housing project is or is not desirable. The concept of the public welfare is broad and inclusive. . . . The values it represents are spiritual as well as physical, aesthetic as well as monetary. It is within the power

of the legislature to determine that the community should be beautiful as well as healthy, spacious as well as clean, well-balanced as well as carefully patrolled." *Id.,* 32-33.

If the ordinance segregated one area only for one race, it would immediately be suspect under the reasoning of *Buchanan v. Warley,* 245 U.S. 60, where the Court invalidated a city ordinance barring a Black from acquiring real property in a white residential area by reason of an 1866 Act of Congress, 14 Stat. 27, 42 U.S.C. § 1982 and an 1870 Act, 16 Stat. 144, both enforcing the Fourteenth Amendment. *Id.,* 78-82. See *Jones v. Alfred H. Mayer Co.,* 392 U.S. 409.

In *Seattle Title Trust Co. v. Roberge,* 278 U.S. 116, Seattle had a zoning ordinance that permitted a "philanthropic home for children or for old people" in a particular district "when the written consent shall have been obtained of the owners of two thirds of the property within four hundred (400) feet of the proposed building." *Id.,* at 118. The Court held that provision of the ordinance unconstitutional saying that the existing owners could "withhold consent for selfish reasons or arbitrarily and may subject the trustee [owner] to their will or caprice." *Id.,* at 122. Unlike the billboard cases (*Cusack Co. v. City of Chicago,* 242 U.S. 526), the Court concluded that the Seattle ordinance was invalid since the proposed home for the aged poor was not shown by its maintenance and construction "to work any injury, inconvenience or annoyance to the community, the district or any person." *Id.,* 278 U.S., at 122.

The present ordinance is challenged on several grounds: that it interferes with a person's right to travel; that it interferes with the right to migrate to and settle within a State; that it bars people who are uncongenial to the present residents; that the ordinance expresses the social preferences of the residents for groups that will be congenial to them; that social homogeneity is not a legitimate interest of government; that the restriction of those whom the neighbors do not like trenches on the newcomers' rights of privacy; that it is of no rightful concern to villagers whether the residents are married or unmarried; that the ordinance is antithetical to the Nation's experience, ideology and self-perception as an open, egalitarian, and integrated society.

We find none of these reasons in the record before us. It is not aimed at transients. Cf. *Shapiro v. Thompson,* 394 U.S. 618. It involves no procedural disparity inflicted on some but not on others such as was presented by *Griffin v. Illinois,* 351 U.S. 12. It involves no "fundamental" right guaranteed by the Constitution, such as voting, *Harper v. Virginia State Board,* 383 U.S. 663; the right of association, *NAACP v. Alabama ex rel. Patterson,* 357 U.S. 449; the right of access to the courts, *NAACP v. Button,* 371 U.S. 415; or any rights of privacy, cf. *Griswold v. Connecticut,* 381 U.S. 479;

Eisenstadt v. Baird, 405 U.S. 438, 453-454. We deal with economic and social legislation where legislatures have historically drawn lines which we respect against the charge of violation of the Equal Protection Clause if the law be "reasonable, not arbitrary" (quoting *F. S. Royster Guano Co. v. Virginia,* 253 U.S. 412, 415) and bears "a rational relationship to a [permissible] state objective." *Reed v. Reed,* 404 U.S. 71, 76.

It is said, however, that if two unmarried people can constitute a "family," there is no reason why three or four may not. But every line drawn by a legislature leaves some out that might well have been included. That exercise of discretion, however, is a legislative not a judicial function.

It is said that the Belle Terre ordinance reeks with an animosity to unmarried couples who live together. There is no evidence to support it; and the provision of the ordinance bringing within the definition of a "family" two unmarried people belies the charge.

The ordinance places no ban on other forms of association, for a "family" may, so far as the ordinance is concerned, entertain whomever they like.

The regimes of boarding houses, fraternity houses, and the like present urban problems. More people occupy a given space; more cars rather continuously pass by; more cars are parked; noise travels with crowds.

A quiet place where yards are wide, people few, and motor vehicles restricted are legitimate guidelines in a land use project addressed to family needs. This goal is a permissible one within *Berman v. Parker, supra.* The police power is not confined to elimination of filth, stench, and unhealthy places. It is ample to lay out zones where family values, youth values, and the blessings of quiet seclusion, and clean air make the area a sanctuary for people.

The suggestion that the case may be moot need not detain us. A zoning ordinance usually has an impact on the value of the property which it regulates. But in spite of the fact that the precise impact of the ordinance sustained in *Euclid* on a given piece of property was not known, 272 U.S., at 397, the Court, considering the matter a controversy in the realm of city planning, sustained the ordinance. Here we are a step closer to the impact of the ordinance on the value of the lessor's property. He has not only lost six tenants and acquired only two in their place; it is obvious that the scale of rental values rides on what we decide today. When *Berman* reached us it was not certain whether an entire tract would be taken or only the buildings on it and a scenic easement. 348 U.S., at 36. But that did not make the case any the less a controversy in the constitutional sense. When Mr. Justice Holmes said for the Court in *Block v. Hirsh,* 256 U.S. 135, 155, "property rights may be cut down, and to that extent taken, without pay," he stated the issue here. As is true in most zoning cases, the precise impact on value may, at the threshold of litigation over validity, not yet be known.

Reversed.

MR. JUSTICE BRENNAN, dissenting. . . .

[Justice Brennan found that no case or controversy existed. The tenants had moved out, and he would hold that the landlord does not have standing to assert the rights of his tenants. — Eds.]

MR. JUSTICE MARSHALL, dissenting.

. . . In my view, the disputed classification burdens the students' fundamental rights of association and privacy guaranteed by the First and Fourteenth Amendments. Because the application of strict equal protection scrutiny is therefore required, I am at odds with my brethren's conclusion that the ordinance may be sustained on a showing that it bears a rational relationship to the accomplishment of legitimate governmental objectives.

. . . .

My disagreement with the Court today is based upon my view that the ordinance in this case unnecessarily burdens appellees' First Amendment freedom of association and their constitutionally guaranteed right to privacy. Our decisions establish that the First and Fourteenth Amendments protect the freedom to choose one's associates. Constitutional protection is extended not only to modes of association that are political in the usual sense, but also to those that pertain to the social and economic benefit of the members. . . . The selection of one's living companions involves similar choices as to the emotional, social, or economic benefits to be derived from alternative living arrangements.

The freedom of association is often inextricably entwined with the constitutionally guaranteed right of privacy. The right to "establish a home" is an essential part of the liberty guaranteed by the Fourteenth Amendment. . . . And the Constitution secures to an individual a freedom "to satisfy his intellectual and emotional needs within the privacy of his own home." *Stanley v. Georgia,* 394 U.S. 557 (1969). . . . Constitutionally protected privacy is, in Mr. Justice Brandeis' words, "as against the government, the right to be let alone . . . the right most valued by civilized man." *Olmstead v. United States,* 277 U.S. 438 (1928) (dissenting opinion). The choice of household companions — of whether a person's "intellectual and emotional needs" are best met by living with family, friends, professional associates or others — involves deeply personal considerations as to the kind and quality of intimate relationships within the home. That decision surely falls within the ambit of the right to privacy protected by the Constitution. . . .

The instant ordinance discriminates on the basis of just such a personal lifestyle choice as to household companions. It permits any number of persons related by blood or marriage, be it two or twenty, to live in a single household, but it limits to two the number of unrelated persons bound by profession, love, friendship, religious or political affiliation or mere economics who can occupy a single home. Belle Terre imposes upon those who deviate from the community norm in their choice of living companions significantly greater restrictions than are applied to residential groups who are related by blood or marriage, and comprise the established order with the community. The town has, in effect, acted to fence out those individuals whose choice of lifestyle differs from that of its current residents.

This is not a case where the Court is being asked to nullify a township's sincere efforts to maintain its residential character by preventing the operation of rooming houses, fraternity houses or other commercial or high-density residential uses. Unquestionably, a town is free to restrict such uses. Moreover, as a general proposition, I see no constitutional infirmity in a town limiting the density of use in residential areas by zoning regulations which do not discriminate on the basis of constitutionally suspect criteria. This ordinance, however, limits the density of occupancy of only those homes occupied by unrelated persons. It thus reaches beyond control of the use of land or the density of population, and undertakes to regulate the way people choose to associate with each other within the privacy of their own homes.

It is no answer to say, as does the majority that associational interests are not infringed because Belle Terre residents may entertain whomever they choose. Only last Term Mr. Justice Douglas indicated in concurrence that he saw the right of association protected by the First Amendment as involving far more than the right to entertain visitors. He found that right infringed by a restriction on food stamp assistance, penalizing households of "unrelated persons." As Mr. Justice Douglas there said, freedom of association encompasses the "right to invite a stranger into one's home" not only for "entertainment" but to join the household as well. *Moreno v. Department of Agriculture,* 413 U.S. 528 (1973) (Douglas, J., concurring). I am still persuaded that the choice of those who will form one's household implicates constitutionally protected rights.

Because I believe that this zoning ordinance creates a classification which impinges upon fundamental personal rights, it can withstand constitutional scrutiny only upon a clear showing that the burden imposed is necessary to protect a compelling and substantial governmental interest, . . . And, once it be determined that a burden has been placed upon a constitutional right, the onus of demonstrating that no less intrusive means will adequately protect the compelling state interest and that the challenged statute is sufficiently narrowly drawn, is upon the party seeking to justify the burden. . . .

A variety of justifications have been proffered in support of the village's ordinance. It is claimed that the ordinance controls population density, prevents noise, traffic and parking problems, and preserves the rent structure of the community and its attractiveness to families. As I noted earlier, these are all legitimate and substantial interests of government. But I think it clear that the means chosen to accomplish these purposes are both over- and under-inclusive, and that the asserted goals could be as effectively achieved by means of an ordinance that did not discriminate on the basis of constitutionally protected choices of life style. The ordinance imposes no restriction whatsoever on the number of persons who may live in a house, as long as they are related by marital or sanguinary bonds — presumably no matter how distant their relationship. Nor does the ordinance restrict the number of income earners who may contribute to rent in such a household, or the number of automobiles that may be maintained by its occupants. In that sense the ordinance is under-inclusive. On the other hand, the statute restricts the number of unrelated persons who may live in a home to no more than two. It would therefore prevent three unrelated people from occupying a dwelling even if among them they had but one income and no vehicles. While an extended family of a dozen or more might live in a small bungalow, three elderly and retired persons could not occupy the large manor house next door. Thus the statute is also grossly over-inclusive to accomplish its intended purposes.

There are some 220 residences in Belle Terre occupied by about 700 persons. The density is therefore just above three per household. The village is justifiably concerned with density of population and the related problems of noise, traffic, and the like. It could deal with those problems by limiting each household to a specified number of adults, two or three perhaps, without limitation on the number of dependent children. The burden of such an ordinance would fall equally upon all segments of the community. It would surely be better tailored to the goals asserted by the township than the ordinance before us today, for it would more realistically restrict population density and growth and their attendant environmental costs. Various other statutory mechanisms also suggest themselves as solutions to Belle Terre's problems — rent control, limits on the number of vehicles per household, and so forth, but, of course, such schemes are matters of legislative judgment and not for this Court. Appellants also refer to the necessity of maintaining the family character of the village. There is not a shred of evidence in the record indicating that if Belle Terre permitted a limited number of unrelated persons to live together, the residential, familial character of the community would be fundamentally affected.

By limiting unrelated households to two persons while placing no limitation on households of related individuals, the village has embarked upon its commendable course in a constitutionally faulty vessel. . . . I would find the challenged ordinance unconstitutional. But I would not ask the village to abandon its goal of providing quiet streets, little traffic, and a pleasant and reasonably priced environment in which families might raise their children. Rather, I would commend the town to continue to pursue those purposes but by means of more carefully drawn and even-handed legislation.

I respectfully dissent.

———————

Comments: 1. *Belle Terre* was the first zoning case to be reviewed by the United States Supreme Court since the late 1920's. The District Court had upheld Belle Terre's definition of "family" on the ground that the interest of conventional "families" in limiting residential areas to occupancy by their own kind was a "legally protectable affirmative interest," and thus was by itself a legitimate goal of zoning. The Second Circuit's majority explicitly repudiated that ground, stating:

> [W]e start by examination of the sole ground upon which it was upheld by the district court, namely the interest of the local community in the protection and maintenance of the prevailing traditional family pattern which consists of occupancy of one-family houses by families based on consanguinity or legal affinity. In our view such a goal fails to fall within the proper exercise of state police power. It can hardly be disputed — and the district court so found — that the ordinance has the purpose and effect of permitting existing inhabitants to compel all others who would take up residence in the community to conform to its prevailing ideas of life-style, thus insuring that the community will be structured socially on a fairly homogeneous basis. Such social preferences, however, while permissible in a private club, have no relevance to public health, safety or welfare.
>
> The effect of the Belle Terre ordinance would be to exclude from the community, without any rational basis, unmarried groups seeking to live together, whether they be three college students, three single nurses, three priests, or three single judges. Although local communities are given wide latitude in achieving legitimate zoning needs, they cannot under the mask of zoning ordinances impose social preferences of this character upon their fellow citizens.

476 F.2d 806, at 815.

2. Two things are striking about the majority opinion in this case [*Belle Terre*]. The first is . . . that Douglas clearly regarded this case as merely involving conventional social and economic regulation of an owner's . . . property rights, and not as raising any civil liberties issues of any kind. The second is that the text of the opinion clearly documents the Supreme Court's unfamiliarity with zoning matters. True, the opinion starts off in a tone which implies that deciding this case merely involved filling in a previously unnoted gap in a long worked-over mosaic. . . . Along with some cases on tangential points, the opinion cited four cases having to do with land use controls — Euclid in 1926, Roberge in 1927, and Cusack in 1915, all on zoning — and one case (Berman) involving the use of eminent domain in the District of Columbia. An examination of these opinions is hardly an apt way for the Court to learn about what has been going on in the massive evolution of recent zoning law; the most recent of these three zoning cases was decided 46 years ago.

Moreover, the opinion is not surprising when considered against the background of Douglas's opinion in Berman, for in both cases he clearly regarded the main problem . . . as one of encouraging and protecting a pleasant and livable residential environment. In other words, Douglas (and the Supreme Court generally) are still living in a period when the important constitutional function of the courts is to vindicate the right of communities to control their own land, for various beneficent purposes; there is no trace in the majority opinion of the notion that there may be a widespread pattern involving the use of such local powers for antisocial purposes. . . .

3 N. Williams, American Land Planning Law 99-101 (1975).

3. Many of the state court decisions dealing with "single-family" zoning classifications are reviewed in the footnotes to Justice Stevens' opinion. As Justice Stevens indicated, fraternities, sororities, and retirement homes have not fared well in the state courts under "single-family" zoning provisions. *Accord, Pettis v. Alpha Alpha Chapter of Phi Beta Pi,* 213 N.W. 835 (Neb. 1927). The state courts have been divided with respect to the application of "single-family" zoning classifications to group homes for juveniles or mentally retarded adults and to drug treatment centers. In addition to *Browndale Int'l, Ltd. v. Board of Adjustment,* cited in n. 15 to Justice Stevens' opinion, see *Planning and Zoning Comm'n v. Synanon,* 216 A.2d 442 (Conn. 1966) (provision allowing "[o]ne detached dwelling for occupancy by one family per lot" held not to encompass an institution for rehabilitation of drug addicts, which would shelter "an ever-changing aggregate of individuals"). *Cf. Abbot House v. Village of Tarrytown,* 312 N.Y.S.2d 841 (N.Y. App. Div. 1970); *State ex rel. Ellis v. Liddle,* 520 S.W.2d 644 (Mo. App. 1975) (in both cases, group foster homes for juveniles were held permissible in "single-family" districts). In *Robertson v. Western Baptist Hosp.,* 267 S.W.2d 395 (Ky. 1954), cited in a footnote to Justice Stevens' opinion, twenty nurses living together were held to be a "family" under a zoning ordinance defining a "family" as "one or more persons living as a single housekeeping unit, as distinguished from a group occupying a hotel, club, fraternity or sorority house."

The state courts have generally been much more favorable to religious groups living together in a "single-family" district. In *Carroll v. City of Miami Beach,* 198 So.2d 643 (Fla. Dist. Ct. App. 1967), cited in a footnote to Justice Stevens' opinion, a group of novices living together with a Mother Superior as a single housekeeping unit was held to be a "family." In *Missionaries of Our Lady of La Sallette v. Village of Whitefish Bay,* 66 N.W.2d 627 (Wis. 1954), a group of up to eight priests and lay brothers living together in a large house in a suburb of Milwaukee was held to be a single family under an ordinance which did not require that members of a "family" be related. And a four-story dormitory for sixty students in a Roman Catholic college in New Rochelle was held to be a single-family house in *Laporte v. City of New Rochelle,* 152 N.Y.S.2d 916 (N.Y. App. Div. 1956), *aff'd,* 141 N.E.2d 917 (N.Y. 1957).

4. In addition to the *Ellis* case, *supra,* and the *City of White Plains* case, cited in footnote 17 of the *Moore* opinion, other state courts post-*Belle Terre* have refused to extend the reasoning of the case to uphold local ordinances defining "family" to exclude various kinds of group living arrangements. *See, e.g., Berger v. State,* 364 A.2d 993 (N.J. 1976) (group home for multi-handicapped, preschool children). The holding in the *Berger* case technically was dictum; the home was leased by the state and the court was able to apply the rule that state agencies are generally immune from local zoning ordinances. *See* Note, Governmental Immunity from Local Zoning Ordinances, 84 Harv. L. Rev. 869 (1971). Nevertheless, the New Jersey court was quite clear in rejecting the *Belle Terre* holding on state substantive due process grounds, and suggested that municipalities could maintain a family environment by restricting "single family dwellings to a reasonable number of persons who constitute a *bona fide* single housekeeping unit." *Id.* at 1003. Since in many of these cases the group homes are either leased or licensed by a state agency the state immunity ground provides an alternative basis for finding a local ordinance containing a restrictive family definition inapplicable. *But see Town of Durham v. White Enterprises, Inc.,* 348 A.2d 706 (N.H. 1975) (following *Belle Terre*). For critical commentary on zoning ordinances excluding group living arrangements see Note, "Burning the House to Roast the Pig": Unrelated Individuals and Single Family Zoning's Blood Relation Criterion, 58 Cornell L. Rev. 138 (1972).

MOORE v. CITY OF EAST CLEVELAND, OHIO

Supreme Court of the United States
431 U.S. 494, 52 L. Ed. 2d 531, 97 S. Ct. 1932 (1977)

Mr. Justice Powell announced the judgment of the Court, and delivered an opinion in which Mr. Justice Brennan, Mr. Justice Marshall, and Mr. Justice Blackmun joined.

East Cleveland's housing ordinance, like many throughout the country, limits occupancy of a dwelling unit to members of a single family. § 1351.02. But the ordinance contains an unusual and complicated definitional section that recognizes as a "family" only a few categories of related individuals, § 1341.08.[18] Because her

---

[18] Section 1341.08 provides:

" 'Family' means a number of individuals related to the nominal head of the household or to the spouse of the nominal head of the household living as a single housekeeping unit in a single dwelling unit, but limited to the following:

"(a) Husband or wife of the nominal head of the household.

"(b) Unmarried children of the nominal head of the household or of the spouse of the nominal head of the household, provided, however, that such unmarried children have no children residing with them.

"(c) Father or mother of the nominal head of the household or of the spouse of the nominal head of the household.

"(d) Notwithstanding the provisions of subsection (b) hereof, a family may include not more than one dependent married or unmarried child of the nominal

family, living together in her home, fits none of those categories, appellant stands convicted of a criminal offense. The question in this case is whether the ordinance violates the Due Process Clause of the Fourteenth Amendment.[19]

I

Appellant, Mrs. Inez Moore, lives in her East Cleveland home together with her son, Dale Moore, Sr., and her two grandsons, Dale, Jr., and John Moore, Jr. The two boys are first cousins rather than brothers; we are told that John came to live with his grandmother and with the elder and younger Dale Moores after his mother's death.

In early 1973, Mrs. Moore received a notice of violation from the city, stating that John was an "illegal occupant" and directing her to comply with the ordinance. When she failed to remove him from her home, the city filed a criminal charge. Mrs. Moore moved to dismiss, claiming that the ordinance was constitutionally invalid on its face. Her motion was overruled, and upon conviction she was sentenced to five days in jail and a $25 fine. The Ohio Court of Appeals affirmed after giving full consideration to her constitutional claims, and the Ohio Supreme Court denied review. We noted probable jurisdiction of her appeal, 425 U. S. 949 (1976).

II

The city argues that our decision in *Village of Belle Terre v. Boraas,* 416 U.S. 1 (1974), requires us to sustain the ordinance attacked here. Belle Terre, like East Cleveland, imposed limits on the types of groups that could occupy a single dwelling unit. Applying the constitutional standard announced in this Court's leading land-use case, *Euclid v. Ambler Realty Co.,* 272 U. S. 365 (1926), we sustained the Belle Terre ordinance on the ground that it bore a rational relationship to permissible state objectives.

But one overriding factor sets this case apart from *Belle Terre.* The ordinance there affected only *unrelated* individuals. It expressly allowed all who were related by "blood, adoption, or marriage" to live together, and in sustaining the ordinance we were careful to note

---

head of the household or of the spouse of the nominal head of the household and the spouse and dependent children of such dependent child. For the purpose of this subsection, a dependent person is one who has more than fifty percent of his total support furnished for him by the nominal head of the household and the spouse of the nominal head of the household.

"(e) A family may consist of one individual."

[19] Appellant also claims that the ordinance contravenes the Equal Protection Clause, but it is not necessary for us to reach that contention.

that it promoted "family needs" and "family values." 416 U. S., at 9. East Cleveland, in contrast, has chosen to regulate the occupancy of its housing by slicing deeply into the family itself. This is no mere incidental result of the ordinance. On its face it selects certain categories of relatives who may live together and declares that others may not. In particular, it makes a crime of a grandmother's choice to live with her grandson in circumstances like those presented here.

When a city undertakes such intrusive regulation of the family, neither *Belle Terre* nor *Euclid* governs; the usual judicial deference to the legislature is inappropriate. "This Court has long recognized that freedom of personal choice in matters of marriage and family life is one of the liberties protected by the Due Process Clause of the Fourteenth Amendment." *Cleveland Board of Education v. LaFleur,* 414 U. S. 632, 639-640 (1974). A host of cases, tracing their lineage to *Meyer v. Nebraska,* 262 U. S. 390, 399-401 (1923), and *Pierce v. Society of Sisters,* 268 U. S. 510, 534-535 (1925), have consistently acknowledged a "private realm of family life which the state cannot enter." *Prince v. Massachusetts,* 321 U. S. 158, 166 (1944). . . . Of course, the family is not beyond regulation. See *Prince v. Massachusetts, supra,* at 166. But when the government intrudes on choices concerning family living arrangements, this Court must examine carefully the importance of the governmental interests advanced and the extent to which they are served by the challenged regulation. See *Poe v. Ullman, supra,* at 554 (Harlan, J., dissenting).

When thus examined, this ordinance cannot survive. The city seeks to justify it as a means of preventing overcrowding, minimizing traffic and parking congestion, and avoiding an undue financial burden on East Cleveland's school system. Although these are legitimate goals, the ordinance before us serves them marginally, at best.[20] For example, the ordinance permits any family consisting only of husband, wife, and unmarried children to live together, even if the family contains a half-dozen licensed drivers, each with his or her own car. At the same time it forbids an adult brother and sister to share a household, even if both faithfully use public transportation. The ordinance would permit a grandmother to live with a single dependent son and children, even if his school-age children number a dozen, yet it forces Mrs. Moore to find another dwelling for her grandson John, simply because of the presence of his uncle and cousin in the same household. We need not labor the point. Section

---

[20] It is significant that East Cleveland has another ordinance specifically addressed to the problem of overcrowding. See *Department of Agriculture v. Moreno,* 413 U. S. 528, 536-537 (1973). Section 1351.03 limits population density directly, tying the maximum permissible occupancy of a dwelling to the habitable floor area. Even if John, Jr., and his father both remain in Mrs. Moore's household, the family stays well within these limits.

1341.08 has but a tenuous relation to alleviation of the conditions mentioned by the city.

III

The city would distinguish the cases based on *Meyer* and *Pierce*. It points out that none of them "gives grandmothers any fundamental rights with respect to grandsons." Brief, at 18, and suggests that any constitutional right to live together as a family extends only to the nuclear family — essentially a couple and its dependent children.

To be sure, these cases did not expressly consider the family relationship presented here. They were immediately concerned with freedom of choice with respect to childbearing, . . . or with the rights of parents to the custody and companionship of their own children, . . . or with traditional parental authority in matters of child rearing and education. . . . But unless we close our eyes to the basic reasons why certain rights associated with the family have been accorded shelter under the Fourteenth Amendment's Due Process Clause, we cannot avoid applying the force and rationale of these precedents to the family choice involved in this case.

Understanding those reasons requires careful attention to this Court's function under the Due Process Clause. Mr. Justice Harlan described it eloquently:

> "Due process has not been reduced to any formula; its content cannot be determined by reference to any code. The best that can be said is that through the course of this Court's decisions it has represented the balance which our Nation, built upon postulates of respect for the liberty of the individual, has struck between that liberty and the demands of organized society. If the supplying of content to this Constitutional concept has of necessity been a rational process, it certainly has not been one where judges have felt free to roam where unguided speculation might take them. The balance of which I speak is the balance struck by this country, having regard to what history teaches are the traditions from which it developed as well as the traditions from which it broke. That tradition is a living thing. A decision of this Court which radically departs from it could not long survive, while a decision which builds on what has survived is likely to be sound. No formula could serve as a substitute, in this area, for judgment and restraint.
>
> ". . . [T]he full scope of the liberty guaranteed by the Due Process Clause cannot be found in or limited by the precise terms of the specific guarantees elsewhere provided in the Constitution. This 'liberty' is not a series of isolated points

pricked out in terms of the taking of property; the freedom of speech, press, and religion; the right to keep and bear arms; the freedom from unreasonable searches and seizures; and so on. It is a rational continuum which, broadly speaking, includes a freedom from all substantial arbitrary impositions and purposeless restraints, . . . and which also recognizes, what a reasonable and sensitive judgment must, that certain interests require particularly careful scrutiny of the state needs asserted to justify their abridgment." *Poe v. Ullman,* 367 U. S., at 542-543 (Harlan, J., dissenting).

Substantive due process has at times been a treacherous field for this Court. There *are* risks when the judicial branch gives enhanced protection to certain substantive liberties without the guidance of the more specific provisions of the Bill of Rights. As the history of the *Lochner* era demonstrates, there is reason for concern lest the only limits to such judicial intervention become the predilections of those who happen at the time to be Members of this Court. That history counsels caution and restraint. But it does not counsel abandonment, nor does it require what the city urges here: cutting off any protection of family rights at the first convenient, if arbitrary boundary — the boundary of the nuclear family.

Appropriate limits on substantive due process come not from drawing arbitrary lines but rather from careful "respect for the teachings of history [and] solid recognition of the basic values that underlie our society." *Griswold v. Connecticut,* 381 U. S., at 501 (Harlan, J., concurring). . . . Our decisions establish that the Constitution protects the sanctity of the family precisely because the institution of the family is deeply rooted in this Nation's history and tradition. It is through the family that we inculcate and pass down many of our most cherished values, moral and cultural.

Ours is by no means a tradition limited to respect for the bonds uniting the members of the nuclear family. The tradition of uncles, aunts, cousins, and especially grandparents sharing a household along with parents and children has roots equally venerable and equally deserving of constitutional recognition. Over the years millions of our citizens have grown up in just such an environment, and most, surely, have profited from it. Even if conditions of modern society have brought about a decline in extended family households, they have not erased the accumulated wisdom of civilization, gained over the centuries and honored throughout our history, that supports a larger conception of the family. Out of choice, necessity, or a sense of family responsibility, it has been common for close relatives to draw together and participate in the duties and the satisfactions of a common home. Decisions concerning child rearing, which *Yoder, Meyer, Pierce* and other cases have recognized as entitled to constitutional protection, long have been shared with grandparents or other relatives who occupy the same household — indeed who may take on major responsibility for the rearing of the children. Especially in times of adversity, such as the death of a spouse or economic need, the broader family has tended to come together for mutual sustenance and to maintain or rebuild a secure home life. This is apparently what happened here.

Whether or not such a household is established because of personal tragedy, the choice of relatives in this degree of kinship to live together may not lightly be denied by the State. *Pierce* struck down an Oregon law requiring all children to attend the State's public schools, holding that the Constitution "excludes any general power of the State to standardize its children by forcing them to accept instruction from public teachers only." 268 U. S., at 535. By the same token the Constitution prevents East Cleveland from standardizing its children — and its adults — by forcing all to live in certain narrowly defined family patterns.

Reversed.

MR. JUSTICE BRENNAN, with whom MR. JUSTICE MARSHALL joins, concurring.

. . . .

[Justice Brennan noted that "[t]he Court's opinion conclusively demonstrates that classifying family patterns in this eccentric way [as in the East Cleveland ordinance — Eds.] is not a rational means of achieving the ends East Cleveland claims for its ordinance. . . ." He then noted the impact that the ordinance could be expected to have on black families:]

The "extended" form is especially familiar among black families. We may suppose that this reflects the truism that black citizens, like generations of white immigrants before them, have been victims of economic and other disadvantages that would worsen if they were compelled to abandon extended for nuclear living patterns. Even in husband and wife households, 13% of black families compared with 3% of white families include relatives under 18 years old, in addition to the couple's own children. In black households whose head is an elderly woman, as in this case, the contrast is even more striking: 48% of such black households, compared with 10% of counterpart white households, include related minor children not offspring of the head of the household.

I do not wish to be understood as implying that East Cleveland's enforcement of its ordinance is motivated by a racially discriminatory purpose: the record of this case would not support that implication. But the prominence of other than nuclear families among ethnic and racial minority groups, including our black citizens, surely demonstrates that the "extended family" pattern remains a vital tenet of our society. It suffices that in prohibiting this pattern of family living as a means of achieving its objectives, appellee city has chosen a device that deeply intrudes into family associational rights that historically have been central, and today remain central, to a large proportion of our population.

. . . .

[Justice Brennan also noted that the *Belle Terre* case supported the Court's decision because in *Belle Terre* "[t]he village took special care in its brief to emphasize that its ordinance did not in any manner inhibit the choice of *related* individuals to constitute a family, whether in the 'nuclear' or 'extended' form." (Emphasis by the Court.)]

MR. JUSTICE STEVENS, concurring in the judgment.

. . . .

Litigation involving single-family zoning ordinances is common. Although there appear to be almost endless differences in the language used in these ordinances, they contain three principal types of restrictions. First, they define the kind of structure that may be erected on vacant land. Second, they require that a single-family home be occupied only by a "single housekeeping unit." Third, they often require that the housekeeping unit be made up of persons related by blood, adoption, or marriage, with certain limited exceptions.

Although the legitimacy of the first two types of restrictions is well settled, attempts to limit occupancy to related persons have not been successful. The state courts have recognized a valid community interest in preserving the stable character of residential neighborhoods which justifies a prohibition against transient occupancy.[21] Nevertheless, in well reasoned opinions, the courts of Illinois,[22] New York,[23] New Jersey,[24] California,[25] Connecticut,[26]

---

[21] Types of group living which have not fared well under single-family ordinances include fraternities, *City of Schenectady v. Delta Chi Fraternity,* 5 App. Div. 2d 14, 168 N. Y. S. 2d 754 (1957), sororities, *Cassidy v. Triebel,* 337 Ill. App. 117, 85 N. E. 2d 461 (1948), a retirement home designed for over 20 people, *Kellogg v. Joint Council of Women's Auxiliaries Welfare Assn.,* 265 S. W. 2d 374 (S. C. of Mo. 1954), and a commercial therapeutic home for emotionally disturbed children, *Browndale International, Ltd. v. Board of Adjustment,* 60 Wis. 2d 182, 208 N. W. 2d 121 (Wis. 1973). These institutional uses are not only inconsistent with the single-housekeeping unit concept but include many more people than would normally inhabit a single-family dwelling.

[22] [Citing *City of Des Plaines v. Trottner,* 216 N.E.2d 116 (Ill. 1966). — Eds.]

[23] [Citing *City of White Plains v. Ferraioli,* 313 N.E.2d 756 (N.Y. 1974). — Eds.]

[24] [Citing *Kirsch Holding Co. v. Borough of Manasquan,* 281 A.2d 513 (N.J. 1971). — Eds.]

[25] [*Brady v. Superior Court,* 19 Cal. Rptr. 242 (Cal. App. 1962). — Eds.]

[26] [*Neptune Park Ass'n v. Steinberg,* 84 A.2d 687 (Conn. 1951). — Eds.]

Wisconsin,[27] and other jurisdictions, have permitted unrelated persons to occupy single-family residences notwithstanding an ordinance prohibiting, either expressly or implicitly, such occupancy.

These cases delineate the extent to which the state courts have allowed zoning ordinances to interfere with the right of a property owner to determine the internal composition of his household. The intrusion on that basic property right has not previously gone beyond the point where the ordinance defines a family to include only persons related by blood, marriage or adoption. Indeed, as the cases in the margin demonstrate, state courts have not always allowed the intrusion to penetrate that far. The state decisions have upheld zoning ordinances which regulated the identity, as opposed to the number, of persons who may comprise a household only to the extent that the ordinances require such households to remain nontransient, single-housekeeping units.

There appears to be no precedent for an ordinance which excludes any of an owner's relatives from the group of persons who may occupy his residence on a permanent basis. Nor does there appear to be any justification for such a restriction on an owner's use of his property. The city has failed totally to explain the need for a rule which would allow a homeowner to have two grandchildren live with her if they are brothers, but not if they are cousins. Since this ordinance has not been shown to have any "substantial relation to the public health, safety, morals or general welfare" of the City of East Cleveland, and since it cuts so deeply into a fundamental right normally associated with the ownership of residential property — that of an owner to decide who may reside on her property — it must fall under the limited standard of review of zoning decisions which this Court preserved.... Under that standard, East Cleveland's unprecedented ordinance constitutes a taking of property without due process and without just compensation.

For these reasons, I concur in the Court's judgment.

MR. CHIEF JUSTICE BURGER, dissenting.

[The Chief Justice would not reach the constitutional issues. He held that the appellants had not exhausted their administrative remedies because no effort had been made to apply for a variance as provided in the East Cleveland housing code. — Eds.]

MR. JUSTICE STEWART, with whom MR. JUSTICE REHNQUIST joins, dissenting.

. . . .

In my view, the appellant's claim that the ordinance in question invades constitutionally protected rights of association and privacy is in large part answered by the *Belle Terre* decision. The argument

---

[27] [*Missionaries of Our Lady of La Sallette v. Village of Whitefish Bay*, 66 N.W.2d 627 (Wis. 1954). — Eds.]

was made there that a municipality could not zone its land exclusively for single-family occupancy because to do so would interefere with protected rights of privacy or association. We rejected this contention. . . .

The *Belle Terre* decision thus disposes of the appellant's contentions to the extent they focus not on her blood relationships with her sons and grandsons but on more general notions about the "privacy of the home." Her suggestion that every person has a constitutional right permanently to share his residence with whomever he pleases, and that such choices are "beyond the province of legitimate governmental intrusion," amounts to the same argument that was made and found unpersuasive in *Belle Terre.*

To be sure, the ordinance involved in *Belle Terre* did not prevent blood relatives from occupying the same dwelling, and the Court's decision in that case does not, therefore, foreclose the appellant's arguments based specifically on the ties of kinship present in this case. Nonetheless, I would hold, for the reasons that follow, that the existence of those ties does not elevate either the appellant's claim of associational freedom or her claim of privacy to a level invoking constitutional protection.

To suggest that the biological fact of common ancestry necessarily gives related persons constitutional rights of association superior to those of unrelated persons is to misunderstand the nature of the associational freedoms that the Constitution has been understood to protect. Freedom of association has been constitutionally recognized because it is often indispensable to effectuation of explicit First Amendment guarantees. . . . But the scope of the associational right, until now, at least, has been limited to the constitutional need that created it; obviously not every "association" is for First Amendment purposes or serves to promote the ideological freedom that the First Amendment was designed to protect.

The "association" in this case is not for any purpose relating to the promotion of speech, assembly, the press, or religion. And wherever the outer boundaries of constitutional protection of freedom of association may eventually turn out to be, they surely do not extend to those who assert no interest other than the gratification, convenience, and economy of sharing the same residence.

The appellant is considerably closer to the constitutional mark in asserting that the East Cleveland ordinance intrudes upon "the private realm of family life which the state cannot enter." *Prince v. Massachusetts,* 321 U. S. 158, 166. Several decisions of the Court have identified specific aspects of what might broadly be termed "private family life" that are constitutionally protected against state interference. See, *e. g., Roe v. Wade,* 410 U. S. 113, 152-154 (woman's right to decide whether to terminate pregnancy); *Loving v. Virginia,* 388 U. S. 1, 12 (freedom to marry person of another race); *Griswold v. Connecticut,* 381 U. S. 479; *Eisenstadt v. Baird,* 405 U. S. 438 (right to use contraceptives); *Pierce v. Society of Sisters,* 268 U. S. 510, 534-535 (parents' right to send children to private schools); *Meyer v. Nebraska,* 262 U. S. 390 (parents' right to have children instructed in foreign language).

Although the appellant's desire to share a single-dwelling unit also involves "private family life" in a sense, that desire can hardly be equated with any of the interests protected in the cases just cited. The ordinance about which the appellant complains did not impede her choice to have or not to have children, and it did not dictate to her how her own children were to be nurtured and reared. The ordinance clearly does not prevent parents from living together or living with their unemancipated offspring.

But even though the Court's previous cases are not directly on point, the appellant contends that the importance of the "extended family" in American society requires us to hold that her decision to share her residence with her grandsons may not be interfered with by the State. This decision, like the decisions involved in bearing and raising children, is said to be an aspect of "family life" also entitled to substantive protection under the Constitution. Without pausing to inquire how far under this argument an "extended family" might extend, I cannot agree. When the Court has found that the Fourteenth Amendment placed a substantive limitation on a State's power to regulate, it has been in those rare cases in which the personal interests at issue have been deemed "implicit in the concept of ordered liberty." See *Roe v. Wade, supra,* at 152, quoting *Palko v. Connecticut,* 302 U. S. 319, 325. The interest that the appellant may have in permanently sharing a single kitchen and a suite of contiguous rooms with some of her relatives simply does not rise to that level. To equate this interest with the fundamental decisions to marry and to bear and raise children is to extend the limited substantive contours of the Due Process Clause beyond recognition.

The appellant also challenges the single-family occupancy ordinance on equal protection grounds. Her claim is that the city has drawn an arbitrary and irrational distinction between groups of people who may live together as a "family" and those who may not. While acknowledging the city's right to preclude more than one family from occupying a single dwelling unit, the appellant argues that the purposes of the single-family occupancy law would be equally served by an ordinance that did not prevent her from sharing her residence with her two sons and their sons.

This argument misconceives the nature of the constitutional inquiry. In a case such as this one, where the challenged ordinance intrudes upon no substantively protected constitutional right, it is not the Court's business to decide whether its application in a particular case seems inequitable, or even absurd. The question is not whether some other ordinance, drafted more broadly, might have served the city's ends as well or almost as well. The task, rather, is to determine if East Cleveland's ordinance violates the Equal Protection Clause of the United States Constitution. And in performing that task, it must be borne in mind that "[w]e deal with economic and social legislation where legislatures have historically drawn lines which we respect against the charge of violation of the Equal Protection Clause if the law be ' "reasonable, not arbitrary" ' (quoting *Royster Guano Co. v. Virginia,* 253 U. S. 412, 415) and bears 'a rational relationship to a [permissible] state objective.' *Reed v. Reed,* 404 U. S. 71, 76." *Village of Belle Terre v. Boraas, supra,* at 8. "[E]very line drawn by a legislature leaves some out that might well have been included. That exercise of discretion, however, is a legislative, not a judicial, function." *Ibid.* (footnote omitted).

Viewed in the light of these principles, I do not think East Cleveland's definition of "family" offends the Constitution. The city has undisputed power to ordain single-family residential occupancy. . . . And that power plainly carries with it the power to say what a "family" is. Here the city has defined "family" to include not only father, mother, and dependent children, but several other close relatives as well. The definition is rationally designed to carry out the legitimate governmental purposes identified in the *Belle Terre* opinion: "The police power is not confined to elimination of filth, stench, and unhealthy places. It is ample to lay out zones where family values, youth values, and the blessings of quiet seclusion and clean air make the area a sanctuary for people." 416 U. S., at 9.

. . . .

MR. JUSTICE WHITE, dissenting.

. . . .

[Justice White reviews the development of substantive Due Process doctrine in the Supreme Court, and notes that the Court has moved to a highly deferential view of state and local legislative enactments, especially "with respect to legislation seeking to control or regulate the economic life of the state or Nation." He continues: — Eds.]

There are various "liberties," however, which require that infringing legislation be given closer judicial scrutiny, not only with respect to existence of a purpose and the means employed, but also with respect to the importance of the purpose itself relative to the invaded interest. Some interests would appear almost impregnable to invasion, such as the freedoms of speech, press, and religion, and the freedom from cruel and unusual punishments. Other interests, for example, the right of association, the right to vote, and various claims sometimes referred to under the general rubric of the right to privacy, also weigh very heavily against state claims of authority to regulate. It is this category of interests which, as I understand it, MR. JUSTICE STEWART refers to as "implicit in the concept of ordered liberty.". . . Because he would confine the reach of substantive due process protection to interests such as these and because he would not classify in this category the asserted right to share a house with the relatives involved here, he rejects the due process claim.

Given his premise, he is surely correct. Under our cases, the Due Process Clause extends substantial protection to various phases of family life, but none requires that the claim made here be sustained. I cannot believe that the interest in residing with more than one set of grandchildren is one that calls for any kind of heightened protection under the Due Process Clause. To say that one has a personal right to live with all, rather than some, of one's grandchildren and that this right is implicit in ordered liberty is, as my Brother STEWART says, "to extend the limited substantive contours of the Due Process Clause beyond recognition." . . . The present claim is hardly one of which it could be said that "neither liberty nor justice would exist if [it] were sacrificed." . . .

MR. JUSTICE POWELL would apparently construe the Due Process Clause to protect from all but quite important state regulatory interests any right or privilege that in his estimate is deeply rooted in the country's traditions. For me, this suggests a far too expansive charter for this Court and a far less meaningful and less confining guiding principle than MR. JUSTICE STEWART would use for serious substantive due process review. What the deeply rooted traditions of the country are is arguable; which of them deserve the protection of the Due Process Clause is even more debatable. The suggested view would broaden enormously the horizons of the Clause; and, if the interest involved here is any measure of what the States would be forbidden to regulate, the courts would be substantively weighing and very likely invalidating a wide range of measures that Congress and state legislatures think appropriate to respond to a changing economic and social order.

Mrs. Moore's interest in having the offspring of more than one dependent son live with her qualifies as a liberty protected by the Due Process Clause; but, because of the nature of that particular interest, the demands of the Clause are satisfied once the Court is assured that the challenged proscription is the product of a duly enacted or promulgated statute, ordinance, or regulation and that it is not wholly lacking in purpose or utility. That under this ordinance any number of unmarried children may reside with their mother and that this number might be as destructive of neighborhood values as one or more additional grandchildren is just another argument that children and grandchildren may not constitutionally be distinguished by a local zoning ordinance.

That argument remains unpersuasive to me. Here the head of the household may house himself or herself and spouse, their parents, and any number of their unmarried children. A fourth generation may be represented by only one set of grandchildren and then only if born to a dependent child. The ordinance challenged by petitioner prevents her from living with both sets of grandchildren only in East Cleveland, an area with a radius of three miles and a population of 40,000. Brief for Appellee 16 n. 1. The ordinance thus denies petitioner the opportunity to live with all her grandchildren in this particular suburb; she is free to do so in other parts of the Cleveland metropolitan area. If there is power to maintain the character of a single-family neighborhood, as there surely is, some limit must be placed on the reach of the "family." Had it been our task to legislate, we might have approached the problem in a different manner than did the drafters of this ordinance; but I have no trouble in concluding that the normal goals of zoning regulation are present here and that the ordinance serves these goals by limiting, in identifiable circumstances, the number of people who can occupy a single household. The ordinance does not violate the Due Process Clause.

. . . .

Comment: Although the definition of a "family" before the court in *Moore v. City of East Cleveland* was included in a housing code rather than a "zoning" ordinance, the technical distinction appears to have little significance. Most of the justices seem to have assumed that Mrs. Moore's home was a single-family dwelling, but Justice Stewart's opinion, in a footnote, indicates that it was actually a two-family dwelling.

APPEAL OF GIRSH

Supreme Court of Pennsylvania
437 Pa. 237, 263 A.2d 395 (1970)

OPINION OF THE COURT

ROBERTS, Justice.

By agreement dated July 13, 1964, appellant contracted to purchase a 17½ acre tract of land, presently zoned R-1 Residential,[28] in Nether Providence Township, Delaware County. Appellant agreed to pay a minimum of $110,000 (later changed by agreement to $120,000) for the property. He further agreed to request the

---

[28] R-1 Residential zones require minimum lot sizes of 20,000 square feet. The most common of the permissible land uses under the R-1 Residential classification is a single-family detached dwelling.

Township Board of Commissioners to change the R-1 Residential zoning classification so that a high-rise apartment could be built on the property and to pay $140,000 if this request were granted.

Nether Providence is a first-class township with a population of almost 13,000 persons and an area of 4.64 square miles. Approximately 75% of the Township is zoned either R-1 or R-2 Residential, which permit the construction of single-family dwelling units on areas not less than 20,000 and 14,000 square feet, respectively. Multi-unit apartment buildings, although not *explicitly* prohibited, are not provided for in the ordinance. The Township contains the customary commercial and industrial districts, as well as two areas where apartments have been permitted and constructed only after variances were secured.

After the Board refused to amend the zoning ordinance, appellant sought a building permit to construct two nine-story luxury apartments, each containing 280 units.[29] The permit was refused since the R-1 Residential classification does not permit multiple dwellings. Appellant appealed to the Zoning Board of Adjustment and announced that he would attack the constitutionality of the zoning ordinance in lieu of seeking a variance. The Zoning Board sustained the ordinance and denied relief. The Court of Common Pleas of Delaware County affirmed, and appellant took this appeal. We hold that the failure of appellee-township's zoning scheme to provide for apartments is unconstitutional and reverse the decree of the court below.

Initially, it is plain that appellee's zoning ordinance indeed makes no provision for apartment uses. Appellee argues that nonetheless apartments are not explicitly *prohibited* by the zoning ordinance. Appellee reasons that although only single-family residential uses are provided for, nowhere does the ordinance say that there shall be no apartments. In theory, an apartment use by variance is available, and appellee urges that this case thus is different from prior cases in which we severely questioned zoning schemes that did not allow given uses in an *entire* municipality. See *Exton Quarries, Inc. v. Zoning Board of Adjustment,* 425 Pa. 43, 228 A.2d 169 (1967); *Ammon R. Smith Auto Co. Appeal,* 423 Pa. 493, 223 A.2d 683 (1966); *Norate Corp. v. Zoning Board of Adjustment,* 417 Pa. 397, 207 A.2d 890 (1965).

Appellee's argument, although perhaps initially appealing, cannot withstand analysis. It is settled law that a variance is available *only* on narrow grounds, i. e., "where the property is subjected to an unnecessary hardship, unique or peculiar to itself, and where the

---

[29] Appellant stated in court that he would reduce the number of units per building to 216.

grant thereof will not be contrary to the public interest. The reasons to justify the granting of a variance must be 'substantial, serious and compelling.' " *Poster Advertising Company, Inc. v. Zoning Board of Adjustment,* 408 Pa. 248, 251, 182 A.2d 521, 523 (1962). In light of this standard, appellee's landuse restriction in the case before us cannot be upheld against constitutional attack because of the *possibility* that an *occasional* property owner may carry the heavy burden of proving sufficient hardship to receive a variance. To be constitutionally sustained, appellee's land-use restriction must be reasonable. If the failure to make allowance in the Township's zoning plan for apartment uses is unreasonable, that restriction does not become any the more reasonable because once in a while, a developer may be able to show the hardship necessary to sustain a petition for a variance.[30] At least for the purposes of this case, the failure to provide for apartments anywhere within the Township must be viewed as the legal equivalent of an explicit total prohibition of apartment houses in the zoning ordinance.

Were we to accept appellee's argument, we would encourage the Township in effect to spot-zone a given use on variance-hardship grounds. This approach distorts the question before us, which is whether appellee must provide for apartment living as part of its *plan* of development. . . .

By emphasizing the possibility that a given land owner *could* obtain a variance, the Township overlooks the broader question that is presented by this case. In refusing to allow apartment development as part of its zoning scheme, appellee has in effect decided to zone *out* the people who would be able to live in the Township if apartments were available. Cf. *National Land and Investment Co. v. Easttown Twp. Board of Adjustment,* 419 Pa. 504, 532, 215 A.2d 597, 612 (1965): "The question posed is whether the township can stand in the way of the natural forces which send our growing population into hitherto undeveloped areas in search of a comfortable place to live. We have concluded not. A zoning ordinance whose primary purpose is to prevent the entrance of newcomers in order to avoid future burdens, economic and otherwise, upon the administration of public services and facilities can not be held valid." [The *National Land* case is reproduced *infra* p.432.— Eds.]

---

[30] . . . If the zoning ordinance is unreasonable, it is no saving that some people may show the requisite degree of hardship to obtain a variance. The hardship necessary to sustain an application for a variance borders on economic disaster, but this provides no protection for the individual who is disadvantaged to a substantial, but lesser, extent. This infringement on this latter individual's right to use his own property cannot be allowed unless it is reasonable.

We emphasize that we are not here faced with the question whether we can compel appellee to zone *all* of its land to permit apartment development, since this is a case where *nowhere* in the Township are apartments permitted. Instead, we are guided by the reasoning that controlled in *Exton Quarries,* supra. We there stated that "The constitutionality of zoning ordinances which totally prohibit legitimate businesses ... from an entire community should be regarded with particular circumspection; for unlike the constitutionality of most restrictions on property rights imposed by other ordinances, the constitutionality of total prohibitions of legitimate businesses cannot be premised on the fundamental reasonableness of allocating to each type of activity a particular location in the community." 425 Pa. at 58, 228 A.2d at 179. In *Exton Quarries* we struck down an ordinance which did not allow quarrying anywhere in the municipality, just as in *Ammon R. Smith Auto Co. Appeal,* supra, we did not tolerate a total ban on flashing signs and in *Norate Corp.,* supra, we struck down a prohibition on billboards everywhere in the municipality. Here we are faced with a similar case, but its implications are even more critical, for we are here dealing with the crucial problem of population, not with billboards or quarries. Just as we held in *Exton Quarries, Ammon R. Smith,* and *Norate* that the governing bodies must make some provision for the use in question, we today follow those cases and hold that appellee cannot have a zoning scheme that makes no reasonable provision for apartment uses.

Appellee argues that apartment uses would cause a significant population increase with a resulting strain on available municipal services and roads, and would clash with the existing residential neighborhood. But we *explicitly* rejected both these claims in *National Land,* supra: "Zoning is a tool in the hands of governmental bodies which enables them to more effectively meet the demands of evolving and growing communities. It must not and can not be used by those officials as an instrument by which they may shirk their responsibilities. Zoning is a means by which a governmental body can plan for the future — it may not be used as a means to deny the future. . . . Zoning provisions may not be used . . . to avoid the increased responsibilities and economic burdens which time and natural growth invariably bring." 419 Pa. at 527-528, 215 A.2d at 610. . . . That reasoning applies equally here. Likewise we reaffirm our holding in *National Land* that protecting the character — really the aesthetic nature — of the municipality is not sufficient justification for an exclusionary zoning technique. 419 Pa. at 528-529, 215 A.2d at 610-611.

This case presents a situation where, no less than in *National Land,* the Township is trying to "stand in the way of the natural forces which send out growing population into hitherto undeveloped areas in search of a comfortable place to live." Appellee here has simply made a decision that it is content with things as they are, and that the expense or change in character that would result from people moving in to find "a comfortable place to live" are for someone else to worry about. That decision is unacceptable. Statistics indicate that people are attempting to move away from the urban core areas, relieving the grossly over-crowded conditions that exist in most of our major cities. Figures show that most jobs that are being created in urban areas, including the one here in question, are in the suburbs. New York Times, June 29, 1969, p. 39 (City Edition). Thus the suburbs, which at one time were merely "bedrooms" for those who worked in the urban core, are now becoming active business areas in their own right. It follows then that formerly "outlying", somewhat rural communities, are becoming logical areas for development and population growth — in a sense, suburbs to the suburbs. With improvements in regional transportation systems, these areas also are now more accessible to the central city.

In light of this, Nether Providence Township may not permissibly choose to only take as many people as can live in single-family housing, in effect freezing the population at near present levels. Obviously if every municipality took that view, population spread would be completely frustrated. Municipal services must be provided *somewhere,* and if Nether Providence is a logical place for development to take place, it should not be heard to say that it will not bear its rightful part of the burden.[31] Certainly it can protect its attractive character by requiring apartments to be built in accordance with (reasonable) set-back, open space, height, and other light-and-air requirements,[32] but it cannot refuse to make any provision for apartment living. The simple fact that someone is anxious to build apartments is strong indication that the location of

[31] Perhaps in an ideal world, planning and zoning would be done on a *regional* basis, so that a given community would have apartments, while an adjoining community would not. But as long as we allow zoning to be done community by community, it is intolerable to allow one municipality (or many municipalities) to close its doors at the expense of surrounding communities and the central city.

[32] As appellants indicate, the apartments here in question would cover only 2.7 acres of a 17.7 acre tract, would be located far back from the road and adjacent properties, and would be screened by existing high trees. Over half of the trees now on the tract would be saved.

It should be pointed out that much of the opposition to apartment uses in suburban communities is based on fictitious emotional appeals which insist on categorizing all apartments as being equivalent to the worst big-city tenements. See Babcock and Bosselman, Suburban Zoning and the Apartment Boom, 111 U.Pa.L.Rev. 1040, 1051-1072 (1963), wherein the authors also convincingly refute the arguments that apartments necessarily will: not "pay their own way"; cut off light and air; become slums; reduce property values; be destructive to the "character of the community"; and bring in "low-class" people.

this township is such that people are desirous of moving in, and we do not believe Nether Providence can close its doors to those people.

It is not true that the logical result of our holding today is that a municipality must provide for all types of land use. This case deals with the right of people to *live on land,* a very different problem than whether appellee must allow certain industrial uses within its borders.[33] Apartment living is a fact of life that communities like Nether Providence must learn to accept. If Nether Providence is located so that it is a place where apartment living is in demand, it must provide for apartments in its plan for future growth; it cannot be allowed to close its doors to others seeking a "comfortable place to live."

The order of the Court of Common Pleas of Delaware County is reversed.

BELL, C. J., files a concurring opinion.

[The opinion of Bell, C. J., is omitted. — Eds.]

JONES, Justice (dissenting).

Appellant attacks the constitutionality of the zoning ordinance in question on two levels. First, he maintains that it is unconstitutional for the Township to prohibit the construction of apartment buildings throughout the entire township. Second, he argues that the ordinance as applied to the Duer Tract in particular is unconstitutional because the property cannot reasonably be graded and developed for single-family residences.

. . . .

Appellant's first argument is that the zoning ordinance is unconstitutional in that it makes no provision for apartment buildings anywhere in the township. Appellant maintains that this Court looks askance at zoning ordinances which totally prohibit a legitimate use anywhere within the municipality, citing *Exton Quarries, Inc. v. Zoning Board of Adjustment,* 425 Pa. 43, 228 A.2d 169 (1967); *Ammon R. Smith Auto Co. Appeal,* 423 Pa. 493, 223 A.2d 683 (1966); *Norate Corp. v. Zoning Board of Adjustment,* 417 Pa. 397, 207 A.2d 890 (1965); *Eller v. Board of Adjustment,* 414 Pa.

---

[33] Even in the latter case, if the Township instituted a total ban on a given use, that decision would be open to at least considerable question under our decision in *Exton Quarries,* supra.

In addition, at least hypothetically, appellee could show that apartments are not appropriate on the site where appellant wishes to build, but that question is not before us as long as the zoning ordinance in question is fatally defective on its face. Appellee could properly decide that apartments are more appropriate in one part of the Township than in another, but it cannot decide that apartments can fit in *no* part of the Township.

1, 198 A.2d 863 (1964). Of these four cases, the authority most in point is *Exton.* In *Exton* we struck down a zoning ordinance as unconstitutional which prohibited any and all quarrying within the township. We noted that the township was sparsely settled and that the proposed quarry would be located some distance from the nearest residential neighborhood. We held that "a zoning ordinance which totally excludes a particular business from an entire municipality must bear a more substantial relationship to the public health, safety, morals and general welfare than an ordinance which merely confines that business to a certain area in the municipality." (425 Pa. at 60, 228 A.2d at 179.)

. . . .

Exton, upon which the majority opinion places the most reliance, can be distinguished on two grounds. First, *Exton* involved the total prohibition of a valid use. The ordinance now before us does not involve a total prohibition; the ordinance simply does not make provision for apartment buildings. While at first blush this might appear to be a distinction without a difference, there is, in reality, an important difference. Apartment buildings are permissible — and, in fact, have been constructed — if a variance is granted. Therefore, it is not correct to say that the Township totally prohibits the construction of apartment buildings.

Second, the natural expansion of the majority's conclusion is that Nether Providence must provide for all types of high-density, residential land use. This is an unsound result. It makes no more sense to require a rural township to provide for high-rise apartments than to provide for industrial zones; likewise, it would not make sense to require an industrial municipality to provide for agricultural uses. By concluding that the township must provide for high-rise apartments, the majority also impliedly holds that every possible use, having no greater detrimental effect, must also be allowed. In my opinion, this decision places us in the position of a "super board of adjustment" or "planning commission of last resort," a position which we have heretofore specifically rejected. *National Land and Investment Co. v. Easttown Twp. Bd. of Adjustment,* 419 Pa. 504, 521-22, 215 A.2d 597, 606-607 (1965).

Even if I were to accept appellant's logic, it must still be affirmatively demonstrated that high-rise apartment buildings are a *suitable* land use within the township. The court below held that appellant had failed to carry his burden of proof, and I find no fault in this decision. The evidence indicates that 90% of the township is presently already developed. A land planner and municipal consultant testified that he had studied the remaining undeveloped properties within the township and concluded that none of them was suitable for high-rise apartments. Furthermore, the township is residential in nature with a relatively sparse population. A high-rise apartment project would produce a significant increase in population which would tax the limited municipal services available in the township. Accordingly, I find it impossible to say on the face of this record that a township such as Nether Providence is constitutionally required to make provision for high-rise apartments in its zoning ordinances.

I turn now to appellant's second contention, *viz.,* that the zoning ordinance permitting only single-family dwellings is unconstitutional as applied to the Duer Tract in particular. Appellant's first argument under this heading is that the ordinance has no relation to the public health, safety and welfare. I cannot agree. The proposed apartment complex would be the largest of its kind in Delaware County, housing an estimated 1,600 persons, and would increase the population of the township by 13%. We cannot refute the conclusion that such a large and rapid increase in population would place a strain on the township's limited municipal services and rural roads. Furthermore, except for the railroad tracks, the area sourrounding the Duer Tract is composed exclusively of single-family dwellings. The proposed apartment towers would be incompatible with the existing residential neighborhood and would introduce a structure completely out of proportion to any other building in the township. Furthermore, the complex would present a density problem in this area of the township. The First Class Township Code specifically empowers local municipalities to zone for density; I conclude that the ordinance in question is a proper application of that power.

Appellant's second argument is that the ordinance is unreasonable, arbitrary and discriminatory as applied to the Duer Tract because of the prohibitive expense involved in grading and preparing the land for single-family residences. There is no question that the property contains some topographical features which are less than desirable for the construction of single-family homes. The record is replete with conflicting testimony, however, as to how much expense would be required to grade the tract and divert the creek which runs through the property. There is evidence in the record to support the court's conclusion that these preparatory expenses would not make the cost of the homes prohibitively expensive. The court pointed out that a development of single-family houses is now being constructed on a neighboring tract which is very similar topographically to the Duer Tract. Furthermore, appellant made a firm commitment to buy the property regardless of whether he was successful in having the zoning classification changed. Apparently when he purchased the property, therefore, appellant concluded that he could successfully build and sell single-family homes on the tract.

Therefore, I would hold that the Township is *not* constitutionally required to provide for multiple-unit apartment buildings in its zoning ordinance and that the ordinance in question is not unconstitutional as applied to the Duer Tract.

I dissent.

COHEN and POMEROY, JJ., join in this dissenting opinion.

_____

Comments: 1. As the dissenting opinion indicates, there was evidence in the record to support the trial court's conclusion that the cost of grading and other expenses required to prepare the Duer Tract for single-family house construction "would not make the cost of the homes prohibitively expensive." Indeed, the appellant-developer apparently did not even show that apartment construction would be more profitable than single-family development. Did the court hold the zoning ordinance unconstitutional because it deprived the appellant of property without due process of law? Or because the zoning ordinance was *ultra vires*? Or was the court primarily concerned, not with the appellant's property rights, but with the inability of persons desiring to live in apartments to move to Nether Providence Township? Did the appellant have standing to represent the interests of "outsiders" excluded by the zoning ordinance? And why should the court be concerned about the exclusion of persons desiring to live in "luxury apartments"? What constitutional rights of "outsiders" desiring to live in "luxury apartments" were infringed by the ordinance? For an excellent discussion of the *Girsh* decision see Washburn, Apartments in the Suburbs, 74 Dick. L. Rev. 634 (1970).

The judicial approach to prohibition of residential building types established in *Girsh* was applied to "townhouses" in *Camp Hill Dev. Co. v. Zoning Bd. of Adjustment,* 319 A.2d 197 (Pa. Commw. Ct. 1974), where the court held that an ordinance prohibiting townhouses anywhere in the municipality was unconstitutional because it unreasonably failed to provide for a legitimate and needed residential use. The court said, *inter alia,* that it had not

> neglected the Borough's contention that the *Girsh* rule is not violated because apartments are permitted in the R-2 district, although limited to such as do not have more than one wall in common with another apartment. But ... townhouses are an accepted form of development entitled .... to the same recognition accorded by *Girsh* to apartments.

Id. at 200. In *Dublin Properties v. Board of Comm'rs,* 342 A.2d 821 (Pa. Commw. Ct. 1975), a zoning ordinance that did not allow townhouses as a matter of right anywhere in the township was held unconstitutional, although "the Township had permitted townhouses to be built in AH-Apartment Districts" (presumably by granting variances).

In *Appeal of Baker,* 339 A.2d 131 (Pa. Commw. Ct. 1975), however, it was held that prohibition of more than six townhouse units per acre was not unconstitutional either on the theory that it bore no reasonable relationship to the traditional police power goals of zoning or on the theory that it constituted *de facto* exclusionary zoning. And in *Kaiserman v. Springfield Township,* 348 A.2d 467 (Pa. Commw. Ct. 1976), it was held that the record did not sustain the allegation of *de facto* exclusion of multifamily dwellings. *Inter alia,* the court rejected an argument that the zoning ordinance provision requiring grant of a special exception before multifamily housing could be constructed foreclosed, as a practical matter, the possibility of building multifamily dwellings in the township. The court said:

> A use which requires a special exception is a *permitted use* in an area, and the burden is on the township, if it seeks to deny the petition, to show that the use would adversely affect the health, safety, and morals of the community.... An application for a variance, on the other hand, places the burden on the applicant to show that, even though the use is prohibited, a unique hardship is imposed on the particular property as a result of the zoning restrictions.... Persons claiming that a township has used an unreasonably restrictive standard in denying a special exception have recourse to a reviewing court for their remedy.

Id. at 471-72. Note: Townhouses are a series of dwellings, usually two or three stories in height, that are built for single-family occupancy and that share common side walls. They are usually built in linear groups of three or more.

2. In the principal case the appellant-developer did not try to obtain a variance after failing to persuade the township governing body to rezone the Duer Tract to permit apartment construction. Although the court did not expressly address the "exhaustion of remedies" issue, it seems clear that no variance to permit apartment construction could properly have been granted. The appellant-developer certainly did not "show the requisite degree of hardship to obtain a variance" as defined in footnote 24 to the majority opinion. Moreover, there was no showing that the appellant's hardship, if any, was due to "peculiar" or "unique" circumstances that only affected the Duer Tract. So any attempt to obtain a variance to permit apartment construction would have been futile if the township board of adjustment applied the usual standards in passing on the variance application.

But, why did the appellant-developer appeal to the zoning board of adjustment and announce "that he would attack the constitutionality of the zoning ordinance in lieu of seeking a variance"? In most jurisdictions the zoning board of adjustment (or appeals) has no authority to entertain a constitutional attack on the zoning ordinance. In Pennsylvania, however, it came to be held that a landowner who is not seeking a variance cannot attack the validity of a zoning ordinance on substantive grounds unless he applies for a building permit, is denied, and then pursues an appeal, first to the zoning board of adjustment, and then to the courts. *Home Life Ins. Co. v. Board of Adjustment,* 143 A.2d 21 (Pa. 1958); *Jacobs v. Fetzer,* 112 A.2d 356 (Pa. 1955).

The Pennsylvania Municipalities Planning Code § 1004 (1) (a) (enacted in 1968 and amended in 1972), Pa. Stat. Ann. tit. 53, § 11004(1)(a) (1972), in effect authorized the continuance of the old practice; it provides that "[a] landowner who, on substantive grounds, desires to challenge the validity of an ordinance or map or any provision thereof which prohibits or restricts the use or development of land in which he has an interest shall submit the challenge ... (a) To the zoning hearing board for a report thereon ...." MPC § 910, Pa. Stat. Ann. tit. 53, § 10910 (1972) provides that

The board shall hear challenges to the validity of a zoning ordinance or map . . . . In all such challenges, the board shall take evidence and make a record thereon . . . . At the conclusion of the hearing, the board shall decide all contested questions and shall make findings on all relevant issues of fact which shall become part of the record on appeal to the court.

MPC §§ 1008 through 1011, Pa. Stat. Ann. tit. 53, §§ 11008 through 11011 (1972), deal with judicial review upon such appeal.

3. As previously indicated, a judicial decision invalidating a zoning ordinance as applied to a particular tract of land does not necessarily assure that the land will be rezoned to permit the use desired by the landowner. This is equally true where, as in *Girsh,* the landowner (or developer) attacks the zoning ordinance "as a whole." In fact, after the decision in *Girsh,* Nether Providence Township amended its zoning ordinance so as to include a multifamily residential use classification and rezoned several parcels of land for multifamily use; but the appellant's property was not rezoned. Subsequently, the appellant attempted to obtain a variance and a building permit for the proposed luxury apartment development, but the application was denied. The appellant then petitioned the court for further relief, and the court ordered the issuance of a building permit. Order No. MP-12, 271 (Aug. 29, 1972) (unpublished). *See Casey v. Zoning Hearing Bd.,* 328 A.2d 464, 468 n. 10 (Pa. 1970). But the appellant's attempt to build apartments in Nether Township was again frustrated, at least temporarily, by the township's undertaking to condemn the appellant's tract for an open-space area. *See* Krasnowiecki, Zoning Litigation and the New Pennsylvania Procedures, 120 U. Pa. L. Rev. 1029, 1080-82 (1972).

4. As an alternative to challenging the validity of a zoning ordinance on substantive grounds before the zoning hearing board, one with an interest in land restricted by the ordinance may submit a challenge to the local governing body, together with a request for a "curative amendment," under Pennsylvania Municipalities Planning Code §§ 609.1, 1004(1)(b), Pa. Stat. Ann. tit. 53, §§ 10609.1, 11004(1)(b) (1972). Post-1972 decisions establish the applicability of the new procedure where "the validity of an entire zoning ordinance" is challenged as "exclusionary," as well as where the landowner makes a "due process" attack on the ground that his land is too severely restricted by the ordinance. *Robin Corp. v. Lower Paxton Township,* 332 A.2d 841, 846 (Pa. Commw. Ct. 1975). It also appears that the new procedure gives the landowner or developer a good chance to obtain effective relief, either through adoption of the proposed curative amendment by the local governing body or by the court on appeal. If the local governing body denies the request for a curative amendment and the court, on appeal, finds that the zoning ordinance or map unlawfully prevents or restricts a use or development of the land described in plans or other materials submitted to the local governing body along with the proposed curative amendment, the court may order the described use or development approved as to all elements or order approval only as to some elements and refer other elements to the governing body for further proceedings, including the adoption of alternative restrictions, in accordance with the court's opinion and order. *See* Pa. Stat. Ann. tit. 53, §§ 11004(1)(b), (2)(c), (e)(4) (1972). While the governing body may formulate its own "curative amendment" rather than simply adopting the one proposed by the landowner or developer, it would seem that the local governing body will not find it more difficult to frustrate the successful challenger by zoning around him. *See Casey v. Zoning Hearing Bd.,* 328 A.2d 464 (Pa. 1974); *Ellick v. Board of Supervisors,* 333 A.2d 239 (Pa. Commw. Ct. 1975); Henszey & Novak, Substantive Validity Challenges Under the Pennsylvania Municipalities Planning Code: The Practitioner and the New Procedures, 21 Vill. L. Rev. 187 (1976); Hyson, The Problem of Relief in Developer-Initiated Zoning Litigation, 12 Urb. L. Ann. 21 (1976); Krasnowiecki, *supra* Comment 5; Rosenzweig, the Curative Amendment Procedure in Pennsylvania: The Landowners Challenge to the Substantive Validity of Zoning Restrictions, 80 Dick. L. Rev. 43 (1975).

5. Without any specific statutory authorization, the Illinois courts have provided relief similar to the relief now available under the Pennsylvania Municipalities Planning Code of 1972. The leading case is *Sinclair Pipe Line Co. v. Village of Richton Park,* 167 N.E.2d 406 (Ill. 1960), where the court said:

> [T]wo equally undesirable consequences may ensue if the property is left unzoned as the result of a decree declaring a zoning ordinance void. The municipality may rezone the property to another use classification that still excludes the one proposed, thus making further litigation necessary as to the validity of the new classification.... The present case illustrates the other possibility: — that a decree which was induced by evidence which depicted a proposed use in a highly favorable light would not restrict the property owner to that use, and he might thereafter use the property for an entirely different purpose.
>
> In our opinion, it is appropriate for the court to avoid these difficulties by framing its decree with reference to the record before it, and particularly with reference to the evidence offered at the trial. In most of the cases that have come before us in recent years, a specific use was contemplated and the record was shaped in terms of that use. In such cases the relief awarded may guarantee that the owner will be allowed to proceed with that use without further litigation and that he will not proceed with a different use....

Id. at 411.

Subsequent Illinois appellate cases have held that the specific use authorized under the *Sinclair Pipe Line* rule may not be framed in terms that are too broad, but that it is proper to authorize the proposed use on the basis of site plans showing its general design and layout. *E.g., Tomasek v. City of Des Plaines,* 325 N.E.2d 345 (Ill. App. 1975); *Bass v. City of Joliet,* 295 N.E.2d 53 (Ill. App. 1973); *Fiore v. City of Highland Park,* 221 N.E.2d 323 (Ill. App. 1966).

The appellate courts in Florida and Virginia will also grant a form of site-specific relief to developers successfully challenging zoning restrictions. *See Burritt v. Harris,* 172 So. 2d 820 (Fla. 1965); *City of Richmond v. Randall,* 211 S.E.2d 56 (Va. 1975); Note, Beyond Validation: The Judicial Power to Zone, 9 Urb. L. Ann. 159 (1975). The question of judicial competence to award site-specific relief has also become important in exclusionary zoning cases. See *infra* p. 445.

6. It is clear that a municipality which already has a substantial amount of apartment development may justifiably decide to prohibit further apartment construction. *Fanale v. Hasbrouck Heights,* 139 A.2d 749 (N.J. 1958). But the efforts of suburban communities like Nether Providence Township with substantial undeveloped land areas to exclude or severely restrict the construction of apartments presents a much more difficult issue. Perhaps the best discussion of the entire problem is to be found in Babcock & Bosselman, Suburban Zoning and the Apartment Boom, 111 U. Pa. L. Rev. 1040 (1963).

Why do you think Nether Providence Township sought to exclude apartments? Was it primarily because of the fear that apartments would not "pay their way" and that apartment construction would therefore result in property tax increases? Would such a fear be rational with respect to the proposed "luxury apartments"? Or was the exclusion of apartments an attempt to maintain the existing "character" of the township as a semi-rural suburban area? Would high-rise "luxury apartments" be inconsistent with maintaining the "character" of the community?

For a different slant on the problem of apartment construction in suburban communities, see Neutze, The Suburban Apartment Boom 45 (1968):

> In Montgomery County, Maryland, in the 1963-66 period it seems to have been relatively easy to have land rezoned for apartments. In fact, it appeared that the legal costs of a good zoning lawyer could possibly be regarded as the cost of getting rezoning. Land already zoned for apartments was relatively unattractive because its owners had already put a premium on their selling price, but land zoned for single-family housing or even for agricultural purposes could be bought much more cheaply, even if the purchase was, as quite commonly, conditional upon rezoning being granted. As long as the area could be construed as in some sense suitable for apartments, there would be a good chance of rezoning being granted, at least in the 1963-66 period. It almost appeared that the best way to keep apartments out of an area was for the Planning Commission to take the initiative in rezoning it for apartments — the current owner would then reap the capital gain and the area would be made less attractive to apartment builder-speculators. Of course, this was an unstable situation and resulted from the expectation that the liberality of the rezoning policy would not continue. The political opposition to it was ample justification for this belief.
>
> Despite the arguments about overcrowded schools and roads, there is a good deal of evidence that apartments, compared to single-family houses, do in fact contribute more to revenue than to public expenditure. Certainly zoning lawyers have frequently claimed this in applying for rezoning. They may well have convinced the government bodies who made the decisions that rezoning will reduce the level of taxation on the rest of the community.

Recent, in-depth studies do indicate that many types of apartment development are more beneficial to communities fiscally than single-family development, especially if the local zoning process can be manipulated to restrict substantially the number of apartment units with more than one bedroom. *See* New Jersey County & Municipal Gov't Study Comm'n, Housing and Suburbs: Fiscal and Social Impact of Multifamily Development, ch. 1 (9th Rep. 1974). Nevertheless, other nonfiscal and overwhelmingly negative objections to apartment development lead to restrictive suburban apartment zoning policies, as the following table from the New Jersey report indicates:

SUBURBAN ATTITUDES TOWARD APARTMENTS AND THEIR OCCUPANTS

1. Apartments are undesirable housing types (look bad; don't fit into community; too urban; density too high)	23.3%
2. Apartments are fiscally damaging to the community (don't pay fair share of taxes; don't pay their way)	20.8%
3. Residents of apartments are transients, and don't care about community (don't care about local issues; outsiders; don't get involved)	20.0%
4. Residents of apartments have too many schoolchildren; place too much burden on local schools	12.5%
5. Residents of apartments are socially undesirable (on welfare; criminals; wild parties)	9.2%
6. Apartments place particular burdens on municipal services (traffic problems; fire problems)	5.0%
Other negative comments	6.7%
Positive comments	2.5%

Id. at xi.

When negative attitudes toward apartment development lead to a wholesale zoning out of multifamily development the entire local zoning ordinance becomes subject to attack as exclusionary. For a discussion of these issues see Section D of this chapter, *infra* p. 445. For more on the development of multifamily housing in the suburbs see R. Schafer, The Suburbanization of Multifamily Housing (1974).

VICKERS v. TOWNSHIP COMMITTEE OF GLOUCESTER TOWNSHIP

Supreme Court of New Jersey
37 N.J. 232, 181 A.2d 129 (1962), *cert. denied,* 371 U.S. 233 (1963)

[Plaintiff bought ten acres in an industrial district. "Trailer camps" (mobile home parks) were permitted in that district. Plaintiff applied for a permit to establish a trailer camp, but he failed to meet health department standards. He then submitted an amended plan. Four days later, without acting on his application, the township amended its zoning ordinance to bar trailer camps from industrial districts, having previously barred them from all other districts. The township, a largely rural community of about 23 square miles, wished to improve the appearance of potential industrial sites and to attract industry. The area around plaintiff's tract was relatively undeveloped and several of the existing buildings in the area were rather dilapidated. The township's population was beginning to grow, but not in the area where plaintiff's tract was located. Plaintiff's challenge to the validity of the amendment excluding trailer camps from industrial districts was rejected by the trial court, but the intermediate appellate court reversed, saying: "Surely in this vast rural area, there must be some portion in which the operation of a trailer park would be compatible with the scheme of zoning the township has seen fit to erect." — Eds.]

PROCTOR, J. . . .

. . . The role of the judiciary in reviewing zoning ordinances adopted pursuant to the statutory grant of power is narrow. The court cannot pass upon the wisdom or unwisdom of an ordinance, but may act only if the presumption in favor of the validity of the ordinance is overcome by an affirmative showing that it is unreasonable or arbitrary. *Kozesnik v. Township of Montgomery,* 24 N.J. 154, 167, 134 A.2d 1 (1957); see Cunningham, "Control of Land Use in New Jersey," 14 Rutgers L.Rev. 37, 48 (1959). By these standards which control judicial review, the plaintiff to prevail must show beyond debate that the township in adopting the challenged amendment transgressed the standards of R.S. 40:55-32. In other words, if the amendment presented a debatable issue we cannot nullify the township's decision that its welfare would be advanced by the action it took.

"It cannot be said that every municipality must provide for every use somewhere within its borders." *Fanale v. Borough of Hasbrouck Heights,* 26 N.J. 320, 325, 139 A.2d 749, 752 (1958). The fact that a municipality is largely undeveloped does not impose a contrary obligation. Sound planning and zoning look beyond the present into what lies ahead in the hopes of the planners. "It requires as much official watchfulness to anticipate and prevent suburban blight as it does to eradicate city slums." *Lionshead Lake, Inc. v. Township of Wayne,* 10 N.J. 165, 173, 89 A.2d 693, 697 (1952), appeal dismissed 344 U.S. 919, 73 S.Ct. 386, 97 L.Ed. 708 (1953).

This court has considered several cases in which a municipality's zoning ordinance was attacked as unreasonable because it prohibited certain structures or uses.

. . . .

In *Lionshead Lake, Inc. v. Township of Wayne,* supra, this court sustained a zoning ordinance provision barring the construction anywhere in the township (which included residential, business and industrial districts) of dwellings containing less than 768 square feet of living area. After alluding to health factors, the court said, at p. 174 of 10 N.J., at p. 697 of 89 A.2d:

"But quite apart from these considerations of public health which cannot be overlooked, minimum floor-area standards are justified on the ground that they promote the general welfare of the community and . . . the courts in conformance with the constitutional provisions and the statutes hereinbefore cited take a broad view of what constitutes general welfare. The size of the dwellings in any community inevitably affects the character of the community and does much to determine whether or not it is a desirable place in which to live."

In *Fischer v. Township of Bedminster,* 11 N.J. 194, 93 A.2d 378 (1952), this court upheld a zoning ordinance which placed most of the township in a residence zone with a minimum lot size of five acres for each residence. The court said, at p. 204: "As much foresight is now required to preserve the countryside for its best use as has been needed to save what could be salvaged of our cities."

. . . .

In *Fanale v. Borough of Hasbrouck Heights, supra,* the validity of the zoning ordinance prohibiting the construction of apartment houses anywhere in the borough was under attack. The borough was zoned for residence, business and industry. The plaintiff sought to construct an apartment house in the business district on a lot which contained a dilapidated residence. The plaintiff contended *inter alia* the ordinance was invalid because one- and two-family houses were permitted in the industrial zone, while apartment houses were excluded. In sustaining the ordinance, we said, at p. 328 of 26 N.J., at p. 753 of 139 A.2d:

"True, as the ordinance now stands, one- and two-family homes may be erected in those districts. Nonetheless, and apart from the unlikelihood of that development, a multi-family structure in an industrial setting would grossly accentuate the resulting problems. The matter is one of classification, and we cannot say a distinction between one- and two-family houses as against multi-family ones even in industrial districts is devoid of reasonable factual support."

In *Napierkowski v. Township of Gloucester* [29 N.J. 481, 150 A. 2d 481 (1959)], the provisions of this township's zoning ordinance which prohibited trailers and trailer parks from the residential, business and agricultural districts were under attack. The plaintiff wanted to place a trailer on her four-acre tract for use as her permanent residence. Although the land was situated in a residential zone, the area about her plot was mainly rural and was likely to remain so for the reasonably foreseeable future. After noting that: (1) some states have upheld regulations limiting the time during which a trailer could remain in a municipality to short intervals thus making them strictly temporary abodes and effectively eliminating trailer parks which cater to trailers used as permanent residences; (2) other states have permitted municipalities to apply their house building codes to trailers, thus effectively barring all trailers since none could possibly comply; and (3) some states have permitted the unequivocal prohibition of trailers throughout the municipality, we said, at p. 493 of 29 N.J., at p. 487 of 150 A.2d:

"The decisions elsewhere highlight the fact that the use of trailers as permanent residences present [sic] problems which are ofttimes inimical to the general welfare. . . . And from the point of view of aesthetic considerations (which are inextricably intertwined with conservation of the value of property) trailers may mar the local landscape."

We concluded that the Township of Gloucester had the power to prohibit trailers from all residential districts, even though those districts include rural areas which will remain undeveloped for the reasonably foreseeable future. We said, at p. 494 of 29 N.J., at p. 488 of 150 A. 2d: "Zoning must subserve the long-range needs of the future as well as the immediate needs of the present and the reasonably foreseeable future. It is, in short, an implementing tool of sound planning."

. . . .

[The court then noted that the township had been growing and that accelerated growth was likely to continue. No significant industry had located in the township but it was likely to do so and the township's planning should accommodate this possibility. If industry was to move into the township it was also important to provide exclusively zoned areas in which it might locate because industries might shun areas in which discordant uses existed side by side. Trailer camps bring a host of problems, including congestion, and the township could properly conclude that for this reason they should be excluded from industrial areas. This exclusion could be sustained even though single family houses are not excluded from industrial districts, the township governing body having determined that single family homes would be compatible with industrial uses. — Eds.]

Since, as this court has held, municipalities can properly determine that the construction of small houses, *Lionshead Lake,* apartment houses, *Fanale,* and motels, *Pierro,* may have an adverse effect upon other properties throughout those municipalities (including industrial districts), and that living units which produce congestion can be excluded, we would be flying in the face of the broad powers granted to municipalities by the Constitution and zoning statutes as interpreted by our decisions if we held that the township in the present case must, against the will of its governing body, allow the construction and operation of trailer camps in its industrial district. Accordingly, we hold the plaintiff has failed to show the township acted unreasonably in amending its zoning ordinance to exclude trailer camps from its industrial district.

Since trailer camps are not permitted in the other districts, the effect of the amending ordinance prohibiting them in the industrial district is to bar them from the entire municipality. There are no trailer camps in the township at present. Plaintiff contends that total prohibition is illegal. However, we have held that a municipality need not provide a place for every use. *Fanale v. Borough of Hasbrouck Heights, supra.* We do not think that a municipality must open its borders to a use which it reasonably believes should be excluded as repugnant to its planning scheme. It must be remembered that once a use is legally established, even though conditions impel a revision of the zoning ordinance and the use strikes a jarring note, it cannot be eliminated by such a revision under existing law. See R.S. 40:55-48. If through foresight a municipality is able to anticipate the adverse effects of particular uses and its resulting actions are reasonable, it should be permitted to develop without the burdens of such uses.

. . . .

It is of no significance that plaintiff's proposed trailer camp would not be detrimental to his immediate neighborhood as it now exists. The validity of a zoning ordinance is not to be determined by reference to an individual parcel of land. . . . Moreover, the township has embarked upon an active program designed to eliminate the blighted structures which are near plaintiff's property. We repeat what we said in *Napierkowski v. Township of Gloucester, supra,* 29 N.J. at p. 494, 150 A.2d at p. 488: "Zoning must subserve the long-range needs of the future as well as the immediate needs of the present and the reasonably foreseeable future." The township officials have a basis to expect plaintiff's neighborhood will not remain in its present run-down condition and they are justified in considering the envisioned betterment.

The only decision of an appellate court cited by the plaintiff to sustain his contention that total prohibition of trailer camps in a municipality is beyond the zoning power is *Gust v. Township of Canton,* 342 Mich. 436, 70 N.W.2d 772 (Sup.Ct.1955). There the court said, "The test of validity is not whether the prohibition may *at some time in the future* bear a real and substantial relationship to the public health, safety, morals or general welfare, but whether it does so *now.* (Italics supplied.) 70 N.W.2d 774, 775. This view is contrary to our concept of zoning which requires a looking beyond an immediate "now." *Napierkowski v. Township of Gloucester, supra,* at p. 494. Therefore, we are not persuaded by a result based on the philosophy of the court in *Gust.*

. . . .

In light of the above, we hold that the township zoning ordinance amendment barring trailer camps from its industrial district was a valid exercise of its zoning power and was adopted in conformity with the statutory requirements.

The judgment of the Appellate Division is reversed and the judgment of the Law Division is reinstated.

HALL, J. (dissenting). The majority decides that this particular municipality may constitutionally say, through exercise of the zoning power, that its residents may not live in trailers — or in mobile homes, to use a more descriptive term. I am convinced such a conclusion in this case is manifestly wrong. Of even greater concern is the judicial process by which it is reached and the breadth of the rationale. The import of the holding gives almost boundless freedom to developing municipalities to erect exclusionary walls on their boundaries, according to local whim or selfish desire, and to use the zoning power for aims beyond its legitimate purposes. Prohibition of mobile home parks, although an important issue in itself, becomes, in this larger aspect, somewhat a symbol.[34]

. . . .

We should not forget some fundamentals. Zoning is land use control by *physical* planning to bring about physical results for public, not private, welfare. It is not a device to be used to accomplish any and all purportedly desirable *social* results unrelated to the statutorily stated purposes. The basic definition by the first authority in the field still holds good: "Zoning is the regulation by districts under the police power of the height, bulk and use of buildings, the use of land and the density of population." Bassett, Zoning 45 (1940). The purpose "to promote . . . the general welfare" does not stand alone in the statute. Its meaning and scope must have some relation to the other specified standards and the whole authorized scheme. Certainly "general welfare" does not automatically mean whatever the municipality says it does, regardless of who is hurt and how much.

. . . .

Trailer living is a perfectly respectable, healthy and useful kind of housing, adopted by choice of several million people in this country today. Municipalities and courts can no longer refuse to recognize its proper and significant place in today's society and should stop acting on the basis of old wives' tales.

In the face of these facts, it is arbitrary to permit the prohibition of mobile home parks completely in a municipality where they can be placed in appropriate districts and in which there is a need or demand for them. To hold otherwise would be to allow any method of housing to be outlawed by local whim. I cannot understand how, in a large and roomy township, a properly situated and regulated mobile home park can have a detrimental effect on the value of all the property in the township or on its overall attractiveness any more than industrial and commercial districts or even small lot housing developments.

. . . .

---

[34] Justice Hall's well-known dissent in the *Vickers* decision is best known for its indictment of exclusionary suburban zoning, a subject which Justice Hall addresses with even greater force in the *Mount Laurel* decision, reproduced *infra* p. 454. —Eds.

I would affirm the judgment of the Appellate Division. Justice SCHETTINO joins in this opinion.

For reversal — Chief Justice WEINTRAUB, and Justices JACOBS, FRANCIS, PROCTOR and HANEMAN — 5.

For affirmance — Justices HALL and SCHETTINO — 2.

Comments: 1. For critical comment on the principal case, see 61 Mich. L. Rev. 1010 (1963). Commentators have almost unanimously praised the dissenting opinion of Justice Hall for its clear recognition of the problems generated by population growth and land development trends in suburban areas and for its ringing declaration that " 'general welfare' transcends the artificial limits of political subdivisions and cannot embrace merely narrow local desires." Justice Hall's opinion is also notable for its assertion that, since the presumption that a zoning ordinance is valid "may be overcome or rebutted not only by clear evidence *aliunde,* but also by a showing on its face or in the light of facts of which judicial notice may be taken," it is appropriate in cases where private citizens seek judicial determination of their rights, "to require the municipality, with all its resources, to assume the burden of going forward when the challenged measure gives good possibility on the surface of going to a doubtful extreme." Justice Hall's views, as expressed in the *Vickers* dissent, finally gained the support of a majority of the New Jersey Supreme Court in *Southern Burlington County NAACP v. Township of Mount Laurel,* 336 A.2d 713 (N.J.), *cert. denied,* 423 U.S. 808 (1975). The *Mount Laurel* case is reprinted *infra* in the section on "Exclusionary Zoning."

2. The majority opinion in the principal case consistently refers to the excluded dwelling units as "trailers." A more accurate description would be "mobile homes." As the President's Committee on Urban Housing pointed out in 1968:

> Mobile homes are built more like houses than like automobiles. Although the base is a steel undercarriage vital for safe transportation, framing members are typically of wood .... Aluminum sheeting is the normal exterior covering material. Efficiencies achieved through assembly line production usually cut direct labor costs of the finished unit to less than 10 percent of the retail price.
>
> To qualify as a mobile home (as opposed to a "travel trailer") for statistical purposes, the structure must be over 8 feet in width, 30 feet in length, and 4,500 pounds in weight. The largest mobile homes (12 x 75 feet) are roughly the same size (900 square feet) as the average new single-family home insured by FHA in 1950. The effective size of the mobile homes may be further increased through use of expandable sections pulled out from the main units, or, as with a sectionalized home, through on-site connection of two or more main units. The key determinants of unit widths are transportation restrictions on highway use....
>
> Although designed for mobility, mobile homes once positioned are rarely moved....

Report of the President's Comm. on Urban Housing, A Decent Home 156-57 (1968).

3. The number of cases involving regulation of mobile homes is quite large. In the early cases, courts often used a "nuisance" rationale to uphold severe restrictions on mobile homes and mobile home parks. *See* 2 R. Anderson, American Law of Zoning § 11.49 (2d ed. 1976); 2 N. Williams, American Land Planning Law § 57.08 (1974). Williams summarizes the objections to mobile homes as follows: (1) special health and sanitary problems; (2) problems of high-density development generally; (3) aesthetic shortcomings; (4) less stable occupancy; (5) the unfavorable effect of mobile homes on "residential" (*i.e.,* conventional residential) and other developments; (6) effect on property values; (7) need for expensive municipal services; and (8) inadequate tax revenues from such homes. More recently, some courts have expressed much more sympathetic attitudes toward mobile homes as a result of an increasing recognition that mobile homes are really the only form of low-cost housing now available in the United States. See Housing in the Seventies 223-26 (U.S. Dept. Housing & Urban Dev. 1975) for an analysis of housing costs and mobile homes.

In Michigan the courts have consistently struck down attempts by local governments to exclude mobile home parks. *See, e.g., Gust v. Township of Canton,* 70 N.W.2d 772 (Mich. 1955); *Knibbe v. City of Warren,* 109 N.W.2d 766 (Mich. 1961); *Dequindre Dev. Co. v. Charter Township of Warren,* 103 N.W.2d 600 (Mich. 1960); *Green v. Lima Township,* 199 N.W.2d 243 (Mich. App. 1972); *Bristow v. City of Woodhaven,* 192 N.W.2d 322 (Mich. App. 1971). In the *Bristow* and *Green* cases, the court held that mobile homes are a "preferred use" because they meet the need for low-cost housing. The "preferred use" concept was rejected by the Michigan Supreme Court in *Kropf v. City of Sterling Heights,* 215 N.W.2d 179 (Mich. 1974), although the court said that, "[o]n its face, an ordinance which *totally* excludes from a municipality a use recognized by the constitution or other laws of this state as legitimate also carries with it a strong taint of unlawful discrimination and a denial of equal protection of the law as to the excluded use." *Id.* at 185.

The Illinois appellate court has also recognized that where certain land uses are concerned the term "general welfare" must be defined to meet the exigencies of an urban society and that the need for low-cost housing is a factor that must be considered in determining the reasonableness of excluding "trailer camps" from all or major portions of a community. *Lakeland Bluffs, Inc. v. County of Will,* 252 N.E.2d 765 (Ill. App. 1969). *See also High Meadows Park, Inc. v. City of Aurora,* 250 N.E.2d 517 (Ill. App. 1969). But it is generally held that a zoning ordinance is a valid exercise of the police power when it limits mobile homes to designated mobile home parks so as to facilitate police and fire protection and to regulate health conditions, as well as to facilitate provision of water, sewage, and lighting services. *See, e.g., State v. Larson,* 195 N.W.2d 180 (Minn. 1972).

In *Town of Glocester v. Olivo's Mobile Home Court, Inc.,* 300 A.2d 465 (R.I. 1973), the court invalidated a zoning ordinance that prohibited the use of land for a mobile home park except that any mobile home park already in existence could continue and expand, provided that its expansion should be subject to the 30-unit maximum for each mobile home park imposed by the town's licensing ordinance. When the zoning ordinance was enacted, there were only three mobile home parks in the town, one of which was owned and operated by the defendant on a site containing about 38 acres. The town sought to enjoin the defendant from violating the 30-unit limitation and the defendant filed an answer challenging the constitutionality of the 30-unit limitation and asking that the town be enjoined from interfering with "its right" to operate a mobile home park containing more than 30 units. The court said:

> We cannot assume that an occupant of a mobile home poses any greater threat to the public safety than the other inhabitants of a municipality who might live in a more conventional type of residence. . . . The municipality's contention, that its limitation of 30 units constitutes an effort to lessen congestion, seem to be a diplomatic way of expressing its real concern, that of finding some way to maintain the population of its schools at a point where a stable tax rate can be preserved. We do not believe that a zoning restriction was ever intended to fulfill such a function. . . . Even though we have stated that the location and use of a mobile home is subject to a valid exercise of the police power, the limitation of 30 mobile homes found in the Glocester zoning ordinance and its licensing counterpart, at least as it applies to Olivo's property, fails to satisfy the requisite constitutional standards.

Id. at 468-69, 470.

It can be inferred that the court believed that only health and safety considerations would justify limitations on the number of units permitted in a mobile home park in a rural municipality like Glocester. The court pointed out that the bulk of the town was zoned for agriculture and that, although the zoning ordinance provided an industrial use classification, no part of the town was actually zoned industrial.

Relatively undeveloped rural-residential communities seem to present the most difficult cases when exclusion or severe restriction of mobile home parks is challenged in the courts. Exclusion in established residential areas and in commercial and industrial areas has generally been sustained. On the other hand, many zoning ordinances relegate mobile homes and mobile home parks to commercial or industrial districts, especially commercial districts located along major highways. The problem of locating mobile homes and mobile home parks is often handled by listing such land uses as "special exceptions" and requiring approval by the zoning board of adjustment (or appeals). *See, e.g., Keiger v. Winston-Salem Bd. of Adjustment,* 174 S.E.2d 852 (N.C. App.), *rev'd,* 178 S.E.2d 616 (N.C. 1970); *Jackson v. Guilford County Bd. of Adjustment,* 163 S.E.2d 265 (N.C. App. 1968); *Hester v. Timothy,* 275 A.2d 637 (R.I. 1971).

See J. Carter, Problems in the Regulation and Taxation of Mobile Homes, 48 Iowa L. Rev. 16 (1962); Hodes & Roberson, The Law of Mobile Homes (1964); Modular Housing, Including Mobile Homes: A Survey of Regulatory Practices and Planners' Opinions (American Soc'y of Planning Officials, Planning Advisory Service Rep. No. 265, 1971); 2 Anderson, American Law of Zoning §§ 11.49 — 11.58 (2d ed. 1976); 2 N. Williams, American Land Planning Law, ch. 56 (1974).

4. In the principal case, the majority opinion cited and relied on the *Lionshead Lake* case, where minimum house-size requirements were upheld, while Justice Hall's dissenting opinion is extremely critical of *Lionshead Lake*. The Wayne Township zoning ordinance sustained in *Lionshead Lake* required "living-floor space . . . of not less than 768 square feet for a one story dwelling; of not less than 1000 square feet for a two story dwelling having an attached garage; [and] of not less than 1200 square feet for a two story dwelling not having an attached garage."

In a concurring opinion, Justice Jacobs placed emphasis on evidence in the record supporting the view that "adequate living space must be considered as having reasonable relation to health, particularly mental and emotional health." He also observed that "[t]he provisions with respect to two-story dwellings were influenced in considerable part by aesthetic considerations" which he believed "to be entirely proper," and he quoted from an earlier opinion in which he expressed the view that "it is in the public interest that our communities, so far as feasible, should be made pleasant and inviting and that primary considerations of attractiveness and beauty might well be frankly acknowledged as appropriate, under certain circumstances, in the promotion of the general welfare of our people." Plaintiff's appeal to the United States Supreme Court was dismissed for want of a substantial federal question, 344 U.S. 919 (1953).

For vigorous comment pro and con on the *Lionshead Lake* case, see Haar, Zoning for Minimum Standards: The Wayne Township Case, 66 Harv. L. Rev. 1051 (1953) (very critical); Nolan & Horack, How Small a House? — Zoning for Minimum Space Requirements, 67 Harv. L. Rev. 967 (1954) (approving); Haar, Wayne Township: Zoning for Whom? — In Brief Reply, 67 Harv. L. Rev. 986 (1954). A subsequent survey of local zoning practices in Wayne Township indicates that the decision did not have a notable effect on local practice. Williams & Wacks, Segregation in Residential Areas Along Economic Lines: Lionshead Lake Revisited, 1969 Wis. L. Rev. 827.

In other states minimum building size requirements have had a mixed reception. They were sustained in *De Mars v. Zoning Comm'n,* 115 A.2d 653 (Conn. 1955); *Flower Hill Bldg. Corp. v. Village of Flower Hill,* 100 N.Y.S.2d 903 (N.Y. Sup. Ct. 1950) (trial court); *Dundee Realty Co. v. Omaha,* 13 N.W.2d 634 (Neb. 1944); and *Thompson v. Carrollton,* 211 S.W.2d 970 (Tex. Civ. App. 1948). But such requirements were held invalid in *Elizabeth Lakes Estates v. Waterford Township,* 26 N.W.2d 788 (Mich. 1947), and *Medinger Appeal,* 104 A.2d 118 (Pa. 1954). A survey of the decisions yields the pragmatic rule that the success of house-size restrictions appears to be related to the average size of single-family dwellings insured under federally assisted mortgage programs. Ordinances that have been sustained have generally required a house size less than the average required for federal mortgage insurance.

According to the majority opinion in *Lionshead Lake,* "[a] survey made by the [New Jersey] Department of Conservation and Economic Development in 1951 disclosed that 64 municipalities out of the 138 reporting had minimum dwelling requirements." In 1970, Norman Williams, Jr., reported that

> In some counties in northern New Jersey, of the vacant land which
> is zoned for residence and readily developable for that purpose,

about 75 percent is zoned to require houses of not less than 1,200 square feet, and substantial areas are zoned for houses of at least 1,600 square feet.

N. Williams, The Three Systems of Land Use Control, 25 Rutgers L. Rev. 80, 92 (1970). Elsewhere, Williams notes that minimum house size restrictions — which he castigates as designed simply to force up the cost of housing — are apparently less common in the rest of the country than in the Northeast corridor, and especially in New Jersey. 2 N. Williams, American Land Planning Law § 63.12 (1974). A nation-wide study published in 1968 revealed that only 11.4 percent of even the smaller sized municipalities within metropolitan areas required minimum house sizes of 1,000 square feet or more. National Comm'n on Urban Problems, Building the American City 216 (1968). The best discussion of minimum house size regulations is to be found in 2 N. Williams, American Land Planning Law, ch. 63 (1974).

What justification is there for including a regulation on minimum house size in a zoning ordinance? Note also that the size of a house is somewhat proportionately related to cost, so that a minimum house size requirement is in reality a disguised cost control. Do Justice Jacobs' reasons for advocating minimum house size controls completely overcome objections to these controls that they may have an exclusionary effect?

5. Commercial and Industrial "Use" Classifications

KOZESNIK v. TOWNSHIP OF MONTGOMERY

Supreme Court of New Jersey
24 N.J. 154, 131 A.2d 1 (1957)

WEINTRAUB, J. Plaintiffs challenge the validity of amendments to the zoning ordinances of the Township of Hillsborough and the Township of Montgomery. The trial court upheld the measures. On our own motion we certified appeals prosecuted to the Appellate Division. . . .

[The challenged amendments were adopted by Hillsborough and Montgomery townships in order to facilitate an integrated, across-the-municipal boundary, quarrying and rock-processing operation by Minnesota Mining and Manufacturing Company. The amendments created limited industrial districts in both townships, the Hillsborough district being restricted to residential and agricultural uses (previously permitted) and the quarrying and crushing of rock, and the Montgomery district being restricted to "processing of the products of a stone or rock excavating operation when such processing is physically and operationally integrated with the extracting or quarrying use." 3M proposed to quarry diabase rock on land it owned in the Hillsborough limited industrial district and to process it at a nearby site in the Montgomery limited industrial district. The Hillsborough ordinance conditioned the right to quarry upon the issuance of a permit by the township committee, in accordance with standards which included the following:

(1) No quarry shall be conducted on less than 200 contiguous acres within the zone.

(2) Both a quarry and a processing plant shall not be conducted on less than 400 contiguous acres within the zone.

(3) No part of any of the use, except a railroad spur and approved access roads, shall be (a) within 100 feet from a boundary of the zone, or (b) within 400 feet from the nearest right-of-way "of any public road or highway now maintained by public authority," or within 400 feet "from any dwelling existing at the introduction of this Ordinance."

(4) No quarry excavating shall be done within 500 feet "from any such zone boundary or right-of-way line," nor within 1,000 feet "from any such dwelling," provided that the distance limitation with respect to any such zone boundary shall not apply if the boundary is contiguous to a boundary of a zone in which quarrying or processing of quarry products or both is permitted in an adjoining municipality.

[The Hillsborough ordinance further provided that "No quarry shall be permitted whose primary use of the product extracted shall be the sale of the extracted product in an unprocessed state for road building or the manufacture of concrete." This restriction was intended to confine quarrying to rock having sufficient value to bear the cost of the protective measures required under the ordinance to safeguard the public interest, and apparently also to preclude general quarrying which would lead to substantial trucking operations through the community to meet relatively local demands. — Eds.]

The Hillsborough Ordinance

. . . .

Various challenges are bottomed upon R.S. 40:55-32 which reads:

"Such regulations shall be in accordance with a comprehensive plan and designed for one or more of the following purposes: to lessen congestion in the streets; secure safety from fire, panic and other dangers; promote health, morals or the general welfare; provide adequate light and air; prevent the overcrowding of land or buildings; avoid undue concentration of population. Such regulations shall be made with reasonable consideration, among other things, to the character of the district and its peculiar suitability for particular uses, and with a view of conserving the value of property and encouraging the most appropriate use of land throughout such municipality."

I.

[The court here considered the plaintiff's argument that the zoning amendment was not "in accordance with a comprehensive plan" because "there can be no comprehensive plan unless it is evidenced in writing *dehors* the zoning ordinance itself," which was not the case here. For discussion of this problem see *infra* p. —. — Eds.]

II.

It is asserted that the authorization to quarry and process rock is incompatible with the purposes set forth in R.S. 40:55-32, and hence not part of a "comprehensive plan."

. . . .

Nothing in the zoning statute intimates that natural resources may not be tapped. The power to authorize quarrying and processing of rock must surely exist, and the Planning Act of 1953 lists "mining" and "other like matters" within the scope of proposals for a master plan. N.J.S.A. 40:55-1.11. Hence the issue is whether Hillsborough's determination that its welfare would be advanced by the action it took must be condemned on the standard which controls judicial review.

There assuredly are considerations *pro* and *con.* On the plus side are the economic gains to the municipality consequent upon the industrial activity, including substantial tax revenues in an area which has had a fairly high incidence of tax delinquency; the benefit to the vicinity, State and eastern part of our Nation from access to the natural resource; the circumstance that the property is peculiarly suitable for the particular use and that the amendment authorizes the most appropriate use of the lands involved, a purpose which the statute encourages so long as it is not incompatible with total local welfare.

On the minus side appear a number of considerations, the evaluation of which is sharply disputed. The statute commands that the regulations be made "with a view of conserving the value of property and encouraging the most appropriate use of land throughout" the municipality. The record well supports a finding that by reason of the rural nature of the community and the remoteness of the site, the impact upon property values in other districts will be slight. There will be some increase in traffic, as of course inevitably follows any utilization of land, but the increase will be moderate. There will be no appreciable hazard from fire or panic, or overcrowding of land or buildings, or undue concentration of population. There inheres in quarrying an element of annoyance from sound and concussion, but state legislation and provisions of the ordinance itself serve to confine it. Dust will be emitted but again the testimony justifies a finding that the pollution will not be significant in the light of available techniques. There will be some esthetic impairment of a mountain of unquestioned beauty.

We are not confronted with the question whether any or all of the foregoing would justify a refusal to permit the quarrying operation. Rather, the question is whether we can say that Hillsborough's decision to permit it has been shown to be arbitrary or unreasonable. It seems to us that the amendment presented a fairly debatable issue, and hence we cannot interfere with the legislative judgment that the purposes of R.S. 40:55-32 will be served and that the authorization of the industrial use is appropriately a part of the comprehensive plan.

III.

It is urged that if quarrying is permitted, it is arbitrary to exclude other industrial uses and so-called "higher" uses, such as commercial ones.

We are not unmindful that in the infancy of zoning it was the general practice to permit higher uses in the less restricted district. The statute, however, does not so command. Rather, it broadly permits any reasonable scheme which comports with the legislative standards and thus leaves ample room for new ideas. Experience has satisfied many that, for example, homes are no more appropriate in an industrial district than industry in a residential one. In both situations the baleful influences upon residences are the same. Moreover, industry may prefer to avoid the frictions which ensue when discordant uses are side by side. Hence, in seeking a well-balanced community, . . . a municipality may conclude its welfare is better served by avoiding motley activities within districts. See *Roney v. Board of Supervisors of Contra Costa County,* 138 Cal.App.2d 740, 292 P.2d 529 (Ct.App. 1956). In every case the question is one of reasonableness under the circumstances. The point sufficient for the present is that there is no rule of law, statutory or constitutional, which ordains that any use has an exalted position in a zoning scheme entitling it to move everywhere as of right.

The problem is the familiar one of classification. Thus where the facts were found to demonstrate that it was unreasonable to exclude commercial activity from a light industrial district, the restriction was held invalid, *Katobimar Realty Co. v. Webster,* 20 N.J. 114, 118 A.2d 824 (1955), whereas when a reasonable basis existed for differentiating between motels and boarding or rooming houses, the exclusion of the former was upheld. *Pierro v. Baxendale,* supra (20 N.J. 17, 118 A.2d 401). In both cases this court divided 4 to 3, but the division did not reflect disagreement as to basic principle but rather as to the application of the principle to the facts of the case.

It should be noted that we do not have before us the question whether over objection of an owner his property may be zoned solely for one specific use. See for example *Vernon Park Realty Inc. v. City of Mt. Vernon,* 307 N.Y. 493, 121 N.E.2d 517 (Ct.App.1954), where a parcel was zoned solely for automobile parking and a service station, and *McCarthy v. City of Manhattan Beach,* 41 Cal.2d 879, 264 P.2d 932 (Sup.Ct.1953), certiorari denied 348 U.S. 817, 75 S.Ct. 29, 99 L.Ed. 644 (1954), where property was zoned solely for beach recreational purposes. Here the property in the limited industrial district may continue to be used for residential and agricultural purposes, the ordinance merely authorizing the additional activity here challenged. Hence, the question is whether the quarrying operation may constitute a class apart from other industrial activities and be the sole such activity permitted in addition to agricultural and residential uses.

Ordinarily a single industrial activity would not constitute a defensible class, but the proposition is general and not universal. It is true that where a municipality determines a district is suitable for general industrial uses, it may not reserve the power to decide upon individual applications which industrial uses will be admitted. *Rockhill v. Township of Chesterfield,* 23 N.J. 117, 128 A.2d 473 (1957). Such, however, is not the situation before us. Hillsborough did not conclude that the area in question could advantageously be devoted to general industrial development. It found to the contrary and authorized quarrying operations solely because the natural resource was there.

There are a number of considerations which justify a decision to admit this industrial activity and no other. The determination to authorize quarrying operations in itself involved a nice balancing of advantages against detriments. If, however, all industrial uses were permitted, the total impact upon the abutting areas might be such that the point of diminishing returns would quickly be reached and passed. For one thing, the rock area does not now have local services such as water, sewage disposal, fire or police protection, or improved roads. Quarrying can be conducted without expense to Hillsborough in these respects, whereas other industrial activities might well need these local services at a forbidding cost. It is difficult to conceive of other industry being attracted to that terrain, but if it would, yet other areas are better suited for it and are so zoned. Hillsborough is entitled to encourage industry where it will best advance the community's interest. It would be unreasonable to say it may exploit natural resources only if it was willing to accept the burden of all industrial activity in a place where general industry does not belong. We see no reason for an all-or-nothing proposition.

It may be that there is some other specific industry which could co-exist harmoniously with quarrying and without generating appreciable problems. But the validity of a legislative classification may not be impugned on the basis of attenuated possibilities; otherwise the power to classify would be hampered beyond usefulness. If it should ever appear that another specific use is compatible and desirous of moving into the district, it will then be time enough to consider whether it is arbitrary to exclude it.

. . . .

Hillsborough manifestly found that quarry operations hold a significant potential for deleterious influence upon the enjoyment of neighboring property. This is at least one basis of the acreage requirement and is the basis of the restrictions recited at the outset of this opinion fixing certain distances between phases of the operations and homes. The difficulty is that protection is afforded only for "any dwelling *existing at the introduction of this ordinance.*" The owners of the remaining acreage are entitled to like protection to the end that the authorized uses may reasonably be pursued. The record does not clearly reveal the precise location of the parcels not controlled by 3M. We gather there are five such parcels, of which four are unimproved (the fifth, owned by plaintiffs, Slover, is largely in another zone with a small triangular rear portion jutting into the limited industrial zone). The exact location of 3M's holdings was frankly obscured for private reasons not here pertinent. But whatever the physical relation of the other parcels to 3M's, it is plain that under the ordinance 3M could carry on its activities within the very distances of those parcels which Hillsborough has found to be necessary to protect housing use.

We are not here concerned with that incidental and unremediable loss of value which is inevitably experienced by property abutting another zone in which lesser uses are authorized and which must be accepted for the common good. . . . Rather, we have a situation in which some property owners are required for the special benefit of another proprietor to absorb part of the burden of an industrial use of acknowledged capacity to harm, and this upon the irrelevant circumstance whether their properties are or are not improved at the time of the introduction of the ordinance. The imposition is unreasonable and the classification arbitrary.

It is true that where a nuisance results, it is no defense that the zoning ordinance authorized the operation and hence judicial relief may be had . . . . Nonetheless, when a zoning ordinance is being prepared, and as here the potential nuisance is recognized unless the operation be isolated, the ordinance should require the quarry operator to provide the necessary buffer and not cast the burden on the neighboring owner. If the ordinance expressly said that a property owner may not improve his land within a given distance of the quarry or processing plant, the appropriation of his property for the benefit of the quarry operator would be apparent. . . . Principle is no less offended when the ordinance purports to place the burden upon the quarry operator but as a practical matter transfers it to neighboring owners who, while ostensibly permitted to utilize their properties, must provide their own setbacks or experience an exposure capable of hindering enjoyment. Whatever the reasonable distances may be, they should be measured from adjoining property lines whether or not the parcels are now improved.

We appreciate the lands are of marginal quality. Yet we cannot assume that their owners have the single prospect of paying taxes. Perhaps their marginal character requires all the more that reasonable protection be afforded. At any rate, in sustaining the acreage requirements despite the circumstance that the other owners may not quarry, we assumed with defendants that those other properties are in fact usable for the other authorized purposes and are not legislated into idleness. We cannot discard that assumption in measuring the reasonableness of the aspect we are now considering.

Defendants question the status of plaintiffs to challenge the validity of the ordinance, urging that if the ordinance is invalid as to any parcel, it concerns only that owner and he may not attack it until he has exhausted his administrative remedy before the board of adjustment. This proposition will be discussed below in connection with the Montgomery matter. Here, however, the challenge involves the entire district because the unreasonableness lies not in the inclusion within the district of the five parcels held other than by 3M but rather in the failure so to condition quarrying activities as to afford proper protection for other properties. The administrative remedy could not overcome the infirmity. And we need not stop to consider the *quantum* of detriment to the Slovers (the only property owners within the limited industrial district who are parties plaintiffs), since we have recognized a broad right in taxpayers and citizens of a municipality to seek review of local legislative action without proof of unique financial detriment to them. . . . The community-at-large has an interest in the integrity of the zoning plan, . . . sufficient to justify an attack which goes to the validity of the entire district. . . .

The Montgomery Ordinance

Montgomery adopted its zoning ordinance on May 25, 1940, and as amended on March 4, 1941, it divided the township into residential districts and business districts. In June 1951 Montgomery retained the Institute of Local and State Government of the University of Pennsylvania to assist in the preparation of a master plan and the revision of the ordinance. There were numerous meetings of the planning board to consider recommendations but nothing had been finalized when 3M submitted its proposal in

January 1953. The Institute had prior thereto recommended that quarrying be permitted in the region here involved on the basis of special exception rather than as an authorized use, which proposal had not been accepted as of the time of the advent of 3M.

The ordinance as finally adopted and now before us substantially revised the existing ordinance and created five classes of districts: (1) agricultural, (2) rural residence, (3) commercial, (4) manufacturing, and (5) limited industrial. One limited industrial district was created embracing 450 acres. On the west it abuts the limited industrial district in Hillsborough. To the north and south of it are agricultural districts. On the east are rural residential districts, between which the limited industrial zone extends as a corridor leading to the Pennsylvania and Reading Railroad facilities. . . .

The Montgomery ordinance does not permit residential or agricultural use in the limited industrial district and hence, unlike the Hillsborough ordinance, authorizes but a single use, to wit:

"Processing of the products of a stone or rock excavating operation when such processing is *physically and operationally integrated with the extracting or quarrying use*" (Italics added)

and uses accessory thereto. Since quarrying is not permitted in Montgomery, the integration can only be with quarrying in Hillsborough. Thus the sole use permitted is conditioned upon affiliation with a quarrying operation elsewhere. 3M alone can meet the requirement.

It should be noted that we do not have before us the question whether a district may be restricted to a single specific use. There are but two owners of property within the district and neither raises the question. 3M does not complain; it in fact invited the restriction. Kozesnik presses a different attack which will be considered below. We of course recognize the community's interest in a zoning scheme, but here the suggested issue, if sought to be advanced on that basis, would be academic since there is no prospect that 3M would utilize its lands for any use other than the authorized use.

Kozesnik complains that his property cannot be put to the single authorized use since he cannot associate it with a quarrying operation in Hillsborough and hence the ordinance is invalid as to his property. It was frankly conceded before us that there is nothing he can do with his property. That a restraint against all uses is confiscatory and beyond the police power and statutory authorization is too apparent to require discussion. . . .

Ordinarily the invalidity of an ordinance as to a small parcel will not vitiate the treatment of the entire district within which it is situated. . . . This principle is applicable where it may reasonably be assumed that the local legislative body would have intended the district to remain as legislated notwithstanding such partial invalidity. Here, however, the physical circumstances are such that we cannot say with assurance that the township would have so intended. We are dealing with a fairly substantial parcel of 20 acres running for 1,250 feet along the common boundary of the limited industrial districts of both townships, with a portion of the limited industrial district lying above and below the parcel along the mentioned boundary. Moreover, the ordinance provides that no processing plant or any use incidental thereto shall be located within 500 feet of a boundary of an agricultural or residential zone, thus evidencing, as in the case of the Hillsborough ordinance, a finding that the industrial operation has a potential for harmful influence requiring protection for other properties. Since Kozesnik's acreage is not within an agricultural or residential district, it is not afforded that protection, and we of course cannot amend the ordinance to provide it, even if we could somehow conclude that Montgomery would want an ordinance thus reframed. Hence, we must conclude that the ordinance is invalid insofar as it relates to the limited industrial district and leave it to the local legislative body to decide whether in the light of our conclusions it desires to adopt an amendatory ordinance not inconsistent therewith. . . .

Conclusion

As stated above, we are satisfied that the townships may lawfully achieve the common purpose to which the ordinances were addressed, but since both ordinances have an infirmity we find to be vitiating, they must be declared to be invalid with respect to the limited industrial districts they create, and accordingly the judgments sustaining the ordinances are reversed.

HEHER, J. (concurring). The "Limited Industrial Zone" delineated by the amendment to the Hillsborough zoning ordinance comprises 684.32 acres owned by the Minnesota Mining and Manufacturing Company and 266 acres owned by others, but so divided as not to be usable by the individual owners for quarrying under the terms of the pertinent regulations. It is stipulated that in view of the provision of the ordinance that a "quarry permit" may be had only by an owner of "at least 200 contiguous acres" in the Limited Industrial Zone, a quarry permit can be had only by Minnesota; and so it is that the 266 acres were made subject to the "quarry use" (although the individual ownerships were such as to render this a purely nominal right) and the alternative preexisting residence and agricultural uses, said to be "worthless" in the circumstances. Indeed, it is affirmed that the Limited Industrial Zone has "the exact area requested by Minnesota Mining, and was not arrived at by any independent comprehensive study," but "to benefit one corporate landowner," and the "terms of the amendment are such that no business or industry other than that of Minnesota Mining can operate in the zone." And a member of the local planning board, when asked if the board had considered whether the Limited Industrial Zone "should be bigger, smaller or in this area or some other area," replied: "This was the area that was requested by Minnesota Mining to be rezoned as a limited industrial zone."

The exclusion of business and trade from residential districts bears a rational relation to the health and safety of the community. *Euclid, Ohio v. Ambler Realty Co.,* 272 U.S. 365, 47 S.Ct. 114, 71 L.Ed. 303 (1926). But the restriction of this district, zoned for "limited industrial" uses, to stone quarries, residences and agricultural pursuits, excluding light and other industrial uses, not to mention business, is plainly illusory when assessed in the context of the constitutional and statutory considerations to be served by zoning. The amendment to the ordinance is so framed that no business or industry other than Minnesota's quarrying operation is permissible in the zone and particularly in the area of 266 acres, and thus the classification is arbitrary. As just said, it is conceded that no person or corporation other than Minnesota "could meet the acreage requirement . . . for a quarry permit" in this use district. And Minnesota has a permit, not only to operate a quarry in that zone, but also to erect a large rock crushing plant at a cost in excess of two million dollars.

One of defendants' own witnesses, Mr. Hugh R. Pomeroy, director of the Westchester County Department of Planning and also a recognized specialist in the field, testified that "rock crushing" is "a part of a quarrying operation" and is to be "regarded as heavy industry of a natural productive type of use"; and he agreed that the land is "submarginal for agricultural purposes" and "not conducive to residential development," and that "for all practical purposes" the plan would "place the owners of such properties in a position where they have land that is not readily usable for agricultural or residential purposes, and yet under the ordinance no use would be permitted." And he also conceded that a "nonnuisance-laboratory-type building employing a few employees" would not have "any more unfavorable impact on this community than the quarry use permitted." . . .

The use exclusions from this Limited Industrial Zone bear no rational relation to the field of police action comprehended in zoning. The classification is unreasonable and unduly discriminatory, not in keeping with zoning principle and policy. It is fundamental that land use restrictions cannot exceed the public need and the fair requirements of the general good and welfare.

I do not agree that the determination of the particular question should await an application for "another [compatible] specific use."

We are concerned now with basic zoning power; and the issue is ripe for decision.

I concur in the result otherwise, and in the Montgomery Township case as well.

Comments: 1. The meaning of the "comprehensive plan" requirement in zoning will be treated in more detail *infra* p. 741.

2. Why should the court feel obliged to refer to the listing of "mining" and "other like matters" in the New Jersey Planning Act of 1953 as a basis for the "power to authorize quarrying and the processing of rock"? Were the plaintiffs really arguing that New Jersey municipalities did not have the power to "authorize" such uses under the New Jersey zoning enabling act, which was practically identical to the Standard Act?

3. The zoning ordinances of the 1920-50 period adopted the "cumulative" or "progressive" technique sustained in the *Euclid* case. These ordinances excluded the so-called "lower" uses — *e.g.*, commercial and industrial uses — from "higher" use districts — *e.g.*, single-family, two-family, and general residence zones. Indeed, as we have seen, both two-family dwelling and multifamily dwellings were often excluded from single family districts. But "higher" uses were not excluded from "lower" use districts; all kinds of residential uses were generally permitted in commercial and industrial zones. Edward Bassett, the "father of zoning," explained this on the ground that, although "the surroundings are unhealthful and residences in such locations are almost sure to become neglected and unsanitary, the residences do not hurt the neighboring factories, and the grounds of prohibition cannot be based on the maxim that one should so use his own as not to injure another." E. Bassett, Zoning, 9 Nat. Municipal Rev. 315, 325 (1920).

4. Since World War II local governing bodies have become increasingly aware of the disadvantages of permitting the intrusion of residential uses into areas where industrial uses are permitted and the advantages to be gained from the creation of "exclusive" industrial districts. For a powerful argument in favor of "exclusive" industrial zoning, see Mott & Wehrly, The Prohibition of Residential Developments in Industrial Districts, Urban Land Institute Technical Bulletin No. 10 (November 1948), from which the following excerpt is drawn:

> The theory that residential areas can be allowed to occupy potential industrial areas until such time as needed, and that industry will then come in and acquire the land for industrial use, has proved to be largely erroneous. There are several things wrong with this theory: 1. Cost of acquiring the improvements to be torn down becomes prohibitive. . . . 2. A pattern of utilities and streets has become established which is seldom adapted to industrial use. 3. Greater difficulties are encountered in land acquisition because of the multiplicity of ownerships and vested interests in homes. 4. Residential uses in industrial areas are the first to become blighted. This point is one which should be given the utmost consideration. The net result of permitting residential

development to locate in an industrial district is to set the stage for a more accentuated condition than would normally occur without any zoning at all. It was to prevent this very condition that zoning first developed. To dismiss this by saying that the occupant should have been aware of this danger is to overlook the fact that, on any such scale, such development becomes of public rather than individual concern.

The reasonableness of excluding more restricted uses from industrial districts should not be too difficult to establish. In the first place, the amount of land designated for an industrial district is, or should be, based on exactly the same kind of assumption as that for residential or commercial districts — existing use, plus estimated future need. Therefore the validity of zoning for industry can be assumed to [be] just as much or as little as for other districts. Secondly, if industrial uses are objectionable near residential development because of smoke, fumes, fire or health hazards, the reverse is equally true. . . . How can the courts then consistently hold that the prohibition of commercial or industrial uses in a residential district is reasonable while the prohibition of residential uses in a commercial or industrial district is not?

There is another aspect to this problem which cities now struggling with difficulties of income can ill afford to overlook. Traditionally residential development has been subsidized by the industrial and commercial tax dollar. While the amount of commercial zoning has been excessive in many cities, much of it is misplaced. Industrial zoning has more often been both inadequate and improperly located. This fact, together with the intrusion of other uses, and with public resistance often directed against further desirable increases, has contributed to the decentralization of industry into districts where adequate areas can be acquired and modern plants erected without the difficulties attending piecemeal acquisition of land already developed for other uses.

. . . .

What has been said regarding the exclusion of residential uses might also apply to certain types of commercial development. Baseball parks, skating rinks and similar enterprises needing large sites will often seek locations in industrial districts either because they are prohibited elsewhere or because of land area requirements. The net effect is the same as in residential developments — diversion of land designated for industrial uses to other purposes. . . .

5. What do you think of the following contrary argument:

Exclusive industrial zoning should be faulted, not because of any theories thought inherent in the zoning process, but because of the effect it has on land values and on the implementation of the comprehensive plan. Zoning of this type creates monopoly values, leads to land holding practices, and frustrates developers looking for industrial sites. Probably the best way to stymie industrial development in a community is to zone the best sites exclusively for industrial purposes.

What possible alternatives does this argument overlook? Why not simply overzone for exclusive industrial use? That will at least hold down land values.

6. In *Katobimar Realty Co. v. Webster,* 118 A.2d 824 (N.J. 1955), cited in the principal case, the court invalidated a light industrial classification insofar as it excluded all retail business uses. The court said:

> It is difficult to perceive a rational distinction referable to the fulfillment of the statutory zoning considerations . . . between the contemplated shopping center and the uses permissible in the limited industrial district now before us. . . . The projected business center and light industrial uses are not incompatible in nature; they are generally, so far as zoning policy goes, wholly congruous uses, and if in special circumstances a distinction may reasonably be made to serve an overriding public interest, such showing is not made here. There is no reasonable basis for the classification. Retail commercial uses would not conflict with industrial uses. There must be a reasonable exercise of the grouping power; such is the essence of comprehensive zoning.

Id. at 830, 831. Did the two municipalities show "an overriding public interest" in the principal (*Kozesnik*) case?

Compare *Corthouts v. Town of Newington,* 99 A.2d 112 (1953), invalidating as "confiscatory" a zoning amendment which prohibited residential land use in a "heavy" industrial district but permitted residential use in the "light" industrial district. The court held that residential use was "the highest and best use" to which plaintiff's land could be put, and stated that in all probability the land would remain unused for many years if not developed for residential use. Moreover, the exclusion of residential use was arbitrary since hotels, hospitals, schools and public playgrounds were allowed in the "heavy" industrial district. A careful reading of the *Corthouts* opinion suggests that the heavily overzoned exclusive industrial district may either have been intended as a barrier against new residential development or as the basis for an overly optimistic economic growth policy.

In *Roney v. Board of Supervisors,* 292 P.2d 529 (Cal.App. 1956), where the court upheld an "exclusive" industrial classification, there was no showing that the land thus restricted was unusable for industrial development within a reasonable time. The *Roney* court said:

> [I]t cannot be held that there is anything arbitrary or unreasonable per se in the plan of zoning to prevent the so-called "higher" uses from invading a "lower" use area, a plan described by respondent as "exclusive industrial zoning." In fact, the term "higher" as applied to residential uses, or to uses closer than others to domestic purposes, is not an accurate one; for, although the use of property for homes is "higher" in the sense that commercial and industrial uses exist for the purpose of serving family life, the better these secondary uses can accomplish their purpose, the better is the primary use of the property served. Moreover, the early decline of the new residential districts into blighted areas by their being surrounded by heavy industry is prevented. These considerations, added to those of public health and safety by removing residences from fumes, as set forth above, and viewed in the light of the law that regards the police power as capable of

expansion to meet existing conditions of modern life, . . . place the ordinance with its exclusive industrial feature and the decision of the governing authorities well within the limits of those legislative and administrative acts which are acts where reasonable minds might differ, and therefore, not subject to judicial interference.

Id. at 532.

Since the mid-1950's all the cases accept the validity of "exclusive" industrial zoning in principle, although some cases hold it to be invalid on the facts. Most of the cases not only recognize health and safety factors as a justification for such zoning but also recognize that "industry and commerce are . . . necessary and desirable and that a proper environment for them will promote the general welfare of the public." *Skokie Town House Builders v. Morton Grove,* 157 N.E.2d 33, 36 (Ill. 1959). A few cases even recognize that

a zoning scheme seeking balanced land use to obtain a sound municipal economy by encouraging industry on which taxes may be levied to help meet the deficit in the cost of municipal services to home owners is a proper exercise of the zoning power, subject always to the reasonableness of the classification and regulations enacted to achieve the end both generally and with respect to particular property.

Newark Milk & Cream Co. v. Parsippany-Troy Hills Township, 135 A.2d 682, 695 (N.J.L. 1957, per Hall, J.). *Accord, Gruber v. Raritan Township,* 186 A.2d 489 (N.J. 1962); *Ward v. Montgomery Township,* 147 A.2d 248 (N.J. 1959).

7. In *Grubel v. MacLaughlin,* 286 F.Supp. 24 (D.C.V.I. 1968), the court sustained a commercial use classification which excluded all residential uses as well as all industrial uses, citing cases dealing with the "exclusive" industrial zoning issue. The court's rationale was as follows:

The growing complexity of our civilization, the multiplying forms of industry, the dangers of heavy traffic in mixed residential and commercial districts, the noise, the fumes — are all factors which may well justify the allocation of industries, commercial businesses and dwellings to separate districts in order to promote and preserve the general welfare of the community.

Id. at 28.

FORTE v. BOROUGH OF TENAFLY

Superior Court of New Jersey, Appellate Division
106 N.J. Super. 346, 255 A.2d 804, *petition for certification denied,*
54 N.J. 560, 258 A.2d 13 (1969)

GAULKIN, S. J. A. D. Defendants (hereafter Tenafly) appeal from a judgment declaring Tenafly's amended zoning ordinance unconstitutional insofar as it forbade the construction of a supermarket upon plaintiffs' lands.

Prior to August 1967 the zoning ordinance permitted such a use in the zone in which plaintiffs' lands were situated. Early in 1967 plaintiffs applied to the building inspector for a permit to build the building, and to the planning board (board) for approval of its site plan and parking area. The board, aided by Kendree and Shepherd, planning consultants, was then engaged in a planning study of the borough with a view toward a comprehensive master plan. The consultants had recommended and the board agreed that the "central business core" of the borough should not only be preserved as the borough's retail shopping area, but strengthened and improved. This was to be done principally by improving the roads and the traffic pattern in said core to eliminate through-traffic and traffic congestion, and by forbidding retail businesses in the rest of the borough. This the board and its advisers felt would encourage retail businesses in the area to remain and improve and expand their properties, thus improving the appearance and enhancing the value of all properties in the business area, and providing the borough with an inviting "downtown" center. If retail businesses were allowed to spread along the roads throughout the borough, it was believed the central business area would deteriorate and decay. Therefore, instead of approving plaintiffs' application, the board adopted a resolution asking "that an interim zoning ordinance amendment be adopted in order to create a new district known as the C-2 District in order to discourage and restrict the spread of retail business beyond the downtown business core . . . ." Shepherd, the borough's planning consultant, testified that 93% of all of the borough's retail business establishments were in the central business core.

The governing body agreed and, on November 28, 1967, passed ordinance #939. The ordinance recited the resolution of the planning board and created the C-2 District, stating

"A. Intent — This district is intended for commercial and wholesale services and small local convenience neighborhood service establishments and other businesses not suited to the general retail business zone, and to provide uses which will not have an adverse effect upon the downtown business core."

The C-2 District included plaintiffs' property.

That portion of the C-2 zone here involved included all the lands previously contained in the business zone on the west side of County Road north of Mahan Street to the Cresskill border. Plaintiffs' lands were on said side of County Road, beginning at Prospect Terrace, the street north of and parallel to Mahan Street. At the time of the passage of the amendment there were a number of businesses in the new C-2 zone. Coming south from the Cresskill border on said side of County Road there was a Robert Hall clothing store. In the next block, between Summit Street and Hudson Avenue there was an Esso Service Station, Midtown County Rambler (selling new and used cars), County Auto Parts, an unoccupied but recently renovated business building and a funeral home. Continuing south, in the next block there was Lamb Studios (manufacturers of ceramics) and property occupied jointly by Stryker Drafting and Manufacturing Company and Poretta Plumbing and Heating Company. Then came plaintiffs' lots. Below Prospect Terrace there was a barber and beauty shop, a tavern with a catering service, a TV repair shop and a small grocery store with living quarters on the second floor. On the easterly side of County Road, opposite the premises in question, (zoned residential), there is a Ford automobile agency at the corner of Summit Street, a gasoline station at the corner of Hudson Avenue, between Hudson and Prospect a dance school and studio, and on the corner of Prospect and County Road a cocktail lounge. The land abutting plaintiffs' property to the rear is in the M-1 industrial zone.

Plaintiffs immediately instituted this action to have the ordinance declared invalid. Defendants contend that the action should have been dismissed because plaintiffs failed to first apply for a variance. Under the circumstances here presented, it would have been futile to apply for a variance and therefore it was proper for plaintiffs to proceed as they did.

After a full trial, the trial court entered the judgment appealed from.

Defendants made some effort before the trial court to justify the elimination of retail stores in the C-2 zone on the ground that such uses would increase traffic on County Road, and so forth. The trial judge ruled, in effect, that since the true reasons were those expressed in the ordinance itself, it was not necessary to pass on the other alleged justifications. We agree, but add that the evidence does not establish any other justification. In other words, if the intention to preserve, rehabilitate and improve the central business area does not sustain the ordinance, it must fall.

The first question, then, is this: May a municipality which wishes to preserve, rehabilitate and improve an established business area devoted chiefly to retail stores, zone the rest of the municipality against retail sales? We hold that it may.

Plaintiffs admit that if Tenafly were writing on a clean slate it could zone one part of the borough for retail stores and forbid all but residential use in the remainder or the borough. However, they argue that here Tenafly did not write on a clean slate; before the amendment of the ordinance they were in the same zone and had the same rights as those in the so-called central business core; much of the land in the C-2 District was already devoted to commercial uses, including retail, and since the ordinance was tailored to permit nearly all of them to continue as nonforming uses, the amendment was a sham directed against them alone, solely because they wanted to build a supermarket. Plaintiffs insist it was passed for the sole benefit of the merchants in the central business core; therefore it was unlawfully oppressive, discriminatory and unconstitutional. Furthermore, even assuming that Tenafly would have had the right to forbid retail stores in an area not already commercial, it was arbitrary and unreasonable to do so in this area, already largely commercial (including retail) and abutting commercial and industrial zones. They point out that the Robert Hall store sells only at retail, the gas station and the auto parts store are of course retail, and the manufacturers of ceramics may be selling at retail, as may the plumbing and heating and barber and beauty shops, the tavern and the TV repair store. The small grocery store admittedly sells only at retail.

The trial judge ruled, in effect, that since the avowed purpose of the ordinance was "to protect the business district" it was invalid. We think that was too narrow a view. Zones are often created or uses therein curtailed in a manner which benefits other zones. The mere fact that this is one of the purposes of the ordinance does not make it invalid. An area desirable for industry may be zoned otherwise because industry would damage a nearby residential or business zone. Conversely, residential uses may be forbidden in or near industrial areas to encourage the full expansion of industrial plants therein without fear of complaint of nuisance. It is true that a municipality may not, by zoning or otherwise, exclude a particular use only because it will compete with an existing business or businesses . . ., but if the exclusion of competition happens to be an incident or effect of otherwise valid zoning, it does not invalidate it.

Tenafly has what it considers to be a decaying central business core, choked by poor parking and traffic facilities. We take judicial notice that this is a problem which today faces many municipalities. Tenafly could have permitted the deterioration to continue into blight, hoping that new and desirable retail business areas would develop elsewhere. Instead, it appears that it wishes to make a strong effort to revitalize the present area. It elected to do so upon the recommendation of the planning consultants and the planning board. We hold that it has the right to do so, and the fact that the ordinance may give the central area a virtual monopoly over retail business does not invalidate it.

There is no evidence that Tenafly is trying to keep out supermarkets, or to benefit any particular business or businesses in the central business core. Tenafly is perfectly willing for supermarkets to open in C-1 zones, where such uses are permitted, although it concedes that there may be difficulty in finding or assembling therein the necessary land.

Assuming that the ordinance is generally valid, it leaves the question whether it is unreasonable and therefore invalid insofar as it applies to plaintiffs' property. Plaintiffs contend that it is unreasonable for the ordinance to take away from them the right to sell at retail because nearly every one of their neighbors in the C-2 zone sells at retail — some, like Robert Hall and the grocery, only at retail. They argue that the neighbors will continue to sell at retail either as permitted, accessory or nonconforming uses; hence it is discriminatory, arbitrary and unreasonable not to let them do likewise. But plaintiffs may use their property for the many purposes allowed by the ordinance. If they do, they will have the same rights to make incidental or accessory retail sales as those already carrying on similar businesses in the C-2 zone. The non-conforming retail stores are not so numerous as to make the ordinance unreasonable.

The judgment is reversed.

FOGG v. CITY OF SOUTH MIAMI

District Court of Appeal of Florida
183 So. 2d 219 (1966)

TILLMAN PEARSON, Judge. The appellant owns property in the City of South Miami. The property is zoned for business, but its C-1 classification is subject to a provision which prohibits "a drive-in operation." The appellant was denied a building permit to build a dairy products retail store because the type of store planned was one where the customer drives in and purchases the products without getting out of his car. Appellant filed a complaint in chancery seeking a declaration that: (1) the provision against a "drive-in operation" was void because it was arbitrary and unreasonable, and (2) the operation of a Farm Store retail dairy establishment is a C-1 Business District usage under the zoning ordinance. The chancellor held that the ordinance was valid and that a Farm Store was prohibited by the ordinance. This appeal is from that decree. We reverse upon a holding that the ordinance, as applied to this particular business, has no relation to public welfare.

The chancellor defined a "drive-in operation" as a place where people can drive up in an automobile and be served without having to alight from the automobile. We find nothing in this record upon which this definition could be predicated, but without a doubt, it is a good one. . . . We hold that the chancellor did not err in holding that the ordinance purported to exclude all business activities where the customer does not alight from his car.

The record indicates that the City made no contention that public safety or public health was involved, but relied entirely upon the opinion of its expert witnesses that the provision prohibiting "drive-in operations" contributed to the public welfare of the City by providing a sort of "continuity" to the retail business section of the City. It was urged that all of the merchants benefit by a requirement that the customer alight from his car to make a purchase because once the customer is out of his car he is a prospective customer of all the merchants.

The chancellor set forth the essential question thus presented:

"Now, the only question in the world here is may the City constitutionally pass an ordinance which limits this particular plaintiff from building a drive-in on this area because to build a drive-in in the area would react to the disadvantage of all business people located within the C-1 zone and would tend to detract from the development of the zone because it would cause other people not to want to develop retail stores there because they know that it's easier for somebody to drive in and buy their milk than it is by walking in. This is the real constitutional question involved. Can it be done constitutionally?

"The City's position, it's finally disclosed, is that people who buy, invest and build retail stores in the C-1 zone understand that when somebody goes down there to buy a pair of shoes for the kids, that while there they walk next door to the drug store and buy some liniment, and then while there they walk next door and go into the little retail store and buy a gallon of milk, and that this is what they call continuity of something or another, and this is very advantageous. I assume they are talking about to the business people because it depends on the woman whether she wants to go next door or drive into the drive-in. So they must be talking about economics and regulation of competition through zoning. This is really what you're saying."

While we agree with the chancellor's statement of the question, we must disagree with his answer.[35] The "public welfare" with which

---

[35] The chancellor held:

"The pivotal question before the Court (as defined by the pleadings and the testimony presented thereon) is whether or not a Zoning Ordinance which has for its purpose the protection of the value and usefulness of urban land — or more particularly, the promotion of the communities economic prosperity by the establishment of commercial development patterns within a business district — is related to the general welfare. If so, it is a valid exercise of the municipal power. There is authority in this State for the proposition that such an Ordinance is reasonably related to the general welfare. The question here is not whether the Court considers that it would be more convenient for a busy housewife to be served in her car *in the zone under discussion* than it would be for her to alight from her car and trudge into the store to purchase her family's daily needs.

"The ordinance under attack meets the 'fairly debatable' rule. The effect of this

the City and the courts must be concerned is the welfare of the whole community. A benefit or anticipated benefit to a special group within the City is not enough. . . .

It was disclosed that the City made exceptions by permitting drive-in operations in the area in question for a gasoline service station, a bank and a savings and loan business. To permit drive-in operations for such business and deny it to a dairy products store would appear to be arbitrary and discriminatory. This is so, because as stated above, as to such businesses the City made no showing that the prohibition against drive-in operations had any relation to the health, morals and general welfare. This is not to say that as to some other businesses authorized to be conducted in the area, as to which a drive-in operation would bring about excess traffic, noise in late hours, or tend to promote the gathering of unsavory elements or rowdyism, the City would not then have sufficient reasons of public policy to enforce the restriction against such drive-in operations. Clearly the proposed dairy product store drive-in operation was not shown to be in that category.

Having concluded that the exclusion of the use in question, as to plaintiff's business, has no substantial relation to the general welfare, we hold that the chancellor erred in holding that the prohibition against drive-in retail dairy products stores was not invalid. Wherefore, we reverse the decree in part and remand the cause for the entry of a decree in accordance with the views herein expressed.

Reversed and remanded.

HENDRY, Chief Judge (dissenting). I cannot concur with the majority opinion. The plaintiff has attacked the validity of the ordinance, not merely as it applies to any specific property, and the wisdom of the municipality in enacting this ordinance for the general welfare of the community has been shown to be debatable. Therefore, it is my view that the chancellor's decree should be affirmed under the "fairly debatable" rule.

———

Comments: For a case holding in accord with the principal case see *Frost v. Village of Glen Ellyn*, 195 N.E.2d 616, 619 (Ill. 1964): "We fail to see how a drive-in restaurant of the nature here planned is significantly more detrimental to the public health, safety, welfare or morals than a restaurant fully enclosed within four walls." Assume that an ordinance similar to that considered in the principal case is adopted in order to preserve the

———

Ordinance on the zoning plan and the economic welfare of the City — as well as its effect upon the housewife's quest for milk — is for the elected officials of the City to decide. The Courts should not invade the authority of those elected officials absent a paramount constitutional right and duty to do so. Such right and duty have not been shown in this case."

approaches to an important historic and cultural district in the community. The applicable zoning, while permitting hotels and motels, excludes banks and office buildings. Antique shops are permitted but not stores selling antique reproductions. Is the ordinance constitutional? *See Board of Supervisors v. Rowe,* 216 S.E.2d 199, 211-12 (1975) (held unconstitutional).

MANDELKER, CONTROL OF COMPETITION AS A PROPER PURPOSE IN ZONING, 14 Zoning Digest 33, 34-38, 41 (1962)

In the kind of case under consideration, then, the effect of the proposed use on commercial competition is an element in the zoning decision. Two different types of cases will be treated under this heading. One type raises a proximity question. No question of fulfilling community demand is presented, but an application is denied because another filling station or shopping center is located close by. Were the application granted, the service areas of the two stations (or centers) would overlap, and neither would be completely successful. The second type of case raises a demand question, and in this instance an application will be refused because the community already has a sufficient number of filling stations or shopping facilities. . . .

A survey of the opinions reveals that the courts have been far from unanimous in the weight they have given to the competition factor, and that they have not differentiated between questions of proximity and of demand in their consideration of that factor. At least five approaches can be distinguished:

1. *Control of competition ultra vires or unconstitutional in zoning.* This is the extreme view. It has been adopted in several jurisdictions, and has been reiterated most frequently in lower court New York and Ohio decisions, although the New York cases have not been consistent. Usually, no reason is given for the objection, nor is it always clear whether a consideration of competition is merely ultra vires the enabling act, or is an unconstitutional exercise of the police power. In some cases, the objection is based on the point that the control of competition is a matter for the market, and not for the regulating agency.

Perhaps the most satisfactory explanation for this point of view is found in Circle Lounge & Grille, Inc. v. Board of Appeal, [324 Mass. 427, 86 N.E.2d 290 (1949)] a Massachusetts case, in which the issue was raised obliquely. The Circle Lounge protested a variance which allowed the construction of a Howard Johnson restaurant across the street. Although the Circle Lounge lies in a commercial zone, the new restaurant would be located in a residential zone bordering part of the street. This case came up as a standing question. Did the Circle Lounge have standing to appeal the Howard Johnson variance?

In answering the standing question, the Massachusetts court indicated its attitude toward the role of competition in the zoning process. It found that competition alone did not give the Circle Lounge sufficient standing to appeal the variance. The purpose of zoning is to protect the conformity of uses. Residential owners in the residential zone might object to the intrusion of a commercial use. But a commercial use in an adjacent commercial zone may not object to the conversion of a neighboring residential zone to a commercial use which would be no less restrictive.

2. *Businesses may not be licensed under the zoning power.* Some of the decisions make an additional objection to the consideration of the competitive factor in a zoning decision. They point out that filling stations and shopping centers are not sufficiently affected with the public interest to be subjected to utility-type regulation. Again, the cases are not clear whether a vires or a constitutional question is involved. As the issue arises in a zoning context, the point seems to be that the zoning power is not the licensing power, and so may be used to regulate but not to prohibit, whatever that differentiation may mean. This defect could be cured by statutory authority to license shopping centers and filling stations under utility-type regulations based on need. Whether a statutory licensing scheme would be upheld is another question.

Whatever the basis for the cases that make the licensing objection, they fail to note that the land use questions have been obscured by the presentation of the issue as a conflict between competitors. Nevertheless, land use questions have not necessarily been removed from the case.

3. *Control of competition may not be the dominant purpose in zoning.* In all of the remaining categories, the cases give control of competition some weight as a factor in the zoning process. A dominant purpose rationale was adopted in *Appeal of Lieb*, [179 Pa. Super. 318, 116 A.2d 860 (1955)] a proximity case, in which a competitor challenged a rezoning for a shopping center. The court admitted that under some circumstances zoning limits competition by restricting the area within which it can be conducted. This is but a byproduct of zoning, and does not make the regulation unlawful. But zoning is not like public utility regulation, and so the "purpose" of zoning may not be the restriction of competition. *Lieb* is sensible in its recognition of the practical impact of a zoning ordinance, but its approach seems a little unrealistic.

4. *Control of competition may be a factor in zoning.* In many of the cases in this category, the competitive factor is not the only reason advanced for rejecting the application. Particularly in the filling station cases, traffic and safety objections may be advanced. Asked to pass on the refusal of a variance (or exception) for a filling station, a court may uphold the denial, noting that lack of need for the station in the area may properly be one of the reasons for refusal.

Most of the cases which take this position are filling station appeals. The New Jersey cases have been most consistent in this point of view.

One problem with the filling station cases is that the application at hand may have been prompted by the presence of other stations in the immediate area. If there are many neighboring stations, the traffic and safety objections to the addition of one more station may not be too persuasive. In these cases, the absence of demand sufficient to support an additional station may be the dominant reason behind the refusal. But the court may avoid coming to grips with this issue by ostensibly shifting its approval of the rejection to a more conventional basis. Particularly in a variance or exception case, the board can then be affirmed on the ground that it did not abuse its discretion. . . .

We are not yet running out of land for urban development, but we are developing land scarcities of a different order. As metropolitan centers expand, the competition for desirable sites becomes more intense as size forces increasing attention to travel, distance, and locational factors. Because it does not make allowances for the community's point of view, the market cannot be relied upon to make the most economic use of available sites. Under conditions of comparative land scarcity, planning will have to see to it that the right choices are made. Commercial facilities should not be built if the community does not need them, and a proper locational balance should be maintained between competing commercial uses.

––––––––––

Comments: 1. Recent decisions continue to deny recognition to interests based on competition. *Swain v. County of Winnebago,* 250 N.E.2d 439 (Ill. App. 1969). Downtown business merchants in Rockford were denied standing to challenge a rezoning for a regional shopping center in the surrounding county, and at some distance from downtown Rockford. The court found that the only special damage suffered by complainants stemmed from the potential of increased competition. "Free and open competition has always been a strong pillar in the foundation of our society. A person can have no vested or special property right in either the monopoly or competitive advantage accorded by zoning restrictions at a given time." *Id.* at 444.

But see Van Sicklen v. Browne, 92 Cal. Rptr. 786 (Cal. App. 1971). The planning commission had turned down a conditional use permit for a gasoline filling station, in part because "There is no demonstrated need for an additional service station in this neighborhood at this time." Affirmed. While recognizing that zoning may not be used to regulate economic competition, the court noted that

> planning and zoning ordinances traditionally seek to maintain property values, protect tax revenues, provide neighborhood social and economic stability, attract business and industry and encourage conditions which make a community a pleasant place

to live and work. Whether these be classified as "planning considerations" or "economic considerations," we hold that so long as the primary purpose of the zoning ordinance is not to regulate economic competition, but to subserve a valid objective pursuant to a city's police powers, such ordinance is not invalid even though it might have an indirect impact on economic competition.

Id. at 790.

2. Assume that a municipality adopts a comprehensive plan in which it determines that only one major shopping center is needed in the community and that, for a variety of planning reasons, this center should be located in a certain area of the community. A developer seeking to build a shopping center in another section of the community then brings an action attacking the single-family zoning applicable to his property, having first applied for and having been refused a rezoning to commercial on the ground that the comprehensive plan had designated the only shopping center site elsewhere. The developer makes an agrument that the refusal to rezone his property is an improper control of competition. For a case rejecting this challenge in a comparable fact situation see *Ensign Bickford Realty Corp. v. City Council,* 137 Cal. Rptr. 304 (Cal. App. 1977). The court noted, "[b]y its very nature, a zoning ordinance may be expected to depress the value of some land while it operates, in its total effect, to achieve an end which will benefit the whole community." *Id.* at 310.

3. As an alternative to the zoning ordinance adopted in the *Fogg* case, what if a municipality adopted a commercial zoning district prohibiting drive-in businesses as of right but then providing that a drive-in business could be allowed in that district as a conditional use. Would that make a difference? *See Gino's of Maryland, Inc. v. City of Baltimore,* 244 A.2d 218 (Md. 1968) (upholding ordinance of this type but not considering the arbitrary classification problem). For more on conditional uses see *infra* p. 655.

4. Another approach to the problem of the *Fogg* case is to create two business districts, placing the more offensive and intensive commercial uses in one district and excluding them from the other. This was done in *State ex rel. American Oil Co. v. Bessent,* 135 N.W.2d 317 (Wis. 1965). The village created a limited business district, and a general business district. Gasoline service stations were excluded from the limited district, but permitted in the general district. Both sides of a major road had been zoned as a general business district for a distance of three blocks. The oil company's property was on a corner at the edge of the general business district and adjacent to a residential district. This corner had been zoned as a limited business district to act as a buffer between the general business district and the residence district. However, there was a filling station across the street on a corner which was in the general business district, and on the oil company's property there was a nonconforming blacksmith and metal shop.

The oil company did not attack the constitutionality of the zoning at its site, but attacked the validity of the classification in the ordinance on Equal Protection grounds. While the court was troubled by the justification for the two districts, it sustained the ordinance, relying on the point it was a comprehensive zoning ordinance, which is viewed "somewhat differently" than an ordinance dealing solely with the regulation of a single business. A comprehensive ordinance "rests upon the interdependency of adjoining parcels of land in a community and the appreciation that the value and usefulness of each parcel to the owner and to the community are affected by the use made of the adjoining parcel." *Id.* at 322. The court also sustained against delegation of power objections another section of the ordinance which required plan commission approval of the location and plan of operation of commercial uses.

5. A very restrictive commercial or business use classification is sometimes established for the purpose of providing a "buffer" between more intensive commercial or business districts and adjacent residential districts. But see *City of Tulsa v. Swanson,* 366 P.2d 629 (Okla. 1961). To provide a buffer, the Swanson property was placed in a district which permitted no commercial uses other than a professional office building which could occupy no more than 20 percent of the lot area and which was limited to one story in height. (See map.) In an opinion which was critical of the buffer zone concept, the court invalidated the zoning on the basis of the "physical facts." It noted that a hedge several feet high protected the residence to the east. The court also appeared skeptical of the use of streets as dividing lines. But see on this last point *Carlson v. City of Bellevue,* 435 P.2d 957 (Wash. 1968); *Perron v. Village of New Brighton,* 145 N.W.2d 425 (Minn. 1966).

6. Strip commercial development along arterial streets, of the kind illustrated by the map of the *Swanson* case, has proved to be a very difficult zoning problem to handle. Heavy street traffic makes residential development unattractive, and the existing commercial uses provide an easy argument for property owners wishing to establish new commercial uses and who can argue that the character of the street frontage has already been committed to commercial development. The *Swanson* case illustrates the pressures most courts feel to extend or to allow additional commercial uses in commercial strips along busy streets. A few courts, however, have supported local zoning efforts to resist ribbon commercial development, whose disadvantages are detailed in 4 N. Williams, American Land Planning Law § 90.01 (1974). Thus, in an important Arizona case, *City of Tempe v. Rasor,* 536 P.2d 239 (Ariz. App. 1975), the court refused to allow an "infilling" of an arterial commercial strip in order to support a zoned and partly built industrial park in the immediate area. For another leading Arizona case upholding a local zoning ordinance aimed at reducing commercial strip zoning see *City of Phoenix v. Fehlner,* 363 P.2d 607 (Ariz. 1961).

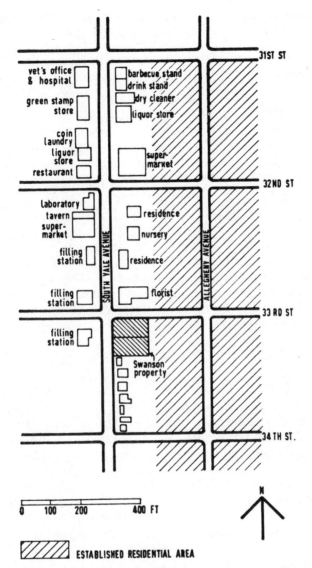

CITY OF TULSA v. SWANSON, OKLAHOMA, 1961

A NOTE ON ZONING CONTROL OF "SEX BUSINESSES"

Local governments and the general public have been concerned in recent years about the proliferation of sexually-oriented commercial establishments of various kinds — "adult" moving picture theatres, "pornshops," and "massage parlors." Many municipalities have adopted amendments to their zoning ordinances aimed at limiting and controlling such establishments. Most of these amendatory ordinances have not yet been tested in the courts. But the chances that a given ordinance will meet constitutional challenges based on the First Amendment ("free speech") and the Fourteenth Amendment ("equal protection" and "due process") would seem to depend upon whether the ordinance meets the standards laid down in *Young v. American Mini Theatres, Inc.,* 427 U.S. 50 (1976). In *American Mini Theatres* the Supreme Court, by a 5-4 vote, sustained Detroit's use of its zoning ordinance to control the locational pattern of "adult" sex businesses.

THE SUPREME COURT, 1975 TERM, 90 Harv. L. Rev. 1, 196-204 (1976)

American Mini Theatres, Inc., sought a certificate of occupancy for a theatre in Detroit to be devoted to showing "adult" movies. The city denied the certificate, citing a zoning ordinance prohibiting new "adult" theatres in proximity to certain other land uses in order to avoid neighborhood deterioration. Mini Theatres challenged the constitutionality of the ordinance in federal court. The district court granted the city's motion for summary judgment, but the Sixth Circuit reversed, holding that the ordinance was an impermissible regulation of speech on the basis of its content. The Supreme Court reversed, 5-4, reinstating the summary judgment for defendants.

Justice Stevens, writing for the Court, first held that the plaintiffs — to whom the ordinance clearly applied — lacked standing to challenge it as unconstitutionally vague. He then turned to Mini Theatres' claim that the ordinance impermissibly discriminated against some speech on the basis of its content. Now writing for only a plurality of the court, Justice Stevens acknowledged the strong constitutional principle forbidding content-based regulation of expression. However, he maintained that this principle had been qualified in several contexts and gave two reasons why it does not absolutely forbid the passage of an ordinance like Detroit's. First, the ordinance did not "violat[e] the Government's paramount obligation of neutrality," since it did not regulate particular speech on the basis of government approval or disapproval of the expression's "point of view." Second, society's interest in sexually explicit "adult" expression is "of a wholly different, and lesser, magnitude than the interest in untrammeled political debate . . . ." Justice Stevens commented in explanation that "few of us would march our sons and daughters off to war to preserve the citizen's right to see 'Specified Sexual Activities' exhibited in the theaters of our choice."

Having found that the ordinance's classification was not absolutely forbidden, the plurality noted that Detroit had a "factual basis" for believing that the scheme would serve its interest in "attempting to preserve the quality of urban life" — an interest entitled to "high respect." Since the ordinance left a sufficient number of sites for "adult" theaters to accommodate all patrons, it did not "greatly restrict access" to "adult" films, and was therefore constitutional.

Justice Powell's concurring opinion rejected the plurality's contention that sexually explicit materials should "be treated differently under First Amendment principles from other forms of protected expression." Instead, he emphasized that the Court had generally upheld innovative exercises of the zoning power. Focusing on the citywide distribution of "adult" materials, Justice Powell determined that the zoning ordinance interfered only "incidentally" with the two most vital first amendment concerns. It neither limited film creators' freedom of expression, nor threatened movie patrons' freedom to receive this form of expression. Moreover, Detroit's intent had not been to regulate or suppress "adult" expression as an end in itself, but only to control the "secondary effects" of such expression on neighborhoods. Accordingly, Justice Powell applied the four-part test of *United States v. O'Brien* [391 U.S. 367 (1968)] for determining if an "incidental" interference is constitutional, and concluded that the ordinance was.

Four Justices joined each of two dissenting opinions. One dissent, written by Justice Blackmun, argued that the plaintiffs had met the Court's test for standing to assert vagueness, and went on to find many aspects of the ordinance unconstitutionally vague. A second dissent, written by Justice Stewart, found the ordinance's content-based distinction unconstitutional as a form of selective control of "offensive" speech. He characterized the plurality's value judgments in *American Mini Theatres* as "wholly alien to the First Amendment," particularly since the Court had previously considered sex " 'one of the vital problems of human interest and public concern.' "

American Mini Theatres is the first case in which the Supreme Court has upheld general governmental regulation of the distribution of protected speech on the basis of its content. Four Justices justified their support for that outcome in part with the novel suggestion that sexually explicit speech has "lesser" value than other protected speech and therefore constitutes a category of expression subject to increased regulation but not suppression. Admittedly, there already exist two such "regulable" categories — libel and commercial speech. But hitherto, the Court has never altered its sharp distinction between sexually explicit expression that has social value and thus merits full constitutional protection, and expression that lacks any such value, and is thus obscene and deserving of no protection at all.

. . . .

Thus far, of course, neither Justice Powell's nor the plurality's rationale for upholding content-based regulation commands the support of a majority of the Court. Moreover, the *American Mini Theatres* majority continues to respect *Erzoznik v. City of Jacksonville* [422 U.S. 205 (1975)], in which Justice Powell and five other Justices struck down an ordinance prohibiting drive-in theatres from displaying nude scenes visible to passersby. The Court there rejected peremptorily Jacksonville's efforts to justify its ordinance as a means of "protecting" citizens from "offensive" speech and preventing traffic accidents. For the moment, therefore, *American Mini Theatres* may signal only the willingness of a majority to accept mild regulation of speech in the service of a city's demonstrated need, like Detroit's, to protect the quality of life in its neighborhoods. This relatively narrow reading is consistent with the Court's willingness in *Village of Belle Terre v. Boraas* [416 U.S. 1 (1974)] to allow a town to exclude nontraditional family units in order to preserve its distinctive ambiance, and Chief Justice Burger's assertion in *Paris Adult Theatres I v. Slaton* [413 U.S. 49 (1973)] that the state may control private showings of obscene films to implement the "interests of the public in the quality of life and total community environment . . . ." Thus construed, *American Mini Theatres* extends neither to zoning schemes justified only by distaste for expression, such as geographic constraints on the exhibition of non-obscene movies unconnected to the general zoning scheme, nor to regulation that significantly restricts the distribution of protected adult materials, such as special taxes, restrictive licensing requirements, or denials of routine government services.

Comments: 1. The zoning ordinance provisions challenged in *American Mini Theatres* were added by a 1972 amendment to an "Anti-Skid Row" ordinance enacted in 1962. The latter barred the establishment of certain designated kinds of businesses, including bars, hotels, poolrooms and similar businesses, within 1,000 feet of one another. The 1972 amendment added to the list of regulated businesses the following: "Adult Book Stores," "Adult Motion Picture Theaters," "Adult Mini Motion Picture Theaters," and "Group D Caberets," all defined in the ordinance as having a predominant "emphasis" upon specified sexual activities and specified anatomical areas. Under the 1972 amendment, establishment of more than two of the designated uses within 1,000 feet of one another, or within 500 feet of a residential dwelling or rooming house, was prohibited.

2. The *American Mini Theatres* case is explicated and its implications assessed in F. Strom, Zoning Control of Sex Businesses (1977), reprinted in part in 1 Zoning and Planning Law Report 9-14 (1977). Strom states that many municipalities and counties have enacted "sex business" zoning ordinances since the *American Mini Theatres* decision; some of these ordinances copy the Detroit ordinance fairly closely and others depart substantially from the Detroit model. For example, the Boston and Seattle ordinances concentrate "sex businesses" instead of dispersing them; the Boston and Indianapolis ordinances define "sex businesses" on the basis of exclusion of minors rather than the sexual emphasis of their services or wares; the Los Angeles and Kansas City, Missouri ordinances contain more comprehensive listings of regulated "sex businesses"; Oakland and Indianapolis subject all "sex businesses" to special or conditional use permit requirements; the Chicago ordinance regulates signs and storefront appearance; the Oakland and Indianapolis ordinances provide for the amortization of preexisting nonconforming "sex businesses"; and the Chicago and Dallas ordinances limit the proximity of "sex businesses" to civic buildings such as churches. For the text of these and other ordinances, see F. Strom, *supra* at 47-133.

3. Strom concludes that zoning control of "sex businesses" is most likely to be sustained against constitutional challenge if the following conditions are met: (a) the locational restrictions are not too strict, so that numerous sites for "sex businesses" are available and access thereto is "essentially unrestricted"; (b) there is an obvious and rational relationship between the restrictions on "sex businesses" and legitimate zoning purposes such as preservation of residential neighborhoods and separation of incompatible uses; (c) the definitions of the regulated "sex businesses" are definite enough so that the ordinance's coverage is clear; and (d) the ordinance either allows "sex businesses" to be established as a matter of right in accordance with the restrictions set out in the ordinance or, if a special or conditional use permit system is used, the standards for granting a permit are as objective as possible. 1 Zoning and Planning Law Report 13-14 (1977).

4. For additional comment on the *American Mini Theatres* case and its implications, see W. Toner, Regulating Sex Businesses (American Soc'y of Planning Officials, Planning Advisory Service Rep. No. 327, 1977); Note, Constitutional Law: Municipal Zoning Ordinance May Restrict Location of Adult Motion Picture Theatres, 16 Washburn L.J. 479 (1977); Note, Equal Protection and the First Amendment: Zoning Away Skid Row, 31 U. Miami L. Rev. 713 (1977); Note, Using Constitutional Zoning to Neutralize Adult Entertainment — Detroit to New York, 5 Fordham Urb. L.J. 455 (1977).

6. Bulk and Density Controls

a. In the City Core

Restrictions on the height of buildings are one of the oldest forms of land use control in the United States. In at least three major cities, New York, Boston, and Baltimore, such restrictions were adopted, long before there were any comprehensive zoning ordinances, as a first attempt to deal with the growing congestion of cities in the late nineteenth century. Since *Welch v. Swasey,* 79 N.E. 745 (Mass. 1907), *aff'd,* 214 U.S. 91 (1909), there has been no doubt about the constitutional power of a municipality to set maximum building heights and to create different districts with differ-maximum height limits. But the reasonableness of particular height limits has always been subject to judicial review. Although height limits in business districts have more often been upheld, many cases have sustained maximum height limits for residential structures. But minimum height limits for residential structures have generally been held invalid.

The New York City Building Zone Resolution of 1916 was, in part, the result of concern over the increasing height and number of skyscraper buildings in lower Manhattan. *See generally,* Toll, Zoned

American (1969). The 1916 New York City Building Zone Resolution provided for three separate classes of districts based on "use," "height," and "land coverage," respectively. The "height" and "land coverage" regulations were primarily intended to assure adequate light and air, and were based on "light angles." The theory of the "light angle" was that building walls must stay behind an inclined plane which rose from the center of the street and, by "leaning against the building," defined an angle of light coming down into the street. The 1916 Building Zone Resolution also included requirements for yards and courts in its "land coverage" regulations. (A variation of "light angle" controls is still used in England and in some of the Commonwealth countries.)

Shortly after its decision in *Euclid,* the United States Supreme Court sustained an ordinance of Roanoke, Virginia, which created a setback or building line, with relation to streets, to which all buildings subsequently erected were required to conform. The ordinance required a setback from the street as great as that of 60 percent of the existing houses in a block. The petitioner sought by mandamus to compel the city council to issue a permit to build out to the street line, alleging the unconstitutionality of the setback ordinance under the due process and equal protection clauses of the Fourteenth Amendment to the United States Constitution. The court upheld the ordinance in *Gorieb v. Fox,* 274 U.S. 603 (1927). The court said:

> It is hard to see any controlling difference between regulations which require the lot owner to leave open areas at the sides and rear of his house and limit the extent of his use of the space above his lot and a regulation which requires him to set his building back a reasonable distance from the street. Each interferes in the same way, if not to the same extent, with the owner's general right of dominion over his property. All rest for their justification upon the same reasons which have arisen in recent times as a result of population in urban communities and the vast changes in the extent and complexity of the problems of modern city life. . . .
>
> The property here involved forms part of a residential district. . . . The members of the city council, as a basis for the ordinance, set forth in their answer that front yards afford room for lawns and trees, keep the dwellings farther from the dust, noise, and fumes of the street, add to the attractiveness and comfort of a residential district, create a better home environment, and, by securing a greater distance between houses on opposite sides of the street, reduce the fire hazard: that the projection of a building beyond the front line of the adjacent dwellings cuts off light and air from them, and, by interfering with the view of street

corners, constitutes a danger in the operation of automobiles. We cannot deny the existence of these grounds—indeed, they seem obvious. . . . .

Since upon consideration we are unable to say that the ordinance under review is "clearly arbitrary and unreasonable, having no substantial relation to the public health, safety, morals, or general welfare," we are bound to sustain it as constitutional.

Id. at 608-09.

Many zoning ordinances now in force control the intensity of land uses by a variety of devices: *height limits* on buildings, *setback* and *side and rear yard lines, minimum lot frontage* regulations, *minimum lot area* regulations, and limitations on the *percentage of the lot area* which may be covered by structures. In some of the larger cities, even more sophisticated devices such as *floor area ratios* and *open space ratios* are now in use.

LA SALLE NATIONAL BANK v. CITY OF EVANSTON

Supreme Court of Illinois
57 Ill.2d 415, 312 N.E.2d 625 (1974)

KLUCZYNSKI, Justice.

This appeal involves the propriety of a zoning classification on certain property located in the City of Evanston, defendant herein. Plaintiffs, La Salle National Bank, as trustee of the property, and James Investment Corporation (hereafter Corporation), as the sole beneficiary of the trust, filed an action in the circuit court of Cook County seeking declaratory and injunctive relief. The circuit court ruled that the present zoning of plaintiffs' property was invalid and further held that the Corporation might construct the multi-unit apartment building which they requested. The appellate court affirmed . . ., and we granted leave to appeal. The primary question concerns whether plaintiffs presented sufficient evidence to permit the invalidation of the present zoning ordinance.

Plaintiffs' property is a vacant lot at 1746 Hinman Avenue consisting of 52,800 square feet. It is located at the southwest corner of Hinman and Clark Street in Evanston. In February, 1968, the Corporation and owners of the majority of property situated on the eastern side of the 1700 block of Hinman Avenue filed a petition to amend the municipal zoning ordinance. They sought to have both sides of the 1700 block of Hinman Avenue reclassified from R-1 (single-family-residence district prohibiting structures in excess of 35 feet in height) to R-7 (general-residence district allowing structural height to 85 feet). A similar attempt had been unsuccessful in 1960.

It would appear from the record that extensive testimonial and documentary evidence was presented to the Evanston Zoning

LaSalle National Bank v. City of Evanston
ILLINOIS SUPREME COURT   1974

Lake

Park

La Salle property

parking lot R7

undeveloped R-1

apartment buildings R7

CENTRAL BUSINESS DISTRICT

U-2

R-1

Amendment Committee in favor of as well as in opposition to the modification. Pertinent to this appeal was the testimony of Kenneth James, an officer of the Corporation, who disclosed plans to develop the property presently at issue by constructing a large luxury apartment building which would be 85 feet in height. The Committee found that "The characteristics of the subject area itself, together with the higher intensity, nonsingle family residence uses which completely surround it, make the present R-1 Single-Family Residence District unreasonable. There are, however, other alternatives for rezoning the property which ought to be considered in addition to the R-7 General Residence District requested by the petitioners." It enumerated the chief arguments against the R-7 classification as Evanston's "policy objectives designed to discourage (a) increased residential density, (b) the encroachment of high rise buildings on existing single-family neighborhoods." The Committee, therefore, recommended that an R-5A (general-residence district permitting multi-family structures not in excess of 35 feet in height) be established for the Hinman Avenue properties because this zoning category would "(a) be much more compatible with the land use and zoning surrounding the west side of the street [Hinman] than is the existing R-1 Single-Family Residence District Zoning, and be compatible with land use and zoning surrounding the east side of the street, (b) reflect the existing character of the south portion of the west side of the street, the blocks to the north and northwest, [and] west side of the 1700 block of Judson Avenue, (c) take advantage of the value of the site to the City as a whole for the development of high quality housing, (d) provide a transition from the development and zoning on the west and southwest to the lower density uses to the southeast and east near the lakefront, (e) allow the same regulations to apply to both sides of the street, and (f) provide for redevelopment of the west side of the street and long range future redevelopment of the east side of the street which would be much more compatible with the remaining single family homes on the east side of the street." The Committee rejected reclassification of the west side of Hinman to R-7 and the east side to R-5A because it would be difficult to permanently implement less than an R-7 use on the east side of Hinman if the higher density R-7 was granted to properties on the west side of the street. The Committee concluded that "rezoning the area to R-5A would allow a reasonable return on the land to the chief petitioner [Corporation] and would allow good advantage to be taken, for the benefit of the City as a whole, of the special features of the area, without the hazard of setting a dangerous precedent for encroachment of high rise apartments on single-family neighborhoods and on the lakefront."

The committee report was submitted to the Evanston city council after the Corporation filed objections thereto. The city council adopted the committee recommendation insofar as it suggested that the west side of the 1700 block of Hinman be rezoned to R-5A. Plaintiffs then commenced this action.

Various area photos and diagrams depicting the zoning classifications and building heights of structures in the vicinity of plaintiffs' property were part of the exhibits submitted to supplement the testimony presented in the circuit court. The property at issue is situated between the central business district of Evanston, which generally lies to the west and southwest, and park land to the east which abuts Lake Michigan. Much of the property located to the north of the subject site is owned by or related to the operation of Northwestern University.

The property on the east side of the 1700 block of Hinman that retained its R-1 classification consists of seven parcels of property on which are located one or more older structures which appear to be substantial in character and which reflect the attributes of their present zoning classification. On the southeast corner of Hinman and Clark directly across from the subject property is a large home owned by the Westminster Presbyterian Church which is used as a religious center. One family also resides at this location. The remainder of this block has six single-family homes, one with a coach house. On the west side of the 1700 block of Hinman, immediately south of plaintiffs' property, is a single-family home with a coach house. Next to this structure is headquarters for a national fraternity whose operations are conducted in a 2½-story "colonial-style" building. At the corner is the University Club, which is a 3-story brick structure.

East of the 1700 block of Hinman is Judson Avenue. The east side of Judson has a triangular-shaped park located thereon. The west side of Judson consists of several houses comparable in structure to those located on the east side of Hinman. Two are used by the University, another is a sorority house. The remaining structure is a building of limited height and a more modern architectural design. It is owned by a Jewish organization. Further to the east of Judson is the lakefront and another park. The area herein described is an R-1 classification.

To the north of the subject property beyond Clark Street are many structures primarily owned by the University and used for administrative purposes. Most of the buildings are large houses which have been adapted for their present purpose. On the northeast corner of Hinman and Clark is a 2½-story building used by a medical group. Its design resembles that of the national fraternity headquarters previously described. The northern area is zoned U-2 (university district). This classification would prohibit the heights of structures to exceed 35 feet with the exception that a school building might rise to 50 feet if, under certain circumstances, the side and rear yards were correspondingly increased. Student or faculty residences might also be constructed by the University in this area, although there was no evidence that this had been done.

West of the subject property is an alley which abuts a lot containing two older structures for single-family residence. South of this, the remainder of the block is occupied by a ground-level city parking lot. The property herein described is zoned R-7, as are properties located for one block further west. Beyond this point is the business district.

Commencing about one block southwest of plaintiffs' property is the business district. Several blocks from plaintiffs' land in this area is a new 20-story office building.

Directly south, the 1600 block of Hinman Avenue is zoned R-7, and it contains numerous older structures. Located on the west side of this block is a church, a 7-story apartment building consisting of 25 units, and a "court-like building" with 4 floors of apartments totaling 76 units. On the east side of this block are two buildings eight stories high. One is a hotel for elderly men and the other a home for elderly women. The remaining two structures are at the north end of this block. These consist of apartment buildings of substantially lesser height containing 9 and 18 units respectively. It would appear from the record that no structure on this block was 85 feet in height.

Beginning about one block in a southeasterly direction from the property at issue, and continuing as such to the lakefront, is a vast area which is zoned for R-1 use.

Kenneth James, vice president of the Corporation, testified that the property at issue had been purchased in 1952 for $50,000. At that time the land was improved by a "mansion" and coach house with two apartments. Rather than place the mansion in compliance with defendant's building code, it was torn down several years later. The coach-house facilities were rented for many years but it, too, was subsequently removed. James related the Corporation's desire to construct a 10-story apartment building on the property containing 114 units of varying sizes. There would be 84 indoor parking spaces and 30 in back of the building. The structure would rise to a height of 85 feet, and at that time the estimated cost of construction was $3,500,000. He explained that this construction was dependent upon an R-7 zoning use, which would permit a maximum height of 85 feet and allow 65% maximum ground coverage of the property, although slightly less coverage was actually contemplated. The R-5A classification granted by defendant would permit construction of only a 3-story building consisting of 42 units. This zoning use would permit only 50% coverage.

George Kranenberg, a planning and zoning consultant, was called on behalf of plaintiffs. After describing the immediate area, he concluded that there existed a variety of uses within the vicinity. He said that an R-7 was the best use and this classification would be in accord with the property to the west and south that was also R-7. He based his opinion on the fact that to the north, west and south of the property greater density and height limits were permitted and that the property to the east was totally out of character to R-1 zoning due to certain deviations from the use normally attendant to an R-1 district. Moreover, he suggested that the construction of the 85-foot-high apartment building would have no deleterious effect upon the area and specifically upon houses on the east side of Hinman Avenue, for the harm to the latter, if any, had already occurred. He opined that the proper dividing line for the R-1 classification should be drawn one block south of plaintiffs' property.

On cross-examination Kranenberg conceded that an R-5A use was not incompatible with the property on the east side of Hinman, that this use was not detrimental to others permitted in the area and that the lakefront could properly be considered an open area. He agreed that it was generally a sound principle to decrease residential population densities as one proceeded away from the central business district and that an alley might properly demarcate different zoning areas. He adhered to his testimony in a prior case in which he had said "that as density increases the compatibility and relationship of dwelling units is lost; that the detriment increases in direct proportion to the density, and that density affects the number of people in an area, the traffic, the transportation, and all the public utilities provided within the city, such as sewer, water, electricity and gas." (*Lapkus Builders, Inc. v. City of Chicago,* 30 Ill.2d 304, 308, 196 N.E.2d 682, 685.) However, he attempted to explain that his statement in *Lapkus* was based on his examination of the proposed population density that would have occurred in *Lapkus,* and had no relationship to the present case. He then admitted that in this instance he had not computed this density in the immediate vicinity of plaintiffs' property.

. . . .

[The Illinois appellate courts usually summarize the expert testimony presented in zoning cases at length. Some of the testimony in this case is repetitive and has been omitted.—Eds.]

Wayne F. Anderson, the city manager of Evanston, was called by plaintiffs as an adverse witness. (Ill.Rev.Stat.1969, ch. 110, par. 60.) Primary inquiry was directed to his knowledge of any plan by defendant to develop the air rights over the parking lot which was zoned for R-7 use and located to the west directly across the alley from plaintiffs' lot. Anderson said that Evanston had acquired the property between 1960-1963. Several developers had apparently submitted proposals for the lot and other city-owned properties; however, usually just inquiries were made concerning the property.

He disclaimed knowledge of any current official interest or plans for development.

. . . .

Defendant called Richard Carter, its director of planning. He described the area with reference to the height of the structures in the vicinity. To the south in the 1600 block of Hinman the nearest structure exceeding five stories in height was about a block in distance from the southern boundary of plaintiffs' lot. He was of the opinion that the best use of the property at issue was for a "townhouse multiple family development." He based his conclusion on the fact that the character of the neighborhood was evidenced by the single-family residences on the east side of Hinman opposite plaintiffs' tract and the structures in the university area to the north. He said that the R-5A use would be compatible to the height and density of these properties. Moreover, he expressed the desire of the City of Evanston to have a tapering effect for buildings in the business district to the lakefront. This would gradually grade down the building heights before reaching the level, open areas contiguous to the lake. He claimed that plaintiffs' development plans would be detrimental to the area particularly on single-family residences situated on large lots whose owners should not be subject to rezoning speculation.

On cross-examination Carter adhered to the tapering concept beginning in the City's core which was being applied in this instance by effecting an R-5A use. He said his opinion would not be modified even to the extent that an 85-foot building might be constructed on the city parking lot although no evidence was ever presented to support the assertion that a structure of this nature was contemplated. Moreover, this witness suggested that an alley might be a proper boundary for differing zoning districts. He further testified that the structures on the university property to the north (U-2 district) might in particular instances reach 50 feet in height, but due to other zoning limitations all the structures would have to be demolished and rebuilt in order to exceed 35 feet. He did not anticipate that any construction of this type would occur for at least a decade because the University had informed his department of its construction plans during this period.

Carter further testified that all the uses of the property sites on Judson, east of plaintiffs' tract, had been established between 1949 and 1952 with the Jewish organization and University. Defendant and the sorority had entered into a consent decree which, in part, provided that no exterior alterations would be made to the sorority house located on Judson. These events occurred prior to the enactment of the present Evanston zoning ordinance in 1960.

F. Gregory Opelka testified on behalf of defendant. This witness possessed extensive experience as a professional real-estate appraiser and he evaluated the single-family homes on Hinman at $40,000-$70,000. He said that the highest and best use of the subject property was under the R-5A classification because of the established character of the surrounding area and lower level of houses which it contained. The apartment complex constructed in accordance with an R-5A use would complement the present height of the surrounding structures which were 2- or 2½-story buildings. He asserted that the proposed 10-story building would lessen the sunlight to some of the structures on the opposite side of Hinman, result in a 5 — 10% devaluation of the homes as single-family residences that are located directly across the street, drastically change the nature of the area by creating a less desirable residential environment and lead to conversion of remaining properties to other uses. He placed the value of plaintiffs' land at $300,000 for R-5A use and between $550,000 and $600,000 if an R-7 classification was granted.

. . . .

William S. Lawrence was called by defendant. The parties stipulated that he was an expert in matters pertaining to city zoning and planning. He defined the highest and best use of property as that which does not unduly affect adjoining or surrounding uses yet provides a reasonable financial profit. . . . He noted that . . . a 10-story building would be vastly dissimilar, thereby changing the area's aesthetic character. It would further have an adverse effect on the area by casting shadows on nearby property and generally diluting the quality of living. He asserted that the area would not be affected by construction of a building under R-7 specifications on the site of the city parking lot.

Initially, we are confronted with defendant's contention that this action was premature, for plaintiffs had failed to exhaust their administrative remedies. . . . Defendant concludes that the trial court erred in failing to grant its motion to dismiss on this ground. The argument is premised on the fact that the Evanston city council had never separately considered rezoning the subject property from R-5A to R-7 and, until such determination is made, plaintiffs may not commence litigation.

Under the circumstances of this case we find this contention to be without merit. It is clear that substantial evidence was presented to the Zoning Committee, including plaintiffs' plan to construct a luxury 10-story structure upon the property. The Zoning Committee made extensive findings regarding reclassification of the entire 1700 block of Hinman to R-7 use. Its report to the Evanston city council was detailed and its recommendation specific. We conclude from the record before us that a further attempt to seek reclassification of the subject property to R-7 use would have been futile, thereby rendering the Bright doctrine inapplicable. . . .

[Compare the court's treatment of the exhaustion problem with the doctrinal rules usually applicable to this question. *See supra* p. 281. — Eds.]

Defendant asserts that it is attempting to maintain a reasonable density of multiple development on a tract of land which faces a substantial single-family development immediately across the street and to maintain a 3-story height limitation in an area characterized by buildings of 2½ stories or less. We understand plaintiffs' argument to be that the area consists of varying uses and is not predominantly single-family in nature. They argue that the public health, safety and welfare would not be adversely affected by the height and density of an R-7 use. Throughout much of plaintiffs' brief is woven the common thread that there exists a substantial loss in property value under the present R-5A classification. Thus they conclude that the R-5A use is arbitrary and unreasonable.

The law governing the disposition of contentions challenging zoning classifications has been set forth in numerous decisions. As stated in *Exchange National Bank of Chicago v. County of Cook,* 25 Ill.2d 434, 439-440, 185 N.E.2d 250, 253, "It is always presumed, in an attack upon an ordinance, that the enactment is valid, and the burden of proving its invalidity falls upon the one who attacks the ordinance. . . . Before a court will intervene it must be established by clear and convincing evidence that the ordinance, as applied to plaintiffs, is arbitrary and unreasonable and has no substantial relation to the public health, safety or welfare. These rules are based upon a recognition that zoning is primarily a legislative function, subject to court review only for the purpose of determining whether the power, as exercised, involves an undue invasion of private constitutional rights without a reasonable justification in relation to the public welfare. . . . Where it appears, from all the facts, that room exists for a difference of opinion concerning the reasonableness of a classification, the legislative judgment must be conclusive. . . . In *La Salle Nat. Bank of Chicago v. Cook County,* 12 Ill.2d 40, 145 N.E.2d 65, we reviewed the considerations determining the validity of an ordinance as applied to a particular property and stated that "among the facts which may be taken into consideration in determining the validity of an ordinance are the following: (1) The existing uses and zoning of nearby property [citing cases], (2) the extent to which property values are diminished by the particular zoning restrictions [citing cases], (3) the extent to which the destruction of property values of plaintiff promotes the health, safety, morals or general welfare of the public [citing cases], (4) the relative gain to the public as compared to the hardship imposed upon the individual property owner [citing cases], (5) the suitability of the subject property for the zoned purposes [citing cases], and (6) the length of time the property has been vacant as zoned considered in the context of land development in the area in the vicinity of the subject property. [Citing cases.]" . . . The parties herein have cited decisions of this court and various appellate courts in support of their respective positions and they would appear to be in agreement that a determination must be made upon the particular facts of the present case. . . .

Evidence was presented to demonstrate that the single-family use was no longer the predominant characteristic of the area. The Zoning Committee report to the Evanston city council amply establishes this recognition in its recommendation for R-5A multi-family zoning. The record sustains the conclusion that the mere unsuitability of the site for R-1 zoning does not require the adoption of the opposite zoning extreme which plaintiffs advance.

[This highly specified factual approach to the constitutionality of zoning restrictions is generally utilized in the Illinois cases. While this particular set of factual categories has not explicitly been adopted elsewhere, it is nonetheless typical of how courts review zoning classifications in other jurisdictions. — Eds.]

While evidence of the possible loss of property values to the home owners of R-1 property on the east side of the 1700 block of Hinman if the Corporation's project is permitted to be constructed is in conflict, it is undisputed that the present value of plaintiffs' property will be substantially increased if an R-7 zoning classification is allowed. However, it is recognized that land zoned for a more intensive purpose normally provides an appreciation in property valuation. . . . Here, plaintiffs will realize a sixfold profit on the property if R-5A multi-family development is upheld while the financial gain will be even more enlarged if the most intensive multi-family luxury use is allowed. At the time the Corporation purchased this land in 1952 it was fully aware of the R-1 single-family use then permitted under the applicable zoning restriction, which we assume would render the value less than under the existing R-5A limitation. It has been noted that a contention as to loss of value is of diminished persuasion when a purchaser acquires land under circumstances similar to this case and then asserts the expectant loss resulting from the present zoning as a basis for his attack thereon. . . .

The parties herein do not suggest that plaintiffs' property is not suited for R-5A development. The uncontroverted testimony introduced supports the feasibility of such use.

A municipality may reasonably restrict increase of population density as necessary for its health, safety and welfare. . . and in the present case Kranenberg was in agreement that as proximity to the central business district lessened, density could also properly decrease. There is no evidence that the structural height or residential density in the immediate vicinity is presently comparable to that envisioned in the Corporation's construction plans and this would include properties located on the 1600 block of Hinman.

Additionally related to the issue of excessive density is the evidence presented as to the impact that the Corporation's proposed development would have on present zoning in the area. We find Opelka's testimony persuasive that an R-7 use would permit the transformation of remaining properties to other uses. It is possible to assume that this rezoning would be directed to an attempt to establish additional multi-family structures permitted under R-7 zoning with the correspondingly substantial increase in density. This inference is reasonably supported not only due to the action of the majority of property owners on the east side of the 1700 block of Hinman, who joined with the Corporation in an attempt to have the entire block rezoned to an R-7 use but is also reflected in the Zoning Committee report.

Plaintiffs have attempted to infer that construction of a building similar to that proposed may occur on the site of the city parking lot directly west of a portion of the subject land. There is no evidence to support this position other than the present R-7 zoning of the parking lot, and the same may be said as to future development in the U-2 area to the north. But even had plans for development of the parking lot to the full extent of R-7 zoning been introduced, we do not believe that this would be of controlling importance. Evidence tended to establish that such a building would not have significant impact on the houses on the east side of the 1700 block of Hinman or the surrounding area. Moreover, zoning boundaries must be drawn and the mere fact that property is adjacent to a district permitting less restricted use does not render the former's classification invalid. . . .

Plaintiffs have relied upon the use variation of the immediately surrounding properties, but it is clear that present area usage does not approach the extent which plaintiffs seek in relation to height and density. While the present or immediate future usage would justify multi-family zoning, plaintiffs, at most, have merely established that a reasonable disagreement exists as to the degree of multi-family use.

In addition to the aforementioned considerations, we note that there was substantial evidence that the building contemplated by the Corporation would be significantly dissimilar to any structure in the immediate vicinity and would alter the area's character. It would also disrupt the defendant's present attempts to have a gradual tapering of building heights toward an open lakefront and park area which could be used for recreational purposes. As was said in *Trust Co. of Chicago v. City of Chicago,* 408 Ill. 91, 100, 96 N.E.2d 499, 504, "A zoning ordinance may not be based alone on aesthetic considerations [citation], although it is no objection to such an ordinance that it tends to promote an aesthetic purpose, if its reasonableness may be sustained on other grounds." Thus prior decisions of this court, while recognizing aesthetic elements, have not deemed them to be controlling in zoning cases. . . . We are of the opinion that in the present case aesthetic qualities are a properly cognizable feature and that the evidence presented is supportive of defendant's position that the R-5A use is not arbitrary or unreasonable and is in accord with the general public welfare. . . .

[For additional discussion of aesthetic controls see Chapter 6, Part B. — Eds.]

After consideration of the aforementioned factors, we conclude that the appellate court and circuit court erred in granting judgment for plaintiffs and their decisions were contrary to the manifest weight of the evidence. Plaintiffs have failed to negate the presumption of validity attendant to the present R-5A zoning classification limiting the construction of luxury residential apartment units to one-third the number planned by the Corporation.

Accordingly, the judgments of the appellate court and the circuit court of Cook County are reversed.

Judgments reversed.

Comments: 1. The "density" controls used in the Evanston zoning ordinance apparently consisted of height limits and limits on the percentage of a lot which could be covered by structures. The opinion in the principal case indicates the kind of testimony commonly offered by the parties in litigation involving the "reasonableness" of particular zoning classification based on different "density" regulations. See also *Chicago City Bank & Trust Co. v. Highland Park,* 137 N.E.2d 835 (Ill. 1956), sustaining central business district zoning regulations requiring 1,500 square feet of lot area per family for residential buildings and limiting the height of structures to three stories or 45 feet. The court held that the trial court had erred in concluding that "intensity" controls could properly be applied only to residentially zoned areas, pointing out that

> [O]ne of the purposes of such a regulation is to protect the public facilities from excessive use. In view of the heavy demands put on such public facilities as water mains, sewers and streets, by commercial users, restrictions upon intensity of use are no less necessary in central business areas than in wholly residential areas.

Id. at 837.

2. In most of New York City the "bulk envelope" established by the 1916 Building Zone Resolution was so loose as to have relatively little impact on actual building sizes or shapes. But in midtown Manhattan the effect of the height and lot coverage regulations was to create what Norman Williams, Jr., has called "a new, inefficient and remarkably ugly type of architecture, for both office buildings and apartment houses — the so-called wedding cake or ziggurat style." 3 N. Williams, American Land Planning Law § 70.02 (1975). It was only by using this shape that a speculative builder could achieve the maximum rentable floor space on a given site, except in the relatively rare case where he could utilize the "tower privilege," permitting unlimited height for a tower covering no more than 25 percent of the lot area.

3. The 1950 proposal for a comprehensive rezoning of New York City would have made important changes in the bulk and density controls imposed by the 1916 Building Zone Resolution. The proposed controls included the following:

(a) Use of the *floor area ratio* (FAR) as the basic control. The FAR regulates the amount of floor space on any given lot by specifying a mathematical relationship between the area of that lot and the floor space area allowed on that — *i.e.,* the FAR is equal to height a building in stories times lot coverage in percentage. Thus, an FAR of 1.0 would permit either a one-story building covering the entire lot, or a two-story building covering 50 percent of the lot, or a ten-story building covering ten percent of the lot. In the 1950 proposal, FAR's ran from .5 for the lowest-density general residence district to 10 for upper-midtown Manhattan and 15 for office buildings in midtown and downtown Manhattan.

(b) *Averaging the light angle* across the frontage of the lot. *E.g.,* if the light angle in the district was 45 degrees, the proposal would have allowed one-half of the lot frontage to be developed with tall buildings producing a light angle of 60 degrees, and one-half of the lot frontage with lower buildings producing a light angle of 30 degrees.

(c) *Area of light access* controls in place of the older "court" controls. The 1950 proposal envisaged a fan-shaped area extending (in residence districts) for 60 feet from all legally-required windows, and required that a specified percentage of this fan-shaped area located between 40 and 60 feet from such windows be left open and unobstructed.

(d) A 30-foot rear yard for all residential buildings, to insure that available light at the rear would be the same as that available at the building's front on a normal 60-foot residential side street.

(e) *Usable open space* for each dwelling unit, with the requirements varying inversely with the density levels in the various proposed residential districts and, in the higher density districts, allowances for roof and balcony space.

As finally adopted in 1960-61, the revised New York City comprehensive zoning ordinance retained the proposed FAR controls, combined with a requirement for stated amounts of lot area per room in each dwelling unit. The "light angle averaging" proposal was abandoned and the "area of light access" proposal was replaced by a simple requirement that a court must be at least as wide as it is deep. The "usable open space" proposal was replaced by a required *open space ratio* (OSR) — the mathematical ratio between the amount of floor space on a lot and the area left open, including parking areas — with "bonuses" for additional open space at ground level provided by relaxation of the FAR and the lot area per room requirement.

4. Sophisticated density controls like the proposed New York City system and the Floor Area Ratio have primarily been used for high density commercial and residential development. Suggestions have also been made for adapting density performance standards of this type for multifamily development as an alternative to the usual zoning controls, which employ

FLOOR AREA RATIO (F.A.R.) CONCEPT

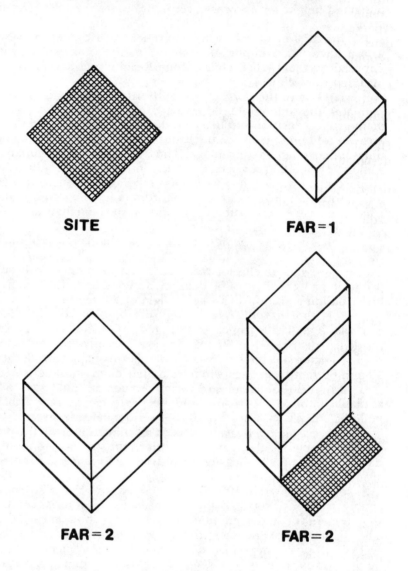

SITE

FAR=1

FAR=2

FAR=2

the standard lot size and setback requirements. (See the model zoning ordinance, *supra* p. 227.) To meet this need the U.S. Federal Housing Administration (FHA) developed a performance standard system of this type known as the Land Use Intensity (LUI) system, and combining the density ratios suggested in the New York study along with others to provide a zoning envelope for multifamily housing. The LUI system, which has since been revised, is explained in Hanke, Planned Unit Development and Land Use Intensity, 114 U. Pa. L. Rev. 15 (1965).

While the LUI system is used by the FHA in setting site standards for multifamily projects insured by the agency, it can and has been adapted for use in local zoning ordinances in many cities, most notably in Honolulu, Hawaii. Densities are set in the zoning ordinance under this approach by designating a range of multifamily densities as determined by the LUI scale for various sectors of the municipality. The LUI scale is then used to determine the density at which a multifamily project can be built. The present form of the LUI system and methods for applying it in local zoning ordinances are explained in F. Bair, Intensity Zoning: Regulating Townhouses, Apartments, and Planned Developments (American Soc'y of Planning Officials, Planning Advisory Service Rep. No. 314, 1976).

The Land Use Intensity system utilizes the following ratios:

(a) Floor area ratio (FAR), as explained above.

(b) Open space ratio (OSR), as explained above.

(c) Living space ratio (LSR) — the minimum amount of open space, not used for parking, which is required for each square foot of floor area.

(d) Recreation space ratio (RSR) — the minimum amount of recreation space which is required for each square foot of floor area.

(e) Total car ratio (TCR) — the minimum amount of parking space required for each living unit, *i.e.,* the total open space (OSR) less the living space (LSR).

(f) Occupant-car ratio (OCR) — the minimum amount of parking space required for each occupant of a building, to be used without time limits on parking, *i.e.,* the total car ratio (TCR) less the parking provided for visitors and tradesmen.

All of these six ratios can be expressed in a single figure, the *land use intensity ratio-scale.*

5. The use of floor area ratio (FAR) controls to regulate residential density has also been increasing in recent years, particularly in the larger cities, and in the higher-density districts in these cities. FAR controls are often combined with lot area per dwelling unit requirements, and occasionally with other bulk and density controls. Lot area per dwelling unit requirements are the most common form of bulk and density control in the higher density residential districts in the suburbs. Such requirements, in the form of minimum lot sizes, are also the most common form of density control in the lower density residential districts in the suburbs. Residential density performance standards similar to the FAR and LUI are also used in planned unit development regulations. *See infra* p. 854.

A NOTE ON BONUS OR INCENTIVE ZONING TECHNIQUES

In recent years several of our larger cities have developed new bonus or incentive zoning techniques designed to encourage private investment in the city core while maintaining relatively tight controls on density and bulk. In addition, these techniques use a carrot approach in the form of higher density bonuses in order to encourage office and commercial developers to provide a variety of public amenities, such as ground level plazas, in return for the higher density that is made available. A set of essays describing these techniques is contained in The New Zoning (N. Marcus & M. Groves eds. 1970). In the following selection the operation of these techniques, their problems, and experience with them in several cities is described.

TEAM FOUR, INC. [CITY OF ST. LOUIS, MISSOURI], DOWNTOWN IMPLEMENTATION STRATEGY: THE INTERIM COMPREHENSIVE PLAN 5-10 (1974) *

Bonus incentive techniques are contained in municipal zoning ordinances. These provisions basically exchange increased development rights for the construction of desired development amenities or even specific improvements. The "trade-off" is based upon the private developer providing selected public amenities such as increased open space, improved pedestrian and automobile circulation or special uses. In return, the municipality generally grants the developer the right to build at higher densities than are normally permitted. The extent and sophistication of bonus systems vary considerably. . . .

If a true bonus approach were to be developed . . . , four general steps would have to be taken in drafting the bonus provisions. They are:

1. Establishing the specific purposes of the ordinance;
2. Selecting the amenities which are most desired for downtown;
3. Determining the extent and impact of bonuses to be granted; and
4. Deciding upon the administrative mechanisms to be used in allocating the bonuses and controlling the system.

As actually implemented in some municipalities, a number of variations have been used. In Boston, for example, bonus provisions are used to encourage the construction of off-street parking and to create open space amenities. The bonus offered is a direct increase in the permitted floor area ratio (FAR). Chicago offers similar bonuses but puts particular emphasis on open space and therefore on developments with increased setbacks. Cincinnati, with much the same goals, adds reduced lot area requirements as a potential bonus. Minneapolis' provisions focus on improving pedestrian movement and amenities, while New York, which has the most highly sophisticated system, uses bonuses to induce features such as arcades, plazas and special uses. San Francisco, Honolulu, Milwaukee, Philadelphia and Seattle are other examples of cities that have worked with bonus provisions.

_____

*On file with the authors.

Density Bonus Ordinance Problems

As evidenced by the above list, density bonus provisions have been widely used and even with some success. Yet, the system has a number of drawbacks . . . . The inherent flaw in the bonus system is the difficulty of developing and administering such a program. An initial administrative problem is how to determine the extent of the bonus. Providing meaningful results requires exhaustive technical analysis of the public benefit derived from the amenity as well as the economic benefit which accrues to the developer via the bonuses. To withstand legal challenges, the bonus must also be based on the equivalent public advantage gained from the amenity. At the same time, if it is to induce private development, the bonus must be large enough to offset the developer's cost in providing the triggering amenity. Achieving a balance is difficult.

In addition to the obvious technical and legal difficulties in determining precise amenity/bonus relationships, the equity of each trade-off made must also concern the city. Without a finely tuned, fixed bonus system, challenges may be brought by individual developers protesting the comparative inequity of a particular bonus granted. Citizen groups may react negatively if they conclude that the furnishing of a particular amenity does not justify granting exceptions to density standards initially enacted to protect the "general welfare."

Solution? Automatic Bonus

To cope with such difficulties, a number of municipalities have adopted a procedure based on a bonus ordinance which grants density bonuses " as of right." This system is generally administered by setting out in the appropriate section of the zoning ordinance a list of specific amenities the city desires along with the corresponding bonus that is earned by providing each of the amenities. As a result, the developer knows exactly the extent of the bonus he has a "right" to take in return for the amenity he is providing. For example, by agreeing to provide an additional 50 square feet of open space at ground level, a developer in Cincinnati is *automatically* entitled to a predetermined bonus of 250 square feet of added floor space which normal zoning density restrictions would otherwise have prohibited. However, the automatic system is not without flaws either. Developers and city officials have both complained that this approach, while assuring equity and predictability, has not assured the quality integrated revitalization of the downtown fabric because of its automatic nature.

Discretionary Bonus Systems

To overcome these problems, an alternative to automatic bonuses has been developed which administers the bonus program with considerable discretion retained by the public sector. However, a number of case studies, including reports on the New York and San

AUTOMATIC DENSITY BONUS CONCEPT*

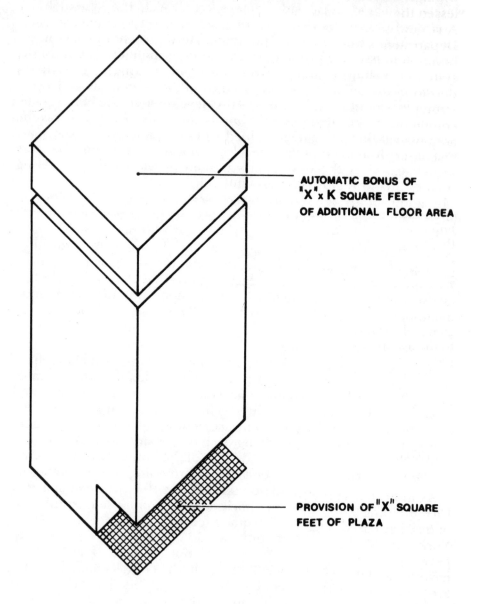

AUTOMATIC BONUS OF
"X" x K SQUARE FEET
OF ADDITIONAL FLOOR AREA

PROVISION OF "X" SQUARE
FEET OF PLAZA

* as used in Cincinnati

Francisco systems, have documented how local governments have willingly chosen to part with this discretionary power in order to lessen the likelihood of bonus allocation decisions being challenged. A review of San Francisco's system offered by that city's Planning Department indicates, for example, that a proposed discretionary bonus system was rejected in favor of an across the board automatic system. The latter was not only predictable and attractive for developers but avoided "emasculating" appeals. Thus, given a strong market as well as a sophisticated planning and development community like that in San Francisco, the complications of administering a discretionary bonus ordinance apparently discouraged its use.

Comments: What possible legal problems are presented by density bonus systems? One problem arises from the need to create a real incentive that will encourage the developer to participate in the trade-off process. If the existing zoning applicable to its site is already sufficient for its project, there will be no incentive to participate. If the intensity of the zoning on the site is reduced in order to encourage the developer to participate, would it then be vulnerable to constitutional attack? What happens if the municipality successively rezones sites in a downtown area in return for ground level plazas and the like? Can owners of remaining sites still subject to the less intensive zoning now bring an action challenging that zoning on the ground that successive upzonings in the area have undercut the validity of the original zone? How does the municipality work itself out of these dilemmas? For discussion of these problems see Mandelker, The Basic Philosophy of Zoning: Incentive or Restraint? in The New Zoning, *supra* at 14.

A NOTE ON "BUILDING BLOCK ZONING": AN OLD IDEA WHOSE TIME HAS COME AGAIN

As indicated at the beginning of this section, the 1916 New York City Building Zone Resolution provided for three separate classes of districts based on "use," "height," and "land coverage." The New York City scheme was frequently followed elsewhere during the period prior to World War II, but since then most zoning ordinances have created districts in which "use" and "bulk and density" controls are combined in a single set of regulations. Recently, however, several California counties have begun to use a scheme of "building block zoning" which bears considerable resemblance to the 1916 New York City scheme.

SEDWAY AND LOYD, BUILDING BLOCK ZONING PROVIDES FLEXIBILITY, Practicing Planner, September 1977, at 26-29

. . . A new approach called Building Block Zoning separates the package of regulations for each zone into three independent units to create greater flexibility. The approach is being officially considered in three California counties whose regulatory needs substantially differ. San Diego County struggles to balance the demands of burgeoning growth with the need to preserve the coast, mountains and desert. Fresno County is more concerned with agricultural preservation, rural commercial centers and resource management. Orange County confronts large scale development and density zoning. Housing characteristics and physical form attract more public interest there. The building block approach can be adapted to all of these needs.

. . . .

Conventional zoning. In traditional zoning all regulations are encompassed in a handful of overworked zones. Individual zones, such as R-1 residential, must be applied uniformly to a broad range of sites throughout a jurisdiction, but these zones do not always respond to local site and social conditions. Drafting completely new zones is sometimes impractical because it requires staff time, hearings, approvals and consolidation. This situation often leads to overcontrol; adding regulations to a single zone to address a problem in one area means imposing the same regulations in many areas throughout the jurisdiction that may not need them.

Each zone is a complete and inseparable package of requirements for use, structure, setback, height, open space, parking and landscaping. Yet in many planning situations each of these elements should be considered individually. Perhaps density should be limited because of site constraints. Perhaps greater flexibility in housing design is needed in newly developing areas. Tighter controls may be appropriate in developed areas to protect the existing neighborhood character.

Perhaps open space requirements should change because of the age of residents or the lack of nearby parks.

. . . .

A new approach. The Building Block Zoning system uses the customary ingredients of zoning but arranges and applies them in new ways. Separate decisions can be made about the type of use, density, building form, setbacks, heights, coverage, open space and so on. These can be shaped into the most appropriate combination for a specific neighborhood.

In the building block approach, regulations are split into three major parts: 1) Use unit; 2) Development unit; and 3) Special Area unit.

The regulations for each unit are written separately; then zones are created by combining these three units. The major payoff of this approach is flexibility. Zones can be tailored to individual locations without the turmoil of drafting totally new zones. Regulations can be made as specific or as general as needed without legislative overload or widespread public controversy.

The first part of Building Block Zoning, the use unit, is the most fundamental element. It defines what uses are permitted in the zone. San Diego, for example, has six basic types of use: residential, commercial, industrial, civic, agricultural and extractive. . . . Each use unit can accommodate several diverse but compatible use types. . . .

The second building block, the development unit, specifies how uses can be developed. It sets physical ranges and limits for builders and developers for variables such as density, lot size, building form, bulk, floor area ratio, height, coverage, setback and open space. Other standards can be included, substituted or added in the future; parking, animals and landscaping are some that concern many communities.

. . . Development standards can be listed in tables, such as the Height Schedule. Selections can be made from each of the tables to create a set of regulations fitted to a particular neighborhood.

Height Schedule
(partial listing)

Designator	Maximum Height (feet)	Maximum Number of Stories
A	15	1
B	20	2
C	25	2
D	25	3
E	30	2
F	30	3
G	35	2
H	35	3
I	35	4
J	40	3
K	40	4
L	45	4

Apart from some general guidelines, the makeup of the development unit is independent of the use unit. This provides flexibility unknown in current zoning. Two neighborhoods may be designated R-10 residential use unit, but one may be zoned for a density of four units per acre with detached structures as the building form, while the other may be zoned for eight units per acre with attached and semidetached structures. Under usual zoning practice, two areas labelled R-10 would have exactly the same requirements.

PROTOTYPICAL AREAS

Prior Physical Conditions

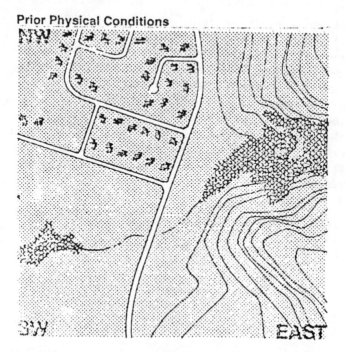

Prior Physical Conditions

Recommended Zoning and Ultimate Development

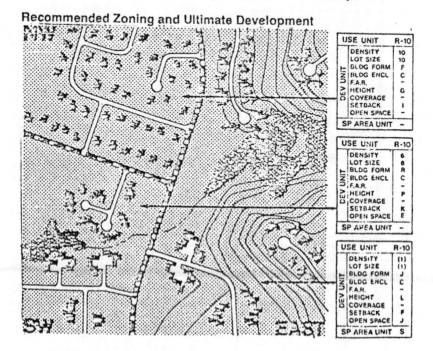

Recommended Zoning and Ultimate Development

The third building block is the special area unit. It is similar to many overlay or additive zones already used in zoning ordinances. A special area unit applies to sites that have unusual geologic, topographic, scenic or development characteristics. . . . Flood plains, flood channels, scenic areas, beaches, bluffs and planned development areas are possible special areas. Extra standards are written for these sensitive locations. For instance, on coastal bluffs the county may require all buildings to be set back 50 feet from the edge. On ocean beaches construction may be limited to life guard stations, concession stands and changing rooms. Construction may be banned within a zone along faults, and special building methods may be required in other nearby earthquake prone areas. The special area regulations also are independently variable from use and development restrictions.

. . . .

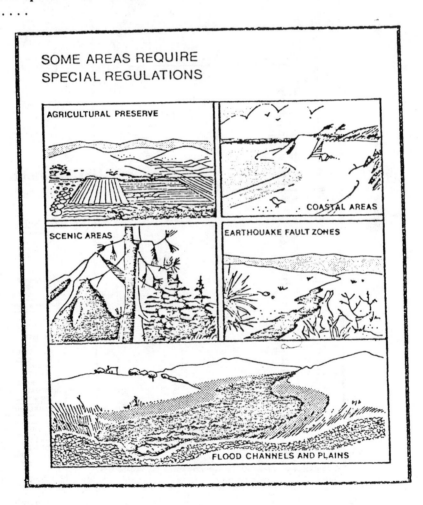

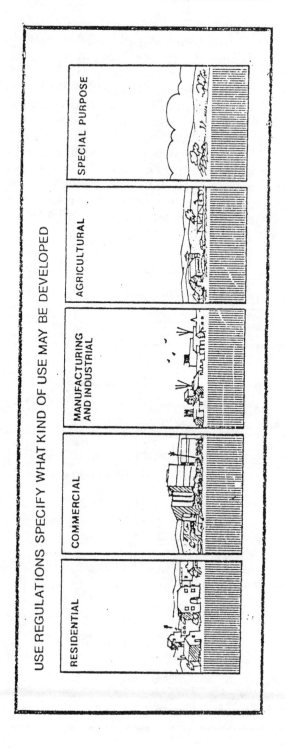

Comments: The building block zoning technique clearly has application outside the city core, and appears especially useful as a method for handling densities and development requirements in suburban and in environmentally fragile areas. It should be contrasted with large lot zoning, which is considered in the next section as the most commonly used method for controlling residential density in suburban areas.

b. In the Suburban Fringe

SIMON v. NEEDHAM

Supreme Judicial Court of Massachusetts
311 Mass. 560, 42 N.E.2d 516 (1942)

RONAN, J. This is a petition filed in the Land Court in accordance with G. L. (Ter. Ed.) c. 240, § 14A and c. 185, § 1 (j½), both as inserted by St. 1934, c. 263, to determine the validity and extent of a zoning by-law which prescribed a minimum area of one acre for house lots in the residential district in which the petitioner's land was located. The judge of the Land Court made a written decision which included findings of fact and rulings of law. He ordered the petition dismissed. The petitioner excepted to certain rulings, to the refusal to give the rulings requested by him, and to the order dismissing the petition.

Needham is a suburb of Boston located twelve miles from the center of Boston, having an area of about eight thousand one hundred sixty-two acres, and a population of approximately thirteen thousand which has been steadily increasing for the last twelve years. It is essentially a residential community with a few manufacturing plants. It has two local business centers and also a small business district containing a number of garages in the northeasterly part of the town where a main traffic route intersects one of the principal highways of the town. A branch line of a railroad having five stations serves the town as do also three bus lines.

The land now owned by the petitioner has been in a single residence district since the adoption of a zoning by-law by the town in 1925. There was no minimum house lot area for the district until 1931, when an area of seven thousand square feet was established. This area was increased in 1939 to ten thousand square feet. The by-law contains a provision authorizing the board of appeals to permit the use of a smaller lot in certain instances. This by-law was amended on July 21, 1941, by dividing the single residence zone into two districts, A and B. All the building lots in district A, which included nearly all of the south side of the town, were required to be at least an acre in area. This new district then comprised one hundred eighty-nine lots, thirty-three of them having an area of less than an acre and others having an area of many acres. The petitioner's land was located in district A.

Early in June, 1941, the petitioner entered into an agreement to purchase a triangular parcel of land, which was bounded on each side by a public highway, and contained about twenty-four and one half acres. He had a plan prepared showing the subdivision of this parcel into fifty-eight lots, varying in area from thirteen thousand five hundred to twenty-seven thousand square feet, and submitted the plan at a hearing before the planning board, which took the matter under advisement. He then recorded this plan and a later plan in the registry of deeds. The transfer of the land to him was recorded later in July, 1941. The planning board on August 19, 1941, disapproved the plan submitted to it because the lots did not comply with the by-law as amended.

The petitioner's lot is covered with a small growth of pine, scrub oak and birches and is suitably adapted for the construction of dwellings. It is located in a stretch of rolling country side, which comprises undeveloped woodland, tillage and pasture land, except for swamp land where the land slopes down to the Charles River. The Charles River and Sabrina Lake districts are the sites of country estates, with expensive buildings and large acreages. The land in question is about three quarters of a mile distant from these districts.

There was evidence tending to show a steady demand for new homes in the town. During the four years commencing with January 1, 1937, more than four hundred fifty permits have been issued by the building inspector for the construction of dwellings. There was also evidence that the value of the petitioner's land had been diminished by reason of the requirement that the area of house lots should be at least an acre.

The issue presented for decision is whether the town had the power to prescribe this minimum area for lots in the residential district in which the petitioner's land is located.

A city or town is expressly empowered to adopt zoning ordinances or by-laws "For the purpose of promoting the health, safety, convenience, morals or welfare of its inhabitants" and to "regulate ... the size and width of lots." G. L. (Ter. Ed.) c. 40, § 25, as appearing in St. 1933, c. 269, § 1. Municipalities have the right to determine whether the public interests demand an exercise of the power and, if so, to select the measures that are necessary for the protection of such interests. A city or town is justified in asserting the power where the interests of the public require such action and where the means employed are reasonably necessary for the accomplishment of the purpose. The authority of the respondent town to regulate the size of house lots is not challenged, but its authority to fix the area at a minimum of an acre is assailed. We have upheld regulations establishing one-family residential districts, ... and those prescribing open spaces of certain sizes in the front, sides and rear of a dwelling. . . .

The physical characteristics of the district itself, considered in conjunction with those of the town, strongly indicate that the district is admirably suited for one family residences. Its nearness to Boston and other densely populated areas makes it available for residential purposes for those who desire the advantages of the quiet and beauty of rural surroundings. The evidence shows a steady demand for homes in the town, and that the development of different areas for the construction of homes has already begun and will probably continue. The establishment of a neighborhood of homes in such a way as to avoid congestion in the streets, to secure safety from fire and other dangers, to prevent overcrowding of land, to obtain adequate light, air and sunshine, and to enable it to be furnished with transportation, water, light, sewer and other public necessities, which when established would tend to improve and beautify the town and would harmonize with the natural characteristics of the locality, could be materially facilitated by a regulation that prescribed a reasonable minimum area for house lots. The area was to be determined not only in the light of present needs of the public but also with a view to the probable requirements of the public that would arise in the immediate future from the normal development of the land. The advantages enjoyed by those living in one family dwellings located upon an acre lot might be thought to exceed those possessed by persons living upon a lot of ten thousand square feet. More freedom from noise and traffic might result. The danger from fire from outside sources might be reduced. A better opportunity for rest and relaxation might be afforded. Greater facilities for children to play on the premises and not in the streets would be available. There may perhaps be more inducement for one to attempt something in the way of the cultivation of flowers, shrubs and vegetables. There may be other advantages accruing to the occupants of the larger lots. The benefits derived by those living in such a neighborhood must be considered with the benefit that would accrue to the public generally who resided in Needham by the presence of such a neighborhood. In the four towns that adjoin Needham the minimum area restrictions for some residential lots have been fixed in one at twenty thousand square feet, in two others at forty thousand square feet, and in the fourth at an acre. Of eight other towns within a short distance from Needham, six have prescribed a minimum area of forty thousand square feet for house lots, and two others have fixed the minimum area as an acre. Such evidence is not decisive that the imposition of a restriction of an area of an acre is reasonable and proper, but it is persuasive that many other communities when faced with an apparently similar problem have determined that the public interest was best served by the adoption of a restriction in some instances identical and in others nearly identical with that imposed by the respondent town. . . .

There may be a difference of opinion as to the real advantages that will accrue from the larger lots and whether they are such as to lead one to the conclusion that the adoption of the acre area will result in a real and genuine enhancement of the public interests. It seems to us that a belief that such a result may be realized in this instance is not unreasonable. It seems to be supported to some extent by what has already been decided in *Brett* v. *Building Commissioner of Brookline,* 250 Mass. 73, 145 N. E. 269. If the question is fairly debatable we cannot substitute our judgment for that of the citizens who voted in favor of the amendment, and, whatever our personal opinions may be as to the wisdom of the amendment, we cannot pronounce the measure invalid. . . .

The by-law does not prohibit the petitioner from developing his land as a site for homes, and although the restriction as to area might not permit him to secure as much profit as he would if the by-law had not been amended, yet this factor, while entitled to consideration in passing upon the reasonableness of the amendment, does not afford sufficient ground for striking down the by-law in the absence of a showing that it goes beyond what the protection of the public interests requires. . . .

The planning board of the town reported, at the special town meeting that adopted the amendment, recommending the passage of the amendment on the ground that the town was receiving more than $60,000 in taxes from district A, that on account of the small amount of municipal service required by the district a tax profit of nearly $50,000 or $2 on the tax rate had resulted, and that there would be a much higher tax rate if the district was developed with low cost houses. The expense that might be incurred by a town in furnishing police and fire protection, the construction and maintenance of public ways, schoolhouses, water mains and sewers and other public conveniences might be considered as an element, more or less incidentally involved, in the adoption of a zoning by-law that will promote the health, safety, convenience, morals or welfare of the inhabitants of the town without imposing any unreasonable and arbitrary burden upon the landowners. A zoning by-law cannot be adopted for the purpose of setting up a barrier against the influx of thrifty and respectable citizens who desire to live there and who are able and willing to erect homes upon lots upon which fair and reasonable restrictions have been imposed nor for the purpose of protecting the large estates that are already located in the district. The strictly local interests of the town must yield if it appears that they are plainly in conflict with the general interests of the public at large, and in such instances the interest of "the municipality would not be allowed to stand in the way." *Euclid* v. *Ambler Realty Co.,* 272 U. S. 365, 390. . . . We assume in favor of the petitioner that a zoning by-law cannot be used primarily as a device to maintain a low tax rate.

It does not appear that it was so used here. It cannot be assumed that the voters in following the recommendations of the board were activated by the reasons mentioned by the board. . . . These reasons dealt with merely one phase of a subject under discussion at the town meeting. We do not know what other considerations were advanced for the passage of the amendment. The citizens of the town were undoubtedly familiar with the locality and with all the material factors involved in the necessity, character and degree of regulation that should be adopted in the public interest. The action of the voters is not to be invalidated simply because someone presented a reason that was unsound or insufficient in law to support the conclusion for which it was urged. It was said in *Attorney General* v. *Williams,* 178 Mass. 330, 335, 52 N. E. 812, 813, in reference to a statute, that it was the duty of this court to sustain it if a reasonable construction shows it to be valid "even if it appeared that in the endeavors which suggested the legislation, considerations were presented to the Legislature which would not be a sufficient constitutional justification for such an enactment.". . .

The ruling dismissing the petition necessarily included an implied ruling that the by-law was valid. There was no error in refusing the rulings requested. The petitioner properly does not now contend that any rights accrued to him by filing his plans of the subdivision of the land in the registry of deeds without securing their approval by the planning board. We cannot quite pronounce the instant by-law invalid when applied to the petitioner's land in all the circumstances disclosed by this record. We make no intimation that, if the lots were required to be larger than an acre or if the circumstances were even slightly different, the same result would be reached. It will be time enough to determine that question when it is presented.

Exceptions overruled.

Comments: 1. A number of justifications for one-acre zoning were advanced in the principal case. While it may be conceded that large lots will reduce "congestion in the streets" by keeping the density of population relatively low, what do you think of the argument that one-acre lot minimums will operate "to secure safety from fire and other dangers, to prevent overcrowding of land, to obtain adequate light, air and sunshine, and to enable it [the land] to be furnished with transportation, light, sewer and other public necessities"? Assuming, *arguendo,* that quarter-acre lots would be adequate to achieve all these objectives, what justification is there for requiring one-acre lots? In any case, how can large lot zoning aid the municipality in providing adequate "transportation, light, sewer and other public necessities" in light of the fact that more miles of streets, sewer lines, water mains, and the like must be constructed to provide for a given population when land development occurs at low densities? Can one-acre lot minimums be justified on the suggested theories that they will provide more freedom from noise, a better opportunity for rest and relaxation, greater facilities for children to play on the premises rather than in the streets, and more inducement for residents to attempt something in the way of cultivation of flowers, shrubs and vegetables? If these desirable objectives fall within the concept of "general welfare," should the entire municipal area not be zoned for one-acre minimum lot sizes?

2. What about the fiscal considerations mentioned by the court in the principal case? Granted that the total cost of "furnishing police and fire protection" and "the construction and maintenance of public ways, schoolhouses, water mains and sewers and other public conveniences" would be greater if development occurs at higher densities, what evidence is there that the cost per house will be greater? Why should there be a higher tax rate if "district A" were to be developed at a higher density than one house per acre? Why should the houses constructed on half-acre or quarter-acre lots necessarily be "low cost houses"? If a "zoning by-law" cannot be used *primarily* as a device to maintain a low tax rate, how much weight should the court give to fiscal considerations in determining the validity of large lot zoning?

3. In addition to the justifications for large lot requirements advanced in the principal case — most of which may also be found in the opinions of other courts — various courts in approving large minimum lot sizes have suggested the following justifications:

(a) Preservation of the semi-rural character and appearance of a suburban community by assuring sufficient open space around buildings to creat a dominant visual impression of open space rather than structures. The court may have had this in mind in the principal case when it referred to "the advantages of the . . . beauty of rural surroundings." The rationale is more fully developed in *Gignoux v. Village of Kings Point,* 99 N.Y.S.2d 280 (N.Y. Sup.Ct. 1950) (one acre). *See also Levitt v. Village of Sands Point,* 160 N.E.2d 501 (N.Y. 1959) (two acres); *Senior v. Zoning Comm'n,* 153 A.2d 415 (Conn. 1959), *appeal dismissed,* 363 U.S. 143 (1960) (four acres); *Fischer v. Bedminster Township,* 93 A.2d 378 (N.J. 1952) (five acres); *Flora Realty & Inv. Co. v. City of Ladue,* 246 S.W.2d 771 (Mo.), *appeal dismissed,* 344 U.S. 802 (1952) (three acres).

(b) Preservation of specific historic sites and buildings in their historic settings. *County Comm'rs v. Miles,* 228 A.2d 450 (Md. 1967) (five acres).

(c) Preservation for low density development sites which, because of their topography, are not easily buildable for higher density development. *Metropolitan Homes, Inc. v. Town Plan & Zoning Comm'n,* 202 A.2d 241 (Conn. 1964) (30,000 sq. ft.). *See also Senior v. Zoning Comm'n, supra* at para. (a); *Larsen v. Zoning Comm'n,* 217 A.2d 715 (Conn. 1966) (one acre); *Fischer v. Bedminster Township, supra* at para. (a); *Bogert v. Washington Township,* 135 A.2d 1 (N.J. 1957) (one acre); *Honeck v. County of Cook,* 146 N.E.2d 35 (Ill. 1957) (five acres); *Flora Realty & Inv. Co. v. City of Ladue, supra* at para. (a).

(d) Provision of large enough building sites to assure a safe water supply and safe sewage disposal in areas without a public water supply and/or without public sanitary sewers. *De Mars v. Zoning Comm'n,* 115 A.2d 653 (Conn. 1955) (one acre); *Zygmont v. Planning & Zoning Comm'n,*

210 A.2d 172 (Conn. 1965) (four acres); *Carruthers v. Board of Adjustment,* 290 S.W.2d 340 (Tex. Civ. App. 1956) (one acre); *Salamar Builders Corp. v. Tuttle,* 275 N.E.2d 585 (N.Y. 1971) (two acres).

(e) Preservation of the natural capacity of the soil to absorb rainfall by limiting the area built upon, and thus to provide protection against flooding and soil erosion after heavy rains. *Bogert v. Washington Township, supra* at para. (c).

(f) Regulation of the rate and pattern of suburban growth to assure orderly, efficient, and economical expansion of necessary public facilities. *Rockaway Estates v. Rockaway Township,* 119 A.2d 461 (N.J. Super. 1955); *Flora Realty & Inv. Co. v. City of Ladue, supra* at para. (a).

(g) Implementation of specific planning principles as to proper organization of residential areas. *Padover v. Farmington Township,* 132 N.W.2d 687 (Mich. 1965) (20,000 sq. ft., based on "neighborhoods of the optimum size" to "support an elementary school of an ideal size and ... location").

(h) Preservation of community identity by providing predominantly open areas ("green belts") between communities. *Norbeck Village Joint Venture v. Montgomery County Council,* 254 A.2d 700 (Md. 1969) (two acres). *See also Morse v. County of San Luis Obispo,* 55 Cal. Rptr. 710 (Cal. App. 1967).

(i) Provision of some "high class" low-density residential areas, viewed as essential to the local economy, and prevention of the "blanketing" of the community with small, low-cost houses. *Clary v. Borough of Eatontown,* 124 A.2d 54 (N.J. App. Div. 1956) (half an acre).

(j) Protection of the value of houses previously constructed on large lots against the depreciation that would result "if sections here and there are developed with smaller lots." *Flora Realty & Inv. Co. v. City of Ladue, supra* at para. (a).

4. Assuming that Needham still allowed houses on 10,000 square foot lots in its residence district "B," would it have been relevant in the principal case to ascertain how much of the undeveloped land in Needham was placed in district "A" and how much in district "B"?

In *Flora Realty & Inv. Co. v. City of Ladue, supra* Comment 3, para. (a), the city's area was zoned as follows: 22 percent for three-acre lots, 32 percent for 1.8 acre lots, 18 percent for 30,000 sq. ft. lots, 7 percent for 15,000 sq. ft. lots, and 2 percent for 10,000 sq. ft. lots. About one half of the area zoned for three acre and 1.8 acre lots was already developed, with an average lot size of about five acres in recent developments in the three acre district. The three acre lot minimums were held valid as applied to a tract located on high and rolling terrain and surrounded by houses already constructed on large (mostly five acre) lots.

In *Senior v. Zoning Comm'n, supra* Comment 3, para. (a), 14 percent of the undeveloped building sites were in a four acre zone; 42 percent were in a two acre zone; 17 percent were in a one acre zone; two percent were in a half acre zone; and 25 percent were in zones requiring less than one half an acre. The court sustained the four acre lot minimums, and said: "[h]aving in mind New Canaan's present population of under 16,000, we cannot say ... that the effect of upgrading of the zone [to four acre minimums] is to limit ownership of new homes in the town to the wealthy." *Id.* at 418.

5. As the previous Comment indicates, most communities adopting large lot zoning usually enact variable lot size requirements; minimums vary in different sectors of the community. This practice would appear to be open to an equal protection objection but has seldom been challenged. In *Medinger Appeal*, 104 A.2d 118 (Pa. 1954), the Pennsylvania court held unconstitutional a variable minimum house size requirement; see *supra* p. 369. It noted:

> But if a 1000-minimum habitable square feet is reasonable and proper for every home in one district and does not adversely affect the health, morals or safety of the occupants of such house, 1125 square feet of habitable floor area in a nearby house cannot adversely affect the health, morals or safety of that house or that community.

Id. at 122. Are these comments applicable to variable minimum lot sizes?

NATIONAL LAND & INVESTMENT CO. v. KOHN

Supreme Court of Pennsylvania
419 Pa. 504, 215 A.2d 597 (1965)

ROBERTS, Justice.

These appeals are taken from an order of the Court of Common Pleas of Chester County which held unconstitutional a provision of the Easttown Township zoning ordinance which required a minimum area of four acres per building lot in certain residential districts in the township.

. . . .

[The court's discussion of procedural issues is omitted. — Eds.]

II. Validity of Four Acre Zoning

Easttown Township has an area of 8.2 square miles devoted almost exclusively to residential use. It is traversed in the north by the Main Line of the Pennsylvania Railroad as well as by U. S. Route 30, a heavily traveled highway which emanates in Philadelphia, 20 miles to the east, and heads west to Lancaster and eventually to the West Coast. It is along this strip that the township's sole commercial activity is conducted and where its two small industrial concerns are located.

The township finds itself in the path of a population expansion approaching from two directions. From the east, suburbs closer to the center of Philadelphia are reaching capacity and residential development is extending further west to Easttown. In addition, a market for residential sites is being generated by the fast growing industrial-commercial complex in the King of Prussia-Valley Forge area to the north of Easttown Township.

Easttown's vital statistics provide a good indication of its character. At present, about 60% of the township's population resides in an area of about 20% of the township. The remaining 40% of the population occupies the balance of about 80% of its area. Privately imposed restrictions limit lot areas to four, five and ten acre minimums on approximately 10% of the total area of the township, consisting of land located in the southern and western sections. Of the total 5,157 acres in the township, some 898, or about 17%, have been restricted by the new zoning ordinance to minimum lots of two acres. Approximately 1,565 acres composing about 30% of the township are restricted by the zoning ordinance to lots of four acres minimum area. About 5% of the population live in the areas zoned for two and four acre sites which together constitute about 47% of the township. Some 1,835 acres, representing about 35% of the township, remain unaffected by the new zoning and continue, under the township's original zoning classification, to be zoned for building sites with a minimum area of one acre.

Before 1959 most of the northeast quadrant of the township, as well as various other areas, had either been built up or prepared for development. In 1959 sporadic developments occurred in the south and central parts of the township, followed by several others in the south and southeast portions in 1960. In 1961 other developments occurred in the northeast and southwest sections, followed by lesser numbers in smaller areas of the north and central sections in 1962 and 1963.

U. S. Census figures show that Easttown's population grew from 2,307 in 1920 to 6,907 in 1960. As of April, 1963, the population estimate was 8,400. Public school population through the sixth grade grew from 498 in the school year 1955-56 to 1,052 in the school year 1963-64 and, as projected, will be about 1,680 in 1969-70.

New residential construction from 1951 through the first eight months of 1963, a twelve year period, consisted of 1,149 units at an estimated cost of about $21,000,000, with an average of 100 building permits annually. At this rate of growth, allowing four persons per housing unit in Easttown,[36] its population, related to new residences, would grow under the previous one acre minimum zoning at the rate of about 400 persons per annum.

Despite the growth and development of Easttown Township, much of the land in the central, southern and western sections continues to be held in parcels of considerable acreage. "Sweetbriar", located on the southern boundary of the township, is one of these large parcels. There is discussion in the briefs as to whether the township, and particularly those sections zoned for four acres, is rural. Such semantic disputes are of little relevance in zoning cases since realities, rather than the label which, for convenience sake, is applied

---

[36] U. S. Census figures from 1960 show 210,680 inhabitants in Chester County with an average of 3.5 individuals occupying each of the county's 58,947 housing units.

to them, are determinative of the issue. However, if a catch-all designation is to be applied, "semi-rural" or "estate rural" probably best describes the portions of the township zoned for minimum lots of four acres.

The task of considering the Easttown Township zoning ordinance and passing upon the constitutionality of its four acre minimum area requirement as applied to appellees' property is not an easy one. . . . The zoning power is one of the tools of government which, in order to be effective, must not be subjected to judicial interference unless clearly necessary. For this reason, a presumption of validity attaches to a zoning ordinance which imposes the burden to prove its invalidity upon the one who challenges it. . . .

While recognizing this presumption, we must also appreciate the fact that zoning involves governmental restrictions upon a landowner's constitutionally guaranteed right to use his property, unfettered, except in very specific instances, by governmental restrictions. The time must never come when, because of frustration with concepts foreign to their legal training, courts abdicate their judicial responsibility to protect the constitutional rights of individual citizens. Thus, the burden of proof imposed upon one who challenges the validity of a zoning regulation must never be made so onerous as to foreclose, for all practical purposes, a landowner's avenue of redress against the infringement of constitutionally protected rights.

The oft repeated, although ill defined, limitation upon the exercise of the zoning power requires that zoning ordinances be enacted for the health, safety, morals or general welfare of the community. . . . Such ordinances must bear a substantial relationship to those police power purposes. . . . Regulations adopted pursuant to that power must not be unreasonable, arbitrary or confiscatory. . . .

. . . .

There is no doubt that in Pennsylvania, zoning for density is a legitimate exercise of the police power. . . . Every zoning case involves a different set of facts and circumstances in light of which the constitutionality of a zoning ordinance must be tested. Therefore, it is impossible for us to say that any minimum acreage requirement is unconstitutional per se. See Annot., 95 A.L.R. 2d 716 (1964).[37]

The relative advantages of a one acre lot over a one-half acre lot are easy to comprehend. Similarly, a two acre lot has advantages over

---

[37] Both appellants and appellees refer us to cases in other jurisdictions which have both sustained and invalidated the type of low density zoning at issue in the present case. While we accept those cases for the proposition that four acre zoning is not per se unconstitutional, we consider them of little value on the specific issues involved here.

a one acre lot and three acres may be preferred over two acres or ten acres over three. The greater the amount of land, the more room for children, the less congestion, the easier to handle water supply and sewage, and the fewer municipal services which must be provided. At some point along the spectrum, however, the size of lots ceases to be a concern requiring public regulation and becomes simply a matter of private preference. The point at which legitimate public interest ceases is not a constant one, but one which varies with the land involved and the circumstances of each case.

We turn, then, to the question of the constitutionality of a four acre minimum in the factual context of the instant case. Quite obviously, appellees will be deprived of part of the value of their property if they are limited in the use of it to four acre lots.[38] When divided into one acre lots as originally planned, the value of "Sweetbriar" for residential building was approximately $260,000. When the four acre restriction was imposed, the number of available building sites in "Sweetbriar" was reduced by 75% and the value of the land, under the most optimistic appraisal, fell to $175,000. The four acre minimum greatly restricts the marketability of this tract because, with fewer potential lots, the cost of improvements such as curbing, streets and other facilities is thus greater on each lot. In addition, each building lot being larger, the cost per lot is automatically increased. The desire of many buyers not to be burdened with the upkeep of a four acre lot also makes "Sweetbriar", so restricted, less desirable. Although there was some evidence in the record that lots of four acres or more could eventually be sold, it is clear that there is not a readily available market for such offerings.

Against this deprivation of value, the alleged public purposes cited as justification for the imposition of a four acre minimum area requirement upon appellees' land must be examined. Appellants contend that the four acre minimum is necessary to insure proper sewage disposal in the township and to protect township water from pollution. At present, only a very small portion of the township in the densely populated northern section is served by a sewage system. The remainder of the lots in the township utilize on-site sewage disposal. With regard to water supply, the evidence was fairly conclusive that the Philadelphia Suburban Water Company serves most, if not all, of the township and that it would furnish water to a development in "Sweetbriar".

. . . .

The township engineer's testimony on the subject of drainage and

---

[38] The mere fact that appellees suffer an economic loss is not sufficient reason to declare the zoning unconstitutional. *Tidewater Oil Co. v. Poore,* 395 Pa. 89, 149 A. 2d 636 (1959). Nevertheless, it is relevant to consider the economic effect of a zoning restriction on the landowner as an aspect of assessing the constitutionality of the ordinance. See Annot., 95 A.L.R. 2d 716, 732-34 (1964).

sewage was vague and unconvincing, consisting, as it did, of the bald statement that he felt that there was a danger of pollution. In addition, this opinion was based upon the hypothetical case of the *entire* township being developed on the basis of one acre lots *maximum,* a situation very unlikely to occur in the near future and probably never.

We can not help but note also that the Second Class Township Code provides for establishing sanitary regulations which can be enforced by a "sanitary board" regardless of the zoning for the area. The Code also provides for the installation and maintenance of sewer systems but the township has made no plans in this regard. In addition, under the township subdivision regulations, the zoning officer may require lots larger than the minimum permitted by the zoning ordinance if the result of percolation tests upon the land show that a larger land area is needed for proper drainage and disposal of sewage. These legislatively sanctioned methods for dealing with the sewage problem compel the conclusion that a four acre minimum is neither a necessary nor a reasonable method by which Easttown can protect itself from the menace of pollution.

In addition to the alleged problem of sewage disposal as justifying the four acre minimum, appellants cite the inadequacy of township roads and the burden which continued one acre zoning for the entire township would impose upon that road system.

As an adjunct to their argument regarding the inadequacy of the road system, appellants maintain that the four acre minimum zoning is warranted because of the difficulty of providing fire protection over the township roads. Because of the narrowness of the roads, their winding nature and the volume of traffic which they presently bear, a fire official responsible for the portion of Easttown Township in which "Sweetbriar" is located testified that difficulty is frequently encountered in getting equipment to a fire.

According to the experts produced for both sides, Easttown's present road network as a whole is capable, with normal maintenance and improvement, of serving a population up to 13,000. This is 4,600 more than the population of the township in April, 1963. On the basis of the former one acre zoning, resulting in a population increase of 400 persons per year, that figure would not be reached until after 1972 or later.

It can be seen, therefore, that the restriction to four acre lots, so far as traffic is concerned, is based upon possible future conditions. Zoning is a tool in the hands of governmental bodies which enables them to more effectively meet the demands of evolving and growing communities. It must not and can not be used by those officials as an instrument by which they may shirk their responsibilities. Zoning is a means by which a governmental body can plan for the future —

it may not be used as a means to deny the future.[39] The evidence on the record indicates that for the present and the immediate future the road system of Easttown Township is adequate to handle the traffic load. It is also quite convincing that the roads will become increasingly inadequate as time goes by and that improvements and additions will eventually have to be made. Zoning provisions may not be used, however, to avoid the increased responsibilities and economic burdens which time and natural growth invariably bring.

It is not difficult to envision the tremendous hardship, as well as the chaotic conditions, which would result if all the townships in this area decided to deny to a growing population sites for residential development within the means of at least a significant segment of the people.

The third justification for rezoning, and one urged upon us most assiduously, deals with the preservation of the "character" of this area.[40] The photographic exhibits placed in the record by appellants attest to the fact that this is an area of great beauty containing old homes surrounded by beautiful pasture, farm and woodland. It is a very desirable and attractive place in which to live.

Involved in preserving Easttown's "character" are four aspects of concern which the township gives for desiring four acre minimum zoning. First, they cite the preservation of open space and the creation of a "greenbelt" which, as most present day commentators impress upon us, are worthy goals. While in full agreement with these goals, we are convinced that four acre minimum zoning does not achieve the creation of a greenbelt in its technical sense and, to the limited extent that open space is so preserved, such zoning as is here involved is not a permissible means to that end.

By suggesting that the creation of a greenbelt is a purpose behind this zoning, appellants betray their argument that there is a ready market for four acre plots. Only if there is no market for four acre lots will the land continue to be open and undeveloped and a greenbelt created. This, however, would amount to confiscation of

---

[39] "*Any* traffic increase with its attendant noise, dirt, danger and hazards is unpleasant, yet, such increase is one of the 'inevitable accompaniments of suburban progress and of our constantly expanding population' which, *standing alone,* does not constitute a sufficient reason to refuse a property owner the legitimate use of his land . . . ." *Archbishop O'Hara's Appeal,* 389 Pa. 35, 54, 131 A. 2d 587, 596 (1957).

[40] Zoning may not be sustained *solely* on the basis of aesthetic considerations. See *Rogalski v. Upper Chichester Twp.,* 406 Pa. 550, 178 A. 2d 712 (1962). See also *Anstine v. Zoning Bd. of Adjustment,* 411 Pa. 33, 43, 190 A. 2d 712, 717 (1963). In the instant case, however, there is nothing inherently unaesthetic about one acre zoning which makes it less desirable than four acre zoning. For this reason, "character zoning" involves considerations which differ somewhat from those involved with zoning for aesthetics.

the property of Easttown landowners for which they must be compensated.

If the preservation of open spaces is the township objective, there are means by which this can be accomplished which include authorization for "cluster zoning" or condemnation of development rights with compensation paid for that which is taken. A four acre minimum acreage requirement is not a reasonable method by which the stated end can be achieved.

Next, the township urges us to consider the historical sites in the township and the need to present them in the proper setting. We are unmoved by this contention since it appears to be purely and simply a makeweight. First, an examination of the map of historical sites in the township demonstrates that the overwhelming majority of such sites, located in areas of dense population, can hardly be provided with proper settings by four acre zoning elsewhere in the township. . . .

Closely related to the goal of protecting historic monuments is the expressed desire to protect the "setting" for a number of old homes in Easttown, some dating back to the early days of our Commonwealth. Appellants denominate this goal as falling within the ambit of promoting the "general welfare". Unfortunately, the concept of the general welfare defies meaningful capsule definition and constitutes an exceedingly difficult standard against which to test the validity of legislation. However, it must always be ascertained at the outset whether, in fact, it is the *public* welfare which is being benefited or whether, disguised as legislation for the public welfare, a zoning ordinance actually serves purely private interests.

There is no doubt that many of the residents of this area are highly desirous of keeping it the way it is, preferring, quite naturally, to look out upon land in its natural state rather than on other homes. These desires, however, do not rise to the level of public welfare. This is purely a matter of private desire which zoning regulation may not be employed to effectuate.

Appellants make some attempt to impose upon this area an aura of historic significance which deserves the protection of the township. Of course, the fact that these houses are old makes them architecturally and historically interesting. But it does not justify the creation of a special setting for them. They are all privately owned; most are already surrounded by substantial land holdings which, if their owners so desire, serve as protection against being "fenced in" by new residential development. In addition, there is nothing about south Easttown which differentiates it from any other area in the southeastern section of Pennsylvania. Surely, no one would seriously maintain that the entire southeast corner of the state should be declared immune from further development on areas of less than four acres simply because there are many old homes located there.

The fourth argument advanced by appellants, and one closely analogous to the preceding one, is that the rural character of the area must be preserved. If the township were developed on the basis of this zoning, however, it could not be seriously contended that the land would retain its rural character — it would simply be dotted with larger homes on larger lots.

Appellants point to the fact that the surrounding townships have similar low density zoning provisions. Although the zoning of the surrounding area is frequently a relevant consideration in assessing the validity of a zoning regulation, . . . it is not controlling on the issue presented. This is particularly so when we are dealing with a unique zoning classification such as is involved here. With most zoning classifications, there can be little question as to their suitability in any political subdivision; the only issue concerns their placement. With these classifications, the surrounding zoning is particularly relevant. As the classification itself becomes more questionable, however, similar classifications in surrounding districts become of less significance in supporting the validity of the restriction.

The briefs submitted by each appellant in this case are revealing in that they point up the two factors which appear to lie at the heart of their fight for four acre zoning.

The township's brief raises (but, unfortunately, does not attempt to answer) the interesting issue of the township's responsibility to those who do not yet live in the township but who are part, or may become part, of the population expansion to the suburbs. Four acre zoning represents Easttown's position that it does not desire to accommodate those who are pressing for admittance to the township unless such admittance will not create any additional burdens upon governmental functions and services. The question posed is whether the township can stand in the way of the natural forces which send our growing population into hitherto undeveloped areas in search of a comfortable place to live. We have concluded not. A zoning ordinance whose primary purpose is to prevent the entrance of newcomers in order to avoid future burdens, economic and otherwise, upon the administration of public services and facilities can not be held valid. Of course, we do not mean to imply that a governmental body may not utilize its zoning power in order to insure that the municipal services which the community requires are provided in an orderly and rational manner.

The brief of the appellant-intervenors creates less of a problem but points up the factors which sometime lurk behind the espoused motives for zoning. What basically appears to bother intervenors is that a small number of lovely old homes will have to start keeping company with a growing number of smaller, less expensive, more densely located houses. It is clear, however, that the general welfare is not fostered or promoted by a zoning ordinance designed to be exclusive and exclusionary.[41] But this does not mean that individual action is foreclosed. "An owner of land may constitutionally make his property as large and as private or secluded or exclusive as he desires and his purse can afford. He may, for example, singly or with his neighbors, purchase sufficient neighboring land to protect and preserve by restrictions in deeds or by covenants inter se, the privacy, a minimum acreage, the quiet, peaceful atmosphere and the tone and character of the community which existed when he or they moved there."

In light of the foregoing, therefore, we are compelled to conclude that the board of adjustment committed an error of law in upholding the constitutionality of the Easttown Township four acre minimum requirement as applied to appellees' property. We therefore affirm the order of the Court of Common Pleas of Chester County.

Order affirmed.

Mr. Justice Jones dissents.

Dissenting Opinion by Mr. Justice Cohen:

. . . .

The majority recognizes that "The task of considering the Easttown Township zoning ordinance and passing upon the constitutionality of its four acre minimum area requirement as applied to appellees' property is not an easy one." To me it becomes very easy to uphold the constitutionality when one recognizes, as the record discloses, that the legislative authority of Easttown Township gave the overall planning of the township considerable study. The four acre restriction was not applied to the entire township, but was only one part of a three part class "A" residential zoning enactment — one of four acres, one of two acres, and one of one acre. This zoning determination for type "A" residential properties included 3,297 acres of the 5,157 acre township and included 2,468 acres of undeveloped property for which no public sewage was available and which also included areas of poor natural drainage and varied stream pollution. It seems a reasonable and proper exercise of the legislative function for the township commissioners to take what is comparatively a small area (3,297 acres), divide it into residential zones and restrict a certain number of the residential zones to four acre lots — some to two and some to one.

Hence, I differ with the majority in three basic areas: (1) I would never get to the constitutional issue by the exercise of proper judicial restraint; (2) I would not permit this Court to become township supervisors and legislate a zoning law as it does, and (3) I would not

---

[41] "And, of course, minimum lot areas may not be ordained so large as to be exclusionary in effect and, thereby, serve a private rather than the public interest." *Bilbar Constr. Co. v. Easttown Twp. Bd. of Adjustment,* 393 Pa. 62, 76, 141 A. 2d 851, 858 (1958); accord, *Simon v. Needham,* 311 Mass. 560, 42 N.E. 2d 516 (1942).

hold a properly enacted zoning code to be unconstitutional when the only argument in support of so doing is the appellees' loss of profits.

I dissent.

Comments: 1. In an earlier case from Easttown, the Pennsylvania Supreme Court first struck down a one-acre minimum lot size requirement and then, after reargument, sustained it by a 4-3 vote. *Bilbar Constr. Co. v. Easttown Township Bd. of Adjustment,* 141 A.2d 851 (Pa. 1958). The Easttown zoning ordinance then provided for a sliding scale of minimum lot areas for various residential districts — 5,000 square feet, 8,500 square feet, 14,000 square feet, 21,000 square feet, and one acre. There was evidence that the soil and drainage of plaintiff's land was adequate for on-site sewage disposal on smaller lots. The township commissioners contended that the one acre zoning was needed because "any less area would (a) substantially increase taxes, and (b) eventually necessitate additional police, a new fire engine, and an addition to or the construction of a new school, and (c) create a density of population which would be injurious to safety in the event of an atomic attack." On the rehearing, the majority applied the usual presumption in favor of the validity of zoning regulations and held that plaintiff had introduced no evidence to rebut the presumption.

2. After the principal case, the Pennsylvania court struck down two and three acre lot minimums in *Concord Township Appeal,* 268 A.2d 765 (Pa. 1970) (reported unofficially as *Appeal of Kit-Mar Builders, Inc.*). The decision was by a 4-3 vote, but Chief Justice Bell only concurred in the result, and did not specifically concur in the "principal opinion" by Justice Roberts, which seems to hold that lot minimums higher than one acre are invalid *per se.* The Roberts opinion includes the following passages:

> The two and three acre minimums imposed in this case are no more reasonable than the four acre requirements struck down in *National Land.* . . . [M]inimum lot sizes of the magnitude required by this ordinance are a great deal larger than what should be considered as a *necessary* size for the building of a house, and are therefore not the proper subjects of public regulation. . . . Absent some extraordinary justification, a zoning ordinance with minimum lot sizes such as those in this case is completely unreasonable. . . .
>
> . . .[W]e cannot ignore the fact that in the narrow confines of the case before us, Concord Township's argument that three-acre minimum zoning is necessary for adequate on-site sewerage is patently ridiculous. . . . This argument assumes that all of the lot where the house is not is necessary for waste effluence, which simply is not what happens. The difference in size between a three-acre lot and a one-acre lot is irrelevant to the problem of sewage disposal, absent the construction of a house of an unimaginably enormous magnitude. . . .
>
> Thinly veiled justifications for exclusionary zoning will not be countenanced by this Court. . . .

Id. at 766, 767, 769, 770.

The *Concord Township Appeal* "principal opinion" is remarkable in its failure to marshal relevant facts to support the "exclusionary zoning" argument. As Norman Williams, Jr., has pointed out,

> There is no indication as to how large an area was so zoned (a few tracts or most of the township?), or on what type of terrain; there is no discussion of the land use pattern, the housing market, or the distribution of income in the township; there is no analysis of the relation between land cost and housing cost; there is not even any indication of the location of the township, and of the land in question, in relation to metropolitan growth patterns. The case was decided on abstract principle, as if the Brandeis-brief technique had not yet been invented.

2 N. Williams, American Land Planning Law 105 (1974).

In his dissenting opinion in *Concord Township Appeal,* Justice Jones noted that there was at least substantial evidence in the record from expert witnesses to indicate the possibility of a public health threat from development of the tract in question on one-acre lots, at least as to a substantial part of the tract. In addition, Justice Jones said:

> Concord Township has no municipal sewerage system. If we strike down this zoning ordinance and if the sewerage problem is such that on-site systems would not be feasible, then the Township will be forced to incur the expense of installing a municipal system. Rural and suburban townships have relatively limited tax resources for the obvious reason that they are composed primarily of single-family residences, properties which do not yield high real estate tax revenues. To require these municipalities to incur the great expense of installing sewerage systems and to augment their limited municipal services to meet a population which is increasing more rapidly than anticipated, does not appear to me to be a sound way to face what is admittedly a serious problem of providing residential communities for a rapidly-growing population.

Id. at 478.

DeCaro v. Washington Township, Berks County, 344 A.2d 725 (Pa. Commw. Ct. 1975), indicates that the Pennsylvania intermediate appellate court does not read *Concord Township Appeal* and *National Land* as absolutely prohibiting minimum lot sizes in excess of one acre. In *DeCaro* the court held that a three acre lot minimum was valid, and distinguished *National Land* and *Concord* on the following ground:

> [W]e start with a presumption that the three-acre minimum lot size . . . is constitutional and the burden was upon DeCaro to prove otherwise. *National Land, supra.* To carry this burden, DeCaro had to prove that the three-acre requirement bears no reasonable relationship to the protection of the public health, safety, or welfare, and that it had an exclusionary purpose or effect. This he did not do. . . .
>
> *National Land* and *Concord* contain reference after reference to the exclusionary effect of the ordinances under attack. . . . It was the *exclusionary purpose and effects* of the ordinances that were condemned by the Supreme Court in those cases. In the instant case there is *no* evidence to support an argument that there is an anticipated population growth beyond that which can be

accommodated under present zoning, with minimum lot sizes as low as one-quarter acre prevailing in most of the Township. The factfinders found that, with over 2,800 acres of developable land presently requiring lot sizes of 40,000 square feet or less, only 800 acres will be needed to accomodate the growth anticipated by the year 2010.

Id. at 728-29.

In *Delaware County Inv. Corp. v. Zoning Hearing Bd.,* 347 A.2d 513 (Pa. Commw. Ct. 1975), it was held that the township's refusal to grant a variance to permit minimum mobile home lot sizes of less than the 20,000 square feet minimum required for single-family dwellings was not unreasonable in the absence of a showing of any unique physical conditions peculiar to the property that would prohibit its development in accordance with the 20,000 square feet minimum. Although Pennsylvania law allowed the landowner to attack the constitutionality of the zoning restriction on appeal from denial of the variance request, the majority of the court said that, "there being no municipality-wide prohibition, the presumption of the ordinance's validity persists," and that the appellant "simply failed to carry its heavy burden of proof on this contention." The majority also rejected the appellant's argument that the lot size minimum unconstitutionally denied mobile home owners the "right of travel." The dissenting justice thought the 20,000 square feet minimum for mobile home lots was clearly unreasonable.

3. In *Aronson v. Town of Sharon,* 195 N.E.2d 341 (Mass. 1964), the court invalidated a minimum lot size requirement of 100,000 square feet in a "Single Residence District Rural." Sharon was a residential community with one small industry and two business centers. There was no public sewer system and the public water system did not extend to most of the 100,000 sq. ft. minimum lot zones. The nearest school was over three miles from the land in question and much of the land was inaccessible by road. There were no large country estates and little residential development in the area. The town argued that the 100,000 square foot minimum lot size requirements would help preserve "all that has made Sharon beautiful" by encouraging land to be left in its natural state, thus providing "amenities that are fundamental to mental and physical health." But the Massachusetts court said that, "however worthy the objectives, the by-law attempts to achieve a result which properly should be the subject of eminent domain." The court conceded that *Simon v. Needham, supra,* held there were certain advantages in living upon a one acre lot as compared with a 10,000 square foot lot, but the court went on to say that:

> While initially an increase in lot size might have the effects there noted, the law of diminishing returns will set in at some point. As applied to the petitioners' property, the attainment of such advantages does not reasonably require lots of 100,000 square feet. Nor would they be attained by keeping the rural district undeveloped, even though this might contribute to the welfare of each inhabitant. Granting the value of recreational areas to the community as a whole, the burden of providing them should not be borne by the individual property owner unless he is compensated.

Id. at 345.

4. In *Board of County Supervisors v. Carper,* 107 S.E.2d 390 (Va. 1959), the court struck down the two-acre lot minimums imposed on the western two thirds of Fairfax County, which was mostly undeveloped and without public water and sewer facilities. The two-acre minimum lot size requirement was defended by the county on several grounds: that it would prevent exhaustion of ground water supplies, protect public health by providing adequate lot areas for septic tank operation, and channel current development into the eastern third of the county where public facilities were available or could be most economically provided. But the court viewed the two-acre minimum lot size requirement as practically preventing low-income people from living in the western two thirds of the county and held that the restriction on lot size was not a valid exercise of the police power. Moreover, since an unusually generous grace period provision in the ordinance would permit many developments to proceed on half acre lots, the zoning was held to violate the uniformity requirement. Fairfax County is located on the outer edge of the Washington, D.C., metropolitan area, and at the time of the *Carper* case was undergoing rapid urbanization.

5. What attitudes should we take toward large lot zoning as a matter of social policy? We might first note that substantial areas in the suburban and urbanizing portions of many metropolitan regions are covered by zoning ordinances requiring very large lot sizes. For example, a comprehensive survey in Connecticut indicated that about 60 percent of all the undeveloped land in the state which was zoned residential was zoned to lot sizes of one acre or more.[42] Moreover, the tendency is in the direction of increasing rather than reducing lot sizes, and the courts in many states have tended to uphold this kind of downzoning.[43] At the same time, it is not clear that large lot zoning standing alone will significantly increase housing costs. For discussion of this problem see *infra* p. 446-48.

6. A fascinating analysis of possible legal approaches to large lot zoning problems is presented in Comment, Large Lot Zoning, 78 Yale L.J. 1418 (1969). The author discusses the impact of large lot zoning in terms of its effects on existing homeowners in the zoned community, homeowners who are allowed to buy in the community, and potential homeowners who are excluded by the large lot zoning. Of course, the interests of these groups conflict, but the author points out that smaller lot sizes and higher densities will have important and positive effects to the extent that this policy will tend to open up the suburbs to excluded groups, who may be expected to be at the low end of the income scale.

---

[42] American Soc'y of Planning Officials, New Directions in Connecticut Planning Legislation 186 (1967).

[43] *Id.,* at 218. *See Chucta v. Planning & Zoning Comm'n,* 225 A.2d 822 (Conn. 1967), upholding an increase in lot size in view of existing schools and other public facilities, and to provide adequately for a safe water supply and proper disposition of sewage. *Contra, Bismark v. Incorporated Village of Bayville,* 267 N.Y.S.2d 1002 (N.Y. Sup. Ct. 1966) (trial court), invalidating an upzoning from 15,000 to 40,000 square foot lots of a comparatively small tract surrounded by land zoned at higher densities. Downzoning problems are discussed *infra.*

Nevertheless, excluded groups do not get a hearing in court cases challenging large lot zoning restrictions. Judicial treatment of large lot zoning has been "gentle," and an unspoken "rule of reason" appears to have emerged. *Id.* at 1436, 1437. In addition, the author observes that courts have sometimes been suspicious of large lot zoning when it exceeds the lot size of nearby homes. But his principal point is that "The adversary process [in large lot zoning cases] brings before the judge a suburb and a developer or land speculator, not the homebuyers or city dwellers." *Id.* at 1436. That is, groups excluded by the large lot zoning are not represented. If this is so, then perhaps the usual judicial presumptions in large lot zoning cases should be reversed.

If *Concord Township Appeal, supra* Comment 2, does not establish in Pennsylvania the rule that minimum lot sizes in excess of one acre are invalid *per se,* it at least reverses the usual presumption that zoning regulations are valid. Chief Justice Bell, in his concurring opinion, said that "[t]his is one of those debatable cases which leave me in 'no man's land' " and then concluded that the minimum lot size regulations had "no substantial relationship to health or safety or morals," was "an unconstitutional restriction upon an owner's basic right of the ownership and use of his property," and could "not be sustained under the theory . . . of 'general welfare.' "

7. The large minimum lot size zoning cases prior to 1964 are collected and discussed in Note, 95 A.L.R.2d 716 (1964). For discussion of the major arguments advanced in favor of large minimum lot size requirements and critiques thereof, together with a thorough and detailed analysis of the major cases, see 2 N. Williams, American Land Planning Law, chs. 38, 39 (1974). *See also* Aloi, Goldberg, and White, Racial and Economic Segregation by Zoning: Death Knell for Home Rule, 1 Tol. L. Rev. 65 (1969); Sager, Tight Little Islands: Exclusionary Zoning, Equal Protection, and the Indigent, 21 Stan. L. Rev. 767 (1969) (discussing a constitutional equal protection approach).

D. EXCLUSIONARY AND INCLUSIONARY ZONING IN THE SUBURBS

The past decade has seen a judicial explosion in that area of social concern generally subsumed under the rubric "exclusionary zoning." This refers to the array of local zoning practices which, singly or in combination, results in the exclusion of housing for low- and moderate-income groups from the suburban communities where most of the growth in employment opportunities has occurred in the past decade. Exclusionary zoning practices are incisively analyzed in 2 N. Williams, American Land Planning Law, chs. 62-65 (1974), 3 N. Williams, American Land Planning Law, ch. 66 (1975). *See also* Williams & Norman, Exclusionary Land-Use Controls: The Case of Northeastern New Jersey, 22 Syracuse L. Rev. 475 (1971), reprinted in part in D. Mandelker & R. Montgomery, Housing in America 431-43 (1973); Williams, The Three Systems of Land-Use Control (Or, Exclusionary Zoning and Revision of the Enabling Legislation), 25 Rutgers L. Rev. 80 (1970). For additional background, see R.

Babcock & F. Bosselman, Exclusionary Zoning: Land Use Regulation and Housing in the 1970s (1973); E. Bergman et al., External Validity of Policy Related Research on Development Controls and Housing Costs (Dept. of City and Regional Planning, Univ. of North Carolina, 1974).

Williams lists six major exclusionary devices: (1) exclusion of multiple family dwellings; (2) restrictions on the number of bedrooms in multiple family dwellings; (3) exclusion of mobile homes; (4) minimum building size requirements; (5) minimum lot size requirements; and (6) minimum lot width requirements. (See articles and treatise cited above.) It seems clear that the first three have the most significant exclusionary effect, for under present market conditions the most promising possibilities for new low- and moderate-cost housing lie in multiple family dwellings and mobile homes. The practice of restricting the number of bedrooms in multiple family dwelling units amounts almost to an express exclusion of renter-families who have children. Mobile homes are now the most important — and probably the most popular — form of prefabricated housing available at a relatively low price to persons seeking to move into suburban areas.

The last three of the zoning devices listed above apply only to single-family detached dwellings, and are probably less significant in terms of exclusion than the first three devices. Of these last three devices, minimum building size requirements appear to be the most "exclusionary." Unless such requirements are set very low, they inevitably increase the cost of single-family detached dwellings above the minimum that a free market in housing would otherwise produce. High minimum lot width requirements may also have significant effects in increasing the cost of single-family housing, since the cost of improvements normally required by subdivision control ordinances — e.g., street paving, sanitary sewers, and storm sewers — is substantial. However, most of the extensive discussion of exclusionary zoning in the legal periodicals has focused on large minimum lot size requirements ("acreage zoning") as a major cost-increasing factor. Yet the effect of large-lot zoning on the cost of housing is far from clear. Three major studies during the period 1956-66 [44] fail to confirm the oft-stated hypothesis that such zoning

---

[44] Urban Land Institute, The Effects of Large Lot Sizes on Residential Development, Technical Bulletin No. 32 (1958) (study covered 11 suburban towns west of Boston, Mass.) ("Much more important, costwise, are the frontage requirements, the number of improvements, and the character standard or level of these improvements" required by subdivision regulations); Coke & Liebman, Political Values and Population Density Control, 37 Land Econ. 347 (1961) (study covered part of the Philadelphia, Pa., metropolitan area, 1956-60); American Soc'y of Planning Officials, New Directions in Connecticut Planning Legislation (1967). A good summary of the results of these studies may be found in 2 N. Williams, American Land Planning Law 672-86 (1974).

is a major factor in preventing construction of low- and moderate-cost housing in the suburbs. The 1966 study, conducted by the American Society of Planning Officials (ASPO) for the Connecticut legislature and covering all of Connecticut, was quite categorical in its conclusion that the increased cost of larger lots was not a significant factor directly influencing the cost of housing. But, the indirect effects of large-lot zoning were found to be significant. Assuming that larger lots are also considerably wider in most cases, the added costs for street improvements required by local subdivision ordinances were found to be larger than the differences in land costs. Moreover, the Connecticut study concluded,

> Large-lot zoning disperses development, wastes valuable land resources, raises the cost of both public and private services, and magnifies transportation problems. The large lot is necessarily far from community services: employment, schools, shopping, recreation. It may not raise the purchase price of the home significantly, but it raises the cost of occupying it. These costs come back to haunt the home owner not only in the form of additional private services which he has to perform (such as buying a second car) but also in the form of higher taxes to pay for additional public services, more streets and expressways, parking areas, and extended utility lines.
>
> There is still another indirect effect when the ratio of large to small lots in a community is badly out of balance with the market demand. When there is a shortage of small lots because most of the undeveloped land is zoned for large lots, the price of the small lots soars to unreasonable heights. The consultants were told of several instances where the price of a quarter-acre lot was much higher than the price of one- and two-acre lots in the same town.[45]

More recent studies tend to find a more significant relation between large-lot zoning and housing costs. The 1968 Douglas Commission Report [46] concluded that large-lot zoning frequently "can have significant effects on the cost of housing" for three reasons: (1) because it creates an overall suburban land shortage, especially a shortage of small lots; (2) because some home builders tend to build larger houses on larger lots; and (3) because larger (and presumably wider) lots require added costs for street improvements required by subdivision ordinances." [47] A 1973 study of the effect

---

[45] American Soc'y of Planning Officials, New Directions in Connecticut Planning Legislation 215 (1967).

[46] Report of the Nat'l Comm'n on Urban Problems to the Congress and the President of the United States, Building the American City, HR Doc. No. 9134, 91st Cong., 1st Sess. (1968).

[47] Id. at 213-16.

of publicly imposed land use controls on the cost of single family dwellings in New Jersey [48] concluded that "large-lot zoning *alone* does not produce expensive housing," but that lot size and width requirements had the greatest effect on single-family housing costs, next to minimum house size requirements, because of the high cost of street improvements and the correlation between large lots and large homes. And the report by Bergman et al., *supra,* — based on an analysis of 12 previous studies [49] — concluded that "a dependence of housing costs on lot size" is "firmly" established by the evidence, although the authors conceded that lot size and land cost *per acre* are "inversely related . . . for single-family zoning uses." [50] The relationships between land cost *per lot* and density, housing package cost *per lot* and density, and land cost *per acre* and density are shown in the following charts.[51] The authors state that the inverse relationship between the latter points directly to an hypothesis frequently advanced in the literature.

> This hypothesis holds that zoning produces imbalances in the supply of land for various uses by systematically overzoning for low-density residential uses and underzoning for high-density residential uses, thereby causing the per unit price of the former to be unduly low and the latter to be inordinately high.[52]

However, the authors also indicate that they were not convinced that the research design of any of the studies they reviewed was framed properly to test this hypothesis.[53]

---

[48] Sternlieb & Sagalyn, Zoning and Housing Costs (1971).

[49] Bergman et al., *supra* at 192.

[50] *Id.* at 212.

[51] These are drawn from *id.* at 200-02.

[52] *Id.* at 213.

[53] *Ibid.*

CHART 1
LAND COST PER LOT BY DENSITY

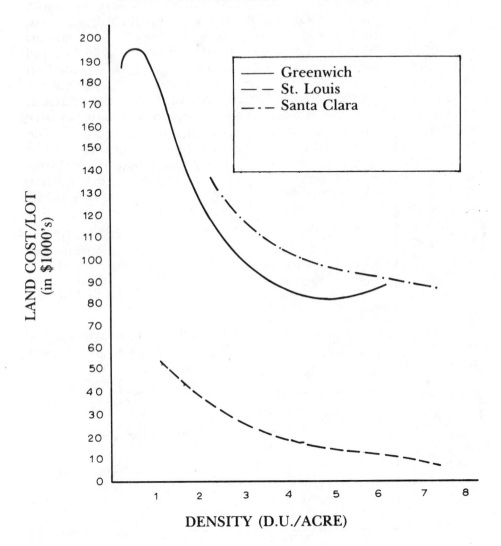

CHART 2
PACKAGE COST PER LOT BY DENSITY

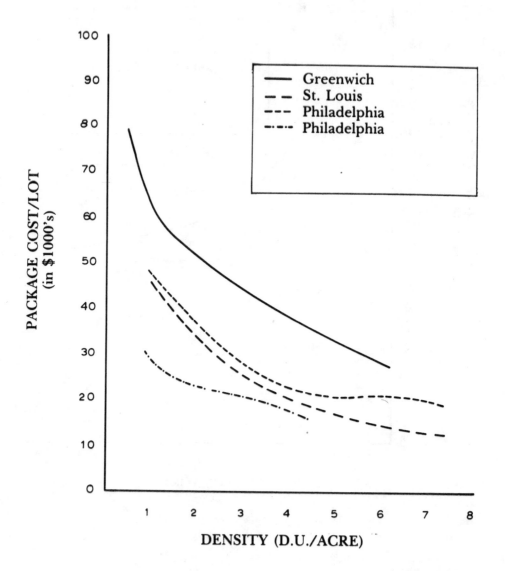

CHART 3
LAND COST PER ACRE BY DENSITY

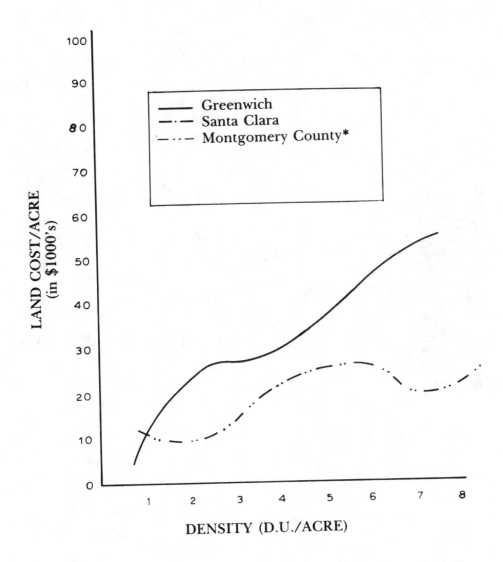

*Add the constant 20.0 to each value of the density along the horizontal axis. Data taken from (6), p. 77.

CHART 4

PACKAGE COST PER ACRE BY DENSITY

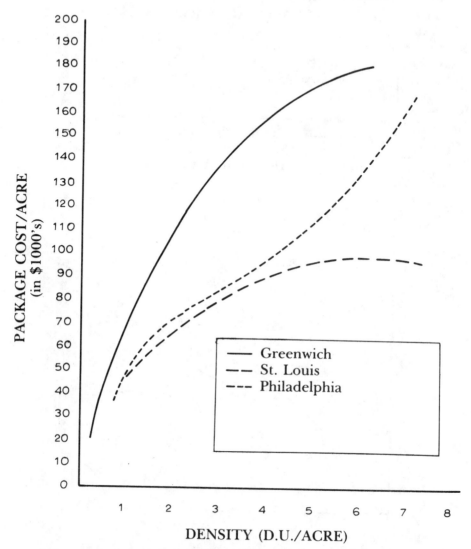

Large-lot zoning may be one technique that excludes lower income housing from the suburbs, but the question that next arises is whether opening up the suburbs for lower income housing is a social goal that ought to be pursued through zoning policy. The arguments in favor of providing lower income housing in the suburbs are stated in W. Grigsby & L. Rosenburg, Urban Housing Policy 115-25 (1975). The arguments are that opening up the suburbs to lower income housing would achieve the following: 1) promote educational opportunity; 2) reduce the problems of the poor through dispersal of poor families; 3) enable persons to live and work in the same community; 4) increase housing opportunities for blacks; 5) eliminate the spatial mismatch of jobs and housing; 6) improve central-city finances; 7) retard the forces of decay; and 8) promote a more healthy, open society.

Among these objectives, improving the spatial mismatch between jobs and housing has figured prominently in discussions about exclusionary zoning and has found a place in judicial examination of exclusionary zoning problems, as the cases that follow will indicate. The jobs and housing mismatch problem has been explained as follows:

> By greatly increasing the barriers to the outward movement of lower-income groups, the exclusionary policies of suburban governments have played a major role in the growing separation of the poor and blacks from jobs in the decentralizing economy of the metropolis. Especially in the larger metropolitan areas, the dispersal of jobs to the suburbs combines with restrictions which limit the supply of inexpensive housing to break the historical connection between urban growth and economic opportunity for the disadvantaged. Before the exodus of employment from the central city, housing available to the urban poor was close to the bulk of industrial and service jobs, and the unskilled worker usually could reach his job relatively quickly and cheaply by walking or riding on public transportation. In the decentralized metropolis, jobs increasingly are located far from the residences of the poor. More and more employment is situated in areas which lack moderately priced housing. Public transportation between the central city and these dispersed suburban job locations often is nonexistent. As a result, suburban job seekers and commuters from inner-city residences to employment in the suburbs must depend heavily on the private automobile. Many of the suburban jobs available to the lower-income groups denied access to housing in the suburbs, however, do not pay enough to make the long and expensive trip from inner city to suburb worthwhile. And the travel burdens for those isolated from economic opportunity are bound to grow in an era of rising fuel costs.

M. Danielson, The Politics of Exclusion 23-24 (1976).

Grigsby & Rosenburg, *supra* at 121-22, challenge the mismatch argument. They note that the inner-city/suburban distinction is statistical, and that in small metropolitan areas commuting distances out to the suburbs are not that far. In addition, a move to the suburb may not necessarily reduce the need for private transportation; a car may be necessary to get to a suburban job even though the worker lives in the suburbs. There is also some evidence that the shift of industrial jobs to the suburbs has been balanced to some extent by an increase in service and governmental jobs in inner-city areas.

What if it appears that all workers in a metropolitan area are able to live relatively near their work, even though they are excluded from some municipalities in the area? One study of housing and commuting patterns in an area in the northeast indicates that this situation does prevail. Burchell, Listokin, & James, Exclusionary Zoning: Pitfalls of the Regional Remedy, 7 Urb. L. 262 (1975). Some municipalities in this area were nevertheless found to be exclusionary; blue collar workers who worked in these communities could not live there. Since there is really no housing and jobs mismatch on the regional level, what basis is there for challenging the exclusionary zoning policies of these municipalities?

The arguments for the open suburbs movement have been put most forcefully in A. Downs, Opening Up the Suburbs (1973). *See also* Tarlock, Book Review, 83 Yale L.J. 637 (1974).

The armory of exclusionary zoning devices discussed above has come under attack in both the state and federal courts, and in a variety of litigational settings. In this section we look first at recent state court cases and then at recent federal court cases. We conclude with an analysis of recent state and local planning and legislative efforts to deal in a more comprehensive manner with the exclusionary zoning problem by means of "inclusionary" techniques.

1. State Cases

SOUTHERN BURLINGTON COUNTY NAACP v. TOWNSHIP OF MOUNT LAUREL

Supreme Court of New Jersey

67 N.J. 151, 336 A.2d 713, *appeal dismissed and cert. denied,*
423 U.S. 808 (1975)

HALL, J.

This case attacks the system of land use regulation by defendant Township of Mount Laurel on the ground that low and moderate income families are thereby unlawfully excluded from the municipality. The trial court so found, 119 N.J.Super. 164, 290 A.2d 465 (Law Div.1972), and declared the township zoning ordinance totally invalid. Its judgment went on, in line with the requests for affirmative relief, to order the municipality to make studies of the housing needs of low and moderate income persons presently or formerly residing in the community in substandard housing, as well as those in such income classifications presently employed in the township and living elsewhere or reasonably expected to be employed therein in the future, and to present a plan of affirmative public action designed "to enable and encourage the satisfaction of the indicated needs." Jurisdiction was retained for judicial consideration and approval of such a plan and for the entry of a final order requiring its implementation.

The township appealed to the Appellate Division and those plaintiffs, not present or former residents, cross-appealed on the basis that the judgment should have directed that the prescribed plan take into account as well a fair share of the regional housing needs of low and moderate income families without limitation to those having past, present or prospective connection with the township. The appeals were certified on our own motion before argument in the Division. R. 2:12-1.[54]

The implications of the issue presented are indeed broad and far-reaching, extending much beyond these particular plaintiffs and the boundaries of this particular municipality.

There is not the slightest doubt that New Jersey has been, and continues to be, faced with a desperate need for housing, especially of decent living accommodations economically suitable for low and moderate income families.[55] The situation was characterized as a "crisis" and fully explored and documented by Governor Cahill in two special messages to the Legislature — *A Blueprint for Housing in New Jersey* (1970) and *New Horizons in Housing* (1972).

Plaintiffs represent the minority group poor (black and Hispanic)[56]

---

[54] The judgment stayed the declaration of invalidity of the zoning ordinance until the court should decide "that sufficient time has elapsed to enable the municipality to enact new and proper regulations." The other provisions of the judgment were stayed pending appeal by subsequent order of the trial court.

[55] "Low income" was used in this case to refer to those persons or families eligible, by virtue of limited income, for occupancy in public housing units or units receiving rent supplement subsidies according to formulas therefor in effect in the area. "Moderate income" was similarly used to refer to those eligible for occupancy in housing units receiving so-called Section 235 or 236 or like subsidies. In another case, *Oakwood at Madison v. Township of Madison*, 128 N.J. Super. 438, 445, 320 A.2d 223 (Law Div. 1974), the figures of income up to $7,000 a year for the first category and up to $10,000—$12,000 for the second were projected. While the formula figures vary depending on family size, the dollar amounts mentioned are close enough to represent the top income in each classification for present purposes. "Middle income" and "upper income" are the designations of higher income categories.

[56] Plaintiffs fall into four categories: (1) present residents of the township residing in dilapidated or substandard housing; (2) former residents who were forced to move elsewhere because of the absence of suitable housing; (3) nonresidents living in central city substandard housing in the region who desire to secure decent housing and accompanying advantages within their means elsewhere; (4) three organizations representing the housing and other interests of racial minorities. The township originally challenged plaintiffs' standing to bring this action. The trial court properly held (119 N.J. Super. at 166, 290 A.2d 465) that the resident plaintiffs

seeking such quarters. But they are not the only category of persons barred from so many municipalities by reason of restrictive land use regulations. We have reference to young and elderly couples, single persons and large, growing families not in the poverty class, but who still cannot afford the only kinds of housing realistically permitted in most places — relatively high-priced, single-family detached dwellings on sizeable lots and, in some municipalities, expensive apartments. We will, therefore, consider the case from the wider viewpoint that the effect of Mount Laurel's land use regulation has been to prevent various categories of persons from living in the township because of the limited extent of their income and resources. In this connection, we accept the representation of the municipality's counsel at oral argument that the regulatory scheme was not adopted with any desire or intent to exclude prospective residents on the obviously illegal bases of race, origin or believed social incompatibility.

As already intimated, the issue here is not confined to Mount Laurel. The same question arises with respect to any number of other municipalities of sizeable land area outside the central cities and older built-up suburbs of our North and South Jersey metropolitan areas (and surrounding some of the smaller cities outside those areas as well) which, like Mount Laurel, have substantially shed rural characteristics and have undergone great population increase since World War II, or are now in the process of doing so, but still are not completely developed and remain in the path of inevitable future residential, commercial and industrial demand and growth. Most such municipalities, with but relatively insignificant variation in details, present generally comparable physical situations, courses of municipal policies, practices, enactments and results and human, governmental and legal problems arising therefrom. It is in the context of communities now of this type or which become so in the future, rather than with central cities or older built-up suburbs or areas still rural and likely to continue to be for some time yet, that we deal with the question raised.

Extensive oral and documentary evidence was introduced at the trial, largely informational, dealing with the development of Mount

---

had adequate standing to ground the entire action and found it unnecessary to pass on that of the other plaintiffs. The issue has not been raised on appeal. We merely add that both categories of nonresident individuals likewise have standing. N.J.S.A. 40:55-47.1; cf. *Walker v. Borough of Stanhope,* 23 N.J. 657, 130 A.2d 372 (1957). No opinion is expressed as to the standing of the organizations.

Laurel, including the nature and effect of municipal regulation, the details of the region of which it is a part and the recent history thereof, and some of the basics of housing, special reference being directed to that for low and moderate income families. . . .

This evidence was not contradicted by the township, except in a few unimportant details. Its candid position is that, conceding its land use regulation was intended to result and has resulted in economic discrimination and exclusion of substantial segments of the area population, its policies and practices are in the best present and future fiscal interest of the municipality and its inhabitants and are legally permissible and justified. It further asserts that the trial court was without power to direct the affirmative relief it did.

I

The Facts

Mount Laurel is a flat, sprawling township, 22 square miles, or about 14,000 acres, in area, on the west central edge of Burlington County. . . .

In 1950, the township had a population of 2817, only about 600 more people than it had in 1940. It was then, as it had been for decades, primarily a rural agricultural area with no sizeable settlements or commercial or industrial enterprises. The populace generally lived in individual houses scattered along country roads. There were several pockets of poverty, with deteriorating or dilapidated housing (apparently 300 or so units of which remain today in equally poor condition). After 1950, as in so many other municipalities similarly situated, residential development and some commerce and industry began to come in. By 1960 the population had almost doubled to 5249 and by 1970 had more than doubled again to 11,221. These new residents were, of course, "outsiders" from the nearby central cities and older suburbs or from more distant places drawn here by reason of employment in the region. The township is now definitely a part of the outer ring of the South Jersey metropolitan area, which area we define as those portions of Camden, Burlington and Gloucester Counties within a semicircle having a radius of 20 miles or so from the heart of Camden city. And 65% of the township is still vacant land or in agricultural use.

The growth of the township has been spurred by the construction or improvement of main highways through or near it. . . . This highway network gives the township a most strategic location from the standpoint of transport of goods and people by truck and private car. There is no other means of transportation.

The location and nature of development has been, as usual, controlled by the local zoning enactments. The general ordinance presently in force, which was declared invalid by the trial court, was adopted in 1964. We understand that earlier enactments provided, however, basically the same scheme but were less restrictive as to residential development. The growth pattern dictated by the ordinance is typical.

Under the present ordinance, 29.2% of all the land in the township, or 4,121 acres, is zoned for industry. . . . Only industry meeting specified performance standards is permitted. The effect is to limit the use substantially to light manufacturing, research, distribution of goods, offices and the like. Some nonindustrial uses, such as agriculture, farm dwellings, motels, a harness racetrack, and certain retail sales and service establishments, are permitted in this zone. At the time of trial no more than 100 acres, mostly in the southwesterly corner along route 73 adjacent to the turnpike and I-295 interchanges, were actually occupied by industrial uses. They had been constructed in recent years, mostly in several industrial parks, and involved tax ratables of about 16 million dollars. The rest of the land so zoned has remained undeveloped. If it were fully utilized, the testimony was that about 43,500 industrial jobs would be created, but it appeared clear that, as happens in the case of so many municipalities, much more land has been so zoned than the reasonable potential for industrial movement or expansion warrants. At the same time, however, the land cannot be used for residential development under the general ordinance.

The amount of land zoned for retail business use under the general ordinance is relatively small — 169 acres, or 1.2% of the total. . . .

The balance of the land area, almost 10,000 acres, has been developed until recently in the conventional form of major subdivisions. The general ordinance provides for four residential zones, designated R-1, R-1D, R-2 and R-3. All permit only single-family, detached dwellings, one house per lot — the usual form of grid development. . . . This dwelling development, resulting in the previously mentioned quadrupling of the population, has been largely confined to the R-1 and R-2 districts in two sections. . . . The result has been quite intensive development of these sections, but at a low density. The dwellings are substantial; the average value in 1971 was $32,500 and is undoubtedly much higher today.

The general ordinance requirements, while not as restrictive as those in many similar municipalities, nonetheless realistically allow only homes within the financial reach of persons of at least middle income. The R-1 zone requires a mimimum lot area of 9,375 square feet, a minimum lot width of 75 feet at the building line, and a minimum dwelling floor area of 1,100 square feet if a one-story building and 1,300 square feet if one and one-half stories or higher. Originally this zone comprised about 2,500 acres. Most of the subdivisions have been constructed within it so that only a few hundred acres remain (the testimony was at variance as to the exact amount). The R-2 zone, comprising a single district of 141 acres in the northeasterly corner, has been completely developed. While it only required a minimum floor area of 900 square feet for a one-story dwelling, the minimum lot size was 11,000 square feet; otherwise the requisites were the same as in the R-1 zone.

The general ordinance places the remainder of the township, outside of the industrial and commercial zones and the R-1D district (to be mentioned shortly), in the R-3 zone. This zone comprises over 7,000 acres — slightly more than half of the total municipal area. . . . The testimony was that about 4,600 acres of it then remained available for housing development. Ordinance requirements are substantially higher, however, in that the minimum lot size is increased to about one-half acre (20,000 square feet). (We understand that sewer and water utilities have not generally been installed, but, of course, they can be.) Lot width at the building line must be 100 feet. Minimum dwelling floor area is as in the R-1 zone. Presently this section is primarily in agricultural use; it contains as well most of the municipality's substandard housing.

The R-1D district was created by ordinance amendment in 1968. The area is composed of a piece of what was formerly R-3 land in the western part of that zone. The district is a so-called "cluster" zone. See generally 2 Williams, American Planning Law: Land Use and the Police Power, §§ 47.01-47.05 (1974). That writer defines the concept as follows:

> . . . Under the usual cluster-zoning provisions, both the size and the width of individual residential lots in a large (or medium-sized) development may be reduced, provided (usually) that the overall density of the entire tract remains constant — provided, that is, that an area equivalent to the total of the areas thus "saved" from each individual lot is pooled and retained as common open space. The most obvious advantages include a better use of many sites, and relief from the monotony of continuous development. § 47.01, pp. 212-213.

Here this concept is implemented by reduction of the minimum lot area from 20,000 square feet required in the R-3 zone to 10,000 square feet (12,000 square feet for corner lots) but with the proviso that one-family houses — the single permitted dwelling use — "shall not be erected in excess of an allowable development density of 2.25 dwelling units per gross acre." The minimum lot width at the building line must be 80 feet and the minimum dwelling floor area is the same as in the R-3 zone. . . . Some dwelling development has taken place in this district, the exact extent of which is not disclosed by the record. It is apparent that the dwellings are comparable in character and value to those in the other residential zones. The testimony was that 486 acres remained available in the district.[57]

A variation from conventional development has recently occurred in some parts of Mount Laurel, as in a number of other similar municipalities, by use of the land use regulation device known as "planned unit development" (PUD). This scheme differs from the traditional in that the type, density and placement of land uses and buildings, instead of being detailed and confined to specified districts by local legislation in advance, is determined by contract, or "deal," as to each development between the developer and the municipal administrative authority, under broad guidelines laid down by state enabling legislation and an implementing local ordinance. The stress is on regulation of density and permitted mixture of uses within the same area, including various kinds of living accommodations with or without commercial and industrial enterprises. . . . While the [Mount Laurel PUD] ordinance was repealed early in 1971, the township governing body in the interim had approved four PUB projects, which were specifically saved from extinction by the repealer.[58]

These projects, three in the southwesterly sector and one in the northeasterly sector, are very substantial and involve at least 10,000 sale and rental housing units of various types to be erected over a period of years. Their bounds were created by agreement rather than legislative specification on the zoning map, invading industrial, R-1, R-1D, R-3 and even flood plain zones. If completed as planned, they will in themselves ultimately quadruple the 1970 township

---

[57] The validity of cluster zoning and of particular ordinance provisions, including, as here, those requiring the dedication of open space for public uses, has never been passed upon by this court. See generally 2 Williams, *supra*, §§ 47.02, 47.03, 47.05.

[58] The ordinance was held, in a taxpayer's suit, to be unconstitutional under the zoning section of the state constitution (Art. IV, sec. VI, par. 2) and violative of the general zoning enabling act (N.J.S.A. 40:55-30 et seq.). Rudderow v. Township Committee of Mount Laurel Township, 114 N.J.Super. 104, 274 A.2d 854, decided in March 1971 by the same judge who determined the instant case. His judgment was reversed by the Appellate Division in December 1972, 121 N.J.Super. 409, 297 A.2d 583, after the ordinance had been repealed and the instant case heard and decided at the trial level. This court has never passed upon the PUD enabling legislation, any local implementing ordinance or any municipal approval of a PUD project. The basic legal questions involved in *Rudderow,* which include among other the matter of what requirements a municipal authority may, in effect, impose upon a developer as a condition of approval, are serious and not all easy of solution. We refer to the Mount Laurel PUD projects as part of the picture of land use regulation in the township and its effect. It may be noted that, at a hearing on the PUD ordinance, the then township attorney stated that ". . . providing for apartments in a PUD ordinance in effect would seem to overcome any court objection that the Township was not properly zoning in denying apartments." [For more on PUD controls see *infra* p. 854. — Eds.]

population, but still leave a good part of the township undeveloped. (The record does not indicate how far development in each of the projects has progressed.) While multi-family housing in the form of rental garden, medium rise and high rise apartments and attached townhouses is for the first time provided for, as well as single-family detached dwellings for sale, it is not designed to accommodate and is beyond the financial reach of low and moderate income families, especially those with young children. The aim is quite the contrary; as with the single-family homes in the older conventional subdivisions, only persons of medium and upper income are sought as residents.

A few details will furnish sufficient documentation. Each of the resolutions of tentative approval of the projects contains a similar fact finding to the effect that the development will attract a highly educated and trained population base to support the nearby industrial parks in the township as well as the business and commercial facilities. The approvals also sharply limit the number of apartments having more than one bedroom. Further, they require that the developer must provide in its leases that no school-age children shall be permitted to occupy any one-bedroom apartment and that no more than two such children shall reside in any two-bedroom unit. The developer is also required, prior to the issuance of the first building permit, to record a covenant, running with all land on which multi-family housing is to be constructed, providing that in the event more than .3 school children per multi-family unit shall attend the township school system in any one year, the developer will pay the cost of tuition and other school expenses of all such excess numbers of children. In addition, low density, required amenities, such as central air conditioning, and specified developer contributions help to push rents and sales prices to high levels. These contributions include fire apparatus, ambulances, fire houses, and very large sums of money for educational facilities, a cultural center and the township library.[59]

Still another restrictive land use regulation was adopted by the township through a supplement to the general zoning ordinance enacted in September 1972 creating a new zone, R-4, Planned Adult Retirement Community (PARC). The supplementary enactment designated a sizeable area as the zone — perhaps 200 acres — carved out of the R-1D and R-3 districts in the southwesterly sector. The enactment recited a critical shortage of adequate housing in the township suitable "for the needs and desires of senior citizens and

---

[59] The current township attorney, at oral argument, conceded, without specification, that many of these various conditions which had been required of developers were illegal.

certain other adults over the age of 52." The permission was essentially for single ownership development of the zone for multi-family housing (townhouses and apartments), thereafter to be either rented or sold as cooperatives or condominiums. The extensive development requirements detailed in the ordinance make it apparent that the scheme was not designed for, and would be beyond the means of, low and moderate income retirees. The highly restricted nature of the zone is found in the requirement that all permanent residents must be at least 52 years of age (except a spouse, immediate family member other than a child, live-in domestic, companion or nurse.) Children are limited to a maximum of one, over age 18, residing with a parent and there may be no more than three permanent residents in any one dwelling unit.[60]

All this affirmative action for the benefit of certain segments of the population is in sharp contrast to the lack of action, and indeed hostility, with respect to affording any opportunity for decent housing for the township's own poor living in substandard accommodations, found largely in the section known as Springville (R-3 zone). The 1969 Master Plan Report recognized it and recommended positive action. The continuous official reaction has been rather a negative policy of waiting for dilapidated premises to be vacated and then forbidding further occupancy. An earlier non-governmental effort to improve conditions had been effectively thwarted. In 1968 a private non-profit association sought to build subsidized, multi-family housing in the Springville section with funds to be granted by a higher level governmental agency. Advance municipal approval of the project was required. The Township Committee responded with a purportedly approving resolution, which found a need for "moderate" income housing in the area, but went on to specify that such housing must be constructed subject to all zoning, planning, building and other applicable ordinances and codes. This meant single-family detached dwellings on 20,000 square foot lots. (Fear was also expressed that such housing would attract low income families from outside the township.) Needless to say, such requirements killed realistic housing for this group of low and moderate income families.[61]

---

[60] This court has not yet passed on the validity of any land use regulation which restricts residence on the basis of occupant age.

[61] The record is replete with uncontradicted evidence that, factually, low and moderate income housing cannot be built without some form of contribution, concession or incentive by some level of government. Such, under various state and federal methods, may take the form of public construction or some sort of governmental assistance or encouragement to private building. Multi-family rental units, at a high density, or, at most, low cost single-family units on very small lots, are economically necessary and in turn require appropriate local land use regulations.

The record thoroughly substantiates the findings of the trial court that over the years Mount Laurel "has acted affirmatively to control development and to attract a selective type of growth" (119 N.J.Super. at 168, 290 A.2d at 467) and that "through its zoning ordinances has exhibited economic discrimination in that the poor have been deprived of adequate housing and the opportunity to secure the construction of subsidized housing, and has used federal, state, county and local finances and resources[62] solely for the betterment of middle and upper-income persons." (119 N.J.Super. at 178, 290 A.2d at 473).

There cannot be the slightest doubt that the reason for this course of conduct has been to keep down local taxes on *property* (Mount Laurel is not a high tax municipality) and that the policy was carried out without regard for non-fiscal considerations with respect to *people,* either within or without its boundaries. This conclusion is demonstrated not only by what was done and what happened, as we have related, but also by innumerable direct statements of municipal officials at public meetings over the years which are found in the exhibits. The trial court referred to a number of them. 119 N.J.Super. at 169-170, 290 A.2d 465. No official testified to the contrary.

This policy of land use regulation for a fiscal end derives from New Jersey's tax structure, which has imposed on local real estate most of the cost of municipal and county government and of the primary and secondary education of the municipality's children. The latter expense is much the largest, so, basically, the fewer the school children, the lower the tax rate. Sizeable industrial and commercial ratables are eagerly sought and homes and the lots on which they are situate are required to be large enough, through minimum lot sizes and minimum floor areas, to have substantial value in order to produce greater tax revenues to meet school costs. Large families who cannot afford to buy large houses and must live in cheaper rental accommodations are definitely not wanted, so we find drastic bedroom restrictions for, or complete prohibition of, multi-family or other feasible housing for those of lesser income.

This pattern of land use regulation has been adopted for the same purpose in developing municipality after developing municipality. Almost every one acts solely in its own selfish and parochial interest

---

[62] Such "finances and resources" has reference to monies spent by various agencies on highways within the municipality, loans and grants for water and sewer systems and for planning, federal guarantees of mortgages on new home construction, and the like.

and in effect builds a wall around itself to keep out those people or entities not adding favorably to the tax base, despite the location of the municipality or the demand for varied kinds of housing. There has been no effective intermunicipal or area planning or land use regulation. All of this is amply demonstrated by the evidence in this case as to Camden, Burlington and Gloucester counties. As to the similar situation generally in the state, see New Jersey Department of Community Affairs, Division of State and Regional Planning, *Land Use Regulation, The Residential Land Supply* (April 1972) (a study assembling and examining the nature and extent of municipal zoning practices in 16 counties as affecting residential land available for low and moderate income housing) and Williams and Norman, Exclusionary Land Use Controls: The Case of North-Eastern New Jersey, 22 Syracuse L. Rev. 475, 486-487 (1971). One incongruous result is the picture of developing municipalities rendering it impossible for lower paid employees of industries they have eagerly sought and welcomed with open arms (and, in Mount Laurel's case, even some of its own lower paid municipal employees) to live in the community where they work.

The other end of the spectrum should also be mentioned because it shows the source of some of the demand for cheaper housing than the developing municipalities have permitted. Core cities were originally the location of most commerce and industry. Many of those facilities furnished employment for the unskilled and semiskilled. These employees lived relatively near their work, so sections of cities always have housed the majority of people of low and moderate income, generally in old and deteriorating housing. Despite the municipally confined tax structure, commercial and industrial ratables generally used to supply enough revenue to provide and maintain municipal services equal or superior to those furnished in most suburban and rural areas.

The situation has become exactly the opposite since the end of World War II. Much industry and retail business, and even the professions, have left the cities. Camden is a typical example. The testimonial and documentary evidence in this case as to what has happened to that city is depressing indeed. For various reasons, it lost thousands of jobs between 1950 and 1970, including more than half of its manufacturing jobs (a reduction from 43,267 to 20,671, while all jobs in the entire area labor market increased from 94,507 to 197,037). A large segment of retail business faded away with the erection of large suburban shopping centers. The economically better situated city residents helped fill up the miles of sprawling new housing developments, not fully served by public transit. In a society which came to depend more and more on expensive individual motor vehicle transportation for all purposes, low income employees very frequently could not afford to reach outlying places of suitable employment and they certainly could not afford the permissible housing near such locations. These people have great difficulty in obtaining work and have been forced to remain in housing which is overcrowded, and has become more and more substandard and less and less tax productive. There has been a consequent critical erosion of the city tax base and inability to provide the amount and quality of those governmental services — education, health, police, fire, housing and the like — so necessary to the very existence of safe and decent city life. This category of city dwellers desperately needs much better housing and living conditions than is available to them now, both in a rehabilitated city and in outlying municipalities. They make up, along with the other classes of persons earlier mentioned who also cannot afford the only generally permitted housing in the developing municipalities, the acknowledged great demand for low and moderate income housing.

II

The Legal Issue

The legal question before us, as earlier indicated, is whether a developing municipality like Mount Laurel may validly, by a system of land use regulation, make it physically and economically impossible to provide low and moderate income housing in the municipality for the various categories of persons who need and want it and thereby, as Mount Laurel has, exclude such people from living within its confines because of the limited extent of their income and resources. Necessarily implicated are the broader questions of the right of such municipalities to limit the kinds of available housing and of any obligation to make possible a variety and choice of types of living accommodations.

We conclude that every such municipality must, by its land use regulations, presumptively make realistically possible an appropriate variety and choice of housing. More specifically, presumptively it cannot foreclose the opportunity of the classes of people mentioned for low and moderate income housing and in its regulations must affirmatively afford that opportunity, at least to the extent of the municipality's fair share of the present and prospective regional need therefor. These obligations must be met unless the particular municipality can sustain the heavy burden of demonstrating peculiar circumstances which dictate that it should not be required so to do.[63]

---

[63] While, as the trial court found, Mount Laurel's actions were deliberate, we are of the view that the identical conclusion follows even when municipal conduct is not shown to be intentional, but the effect is substantially the same as if it were.

We reach this conclusion under state law and so do not find it necessary to consider federal constitutional grounds urged by plaintiffs. We begin with some fundamental principles as applied to the scene before us.

Land use regulation is encompassed within the state's police power. Our constitutions have expressly so provided since an amendment in 1927. . . .

It is elementary theory that all police power enactments, no matter at what level of government, must conform to the basic state constitutional requirements of substantive due process and equal protection of the laws. These are inherent in Art. I, par. 1 of our Constitution,[64] the requirements of which may be more demanding than those of the federal Constitution. . . . It is required that, affirmatively, a zoning regulation, like any police power enactment, must promote public health, safety, morals or the general welfare. (The last term seems broad enough to encompass the others.) Conversely, a zoning enactment which is contrary to the general welfare is invalid. . . . Indeed these considerations are specifically set forth in the zoning enabling act as among the various purposes of zoning for which regulations must be designed. N.J.S.A. 40:55-32. Their inclusion therein really adds little; the same requirement would exist even if they were omitted. If a zoning regulation violates the enabling act in this respect, it is also theoretically invalid under the state constitution. We say "theoretically" because, as a matter of policy, we do not treat the validity of most land use ordinance provisions as involving matters of constitutional dimension; that classification is confined to major questions of fundamental import. . . . We consider the basic importance of housing and local regulations restricting its availability to substantial segments of the population to fall within the latter category.

The demarcation between the valid and the invalid in the field of land use regulation is difficult to determine, not always clear and subject to change. This was recognized almost fifty years ago in the basic case of *Village of Euclid v. Ambler Realty Co.,* 272 U.S. 365, 47 S.Ct. 114, 71 L.Ed. 303 (1926). . . .

This court has also said as much and has plainly warned, even in cases decided some years ago sanctioning a broad measure of restrictive municipal decisions, of the inevitability of change in

---

[64] The paragraph reads:

All persons are by nature free and independent, and have certain natural and unalienable rights, among which are those of enjoying and defending life and liberty, of acquiring, possessing, and protecting property, and of pursuing and obtaining safety and happiness.

judicial approach and view as mandated by change in the world around us. . . .

The warning implicates the matter of *whose* general welfare must be served or not violated in the field of land use regulation. Frequently the decisions in this state, including those just cited, have spoken only in terms of the interest of the enacting municipality, so that it has been thought, at least in some quarters, that such was the only welfare requiring consideration. It is, of course, true that many cases have dealt only with regulations having little, if any, outside impact where the local decision is ordinarily entitled to prevail. However, it is fundamental and not to be forgotten that the zoning power is a police power of the state and the local authority is acting only as a delegate of that power and is restricted in the same manner as is the state. So, when regulation does have a substantial external impact, the welfare of the state's citizens beyond the borders of the particular municipality cannot be disregarded and must be recognized and served.

This essential was distinctly pointed out in *Euclid,* where Mr. Justice Sutherland specifically referred to ". . . the possibility of cases where the general public interest would so far outweigh the interest of the municipality that the municipality would not be allowed to stand in the way." (272 U.S. at 390, 47 S.Ct. at 119, 71 L.Ed. at 311). Chief Justice Vanderbilt said essentially the same thing, in a different factual context, in the early leading case of *Duffcon Concrete Products, Inc. v. Borough of Cresskill,* 1 N.J. 509, 64 A.2d 347 (1949), when he spoke of the necessity of regional considerations in zoning. . . .

In recent years this court has once again stressed this non-local approach to the meaning of "general welfare" in cases involving zoning as to facilities of broad public benefit as distinct from purely parochial interest. See *Roman Catholic Diocese of Newark v. Ho-Ho-Kus Borough,* 42 N.J. 556, 566, 202 A.2d 161 (1964), Id., 47 N.J. 211, 220 A.2d 97 (1966). In this case we pointed out local action with respect to private educational projects largely benefitting those residing outside the borough must be exercised "with due concern for values which transcend municipal lines." (47 N.J. at 218, 220 A.2d at 101). Likewise in *Kunzler v. Hoffman,* 48 N.J. 277, 225 A.2d 321 (1966), a case unsuccessfully attacking a use variance granted a private hospital to serve the emotionally disturbed in a wide area of the state, we rejected the contention that local zoning authorities are limited to a consideration of only those benefits to the general welfare which would be received by residents of the municipality, pointing out that "general welfare" in the context there involved "comprehends the benefits not merely within municipal boundaries but also those to the regions of the State relevant to the public interest to be served." 48 N.J. at 288, 225 A.2d at 327.

. . . .

It is plain beyond dispute that proper provision for adequate housing of all categories of people is certainly an absolute essential in promotion of the general welfare required in all local land use regulation. Further the universal and constant need for such housing is so important and of such broad public interest that the general welfare which developing municipalities like Mount Laurel must consider extends beyond their boundaries and cannot be parochially confined to the claimed good of the particular municipality. It has to follow that, broadly speaking, the presumptive obligation arises for each such municipality affirmatively to plan and provide, by its land use regulations, the reasonable opportunity for an appropriate variety and choice of housing, including, of course, low and moderate cost housing, to meet the needs, desires and resources of all categories of people who may desire to live within its boundaries. Negatively, it may not adopt regulations or policies which thwart or preclude that opportunity.

It is also entirely clear, as we pointed out earlier, that most developing municipalities, including Mount Laurel, have not met their affirmative or negative obligations, primarily for local fiscal reasons. . . .

In sum, we are satisfied beyond any doubt that, by reason of the basic importance of appropriate housing and the longstanding pressing need for it, especially in the low and moderate cost category, and of the exclusionary zoning practices of so many municipalities, conditions have changed, . . . judicial attitudes must be altered from that espoused in that and other cases cited earlier, to require, as we have just said, a broader view of the general welfare and the presumptive obligation on the part of developing municipalities at least to afford the opportunity by land use regulations for appropriate housing for all.

We have spoken of this obligation of such municipalities as "presumptive." The term has two aspects, procedural and substantive. Procedurally, we think the basic importance of appropriate housing for all dictates that, when it is shown that a developing municipality in its land use regulations has not made realistically possible a variety and choice of housing, including adequate provision to afford the opportunity for low and moderate income housing or has expressly prescribed requirements or restrictions which preclude or substantially hinder it, a facial showing of violation of substantive due process or equal protection under the state constitution has been made out and the burden, and it is a heavy one, shifts to the municipality to establish a valid basis for its action or non-action. . . . The substantive aspect of "presumptive" relates to the specifics, on the one hand, of what municipal land use regulation provisions, or the absence thereof, will evidence invalidity and shift the burden of proof and, on the other hand, of what bases and considerations will carry the municipality's burden and sustain what it has done or failed to do. Both kinds of specifics may well vary between municipalities according to peculiar circumstances.

We turn to application of these principles in appraisal of Mount Laurel's zoning ordinance, useful as well, we think, as guidelines for future application in other municipalities.

The township's general zoning ordinance (including the cluster zone provision) permits, as we have said, only one type of housing — single-family detached dwellings. This means that all other types — multi-family including garden apartments and other kinds housing more than one family, town (row) houses, mobile home parks — are prohibited.[65] Concededly, low and moderate income housing has been intentionally excluded. While a large percentage of the population living outside of cities prefers a one-family house on its own sizeable lot, a substantial proportion do not for various reasons. Moreover, single-family dwellings are the most expensive type of quarters and a great number of families cannot afford them.[66] Certainly they are not pecuniarily feasible for low and moderate income families, most young people and many elderly and retired persons, except for some of moderate income by the use of low cost construction on small lots.

As previously indicated, Mount Laurel has allowed some multi-family housing by agreement in planned unit developments, but only for the relatively affluent and of no benefit to low and moderate income families. And even here, the contractual agreements between municipality and developer sharply limit the

---

[65] Zoning ordinance restriction of housing to single-family dwellings is very common in New Jersey. Excluding six large, clearly rural townships, the percentage of remaining land zoned for multi-family use is only just over 1% of the net residential land supply in 16 of New Jersey's 21 counties (not included are Atlantic, Cumberland, Cape May, Salem and Hudson counties). See *Land Use Regulation, The Residential Land Supply, supra,* pp. 10-13. (It is well known that considerable numbers of privately built apartments have been constructed in recent years in municipalities throughout the state, not allowed by ordinance, by the use variance procedure. N.J.S.A. 40:55-39(d). While the special exception method, N.J.S.A. 40:55-39(b), is frequently appropriate for the handling of such uses, it would indeed be the rare case where proper "special reasons" could be found to validly support a subsection (d) variance for such privately built housing.) Pennsylvania has held it unconstitutional for a developing municipality to fail to provide for apartments anywhere within it. *Appeal of Girsh,* 437 Pa. 237, 263 A.2d 395 (1970).

[66] Some authorities suggest that such dwellings are rapidly becoming financially possible only for those of relatively high income. See New Jersey Trends, ch. 24, *Sternlieb, Introduction: Is This The End of the American Dream House,* p. 302 (Institute for Environmental Studies, Rutgers University, 1974).

number of apartments having more than one bedroom.[67] While the township's PUD ordinance has been repealed, we mention the subject of bedroom restriction because, assuming the overall validity of the PUD technique (see footnote (5), *supra*), the measure could be reenacted and the subject is of importance generally. The design of such limitations is obviously to restrict the number of families in the municipality having school age children and thereby keep down local education costs. Such restrictions are so clearly contrary to the general welfare as not to require further discussion. . . .

Mount Laurel's zoning ordinance is also so restrictive in its minimum lot area, lot frontage and building size requirements, earlier detailed, as to preclude single-family housing for even moderate income families. Required lot area of at least 9,375 square feet in one remaining regular residential zone and 20,000 square feet (almost half an acre) in the other, with required frontage of 75 and 100 feet, respectively, cannot be called small lots and amounts to low density zoning, very definitely increasing the cost of purchasing and improving land and so affecting the cost of housing.[68] As to building size, the township's general requirements of a minimum dwelling floor area of 1,100 square feet for all one-story houses and 1,300 square feet for all of one and one-half stories or higher is without regard to required minimum lot size or frontage or the number of occupants (see *Sente v. Mayor and Municipal Council of City of Clifton,* 66 N.J. 204, 208-209, 330 A.2d 321 (1974)). In most aspects these requirements are greater than those approved in Lionshead Lake, Inc. v. Township of Wayne, . . . 10 N.J. 165, 89 A.2d 693 [1952], almost 24 years ago and before population decentralization, outer suburban development and exclusionary zoning had attained today's condition. See also Williams and Wacks, Segregation of Residential Areas Along Economic Lines: Lionshead Lake Revisited,

---

[67] Apartment bedroom restrictions are also common in municipalities of the state which do allow multi-family housing. About 60% of the area zoned to permit multi-family dwellings is restricted to efficiency or one-bedroom apartments; another 20% permits two-bedroom units and only the remaining 20% allows units of three bedrooms or larger. See *Land Use Regulation, The Residential Land Supply, supra,* pp. 11-12.

[68] These restrictions are typical throughout the state. As shown in *Land Use Regulation, The Residential Land Supply, supra,* pp. 14-16, in the 16 counties covered by that study, only 14.1% of the available single-family land is allowed to be in lots of less than one-half acre, only 5.1% (and that mostly in urban counties) in those of less than 10,000 square feet, and 54.7% of it requires lots of from one to three acres.

The same study, pp. 17-18, demonstrates that only as to 13.5% of the available single-family land is a frontage of less than 100 feet required, 32.2% requires 100-149 feet, 23.3%, 150-199 feet and 31%, 200 feet or more.

1969 Wis.L.Rev. 827.[69] Again it is evident these requirements increase the size and so the cost of housing. The conclusion is irresistible that Mount Laurel permits only such middle and upper income housing as it believes will have sufficient taxable value to come close to paying its own governmental way.

Akin to large lot, single-family zoning restricting the population is the zoning of very large amounts of land for industrial and related uses. Mount Laurel has set aside almost 30% of its area, over 4,100 acres, for that purpose; the only residential use allowed is for farm dwellings. In almost a decade only about 100 acres have been developed industrially. Despite the township's strategic location for motor transportation purposes, as intimated earlier, it seems plain that the likelihood of anywhere near the whole of the zoned area being used for the intended purpose in the foreseeable future is remote indeed and that an unreasonable amount of land has thereby been removed from possible residential development, again seemingly for local fiscal reasons.[70]

Without further elaboration at this point, our opinion is that Mount Laurel's zoning ordinance is presumptively contrary to the general welfare and outside the intended scope of the zoning power in the particulars mentioned. A facial showing of invalidity is thus established, shifting to the municipality the burden of establishing valid superseding reasons for its action and non-action.[71] We now examine the reasons it advances.

The township's principal reason in support of its zoning plan and ordinance housing provisions, advanced especially strongly at oral argument, is the fiscal one previously adverted to, *i. e.,* that by reason of New Jersey's tax structure which substantially finances municipal governmental and educational costs from taxes on local real property, every municipality may, by the exercise of the zoning

---

[69] Minimum floor area requirements exist as to all but 8% of the available residential land supply in the 16 counties studied in *Land Use Regulation, The Residential Land Supply, supra,* pp. 18-20; the Mount Laurel dimensions are representative of those most commonly imposed.

[70] *Land Use Regulation, The Residential Land Supply, supra,* pp. 6-8, shows that in the 16 county area only 14.7% of the net land supply is zoned for industrial uses (including offices and research laboratories). 3.6% is zoned for commercial uses and the remainder (81.7%) for residential uses of all types.

[71] The township has not been deprived of the opportunity to present its defense on this thesis, since the case was very thoroughly tried out with voluminous evidence on all aspects on both sides.

power, allow only such uses and to such extent as will be beneficial to the local tax rate. In other words, the position is that any municipality may zone extensively to seek and encourage the "good" tax ratables of industry and commerce and limit the permissible types of housing to those having the fewest school children or to those providing sufficient value to attain or approach paying their own way taxwise.

We have previously held that a developing municipality may properly zone for and seek industrial ratables to create a better economic balance for the community *vis-a-vis* educational and governmental costs engendered by residential development, provided that such was "... done reasonably as part of and in furtherance of a legitimate comprehensive plan for the zoning of the entire municipality." *Gruber v. Mayor and Township Committee of Raritan Township,* 39 N.J. 1, 9-11, 186 A.2d 489, 493 (1962). We adhere to that view today. But we were not there concerned with, and did not pass upon, the validity of municipal exclusion by zoning of types of housing and kinds of people for the same local financial end. We have no hesitancy in now saying, and do so emphatically, that, considering the basic importance of the opportunity for appropriate housing for all classes of our citizenry, no municipality may exclude or limit categories of housing for that reason or purpose. While we fully recognize the increasingly heavy burden of local taxes for municipal governmental and school costs on homeowners, relief from the consequences of this tax system will have to be furnished by other branches of government. It cannot legitimately be accomplished by restricting types of housing through the zoning process in developing municipalities.

The propriety of zoning ordinance limitations on housing for ecological or environmental reasons seems also to be suggested by Mount Laurel in support of the one-half acre minimum lot size in that very considerable portion of the township still available for residential development. It is said that the area is without sewer or water utilities and that the soil is such that this plot size is required for safe individual lot sewage disposal and water supply. The short answer is that, this being flat land and readily amenable to such utility installations, the township could require them as improvements by developers or install them under the special assessment or other appropriate statutory procedure. The present environmental situation of the area is, therefore, no sufficient excuse in itself for limiting housing therein to single-family dwelling on large lots. *Cf. National Land and Investment Co. v. Kohn,* 419 Pa. 504, 215 A.2d 597 (1965). This is not to say that land use regulations should not take due account of ecological or environmental factors or problems. Quite the contrary. Their importance, at last being recognized, should always be considered. Generally only a relatively small

portion of a developing municipality will be involved, for, to have a valid effect, the danger and impact must be substantial and very real (the construction of every building or the improvement of every plot has some environmental impact) — not simply a makeweight to support exclusionary housing measures or preclude growth — and the regulation adopted must be only that reasonably necessary for public protection of a vital interest. Otherwise difficult additional problems relating to a "taking" of a property owner's land may arise.
. . .

By way of summary, what we have said comes down to this. As a developing municipality, Mount Laurel must, by its land use regulations, make realistically possible the opportunity for an appropriate variety and choice of housing for all categories of people who may desire to live there, of course including those of low and moderate income. It must permit multi-family housing, without bedroom or similar restrictions, as well as small dwellings on very small lots, low cost housing of other types and, in general, high density zoning, without artificial and unjustifiable minimum requirements as to lot size, building size and the like, to meet the full panoply of these needs. Certainly when a municipality zones for industry and commerce for local tax benefit purposes, it without question must zone to permit adequate housing within the means of the employees involved in such uses. (If planned unit developments are authorized, one would assume that each must include a reasonable amount of low and moderate income housing in its residential "mix," unless opportunity for such housing has already been realistically provided for elsewhere in the municipality.) The amount of land removed from residential use by allocation to industrial and commercial purposes must be reasonably related to the present and future potential for such purposes. In other words, such municipalities must zone primarily for the living welfare of people and not for the benefit of the local tax rate.[72]

We have earlier stated that a developing municipality's obligation to afford the opportunity for decent and adequate low and moderate income housing extends at least to ". . . that municipality's fair share

---

[72] This case does not properly present the question of whether a developing municipality may time its growth and, if so, how. See, *e. g., Golden v. Planning Board of Town of Ramapo,* 30 N.Y.2d 359, 334 N.Y.S.2d 138, 285 N.E.2d 291 (1972), appeal dismissed 409 U.S. 1003, 93 S.Ct. 436, 440, 34 L.Ed.2d 294 (1972); *Construction Industry Association of Sonoma County v. City of Petaluma,* 375 F.Supp. 574 (N.D.Cal.1974), appeal pending (citation of these cases is not intended to indicate either agreement or disagreement with their conclusions). We now say only that, assuming some type of timed growth is permissible, it cannot be utilized as an exclusionary device or to stop all further development and must include early provision for low and moderate income housing.

of the present and prospective regional need therefor." [73] Some comment on that conclusion is in order at this point. Frequently it might be sounder to have more of such housing, like some specialized land uses, in one municipality in a region than in another, because of greater availability of suitable land, location of employment, accessibility of public transportation or some other significant reason. But, under present New Jersey legislation, zoning must be on an individual municipal basis, rather than regionally.[74]

---

[73] This was said with the realization that most of such housing will require some form of governmental subsidy or assistance at some level to construct and, if the present tax structure remains unchanged, perhaps also some assistance to the municipality itself in connection with the furnishing of the additional local services required. See recommendations, *Housing & Suburbs, Fiscal & Social Impact of Multifamily Development, supra,* p. 123 et seq.

We further agree with the statement in the separate summary of the cited study, p. 2: "We recognize that new development, whatever the pace of construction, will never be the source of housing for more than a small part of the State's population. The greater part of New Jersey's housing stock is found and will continue to be found in the central cities and older surburbs of the State . . . ." (Substantial housing rehabilitation, as well as general overall revitalization of the cities, is, of course, indicated.) So, while what we decide today will produce no mass or sudden emigration of those of low and moderate income from the central cities and older suburbs to the developing municipalities, our conception of state law as applied to land use regulation affecting housing requires that the fair opportunity therefor be afforded at once, with the expectation and purpose that the opportunity will come to fruition in the near future through private or public enterprises, or both, and result in available housing in the developing municipalities for a goodly number of the various categories of people of low and moderate income who desire to live therein and now cannot.

[74] This court long ago pointed out ". . . the unreality in dealing with zoning problems on the basis of the territorial limits of a municipality." *Duffcon Concrete Products, Inc. v. Borough of Cresskill, supra* (1 N.J. at 513, 64 A.2d at 350). It is now clear that the Legislature accepts the fact that at least land use *planning,* to be of any value, must be done on a much broader basis than each municipality separately. Note the statutes establishing county planning boards, with the duty to prepare a county master plan and requiring that board's review and approval of certain subdivisions, N.J.S.A. 40:27-1 to 8; authorizing voluntary regional planning boards, N.J.S.A. 40:27-9 to 11; creating state planning and coordinating functions in the Department of Community Affairs and its Division of State and Regional Planning, N.J.S.A. 52:27D-6 and 9 and 13:1B-5.1 and 15.52; and providing for New Jersey to join with New York and Connecticut in the establishment of the Tri-State Regional Planning Commission with extensive area planning functions, N.J.S.A. 32:22B-1 et seq. (Federal statutes and regulations require many federal grants for local public works and installations to have the approval of regional planning agencies, consistent with comprehensive area plans.) Authorization for regional *zoning* — the implementation of planning —, or at least regulation of land uses having a substantial external impact by some agency beyond the local municipality, would seem to be logical and desirable as the next legislative step.

So long as that situation persists under the present tax structure, or in the absence of some kind of binding agreement among all the municipalities of a region, we feel that every municipality therein must bear its fair share of the regional burden. (In this respect our holding is broader than that of the trial court, which was limited to Mount Laurel-related low and moderate income housing needs.)

The composition of the applicable "region" will necessarily vary from situation to situation and probably no hard and fast rule will serve to furnish the answer in every case. Confinement to or within a certain county appears not to be realistic, but restriction within the boundaries of the state seems practical and advisable. (This is not to say that a developing municipality can ignore a demand for housing within its boundaries on the part of people who commute to work in another state.) Here we have already defined the region at present as "those portions of Camden, Burlington and Gloucester Counties within a semicircle having a radius of 20 miles or so from the heart of Camden City." The concept of "fair share" is coming into more general use and, through the expertise of the municipal planning adviser, the county planning boards and the state planning agency, a reasonable figure for Mount Laurel can be determined, which can then be translated to the allocation of sufficient land therefor on the zoning map. See generally, New Jersey Trends, ch. 27, *Listokin, Fair Share Housing Distribution: An Idea Whose Time Has Come?,* p. 353. We may add that we think that, in arriving at such a determination, the type of information and estimates, which the trial judge (119 N.J.Super. at 178, 290 A.2d 465) directed the township to compile and furnish to him, concerning the housing needs of persons of low and moderate income now or formerly residing in the township in substandard dwellings and those presently employed or reasonably expected to be employed therein, will be pertinent.

There is no reason why developing municipalities like Mount Laurel, required by this opinion to afford the opportunity for all types of housing to meet the needs of various categories of people, may not become and remain attractive, viable communities providing good living and adequate services for all their residents in the kind of atmosphere which a democracy and free institutions demand. They can have industrial sections, commercial sections and sections for every kind of housing from low cost and multi-family to lots of more than an acre with very expensive homes. Proper planning and governmental cooperation can prevent over-intensive and too sudden development, insure against future suburban sprawl and slums and assure the preservation of open space and local beauty. We do not intend that developing municipalities shall be overwhelmed by voracious land speculators and developers if they use the powers which they have intelligently and in the broad public interest. Under our holdings today, they can be better communities for all than they previously have been.

III

The Remedy

As outlined at the outset of this opinion, the trial court invalidated the zoning ordinance *in toto* and ordered the township to make certain studies and investigations and to present to the court a plan of affirmative public action designed "to enable and encourage the satisfaction of the indicated needs" for township related low and moderate income housing. Jurisdiction was retained for judicial consideration and approval of such a plan and for the entry of a final order requiring its implementation.

We are of the view that the trial court's judgment should be modified in certain respects. We see no reason why the entire zoning ordinance should be nullified. Therefore we declare it to be invalid only to the extent and in the particulars set forth in this opinion. The township is granted 90 days from the date hereof, or such additional time as the trial court may find it reasonable and necessary to allow, to adopt amendments to correct the deficiencies herein specified. It is the local function and responsibility, in the first instance at least, rather than the court's, to decide on the details of the same within the guidelines we have laid down. If plaintiffs desire to attack such amendments, they may do so by supplemental complaint filed in this cause within 30 days of the final adoption of the amendments.

We are not at all sure what the trial judge had in mind as ultimate action with reference to the approval of a plan for affirmative public action concerning the satisfaction of indicated housing needs and the entry of a final order requiring implementation thereof. Courts do not build housing nor do municipalities. That function is performed by private builders, various kinds of associations, or, for public housing, by special agencies created for that purpose at various levels of government. The municipal function is initially to provide the opportunity through appropriate land use regulations and we have spelled out what Mount Laurel must do in that regard. It is not appropriate at this time, particularly in view of the advanced view of zoning law as applied to housing laid down by this opinion, to deal with the matter of the further extent of judicial power in the field or to exercise any such power. See, however, *Pascack Association v. Mayor and Council of Township of Washington,* 131 N.J.Super. 195, 329 A.2d 89 (Law Div.1974), and cases therein cited, for a discussion of this question. The municipality should first have full opportunity to itself act without judicial supervision. We trust it will do so in the spirit we have suggested, both by appropriate zoning ordinance amendments and whatever additional action encouraging the fulfillment of its fair share of the regional need for low and moderate income housing may be indicated as necessary and advisable. (We have in mind that there is at least a moral obligation in a municipality to establish a local housing agency pursuant to state law to provide housing for its resident poor now living in dilapidated, unhealthy quarters.) The portion of the trial court's judgment ordering the preparation and submission of the aforesaid study, report and plan to it for further action is therefore vacated as at least premature. Should Mount Laurel not perform as we expect, further judicial action may be sought by supplemental pleading in this cause.

The judgment of the Law Division is modified as set forth herein. No costs.

MOUNTAIN and PASHMAN, JJ., concurring in the result.

For modification: Chief Justice HUGHES and Justices JACOBS, HALL, MOUNTAIN, SULLIVAN, PASHMAN and CLIFFORD — 7.

Opposed: None.

[The concurring opinion of Justice Mountain is omitted.]

PASHMAN, J. (concurring).

With this decision, the Court begins to cope with the dark side of municipal land use regulation — the use of the zoning power to advance the parochial interests of the municipality at the expense of the surrounding region and to establish and perpetuate social and economic segregation.

. . . .

The misuse of the municipal zoning power at issue in this case, generically described as "exclusionary zoning," *see, e. g., Brooks, Exclusionary Zoning* 3 (Am. Soc'y. of Planning Officials 1970), involves two distinct but interrelated practices: (1) the use of the zoning power by municipalities to take advantage of the benefits of regional development without having to bear the burdens of such development; and (2) the use of the zoning power by municipalities to maintain themselves as enclaves of affluence or of social homogeneity.

. . . .

Every developing municipality has at least a duty to consider regional housing needs in all its planning activities, both formal and informal, including its formulation of the comprehensive plan underlying its zoning ordinance, N.J.S.A. 40:55-21, its adoption of a master plan, N.J.S.A. 40:55-1.10 and its consideration of applications for zoning variances, N.J.S.A. 40:55-39, and for approval of subdivision plats, N.J.S.A. 40:55-1.14.[75] In addition, since effective

---

[75] While this opinion is principally directed towards municipalities, the same considerations also apply to planning at the county level when the county has chosen to exercise power to regulate land use permitted it by N.J.S.A. 40:27-1 et seq.

planning for regional needs is virtually impossible without some degree of intergovernmental cooperation, all developing municipalities also have an affirmative obligation to cooperate, where appropriate, in regional planning efforts, to cooperate, for example, with regional planning boards established pursuant to N.J.S.A. 40:27-9 and in area review procedures established under the Intergovernmental Cooperation Act, 42 U.S.C. § 4231 and implemented by U.S. Office of Management and Budget Circular A-95 (July 24, 1969) and N.J.A.C. 5:42-1.1 et seq. *See generally Babcock & Bosselman, Exclusionary Zoning: Land Use Regulation and Housing in the 1970s,* 135-47 (1973).

There is little hope that the private housing construction industry will be able to satisfy the State's housing needs in the foreseeable future, even if all exclusionary barriers are removed. *Building the American City, supra,* at 93. To meet these needs, State or federal assistance will be required. This act has been recognized by both the State Legislature and Congress in a lengthy series of statutes providing governmental subsidies for private construction and ownership of low and moderate income housing. . . . To a greater or lesser degree, all of the programs require active municipal cooperation. Failure to actively cooperate in the implementation of such programs as effectively thwarts the meeting of regional needs for low and moderate income housing as does outright exclusion. . . . Developing municipalities have a duty to make all reasonable efforts to encourage and facilitate private efforts to take advantage of these programs.

Finally, there may be circumstances in which the municipality has an affirmative duty to provide housing for persons with low and moderate incomes through public construction, ownership, or management.

. . . .

There are certain important limitations on the scope of these affirmative obligations. While municipalities must plan and provide for regional housing needs, no municipality need assume responsibility for more than its fair share of these needs. The purpose of land use regulation is to create pleasant, well-balanced communities, not to recreate slums in new locations. It is beyond dispute that when the racial and socioeconomic composition of the population of a community shifts beyond a certain point, the white and affluent begin to abandon the community. While the attitudes underlying this "tipping" effect must not be catered to, the phenomenon must be recognized as a reality. . . . Municipalities have a legitimate interest in placing an upper limit on the extent of uses which, if permitted to expand without limit, might reasonably be feared to operate to the general detriment. *Tidewater Oil Co. v. Carteret,* 84 N.J.Super. 525, 202 A.2d 865 (App.Div.1965), aff'd 44 N.J. 338, 209 A.2d 105 (1965). The limitation of the municipality's affirmative duty to one of providing for its fair share of reasonable needs responds to this interest. *Cf.* Mass.Gen.Laws Ann., c. 40B, §§ 20-23 (a statute authorizing the state to override local zoning restrictions for low and moderate income housing projects, but limiting the municipality's obligations to fixed annual and total maxima). A number of regions have, in response to the problem of exclusionary zoning, voluntarily sought to put such fair share housing plans into effect. *See Babcock & Bosselman, supra* at 109-13.

Nor need a municipality altogether give up control of the pace and sequence of development. A municipality has a legitimate interest in insuring that residential development proceeds in an orderly and planned fashion, that the burdens upon municipal services do not increase faster than the practical ability of the municipality to expand the capacity of those services, and that exceptional environmental and historical features are not simply concreted over. *See, e. g., Golden v. Ramapo Planning Board,* 30 N.Y.2d 359, 334 N.Y.S.2d 138, 285 N.E.2d 291 (1972), appeal dismissed 409 U.S. 1003, 93 S.Ct. 436, 34 L.Ed.2d 294 (1972); *Construction Industry Ass'n of Sonoma County v. Petaluma,* 375 F.Supp. 574 (N.D.Cal.1974); Mass.Gen.Laws Ann., c. 40B, §§ 20, 23. On the other hand, such regulations must be reasonable, substantially related to the purpose which they seek to achieve, and must adopt the least exclusionary means practical. "Zoning is a means by which a governmental body can plan for the future — it may not be used as a means to deny the future." *National Land and Investment Co. v. Kohn,* 419 Pa. 504, 528, 215 A.2d 597, 610 (Pa.Sup.Ct.1965). By way of illustration, large lot zoning is commonly rationalized as a device for preventing premature development. Such zoning, it is claimed, merely creates holding zones. In practice, however, it appears that land zoned for large lots, even where intended as an interim holding zone, tends to become frozen in a pattern of low density development. . . . Such zoning is not a reasonable device for regulating the pace and sequence of development. Its effects on development, if any, are merely exclusionary.

Finally, the affirmative duty to plan and provide for regional needs does not require the municipality to make any specific piece of property available for low or moderate income housing, absent a showing that there are inadequate alternative sites realistically available for that type of development. A municipality must zone in accordance with a comprehensive plan. N.J.S.A. 40:55-32. Once it has adopted a comprehensive plan which properly provides for the community's fair share of the regional housing needs, it is entitled to be able to enforce that plan through its zoning ordinances. To permit a developer to come in at a later date and demand, as a matter of right, that a piece of property not presently zoned to permit development of low or moderate cost housing be so zoned, is to undermine the entire premise of land use regulations. *Williams, supra* at § 66.15; *See Confederacion de la Raza Unida v. Morgan Hill,* 324 F.Supp. 895 (N.D.Cal.1971). The one exception to this principle is the situation in which the developer can show that as a matter of practical fact, sufficient land is not available for development in the areas zoned for low or moderate income housing. *See, e. g., Kennedy Park Homes Association v. Lackawanna,* 318 F.Supp. 669 (W.D.N.Y.1970), aff'd 436 F.2d 108 (2 Cir. 1970), cert. den. 401 U.S. 1010, 91 S.Ct. 1256, 28 L.Ed.2d 546 (1971) (construction of multi-family housing in area zoned for it would perpetuate a segregated housing pattern and add to existing problem of overcrowding); *Pascack Ass'n v. Washington Tp.,* 131 N.J.Super. 195, 329 A.2d 89 (Law Div.1974) (area zoned for multi-family housing was already largely occupied by other, non-residential uses, and was burdened with other zoning requirements that made construction of low or moderate income housing impractical).

The affirmative obligations of developing municipalities so far discussed are legally binding and judicially enforceable. It is a truism that courts have no inherent expertise in matters of land use planning. They are not equipped to sit as higher planning boards and substitute their judgment for municipal bodies lawfully established for the purpose of making planning and zoning decisions. . . . The decision as to how the municipality should go about performing the affirmative duties set out above is one initially to be made by the officials of the municipality itself. Nevertheless, if the municipality has failed to take affirmative steps to make realistically possible a variety and choice of housing so as to meet its fair share of the regional housing needs, its actions are presumptively illegal and the burden shifts to the municipality to justify them. The mere fact that local land use control issues are involved does not preclude the court from making such determinations, nor, if a court finds that the municipality has failed to meet its obligation, from exercising the full panoply of equitable powers to remedy the situation. . . .

Judicial enforcement of municipal obligations, both negative and affirmative, to plan and provide for a fair share of regional housing needs, even if only directed to one municipality, necessarily has grave implications for the entire region. In dealing with such cases courts must act both deliberately and imaginatively. In administering such relief the trial court ought to proceed in four steps:

(1) identify the relevant region; [76]

(2) determine the present and future housing needs of the region;

(3) allocate these needs among the various municipalities in the region; [77] and

(4) shape a suitable remedial order.

. . . .

Since conflicting decisions within a given region would be highly undesirable, all municipalities in the region should be joined as parties at the earliest practical point in the proceedings, if not at the instance of one of the parties, then on the motion of the court. R. 4:28-1, 4:30.

. . . .

Comments: 1. The outpouring of commentary on the *Mount Laurel* case has been enormous. Much of this commentary is cited in footnote 80 in the next principal case. In addition, see Buchsbaum, The Irrelevance of the "Developing Municipality" Concept — A Reply to Professors Rose and Levin, 5 Real Est. L.J. 280 (1977); Rose, The Trickle Before the Deluge from *Mount Laurel,* 5 Real Est. L.J. 69 (1976); Kelly, Will the Housing Market

---

[76] Relevant considerations might include: the area included in the interdependent residential housing market; the area encompassed by significant patterns of commutation; the area served by major public services and facilities, *e. g.,* parks, hospitals, cultural facilities, etc.; the area in which the housing problem can be solved. All of these considerations must be evaluated in terms of both present facts and projections of future development.

[77] The following factors were considered in developing a fair share plan for the Dayton, Ohio area:

[T]he needed low and moderate income dwelling units were assigned to the planning units using a composite of numbers resulting from six calculation methods: (1) equal share; (2) proportionate share of the county's households; (3) proportionate share of the county's households making less than $10,000 annually (or less than $7,000 in the three more rural counties); (4) the inverse of #3; (5) a share based on the assessed valuation per pupil of the school districts covering the planning units; and (6) a share based on the relative over-crowding of the school districts involved.

. . . .

The six factors used in the calculations, however, seemed to reflect some very basic determinations: the possibility of each subarea being treated equally, the existing distribution of each county's households and lower income households, and two indicators of the receiving school districts' ability to accept new students. The latter two were used because the school question emerged as a critical concern whenever low and moderate income housing was mentioned for placement in a given area.

[Bertsch & Shafer "A Regional Housing Plan: The Miami Valley Regional Planning Commission Experience," 1 Planners Notebook No. 1 (1971) quoted in *Williams, supra* § 66.36.]

Evaluation Model Be the Solution to Exclusionary Zoning? 3 Real Est. L.J. 373 (1975). *See also* Rose, The Mandatory Percentage of Moderately Priced Dwelling Ordinance (MPMPD) Is the Latest Technique of Inclusionary Zoning, 3 Real Est. L.J. 176 (1974); Listokin, Fair Share Housing Distribution: Will It Open the Suburbs to Apartment Development? 2 Real Est. L.J. 739 (1974). Many of the articles commenting on *Mount Laurel* were originally presented as papers at a symposium held at the Rutgers-Newark Law School. All the symposium papers (including many not published elsewhere) have recently been published in After *Mount Laurel:* The New Suburban Zoning (J. Rose and R. Rothman eds. 1977).

2. In the principal case, as the court noted in footnote [56], the defendant township originally challenged the plaintiffs' standing to bring the action and the trial court held that the resident plaintiffs had adequate standing to ground the entire action, thus finding it unnecessary to pass on the standing of the other plaintiffs. The Supreme Court in the principal case then volunteered the opinion "that both categories of nonresident individuals likewise have standing," but expressed "no opinion" as to the standing of the organizations. The relaxed attitude of the New Jersey courts with regard to standing in exclusionary zoning cases is further illustrated by *Urban League v. Mayor & Council,* 359 A.2d 526 (N.J. Super. 1976), and *Urban League v. Township of Mahwah,* 370 A.2d 521 (N.J. Super. 1977).

In the *Carteret* case the court held that all the plaintiffs — the Urban League and five persons who sued individually and as representatives of others similarly situated — had standing under New Jersey law to challenge the zoning ordinances of 23 of the 25 municipalities in Middlesex County on the ground that these ordinances did not permit the municipalities to accept their fair share of the low- and moderate-income housing needed in the region. The court cited *Crescent Park Tenants Ass'n v. Realty Equity Corp.,* 275 A.2d 433 (N.J. 1971) in support of the Urban League's standing. It is interesting that one of the individual plaintiffs was a white person who objected to the racial and economic imbalance in South Brunswick, the predominantly white municipality in which he resided with his family, including two children attending public schools. The court held that the suit was maintainable as a class action.

In the *Mahwah* case, the court held that two of the individual plaintiffs had standing to challenge the Mahwah zoning ordinance and the zoning ordinances of three nearby municipalities because of their alleged discriminatory effect in excluding potential residents on the basis of race, national origin, and economic status. These two plaintiffs worked at the Ford plant in Mahwah and asserted that they were required to commute substantial distances (from New York City) to their jobs due to the absence of decent, adequate, and affordable housing in the defendant municipalities. The court did not express any opinion as to the standing of the other two individual plaintiffs or the two nonprofit corporate plaintiffs; but the court emphasized that New Jersey "is not . . . bound by federal rules of standing, particularly where rights under the State Constitution are brought into issue" and again cited the *Crescent Tenants Ass'n* case.

3. On the "standing" issue, see also *Suffolk Hous. Serv., Inc. v. Town of Brookhaven,* 397 N.Y.S.2d 302 (N.Y. Sup. Ct. 1977) (trial court), where a suit to invalidate zoning ordinance restrictions on multiple-family housing

development was brought by a group of unpropertied, low-income residents of the town; one individual who alleged she was forced to leave the town because she could not locate adequate housing for herself and her two children; the President of the Borough of Manhattan in New York City; and three nonprofit corporate plaintiffs. The court held that the unpropertied low-income residents, as well as the individual who allegedly was forced to leave the town and locate elsewhere in inadequate housing, had standing to challenge the zoning restrictions as having a disportionately harsh impact on low-income groups who must rent rather than purchase. The resident taxpayers, however, were held to lack standing because their "federal claims" had been rejected in the federal courts when advanced by others and they claimed no injury judicially cognizable under New York law. The court said, in so holding, that while zoning cases have traditionally imposed a rather loose standing requirement, a plaintiff is still required to show some injury or deprivation of right. The court also held that the Manhattan Borough President, who claimed to represent minority citizens living in the New York City "slum ghetto" who could not relocate in Brookhaven because affordable housing was unavailable, was "also merely a concerned bystander who asserts no direct interest in the litigation." Therefore, he was also without standing to bring the action. But the nonprofit corporate plaintiffs were held to have standing to challenge the zoning ordinance as violative of both state and federal equal protection clauses and various statutes. On appeal, the Appellate Division held that the resident taxpayers plaintiffs had standing "to challenge the adequacy of the zoning ordinance as to whether it provides an orderly plan for balanced growth." 405 N.Y.S.2d 302-303 (N.Y.App.Div. 1978).

4. With the exception of New Jersey and perhaps New York, the state courts have generally held that a party must demonstrate that the municipal zoning regulations invade a personal legal right in order to have standing to challenge the validity of the regulations. Under this restrictive standing rule, the only parties with standing to challenge zoning regulations are the owners of the land directly affected by the challenged regulations and the owners of other land indirectly affected thereby. In many states a sufficient invasion of legal right to create standing is presumed (pursuant to statute or judicial decision) in favor of any owner of land adjacent or reasonably close to the land that is subject to the challenged zoning regulations. But owners of land not within a reasonable distance of the subject property must prove special injury to their property rights in order to establish standing to challenge the zoning regulations. A mere generalized claim that the zoning regulations are harmful to a landowner as a member of the community or taxpayer is not sufficient. Although § 7 of the Standard State Zoning Enabling Act (see *supra* p. 219) expressly conferred standing on "any taxpayer," less than one half the states which substantially enacted the Standard Act retained this provision; and even in the states which retained it, the courts have generally required a showing of special injury to a property interest as a prerequisite to finding that a landowner has standing. Persons not owning land within the municipality have generally been denied standing to challenge municipal zoning regulations. For a concise but somewhat fuller discussion of the standing problem in state courts, see

Housing for All Under Law 98-104 (R. Fishman ed. 1977) (Report of the American Bar Ass'n Advisory Comm'n on Housing and Urban Growth).

5. On the merits, it was held in *Carteret* that the zoning ordinances of 11 of the 23 defendant municipalities were invalid because they did not permit these municipalities to accept their fair share of the low- and moderate-income housing needed in the region; and that each of these municipalities must rezone to accept enough housing units so that the total number of low- and moderate-income units available in the region would beet the projected need for such units in 1985. The court found that Middlesex County, which was a standard metropolitan statistical area, which contained 20 of the county's 25 municipalities joining in a community block grant application under the terms of the Housing and Community Development Act of 1974, which had a county master plan, and was "within the sweep of suburbia," was a "region" for purposes of determining if the various municipalities were affording opportunities for their fair shares of low- and moderate-income housing. The court apparently thought the 11 municipalities in question were "developing" communities within the meaning of the term as used in *Mount Laurel,* although the court said by way of dictum that "a municipality is not exempt from the constitutional standards of reasonableness in its zoning because it is not 'developing' within *Mount Laurel.*"

6. In the *Suffolk Hous. Serv.* case, *supra,* the court sustained the complaint, as against a motion to dismiss, on the ground that it adequately pleaded that the town's zoning policies contravened the New York zoning enabling act because they did not promote the general welfare and did not provide for a properly balanced, well-ordered plan for meeting the community's present and future needs. In so holding, the court relied heavily on *Berenson v. Town of New Castle,* 341 N.E.2d 236 (N.Y. 1975). The *Suffolk Hous. Serv.* opinion summarizes the *Berenson* case as follows:

> *Berenson* involved an attack on the validity of the entire New Castle zoning ordinance because it excluded multi-family housing throughout the Town. The case was traditionally postured with landowning plaintiffs who had failed to obtain approval for a multi-family condominium development — clearly not intended for low or moderate income occupants — on a 50-acre site in a one-acre single family zoning district. Cross motions for summary judgment were denied because Special Term and the Appellate Division found the existence of fact issues as to whether the need for multi-family housing in New Castle "is so compelling as to amount to a deprivation of the constitutional rights of those people who are presently, or would if economically feasible, become residents of the Town." ...
>
> Disagreeing with this formulation of constitutional issues and relying upon the general welfare provision of Town Law 261, [the zoning enabling act — Eds.] the Court of Appeals enunciated a two-tiered doctrine under which the New Castle Town Board was held obligated 1) to provide a properly balanced and well-ordered plan for the community which meets its present and future needs, and 2) to consider regional needs and requirements in view of the needs of Westchester County [where the town is located — Eds.] and New York metropolitan region residents who require multi-family housing in the New Castle area to be near their

employment or for a variety of other social and economic reasons. The court stopped far short of the "fair share" doctrine posited by the New Jersey Supreme Court to the effect that each municipality must provide the opportunity to meet a fair share of regional requirements ... and declared instead that there is no municipal obligation to provide for local or regional needs if those needs are already being met by other nearby communities. As in Pennsylvania, where the plaintiffs also have been landowners and developers, the constitutional question of equal protection was avoided ... by the Court of Appeals.

7. On remand of the *Berenson* case, *supra,* Comment 6, the trial court found that the New Castle zoning ordinance (a) did not provide a properly balanced and well-ordered plan to meet the present and future needs of the community, and (b) that regional needs for multiple-family housing were not being met by other nearby communities. The court then proceeded to work out "the appropriate remedy" for the exclusionary zoning problem it found to exist. The opinion on remand is reprinted *infra* p. 554.

8. In *Township of Willistown v. Chesterdale Farms, Inc.,* 341 A.2d 466 (Pa. 1975), the Pennsylvania Supreme Court adopted a novel application of the *Mount Laurel* "fair share" requirement. The following discussion of the *Willistown* case is drawn from 13 Urb. L. Ann. 277, 278-86 (1977):

In *Willistown* plaintiff-developer proposed to build apartments on a parcel of land located in the township. The township zoning ordinance had been amended in accordance with the landmark Pennsylvania case *Appeal of Girsh* [reprinted as a principal case, *supra* p. 347. — Eds.] to permit apartments in an eighty acre area. This area did not, however, include plaintiff-developer's land. After his request for a building permit was denied by the local zoning hearing board, the developer appealed to the court of common pleas which upheld the hearing board decision but declared the amended zoning ordinance unconstitutional. On allocatur, the Pennsylvania Supreme Court held the rezoning to be "mere tokenism" in violation of the restrictions on exclusionary land use regulations set forth in *Girsh* and " 'exclusionary' in that it does not provide for a fair share of the township acreage for apartment construction." The court directed that zoning approval be granted and that a building permit be issued to plaintiff-developer. . . .

The more recent exclusionary zoning cases have examined the effects of zoning ordinances from a regional perspective. The courts consider a wider range of interests, including those of neighboring communities and potential residents, to be within the general welfare when reviewing challenged zoning ordinances. New Jersey has been at the center of exclusionary zoning litigation.
. . .

Mount Laurel left several questions unanswered: how to determine "regional need" and "fair share" and the extent to which courts should grant affirmative relief in exclusionary zoning cases. These issues were raised but not confronted in *Willistown,* which was based almost entirely on *Girsh* and *Mount Laurel.* The court found that "the rezoning of only eighty acres out of 11,589 acres in the township constitute[d] 'tokenism,' and was an exclusionary land use restriction not meeting the *Girsh* standard." The court then relied on *Mount Laurel* to hold that the township zoning ordinance continued to be exclusionary because "it did not provide for a fair share of the township acreage for apartment construction."

The court's characterization of the township's zoning as an unacceptable token response to *Girsh* is questionable. *Girsh* simply held a total exclusion of apartment use to be an impermissible restraint on population growth, and required zoning schemes to make "reasonable provision" for such uses. The *Willistown* court apparently considered an eighty acre rezoning (less than one percent of the total township acreage) to be unreasonable and tantamount to a total exclusion under *Girsh*. The dissent, however, noted that the rezoning for apartment use in the predominantly rural township would have provided for the construction of 800 to 1040 apartment units which could have housed 1600 to 3120 persons. The 3120-person figure represented a potential increase of over one third the township population at the time of rezoning, which is arguably neither a token increase nor a de facto exclusion.

The courts have attempted to substantively define regional need and fair share. *Mount Laurel* and several recent Pennsylvania cases have applied socioeconomic criteria to determine a municipality's fair share of low and moderate income housing. *Mount Laurel*, however, considered "fair share" in the context of "regional need." The *Willistown* court did not consider regional housing needs but instead looked only to the fact that less than one percent of the township acreage was zoned to permit apartments. . . . .

The transformation of a courtroom victory into actual housing has been rare. . . . Controversy has developed over the extent to which courts should order affirmative relief. The court in *Willistown* granted zoning approval to plaintiff-developer and directed that a building permit be issued, contingent upon developer "compliance with the administrative requirements of the zoning ordinance and other reasonable controls." . . .

Willistown may represent an overreaction of the Pennsylvania Supreme Court to the frustration of its decision in *Girsh* and to the attention given to *Mount Laurel*. While a charge of "tokenism" is undoubtedly valid in some circumstances, it is possible that the court has misapplied this characterization in *Willistown*. Willistown Township may in fact have complied with the mandate of *Girsh*. However, the validity of a finding of exclusionary purpose and effect based solely on the acreage alloted for apartment use is questionable. Consideration of percentage of township land alone is an inadequate basis from which to determine fair share or regional need.

9. The implications of the *Willistown* case for exclusionary zoning in Pennsylvania were clarified in *Surrick v. Zoning Bd.*, 382 A.2d 105 (Pa. 1977). In this case a challenge was brought by a developer who had requested a variance for apartment use in a township which practically excluded all multifamily development from its limits. Apartments were allowed only in the business district, along with other uses. This district occupied only 1.14 percent of the land area of the township and was almost fully developed. The township was located on the periphery of the Philadelphia metropolitan area and was about one quarter undeveloped.

The Pennsylvania Supreme Court struck down the ordinance in an opinion which it viewed as confirming the trend of its authority in cases such as *Willistown, Girsh, supra* p. 347, and *National Land, supra* p. 432. As the court noted, it had "employed a substantive due process analysis in reviewing zoning schemes and ha[d] concluded implicitly that exclusionary or unduly restrictive zoning techniques do not have the requisite substantial relationship to the public welfare." *Id.* at 108. *Willistown* was viewed as having "adopted the 'fair share' principle, which requires local political units to plan for and provide land-use regulations which meet the legitimate needs of all categories of people who may desire to live within its boundaries," a statement somewhat contradicted by a later assertion by the court that the Pennsylvania cases had been concerned, not with the exclusion of people, but with use exclusions.

In response to commentary that judicial review of exclusionary zoning improperly intruded courts into the local decision-making process, the Pennsylvania court next noted that it would only review to determine whether local zoning ordinances "reflect a balanced and heightened consideration of the many factors which bear upon local and regional housing needs and development." The "vast expansion" of zoning principles brought about by *Mount Laurel* was foresworn, and the fair share approach was seen only as an "analytical strand" in the application of the conventional due process substantial relationship test.

The court next outlined the nature of the inquiry to be conducted in exclusionary zoning cases:

> The initial inquiry must focus upon whether the community in question is a logical area for development and population growth. . . . The community's proximity to a large metropolis and the community's and region's projected population growth figures are factors which courts have considered in answering this inquiry. . . .
> Having determined that a particular community is in the path of urban-suburban growth, the present level of development within the particular community must be examined. Population density data and the percentage of total undeveloped land and the percentage available for the development of multi-family dwellings are factors highly relevant to this inquiry. . . .

Id. at 110. The court then noted that their inquiry did not require an analysis of the purpose of the zoning ordinance; exclusionary impact was the issue to be considered. In evaluating this impact a distinction was to be made between total and partial exclusions. Partial exclusion cases required consideration of local and regional growth pressures in light of the total undeveloped land within the community. When the amount of zoned land available for multifamily development was disproportionately small, the ordinance must be held unconstitutional as exclusionary. In this case, the court had no difficulty in reaching this result.

Note that the Pennsylvania Supreme Court made no reference to the *Oakwood at Madison* case in New Jersey, which is reproduced *infra* and which elaborates on the *Mount Laurel* fair share requirement. However, the simplified factor test adopted in *Surrick* appears to be an attempt by the Pennsylvania court to escape some of the difficult policy dilemmas posed by the *Mount Laurel* opinion. Has the Pennsylvania court been successful in providing a more easily manageable test for exclusionary zoning? *See also Save a Valuable Environment v. City of Bothell,* 576 P.2d 401 (Wash. 1978) (regional general welfare test applied in shopping center rezoning).

    10. In *Mount Laurel* the New Jersey court said that definition of the relevant "region" and determination of the municipality's "fair share" of low and moderate income housing "are more fully involved in *Oakwood at Madison v. Township of Madison,* . . . appeal pending unheard in this court." (336 A.2d n. 23, at 733.) We reprint, as the next principal case, the New Jersey Supreme Court's opinion(s) in *Oakwood at Madison.* The trial court's opinion on remand in the *Mt. Laurel* case is discussed *infra* pp. 538-39 following the *Oakwood* opinion.

OAKWOOD AT MADISON, INC. v. TOWNSHIP OF MADISON

Supreme Court of New Jersey
72 N.J. 481, 371 A.2d 1192 (1977)

CONFORD, P. J. A. D., Temporarily Assigned.

    We today review the decision of Judge Furman invalidating the 1973 amendatory zoning ordinance of defendant Township of Madison.[78] 128 N.J.Super. 438, 320 A.2d 223 (Law Div.1974). That determination culminated an action instituted by plaintiffs in November 1970 challenging the validity of a zoning ordinance adopted by the township in September 1970 to replace a previous one in effect since 1964.[79] Judge Furman had invalidated the 1970 ordinance in *Oakwood at Madison, Inc. v. Tp. of Madison,* 117 N.J.Super. 11, 21, 283 A.2d 353 (Law Div. 1971), but at the same time rejected an attack by plaintiffs on the constitutionality of the enabling zoning statute, N.J.S.A. 40:55-30 *et seq. Id.* at 16.

    Defendant obtained a stay of judgment pending its appeal to the Appellate Division, and plaintiffs filed a cross-appeal as to that part

---

   [78] Since the last oral argument the name of the municipality was changed to Old Bridge. For convenience and conformity with the record we use the former name, Madison, in this opinion.

   [79] In 1969, prior to adoption of the 1970 ordinance, the township declared a moratorium on all residential construction other than owner-occupied single family dwellings pending the adoption of a new master plan and zoning ordinance. As a result of litigation challenging the moratorium, the Superior Court in Middlesex County, in *Verterre Corp. v. Township Comm. of Twp. of Madison* (Docket No. L-13820-68 P.W., 7/30/69), ordered the submission to the Township of a new master plan by January 1, 1970 and adoption of a new zoning ordinance by July 1, 1970.

of the judgment sustaining the validity of the statute. On plaintiffs' motion, and because of the importance of the case, we certified the appeals pending unheard in the Appellate Division pursuant to R. 2:12-2. 62 N.J. 185, 299 A.2d 720 (1972).

Oral argument was originally heard by the court on March 5, 1973, and additional argument was requested for January 8, 1974. However, on October 1, 1973 Madison Township adopted a major amendment to the 1970 ordinance. Consequently, on January 8, 1974, while retaining jurisdiction, we remanded the action to the trial court for a trial and ruling on the ordinance as amended, with the result stated above.

Oral argument on the present phase of the appeal has been had twice, emphasis being placed on the effect on the issues herein of our intervening decision in *So. Burl. Cty. N. A. A. C. P. v. Tp. of Mt. Laurel,* 67 N.J. 151, 336 A.2d 713, app. dism. and cert. den. 423 U.S. 808, 96 S.Ct. 18, 46 L.Ed.2d 28 (1975) (*"Mount Laurel"* hereinafter). We have received and considered supplemental briefs and materials.

Plaintiffs herein comprise two groups. Oakwood at Madison, Inc. and Beren Corporation (hereinafter "corporate plaintiffs"), both New Jersey corporations, were developers owning a tract of vacant developable land of some 400 acres, the disputed Oakwood-Beren tract. Six individuals were low income persons acknowledged by the trial judge as "representing as a class those who reside outside the township and have sought housing there unsuccessfully." *Oakwood at Madison, Inc. v. Tp. of Madison, supra* (117 N.J.Super. at 14, 283 A.2d at 354). Plaintiffs alleged, *inter alia,* (a) that the exclusionary nature of the ordinance rendered it unconstitutional; (b) that the enabling legislation was unconstitutional in its failure to provide adequate standards for municipal exercise of the zoning power; and (c) that the restrictive effect of the ordinance as applied to corporate plaintiffs' property rendered it confiscatory.

The trial court invalidated the 1970 ordinance, primarily on the grounds that in zoning massive areas of vacant developable land for one- and two-acre single family residences, beyond the reach of 90% of the population, and in allocating only "miniscule" acreage for multi-family dwelling units, it ignored the housing needs of the township and the region, and failed "to promote reasonably a balanced community in accordance with the general welfare." 117 N.J.Super. at 20-21, 283 A.2d at 358. The court upheld the constitutionality of the enabling legislation; it did not reach the issue of confiscation, apparently regarding the invalidation of the entire ordinance as rendering that matter moot.

While the 1973 amendatory ordinance transferred substantial areas from large lot to smaller lot zoning, made more land available for multi-family development and provided for planned unit development (PUD) and "cluster" zones, the evidence in the case convinced the court that the municipality still was not satisfying its obligation to "provide its fair share of the housing needs of its region", particularly in relation to the low-income and moderate-income population. 128 N.J.Super. at 447, 320 A.2d at 227. The amended ordinance was therefore again struck down in its entirety. *Ibid.*

The main lines of the Law Division opinion striking down the 1973 ordinance may be summarized as follows. A crisis in housing needs continues, most serious for those of low and moderate income. The region, whose housing needs must reasonably be provided for by such municipalities as Madison, is not necessarily coextensive with Middlesex County. "Rather, it is the area from which, in view of available employment and transportation, the population of the township would be drawn, absent invalidly exclusionary zoning". 128 N.J.Super. at 441, 320 A.2d at 224. Almost all of Madison's employed residents work outside the township, 50% in the county, 15% in New York City, 10% in Essex County, and the remainder in nearby counties, including 7% in Monmouth County. After an analysis of the testimony concerning the number of housing units which could be expected, under the amended ordinance, to be produced and to be affordable by low and moderate income households, the court said:

> Of the total 20,000 to 30,000 housing units which may be built in Madison Township under the 1970 zoning ordinance as amended, about 3500 [12% to 17%] at most would be within the reach of households with incomes of $10,000 a year, the upper limit of moderate incomes, and virtually none within the reach of households with incomes of $9,000 a year or less. This contrasts with the present township population, approximately 12% low income and 19% moderate income. *Id.* at 446, 320 A.2d at 227.

The court assessed Madison Township's obligation to provide its fair share of regional housing needs as follows:

> Without the rigidity of a mathematical formula this court holds that Madison Township's obligation to provide its fair share of the housing needs of its region is not met unless its zoning ordinance approximates in additional housing unit capacity the same proportion of low-income housing as its present low-income population, about 12%, and the same proportion of moderate-income housing as its present moderate-income population, about 19%. The amended zoning ordinance under review falls palpably short and must be struck down in its entirety. *Id.* at 447, 320 A.2d at 227.

The court did not specify any absolute numerical quota of low and moderate income units the ordinance would be expected to render possible, but found that annual needs "into the 1980's were 750 to 1000 units, 500 to 600 of those low and moderate income." *Id.* at 442, 320 A.2d at 225.

The court dealt with the defendants' argument that ecological and environmental factors justified the RP, R-80 (2 acre lot minimum) and R-40 (1 acre lot minimum) zones by pointing out that such problems had "no bearing" except in specified limited areas and that "ample land outside these areas is available" with which the township could meet its obligation to provide its fair share of needed housing. 128 N.J.Super. at 447, 320 A.2d at 228.

It should be stated at the outset that the basic rationale embraced by Judge Furman in both of his opinions in the case is substantially that adopted by this court in *Mount Laurel,* with the qualification that our determination there rested on the state constitutional ground that due process and equal protection are denied if "substantial segments of the population" are improperly precluded from residing within the municipality because of local zoning regulations. 67 N.J. at 175, 336 A.2d 713. The "substantial" segments thus identified were those low and moderate income people of the region economically unable to afford suitable housing in developing municipalities of the region because of their highly cost-generating zoning restrictions. . . .[80]

---

[80] Since *Mount Laurel* is based on State constitutional grounds, its requirements are not affected by the less restrictive federal concept of equal protection in this area. See *Arlington Heights v. Metropolitan Housing Development Corp.,* 429 U.S. 252, 97 S.Ct. 555, 50 L.Ed.2d 450 (1977).

Mount Laurel has been the subject of extensive discussion in the literature. See Ackerman, "The *Mount Laurel* Decision: Expanding the Boundaries of Zoning Reform", 1976 *U. of Ill. Law Forum* 1; Payne, "Delegation Doctrine in the Reform of Local Government Law: The Case of Exclusionary Zoning", 29 *Rutgers L.Rev.* 803, 805-819, 859-866 (1976); Williams, *American Land Planning Law* (1975) Addendum Ch. 66; Rose, "The *Mount Laurel* Decision: Is It Based on Wishful Thinking?", 4 *Real Estate L.J.* 61 (1975); Mytelka and Mytelka, "Exclusionary Zoning: A Consideration of Remedies," 7 *Seton Hall L.Rev.* 1, 3-4 (1975); Kushner, "Land Use Litigation and Low Income Housing: Mandating Regional Fair Share Plans," 9 *Clearinghouse Rev.* 10 (1975) (terming *Mount Laurel* the "Magna Carta of suburban low and moderate income housing"); Rohan, "Property Planning and the Search for a Comprehensive Housing Policy — The View from *Mount Laurel*", 49 *St. Johns L.Rev.* 653 (1975); Williams and Doughty, "Studies on Legal Realism: *Mount Laurel, Belle Terre* and *Berman*", 29 *Rutgers L.Rev.* 73 (1975) (calling *Mount Laurel* a "major turnaround on a major current problem"); Mallach, "Do Law Suits Build Housing? The Implications of Exclusionary Zoning Litigation", 6 *Rutgers-Camden L.J.* 653 (1975); Rose, "Exclusionary Zoning and Managed Growth: Some Unresolved Issues", 6 *Rutgers-Camden L.J.* 689 (1975); 6 Powell, *Real Property,* § 872.1[2][g] (1975); Rose and Levin, "What is a 'Developing Municipality' Within the Meaning of the *Mount Laurel* Decision?", 4 *Real Estate L.J.* 359 (1976). See also Berger, *Land Ownership and Use* 790-799 (2d ed. 1975). For

After the last argument in this matter the Legislature revised the zoning statutes of this State by enactment of the "Municipal Land Use Law", *L.* 1975, c. 291, which by its terms became operative August 1, 1976. We invited and have received from counsel supplemental comment as to any effect of the new law on the issues herein, particularly as to the continued viability of *Mount Laurel.* We find nothing in the statute inconsistent with the doctrine there laid down. (The decision would control, in any event, in view of its constitutional underpinning.) . . .

At the same time, the new law reminds us, as we emphasized in *Mount Laurel,* that out of a proper concern for adequate housing there should not and need not be overintensive and too sudden development, future suburban sprawl and slums, or sacrifice of open space and local beauty. 67 N.J. at 191, 336 A.2d 713. . . .

I

Outline of Major Issues

The judgment of the trial court, the intervention of our decision in *Mount Laurel* and the nature of the record and briefs before us combine to cast the issues for determination as follows:

1. Is the Madison 1973 zoning ordinance exclusionary, *i.e.,* whether or not so intended, does it operate in fact to preclude the opportunity to supply any substantial amounts of new housing for low and moderate income households now and prospectively needed in the municipality and in the appropriate region of which it forms a part?

2. If, as we have concluded, the affirmative response to the foregoing question by the trial court should be sustained is it incumbent upon the courts, pursuant to *Mount Laurel,* to demarcate a pertinent region and to fix a specific number of lower-cost housing units as the "fair share" of the regional need therefor to be made possible by the Madison ordinance?

3. If, as we have concluded, the foregoing question should be answered in the negative, what kind of an order should be made to assure Madison's compliance, as a developing municipality, with *Mount Laurel's* mandate that its zoning ordinance "afford the opportunity" for at least "the municipality's fair share of the present and prospective regional need" for "decent and adequate low and moderate income housing"? 67 N.J. at 188, 336 A.2d at 732.

---

a journalistic appraisal, see "U.S. Journal: Mount Laurel, N.J. — Some Thoughts on Where Lines are Drawn", *New Yorker,* 69 (Feb. 2, 1976). See also Note, "The Inadequacy of Judicial Remedies in Cases of Exclusionary Zoning", 74 *Mich.L.Rev.* 760 (1976).

II

"Fair Share" and "Region" — Preliminary Considerations

As noted above, the prime question before us, in *Mount Laurel* terms, is whether the trial court has correctly found that Madison's zoning ordinance does not provide the opportunity to meet a fair share of the regional burden for low and moderate income housing needs. We have seen that the trial court did not specify the precise boundaries of the applicable region nor fix an absolute number of appropriate housing units to be provided. It merely described the pertinent region as the area from which the population of the township would be drawn, absent exclusionary zoning.

A substantial body of evidence was adduced by the defendant below purporting to specify Madison's fair share of Middlesex County's unmet need for low and moderate income housing as of 1975. Moreover, the record before us, the briefs and the literature in the field supply abundant data concerning methods and techniques for estimating a municipality's fair share of a regional housing need. We propose to comment on these matters hereinafter, for three purposes: (a) to explain our conclusion that the evidence concerning fair share adduced by defendant does not refute the trial court determination that the Madison ordinance is deficient in the respects noted; (b) to elucidate the considerations relating to the appropriate "region" whose housing needs are relevant to this action; and (c) to furnish guidance to courts, counsel and expert witnesses in this area in applying the principles of *Mount Laurel* to litigated controversies generally.

However, we deem it well to establish at the outset that we do not regard it as mandatory for developing municipalities whose ordinances are challenged as exclusionary to devise specific formulae for estimating their precise fair share of the lower income [81] housing needs of a specifically demarcated region. Nor do we conceive it as necessary for a trial court to make findings of that nature in a contested case. First, numerical housing goals are not realistically translatable into specific substantive changes in a zoning ordinance by any technique revealed to us by our study of the data before us. There are too many imponderables between a zone change and the actual production of housing on sites as zoned, not to mention the production of a specific number of lower cost units in a given period of time. Municipalities do not themselves have the duty to build or subsidize housing. Secondly, the breadth of approach by the experts to the factor of the appropriate region and to the criteria for allocation of regional housing goals to municipal "subregions" is so

---

[81] "Lower income" is intended as a generic reference to low and moderate income, collectively.

great and the pertinent economic and sociological considerations so diverse as to preclude judicial dictation or acceptance of any one solution as authoritative. For the same reasons, we would not mandate the formula approach as obligatory on any municipality seeking to correct a fair share deficiency.

We are convinced from the record and data before us that attention by those concerned, whether courts or local governing bodies, to the *substance* of a zoning ordinance under challenge and to *bona fide* efforts toward the elimination or minimization of undue cost-generating requirements in respect of reasonable areas of a developing municipality represents the best promise for adequate productiveness without resort to formulaic estimates of specific unit "fair shares" of lower cost housing by any of the complex and controversial allocation "models" now coming into vogue.[82]

It is desirable that administrative agencies acting under legislative authorization assume the regulation of the housing distribution problem. Until then, in the current post-*Mount Laurel* period judicial emphasis on approaches such as those just outlined, and exemplified in the remedial section of this opinion, will, it is hoped, suffice to move the State toward the objective of "available housing in the developing municipalities for a goodly number of the various categories of people of low and moderate income who desire to live therein and now cannot." *Mount Laurel,* 67 N.J. at 188, n. 21, 336 A.2d at 732.

III

Madison-Its Growth and Development

Madison Township consists of approximately 42 square miles, or 25,000 acres, in the southeast corner of Middlesex County, of which almost 40% is vacant developable land. Its location within the gap between the metropolitan centers of New York and Philadelphia is a strategic one: this "Atlantic urban region" gap is expected to be bridged within the next 25 years, with a concomitant population

---

[82] See notes 102, 103, *infra.* We of course do not deprecate regional "fair share" studies by official or quasi-official governmental agencies or commissions such as those discussed hereinafter. Indeed, as will be emphasized, the basic underlying social problem is far better addressed by administrative action than litigation. In any case, the setting of numerical housing goals is only an incidental phase of the solution. The effective substantive revision of restrictive ordinances and governmental desire to implement such goals affirmatively are the essential prerequisites for housing relief.

We recognize, moreover, that fair share studies by expert witnesses may be of substantial evidential value to a trial court confronted with a litigated issue like the present one.

increase of 75%. The Tri-State Regional Planning Association (covering counties in New York, New Jersey and Connecticut and including Middlesex) predicts that Middlesex will be one of four counties to experience the greatest rates of growth in the tri-state area from 1970 to 2000.

Parts of the township lie within 20 miles of the highly urbanized areas of Elizabeth and Newark. . . . The accessibility of the township is readily illustrated by the status of the community as a commutershed. Only 1% of Madison's employed residents work within the township. As found by the trial court, 50% of the work force are employed in Middlesex County, 15% in New York City, 10% in Essex County, 9-12% in Union County and 7% in Monmouth County.

Madison is an archetypal "developing" municipality within the contemplation of the *Mount Laurel* specifications. 67 N.J. at 173, 187, 336 A.2d 713. During the past 25 years, it has experienced explosive growth. Its population increased over two decades by 561%, from 7,366 in 1950 to 48,715 in 1970. This boom has continued, with the population climbing to 50,000 by the time of the first trial and 55,000 by the second in 1974. With the growth and concomitant municipal problems came a steady rise in tax rates.

Even in light of this period of great expansion, Madison still has large potential for further growth.[83] Among the twenty-five municipalities in Middlesex County, Madison in 1970 ranked 20th lowest both in population density and housing density. Vacant acreage is plentiful; of the township's 25,000 acres, between 8,143 and 11,000 are vacant and developable. The township is a sprawling municipality marked by little continuity and spotty development. The area is laced by a network of streams and rivers eventually feeding into South River to the north. Cheesequake State Park occupies a sizeable portion of land in the eastern part of the town.

. . . .

Construction within the township fell off from 1970 to 1973. Comparing Madison with four nearby municipalities of generally similar characteristics (with large undeveloped areas) for the said three year period, Madison issued an average of only 53 dwelling unit building permits per year as against 368 in East Brunswick, 309 in Monroe, 89 in Sayreville and 212 in South Brunswick. Although

---

[83] Our discussion of the facts is not to be taken as laudation of growth *per se*. The fact and extent of anticipated growth are circumstances material to the need for housing all segments of the population. The control of growth is attracting widespread attention as vital to the maintenance of an acceptable environment. See *Federal Environmental Law* (1974) at pp. 1420-1426. See also 3 Williams, *American Land Planning Law* (1975), Ch. 73, "Timing of Development", p. 345 *et seq.; Mount Laurel,* 67 N.J. at 191, 336 A.2d 713; *id.* at 213, 336 A.2d 713 (Pashman, J., concurring).

Madison contains 20% of the county's vacant residentially zoned land, and from 1960 to 1970 issued 15% of all the building permits, from 1970 to 1972 its percentage of county building starts fell to 6%.

From 1950 to 1970 the housing growth in the township was characterized by construction of single family homes built on lots of 15,000 square feet or less and of a number of multi-family garden apartment developments. Virtually all the apartment units in the township, however, were constructed after 1963, and by April 1969 they comprised 3,700 or 27.4% of the total of 13,499 housing units in the township. In 1970, 56% of the single family dwellings in the township were valued at $25,000 or less. Figures from the 1970 census show that, in terms of statewide quintiles (20%) of income category, 12% of the township's households had income below $6,627, 19% between $6,627 and $9,936, 24% between $13,088 and $19,236, and 18% above $19,236. As of 1970, existing land uses were predominantly residential: 68% of all realty taxes were paid by single family homeowners, 16% by apartments and condominiums and the rest by commercial users, farms and industry.

Thus the overall pattern of land use confronting Madison Township planners and officials in 1970 was one of substantial but scattered residential growth, with little industrial and commercial development. The 1970 ordinance was a hurried effort to slow population growth and the accompanying rise in the tax rate and largely to confine new population to designated areas. See 117 N.J.Super. at 14, 283 A.2d 353.

IV

The Zoning Ordinances

A. The 1970 Ordinance

For present purposes the salient provisions of the 1970 ordinance are adequately summarized in the first opinion of the trial court. 117 N.J.Super. 16-17, 283 A.2d 353. The patent intent and effect of the ordinance was to prevent construction of a substantial number of homes or apartments, particularly at low cost. Most of the land area was zoned for one- or two-acre single family homes — uses not only beyond the reach of 90% of the general population but also responsive to little if any existing market. *Ibid.* It goes without saying that the ordinance was clearly violative of the principles later enunciated in *Mount Laurel.* Judge Furman properly condemned it as pure "fiscal zoning", not taking into consideration "[h]ousing needs of the region" and failing to promote "reasonably a balanced and well ordered plan for the entire municipality". 117 N.J.Super. at 18, 283 A.2d at 357.

B. The 1973 Ordinance

The 1973 ordinance extensively revised the land use restrictions of the prior ordinance. The amount of land zoned nonresidential (commercial, office and industrial) was decreased by 760 acres from 19.80% to 16.70% of the total. A new "open space" zone — RP or Recreation-Preservation — was created. This encompassed the areas deemed environmentally sensitive by the township: Cheesequake State Park, the Old Bridge sands area, Burnt Fly Bog, the meadowlands adjacent to Deep Run (the latter three containing underground water resources areas), and the Raritan beachfront. The RP and the RR zone (also an open space area devoted to substantial preservation in a natural condition) were permitted to be developed as R-80 on two-acre lots until acquired by the municipality.

Although the fact was not stressed at trial, Madison has placed more than 4,000 acres in zones restricted to industrial and office uses despite the fact that only some 600 acres have ever been devoted to that use. By comparison, we critized *Mount Laurel* for zoning 4,100 acres industrial although only 100 acres had even been so used. 67 N.J. at 162-163, 184, 336 A.2d 713.

The 1973 ordinance considerably increased the facial housing potential of the prior ordinance. It enlarged the total acreage available therefor by 800 acres and the potential housing capacity, inclusive of existing housing, by 16,000 units or 46,000 persons. These figures, supplied by the Madison Township Housing Study, may be misleading, as they assume all acreage zoned residential is or will be developed to its maximum permissible density whereas some of it is already developed, either nonresidential or below permissible density, or is undevelopable.

Under the 1973 ordinance, there are five single-family zones, accounting for 72% of the total vacant residential area.[84] The most restrictive zone, the R-80, with a minimum lot size of two acres, was reduced from 9,134 to 3,040 acres. The R-40 zone (one acre minimum lot size) was increased from 5,557 to 7,511 acres. Together, however, these two zones account for 42% of the total acreage within the township, 58% of its vacant developable acreage, 70% of the total acreage zoned single-family, and 80% of vacant

---

[84] Trial figures on the amount of acreage in each zone, both total and vacant developable, were often in conflict. However, unless otherwise stated, the statistics cited herein for total acreage, total units and total population are those submitted by the township's planning firm. The vacant developable acreage figures are those of defendant's expert witness Dennis Lanning, and, with the exception of the AF zone, were stipulated by the parties.

developable single family acreage.[85] The R-20 zone, 1,977 total or 1,285 vacant developable acres, requires a 20,000 square foot minimum lot size.

These three zones (R-20, R-40 and R-80) may be compared with the zones considered exclusionary in *Mount Laurel.* There more than half the township was zoned R-3, requiring single family homes on half acre lots; in the instant case, over 50% of the township is zoned for half acre lots or larger, and 42% for one- or two-acre lots. Considering only vacant developable acreage, the total for the three zones is over 65%, 58% comprising R-40 and R-80.[86]

The R-15 zone [87] and R-10 zones, requiring 15,000 and 10,000 square foot lots respectively, account for another 5% of the land. Both are more restrictive than the R-1 zone (9,375 square foot, 75' wide lots) involved in *Mount Laurel.* Calling for some "very small lot" zoning in a developing municipality, 67 N.J. at 170, n.8, 187, 336 A.2d 713, Justice Hall noted that minimum size lots of 9,375 to 20,000 square feet "cannot be called small lots and amounts to low density zoning." 67 N.J. at 183, 336 A.2d at 730. Yet almost 70% of Madison Township is zoned at such or lower densities (including the RP and RR zones).

Only the R-7 zone allows residential single family development on lots smaller than those found in *Mount Laurel* to constitute low density zoning. It allows 7,500 square foot lots and two-family dwellings. However it accounts for only 5.8% of the total acreage and 2% of the vacant developable acreage in the township.

The AF or multi-family apartment zone was enlarged by 150 acres. The prescribed bedroom ratio of the prior ordinance (80% one bedroom, 20% two bedroom) was deleted and replaced by a floor area ratio (FAR) limiting construction to a maximum of 10,000 square feet per acre. Although the ordinance presumably allows any

---

[85] The minimum floor space limitations in the R-40 and R-80 zones were eliminated, and minimum floor space limitations per room were established in all residential zones. With respect to the R-40 and R-80 zones, however, these changes have no effect on provision of low cost housing.

[86] We have no intent to impugn large lot zoning *per se.* If a developing municipality adequately provides by zoning for lower income housing it may zone otherwise for large lots to the extent that the owners of property so zoned have no other legitimate grievance therewith. *Cf.* Berger, *Land Ownership and Use* 735, 756 (2d ed. 1975).

[87] The R-15 is a new zone on the outskirts of existing high density development and contains a little over 500 acres. The 1964 ordinance had a majority residential area similar to the R-15 in which there were more than 3,000 vacant and developable acres compared to 168 acres under the 1973 ordinance. Thus although the R-15 has been restored, it is reduced to a small fraction of its original size.

size units in any combination, up to the maximum FAR, the impact of the building area ratio combined with the profit incentive which motivates developers is such that, according to the proofs, only small units (efficiencies and one bedrooms) will be constructed.[88]

Of the 676 acres zoned AF (2.7% of the total township acreage) at most only 193 acres are vacant and developable (2.3% of township total). The true figure, however, as indicated by Judge Furman, is more likely to approximate 120 acres (or 1.5% of township total).[89] The AF zone is limited to the development of parcels of six or more acres. The parties agreed that the AF zone could hold at least 800 housing units, but defendant maintains the maximum capacity is 1,700. However, as against township planner Abeles's estimate of 15,600 to 20,700 total additional units of all kinds possible under the ordinance, the potential AF units constitute only 5.1% to 8.2% thereof.[90]

Madison Township relies heavily on provisions in the 1973 ordinance for PUDs (planned unit developments) and clustering to satisfy its obligation with respect to low and moderate income housing. On the evidence, that reliance is illusory.

. . . .

[The PUD or planned unit development procedure is discussed *infra* Chapter 6, Part A. Generally, it contemplates an administrative process for the approval of an entire residential development as an

---

[88] Taken in entirety, the record herein justifies the following conclusions. Using the allowable 10,000 square foot figure, it would be possible to build 16 efficiencies per acre, which, at an average rental of $180 per month, would yield a total rental income per acre of $2880 per month. An acre can alternatively accommodate twelve one- and two-bedroom apartments on an 80-20 ratio, which, at rentals of $200 and $240 per month respectively, yields a monthly rental income per acre of $2496. If three-bedroom units were built, only 7 to 8 units would be possible, which, at a monthly rent of $280 per month, gross only $1960 or $2,240 per acre per month. Obviously, given equal marketability of all units, it is more profitable to develop efficiencies. Consequently we find justified Judge Furman's acceptance of plaintiffs' witness' testimony that under the restricted FAR provision, and without a maximum density per acre, efficiencies and one bedroom apartments will predominate. 128 N.J.Super. at 443, 320 A.2d 223.

All income, sale or rental figures set forth in this opinion, unless otherwise indicated, reflect economic conditions as of 1974 when the case was tried.

[89] The township tax assessor gave two figures for the vacant developable acreage in the AF — 112 and 125 acres. Plaintiffs contend the figure is closer to 67 acres.

[90] Based on other figures adduced at trial which were more favorable to the township, Judge Furman found a total additional capacity under the ordinance of 20,000 to 30,000 units. 128 N.J.Super. at 446, 320 A.2d 223. Using this capacity range, the percentage range is 4% to 5.7%.

entity. Density increases may be allowed in return for the provision by the developer of open spaces and other site amenities. However, the allowable densities in the township's PUD regulations were relatively low; the court doubted whether a density greater than 4.25 units per acre would be achieved. In addition, a variety of requirements were imposed on PUD developers that substantially increased housing costs. Streets and utility hookups had to be provided and developers had to build a school large enough to accommodate .5 children per dwelling unit. — Eds.]

The distribution of vacant and developable acreage (and total acreage) among the various zones under the ordinance shows that low density, middle and high income residential uses are strongly favored. Only a maximum of 2.37% of the town's vacant developable residential acreage is zoned for multi-family apartments (AF), and the correct figure may be as low as 1.02% or 0.84%. An additional 2% is zoned R-7 for small lot attached double houses. Though 9.9% is zoned for PUD development, the location of two of the three PUD tracts makes their development highly unlikely. Using the township planner's estimates of the potential future building capacity under the 1973 ordinance, the R-7 and AF zones account for a maximum of 16% of all housing units. By contrast, the R-80, R-40 and open space zones account for over 71% of the vacant developable residential acreage and over 41% of the housing units. If the R-15 and R-20 zones are counted, the large-lot single-family acreage figure increases to 82% and the unit figure to almost 50%.

V

"Least Cost" versus "Low and Moderate Income" Housing

A key consideration in this particular case as well as a factor integral to the entire problem, generally, is the well-known fact, amply corroborated by this record, that private enterprise will not in the current and prospective economy without subsidization or external incentive of some kind construct new housing affordable by the low income population and by a large proportion of those of moderate income.[91] We recognized this fact in *Mount Laurel.* 67 N.J.

---

[91] Kleven, "Inclusionary Ordinances — Policy and Legal Issues in Requiring Private Developers to Build Low Cost Housing", 21 *U.C.L.A.L. Rev.* 1432, 1434, 1451, 1456, 1466 (1974); Rose, "The *Mount Laurel* Decision: Is It Based on Wishful Thinking?", 4 *Real Estate L.J.* 61, 68 (1975); Mallach, "Exclusionary Zoning and Managed Growth: Some Unresolved Issues", 6 *Rutgers-Camden L.J.* 653, 660 (1975). See generally, HUD, *Housing in the Seventies* (1974), for a detailed discussion of housing costs, housing consumption by income groups, and the impact of subsidy programs.

at 170, n. 8; 188, n. 21, 336 A.2d 713. The amount and kind of governmental subsidies available for housing has always been fragmentary, and federal sources have recently been restricted. What can legally be required of municipalities by way of initiation of public housing programs and provision of zoning incentives for production of lower income housing will be discussed *infra*. But it will be apparent that sources extraneous to the unaided private building industry cannot be depended upon to produce any substantial proportion of the housing needed and affordable by most of the lower income population.

In view of the foregoing, defendant implies that the mandate of *Mount Laurel* is impracticable in the current economy and that litigation to enforce it is futile. Thus defendant flatly asserts in a supplemental brief: "We do not believe that substantial low and moderate income housing can be created by zoning." However, it goes on to make an observation which appears to us to provide the clue to the only acceptable alternative recourse if in fact private enterprise cannot economically construct the housing needed for lower income families. It states:

> Planned Unit Development can help by providing large amounts of additional housing some of which is in the moderate income range. The effect of new construction is also to create filtering whereby families in the moderate income group move into new housing created in the PUD zone making available existing housing for lower income families who cannot afford the new. Without subsidization, this is undoubtedly the most reasonable and certain method of creating housing opportunities for low income families.

To the extent that the builders of housing in a developing municipality like Madison cannot through publicly assisted means or appropriately legislated incentives (as to which, see *infra)* provide the municipality's fair share of the regional need for lower income housing, it is incumbent on the governing body to adjust its zoning regulations so as to render possible and feasible the "least cost" housing, consistent with minimum standards of health and safety, which private industry will undertake, and in amounts sufficient to satisfy the deficit in the hypothesized fair share. As the matter was put in a supplemental *amicus* brief of The Public Advocate:

> ... for now, and in the foreseeable future, it is absolutely essential to build a substantial amount of housing units at the lowest cost feasible and consistent with health and safety. Builders now must be given the opportunity to build as inexpensively as possible in order to accommodate the low, moderate-subsidized and, especially, moderate-conventional population. Thus, in one sense, future

disparities in the increases in housing cost and median income are not relevant; that is, we should be building at the lowest cost feasible now.

. . . .

Nothing less than zoning for least cost housing [92] will, in the indicated circumstances, satisfy the mandate of *Mount Laurel.* While compliance with that direction may not provide *newly constructed* housing for all in the lower income categories mentioned, it will nevertheless through the "filtering down" process referred to by defendant tend to augment the total supply of available housing in such manner as will indirectly provide additional and better housing for the insufficiently and inadequate housed of the region's lower income population. See also *Mount Laurel,* 67 N.J. at 205, 336 A.2d 713. (Pashman, J., concurring).[93]

---

[92] The concept of least cost housing is not to be understood as contemplating construction which could readily deteriorate into slums. We have emphasized the necessity for consistency of such housing with official health and safety requirements. The recently enacted State Uniform Construction Code Act, *L.*1975, c. 217 (*N.J.S.A.* 52:27D-119 *et seq.*) states among its purposes "to encourage innovation and economy in construction . . ." and "to eliminate . . . construction regulations that tend to unnecessarily increase construction costs . . .", yet be "consistent with reasonable requirements for the health, safety, and welfare of occupants or users of buildings and structures". Sec. 2.

We envisage zoning provisions which will permit construction of housing, in reasonable amounts, at the least cost consistent with such standards. Observation in many areas of the State confirms that low cost housing can be maintained without becoming a slum. See also *Mount Laurel,* 67 N.J. at 191, 336 A.2d 713.

[93] See Lansing, Clifton and Morgan, *New Homes and Poor People: A Study of Chains of Moves* (1969) (a study of the construction of over 1,000 new units in 17 metropolitan areas and its effects, especially on lowest income groups); Grigsby, *Housing Markets and Public Policy* 84-130 (1963); Fisher & Winnick, "A Reformulation of the Filtering Concept," 1951 *Journal of Social Issues* 47-58; Mallach, "Do Lawsuits Build Housing? The Implications of Exclusionary Zoning Litigation", 6 *Rutgers-Camden L.J.* 653, 666 (1975) (emphasizing filtering process may take a lifetime to occur). ·

The "filtering down" or "trickling down" theory has also been advocated in support of subsidies for middle income housing. See HUD, *Housing in the Seventies* 172-173 (1974).

Added support for this "filtering down" theory was adduced at the trial by Peter Abeles, township planner, who acknowledged that the movement of upper moderate or middle income families to newly constructed housing would leave their former housing available for families lower in the income scale. This movement can comprise a chain of families "moving up". The shorter the chain, the sooner the needs of the lowest income families are met and presumably the better the facilities made available to them. The shortness of the chain obviously depends on the inexpensiveness of the most recently constructed housing. *Lansing et al., supra,* at pp. 5, 65.

It will be apparent from our survey of the facts and the discussion hereinafter that the 1973 ordinance under review not only fails to provide directly for Madison's fair share of the region's low and moderate income housing needs but also is not geared to satisfy such a share in terms of "least cost" housing in the sense just described. The failure will be seen to be both quantitative and qualitative. Insufficient areas are zoned to permit such housing, and the zoning restrictions are such as to prevent production of units at least cost consistent with health and safety requirements.

VI

Incapacity of the 1973 Ordinance to Effect Adequate Lower Income Housing

As we shall indicate hereinafter, Madison's planners have, for purposes of this litigation, formulated a study purporting to demonstrate an unmet need in Madison for low and moderate income housing, as its share of a larger Middlesex County regional need therefor, of some 1800 housing units as of 1975.[94] Assuming, for present purposes, the legitimacy of that estimate — a matter for discussion in a later section of this opinion — the evidence is convincing that the 1973 zoning ordinance does not hold the promise of an opportunity to meet that need and at the same time satisfy the prospective continuing need in the foreseeable period following 1975. This, in effect, was the substance of Judge Furman's holding, quoted earlier herein. From his conclusions,[95] amply supported by the record, it appears that no new housing is feasible under the ordinance for persons in the bottom income third of the population (under $9,000); that at most 12% (3500/30,000) to 17% (3500/20,000) of all new housing units are attainable by persons earning $10,000 [96] a year; so that 83% to 88% of the feasible future units would be zoned out of the reach of the lowest 40% of the population.

The anatomy of these failures is apparent.

---

[94] This is without regard to a share of the prospective need for the foreseeable future thereafter.

[95] Judge Furman's finding that 80% of vacant developable residential land is zoned R-40 and R-80 and 4% is zoned R-7 and R-10 is based on acreage in the single family zones only. See *supra* (pp. 1203-1204).

[96] This was the figure used at trial for the upper limit of moderate income families, based on the 1972 median income in New Jersey of $11,600. Low income was set at below $7,000. Based on 1974 statistics of the Newark area, a low income family of four earns below $8,150 and a moderate income family earns between $8,150 and $13,050.

In our analysis of the minimum lot single-family and multi-family zones in IV B, *supra,* the *prima facie* disproportion of land zoned for high cost residences *vis-à-vis* that zoned for lower cost residences and multi-family units was fully canvassed. According to the proofs here adduced, there is little or no present market for the R-80 and R-40 zoning as such. . . . While the R-7 zone may permit a marginal amount of moderate income housing, new home ownership in that zone is precluded for the low income population. While the latter condition may be economically unavoidable (see V, *supra*), Madison has provided for no home ownership at all on "very small lots", as mandated by *Mount Laurel.* 67 N.J. at 187, 336 A.2d 713. Clearly no effort was made to permit "least cost" single family homes — and certainly not in reasonable numbers.

We have further seen that the multi-family zoning regulations are not only substantially deficient in areas of developable vacant land made available therefor, but also defective in their susceptibility to entrepreneurial concentration in one- and two-bedroom configurations.

. . . Although the express bedroom restrictions of the 1970 Madison ordinance were excised in 1973, the maximum bulk and density regulations in the AF and PUD zones (the sole sites of multi-family units),[97] when combined with the economics of building, effectively dictate development on an 80% one bedroom, 20% two bedroom mix, and such a combination was within the contemplation of the township planners. This is not an inevitable result of zoning and economics, for a municipality through the zoning power can and should affirmatively act to encourage a reasonable supply of multi-bedroom units affordable by at least some of the lower income population. Such action should include a combination of bulk and density restrictions, utilization of density bonuses,[98] minimum bedroom provisions and expansion of the FAR ratio and the AF zone to encourage and permit larger units.

Although the validity of a zoning provision for density bonuses in the sense stated in note [98], *supra* (as distinguished from unit bonuses for rental concessions — *i.e.,* "rent skewing"), has not been argued in this case, we see no objection to it in principle. Comparable bonuses are expressly permitted by the statute in relation to PUDs and clustering. *N.J.S.A.* 40:55-57(b)(2) and (3). While there is no

---

[97] Except for the AR zone, a small zone restricted to senior citizens housing.

[98] The density bonus indicated in this context is the bonus of, for example, an additional single-bedroom or efficiency (in addition to those densities generally permitted) for every three- or four-bedroom unit constructed. Compare this to density bonuses as incentives for construction of subsidized or lower income housing discussed *infra,* n. 28 and accompanying text.

express statutory sanction for a density bonus provision outside the PUD context, this type of regulation is directly tied to the physical use of the property and is thus within the recognized ambit of the zoning power. There was unanimity of opinion among the experts at the trial herein that such a device is a vital weapon in the armament of affirmative zoning for adequate housing of families in all income categories. Recognizing that the objectives of *Mount Laurel* are essential to the effectuation of the general welfare, and are within the broad legislative delegation to municipalities of both the zoning and the general police power, . . . we hold that provision for density bonuses in the sense indicated is within the municipal zoning power, and, in situations such as that here presented, is a necessary implement in the encouragement of builders to provide multi-family housing for those of lower income. *Cf. Mount Laurel*, 67 N.J. at 170, n. 8, 336 A.2d 713.

We are constrained to take a more reserved position as to the validity of zoning provisions for "rent skewing", or the allowance of greater density in either sale or rental accommodations in exchange for special concessions by the developer of rental or sale price of a limited number of units. Although this is also a widely recommended zoning technique for handling the problem of encouraging private construction of lower income housing,[99] we discern serious problems with the exercise of local zoning power in such a manner without express legislative authorization. . . . We will not here resolve the

---

[99] "Rent skewing" is a generic term referring to the imposition of a greater proportion of land, construction or other costs on one group of units in a development in order to lower the eventual rental or sale price of another group of units therein. Rent skewing can be encouraged by a municipality in two ways: requiring that a mandatory percentage of moderately priced dwellings be constructed (this is often referred to as an MPMPD ordinance) or allowing a developer a density bonus enabling him to build, for example, one conventional unit for every two low or moderate income units constructed. See Kleven, "Inclusionary Ordinances — Policy and Legal Issues in Requiring Private Developers to Build Low Cost Housing", 21 *U.C.L.A. L. Rev.* 1432 (1974).

Various alternatives have been suggested for satisfying the low and moderate income requirement: constructing federally subsidized housing, renting to low income families under a rent subsidy program, constructing units selling or renting at or below maximums fixed in the ordinance, conveying land to the county or its designee, selling or leasing units to a redevelopment or housing authority or giving the authority first refusal to rent or buy. See Kleven, *supra,* at 139-147.

On density bonuses or MPMPD's generally, see Rose, "The Mandatory Percentage of Moderately Priced Dwelling Ordinance (MPMPD) Is the Latest Technique of Inclusionary Zoning", 3 *Real Estate L.J.* 176 (1974); Rose, "The *Mount Laurel* Decision: Is It Based on Wishful Thinking?", 4 *Real Estate L.J.* 61, 68-9 (1975); Brooks, *Lower Income Housing: The Planner's Response,* ASPO Report No. 282 (Am. Socy. of Planning Officials, July-August 1972).

issue in the absence of adequate argument on the matter. However, we are not to be understood as discouraging local initiative in this area; the question, moreover, deserves legislative study and attention.

It seems useful to point out, in connection with the revision of the ordinance which will be required by our judgment herein, that sound planning calls for providing for a reasonable cushion over the number of contemplated least cost units deemed necessary and believed theoretically possible under a particular revision. . . . The reasons are evident. Many owners of land zoned for least cost housing may not choose to use it for that purpose. And developers of least cost housing may not select all of the zoned land available therefor, or at least not within the anticipated period of need. Thus overzoning for the category desired tends to solve the problem.[100]

. . . .

[The court then held that the PUD provisions of the ordinance were unacceptable. Contributions required for schools and the like were excessive. The land allocated for PUD's was located in remote areas and made up only nine percent of the vacant land available for residential development. Developers would thus have to bring in roads and utilities to remote PUD sites at great expense and would have to make off-site improvements benefiting other property owners who would not help pay for them. The PUD approval procedures were lengthy and "will add greatly to the cost of any project and hence may tend to render development prohibitive to lower income users." — Eds.]

---

[100] Of further significance, there is the possibility that low cost units actually built will not be utilized by persons needing low cost housing, but will be inhabited instead by higher income persons wishing to economize. According to the township's housing study statistics, 31% of its households are low or moderate income, yet 62.4% of its housing stock can be categorized as low and moderate income housing. These figures seem to support the inference that since not all inexpensive dwellings will be inhabited by households economically requiring such accommodations, a municipality should overzone to meet the requirements of those who do. See Mallach, "Exclusionary Zoning and Managed Growth: Some Unresolved Issues," 6 *Rutgers-Camden L.J.* 660, 668 (1975).

Finally, in this connection, it is obvious that a zoning ordinance may be revised periodically if experience shows that the allocations for a particular type of housing are excessive or impracticable. Note that the new statutory zoning revision, see *supra* (p. 1199) calls for a general reexamination at least every six years of a master plan and development regulations. *L.*1975 c. 291, Sec. 76.

VII

The "Fair Share" Approach of the Defendant

We made the preliminary observation in II, *supra,* that although we would neither make nor require a finding of fact as to a given number of lower income housing units to be made possible by the Madison Zoning Ordinance, we would, for the purposes there enunciated, nevertheless discuss the evidence herein concerning Madison's fair share of a regional need for such housing. . . . We intend that our judgment herein shall subserve that principle notwithstanding that we do not propose to, nor require that the trial court shall demarcate specific boundaries for a pertinent region or fix a specific unit goal as defendants' fair share of such housing needs.

Defendant undertook at the trial to establish what would constitute a fair share of the regional need for low and moderate income housing for Madison's zoning ordinance to render possible. It relied upon two allocation studies. . . . [These studies were rejected as inadequate and self-serving. — Eds.]

VIII

"Fair Share" and "Region" — General Considerations

The probative value of the . . . fair share studies should be appraised against the background of the substantial body of experience that has been developed by governmental planning bodies in recent years in devising fair share plans for voluntary housing planning purposes as distinguished from litigation. All of them involve realistic housing market areas larger and functionally more appropriate, in *Mount Laurel* terms, than the small Middlesex County region. Before discussing those specific plans, some preliminary observations as to the concepts of "fair share" and "region" seem appropriate by way of background.

Of primary significance is the difference between the situation of an administrative planning agency functioning under authorizing legislation and that of a court dealing with an attack by litigation on the adequacy of the zoning ordinance of an isolated municipality. The former is dealing with a comprehensive, predetermined region and can render or delegate the making of allocations with relative fairness to all of the constituent municipalities or other subregions within its jurisdiction.[101] Moreover, it presumably has expertise

---

[101] A preliminary but comprehensive housing allocation plan for the entire State has just been published by the State Division of State and Regional Planning. "A Statewide Housing Allocation Plan for New Jersey", op. cit. supra, note 35. This

suited to the task. The correlative disadvantages of a court adjudicating an individual dispute are obvious.

---

undertaking, which is subject to public hearings and further review, was directed by Governor Byrne's Executive Order No. 35, dated April 2, 1976. That order acknowledged the impetus of our decision in *Mount Laurel,* and it directed that the State Division of State and Region Planning prepare State housing goals "to guide municipalities in adjusting their municipal land-use regulations in order to provide a reasonable opportunity for the development of an appropriate variety and choice of housing to meet the needs of the residents of New Jersey." County planning boards were permitted to be enlisted in the studies for regions, which could consist of counties or groups of counties. The order states the "law of the State of New Jersey" in language tracking the fair share-regional concept set forth in *Mount Laurel.*

In allocating regional goals the Division was directed to take into account: (1) the extent of housing need in the region; (2) the extent of employment growth or decline; (3) fiscal capacity to absorb the housing goal; (4) availability of appropriate sites for the housing goal; (5) "Other factors as may be necessary and appropriate."

The resulting State Division study is presented in four sections: (1) present housing needs: 1970; (2) prospective housing needs: 1970-1990; (3) substate regions for housing allocation; and (4) housing allocation methodology. The study culminates in tables setting forth a "fair share" number of housing units for low and moderate income households to meet present and prospective housing needs allocated to every municipality in the State.

Present housing needs are estimated by the criteria of (1) dilapidated units; (2) overcrowded units and (3) necessary vacant units, as of 1970. p. 13.

Prospective housing needs are based upon estimates of growth of housing units from 1970 to 1990. pp. 13-15.

The criteria for fixing regions were: (1) sharing housing needs; (2) socio-economic interdependence; (3) data availability; (4) the intent of Executive Order No. 35; pp. 7-8. There are 12 resulting regions: one for the eight northeastern counties (including Middlesex); one for Camden, Gloucester and Burlington; and one for each of the other ten counties of the State. pp. 10-11.

Allocation of fair shares to municipalities was developed separately for present housing needs and prospective housing needs. The method used for allocating present housing needs is to take the percentage of present housing needs of the region to the region's total housing stock and then apply that percentage to each municipality's housing stock. p. 13. The method used for allocating prospective housing needs was to apply an average of four indexes, being: (1) vacant developable land; (2) employment growth; (3) municipal fiscal capability (in terms of growth of non-residential ratables); and (4) personal income per capita. pp. 14-15.

Each municipality's fair share is thus the sum of the two fair shares arrived at as aforesaid. p. 15.

By Executive Order No. 46, dated December 8, 1976, Governor Byrne has ordered postponement of hearings and final review of the preliminary study until after November 1977.

The formulation of a plan for the fixing of the fair share of the regional need for lower income housing attributable to a particular developing municipality, although clearly envisaged in *Mount Laurel,* 67 N.J. at 162, 189-190, 336 A.2d 713, involves highly controversial economic, sociological and policy questions of innate difficulty and complexity. Where predictive responses are called for they are apt to be speculative or conjectural.[102] These observations are supported not only by the published literature [103] but by the proofs and comprehensive briefs supplied us by the parties and *amici.*

Some of the problems catalogued above were touched upon in *Mount Laurel, e. g.,* "region", 67 N.J. at 162, 189-190, 336 A.2d 713; incidence of subsidized construction in contemplation, *id.* at 170, n. 8, 188, n. 21, 336 A.2d 713; sources of reliance for "fair share" guidance, *id.* at 190, 336 A.2d 713; quantity of needed housing reasonably expectable under proper zoning, *id.* at 188, n. 21, 336 A.2d 713. We take this occasion to make explicit what we adumbrated in *Mount Laurel* and have intimated above — that the governmental-sociological-economic enterprise of seeing to the provision and allocation throughout appropriate regions of adequate and suitable housing for all categories of the population

---

[102] One commentator has specifically warned that because of the conjecture nature of such calculations, utilization of the court as the forum for determining a municipality's fair share may result in "statistical warfare" between the litigants. Rose, "The *Mount Laurel* Decision: Is It Based on Wishful Thinking?", 4 *Real Estate L.J.* 61, 67 (1975).

[103] The recent literature on "fair share" methodologies is considerable. The leading theoretical analysis of fair share plans is found in Brooks, *Lower Income Housing: The Planner's Response,* ASPO Report No. 282 (Am. Socy. of Planning Officials, July-August 1972). In addition to Brooks, and the commentaries on *Mount Laurel* cited in note 3 *supra,* a representative sampling of fair share literature includes: Kelly, "Will the Housing Market Evaluation Model Be The Solution to Exclusionary Zoning?" 3 *Real Estate L.J.* 373 (1975); Listokin, "Fair-Share Housing Distribution: Will It Open the Suburbs to Apartment Development?" 2 *Real Estate L.J.* 739 (1974); Listokin, "Fair Share Housing Distribution: An Idea Whose Time Has Come?" in *New Jersey Trends* 353 (T. Norman, ed., 1974); Lindbloom, "Defining 'Fair Share' of 'Regional Need': A Planner's Application of Mount Laurel", 98 *N.J.L.J.* 633 (1975); Moskowitz, "Regional Housing Allocation Plans: A Case History of the Delaware Valley Regional Plan," 7 *J. Urban Law* 292 (1975); National Committee Against Discrimination in Housing (NCDH), " 'Fair Share' Idea Begins to Spread", *Trends in Housing,* vol. 16, no. 2, pp. 2-3 (July 1972); NCD, " 'Fair Share Evolves' ", *Trends in Housing,* vol. 16, no. 3, pp. 1-2 (Fall 1972); Holmgren & Erber, "Fair Share Formulas", 4 *HUD Challenge* 22 (April 1973).

See also, Erber & Prior, *Housing Allocation Planning: An Annotated Bibliography,* Council of Planning Librarians Exchange Bibliography No. 547 (March 1974).

is much more appropriately a legislative and administrative function rather than a judicial function to be exercised in the disposition of isolated cases. *Cf.* 67 N.J. at 189, n. 22, 190, 336 A.2d 713. Fortunately, the other branches of government are giving the matter their attention. But unless and until other appropriate governmental machinery is effectively brought to bear the courts have no choice, when an ordinance is challenged on *Mount Laurel* grounds, but to deal with this vital-public welfare matter as effectively as is consistent with the limitations of the judicial process.

We address the question, implicated by defendant's evidential studies, of the appropriate concept of a "region" in the context of a litigation challenging the housing adequacy of a particular zoning ordinance. Defendant purports to justify its fair share allocation on the basis of a single county as a region. However, . . . it does appear that . . . [the township's studies] envisaged a need emanating beyond the county boundaries.

. . . .

In broad principle, we believe Judge Furman was correct in conceiving the appropriate region for Madison Township as "the area from which, in view of available employment and transportation, the population of the township would be drawn, absent invalidly exclusionary zoning". 128 N.J.Super. at 441, 320 A.2d at 224. This is essentially like the housing market area concept espoused in the Abeles report as sound in principle, although not directly employed in the Abeles fair share study.

The concept of a county *per se* as the appropriate region was thought not to be "realistic" by Justice Hall in writing *Mount Laurel.* . . .

Justice Hall defined the region applicable there as "the outer ring of the South Jersey metropolitan area, which area we define as those portions of Camden, Burlington and Gloucester Counties within a semicircle having a radius of 20 miles or so from the heart of Camden city." 67 N.J. at 162, 190, 336 A.2d at 718. What was material to that determination was the proximity of Mount Laurel to the highly urbanized Camden area, its residential development due to the influx of new residents from nearby central cities, existing and projected employment patterns, the "highway network" linking Mount Laurel with all parts of the Camden area and the contrast of its vacant acreage (65%) with the land supply situation in those nearby central cities. See 67 N.J. at 161-162, 336 A.2d 713. . . .[104]

---

[104] We do not fully accord such status to the preliminary statewide housing allocation plan of the State Division of State and Regional Planning as it is only tentative and subject to further public hearings and review. See notes 37 and 42 *supra.*

. . . .

For examples of regions large enough and sufficiently integrated economically to form legitimately functional housing market areas, we turn to some of the pioneering fair share allocation plans executed under official or quasi-official auspices. The Miami Valley (Dayton, Ohio) Regional Planning Commission includes five counties and 31 municipalities as far as 60 miles from the center of Dayton. The Metropolitan Washington COG (see *supra* pp. 1215-1216) covers 15 counties and local governmental jurisdictions, including the District of Columbia. San Bernardino County, California, although a county, occupies 20,000 square miles. The Metropolitan Council of the Twin Cities (Minneapolis-St. Paul) covers 7 counties, including almost 300 jurisdictions, with a total population of 1.9 million. The DVRPC, as already shown, comprises nine counties in Pennsylvania and New Jersey. The present significance of the cited plans is that their regions are of such size that it is difficult to conceive of a *substantial* demand for housing therein coming from any one locality *outside* the jurisdictional region, even absent exclusionary zoning. The essence of the cited plans is "to provide families in those economic categories [low and moderate] a choice of location." 16 *Trends on Housing,* No. 2 p. 2 (1972).

We thus proceed to formulation of our position as to the concept of region in the context of an *ad hoc* application of *Mount Laurel* principles to a single litigated ordinance, having in mind our determination in II, *supra,* that it would not generally be serviceable

---

To date a number of fair share plans have been proposed or implemented by governmental or regional bodies. The plans vary, depending upon the type of body selected to formulate or implement the plan, the geographical areas encompassed, and the type of housing being allocated (*e. g.,* subsidized or total low income). See Listokin, "Fair Share Housing Distribution: Will It Open the Suburbs to Apartment Development?", 2 *Real Estate L.J.* 739, 743 (1974). The most noted of those plans which have been actually implemented include the following: Miami Valley (Dayton, Ohio area) Regional Planning Commission, *The Miami Valley Region's Housing Plan* (1973) (updating its 1970 housing allocation plan); Metropolitan Washington (D.C. area) Council of Governments, *Fair Share Housing Formula* (1972); San Bernardino County (California) Planning Department, *Government Subsidized Distribution Model for Valley Portion of San Bernardino County* (1972); Metropolitan Council of the Twin Cities Area (Minneapolis-St. Paul), *Housing: Plan, Policy, Program* (1973); *Delaware Valley Regional Plan,* see *supra* note 37.

The utility of almost all these plans is that they are intended to subserve the actual construction or subsidization of low cost housing. By contrast, a plan for a *Mount Laurel* type litigation, as the present, is not capable of direct utilization by the affected municipality or by the court.

For a list of twenty-five additional plans, see Erber and Prior, *Housing Allocation Planning: An Annotated Bibliography* (Council of Planning Librarians Exchange Bibliography # 547, 1974).

to employ a formulaic approach to determination of a particular municipality's fair share. We conclude that, in general, there is no specific geographical area which is necessarily the authoritative region as to any single municipality in litigation. Different experts may quite reasonably differ in their concepts of the pertinent region. See Lindbloom, "Defining 'Fair Share' of 'Regional Need' ", 98 *N.J.L.J.* 633-644 (July 24, 1975). But in evaluating any expert testimony in terms of the *Mount Laurel* rationale, weight should be given to the degree to which the expert gives consideration to the areas from which the lower income population of the municipality would *substantially* be drawn absent exclusionary zoning. (Evidence of the historical sources of a municipality's population, among other indicia, is relevant thereto). This is broadly comparable to the concept of the relevant housing market area, to which there has been prior reference herein.

The factors which draw most candidates for residence to a municipality include not only, for employed persons and those seeking employment, reasonable proximity thereto of jobs and availability of transportation to jobs, as mentioned by Judge Furman and stressed by most of the experts,[105] but proximity to and

---

[105] The criteria relevant for determining "region" have not received the same attention as those used to measure fair share, see note [106] *infra,* because of the fact that most of the fair share plans under discussion have accepted the geographic area within the jurisdiction of the planning agency as the appropriate region. Moreover, urban literature on derivation of regional boundaries often pertains to subject matter other than housing allocation, *e. g.,* water supply, environment, transportation, etc. However, suggestions do emerge from fair share discussions as to the criteria for determining the appropriate region. The most mentioned is that of journey to work. Rose, "Exclusionary Zoning and Managed Growth: Some Unresolved Issues", 6 *Rutgers-Camden L.J.* 689, 717-720 (1975); Lustig and Pack, "A Standard for Residential Zoning Based Upon the Location of Jobs", 1974 *AIP Journal* 333 (1974); Burchell, Listokin and James, "Exclusionary Zoning: Pitfalls of the Regional Remedy", 7 *Urban Lawyer* 262, 271 (1975). This implicates existing job and transportation patterns. *Burchell, et al., supra.*

The Federal Housing Authority (FHA) has defined a housing market region as the geographic entity within which non-farm dwelling units are in mutual competition, HUD, FHA Economic and Market Analysis Division, *FHA Techniques of Housing Market Analysis* 12, and hence the location of actual and prospective business centers and the availability of transportation facilities are important. *Id.*

Rubinowitz has suggested that the relevant region should be the area in which development and movement are or will be taking place, places where middle income families have already exercised the option to move and which would be desirable to low and moderate income groups if housing were available. "Exclusionary Zoning: A Wrong in Search of a Remedy", 6 *Mich.J.L.Reform* 625, 654-5 (1973).

The Department of Community Affairs in its November 26, 1975 status report (see note 42 *supra*) rejected journey to work as the sole criterion for delineation of regions in northern New Jersey, suggesting demarcation of regions "which are

convenience of shopping, schools and other amenities. Retired people, who represent a substantial part of the lower to moderate income population, might be attracted from a greater distance than employed people.

Finally, we submit general observations as to the techniques of "fair share" allocation to municipalities within an assumedly valid region. There is much greater diversity among the experts in this regard than in relation to determining pertinent regions. Moreover, as already noted herein, harm to the objective of securing adequate opportunity for lower income housing is less likely from imperfect allocation models than from undue restriction of the pertinent region. The essential thing from that standpoint is that the true regional need be adequately quantified.

The trial court specified that for Madison to meet its fair share of the housing needs of the region its zoning ordinance must approximate "in additional housing unit capacity the same proportion of low-income housing as its present low-income population, about 12%, and the same proportion of moderate-income housing as its moderate-income population, about 19%." The 1973 ordinance was held "palpably short" of these requirements. 128 N.J.Super. at 447, 320 A.2d 223.

Mount Laurel devised no formula for estimating "fair share," but the matter was left for the municipality to apply the expertise of the "municipal planning adviser, the county planning boards and the state planning agency." 67 N.J. at 190, 336 A.2d at 733.

The number and variety of considerations which have been deemed relevant in the formulation of fair share plans is such as to underscore our earlier observation that the entire problem involved is essentially and functionally a legislative and administrative, not a judicial one.[106]

---

large enough or within which a burden may be shared." Plaintiffs' witness Paul Davidoff suggested three factors for determining the relevant region: (1) the volume of transactions (communications, trade, employment) between component sections of the region; (2) the demand exerted for housing within the region; and (3) the area within which a satisfactory solution of the housing need may be found.

[106] The most frequently mentioned fair share criteria have been grouped under four headings. We list them for informational purposes without necessarily implying our approval.

"Equal share" criteria have as their objective equal distribution of housing, *e.g.*, by establishing a minimum percentage of low and moderate income housing units to be contained within each community.

"Need" criteria allocate housing to regions where there is the greatest need, but have been criticized as perpetuating slums.

"Distribution" criteria allocate low and moderate income units to areas lacking the same in order to achieve a greater income and racial mix.

The formula specified by the trial court would not necessarily be properly utilizable in other contexts. Some municipalities might have such very high or very low existing proportions of lower-income families in their population make-up as to render such a formula patently unfair. If the existing municipal proportions correspond at least roughly with the proportions of the appropriate region the formula would appear *prima facie* fair. The evidence herein is that the stated municipal proportions approximate those of the county of Middlesex. We are without data as to the comparative proportions of such a larger area as would include the more urban counties in the northeast New Jersey region.

Harking back to our statement in II as to why we proposed in this opinion to discuss the concepts of fair share and region notwithstanding that we would not, nor would we require the trial court to specify a pertinent region or fix a fair share housing quota for Madison, we summarize the observations in VII and VIII as follows:

1. Based upon our analysis and findings in IV and VI, the 1973 ordinance is clearly deficient in meeting Madison's obligation to share in providing the opportunity for lower cost housing needed

---

"Suitability" criteria select areas containing the most sutable housing sites based on physical and fiscal capacity. Kelly, "Will the Housing Market Evaluation Model Be the Solution to Exclusionary Zoning?", 3 *Real Estate L.J.* 373 (1975); Brooks, *Lower Income Housing: The Planner's Response, op. cit. supra,* n. 40; Listokin, "Fair-Share Housing Distribution: Will it Open the Suburbs to Apartment Development?" 2 *Real Estate L.J.* 739, 746 (1974).

The most important single criterion emerging from fair share literature is the amount of vacant developable land, as "access to land is the basic issue in exclusionary zoning." Rubinowitz, "Exclusionary Zoning: A Wrong in Search of a Remedy", 6 *Mich.J.L.Reform* 625, 661 (1973). Other basic criteria include employment opportunity, fiscal measures (including per capita income, equalized assessed valuation per pupil, degree of underutilization of classrooms) and existing housing or population density. See generally, Brooks, *supra;* Listokin, *supra;* Kelly, "Will the Housing Market Evaluation Model be the Solution to Exclusionary Zoning?", 3 *Real Estate L.J.* 373 (1975); Rubinowitz, *supra;* authorities cited *supra* note 39.

It has been emphasized that many of the potential fair share criteria measure the same factors, Rubinowitz, *supra,* 6 *Mich.J.L.Reform* at 660-661, and the effort should be made to keep the formula factors simple to avoid duplication and the "statistical warfare" which may otherwise result from over-sophisticated formulae. *Cf.* Rose, "The *Mount Laurel* Decision: Is It Based on Wishful Thinking?", 4 *Real Estate L.J.* 61, 67 (1975).

The Delaware Valley Regional Planning Board adopted a formula equally weighing only three criteria: relative wealth (based upon the market value of all taxable real estate in the county compared to the region total); equalization criteria (would give each county the same proportion of income groups); and projected employment opportunities. See Moskowitz, "Regional Housing Allocation Plans: A Case History of the Delaware Valley Regional Plan", 7 *Urban Lawyer* 292 (1975).

in the region, whether or not the specific fair share estimates submitted by defendant are acceptable. Those estimates are, in any event, defective at least in not including prospective need beyond 1975.

2. The objective of a court before which a zoning ordinance is challenged on *Mount Laurel* grounds is to determine whether it realistically permits the opportunity to provide a fair and reasonable share of the region's need for housing for the lower income population.

3. The region referred to in 2 is that general area which constitutes, more or less, the housing market area of which the subject municipality is a part, and from which the prospective population of the municipality would substantially be drawn, in the absence of exclusionary zoning.

4. Fair share allocation studies submitted in evidence may be given such weight as they appear to merit in the light of statements 2 and 3 above. But the court is not required, in the determination of the matter, itself to adopt fair share housing quotas for the municipality in question or to make findings in reference thereto.

IX

Environmental Considerations

As noted above, a considerable amount of vacant acreage in Madison borders certain streams or comprises important aquifer storage and discharge areas. Depositions and counter-depositions were taken by defendant and plaintiffs, respectively, bearing upon the effect of development of varying kinds on such areas as Burnt Fly Bog, the Old Bridge Sands, Raritan Bay beachfront, the salt marshes behind Raritan Bay and the four streams flowing into South River. Defendant offered the depositions at the trial to establish that certain areas zoned R-80, R-40 and RP were so sensitive to flood, water contamination and related problems that they should be kept from development at all or restricted to very low residential density. The trial judge declined to consider this evidence on the ground that considerable other land, free from such ecological considerations, and amenable to higher density development, was available within the township with which it could meet its fair share obligation for its own and the region's housing needs. 128 N.J.Super. at 447, 320 A.2d 223.

Plaintiffs' experts testified on depositions that the answer to the ecological problems posed was not prohibition or regulation of the density of development *per se* but careful use of the land, with adequate controls in respect of construction, sewerage, water control and treatment, sufficient open space per structure and other services.

Ecological and environmental considerations were also advanced by the municipality in *Mount Laurel* to justify large lot zoning throughout the township. We pointed out there that while such factors and problems were always to be given consideration in zoning (see 3 Williams, *American Land Planning Law* (1975) § 66.12, pp. 30, 34-35), "the danger and impact must be substantial and very real (the construction of every building or the improvement of every plot has some environmental impact) — not simply a makeweight to support exclusionary housing measures or preclude growth . . .". 67 N.J. at 187, 336 A.2d at 731.

Notwithstanding the foregoing, we conclude the trial court erred in not receiving in evidence and giving consideration to the environmental depositions mentioned. It is not an answer to say there is ample other land capable of being deployed for lower income housing. The municipality has the option of zoning areas for such housing anywhere within its borders consistent with all relevant considerations as to suitability. There are proponents of scattering lower income housing widely throughout a municipality as well as adherents of segregating such housing in limited areas. Since the municipal fathers should have the widest latitude of judgment in that regard, it is in the interests both of the municipality and the plaintiffs that the parties have the benefit of findings by the court, from the proofs, as to exactly which of the allegedly environmentally sensitive areas, if any, are in fact not susceptible of housing development at all; which, of only low density development; and which are free of any environmental constraints in respect of density or type of housing.

We shall, in the remedial portion of this opinion, be directing amendment of the ordinance to add substantial areas to districts zoned for multi-family housing and for single-family homes on very small lots. It therefore will be necessary for the governing body of defendant to be apprised, from the findings of the court in the respects just noted, what part of the areas claimed by defendant to be environmentally unsuited for such zoning need not be resorted to for that purpose.

The court may in its discretion, permit the depositions to be amplified at a hearing on remand, but any such hearings and the added findings here directed to be made shall be expedited.

In concluding this point, however, we find no basis in the record for determining that, in any view of the environmental proofs, defendant does not have sufficient vacant developable land free from disabling ecological considerations to enable it to create the zoning opportunity for its fair share of the region's need for least cost housing.[107]

X

"Affirmative Action" for Lower Income Housing

Plaintiffs and supporting *amici* press for a judicial mandate that developing municipalities be required affirmatively to act for creation of additional lower income housing in more ways than by eliminating zoning restrictions militating against that objective. Of the devices which have been suggested to this end, tax concessions and mandatory sponsorship of or membership in public housing projects must be summarily rejected. Tax concessions would unquestionably require enabling legislation and perhaps constitutional amendment. While we have described the sponsorship of public housing projects as a moral obligation of the municipality in certain specified circumstances, *Mount Laurel,* 67 N.J. at 192, 336 A.2d 713, we have no lawful basis for imposing such action as obligatory. It goes without saying, however, that the zoning in every developing municipality must erect no bar or impediment to the creation and administration of public housing projects in appropriate districts. See also *id.* at 211-212, 336 A.2d 713 (Pashman, J., concurring).

We have hereinabove indicated that provision by zoning for density bonuses keyed to quantitative or bulk concessions by the builder (*e.g.,* added bedrooms) is both valid and mandatory where necessary to achieve sufficient suitable least-cost housing, but that we are not prepared presently to pass upon the validity of zoning for bonuses keyed to rental or sale price concessions.

Various additional suggestions for encouraging the proliferation of lower cost housing on municipal initiative are set forth in the supplemental *amicus* brief of The Public Advocate but are not deemed to require comment here as none warrant mandatory imposition in any revised Madison ordinance. See also *Mount Laurel,* 67 N.J. 209-213, 336 A.2d 713 (Pashman, J., concurring).

XI

The Validity of the Zoning Statute

Plaintiffs' original cross-appeal from the trial court's first determination assailed that portion of the court's decision upholding the constitutionality of the zoning enabling act, *N.J.S.A.* 40:55-30 *et seq.,* and their second brief to this court incorporates the supporting

---

[107] See generally Ackerman, "The *Mount Laurel* Decision: Expanding the Boundaries of Zoning Reform," 1976 *U. of Ill. Law Forum* 1, 43-71 (1976).

arguments. Plaintiffs' novel contention is that the general zoning purposes stated in *N.J.S.A* 40:55-32, although adequate when enacted in 1928, today fail to provide detailed standards to guide municipalities in their exercise of the zoning power, to wit, they fail to direct that a municipality must be racially and economically "inclusionary" rather than exclusionary.

The stated argument was formulated before we decided *Mount Laurel* and is basically mooted by our holding there, in effect, that the zoning statute is to be construed to conform with state due process and equal protection so as to compel zoning in developing municipalities to affirmatively combat exclusion of the lower income population needing housing.[108]

. . . .

It goes without saying that the statutory and constitutional prohibition, by judicial construction, of zoning to exclude, encompasses exclusion by race as well as by economic circumstances.

The statute is valid.

XII

Relief for Corporate Plaintiffs

The corporate plaintiffs contend that the 1973 ordinance is invalid not only generally, as exclusionary of lower income housing, but specifically as to their own tract of land because of zoning restrictions which are confiscatory. They therefore ask that the court specifically order the township to place their property in an appropriate multi-family or PUD zone to be created — in effect, to grant them a permit to build the kind of moderate-to-middle income housing they have in mind.[109]

Plaintiffs' expert witnesses testified that the restrictions upon their land (originally encompassing about 400 acres, but later reduced by a "Green Acres" taking to about 200 acres in the R-40 zone) were such that even using the clustering device the residences to be produced would have to sell for about $63,000, for which there was

---

[108] In addition, it should be noted that on January 14, 1976 a new zoning statute, *L.* 1975, *c.* 291, was enacted to supersede the one under consideration, and took effect August 1, 1976. Under this statute, housing needs, regional needs and low cost development are specified as among the concerns of zoning. *L.* 1975, *c.* 291, § 2(a), (d), (e), (g), (m).

[109] Plaintiffs offered purported proof, and contend that if their land were appropriately zoned they could develop 20% of their proposed housing for families of moderate income.

no feasible market in the number producible on the property. Plaintiffs' witness Chester conceded that if only 30 or 40 units were involved they might be marketable, but not the hundreds contemplated by plaintiffs' project. We cannot render an assured determination that the zoning is confiscatory against corporate plaintiffs on such proofs. Plaintiffs are not necessarily entitled to zoning feasible for their holdings as an entirety if they are reasonably utilizable as divided in separate ownerships. Nor are they entitled to zoning permitting the most profitable development of the property. . . . Yet it appears that even if divided into smaller ownerships it would be difficult to market the property for residential uses under the zoning restrictions as they stand, having in mind the historical absence of any large lot development in the area. . . .

A consideration pertinent to the interests of justice in this situation, however, is the fact that corporate plaintiffs have borne the stress and expense of this public-interest litigation, albeit for private purposes, for six years and have prevailed in two trials and on this extended appeal, yet stand in danger of having won but a pyrrhic victory. A mere invalidation of the ordinance, if followed only by more zoning for multi-family or lower income housing elsewhere in the township, could well leave corporate plaintiffs unable to execute their project. There is a respectable point of view that in such circumstances a successful litigant like the corporate plaintiffs should be awarded specific relief. . . .

There is also judicial precedent for such action. *In Appeal of Girsh,* 437 Pa. 237, 263 A.2d 395 (Sup.Ct.1970), a builder succeeded in obtaining an adjudication of the invalidity of an ordinance precluding apartment development. The municipality rezoned to create an apartment district but did not include plaintiff's land. The plaintiff then sought to compel issuance of a permit, but the town announced the property would be condemned for a park. When plaintiff sued to enjoin condemnation, the Supreme Court ordered issuance of a permit. Order No. MP-12, 271 (August 29, 1972). . . . The same court took similar action in *Township of Williston v. Chesterdale Farms, Inc.,* 462 Pa. 445, 341 A.2d 466 (Sup.Ct.1975). See also *Franklin v. Village of Franklin Park,* 19 Ill.2d 381, 167 N.E.2d 195 (Sup.Ct.1960).

Such judicial action, moreover, creates an incentive for the institution of socially beneficial but costly litigation such as this and *Mount Laurel,* and serves the utilitarian purpose of getting on with the provision of needed housing for at least some portion of the moderate income elements of the population. We have hereinabove referred to the indirect housing benefits to low income families from the ample provision of new moderate and middle income housing. Point V.

The foregoing considerations have persuaded us of the appropriateness in this case of directing the issuance to the corporate plaintiffs, subject to the conditions stated *infra,* of a permit for the development on their property of the housing project they proposed to the township prior to or during the pendency of the action, pursuant to plans which, as they originally represented, will guarantee the allocation of at least 20% of the units to low or moderate income families.[110] This direction will be executed under the enforcement and supervision of the trial judgment in such manner as to assure compliance with reasonable building code, site-plan, water, sewerage and other requirements and considerations of health and safety. *Cf. Township of Williston v. Chesterdale Farms, Inc., supra* (341 A.2d at 468-469).

An express condition of this holding, moreover, is that the trial court, after consideration of the ecological and environmental proofs referred to in IX, *supra,* determine that the plaintiff's land is environmentally suited to the degree of density and type of development plaintiffs propose. Subject to these conditions it is our purpose to assure the issuance of a building permit to corporate plaintiffs within the very early future.[111]

XIII

Remedy and Remand

We herewith modify the judgment entered in the Law Division to hold, as we did in *Mount Laurel* as to the ordinance there involved, that the 1973 zoning ordinance is invalid, not *in toto,* but only "to the extent and in the particulars set forth in this opinion". *Mount Laurel,* 67 N.J. at 191, 336 A.2d at 734. For the reasons elaborated above the ordinance is presumptively contrary to the general welfare

---

[110] The income standards specified are to accord with data applicable as of the date of the completion of the buildings.

The "Statewide Housing Allocation Plan for New Jersey" study, *op. cit. supra,* n. 35, sets 1970 ranges for low income households as up to $5,568/year and moderate income household as $5,569-$8,567/year. As of 1976 the estimate for low and moderate income households is stated as "up to approximately $13,000". Pp. 1196-1197.

[111] This determination is not to be taken as a precedent for an automatic right to a permit on the part of any builder-plaintiff who is successful in having a zoning ordinance declared unconstitutional. Such relief will ordinarily be rare, and will generally rest in the discretion of the court, to be exercised in the light of all attendant circumstances.

and beyond the scope of the zoning power in the particulars mentioned. *Mount Laurel,* 67 N.J. at 185, 336 A.2d 713. The municipality has not borne its consequent burden of establishing valid reasons for the deficiencies of the ordinance. *Id.* at 185, 336 A.2d 713. It is obvious that a revision of the residential provisions of the ordinance is called for in order to provide the opportunity for that amount of least-cost housing in the township which will comply with the directions contained in this opinion.

In *Mount Laurel* we elected not to impose direct judicial supervision of compliance with the judgment "in view of the advanced view of zoning law as applied to housing laid down by [the] opinion". 67 N.J. at 192, 336 A.2d at 734. The present case is different. The basic law is by now settled. Further, the defendant was correctly advised by the trial court as to its responsibilities in respect of regional housing needs in October 1971, over five years ago. 117 N.J.Super. 11, 283 A.2d 353. It came forth with an amended ordinance which has been found to fall short of its obligation. Considerations bearing upon the public interest, justice to plaintiffs and efficient judicial administration preclude another generalized remand for another unsupervised effort by the defendant to produce a satisfactory ordinance. The focus of the judicial effort after six years of litigation must now be transferred from theorizing over zoning to assurance of the zoning opportunity for production of least cost housing. See Mytelka and Mytelka, "Exclusionary Zoning: A Consideration of Remedies", 7 *Seton Hall L.Rev.* 1, 18, 23 (1975).

The trial court on remand shall execute the directions in IX and XII above and render its findings thereon with the reasonable dispatch appropriate to the age of this litigation. It shall become the obligation of the defendant, within 90 days thereafter, unless more time is allowed by the trial court, to submit to the trial court for its approval a revised ordinance.

The revision shall zone, in the manner specified in this opinion, to create the opportunity for a fair and reasonable share of the least cost housing needs of Madison's region, the concept of "region" to be understood as generally set forth in II and VIII hereinabove. While no formulaic determination or numerical specification of such a fair and reasonable share is required, we do not preclude it if the municipal planning advisors deem it useful. The revision shall, as *minima:* (a) allocate substantial areas for single-family dwellings on very small lots; (b) substantially enlarge the areas for dwellings on moderate sized lots; (c) substantially enlarge the AF district or create other enlarged multi-family zones; (d) reduce the RP, R-80 and R-40 zones to the extent necessary to effect the foregoing, subject to the directions in IX, *supra;* (e) modify the restrictions in the AF zones and PUD areas discussed hereinabove which discourage the construction of apartments of more than two bedrooms; (f) modify the PUD regulations to eliminate the undue cost-generating requirements specified above; and (g) generally eliminate and reduce undue cost-generating restrictions in the zones allocated to the achievement of lower income housing in accordance with the principles of least cost zoning set forth in V hereinabove.

The trial court shall have discretion, in the event of undue delay in compliance with this opinion or of a finding by the court that any zoning revision submitted by defendant fails to comply with this opinion, to appoint an impartial zoning and planning expert or experts. Such expert may be directed to file a report or to testify, as the court may deem appropriate, as to a recommendation for the achievement by defendant of compliance with this opinion or with any further directions by the court pursuant thereto. See *Mount Laurel,* 67 N.J. at 216, 336 A.2d 713 (Pashman, J., concurring); *Pascack Assoc. v. Mayor, Coun. Tp. of Washington,* 131 N.J.Super. 195, 329 A.2d 89 (Law Div.1974); Mytelka and Mytelka, "Exclusionary Zoning: A Consideration of Remedies", 7 *Seton Hall L.J.* 1, 31 (1975); Hartman, "Beyond Invalidation: The Judicial Power to Zone", 9 *Urban L.An.* 159, 171-173 (1975); Rubinowitz, "Exclusionary Zoning: A Wrong in Search of a Remedy", 6 *Mich.J.L.Ref.* 625, 656-657 (1973).

Judgment modified, and affirmed as modified; no costs.

For affirmance and remandment as modified: Chief Justice HUGHES, Justices SULLIVAN and CLIFFORD and Judge CONFORD — 4.

Concurring in part and dissenting in part: Justices MOUNTAIN, PASHMAN and SCHREIBER — 3.

PASHMAN, J., concurring and dissenting.

[Justice Pashman's opinion, except for its conclusion, is omitted; but its flavor can be gathered from the following outline of the entire opinion:]

I Limited Agreement with Majority
II The Need for Affirmative Relief
III The Nature of Affirmative Judicial Relief
   (A) Remedial Objectives
   (B) Procedural Approach
   (C) Calculation of the Municipal "Fair Share" of Regional Housing Needs
   (D) Imposition of Remedial Devices
      (1) Award Specific Relief to Corporate Plaintiffs
      (2) Enjoin Interference with Construction of Low and Moderate Income Housing
      (3) Establish "Set-Aside" or "Override" Procedures to Facilitate Construction of Low and Moderate Income Housing
      (4) Declare that Regional Housing Needs Constitute a "Special Reason" for Granting Use Variances
      (5) Order Specific Changes in the Zoning Ordinance
      (6) Enjoin Municipal Approval of Other Forms of Development

(7) Order Municipality to Provide Density Bonuses and Other Incentives for Building Lower Income Housing

(8) Order Municipality to Impose Subdivision Conditions and Other Inclusionary Devices

(9) Order the Municipal Government to Establish a Local Housing Authority

IV Conclusion

. . . .

Because the Court has satisfied itself with declaring exclusionary zoning unconstitutional and relying upon generalized notions of "fair share" and regional considerations, I am fearful that it has stopped short of taking steps which are needed to implement today's decision requiring Madison Township to meet regional housing needs. Unlike decisions declaring specific exclusionary devices unconstitutional, enforcement of an affirmative obligation to provide multifamily housing requires an ongoing process of judicial vigilance coupled with strong corrective measures.

Only by taking upon ourselves the task of fashioning affirmative judicial relief will we make exclusionary suburbs responsive to the needs of our democratic society. Only through such direct and forceful action will the evils of a segregated society and economic bigotry be thwarted and the barriers of exclusionary zoning permanently breached.

SCHREIBER, J. (concurring in part and dissenting in part).

[A major part of Justice Schreiber's opinion is omitted. — Eds.]

Obviously, an effective remedy to alleviate the evil which *Mt. Laurel* has exposed is one which strikes at its root causes, such as revitalization of the cities with new commercial and industrial enterprises which would add substantial ratables to the local tax base, or reformation of New Jersey's tax structure, or both, so that, as Justice Hall wrote, municipalities would "zone primarily for the living welfare of people and not for the benefit of the local tax rate." *Id.* at 188, 336 A.2d at 732 (footnote omitted). Most would readily concede that the legislature and not the courts is the proper body to exercise such relief. The Public School Education Act of 1975, *N.J.S.A.* 18A:7A-1 *et seq.,* as funded, *N.J.S.A.* 54A:1-1 *et seq.,* will have some effect on the local tax rate, but most public educational costs, expenses for police and fire departments, municipal aid to the poor, and expenditures for other local related services are still borne by local taxes with urban areas having disproportionately greater costs in these respects. *See Robinson v. Cahill,* 67 N.J. 333, 369-370, 339 A.2d 193 (1975) (Pashman, J., concurring in part and dissenting), *cert. denied,* 423 U.S. 913, 96 S.Ct. 217, 46 L.Ed.2d 141 (1975). No party in these proceedings has advocated that the judicial remedy be directed toward elimination of the causes. Instead efforts, following the lead of *Mt. Laurel,* have been directed toward the amelioration or elimination of the result, namely modification of the exclusionary provisions of the zoning ordinance.

The judicial remedial guideline suggested in *Mt. Laurel* was that a municipality must bear its "fair share" of low and moderate income housing in the "region". Problems inherent in the "fair share" of the "region" formula have been expressed by the majority as well as Justice Mountain and need not be repeated. Clearly the legislature or an administrative agency with the necessary expertise would unquestionably be in a far superior position than the courts to receive all relevant information and data and reach legitimate results using the concepts of "fair share" and "region".[112] Furthermore, the Court should not be and is not limited to solutions within that framework. The opportunity to construct low or moderate income housing predicated upon projected population growth (municipal, county, regional or area), geological, geographical, environmental, ecological conditions or on other rational bases may satisfy the *Mt. Laurel* mandate.[113]

There is broad language in *Mt. Laurel* to the effect that a "developing" municipality must provide by its land use regulations the reasonable opportunity for an appropriate variety and choice of housing for *all* categories of people who may desire to live within its boundaries. 67 N.J. at 179, 336 A.2d 713. I do not accept that generalization. The general welfare calls for adequate housing of all types, but not necessarily within any particular municipality. *Fanale v. Hasbrouck Heights,* 26 N.J. 320, 139 A.2d 749 (1958). Environmental, ecological, geological, geographical, demographic, regional or other factors may justify exclusion of certain types of housing, be it two-acre or multifamily. *See N.J.S.A.* 50:55D-2 c, i, j, k. It should be noted that the general welfare includes "public health safety, morals and welfare by means of adequate light and air, the avoidance of overcrowding of land and buildings and the undue concentration of population; these among other considerations related to the essential common good, the basic principle of civilized

---

[112] *See Division of State and Regional Planning, A Statewide Housing Allocation Plan for New Jersey* (preliminary draft, 1976), which commented that court decisions have attempted to deal with "fair shares" and related issues, but not on a uniform basis. *Id.* at 2. The study allocated low and moderate income housing needs among the municipalities, using factors such as municipal fiscal capability, employment growth, vacant developable land and personal income. *Id.* at 13-15.

[113] Judge Conford in the majority opinion and Justice Pashman in his concurring and dissenting opinion recognize the need for flexibility in determining "region" and "fair share", but even then, the "fair share" — "region" principle may unduly circumscribe a municipality in its efforts to satisfy the constitutional requirement that a zoning ordinance be consonant with the general welfare.

society." *San-Lan Builders, Inc. v. Baxendale,* 28 N.J. 148, 157, 145 A.2d 457, 462 (1958). . . .

Madison Township's zoning ordinance, as amended, is facially exclusionary to the extent delineated in the majority opinion. It was the Township's burden to justify the exclusionary provisions of its amended ordinance on a reasonable basis such as projected population growth, regional requirements, geological, geographical, environmental or ecological considerations. This it has not done. Accordingly, I would remand to permit the municipality to present evidence to justify the extent to which its ordinance now permits construction of low and moderate income housing to meet the criteria set forth herein or to revise its ordinance in accordance with the minimum requirements projected in Part XIII of the majority opinion. I also agree with Part XII with respect to relief for the corporate plaintiffs at this time under the unusual circumstances of this case. Lastly, I agree with the majority that the trial court erred in not receiving in evidence the environmental depositions. On the remand these should be admitted and additional relevant evidence in connection with that subject matter, if offered by any of the parties, should be considered.

I concur in the remand consistent with the provisions stated herein.

MOUNTAIN, J. concurring and dissenting.

[A major part of Justice Mountain's opinion is omitted. — Eds.]

As lawyers, judges, scholars and concerned citizens have quickly come to realize, the decision of this Court in *Mount Laurel* has raised problems that defy easy answer.

. . . .

The opinion in *Mount Laurel* laid upon each developing municipality in the State an obligation to exercise its zoning power in such a way as to provide for its "fair share" of the housing needs of the lower- and moderate-income persons resident within the "region" within which the municipality was found to lie. It now seems to me, as it has come to seem to many others, that neither "fair share" nor "region" can be determined with even approximate accuracy in any given case and that neither concept provides a really workable tool to aid in the resolution of this difficult problem. For instance, the majority adopts the trial court's definition of "region" as being "the area from which, in view of available employment and transportation, the population of the township would be drawn, absent, invalidly exclusionary zoning." . . . As soon as one seeks to apply this definition it is seen that it rests upon circular reasoning. A predicate of exclusionary zoning is a finding that a municipality is contributing less than its fair share of particular housing needs of its region. So before we can know whether zoning is exclusionary we must first find the region to whose housing needs it is allegedly making an inadequate contribution. But by the foregoing definition a determination of region implicates a prior finding of exclusionary zoning. Where is one to begin?

Actually, in light of the rule announced by the majority, it seems no longer necessary to define either "region" or "fair share." The opinion states very clearly that a reviewing tribunal henceforth need not specify a particular region nor fix a fair share quota. . . . It would seem implicit that a municipality also need not do so. In place of the fair share-regional approach, the majority now postulates a rule directing attention to the *substance* of zoning ordinances and to the *bona fide* efforts of those responsible for the administration of plans of land use regulation. . . . This is undoubtedly a very great improvement; and yet it carries its own particular weaknesses. Implicit in this rule is the likelihood of *ad hoc* determinations rather than uniform application of a well understood governing principle. Furthermore, and perhaps somewhat naively, it places what I fear is undue reliance upon good faith effort, despite the fact that, for understandable if not laudable reasons, any such effort has thus far been conspicuous by its almost total absence. Nevertheless, there is probably nothing better to offer as a judicially devised alternative.

Quite apart from the uncertain efficacy of this newly formulated rule, there are a number of reasons why courts should abstain from seeking ultimate solutions in this area, but should rather urge a legislative, or legislative-administrative approach. In the first place courts are not equipped for the task. If a court goes beyond a declaration of validity or invalidity with respect to the land use legislation of a particular municipal body, it invites the fairly certain prospect of being required itself to undertake the task of rezoning. Of course it has neither the time, the competence nor the resources to enter upon such an undertaking. It must therefore appoint planning experts to do the work for it. Such a course was followed in *Pascack Association Ltd. v. Mayor and Council of Washington Twp.*, 131 N.J.Super. 195, 329 A.2d 89 (Law Div. 1974), certif. granted 69 N.J. 73, 351 A.2d 2 (1975). A principal weakness inherent in this approach is that no authoritative guidelines exist at the present time to aid the trial judge and the planning experts he has appointed, and to which the law would require that they adhere. Therefore a land use plan so devised will reflect rather the informed judgment of the chosen expert than a judicial application of settled principle to particular facts. Full realization of this is likely further to diminish the probability of community acceptance.

. . . .

A second, and at least equally important reason why courts should not rezone, lies in the fact that in so doing they must inevitably make policy decisions that have traditionally been the prerogative of a democratically selected branch of government. Judicial rezoning, like all other zoning, implicates a choice among competing, often mutually exclusive uses. While a court may rightfully challenge a municipality's parochialism, it may at the same time find that its own activism constitutes an intrusion upon a legitimate political debate as to how the limited supply of land in a developing municipality is to be regulated. *Id.* at 779. Many others have expressed a like concern. Professor John M. Payne, for instance, has recently drawn attention to the undesirability of seeking ultimate answers to problems of exclusionary zoning through the application of judicially fashioned remedies. *Payne, Delegation Doctrine in the Reform of Local Government Law: The Case of Exclusionary Zoning,* 29 *Rutgers L.Rev.* 803 (1976). Speaking directly to the current tendency of New Jersey courts to seek final remedies where zoning imbalance is perceived, he says,

> This expansive judicial role raises grave constitutional problems going to the inherent limitations on the ability of a court to encroach upon legislative and executive prerogatives, since the structural issues being addressed by the current litigation can seldom be remedied without either legislative and executive cooperation or judicial action that is essentially legislative in scope. Assuming (all other things being reasonably equal) that the law reform decisions under discussion here ought to be framed in terms that are as minimally intrusive of the ordinary democractic process as possible, it appears that the trend of recent decisions seriously and unnecessarily violates that norm of non-intrusiveness.
> [*Id.* at 804-05]

He further points out that such action on the part of the courts may not only exceed the boundaries of judicial skill but also those of "political tolerance." *Id.* at 805. Such activity "cuts too closely to the political core of our society." *Id.* at 817.

No one questions that zoning is a legislative function. When the judiciary — for whatever reason — undertakes to move in this field, it immediately places in issue its power of legitimacy. I suggest that such intrusion may be especially resented, and hence more likely to be denied acceptance, where the subject matter is as controversial and potentially inflammatory as are many questions of zoning. How much better were the Legislature to take steps that would obviate this problem altogether!

A chief obstacle to achieving a rational, useful and adequate answer to our problem inheres in the fact that the zoning power today rests — potentially at least — with 567 different entities. Any municipality in the State is at liberty to adopt a zoning ordinance or plan of land use regulation, and presumably most have done so. Of these municipalities a goodly number must surely qualify — albeit reluctantly — as "developing." Their land use plans are therefore required to meet the test of *Mt. Laurel.* But it must be obvious that the housing needs with which we are concerned can be better met in some municipalities within the region than in others. From a purely rational point of view, it makes little sense to apportion the regional obligation, willy-nilly, among some number of diverse political entities, set off from one another by boundary lines placed where they are by historical accident. . . .

Any comprehensive review of our zoning problems should take account of a statewide or regional allocation of zoning power as a possibly preferable alternative to present arrangements. The strength of the home rule tradition in New Jersey as well as other rather securely built-in forces will almost certainly provoke immediate opposition to any such proposal. And yet it should be carefully considered, despite the almost certain necessity of constitutional revision that would be entailed.

In *Mount Laurel* we said, "Courts do not build housing nor do municipalities." 67 N.J. at 192, 336 A.2d at 734. Today the majority repeats, "Municipalities do not themselves have the duty to build or subsidize housing." (P. 1200). This I take to be settled doctrine, which should not, I submit, be altered in any way except by legislation. This comment is provoked by the plethora of suggestions that have arisen on all sides demanding various kinds of immediate and far-reaching affirmative action — kinds of action that if undertaken would require the exercise of some unspecified municipal power, but certainly not the zoning power.

There is no real likelihood that any of the problems to which I have adverted will yield to unaided judicial ingenuity. There is, on the other hand, very legitimate hope that our zoning difficulties and land use problems — centered as they are today around the injustice of exclusionary zoning, but by no means limited to that — can be ameliorated and eventually solved by careful and imaginative legislative action. The Legislature can recruit the expertise, hear all sides of each strand of the tangled web, view the State regionally or as a whole, experiment if need be, and develop a land use program responsive to the needs of all its citizens. I am satisfied this is a feat of which the courts are incapable.

In the meantime this case must be decided. Courts cannot pass. I agree that the case should be remanded to the trial court, but I disagree strongly with the proposed terms of remand. They seem to me unfair to the municipality. The majority has today announced a new rule henceforth to govern the determination as to whether or not a municipality is guilty of exclusionary zoning. The defendant has had no opportunity to address the issue as so propounded. It should have that opportunity, which should include the right to present not only argument but further testimony as well. Without going into detail, I wish simply to register my disagreement with everything appearing in Point XIII of the majority opinion.

. . . .

CLIFFORD, J. (concurring).

[A major part of Justice Clifford's opinion is omitted. — Eds.]

Sometimes judges decide cases with their fingers crossed. I confess that my vote with the majority opinion is cast with a discomforting feeling that this *judicial* effort to meet the imperative of *Mount Laurel,* from which I would not retreat, is neither entirely satisfactory nor wholly successful.

. . . .

Some of the shortcomings of the Court's response to the problems presented are laid bare in Justice Mountain's concurring and dissenting opinion. While I am inclined to agree with much of his gentle probing of the vulnerable areas, I tend to look upon whatever infirmity may inhere in our position not as the result of flawed analysis but rather as an unfortunate but inescapable by-product of the *judicial* function being called upon to solve the extraordinarily complex problems underlying this litigation — problems whose solution, it may be plausibly argued, should be undertaken elsewhere.

. . . .

Let me narrow the focus. What I seek to emphasize is this: society has yet to achieve agreement on the basic question of what it is our courts are expected to do; as a result of this uncertainty we may be accepting litigational burdens which, according to one commentator, are beyond the institutional capacity of the tribunals and the "cranial capacity" of the judges. This, from former Judge Simon H. Rifkind, who points out in his penetrating article, "Are We Asking Too Much of Our Courts?," 15 *Judges' J.* 43 (1976) (Address of Judge Rifkind at the April, 1976 "National Conference on the Causes of Popular Dissatisfaction with the Administration of Justice") (hereinafter "Rifkind"), that the judiciary has increasingly been solicited to become the problem solver of our society, sort of its all-around handyman.

. . . .

The thrust of the Rifkind essay is that courts, being institutions of last resort, should be required to do nothing which other, less irreplaceable institutions can do as well, and should be preserved for doing that which cannot be done elsewhere.

. . . .

In developing his theme Judge Rifkind dwells on the distinction between the traditional judicial function of "dispute-resolving," with its well-placed reliance on the adversary process, and "problem-solving," for which the adversary system is conspicuously ill adapted. . . .

As Justice Mountain has observed, the gravitation into the judicial machinery of causes better and more effectively dealt with elsewhere surely jeopardizes the judiciary's "power of legitimacy." See Mountain, J., concurring and dissenting, *ante* at 1266; *cf. Robinson v. Cahill,* 70 N.J. 155, 163-64, 358 A.2d 457 (dissenting opinion of Mountain, J.). The concern he expresses is shared by many others. . . .

There is an additional point perhaps worth making here, and that is that in many instances the law is becoming "excessively complex, excessively sophisticated, unduly mysterious." Rifkind, *supra* at 50. The author refers specifically to the field of taxes, sensibly acknowledging that "[a]fter 50 years of practice, I would no more have the audacity to formulate my own tax return than I would engage in open heart surgery." *Id.*

It may be that the same excessive complexities and compounded anfractuosities are finding their way into our zoning-planning law. And elsewhere. I have no ready answer as to how that dilemma may be avoided as long, again, as the courts are looked to for ultimate solution of the kinds of problems presented by this case. An attempted solution too often seems to defy its articulation in a judicial opinion unfettered by distracting obfuscation. Reality thus becomes camouflaged.

. . . .

Because the majority opinon seems to me to represent the best judicial accommodation of the present controversy to *Mount Laurel's* essential principles, I vote with it.

Comments: 1. *Oakwood at Madison* was eagerly awaited by those who anticipated that it would eliminate much of the uncertainty generated by *Mount Laurel.* But the *Oakwood at Madison* decision has done little to remove that uncertainty. Rose suggests that the court's statement the local zoning is invalid if it will "preclude the opportunity to supply any substantial amounts of new housing for low and moderate income households" was intended "to enable a trial court to determine whether a municipal zoning ordinance is exclusionary without having to engage in the 'controversial,' 'speculative,' or 'conjectural' calculations required to determine fair-share allocations of regional housing needs." Rose, A New Test for Exclusionary Zoning: Does It Preclude the Opportunity for "Least Cost" Housing? 6 Real Est. L.J. 91, 94 (1977), reprinted in *After "Mount Laurel": The New Suburban Zoning* 230, 232 (J. Rose & R. Rothman eds. 1977). But in summarizing the discussion prior to taking up "environmental considerations," the *Oakwood at Madison* opinion asserts that the test of validity of local zoning is "whether it realistically permits the opportunity to provide a fair share of the region's need for housing for the lower income population" — a reiteration of the original *Mount Laurel* formula. In any case, Rose seems correct in his further observation that "it seems unlikely that a trial court will be able to determine whether a given zoning ordinance precludes the opportunity for the required types and amounts of housing without evidence relating to fair share of housing needs." *Id.*

2. The *Oakwood at Madison* opinion seems to substitute "least cost" housing for "low and moderate income" housing in the *Mount Laurel* formula. Is this really anything more than a recognition of the fact (as the court states) that "[t]he amount and kind of governmental subsidies available for housing has always been fragmentary," that "federal sources have recently been restricted," and that "sources extraneous to the unaided private building industry cannot be depended upon to produce any substantial proportion of the housing needed and affordable by most of the lower income population"? What do you think of the court's acceptance of the theory that construction of new "least cost" housing "will . . . through the 'filtering down' process referred to by defendant tend to augment the total supply of available housing in such manner as will indirectly provide additional and better housing for the . . . inadequately housed of the region's lower income population"?

3. The *Mount Laurel* and *Oakwood at Madison* decisions appear to require all "developing" municipalities to allocate land in their zoning ordinances for "least cost" housing and — so far as is feasible — for "low income" households. What do you think of Rose's statement that:

> It can be argued that a municipality that has few jobs, no public transportation, insufficient educational, medical, and social services, and a high property tax, or a combination of the above, would be inappropriate for low-income persons and that the failure to provide for low-income persons should not be a reason to characterize the land use regulations as "exclusionary"?

Rose, *supra* at 96, reprinted in *After "Mount Laurel," supra* at 234.

4. Assuming that estimation of the *present* housing needs of a *municipality* is possible within an acceptable margin for error, how should a local governing body go about estimating the amount of low- and moderate-income housing "*prospectively* needed in the . . . *appropriate region*"? (Emphasis added.) A determination of the boundaries of the "appropriate region" is obviously necessary, but *Oakwood at Madison* does not provide much guidance on this point. The court states that it will not, and will not require the trial court, to "specify a pertinent region." Instead, the court merely indicated its approval of Judge Furman's definition of "the appropriate region" for Madison Township as "the area from which, in view of available employment and transportation, the population of the township would be drawn absent exclusionary zoning," and Justice Hall's observation in *Mount Laurel* that "confinement to or within a certain county appears not to be realistic, but restriction within the boundaries of the state seems practical and advisable." This provides little guidance for local governing bodies seeking to follow the mandates of *Mount Laurel* and *Oakwood at Madison,* especially in light of Judge Conford's further assertion that, "in general, there is no specific geographic area which is necessarily the authoritative region as to any single municipality in litigation. Different experts may quite reasonably differ in their concepts of the pertinent region." Perhaps local governing bodies can derive a little comfort from

Judge Conford's statement that the court "might conceivably regard a 'region' . . . constructed" on the basis of "an official fair share housing study of a group of counties or municipalities conducted under such auspices as . . . [a regional planning agency] or the planning boards of a county or group of counties functioning under Executive Order No. 35" as meriting "*prima facie* judicial acceptance." (For the full text of Executive Order No. 35, see After *Mount Laurel, supra* at 273.) But determination of *future* needs still presents a difficult problem, even if "the appropriate region" can be defined.

5. The following methodology was adopted by the New Jersey Division of State and Regional Planning for estimation of the *future* needs of a region:

Step 1. *Predict* the population for a given date in the future.

Step 2. *Predict* the average household size at that date.

Step 3. Divide the *predicted* population by the *predicted* average household size. The quotient is the *predicted* number of households at the given date.

Step 4. Subtract the present number of households from the *predicted* number of households. The difference represents the total household growth for the period.

Step 5. *Predict* the percentage of future households that will have low- and moderate-income.

Step 6. Multiply the predicted household growth for the period by the *predicted* percentage of low- and moderate-income households. The product is the *predicted* prospective housing needs for low- and moderate-income households at the given date in the future.

New Jersey Division of State and Regional Planning, prospective Housing Needs Report (Draft Report 1976), as set out in Rose, *supra* Comment 1, at 97. As Rose observes,

> [I]n predicting future population growth, the New Jersey Department of Labor and Industry has proposed four different population projections for estimating future levels of growth. The projections make different assumptions relating to fertility-birth rates, mortality rates, and in-out-migration from the state . . . [and] different assumptions relating to long-term trends, economic events, and so on. . . . Each of the assumptions differs significantly and the selection of one rather than another will have a significant effect on the prediction of future housing needs. Similar variations will result from the selection of other assumptions (e.g., future average household size) in the process of computation.

It would seem that Rose is justified in his conclusion that "the requirement that future housing needs be considered in the process of determining whether a municipality's land use regulations are exclusionary requires speculative and conjectural calculations and will involve the courts in battles of statistical warfare that the New Jersey Supreme Court had hoped to avoid." *See id.* at 98.

6. We now know that Judge Furman's specification of Madison Township's "fair share" of regional housing needs — approximately "the same proportion of low-income housing as its present low-income

population, about 12%, and the same proportion of moderate-income housing as its moderate-income population, about 19%" — meets the *Mount Laurel* test, although Judge Furman's opinion provides no rational basis for such a specification. *See* 320 A.2d at 227. And the Supreme Court's opinion absolves New Jersey trial judges of any obligation, themselves, "to adopt fair share housing quotas for the municipality in question or to make findings in reference thereto." Does this leave New Jersey trial courts unconstrained by judicially established standards as to "fair share" allocations? Granted that (as the Supreme Court said in *Oakwood at Madison*) "the entire problem involved is essentially and functionally a legislative and administrative, not a judicial one," how should New Jersey trial courts proceed in exclusionary zoning cases prior to the time when New Jersey's legislative and administrative bodies fulfill their responsibilities with respect to "fair share" allocations? And what guidelines do New Jersey local governing bodies have in attempting to make such allocations?

The *Oakwood at Madison* opinion includes a discussion of "fair share criteria" in footnote [106] *supra.* In addition to the four criteria listed there, Rose discusses as possible additional criteria the following: (a) allocation based on population proportions within the region; (b) allocation based upon proportion of existing jobs within the region; (c) allocation based upon proportion of jobs within the region; (d) allocation based upon suitability of the municipality for low- and moderate-income housing; and (e) allocation based upon the obligation of every municipality to take care of the housing needs of its own constituents. Rose, Is There a Fair Share Housing Allocation Plan That Is Acceptable to Suburban Municipalities in *After "Mount Laurel," supra* at 114, 120-24.

In *Urban League v. Mayor & Council,* 359 A.2d 526 (N.J. Super. 1976), Judge Furman (the trial judge in *Oakwood at Madison*) made a "fair share" allocation as follows:

> The initial fair share allocation must be to correct the present imbalance, that is, to bring each defendant municipality up to the county proportion of 15% low and 19% moderate-income population. The county proportion rather than the state proportion of 20% low and 20% moderate-income is determined upon. The historic trend of urban dispersal from New York and Philadelphia is that per capita incomes in counties are higher in inverse ratio to distance from the central city. The allocation to correct imbalance results in the following additional low and moderate-income housing units.
>
> Cranbury 18
> East Brunswick 1,316
> Edison 1,292
> Monroe 23
> North Brunswick 180
> Old Bridge 301
> Piscataway 0
> Plainsboro 0
> Sayreville 328
> South Brunswick 156
> South Plainfield 416
>   4,030

Subtracting 4,030 from the 18,697 low and moderate-income housing units needed in the county to 1985, the balance is 14,667 or approximately 1,333 per municipality. There is no basis not to apportion these units equally. Each municipality has vacant suitable land far in excess of its fair share requirement without impairing the established residential character of neighborhoods. Land to be protected for environmental considerations has been subtracted from vacant acreage totals. No special factor, such as relative access to employment, justifies a deviation from an allocation of 1,333 low and moderate housing units, plus the allocation to correct imbalance, to each of the 11 municipalities.

Low and moderate-income housing units should be divided 45% low and 55% moderate. Low income is defined as up to 50% of median income in the county, and moderate income as 50% to 80% of median income, according to current data of the county planning board. Within each municipality there may be flexibility — for example, multi-family housing at densities of ten or more units an acre, multi-family housing encompassing a diversity of housing but with mandatory minimums of low and moderate-income units; mobile homes at densities of five to eight units an acre, and single-family housing at densities of four or more units an acre. A combination of these alternatives may be arrived at. Each municipality would receive credit for pending low and moderate income construction for which certificates of occupancy have not been granted as of the date of this judgment.

After the allocation to correct imbalance, Cranbury, East Brunswick, Edison, North Brunswick, Piscataway, Plainsboro, Sayreville and South Plainfield are ordered to rezone their respective net vacant acreage suitable for housing, as shown in the fourth table *supra*, 15% for low income and 19% for moderate income on the basis of 100% zoning for housing (which this judgment does not require). The housing units thus afforded should approximate the allocation of 1,333 units each. As to any municipality, if it appears that such rezoning would fall significantly short of the allocation of 1,333 units, plus the allocation to correct imbalance, application to modify this judgment may be brought.

Monroe, Old Bridge and South Brunswick, all with net vacant land suitable for housing exceeding 10,000 acres, are ordered to rezone to provide their respective allocations of 1,333 units, plus their respective allocations to correct imbalance, by any combination of multi-family, mobile home or single-family housing.

359 A.2d at 541-42.

7. What standards should the trial judge apply, on remand of *Oakwood at Madison,* in making findings as to "what part of the areas claimed by defendant to be environmentally unsuited for . . . zoning [for multifamily housing and for single-family homes on very small lots] need not be resorted to for that purpose"? Was it sufficient for the Supreme Court to remind the trial judge that (as it said in *Mount Laurel*) "the danger and impact [of housing development] must be substantial and very real (the construction of every building or the improvement of every plot has some environmental impact) — not simply a makeweight to support exclusionary housing measures or preclude growth . . ."? *Cf.* the following excerpt from English, The General Welfare and Environmental Considerations:

> The first thing to do is to determine the maximum population which the environmental constraints will permit to live in the town without adverse effect within or without the municipal boundaries. Indeed, this seems to be called for by the new Municipal Land Use Law. It is now ordained that a zoning ordinance "shall be adopted after the planning board has adopted the land use plan element of a municipal master plan." The land use plan element of a municipal master plan is to take into account "natural conditions including, but not necessarily limited to, topography, soil conditions, water supply, drainage, floodplain areas, marshes, and woodlands." The master plan is also to include a conservation plan element. It should also be pointed out that the legislature has provided for municipal environment commissions which have powers of recommendation. One member of the environmental commission shall be a member of the planning board. Thus the legislature has tried to ensure that environmental factors be reflected in the master plan. Moreover, a zoning ordinance must "either be substantially consistent with the land use element of the master plan or designed to effectuate such plan element," or the reasons for not doing so must be stated in the minutes. In short, a zoning ordinance is now supposed to be based, among other things, upon environmental constraints.
>
> The process of preparing a natural resource inventory and a master plan based thereon should result in the identification of such areas of undeveloped land that are unbuildable because of steep slopes, floodplain, marshland, or publicly-owned open space. It should also identify any areas that should remain undeveloped in order to protect the public water supply, or otherwise further the general welfare. This process will, in effect, define the areas which remain available for development. The acreage thus determined as developable, and the application of the considerations listed in . . . [the statute] will suggest appropriate limits on future population growth, and hence the ultimate maximum population of the municipality.
>
> It is important to check the projected future population growth against available water supply and sewage disposal capacity. The state of New Jersey is presently embarking upon the preparation of a state-wide master plan of water supply, which, when completed, may suggest allocations of water that will not permit unrestrained population growth everywhere in the state.
>
> Pursuant to the Federal Water Pollution Control Act Amendments of 1972, planning . . . is underway in New Jersey, but not yet completed. It is apparent, however, that the planning process when combined with the permit system for controlling discharges into streams, will result in waste load allocations being assigned to sewerage treatment plants which will in effect limit the size of such plants and hence the number of people who can be served thereby. These limitations may well be drastic in the case of municipalities located in the headwaters of the Passaic and Raritan river basins and in areas located over aquifers or where wells are readily susceptible to pollution. In particular situations,

these limitations may curtail further population growth in the municipality to the extent that what would otherwise be regarded as its fair share of regional housing needs will have to be reduced.

For municipalities located in the pinelands or in certain coastal areas, a formulation of fair share that is based upon housing and job relationships may have to be modified in order to comply with the regional planning required . . . so as to protect what the legislature has declared to be important environmental interests.

After "Mount Laurel," supra at 195, 204-05. For more detailed consideration of environmental land use controls and state and regional planning and development control, see *infra* Chapters 8 and 9.

8. In *Associated Homebuilders of Greater Eastbay, Inc. v. City of Livermore,* 557 P.2d 473 (Cal. 1976), decided after *Mount Laurel* but before *Oakwood,* the California Supreme Court upheld a growth moratorium imposed by an initiative ordinance. In the concluding pages of the opinion the court, while rejecting cases like *Mount Laurel* because they rested "upon principles of state law inapplicable in California, . . . [and] involve ordinances which impede the ability of low or moderate income persons to immigrate to a community but permit largely unimpeded entry by wealthier persons," *id.* at 487, nevertheless adopted a regional view of zoning ordinances to be applied when the ordinance "may strongly influence the supply and distribution of housing for an entire metropolitan region." *Id.* The criteria to be applied under the regional standard were stated as follows:

> We explain the process by which a trial court may determine whether a challenged restriction reasonably relates to the regional welfare. The first step in that analysis is to forecast the probable effect and duration of the restriction. . . .
>
> The second step is to identify the competing interests affected by the restriction. We touch in this area deep social antagonisms. We allude to the conflict between the environmental protectionists and the egalitarian humanists; a collision between the forces that would save the benefits of nature and those that would preserve the opportunity of people in general to settle. Suburban residents who seek to overcome problems of inadequate schools and public facilities to secure "the blessing of quiet seclusion and clean air" and to "make the area a sanctuary for people" (*Village of Belle Terre v. Boraas,* . . .) may assert a vital interest in limiting immigration to their community. Outsiders searching for a place to live in the face of a growing shortage of adequate housing, and hoping to share in the perceived benefits of suburban life, may present a countervailing interest opposing barriers to immigration.
>
> Having identified and weighed the competing interests, the final step is to determine whether the ordinance, in light of its probable impact, represents a reasonable accommodation of the competing interests. We do not hold that a court in inquiring whether an ordinance reasonably relates to the regional welfare, cannot defer to the judgment of the municipality's legislative body. But judicial deference is not judicial abdication. The ordinance must have a *real and substantial* relation to the public welfare. . . . There must be a reasonable basis in fact, not in fancy, to support the legislative

determination. . . . Although in many cases it will be "fairly debatable" that the ordinance reasonably relates to the regional welfare, it cannot be assumed that a land use ordinance can *never* be invalidated as an enactment in excess of the police power.

The burden rests with the party challenging the constitutionality of an ordinance to present the evidence and documentation which the court will require in undertaking this constitutional analysis.

Id. at 488-89.

Many commentators have also urged that the Right to Travel doctrine articulated in United States Supreme Court cases can provide a basis for invalidating exclusionary local zoning ordinances. However, as the *Livermore* case noted, "[b]oth the Supreme Court [in *Belle Terre* — Eds.] and this court have refused to apply the strict constitutional test [arising out of the Right to Travel doctrine — Eds.] to legislation, such as the present ordinance, which does not penalize travel and resettlement but merely makes it more difficult for the outsider to establish his residence in the place of his choosing." *Id.* at 484. For discussion see Note, The Right to Travel and Exclusionary Zoning, 26 Hastings L.J. 849 (1975).

9. The practical outcome of *Oakwood at Madison* is reported in the following story by Oser, from the New York Times for January 27, 1978, p. A15, col. 1:

OLD BRIDGE, N. J. — In the last seven years a development project known as Oakwood at Madison has become synonomous with zoning controversy. It has made no small contribution to the complex legal edifice that New Jersey courts have built in decisions that generally seek to prevent towns from "zoning out" people of lower or moderate income.

Last year the builder, Kaplan & Sons of Highland Park, reached a settlement with the township, which by then had changed its name to Old Bridge. The builder had proposed to put up 2,400 units of housing, with 480 set aside as low or moderate income housing. The settlement called for 1,750 units of housing, with 350 of them for low or moderate income pelple [people]. Half of the 350 are to be for the elderly.

This week spokesmen for the builder made public details of their proposed new subdivision and site plan for Oakwood at Madison. They hope to go into production this year. Town approval of the plans is required, however, and there may be negotiations on revisions.

The plan is interesting as an expression of where the "exclusionary zoning" issue is leading in actual development terms. Not, in the first instance, to housing either for the poor or for "moderate" income people (defined by the court as $13,000 a year for a family of four in 1976), but rather to higher-density housing for the middle class. The average unit contemplated at Oakwood at present, if built this year, would cost $50,000, the builders say.

Oakwood at Madison would be the first of the projects litigated on exclusionary zoning grounds to go into production, if final clearances are forthcoming. The builder plans 275 units of cluster houses and 320 patio houses, plus 220 townhouses and 200 apartments.

Then there are to be 385 single-family detached houses, 295 of them on lots of 7,500 square feet and the rest on lots of 12,000 or 15,000 square feet. The site is 400 acres.

. . . .

From a price standpoint, Oakwood's prices if it was built today would range from $35,000 to $45,000 for townhouses, $42,000 to $52,000 for patios, $48,000 to $58,000 for clusters, and $55,000 to $72,000 for single-family units, builder spokesman said. Full construction should take four to five years, so actual prices might be higher.

Of the 350 theoretical lower-income or moderate-income units, half are to be for senior citizens and half for families. Fred Mezey, counsel to Kaplan & Sons, said that he expected these to be moderate-income units, built with "whatever subsidy is available to get the housing cost down to $35,000 a unit." There are no current plans on who will build these or when, he said.

In sum, this is to be a $160 million development of far higher density than the builder conceived in 1969, when a new town council blocked his subdivision plan for 300 houses on half-acre lots. At that time the town's population had doubled in a few years with the spread of single-family houses, especially astride Route 9.

Ironies and curiosities abound. Eight years ago the conventional subdivision of single-family home was fought in part on the ground that the township could not stand the added tax burden of an infusion of so many more families. Today Courtney Powell, the Old Bridge assessor, says that since school enrollment has been dropping the town already has the school facilities to handle what rise there may be from Oakwood at Madison. From a tax standpoint, the development may not produce a "negative situation."

The former town counsel who represented Madison in the case, Richard Plechner, expressed pleasure at the settlement, which is "going to make a lot of rich people richer." He expresses fear that the concept of "fair share" housing that emerged in the *Mount Laurel* zoning case will open the door to the kind of "shoddy" multifamily development that was built in the state in the late 1940's.

10. *Oakwood* had been decided by the time the trial court handed down its opinion on remand in the *Mt. Laurel* case, 391 A.2d 935 (N.J. L. 1978). At issue on remand was a revision to the Mt. Laurel ordinance which zoned 20 acres out of a total of 22.4 square miles in the township for higher density housing. Plaintiffs attacked this rezoning as an inadequate reponse to the Supreme Court's decision in *Mt. Laurel* but the trial judge held for the township.

First at issue was the regional fair share allocation the township had made to determine its share of lower income housing. Although this allocation was alleged to be woefully inadequate as measured against a fair share allocation made by the regional planning agency, the trial court noted the difficulties in making fair share determinations as recognized in *Oakwood* and accepted the township's figures. The rezoning was upheld even though it was alleged that the sites rezoned were inappropriate and even though each was held by a single owner and might not be placed on the market.

For example, one of the rezoned sites was criticized because it was located near an industrial area. This location was defended by the township because it would locate lower cost housing near employment opportunities. In addition, the site was near a proposed rail commuter line that would provide public transportation.

Cost-generating provisions in the township's PUD ordinance had been waived for one of the rezoned sites which was subject to the PUD provisions, but the court refused to declare the entire PUD ordinance unconstitutional, noting that the Supreme Court had not done so. The trial court also relied on testimony from the township that over 10,000 dwelling units were or would be made available in PUD's completed or under construction. These units would be available at reasonable rents and prices and in any event would eventually help eliminate the township's housing problem through the filtering down process. While many zones zoned for higher income housing remained unchanged, the trial court indicated that no such change was required by the Supreme Court, which expressly noted that the township could meet its lower income housing obligations while still providing a variety of housing types.

An intervenor in the litigation who had been refused permission to build a mobile home park attacked the exclusion of mobile homes by the zoning ordinance. Overruling *Vickers, supra* p. 360, the trial court held that the time had come when mobile homes must be considered an appropriate housing use.

PASCACK ASSOCIATION, LIMITED v. MAYOR AND COUNCIL OF TOWNSHIP OF WASHINGTON

Supreme Court of New Jersey
74 N.J. 470, 379 A.2d 6 (1977)

CONFORD, P. J. A. D., Temporarily Assigned.
This appeal projects the significant issue as to whether, in the wake of the decisions of this court imposing upon developing municipalities the obligation of providing by zoning for the opportunity to create housing for the low and moderate income segments of the population . . . all municipalities, regardless of the state or character of their development, have an obligation to zone for multi-family housing on behalf of middle income occupants if there is a local and regional shortage of multi-family housing in general. More specifically, the issue is whether there is such an obligation on the part of a small municipality, developed substantially fully upon detached single-family dwellings and restricted accordingly in the residential provisions of its zoning ordinance.
. . . .

[This action was filed in 1970 by Pascack, which sought to set aside the township's refusal to grant a variance for a 520-unit garden apartment project on its property, and which challenged the zoning ordinance for failing to make any provision for multifamily housing.

The trial court decision, as amended, invalidated the prohibition of multifamily housing and nullified the lot size restriction. Subsequently, the township rezoned a different 34-acre tract for multifamily use and its board of adjustment again denied the variance. Pascack then moved to compel the township to issue it a building permit, claiming that in practical terms only five acres in the township were available for multifamily construction and that the zoning restrictions on this construction "precluded construction meeting the economic and social needs of the area." Agreeing with this position, the court ordered the township to complete within 60 days all rezoning required by its prior judgment. When no timely rezoning occurred, Pascack again moved for an order directing the township to issue a building permit. In response, the court appointed two planning experts to advise the court on whether the township had complied with its order, "and, if not, to recommend a zoning plan which would so comply." — Eds.]

On January 9, 1974 the experts submitted their report and recommendations. They concluded that Ordinance 73-1 did not comply with the judgment and recommended inclusion of the plaintiffs' tract in the multi-family zone. In addition, they recommended densities in the multi-family zone of at least 6 and up to 9 units per acre. After a hearing on the report the trial court on February 26, 1974 filed an opinion, 131 N.J.Super. 195, 329 A.2d 89, ordering:

1) The issuance of a building permit to plaintiffs for construction of a two story garden apartment complex upon proper application by plaintiffs to all necessary agencies for site plan review;

2) The "maximum number" (*sic*) of multi-family units permitted plaintiff as a matter of right should be no less than 9 per acre;

3) Certain specified regulatory provisions (*e.g.*, minimum off-street parking facilities, number of bedrooms, minimum floor area) were attached to plaintiffs' permit.

. . . .

Defendant township filed another appeal from the January 12, 1973 judgment and the July 9, 1973 order, as well as from the February 6, 1974 order. Plaintiffs cross-appealed from the apartment specifications set forth in the court's judgment.

. . . .

Pending the appeal herein, this court decided *Mount Laurel* in March 1975. The Appellate Division invited supplemental briefs as to the effect of that ruling on the trial court's determination of the invalidity of the ordinance for failure to zone for multi-family housing. In reversing, the Appellate Division, in an unreported *per curiam* opinion, held that *Mount Laurel* was not applicable, primarily for the reason that that decision was not authoritative except as to developing municipalities — a category not represented by the township. We have concluded that that determination was essentially correct, and affirm to that extent.

I

We direct our attention first to the trial court holding that the ordinance was defective in not providing for multi-family housing. This determination rested on certain essentially undisputed operative facts. The township comprises 1,984 acres or $3^{1}/_{4}$ square miles. It is one of a group of Bergen County residential communities popularly referred to as the Pascack Valley, of which Washington Township is southernmost. The residential nature of the township is almost exclusively single family, on lots ranging from 5000 sq. ft. to two acres or more. These residences take up 94.5% of the land; commercial uses occupy 3.25%, and there are no industrial or multi-family residential uses (except a few two-family houses). The remaining 2.3% is vacant land, there being no single parcel larger than that here involved.

The 1970 census population was 10,577, with a projection for 1980 on the master plan (made in 1963) of 10,800. There were in 1970 2,742 dwelling units. The growth of population since 1960 has been rapid, outstripping the rate of increase in surrounding municipalities. Housing density has increased from 41 units per square mile in 1950 to 862 in 1970. The average house was valued at $37,508 in 1970. Most houses are on lots of 75 X 100 feet or 100 X 100 feet, but there are many on half-acre lots and a considerable number larger.

In April 1970, 10% of the total single-family homes were renter occupied. In 1971 Bergen County had approximately 283,700 housing units, of which 90,360, or 31.9%, were rental. This may be compared with 5% for the Pascack Valley region. Five of the eight municipalities in the Pascack Valley region have no multi-family units, and the ratio of single-family units to all others is higher in the county than in the State as a whole.

The subject property is the largest undeveloped tract in the township. The plot is roughly rectangular in shape and, except for a few small lots, takes up the whole of the southeast corner of Pascack Road and Washington Avenue, with a total frontage of 774 feet on the former and 370 feet on the latter. On the east the tract abuts a single-family residential area on 7,500 and 10,000 square foot lots. To the west across Pascack Road is a restaurant and a bank followed by single-family residences in both directions. Proceeding west on Washington Avenue near plaintiff's property is a gas station, followed by a small used car lot and another gas station. Going east along Washington Avenue is a municipal firehouse followed by single-family residences. Aside from a vacant 9-acre parcel to the south, the tract mainly abuts single-family homes.

Although the plaintiffs' project has been represented by them at various times to be designed to accommodate middle to moderate income renters, they firmly took the position at the hearing in January 1974 that if limited to a density of nine units per acre (as provided in the final judgment) they would not be able to provide rental units but only condominiums at a sale price of $50,000. In that event, moreover, there would be approximately 270 rather than 520 units.

. . . .

III

The determination of the trial court as to invalidity of the ordinance in respect of absence of provision for multi-family housing was based upon the shortage of housing in Bergen County and the Pascack Valley region. The court found this condition operated to create a scarcity of dwelling accommodations affordable by persons, in and out of Washington Township, who needed housing but who were not able to make the average down payment of $8,000, or did not have the $19,000 minimum income requisite to meet bank standards for a loan needed to purchase the average priced home for sale in the township.

The opinion of the court was that "All segments of the population should have a reasonable choice of living environments to the extent that it is possible . . ."; and that where, as in this part of Bergen County, there is a need for multi-family housing, there is "a statutory requirement to provide as part of a comprehensive plan for a well-balanced community at least some area, however limited it must be under the circumstances present here, where such housing may be constructed." Throughout the opinion zoning not providing for multi-family housing is described as "exclusionary zoning."

The trial opinion and judgment here was rendered prior to this court's determination in *Mount Laurel,* but plaintiffs bring to their aid the thesis that that case supports the trial court's rationale. However, the relevance of *Mount Laurel* here is affected by two important considerations: (1) the population category effectively excluded by the ordinance involved in *Mount Laurel* — and the class intended to be relieved by our decision therein — was that of persons of low and moderate income; (2) the municipal category subjected to the mandate of the decision was that of the "developing municipality." It required the combined circumstances of the economic helplessness of the lower income classes to find adequate housing and the wantonness of foreclosing them therefrom by zoning in municipalities in a state of ongoing development with sizeable areas of remaining vacant developable land that moved this court to a decision which we frankly acknowledged as "the advanced view of zoning law as applied to housing laid down by this opinion." 67 N.J. at 192, 336 A.2d at 734.

We have recently reaffirmed and faithfully enforced the principles of *Mount Laurel* in an appropriate fact situation. See *Oakwood at Madison* .... But it would be a mistake to interpret *Mount Laurel* as a comprehensive displacement of sound and long established principles concerning judicial respect for local policy decisions in the zoning field. What we said recently in this regard in *Bow & Arrow Manor v. Town of West Orange,* 63 N.J. 335, 343, 307 A.2d 563, 567 (1973), is worth repeating as continuing sound law:

It is fundamental that zoning is a municipal legislative function, beyond the purview of interference by the courts unless an ordinance is seen in whole or in application to any particular property to be clearly arbitrary, capricious or unreasonable, or plainly contrary to fundamental principles of zoning or the statute. *N.J.S.A.* 40:55 — 31, 32. It is commonplace in municipal planning and zoning that there is frequently, and certainly here, a variety of possible zoning plans, districts, boundaries, and use restriction classifications, any of which would represent a defensible exercise of the municipal legislative judgment. It is not the function of the court to rewrite or annul a particular zoning scheme duly adopted by a governing body merely because the court would have done it differently or because the preponderance of the weight of the expert testimony adduced at a trial is at variance with the local legislative judgment. If the latter is at least debatable it is to be sustained.

. . . .

There is no *per se* principle in this State mandating zoning for multi-family housing by every municipality regardless of its circumstances with respect to degree or nature of development. This court confronted a cognate problem in *Fanale v. Hasbrouck Heights,* 26 N.J. 320, 139 A.2d 749 (1958). We there reversed a trial court decision invalidating an ordinance prohibiting any further construction of apartment houses in the entire borough. We said (at 325-326, 139 A.2d at 752):

It cannot be said that every municipality must provide for every use somewhere within its borders.... Whether a use may be wholly prohibited depends upon its compatibility with the circumstances of the particular municipality, judged in the light of the standards for zoning set forth in *R.S.* 40:55 — 32.

Apartment houses are not inherently benign. On the contrary, they present problems of congestion and may have a deleterious impact upon other uses. . . . Accordingly, an ordinance has been upheld although it confined apartment houses to a small portion of the municipality. . . . And elsewhere it has been broadly said that circumstances may permit a municipality to zone for a single use to retain its residential character. . . . No definitive pattern can be judicially prescribed; each case must turn upon its own facts.

While it is true that in *Fanale,* as contrasted with the factual situation here, the municipality already had a substantial number of apartments when the prohibitory ordinance was adopted, the principles enunciated in the foregoing excerpt from *Fanale* are nevertheless pertinent here. It is obvious that among the 567 municipalities in the State there is an infinite variety of circumstances and conditions, including kinds and degrees of development of all sorts, germane to the advisability and suitability of any particular zoning scheme and plan in the general interest. There must necessarily be corresponding breadth in the legitimate range of discretionary decision by local legislative bodies as to regulation and restriction of uses by zoning. The legislative designation of the purposes and criteria of zoning, as set forth in *N.J.S.A.* 40:55-32, is broad and comprehensive, its most dominant notes being (a) avoidance of undue crowding of uses: *e. g.,* "lessen congestion in the streets; . . . provide adequate light and air; prevent the overcrowding of land or buildings; avoid undue concentration of population . . ."; and (b) consideration of the character of the district and its peculiar suitability for particular uses and encouraging the most appropriate use of land throughout the municipality.[114]

Beyond the judicial strictures against arbitrariness or patent unreasonableness, it is merely required that there be a substantial relation between the restraints put upon the use of the lands and the public health, safety, morals, or the general good and welfare in *one or more* of the particulars involved in the exercise of the use-zoning process specified in the statute. . . .

Without in any way deprecating the recent salutary judicial, executive and legislative efforts at promoting the construction of multi-family housing to meet an obvious and urgent need therefor, see *Mount Laurel, supra,* 67 N.J. at 178—180, 336 A.2d 727—728; *Oakwood at Madison, supra,* 72 N.J. at 531 — 532, 535, 371 A.2d at 1217 — 1218, 1219, there has been no fundamental change, beyond the holding in *Mount Laurel* itself, in the statutory and constitutional policy of this State to vest basic local zoning policy in local legislative officials. *N.J. Const.* 1947, Art. 4, § 6, par. 2; *cf.* Art. 4, § 7, par. 11 (liberal construction of powers of municipal corporations). Thus, maintaining the character of a fully developed,

---

[114] The purposes and objects of zoning reflected by the new Municipal Land Use Law, *L.* 1975, *c.* 291 (effective August 1, 1976) *N.J.S.A.* 40:55D-1 *et seq.,* although broadened in several respects, are not essentially dissimilar from those enunciated above. See *N.J.S.A.* 40:55D-2 a., c., e., g., j., 49 a., 52 b. And see *Oakwood at Madison, supra,* 72 N.J. at 499, at 1200.

predominantly single-family residential community constitutes an appropriate desideratum of zoning to which a municipal governing body may legitimately give substantial weight in arriving at a policy legislative decision as to whether, or to what extent, to admit multi-family housing in such vacant land areas as remain in such a community. . . .

Unless there is something in *Mount Laurel,* either directly or by compelling analogy, to persuade otherwise, the long held principles just stated must be controlling here. During the period of development of Washington Township it served a widespread contemporaneous demand of people employed elsewhere for single-family residential housing — a kind of housing traditionally highly valued by the American family — and until fairly recent years affordable by the average family. Such development was characteristic of many communities. It served a basic social and regional need. There was thus nothing invidious about such development or about the decision of the township municipal planners in 1963 to continue that basic scheme of development in order to maintain the established character of the community. Such a determination fully accorded with the statutory criteria of consideration of the character of the municipality and the most appropriate use of land throughout the municipality. As to the potential deleterious zoning effects of emplacing apartment house projects amidst solid single-family development, as here, see *Leimann v. Board of Adjustment, Cranford Tp.,* 9 N.J. 336, 341-342, 88 A.2d 337 (1952); *Shipman v. Town of Montclair,* 16 N.J.Super 365, 370, 84 A.2d 652 (App.Div.1951). In the same tenor, in part, was the report of the planning experts appointed by the trial court and the testimony of the opposing planning experts herein.

The decision of the municipal legislators, prior to the institution of the present litigation, to keep the municipality free from multi-family development, was, for the reasons stated above, not an arbitrary one, although, concededly, respectable arguments could be mounted for a different policy determination.

Nor is the reasonableness of the municipal residential zoning policy affected by the experimental and defensible zoning decision to try to attract commercial ratables by expanding the permitted uses of some areas, including the instant property, for professional, office and research purposes. . . . Whether that regulation was so factually unjustified as to merit judicial nullification was not decided by the trial court and is not an issue here.

But the overriding point we make is that it is not for the courts to substitute their conception of what the public welfare requires by way of zoning for the views of those in whom the Legislature and the local electorate have vested that responsibility. The judicial role is circumscribed by the limitations stated by this court in such decisions as *Bow & Arrow Manor*. . . . In short, it is limited to the assessment of a claim that the restrictions of the ordinance are patently arbitrary or unreasonable or violative of the statute, not that they do not match the plaintiff's or the court's conception of the requirements of the general welfare, whether within the town or the region.

The Public Advocate argues that the lesson of *Mount Laurel* and the implications of such decisions as *Sente v. Mayor and Mun. Coun. Clifton*, 66 N.J. 204, 330 A.2d 321 (1974) and *DeSimone v. Greater Englewood Housing Corp. No. 1*, 56 N.J. 428, 267 A.2d 31 (1970), are that housing needs of all segments of the population are a priority charge on the zoning regulations of *all* municipalities, whether or not developed. There is no such implication in the cases cited, individually or collectively. None of them stands for the proposition that because of the conceded general shortage of multi-family housing the zoning statute has, in effect, been amended to render such housing an absolutely mandatory component of every zoning ordinance — as virtually contended for by plaintiffs and the Public Advocate. In this regard, it is significant that the Legislature has just completed a comprehensive revision of the zoning statute and has made no change approaching the impact of the proposition just stated.[115]. . .

There are allusions in the briefs to approving references in our cases to zoning for an appropriate variety and choice of housing, see, *e. g., Mount Laurel*, 67 N.J. at 174, 179, 187, 336 A.2d 713, and corollary arguments that such references support the thesis that *all* municipalities must zone for housing for all categories of the population, middle and upper classes as well as low and moderate income. A moment's reflection will suffice to confirm the fact that such references contemplate fairly sizeable developing, not fully developed municipalities — particularly small ones — which may vary in character from such a tiny municipality as Winfield in Union County, developed in a dense, moderate-income, multi-family residential pattern, to one like the subject municipality, homogeneously and completely developed as a middle-upper income, moderate to low density, single-family community. The ideal of the well balanced community, providing all kinds of housing for

---

[115] The only apparent substantive use change in the recent Municipal Land Use Law specifically dealing with housing density is that authorizing "senior citizen community housing construction consistent with provisions permitting other residential uses of a similar density in the same zoning district." *N.J.S.A.* 40:55D-21; 52 g. See *Taxpayers Association of Weymouth v. Weymouth Tp.*, 71 N.J. 249, 288 — 289, 296 — 297, 364 A.2d 1016 (1976).

. . . .

a cross-section of the regional population pattern, is, quite obviously, realizable physically only in the kind of developing municipality of sizeable area identified in *Mount Laurel* as such, see 67 N.J. at 160, 336 A.2d 713 or perhaps in a developed municipality undergoing thorough-going redevelopment of blighted areas.[116]

What Justice Hall probably had in mind, in this regard, when writing for the court in *Mount Laurel, supra,* was foreshadowed when he said, in his noted dissent in *Vickers v. Tp. Com. of Gloucester Tp., supra* (37 N.J. at 252, 253, 181 A.2d at 140):

> The instant case, both in its physical setting and in the issues raised, is typical of land use controversies now current in so many New Jersey municipalities on the outer ring of the built up urban and suburban areas. These are municipalities with relatively few people and a lot of open space, but in the throes, or soon to be reached by the inevitable tide, of industrial and commercial decentralization and mass population migration from the already densely settled central cores. *They are not small, homogeneous communities with permanent character already established, like the settled suburbs surrounding the cities in which planning and zoning may properly be geared around things as they are and as they will pretty much continue to be.* (emphasis added).

We are, of course, not insensitive to the current social need for larger quantities of affordable housing of all kinds for the general population. . . . A possibility of some relief in that regard is contained within the statutory special exception or variance processes. See *Mount Laurel,* 67 N.J. at 181-182, n. 12, 336 A.2d 713. But insofar as review of the validity of a zoning ordinance is concerned, the judicial branch is not suited to the role of an *ad hoc* super zoning legislature, particularly in the area of adjusting claims for satisfaction by individual municipalities of regional needs, whether as to housing or any other important social need affected by zoning. The closely contested expert planning proofs before the trial court with respect to the utility of the subject tract for various kinds of housing, office and research uses, hospitals and nursing homes, banks and public recreational facilities, is illustrative of the reasonable differences of opinion in this area. We went as far in that general direction as

---

[116] Planning experts Rose and Levin, after applauding the movement in *Mount Laurel* toward zoning requirements for regional housing needs, argue that to "balance" this decision there is needed "an equally forceful judicial expression of the importance of another planning constraint, *i. e.,* the *suitability* of each municipality to accommodate the required housing units". (emphasis the authors'). "What is a 'Developing Municipality' within the Meaning of the *Mount Laurel* Decision?", 4 *Real Est.L.J.* 359, 386 (1976).

comports with the limitations of the judicial function, in our determinations in *Mount Laurel, supra,* and *Oakwood at Madison, supra.* The sociological problems presented by this and similar cases, and of concern not only to our dissenting brother, but ourselves, call for legislation vesting appropriate developmental control in State or regional administrative agencies. See A.L.I. Model Land Development Code (Proposed Official Draft 1975) Commentary on Article 7, pp. 284 — 291; Proposed "Comprehensive and Balanced Housing Plan Act", Senate No. 3139 (1977), (Sens. Greenberg, Merlino and McGahn); *cf. Oakwood at Madison, supra,* 72 N.J. at 499, 531 — 532, 371 A.2d at 1200, 1217 — 1218. The problem is not an appropriate subject of judicial superintendence. Clearly the legislature, and the executive within proper delegation, have the power to impose zoning housing regulations on a regional basis which would ignore municipal boundary lines and provide recourse to all developable land wherever situated, *Oakwood at Madison, ubi cit. supra.* Nothing in this opinion, contrary to the assertion in the dissent (pp. 28 — 29), is calculated to preclude that salutary course.

We concur in the Appellate Division judgment setting aside the trial court adjudication of illegality of the Washington ordinance for failure to zone for multi-family residential use.

This conclusion renders it unnecessary to deal with the orders of the trial court enforcing that determination, *i. e.,* the appointment of experts in aid of the court's judgment and the remedy of ordering the grant of a building permit to the plaintiffs. Those actions of course fall with the setting aside of the underlying adjudication by the trial court.

. . . .

[The court then held that a 1967 amendment to the zoning ordinance increasing the minimum lot size requirements for the Pascack property from 10,000 square feet to two acres was invalid as piecemeal and haphazard zoning. — Eds.]

Judgment modified in accordance with this opinion. No costs, but the order of the trial court with respect to defrayal of costs of the report of the experts is to stand.

SULLIVAN and SCHREIBER, JJ., concurring in the result.

For modification: Chief Justice HUGHES, Justices MOUNTAIN, SULLIVAN, CLIFFORD and SCHREIBER and Judge CONFORD — 6.

Dissenting: Justice PASHMAN — 1.

SULLIVAN, J. (concurring).

I am in general agreement that this is not a *Mount Laurel* case for two reasons. First, the Township of Washington is not a developing municipality. Second, the proposed housing is not for low or moderate income families. The trial judge, while he properly struck down the 1967 amendment to the zoning ordinance which increased the minimum lot requirements of the property in question from 10,000 square feet to two acres, unnecessarily became enmeshed in rezoning in order to allow for multi-family housing on plaintiff Waldy's 30-acre tract of land.

. . . .

This case points up the inherent weakness in the present statutory provisions which, with few exceptions, vest exclusive control over zoning in the particular municipal government. Pascack Valley is a typical example. There is an admitted need for multi-family housing in this area yet five of the eight municipalities in the Valley do not permit this type of housing unit. However, if you consider each one of these municipalities separately, some basis can be demonstrated for the particular zone plan. Until regional zoning is established based on comprehensive planning, the problems we are now grappling with cannot be resolved except on an *ad hoc* basis.

. . . Our decision in *Mount Laurel* and its progeny admittedly deal with difficult and farreaching problems involving the public welfare. I wonder, though, if the opinions we are handing down in this area of the law of zoning have not become so complicated that they are beyond the comprehension of the average member of a local planning board, board of adjustment or governing body (not to mention many members of the bench and bar). In directing local government as to how it must exercise its zoning power pursuant to law, it is essential that we speak with more clarity, directness and simplicity.

I join in the modification of the Appellate Division judgment and the affirmance of that judgment as modified.

SCHREIBER, J., concurring.

The *Mt. Laurel* principle, as I view it, of prohibiting a municipality from utilizing its zoning power to exclude low and moderate income families in order to escape an adverse financial impact, should be applicable to *all* municipalities. . . . Equitably I cannot envision any sound policy which would justify a differentiation in the *duty* owed by a developing or a fully developed community. If a municipality, motivated by fiscal reasons, has zoned to exclude low and moderate income people and has successfully accomplished that end, contrary to the general welfare, the courts should not absolve that municipality from its underlying duty simply because it has already completed its illegal objective.

The fact that a settled and developed community may not have any vacant or undeveloped land does not and should not bar fulfillment of that obligation once it is found that the zoning has been enacted with fiscal considerations in mind. As soon as the wrong is adjudicated, the municipality must rezone. The municipality's duty, as Justice Hall stated in *Mt. Laurel,* would be satisfied if its zoning afforded the *opportunity* for low and moderate income housing. . . . Although rezoning undeveloped land for this purpose may be desirable, developed acreage may likewise be utilized. In each of these developed communities there appear to be some vacant tracts, and, in addition, some sections may be ripe for redevelopment. Irrespective of sufficient vacant land and areas in need of redevelopment, the municipality should rezone whatever area is needed to permit the construction of low and moderate income housing, even though those projects may not become economically feasible until sometime in the future. In this manner, the municipality will acquit its obligation.

However, the enactment of zoning ordinances in some municipalities, such as in the Township of Washington, was not motivated by fiscal considerations. . . . Its initial zoning ordinance in 1941 encouraged construction of single-family homes, and the 1963 master plan recognized the municipality had and was "predominantly developed" as a single-family community. Thus we find that the invidious motive condemned by *Mt. Laurel* is nonexistent and its principle inapplicable.

I concur and join in the judgment as modified by the majority.

PASHMAN, J., dissenting.

[Most of Justice Pashman's dissenting opinion is omitted. The conclusion of his opinion is reprinted below. — Eds.]

The majority today effectively neutralizes our holding in *Mt. Laurel.* The Court neglects to consider the troublesome effect that its decision will have on "fair share" allocations and defining appropriate regions; by exempting from any affirmative obligations under *Mt. Laurel* a significant number of municipalities, the majority makes an equitable distribution of the burdens of providing for low and moderate family housing impossible. Rather than order a sharing of responsibilities under *Mt. Laurel,* the majority fragmentizes the State by selectively targeting areas which must affirmatively provide for multi-family housing.

Furthermore, today's opinion seriously underestimates the depth and magnitude of the measures needed to correct decades of exclusionary development. I have referred to the tactics of municipalities in avoiding their "fair share," . . .; and the reluctance of courts to forcefully implement our decision in *Mt. Laurel, supra.* . . . Today's decision can only provide new incentives to communities which seek to escape their constitutional and statutory duties. Consequently, we can offer no hope that new advances will be made in our efforts against exclusionary zoning.

Unfortunately, the effect of today's decision will be long lasting. State regulation embodied in the zoning power deeply affects the racial, economic, and social structure of our society, and locks people into an environment over which they have no control. Generations of children are relegated to a slum schooling and playing in the overcrowded and congested streets of the inner cities. Men and women seeking to earn a living for themselves and their families are barred by distance from job markets. Society as a whole suffers the failure to solve the economic and social problems which exclusionary zoning creates; we live daily with the failure of our democratic institutions to eradicate class distinctions. Inevitably, the dream of a pluralistic society begins to fade.

This Court has been in the vanguard declaring the right of children to a thorough and efficient education, *Robinson v. Cahill,* 62 N.J. 473, 303 A.2d 273 (1973); the right of all persons to acquire, own, and dispose of real property, *Jones v. Haridor Realty Corp.,* 37 N.J. 384, 391, 181 A.2d 481 (1962); and the right of all persons to share equal access to the State's resources, *Neptune City v. Avon,* 61 N.J. 296, 294 A.2d 47 (1972). Today we make a mockery of those rights by perpetuating a ghetto system in which residents live in inferior and often degrading conditions. Unless and until we open up the suburbs to all citizens of the State on an equal basis, the cherished ideals of our constitutional rights will remain illusive and unattainable.

Comments: 1. The New Jersey Supreme Court decided a companion case, *Fobe Assocs. v. Mayor & Council & Bd. of Adjustment,* 379 A.2d 31 (N.J. 1977), on the same day as *Pascack.* After the borough board of adjustment refused to recommend a variance to permit developer to build apartment house in single-family residential district, the developer sought an adjudication that the denial of the recommendation was arbitrary and unreasonable and that the relevant zoning ordinance was invalid. The trial court entered judgment for defendants and the Superior Court, Appellate Division, affirmed. Certification was granted, and the Supreme Court, Conford, P. J. A. D., temporarily assigned, held that: (1) the borough zoning ordinance was not invalid by reason of its absolute prohibition of multifamily residential buildings; (2) even if the provision of multifamily housing in the borough was inherently for the general welfare, the board of adjustment's decision to deny the variance was not arbitrary or unsupported by record evidence where the determination was based on a finding that granting the variance would substantially impair the intent and purpose of the zone plan and zoning ordinance and that the zoning benefits would not outweigh the zoning harms consequent on a variance, and (3) the board of adjustment did not err in accepting in evidence a disapproving resolution submitted by the borough planning board.

In dealing with the validity of the Demarest zoning ordinance, the court said:

> There is no essential difference between the facts here and those in *Pascack Association* in respect of the contention of invalidity

advanced in both cases. That position was that in view of the essentiality of housing for all categories of people and families and the current shortage of multi-family housing in and around the environs and regions of Washington and Demarest, respectively, it is mandatory that every municipality in those regions, regardless of the nature and extent of its current development, provide by its zoning ordinance the opportunity for some degree of multi-family residential development. We rejected that contention in *Pascack Association.* . . .

. . . How best to use the few isolated parcels of vacant land remaining in Demarest is a matter for the local governmental bodies unless and until the Legislature expressly ordains any specific disposition (within constitutional limitations). The Demarest ordinance is not invalid on the grounds advanced by plaintiff.

Id. at 34-35.

In *Fobe* the plaintiff sought a variance under N.J. Stat. Ann. § 40:55-39(d) (Supp. 1977), which authorizes the grant of a "use" variance "in particular cases" upon an affirmative finding of "special reasons," together with the negative findings, applicable in all New Jersey zoning relief situations, that the "relief can be granted without substantial detriment to the public good and will not substantially impair the intent and purpose of the zone plan and zoning ordinance." It had long been settled in New Jersey that a "special reasons" variance could be granted without a showing that the particular property could not feasibly be used for a permitted use or that other hardship existed, and that such variances could be granted simply to promote the general purposes of zoning. In fact, most of the "special reasons" variance previously approved by the New Jersey appellate courts were for public and semi-public uses deemed to further "the general welfare" — *e.g.,* a parochial school in a residential zone, a private school in a residential zone, a telephone equipment building in a residential zone, a private hospital for the emotionally disturbed in a residential zone, and semi-public low-income housing in a residential zone. The *Fobe* court said:

> . . . [O]ne is hard put to respond to the insistence that if "adequate housing of all categories of people is . . . an absolute essential in promotion of the general welfare required in all local land use regulation", as stated in *Mount Laurel,* . . . (whether or not the statement constituted a strict holding, as to which see our opinion in *Pascack Association v. Mayor and Council of Washington,* . . .), a variance to provide additional rental housing in a region which plainly needs it is "inherently" for the general welfare, in the *Kohl* sense of the concept.
>
> We propose to leave definitive resolution of this knotty problem to a future case which will compel it; the instant one does not. For reasons which follow, we conclude that even if the provision of multifamily housing in Demarest is inherently for the general welfare, so as to affirmatively authorize a d. variance *if the negative criteria of* N.J.S.A. 40:55-39 *were met,* the decision of the board of adjustment to deny the variance should be upheld. That determination was based on a finding that the grant would substantially impair the intent and purpose of the zone plan and

zoning ordinance, and also, impliedly, that the zoning benefits would not outweigh the zoning harms consequent upon a variance. We cannot find these determinations to be arbitrary or without substantial support by evidence in the record.

. . . .

It is apparent that in many, if not most, cases the decision of a board of adjustment on a contested d. variance application is an amalgam of resolution of fact and exercise of discretion. . . .

Having in mind that in the administration of the law on this subject there is always a particular concern over the judicial overruling of a denial of a variance, as distinguished from a grant, . . . the foregoing principles dictate an affirmance of the concordant determinations of the Law and Appellate Divisions not to disturb the denial of a recommendation for a variance by the board of adjustment. We have already found that the conclusion that the grant would substantially affect the zone scheme and plan adversely is supported by substantial evidence. We add that the implied, discretionary determination that whatever zoning benefits might accrue from the variance sought are outweighed by the zoning harm envisaged by the board cannot, on this record, be adjudged arbitrary or capricious.

Id. at 40-41.

In *Fobe,* Sullivan and Schreiber, JJ., concurred in the result; Sullivan, J., also concurred in the majority opinion, subject to his comments in the companion *Pascack* case. Pashman, J., dissented; the conclusion of his dissenting opinion was as follows:

Today's decision by the Court will neither further the legislative intent in enacting the (d) variance nor provide any remedy for exclusionary zoning. Instead, it merely reinforces the unbridled power which is currently exercised by local governing bodies — including the ability to pass exclusionary zoning measures and to needlessly restrict housing development. Contrary to the expressed purpose of zoning and the (d) variance, the majority today legitimates planning decisions based on exclusionary principles, and relegates the zoning purposes which the Legislature specifically enacted within *N.J.S.A.* 40:55-32 to secondary importance.

Id. at 53.

2. Do you think *Pascack* and *Fobe* represent a significant retreat by the New Jersey Supreme Court from the principles enunciated in *Mount Laurel* and *Oakwood at Madison? See also Dolan v. Borough of Tenafly,* 380 A.2d 1119 (N.J. 1977). In this case the borough acquired for open space purposes the last substantial unimproved residentially zoned tract of land within its limits. Noting that the acquisition had been made under the state's open space acquisition program and with a state grant, the court held that the acquisition did not violate *Mount Laurel.*

In *Home Builders League of South Jersey, Inc. v. Township of Berlin,* 385 A.2d 295 (L. Div. 1978), a home builders' association and others challenged the minimum floor area requirements in the zoning ordinances of four municipalities, each a "developing community" in a regional housing market. The court invalidated the minimum floor area requirements on the ground that they bore no relation to the health, safety, morals, or general welfare of the municipalities' residents or the public at large. The court noted that the New Jersey zoning enabling act did not recognize preservation of the character of a neighborhood or the conservation of property values as a proper objective of zoning, and also found that smaller houses would not adversely affect the value of larger houses because smaller houses could be equal in quality and attractiveness to larger houses. The court characterized the minimum floor area restrictions as "snob zoning," and held that they were *ultra vires*. Distinguishing *Mount Laurel,* the court said that the case before it cut across economic lines, and that people should be free to build houses of a size best fitted to their needs in either "developing" or "developed" communities, regardless of income.

In *Windmill Estates, Inc. v. Zoning Bd. of Adjustment,* 385 A.2d 924 (N.J. App. Div. 1978), where a zoning ordinance was challenged because it prevented plaintiffs from developing townhouses on its property, the trial court held there was no violation of the *Mount Laurel* doctrine because the municipality was not a "developing community," but that the ordinance did violate the New Jersey Municipal Land Use Law because the latter had adopted the principles of *Mount Laurel* without excluding "nondeveloping communities" from their application. However, the intermediate appellate court reversed and declared the ordinance valid under the Municipal Land Use Law. The court held that, except with respect to density zoning for senior citizens' housing, the Municipal Land Use Law did not change the application of the *Mount Laurel* doctrine.

Governor Byrne recently released a low- and moderate-income housing plan for most municipalities in New Jersey, calling for 429,000 new housing units for low- and moderate-income families by 1990. The plan establishes housing quotas, but Governor Byrne emphasized that "whether such housing is in fact built depends on a whole series of outside factors such as land and development costs and financing and market demands." The Governor also emphasized that the *Mount Laurel* opinion and subsequent lower court opinions said that "a town had an obligation to provide housing opportunities, but it was not obligated to provide for the housing itself." Quotas were not set for all New Jersey municipalities because of the need to preserve farmland and open space and because some municipalities have little or no undeveloped land.

A recent study conducted by the Middlesex-Mercer Regional Study Council found that only a handful of communities in the region have so far undertaken to address the "fair share" requirement laid down in *Mount Laurel.*

BERENSON v. TOWN OF NEW CASTLE

New York Supreme Court
Unpublished trial court opinion (1977)

TRAINOR, J.

Plaintiffs attack the zoning ordinance of the Town of New Castle as unconstitutional in its entirety, in that no provision is, or ever had been, made permitting any form of multi-family housing in the Town. Plaintiffs are the fee owners of a parcel of 50 acres of land which they allege cannot reasonably be developed under existing zoning regulations and which is suitable for multi-family residential development.

The Plaintiffs commenced this action by the service of a summons and verified complaint seeking, inter alia, a declaratory judgment that the zoning ordinance of the Town is unconstitutional, in general and in particular as it applies to Plaintiffs' real property. Issue was joined by the serving of an answer which included a general denial and certain affirmative defenses.

The Plaintiffs moved for summary judgment pursuant to CPLR 3212; Defendants opposed this motion and cross-moved for summary judgment dismissing the complaint pursuant to CPLR 3211 and 3212. Both motions were denied. Special term held that there was a triable issue of fact with respect to the need for multi-family housing in New Castle.

Both parties appealed to the Appellate Division, Second Department, which upheld the decision below, and certified that issue to the Court of Appeals.

The Court of Appeals unanimously affirmed the decision below, 38 N.Y. 2d 102 (1975), and remanded the matter to this Court for trial. The Court of Appeals reviewed the general considerations which affect the validity of zoning ordinances and then set forth at length its views as to the proper factual issues to be considered upon the trial and the specific legal criteria by which the constitutionality of New Castle's zoning ordinance is to be determined by this Court, citing New York, Federal and cases from other jurisdictions.

. . . .

[The trial court next reviewed the decision of the Court of Appeals, which is discussed *supra* p. 484. The trial court then determined that there was a substantial unmet housing need in New Castle, primarily for families working within the town whose incomes are no greater than $15,000. There was an insignificant amount of rental housing in the town and the average price of housing for sale was $89,750. Since the town was practically all zoned for one- or two-acre residential development, it was virtually a "one-use" community. Applying the tests adopted by the Court of Appeals, the trial court found that the town had failed to provide a " 'properly balanced and well-ordered plan for the community.' " Reviewing housing needs in the surrounding region, the court also found that the town had failed, as required by the Court of Appeals, to take that regional need into account. Some nearby communities had recently completed subsidized multifamily housing developments, and private, unsubsidized projects also existed in those communities. However, other nearby communities had equally restrictive zoning ordinances.

There was also a severe shortage of multifamily units in the region available to lower income families. — Eds.]

Based on these considerations, the Court finds that the regional needs are not being met by the communities which are New Castle's neighbors, further, if the present exclusionary zoning policies of New Castle and the other now-undeveloped communities in northern Westchester are permitted to continue without change, it will be impossible to supply the housing needs of the county during the next decade.

 . . . .

This Court is convinced from the testimony given at the trial by public officials and planning experts, including the planning commissioner of Westchester County, that it would be unrealistic to expect multi-family housing to be built in the future unless provision is made now to set aside adequate lands for that purpose and to create a land-use decision-making process that will accommodate present and prospective local and regional housing needs. The testimony further establishes that the present housing shortage of two million units in the Tri-State Regional Area will increase over the next decade, the period most commonly used by planners in projecting such needs. Taking these factors into account, the most conservative estimate of what will be required of New Castle over the next ten years to supply its own needs for multi-family housing and to meet its share of the regional needs for such housing is not less than 3,500 multi-family housing units. While proper zoning cannot guarantee that such units will be built in fact, the absence of such zoning absolutely precludes any such construction.

The Court notes that during the pendency of this action, the Town amended its zoning ordinance to permit the construction of some apartments in commercial structures in business districts. However, an analysis of the actual effect of this amendment taking into account the existing buildings and character of uses, physical conditions, and limitations set forth in the amendment itself, demonstrates that only an insignificant number of rental units could possibly result. This measure is wholly inadequate to meet the needs found to exist by this Court from New Castle alone and thereby clearly establishes the failure of the Town to consider the needs of the region as well as its own needs, under the second branch of the standards set forth by the Court of Appeals. This failure on the part of the Town is not merely a result of indifference to such needs. The uncontradicted evidence amply proves that the Town has continuously and actively opposed any planning or program that would suggest the assumption by it of any responsibility to meet local or regional housing needs. In 1949, New Castle refused to participate in the earliest regional plan for northern Westchester. In 1976 Westchester County applied for a Federal Community Development Block Grant under Title 1 of the Housing and Community Development Act of 1974. The Town of New Castle refused to cooperate with the County to assist it in establishing its eligibility for a $500,000 grant for planning and housing studies. New Castle has further totally disregarded Westchester County's recommended policy for housing distribution and density, and its planning policy has been inconsistent with the County's. The Town effectively thwarted the introduction of a small one hundred-unit subsidized rental housing development by the New York State Urban Development Corporation. See *Evans v. Lynn,* 376 F. Supp. 327, 330 (S.D.N.Y. 1974) *aff'd* 537 F. 2d 571 (2d Cir. 1975). The Town has even refused to hold public hearings on plaintiffs' rezoning applications for multi-family use. The defendant has not simply *failed* to consider local and regional housing needs; it has *refused* to consider them.

There remains the difficult question as to the appropriate remedy in a case of this nature.

The plaintiffs have sought specific relief affecting their parcel of land and requested that it be rezoned to permit the multi-family use they propose. In the first instance, the Court is faced with the question of what can be done to persuade the defendant Town to amend its ordinance and map comprehensively to accommodate identified local and regional housing needs which would encompass the plaintiffs' parcel.

The Court concludes that the plaintiffs have sustained the burden of demonstrating the invalidity of the Town's zoning as it affects their parcel and the development of that parcel for multi-family use would contribute to meeting the needs identified upon the trial. The rezoning of such land for multi-family use subject only to such standards as are reasonably related to protecting the health and safety of the community and the occupants of the plaintiffs' development is hereby recommended. Westchester County's "Assumptions, Goals and Urban Form" (Exh. F) designates New Castle as a "Medium Density Suburban Area" with recommended densities of one to sixteen units per acre. Such rezoning should provide for a density of development in the middle of that range. The defendant should adopt the necessary amendments to its Zoning Ordinance within six (6) months after entry of this order. Upon compliance therewith, a building permit shall be issued to the plaintiffs.

In reaching this conclusion, the Court is not exercising any legislative function. There is a distinction between the role of the Town Board acting on a matter involving the zoning of a specific parcel and its role in adopting a comprehensive zoning ordinance or plan. In the former role it would act in a quasi-judicial or administrative capacity, and the Court's order effecting the parcel carries out a supervisory role traditional for Courts to undertake. . . .

This distinction between specific site-classifications or reclassifications which are quasi-judicial or administrative in character, and comprehensive decision-making affecting the entire locality or large portions of it has been drawn by other Courts. . . .

The evidence in this case has demonstrated that the refusal of the Town to rezone plaintiffs' parcel for multi-family use would be arbitrary and capricious and without any reasonable relationship to the general welfare of the Town or the region in which it is a part. Under these circumstances it would be a Pyrrhic victory indeed after prolonged and complex litigation for the plaintiffs to win a comprehensive remedy that did not encompass their land. The Supreme Court of New Jersey faced with this very issue, has authorized trial courts in that state to issue specific relief to avoid this problem. . . . [Here the court quotes from *Oakwood at Madison.* — Eds.]

The Court concludes that this case is analogous to the *Oakwood at Madison* situation and that specific relief is required to make standards set forth by our Court of Appeals meaningful and effective. Such relief is particularly appropriate in light of voluminous evidence produced that the plaintiffs' proposed development will not be inconsistent with the needs of the Town or the region. This assures that specific relief could not be regarded as a "piecemeal" decision divorced from broader considerations.

There remains the issue of more comprehensive relief requested by the plaintiffs, affecting the Town's zoning and land use policy generally.

Although this case and other similar land-use cases are brought by private parties concerned with unreasonable restraints on the use of their land, our Court of Appeals has noted that the rights of a landowner or developer "cannot realistically speaking, be viewed separately and apart from the rights of others in search of a [more] comfortable place to live." . . . Just as the rights of the landowner cannot be separated from those of the future residences, so the remedy must recognize the rights of future residents. It would impose a great burden on the Courts and the parties to conduct extensive litigation on the reasonableness of a local land use policy as it affects the general welfare of the region if the only remedy were specific to the same project. This would leave to future litigants and courts the expensive and wasteful burden of traversing the same legal ground for the purpose of granting zoning relief on a parcel-by-parcel basis.

The Court believes that the Court of Appeals mandated standards for local government land-use controls in order to promote compliance that is not dependent on repetitive litigation of the basic substantive issues.[117] The legal predicate for broader relief is found not only in the Court of Appeals mandate in this case, but also in two decisions of the New Jersey Supreme Court, *Southern Burlington NAACP v. Tp. of Mount Laurel,* ... [and] *Oakwood at Madison, Inc. v. Township of Madison.* ...

The Court has already found, on the basis of the evidence adduced at trial, that not less than 3,500 multi-family housing units will be needed in New Castle over the next ten years to supply its own needs and that of the region. This figure is not a "formuliac determination of numerical speculation of . . . a fair share," eschewed by the New Jersey Supreme Court in its *Oakwood* decision. It is a realistic planning goal that recognized the minimum needs established by the evidence in this case. Although the plaintiffs' proposed project will contribute to meeting such needs, another trial should not be required to establish the right of each successive developer to contribute to meeting those needs if the Town fails to accommodate them in its land-use decision-making process.

The Court determines that the Town of New Castle should affirmatively afford the opportunity to meet such needs and that its current planning and zoning policies to the extent they frustrate private efforts to do so, are invalid.

Accordingly, the Court, in the first phase of declaratory relief, holds that the Town, under its existing planning and land-use control system, has a heavy burden of showing compelling reasons to justify the exclusion of future proposals of multi-family housing up to 3,500 units of such housing over the next ten years. This shifting to the Town the burden of showing a compelling public interest in order to deny future proposals which meet judicially established housing goals is an essential element of the remedy developed by the New Jersey Supreme Court in the *Mount Laurel* and *Oakwood* cases. ... Should the Town fail to adopt adequate changes in its zoning, planning and land use regulatory policies, a party desiring to construct such housing need show only that the proposed development will contribute to meeting such goals and that the Town has frustrated that objective for less than compelling reasons. Upon this showing, specific relief may be ordered for such proposed development, subject to similar conditions as are provided for with respect to specific relief granted in the instant case.

The foregoing declaratory relief shall be regarded as interim relief pending the revision of the Town's planning and zoning policies to

---

[117] "Zoning, as we have previously noted, is essentially a legislative act. Thus, it is quite anomalous that a Court should be required to perform the tasks of a regional planner. In the end, we look to the Legislature to make appropriate changes in order to foster the development of programs designed to achieve sound regional planning." *Berensen, supra* p. 111.

accommodate the needed housing. Upon the adoption of a satisfactory plan and comprehensive zoning ordinance and map, the traditional presumption of validity enjoyed by local legislative judgment shall be reinstated with regard to the Town's action.

The Court will retain jurisdiction for the purpose of determining whether the interim declaratory relief should be lifted because of the Town's adoption of a satisfactory zoning, planning and land-use regulatory policy in regard to needed housing. To afford the Town an opportunity to comply with this more comprehensive requirement such interim declaratory relief shall not become effective prior to six (6) months from the entry of the Court's judgment herein. After the six (6) month period, however, the interim declaratory relief shall become effective in the event the Town has not adopted a zoning amendment and a planning and land-use regulatory policy which meets the local and regional housing needs as found by the Court.

In considering the degree to which affirmative relief is appropriate in this matter, the Court is mindful of the natural and well taken reluctance of the judiciary to take any action which can be viewed as a usurpation of other governmental powers or functions. Therefore, this Court will not attempt to exercise the legislative powers delegated to the Town by the State Legislature. Rather, the Court recommends the Town exercise those powers which it possesses in a manner consistent with this decision and the standards enunciated in the opinion of the Court of Appeals in this case. Moreover, it is in the interest of the Town that its legislative power be used to establish clear standards for the implementation of this Court's decision. This will shield the Town against the consequences of multiple *ad hoc,* litigation which would otherwise inevitably result from the absence of a comprehensive local zoning law.

The Town Board in the first instance shall be given the opportunity to prepare and submit to the Court the proposed revision of the Town Plan, Zoning Ordinance and Map. Throughout the planning process, it is suggested that the Town consult with officials and staff of the Westchester County Planning Department as to appropriate housing densities, types, locations and sites.

The Town shall not adopt laws or regulations that result in unnecessary costs for development of multi-family housing, such as unreasonable lot coverage and set-back requirements for excessive utility connections and other similar restrictions.

Guidelines for the Town's plan and ordinance should express a statement of policy indicating its intention to permit the development of the needed multi-family housing within its jurisdiction. Such a policy statement should include, at a minimum, the following:

(a) A declaration that the Town intends to encourage newly constructed multi-family housing to meet the needs of the indicated households in the amount of at least 3,500 units by 1988;

(b) A schedule of the pace of such development and the reasons therefor;

(c) The types of area or areas where proposals for such development will be sympathetically considered and why those areas have been selected; and

(d) The willingness of the community to assist in meeting regional housing goals as determined by the Westchester County Planning Department.

The Town should develop laws and regulations for meeting the described needs and may create a "floating" zone, a conditional use for other special permit process for such housing that is not located geographically or mapped until the specific development proposal is approved in accordance with the prestated inclusionary policy statement. This will avoid the problem of mapping such districts with such specificity that land prices may escalate to such an extent that interferes with the economic feasibility of proposed development. Refusal of development permission may be justified only for inconsistency with the Town's inclusionary policy statement. Alternatively, if and to the extent that the Town should decide to locate the zones for needed housing geographically in advance, it may "over-zone" for this purpose to avoid inflated land values or the possibility that such land may instead be used up for lower density housing. See *Oakwood at Madison.* . . .

The Town may provide an incentive to developers of needed multi-family housing to encourage the inclusion of lower cost rental units in their development, by density bonuses or by relaxing other requirements normally applicable.

The foregoing guidelines provide great flexibility to the Town to control its future while at the same time contributing appropriately to the housing market for the area of which it is a part. "Indeed sound planning inherently calls for recognition of the dynamics of change" *Town of Bedford v. Village of Mt. Kisco,* 33 N.Y. 2d 178, 351 N.Y.S. 2d 129 (1973). The change for New Castle can preserve autonomy with regard to the controls over specific development, within the standards set forth within the policy statement.

The affirmative land use obligation placed on New Castle is consistent with, and is not intended to override, the maintenance and attainment of attractive environment with good living accommodations and adequate services for a wide variety of people living in a wide assortment of decent housing. New Castle will always include large amounts of low density housing occupied by affluent households. It can retain this character and still accommodate regionally needed housing at higher densities to achieve the balance required by the Court of Appeals.

An official inclusionary policy statement, pre-stated requirements for housing at higher densities, and the creation of a process for granting development permission for proposals for meeting such standards (or in the alternative "over-zoning" for such housing) will establish a land-use decision-making process that will provide standards for judicial review in the future, should any be necessary.

The inclusionary policy statement will evidence the community's forethought to its land-use problems and become a major element of the comprehensive planning process that is a predicate for the existence of the Town's zoning power under the principals of *Udell v. Haas,* 21 N.Y. 2d 463, 288 N.Y.S. 2d 888 (1969). As the Court of Appeals noted, the comprehensive plan, by evidencing the community's deliberate policy choices in advance of specific proposals, also "protects the landowner from arbitrary restrictions on the use of his property which can result from the pressures which outraged voters can bring to bear on public officers" *id.* at 469. While it protects the landowner it also protects the community from opening itself to undue pressures for rezoning beyond the areas consistent with the pre-stated policy on the ground that the character of an area and surrounding land uses are affected by multi-family zoning. With the policy statement meeting the aforesaid guidelines, New Castle will accommodate local and regional needs. New Castle will not run the risk that its multi-family developments will change the character of a neighborhood or permit multi-family housing in excess of the basic policy limits. This will permit rational intermingling of land uses that would otherwise become difficult to control.

Comments: Judicial remedies in exclusionary zoning cases are considered in Housing for All Under Law, ch. 3 (R. Fishman ed. 1978) (Report of the American Bar Ass'n Advisory Comm'n on Urban Growth). Three approaches to rezoning to accommodate low-income housing are suggested. *Id.* at 178-81. Under the first, a portion of the jurisdiction is zoned to permit high-density development, but it is suggested that this approach will drive up the price of the rezoned land if there is substantial demand for upper-income apartments and force out developers of low-income housing.

A second approach is to create a zone in which low-income housing is the sole permitted use, but this approach is said to raise substantial constitutional questions. What are they? In view of these two suggestions, how would the town in *Berenson* implement the court's direction to indicate "types of . . . areas where proposals for . . . [multifamily] development will be sympathetically considered" ? The third approach recommended is a flexible regulatory technique such as the floating zone, which is also recommended by the *Berenson* opinion. Floating zones and similar administrative techniques are discussed *infra* p. 706. See also the discussion of judicial remedies for correcting zoning ordinances held unconstitutional which follows the *Girsh* decision, *supra* p. 347.

2. Federal Cases

Unlike state governments, the federal government has only delegated, not plenary powers. But the Fourteenth Amendment incorporates substantial restraints upon state governmental action. In the field of "exclusionary zoning," those who challenge local zoning regulations as "exclusionary" usually rely on the "equal protection" clause of the Fourteenth Amendment when the regulations are challenged in the federal courts. Some of the more recent cases also rely on the Fair Housing Act, 42 U.S.C.A. §§ 3601 et seq. (1976). The state court cases reprinted above treat the exclusion of low- and moderate-income housing as a violation of state constitutional provisions because they result in the exclusion of lower income households from the municipality. Since *James v. Valtierra,* 402 U.S. 137 (1971), however, it is clear that "discrimination against the poor" does not violate the United States Constitution, and that "exclusionary zoning" can be attacked in the federal courts only on the ground that it directly or indirectly results in racial (not economic) discrimination.

BOSSELMAN, COMMENTARY ON *JAMES v. VALTIERRA,* 23 Zoning Digest 117 (1971)

The Supreme Court's decision in *James v. Valtierra* is at best a step backward and at worst a headlong retreat from the Court's stand in favor of integrated housing. Does it foretell a basic shift in the Court's direction? Or can it be explained on less ominous grounds?

. . . .

Regarding racial discrimination in housing, . . . the Court has followed a course of vigilant activism that has led it inevitably closer to a confrontation with local governments. Beginning with racial restrictive covenants, which it outlawed in *Shelley v. Kraemer,* 334 U.S. 4, and culminating in the broad holding of *Jones v. Mayer,* 392 U.S. 409, the Court took a firm position against private racial discrimination in the sale or rental of housing. State and local government actions which directly encouraged such discrimination were also held invalid: Thus when a state outlawed open occupancy ordinances the Court found the state action unconstitutional (*Reitman v. Mulkey,* 387 U.S. 369) and when a city required that any open occupancy ordinance be submitted to a referendum the Court struck down this requirement (*Hunter v. Erickson,* 393 U.S. 385).

All of these cases involved an explicit issue of *racial* discrimination. At the same time, however, another line of cases was developing in which the Court found that it was unconstitutional for state or local governments to discriminate against the poor by requiring them to pay a poll tax (*Harper v. Virginia Board of Elections,* 383 U.S. 663) or forcing them to purchase a transcript of their trial in order to appeal (*Griffin v. Illinois,* 351 U.S. 12). These cases involved no racial issue, and seemed to be creating a separate body of constitutional doctrine involving "discrimination against the poor" — a phrase that, as Frank Michelman has shown, is appealing in its simplicity but bewildering in its implications. (See 83 Harvard Law Review 7 (1969).)

The line of race-housing cases and the line of poor-discrimination cases were developing separately, but civil rights lawyers thought they saw a chance to merge them. It is well known that many local governments use discrimination against low-income housing as a means of indirectly excluding racial minorities, thus preserving the racially segregated housing patterns the Court appeared to abhor, through the use of a means (discrimination against the poor) upon which the Court had frowned. Therefore, would not the Court hold local regulations unconstitutional if they allowed only housing for rich people?

Unfortunately, however, the first case to reach the Supreme Court involved a referendum — an unusual law — a provision of the California Constitution requiring the local voters to approve the location of every low-income housing project. Now everyone familiar with the low-income housing problem knows that referenda are not the central issue. In the relatively few places where referenda are required the developer does not reach the referendum until he has obtained the approval of the local city council, which is the crucial hurdle. In towns where the residents want to keep out poor people their elected representatives are not likely to vote against the wishes of the electorate.

So the *Valtierra* case involved a distracting and largely extraneous issue. The Ninth Circuit Court of Appeals had seen the irrelevance of the referendum issue in a well-prepared case brought by Dick Bellman of the National Committee Against Discrimination in Housing. *SASSO v. City of Union City,* 424 F.2d 291. The Court held that a local government could not discriminate against its poor citizens by refusing to provide housing for them, whether the refusal took the form of a referendum or an ordinary legislative action.

But it was the *Valtierra* case, not *SASSO,* that came up to the Supreme Court, and it came up on summary judgment, with a meager factual record. And it came before a Supreme Court remarkably unsophisticated in the devious jungle of local government, a Court that had barely brushed against a building code or zoning ordinance since the 1920's and had little familiarity with this entire sphere of law. Furthermore, it was a Court that had just decided a revolutionary series of legislative reapportionment cases in which it had strongly espoused the principle of "one-man one-vote" — a principle that reaches its epitome in the referendum.

The result was disastrous. The Court refused to grant "the poor" the privileged status they had received in the poll tax and criminal appeals cases. It dismissed the poor as one "of the diverse and shifting groups that make up the American people." Nor did the Court find racial discrimination. The law required a referendum for all public housing, said the Court, not just for projects to be occupied by minority groups. It held that "the record here would not support" a finding that the law was aimed at racial minorities.

The Court's opinion was written by Mr. Justice Black, who has long held strong convictions about popular democracy. He had seen the doctrine of "one-man one-vote" arise out of his dissenting opinions (*Colegrove v. Green,* 328 U.S. 549, 566) to become the law of the land. (*Baker v. Carr,* 369 U.S. 186). In ringing maxims he now wrote that "referendums demonstrate devotion to democracy, not to bias, discrimination or prejudice," and that they ensure "that all the people of a community will have a voice in decisions that will affect the future development of their own community."

The opinion demonstrates that traditional liberal principles combined with ignorance of the facts can produce tragic results. Given a meager record and a lack of familiarity with the social milieu with which the case dealt, it is perhaps understandable that the Court apparently failed to recognize the fallacy of its cliches. How can the poor be "one of the diverse and shifting groups that make up the American people" if local restrictions on housing give them no place to shift? The right of "all the people of a community" to decide the future of "their own community" merely means that those who got there first are now privileged to keep out the less fortunate.

What does *James v. Valtierra* do? It clearly does not overturn cases in which local building or zoning codes are applied with a demonstrable motive of racial discrimination (*e.g., Dailey v. City of Lawton,* 425 F.2d 1037, *Kennedy Park Homes Ass'n v. City of Lackawanna,* 318 F. Supp. 669). And it does not necessarily overturn cases such as *SASSO, supra,* or *Norwalk CORE v. Norwalk Redevelopment Agency,* 395 F.2d 920, in which the lower federal courts held that a community may not reduce the housing opportunities for poor people who are already there — though it surely casts a shadow over those cases.

Nor does this case weaken the position of state courts who choose to follow the lead of the Supreme Court of Pennsylvania and find that "It is not for any given township to say who may or may not live within its confines, while disregarding the interests of the entire area," (*Appeal of Kit-Mar Builders*, 268 A. 2d 765) for these cases are decided on state law grounds not reviewable in the Supreme Court.

The real tragedy of *Valtierra* is not its immediate effect, but the suspicion it creates that the Supreme Court is blind to the real facts of racial discrimination. Hopefully future cases can be brought to the Court on factual records that clearly demonstrate the connection between local restrictions on housing and the disadvantaged status of minorities.

Comments: 1. Actually, the *SASSO* case was lost when the Court of Appeals refused a preliminary injunction to enjoin a referendum nullifying the rezoning for the project in question. *Southern Alameda Spanish Speaking Organ. v. City of Union City*, 424 F.2d 291 (9th Cir. 1970). On remand, the District Court concurred. 357 F. Supp. 1188 (N.D. Cal. 1970). However, the District Court noted that plaintiffs be granted "relief insofar as they pray that the City take steps necessary and reasonably feasible under the law to accommodate within a reasonable time the needs of low-income residents of Union City". *Id.* at 1199. These steps were to include the encouragement of privately built but subsidized housing as well as public housing programs to be undertaken by the city. Ground has apparently been broken for this project since the ruling in this case. For a case refusing to enjoin the holding of a referendum on a zoning change for a low-income housing project, see *Ranjel v. City of Lansing*, 417 F.2d 321 (6th Cir. 1969), *cert. denied*, 397 U.S. 980 (1970).

2. For discussions of the impact of the *Valtierra* case, see Comment, *James v. Valtierra:* Housing Discrimination by Referendum?, 39 U. Chi. L. Rev. 115 (1971); Note, The Equal Protection Clause and Exclusionary Zoning After *Valtierra* and *Dandridge*, 81 Yale L.J. 61 (1971).

DAILEY v. CITY OF LAWTON

United States Court of Appeals
425 F.2d 1037 (10th Cir. 1970)

Before LEWIS, Chief Judge, and BREITENSTEIN and SETH, Circuit Judges.

BREITENSTEIN, Circuit Judge. Columbia Square, Inc., plaintiff-appellee, proposed to construct a privately sponsored low-income housing project in a predominantly white residential section of Lawton, Oklahoma. Plaintiff-appellee Willie Mae Dailey is a Negro and a potential renter of project space. The defendants-appellants, the City of Lawton and some of its employees, refused to issue a building permit without a zone change. Columbia Square's request for a zone change was denied. This action was then brought under 28 U.S.C. § 1343 and 42 U.S.C. § 1983. The district court enjoined the appellants from denying the building permit on the ground of a zoning violation. *Dailey v. City of Lawton,* W.D.Okl., 296 F. Supp. 266. We affirm.

We are concerned with Block 26 in the North Addition to Lawton. The Block was patented to the City for school purposes and was so used until about 1954. In 1962 the School District, which had acquired the land from the City, conveyed it to the Catholic Bishop. The Church used the premises for a parochial school until 1966. The Church then decided to use the property for a low-income housing project and arranged for the formation of Columbia Square, Inc., a non-profit corporation which would manage the project under the federal rent supplement program, 12 U.S.C. § 1701s.

The record does not show any zoning restriction on Block 26, at the time of its acquisition by the Bishop, which would prevent its use for the proposed project. In 1964 a new zoning ordinance was passed and the Block was classified as PF, a designation for public facilities. At the time the land was owned by the Church and not by any public agency. The area surrounding Block 26 and about three-fourths of the North Addition was zoned R-4, high density residential, in the 1964 ordinance. Most of the area around the Block consisted of single dwellings in some of which rooms were rented.

City officials told representatives of Columbia Square that a building permit would not be issued for the project without a change of the zone to R-4. Columbia Square then applied to the Lawton Metropolitan Area Planning Commission for the required zone change. Certain residents of the North Addition circulated petitions opposing the change and obtained the signatures of about 250 people, all of them white. The Planning Commission denied the application. Columbia Square then unsuccessfully appealed to the Lawton City Council.

The district court held that the actions of the Planning Commission and the City Council were racially motivated, arbitrary, and unreasonable. The judgment enjoined the City and its employees from refusing to issue a building permit for the project under an R-4 authorization. 296 F. Supp. at 269. . . .

After making many specific findings, the district court held that the actions of the Planning Commission and City Council were "a direct result of the bias and prejudice on the part of the owners of other property in North Addition, which feeling carried over" to the members of those bodies; that the motivation for the denial of the zoning change "was to keep a large concentration of Negroes and other minority groups from living in North Addition . . . and the fear of the property owners . . . that . . . such project as proposed by the plaintiff would bring about a depreciation in property values in the district." 296 F.Supp. at 268-269. The court also found that the

Planning Commission and the City Council "acted arbitrarily and unreasonably in refusing to re-zone the property and to issue the building permit requested."

The prime question is whether the record supports the findings of the trial court that the appellants violated the rights of the appellees under the Constitution and laws of the United States. We must review the evidence and the findings in the light of the clearly erroneous standard. Rule 52(a), F.R.Civ.P.

Except for military personnel from Fort Sill, Lawton is in large measure a racially segregated city. The North Addition is predominately white. The housing project is designed to serve low-income groups which consist of Negroes, Spanish-Americans, and poor whites. The signers of the petitions in opposition were all white. The racial situation was discussed in connection with the circulation of the petitions. The project sponsors received numerous anonymous phone calls which opposed the project on a racial basis. The one dissenting member of the Planning Commission testified that the opposition was based on racial bias. The evidence is sufficient to show that the public bodies acted as they did because of the opposition to the project by the residents of the North Addition.

The appellants point out that the race issue was not discussed at any of the public meetings and that there was no evidence of racial prejudice on the part of any city official. If proof of a civil right violation depends on an open statement by an official of an intent to discriminate, the Fourteenth Amendment offers little solace to those seeking its protection. In our opinion it is enough for the complaining parties to show that the local officials are effectuating the discriminatory designs of private individuals. See e.g. *Shelley v. Kraemer,* 334 U.S. 1, 68 S. Ct. 836, 92 L.Ed. 1161, holding unconstitutional the judicial enforcement of restrictive covenants contained in deeds, and *Reitman v. Mulkey,* 387 U.S. 369, 87 S. Ct. 1627, 18 L.Ed.2d 830, holding unconstitutional an initiated amendment to the California constitution effectively permitting discriminatory practices in the housing market.

The appellants argue that a finding of discriminatory intent is barred because the project was opposed on the grounds of overcrowding of the neighborhood, the local schools, and the recreational facilities and the overburdening of the local fire fighting capabilities. The testimony in this regard was vague and general. No school, fire, recreational, traffic or other official testified in support of the appellants' claims. The racial prejudice alleged and established by the plaintiffs must be met by something more than bald, conclusory assertions that the action was taken for other than discriminatory reasons. . . .

There is no escape from the fact that the area immediately surrounding Block 26 is classified R-4, high density residential. The plaintiffs want the same zone designation for Block 26 that the neighboring property has. Both the present and the former director for the Planning Commission testified that from a zoning standpoint there was no reason why Block 26 should not be classified R-4. In the circumstances presented, the claims of overcrowding of municipal facilities are unpersuasive.

The appellants argue that the property owners in the vicinity of Block 26 have the right to a continuation of the use of that block for school purposes. The patent from the United States conveyed the Block to the City of Lawton for school purposes. Such use had been abandoned some years before the conveyance to the Bishop. A land gift by the United States to a local government is absolute and the recipient has full power to sell and convey the land to private individuals for private use. *Alabama v. Schmidt,* 232 U.S. 168, 173-174, 34 S. Ct. 301, 58 L.Ed. 555, and *Cooper v. Roberts,* 59 U.S. (18 How.) 173, 181-182, 15 L.Ed. 338. The phrase "according to the recorded plate thereof" found in the deed to the Bishop is descriptive only and is not a restriction on use. . . .

. . . In our opinion the record sustains the holding of racial motivation and of arbitrary and unreasonable action in violation of the Fourteenth Amendment and of § 1983. The injunctive relief granted was necessary and appropriate to protect the rights of the plaintiffs. . . .

Affirmed.

Comments: 1. In *Kennedy Park Homes Ass'n v. City of Lackawanna,* 318 F. Supp. 669 (W.D.N.Y.), *aff'd,* 436 F.2d 108 (2d Cir. 1970), *cert. denied,* 401 U.S. 1010 (1971), the Lackawanna city council had amended its zoning ordinance to rezone land originally intended for use as a low-income housing project site; it was rezoned for exclusive use as a park and recreation area. The federal district court applied a modified "rigid scrutiny" equal protection standard and held that the effect of the rezoning was to deny equal protection to low-income groups. The fact that sewage disposal problems would be aggravated by the use of the site for low-income housing was held to be an insufficient "state interest" to justify removing the site from use for low-income housing. The Court of Appeals affirmed, emphasizing that almost all black residents of Lackawanna were concentrated in one ward. The city's rezoning of the site and its failure to provide improved sewage disposal facilities, despite the recommendations of city planners, were found to constitute "specific authorization and continuous encouragement of racial discrimination, if not almost complete racial segregation"; and the city's action in rezoning the site was held unconstitutional as a denial of equal protection under the Fourteenth Amendment. Even if the discrimination were inadvertent, the court held, the city could not constitutionally place its minorities at a severe disadvantage in acquiring housing without demonstrating some "compelling governmental interest" as justification.

2. In *Park View Heights Corp. v. City of Black Jack,* 467 F.2d 1208 (8th Cir. 1972), the Court of Appeals for the Eighth Circuit remanded the case for trial of the issue whether the newly formed suburb of Black Jack, Missouri, could legally exclude a low- to moderate-income housing project through the use of the zoning power. Inter-religious Center for Urban Affairs, Inc. (ICUA) had contracted to buy the land in question when it was located in an unincorporated area of St. Louis County, and had then assigned its contract rights to Parkview Heights Corporation to use as a site for the housing project. After financing, legal, and organizational plans had been completed, citizens in the area of the proposed housing project petitioned for incorporation of the area. After incorporation the new city council adopted a zoning ordinance which prohibited construction of any new multifamily housing. ICUA, Parkview, and eight individuals desiring to live in the proposed housing project brought suit to challenge the validity of the ordinance. The plaintiffs charged that the zoning ordinance was adopted specifically to stop construction of the housing project, whose sponsors had promised that it would be racially integrated, and that this violated the plaintiffs' rights under the Thirteenth and Fourteenth Amendments. The defendant city sought to justify its adoption of the prohibition against multifamily housing construction on the grounds that prior construction of apartment developments in the area had already caused serious overcrowding in the schools, had overburdened the local roads, and had overburdened local taxpayers because apartments do not pay their "fair share" of property taxes. The District Court dismissed the action on the grounds that ICUA and Parkview did not have "standing" to raise the constitutional issues and that the controversy was not yet "ripe" for adjudication. The Court of Appeals disagreed with the District Court on both of these points and remanded the case for trial on the merits.

While the *Park View Heights* case was in litigation, the United States also brought a suit against Black Jack to invalidate the zoning ordinance insofar as it excluded multifamily housing. This suit alleged that the Black Jack zoning resulted in racial discrimination in violation of the Fair Housing Act of 1968, 42 U.S.C.A. §§ 3601 et seq. (1976). The trial judge found that the exclusion of multifamily housing was not racially motivated and dismissed the suit. 372 F. Supp. 319 (E.D. Mo. 1974). On appeal, however, the Court of Appeals reversed, holding that effect rather than motive was the touchstone in making out a case of racial discrimination under the Fair Housing Act; that since the Black Jack ordinance was shown to have a racially discriminatory effect, it could only be justified by a showing of compelling governmental interest; and that the asserted governmental interests in road and traffic control, prevention of school overcrowding, and devaluation of adjacent single-family homes did not rise to the level of a compelling governmental interest where there was no factual basis for the assertion that such interests were furthered by the ordinance. *United States v. City of Black Jack,* 508 F.2d 1179 (8th Cir. 1974), *cert. denied,* 412 U.S. 1042 (1975). For further consideration of racially discriminatory effect as the basis for suit under the Fair Housing Act, see *Metropolitan Hous. Dev. Corp. v. Village of Arlington Heights,* reprinted as a principal case *infra* p. 591.

3. It is now clear that allegedly racially discriminatory zoning regulations can only be attacked in actions by developers of federally subsidized housing seeking site-specific relief from local zoning restrictions, as in *Dailey v. Lawton.* Any broad challenge by civil rights organizations or low-income housing sponsors to the validity of a zoning ordinance on the ground that it is "exclusionary" in its overall effect is practically foreclosed by the decision of the United States Supreme Court in *Warth v. Seldin,* 422 U.S. 490 (1975). *Seldin* is summarized in the following syllabus "prepared by the Reporter of Decisions for the convenience of the reader":

> This action for declaratory and injunctive relief and damages was brought by certain of the petitioners against respondent town of Penfield (a suburb of Rochester, N.Y.), and respondent members of Penfield's Zoning, Planning, and Town Boards, claiming that the town's zoning ordinance, by its terms and as enforced, effectively excluded persons of low and moderate income from living in the town, in violation of petitioners' constitutional rights and of 42 U.S.C. §§ 1981, 1982, and 1983. Petitioners consist of both the original plaintiffs— (1) Metro-Act of Rochester, a not-for-profit corporation among whose purposes is fostering action to alleviate the housing shortage for low- and moderate-income persons in the Rochester area; (2) several individual Rochester taxpayers; and (3) several Rochester area residents with low or moderate incomes who are also members of minority racial or ethnic groups—and Rochester Home Builders Association (Home Builders), embracing a number of residential construction firms in the Rochester area, which unsuccessfully sought to intervene as a party-plaintiff, and the Housing Council in the Monroe County Area (Housing Council), a not-for-profit corporation consisting of a number of organizations interested in housing problems, which was unsuccessfully sought to be added as a party-plaintiff. The District Court dismissed the complaint on the ground, *inter alia,* that petitioners lacked standing to prosecute the action, and the Court of Appeals affirmed. *Held:* Whether the rules of standing are considered as aspects of the constitutional requirement that a plaintiff must make out a "case or controversy" within the meaning of Art. III, or, apart from such requirement, as prudential limitations on the courts' role in resolving disputes involving "generalized grievances" or third parties' legal rights or interests, none of the petitioners has met the threshold requirement of such rules that to have standing a complainant must clearly allege facts demonstrating that he is a proper party to invoke judicial resolution of the dispute and the exercise of the court's remedial powers. [See 422 U.S. at 498-518. — Eds.]

> (a) As to petitioner Rochester residents who assert standing as persons of low or moderate income and, coincidentally, as members of minority racial or ethnic groups, the facts alleged fail to support an actionable causal relationship between Penfield's zoning practices and these petitioners' alleged injury. A plaintiff who seeks to challenge exclusionary zoning practices must allege

specific, concrete facts demonstrating that such practices harm *him,* and that he personally would benefit in a tangible way from the court's intervention. Here, these petitioners rely on little more than the remote possibility, unsubstantiated by allegations of fact, that their situation might have been better had respondents acted otherwise, and might improve were the court to afford relief. [See *id.* at 502-08. — Eds.]

(b) With respect to petitioners who assert standing on the basis of their status as Rochester taxpayers, claiming that they are suffering economic injury through increased taxes resulting from Penfield's zoning practices having forced Rochester to provide more tax-abated low- or moderate-cost housing than it otherwise would have done, the line of causation between Penfield's actions and such injury is not apparent. But even assuming that these petitioners could establish that the zoning practices harm them, the basis of their claim is that the practices violate the constitutional and statutory rights of third parties—persons of low and moderate income who allegedly are excluded from Penfield. Hence, their claim falls squarely within the prudential standing rule that normally bars litigants from asserting the rights or legal interests of others in order to obtain relief from injury to themselves. [See *id.* at 508-10. — Eds.]

(c) Petitioner Metro-Act's claims to standing as a Rochester taxpayer and on behalf of its members who are Rochester taxpayers or persons of low or moderate income, are precluded for the reasons applying to the denial of standing to the individual petitioner Rochester taxpayers and persons of low and moderate income. In addition, with respect to Metro-Act's claim to standing because 9% of its membership is composed of Penfield residents, prudential considerations strongly counsel against according such residents or Metro-Act standing, where the complaint is that they have been harmed indirectly by the exclusion of others, thus attempting, in the absence of a showing of any exception allowing such a claim, to raise the putative rights of third parties. *Trafficante v. Metropolitan Life Ins.,* 409 U.S. 205, 93 S. Ct. 364, 34 L.Ed.2d 415, distinguished. [See *id.* at 512-14. — Eds.]

(d) Petitioner Home Builders, which alleges no monetary injury to itself, has no standing to claim damages on behalf of its members, since whatever injury may have been suffered is peculiar to the individual member concerned, thus requiring individualized proof of both the fact and extent of injury and individual awards. Nor does Home Builders have standing to claim prospective relief, absent any allegation of facts sufficient to show the existence of any injury to members of sufficient immediacy and ripeness to warrant judicial intervention. [See *id.* at 514-16. — Eds.]

(e) Petitioner Housing Council has no standing, where the complaint and record do not indicate that any of its members, with one exception, has made any effort involving Penfield, has taken any steps toward building there, or had any dealings with respondents. With respect to the one exception, this petitioner averred no basis for inferring that an earlier controversy between it and respondents remained a live, concrete dispute. [See *id.* at 516-17. — Eds.]

For commentary on *Warth v. Seldin* see Note, Alternatives to *Warth v. Seldin*: The Potential Resident Challenger of an Exclusionary Zoning Scheme, 11 Urb. L. Ann. 223 (1976).

4. In *Cornelius v. City of Parma,* 374 F. Supp. 730 (N.D. Ohio 1974), the court refused to allow plaintiffs to attack a local referendum requirement in the absence of a housing project alleged to be affected by that requirement, even though there were allegations that the requirement was having a "chilling" effect on developers interested in building subsidized housing in the city. On appeal, the case was vacated and remanded, 506 F.2d 1400 (6th Cir. 1974), the Supreme Court remanded for consideration in light of *Warth v. Seldin,* 422 U.S. 1052, and the Sixth Circuit again remanded, 521 F.2d 1401 (6th Cir. 1975), *cert. denied,* 424 U.S. 955 (1976). Is the *Parma* result consistent with *Warth?*

5. *United States Gen., Inc. v. City of Joliet,* 432 F. Supp. 346 (E.D. Ill. 1977), was an action by a developer of low-income housing seeking damages from the City of Joliet because of its refusal to issue building permits for two low-income housing projects. The developer had expended time and money in planning and had acquired outright or bought options on specific parcels of land and had sought to have these parcels rezoned to allow construction of the housing projects. The City Council refused to rezone, however, and instructed the City Building Department "to withhold all building permits for Federal housing projects until the entire plan of the Housing Authority can be reviewed." The developer's application for building permits was then denied, and the developer filed a seven-count complaint for damages based on the Fifth and Fourteenth Amendments to the United States Constitution, various federal civil rights statutes including the Fair Housing Act of 1968, and Article I, § 17 of the Illinois Constitution. The court accepted as true (for purposes of ruling on motions to dismiss) the following facts:

> . . . . The City of Joliet is a racially segregated community. In 1970, it had a minority population of black and Mexican Americans numbering 18,111, approximately 12% of the total population. By 1973, the Housing Authority of Joliet (HAJ) constructed and operated about 450 units of public housing for low-income families and about 850 units of public housing for the elderly. Virtually all occupants of the family units were black or Mexican, but only 10% of the units for the elderly were rented by members of either of these two minority groups. It is claimed that the sites of these public housing buildings were selected to perpetuate the pattern of racially segregated housing in Joliet.

Several of the defendant's motions to dismiss were based on the assertion that the developer did not have standing to bring the action. With respect to the standing issues, the court held that (1) where the developer was asserting its own legal rights and not the rights of others, alleging tortious interference with the developer's own contract rights, and alleging that the developer itself detrimentally relied on the ordinances of the defendant, the developer had standing to bring the action; (2) the developer lacked standing to bring the action on the civil rights counts solely as a result of the indirect relationship between the developer and minority group families "who would ultimately have resided in the proposed public housing units"; (3) none of the general civil rights statutes relied on by the developer waived the "prudential rule" barring third-party standing in cases where, as here, "the relationship between plaintiff and the third parties is extremely attenuated if it exists at all" and the relief sought by plaintiff would not benefit the third parties in any way; and (4) the developer had standing to bring the action under the Fair Housing Act of 1968. The court recognized that, if the developer prevailed under the Fair Housing Act, it would recover for its own injury and not for the injury to the third parties—prospective minority tenants in Joliet public housing. The court said the controlling factors were twofold: "[f]irst, Congress intended to expand standing under [42 U.S.C.A.] § 3617, and created an exception to the prudential rule. Second, developers are essential participants in the growth of integrated public housing, and it is consistent with the broad sweep of the Act to permit them to inforce its prohibitions." *Id.* at 353-54.

VILLAGE OF ARLINGTON HEIGHTS v. METROPOLITAN HOUSING DEVELOPMENT CORPORATION

Supreme Court of the United States
429 U.S. 252, 50 L. Ed. 2d 450, 97 S. Ct. 555 (1977)

Mr. Justice POWELL delivered the opinion of the Court.

In 1971 respondent Metropolitan Housing Development Corporation (MHDC) applied to petitioner, the Village of Arlington Heights, Ill., for the rezoning of a 15-acre parcel from single-family to multiple-family classification. Using federal financial assistance, MHDC planned to build 190 clustered townhouse units for low and moderate income tenants. The Village denied the rezoning request. MHDC, joined by other plaintiffs who are also respondents here, brought suit in the United States District Court for the Northern District of Illinois.[118] They alleged that the denial was racially discriminatory and that it violated, *inter alia,* the Fourteenth Amendment and the Fair Housing Act of 1968, 42 U.S.C. § 3601 *et seq.* Following a bench trial, the District Court entered judgment for the Village, 373 F. Supp. 208 (1974), and respondents appealed. The Court of Appeals for the Seventh Circuit reversed, finding that the "ultimate effect" of the denial was racially discriminatory, and that the refusal to rezone therefore violated the Fourteenth Amendment. 517 F.2d 409 (1975). We granted the Village's petition for certiorari, 423 U.S. 1030 (1975), and now reverse.

---

[118] Respondents named as defendants both the Village and a number of its officials, sued in their official capacity. The latter were the Mayor, the Village Manager, the Director of Building and Zoning, and the entire Village Board of Trustees. For convenience, we will occasionally refer to all the petitioners collectively as "the Village."

I

Arlington Heights is a suburb of Chicago, located about 26 miles northwest of the downtown Loop area. Most of the land in Arlington Heights is zoned for detached single-family homes, and this is in fact the prevailing land use. The Village experienced substantial growth during the 1960's, but, like other communities in northwest Cook County, its population of racial minority groups remained quite low. According to the 1970 census, only 27 of the Village's 64,000 residents were black.

The Clerics of St. Viator, a religious order (the Order), own an 80-acre parcel just east of the center of Arlington Heights. Part of the site is occupied by the Viatorian high school, and part by the Order's three-story novitiate building, which houses dormitories and a Montessori school. Much of the site, however, remains vacant. Since 1959, when the Village first adopted a zoning ordinance, all the land surrounding the Viatorian property has been zoned R-3, a single-family specification with relatively small minimum lot size requirements. On three sides of the Viatorian land there are single-family homes just across a street; to the east the Viatorian property directly adjoins the back yards of other single-family homes.

The Order decided in 1970 to devote some of its land to low and moderate income housing. Investigation revealed that the most expeditious way to build such housing was to work through a nonprofit developer experienced in the use of federal housing subsidies under § 236 of the National Housing Act, 12 U.S.C. § 1715z-1.[119]

---

[119] Section 236 provides for "interest reduction payments" to owners of rental housing projects which meet the Act's requirements, if the savings are passed on to the tenants in accordance with a rather complex formula. Qualifying owners effectively pay one percent interest on money borrowed to construct, rehabilitate or purchase their properties. (Section 236 has been amended frequently in minor respects since this litigation began. See 12 U.S.C. § 1715z-1 (1970 ed., Supp. V), and the Housing Authorization Act of 1976, Pub. L. No. 94-375, § 4, 90 Stat. 1070.)

New commitments under § 236 were suspended in 1973 by executive decision, and they have not been revived. Projects which formerly could claim § 236 assistance, however, will now generally be eligible for aid under § 8 of the Housing and Community Development Act of 1974, 42 U.S.C. § 1437f (1970 ed., Supp. V), as amended by Housing Authorization Act of 1976, Pub. L. No. 94-375, § 2, 90 Stat. 1068. Under the § 8 program, the Department of Housing and Urban Development contracts to pay the owner of the housing units a sum which will make up the difference between a fair market rent for the area and the amount contributed by the low-income tenant. The eligible tenant family pays between 15 and 25% of its gross income for rent. Respondents indicated at oral argument that, despite the demise of the § 236 program, construction of the MHDC project could proceed under § 8 if zoning clearance is now granted.

MHDC is such a developer. It was organized in 1968 by several prominent Chicago citizens for the purpose of building low and moderate income housing throughout the Chicago area. In 1970 MHDC was in the process of building one § 236 development near Arlington Heights and already had provided some federally assisted housing on a smaller scale in other parts of the Chicago area.

After some negotiation, MHDC and the Order entered into a 99-year lease and an accompanying agreement of sale covering a 15-acre site in the southeast corner of the Viatorian property. MHDC became the lessee immediately, but the sale agreement was contingent upon MHDC's securing zoning clearances from the Village and § 236 housing assistance from the Federal Government. If MHDC proved unsuccessful in securing either, both the lease and the contract of sale would lapse. The agreement established a bargain purchase price of $300,000, low enough to comply with federal limitations governing land acquisition costs for § 236 housing.

MHDC engaged an architect and proceeded with the project, to be known as Lincoln Green. The plans called for 20 two-story buildings with a total of 190 units, each unit having its own private entrance from outside. One hundred of the units would have a single bedroom, thought likely to attract elderly citizens. The remainder would have two, three or four bedrooms. A large portion of the site would remain open, with shrubs and trees to screen the homes abutting the property to the east.

The planned development did not conform to the Village's zoning ordinance and could not be built unless Arlington Heights rezoned the parcel to R-5, its multiple-family housing classification. Accordingly, MHDC filed with the Village Plan Commission a petition for rezoning, accompanied by supporting materials describing the development and specifying that it would be subsidized under § 236. The materials made clear that one requirement under § 236 is an affirmative marketing plan designed to assure that a subsidized development is racially integrated. MHDC also submitted studies demonstrating the need for housing of this type and analyzing the probable impact of the development. To prepare for the hearings before the Plan Commission and to assure compliance with the Village building code, fire regulations, and related requirements, MHDC consulted with the Village staff for preliminary review of the development. The parties have stipulated that every change recommended during such consultations was incorporated into the plans.

During the Spring of 1971, the Plan Commission considered the proposal at a series of three public meetings, which drew large crowds. Although many of those attending were quite vocal and demonstrative in opposition to Lincoln Green, a number of individuals and representatives of community groups spoke in support of rezoning. Some of the comments, both from opponents and supporters, addressed what was referred to as the "social issue" — the desirability or undesirability of introducing at this location in Arlington Heights low and moderate income housing, housing that would probably be racially integrated.

Many of the opponents, however, focused on the zoning aspects of the petition, stressing two arguments. First, the area always had been zoned single-family, and the neighboring citizens had built or purchased there in reliance on that classification. Rezoning threatened to cause a measurable drop in property value for neighboring sites. Second, the Village's apartment policy, adopted by the Village Board in 1962 and amended in 1970, called for R-5 zoning primarily to serve as a buffer between single-family development and land uses thought incompatible, such as commercial or manufacturing districts. Lincoln Green did not meet this requirement, as it adjoined no commercial or manufacturing district.

At the close of the third meeting, the Plan Commission adopted a motion to recommend to the Village's Board of Trustees that it deny the request. The motion stated: "While the need for low and moderate income housing may exist in Arlington Heights or its environs, the Plan Commission would be derelict in recommending it at the proposed location." Two members voted against the motion and submitted a minority report, stressing that in their view the change to accommodate Lincoln Green represented "good zoning." The Village Board met on September 28, 1971, to consider MHDC's request and the recommendation of the Plan Commission. After a public hearing, the Board denied the rezoning by a 6-1 vote.

The following June MHDC and three Negro individuals filed this lawsuit against the Village, seeking declaratory and injunctive relief.[120] A second nonprofit corporation and an individual of Mexican-American descent intervened as plaintiffs. The trial resulted in a judgment for petitioners. Assuming that MHDC had standing to bring the suit, the District Court held that the petitioners were not motivated by racial discrimination or intent to discriminate against low income groups when they denied rezoning, but rather by a desire "to protect property values and the integrity of the Village's zoning plan." 373 F. Supp., at 211. The District Court concluded also that the denial would not have a racially discriminatory effect.

---

[120] The individual plaintiffs sought certification of the action as a class action pursuant to Fed.Rule Civ.Proc. 23 but the District Court declined to certify. 373 F.Supp., at 209.

A divided Court of Appeals reversed. It first approved the District Court's finding that the defendants were motivated by a concern for the integrity of the zoning plan, rather than by racial discrimination. Deciding whether their refusal to rezone would have discriminatory effects was more complex. The court observed that the refusal would have a disproportionate impact on blacks. Based upon family income, blacks constituted 40% of those Chicago area residents who were eligible to become tenants of Lincoln Green, although they comprised a far lower percentage of total area population. The court reasoned, however, that under our decision in *James v. Valtierra,* 402 U.S. 137 (1971), such a disparity in racial impact alone does not call for strict scrutiny of a municipality's decision that prevents the construction of the low-cost housing.[121]

There was another level to the court's analysis of allegedly discriminatory results. Invoking language from *Kennedy Park Homes Association v. City of Lackawanna,* 436 F.2d 108, 112 (C.A.2 1970), cert. denied, 401 U.S. 1010 (1970), the Court of Appeals ruled that the denial of rezoning must be examined in light of its "historical context and ultimate effect."[122] Northwest Cook County was enjoying rapid growth in employment opportunities and population, but it continued to exhibit a high degree of residential segregation. The court held that Arlington Heights could not simply ignore this problem. Indeed, it found that the Village had been "exploiting" the situation by allowing itself to become a nearly all white community. 517 F.2d, at 414. The Village had no other current plans for building low and moderate income housing, and no other R-5 parcels in the Village were available to MHDC at an economically feasible price.

Against this background, the Court of Appeals ruled that the denial of the Lincoln Green proposal had racially discriminatory effects and could be tolerated only if it served compelling interests. Neither the buffer policy nor the desire the protect property values met this exacting standard. The court therefore concluded that the denial violated the Equal Protection Clause of the Fourteenth Amendment.

---

[121] Nor is there reason to subject the Village's action to more stringent review simply because it involves respondents' interest in securing housing. *Lindsey v. Normet,* 405 U.S. 56, 73-74, 92 S. Ct. 862, 874, 31 L. Ed. 2d 36 (1972). See generally *San Antonio Independent School District v. Rodriguez,* 411 U.S. 1, 18-39, 93 S. Ct. 1278, 1288-1300, 36 L.Ed.2d 16 (1973).

[122] This language apparently derived from our decision in *Reitman v. Mulkey,* 387 U.S. 369, 373, 87 S. Ct. 1627, 1629, 18 L.Ed.2d 830 (1967) (quoting from the opinion of the California Supreme Court in the case then under review).

II

At the outset, petitioners challenge the respondents' standing to bring the suit. It is not clear that this challenge was pressed in the Court of Appeals, but since our jurisdiction to decide the case is implicated, . . . we shall consider it.

In *Warth v. Seldin,* 422 U.S. 490 (1975), a case similar in some respects to this one, we reviewed the constitutional limitations and prudential considerations that guide a court in determining a party's standing, and we need not repeat that discussion here. The essence of the standing question, in its constitutional dimension, "is whether the plaintiff has 'alleged such a personal stake in the outcome of the controversy' [as] to warrant *his* invocation of federal-court jurisdiction and to justify exercise of the court's remedial powers on his behalf." *Id.,* at 498-499, quoting *Baker v. Carr,* 369 U.S. 186, 204 (1962). The plaintiff must show that he himself is injured by the challenged action of the defendant. The injury may be indirect, . . . but the complaint must indicate that the injury is indeed fairly traceable to the defendant's acts or omissions. . . .

A

Here there can be little doubt that MHDC meets the constitutional standing requirements. The challenged action of the petitioners stands as an absolute barrier to constructing the housing MHDC had contracted to place on the Viatorian site. If MHDC secures the injunctive relief it seeks, that barrier will be removed. An injunction would not, of course, guarantee that Lincoln Green will be built. MHDC would still have to secure financing, qualify for federal subsidies,[123] and carry through with construction. But all housing developments are subject to some extent to similar uncertainties. When a project is as detailed and specific as Lincoln Green, a court is not required to engage in undue speculation as a predicate for finding that the plaintiff has the requisite personal stake in the controversy. MHDC has shown an injury to itself that is "likely to be redressed by a favorable decision." *Simon v. Eastern Kentucky Welfare Rights Org.,* 426 U.S., at 38.

Petitioners nonetheless appear to argue that MHDC lacks standing because it has suffered no economic injury. MHDC, they point out,

---

[123] Petitioners suggest that the suspension of the § 236 housing assistance program makes it impossible for MHDC to carry out its proposed project and therefore deprives MHDC of standing. The District Court also expressed doubts about MHDC's position in the case in light of the suspension. 373 F.Supp., at 211. Whether termination of all available assistance programs would preclude standing is not a matter we need to decide, in view of the current likelihood that subsidies may be secured under § 8 of the Housing and Community Development Act of 1974. See n. 119, *supra.*

is not the owner of the property in question. Its contract of purchase is contingent upon securing rezoning.[124] MHDC owes the owners nothing if rezoning is denied.

We cannot accept petitioners' argument. In the first place, it is inaccurate to say that MHDC suffers no economic injury from a refusal to rezone, despite the contingency provisions in its contract. MHDC has expended thousands of dollars on the plans for Lincoln Green and on the studies submitted to the Village in support of the petition for rezoning. Unless rezoning is granted, many of these plans and studies will be worthless even if MHDC finds another site at an equally attractive price.

Petitioners' argument also misconceives our standing requirements. It has long been clear that economic injury is not the only kind of injury that can support a plaintiff's standing. . . . MHDC is a nonprofit corporation. Its interest in building Lincoln Green stems not from a desire for economic gain, but rather from an interest in making suitable low-cost housing available in areas where such housing is scarce. This is not mere abstract concern about a problem of general interest. See *Sierra Club v. Morton,* 405 U.S., at 739. The specific project MHDC intends to build, whether or not it will generate profits, provides that "essential dimension of specificity" that informs judicial decisionmaking. *Schlesinger v. Reservists Committee to Stop the War,* 418 U.S. 208 (1974).

B

Clearly MHDC has met the constitutional requirements and it therefore has standing to assert its own rights. Foremost among them is MHDC's right to be free of arbitrary or irrational zoning actions. See *Euclid v. Ambler Realty Co.,* 272 U.S. 365 (1926); *Nectow v. Cambridge,* 277 U.S. 183 (1928); *Village of Belle Terre v. Boraas,* 416 U.S. 1 (1974). But the heart of this litigation has never been the claim that the Village's decision fails the generous *Euclid* test, recently reaffirmed in *Belle Terre.* Instead it has been the claim that the Village's refusal to rezone discriminates against racial minorities

---

[124] Petitioners contend that MHDC lacks standing to pursue its claim here because a contract purchaser whose contract is contingent upon rezoning cannot contest a zoning decision in the Illinois courts. Under the law of Illinois, only the owner of the property has standing to pursue such an action. . . .

State law of standing, however, does not govern such determination in the federal courts. The constitutional and prudential considerations canvassed at length in *Warth v. Seldin,* 422 U.S. 490 (1975), respond to concerns that are peculiarly federal in nature. Illinois may choose to close its courts to applicants for rezoning unless they have an interest more direct than MHDC's, but this choice does not necessarily disqualify MHDC from seeking relief in federal courts for an asserted injury to its federal rights.

in violation of the Fourteenth Amendment. As a corporation, MHDC has no racial identity and cannot be the direct target of the petitioners' alleged discrimination. In the ordinary case, a party is denied standing to assert the rights of third persons. *Warth v. Seldin,* 422 U.S., at 499. But we need not decide whether the circumstances of this case would justify departure from that prudential limitation and permit MHDC to assert the constitutional rights of its prospective minority tenants. . . . For we have at least one individual plaintiff who has demonstrated standing to assert these rights as his own.[125]

Respondent Ransom, a Negro, works at the Honeywell factory in Arlington Heights and lives approximately 20 miles away in Evanston in a 5-room house with his mother and his son. The complaint alleged that he seeks and would qualify for the housing MHDC wants to build in Arlington Heights. Ransom testified at trial that if Lincoln Green were built he would probably move there, since it is closer to his job.

The injury Ransom asserts is that his quest for housing nearer his employment has been thwarted by official action that is racially discriminatory. If a court grants the relief he seeks, there is at least a "substantial probability," *Warth v. Seldin,* 422 U.S., at 504, that the Lincoln Green project will materialize, affording Ransom the housing opportunity he desires in Arlington Heights. His is not a generalized grievance. Instead, as we suggested in *Warth, id.,* at 507, 508 n. 18, it focuses on a particular project and is not dependent on speculation about the possible actions of third parties not before the court. See *id.,* at 505; *Simon v. Eastern Kentucky Welfare Rights Org.,* 426 U.S., at 41-42. Unlike the individual plaintiffs in *Warth,* Ransom has adequately averred an "actionable causal relationship" between Arlington Heights' zoning practices and his asserted injury. *Warth v. Seldin,* 422 U.S., at 507. We therefore proceed to the merits.

III

Our decision last Term in *Washington v. Davis,* 426 U.S. 229 (1976), made it clear that official action will not be held unconstitutional solely because it results in a racially disproportionate impact. "Disproportionate impact is not irrelevant, but it is not the sole touchstone of an invidious racial discrimination." *Id.,* at 242. Proof of racially discriminatory intent or purpose is required to show a violation of the Equal Protection Clause. Although some contrary indications may be drawn from some of our

---

[125] Because of the presence of this plaintiff, we need not consider whether the other individual and corporate plaintiffs have standing to maintain the suit.

cases, the holding in *Davis* reaffirmed a principle well established in a variety of contexts. . . .

Davis does not require a plaintiff to prove that the challenged action rested solely on racially discriminatory purposes. Rarely can it be said that a legislature or administrative body operating under a broad mandate made a decision motivated solely by a single concern, or even that a particular purpose was the "dominant" or "primary" one. In fact, it is because legislators and administrators are properly concerned with balancing numerous competing considerations that courts refrain from reviewing the merits of their decisions, absent a showing of arbitrariness or irrationality. But racial discrimination is not just another competing consideration. When there is a proof that a discriminatory purpose has been a motivating factor in the decision, this judicial deference is no longer justified.

Determining whether invidious discriminatory purpose was a motivating factor demands a sensitive inquiry into such circumstantial and direct evidence of intent as may be available. The impact of the official action — whether it "bears more heavily on one race than another," *Washington v. Davis,* 426 U.S., at 242 — may provide an important starting point. Sometimes a clear pattern, unexplainable on grounds other than race, emerges from the effect of the state action even when the governing legislation appears neutral on its face. . . . The evidentiary inquiry is then relatively easy. But such cases are rare. Absent a pattern as stark as that in *Gomillion* [364 U.S. 339 (1960)] or *Yick Wo* [118 U.S. 356 (1886)] impact alone is not determinative, and the Court must look to other evidence.[126]

The historical background of the decision is one evidentiary source, particularly if it reveals a series of official actions taken for invidious purposes. . . . The specific sequence of events leading up to the challenged decision also may shed some light on the decisionmaker's purposes. . . . For example, if the property involved here always had been zoned R-5 but suddenly was changed to R-3 when the town learned of MHDC's plans to erect integrated housing,[127] we would have a far different case. Departures from the normal procedural sequence also might afford evidence that

---

[126] In many instances, to recognize the limited probative value of disproportionate impact is merely to acknowledge the "heterogeneity" of the nation's population. . . .

[127] See, *e. g., Progress Development Corp. v. Mitchell,* 286 F.2d 222 (C.A.7 1961) (park board allegedly condemned plaintiffs' land for a park upon learning that the homes plaintiffs were erecting there would be sold under a marketing plan designed to assure integration); *Kennedy Park Homes Association, Inc. v. City of Lackawanna,* 436 F.2d 108 (C.A.2 1970), cert. denied, 401 U.S. 1010 (1971) (town declared moratorium on new subdivisions and rezoned area for park land shortly after learning of plaintiffs' plans to build low income housing). To the extent that the decision in *Kennedy Park Homes* rested solely on a finding of discriminatory impact, we have indicated our disagreement. *Washington v. Davis,* 426 U.S., at 244-245.

improper purposes are playing a role. Substantive departures too may be relevant, particularly if the factors usually considered important by the decisionmaker strongly favor a decision contrary to the one reached.[128]

The legislative or administrative history may be highly relevant, especially where there are contemporary statements by members of the decisionmaking body, minutes of its meetings, or reports. In some extraordinary instances the members might be called to the stand at trial to testify concerning the purpose of the official action, although even then such testimony frequently will be barred by privilege. . . .

The foregoing summary identifies, without purporting to be exhaustive, subjects of proper inquiry in determining whether racially discriminatory intent existed. With these in mind, we now address the case before us.

IV

This case was tried in the District Court and reviewed in the Court of Appeals before our decision in *Washington v. Davis, supra.* The respondents proceeded on the erroneous theory that the Village's refusal to rezone carried a racially discriminatory effect and was, without more, unconstitutional. But both courts below understood that at least part of their function was to examine the purpose underlying the decision. In making its findings on this issue, the District Court noted that some of the opponents of Lincoln Green who spoke at the various hearings might have been motivated by opposition to minority groups. The court held, however, that the evidence "does not warrant the conclusion that this motivated the defendants." 373 F.Supp., at 211.

On appeal the Court of Appeals focused primarily on respondents' claim that the Village's buffer policy had not been consistently applied and was being invoked with a strictness here that could only demonstrate some other underlying motive. The court concluded that the buffer policy, though not always applied with perfect consistency, had on several occasions formed the basis for the Board's decision to deny other rezoning proposals. "The evidence does not necessitate a finding that Arlington Heights administered this policy in a discriminatory manner." 517 F.2d, at 412. The Court of Appeals therefore approved the District Court's findings concerning the Village's purposes in denying rezoning to MHDC.

We also have reviewed the evidence. The impact of the Village's decision does arguably bear more heavily on racial minorities. Minorities comprise 18% of the Chicago area population, and 40% of the income groups said to be eligible for Lincoln Green. But there

---

[128] See *Dailey v. City of Lawton,* 425 F.2d 1037 (C.A.10 1970). . . .

is little about the sequence of events leading up to the decision that would spark suspicion. The area around the Viatorian property has been zoned R-3 since 1959, the year when Arlington Heights first adopted a zoning map. Single-family homes surround the 80-acre site, and the Village is undeniably committed to single-family homes as its dominant residential land use. The rezoning request progressed according to the usual procedures.[129] The Plan Commission even scheduled two additional hearings, at least in part to accommodate MHDC and permit it to supplement its presentation with answers to questions generated at the first hearing.

The statements by the Plan Commission and Village Board members, as reflected in the official minutes, focused almost exclusively on the zoning aspects of the MHDC petition, and the zoning factors on which they relied are not novel criteria in the Village's rezoning decisions. There is no reason to doubt that there has been reliance by some neighboring property owners on the maintenance of single-family zoning in the vicinity. The Village originally adopted its buffer policy long before MHDC entered the picture and has applied the policy too consistently for us to infer discriminatory purpose from its application in this case. Finally, MHDC called one member of the Village Board to the stand at trial. Nothing in her testimony supports an inference of invidious purpose.[130]

In sum, the evidence does not warrant overturning the concurrent findings of both courts below. Respondents simply failed to carry their burden of proving that discriminatory purpose was a motivating factor in the Village's decision.[131] This conclusion ends the

_____

[129] Respondents have made much of one apparent procedural departure. The parties stipulated that the Village Planner, the staff member whose primary responsibility covered zoning and planning matters, was never asked for his written or oral opinion of the rezoning request. The omission does seem curious, but respondents failed to prove at trial what role the Planner customarily played in rezoning decisions, or whether his opinion would be relevant to respondents' claims.

[130] Respondents complain that the District Court unduly limited their efforts to prove that the Village Board acted for discriminatory purposes, since it forbade questioning Board members about their motivation at the time they cast their votes. We perceive no abuse of discretion in the circumstances of this case, even if such an inquiry into motivation would otherwise have been proper. See n. 18, *supra*. Respondents were allowed, both during the discovery phase and at trial, to question Board members fully about materials and information available to them at the time of decision. In light of respondents' repeated insistence that it was effect and not motivation which would make out a constitutional violation, the District Court's action was not improper.

[131] Proof that the decision by the Village was motivated in part by a racially discriminatory purpose would not necessarily have required invalidation of the challenged decision. Such proof would, however, have shifted to the Village the burden of establishing that the same decision would have resulted even had the

constitutional inquiry. The Court of Appeals' further finding that the Village's decision carried a discriminatory "ultimate effect" is without independent constitutional significance.

V

Respondents' complaint also alleged that the refusal to rezone violated the Fair Housing Act, 42 U.S.C. § 3601 *et seq.* They continue to urge here that a zoning decision made by a public body may, and that petitioners' action did, violate § 3604 or § 3617. The Court of Appeals, however, proceeding in a somewhat unorthodox fashion, did not decide the statutory question. We remand the case for further consideration of respondents' statutory claims.

Reversed and remanded.

Mr. Justice Stevens took no part in the consideration or decision of this case.

Mr. Justice Marshall, with whom Mr. Justice Brennan joins, concurring in part and dissenting in part.

I concur in Parts I-III of the Court's opinion. However, I believe the proper result would be to remand this entire case to the Court of Appeals for further proceedings consistent with *Washington v. Davis,* 426 U.S. 229 (1976), and today's opinion. The Court of Appeals is better situated than this Court both to reassess the significance of the evidence developed below in light of the standards we have set forth and to determine whether the interests of justice require further District Court proceedings directed towards those standards.

Mr. Justice White, dissenting.

[Justice White would have remanded in order to allow the Court of Appeals to reconsider the case in light of the intervening decision in *Washington v. Davis,* and to consider the statutory claim. He also believed that it was improper for the Court "to list various 'evidentiary sources' or 'subjects of proper inquiry' in determining whether a racially discriminatory purpose existed" because the Court of Appeals had accepted the finding that the Village's decision to deny the rezoning was legitimate. — Eds.]

---

impermissible purpose not been considered. If this were established, the complaining party in a case of this kind no longer fairly could attribute the injury complained of to improper consideration of a discriminatory purpose. In such circumstances, there would be no justification for judicial interference with the challenged decision. But in this case respondents failed to make the required threshold showing. See *Mt. Healthy City School Dist. Bd. of Education v. Doyle,* 429 U.S. 274.

Comments: *Joseph Skillken & Co. v. City of Toledo,* 528 F.2d 867 (6th Cir. 1975), was a case in which a real estate developer and a group of low-income minority persons (on behalf of themselves and others similarly situated) sued the City of Toledo and others seeking declaratory and permanent injunctive relief on the ground that the city's refusal to rezone a certain area to permit construction of low-rent housing projects violated the plaintiffs' civil and constitutional rights under the Housing Act of 1937, the Civil Rights Act of 1964, the Fair Housing Act of 1968, and the Fourteenth Amendment. The District Court held that the evidence was sufficient to show that the actions of the defendants were motivated by racial discrimination and that there was no compelling governmental interest which was promoted by such actions. After entering judgment for the plaintiffs, 380 F.Supp. 228 (N.D. Ohio 1974), the District Court issued an order (not included in its published opinion) requiring the City Council to submit to the court, within 90 days, a comprehensive plan for the integration of the residential neighborhoods of Toledo. On appeal, the Court of Appeals reversed and remanded. *Inter alia,* it said:

> The zoning laws in the present case are not inherently suspect. To apply the compelling state interest test would virtually invalidate all forms of state legislation where people are affected differently.
>
> The compelling interest rule was rejected in *Village of Belle Terre v. Boraas,* . . . .
>
> It is significant that no attack has been made here on Toledo's comprehensive zoning ordinance. It was neutral legislation enacted long before the controversy in the present case arose. . . .
>
> Under this broad order [of the District Court] all zoning laws in conflict therewise would be invalidated. Low cost public housing could move into the most exclusive neighborhoods in the metropolitan area and property values would be slaughtered. Innocent people who labored hard all of their lives and saved their money to purchase homes in nice residential neighborhoods, and who never discriminated against anyone, would be faced with a total change in their neighborhoods, with the values of their properties slashed. All this would be accomplished simply by an order of a Federal Judge, and at the expense of the taxpayers.
>
> It is submitted that Congress never vested any such power in Federal Judges.
>
> Members of the City Council did not cause nor create the concentration of black people in Toledo, and they are under no legal obligation to deconcentrate the area or to change the zoning laws to bring about deconcentration.
>
> Nor are the city officials responsible for private discrimination, most of which . . . occurred prior to Ohio's Civil Rights Act . . . and the decision of the Supreme Court in *Jones v. Alfred H. Mayer Co.,* 392 U.S. 409, 88 S.Ct. 2186, 20 L.Ed.2d 1189 (1968), which afford adequate remedies for private racial discrimination in housing. . . . .
>
> Nor do we regard the refusal to the City Council to rezone . . . as obstructing the rights of minorities to housing, upon which an inference of discrimination "in effect" may be drawn against . . . [the council].

. . . .

We live in a free society. The time has not yet arrived for the courts to strike down state zoning laws which are neutral on their face and valid when passed, in order to permit the construction at public expense of large numbers of low cost public housing units in a neighborhood where they do not belong, and where the property owners, relying on the zoning laws, have spent large sums of money to build fine homes for the enjoyment of their families.

A federal court ought not to exercise state legislative functions. It is without power to do so, and furthermore it has not developed proficiency in that field.

528 F.2d at 879-81.

The United States Supreme Court vacated the judgment of the Court of Appeals and remanded the case for further consideration in light of the Supreme Court's decision in *Village of Arlington Heights v. Metropolitan Hous. Dev. Corp.,* reprinted *supra,* and *Washington v. Davis,* discussed in the *Arlington Heights* case. 429 U.S. 1068 (1977). On remand, the Court of Appeals adhered to its original opinion. 558 F.2d 350 (6th Cir. 1977).

MANDELKER, RACIAL DISCRIMINATION AND EXCLUSIONARY ZONING: A PERSPECTIVE ON *ARLINGTON HEIGHTS,* 55 Texas Law Review 1217, 1245-49 (1977)

The *Arlington Heights* decision preserves the significance of demonstrating racially correlated effects in zoning cases, at least insofar as abrupt changes in local zoning policy and a history of racial discrimination in the execution of that policy constitute proof of the constitutionally requisite racial motive or intent. Proof of racially discriminatory intent arises from an examination of the process by which the zoning ordinance is administered, not from an analysis of the substantive criteria on which it is based. Although state courts usually will not consider the local zoning history in their appraisal of the validity of zoning under state constitutional principles, the Supreme Court's willingness to allow consideration of this kind of evidence in *Arlington Heights* conforms with its treatment of similar methods of historic proof of constitutional violations arising in other contexts. Considering historic patterns of zoning administration also provides the Court with some leverage over the local zoning process in racial discrimination cases independent of state constitutional law principles that ordinarily prove supportive of the zoning decision. The difficulty is that super-cautious local zoning officials are likely to develop sufficient sophistication to administer their zoning ordinances without allowing this kind of evidence to become available to litigants. The immunity of local zoning from attack on racial grounds when there is no evidence of racial unfairness in its administration is synonymous with stating that local zoning is virtually immune from an attack based on objections to the zoning process.

The Supreme Court's use of the normal "zoning factors" as a rationale for the *Arlington Heights* decision also suggests that the Court will not question the substantive bases for local zoning decisions as long as application of the ordinance does not suggest the presence of a racially discriminatory intent. As a consequence, consistently applied municipal zoning may be immune from attack on racial discrimination grounds. In theory, any municipality may foreclose judicial consideration of its zoning based on racial grounds simply by adopting and consistently applying a highly exclusionary set of zoning restrictions. Such a conclusion is not compelled by the *Arlington Heights* decision, however, since properly zoned vacant land sufficient to accommodate substantial numbers of apartment units existed in the village, a fact suggesting that the village's zoning may not have been exclusionary.

Thus, the availability of zoned but vacant land for apartments provides another reason for suggesting that local zoning that is consistently applied will withstand a fourteenth amendment challenge. . . . [T]he district court in *Arlington Heights* cited the availability of alternate sites for the proposed housing project as a reason for not finding racial discrimination in the municipality's refusal to rezone. Presumably, if other courts follow the district court's analysis, a consistent refusal to rezone when other suitably zoned sites are available will also help defeat a claim of racially discriminatory intent.

Since the fundamental issue in racial exclusionary zoning cases concerns minority access to the community and not the propriety of a rezoning at any one location in the community, the district court's handling of the alternative-site problem appears consistent with the fourteenth amendment. The developer's claim in *Arlington Heights* that alternative sites were too expensive to build on suggests the need for an adjustment in the housing subsidies available for the project and not a distortion in the municipal zoning, assuming the compatibility of zoning restrictions on the alternative sites with the proposed development. In any event, to review the alternative development possibilities within a municipality would force the federal courts to evaluate local zoning policy and to second-guess municipal decisions concerning the proper location of competing uses within the municipality — a task for which the Federal judiciary is ill-suited.

Post-*Arlington Heights* therefore, a federal court wanting to appraise the constitutionality of zoning from a racial perspective will have to do more than merely examine whether the municipality has applied its zoning in an internally consistent manner. An appraisal of the acceptability of municipal zoning in a broader context is required, and necessarily must survey the entire region containing the municipality. Only by employing a regional perspective can a court obtain more leverage on the racial impacts of municipal zoning than an appraisal of internal consistency permits. This perception may have prompted the Seventh Circuit Court of Appeals in *Arlington Heights* to evaluate the regional impact of the village's refusal to rezone, an approach not explicitly foreclosed by the Supreme Court's opinion.

. . . .

State courts that have more courageously entered this arena have encountered similar difficulties in implementing a regionally based review of local zoning ordinances. After several pathbreaking decisions, for example, the New Jersey Supreme Court retreated from an earlier opinion that imposed a duty on municipalites to accept their fair share of the regional housing need. Although the New Jersey court still adheres to the regional need concept, it no longer demands municipal compliance with a specific fair share formula for meeting that need, it has called for "least-cost zoning" that will encourage the construction of low-income housing, and it has awarded site-specific relief to a developer for what appear to be *ad hoc* reasons. Whatever the acceptability of this approach to the exclusionary zoning problem in the state courts, it is much more difficult to implement in federal courts, which, because of their lack of plenary jurisdiction over the content of local zoning policy, have only limited opportunities for formulating remedies to eliminate racial discrimination in zoning practices. This perception may have hastened the Supreme Court's retreat from more active supervision of municipal zoning in the *Arlington Heights* case.

. . . .

Nonetheless, an argument still persists that the prohibition against racial discrimination in the fourteenth amendment demands a more activist federal judicial role and that the courts should strike down local zoning whenever it proves racially exclusionary. Many commentators argue against this position, contending on both constitutional and philosophical grounds that intervention by the federal judiciary in the resolution of major policy conflicts is an unwise use of the supervisory judical power to review the conformity of governmental policy decisions with the federal constitution.[132]

---

[132] *See* Cox, *The New Dimensions of Constitutional Adjudication*, 51 Wash. L. Rev. 791 (1976) Professor Cox offers the following admonition in conclusion:
    Constitutional adjudication depends upon a delicate, symbiotic relation. The Court must sometimes be the voice of the spirit, telling us what we are by reminding us of what we may be. But while the opinions of the Court can help to shape our national understanding of ourselves, the roots of its decisions must be already in the Nation. The aspirations voiced by the Court must be those the community is willing not to avow but in the end to live by. In the end, I think, the power of the great constitutional decisions rests upon the accuracy of the Court's perception of this kind of common will and upon the Court's resulting ability, by expressing its

Whatever the philosophical and constitutional merits of this argument, the proper limits of judicial invervention in policy-oriented decision-making depend as much on the contextual setting of the dispute presented for resolution as they do on abstract conceptions of the reach of the judical power. This article has argued that the responsibility for ongoing judicial supervision of community zoning and land use planning more appropriately rests with the state courts, which are empowered to exercise plenary jurisdiction over the reach of the zoning power, than it does with a federal judiciary that may intervene actively in these zoning disputes only when a claim of racial discrimination has been asserted. A more activist stance by the federal judiciary would place the federal courts in a remedial policymaking role in community land use decisions — a role for which they are not notably equipped. Tired from the struggles in the school intergration cases, the federal courts may have had enough.

Alternative formulations of the Seventh Circuit's regional housing need approach might, nevertheless, alleviate these problems. If, as the Seventh Circuit's opinion suggests, the real issue in racial discrimination zoning cases concerns minority access to communities from which they are excluded rather than the availability of a rezoning on a specific site, then the federal courts could formulate easily applicable definitions of minority access for use in zoning litigation. A municipality's failure to satisfy the minority-access test would then provide evidence that the municipality had zoned with a racially discriminatory motive and intent.

Several formulations of a minority-access criterion are possible. Comparing the proportion of minorities in the regional population with the proportion of minorities in the municipality whose zoning is under challenge is one possibility; evidence of this approach appears in the Seventh Circuit opinion. Under this approach, the proportion of minorities in any community would have to equal the proportion of minorities in the metropolitan area. Certain difficulties emerge under this test, however. If the median income in the community under challenge exceeds the median income in the metropolitan area, the proportionality rule would require an adjustment taking this fact into account. One such reformulated rule might require communities to provide housing sufficient to accomodate the proportion of minorities living in the region with income levels corresponding to the income groups currently living in the community. This test suffers from a circularity problem, however, because the prior existence of restrictive zoning in the community may have limited the proportion of less affluent groups

---

perception, ultimately to command not merely a passive but a supportive consensus.

Id. at 829.

living in the community population. Federal courts would have to determine optimal minority population distribution patterns in metropolitan areas to evaluate a community's zoning. Once more, the presence of major land use allocation issues in the analysis of racially discriminatory zoning practices militates against active judicial intervention at the federal level.

METROPOLITAN HOUSING DEVELOPMENT CORP. v. VILLAGE OF ARLINGTON HEIGHTS

United States Court of Appeals, Seventh Circuit
558 F.2d 1283 (1977)
Cert. denied, 98 S. Ct. 752 (1978)

Before FAIRCHILD, Chief Judge, and SWYGERT and SPRECHER, Circuit Judges.

SWYGERT, Circuit Judge.

In this case plaintiffs seek to compel defendant, the Village of Arlington Heights, Illinois ("the Village"), to rezone plaintiffs' property to permit the construction of federally financed low-cost housing. Plaintiffs contend that defendant's refusal to rezone the property was racially discriminatory. The Supreme Court has determined that defendant's action did not violate the Equal Protection Clause. The remaining issue is whether the refusal to rezone was illegal under the Fair Housing Act, 42 U.S.C. §§ 3601 *et seq.* We hold that under the circumstances of this case defendant has a statutory obligation to refrain from zoning policies that effectively foreclose the construction of any low-cost housing within its corporate boundaries, and remand the case to the district court for a determination of whether defendant has done so.

I

We will briefly review the history of this case, which has been well documented in previously reported decisions.

. . . [The court then reviewed the facts and the history of the case. — Eds.]

II

The Fair Housing Act, 42 U.S.C. §§ 3601 *et seq.*, was enacted as Title VIII of the Civil Rights Act of 1968. Plaintiffs contend that the Village's refusal to rezone violated two of the Act's provisions. The first is 42 U.S.C. § 3604(a), which provides in part that "it shall be unlawful . . . [t]o make unavailable or deny . . . a dwelling to any person because of race, color, religion, or national origin." The second is 42 U.S.C. § 3617, which states:

> It shall be unlawful to coerce, intimidate, threaten, or interfere with any person in the exercise or enjoyment of, or on account of his having exercised or enjoyed, or on account of his having aided or encouraged any other person in the exercise or enjoyment of, any right granted or protected by section 3603, 3604, 3605, or 3606 of this title. This section may be enforced by appropriate civil action.

Defendant argues that these claims are barred by the Act's statute of limitations, which provides that civil actions to enforce rights granted by section 3604 must be commenced within 180 days after the alleged discriminatory housing practice occurred. 42 U.S.C. § 3612(a). It maintains that plaintiffs failed to file this suit within 180 days after the petition for rezoning was denied.

However, we need not decide whether the complaint was timely under section 3612(a) because defendant failed to raise this issue in the pleadings. A claim that the statute of limitations bars a lawsuit is an affirmative defense, and it must be pleaded or it will be considered waived. . . . Accordingly, we will proceed to the merits of this case.

III

In determining whether the Village's failure to rezone violated the Fair Housing Act, it is important to note that the Supreme Court's decision does not require us to change our previous conclusion that the Village's action had a racially discriminatory effect. What the Court held is that under the Equal Protection Clause that conclusion is irrelevant.

We reaffirm our earlier holding that the Village's refusal to rezone had a discriminatory effect. The construction of Lincoln Green would create a substantial number of federally subsidized low-cost housing units which are not presently available in Arlington Heights. Because a greater number of black people than white people in the Chicago metropolitan area satisfy the income requirements for federally subsidized housing, the Village's refusal to permit MHDC to construct the project had a geater impact on black people than on white people. Moreover, Arlington Heights remains almost totally white in a metropolitan area with a significant percentage of black people. Since Lincoln Green would have to be racially integrated in order to qualify for federal subsidization, the Village's action in preventing the project from being built had the effect of perpetuating segregation in Arlington Heights.

The basic question we must answer is whether the village's action violated sections 3604(a) or 3617 because it had discriminatory effects when that action was taken without discriminatory intent. Since the violation of section 3617 alleged in this case depends upon a finding that the Village interfered with rights granted or protected by section 3604(a), we can confine our inquiry to whether the refusal to rezone made unavailable or denied a dwelling to any person because of race within the meaning of section 3604(a). In resolving this issue we must address ourselves to two preliminary subissues: first, whether a finding that an action has a discriminatory effect, without a concomitant finding that the action was taken with discriminatory intent, is ever enough to support the conclusion that the action violated section 3604(a); and, if so, under what factual circumstances will it be enough?

A.

The major obstacle to concluding that action taken without discriminatory intent can violate section 3604(a) is the phrase "because of race" contained in the statutory provision. The narrow view of the phrase is that a party cannot commit an act "because of race" unless he intends to discriminate between races. By hypothesis, this approach would excuse the Village from liability because it acted without discriminatory intent. The broad view is that a party commits an act "because of race" whenever the natural and foreseeable consequence of that act is to discriminate between races, regardless of his intent. Under this statistical, effect-oriented view of causality, the Village could be liable since the natural and foreseeable consequence of its failure to rezone was to adversely affect black people seeking low-cost housing and to perpetuate segregation in Arlington Heights.

The Supreme Court adopted the narrow view for equal protection purposes in *Washington v. Davis,* and defendant argues that that decision should bind us in this case as well. However, *Washington* undercuts more than it supports defendant's position. In that case, the Court created a dichotomy between the Equal Protection Clause and Title VII of the Civil Rights Act of 1964, 42 U.S.C. §§ 2000e *et seq.* Although the Court announced its new intent requirement for equal protection cases, it reaffirmed the viability of *Griggs v. Duke Power Co.,* 401 U.S. 424, 91 S.Ct. 849, 28 L.Ed.2d 158 (1971), in which it had previously held that an employment practice that produced a racially discriminatory effect was invalid under Title VII unless it was shown to be job-related. 426 U.S. at 238-39, 246-48, 96 S.Ct. 2040. Thus, a prima facie case of employment discrimination can still be established under Title VII by statistical evidence of discriminatory impact, without a showing of discriminatory intent. *United States v. City of Chicago,* 549 F.2d 415, 435 (7th Cir. 1977).

Defendant asserts that Title VII is distinguishable from the Fair Housing Act because Congress in Title VII mandated a more probing standard of review than it did under the Fair Housing Act. An examination of the two statutes, however, does not indicate Congress intended that proof of discriminatory intent was unnecessary under one but necessary under the other. Section 703(h) of Title VII, codified at 42 U.S.C. § 2000e-2(h), states in relevant part:

> [N]or shall it be an unlawful practice for an employer to give and to act upon the results of any professionally developed ability test provided that such test, its administration or action upon the results is not designed, intended or used to discriminate because of race, color, religion, sex or national origin.

The Supreme Court in *Griggs* held that this provision did not sanction all employment tests administered without discriminatory intent, in spite of the "because of race" language that it contains. Rather, the Court looked to the general congressional purpose in enacting Title VII — which was to achieve equality of employment opportunities — and interpreted section 703(h) in a broad fashion in order to effectuate that purpose.[133] 401 U.S. at 429-36, 91 S.Ct. 849.

The purpose of Congress in enacting the Fair Housing Act was "to provide, within constitutional limitations, for fair housing throughout the United States." 42 U.S.C. § 3601. The Second Circuit has observed that the Act was intended to promote "open, integrated residential housing patterns and to prevent the increase of segregation, in ghettos, of racial groups whose lack of opportunities the Act was designed to combat." *Otero v. New York City Housing Authority,* 484 F.2d 1122, 1134 (2d Cir. 1973). Other courts have responded to the congressional statement of policy by

---

[133] The Court did not directly construe the "because of race" language in section 703(h). Instead, it held that "any professionally developed ability test" only included tests that were job-related. 401 U.S. at 436, 91 S.Ct. 849, 854. By reading the statutory language in this manner the Court rendered the second half of the provision superfluous since a job-related test would never be "designed, intended or used to discriminate because of race."

The important point to be derived from *Griggs* is that the Court did not find the "because of race" language to be an obstacle to its ultimate holding that intent was not required under Title VII. It looked to the broad purposes underlying the Act rather than attempting to discern the meaning of this provision from its plain language.

holding that the Act must be interpreted broadly. *See, e.g., Trafficante v. Metropolitan Life Ins. Co.,* 409 U.S. 205, 93 S.Ct. 364, 34 L.Ed.2d 415 (1972); . . . .

In light of the declaration of congressional intent provided by section 3601 and the need to construe the Act expansively in order to implement that goal, we decline to take a narrow view of the phrase "because of race" contained in section 3604(a). Conduct that has the necessary and foreseeable consequence of perpetuating segregation can be as deleterious as purposefully discriminatory conduct in frustrating the national commitment "to replace the ghettos 'by truly integrated and balanced living patterns.' " *Trafficante,* 409 U.S. at 211, 93 S.Ct. at 368, *citing* 114 Cong. Rec. 3422 (remarks of Sen. Mondale). Moreover, a requirement that the plaintiff prove discriminatory intent before relief can be granted under the statute is often a burden that is impossible to satisfy. "[I]ntent, motive and purpose are elusive subjective concepts," *Hawkins v. Town of Shaw,* 461 F.2d 1171, 1172 (5th Cir. 1972) (*en banc*) (*per curiam*), and attempts to discern the intent of an entity such as a municipality are at best problematic. . . . A strict focus on intent permits racial discrimination to go unpunished in the absence of evidence of overt bigotry. As overtly bigoted behavior has become more unfashionable, evidence of intent has become harder to find. But this does not mean that racial discrimination has disappeared. We cannot agree that Congress in enacting the Fair Housing Act intended to permit municipalities to systematically deprive minorities of housing opportunities simply because those municipalities act discreetly. *See* Brest, *The Supreme Court, 1975 Term — Foreword: In Defense of the Antidiscrimination Principle,* 90 Harv.L.Rev. 1, 28-29 (1976).

We therefore hold that at least under some circumstances a violation of section 3604(a) can be established by a showing of discriminatory effect without a showing of discriminatory intent. A number of courts have agreed. . . .

B.

Plaintiffs contend that once a racially discriminatory effect is shown a violation of section 3604(a) is necessarily established. We decline to extend the reach of the Fair Housing Act this far. Although we agree that a showing of discriminatory intent is not required under section 3604(a), we refuse to conclude that every action which produces discriminatory effects is illegal. Such a per se rule would go beyond the intent of Congress and would lead courts into untenable results in specific cases. *See* Brest, *Foreword,* 90 Harv.L.Rev. at 29. Rather, the courts must use their discretion in deciding whether, given the particular circumstances of each case, relief should be granted under the statute.

We turn now to determining under what circumstances conduct that produces a discriminatory impact but which was taken without discriminatory intent will violate section 3604(a). Four critical factors are discernible from previous cases. They are: (1) how strong is the plaintiff's showing of discriminatory effect; (2) is there some evidence of discriminatory intent, though not enough to satisfy the constitutional standard of *Washington v. Davis;* (3) what is the defendant's interest in taking the action complained of; and (4) does the plaintiff seek to compel the defendant to affirmatively provide housing for members of minority groups or merely to restrain the defendant from interfering with individual property owners who wish to provide such housing. We shall examine each of these factors separately.

1. There are two kinds of racially discriminatory effects which a facially neutral decision about housing can produce. The first occurs when that decision has a greater adverse impact on one racial group than on another. The second is the effect which the decision has on the community involved; if it perpetuates segregation and thereby prevents interracial association it will be considered invidious under the Fair Housing Act independently of the extent to which it produces a disparate effect on different racial groups. *See Trafficante,* 409 U.S. at 209-10, 93 S.Ct. 364.

In this case the discriminatory effect in the first sense was relatively weak. It is true that the Village's refusal to rezone had an adverse impact on a significantly greater percentage of the nonwhite people in the Chicago area than of the white people in that area. But it is also true that the class disadvantaged by the Village's action was not predominantly nonwhite, because sixty percent of the people in the Chicago area eligible for federal housing subsidization in 1970 were white. The argument for *racial* discrimination is therefore not as strong as it would be if all or most of the group adversely affected was nonwhite. *Compare Resident Advisory Board v. Rizzo,* 425 F.Supp. 987, 1018 (E.D.Pa.1976), in which plaintiffs sought to compel the construction of public housing in a predominantly white neighborhood of Philadelphia. Since ninety-five percent of the individuals on the waiting list for public housing in Philadelphia were members of minority groups, the failure to build public housing had a much greater adverse effect on nonwhite people than on white people.

The fact that the conduct complained of adversely affected white as well as nonwhite people, however, is not by itself an obstacle to relief under the Fair Housing Act. *See United States v. City of Black Jack,* 508 F.2d 1179 (8th Cir. 1974), *cert. denied,* 422 U.S. 1042, 95 S.Ct. 2656, 45 L.Ed.2d 694 (1975); *Kennedy Park Homes Assoc., Inc. v. City of Lackawanna,* 436 F.2d 108 (2d Cir. 1970), *cert. denied,* 401 U.S. 1010, 91 S.Ct. 1256, 28 L.Ed.2d 546 (1971). In both of these cases, local zoning ordinances prevented the construction of low-income housing projects which would not have been limited to nonwhite people. Both courts nonetheless found a racially discriminatory effect.

What was present in *Black Jack* and *Kennedy Park* was a strong argument supporting racially discriminatory impact in the second sense. In each case the municipality or section of the municipality in which the proposed project was to be built was overwhelmingly white.[134] Moreover, in each case construction of low-cost housing was effectively precluded throughout the municipality or section of the municipality which was rigidly segregated.[135] Thus, the effect of the municipal action in both cases was to foreclose the possibility of ending racial segregation in housing within those municipalities.

It is unclear in this case whether the Village's refusal to rezone would necessarily perpetuate segregated housing in Arlington Heights. The Village remains overwhelmingly white at the present time,[136] and the construction of Lincoln Green would be a significant step toward integrating the community. The Village asserts, however, that there is a substantial amount of land within its corporate limits which is properly zoned for multiple family dwellings and on which it would have no objection to the construction of a low-cost housing project. Plaintiffs reply that all other sites within the Village limits are unsuitable under federal guidelines governing subsidized housing. The district court never resolved this issue.

---

[134] The area of St. Louis County which included the City of Black Jack was approximately ninety-nine percent white. 508 F.2d at 1183.

The City of Lackawanna has three wards. 98.9 percent of Lackawanna's nonwhite citizens lived in the First Ward, and they constituted 35.4 percent of that ward's population. The Third Ward, where the proposed project was to be built, had 12,229 residents, of whom twenty-nine were black. 436 F.2d at 110; 318 F.Supp. at 674.

[135] In *Black Jack,* the city had enacted a zoning ordinance prohibiting the construction of new multiple family dwellings. 508 F.2d at 1183. In *Kennedy Park,* the city imposed a moratorium on the construction of new subdivisions, a category into which the proposed project fell. 436 F.2d at 111.

[136] Defendant asserts that the minority population of Arlington Heights has grown substantially since 1970. It contends that a special census in 1976 showed a black population of 200 and a total nonwhite population of 848. Defendant does not inform us what the total population of the Village now is, but even assuming that it has remained the same since 1970 and that defendant's statements about the 1976 census are accurate, Arlington Heights would be approximately ninety-nine percent white. We find these numbers to be evidence of "overwhelming" racial segregation.

2. The second factor which appears to have been important in previous Fair Housing Act cases which focused on the discriminatory effect of the defendant's conduct was the presence of some evidence of discriminatory intent. In three cases this evidence was insufficient to independently support the relief which the plaintiff sought. *See Smith v. Anchor Bldg. Corp.,* 536 F.2d 231 (8th Cir. 1976); *Black Jack,* 508 F.2d at 1185 n. 3; *Resident Advisory Board v. Rizzo,* 425 F.Supp. at 1021-25 (E.D.Pa.1976).[137] In another case the court found the defendant liable on both a discriminatory intent and a discriminatory impact theory. *See Kennedy Park,* 436 F.2d at 112-14, *aff'g,* 318 F.Supp. at 694-95.

These courts did not address the role that evidence of intent ought to play in determining whether liability should be imposed because of discriminatory impact. But it is evident that the equitable argument for relief is stronger when there is some direct evidence that the defendant purposefully discriminated against members of minority groups because that evidence supports the inference that the defendant is a wrongdoer. Thus, the absence of any such evidence in this case is a factor buttressing the Village's contention that relief should be denied.

We conclude, however, that this criterion is the least important of the four factors that we are examining. By hypothesis, we are dealing with a situation in which the evidence of intent constitutes an insufficient basis on which to ground relief. If we were to place great emphasis on partial evidence of purposeful discrimination we would be relying on an inference — that the defendant is a wrongdoer — which is at best conjectural. In addition, the problems associated with requiring conclusive proof of discriminatory intent which we earlier discussed remain troublesome in any attempt to weigh partial evidence of intent.

The difficulties which arise from taking account of partial evidence of intent can be illuminated by comparing this case to *Black Jack.* In *Black Jack* plaintiffs proposed to build a low-cost integrated housing project in an overwhelmingly white unincorporated area of St. Louis County. The residents of the area blocked the construction of the project by incorporating the area into a city and then enacting a zoning ordinance prohibiting the construction of new multiple family dwellings. The court referred to evidence that opposition to the project was expressed in racial terms by the leaders of the incorporation movement and by the zoning commissioners themselves. 508 F.2d at 1185 n. 3. Moreover, the fact that the zoning

---

[137] In *Rizzo* some of the defendants were found liable without a finding of discriminatory intent while other defendants were held liable on both an intent and an impact theory.

ordinance was not enacted until after plans for the project were revealed is further evidence of discriminatory intent which is absent from the case at bar.

It is undeniable that this partial evidence of discriminatory intent undermined the equitable position of the city of Black Jack. In cases such as these, which place broad national goals in conflict with heretofore established local prerogatives, courts must take account of the facts particular to each case. But too much reliance on this evidence would be unfounded. The bigoted comments of a few citizens, even those with power, should not invalidate action which in fact has a legitimate basis. *See Washington v. Davis,* 426 U.S. at 253, 96 S.Ct. 2040 (Stevens, J., concurring). If the goal of most of the residents of Black Jack was to protect local property values rather than to exclude black people, it would be unfair to substantially distinguish between Black Jack and Arlington Heights. Nor is it clear that Black Jack acted with more discriminatory intent than Arlington Heights because Black Jack's zoning ordinance was enacted in reaction to a proposed integrated development while Arlington Heights' zoning ordinance was enacted years in advance of the plans to build Lincoln Green. If the effect of a zoning scheme is to perpetuate segregated housing,[138] neither common sense nor the rationale of the Fair Housing Act dictates that the preclusion of minorities in advance should be favored over the preclusion of minorities in reaction to a plan which would create integration.

3. The third factor which we find to be important is the interest of the defendant in taking the action which produces a discriminatory impact. If the defendant is a private individual or a group of private individuals seeking to protect private rights, the courts cannot be overly solicitous when the effect is to perpetuate segregated housing. *See Smith v. Anchor Bldg. Corp.,* 536 F.2d 231 (8th Cir. 1976). Similarly, if the defendant is a governmental body acting outside the scope of its authority or abusing its power, it is not entitled to the deference which courts must pay to legitimate governmental action. *See Kennedy Park,* 436 F.2d at 113-14. . . . On the other hand, if the defendant is a governmental body acting within the ambit of legitimately derived authority, we will less readily find that its action violates the Fair Housing Act. *See Joseph Skillken & Co. v. City of Toledo,* 528 F.2d 867, 876-77 (6th Cir. 1975), *vacated and remanded,* 429 U.S. 1068, 97 S.Ct. 800, 50 L.Ed.2d 786 (1977).

---

[138] As we have already noted, it is unclear from the record whether the effect of the Village's zoning scheme, combined with its refusal to rezone the land in question, is, to preclude the construction of low-cost housing in Arlington Heights and therefore to perpetuate segregated housing. There was no question about the discriminatory effect of the zoning ordinance in *Black Jack.*

In this case the Village was acting within the scope of the authority to zone granted it by Illinois law. *See* Ill.Rev.Stat. Ch. 24, §§ 11-13-1 *et seq.* Moreover, municipalities are traditionally afforded wide discretion in zoning. *Village of Belle Terre v. Boraas,* 416 U.S. 1, 94 S.Ct. 1536, 39 L.Ed.2d 797 (1974). Therefore, this factor weakens plaintiffs' case for relief.

4. The final criterion which will inform the exercise of our discretion is the nature of the relief which the plaintiff seeks. The courts ought to be more reluctant to grant relief when the plaintiff seeks to compel the defendant to construct integrated housing or take affirmative steps to ensure that integrated housing is built than when the plaintiff is attempting to build integrated housing on his own land and merely seeks to enjoin the defendant from interfering with that construction. To require a defendant to appropriate money, utilize his land for a particular purpose, or take other affirmative steps toward integrated housing is a massive judicial intrusion on private autonomy. By contrast, the courts are far more willing to prohibit even nonintentional action by the state which interferes with an individual's plan to use his own land to provide integrated housing. . . . The Second Circuit has explicitly relied on the distinction between requiring affirmative action on the part of the defendant and preventing the defendant from interfering with the plaintiff's attempt to build integrated housing in deciding whether to grant relief under the Fair Housing Act. . . .

This factor favors plaintiffs in this case. They own the land on which Lincoln Green would be built and do not seek any affirmative help from the Village in aid of the project's construction. Rather, they seek to enjoin the Village from interfering with their plans to dedicate their land to furthering the congressionally sanctioned goal of integrated housing.

C.

Analysis of the four factors that we have enumerated reveals that this is a close case. The Village is acting pursuant to a legitimate grant of authority and there is no evidence that its refusal to rezone was the result of intentional racial discrimination. On the other hand, plaintiffs are seeking to effectuate the national goal of integrated housing within Arlington Heights and are asking nothing more of the Village than that they be allowed to pursue that objective. Whether the Village's refusal to rezone has a strong discriminatory impact because it effectively assures that Arlington Heights will remain a segregated community is unclear from the record.

In our judgment the resolution of this case turns on clarification of the discriminatory effect of the Village's zoning decision. We hold that, if there is no land other than plaintiffs' property within

Arlington Heights which is both properly zoned and suitable for federally subsidized low-cost housing, the Village's refusal to rezone constituted a violation of section 3604(a). Accordingly, we remand the case to the district court for a determination of this question subject to the guidelines which we shall lay down. Since the Village's zoning powers must give way to the Fair Housing Act, the district court should grant plaintiffs the relief they request if it finds that the Act has been violated.[139]

We realize that, even assuming that plaintiffs are able to show a strong discriminatory effect, only two of the four criteria on which we have focused point toward the granting of relief. As we have already noted, however, the factor of whether there is some evidence of discriminatory intent should be partially discounted. Moreover, if we are to liberally construe the Fair Housing Act, we must decide close cases in favor of integrated housing.

IV

We shall now describe the procedure which the district court should follow on remand.

The district court must first determine whether this case is moot. The original federal subsidy for Lincoln Green was to be obtained pursuant to section 236 of the National Housing Act, 12 U.S.C. § 1715z-1. In 1973, however, the Government suspended new commitments for section 236 payments. Therefore, Lincoln Green can only be built if plaintiffs can obtain another subsidy.

Plaintiffs contended before the Supreme Court that alternative subsidization would be available under section 8 of the United States Housing Act of 1937, 42 U.S.C. § 1437f. They carry the burden of proving this assertion in the district court.

Plaintiffs must also demonstrate to the district court that Lincoln Green would be racially integrated. They had previously discharged this burden by relying on the requirement of racial integration imposed by section 236. Since section 236 is no longer applicable, plaintiffs must either show that section 8 imposes a similar requirement or otherwise satisfy the court that the tenants of the project would be substantially nonwhite.

Assuming that section 8 funds are available, the district court must then determine whether there is any land in Arlington Heights that

---

[139] We note that Lincoln Green would conform with the standard set by the Village's multiple family zoning classification. We need not reach the question of whether plaintiffs would have been entitled to relief if Lincoln Green had been out of conformance with the Village's multiple family zoning classification as well as its single family zoning classification.

is both zoned R-5 and suitable for federally subsidized low-cost housing. The decision as to whether a parcel of land is "suitable" will be greatly simplified by section 8 itself. Section 8(e) sets out restrictions on subsidies granted under section 8, and section 8(e)(3) states: "[t]he construction or substantial rehabilitation of dwelling units to be assisted under this section shall be eligible for financing with mortgages insured under the National Housing Act." The National Housing Act, 12 U.S.C. § 1713(c)(3), provides upper limits on the cost of mortgages for housing which is eligible for mortgage insurance. The district court should use these upper limits as guidelines in determining whether the cost of a parcel of land would prohibit the construction of low-cost housing.[140] The court should also take account of any other requirements imposed by federal law.

In conducting its inquiry, the district court should place on defendant the burden of identifying a parcel of land within Arlington Heights which is both properly zoned and suitable for low-cost housing under federal standards.[141] If defendant fails to satisfy this burden, the district court should conclude that the Village's refual to rezone effectively precluded plaintiffs from constructing low-cost housing within Arlington Heights,[142] and should grant plaintiffs the relief they seek.

---

[140] The court will still have some discretion because the statutory limits on mortgage costs cover the combined cost of land and the construction of housing while the court will only be considering the variable of land costs. However, the court should be able to obtain objective evidence of the cost of constructing a development such as Lincoln Green aside from the cost of land. By treating the cost of construction as a constant, the court will be in a position to determine whether the cost of a parcel of land, when added to that constant, exceeds the statutory limits.

[141] The concurrence argues that plaintiffs ought to bear the burden on this issue. Allocating the burden in this fashion, however, would compel plaintiffs to attempt the almost impossible task of proving a negative. It is far easier for defendant to show that a single parcel of land which is suitable does exist than for plaintiffs to show that no suitable land exists.

[142] Defendant asserts that it has fulfilled any obligation with respect to low and moderate-income housing because it is committed to building one hundred fifty units of such housing in the next three years. We disagree. Even assuming that defendant's assertion is accurate and that the commitment will be carried out, Arlington Heights would remain highly segregated. The Village's plan, though laudable, cannot excuse its interference with the plans of individual landowners who are trying to build integrated housing and lessen that segregation.

The cause is remanded for further proceedings consistent with this opinion. Pursuant to Circuit Rule 18, the cause should be heard on remand by a new district judge.

FAIRCHILD, Chief Judge, concurring.

With all respect, I do not subscribe to all the principles and analytical steps described in the opinion prepared for the court by Judge Swygert.

The ultimate question is whether the refusal of the zoning change made a dwelling unavailable to plaintiff Ransom (and others) because of race. If it did, the refusal was unlawful under 42 U.S.C. § 3604(a).

After trial, the district court found that the Village has 60 tracts zoned for R-5 use and some of it is still vacant and available to plaintiff. The proof showed nine undeveloped tracts in excess of 15 acres, zoned R-5. It was not established whether or not these were suitable for low-cost housing under federal standards. A preliminary question arises as to why plaintiffs should have a second chance at this element of the case. I am satisfied that the mandate of the Supreme Court for further consideration of plaintiffs' statutory claim is a reason for affording a second inquiry in this area. The majority's answer appears to be that the Village has the burden on this issue. It seems to be, however, that traditional principles apply and burden should be allocated to plaintiffs.

Arlington Heights is a community of substantial size (64,000 in 1970). It seems clear that housing there is presently almost totally confined to white persons. The substantial percentage of minority persons in the whole metropolitan community and the fact that minority persons are employed in Arlington Heights render it improbable that existing housing segregation there can represent free choice among persons who might reasonably consider living there. Zoning is appropriate for regulating the location of land use within a community. With exceptions, which are rare in this context, it is not appropriate for total exclusion. If on remand it be demonstrated that no suitable site with proper zoning is available, I can accept the conclusion that the denial of a change in zoning was, in the circumstances of this case, unlawful under 42 U.S.C. § 3604(a).

MANDELKER, RACIAL DISCRIMINATION AND EXCLUSIONARY ZONING: A PERSPECTIVE ON *ARLINGTON HEIGHTS,* 55 Texas Law Review 1217, 1250-52 (1977)

Despite its conclusion that plaintiff failed to establish evidence sufficient to prove racial discrimination under the fourteenth amendment, the Supreme Court in *Arlington Heights* remanded the case to determine whether the village's refusal to rezone constituted a violation of Title VIII of the Civil Rights Act of 1968, the Federal Fair Housing Act. This statute is directed primarily at racial discrimination in the renting and selling of real estate, but it also contains sweeping language rendering it unlawful to make housing "otherwise unavailable" for racial and other discriminatory reasons. The Eighth Circuit Court of Appeals relied on an expansive reading of this provision to find a statutory violation in *United States v. Black Jack,* a notorious case in which a suburban community incorporated to frustrate construction of a subsidized housing project. Immediately after its incorporation the community downzoned the project site from the prior zoning classification applicable under the county zoning ordinance, a classification that would have permitted construction of the project. The new zoning adopted by the community did not permit construction of the project. Viewing the municipal downzoning in a regional context and using much the same reasoning as the Seventh Circuit did in *Arlington Heights,* the Eighth Circuit found a Title VIII violation on the ground that the downzoning had a racially discriminatory effect.[143]

Black Jack was not a good case to test the reach of Title VIII in racially discriminatory zoning cases. The abrupt incorporation of the community and the subsequent and blatantly motivated downzoning might well have led to a finding of racial discrimination under the fourteenth amendment. Putting aside the supervening incorporation, and looking solely at the continuity of zoning in the

---

[143] . . . Some federal courts have refused to apply a racial effect test when interpreting Title VIII. *See* Boyd v. Lefrak Organization, 509 F.2d 1110 (2d Cir.) (upholding landlord's rule requiring tenants to have weekly net income equal to 90 per cent of monthly rent), *cert. denied,* 423 U.S. 896 (1975). *Cf.* Joseph Skillken & Co. v. City of Toledo, 528 F.2d 867 (6th Cir. 1975) (refusal of city council to rezone area to permit building of low income housing on smaller lots did not discriminate against minorities), *vacated and remanded,* 429 U.S. 1068 (1976), *aff'd on remand,* 558 F.2d 350 (6th Cir. 1977); Acevedo v. Nassau County, 500 F.2d 1078, 1082 (2d Cir. 1974) (Federal Fair Housing Act does not impose any duty upon a governmental body to construct or to "plan or approve and promote" any low-income housing.

area concerned, *Black Jack* qualifies as an example of the abrupt change category of racial discrimination. The Supreme Court has indicated that a racially discriminatory motive and intent can be inferred from such a local zoning action having a racially discriminatory effect. How Title VIII will fare in less obvious cases of racially discriminatory local zoning remains unclear.

Congress may, of course, explicitly contour the characteristics of a statutory civil rights violation more broadly than the constitutional protection offered by the fourteenth amendment. It has done so in other contexts. One difficulty in the Title VIII context, however, is the failure of the statute explicitly to address racially discriminatory zoning problems. The existence of a meager legislative history that provides little guidance to federal courts seeking to apply the statute to zoning cases would require the federal courts to exercise considerable ingenuity in constructing a statutory framework for evaluating allegedly discriminatory zoning practices. The language of Title VIII permits the exercise of such judicial creativity. Nevertheless, respect for existing state and local competence in an arena in which community land use policies and demands for fair minority treatment conflict, and the difficulty of fashioning judicial remedies in an area as complicated as zoning, argue for explicit congressional legislation detailing the applicability of this statute to municipal zoning problems.

This conclusion is all the more supportable in view of the Eighth Circuit's reliance on a regional perspective to find a Title VIII violation in the *Black Jack* case. The need to employ a regional approach to the statute suggests again that examining the internal consistency of local zoning is inadequate, even under the statutory formula, to ensure that sufficient attention is paid to the impact of municipal zoning on housing opportunities for minority groups. The time may have come for a political rather than a judicial resolution of the policy conflict between unfettered local power to control the distribution of land development opportunities and the growing racially segregated nature of our metropolitan areas that results from restricted minority access to housing.

Comments: How supportable is the Court of Appeals decision? Note that the court reaffirmed its regional view of housing discrimination. This holding, together with its emphasis on the nearly all-white character of Arlington Heights, would seem to push the court toward an analysis of regional fair shares in regional housing allocations, an analysis which compels the court to make complex distributive judgments to some extent foresworn in the New Jersey exclusionary zoning cases. The court's attention to acceptable price levels for available land will also force the court to an appraisal of supply and demand factors in housing markets that requires great sophistication. It there warrant for the court's conclusion that the nature of the relief sought influences a decision on the substantive statutory violation? Another Court of Appeals has taken a somewhat critical view of the Seventh Circuit's analysis of the statutory requirements. *Resident Advisory Bd. v. Rizzo,* 564 F.2d 126 (3d Cir. 1977).

3. Inclusionary Zoning Techniques

While the concern over exclusionary zoning has largely been focused through litigation attacking these practices, concerned observers have also suggested a variety of so-called inclusionary zoning techniques through which both states and municipalities may move positively to provide housing opportunities for lower income families. This section reviews several of these inclusionary zoning techniques that have either been tried or suggested at the state or local level.

a. Mandatory Inclusionary Zoning Techniques

H. FRANKLIN, D. FALK, & A. LEVIN, IN-ZONING: A GUIDE FOR POLICY-MAKERS ON INCLUSIONARY LAND USE PROGRAMS 131-38 (1974)

In a straight-forward attempt to use land use regulations for inclusionary purposes, two suburban Washington, D.C., counties (Fairfax County, Virginia, and Montgomery County, Maryland) and the City of Los Angeles, California, have enacted ordinances *requiring* all new housing developments covered by the ordinance to include a minimum number of units for sale or rental to low- and moderate-income families. Although the details of these ordinances vary greatly . . ., they are similar in certain essential features:

1. Each ordinance applies to multifamily development proposals over a minimum number of units. The minimum is 50 units in the two suburban ordinances and five units for the Los Angeles ordinance. The Fairfax County ordinance, however, exempts apartment buildings of six or more stories.

2. In general, 15% of the new dwelling units in such developments must be sold or rented to low- and moderate-income families. In two of the ordinances (Fairfax and Los Angeles), 6% of the units are reserved for low-income families within the public housing income limits, and an additional 9% are reserved for moderate-income families within the Section 236 income limits. The Montgomery County ordinance does not distinguish between low- and moderate-income families and does not tie the income limits to federal housing programs; instead, the ordinance specifies maximum

income levels for each type of dwelling unit, subject to periodic adjustments.

3. The economic feasibility of the mandatory requirement is sought through two methods: federal housing subsidies to support the low- and moderate-income units, and density bonuses. Two of the ordinances (Fairfax and Los Angeles) would excuse the development from compliance if federal subsidies are not available (subject to the caveats, in Fairfax, that the unavailability of federal subsidies is not attributable to proposed high development costs for the project and, in Los Angeles, that the local housing authority has the option to lease or require the leasing of up to 15% of the units, presumably when federal subsidies later become available). The density bonuses offered in the two suburban ordinances—in Montgomery, one additional market-rent unit for every two low- and moderate-income units up to a 20% overall increase, and in Fairfax, one additional market-rent unit for every low- and moderate-income unit up to a 20% density increase — are intended to lower the land cost attributable to each low- and moderate-income unit so it may continue to be sold or rented at a reasonable profit. The Los Angeles ordinance does not offer a density bonus; on the other hand, it requires all low- and moderate-income units to be rented at "fair market value," in theory assuring that the developer will not bear any cost himself — either the private market or public subsidy will pay the rent.

The ordinances are different from each other in other respects. Only one ordinance (Montgomery) applies to developments of single-family detached homes. One ordinance (Fairfax) authorizes the county to permit the developer to meet his obligation by building low- and moderate-income housing on a separate site; the Montgomery ordinance permits the requirement to be met if the county agrees to accept free title to an undeveloped portion of the developer's site. One ordinance (Montgomery) relaxes other zoning requirements relating to yards, open space, building heights, and parking, and also permits duplexes and townhouses in single family districts. Two ordinances (Montgomery and Los Angeles) contain restrictions on the resale or increased rentals of units reserved for low- and moderate-income families. Only one ordinance (Los Angeles) requires that the low- and moderate-income units are dispersed throughout the development and contain the same average mixture of bedrooms as the market-rate units. The Montgomery ordinance provides, however, that the developer's construction plan must show that the low- and moderate-income units will be built before or along with (but not after) the market-rate units.

The basic purpose of these ordinances has been to increase the supply of low- and moderate-income housing, with a secondary purpose of assuring its dispersal throughout the developing areas of the community. Yet, to date, it has been difficult to evaluate their effectiveness. The Fairfax County ordinance was invalidated by the Supreme Court of Virginia before it had any noticeable impact. [See the *DeGroff* case, which follows. — Eds.] In addition, the federal housing subsidy programs had been terminated before the final enactment of the Montgomery County and Los Angeles ordinances. Compliance in Los Angeles was thus legally excused. Montgomery County is under a state-imposed sewer moratorium, which has virtually blocked all new housing development. Nevertheless, these ordinances have generated considerable interest among planners and lawyers and have prompted some initial speculative analysis in the literature. With the revival of federal housing subsidy programs through leased housing under the Housing and Community Development Act of 1974, the mandatory inclusionary ordinance could assume major importance for communities designing inclusionary programs.

The literature on mandatory ordinances focuses on two questions: whether the mandatory ordinances will meet their objectives and whether they will be upheld by the courts despite the initial adverse ruling in Virginia.

The usefulness of mandatory inclusionary ordinances for increasing the supply of low- and moderate-income housing is thought by commentators to be the greatest in growing communities where, because of traditional exclusionary zoning practices, high land costs and possibly other reasons, only middle- and upper-income housing is being built. But it should be noted that the limited availability of federal subsidy funds and the relatively small percentage of required low- and moderate-income units per development may not permit projected needs for such housing in these communities from being satisfied in the near term. There is no evidence, in this connection, that such ordinances were designed to mesh with regional or local plans when their numerical quotas were established.

Mandatory inclusionary ordinances are seen as causing the dispersal of some lower income households to locations in the community where such housing had never before been built. But the ordinances will not cause great reduction of existing concentrations of lower income families.

Reliance on federal housing subsidies have been seen to give rise to many problems in implementing mandatory inclusionary ordinances. There is, first of all, the uncertain availability of subsidy funds because of inadequate appropriations by Congress, unexpected HUD refusals to carry out programs, or HUD administrative policies that make the subsidies unavailable in practice. These problems were addressed by two of the ordinances that excuse compliance if federal subsidy funds cannot be obtained.

On the other hand, the ordinances do not address the burden of time and expense to many developers of having to deal with HUD and become familiar with its programs and requirements.

More important, there may have been serious structural problems of meshing the mandatory inclusionary requirements with the HUD programs. . . . [The authors then note that some of these problems have been alleviated by the new leased housing subsidy program, which allows the mixing of subsidized and unsubsidized units in the same building. Nevertheless, rents set by HUD under this program may in some cases be too low.—Eds.]

Commentators have felt that experience with the mandatory inclusionary ordinances has been too limited to be able to determine whether they significantly impose additional risks and reduce economic incentives so as to inhibit undertaking new residential construction. One critical issue is whether developers believe that they can sell or rent units at market rates in developments with 15% of the units reserved for low- and moderate-income families. People, they fear, may not buy or rent housing in close proximity to persons of lower income who are paying significantly less for similar housing facilities. Potential buyers of homes also may fear that the 15% requirement will dampen appreciation in the value of their homes. One commentator, who interviewed a number of developers, noted that they did not anticipate unusual marketing difficulties; on the other hand, it was homebuilders who initiated successful litigation against the mandatory ordinance in Fairfax County. Equally uncertain at the present time is the attitude of construction lenders, who provide construction financing only if they believe that the units will be marketable and that the development will be profitable.

Thus, the most important economic question is whether a development with the 15% low- and moderate-income housing requirement can be profitable, assuming no unusual marketing problems. One commentator has analyzed the problem in various hypothetical situations under the three ordinances. He concludes that the economic profitability of any project depends primarily upon (1) the extent of density bonuses granted under the ordinance, (2) the ability of the developer to reduce construction costs by reducing the dimensions and amenities of the low- and moderate-income units, (3) the maximum sales and rent levels set for these units, and (4) whether any losses on the low- and moderate-income units can be recouped from unsubsidized buyers and tenants through higher prices or rents, or from the landowner through a reduced price for the site.

The most favorable situation for sales housing was found to exist under the Montgomery County ordinance. Not only does the ordinance grant a generous density bonus, but also the sales limits established by the ordinance are $4,000 to $5,000 per unit above the limits established under the federal Section 235 home ownership program. . . . [This is a federally subsidized housing program.—Eds.] A developer's percentage return on his investment remained unchanged in the example, while his absolute profit increased because of building 20% more units. Under the less favorable density bonus provision of the Fairfax County ordinance and the lower federal subsidy sales limits, developers could lose money on the 15% subsidized units held for sale, but, even with losses on the subsidized units, the developer could realize an acceptable overall profit on the development.

. . . .

Predictions on how the mandatory inclusionary ordinances will affect developer incentives cannot be made with any confidence. There are too many complex, interrelated variables. Possibly the major determining factor is whether developers have any viable options other than to develop under the mandatory inclusionary ordinances, and, if not, whether they will accept what they perceive as added risks and burdens as an alternative to developing elsewhere or going out of business altogether. The literature on the subject at least suggests, however, that there may be opportunity to make a reasonable profit under a mandatory inclusionary ordinance.

Equally uncertain is the social effect of broadly mixing income levels within a single development. The lack of empirical data on this question would seem to reflect the American custom of developing and marketing new housing for a homogeneous population. Most projects categorized as mixed-income developments consist of subsidized moderate-income families living side-by-side with more deeply subsidized, lower-income families. These projects have, on the whole, been characterized as "successful" on the basis of informed subjective judgments where design, construction, and management have been of good quality. A few of these "successful" mixed-income projects have included middle-income tenants. . . .

However, housing developments financed by the Massachusetts Housing Finance Agency (MHFA) have been studied on this point. That agency is required by its authorizing legislation to assure that a minimum of 25% of the units in each project it finances are rented to low-income families, defined as families that would have to expend more than 25% of their income to rent market-rate units. Since the low-income renters are not permitted to spend more than one-quarter of their incomes for rent in MHFA-financed developments, the fiscal soundness of the development can be preserved without federal or state subsidies only by charging significantly higher rents (but not higher than market rents) for the remaining units. Where subsidy funds are available, the MHFA sometimes has increased the number of units reserved for lower income families.

One conclusion of the MHFA study was that income mixing was not a significant factor in determining the degree of tenant satisfaction with the projects in which they were living. The significant factors to tenants related to the quality of the design, construction, and management of the projects. However, the data base for this study was narrow. Sixteen MHFA-financed projects were studied. Since these were limited to the earliest financed projects, which had achieved some occupancy history, they were almost all garden-type apartments located in suburban areas and in smaller cities. Moreover, the study surprisingly does not disclose the actual range of incomes of tenants; it is possible that this range is not sufficiently broad to permit a meaningful prediction for other mixed-income developments.

The MHFA study did demonstrate that the projects exhibiting the greatest degree of tenant satisfaction were occupied by an almost all-white population, with few children and substantial numbers of market-rate units. Significantly lower levels of tenant satisfaction were registered in projects occupied by poorer families, with more children, where all of the units were subsidized, where most of the minority families included in the study lived, and where the design, construction and management qualities were less evident. The study does show at least that income mixing within a project in suburban areas may not hinder the success of an otherwise well designed, constructed, and managed project.

Other sociological studies referred to in the literature on mandatory inclusionary ordinances suggest, to the contrary, that while considerable heterogeneity will be acceptable within a community, wide spreads of income and cultural characteristics will not be so readily acceptable at the neighborhood or block level. It would seem to follow that heterogeneity within a project would be most difficult of all. On the other hand, these studies were based on attitudinal surveys that might not accurately reflect the reactions of people when actually faced with living in a mixed-income development. In addition, a 15% low and moderate component might not be large enough to threaten the security perceptions of the majority in the development, particularly if the only characteristic differentiating the 15% of the population from the remainder is the magnitude of their incomes. Indeed, the literature contains some suggestion that social problems from mandatory inclusionary ordinances are more likely to arise among the lower income beneficiaries themselves since they exist in numbers too small to provide intra-group support in an environment of higher income people.

Comments: A survey of mandatory inclusionary local zoning ordinances covering ordinances in several additional municipalities can be found in Fox & Davis, Density Bonus Zoning to Provide Low and Moderate Cost Housing, 3 Hastings Const. L.Q. 1015 (1976). These ordinances may raise constitutional problems and problems of statutory authority, as the following case indicates.

BOARD OF SUPERVISORS v. DeGROFF ENTERPRISES, INC.

Virginia Supreme Court
214 Va. 235, 198 S.E.2d 600 (1973)

HARMAN, Justice.

The question presented by this appeal is the validity of amendment 156 (the amendment) to the Fairfax County Zoning Ordinance (ordinance) which became effective on September 1, 1971.

When the amendment, which consists of 39 typewritten pages, is stripped of detail, it requires the developer of fifty or more dwelling units in five zoning districts (RT-5, RTC-5, RT-10, RTC-10 and RM-2G) to commit himself, before rezoning or site plan approval to build at least 15% of these dwelling units as low and moderate income housing within the definitions promulgated from time to time by the Fairfax County Housing and Redevelopment Authority (FCHRA) and the United States Department of Housing and Urban Development (HUD). Under the amendment the housing units designated as low and moderate income units can be sold or rented only to persons of low and moderate income as defined by [FCHRA] and HUD regulations and the sale or rental price for such units cannot exceed the amount established as price guidelines by those agencies.

After a lengthy hearing the trial court found the amendment invalid on the grounds that the Board of Supervisors exceeded its authority under the zoning enabling act, Code § 15.1-486 et seq., that the amendment constituted an improper delegation of legislative authority, and that the amendment was arbitrary and capricious.

The hearing before the trial court clearly demonstrated both a demand and an urgent need for housing units for low and moderate income families in Fairfax County. Indeed, the uncontroverted evidence indicates that the need then existed there for 10,500 such dwelling units.

The Board of Supervisors of Fairfax County (Board) on the basis of this need, would have us hold the amendment valid on the ground that it "facilitates 'creation of a convenient . . . and harmonious community' and is essential to the 'health, safety, . . . [and] general welfare of the public.' " In support of this proposition the Board cites

Code § 15.1-489 in which these purposes for zoning ordinances are enumerated.

That a problem exists in the need for low and moderate income housing has been recognized for many years. In 1937, in an effort to help meet this need, the Congress passed the United States Housing Act, Act of Sept. 1, 1937, c. 896, 50 Stat. 888.

The following year the General Assembly, to implement the low income housing provisions of this federal act, passed the Housing Authorities Law, Acts of Assembly, 1938, c. 310, which now appears, as amended, as Code § 36-1 et seq. In *Mumpower v. Housing Authority,* 176 Va. 426, 11 S.E.2d 732 (1940), we considered the Housing Authorities Law and found it to be a constitutionally valid exercise of the police power. In doing so we recognized that slum eradication and the erection of low income public housing was "a matter of vital concern to the public and to the State." *Id.* at 437, 11 S.E.2d at 735.

Today, as a part of the nationwide effort to solve the housing problem upon which billions of dollars of public funds have been expended, redevelopment and housing authorities exist in most, if not all, of the urban areas of the Commonwealth and in many of the nonurban areas.

Thus it would appear that providing low and moderate income housing serves a legitimate public purpose. The question, then, becomes whether this public purpose can be accomplished by the amendment to the ordinance which rests upon the police power.

. . . .

In [*Board of Supervisors v. Carper,* 200 Va. 653, 107 S.E.2d 390 (1959)], we held invalid a zoning ordinance which had as its purpose the exclusion of low and middle income groups from the western areas of Fairfax County. The effect of this decision is to prohibit socio-economic zoning. We conclude that the legislative intent was to permit localities to enact only traditional zoning ordinances directed to physical characteristics and having the purpose neither to include nor exclude any particular socio-economic group.

In *Boggs v. Board of Supervisors,* 211 Va. 488, 178 S.E.2d 508 (1971), we found that a zoning ordinance which had the effect of completely depriving the owner of the beneficial use of his property by precluding all practical uses to be unreasonable and confiscatory and, therefore, illegal.

More recently in *Fairfax County v. Columbia Pike, Ltd.,* 213 Va. 437, 192 S.E.2d 778 (1972), we followed our earlier holding in *Mooreland v. Young,* 197 Va. 771, 91 S.E.2d 438 (1956), that the zoning enabling act does not authorize the governing body of a county to control compensation for the use of lands or the improvements thereon.

When the amendment is measured by these legal standards, we find it deficient.

The amendment, in establishing maximum rental and sale prices for 15% of the units in the development, exceeds the authority granted by the enabling act to the local governing body because it is socio-economic zoning and attempts to control the compensation for the use of land and the improvements thereon.

Of greater importance, however, is that the amendment requires the developer or owner to rent or sell 15% of the dwelling units in the development to persons of low or moderate income at rental or sale prices not fixed by a free market. Such a scheme violates the guarantee set forth in Section 11 of Article 1 of the Constitution of Virginia, 1971, that no property will be taken or damaged for public purposes without just compensation.

Affirmed.

Comments: 1. The *Carper* case, relied on in the principal case, is the subject of an earlier comment *supra* p. 444. Although the court says (in the principal case) that the purpose of the ordinance invalidated in *Carper* was "the exclusion of low- and middle-income groups from the western areas of Fairfax County," the real purpose of that ordinance seems to have been to establish a "holding zone" in order to channel growth into the eastern part of Fairfax County, where most of the existing population was and where urban services could be provided most economically.

2. The Virginia Supreme Court . . . [in *DeGroff*] held that the state's constitutional provisions against a taking of private property without the payment of just compensation had been violated by requiring a developer to sell or rent 15% of the units at prices not fixed by the free market. This holding seems out of line with most cases, which do not find a public taking of property when the owner is left with some reasonable use for the property. However, one commentator's careful legal analysis of mandatory inclusionary ordinances suggests that they raise difficult legal questions that are not answered by a mechanical measurement of the residual value of the property. [Kleven, Inclusionary Ordinances—Policy and Legal Issues in Requiring Private Developers to Build Low Cost Housing, 21 U.C.L.A. L. Rev. 1432, 1490-1528 (1974). — Eds.] Basically, a mandatory ordinance requires a developer's land to be used, in part, in a manner intended to solve a community-wide housing problem. This is not a problem of the developer's own creation; yet, he, and others developing housing in the community, are being singled out to bear the economic burden of helping solve the problem.

The problem appears in a number of analogous contexts. Most courts uphold subdivision regulations that require a developer to pay for streets, utilities, and even schools, that will serve primarily the population living in the subdivision. Since the subdivision created the demand for the additional public services, it is not unfair to require the subdivision to bear such economic burdens.

On the other hand, the courts often invalidate subdivision regulations that require the developer to bear the cost of public facilities that will not be used primarily by residents of the subdivision. Similarly, zoning by districts has traditionally been justified on the basis that the odors, noise, and congestion from industrial and commercial uses would be unhealthful and destroy the economic value for residential uses of land mixed in with it. Thus, incompatible uses can be separated to prevent the harmful external side-effects of one type of use from impinging on other uses. This is not the rationale for a mandatory requirement for mixing incomes in a housing project. Rather, the objectives are broadly social, and the developer is singled out to bear the burden of achieving them. Mandatory inclusionary ordinances can also be compared to rent and price control measures that have been upheld by courts if they operate fairly. On this basis, however, it also can be questioned whether it is fair to cause a reduction in the economic return of residential developers to solve a problem of community-wide dimension.

This type of analysis leads the commentator to conclude that a mandatory inclusionary ordinance stands a better chance of being upheld by the courts if it contains density bonuses and other relaxations in zoning and building code requirements to eliminate any economic loss resulting from complying with the ordinance. He also expresses the hope that a broader view of the public policy served by these mandatory inclusionary features will persuade the courts to uphold such enactments as within local legislative discretion. At present, however, it cannot be said that such ordinances are assured of judicial acceptance.

H. Franklin, D. Falk, & A. Levin, *supra* at 139-40 (1975). The substance of the excerpt set out above is also to be found in Housing for All Under Law, *supra* p. 562, at 589-92.

    3. Notwithstanding the Virginia decision, a court reviewing an inclusionary land use program ... is likely to be influenced favorably by a community attempting to deal with the housing problems of lower income persons in a manner that is rational and responsible to its residents and to residents of the wider region. When the community is obviously so motivated, its judgment and the legislative policy it adopts will be respected by the courts—particularly if no personal constitutional right is threatened. The *Ramapo* decision in New York state [*Golden v. Planning Board of Town of Ramapo,* reprinted as a principal case in Chapter 7, *infra* p. 1037. — Eds.] stands as evidence of the extent to which a court will go to interpret a state zoning enabling act to authorize novel local land use control techniques if the judges believe that the community is making a good faith effort to deal rationally and fairly with anticipated growth problems. A similar attitude can be anticipated toward communities trying to deal rationally and fairly with their housing problems.

    It is, of course, important that the technical legal principles that have developed in zoning law over the past half century are not permitted to defeat a well-motivated community inclusionary program. The problem requires adjusting the powers granted to localities under traditional state zoning enabling laws to the newly conceived dynamic approaches to the management of urban growth. It is therefore important that the *means* selected by a community to implement an inclusionary program be techniques either approved by the courts in the jurisdiction or at least not invalidated by the courts in an earlier day. Courts are frequently hardened by established dogma and do not lightly ignore past decisions, no matter how sympathetic they may be to underlying public objectives. Therefore, the test is not only to fashion the inclusionary program itself, but to devise its implementation with the law of the state clearly in focus, realizing that different state courts have developed different legal attitudes toward techniques of flexibility in zoning.

H. Franklin, D. Falk, & A. Levin, *supra* at 107-08.

4. Two later decisions in New York and New Jersey, involving the creation of special zoning districts for the elderly, indicate that other state courts may be more receptive to the "inclusionary" zoning concept than was the Virginia court in *DeGroff.* See *Maldini v. Ambro,* 330 N.E.2d 403 (N.Y. 1975); *Taxpayers' Ass'n of Weymouth Township v. Weymouth Township,* 364 A.2d 1016 (N.J. 1976), discussed in Housing for All Under Law, *supra* at 590-92.

b. State Agency Override Zoning Techniques

BOARD OF APPEALS OF HANOVER v. HOUSING APPEALS COMMITTEE

Massachusetts Supreme Judicial Court
363 Mass. 339, 294 N.E.2d 393 (1973)

TAURO, Chief Justice.

This is a reservation and report by a Superior Court judge without decision of two suits in equity brought by (1) the board of appeals of the town of Hanover (Hanover board) and (2) the board of appeals of the town of Concord (Concord board). We have before us the records of the proceedings before both boards and the Housing Appeals Committee (committee) as certified by the committee. The boards denied applications for comprehensive permits to build low and moderate income housing filed pursuant to the provisions of G.L. c. 40B, §§ 20 and 21, and the applicants appealed to the committee pursuant to G.L. c. 40B, § 22. The committee rendered two decisions, in each case reversing the board and ordering the issuance of the permit. The suits, brought under G.L. c. 40B, § 22, and G.L. c. 30A, § 14, seek review of the committee's decisions. The cases were argued together. The bills present similar questions concerning the constitutional validity and the substantive and procedural effects of G.L. c. 40B, §§ 20-23, inserted by St. 1969, c. 774, § 1 (c. 774). The cases are, therefore, decided together.

The Hanover Proceedings.

In April, 1970, Country Village Corporation filed an application with the Hanover board for a comprehensive permit to construct eighty-eight units of low and moderate income housing for the elderly on approximately ten acres of land. After holding public hearings on the application, as required by G.L. c. 40B, § 21, and G.L. c. 40A, § 17, the board refused to issue the permit. The board then filed with the clerk of the town of Hanover its decision denying the permit and the reasons for the denial.[143] In December, 1970, the applicant appealed to the committee. G.L. c. 40B, § 22. The committee, after holding public hearings on the appeal pursuant to G.L. c. 40B, §§ 22 and 23, vacated the decision of the board in July, 1971, and ordered the board to issue a comprehensive permit for the project, subject to specified conditions. The Hanover board then filed this bill for review in the Superior Court.

The Concord Proceedings.

In January, 1971, the Concord Home Owning Corporation filed with the Concord board an application for a comprehensive permit to construct sixty garden apartment units of low and moderate income housing on approximately five and one-half acres of land. The board then held public hearings on the application as required by G.L. c. 40B, § 21, and G.L. c. 40A, § 17, and refused to issue the permit. The board filed with the clerk of the town of Concord its decision denying the permit and the reasons for the denial.[144] In

---

[143] The reason specified by the Hanover board for its denial of the permit were:

"1. The apparent conflict between chapter 774 of the Acts of 1969 and the zoning bylaws of the town of Hanover in regard to zoning districts and permissible uses in different zoning districts;

"2. The apparent conflict between chapter 774 of the Acts of 1969 and the zoning enabling act, G.L. c. 40A;

"3. The applicant does not own the site on which the proposed project it to be built;

"4. The applicant is not a limited-dividend corporation;

"5. The proposed project would increase traffic and would not be acceptable for the present road construction;

"6. The applicant failed to submit adequate drainage and sewerage plans to the appellant [Hanover board] and failed to file revised drainage and sewerage plans with the appellant incorporating changes recommended by the appellant;

"7. The applicant failed to submit to the appellant sewerage plans acceptable to the state department of public health or the Hanover board of health."

[144] The reasons specified by the Concord board for its denial of the permit were:

"(a) the construction of the project would be in violation of the Town of Concord Zoning By-Law, which violation the Board of Appeals was not empowered by G.L. c. 40B, §§ 20 and 21 to authorize, and (b) the denial of the application for a comprehensive permit for the project was 'reasonable and consistent with local needs,' as required by the provisions of G.L. c. 40B, § 23, in that the project could be detrimental to the health and safety of the future occupants of the project and the residents of the Town in the vicinity of the project because of the severe subsurface water conditions affecting the area of the project."

April, 1971, the applicant appealed to the committee. G.L. c. 40B, § 22. After holding the required public hearing on the appeal, the committee vacated the decision of the board and ordered the board to issue the applicant a comprehensive permit for the project, subject to specified conditions. The board then filed this bill for review in the Superior Court.

Issues Presented.

The bills present three issues for resolution concerning the powers and procedures of the boards of appeals and the committee under G.L. c. 774. We must determine:

(a) whether c. 774 confers power upon both the committee and the boards to override zoning regulations which hamper the construction of low and moderate income housing;

(b) whether such power to override zoning regulations, if it exists, is constitutional; and

(c) whether such power to override zoning regulations, if it exists, was properly exercised by the committee in the instant cases.

Chapter 774 permits a qualified applicant [145] interested in building low or moderate income housing to file with a board of appeals an application for a comprehensive permit instead of filing separate applications with each local agency or official having jurisdiction over various aspects of the proposed project. The statute allows the board of appeals to grant a single comprehensive permit for construction after considering the recommendations of the local agencies or officials. General Laws c. 40B, § 21, establishes a specific time period within which the board of appeals must make its decision. If the board makes no decision within this period, "the application shall be deemed to have been allowed and the comprehensive permit or approval shall forthwith issue." § 21. If the board issues a comprehensive permit, any person aggrieved by its decision may appeal to the District or Superior Court as provided in § 21 of G.L. c. 40A.

Whenever the board of appeals denies an application or grants it with conditions which make the building or operation of the proposed housing project "uneconomic," [146] § 22 grants the applicant a right of appeal to the committee. The committee is required to conduct a full hearing with a stenographic record within twenty days of the receipt of the applicant's appeal and it must render

---

[145] General Laws c. 40B, § 20, limits the class of proper applicants under c. 774 to public agencies, nonprofit organizations, and limited dividend organizations. See fn. [147], *infra*.

[146] General Laws c. 40B, § 20, defines "uneconomic" as "any condition brought about by any single factor or combination of factors to the extent that it makes it impossible for a public agency or nonprofit organization to proceed in building or

a written decision "stating its findings of fact, its conclusions and the reasons therefor within thirty days after the termination of the hearing, unless such time shall have been extended by mutual agreement between the committee and the applicant." Section 23 limits the committee's review to determining whether the board of appeals' decision to deny the application was "reasonable and consistent with local needs" as defined by § 20. If the board grants the application subject to conditions, § 23 limits the committee's review to determining whether the conditions make the construction or operation of the housing uneconomic and whether the conditions are consistent with local needs. If the board's decision to deny the permit or to impose uneconomic conditions on its approval is found to be consistent with local needs, the committee must affirm the board's decision. "If the committee finds, in the case of a denial, that the decision of the board of appeals was unreasonable and not consistent with local needs, it shall vacate such decision and shall direct the board to issue a comprehensive permit or approval to the applicant." § 23. If the committee finds that the conditions imposed by the board in approving the application make the building or operation of the housing "uneconomic" and that the board's decision is not consistent with local needs, the committee "shall order such board to modify or remove any such condition or requirement so as to make the proposal no longer uneconomic and to issue any necessary permit or approval." The committee's decision is subject to judicial review in accordance with c. 30A's provisions. G.L. c. 40B, § 22.

1. *Does c. 774 Confer upon both the Committee and the Boards the Power to Override Local Zoning Regulations to the Extent that such Regulations Conflict with the Implementation of c. 774?*

The boards argue that the Legislature did not intend to grant the power to override local zoning by-laws or ordinances to any authority when it enacted c. 774. Thus, their respective decisions to deny comprehensive permits in these cases were reasonable and consistent with local needs because neither they nor the committee had authority to issue comprehensive permits for a use of land not permitted under local zoning by-laws. The boards contend that the Legislature's purpose in enacting c. 774 was merely to provide a streamlined procedure for processing applications for the necessary

---

operating low or moderate income housing without financial loss, or for a limited dividend organization to proceed and still realize a reasonable return in building or operating such housing within the limitations set by the subsidizing agency of government on the size or character of the development or on the amount or nature of the subsidy or on the tenants, rentals and income permissible, and without substantially changing the rent levels and units sizes proposed by the public, nonprofit or limited dividend organizations."

local approvals of construction of low or moderate income housing. Where previously an applicant was forced to negotiate with various local agencies or officials before gaining their approval, c. 774's new time limits expedited the process by allowing the applicant to apply for and obtain a comprehensive permit from a single agency, the board of appeals. The committee argues, to the contrary, that the text, history, and context of c. 774 indicate that the Legislature intended to confer to both the board and the committee the power to override any local requirements and regulations, including zoning by-laws, which prevented the construction of low and moderate income housing when such housing is deemed "consistent with local needs."

To resolve this controversy over c. 774's essential purpose, we must examine its detailed legislative history to determine the nature of the problem that the statute was designed to remedy. The boards' interpretation of the statute rests on their argument that the Legislature was chiefly concerned with speeding up the processing of applications for the construction of low and moderate income housing. However, the legislative history of c. 774 indicates that the Legislature was more concerned with the cities' and towns' possible use of their zoning powers to exclude low and moderate income groups.

The legislative history of c. 774 begins with a 1967 Senate Order, No. 933, which directed the Legislative Research Council (Council) to "undertake a study and investigation relative to the feasibility and implications of restricting the zoning power to cities and county governments with particular emphasis on the possibility that the smaller communities are utilizing the zoning power in an unjust manner with respect to minority groups."

. . . .

What follows is a summary of the Report's conclusions:

(1) Large lot requirements (minimum lot size) have a substantial negative effect on the availability of land in the suburbs which could be used for low and moderate income housing. P. 102. The Report listed twenty-one municipalities, including Hanover, that restricted 50% or more of their territory to large lot zoning. P. 98.

(2) Building height limitations were also found to have a significant negative impact on low and moderate income housing. The Report noted that forty-six municipalities had height limitations and thirty-one, including Hanover, forbade apartment buildings altogether. The Report concluded, "Beyond these height restrictions . . . lies the greater public policy issue of providing sufficient sites in metropolitan areas for adequate multi-family and apartment housing at modest rentals for that portion of the area population which cannot afford to own or to rent a single-family home . . . . To the extent that inner suburban communities prohibit multi-family and

apartment housing, or attach height or other restrictions which make such housing feasible only on a 'luxury' basis, the modest income housing problems of the entire metropolitan area are aggravated." *Id.* at 118.

After determining that seven of the eight local restrictive zoning practices studied had a negative impact on the construction of low and moderate income housing, the Report noted that the housing shortage problem had reached crisis proportions. In 1947, the entire State population could be housed in buildings on land as then zoned. Pp. 32-33. But by 1968, low income persons could not find places to live in the suburbs at prices which they could afford to pay. *Id.* at 87-88. One study estimated that by 1968, 20,000 additional housing units would be needed to accommodate low income families (*id.* at 121; Massachusetts Special Commission on Low-Income Housing, Final Report, 1965 House No. 4040, at 82-83), and that 125,000 new housing units would be needed to meet population increases alone by 1975. Report at 88.

The Report concluded with the dire prediction that if existing exclusionary zoning practices by municipalities were left unregulated, the supply of vacant land would be eliminated by the 1990's (*id.* at 102) because the communities were not inclined to act on their own to alleviate the problem (*id.* at 123) and the courts were unwilling to intervene as long as the discrimination involved in the exclusionary zoning practices was economic. The Council recommended a plan which would leave with cities and towns the general power to direct their own development but would permit, in appropriate cases, the circumvention of exclusionary zoning by-laws where their enforcement would frustrate the State's need for more low and moderate income housing.

The Council's Report prompted the submission of the following bills in the 1969 session of the Legislature: Senate Bills Nos. 1137 and 1141, and House Bills Nos. 2924, 3175 and 3603. All of these bills called for the imposition of State control over the suburbs' exercise of exclusionary zoning practices in order to insure the availability of low and moderate income housing throughout the State. In different ways and to different degrees, these bills provided for the overriding of local zoning ordinances and by-laws which frustrated the construction of low and moderate income housing in the suburbs.

. . . .

The Concord board claims that the Council's Report, the bills submitted in response to it, and the final draft of House Bill No. 5429 which was reported out of the Urban Affairs Committee along with its report are "misleading indication[s] of the intent of the General Court." Although all of the prior legislative history of House Bill No. 5429 reflects a consistent attempt on the Legislature's part to resolve the housing shortage problem by establishing an effective means of circumventing the suburbs' exclusionary zoning provisions, the Concord board claims that this intended approach was eliminated when House Bill No. 5429 was redrafted by the Committee on Ways and Means.

However, a careful examination of the changes made by the Committee on Ways and Means reveals that the Concord board's argument rests on a relatively insignificant rephrasing of language which changed the form but not the substance of the bill. When the bill was reported out by the Committee on Urban Affairs, the section concerning the committee's review of a local board of appeals' decision that imposed "uneconomic" conditions on the permit read, "the commission or the committee shall, unless the action of the board of appeals is found to be consistent with local needs, order such board to issue any necessary permit or approval or to modify or remove any requirement, *including but not limited to zoning or building code requirements*" (emphasis supplied). When the bill was reported out of the Committee on Ways and Means, 1969 House Bill No. 5381, the "including but not limited to" clause had been eliminated so the clause read "it [the committee] shall order such board to modify or remove any such condition or requirement . . . and to issue any necessary permit or approval . . . ." The omission of the superfluous "including but not limited to" phrase which delineated only part but not all of the power granted by the clause which it modified did not negate the Legislature's primary intent to circumvent the suburbs' exclusionary zoning practices. The insignificance of this redrafting is further emphasized by the proviso following that section which establishes minimum construction safety standards for housing built under the statute. This provision would have been unnecessary if in all instances local regulations were to apply.

Examination of the subsequent legislative history of c. 774 as redrafted by the Committee on Ways and Means (renumbered House Bill No. 5581) discloses neither a change of purpose nor a change of method on the part of the Legislature. . . .

In view of the descriptions of the redrafted bill's effect by the legislators themselves, and considering the failure of these amendments, both in the House and Senate, which would have given local communities a veto over application of the statute to their municipality, we conclude that the Legislature's intent in passing c. 774 was to provide relief from exclusionary zoning practices which prevented the construction of badly needed low and moderate income housing.

Our determination of the Legislature's intent enables us to interpret the text of the statute which admittedly is not without its ambiguities. The statute must be construed in a manner that effectuates its intent. With this in mind, we turn to the ambiguities in the statute's text noted by the boards.

The boards claim that the statute's failure to refer specifically to local zoning ordinances or by-laws indicates that no power to override them was in fact conferred. However, c. 40B, § 20, in delineating when a board's decision is consistent with local needs, refers to "requirements and regulations." Though this reference is somewhat ambiguous, the Legislature's clear purpose in passing this statute requires our construction of this term to include local zoning by-laws and ordinances. Although the word "zoning" is not specifically used, the statute's legislative history and avowed purpose to facilitate the construction of low and moderate income housing in areas which have exclusionary zoning practices compel our decision to construe the statute so that zoning ordinances or by-laws are treated like any other local requirements which hamper the construction of low and moderate income housing. All these local "requirements and regulations" will be applicable if they are "consistent with local needs"; if they are not, they must be modified or ignored.

Our decision that the committee has the authority to override local requirements and regulations that are inconsistent with local needs by implication necessitates a construction of the statute which confers this same authority upon the boards. As the Concord board noted, "if anyone has the power to override zoning ordinances or by-laws under G.L. c. 40B, §§ 20-23, then both the Committee and all local boards of appeals have that power. If the result were otherwise, it is obvious that in any case where a proposed project is not permitted by a zoning by-law, the applicant must follow the futile procedure of applying for relief before a forum which has no power to grant the relief being sought." Since we must avoid a construction of statutory language which produces irrational results (*Johnson v. Commissioner of Pub. Safety*, 355 Mass. 94, 99, 243 N.E.2d 157), that portion of § 21 which states that the "board of appeals . . . *shall have the same power* to issue permits or approvals as any local board or official who would otherwise act with respect to such application . . ." (emphasis supplied) cannot be read to exclude the additional power to override local requirements and regulations granted by § 20 and § 23. Thus, we construe § 21 to confer upon boards "the same power . . . as any local board or official" in addition to that power otherwise conferred by the provisions of this act.

We have often stated that a construction of a statute which would completely negate legislative intent should be avoided. *Assessors of Newton v. Pickwick Ltd., Inc.*, 351 Mass. 621, 625, 223 N.E.2d 388. The boards' interpretation of this statute would have exactly this effect. Streamlining local permit procedures could not possibly serve the statute's clear purpose of promoting the construction of low and moderate income housing if the cities and towns retained the unlimited power to enforce restrictive zoning ordinances or by-laws which prevented the construction of such housing. Therefore, we hold that c. 774 confers on boards of appeals and the Housing Appeals Committee the power to override local "requirements and regulations," including zoning ordinances or by-laws, which are not "consistent with local needs."

2. *Does c. 774 Violate the Home Rule Amendment?*

[This section of the opinion is omitted. The court held that local zoning powers "cannot be exercised in a manner which frustrates the purpose or implementation of a general or special law enacted by the Legislature. . . ."—Eds.]

3. *Does the Boards' or Committee's Exercise of their Power to Override Local Zoning Regulations Deemed Inconsistent with Local Needs Constitute Spot Zoning?*

The amici curiae argue that when the committee exercises its power to override local zoning by-laws deemed inconsistent with local needs, it engages in illegal spot zoning because its act singles out a particular parcel of property in a community for treatment different from that given to similar surrounding land indistinguishable from it in character.

However, we have frequently held that a spot zoning violation involves more than a mere finding that a parcel of property is singled out for less restrictive treatment than that of surrounding land of a similar character. If we accepted the amici curiae's test for spot zoning, the State could never exercise its undoubted power to override local zoning ordinances or by-laws for legitimate public purposes because there would always be a disparity of treatment between the area where the local ordinance or by-law is ignored and the rest of that zoning area where it is enforced. Moreover, zoning variances and amendments would also be subject to serious challenge on spot zoning grounds if the test were merely one of dissimilar treatment of similar parcels of property.

We stated the definition of spot zoning in *Lamarre v. Commissioner of Pub. Works of Fall River,* 324 Mass. 542, 87 N.E.2d 211, a case concerning a zoning amendment which converted a parcel of land that had previously been zoned as a single and general (not more than three family housing) residence district into a multi-family residence district. The local housing authority had requested the amendment and it had been approved by the local planning board and the city council because of a shortage of rental housing in Fall River. The facts of the *Lamarre* case are closely analogous to those in the instant case. . . .

We held in the *Lamarre* case at 545-546, 87 N.E.2d at 213, that "it [the zoning amendment] was not an instance of 'spot' zoning. 'It does not appear that there was "a singling out of one lot for different treatment from that accorded to similar surrounding land indistinguishable from it in character, *all for the economic benefit of the owner of that lot." ' Marblehead v. Rosenthal,* 316 Mass. 124, 126, 55 N.E.2d 13, 14; *Whittemore v. Building Inspector of Falmouth,* 313 Mass. 248, 249, 46 N.E.2d 1016. . . ." Our definition of spot zoning is in accord with the general view held by most State courts that spot zoning problems arise where a zoning change is designed solely for the economic benefit of the owner of the property receiving special treatment and is not in accordance with a well considered plan for the public welfare. . . .

Thus, the central question posed by this spot zoning challenge is whether the difference of treatment accorded by c. 774 serves the public welfare or merely affords an economic benefit to the owner of the land receiving special treatment. We decided in the *Lamarre* case that zoning changes affording special treatment to encourage the construction of multi-family residences in cities with housing shortages promote the public welfare. 324 Mass. p. 546, 87 N.E.2d 211. We followed this decision in *Henze v. Building Inspector of Lawrence, Mass.,* 269 N.E.2d 711, where we held that the need for low and moderate income housing justified a zoning reclassification of a parcel of land from a one and two-family residential district to a multi-family residential district. We think these decisions are dispositive of the spot zoning challenge. Chapter 774 reflects the Legislature's judgment that the special treatment accorded to a site proposed for the construction of low and moderate income housing and necessitated by exclusionary zoning practices serves the general welfare by promoting the construction of badly needed housing units in the suburbs. The statute's "consistent with local needs" standard and its provisions for judicial review of the board's and committee's decisions insure that special treatment will be allowed only when it serves the public interest. Thus, we hold that the exercise of c. 774's power to override local zoning by-laws and ordinances deemed inconsistent with local needs does not constitute spot zoning.

4. *Is c. 774 Unconstitutionally Vague?*

The boards contend that c. 774 improperly delegates legislative authority to an administrative agency and is void for vagueness because its provisions fail to provide standards sufficient to guide administrative action and to limit the exercise of untrammeled discretion. See *Smith v. Board of Appeals of Fall River,* 319 Mass. 341, 344, 65 N.E.2d 547. These constitutional claims of "void for vagueness" and unlawful delegation of legislative authority are closely related. . . .

The Concord board claims that "[t]he constitutional defect in G.L. c. 40B, §§ 20-23, is not that the standards provided local boards are not specific enough, but that the statute provides no standards at all for use by such boards in passing on applications for comprehensive permits under G.L. c. 40B, § 21." The boards' claim of lack of standards to guide their decisions rests on their assumption that the "consistent with local needs" and "uneconomic" standards referred to in § 23 and defined in § 20 apply only to the committee's review of the boards' decisions. We cannot agree.

. . . .

Our examination of c. 774 leads us to conclude that the standards to be applied by boards of appeals in deciding whether to issue comprehensive permits are the same as those to be applied by the committee in reviewing the boards' decisions, namely, whether the grant of the permit is "reasonable and consistent with local needs" and whether any conditions imposed on the permit are "uneconomic." It is irrelevant that these standards are set forth in sections (§ 23 and § 20) different from the section dealing expressly with the hearing before the board of appeals (§ 21) because §§ 20-23 must be construed as a whole. . . . If the board's decision does not comply with these standards, its decision will be reversed by the committee on appeal, so by necessary implication its own decision must be based on the same standards. Any other construction of the statute would render the hearing before the board a useless procedure.

Finally, there is no merit to the claim that these standards are impermissibly vague. Section 20 contains detailed definitions of the factors to be considered by both the board of appeals and the committee in determining whether a proposal is "consistent with local needs" or whether conditions which might be imposed would render the construction or operation of the project "uneconomic." The "consistent with local needs" standard requires both the board and the committee to balance the regional need for low and moderate income housing against any objection to the details of the proposed plan. This standard requires the local board to consider the "regional need for low and moderate income housing . . . with the number of low income persons in the city or town affected" and with the local need to "protect the health or safety of the occupants of the proposed housing or of the residents of the city or town, to promote better site and building design in relation to the surroundings, or to preserve open spaces." § 20. In weighing these local concerns, the board must apply municipal requirements and regulations "as equally as possible to both subsidized and unsubsidized housing" applications. § 20.

Moreover, § 20 gives the board of appeals specific guidelines to aid its determination of whether the regional need for low and moderate income housing requires the board to override local "requirements and regulations," including restrictive zoning ordinances or by-laws, which would prevent the board from approving a proposal that is otherwise "reasonable [147] and consistent with local needs." Section 20 provides that the board need not override local "requirements and regulations" where (1) "low or moderate income housing exists which is in excess of ten per cent of the housing units reported in the latest decennial census" or (2) such housing exists "on sites comprising one and one half per cent or more of the total land area zoned for residential, commercial or industrial use" (excluding public land) or (3) "the application before the board would result in the commencement of construction of such housing on sites comprising more than three tenths of one per cent of such land area or ten acres, whichever is larger, in any one calendar year." § 20.

The value of these three specific alternative definitions of when local "requirements and regulations shall be considered consistent with local needs" is that they define precisely the municipality's minimum housing obligations "under the statute and permit it to do some intelligent, long-range planning about how and where the necessary housing should be built." Rodgers, Snob Zoning in Massachusetts, 1970 Ann. Surv.Mass.Law, pp. 487, 490. These precise guidelines set forth in § 20 place a ceiling on the extent to which a local board *must override* local requirements and regulations, including exclusionary zoning laws, where the board decides that the application is reasonable and consistent with local needs.

Our construction of c. 774 does not mean that the board must automatically grant comprehensive permits in all cases where the community has not met its minimum housing obligation as it is specifically defined in § 20. The statute merely prevents the board from relying on local requirements or regulations, including applicable zoning by-laws and ordinances which prevent the use of the site for low and moderate income housing, as the reason for the board's denial of the permit or its grant with uneconomic conditions.

In cases where the locality has not met its minimum housing obligations, the board must rest its decision on whether the required need for low and moderate income housing outweighs the valid

---

[147] Section 23 provides that the committee must decide whether the board's denial of an application or its approval with conditions imposed was "reasonable and consistent with local needs." Since the board's decision could be reasonable only if it was "consistent with local needs" as defined by § 20, the term "reasonable" is surplus verbiage which does not add any substance to the "consistent with local needs" standard. The word "reasonable" appears to be equated with the "consistent with local needs" standard.

planning objections to the details of the proposal such as health, site design, and open spaces (see § 20). If the regional need for such housing outweighs these objections, the board must override any restrictive local requirements and regulations which prevent the construction of the housing and grant the comprehensive permit. However, the municipality's failure to meet its minimum housing obligations, as defined in § 20, will provide compelling evidence that the regional need for housing does in fact outweigh the objections to the proposal. See 7 Harv.J. on Legislation, 246.

However, once the municipality has satisfied its minimum housing obligation, the statute deems local "requirements and regulations," including its restrictive zoning ordinances or by-laws, as "consistent with local needs" and thereby enforceable by the board *if it wants to apply them.* In this situation, only the board retains the power to override these requirements and regulations in order to grant a comprehensive permit. This result reflects the Legislature's desire to preserve local autonomy once the community has satisfied its minimum obligation.[148]

. . . .

5. *Does c. 774 Require a De Novo Hearing before the Committee?*

[The court's discussion of this issue is omitted. The court held that a de novo hearing before the committee is required.—Eds.]

6. *Are the Alternative Methods of Review Afforded an Applicant Who Has Been Denied a Permit and an Aggrieved Person Appealing from the Grant of a Permit Violative of the Equal Protection of the Laws Guaranteed by the Federal and Massachusetts Constitutions?*

The boards argue that the statute's provisions for alternative methods of review, depending upon whether the application has been granted or denied, violates the equal protection of the laws guaranteed by the Federal and the State Constitutions. The thrust of these arguments was premised upon the view that the hearing

---

[148] A recent law review article noted that c. 774, "was designed to motivate concern by the local municipalities for the needs of the public in general without depriving them of their home rules." The author noted that regional considerations were injected into local zoning decisions by the statute's definition of "consistent with local needs" which included a precise "mathematical formula" providing for a bare minimum of low or moderate income housing that must exist in the city or town before exclusionary zoning practices can be enforced. "Thus, through these standards the state has maintained the home rule of the municipalities with regard to zoning, but has imposed minimum standards which must be followed." Comments, 22 Syracuse L.Rev. 465, 592, 593.

before the committee was restricted to an inquiry into whether the board's decision was based upon "substantial evidence" (cf. G.L. c. 30A, §§ 1 [6] and 14 [8] [e]) whereas the hearing before the court afforded an aggrieved person appealing from the grant of a permit is essentially a de novo review. G.L. c. 40B, § 21. G.L. c. 40A, § 21.... Since we hold that the statute requires the committee to hear any evidence relevant to the issue whether the denial of the application was reasonable and consistent with local needs, there are no substantial differences between the alternative methods of review.

7. *If the Committee Decides that the Boards' Decisions Are Incorrect, Must the Committee Remand the Cases to the Boards?*

... Section 23 is explicit in its directives to the committee: "If the committee finds, in the case of a denial, that the decision of the board of appeals was unreasonable and not consistent with local needs, it shall vacate such decision and shall direct the board to issue a comprehensive permit or approval to the applicant." Any notion of a remand procedure (other than ordering the board to carry out the committee's decision) is precluded by the clear language of the statute....

8. *Does the Committee Have the Power to Order the Issuance of Permits Subject to the Conditions as Specified?*

The Hanover board argues that the committee exceeded its authority in ordering the issuance of a permit with conditions that (a) stated that the drainage and sewage disposal systems must be approved by the appropriate State authorities, (b) empowered the board, at its option, to require the applicant to make a full disclosure concerning its leasing arrangements, and (c) set no time limits either for the fulfillment of the four specified conditions or for the commencement or completion of the project. The board maintains that such a conditional permit is impermissible because it constitutes an advisory opinion and only partially commits the committee to the issuance of the permit.

It is clear that the committee may order the issuance of conditional permits. Chapter 774 gives a board the power to issue permits or approvals "including but not limited to the power to attach to said permit or approval conditions and requirements with respect to height, site plan, size or shape, or building materials as are consistent with the terms of this section." G.L. c. 40B, § 21. When a board has denied an application, the committee is empowered to vacate the board's decision if it is unreasonable and not consistent with local needs and to direct the board to issue a comprehensive permit or approval to the applicant. G.L. c. 40B, § 23. Since the committee is issuing an order for the board to act pursuant to the board's own power, and since the board is specifically authorized to issue conditional permits or approvals, it follows that the committee has the power to order the board to issue conditional permits or approvals.

. . . .

The time within which the four conditions must be fulfilled is either stated directly (e. g., the first condition must be fulfilled "[b]efore beginning construction") or is implicitly an on-going process coinciding with the progress of the construction (e. g., the fourth condition provides that "local officials shall carry out compliance inspections in the usual manner"). The completion of the project necessarily depends upon numerous factors, including the outcome of this litigation. In the circumstances of this case it is within the committee's discretion to refuse to set final dates for the completion of the project.

9. *Are the Committee's Decisions Supported by "Substantial Evidence"?*

[The court's discussion of this issue is omitted. The court concluded, "upon consideration of the entire record," that the Committee's decisions in both the Hanover and Concord cases "were supported by substantial evidence."—Eds.]

. . . .

In conclusion, c. 774 represents the Legislature's attempt to satisfy the regional need for housing without stripping municipalities of their power to zone. By creating a "consistent with local needs" criterion which expands the scope of relevant local needs considered by the local boards to include the regional need for low and moderate income housing, the Legislature has given the boards the power to override the local exclusionary zoning practices in order to encourage the construction of such housing in the suburbs. By fixing a ceiling on the extent to which a board must override local zoning regulations, the Legislature has clearly delineated that point where local interests must yield to the general public need for housing. This ceiling establishes the minimum share of responsibility that each community must shoulder in order to alleviate the housing crisis that confronts the Commonwealth.

. . . .

The legislative reports which prompted c. 774's passage demonstrated how local restrictive zoning regulations have set up, in fact if not intentionally, a barrier against the introduction of low and moderate income housing in the suburbs. Moreover, this barrier exists at a time when our housing needs for the low and moderate income groups cannot be met by the "inner cities." This housing crisis demands a legislative and judicial approach that requires "the strictly local interests of the town" to yield to the regional need for the construction of low and moderate income housing. Chapter 774 represents the Legislature's use of its own zoning powers to respond to this problem.

The Legislature's zoning power may be used "where the interests of the public require such action and where the means employed are reasonably necessary for the accomplishment of the purpose." *Simon v. Needham,* 311 Mass. 560, 562, 42 N.E.2d 516, 517. Within these broad limits, the General Court is the sole judge as to how and when the power is to be exercised as long as it acts in accordance with the powers reserved to it by § 8 of the Home Rule Amendment. Our responsibility in examining the Legislature's exercise of its zoning power is limited to the determination of whether the legislation adopts a reasonable means to serve a legitimate public purpose. Our analysis of c. 774's legislative history and text leads us to conclude that the Legislature's adoption of an administrative mechanism designed to supersede, when necessary, local restrictive requirements and regulations, including zoning by-laws and ordinances, in order to promote the construction of low and moderate income housing in cities and towns is a constitutionally valid exercise of the Legislature's zoning power which was properly implemented in the proceedings before us.

In each case, a decree shall be entered in the Superior Court affirming the decision of the Housing Appeals Committee.

So ordered.

Comments: 1. The Massachusetts law was slow in having an effect on the construction of lower income housing, since as one commentator noted "a community blindly opposed to subsidized housing can probably still prevent its development. A full administrative and judicial appeals procedure combined with burdensome inspections at all phases of initial construction will discourage even the most persistent developer." Note, The Massachusetts Zoning Appeals Law: First Breach in the Exclusionary Wall, 54 B.U.L. Rev. 37, 69-70 (1974).

More recent information indicates that the law has been helpful. Permits for about 6,900 units of lower income housing have been issued or ordered under the law for 44 jurisdictions. Of these, 4,317 units were appealed to the state board. A total of 1,389 units were occupied or under construction. Altman, Anti Snob Zoning Law Produces Low Income Housing, Practicing Planner, Dec. 1976, at 31. The author notes that the law has been most effective when local boards have granted the comprehensive building permit required by the law without an appeal to the state. Local boards had granted permits for 2,586 housing units in 20 communities. However, a majority of the units constructed so far have been for the elderly and an overwhelming majority have been occupied by residents of the community. The law has not created new housing opportunities for minorities and the urban poor.

For decisions restricting the authority of the state appeals committee see *Town of Chelmsford v. DiBiase,* 345 N.E.2d 373 (Mass. 1976) (committee powerless to displace local acquisition for conservation purposes of tract on which appeal was pending); *Board of Appeals v. Housing Appeals Comm.,* 357 N.E.2d 936 (Mass. App. Ct. 1976) (committee may not attach condition to permit for lower income housing which displaces state building code). *But see Board of Appeals v. Housing Appeals Comm.,* 345 N.E.2d 382 (Mass. 1976) (upholding committee's permit for lower income housing).

    2. The second form of intervention is the creation of a state urban development corporation empowered to develop subsidized housing by overriding, if necessary, local zoning and building codes. If the creation of the Massachusetts Act may be described as the result of "a combination of political altruism and pettiness," the passage of New York's Urban Development Corporation with its power to override local zoning has been described as resulting from the extraordinary efforts of a powerful and popular governor, combined with public remorse over the contemporaneous assassination of Martin Luther King. The Corporation has formidable powers. It may condemn, clear land, relocate displacees, and engage in replanning and reconstructing substandard areas as well as engage in "land use improvement" projects to prevent the spread of blight. The Corporation and its lessees and successors were specifically exempted from municipal permit-granting powers and certificates of occupancy. In addition, the Corporation was initially authorized to override local laws, ordinances, zoning codes, and construction regulations "when, in the discretion of the corporation . . . compliance is not feasible or practicable."

    The power to override local zoning has been the focus of controversy since the establishment of the Corporation, and it has moved cautiously in invoking it over local opposition. It therefore worked primarily on central city sites in its early programs. When it announced, however, in June 1972 that it had acquired options on sites in nine different areas in Westchester County (suburban New York City) to build 100 units of low- and moderate-income housing on each of the sites over the objections of the suburban jurisdictions, opposition crystallized. Within a year the State Legislature enacted an amendment to the Corporation's enabling legislation to permit suburban exclusion of projects undertaken by the Corporation. The law permits any town or incorporated village [categories that rarely include older core cities] to veto Corporation residential projects *even if* the Corporation were complying with preexisting local zoning and building regulations. The operative provision of this repeal legislation reads as follows:

    Notwithstanding any inconsistent provision of this Act or of any general or special law, no plan for a proposed residential project in a town or incorporated village . . . shall be affirmed if, within thirty days after the public hearing held pursuant to subdivision 2 of Section 16 of this Act . . . the local governing body of such town or village submits in writing to the corporation formal objections to the proposed residential project, unless and until such objections are withdrawn. . . .

The law does not define the term "formal objection," nor does it require that any reasons for such objections be given. It should be noted that such objections may be effectively lodged even if the Corporation is complying with local zoning in the particular project.

H. Franklin, D. Falk, & A. Levin, *supra* at 86-87.

3. New York's Urban Development Corporation fell on evil days in the period 1974-76. The story is told in detail in Osborn, New York's Urban Development Corporation: A Study on the Unchecked Power of a Public Authority, 43 Brooklyn L. Rev. 237 (1977). Sumarizing the situation as of mid-1973, Osborn says:

> . . . UDC, if conceptually stripped of the moral obligation of the State, could not be considered a "going concern," and would not have withstood SEC scrutiny of its registration statement, if forced to adhere to the rigid standards demanded of private business corporations. In its dual role as developer/lender, unchecked by customary governmental or market regulatory mechanisms, the Corporation had committed an aggregate amount of over $1.2 billion in bond proceeds to the financing and/or construction of more than 30,000 housing units. Its ever-expanding level of commitments resulted in a more than directly proportional increase in the aggregate amount of deferred projects costs. And given Mr. Logue's unorthodox financial shortcuts — witness the use of $15 million from bond proceeds, as early as 1971, to pay interest on the Corporation's debt — UDC's negative cash flow became more serious with each new undertaking. [Logue was the head of UDC. — Eds.] Moreover, the authority's total failure to achieve any "track record," as reflected by its failure to complete a single project at the time of the May 1973 [bond] offering, foreclosed not only the possibility of any reversal in cash flow patterns, but also prevented its planners from developing a capacity to formulate accurate projections, such as those relating to the adequacy of mortgage loan revenues.

Id. at 293-94.

The ultimate result of UDC's financial difficulties was a default on its obligations in early 1975; creation by the New York legislature of the Project Finance Agency (PFA), which was authorized to sell its own bonds for the "single purpose" of buying, at a premium, mortgages on existing UDC projects; and execution of a Credit and Loan Agreement between PFA, the New York commercial banks, and the New York State Property and Liability Insurance Fund which, *inter alia,* prohibited UDC from engaging in any activity involving the expenditure of funds for any purposes other than those entailed in completing its build-out [of projects already started], subject to expenditure ceilings. Osborn's conclusion is as follows:

> . . . To the extent that the high-level negotiations — conducted on behalf of both UDC, to save its building program from utter collapse, and the State, to salvage its fiscal credibility — may be viewed as a competitive struggle for the economic "upper hand," the institutional lenders won. The financial institutions have emerged from the bail-out settlements with well-secured investments carrying attractive returns. . . . The State, its taxpayers, and, perhaps, UDC's bondholders have not fared so

well. As of October 1975, the Legislature had appropriated for
UDC's use, through PFA, $245,952,000 in the form of
interest-free, repayable grants, which may never, in fact, be repaid.
To that extent, the State's taxpayers, in the most direct sense, will
have paid. Moreover, New York's investment in Governor
Rockefeller's housing program, which was to cost the taxpayers
nothing, is inadequately secured, and the value of its return — a
rash of housing, civic, and commercial facilities — may be found
wanting, when weighed against the resultant loss of confidence in
the State's overall housing program and, ultimately the State's
credit. Through its financial arrangements, which, though
face-saving in certain respects, effectively violate at least the spirit
of New York's constitution, the State has expended and will
remain contingently liable for massive sums of tax dollars for
programs of arguable worth.

Id. at 353-54.

4. Although the New York Urban Development Corporation
was established in 1968, no other states followed this model. The
Corporation's controversial power to override local regulations
may have had something to do with this. Whatever the
explanation, the subsequent curbing of its powers in this
connection may ironically provide a negative model of far greater
attraction to other states.

The states have, however, moved rapidly into housing
finance. . . .

Although none of the state housing finance agencies has the
powers of the New York State Urban Development Corporation
to set aside local land use regulations, many with direct lending
authority have abandoned the traditional lender's passive role of
waiting for development proposals to be presented for funding
consideration. Rather, they view themselves as responsible for the
implementation of the state's housing objectives, and are
accordingly active in seeking out and "packaging" development
opportunities that will achieve these public purposes. However,
the state agencies possess no legal means to overcome determined
local opposition to their proposed developments.

Some combination of the Massachusetts zoning appeals
mechanism and a state housing finance agency with direct lending
authority would seem to be an effective model for a state
inclusionary policy. The zoning appeals mechanism by itself relies
heavily on the willingness of private developers to invoke its
provisions and their decision as to which sites to seek to develop.
In concert with a state housing program, however, a state housing
plan and state involvement in site selection and zoning appeals
might provide the linkage with ongoing planning and achievement
of state or regional housing objectives that would otherwise be
missing.

H. Franklin, D. Falk, & A. Levin, *supra* at 87-88.

5. Another approach to mandating local recognition of housing needs
is provided by the American Law Institute's Model Land Development Code
§ 7-305 (1976). The Code does not allow local approval of a new
employment facility for 100 or more employees unless the local land
development control agency finds that:

(1) adequate and reasonably accessible housing for prospective employees is available within or without the jurisdiction of the local government; or

(2) the local government has adopted a Land Development Plan designed to make available adequate and reasonably accessible housing within a reasonable time; or

(3) a State Land Development Plan shows that the proposed location is a desirable location for the proposed employment source.

Note that the ALI Code does not specifically require housing for lower income employees, although the Code commentary does indicate that housing made available must be reasonably priced for sale or rent. Note also that the Code allows the municipality to satisfy its obligation for employee housing by relying on housing available in another community. Would this provision be acceptable under *Mount Laurel?*

An attempt to develop a measure for correcting exclusionary zoning that relies on the relationship between housing and workplace can be found in E. Bergman, Eliminating Exclusionary Zoning (1974). Bergman develops and applies a performance standard for exclusionary zoning that requires a one-to-one match between job opportunities and available housing. *See id.* ch. 2.

6. An attempt to mandate local consideration of lower income housing needs is also contained in the federal Housing and Community Development Act of 1974. Communities applying for community development assistance under that Act must prepare a Housing Assistance Plan indicating lower income housing needs and showing general locations for lower income housing projects. 42 U.S.C. § 5304(a)(4) (Supp. 1977). This requirement, like the ALI code provision, is job-linked. The legislative history to the statute indicates that the Housing Assistance Plan was mandated in order to require localities to provide housing for those who might be expected to find employment in the community.

The Housing Assistance Plan requirement has proved difficult to administer, but the federal Department of Housing and Urban Development, which administers the community development program, is increasingly relying on regional planning for housing to assist localities in meeting their lower income housing obligations. Regional planning for lower income housing needs is discussed *infra* p. 1217. The success of these and related efforts to correct suburban exclusionary zoning problems will depend, ultimately, on political acceptance of corrective measures at the state and local level. For a thorough review of exclusionary zoning problems that takes a pessimistic view of the political possibilities for corrective reform see M. Danielson, The Politics of Exclusion (1976).

c. Local Flexible Zoning Techniques

It is possible, of course, for a municipal governing body simply to "pre-zone" substantial areas for "minimum cost" housing. This is apparently what the New Jersey courts are now requiring "developing communities" to do. But large scale "pre-zoning" may well push up the cost of land "pre-zoned" *(e.g.)* for high density multifamily dwellings to the the point where housing for low and/or moderate income families cannot be constructed. On the other hand, if a municipal governing body adopts a "wait and see" policy and rezones specific sites for *(e.g.)* high density multifamily dwellings in response to applications from land developers, it will run the risk that site-specific rezonings will be held, if challenged by neighboring landowners, to be illegal "spot zoning." One possible way out of the dilemma is to utilize the "bonus" or "incentive" zoning technique, which has already been considered in connection with our general treatment of "density" and "bulk" controls, *supra* Part C, Section 7 of this chapter.

Through "bonus" or "incentive" zoning a community offers economic incentives to developers to develop certain desired types of projects or to include certain amenities within projects in exchange for relaxation of various zoning restrictions. "Bonus" or "incentive" zoning has been most frequently used in downtown urban areas in order to encourage the construction of attractive buildings with facilities, such as plazas and arcades, that the public may use and enjoy. But there is no reason why this zoning technique cannot be used to encourage development of "least-cost" housing in suburban areas. Indeed, as you will recall, the New Jersey Supreme Court in *Oakwood at Madison* said that "provision by zoning for density bonuses keyed to quantitative or bulk concessions by the builder (*e.g.,* added bedrooms) is both valid and mandatory where necessary to achieve sufficient suitable least-cost housing," although the court was "not prepared presently to pass upon the validity of zoning for bonuses keyed to rental or sale price concessions." (371 A.2d at 1225.)

> There are not many instances where incentive zoning has been adopted as a procedure for encouraging new housing for low and moderate income families outside of a planned unit development. A planning guideline adopted in Arlington County, Virginia, permits the County Board of Supervisors to increase the height of proposed apartment buildings by up to six stories, or to increase densities by up to 10%, if the development proposal provides that at at least 10% of the dwelling units will be for moderate income families (before application of the incentives) and includes guarantees that these units will remain available for moderate income families. One interesting feature of the guideline is that the developer may provide the moderate income units at some site other than that to which the incentives are applied. ... Subsequent to adoption of the guidelines, the county board agreed to accept cash payments from developers in the amount of $4,500 per moderate income unit in lieu of construction of the units. The cash

payments are added to the county's rent supplement fund, which is used to provide rent and tax relief for the elderly, handicapped or needy working families with children.

The complex legal issues raised by the use of incentive zoning have not been resolved because there has been little litigation involving its use. However, an analogous ordinance enacted by the Town of Bellingham, Massachusetts, was challenged and upheld. [*Cameron v. Zoning Agent of Bellingham*, 260 N.E.2d 143 (Mass. 1970). — Eds.] Although the zoning ordinance in Bellingham established the usual multifamily districts containing the usual requirements on frontage, side and rear yards, open space, and building heights, it also provided that public housing built on land owned by the local housing authority was not subject to any of the restrictions. Moreover, public housing could also be built as of right on any land owned by the local housing authority in any zoning district other than industrial. This ordinance differs from an incentive ordinance for lower income housing in that the benefits were offered only to a public agency and the development of public housing is subject to federally imposed requirements and limitations on building and site design similar to those included in local zoning ordinances. Nevertheless, the fact that the Massachusetts Supreme Judicial Court upheld the Bellingham ordinance suggests that an ordinance relaxing zoning requirements to encourage privately developed housing for lower income families pursuant to a community inclusionary program would also be upheld.

Incentive zoning as a technique for implementing an inclusionary program merits more consideration by communities than it has heretofore received. . . . With a suitably framed incentive zoning provision, a community could increase the economic return to developers to induce their participation in the leased housing program. On the other hand, there is also a risk involved. If the subsidized housing project is not to be stigmatized as being inferior to market-rate projects in structure, design and amenities, the incentive features should be carefully framed to avoid encouraging subsidized housing projects that are markedly more dense and less attractive than other multifamily developments in the surrounding area. The undesired stigmatization could be avoided if incentive bonuses are offered for projects of which only 20% of the units are to be subsidized. . . .

H. Franklin, D. Falk, & A. Levin, *supra* at 122-24 (1975).

Another possible way out of the dilemma posed above is to employ one or more of the "flexible" zoning techniques discussed in more detail in subsequent portions of this chapter and in the next chapter.

These techniques include the "variance," the "special exception" or "special use permit," the "contract" or "conditional" rezoning amendment, the "floating zone" amendment, and the "planned unit development."

E. THE ZONING PROCESS: EUCLIDEAN ZONING GIVES WAY TO FLEXIBLE ZONING

1. The Standard State Zoning Enabling Act's Provisions for Change

In the 1920's and 1930's, control of land use by zoning was generally viewed as a relatively static process, although the Standard State Zoning Enabling Act and the early statutes modeled on it did contain provisions for change in the zoning regulations, as indicated in the following excerpt.

D. MANDELKER, DELEGATION OF POWER AND FUNCTION IN ZONING ADMINISTRATION, 1963 Wash. U.L.Q. 60, 61-63

1. ADMINISTRATIVE STRUCTURE AND ADMINISTRATIVE DISCRETION IN ZONING

As elsewhere in public administration, the basic problem in zoning is to achieve as clear a differentiation as possible between policy-making and policy-application. On this score the Standard State Zoning Enabling Act, on which a majority of the state statutes are modeled, failed to make tenable distinctions. Policy-making was confided to the governing body of the locality, which was given the authority to adopt the zoning ordinance. Administration was given to the zoning administrator, often the building inspector, who has the power to issue zoning permits. But ambiguity comes in the introduction of two agencies, the plan commission and the board of adjustment, known also as the board of zoning appeals. Both the commission and the board exercise functions that are partly legislative and partly administrative.

The plan commission is to advise on the enactment and amendment of the original ordinance. In theory, zoning amendments are to be made in response to substantial changes in environmental conditions or in other instances in which a policy change is indicated. Instead, amendments have often been employed to take care of limited changes in use, usually confined to one lot, a technique that has disapprovingly been called "spot zoning." Spot zoning for one parcel, vigorously opposed by adjacent neighbors, takes on adversary characteristics that give it a distinctly adjudicative cast.

The agency originally intended to provide a safety valve from the zoning ordinance is the board of adjustment. This board was authorized to grant both variances and [special] exceptions. . . . The variance is an administratively-authorized departure from the terms of the zoning ordinance, granted in cases of unique and individual hardship, in which a strict application of the terms of the ordinance would be unconstitutional. The grant of the variance is meant to avoid an unfavorable holding on constitutionality.

By way of contrast, an exception is a use permitted by the ordinance in a district in which it is not necessarily incompatible, but where it might cause harm if not watched. Exceptions are authorized under conditions which will insure their compatibility with surrounding uses. Typically, a use which is the subject of a special exception demands a large amount of land, may be public or semi-public in character and might often be noxious or offensive. Not all of these characteristics will apply to every excepted use, however. Hospitals in residential districts are one example, because of the extensive area they occupy, and because of potential traffic and other problems which may affect a residential neighborhood. A filling station in a light commercial district is another example because of its potentially noxious effects.

a. The Zoning Variance

PURITAN-GREENFIELD IMPROVEMENT ASSOCIATION v. LEO

Court of Appeals of Michigan
7 Mich. App. 659, 153 N.W.2d 162 (1967)

LEVIN, Judge. Defendant-appellant John L. Leo claims the circuit judge erred in setting aside a use variance granted by the Detroit Board of Zoning Appeals.

Leo owns a one-story, one-family dwelling at the northwest corner of Puritan avenue and Prest avenue, located in the northwest section of Detroit in an R-1 (single family residence) zoning district. On application and after hearing, the board granted Leo a variance to permit the use of the property as a dental and medical clinic (an RM-4 use) and to use the side yard for off-street parking on certain conditions.

The order of the board states that immediately to the west of the westerly boundary of Leo's property is a gasoline service station (at the corner of Puritan and Greenfield); that there was testimony Leo had not received any offers from residence-use buyers during the period of over a year the property had been listed and offered for sale; and, in the event a variance was granted, it was intended to preserve the present exterior of the building without significant alteration so that it would continue to appear to be a one-family dwelling.

The appeal board's dominant finding was:

"That the board found unnecessary hardship and practical difficulty because of the heavy traffic and the closeness to the business section immediately to the west."

The board also found that the proposed use would not alter the essential character of the neighborhood, would not be injurious to the contiguous property, would not be detrimental to the surrounding neighborhood, and would not depreciate property values.

Plaintiff-appellee, Puritan-Greenfield Improvement Association, filed a complaint with the circuit court which was treated by the court as one for superintending control. The matter was heard by the circuit judge on the record made before the board. The circuit judge reversed the decision of the board, stating *inter alia* that it had not been shown the land could not yield a reasonable return or be put to a proper economic use if used only for a purpose allowed by existing zoning and that such showing of hardship as had been made was of "self-created" hardship attributable to the character of the structure thereon.

The applicable enabling act provides for a board of zoning appeals authorized to grant a variance upon a showing of practical difficulties or unnecessary hardship. The Detroit ordinance requires evidence of special conditions and unnecessary hardship or practical difficulties.

The enabling act specifies neither a particular procedure for obtaining review of board of zoning appeals' action nor the scope of review. Review is obtained by means of an application for superintending control . . . which replaces certiorari. The minimum constitutional standard establishes the scope of review. The circuit judge and we are required by the Michigan constitution to determine whether the findings of the board and its order are authorized by law and whether they are supported by competent, material, and substantial evidence on the whole record. Const. 1963, art. 6, § 28.

Although there has been a great deal of judicial effort expended in Michigan in considering challenges to the reasonableness or constitutionality of zoning as applied to individual properties, we find no Michigan appellate decisions construing the words "unnecessary hardship or practical difficulties."

The first modern zoning regulations were adopted by the city of New York and phrase "practical difficulties or unnecessary hardship" was fashioned as the applicable standard to guide New York's board of appeals in considering applications for variances. A comparison of the relevant language of the applicable Michigan enabling act with that of the original New York city legislation shows that the Michigan provision authorizing the vesting in a board of zoning appeals the authority to grant variances parallels the corresponding New York city provision.

It appears that most State enabling acts, and ordinances based thereon, use "unnecessary hardship" as the governing standard. In those States (like Michigan and New York) where the applicable standard is "unnecessary hardship *or* practical difficulties," the phrase "practical difficulties" had been regarded as applicable only when an area or a dimension variance is sought, and in determining whether a use variance will be granted the decisive words are "unnecessary hardship." In the light of this history, we have turned for guidance to decisions of other States applying the "unnecessary hardship" standard.

A text writer, Rathkopf, states that courts have held, variously, that a property owner seeking a variance on the ground of "unnecessary hardship" must show credible proof that the property will not yield a reasonable return if used only for a purpose allowed by the ordinance or must establish that the zoning gives rise to hardship amounting to virtual confiscation or the disadvantage must be so great as to deprive the owner of all reasonable use of the property. He concedes that the showing required "is substantially equivalent to that which would warrant a court in declaring the ordinance confiscatory, unreasonable, and unconstitutional in its application to the property involved." 2 Rathkopf, The Law of Zoning and Planning, p. 45-14.

These principles also find expression in the frequently stated generalizations that variances should be sparingly granted, that it is not sufficient to show that the property would be worth more or could be more profitably employed if the restrictions were varied to permit another use, and that the board of appeals, being without legislative power, may not in the guise of a variance amend the zoning ordinance or disregard its provisions.

The judicial attitudes so expressed could well have been influenced by the early history of the boards of zoning appeal and the need to declare more precise standards than the somewhat nebulous "unnecessary hardship." When zoning was in its infancy it was thought by some that without a board of zoning appeals the individual declarations of zoning ordinance invalidity would be so numerous it would become necessary to declare the legislation void as a whole and, thus, "the chief value of the board of appeals in zoning is in protecting the ordinance from attacks upon its constitutionality." That view of the purpose of the board of zoning appeals has been said to require a standard related to the reasonableness of the zoning:

"The hardship contemplated in this legislation has constitutional overtones, and it is the purpose of the variance to immunize zoning legislation against attack on the ground that it may in some instances operate to effect a taking of property without just compensation." *R.N.R. Associates v. City of Providence Zoning Board of Review* (1965), R.I., 210 A.2d 653, 654.

It has been said that the function of a board of zoning appeals is to protect the community against usable land remaining idle and it is that purpose which gives definition to "unnecessary hardship."

"Since the main purpose of allowing variances is to prevent land from being rendered useless, 'unnecessary hardship' can best be defined as a situation where in the absence of a variance no feasible use can be made of the land." 74 Harv. Law Rev. p. 1401; quoted in *State ex rel. Markdale Corporation v. Milwaukee Board of Appeals* (1965), 27 Wis.2d 154, 133 N.W.2d 795, 799.

Whatever the rationale may be, it has been held that a variance should not be granted until it appears the property cannot be put reasonably to a conforming use...; or the application of the ordinance is so unreasonable as to constitute an arbitrary and capricious interference with the basic right of private property...; or that the property cannot be used for a conforming purpose (... *Searles v. Darling* [1951], 46 Del. 263, 83 A.2d 96, 100).

"An unnecessary hardship exists when all the relevant factors taken together convince that the plight of the location concerned is unique in that it cannot be put to a conforming use because of the limitations imposed upon the property by reason of it [sic] classification in a specific zone." *Peterson v. Vasak, supra,* 76 N.W.2d at p. 426.

The authors of a number of scholarly studies appear to agree that an applicant desiring a variance must show

"(a) that if he complies with the provisions of the ordinance, he can secure no reasonable return from, or make no reasonable use of, his property; (b) that the hardship results from the application of the ordinance to his property; (c) that the hardship of which he complains is suffered by his property directly, and not merely by others; (d) that the hardship is not the result of his own actions; and (e) that the hardship is peculiar to the property of the applicant." Green, The Power of the Zoning Board of Adjustment to Grant Variances from the Zoning Ordinance (1951), 29 N.C. Law Rev. 245, 249.

The New York Court of Appeals has stated:

"Before the Board may exercise its discretion and grant a [use] variance upon the ground of unnecessary hardship, the record must show that (1) the land in question cannot yield a reasonable return if used only for a purpose allowed in that zone; (2) that the plight of the owner is due to unique circumstances and not to the general conditions in the neighborhood which may reflect the unreasonableness of the zoning ordinance itself; and (3) that the use to be authorized by the variance will not alter the essential character of the locality." *Otto v. Steinhilber* (1939), 282 N.Y. 71, 24 N.E.2d 851.

The *Otto* definition has been adopted by other courts....

We find overwhelming support for the proposition — expressed in *Otto* — that the hardship must be unique or peculiar to the property for which the variance is sought.

     . . . .

Under these definitions even if the land cannot yield a reasonable return if used only for a purpose permitted by existing zoning, a use variance may not be granted unless the landowner's plight is due to unique circumstances and not to general conditions in the neighborhood that may reflect the unreasonableness of the zoning.

This limitation on the board's powers is related to the third limitation expressed in *Otto* — that a use authorized by a variance shall not alter the essential character of the locality. In this connection we note that the Detroit ordinance prohibits a variance that would be contrary to the public interest or inconsistent with the spirit of the ordinance. . . .

"If it [the hardship] affects a whole area, then his remedy lies in seeking an amendment to the zoning ordinance. This is true even where the applicant's property is situated in an area where none of the properties can be put to any reasonable beneficial use owing to zoning restrictions. It is not for the board in these circumstances to bestow liberties upon one single member of this group of property holders. The legislature must be the body to make decisions of this sort even in cases where the most severe hardship can be shown." Pooley, Planning Zoning in the United States, op. cit. at p. 59.

The Rhode Island Supreme Court has stated that once the right to a variance becomes established the only matter remaining is the scope and character of the relief to be granted, which must be effectuated in a manner consistent with the public interest . . . ; but if a considerable number of property owners are similarly affected, it might well appear contrary to the spirit of the ordinance to grant relief to one while denying it to another, and in such a case it has been said that relief should be withheld until it can be decreed by the governing body or, if necessary, by the courts.

While we have discussed the foregoing statements that the hardship must be unique and that there are limitations on a zoning appeal board's power to frame a rer :dy when the hardship is shared with others — such statements being so inextricably a part of judicial, text and scholarly definitions of "unnecessary hardship" that the construction of that term could not accurately be discussed without reference to those statements — we do not here express our views thereon, as it is not necessary to do so in order to decide this case. We limit our holding to that expressed in the next paragraph.

Our review of the authorities leads us to hold that a use variance should not be granted unless the board of zoning appeals can find on the basis of substantial evidence that the property cannot reasonably be used in a manner consistent with existing zoning. In *Otto* the New York Court of Appeals stated that one seeking a variance must show that the land in question cannot yield a *reasonable return* if used only for a purpose allowed in the relevant zoning district. It will be noted that we have used the word "property" (i.e., including improvements) rather than "land", reserving to a later day the decision whether we wish to adopt that aspect of the *Otto* definition. It will also be noted that our holding speaks in terms of "reasonable use" rather than "reasonable return." Whether property usable in trade or business or held for the production of income can reasonably be used for a purpose consistent with existing zoning will, no doubt, ordinarily turn on whether a reasonable return can be derived from the property as then zoned. While any property, including a single family residence, may be made to produce income if a tenant can be found therefor, it would in our opinion be unrealistic as to all properties (without regard to their varying utility) to resolve the question solely on the basis of the return that can be derived from the property.

In the case of Leo's property, we perceive the question to be whether the property can continue reasonably to be used as a single family residence. The appeal board made no determination in that regard, resting its finding of unnecessary hardship solely on the "heavy traffic and the closeness to the business section immediately to the west."

Leo's property has been used for some time as a single family residence. While the board found there was "testimony" that Leo had not received any offers from residence-use buyers during the period of over a year the property had been listed and offered for sale, the asking price for the house and adjoining lot was $38,500 in a neighborhood where, according to the only record evidence, houses generally sell for $20,000 to $25,000. There was no evidence of efforts to sell the property at any price lower than $38,500; indeed, there was no testimony at all as to the extent of the sales effort or the income that could be derived from the property as zoned. See *Crossroads Recreation, Inc. v. Broz* (1958), 4 N.Y.2d 39, 44, 172 N.Y.S.2d 129, 132, 149 N.E.2d 65; *Forrest v. Evershed* (1959), 7 N.Y.2d 256, 196 N.Y.S.2d 958, 164 N.E.2d 841; *compare Jones v. DeVries*, 326 Mich. 126, 137, 40 N.W.2d 317, et seq. applying the Grand Rapids ordinance.

Testimony that the house and lot could not be sold for $38,500 in a neighborhhod where houses generally sell for substantially less than that amount does not, in our opinion, constitute any evidence that the property could not continue reasonably to be used as a single family residence. . . .

Thus there was not only a failure to find that the property could not reasonably be used in a manner consistent with existing zoning, but, as we read the record, there was no evidence upon which such a finding could have been based. In this connection, it should be remembered that the fact that the property would be worth more if it could be used as a doctor's clinic and that the corner of Puritan and Prest has disadvantages as a place of residence does not authorize the granting of a variance. Heavy traffic is all too typical of innumerable admittedly residential streets. Adjacency to gasoline stations or other commercial development is characteristic of the end of a business or commercial district and the commencement of a residential district. "A district has to end somewhere." *Real Properties, Inc. v. Board of Appeal of Boston* (1946), 319 Mass. 180, 65 N.E.2d 199, 201.

It can readily be seen that unless the power of the board of zoning appeals to grant a use variance is defined by objective standards, the appeal board could [and we do not in any sense mean to suggest this would be deliberate] rezone an entire neighborhood — a lot or two lots at a time. The variance granted in response to one "hardship" may well beget or validate another claim of hardship and justify still another variance. If it is a hardship to be next to a gasoline station, it could be a hardship to be across from one, to be behind one, or diagonally across from one. If heavy traffic is a valid basis, variances might become the rule rather than the sparingly granted exception.

We do not wish to be understood as challenging the judgment of the board of zoning appeals. A doctor's office with the appearance of a single family residence on a busy street which already has other commercial uses may very well be a logical, sensible and unobjectionable use. However the question before us is not whether the board of zoning appeals has acted reasonably, but whether on the proofs and findings the board could grant a variance on the ground of unnecessary hardship. We have concluded that neither the proofs nor the findings justified the variance granted.

We have given careful consideration to the considerable number of cases we found where the result was based on the reviewing court's conclusion that the appeal board had not abused the discretion confided to it. If there is substantial evidence to support the necessary findings, such a decision is, indeed, the correct one. However, there must be such evidence and such findings.

We have considered and rejected appellee's contention that a board of zoning appeals may not grant a use variance. We have also considered appellee's contention that the board's action should be reversed because the hardship alleged by Leo was "self-created." However, the hardship found by the board in this case could not be said to have been self-created — Leo neither created the traffic conditions on Puritan nor the gasoline station immediately to the west of his property.

Affirmed. Costs to appellee.

LESINSKI, C. J., and BURNS, J., concurred.

Comments: 1. The 1917 New York General City Zoning Enabling Act provided merely that a zoning board of appeals should be created with power to "vary the application of zoning regulations in harmony with their general purpose and intent and in accordance with the general or specific rules contained therein." Section 7 of the Standard State Zoning Enabling Act was more specific; it authorized the zoning board of adjustment to:

> [A]uthorize upon appeal in specific cases such variance from the terms of the ordinance as will not be contrary to the public interest, where, owing to special conditions, a literal enforcement of the provisions of the ordinance will result in unnecessary hardship, and so that the spirit of the ordinance shall be observed and substantial justice done.

The dual standard of "practical difficulties or unnecessary hardship" seems to have originated in a 1920 amendment to the General City Law, which provided:

> Where there are practical difficulties in the way of carrying out the strict letter of such ordinance, the board of appeals shall have the power to vary or modify the application of any of the regulations or provisions of such ordinance relating to the use, construction or alteration of buildings or structures, or the use of land, so that the spirit of the ordinance shall be observed, public safety and welfare secured and substantial justice done.

New York Town Law § 267(5) (McKinney Supp. 1978) and New York Village Law § 7-712(2)(c) (McKinney 1973) contain language identical to that set out above. In New York General City Law § 81(4) (McKinney Supp. 1978) the language set out above is slightly altered; instead of "use, construction or alteration of buildings or structures," the statute now says, "use, construction, structural changes in, equipment or alteration of buildings or structures."

2. In the spirit of the principal case, the same court reversed a variance for a high-rise apartment granted by the Detroit board of zoning appeals. *Farah v. Sachs,* 157 N.W.2d 9 (Mich. App. 1968). Strictly speaking, the Farah variance may have been a dimensional rather than a use variance, since apartments up to 50 feet in height were permitted by the applicable zoning restriction. The variance was granted in part because there was a showing of need for apartments in the area, but the court observed that this evidence would go toward a showing of consistency with the public interest, but not toward a showing of hardship. But *cf. Kessler-Allisonville Civic League, Inc. v. Marion County Bd. of Zoning Appeals,* 209 N.E.2d 43 (Ind. App. 1965), affirming a variance for apartments.

3. *Otto v. Steinhilber,* cited and quoted in the principal case, is undoubtedly the leading case on standards for granting zoning variances. In *Steinhilber* the court distinguished situations where a variance should be granted from those where zoning regulations as applied to a substantial area should be held invalid, as follows:

The object of a variance granted by the Board of Appeals in favor of property owners suffering unnecessary hardship in the operation of a zoning law, is to afford relief to an individual property owner laboring under restrictions to which no valid general objection may be made. Where the property owner is unable reasonably to use his land because of zoning restrictions, the fault may lie in the fact that the particular zoning restriction is unreasonable in its application to a certain locality or the oppressive result may be caused by conditions peculiar to a particular piece of land. In the former situation, the relief is by way of direct attack upon the terms of the ordinance. . . . In order to prevent the oppressive operation of the zoning law in particular instances, when the zoning restrictions are otherwise generally reasonable, the zoning laws usually create a safety valve under the control of a Board of Appeals, which may relieve against "unnecessary hardship" in particular instances.

On this point, see also the *Arverne Bay* case, reprinted *supra* p. 236, and Comments 1 and 3 following that case. Most courts have followed the New York decisions in refusing to approve a variance if it appears that the variance is based on conditions general to the neighborhood. *E.g., Priest v. Griffin,* 222 So.2d 353 (Ala. 1969); *Tavares v. Zoning Bd. of Review,* 325 A.2d 883 (R.I. 1967). Of course, where "unnecessary hardship" is a result of conditions general to the neighborhood, it would be proper for the local governing body to amend the ordinance, either on its own initiative or on the request of landowners in the neighborhood.

Although the "unique circumstances" test laid down in *Steinhilber* has generally been accepted by courts in other states, it may well have been repudiated in the state of its origin. In *Jayne Estates, Inc. v. Raynor,* 239 N.E.2d 713 (N.Y. 1968), the court stated (per Keating, J.) that unique hardship arose from the unusual history of negotiations for the development of the land in question, not from general conditions in the area, and then went on to say:

In any case, as a general rule, where the landowner has made the requisite showing of financial hardship and compatibility of his proposed use with the existing land use pattern it would seem preferable to grant the variance. To deny the variance solely on the ground that "unique circumstances" are not shown leaves open the possibility of a successful assault on the zoning ordinance as being confiscatory. . . .

Consequently, the net effect of the denial of the variance might be more detrimental to the community's land use plan because the old less restrictive ordinance [prior to a restrictive amendment] may authorize a far greater range of uses, many of which might be completely unacceptable. In contrast, a variance, wisely used, provides local zoning officials with an excellent means by which they can accommodate a conflict between the requirements of a generally sound zoning ordinance and the needs of a particular situation.

Id. at 717-18. *Sed quaere* whether the New York courts would grant a variance where the landowner has made the requisite showing of financial hardship and also has proved "unique circumstances," but has failed to prove "compatibility of his proposed use with the existing land use pattern." The present status of the *Jayne Estates* dictum in New York is unclear. In *Williams v. Town of Oyster Bay,* 295 N.E.2d 788 (N.Y. 1973), the court quoted the first paragraph from *Jayne Estates* set out above, and then said: "[t]his indicates that only 'financial hardship' — *i.e.,* absence of a 'reasonable return' — and 'compatibility . . . with the existing land pattern' are standards for determining . . . the right to a variance." *Id.* at 790, n. 1 (dictum). Compare *Dauernheim, Inc. v. Town of Hempstead,* 310 N.E.2d 516, 516 (N.Y. 1974), where the court quoted the *Steinhilber* language laying down the threefold test for "hardship" variances and then said, "but see *Williams v. Town of Oyster Bay.*"

The "unique circumstances" requirement is codified in Cal. Gov. Code § 65906 (Deering Supp. 1977):

> Variances from the terms of the zoning ordinance shall be granted only when, because of special circumstances applicable to the property, including size, shape, topography, location or surroundings, the strict application of the zoning ordinance deprives such property of privileges enjoyed by other property in the vicinity and under identical zoning classification.

Proper application of the uniqueness rule would seem to preclude variances based on conditions general to the neighborhood, as the principal case suggests. *See also Priest v. Griffin,* 222 So.2d 353 (Ala. 1969); *Banks v. City of Bethany,* 541 P.2d 178 (Okla. 1975). *Compare Pfile v. Zoning Bd. of Adjustment,* 298 A.2d 598 (Pa. Commw. Ct. 1972).

4. What is the significance of the distinction drawn by Judge Levin, in the principal case, between proof that the land in question "cannot yield a *reasonable return* if used only for a purpose allowed in the relevant zoning district" and proof that no *reasonable use* of the property can be made unless a variance is granted? This distinction is rarely made in the variance cases from other states, and courts seem to use the two formulas interchangeably. Typical of judicial statements with respect to the "unnecessary hardship" test is the following language from *MacLean v. Zoning Bd. of Adjustment,* 185 A.2d 533 (Pa. 1962), where the court affirmed the board's refusal to grant a variance to permit construction of a gasoline service station in a residential area:

> [T]he real owner of this property, testified that the "best use" of this property would be as a gasoline service station, [so] it is obvious that his definition of "best use" is that use which would be most productive of economic profit. An examination of this record clearly shows that the request for a variance is not based upon any lack of feasibility of the use of this property for residential purposes but rather upon the expectation that the property will be productive of greater financial gain if used as a gasoline service station. This is the type of "economic hardship" which time and again we have stated does not constitute an "unnecessary hardship" sufficient to justify the grant of a variance.

Id. at 536. The point of view of the Pennsylvania court was reaffirmed in a carefully reasoned opinion in *Lovely v. Zoning Bd. of Appeals,* 259 A.2d

666 (Me. 1969). *See also Ivancovich v. City of Tucson Bd. of Adjustment,* 529 P.2d 242 (Ariz. App. 1975).

Some state zoning enabling acts are much more specific than the Standard Act with regard to standards for granting "use" variances. Mass. Gen. Laws Ann. tit. VII, ch. 40A, § 15, empowers the zoning board of appeals:

> To authorize upon appeal, or upon petition in cases where a particular use is sought for which no permit is required, with respect to a particular parcel of land or to an existing building thereon a variance from the terms of the applicable zoning ordinance or by-law where, owing to conditions especially affecting such parcel or such building but not affecting generally the zoning district in which it is located, a literal enforcement of the provisions of the ordinance or by-law would involve substantial hardship, financial or otherwise to the appellant, and where desirable relief may be granted without substantial detriment to the public good and without nullifying or substantially derogating from the intent or purpose of such ordinance or by-law, but not otherwise.
>
> In exercising the powers . . . above, the board may impose limitations both of time and of use, and a continuation of the use permitted may be conditioned upon compliance with regulations to be made and amended from time to time thereafter.

5. Since the statutory provision for variances in the Standard State Zoning Enabling Act and most of the zoning enabling acts now in force is a direct authorization to grant variances, the power given to local boards of appeals or adjustment cannot be changed by a local zoning ordinance, which proceeds from a lower level of government. *E.g., Nelson v. Donaldson,* 50 So.2d 244 (Ala. 1951); *Mello v. Board of Review,* 177 A.2d 533, 535 (R.I. 1962). Yet local zoning ordinances often purport to impose more specific standards for granting variances than those embodied in the enabling statute. In many cases, of course, these more specific standards merely summarize judicial decisions interpreting the (usually) vague standards set out in the zoning enabling acts. Although one would suppose that courts would approve ordinance provisions that, in effect, interpret the enabling act in terms compatible with the prevailing tone of the applicable case law, there is little support for this in the cases. Indeed, an ordinance provision that any variance granted must be the minimum variance necessary to provide the landowner with a reasonable return on his investment has been held invalid on the ground that this is an additional standard not set out in the enabling act. *See Celentano, Inc. v. Board of Zoning Appeals,* 184 A.2d 49 (Conn. 1962); *Coderre v. Zoning Bd. of Review,* 230 A.2d 247 (R.I. 1967).

6. If the landowner's hardship is "self-inflicted," courts will set aside any variance granted on the ground of hardship. Hardship is clearly "self-inflicted" if a landowner or developer proceeds to build in willful or accidental violation of the zoning ordinance and the municipal authorities insist that the violation be corrected. Hardship is also "self-inflicted" when it is "manufactured" — *e.g.,* where the landowner or developer has torn down a residential structure and then claims that his property cannot profitably be put to residential use, or where he has deliberately carved a triangular lot out of a larger tract and then claims that development for residential use is not feasible. Similarly, when a developer pays a premium price for land, and then seeks a variance on the ground of financial hardship, the hardship has been held to be simply a case of "self-inflicted" hardship. *Josephson v. Autry,* 96 So.2d 784 (Fla. 1957). In New York and Pennsylvania, however, the courts have repeatedly held that the purchase of property with knowledge of the zoning restrictions gives rise to "self-inflicted" hardship even if, arguably, the vendor could have established sufficient hardship to justify a variance. The leading case is *Thomas v. Board of Standards & Appeals,* 33 N.Y.S.2d 219 (N.Y. App. Div. 1942), *rev'd on other grounds,* 48 N.E.2d 284 (N.Y. 1943). In the *Thomas* case, the existing improvements (a garage and an auto laundry), which made the use of the land unprofitable, had been erected solely to lay the basis for a hardship variance to permit construction of a filling station on the land; thus it was a clear case of "manufactured" hardship, and a variance should not have been granted. But *Thomas* has been cited ever since in New York for the proposition that, if land is purchased with notice of the zoning restrictions, any hardship is "self-inflicted." Such a broad rule is difficult to justify, since it results in a requirement thay any landowner who has a legitimate claim to a hardship variance must himself obtain the variance before selling his property, even though he has no intention of developing the property himself; otherwise, the purchaser will be barred from obtaining a variance and, presumably, must attempt to have the zoning restrictions declared invalid as applied to his property if no reasonable return on a conforming use is possible.

The broad New York and Pennsylvania rules on "self-inflicted" hardship have been followed in several other states, including California, Florida and Maryland. In New Jersey, however, the courts have adopted a different attitude. Most of the New Jersey cases reject the rule that purchase of land with knowledge of zoning restrictions will preclude a finding of hardship, and hold that purchasing with knowledge of zoning restrictions is simply one element that the board of adjustment may properly consider on the issue of hardship. The Delaware and Rhode Island courts have followed New Jersey on this point. Only the Alabama court has held that the fact of purchase with knowledge of zoning restrictions is completely irrelevant. *Arant v. Board of Adjustment,* 126 So.2d 100 (Ala. 1960).

For a good brief discussion of the "self-inflicted" hardship problem, see 5 N. Williams, American Land Planning Law §§ 146.01-146.07 (1975, Supp. 1977). *See also* Note, The Ad Hominem Element in the Treatment of Zoning Problems, 109 U. Pa. L. Rev. 992 (1961).

7. Because of lack of expertise, political influence, and — in some of the larger cities — far too heavy a case load, many zoning boards of adjustment (or appeals) have long shown a regrettable tendency to ignore the standards prescribed by statute and by judicial decision for the granting of variances. Two substantial empirical studies of the variance procedure both concluded that the boards in the communities under study did not, in a majority of cases, insist that the statutory and case law standards for variances be satisfied. See Dukeminier & Stapleton, The Zoning Board of Adjustment: A Case Study in Misrule, 50 Ky. L. J. 273 (1962); Comment, 50 Cal. L. Rev. 101 (1962).

8. So-called "use" variances have been recognized as valid in the great majority of states, and the litigated cases on variances usually involve "use" variances. In a few states, however, the courts have refused to recognize the validity of "use" variances on the ground that to grant a variance that changes the uses permitted in a zoning district is, in substance, to amend the zoning ordinance, and thus to usurp the legislative power of the local governing body. *Josephson v. Autry,* 96 So.2d 784 (Fla. 1957); *Bray v. Beyer,* 166 S.W.2d 290 (Ky. 1942); *Leah v. Board of Adjustment,* 37 S.E.2d 128 (N.C. 1946); *State ex rel. Nigro v. Kansas City,* 27 S.W.2d 1030 (Mo. 1930); *State ex rel. Sheridan v. Hudson,* 400 S.W.2d 425 (Mo. App. 1966); *Texas Consol. Theatres v. Pittillo,* 204 S.W.2d 396 (Tex. Civ. App. 1947). *See also Antrim v. Holht,* 108 N.E.2d 197 (Ind. App. 1952); *Livingston v. Peterson,* 228 N.W. 816 (N.D. 1930). A recent revision of the California zoning enabling act has also prohibited the granting of "use" variances: "[a] variance shall not be granted for a parcel of property which authorizes a use or activity which is not otherwise expressly authorized by the zone regulation governing the parcel of property." Cal. Gov't Code § 65906 (Deering Supp. 1977).

Despite the almost universal criticism of the tendency of zoning boards of adjustment (or appeals) to disregard the statutory and case law standards for granting "use" variances, the American Law Institute's Model Land Development Code §§ 2-202 and 2-204 (1976) makes provision for both "use" and "area or dimension" variances, although the term "special development permit" rather than "variance" is used in the Model Code.

9. Most courts have held that the zoning board of adjustment (or appeals) has the power to attach appropriate conditions to the grant of any variance, although the Standard State Zoning Enabling Act and enabling statutes modeled on it do not expressly confer such power. It is arguable that the power to impose conditions can be implied from the final phrase in the Standard Act's authorization for the granting of variances — "so that the spirit of the ordinance shall be observed and substantial justice be done." Municipal zoning ordinances often expressly authorize the board of adjustment (or appeals) to impose conditions upon the grant of a variance, and in some cases the courts have considered this authorization to be significant. Both the Massachusets enabling act (see *supra* Comment 4) and the California enabling act (set out *supra* in Part B of this chapter) expressly authorize the imposition of conditions. The California statute, however, also contains the following important limitation on the power to impose conditions:

> No local governmental body, or any agency thereof, may condition the issuance of any building or use permit or zone variance on any or all of the following: (1) The dedication of land for any purpose not reasonably related to the use of the property for which the variance, building or use permit is requested. (2) The posting of a bond to guarantee installation of public improvements not reasonably related to the use of the property for which the variance, building, or use permit is requested.

Cal. Gov't Code § 65909 (Deering Supp. 1977). In any case, it is clear that the zoning board of adjustment (or appeal) may not attach conditions unrelated to the purposes of zoning.

Generally, on conditional variance grants, see R. Anderson, American Law of Zoning §§ 18.59-18.69 (2d ed. 1977); Reps, Legal and Administrative Aspects of Conditional Zoning Variances and Exceptions, 2 Syracuse L. Rev. 54 (1951); Comment, Zoning Amendments and Variances Subject to Conditions, 12 Syracuse L. Rev. 230 (1960).

10. As previously indicated in the discussion of *Fobe Assoc. v. Mayor & Council & Bd. of Adjustment, supra* p. 552, New Jersey has a unique provision in its zoning enabling act authorizing the grant of a "use" variance "in particular cases" upon an affirmative finding of "special reasons," together with the negative findings, required in connection with all grants of variances and special exceptions, that "relief can be granted without substantial detriment to the public good and will not substantially impair the intent and purpose of the zone plan and zoning ordinance." N.J. Stat. Ann. § 40:55D-70 (d) (Supp. 1978) (formerly § 40:55-39 (d)). For a good brief treatment of the New Jersey "special reasons" variance, see 5 N. Williams, American Land Planning Law §§ 149.16-149.20 (1975).

Although most of the "special reasons" variances so far approved by the New Jersey appellate courts were for public and quasi-public uses deemed to further the "general welfare," it is clear that, in appropriate cases, a "special reasons" variance may properly be granted by the local board of adjustment in order to permit the construction of high density multifamily housing in an area generally zoned for low density multifamily dwellings or for single family dwellings, in order to make possible the production of "least cost housing" pursuant to the *Oakwood at Madison* mandate. The leading case in support of the use of the "special reasons" variance to make "least cost housing" available is *DeSimone v. Greater Englewood Housing Corp. No. 1,* 267 A.2d 31 (N.J. 1970). The New Jersey "special reasons" variance has the advantage of giving maximum flexibility to the local governing body, since there are no preset standards with respect, *e.g.,* to density or housing types. But this very lack of preset standards also makes the "special reasons" variance subject to abuse.

Compare decisions of the Massachusetts courts, which are reluctant to grant variances for multifamily and subsidized housing under a statute containing the traditional variance criteria. *Kelloway v. Board of Appeal,* 280 N.E.2d 160 (Mass. 1972) (subsidized housing); *Cass v. Board of Appeal,* 317 N.E.2d 77 (Mass. App. Ct. 1974) (multifamily housing). But see the discussion of the Massachusetts zoning appeal law, *supra* p. 649. Moreover, in *Middlesex & Boston St. Ry. v. Board of Aldermen,* 359 N.E.2d 1279 (Mass. 1977), the court struck down a condition attached to a special permit for multifamily housing requiring a percentage of that housing to be leased to the local public housing authority for use as subsidized low-income housing. The court noted that the administrative board issuing the permit "is without power to make the important policy decisions involved in committing a municipality to a program of public housing." *Id.* at 1284. See the discussion of inclusionary zoning techniques, *supra* p. 606.

A NOTE ON AREA, BULK, AND DENSITY VARIANCES

Much of the preceding material on zoning makes it clear that area, bulk, and density regulations are often more important to the land developer than "use" regulations. Especially is this so in apartment development. Many communities, for example, have more than one multifamily apartment zone, and the distinctions between the zones may be based on density rather than use. Density may in turn be controlled in a variety of ways, often used in combination: limitations on the number of dwelling units per acre; height limitations; restrictions on the percentage of the site that can be covered; and provisions requiring a minimum amount of open space for each multifamily dwelling unit. Obviously, getting increases in the allowable density is important to the developer, who sees it as a way of increasing his return. And he may seek density increases through what are known as dimensional, area, or site variances.

An apartment developer may seek a site or density variance for a variety of reasons. He may only be seeking a minor adjustment in the regulations to help facilitate his project. Here it may be noted that the conventional one building-one lot restrictions may trouble him; he may need a variance simply to place more than one building on a single tract. But his search for a variance may represent a quest for higher density. It had been observed in this respect that judicial tests for area variances are simply not as strict as they are for use variances, at least in many courts. As the Court of Appeals explained in *Matter of Hoffman v. Harris,* 216 N.E.2d 326 (N.Y. 1966):

> An applicant for an area variance need not establish special hardship. . . . "A change of area may be granted on the ground of practical difficulties alone, without considering whether or not there is an unnecessary hardship." . . .
>
> There is good reason for the distinction between use and area variances and the requirment of a higher standard of proof of hardship for the former. When the variance is one of area only, there is no change in the character of the zoned district and the neighborhood considerations are not as strong as in a use variance. For example, in *Bronxville* (supra), the question was whether a bank could make the floor area of its new building more than 1 and ½ times the area of its lot despite an ordinance limiting the total floor area of a building to 1 and ½ times the lot. There was no question of change of character of neighborhood since the bank was a proper use. In such a case, it seems fair that only practical difficulties without unique or special hardship need be proved to obtain a variance.

Id. at 329, 330.

In recent years, the courts of several other states have adopted the New York courts' gloss on the zoning enabling act and now make the same distinction between "use" variances — where "unnecessary hardship" must be proved — and "area" variances — where only "practical difficulties" need be proved. An interesting recent case accepting this distinction is *Palmer v. Board of Zoning Adjustment,* 287 A.2d 535 (D.C. Ct. App. 1972). Of course, the "practical difficulties" standard can only be applied when the zoning enabling act uses the phrase "practical difficulties or unnecessary hardship," as it does in New York.

Neither the New York courts nor the courts of other states where the distinction between "use" variances and other variances is now recognized have made very clear what they mean by "practical difficulties." For an excellent treatment of the problem, see 3 R. Anderson, American Law of Zoning §§ 14.45 through 14.51 (2d ed. 1977). Anderson's conclusion is that

> In general, the area variance opinions reflect a practical approach to the problem. The courts appear to consider the size of the deviation that is sought, and to weigh its probable effect on the neighborhood against the harm which will be suffered by the applicant if the variance is refused. Usually, nothing is said about the inability of the owner to derive a reasonable return from his land unless the variance is granted.

Id. § 14.47 at p. 11. Predictability of results in New York "area" variance cases does not seem to have been improved by the court's statement in *Fulling v. Palumbo,* 233 N.E.2d 272 (N.Y. 1967), that "where the property owner will suffer significant economic injury by the application of an area standard ordinance, that standard can be justified only by a showing that the public health, safety and welfare will be served by upholding the standard and denying the variance," and that it is only when such a showing is made that the property owner, in order to obtain an "area" variance, "must demonstrate that the hardship caused is such as to deprive him of any use of the property to which it is reasonably adapted, and that, as a result, the ordinance amounts to a taking of his property." *Id.* at 273-74.

Moreover, it is not clear what the courts mean when they speak of an "area" variance. The New York court has held that a variance is an area variance even though it results in an increase in density. *Wilcox v. Zoning Bd. of Appeals,* 217 N.E.2d 633 (N.Y. 1966). This was an apartment case. Other courts have not been as lenient. *O'Neill v. Zoning Bd. of Adjustment,* 254 A.2d 12 (Pa. 1969). Here the property was located in an apartment zone, but the developer secured a variance permitting him to increase the floor space in his building by two and one half times. While admitting that it might be willing to relax its rules for space variances, the court held that this was not such a case and that a change of this magnitude had to be made legislatively. The variance was set aside. Of similar import is *Mavrantonis v. Board of Adjustment,* 258 A.2d 908 (Del. 1969), where the court set aside a variance which would have reduced the side yard for a 12-story apartment building. The court noted that there were "sound reasons" for side yards. And in *Broadway, Laguna, Ass'n v. Board of Permit Appeals,* 427 P.2d 810 (Cal. 1967), the board had granted a variance from the floor area ratio (FAR) provisions of the zoning ordinance to permit construction of a high-rise apartment. The court overturned the variance and commented:

> The variance requested by the developer, however, did *not* involve a relatively unimportant code provision. On the contrary, the consensus among zoning authorities is that, in terms of controlling population density and structural congestion, the technique of restricting the ratio of a building's rentable floor space to the size of the lot on which it is constructed ... [has advantages] shared by no other method of controlling building bulk or density.

Id. at 813.

If a particular court is willing to treat "density" variances like "area" variances for the purpose of applying the "practical difficulties" standard rather than the "unnecessary hardship" standard, it seems likely that it would treat "bulk" variances in the same manner. But see *Board of Adjustment v. Willie,* 511 S.W.2d 591 (Tex. Civ. Cas. 1974), reversing a height variance granted by the board of adjustment. In *Taylor v. District of Columbia Bd. of Zoning Adjustment,* 308 A.2d 230 (D.C. Ct. App. 1973), the landowner was denied a variance from height, side yard, court and lot occupancy requirements which would have allowed him to build 27 townshouses instead of 10 detached single family dwellings on his property. The court noted that "while the requested variance may not be a use variance in its 'purest form,' it is a hybrid variance which would drastically alter the character of the zoned district" and could be characterized as "a use-area variance." *Id.* at 233.

b. The Special Exception, Special Use Permit, or Conditional Use

DEPUE v. CITY OF CLINTON

Supreme Court of Iowa
160 N.W.2d 860 (1968)

BECKER, Justice.
Plaintiffs, by petition for declaratory judgment and injunctive relief, seek to set aside a resolution of the city council of Clinton, Iowa, granting a special use permit authorizing the construction of a 58 bed nursing home on real estate near or adjacent to residential property owned by plaintiffs. After full hearing on the merits the trial

court declared the action of the city council to be valid and denied injunctive relief. We disagree.

We think this case must turn on our construction of Chapter 414, Code, 1966. We therefore shorten the statement of facts to bare essentials.

Defendant Americana Nursing Homes, Inc. took an option on a 28 room house situated on a three acre tract located quite near downtown Clinton. This home and acreage had been zoned R-1 residential by Clinton's recently adopted 1965 zoning ordinance. The district is entirely residential except for a nearby nursing home and hospital. Due to the topography and wooded nature of the territory the area affords maximum privacy considering its urban location. Plaintiffs are neighboring property owners who were practically unanimous in their protests.

On March 7, 1966 Americana first petitioned the city council to rezone the three acre tract from R-1 (single family residences only) to R-3 (which permits nursing homes). The matter was referred to the city plan commission which recommended against the requested rezoning on April 27, 1966. The council did not act on the petition.

Apparently at the suggestion of one of the councilmen, Americana then applied to the council on May 23, 1966 for a special use permit. This was also referred to the city plan commission. On June 22, 1966 a public hearing, on notice, was held by the commission which, on June 28, 1966, recommended against granting a special use permit.

The city council has a three man planning committee composed wholly of council members. The members of this committee provide council liaison with the city plan commission and attend all the latter's meetings. This committee submitted its own report. Noting that the city plan commission had recommended the request for a special use be denied, the committee then recommended the request be granted.

On July 25, 1966 with all council members present a resolution was passed granting the request. There was no further public hearing before the council itself and the several interested citizens were present when the resolution was passed but did not specifically ask to be heard before the council voted. The matter was never referred to the board of adjustment for any purpose.

I. Chapter 414, Code, 1966 deals with municipal zoning and is the pertinent chapter here. It authorizes the council to adopt comprehensive zoning plans and regulations, and provides for notice and public hearing before the comprehensive laws are adopted and amended.

The chapter mandates the appointment of two official bodies; (1) a zoning commission, the function of which is to make recommendations to the council on adoption of the plan and to make like recommendations in connection with amendments thereto, and (2) a board of adjustment, ordered to be created by section 414.7.

"414.7 ... The council shall provide ... that the said board of adjustment may in appropriate cases and subject to appropriate conditions and safeguards make special exceptions to the terms of the ordinance in harmony with the general purpose and intent and in accordance with general or specific rules therein contained ...."

Section 414.12 states: "... The board of adjustment shall have the following powers:

"....

"... To hear and decide special exceptions to the terms of the ordinance upon which such board is required to pass under such ordinance.

"...."

Section 414.15 provides for review of the decisions of the board of adjustment by way of application for certiorari presented to *a court of record.* The chapter provides for no appeal *to the city council* from the action of the board of adjustment.

When the city adopted its new zoning ordinance in 1965 it provided in section 20 for applications *to the city council* for what were termed "special uses." It also provided in section 22 for creation of a board of adjustment for "special exceptions" to be granted by that board on appeal from action of administrative officers and for variances which could be granted by the board under certain conditions. Both sections are quite long. In the interest of brevity we do not reproduce them here but refer only to their salient factors.

The key issue in this case is whether the statute allows the city to allocate jurisdiction over "special uses" to the council and "special exceptions" to the board of adjustment. First, does the term "special exceptions" include "special uses?" If so, is the jurisdiction of the board of adjustment, conferred by sections 414.7 and 414.12, an exclusive jurisdiction? We think the answers to both questions are affirmative, thus section 20 of the ordinance is invalid and the action of the city council under that section is likewise invalid.

. . . .

We have no doubt that creation of a board of adjustment is mandatory. The board having been created, its jurisdiction is fixed by statute, not by city ordinance. *Deardorf v. Board of Adjustment,* 254 Iowa 380, 118 N.W.2d 78, 80:

"The power to permit variances which the zoning ordinance delegates to the board is less broad than that delegated by the state statute, supra. There can be little doubt that power conferred on the board by state statute may not be limited by city ordinance. Insofar as this ordinance conflicts with section 414.12, subd. 3, the statute controls. ...."

In *Call Bond and Mortgage Co. v. City of Sioux City,* 219 Iowa 572, 259 N.W. 33 after analyzing the position of the board of adjustment we held that the jurisdiction to review nonarbitrary action of the city inspector in revoking a building permit was solely and exclusively in the board of adjustment.

The foregoing cases all indicate an interpretive history for Chapter 414 which would require the city to place what we have called the quasi judicial function of granting special exceptions in the board of adjustment. This interpretation is buttressed by legislative provision for review of the board's action by the *courts,* not by the council.

III. Does the term "special exception" as used in the statute include the term "special use" as used in the ordinance. We hold that it does.

In 2 Rathkopf, The Law of Planning and Zoning, 1966 at page 54-1, the term "special exception use" is used with the following explanatory footnote #1. "Although, in this chapter we adhere to ordinary terminology and use the term 'special exception use' or 'special exception permit,' it should be pointed out in the beginning that this term is a misnomer. As will be made clear in this chapter, no 'exception' is made to the provisions of the ordinance in permitting such use; the permit granted is for a use specifically provided for in the ordinance in the case in which conditions, legislatively prescribed, are also found. A much more accurate description would be 'conditional use' permit."

In *Schultz v. Board of Adjustment,* 258 Iowa 804, 807, 139 N.W.2d 448 in construing our county zoning statute, Chapter 358A, which uses "special exceptions" in exactly the same context as used in Chapter 414, we said: "The term 'conditional use' employed in a zoning ordinance means provisional use for a purpose designated by the ordinance itself; a grant of right for any use specified by the ordinance subject to finding by an administrative officer or board that the use is proper, essential, advantageous or desirable to public good, convenience, health or welfare. It is neither the equivalent of nor should it be confused with 'variances'. *Tustin Heights Assn. v. Board of Supervisors,* 170 Cal.App.2d 619, 339 P.2d 914, 919, and 101 C.J.S. Zoning §§ 272-274, pages 1037-1040."

Also in 50 Iowa Law Review, 367, 399, 400, Land-Use Controls — The State and Local Programs, Professor Cunningham uses the following language: "Since World War II, however, most courts have come to recognize that a 'special exception' permits in a particular district a use not otherwise permitted when certain conditions specifically set out in the ordinance are satisfied by the board to exist. A 'variance,' on the other hand, relaxes the zoning regulations when literal enforcement would result in 'unnecessary hardship.'

". . . .

"The statutory 'special exception' technique seems to provide an effective way to handle land uses whose 'side effects' may affect an entire neighborhood, entire zoning district, or even the entire community, ..." We are satisfied from our examination of the statute and the terminology used by the courts and other authorities in dealing with zoning problems that "special exceptions" includes "special uses", and that both must be placed within the jurisdiction of the board of adjustment.

IV. This construction of our statute is consistent with our interpretation of the fifth sentence of the second paragraph of section 368.2, Code, 1966, which reads: "However statutes which provide a manner or procedure for carrying out their provisions or exercising a given power shall be interpreted as providing the exclusive manner of procedure and shall be given substantial compliance, . . ."

. . . .

Reversed and remanded.

All Justices concur except LeGrand, J., who takes no part.

Comments: 1. The classic statement on the purpose of "special exceptions" under the Standard State Zoning Enabling Act and statutes based thereon is found in Judge Hall's opinion in *Tullo v. Millburn Township,* 149 A.2d 620, 624-25 (N.J. Super. 1959):

> . . . The term might well be said to be a misnomer. "Special uses" or "special use permits" would be more accurate. The theory is that certain uses, considered by the local legislative body to be essential or desirable for the welfare of the community and its citizenry or substantial segments of it, are entirely appropriate and not essentially incompatible with the basic uses in any zone (or in certain particular zones), but not at every or any location therein or without restrictions or conditions being imposed by reason of special problems the use or its particular location in relation to neighboring properties presents from a zoning standpoint, such as traffic congestion, safety, health, noise, and the like. The enabling act therefore permits the local ordinance to require approval of the local administrative agency as to the location of such use within the zone. If the board finds compliance with the standards or requisites set forth in the ordinance, the right to the exception exists, subject to such specific safeguarding conditions as the agency may impose by reason of the nature, location and incidents of the particular use. Without intending here to be inclusive or to prescribe limits, the uses so treated are generally those serving considerable numbers of people, such as private schools, clubs, hospitals and even churches, as distinguished from governmental structures or activities on the one hand and strictly individual residences or businesses on the other. This method of zoning treatment is also frequently extended to certain unusual kinds of strictly private business or activity which, though desirable and compatible, may by their nature present peculiar zoning problems or have unduly unfavorable effect on their neighbors if not specially regulated. Gasoline stations . . . are an example of this second category. The

point is that such special uses are permissive in the particular zone under the ordinance and neither non-conforming nor akin to a variance.

In *Brown Boveri, Inc. v. Township of North Brunswick,* 389 A.2d 483 (N.J. App. Div. 1978), the court held that (1) since automobile showrooms were allowed only as special exceptions in Commercial C-2 districts, permission to use land for an automobile showroom could only be obtained through the special exception procedure and not by means of a "use variance"; and (2) such a special exception could not be granted in an industrial zone in any event, since automobile showrooms were not permitted in such a zone even as a special exception.

2. As Judge Hall said in *Tullo, supra* Comment 1, "special use" or "special use permit" would be a more accurate term than "special exception" to describe the uses specified in the zoning ordinance as permitted in a given district with the approval of a designated local zoning board or agency. The term "conditional use" or "conditional use permit" is sometimes used in zoning enabling acts and local zoning ordinances. *E.g.,* Cal. Gov't Code § 65901 (Deering Supp. 1977), *supra* p. 222; N.J. Stat. Ann. § 40:55D-67 (Supp. 1978). The term "conditional use" also seems to have been used in Oregon prior to the last revision of the Oregon zoning statute. *See Archdiocese of Portland v. County of Washington,* 458 P.2d 682 (Ore. 1969).

3. As Judge Hall pointed out in *Tullo, supra* Comment 1, the New Jersey Supreme Court had previously held that the zoning board of adjustment could properly be given a "merely recommendatory" role by the local ordinance, "with final approval reserved to the governing body." *See Schmidt v. Board of Adjustment,* 88 A.2d 607 (N.J. 1952). The newly enacted New Jersey Municipal Land Use Law, N.J. Stat. Ann. § 40:55D-67 (Supp. 1978), now provides for the granting of "conditional uses" by the planning board; the old provision authorizing the granting of "special exceptions" by the board of adjustment has been eliminated. Cal. Gov't Code § 65901, *supra* Comment 2, provides for the granting of "conditional uses" by the board of adjustment or the zoning administrator, but under *id.* § 65902, if "neither a board of zoning adjustment nor the office of a zoning administrator has been created and established, the planning commission shall exercise all of the functions and duties of said board or administrator." Under the former Oregon zoning enabling act, "conditional uses" appear to have been granted by the county planning commission and the "county court" (a legislative and administrative body). *See Archdiocese of Portland v. County of Washington, supra* Comment 2.

4. It is clear that the zoning pioneers did not intend the "special exception" to be anything more than a supplement to the basic technique of "pre-zoning" a municipality into a number of different "use" and "density" districts. *Rockhill v. Chesterfield Township,* reprinted as a principal case *supra* p. 283, makes it clear that the "special exception" technique, combined with low density "wait-and-see" zoning, cannot be used as the primary method by which a municipality controls its growth and development.

5. Multifamily residential developments have sometimes been handled through "group housing" provisions which are drafted as exceptions in the zoning ordinance. Thus in *LaRue v. Township of East Brunswick,* 172 A.2d 691 (N.J. App. Div. 1961), apartments could be allowed by the board of adjustment as a special exception in five of the township's eleven zoning districts. The board was to apply several standards, including the suitability of the apartment development for the area of the community in which it was to be located, advantage to the community, proximity to community facilities, and similar tests. The court upheld the ordinance provision and found the standards sufficient. It rejected the argument that the ordinance created an invalid "floating" zone since the apartments could only be allowed in certain specified districts. The *LaRue* case suggests that the "special exception" technique may be useful for implementing an "inclusionary" zoning program for "least cost" housing, provided sufficient standards to control the exercise of discretion by the administrative body are included in the ordinance.

See also *High Meadows Park, Inc. v. City of Aurora,* 250 N.E.2d 517 (Ill. App. 1969); ordinance was invalid for totally excluding mobile homes from the municipality, the court suggesting that a special exception for mobile homes would have to be provided, as a minimum measure, to assure the validity of the ordinance. And see *Jackson v. Guilford County Bd. of Adjustment,* 166 S.E.2d 78 (N.C. 1969).

6. Although most state zoning enabling acts provide for "special exceptions," "special use permits," or "conditional uses," not all of them do so. The next principal case considers the questions whether, in the absence of express authority from the enabling act, local governments may nevertheless make provision for this "flexible" zoning technique, and how detailed the standards for granting "special exceptions," etc., must be.

KOTRICH v. COUNTY OF DU PAGE

Supreme Court of Illinois
19 Ill.2d 181, 166 N.E.2d 601
Appeal dismissed, 364 U.S. 475 (1960)

Mr. Justice SCHAEFER delivered the opinion of the court:

This is a declaratory judgment proceeding which involves the validity of a "special use" permit granted by the defendant, the board of supervisors of Du Page County, to the defendant, Salt Creek Club, under the terms of the Du Page County zoning ordinance. The primary issues concern the statutory authority of the county to provide for "special uses" in its zoning ordinance, and, if the authority exists, the conditions that govern its exercise.

The defendant club is a not-for-profit corporation organized for social, educational, and athletic purposes. It owns the property in question, a six-acre parcel of land now zoned for R-2 single family residence use. On this land it proposes to build a clubhouse, a swimming pool, tennis courts and a parking area for use of its anticipated membership of 275 families.

The club applied to the zoning board for a special use permit under the county ordinance, to allow the construction of a private outdoor recreation center on the property. The board conducted a hearing and recommended to the county board that the special use permit be denied. Notwithstanding this recommendation, the county board passed a resolution granting the permit. The plaintiffs, who are adjacent property owners, commenced this suit in the circuit court of Du Page County to challenge the permit and the zoning ordinance under which it was granted. From a judgment sustaining the validity of the ordinance and the permit, they appeal directly to this court. The trial judge has certified that the validity of a county zoning ordinance is involved and that the public interest requires a direct appeal to this court. Ill.Rev.Stat.1959, chap. 110, par. 75.

The special use is a relatively new method of land use control. Zoning ordinances embodying this technique retain the usual residential, commercial, and industrial zones, specifying the uses permitted in each zone. For each zone, however, special uses are also established which are permitted within the zone only if approved by the zoning board or the governing legislative body. The Du Page County ordinance follows this general scheme, and it specifies private outdoor recreational facilities among the special uses which may be permitted in the R-2 single family residence zone. Among other special uses permitted in this zone are colleges and universities, public outdoor recreational centers, rest homes, hospitals and sanitariums, planned developments of not less than 40 acres, and "public service uses" such as electric and telephone substations, filtration plants, and fire and police stations.

The first contention advanced by the plaintiffs is that the County Zoning Enabling Act (Ill.Rev.Stat.1957, chap. 34, par. 152i, et seq.) does not authorize counties to employ this method. In support of this contention they argue that since the special use technique is not mentioned in the act, and indeed did not exist at the time the act was adopted in 1935, the legislature could not have intended to authorize it. Their position is that the legislature must specifically grant counties the power to adopt special use provisions, as it has done in the case of variations and amendments, and as legislatures of some other States have done.

They note also that procedural safeguards limit the exercise of administrative and legislative discretion with respect to variations and amendments. Written findings of fact must accompany every variation, and any variation rejected by the zoning board of appeals can be approved only by a three-fourths majority of the legislative body. The same extraordinary majority is required to approve any amendment if 20% of adjacent landowners object. It is argued that the legislature has thus indicated its intention that deviations from the established zoning pattern should be permitted only by the procedurally restricted methods included in the act.

Carl L. Gardner, a planning and zoning consultant, testified that the special use technique developed as a means of providing for infrequent types of land use which are necessary and desirable but which are potentially incompatible with uses usually allowed in residential, commercial and industrial zones. Such uses generally occupy a rather large tract of land. They can not be categorized in any given use zone without the danger of excluding beneficial uses or including dangerous ones. A typical example was presented in *Illinois Bell Telephone Co. v. Fox,* 402 Ill. 617, 85 N.E.2d 43, where this court affirmed a judgment ordering a special use permit to issue for construction of a telephone exchange in a residential district.

Instead of excluding such uses entirely from certain zones because of the harm they might cause, or, despite the potential harm, including them because of the benefits they will bring, the special use technique allows a more flexible approach. It contemplates that the county board may permit these uses when desirable and, if necessary, impose conditions designed to protect nearby property owners. This seems to be an effective method of dealing with a narrow but difficult problem of land use control. Approximately 25 municipalities and counties in Illinois have incorporated it in their zoning ordinances, and the record shows that its use is increasing.

It is true that the procedural restrictions prescribed for amendments and variations, as well as the standards prescribed for variations, evidence a legislative plan to guarantee property owners some protection from piecemeal changes in the general zoning scheme by ad hoc determinations with respect to particular pieces of property. And since granting a special use permit involves an ad hoc judgment which may affect surrounding property owners in the same way as a variation or an amendment, unlimited application of the special use technique to land uses that can readily be accommodated within the customary categories would undermine the protection contemplated by the statute. But unlimited application of the special use technique is not required to meet the problem it was designed to solve. Only those infrequent uses which are beneficial, but potentially inconsistent with normal uses in the various zones, need be included.

The statute authorizes the board of supervisors "to regulate and restrict the location and use of buildings, structures and land for trade, industry, residence and other uses which may be specified by such board, . . .; to divide the entire county . . . into districts of such number, shape, area and of such different classes, according to the use of land and buildings, . . . as may be deemed best suited to carry out the purposes of this Act; to prohibit uses, buildings or structures incompatible with the character of such districts respectively; . . . ."

(Ill.Rev.Stat.1957, chap. 34, par. 152i.) In our opinion, a residual category of those special uses which can not, without distortion, be included in the customary classifications, is permissible as a means of implementing the powers conferred by the statute.

Applying these criteria, we think that a private country club such as that involved in the present case may properly be classified as a special use in a single family residence zone. Such uses of land are often found in residential areas. Proximity to a club may increase the desirability of land. On the other hand, a club may also produce increased noise from bathers, tennis players, social functions and automobiles. If the parking area is not properly designed, headlights may shine in neighboring houses; if it is not large enough, members' automobiles will overflow onto neighboring streets. Increased traffic may produce safety hazards. Whether these undesirable consequences will occur depends upon the design of the club's facilities and its location within the zone. In such a case, governmental supervision of each situation is justified.

The plaintiffs also contend that the ordinance providing for special uses is invalid because it does not specify standards by which the county board of supervisors is to judge whether a special use permit should be granted. Although the ordinance does not prescribe standards in so many words, it does state that special uses are established for the purpose of providing "for the location of special classes of uses which are deemed desirable for the public welfare within a given district or districts, but which are potentially incompatible with typical uses herein permitted within them . . . ." It also empowers the board of supervisors to impose "such . . . conditions as it considers necessary to protect the public health, safety and welfare." A fair reading of the ordinance shows that it contemplates that the county board will weigh the desirability of the proposed use against its potential adverse impact. Since the board of supervisors is a legislative body, precise standards to govern its determination are not required.

The plaintiffs' next contention is that since the impact of a special use is like the impact of a variation, the statutory requirement that written findings of fact must accompany a variation should be applied to special uses. They also assert, again by analogy to variations, that if the zoning board of appeals rejects a special use, a three-fourths majority of the county board of supervisors should be required to grant the permit. In the present case no finding of facts was adopted by the county board. The special use permit was granted without a three-fourths vote of the county board, although the board of zoning appeals had rejected the club's application, and had found specifically that the proposed use would be incompatible with the general character of the neighborhood and its trend of development would cause considerable depreciation of surrounding property, and would increase traffic congestion.

We recognize that because the special use may have the same impact upon neighboring property as a variation, procedural safeguards similar to those prescribed for variations might be desirable for special uses as well. But the enabling act imposes these safeguards only as to variations, and the two techniques are not identical. The scope of the special use, and its purpose, differ from those of the variation, which is designed to handle cases of practical difficulty or particular hardship to property owners created by zoning restrictions. For this court to impose upon the local legislative body, in dealing with special uses, the procedures required for variations would be to move from interpretation of the act to policy determination and implementation. This is the function not of the court, but of the General Assembly.

Furthermore, the impact of a special use may resemble that of an amendment as well as a variation. Yet the statutory procedures for amendments vary greatly from those for variations. A three-fourths vote of the county board is required if 20% of the adjacent landowners object, but no findings of fact are required since an amendment is considered a legislative act. By analogy to the plaintiffs' contention in this case, it may be argued that amendment procedures, rather than variation procedures, should be required when granting a special use permit. Which, if either, of the statutory procedures is appropriate for the new special use technique that has developed under the statute is a matter for legislative determination.

It is true that in *Rosenfeld v. Zoning Board of Appeals,* 19 Ill.App. 2d 447, 154 N.E.2d 323, the Appellate Court set aside a special use permit in part for lack of written findings of fact, although it recognized that findings were not required by the zoning ordinance or the enabling act. In that case, however, the special use was granted by the zoning board of appeals of Chicago and review was under the Illinois Administrative Review Act. (Ill.Rev.Stat.1959, chap. 110, pars. 264-279.) Review under that act is on the record made in the administrative agency and its findings of fact are to be held *prima facie* true and correct. (Ill.Rev.Stat.1959, chap. 110, par. 274.) Orderly and efficient review procedure under the act may, therefore, require that the administrative agency make written findings. The same reasoning does not apply in the present case where the special use permit was granted by a legislative body and judicial review is had in an independent action on a new record made in court.

The plaintiffs contend, finally, that to allow the club to conduct its proposed activities under a special use permit will deprive them of their property without due process of law. They argue that the damage to their property far outweighs any public benefit the club may produce. Although an expert witness for the plaintiff testified that operation of the club would substantially depreciate the value of surrounding property, two witnesses for the defendants took the opposite view. The county board imposed several restrictions designed to protect nearby houses from excessive light and noise. We think the record shows that the county board's action was not arbitrary and did not deprive the plaintiffs of their property without due process of law.

The judgment is affirmed.

Judgment affirmed.

Mr. Chief Justice HOUSE, dissenting:

The county has only the powers delegated to it, expressly or by necessary implication. There is no specific authority granted by the county zoning enabling act for special use procedure, nor, in my opinion, can the device be justified under the general power to "regulate," "restrict" and "prohibit." How can it be said that a legislative intent was manifested to permit special use procedure when, as the majority opinion recognizes, such procedure was unknown at the date of enactment of the enabling legislation? The fact that statutory restrictions and standards are set up for amendments and variations indicates a legislative intent to the exact contrary.

I agree with the majority that it is a matter for legislative determination whether amendment, variation or other procedure is appropriate for the new special use technique. But, that determination must come from the legislature together with suitable standards fixed for application of the procedure. It should not, as here, be left without restriction to the whim of the local governing body.

In one breath the majority opinion admits that unlimited application of the special use technique would take away the guarantee to property owners which is the very vitals of zoning and in the next approves special use procedure because its unlimited application "is not required." The ingenuity of members of our profession could conceivably conjure up so many "unique" situations which would require applications of special use procedures that ad hoc determination could become the rule rather than the exception.

The *Bell Telephone* case (402 Ill. 617, 85 N.E.2d 43) is readily distinguishable. First, the ordinances involved are entirely different and, second, the special use device was not in question, but the issue was whether area and height restrictions in the volume district were applicable.

From the standpoint of zoning enthusiasts and administrators the special use device provides a flexible method disposing of troublesome "unique" situations. On the other hand, its use in such cases as here (recreation center) is the further limiting of the rights of ownership of property under the guise of the much tortured and misused police power.

Comments: 1. What do you make of Ill.Ann.Stat. ch. 34, § 3156 (Supp. 1977), which authorizes the board of appeals to "hear and decide all matters referred to it or upon which it is required to pass under any ... [county zoning] ordinance or resolution or under the terms of this Act"? The Du Page county zoning ordinance before the court in the *Kotrich* case apparently required applications for "special uses" to be made to the board of appeals — which under the statutory provision quoted above could authorize a "special use" only by the "concurring vote of 4 members of a board consisting of 5 members or the concurring vote of 5 members of a board consisting of 7 members" — but also provided that the county governing body could overrule the decision of the board of appeals by a simple majority vote.

The language from the Illinois zoning enabling act quoted above is derived from the early New York zoning enabling legislation. See, *e.g.,* N.Y. Town Law § 267(2) (1965), which provides that the zoning board of appeals shall "hear and decide all matters referred to it or upon which it is required to pass under any such ordinance." This language, originally adopted in 1926, has been construed in New York to authorize the granting of "special use permits." See R. Anderson, Am. Law of Zoning § 15.01 (2d ed. 1977).

Assuming that the authorization for the board of appeals to "hear and decide all matters referred to it or upon which it is required to pass under any ... ordinance or resolution" of the county governing body does not expressly authorize the granting of "special uses," why do you think the Illinois court approved the "special use" technique despite its admission "that because the special use may have the same impact upon neighboring property as a variation, procedural safeguards similar to those prescribed for variations might be desirable"? Is the case for recognition of the "special use" technique strengthened by the court's observation that "the statutory procedures for amendments vary greatly from those for variations," although "the impact of a special use may resemble that of an amendment as well as a variation"? If, as the court states, "[w]hich, if either of the statutory procedures is appropriate for the new special use technique ... is a matter for legislative determination," is it not strongly arguable that the court should have left validation of the "special use" technique to "legislative determination"?

2. In *Kotrich, supra,* the Illinois court held that "a fair reading of the ordinance" showed that it contemplated "that the county board will weigh the desirability of the proposed use against its potential adverse impact," and further, that since the county board of supervisors was "a legislative body," no "precise standards to govern its determination" were required. Do you agree that the county board was acting "legislatively" in granting or denying "special use permits"? If so, was not the county board really amending the zoning ordinance when it granted a "special use permit"? Since the county board clearly had the power to amend the zoning ordinance and to change the zoning classification of the land in question, why would it choose to use the "special use permit" technique rather than the amendment technique? In connection with this question, consider the following excerpt from *Archdiocese of Portland v. County of Washington*, 458 P.2d 682 (Ore. 1969):

> Experience has demonstrated that frequently zone changes are made by governing boards without adequate consideration of the effect which the change will have on the over-all plan. It is known that zone changes are commonly made simply because the change is requested and no one in the neighborhood has an objection to it. Knowing this it would not be realistic to presume in a particular case that the governing board acted regularly in the sense that it duly considered the effect which the change would have on the comprehensive plan.
>
> The same considerations do not obtain however when, as in the case before us, the governing board passes upon an application for a conditional use. The original ordinance itself expressly provides for the specified "conditional uses" which might be made in the zone. In this sense the granting of an application for a conditional use does not constitute a deviation from the ordinance but is in compliance with it. The Washington County ordinance expressly declares that "A conditional use shall not be construed to be a zone change...."
>
> ....
>
> Thus the Washington County ordinance provides for such compatible uses as auditoriums, boat moorages, cemeteries, churches, colleges, community buildings, golf courses, greenhouses, hospitals, libraries, etc. Because these uses are generally compatible with the design of the zone the possibility that a permitted use will not comport with the comprehensive plan is not as great as it is when a variance or amendment is sought. Nor is there the same likelihood that such uses will be sought for and obtained as a matter of special privilege by those seeking private gain as there is where a variance or amendment is requested.
>
> But more important than these considerations is the fact that the ordinance itself reveals the legislative plan forecasting the likelihood that certain specified uses will be needed to maximize the use of land in the zone for residential purposes. The Board's discretion is thus narrowed to those cases in which an application falls within one of the specified uses. The fact that these permissible uses are pre-defined and have the legislative endorsement of the governing body of the county as a tentative part of the comprehensive plan for the area limits the possibility that the Board's action in granting a permit will be inimical to the interests of the community. The suspicion which is cast upon the approval of a change involving an incompatible use ... is not warranted where the change has been anticipated by the governing body. Therefore, unlike the spot zoning cases the granting of permits for conditional uses is not likely to cause the "erosive effect upon the comprehensive zoning plan" described in *Smith v. County of Washington*, ... [406 P.2d 545 (Ore. 1965)].

Id. at 685-86.

3. It is clear that a zoning board of adjustment (or appeals) acts "administratively" when it grants or denies a "special exception," "special use permit," or "conditional use." Moreover, where the final decision is made by the local governing body upon recommendation of the board of adjustment (or appeals), the courts have generally held that the governing body acts "administratively" rather than "legislatively." Thus, in theory, the zoning ordinance should contain standards adequate to guide the exercise of administrative discretion by the board of adjustment (or appeals). In *Tullo v. Millburn Township,* 149 A.2d 620 (N.J. Super. 1959), the court affirmed the action of the board of adjustment and the local governing body in granting a special exception to a country club to allow construction of an addition to its clubhouse and an outdoor swimming pool adjacent thereto, in an exclusive single family residence district, under the following provision of the local zoning ordinance:

> SCHOOLS, HOSPITALS, CLUBS, COMMUNITY CENTER BUILDINGS, SANITARIUMS & CEMETERIES. Recognizing the necessity for schools, hospitals, clubs, sanitariums and cemeteries, and at the same time the fact that they may be inimical to the public health, safety and general welfare, if located without due consideration of conditions and surroundings, the following procedure is ordained for their establishment:
>
> An application for a permit for a school, other than a public school, a hospital, a club-house, a sanitarium, or a cemetery, shall be made first to the Board of Adjustment, which shall hear the application in the same manner and under the same procedure as the Board of Adjustment is empowered by law and ordinance to hear cases and make exceptions [*sic; reference seems intended to be made to variances*] to the provisions of a zoning ordinance, and the Board of Adjustment may thereafter recommend to the Township Committee that a permit be granted for a school, a hospital, a club-house, a sanitarium, or a cemetery, if in its judgment said school, hospital, club-house, sanitarium or cemetery, as it is proposed to be located, will not be detrimental to the health, safety and general welfare of the community, and is reasonably necessary for the convenience of the community, whereupon the Township Committee may by resolution approve or disapprove such recommendation, and in case such recommendation shall be approved, and all statutory and other municipal requirements shall be complied with, the administrative officer in charge of granting permits shall forthwith issue a permit for such structure or use subject to such requirement as to front, side and rear yards, and other reasonable restrictions as to structure or use as the governing body may see fit to impose.

In *Archdiocese of Portland v. County of Washington, supra* Comment 2, the court upheld the denial of a "conditional use" permit for a church, school, and gymnasium in a residential district, pursuant to a zoning ordinance provision authorizing such uses "in the indicated zones . . . after due notice and a public hearing and finding that such conditional use is not at variance with the various elements or objectives of this code and the comprehensive plan."

While the court may be limited to the criteria specified by the ordinance, it may find the criteria impermissible: In *Pioneer Trust & Savings Bank v. County of McHenry,* 241 N.E.2d 454 (Ill. 1968), a conditional use provision authorized approval of mobile home parks on a finding that they would not have a detrimental effect on surrounding uses, on a finding that adequate facilities and access can be provided, and on a finding of "public necessity." The court held that the necessity test was improper, if lack of necessity is the *only* basis for denying the conditional use. What standards are permissible in a conditional use provision is unclear from the opinion, which appeared to appraise the denial of the conditional use under the conventional police power tests.

See also *Nani v. Zoning Bd. of Review,* 242 A.2d 403 (R.I. 1968): the "public need" test may not be used in a special exception provision for gasoline filling stations. It "smacks" of the improper regulation of competition. And cf. *Waterville Hotel Corp. v. Board of Zoning Appeals,* 241 A.2d 50 (Me. 1968): delegating to the board of appeals the power, without standards, to approve all "major" changes in use is constitutional.

Judicial treatment of ordinance standards for "special exceptions," "special use permits," and "conditional uses" is summarized as follows in American Law Institute, Model Land Development Code, Tentative Draft No. 2, Note to § 2-207 (1970):

> Mandelker's review of cases shows that "nuisance standards" — negatively phrased standards directing that uses will not be allowed as exceptions if they create nuisance type external costs — have been approved overwhelmingly. Ordinances without any standards — simply authorizing an administrative board to issue an exception — generally have been held to delegate legislative authority invalidly. But most zoning ordinances provide general welfare standards and here judicial reaction is mixed. (Usually the ordinance allows the board to permit any of the enumerated special uses if such action would be in accord with the purposes and intent of the ordinance and be conducive to the general welfare.) Many cases sustain such standards without any critical comment. Some courts attempt to evaluate such standards and conclude that they are certain enough in view of the technological complexities of zoning administration. . . . A number of cases hold such standards unconstitutional or ultra vires. Confusingly, courts in the same jurisdiction, and even the same courts, render inconsistent opinions on similar standards in different cases. . . . The problems raised by exceptions are like those raised by variances. At base it is the fear that without somewhat concrete standards landowners will be vulnerable to discrimination. In addition, there is the desire to have policy made by a representative body and to assure neighborhood status quo. And as with variances, courts have not been able to take solace in procedural regularity because enabling acts and ordinances have not required administrative agencies to state in detail the reasons for granting or denying exceptions.

"Mandelker's review of cases" can be found in Mandelker, Delegation of Power and Function in Zoning Administration, 1963 Wash. U.L.Q. 60. N.J. Stat. Ann. § 40:55D-67 (Supp. 1978) now requires that the zoning ordinance shall contain "definite specifications and standards which shall be clearly set forth with sufficient clarity and definiteness to enable the developer to know their limit and extent." Do you think this will effectively prohibit the use of "nuisance" and vague "general welfare" standards?

4. The Illinois court in *Kotrich* held that there is no need for "written findings of fact" when "the special use permit was granted by a legislative body" rather than an administrative body, since in such a case "judicial review is had in an independent action on a new record made in court." Does this make sense? Was the county governing body acting "legislatively" or "administratively" in granting a special use permit? Does it make any difference? Are the standards for judicial review different for "legislative" action than for "administrative" action?

In *Archdiocese of Portland v. County of Washington, supra* Comment 2, the court said:

> Absent the dangers incident to "spot zoning" the presumption of legislative regularity can be given its full effect. Under such circumstances the only function of this court and the trial court in reviewing the action of the Board of County Commissioners is to decide whether the Board acted arbitrarily or capriciously. It is not our function to weigh the evidence for the purpose of determining whether in our judgment the Board correctly decided that the use sought would result in a detriment to the community as a whole. It is possible, as plaintiff contends, that the Board erred in concluding that the proposed use would cause traffic congestion or a fire hazard or other harm to the citizens in that area of the county. But the members of the Board, as representatives of the people who elected them, have the privilege of erring in making their decisions as long as they abide by the required precedures [sic] and their conclusion is not patently irrational. We examine the record of the proceedings before the Board only to determine whether those proceedings were fairly conducted in accordance with the requirements of the ordinance and that there was a rational basis for the Board's decision. It is important to bear in mind that in these cases we and the trial court are reviewing the legislative action of a governmental unit engaged in carrying out a land use policy formulated by it. The basis for that action need not be found in "evidence" as we use that term in connection with the trial of cases before a court. The ordinance requires the Planning Commission to hold a public hearing on all proposed changes and the Board must also hold a public hearing on all appeals from the Planning Commission. But these public hearings are not trials and the views expressed by those who attend are evidence only in the broad sense that the Board may consider the points of view expressed at those hearings in reaching its conclusion.

Id. at 686.

Compare *Tullo v. Millburn Township,* 149 A.2d 620 (N.J. Super. 1959), where the court, in reviewing the "administrative" act of the zoning board of adjustment and the local governing body in granting a "special exception" to allow construction of a clubhouse addition and swimming pool in a single family residence zone, said:

It is, of course, elementary that, similar to the case of a variance, an applicant for a special exception has the burden of producing proofs before the Board of Adjustment to establish that the ordinance and statutory standards are met and the agency must make adequate basic findings of fact from that evidence leading to the ultimate finding or conclusion. The findings need not be in legal language and the ultimate findings or conclusions need not parrot the legislative verbiage. These ultimate requisites may be deduced from what is actually said. It must be kept in mind that the administrative bodies are composed of laymen. The prescribed procedural pattern is a general and flexible one, adaptable to the particular case. . . .

Each application must be considered in its peculiar factual setting and the *quantum* of proof required will necessarily vary. In any special exception case the statutory criterion of absence of substantial impairment of the intent and purpose of the zone plan and ordinance plays a very small part since the ordinance itself makes the proposed use permissive in the particular zone. The other statutory standard of absence of substantial detriment to the public good must have reference in such a case primarily to the weighing of the admitted general utility of the use and the public convenience of the requested location against the effect of disadvantageous factors on other uses in the area. The ordinance requirements of the location being not detrimental to the health, safety and general welfare of the community and being reasonably necessary for community convenience have much the same connotation.

. . . It was peculiarly within the province of the board to determine, in balancing the conflicting interests, whether there was likely to be such effect on property values and greater annoyance to neighbors as to amount to a sufficient detriment to the general welfare of the neighborhood to require the denial of the exception.

We are satisfied beyond any doubt that there was adequate evidence before the board so that, under the particular circumstances here present, it could properly and reasonably find the standards of both statute and ordinance had been sufficiently met and it and the township committee could validly conclude the club was entitled to the requested exception. The function of the judicial branch is not to substitute its judgment for that of the administrative agency to which the Legislature has committed the determination. We can and should only interfere where the result is arbitrary, capricious or illegal in the light of the proofs. . . .

Id. at 627-28.

5. American Law Institute, Model Land Development Code § 2-20 (1976) provides as follows:

(1) A development ordinance may authorize the Land Development Agency to grant special development permission under this Section by using the phrase "special permit to allow compatible use" or any other language signifying a similar intent, and by specifying the types of development that may be permitted after a finding of compatibility. Development so specified may differ from one part of the community to another.

(2) If authorized by ordinance to grant permits under this Section, the Land Development Agency shall grant a special development permit for proposed development if it finds that

    (a) the proposed development will be development that may be permitted after a finding of compatibility under the applicable ordinance provisions; and

    (b) the proposed development is likely to be compatible with development permitted under the general development provisions of the ordinance on substantially all land in the vicinity of the proposed development.

The Reporter's Note states that § 2-207 "is the legislative descendant of the 'special exceptions' or 'special use' or 'conditional use' provisions in existing zoning enabling acts, many of which are based on the provisions in the Standard Zoning Enabling Act authorizing boards of adjustment to make exceptions to the terms of the ordinance 'in harmony with its general purpose and intent and in accordance with general or specific rules' contained in the ordinance."

  6. Compare Model Land Development Code § 2-205 (1975):

    (1) A development ordinance may authorize the Land Development Agency to grant special development permission to review district boundary lines.

    (2) If authorized by the ordinance to grant permits under this Section, the Land Development Agency shall grant a permit if it finds that

    (a) the development will occupy not more than [five] acres of land; and

    (b) the development would be permitted as general development [as of right — Eds.] on some land adjacent to the parcel or separated from the parcel only by the width of a street between them; and

    (c) the development will not significantly interfere with the enjoyment of other land in the vicinity; and

    (d) the development will not be detrimental to the general interest of the community; and

    (e) the development will be consistent with the traffic patterns of the community.

The Reporter's Note states that this section:

> [H]as no counterpart in traditional zoning law. It enables a locality to authorize its administrative agency to make district boundary changes for relatively small parcels. . . . This provision is linked to the special amendment provision contained in § 2-312 that seeks to discourage local legislatures from enacting small parcel amendments. The Institute believes that more inequities flow from legislative "spot zoning" than could possibly result from an administrative procedure requiring reasoned statements for action.

c. The Rezoning Amendment

TREMARCO CORP. v. GARZIO

Supreme Court of New Jersey
32 N.J. 448, 161 A.2d 241 (1960)

The opinion of the court was delivered by
SCHETTINO, J.

This appeal is from a unanimous reversal by the Appellate Division of a judgment of the Superior Court, Law Division ordering defendants to reissue a building permit to plaintiff for the erection of a public garage and a gasoline station. . . .

In the trial court the parties stipulated the facts and agreed to submit the cause on cross motions for summary judgment. The facts are as follows: On June 25, 1957, all of the provisions of the applicable zoning ordinance having been complied with, the Ewing Township building inspector issued to the then owners of the premises in question a valid building permit for the construction of a public garage and gasoline filling station. At that time and up to September 3, 1958 the property was in an area that had been zoned a business district since the enactment of the zoning ordinance of 1950. Until June 5, 1958, public garages and gasoline filling stations were permitted in such business districts subject only to limitations as to proximity to certain buildings and places such as churches, schools and parks and as to the location of the buildings and gasoline pumps on the lot.

Concededly, the right to use the property for a service station increased the value of the property above what it would have been worth as a location for other business purposes and increased its value far above what it would have been worth for residential purposes. Except for the availability of the premises in question for the proposed service station plaintiff, whose sole function is to acquire sites for gasoline service stations for Gulf Oil Corporation, would have had no interest in it. Relying upon the existence of the permit and the provisions of the ordinance under which it had been granted, the plaintiff agreed to purchase the premises for $21,500. Prior to the passing of title the attention of all parties was directed to the fact that Section 7 of the building code provided that any permit issued thereunder would automatically be revoked if the proposed work was not actually begun within three months next after the date on which such permit had been issued. At the expiration date of this permit an assurance was secured from the building inspector that the permit could be renewed. Relying upon such assurance, plaintiff acquired title on October 2, 1957. In accordance with the inspector's commitment, the permit was renewed on October 8, 1957 for an additional 90 days. Prior to the expiration of this 90-day period, plaintiff again applied for and received a reissuance or renewal of the building permit for an additional 90 days. The renewals were granted in the name of Gulf Oil Corporation, plaintiff's principal.

During the period of the renewals of the permit, plaintiff spent $145 for a survey, $647.16 for architect's fees, and entered into a contract in the amount of $31,412 with a contractor for the construction of the building and for the installation of the necessary equipment. During March of 1958 the contractor deposited storage tanks on the premises as the first step in the execution of the contract.

In the month of February 1958 defendant Garzio was appointed to the position of building inspector succeeding the inspector with whom plaintiff had dealt. In March of 1958 plaintiff applied to Garzio for a reissuance or renewal of the building permit, and such a permit was issued on March 27, 1958. Defendants concede the validity of this permit. Garzio knew of the prior permits and had been informed that plaintiff in reliance thereon had entered into the contract for the construction and installation work.

Shortly thereafter, defendant township committee received a petition from certain township residents protesting the issuance of the permit to plaintiff and although there had been no change in the character of the neighborhood since the enactment of the 1950 zoning ordinance, the township committee instructed Garzio to revoke plaintiff's building permit. On March 31, 1958 Garzio, by a personal visit, informed plaintiff's agents that the permit had been revoked and when they refused to acknowledge or accept the revocation, Garzio mailed "official" notification thereof to plaintiff, which was received on April 2, 1958. (At oral argument, defendants admitted that the "revocation" was without legal warrant.)

At a regular township committee meeting on April 3 plaintiff protested the action of the building inspector and asked for the reinstatement of the permit. The minutes of the meeting show that the mayor stated that the committee was in the process of considering the adoption of an ordinance which would require applications to construct service stations to be "appealed" to the board of adjustment before a building permit could be issued. Plaintiff, desiring to cooperate with the municipal officials, accepted the mayor's statement that the only change which the proposed ordinance would work would be the requirement of such an appeal and therefore awaited the passage of the new ordinance. No such ordinance having been introduced prior to April 30, 1958, plaintiff on that date again protested the revocation of the permit. On May

8, 1958 the township solicitor notified plaintiff of the refusal of the township committee to act upon its request for relief.

On May 1, 1958 the committee had introduced and approved on first reading a proposed amendment to the zoning ordinance. The advertisement concerning this amendment stated that it would be further considered on May 15, 1958. At that meeting the planning board made an oral report that it had met on May 8, had disapproved the proposed amendment to the ordinance and had suggested a different ordinance. The committee thereupon rejected the May 1, 1958 amendment and introduced on first reading another amendment which was advertised for further consideration at a meeting to be held on June 5. On that date the committee adopted said ordinance on final hearing. Under its terms the board of adjustment has no power to grant plaintiff a permit for the construction of a gasoline station on plaintiff's lands. On September 3, 1958 the committee passed another amendment to its zoning ordinance changing the area in question from a business zone to a residential zone.

Plaintiff contends that a validly issued building permit cannot be revoked nor can its lands be rezoned adversely to its interests under the permit if there has been "substantial" reliance upon the continued validity of the permit; that there was such reliance and that it is demonstrated by substantial expenditures which were made, by its change of position, by the purchase of the property at a higher price than it would be worth were it to be used for other business or residential purposes and by incurring additional obligations, ... Plaintiff also urges that the beginning of actual construction is not a necessary element in evaluating whether there has been substantial reliance and that the statement in *Crecca v. Nucera,* 52 N.J. Super. 279, 145 A.2d 477 (App.Div.1958), to the effect that substantial reliance pertains to investments or expenditures in connection with the actual commencement of excavation or construction was *dictum* and unnecessary to the result of that case. Plaintiff also contends that even if its reliance had been minimal, defendant municipality abused its police powers in revoking the permit. Generally, it charges defendants with arbitrary, capricious and unreasonable conduct.

Defendants argue that except in those cases where there has been substantial reliance upon a building permit prior to its revocation, the law existing at the time of decision governs the validity of the intended use of the property rather than the law which existed at the time the building permit was issued. *Roselle v. Mayor and Council of Borough of Moonachie,* 49 N.J. Super. 35, 139 A.2d 42 (App.Div.1958), reaffirming 48 N.J. Super. 17, 136 A.2d 773 (App.Div.1957). Defendants insist that here there has been no substantial reliance because that term requires something akin to actual commencement of construction, and that the *dictum* in

Crecca, indicating that actual commencement of excavation or construction is required, was not a departure from the New Jersey holdings, and moreover was completely in line with the weight of authority elsewhere. . . . Lastly, defendants contend that even if there had been substantial reliance upon the building permit by the plaintiff, the permit nevertheless expired by operation of law as plaintiff began no excavation or construction under the original permit or the renewals within the 90-day periods provided for by the ordinance. . . .

This synopsis of the arguments of the parties demonstrates that the main contention centers upon the question of what actions constitute such reliance as would bar revocation of the validly issued building permit. We note at the outset that this case involves an ordinance proposed and enacted after the regular issuance of a building permit. Therefore, we have no occasion to and do not consider what rule of law should be applied to those cases where there is no semblance of compliance by the landowner with the applicable ordinance or authorization for the issuance of such a permit. . . . Nor do we consider or express any opinion as to the proper outcome of what has been characterized as the "race of diligence". . . which often occurs when landowners hasten to acquire permits before a pending ordinance, which would have the effect of prohibiting the intended use, can be enacted. See *Socony-Vacuum Oil Co. v. Mt. Holly Township,* 135 N.J.L. 112, 51 A.2d 19, 169 A.L.R. 579 (Sup.Ct.1947) and *Gold v. Building Committee of Warren Borough,* 334 Pa. 10, 5 A.2d 367 (Sup.Ct.1939) in which permits were refused for this reason. In *Appeal of A. N. "Ab" Young Co.,* 360 Pa. 429, 61 A.2d 839 (Sup.Ct.1948) a permit had been issued and then revoked and a request for a new permit had been refused because the proposed use conflicted with a pending ordinance, and in *Sharrow v. City of Dania,* 83 So.2d 274 (Fla.Sup. Ct.1955) a permit was revoked because of such a conflict. See also Note, 34 Notre Dame Lawyer, 109, 111-113 (1958). Nor, as we view the record, is this a case where a flaw in the zoning scheme was revealed for the first time by plaintiff's application. . . .

In general terms the rule is that where the permit is regularly issued in accordance with the zoning ordinance, it may not be revoked after reliance. It must be determined at what point it can be said that an individual has performed acts which form the wellspring from which certain protectable interests may flow and create a countervailing force which will prevail over the normally paramount authority of the municipality to preserve the desirable characteristics of the community through zoning. . . . As was pointed out by Judge Conford in *Roselle, supra,* 49 N.J. Super. at page 40, 139 A.2d at page 45, the basic problem is "as to the stage of utilization of an individual's property which should be regarded as immunizing it from the ban of a subsequently adopted prohibitory zoning regulation." While that case dealt with an application for a license to operate a trailer park, the following language is especially pertinent here:

". . . In some jurisdictions this point is reached when an application for a permit or license is filed, and subsequent prohibitory legislation is not permitted to affect the applicant's rights, ... The more general view, however, is that the mere right under existing laws and ordinances to make a particular use of property at the time of an application for a permit does not immunize the owner from valid subsequently adopted legislation, state or municipal, . . .

. . . .

". . . The predominant viewpoint goes to the extent of sanctioning the revocation of a permit for a use valid when issued, where a subsequent prohibitory regulation is adopted prior to reliance by the owner upon the permit by substantial investment or expenditure. . . ."

There is no easy formula to resolve issues of this kind. The ultimate objective is fairness to both the public and the individual property owner. We think there is no profit in attempting to fix some precise concept of the nature and *quantum* of reliance which will suffice. Rather a balance must be struck between the interests of the permittee and the right and duty of the municipality through planning and the implementation of that scheme through zoning "to 'make, ordain and establish all manner of wholesome and of reasonable laws, not repugnant to the Constitution,' as may be deemed to be 'for the good and welfare of the commonwealth, and all the subjects of the same.' " *Roselle v. Wright,* 21 N.J. 400, 408-409, 122 A.2d 506, 510 (1956). This right is one of which the permittee is deemed to be aware. . . .

The pertinent factors are these. The municipality in fact knew that plaintiff wanted the property solely for a gasoline service station and intended and did pay a sum substantially in excess of the value of the property for other purposes. Prior to the attempted revocation of the permit, plaintiff entered into the construction and installation contract and thus faces the prospect of a suit for breach of this contract. Before revocation the contractor delivered gasoline storage tanks onto the premises for installation. It expended moneys for title and architectural work. The permit was illegally revoked. There was no superseding ordinance nor in fact a pending one at the time of the attempted revocation. Additionally as to the amendment, plaintiff was lulled into inaction on its construction work by defendants' promise that the zoning change contemplated would not affect plaintiff.

There was no change whatsoever in the characteristics of the area since the adoption of the 1950 zoning plan. The surrounding lands are still substantially undeveloped. There is no suggestion that the governing body suddenly found itself confronted with an ordinance which had become outmoded because of ensuing events. The amendment was provoked by a petition from some of the residents who sought to eliminate gasoline stations out of the zone.

In these circumstances, we are satisfied that the equities strongly predominate in favor of plaintiff. Its right to proceed under the regularly issued permit should therefore be upheld.

Defendants also contend that plaintiff did not comply with the requirement that the work be started within 90 days after the issuance of the permit. It is conceded that on March 27, 1958 defendant Garzio issued a valid permit to plaintiff. The 90-day period thereunder would have expired on June 27, 1958. It cannot be argued that when defendants attempted to revoke plaintiff's permit on April 2, 1958, plaintiff should have insisted on the validity of its permit and have gone ahead with construction. We can readily assume that the municipal police authorities would be called in and action taken. Plaintiff, instead of following a course of conduct which might lead to a breach of peace, filed its complaint in this cause on June 16, 1958, well within the 90-day period. We find no merit in this point.

The judgment of the Appellate Division is reversed and that of the Law Division reinstated.

For reversal: Chief Justice WEINTRAUB, and Justices BURLING, JACOBS, FRANCIS, PROCTOR, HALL and SCHETTINO—7.

For affirmance: None.

———————

Comments: 1. When amendments are made to the zoning map or zoning text they may change the zoning restrictions applicable to properties on which development has commenced which, though allowable under the ordinance before amendment, is not allowable under the ordinance as amended. These cases raise questions of zoning estoppel and vested rights, and the circumstances of the case may lead a court to protect the developer against changes made in the ordinance after his development has been started.

The theory on which relief is awarded in these cases is not entirely clear:

> The defense of estoppel is derived from equity, but the defense of vested rights reflects principles of common and constitutional law. Similarly their elements are different. Estoppel focuses on whether it would be inequitable to allow the government to repudiate its prior conduct; vested rights upon whether the owner acquired real property rights which cannot be taken away by governmental regulation.

Heeter, Zoning Estoppel: Application of the Principles of Equitable Estoppel and Vested Rights to Zoning Disputes, 1971 Urb. L. Ann. 63, 64-65. The vested rights approach is simply an extension of the usual rule, that nonconforming uses are entitled to protection from changes in the zoning ordinance. *See supra* p. 290. While the results in the cases do not appear to vary with the theory that is applied, each theory has different origins and different implications for zoning law. When the court in the principal case indicated that "[t]he ultimate objective is fairness to both the public and the individual property owner," which theory were they applying?

2. Estoppel influences are evident in some of the principles applied to these cases. Most courts, for example, are reluctant to hold local governments, their officers and agencies, to representations made to developers which later are not honored; there is a reluctance to bind governmental agencies to a course of action when there is no overt commitment on the public side. This may be the reason why most courts do not find a zoning estoppel if no building permit is issued, even though the developer would have been entitled to the permit under the zoning ordinance before it was amended. The California Supreme Court has recently reaffirmed this position. *Avco Community Builders, Inc. v. South Coast Regional Comm'n,* 553 P.2d 546 (Cal. 1976). The courts apparently believe that the issuance of the building permit demonstrates some commitment to the developer on which a zoning estoppel may be founded. For a thoughtful critique of the *Avco* case see Hagman, The Vesting Issue: The Rights of Fetal Development Vis-à-Vis the Abortions of Public Whimsy, 7 Envt'l L. 519 (1977). A few states have adopted a minority rule that fully protects the developer once a permit has been issued. In effect, the permit is nonrevocable. *See, e.g., Hull v. Hunt,* 331 P.2d 856 (Wash. 1958).

The requirement that appears in many of the cases, that the developer seeking the protection of a zoning estoppel be in good faith, also reflects the equity influence. Vested right doctrine, however, appears to have produced the requirement that the developer make substantial expenditures in reliance on his permit before he is protected. This influence is also seen in the further requirement that these expenditures be substantial as compared with the total cost of the project. *But see Clackamas County v. Holmes,* 508 P.2d 190 (Ore. 1973) (relaxes substantiality test in favor of equitable factors).

Note the dilemma in which the combination of these requirements often places the developer:

> Prior to the enactment of [a provision in the zoning ordinance making building permits nonrevocable] . . ., even a permit which had achieved administrative finality could be revoked on the basis of a subsequent change in the zoning laws. The permittee could win immunity from such "ex post facto" revocation only by constructing a substantial portion of the structure authorized by his permit in good faith reliance upon the prior law. A permittee who delayed construction in the face of an impending amendment to the zoning laws might find that he had not progressed far enough in time to qualify for immunity; one who proceeded with unseemly haste ran the risk that his conduct might bear the stigma of bad faith. No facile formula informed the permittee how to strike the delicate balance which would afford the desired immunity.

Russian Hill Improvement Ass'n v. Board of Permit Appeals, 423 P.2d 824, 828-29 (Cal. 1967).

3. The *Russian Hill* case construed a savings clause in the local zoning ordinance, a strategy that many communities have adopted to provide more certainty to the rules affecting development in progress when zoning ordinances change. This clause provided:

> Any building or use for which a permit has been lawfully granted prior to the effective date of an amendment to the City Planning Code . . . may be completed and used in accordance with the approved plans, provided that construction is started and diligently prosecuted to completion. . . .

Does this savings clause give away too much? Assume, for example, that a municipality enacts a new height control ordinance lowering the height of buildings to control the intensity of downtown development. Would there be a case for revoking a permit issued under the old ordinance at the old height limit in order to protect the integrity of the new height restriction? Does a savings clause raise an equal protection objection? *See State ex rel. Bolce v. Hauser,* 145 N.E. 851 (Ohio 1924) (objection dismissed). Subdivision control legislation sometimes contains similar provisions. They are discussed *infra* p. 785. For discussion of vested rights and savings clause cases see Annot., 49 A.L.R.3d 13 (1973); 49 A.L.R.3d 1150 (1973).

4. Estoppel and vested rights theories may protect a landowner from a zoning change that will preclude a planned use of his land. Most of the cases in which the validity of zoning changes is litigated, however, are cases where the zoning regulations applicable to a tract of land have been changed and the neighboring landowners seek to have the rezoning invalidated. The next three principal cases are of this type.

KUEHNE v. TOWN OF EAST HARTFORD

Connecticut Supreme Court of Errors
136 Conn. 452, 72 A.2d 747 (1950)

MALTBIE, C.J. . . . [A substantial part of the opinion is omitted.—Eds.]

Main Street in East Hartford runs substantially north and south. The petitioner before the town council, Langlois, owned a piece of land on the east side of it which he had been using for growing fruit and vegetables, and he has had upon it a greenhouse and a roadside stand for the sale of products of the land. The premises, ever since zoning was established in East Hartford in 1927, had been in an A residence district. Langlois made an application to the town council to change to an A business district a portion of the tract fronting on Main Street for about 500 feet and extending to a depth of 150 feet. He intended, if the application was granted, to erect upon the tract a building containing six or eight stores, apparently in the nature of retail stores and small business establishments calculated to serve the needs of residents in the vicinity. Starting at a business district to the north and extending for almost three miles to the town boundary on the south, the land along Main Street and extending to a considerable depth on each side of it has been, ever since zoning was established in the town, in an A residence district, with certain exceptions hereinafter described. Seven hundred feet north of the Langlois property is a small business district lying on both sides of Main Street; the land on the east side is used for a fruit and vegetable stand, a milk bar and a garage and gas station; and the land on the west side, with an area a little larger than the Langlois tract in question, is now unoccupied. About 500 feet south of the Langlois property is another small business district in which is located a grill and restaurant, a drugstore, a cleaning and dyeing business and a large grocery and meat market. Formerly the land about the tract in question was used quite largely for agricultural purposes, but within the last few years a large residential community, comprising some one thousand houses, has grown up in the vicinity.

The application to the town council was based upon the claim that residents in the vicinity need the stores and services which could be located in the building Langlois proposed to erect. There was, for example, a petition filed with the council in support of the application signed by fifty-one of those residents which asked it to allow such a change as might be necessary to permit for their benefit a shopping center on the property. None of the signers, however, owned property on Main Street or in the immediate vicinity of the Langlois property. On the other hand, the application was opposed by the owner of property directly opposite the tract in question and by the owners of the two properties fronting on Main Street immediately south of the Langlois land.

The council voted that the application "be granted for the general welfare and the good of the town in that section." In *Bartram v. Zoning Commission,* 136 Conn. 89, 68 A.2d 308, we recently had before us an appeal from the granting by a zoning commission of an application to change a lot in Bridgeport even smaller than the tract here in question from a residence to a business zone, and we sustained the action of the commission. We said (p. 93): "A limitation upon the powers of zoning authorities which has been in effect ever since zoning statutes were made applicable generally to municipalities in the state is that the regulations they adopt must be made 'in accordance with a comprehensive plan.' Public Acts, 1925, c. 242, § 3 (Rev.1949, § 837). 'A "comprehensive plan" means "a general plan to control and direct the use and development of property in a municipality or a large part of it by dividing it into districts according to the present and potential use of the properties."' *Bishop v. Board of Zoning Appeals,* 133 Conn. 614, 618, 53 A.2d 659; *State ex rel. Spiros v. Payne,* 131 Conn. 647, 652, 41 A.2d 908. Action by a zoning authority which gives to a single lot or a small area privileges which are not extended to other land in the vicinity is in general against sound public policy and obnoxious to the law. It can be justified only when it is done in furtherance of a general plan properly adopted for and designed to serve the best interests of the community as a whole. The vice of spot zoning lies in the fact that it singles out for special treatment a lot or a small area in a way that does not further such a plan. Where, however, in pursuance of it, a zoning commission takes such action, its decision can be assailed only on the ground that it abused the discretion vested in it by the law. To permit business in a small area within a residence zone may fall within the scope of such a plan, and to do so, unless it amounts to unreasonable or arbitrary action, is not unlawful." It appeared in that case that the change was granted by the commission in pursuance of a policy to encourage decentralization of business in the city and to that end to permit neighborhood stores in outlying districts. It is true that we said in that opinion (p. 94) that if the commission decided, "on facts affording a sufficient basis and in the exercise of a proper discretion, that it would serve the best interests of the community as a whole to permit a use of a single lot or small area in a different way than was allowed in surrounding territory, it would not be guilty of spot zoning in any sense obnoxious to the law." We meant by that statement to emphasize the fact that the controlling test must be, not the benefit to a particular individual or group of individuals, but the good of the community as a whole, and we did not mean in any way to derogate from our previous statement that any such change can only be made if it falls within the requirements of a comprehensive plan for the use and development of property in the municipality or a large part of it. See *Parsons v. Wethersfield,* 135 Conn. 24, 29, 60 A.2d 771.

In the case before us it is obvious that the council looked no further than the benefit which might accrue to Langlois and those who resided in the vicinity of his property, and that they gave no consideration to the larger question as to the effect the change would have upon the general plan of zoning in the community. In fact, the controlling consideration seems to have been that Langlois intended to go ahead at once with his building rather than any consideration of the suitability of the particular lot for business uses, because there is no suggestion in the record that the council considered the fact that only some 700 feet away was a tract of land already zoned for business which, as appears from the zoning map in evidence, was more easily accessible to most of the signers of the petition than was the Langlois land.

In *Strain v. Mims,* 123 Conn. 275, 287, 193 A. 754, we said "One of the essential purposes of zoning regulation is to stabilize property uses." In this case it is significant that the change was opposed by the owners of three properties so situated as to be most affected by it, while those who supported it were the owner of the tract and residents who did not live in its immediate vicinity. It should also be noted that the petition they signed contained a provision that it should not be construed as supporting permission for the use of the premises as a liquor outlet, but at the hearing before the council the attorney for Langlois in effect conceded that the zoning regulations permitted such a use in an A business district; and if that is so and the change were granted, it is quite possible that the premises would be sooner or later converted to such a use.

The action of the town council in this case was not in furtherance of any general plan of zoning in the community and cannot be sustained.

. . . .

There is error, the judgment is set aside and the case is remanded to be proceeded with according to law.

. . . .

Comments: 1. Was the Connecticut court persuasive in distinguishing the principal case from *Bartram v. Zoning Comm'n* on the ground that, in *Bartram,* "the change was granted by the commission in pursuance of a policy to encourage decentralization of business in the city and to that end to permit neighborhood stores in outlying districts"? Perusal of the *Bartram* opinion indicates that only one commission member testified that the commission had adopted such a policy; the court, however, said, "nowhere in the record is there any suggestion that this testimony is not true," and apparently gave significant weight to it. Assuming that the zoning commission, in fact, had formulated such a policy in *Bartram,* does it rise to the dignity of "a comprehensive plan" within the meaning of the Standard State Zoning Enabling Act and the Connecticut zoning statute? The *Bartram* opinion does not indicate that the zoning commission had adopted any standards or guidelines to be applied when landowners sought rezoning to permit establishment of business uses in areas zoned for residential use. The zoning commission justified the business rezoning in *Bartram* as follows:

> 1. The location is on Sylvan Avenue, a sixty-foot street, and there is no shopping center within a mile of it. To the north of this tract there is a very large development but only small nonconforming grocery stores to serve people. 2. There is practically only one house, adjacent to this tract on the north, which will be directly affected by this change of zone. 3. Business No. 3 regulations, with their thirty-foot setback and liquor restrictions, were designed to meet conditions like this and help alleviate the great congestion in the centralized shopping districts.

Do any of these findings demonstrate that the land rezoned was, in fact, the best location for a new neighborhood shopping center in the general area involved in the case?

2. Compare the principal case and *Bartram* with *Fritts v. City of Ashland,* 348 S.W.2d 712 (Ky. 1961), where the court said:

> We feel impelled to express briefly our view of the proper theory of zoning as relates to the making of changes in an original comprehensive ordinance. We think the theory is that after the enactment of the original ordinance there should be a continuous or periodic study of the development of property uses, the nature of population trends, and the commercial and industrial growth, both actual and prospective. On the basis of such study changes may be made intelligently, systematically, and according to a coordinated plan designed to promote zoning objectives. An examination of the multitude of zoning cases that have reached this court leads us to the conclusion that the common practice of zoning agencies, after the adoption of an original ordinance, is simply to wait until some property owner finds an opportunity to acquire a financial advantage by devoting his property to a use other than that for which it is zoned, and then struggle with the question of whether some excuse can be found for complying with his request for a rezoning. The result has been that in most of the rezoning cases reaching the courts there actually has been spot zoning and the courts have upheld or invalidated the change according to how flagrant the violation of true zoning principles has been. It is to be hoped that in the future zoning authorities will give recognition to the fact that an essential feature of zoning is *planning.*

Id. at 714-15.

In the *Fritts* case, the local governing body had rezoned a four-acre tract in single ownership from R-2 Residential to I-1 Light Industrial because the owner of a garment factory, which had outgrown its existing location in the city, desired to build a new factory on that tract and threatened to leave the city unless that tract was made available. In holding that the rezoning amendment was invalid, the court said (*inter alia*):

> . . . [T]he general welfare argument is not sound. The providing of employment opportunities is merely one element of general welfare as that term relates to the zoning field. Sociological factors, protection of property values, traffic and safety considerations, preservation of health, providing adequate light and air, all enter into the question of general welfare. . . . If the appellees' argument were carried to its logical conclusion the mere fact that employment would be provided through particular use of land would overcome all other factors, and a boiler factory could be put in the middle of a beautiful residential neighborhood.
>
> The appellees argue that . . . there are no suitable light industry sites in the city other than the Wilson tract. Our answer to that is that if the lack of suitable industrial sites is due to the restrictions of the present zoning ordinance a study and survey of the situation should be made, suitable areas for industrial development selected, and changes made in the zoning ordinance in accordance with systematic planning. On the other hand, if lack of suitable

sites is due to other factors no real solution to the long range problem is reached by momentarily satisfying one particular industry.

Id. at 713-14.

3. In *Fritts* the Kentucky court articulated a more intelligible theory as to the relationship between "zoning" and "planning" than can be found in most of the cases, but the court did not state that zoning and rezoning must be preceded by the formal adoption of a "master" or "general" plan for the municipality, or even the land-use element of such a plan. Courts have generally taken the same view, although most of the original state zoning enabling acts included the Standard State Zoning Enabling Act's provision that zoning regulations "shall be in accordance with a comprehensive plan." (Standard Act § 3.) The draftmen's note to this provision simply states that "this requirement will prevent haphazard or piecemeal zoning. No zoning should be done without such a comprehensive study." [*Sic.*] When the Standard State Zoning Enabling Act was published there was no model planning enabling act authorizing the formulation of a comprehensive plan that could serve as the basis for the zoning regulations, although the Standard City Planning Enabling Act was published a few years later. In most of the states where the zoning enabling act is modeled on the Standard State Zoning Enabling Act, the courts have agreed with the New Jersey court's conclusion in *Kozesnik v. Township of Montgomery*, reprinted as a principal case *supra* p. 370:

> It is thus clear that the "comprehensive plan" of the zoning statute is not identical with the "master plan" of the Planning Act and need not meet the formal requirements of a master plan. The Zoning Act nowhere provides that the comprehensive plan shall exist in some physical form outside the ordinance itself. . . .
>
> There has been little judicial consideration of the precise attributes of a comprehensive plan. . . . Our own decisions emphasize that its office is to prevent a capricious exercise of the legislative power resulting in haphazard or piecemeal zoning. . . . Without venturing an exact definition, it may be said for present purposes that "plan" connotes an integrated product of a rational process and "comprehensive" requires something beyond a piecemeal approach, both to be revealed by the ordinance considered in relation to the physical facts and the purposes authorized by R.S. 40:55-32. Such being the requirements of a comprehensive plan, no reason is perceived why we should infer the Legislature intended by necessary implication that the comprehensive plan be portrayed in some physical form outside the ordinance itself. A plan may readily be revealed in an end-product — here the zoning ordinance — and no more is required by the statute.

131 A.2d at 7-8.

4. The seminal article on the "comprehensive plan" requirement in zoning is Haar, "In Accordance with a Comprehensive Plan," 68 Harv. L. Rev. 1154 (1955). Professor Haar's conclusion is as follows:

> . . . [T]he courts have taken a number of rather different approaches in testing zoning measures for consonance with the

enabling act mandate of "accordance with a comprehensive plan." None of the meanings suggested—broad geographical coverage, "policy" of the planning or zoning commission, the zoning ordinance itself, the rational basis underlying the ordinance—do extreme violence to the statutory wording. But all of them share a common defect: they emphasize the question whether the zoning ordinance is a comprehensive plan. Thus, construed, the enabling act demands little more than that zoning be "reasonable" and impartial in treatment, to satisfy the constitutional conditions for exercise of the state's police power.

Id. at 1173.

PIERREPONT v. ZONING COMMISSION OF TOWN OF RIDGEFIELD

Supreme Court of Connecticut
154 Conn. 463, 226 A.2d 659 (1967)

[The zoning commission is authorized by statute to enact and amend zoning ordinances in Connecticut towns.—Eds.]

COTTER, Associate Justice. The defendant zoning commission, after a public hearing, amended the Ridgefield zoning regulations to include a new residence R5-1 zone and granted a change of zone affecting approximately thirty-three acres from residence R-1 to the new residence R5-1. At the time of the change of zone, permitted uses in a residence R-1 zone included one-family and two-family residences on a minimum lot of one acre, resident professional offices, farming establishments, customary home occupations, church facilities, parks and municipal buildings, and schools. Ridgefield Zoning Regs. § 5 (1961). The new residence R5-1 zone, in addition to the uses allowed in a residence R-1 zone, permits the construction of two-story garden-style apartment buildings, subject to special requirements such as setbacks, maximum land usage, floor area of the dwelling units, and parking facilities. The plaintiffs, who own property in the immediate vicinity, appealed to the Court of Common Pleas, claiming that the action of the commission, on several specific grounds, was illegal, arbitrary and in abuse of the commission's discretion. A prospective developer, Jerry Tuccio, claiming to own a substantial portion of the rezoned property, was allowed to intervene as a party defendant. The present appeal has been taken by the plaintiffs from a judgment dismissing their appeal in the Court of Common Pleas.

The plaintiffs have raised three claims on appeal. The first is that the commission's action in granting the change of zone was inconsistent with the town's comprehensive plan and was not shown to have been justified by any change in conditions. Zoning in Ridgefield is governed by chapter 124 of the General Statutes. As such, it is subject to the implicit requirement of General Statutes

§ 8-2 that any zone change must be in harmony with the comprehensive plan. . . . The comprehensive plan for Ridgefield consists of the zoning regulations themselves and the zoning map which has been established pursuant to those regulations. See *Zandri v. Zoning Commission,* 150 Conn. 646, 649, 192 A.2d 876. The regulations, the zoning map and the record of the public hearing before the commission, a portion of which has been printed in the appendix to the plaintiffs' brief (see Practice Book § 719), reveal the following circumstances. The area in question is a largely undeveloped tract located near the main business center of town. It is bounded on the north by a business B-1 zone and on the east by a light industry B-2 zone, which is the town's least restrictive zoning classification. Several business establishments are situated in the general vicinity to the north and the east, across Grove Street, of the rezoned area. The property to the south consists of two large parcels, one lying in the business B-1 zone and the other in a residence R-1 zone. The Elms Inn, which is a nonconforming business use, is located on the latter parcel. To the west lie Main Street, recognized by the commission, as an historical and aesthetic asset of the community, and, across Main Street, a residence R-1 zone in which are located the homes of the appealing plaintiffs. A tract of seven and one-half acres, rezoned by the commission in 1960 to allow garden-style apartments, is in the immediate vicinity, lying somewhat south and east of the property presently under consideration. This earlier action by the commission was also challenged and was affirmed. See *Zandri v. Zoning Commission,* supra. The entire area is within a short distance of the civic and commercial center of the town.

A number of closely prescribed restrictions have been incorporated into the new zone in an attempt to harmonize any proposed use of the land in question with the surrounding area. As enacted by the commission, the provisions relating to the new zone limit the land area on which buildings may be constructed to 25 percent of the total area involved and allow no more than ten apartment units per acre. In addition, a setback requirement of 250 feet from Main Street is designed to preserve the historical atmosphere of the Main Street area and serves as a buffer between the properties of the plaintiffs and any garden apartments which might be developed as a result of the zone change. In view of the foregoing facts, including the proximity of the rezoned area to properties zoned for commercial and apartment uses, and the restrictive provisions adopted by the commission to preserve the general tenor of the entire area, it cannot be said that the commission's action was in conflict with the town's comprehensive plan.[149]

The plaintiffs also claim that there had not been any change in conditions affecting the area in question which could justify the action taken by the commission. In amending its zoning regulations, and in rezoning this particular property, the commission was acting as a legislative body. . . . When acting in such a capacity, it is subject to the general rule that it may modify its enactments whenever time and experience reasonably indicate the need for revision. . . . A substantial change in the overall character of a town is a change which affects every part of that town. The commission in this case based its action, in part, on a substantial increase in Ridgefield's total population and the resulting need for appropriate housing to accommodate such classes of people as school teachers, retired persons, and executives of certain industries which had recently located in the town. This evolution in the character of the town, not limited in its effect to any one specific area, produced a change in conditions which the zoning commission could properly take into account in amending the zoning regulations. Its action in this case was not shown to be an unreasonable exercise of its discretion in meeting these changing conditions. . . .

The zoning authority acting as a legislative body, may amend or modify zoning ordinances or regulations when the growth and progress of the town require it, or where it is for the general welfare of the community. . . . By necessity a comprehensive plan must undergo changes. "If any zoning plan is to be really comprehensive, it must be kept up to date. . . . A plan may . . . become quite obsolete where there is a refusal to recognize changing conditions in a community." 1 Yokley, Zoning Law and Practice (3d Ed.) § 3-6. Zoning regulations cannot remain static or immutable; changing conditions require orderly changes . . . . The zoning commission is under a duty reasonably to anticipate future conditions which could affect the public welfare. . . .

The plaintiffs also make the claim that the action of the commission constituted spot zoning. The practice of spot zoning, in the sense of an illegal exercise of the zoning power, has been generally defined as the reclassification of a small area of land in such a manner as to disturb the tenor of the surrounding neighborhood. . . . It should be

---

[149] Although there was some evidence before the commission that the town sewerage system could not adequately serve apartments in this location, the commission felt that the necessary facilities were available. In light of the preliminary steps which had been taken toward an expansion of the sewerage plant if it became necessary, we cannot say that the commission abused its discretion in this regard. In addition, the zoning regulations provide that no apartment building shall be erected in an R5-1 zone unless public water and sewer services are available and unless a development plan for the entire premises has been approved by the commission.

clear from what has already been said in relation to the general neighborhood involved in this case, as well as from what we said in *Zandri v. Zoning Commission,* supra, that the characterization of spot zoning is not applicable to the facts of the present case. . . .

There is no error.

In this opinion the other judges concurred.

Comments: 1. It is clear that the Connecticut court gave substantial weight to the "change of conditions" in sustaining the rezoning amendment in the principal case. Compare *Zoning Comm'n v. New Canaan Bldg. Co.,* 148 A.2d 330 (Conn. 1959), were the court invalidated a zoning amendment placing property which had been in an apartment zone for more than fifteen years in a single-family residence zone. Emphasizing that an essential purpose of zoning is to stabilize land uses, the court said: "There is nothing in the finding to indicate a change in the character of the neighborhood which would warrant a reclassification of the area. . . . Before a zoning board rezones property, there should be proof either that there was some mistake in the original zoning or that the character of the neighborhood has changed to such an extent that a reclassification ought properly to be made. . . . Those who buy property in a zoned district have the right to expect that the classification made in the ordinance will not be changed unless a change is required for the public good."

2. Maryland is the state *par excellence* in which a legislative rezoning by amendment must be justified by either an original mistake in the zoning ordinance or by a change in conditions. Between fifty and one hundred cases involving rezonings to allow apartment development have been considered by the Maryland Court of Appeals (highest court) in the last decade or so. These cases were analyzed in D. Mandelker, The Zoning Dilemma 87-105 (1971). A review of these cases appears to indicate that the Court of Appeals gives weight to the following factors when passing on apartment rezonings:

(1) The court accepts the principle that apartments may and should be used as buffers between single family residential development and other nonresidential development, such as commercial development, which is even less "desirable" than apartments.

(2) However, allowing one apartment rezoning as a buffer does not justify the extension of that buffer in a subsequent rezoning.

(3) If another apartment rezoning has been granted in the vicinity of the present rezoning, and if the other apartment zoning has not yet been used, this factor may justify a denial of the present rezoning.

(4) Highways are proper boundaries between areas of more intensive and less intensive land uses. So are interchanges on limited-access highways.

(5) A new highway or substantial street improvement in the vicinity of the rezone site is a change in condition favorable to the granting of an apartment rezone.

(6) A very large tract is its own neighborhood, and internal compatibilities of use are as important to the rezoning as the external relationship of the site to its surroundings.

(7) A mere increase in traffic and in school population does not justify denial of an apartment zoning. On the other hand, if the rezoning will create a traffic hazard it should be rejected.

(8) Improved water and sewer facilities justify apartment development, and a lack of either is a reason for denying an apartment rezone.

The impact that the availability of public facilities has on rezoning is troublesome, for the zoning system will lose its initiative to the extent that its decisions must rest on the adequacy of highway and other public facility programs. Nor can highway planners and highway departments control zoning decisions. This observation simply underscores a point made by many observers: *The most important factors influencing the zoning process lie outside the system.* Cases illustrating the impact of the highway network on the zoning process are noted in the next comment. See also *Malafronte v. Planning and Zoning Bd.,* 230 A.2d 606 (Conn. 1967), holding that the need to find replacement housing for urban renewal displacees helps justify a rezoning for public housing.

3. When courts justify rezoning amendments on the basis of a change in conditions in the area surrounding the zone change, they tend to equate change with intensification of the land uses surrounding the site, and with the provision of improved highways and highway access to support the higher density or traffic-generating uses allowed by the zone change. But as the cases come up for judicial review, usually assisted by a presumption of validity and by the reasonably debatable rule, it is often difficult to tell just what factors the courts consider determinative. The following cases are illustrative:

Ball v. Town Plan & Zoning Comm'n, 151 A.2d 327 (Conn. 1959). The court upheld a rezoning of property to the east and to the west of the Springfield-Hartford expressway from residence to business. Reliance was placed on the proximity of the property to the expressway, and on the fact that the municipality wanted to promote "a logical and reasonable development of the expressway interchange." *Id.* at 329.

Jablon v. Town Planning and Zoning Comm'n, 254 A.2d 914 (Conn. 1969). The court sustained a zoning map amendment to change a 47-acre parcel from an R-1 (farming and residential) to an M-2 (industrial) classification. The court gave substantial weight to the commission's findings:

> The highest and best use of the tract is for light industry, laboratory and office uses. There are at present only two expressway interchanges in Newtown, whereas there is ample undeveloped residential land elsewhere in town, and rezoning this tract should result in a minimum increase in traffic burden to local streets. The trend of industrial construction is to locate near expressway interchanges, and the construction of interstate route 84 with access to Connecticut routes 25 and 6 resulted in a change in the area justifying such a new zonal classification. . . . Also there has been no residential construction in Newtown on land adjacent to interstate route 84 since its opening four and one-half years ago;

residential construction adjacent thereto, if any, is likely to be
marginal in quality; the tract is served by electricity and
high-pressure natural gas; and its topography is appropriate for
low-density industrial uses.

Id. at 917.

Rosko v. City of Marlborough, 242 N.E.2d 857 (Mass. 1968). The court
upheld the rezoning of 800 acres in the vicinity of two interstate highways
for industrial uses. Access to the highways was available. The court
appeared to approve comments by the trial judge that the zoning would
increase property values in the city and aid its economic advancement.

Zopfi v. City of Wilmington, 160 S.E.2d 325 (N.C. 1968). The court
approved the rezoning for shopping center development of a 40-acre parcel
located in a triangle between two expressways.

Finney v. Halle, 216 A.2d 530 (Md. 1966). Construction of an expressway
was found to be an important factor supporting a zoning change to allow
apartments. It was apparently local planning policy to locate apartments
near expressways. *But cf. France v. Shapiro,* 236 A.2d 726 (Md. 1968).

Park Constr. Corp. v. Board of County Comm'rs, 227 A.2d 15 (Md. 1967).
The legislative body's decision to refuse rezoning for apartment
development was affirmed. The court noted that a freeway scheduled to cut
across the property was not to be completed for five years and that its
location was tentative.

4. Even in Maryland, the "original mistake or change of conditions" rule
would apparently not be applied in cases where the local governing body
enacts a comprehensive revision of the original zoning ordinance or
replaces it with a completely new ordinance. All the cases where the rule
was stated involved the rezoning of a comparatively small parcel of land,
usually under single ownership. In Kentucky the courts have differentiated
cases involving the rezoning of a small tract under single ownership—"spot
zoning" cases—from cases involving the rezoning of larger tracts consisting
of parcels owned by several different persons. *See, e.g., Leutenmayer v.
Mathis,* 333 S.W.2d 774 (Ky. 1959). The "original mistake or change of
conditions" rule was expressly rejected in *Levitt v. Village of Sands Point,*
174 N.Y.S.2d 283 (N.Y. App. Div. 1958), and in *Oka v. Cole,* 145 So.2d 233
(Fla. 1962).

5. In Denver, Colorado, a Home Rule City, the zoning ordinance
contains the following provision:

> 1. Declaration of Public Policy. For the purpose of establishing
> and maintaining sound, stable and desirable development within
> the territorial limits of the municipality, this ordinance, and as here
> used the term ordinance shall be deemed to include the official
> map, shall not be amended except to correct a manifest error in
> the ordinance or, because of changed or changing conditions in
> a particular area or in the municipality generally, to rezone an area
> or extend the boundary of an existing district, or [to] change the
> regulations and restrictions thereof, only as reasonably necessary
> to the promotion of the public health, safety or general wel-
> fare. . . .

In *Corper v. City and County of Denver,* 552 P.2d 13 (Colo. 1976), the
court assumed that this ordinance provision was valid, although the

"change-or-mistake" limitation on zoning amendments is apparently not a general component of Colorado zoning law. In the *Corper* case, the court sustained a rezoning amendment to permit expansion of an existing hospital, holding that the rezoning was justified by a finding that there were changing conditions in the municipality generally calling for the hospital expansion, although there was no finding of changing conditions in the particular area.

6. Norman Williams asserts that the "change-or-mistake" rule is based upon a misunderstanding of the nature of the planning process, and further, that there are three situations in which a "piecemeal" zoning change is appropriate without a total reconsideration and comprehensive revision of the zoning ordinance: (a) where the municipality simply changes its land use policy with regard to a relatively small problem—*e.g.,* to allow additional retail shopping facilities; (b) where the municipality changes its land use policy as a result of a more complete understanding of long-established conditions and trends—*e.g.,* a realization that there are new zoning techniques which may provide a better transition between residential and commercial districts; and (c) where the municipality seeks to implement a land use plan over time—*e.g.,* by setting up a sequence of developments for vacant land on the urban fringe—in which case the plan's future zoning classification and the interim classification of some areas will be different and the zoning will be changed to conform to the plan when development is imminent. "In none of the above (except perhaps the last) is comprehensive rezoning really appropriate or necessary." 1 N. Williams, American Land Planning Law § 32.01 (1974).

FASANO v. BOARD OF COUNTY COMMISSIONERS OF WASHINGTON COUNTY

Supreme Court of Oregon
264 Ore. 574, 507 P.2d 23 (1973)

HOWELL, Justice.

The plaintiffs, homeowners in Washington County, unsuccessfully opposed a zone change before the Board of County Commissioners of Washington County. Plaintiffs applied for and received a writ of review of the action of the commissioners allowing the change. The trial court found in favor of plaintiffs, disallowed the zone change, and reversed the commissioners' order. The Court of Appeals affirmed, 489 P.2d 693 (1971), and this court granted review.

The defendants are the Board of County Commissioners and A.G.S. Development Company. A.G.S., the owner of 32 acres which had been zoned R-7 (Single Family Residential), applied for a zone change to P-R (Planned Residential), which allows for the construction of a mobile home park. The change failed to receive a majority vote of the Planning Commission. The Board of County Commissioners approved the change and found, among other matters, that the change allows for "increased densities and different types of housing to meet the needs of urbanization over that allowed by the existing zoning."

The trial court, relying on its interpretation of *Roseta v. County of Washington,* 254 Or. 161, 458 P.2d 405, 40 A.L.R.3d 364 (1969), reversed the order of the commissioners because the commissioners had not shown any change in the character of the neighborhood which would justify the rezoning. The Court of Appeals affirmed for the same reason, but added the additional ground that the defendants failed to show that the change was consistent with the comprehensive plan for Washington county.

According to the briefs, the comprehensive plan of development for Washington county was adopted in 1959 and included classifications in the county for residential, neighborhood commercial, retail commercial, general commercial, industrial park and light industry, general and heavy industry, and agricultural areas.

The land in question, which was designated "residential" by the comprehensive plan, was zoned R-7, Single Family Residential.

Subsequent to the time the comprehensive plan was adopted, Washington county established a Planned Residential (P-R) zoning classification in 1963. The P-R classification was adopted by ordinance and provided that a planned residential unit development could be established and should include open space for utilities, access, and recreation; should not be less than 10 acres in size; and should be located in or adjacent to a residential zone. The P-R zone adopted by the 1963 ordinance is of the type known as a "floating zone," so-called because the ordinance creates a zone classification authorized for future use but not placed on the zoning map until its use at a particular location is approved by the governing body. The R-7 classification for the 32 acres continued until April 1970 when the classification was changed to P-R to permit the defendant A.G.S. to construct the mobile home park on the 32 acres involved.

The defendants argue that (1) the action of the county commissioners approving the change is presumptively valid, requiring plaintiffs to show that the commissioners acted arbitrarily in approving the zone change; (2) it was not necessary to show a change of conditions in the area before a zone change could be accomplished; and (3) the change from R-7 to P-R was in accordance with the Washington county comprehensive plan.

We granted review in this case to consider the questions — by what standards does a county commission exercise its authority in zoning matters; who has the burden of meeting those standards when a request for change of zone is made; and what is the scope of court review of such actions?

Any meaningful decision as to the proper scope of judicial review of a zoning decision must start with a characterization of the nature of that decision. . . .

[The court then reviewed the characterization to be given to zoning amendments. It noted that it would be wrong "to rigidly view all zoning decisions by local governing bodies as legislative acts to be accorded a full presumption of validity and shielded from less than constitutional scrutiny by the theory of separation of powers." The opinion then continued: — Eds.]

Ordinances laying down general policies without regard to a specific piece of property are usually an exercise of legislative authority, are subject to limited review, and may only be attacked upon constitutional grounds for an arbitrary abuse of authority. On the other hand, a determination whether the permissible use of a specific piece of property should be changed is usually an exercise of judicial authority and its propriety is subject to an altogether different test. An illustration of an exercise of legislative authority is the passage of the ordinance by the Washington County Commission in 1963 which provided for the formation of a planned residential classification to be located in or adjacent to any residential zone. An exercise of judicial authority is the county commissioners' determination in this particular matter to change the classification of A.G.S. Development Company's specific piece of property. . . .

We reject the proposition that judicial review of the county commissioners' determination to change the zoning of the particular property in question is limited to a determination whether the change was arbitrary and capricious.

In order to establish a standard of review, it is necessary to delineate certain basic principles relating to land use regulation.

The basic instrument for county or municipal land use planning is the "comprehensive plan." . . . The plan has been described as a general plan to control and direct the use and development of property in a municipality. . . .

In Oregon the county planning commission is required by ORS 215.050 to adopt a comprehensive plan for the use of some or all of the land in the county. Under ORS 215.110(1), after the comprehensive plan has been adopted, the planning commission recommends to the governing body of the county the ordinances necessary to "carry out" the comprehensive plan. The purpose of the zoning ordinances, both under our statute and the general law of land use regulation, is to "carry out" or implement the comprehensive plan. . . . Although we are aware of the analytical distinction between zoning and planning, it is clear that under our statutes the plan adopted by the planning commission and the zoning ordinances enacted by the county governing body are closely related; both are intended to be parts of a single integrated procedure for land use control. The plan embodies policy determinations and guiding principles; the zoning ordinances provide the detailed means of giving effect to those principles.

ORS 215.050 states county planning commissions "shall adopt and may from time to time revise a comprehensive plan." In a hearing of the Senate Committee on Local Government, the proponents of ORS 215.050 described its purpose as follows:

> ". . . The intent here is to require a basic document, geared into population, land use, and economic forecasts, which should be the basis of any zoning or other regulations to be adopted by the county. . . ."

In addition, ORS 215.055 provides:

> "215.055 Standards for plan. (1) The plan and all legislation and regulations authorized by ORS 215.010 to 215.233 shall be designed to promote the public health, safety and general welfare and shall be based on the following considerations, among others: The various characteristics of the various areas in the county, the suitability of the areas for particular land uses and improvements, the land uses and improvements in the areas, trends in land improvement, density of development, property values, the needs of economic enterprises in the future development of the areas, needed access to particular sites in the areas, natural resources of the county and prospective needs for development thereof, and the public need for healthful, safe, aesthetic surroundings and conditions."

We believe that the state legislature has conditioned the county's power to zone upon the prerequisite that the zoning attempt to further the general welfare of the community through consciousness, in a prospective sense, of the factors mentioned above. In other words, except as noted later in this opinion, it must be proved that the change is in conformance with the comprehensive plan.

In proving that the change is in conformance with the comprehensive plan in this case, the proof, at a minimum, should show (1) there is a public need for a change of the kind in question, and (2) that need will be best served by changing the classification of the particular piece of property in question as compared with other available property.

In the instant case the trial court and the Court of Appeals interpreted prior decisions of this court as requiring the county commissions to show a change of conditions within the immediate neighborhood in which the change was sought since the enactment of the comprehensive plan, or a mistake in the comprehensive plan as a condition precedent to the zone change.

. . . .

In *Roseta v. Washington County,* supra, the land in question was classified as residential under the comprehensive plan and had been originally zoned as R-10, Single Family Residential. We held that the commissioners had not sustained the burden of proving that the change was consistent with the comprehensive plan and reversed the order allowing the zone change. In regard to defendants' argument that the change was consistent with the comprehensive plan because the plan designated the areas as "residential" and the term included both single family dwellings and duplex residences, we stated:

> ". . . However, the ordinance established a distinction between the two types of use by classifying one area as R-10 and another area as A-1. It must be assumed that the Board had some purpose in making a distinction between these two classifications. It was for defendant to prove that this distinction was not valid or that the change in the character of the use of the . . . parcel was not inconsistent with the comprehensive plan." 254 Ore. at 169, 458 P.2d 405, at 409.

The instant case could be distinguished from *Roseta* on the basis that we are involved with a floating zone which was not before the court in *Roseta.*

However, *Roseta* should not be interpreted as establishing a rule that a physical change of circumstances within the rezoned neighborhood is the only justification for rezoning. The county governing body is directed by ORS 215.055 to consider a number of other factors when enacting zoning ordinances, and the list there does not purport to be exclusive. The important issues, as *Roseta* recognized, are compliance with the statutory directive and consideration of the proposed change in light of the comprehensive plan.

Because the action of the commission in this instance is an exercise of judicial authority, the burden of proof should be placed, as is usual in judicial proceedings, upon the one seeking change. The more drastic the change, the greater will be the burden of showing that it is in conformance with the comprehensive plan as implemented by the ordinance, that there is a public need for the kind of change in question, and that the need is best met by the proposal under consideration. As the degree of change increases, the burden of showing that the potential impact upon the area in question was carefully considered and weighed will also increase. If other areas have previously been designated for the particular type of development, it must be shown why it is necessary to introduce it into an area not previously contemplated and why the property owners there should bear the burden of the departure.[150]

Although we have said in *Roseta* that zoning changes may be justified without a showing of a mistake in the original plan or ordinance, or of changes in the physical characteristics of an affected area, any of these factors which are present in a particular case would, of course, be relevant. Their importance would depend upon the nature of the precise change under consideration.

By treating the exercise of authority by the commission in this case as the exercise of judicial rather than of legislative authority and thus enlarging the scope of review on appeal, and by placing the burden of the above level of proof upon the one seeking change, we may lay the court open to criticism by legal scholars who think it desirable that planning authorities be vested with the ability to adjust more freely to changed conditions. However, having weighed the dangers of making desirable change more difficult against the dangers of the

---

[150] For example, if an area is designated by the plan as generally appropriate for residential development, the plan may also indicate that some high-density residential development within the area is to be anticipated, without specifying the exact location at which that development is to take place. The comprehensive plan might provide that its goal for residential development is to assure that residential areas are healthful, pleasant and safe places in which to live. The plan might also list the following policies which, among others, are to be pursued in achieving that goal:

1. High-density residential areas should be located close to the urban core area.
2. Residential neighborhoods should be protected from any land use activity involving an excessive level of noise, pollution or traffic volume.
3. High trip-generating multiple family units should have ready access to arterial or collector streets.
4. A variety of living areas and housing types should be provided appropriate to the needs of the special and general groups they are to serve.
5. Residential development at urban densities should be within planned sewer and water service areas and where other utilities can be adequately provided.

Under such a hypothetical plan, property originally zoned for single family dwellings might later be rezoned for duplexes, for garden apartments, or for high-rise apartment buildings. Each of these changes could be shown to be consistent with the plan. Although in addition we would require a showing that the county governing body found a bona fide need for a zone change in order to accommodate new high-density development which at least balanced the disruption shown by the challengers, that requirement would be met in most instances by a record which disclosed that the governing body had considered the facts relevant to this question and exercised its judgment in good faith. However, these changes, while all could be shown to be consistent with the plan, could be expected to have differing impacts on the surrounding area, depending on the nature of that area. As the potential impact on the area in question increases, so will the necessity to show a justification.

almost irresistible pressures that can be asserted by private economic interests on local government, we believe that the latter dangers are more to be feared.

. . . .

When we apply the standards we have adopted to the present case, we find that the burden was not sustained before the commission. The record now before us is insufficient to ascertain whether there was a justifiable basis for the decision. The only evidence in the record, that of the staff report of the Washington County Planning Department, is too conclusory and superficial to support the zoning change. It merely states:

> "The staff finds that the requested use does conform to the residential designation of the Plan of Development. It further finds that the proposed use reflects the urbanization of the County and the necessity to provide increased densities and different types of housing to meet the needs of urbanization over that allowed by the existing zoning. . . ."

Such generalizations and conclusions, without any statement of the facts on which they are based, are insufficient to justify a change of use. Moreover, no portions of the comprehensive plan of Washington county are before us, and we feel it would be improper for us to take judicial notice of the plan without at least some reference to its specifics by counsel.

As there has not been an adequate showing that the change was in accord with the plan, or that the factors listed in ORS 215.055 were given proper consideration, the judgment is affirmed.

BRYSON, Justice (specially concurring). [Omitted.]

Comments: 1. In the *Roseta* case, cited in the principal case, the Oregon Supreme Court held, *inter alia,* that where the county board of commissioners has once established a "use" district and later authorized a change in the character of uses permitted in the district, "the usual presumption of legislative regularity is not recognized and in such a case the Board carries the burden of proving that there has been a change in the neighborhood in order to justify the rezoning of a small tract as an amendment in keeping with the comprehensive plan." The court continued:

> But even viewing the evidence most favorably in support of defendant's position, it was not sufficient to meet the burden of proving that the Board's action was consistent with the comprehensive plan. Moreover, granting that the evidence produced at the trial could support a deviation consistent with the comprehensive plan, we have no way of determining in the absence of written findings by the governing board or its zoning

agency (Planning Commission) whether it made its decision upon that basis. Even where the members of the Board testify at the trial in the circuit court that the Board's action was taken only after a full consideration of its effect upon the comprehensive plan, we have nothing more than a self-serving assertion which may not reflect the actual decision-making process at the time the Board allowed the requested change. Since we cannot properly exercise our function of judicial review without a record of adequate findings by the board or the Planning Commission on which it based its decision to allow a change of use within a zone, it is within our province to require such findings as an essential part of the Board's procedure.

458 P.2d 409-10.

In *Roseta,* the court apparently regarded the action of the county board of supervisors in rezoning by amendment as "legislative" in character. If so, what do you think of the court's reversal of the usual presumption of validity when the amendment was challenged as improper "spot zoning"? What do you think of the Oregon court's requirement that, in order to uphold a "spot zoning" amendment, there must be "written findings by the governing board or its zoning agency (Planning Commission)" because, "even where the members of the Board testify at the trial in the circuit court that the Board's action was taken only after a full consideration of its effect upon the comprehensive plan, we have nothing more than a self-serving assertion which may not reflect the actual decision-making process at the time the Board allowed the requested change"? Is the court on sound ground in citing cases which require a zoning board of adjustment (or appeals) to file written opinions "in every variance case" in support of its holding that "it is within our province to require such findings as an essential part of the Board's procedure"? How can the court's holding be reconciled with the general rule that legislative bodies need not make written findings in support of their legislative acts, and that such acts will be sustained if there is any possible rational basis for them?

2. Although the *Fasano* case technically deals with a "floating zone" amendment, it has been treated in later Oregon cases as applying generally to rezoning by amendment. Given the Oregon Supreme Court's treatment of the rezoning amendment in *Fasano* as "judicial" rather than "legislative" action, the court's reversal of the usual presumption of validity attaching to zoning ordinances as "legislative" acts was inevitable. But the characterization of rezoning by amendment as "judicial" when the tract rezoned is relatively small and is rezoned at the owner's request clearly makes untenable the court's earlier holding, in *Archdiocese of Portland v. County of Washington,* 458 P.2d 682 (Ore. 1969) (discussed *supra* p. 668), that the granting of a "conditional use" permit by the county governing body was a "legislative" act, entitled to the usual presumption of validity. See *Kristensen v. City of Eugene Planning Comm'n,* 544 P.2d 591 (Ore. App. 1976), discussed at length in Comment 2 following *Baker v. City of Milwaukie, infra* p. 754.

3. Note that *Fasano* rejects any implication from *Roseta* that Oregon had adopted the Maryland "original mistake or change of conditions" rule for rezoning amendments. Is some scope for the application of this rule still left by *Fasano*? Note also that the *Fasano* opinion seems to hold that the rezoning at the rezoned site cannot be supported if an alternative site for the proposed use is available. An important case applying this limitation is *Duddles v. City Council,* 535 P.2d 583 (Ore. App. 1975), discussed in Comment 1 following *Baker v. City of Milwaukie, infra* p. 753.

4. The *Fasano* court's characterization of rezoning amendments as "judicial" rather than "legislative" acts led the court to say (in a part of the opinion omitted above) that:

> Parties at the hearing before the county governing body are entitled to an opportunity to be heard, to an opportunity to present and rebut evidence, to a tribunal which is impartial in the matter — i.e., having had no pre-hearing or ex parte contacts concerning the question at issue — and to a record made and adequate findings executed.

507 P.2d at 30. A 1974 survey by the Oregon Local Government Relations Division of the Executive Department of six counties and twelve cities disclosed that all had adopted comprehensive plans and zoning ordinances, and were seeking to cope with the *Fasano* procedural requirements for rezoning amendments. Larger urban areas like Eugene, Portland, and Washington County had adopted formal, very legalistic rules based on an administrative law model in accordance with an opinion of the Oregon Attorney General issued in 1974. (Ore., Att'y Gen. Op. No. 7062.)

In Eugene and Portland, the city councils had shifted responsibility for rezoning hearings from the planning commission to a hearings examiner. This was expressly authorized by 1973 legislation stemming from *Fasano.* See Ore. Rev. Stat. §§ 215.406 (for counties) and 227.165 (for cities) (1975). Other Oregon counties and cities with a large enough volume of rezoning applications were also considering shifting to hearings officers. And certain cities in Washington, Arizona, Maryland, and Ohio have also recently gone to a hearings examiner system, apparently in response to *Fasano* and several similar decisions in other states. In these states, as well as in Oregon, the hearings examiner's jurisdiction generally extends to rezoning amendments, special exceptions or special use permits, zoning variances, subdivision and site plan approvals, and appeals from decisions of the building inspector. The hearings examiner holds hearings on behalf of the local governing body, in effect taking the place of both the zoning board of adjustment and the planning commission.

> The arguments made in behalf of the system include greater efficiency in the conduct of the hearings, elimination of legislative whim and caprice, greater consistency and uniformity of application of zoning laws and general plans, more time for the governing body to deal in broad land use questions, more narrowing of the key issues, promotion of the conduct of quasi-judicial hearings such as preparation of findings of fact and conclusions of law.

Curtin & Shirk, Land Use, Planning and Zoning, 9 Urb. Law. 724, 740 (1977).

5. *Fasano* purports to prohibit "ex parte contacts concerning the question at issue." The 1974 survey by the Oregon Local Government Relations Division, *supra,* showed that in the larger cities and counties where size precludes a close personal relationship between constituents and officials, planning commission members and members of the governing bodies generally had little trouble with the *Fasano* prohibition; they simply refused to talk about pending cases and typically referred the applicants and others to the planning staff. In most of the smaller communities where constituents are well known to officials, redirection of the attempted ex parte contacts proved to be more difficult, although it frequently occurred. In almost all the communities surveyed, however, local officials reported that they were glad to have a good reason not to talk to constituents about pending rezoning decisions. In general, the procedures mandated by *Fasano* seem to have gone largely without additional judicial scrutiny or elaboration, but the ex parte contact problem is an exception. In *Tierney v. Duria,* 536 P.2d 435 (Ore. App. 1975), a rezoning for a shopping center development was involved. In order to satisfy themselves about the attitude of their constituents, two council members made a door-to-door survey. They did not discuss the rezoning with the developer-applicant. The issue was whether the door-to-door survey prior to the completion of the hearing constituted ex parte contacts prohibited by *Fasano.* The court held that they were not, and said:

> In any event, we hold there is no violation of *Fasano* when, as in this case: (1) the "ex parte contacts" were not with the proponents of change or their agents, but, rather, with relatively disinterested persons; (2) the contacts only amounted to an investigation of the merits or demerits of a proposed change; and, most importantly, (3) the occurrence and nature of the contacts were made a matter of record during a quasi-judicial hearing so that parties to the hearing then had an opportunity to respond. . . . As we read *Fasano* its basic requirement is an impartial tribunal; ex parte contacts were just mentioned as one way in which impartiality could be compromised. We conclude that the ex parte contacts revealed by this record are, in the absence of any other claim or evidence of bias, insufficient to establish a lack of impartiality.

Id. at 443.

6. In *Green v. City of Eugene,* 538 P.2d 368 (Ore. App. 1975), three council members who had missed one or more of the earlier meetings at which evidence was taken on a rezoning application participated in the final vote, although they were disqualified by the council's own rules. The case was disposed of on another ground, but the court in a dictum discussed the question whether a lay proponent or opponent of the rezoning who failed to raise the issue of disqualification at the proper time could nevertheless raise it on judicial review:

> *Fasano v. Washington Co. Comm.* tells us that the proceedings before the city council to consider the zone change application were, for some purposes at least, "quasi-judicial" in nature. In a "judicial context, the general rule is that timely objection must be made to allegedly irregular procedure, and that if no objection is made, no claim of irregularity is thereafter cognizable. Should the same rule be applied in this "quasi-judicial" context — proceedings before a local governing body to pass upon individual land-use questions?

Such a holding would arguably strain the *Fasano* "quasi-judicial" analogy to the breaking point. It would amount to a holding that citizens supporting or opposing a requested land use proceed at their own peril unless they retain an attorney who will aggressively interpose any and all possible objections. It would further convert the relatively informal meetings of city councils and county commissions into formal courtroom proceedings. And it must be remembered we are establishing rules for both the largest, most metropolitan, and the smallest, most rural, communities in the state, some of which simply do not contain sufficient legal resources — to say nothing of financial resources — to convert every land-use determination into a formal trial.

Id. at 369-70.

7. Colorado has recently adopted the *Fasano* doctrine. *Snyder v. City of Lakewood,* 542 P.2d 371 (1975); *Colorado Springs v. District Court,* 519 P.2d 325 (Colo. 1974); *Dillon Cos. v. Boulder,* 515 P.2d 627 (Colo. 1973). As the court said in *Snyder,* it now distinguishes "between the adjudicative process involved in enacting a *rezoning* ordinance and the legislative process involved in passing the general zoning ordinance." The *Snyder* court also asserted that, in order to support a finding that the action of a municipal legislative body is quasi-judicial, there must be

(1) a state or local law requiring that the body give adequate notice to the community before acting; (2) a state or local law requiring that the body conduct a public hearing, pursuant to notice, at which time concerned citizens must be given an opportunity to be heard and present evidence; and (3) a state or local law requiring the body to make a determination by applying the facts of a specific case to certain criteria established by law.

Although the zoning ordinance in the *Snyder* case did not contain any requirement that the local legislative body should make its rezoning determination "by applying the facts of a specific case to certain criteria established by law," the court concluded that the general police power criteria in the zoning enabling act (identical with Standard Act § 3, *supra* p. —) were sufficient to make the municipality's action in rezoning a single tract "quasi-judicial" rather than "legislative," since the other two requirements were satisfied. Although any comprehensive revision of a zoning ordinance would presumably also satisfy the three requirements stated in *Snyder,* it seems clear that the "quasi-judicial act" doctrine only applies to single tract rezoning amendments, or at least to rezoning amendments of "localized applicability." In *Corper v. City and County of Denver,* 552 P.2d 13 (Colo. 1976), the court applied the "quasi-judicial act" doctrine in connection with a zoning ordinance provision limiting rezoning amendments to cases of "change-or-mistake." In both *Snyder* and *Corper,* the court held that review of the local legislative body's "quasi-judicial" rezoning amendment should be by certiorari.

8. *Fasano* exhibits a marked distrust of the ability of local governments to resist land developers seeking zoning changes destructive of the policies on which local comprehensive plans are based. See the statement in *Fasano* that, "having weighed the dangers of making desirable change more difficult against the dangers of the almost irresistible pressures that can be asserted by private economic interests on local government, we believe that the latter dangers are more to be feared." In Michigan, however, the *Fasano* doctrine that "a determination whether the permissible use of a specific piece of property should be changed is usually an exercise of judicial authority" was given a reverse twist by Justice Levin in his concurring opinion in *Kropf v. City of Sterling Heights,* 215 N.W.2d 179 (Mich. 1974). Justice Levin started with the factual assumption — no doubt correct — that "[i]n most communities, . . . especially the larger ones, there have been dozens, hundreds and, in some cases, thousands of zoning map changes, exceptions and variances granted." He seems then to have assumed that the existing zoning regulations in such communities cannot be justified as being "in accordance with a plan" designed to promote statutorily defined purposes as required by the Michigan zoning enabling act. This assumption may be correct, in a particular community, because no "plan" was ever formulated, or the original zoning ordinance did not comply with the "plan," or, although the original ordinance complied with the "plan," the current zoning regulations no longer comply because of "spot zoning" amendments, special exceptions, and variances granted over the years. In such communities, Justice Levin concluded, the process of passing upon applications for rezoning amendments should be treated, in substance, as a licensing process in which the criterion for rezoning should be the reasonableness of the use proposed by the applicant "in light of all the circumstances." This appears to be in essence a sophisticated "nuisance" test that would take into account "availability of utilities and roads," "[a]esthetics," and the requirements of "sound communal development," as well as other factors traditionally considered in nuisance litigation. If the applicant carries the burden of proving that his proposed use of the land in question is "reasonable," he would be entitled, under Justice Levin's view, to have the land rezoned to permit that use, regardless of the "reasonableness" of the existing zoning regulations.

It is obvious that the view stated by Justice Levin in *Kropf* goes far beyond the doctrine announced in *Fasano,* where the court could assume that each community has a comprehensive plan. Justice Levin's view, in fact, became the law in Michigan as a result of three subsequent cases where that view prevailed by virtue of 3 to 2 decisions, at a time when there were two vacancies on the seven-member Michigan Supreme Court. *Sabo v. Township of Monroe,* 232 N.W.2d 584 (Mich. 1975); *Nickola v. Township of Grand Blanc,* 232 N.W.2d 604 (Mich. 1975); *Smookler v. Township of Wheatfield,* 232 N.W.2d 616 (Mich. 1975). The triumph of Justice Levin's view was short-lived, however. In *Kirk v. Tyrone Township,* 247 N.W.2d 848 (Mich. 1976), after the vacancies on the court were filled, the Levin doctrine was rejected by a 4 to 3 vote. Speaking for the court, Justice Williams said:

> Upon reflection, it does not seem wise as *Sabo* did to attempt to engraft upon the established legislative scheme of zoning and rezoning, a new system which admittedly requires new legislative action to operate optimally. Should the Legislature choose to revise the approach to zoning amendments in our state [by enacting "an administrative procedure act providing for review of local agency action in contested cases" for use if

local zoning authorities deny a change in zoning], this Court would, of course, view matters differently. But, as of the present time, it seems wisest to return to the [traditional view that no one is entitled to a zoning change if the existing regulations are reasonable].

Id. at 853.

For discussion of the rise and fall of the Levin doctrine in Michigan, see Cunningham, Rezoning by Amendment as an Administrative or Quasi-Judicial Act: The "New Look" in Michigan Zoning, 73 Mich. L. Rev. 1341 (1975); Cunningham, Reflections on Stare Decisis in Michigan: The Rise and Fall of the "Rezoning as Administrative Act" Doctrine, 75 Mich. L. Rev. 983 (1977).

9. The *Fasano* approach has also been expressly rejected in California by the intermediate appellate court and in Georgia by the highest court. In *Ensign Bickford Realty Corp. v. City Council,* 137 Cal. Rptr. 304 (Cal. App. 1977), where a developer attacked the city for failure to make specific findings in denying a zone change from residential to neighborhood commercial, the court held *Fasano* inapplicable because rezoning is a legislative act which need not be based on specific findings. In *Hall Paving Co. v. Hall County,* 226 S.E.2d 728 (Ga. 1976), neighboring landowners contested a zone change from residential to industrial (quarry operation) on the ground that the planning commission had failed to make specific findings; but the court held that rezoning is a legislative act not requiring supportive findings and, like other legislative acts, "when duly adopted, is presumed to be valid."

10. Although the American Law Institute's Model Land Development Code (1976) attempts to discourage participation by the local legislative body in day-to-day regulatory decisions and to commit such decisions to the "land development agency" established by the legislative body, § 2-312 of the Code does provide for "special amendments," as follows:

(1) . . . [T]he local governing body may authorize development by a special amendment. . . . A special amendment is an amendment
   (a) that results in a change limited in effect to a single parcel or to several parcels under related ownership; or
   (b) that changes regulations applicable to an area of [50] acres or less; or
   (c) that permits development specified in a previously adopted ordinance as permissible upon stated criteria after approval by the local governing body.
(2) Prior to the adoption of a special amendment, the Land Development Agency shall hold a hearing. . . and make findings and recommendations on the issues presented in regard to the proposed amendment. A special amendment may be adopted only if
   (a) development at the proposed location is essential or especially appropriate in view of the available alternatives within or without the jurisdiction; or
   (b) the development is development of regional benefit . . .; or
   (c) the development could have been granted a special development permit . . ., whether or not the development

ordinance before the amendment authorized the Land
Development Agency to grant a permit on that basis; or
    (d) there was a mistake in the original ordinance in
regard to property.
    (3) Upon receipt of the findings and recommendations of the
Agency, the governing body may, with or without an additional
hearing, adopt the proposed amendment, or modify the
proposed amendment and adopt it as modified. The governing
body may attach any conditions that could have been attached
to a special development permit under § 2-103. . . .
    (4) The decision of the governing body to adopt a special
amendment shall be supported by findings and conclusions
based upon the record as if a special development permit had
been granted. In any judicial proceeding thereon, the findings
and conclusions shall be those of the agency under subsection
(2) unless the governing body, on the basis of the same record
or a record prepared before it, makes other findings and
conclusions.

The Reporter's Note makes it clear that § 2-312 adopts the *Fasano* doctrine:

    This Section treats amendments applicable to one or a few
pieces of property as if they were applications for special
development permits. While the local governing body is given
the power to approve or reject recommendations of the Land
Development Agency concerning the adoption of special
amendments, the action of the local governing body no longer
carries with it an almost automatic presumption of validity but
is treated under subsection (4) as an administrative decision that
must be supported by findings of fact and reasons; and
therefore, it may be challenged in court on less than
constitutional grounds. . . .

It seems equally clear, however, that § 2-312 does not adopt the extension
of the *Fasano* doctrine advocated by Justice Levin in *Kropf, Sabo, Nickola,*
and *Smookler, supra* Comment 8. (For a definition of development of
regional benefit, see § 2-312(2)(b) *supra,* see *infra* chapter 9.)

2. Newer Forms of Flexible Zoning

a. With Pre-Set Standards: The Floating Zone

RODGERS v. VILLAGE OF TARRYTOWN

Court of Appeals of New York
302 N.Y. 115, 96 N.E.2d 731 (1951)

FULD, Judge. This appeal, here by our permission, involves the
validity of two amendments to the General Zoning Ordinance of the
Village of Tarrytown, a suburban area in the County of Westchester,
within twenty-five miles of New York City.

    Some years ago, Tarrytown enacted a General Zoning Ordinance
dividing the village into seven districts or zones — Residence A for
single family dwellings, Residence B for two-family dwellings,
Residence C for multiple dwellings and apartment houses, three

business districts and an industrial zone. In 1947 and 1948, the board of trustees, the village's legislative body, passed the two amendatory ordinances here under attack.

The 1947 ordinance creates "A new district or class of zone . . . [to] be called 'Residence B-B' ", in which, besides one- and two-family dwellings, buildings for multiple occupancy of fifteen or fewer families were permitted. The boundaries of the new type district were not delineated in the ordinance but were to be "fixed by amendment of the official village building zone map, at such times in the future as such district or class of zone is applied, to properties in this village." The village planning board was empowered to approve such amendments and, in case such approval was withheld, the board of trustees was authorized to grant it by appropriate resolution. In addition, the ordinance erected exacting standards of size and physical layouts for Residence B-B zones: a minimum of ten acres of land and a maximum building height of three stories were mandated; set-back and spacing requirements for structures were carefully prescribed; and no more than 15% of the ground area of the plot was to be occupied by buildings.

A year and a half after the 1947 amendment was enacted, defendant Elizabeth Rubin sought to have her property, consisting of almost ten and a half acres in the Residence A district, placed in a Residence B-B classification. After repeated modification of her plans to meet suggestions of the village planning board, that body gave its approval, and, several months later, in December of 1948, the board of trustees, also approving, passed the second ordinance here under attack. In essence, it provides that the Residence B-B district "is hereby applied to the [Rubin] property . . . and the district or zone of said property is hereby changed to 'Residence B-B' and the official Building Zone Map of the Village of Tarrytown is hereby amended accordingly [by specification of the various parcels and plots involved]."

Plaintiff, who owns a residence on a six-acre plot about a hundred yards from Rubin's property, brought this action to have the two amendments declared invalid and to enjoin defendant Rubin from constructing multiple dwellings on her property. The courts below, adjudging the amendments valid and the action of the trustees proper, dismissed the complaint. We agree with their determination.

While stability and regularity are undoubtedly essential to the operation of zoning plans, zoning is by no means static. Changed or changing conditions call for changed plans, and persons who own property in a particular zone or use district enjoy no eternally vested right to that classification if the public interest demands otherwise. Accordingly, the power of a village to amend its basic zoning ordinance in such a way as reasonably to promote the general welfare cannot be questioned. Just as clearly, decision as to how a community shall be zoned or rezoned, as to how various properties shall be classified or reclassified, rests with the local legislative body; its judgment and determination will be conclusive, beyond interference from the courts, unless shown to be arbitrary, and the burden of establishing such arbitrariness is imposed upon him who asserts it. . . .

By that test, the propriety of the decision here made is not even debatable. In other words, viewing the rezoning in the case before us, as it must be viewed, in the light of the area involved and the present and reasonably foreseeable needs of the community, the conclusion is inescapable that what was done not only accorded with sound zoning principles, not only complied with every requirement of law, but was accomplished in a proper, careful and reasonable manner.

The Tarrytown board of trustees was entitled to find that there was a real need for additional housing facilities; that the creation of Residence B-B districts for garden apartment developments would prevent young families, unable to find accommodations in the village, from moving elsewhere; would attract business to the community; would lighten the tax load of the small home owner, increasingly burdened by the shrinkage of tax revenues resulting from the depreciated value of large estates and the transfer of many such estates to tax-exempt institutions; and would develop otherwise unmarketable and decaying property.

The village's zoning aim being clear, the choice of methods to accomplish it lay with the board. Two such methods were at hand. It could amend the General Zoning Ordinance so as to permit garden apartments on any plot of ten acres or more in Residence A and B zones (the zones more restricted) or it could amend that ordinance so as to invite owners of ten or more acres, who wished to build garden apartments on their properties, to apply for a Residence B-B classification. The board chose to adopt the latter procedure. That it called for separate legislative authorization for each project presents no obstacle or drawback — and so we have already held. . . . Whether we would have made the same choice is not the issue; it is sufficient that the board's decision was neither arbitrary nor unreasonable.

As to the requirement that the applicant own a plot of at least ten acres, we find nothing therein unfair to plaintiff or other owners of smaller parcels. The board undoubtedly found, as it was privileged to find, that garden apartments would blend more attractively and harmoniously with the community setting, would impose less of a burden upon village facilities, if placed upon larger tracts of land rather than scattered about in smaller units. Obviously, some definite acreage had to be chosen, and, so far as the record before us reveals, the choice of ten acres as a minimum plot was well within the range of an unassailable legislative judgment. . . .

Nor did the board, by following the course which it did, divest itself or the planning board of power to regulate future zoning with regard to garden apartments. The mere circumstance that an owner possesses a ten-acre plot and submits plans conforming to the physical requirements prescribed by the 1947 amendment will not entitle him, *ipso facto,* to a Residence B-B classification. It will still be for the board to decide, in the exercise of a reasonable discretion, that the *grant* of such a classification accords with the comprehensive zoning plan and benefits the village as a whole. And — while no such question is here presented — we note that the board may not arbitrarily or unreasonably *deny* applications of other owners for permission to construct garden apartments on their properties. The action of the board must in all cases be reasonable and, whether a particular application be granted or denied, recourse may be had to the courts to correct an arbitrary or capricious determination. . . .

The charge of illegal "spot zoning" — levelled at the creation of a Residence B-B district and the reclassification of defendant's property — is without substance. Defined as the process of singling out a small parcel of land for a use classification totally different from that of the surrounding area, for the benefit of the owner of such property and to the detriment of other owners . . . "spot zoning" is the very antithesis of planned zoning. If, therefore, an ordinance is enacted in accordance with a comprehensive zoning plan, it is not "spot zoning," even though it (1) singles out and affects but one small plot . . ., or (2) creates in the center of a large zone small areas or districts devoted to a different use. . . . Thus, the relevant inquiry is not whether the particular zoning under attack consists of areas fixed within larger areas of different use, but whether it was accomplished for the benefit of individual owners rather than pursuant to a comprehensive plan for the general welfare of the community. Having already noted our conclusion that the ordinances were enacted to promote a comprehensive zoning plan, it is perhaps unnecessary to add that the record negates any claim that they were designed solely for the advantage of defendant or any other particular owner. Quite apart from the circumstance that defendant did not seek the benefit of the 1947 amendment until eighteen months after its passage, the all-significant fact is that that amendment applied to the entire territory of the village and accorded each and every owner of ten or more acres identical rights and privileges.

By the same token, there is no basis for the argument that "what has been done by the board of trustees" constitutes a device for "the granting of a 'variance.' " . . . As we have already shown, the village's zoning aim, the statute's purpose, was not to aid the individual owner but to permit the development of the property for the general welfare of the entire community. That being so, the board of trustees followed approved procedure by changing the General Zoning Ordinance itself. . . . Accordingly, when the board was called upon to consider the reclassification of the Rubin property under the 1947 amendment, it was concerned, not with any issue of hardship, but only with the question of whether the property constituted a desirable location for a garden apartment.

We turn finally to the contention that the 1947 ordinance is invalid because, in proclaiming a Residence B-B district, it set no boundaries for the new district and made no changes on the building zone map. The short answer is that, since the ordinance merely prescribed specifications for a new use district, there was no need for it to do either the one or the other. True, until boundaries are fixed and until zoning map changes are made, no new zone actually comes into being, and neither property nor the rights of any property owner are affected. But it was not the design of the board of trustees by that enactment to bring any additional zone into being or to affect any property or rights; the ordinance merely provided the mechanics pursuant to which property owners might in the future apply for the redistricting of their property. In sum, the 1947 amendment was merely the first step in a reasoned plan of rezoning, and specifically provided for further action on the part of the board. That action was taken by the passage of the 1948 ordinance which fixed the boundaries of the newly created zone and amended the zoning map accordingly. It is indisputable that the two amendments, read together as they must be, fully complied with the requirements of the Village Law and accomplished a rezoning of village property in an unexceptionable manner.

In point of fact, there would have been no question about the validity of what was done had the board simply amended the General Zoning Ordinance so as to permit property in Residence A and Residence B zones — or, for that matter, in the other districts throughout the village — to be used for garden apartments, provided that they were built on ten-acre plots and that the other carefully planned conditions and restrictions were met. It may be conceded that, under the method which the board did adopt, no one will know, from the 1947 ordinance itself, precisely where a Residence B-B district will ultimately be located. But since such a district is simply a garden apartment development, we find nothing unusual or improper in that circumstance. The same uncertainty — as to the location of the various types of structures — would be present if a zoning ordinance were to sanction garden apartments as well as one-family homes in a Residence A district — and yet there would be no doubt as to the propriety of that procedure. . . . Consequently, to condemn the action taken by the board in effectuating a perfectly permissible zoning scheme and to strike down the ordinance designed to carry out that scheme merely because the board had employed two steps to accomplish what may be, and usually is, done in one, would be to exalt form over substance and sacrifice substance to form.

Whether it is generally desirable that garden apartments be freely mingled among private residences under all circumstances, may be arguable. In view, however, of Tarrytown's changing scene and the other substantial reasons for the board's decision, we cannot say that its action was arbitrary or illegal. While hardships may be imposed on this or that owner, "cardinal is the principle that what is best for the body politic in the long run must prevail over the interests of particular individuals." *Shepard v. Village of Skaneateles,* supra, 300 N.Y. 115, 118, 89 N.E.2d 619, 620.

The judgment of the Appellate Division should be affirmed, with costs.

CONWAY, Judge (dissenting). [Omitted.]

Comments: 1. The *Tarrytown* case is a classic, and deserves careful study. What advantage was there, from the municipality's viewpoint, in using the "floating zone" amendment technique to introduce garden apartments into the village instead of simply amending the General Zoning Ordinance "so as to permit property in Residence A and Residence B zones — or, for that matter, in the other districts throughout the village — to be used for garden apartments, provided that they were built on ten-acre plots and that the other carefully planned conditions and restrictions were met"? The court may have supplied a partial answer when it said: "The mere circumstance that an owner possesses a ten-acre plot and submits plans conforming to the physical requirements prescribed by the 1947 amendment will not entitle him, *ipso facto,* to a Residence B-B classification. It will still be for the [planning] board to decide, in the exercise of a reasonable discretion, that the *grant* of such a classification accords with the comprehensive zoning plan and benefits the village as a whole." But what standards are to guide the "exercise of a reasonable discretion"? Is it enough to say, as the New York court did, that "the board may not arbitrarily or unreasonably *deny* applications of other owners for permission to construct garden apartments on their properties"?

It would also appear that Tarrytown adopted the "floating zone" amendment technique, at least in part, to avoid the inevitable charge of illegal "spot zoning" if it should simply rezone individual tracts of land, upon application by landowners, so as to permit garden apartment development, without having previously established "specifications for a new use district."

2. Ordinances similar to the Tarrytown "floating zone" ordinance have been sustained in Connecticut. *Miss Porter's School, Inc. v. Town Plan and Zoning Comm'n,* 198 A.2d 707 (Conn. 1964) ("The expanding population of Farmington and the desirability of apartments to accommodate it were called to the attention of the commission, as well as the fact that the property was close to transportation facilities and shopping areas. The change of zone was in accordance with the comprehensive plan and its logical development"); *DeMeo v. Zoning Comm'n,* 167 A.2d 454 (Conn. 1961) (garden apartments); *Clark v. Town Council,* 144 A.2d 327 (Conn. 1958) (shopping center).

In Maryland, an ordinance creating a kind of hybrid of the "floating zone" and the "special exception" was sustained in *Huff v. Board of Zoning Appeals,* 133 A.2d 83 (Md. 1957) (light manufacturing zone; decision to rezone was made by the zoning commissioner on recommendation of the planning commission, and his decision was reviewable by the board of zoning appeals). In *Beall v. Montgomery County Council,* 212 A.2d 751 (Md. 1965), the Maryland Court of Appeals sustained the county council in rezoning 41.6 acres of land from single-family to multi-family high-rise residential use (R-H). Prior to the application for rezoning, the county council had created the R-H classification as a "floating zone" designed to provide suitable sites for high density housing and to allow numerous types of commercial, recreational and education uses within the zone. The court held that no evidence of original mistake in zoning or of a substantial change in the character of the neighborhood was required to justify rezoning to the new R-H classification "in view of the conclusion of the Technical Staff, adopted by the Planning Commission and the Council, that the applications complied with the purposes of the R-H Zone, and of our decisions in *Costello v. Sieling,* 223 Md. 24, 161 A.2d 824 (1960) and in *Huff v. Board of Zoning Appeals,* 214 Md. 48, 133 A.2d 83 (1957)." The court then reviewed the history of the "floating zone" in Maryland, as follows:

> We followed Huff and treated it as controlling in *Costello* by a unanimous court. In *Costello* three zones called "Tourist Accommodation Districts" had been created. . . . The T-2 district, among other uses, permitted a "trailer coach park." In the T-2 district a minimum lot area of 3 acres was required, a 50 foot set back for any trailer from a street or road, a 20 foot set back from any side line, and a 25 foot set back from a rear line. . . . In 1959, the County Commissioners for Howard County upon the application of the contract purchaser of a 92 acre tract of land, zoned "R" (Residential), reclassified that tract to T-2. The tract in question was surrounded by properties devoted to residential and agricultural uses. . . . The Circuit Court, on appeal *reversed* on the grounds 1) that the T-2 classification was not analogous to a special exception as in *Huff* and 2) there was no substantial evidence before the County Commissioners that there was either a mistake in the original zoning or a substantial change in the character of the neighborhood. We reversed, holding that Huff controlled and that the "mistake-change in conditions" rule was not applicable. . . .
>
> It may be added that neither Huff nor Costello has been overruled or modified by our subsequent opinions. Both cases have been distinguished from the situation arising in Baltimore County in regard to action by the County Board of Appeals in reclassifying land from R-6 (residential, one or two family) to R-A (residential, apartment). . . .
>
> . . .[I]n the Baltimore County cases the R-A zone is not a floating zone like M-R and hence the holding in Huff was held

to be inapplicable. In the case at bar, however, the local legislature has indicated that the new classification and the classification of neighboring property are compatible, hence the holdings in *Costello* and *Huff* do apply and control the decision in the case at bar.

Id. at 759-60, 761-62.

3. The leading case holding the "floating zone" amendment technique impermissible is *Eves v. Zoning Bd.,* 164 A.2d (Pa. 1960). In that case the township had adopted a floating limited industrial district. Detailed site development requirements were included for the district, which could locate anywhere in the township on application and approval by the township board. The court held, in part, that the floating zone was unauthorized by the enabling legislation and noted that "the township supervisors have gone beyond their function of implementing a comprehensive plan with zoning regulations." Only the township board of appeals was authorized to grant "deviations" from the zoning ordinance, and then only through detailed variance or special exception procedures.

The court commented:

> Under the "flexible selective zoning" scheme here under attack, changes in the prevailing zoning regulations are to be made on a case by case basis, . . . by the legislative body, without rigid statutory standards and without any scintilla of notice of potential change as in the case of special exceptions. . . . If the legislature contemplated such a novel scheme of zoning, . . . we are convinced it would have said so. . . .

Id. at 12. *Eves* has now been substantially qualified if not overruled by statutory changes and subsequent judicial decisions. *See Donahue v. Zoning Bd. of Adjustment,* 194 A.2d 610 (Pa. 1963) (floating zone valid if approved shortly after ordinance amended to include floating zone procedure); *Raum v. Board of Supervisors,* 342 A.2d 450 (Pa. Commw. Ct. 1975) (approving floating zone ordinance and explaining *Eves* on grounds that adequate standards were not provided). See also Pa. Stat. Ann. tit. 53, § 10603 (1972), authorizing the governing body to approve conditional uses after recommendation by the planning commission and construed as overruling *Eves* in *Russell v. Pennsylvania Township Planning Comm'n,* 348 A.2d 499 (Pa. Commw. Ct. 1975). Does the subsequent history of *Eves* in Pennsylvania give any clue to what the courts might find troublesome in the floating zone process?

4. Can you see any advantage in the "floating zone" amendment technique as against the "special exception" technique as a means for "flexible" zoning? Or vice versa? Surely the "special exception" technique does not, as the court stated in *Eves,* give any greater advance notice to landowners of the possible intrusion of a new use in an area previously restricted against such use. Nor is the expertise of the zoning board of adjustment, which normally administers the "special exception" procedure, likely to be greater than the combined expertise of the planning board and the local governing body, which usually administer the "floating zone" procedure. And it is hard to see how the standards generally held sufficient to guide the exercise of administrative discretion in "special exception" cases are really more definite than the statutory standards which govern the amending process. Moreover, the "floating zone" procedure results in a change of the zoning map to reflect the change in classification, while the "special exception" procedure does not.

5. It has been suggested that the "floating zone" amendment technique could be used to implement an inclusionary zoning policy designed to increase the supply of "least cost" housing:

> . . .If the ordinance contains a statement of purposes and generalized criteria to govern the granting or denial of applications, landowners and developers will be on notice as to the kinds of development the community favors and under what conditions, while the community's professional staff and local legislative body will have standards against which to review the individual development proposal to determine whether it promotes the community's housing objectives.
>
> . . . .
>
> There is one example in the literature of an inclusionary floating zone ordinance. The town meeting in Lexington, Massachusetts, adopted a floating multifamily district that could be attached to a site only if at least 40% of the units in the proposed development would be federally or state subsidized for low- and moderate-income families. The ordinance states that its purpose is to facilitate the increase in subsidized housing units in the town to a total of approximately 950 units, while at the same time "ensuring compliance with local planning standards and policies concerned with land use, building design, and requirements of health, safety, and welfare of residents of the town of Lexington." To assure that only subsidized housing projects would be able to utilize this floating zone, the ordinance provides that no building permits would be issued until there was an actual federal or state commitment to provide the subsidy funds for the project. However, the first instance in which the town meeting revised the zoning map to apply the floating zone to permit a subsidized housing project to be built was taken to referendum and reversed.

H. Franklin, D. Falk, and A. Levin, In-Zoning: A Guide for Policy-Makers on Inclusionary Land Use Programs 119-20 (1975).

6. As indicated *supra* p. 705, the American Law Institute's Model Land Development Code § 2-312 (1) (c) (1976) authorizes "development by a special amendment . . . that permits development specified in a previously adopted ordinance as permissible upon stated criteria after approval by the local governing body." The Reporter's Note explains:

> Paragraph (c) covers what has been called "floating zoning," in which the ordinance provides somewhat flexible regulations for an unmapped zone, and performance standards determine whether a remapping amendment will be adopted. This is substantially the same as a special permission ordinance, except that final determination is left to the legislature rather than to the agency.

A NOTE ON "X" ZONING, "Q" ZONING, AND "OVERLAY" ZONING

"X" zoning and "Q" zoning are described as follows in a speech by Charles R. Martin to the Planning Department, League of California Cities, Annual Conference, October 14, 1968 (reprinted in D. Hagman, Public Planning and Control of Urban and Land Development 452, 454-55 (1973):

"X" Zoning is a proliferation of the zone classification breakdown and permits a great deal of flexibility with respect to particular developments. It is perhaps a refinement of the Floating Zone concept, and creates, for example, a C-2 Zone minus certain features. If, for example, the C-2 Zone allowed uses #1 through #46, the C-2/X-1 Zone would allow all C-2 uses except, e.g., #8, #17 and #43; or it could be turned the other way and allow only uses #16 and #27. The difficulty with "X" Zoning is that it would greatly increase the bulk of the zoning code.

The "Q" Zone is a new concept which would place a temporary classification on the area involved. If the property is not developed in conjunction with the rough plan . . . the zone classification would fail at the end of the prescribed period; otherwise, if the property were so developed, the zone classification would become permanent. Thus, a piece of property would be rezoned to C-2 or C-2/X-1 with a "Q" classification attached thereto. If the property were so developed within a one-year period . . . , the classification would become permanent; otherwise, the same would fail. There has been no Court test in California of this type of zoning as yet, and therefore the issue of whether such property can be rezoned back to its original state by "default" or whether it is necessary to go through a zone change proceeding has not yet been determined. [On the question of "reversion" to the original zoning classification, see the next principal case.—Eds.]

"Overlay" zoning seems to assume two different forms:

1. The simplest form involves simply placing a tract of land in two different zones—e.g., R-3 and C-2 which would permit the property to be used for either multiple residence or commercial purposes. This form of "overlay" zoning seems designed to accommodate land located in a bona fide transitional zone, i.e., where two competing and rather incompatible uses each have valid claims to the zone. Sometimes the "overlay" zoning is coupled with the "sinking zone" technique, by which, whenever either of the zoned uses is established on the land, the other zoning classification "sinks" out of existence.

2. Another form of "overlay" zoning creates a second mapped zone that imposes a set of requirements in addition to those of the basic use zone. Land in the area covered by both zones may be

developed only in accordance with the regulations applicable in both zones. Meshenberg says that overlay zones of this kind,

> typically are applied when there is a special public interest in a geographic area that does not coincide with the underlying zone boundaries.
>
> Some of the more common uses for such zones relate to special environmental features that restrain development. Floodplain zones and wet soils overlay zones are examples. Other uses are to maintain the integrity of historic areas, to preserve views, to restrict areas to public uses, and to limit building heights in certain portions of a city. . . .
>
> Flexibility enters the process when permissions for development in overlay zones are granted through a special permit process, or where site plan review is required. When administered this way, it is analogous to the amendment process in anchoring a floating zone, except that here the process usually involves an administrative determination. . . .
>
> The use of overlay zones is narrower than that of floating zones, but they avoid some of the objections to the latter since they apply only to specified areas and the regulations are described in the text and the area mapped like conventional zones. For the same reason, they offer less flexibility than floating zones. . . .
>
> Standards are determined by the form of administration, i.e., whether development is permitted as of right or by means of special permits. When special permits are used, they should be specific enough to assure continued vitality of stable and developed neighborhoods, and the range of uses permitted in fringe areas should be limited to minimize potential abuse.
>
> Since overlay zones are tied to the zoning map, the courts are not likely to overturn their provisions if the initial determination of allowable uses is reasonable.

M. Meshenberg, The Administration of Flexible Zoning Techniques 33-35 (American Soc'y of Planning Officials, Planning Advisory Service Rep. No. 318, 1975).

Richard Babcock and John Banta have described some innovative uses of this second type of overlay zoning in New Zoning Techniques for Inner-City Areas 15-16 (American Soc'y of Planning Officials, Planning Advisory Service Rep. No. 297, 1973):

> (a) Boulder, Colorado, overlays three broadly defined districts on top of the conventional use districts. These districts—Established, Redeveloping, and Developing — vary the basic use zone regulations on the basis of the development status of different parts of the city.
>
> (b) Baltimore County, Maryland, "isolates 'the location of automotive-service stations and certain other

vehicle-oriented uses' in an overlay provision which calls for extensive special-permit review before any new service station may be constructed."

(c) In Portland, Oregon, a design zone is superimposed on standard zones by the action of the city council on recommendation of the planning commission. . . . Once designated, such land is subject to the standard district bulk, density, and use regulations and a review by a committee of the planning commission.

(d) In Cincinnati, Ohio, when the overlay provisions are invoked, they grant the power to modify the underlying zoning selectively according to ad hoc standards developed to deal with a specific development proposal. The procedure resembles a special or conditional use permit procedure more than a floating zone procedure because it is entirely administrative; the city council does not engage in the overlay determination unless it decides to exercise its veto right.

(e) In Columbus, Ohio, the overlay technique allows the mapping of special overlay districts, but is not intended as a primary land use control technique. An overlay district establishes special restrictions—e.g., prohibition of most structures in floodways and severe restriction of construction on floodway fringes—applicable to any land use in the district, in addition to the usual use, bulk, area, and density regulations of the underlying districts.

Meshenberg suggests another use for overlay zoning:

> Overlay zones can be used as a device to incorporate special requirements or incentives for the construction of low- or moderate-income housing into zoning ordinances. For example, an overlay zone might be applied to all residentially designated areas of a defined density or size in order to permit low-income or subsidized housing at a higher than usual density. An overlay zone might offer additional incentives to build such housing by relaxing various restrictions in exchange for developing certain types of projects or for providing certain amenities. Such requirements are likely to be administered through a special permit system to afford greater administrative control.

M. Meshenberg, *supra* at 35.

A general discussion of "incentive" or "bonus" zoning techniques will be found *supra* p. 415. For a discussion of the use of such techniques to encourage the construction of "least cost" housing in suburban communities, see *supra* p. 635. As the preceding paragraph of this Note indicates, "overlay" and "incentive" techniques may be combined. "Incentive" provisions in a zoning ordinance may be administered "as of right" or through a special permit procedure, with or without site plan review.

b. Without Pre-Set Standards: Contract and Conditional Zoning

SYLVANIA ELECTRIC PRODUCTS, INC. v. CITY OF NEWTON

Supreme Judicial Court of Massachusetts
344 Mass. 428, 183 N.E.2d 118 (1962)

WHITTEMORE, J. This appeal under G.L. c. 231, § 96, and c. 185, § 15, by landowners in Newton, challenges the decision of the Land Court which held valid an amendment to the Newton zoning ordinance enacted on June 27, 1960. The amendment changed from a single residence A district to a limited manufacturing district the classification of 153.6 acres of land now of the petitioner (Sylvania) situated on the southerly side of Nahanton Street in the southerly end of the city and bounded on the west and south by a strip of land of the metropolitan district commission along the Charles River. The locus is diagonally across the river from the development of the New England Industrial Center in Needham which lies between Route 128 and the river. The limited manufacturing district classification had been added to the ordinance on September 21, 1959. One other parcel had been placed in the classification prior to the amendment.

The judge viewed the locus and its environs. His decision states facts in apparently full detail and incorporates all the exhibits.

1. The validity of the ordinance in all aspects, other than that discussed in point 2 below, is shown by the facts stated in the decision. It was not spot zoning; it did not violate the requirement of uniform classification; it was not invalidated because made after other nearby land had been for a long time classified for residences. . . . It was an appropriate zoning reclassification of the locus in the light of the physical characteristics of the land and very substantial changes in the use of land in the vicinity. . . . We do not reach the issue whether the judge's conclusion in respect of these points must be taken in any event because of his consideration of other facts not stated. . . . The appellants do not contend that the amendment was invalid because fewer acres were reclassified than were described in the proposal of which statutory notice was given. . . .

2. The principal issue is the effect of Sylvania's imposition of restrictions on the locus in connection with the enactment of the amending ordinance and of steps taken by the planning board, and others acting for the city, to cause Sylvania so to do.

In respect of this issue the judge found these facts: Sylvania on April 14, 1960, having an option to purchase a parcel containing 180 acres, inclusive of the rezoned locus, petitioned the board of aldermen (aldermen) to reclassify the parcel. On May 11, 1960, the planning board, after a public hearing held jointly with the aldermen's committee on claims and rules, reported that it had asked the city's planning consultant to review the petition and had decided to withhold action until he should report. On June 2, 1960, the board reported to the aldermen its vote to approve Sylvania's petition except that it recommended retaining in the residence A district a substantial frontage on Nahanton Street, including a parcel of about eighteen and one-half acres on the east side of the parcel adjacent to the property of the Charles River Country Club.

"Meanwhile, Sylvania, in consultation with the planning consultant . . . and members of the planning board and the claims and rules committee . . . , had agreed to certain restrictions upon its use of . . . [the locus],"[151] and had agreed to cede three acres, comprising the southeasterly tip of the parcel, to "Oak Hill Park Association" to be retained in the residence district. The restrictions, to be operative for thirty years from September 1, 1960, were set out in a draft of a deed attached to a proposed option agreement whereby Sylvania would give the city an option to purchase, within a thirty year period, for $300, a strip of land on the west and southwesterly side (the river side) of the parcel, adjacent to the land of the metropolitan district commission, containing thirty and one-half acres. By the option agreement Sylvania would agree to abide by the restrictions in the draft deed during the option term pending the city's exercise thereof. The intention would be to give the city a dominant estate capable of enforcing the restrictions. The deed was to convey the thirty and one-half acres subject to the restriction for the benefit of Sylvania's adjoining premises that for a period of fifty years no buildings or structures (other than fences) should be erected or maintained on the granted premises.

---

[151] The minutes of the planning board meeting of May 25, 1960, after recording the approval of the petition with the exception noted in the opinion above, state as follows:

"The Planning Board also voted to send the following letter to the chairman of the Claims and Rules Committee: 'At a meeting of the Planning Board held May 25, 1960, petition . . . of . . . Sylvania . . . was discussed in great detail and a modified but favorable decision was reached. This decision and a report on the petition are officially submitted in a separate communication to the Board of Aldermen. In considering the change of zone requested by the above petition, the Planning Board respectfully suggests that the following conditions be obtained by agreement with the proper parties concerned, if the Board of Aldermen is favorably disposed to the zone request. . . . [Items 1 to 6, specifying restrictions similar to but not identical with those agreed to and eventually imposed (see text of opinion)].' " [Footnotes are the court's, but have been renumbered. — Ed.]

The proposed restrictions limited the floor area of all buildings to be constructed on the premises to 800,000 square feet; required that sixty per cent of the ground area, or seventy-three and nine-tenths acres, be maintained in open space not occupied by buildings, parking areas or roadways; set back the building line from forty to eighty feet; imposed a sliding scale of height restrictions; called for a buffer zone of comparable size to the three acres to be ceded to Oak Hill Park Association and adjacent thereto, on which no structures might be erected; restricted the number and type of signs and the type of lighting; limited the use of buildings to certain, but not all, of the uses permitted in a limited manufacturing district; and established a pattern for traffic in connection with construction on the premises.

On June 27, 1960, the aldermen's committee on claims and rules reported its approval of the petition as modified by the planning board in its formal vote of approval, except that the committee recommended that the strip on Nahanton Street reserved for the residence district be increased in depth from 140 to 180 feet. There was submitted to the June 27 meeting a memorandum by the planning consultant, adressed to the mayor and to the alderman who was chairman of the committee on claims and rules. This memorandum summarized "the acreage breakdown on the Sylvania site, based upon the tentative deed restrictions as of June 23, 1960," and included a sketch map of the site delineating the areas and restrictions.

Thereafter, at the June 27 meeting, the aldermen enacted the ordinance which approved Sylvania's petition as modified in accordance with its committee's recommendation "and in connection therewith passed [the] order . . . authorizing the mayor to accept the proposed option agreement."

Sylvania took title to the Nahanton Street parcel on July 6, 1960, and thereafter on that day executed the option agreement with attached form of deed. Certified copies of the ordinance of June 27, 1960, which amended the zoning ordinance and of the order which authorized the mayor to accept the option bear the indorsement "Executive Department Approved July 7, 1960." The deed form and option agreement were recorded on July 8, 1960.

In several other jurisdictions votes to rezone on the express condition that the owner impose restrictions (sometimes called "contract zoning") have been held invalid. . . .

Rathkopf, The Law of Zoning and Planning (3d ed.) p. 74-9, states that "The basis of such rule is that the rezoning of a particular parcel of land upon conditions not imposed by the zoning ordinance generally in the particular district into which the land has been rezoned is prima facie evidence of 'spot zoning' in its most maleficent aspect, is not in accordance with a comprehensive plan and is beyond the power of the municipality."

The only decision squarely to the contrary which has come to our attention is *Church v. Islip,* 8 N.Y.2d 254, 259, 203 N.Y.S.2d 866, 869, 168 N.E.2d 680, 683, which the judge in the Land Court found persuasive. The change of zone, sustained in a majority opinion by Desmond, C. J., had been voted on condition that the owners agree that the building should not occupy more than twenty-five per cent of the area, that a six foot fence be erected five feet within the boundary line, and that shrubbery be planted and maintained at fence height. The court said: "Since the Town Board could have, presumably, zoned this ... corner for business without any restrictions, we fail to see how reasonable conditions invalidate the legislation. ... All legislation 'by contract' is invalid in the sense that a Legislature cannot bargain away or sell its powers. But we deal here with actualities, not phrases. To meet increasing needs of Suffolk County's own population explosion, and at the same time to make as gradual and as little of an annoyance as possible the change from residence to business on the main highways, the Town Board imposes conditions. There is nothing unconstitutional about it." ...

We turn to an analysis of what was done in Newton and note that although no condition was imposed by the aldermen in their vote, the conclusion is inescapable that the option proposal was a significant inducement of the zoning amendment and the amendment induced the giving of the option.

It is said that there was a purported, invalid exercise of the zoning power, for the vote operated to subject the locus not only to the restrictions of a limited manufacturing district but also to the restrictions of the option and deed form. But that is not, precisely, what happened. The induced, voluntary action of Sylvania, not the vote of the council, imposed the option restrictions; the vote reclassified land which was being subjected to those restrictions. The zoning decision was that the locus, so restricted by its owner, should be made a limited manufacturing district. That, in form, was an appropriate and untainted exercise of the zoning power.

What was done involved no action contrary to the best interest of the city and hence offensive to general public policy. It involved no extraneous consideration (as, for example, a request to give land for a park elsewhere in the city) which could impeach the enacting vote as a decision solely in respect of rezoning the locus.

We discern no aspect of spot zoning, lack of uniformity, or failure to conform to the comprehensive zoning plan. Even if the restrictions had been made a part of the zoning ordinance, they would not have created spot zoning. The site was all the land in the neighborhood which was proposed for reclassification. The private restrictions in no way made the locus less appropriate for classification as a limited manufacturing district. It is inconsequential that other areas elsewhere in the city, in, or to be put in, such a zoning district, would not have those restrictions. Requirements of uniformity and conformity to a plan do not mean that there must be identity of every relevant aspect in areas given the same zoning classification.

It does not infringe zoning principles that, in connection with a zoning amendment, land use is regulated otherwise than by the amendment. Zoning regulations, as Sylvania points out, exist unaffected by, and do not affect, deed restrictions. . . . The owner of the locus could have imposed restrictions on it prior to the original filing of the petition for rezoning without effect upon the subsequent rezoning vote.

Since the private regulation was, beyond dispute, harmonious, consistent, and beneficial, no hurtful effect requires that we look behind the form of what was done.

It is pointed out that proposals for zoning change can be adopted only after notice and a hearing. G.L. c. 40A, § 6. But the option restrictions did not make the locus a different subject for rezoning from what it was when the notice was given and the hearing held. The voluntary limitations imposed on the use of the land, although relevant in considering the proposal to rezone it, did not call for a new notice and hearing. They could have no adverse effect on anyone other than Sylvania. As noted, none of these restrictions was inconsistent with the requirements for the zoning district. It is far fetched to suggest that citizens opposed to any change might have stayed away from the original hearing in expectation that the proposal would be disapproved. The imposition of these restrictions, subsequent to the hearing, is no more significant than are changes in the zoning proposal itself which are within the scope of the original proposal. Such changes do not require further notice. . . .

It is objected that the council has not determined that the locus, unrestricted, is appropriate to be put in the limited manufacturing district. We agree that the zoning decision applied to the locus as affected by the option agreement. It was not, however, conditioned upon the validity of the option restrictions. The council made an appropriate zoning decision when it determined that the locus, subject to whatever limitations on its use the option effectively placed thereon, be put in the limited manufacturing district. Although not directly in issue, it may be noted that the restrictions appear to have been validly imposed by a sealed and recorded instrument. Sylvania is bound for thirty years even if the option is not exercised. Nothing now turns on an issue of the power of the mayor and council to pay for the dominant estate and take a deed.

The appellants urge that citizens should be able to look with confidence only to the zoning law to ascertain what are the zoning restrictions. The answer is that the option restrictions are not zoning restrictions, and all who have any interest in restrictions in the chain of title may find them of record.

The final objection is that even though the officials acted with good intent, beneficially to the city, and consistently with zoning principles, they were nevertheless making an unauthorized use of the zoning power. Unquestionably the officials let it be known that favorable rezoning depended in great likelihood on the adoption of the option restrictions. The planning board acted as a board when it suggested that "the following conditions be obtained by agreement with the proper parties concerned"; the planning consultant was acting as an adviser in respect of zoning when he submitted to the aldermen and the mayor the memorandum which summarized the proposed restrictions; and the aldermen confirmed their participation as a board by the vote which authorized the mayor to accept the proposed option agreement. This was all extrastatutory but nevertheless, proper activity, precedent to the exercise of the zoning power, not the exercise thereof. Whether the city may have the benefit of the pressures of its officials on Sylvania without adoption of the restrictions into the zoning proposal turns on the effect of the restrictions thereon. Since, as stated, the zoning proposal was not essentially changed, it was not necessary to reinitiate the amending process.

The locus was a unique site which was about to go into a specialized use.[152] It was appropriate and lawful to ask the prospective owner to take consistent action to ameliorate the effect of the pending drastic change of zoning classification.

It is, as other courts have noticed, anomalous for owners of nearby land who object to any change away from the residence district to object on the ground that, contemporaneously, ameliorating restrictions have been imposed. But, since they would be aggrieved by the purported change if it were illegal, we have considered the issue on it merits.

3. It is not necessary to consider Sylvania's appeal from the denial in the Land Court of its motion to dismiss the respondent landowners' appeal.

Decision affirmed.

KIRK, J. I do not agree. The mutual advantages gained by Newton and Sylvania by their arrangement are not in issue. The motives of the participants are not questioned. The central thesis of this dissent is that the method used by Newton to impose restrictions on the use of land owned by Sylvania is invalid. It is, in my opinion, invalid because: (1) the regulation and restriction of land used for "the

---

[152] Among the exhibits is "A Report on the Sylvania Science Center prepared by the Industrial Development Committee of the Newton Chamber of Commerce."

purpose of promoting the health, safety, convenience, morals or welfare" of a city's inhabitants (G.L. c. 40A, § 2) is an exercise of the police power, (2) which reposes in the Legislature, (3) which has exercised this power in G.L. c. 40A, by (4) delegating it to cities and towns within limits and procedures, (5) which Newton has not followed. . . .

We deal, then, with a case of *delegated legislative power.* The delegation is contained in The Zoning Enabling Act, G.L. c. 40A.

General Laws, c. 40A, § 2, provides in part, "For the purpose of promoting the health, safety, convenience, morals or welfare of its inhabitants, any city, except Boston, and any town, may *by a zoning ordinance or by-law* regulate and restrict the height, number of stories, and size of buildings and structures, the size and width of lots, the percentage of lot that may be occupied, the size of yards, courts and other open spaces, the density of population, and the location and use of buildings, structures and land for trade, industry, agriculture, residence or other purposes. . . .

"For any or all such purposes a *zoning ordinance or by-law* may divide the municipality into districts of such number, shape and area as may be deemed best suited to carry out the purposes of this chapter, and within such districts it may regulate and restrict the erection, construction, reconstruction, alteration or use of buildings, and structures, or use of land . . ." (emphasis supplied).

There would seem to be no question (and it appears the majority agrees) that (1) each and every restriction imposed by the "option agreement" (contract)[153] is one which the city is empowered to impose by ordinance under c. 40A, § 2; and (2) each and every restriction imposed by the contract was imposed in order to further the purposes stated in c. 40A, § 2 and § 3. [These are the usual statutory zoning purposes.—Eds.]

With equal certainty it should be clear that when a municipality elects to impose restrictions on the use of land for the purposes set out in c. 40A, §§ 2, 3, it must, under the express provisions of c. 40A, § 2, impose them *"by a zoning ordinance or by-law."* The attempt

---

[153] As the situation stands there are no deed restrictions on Sylvania's land. The restrictions derive from the collateral promises of Sylvania in the option agreement to abide by the "restrictions" in the undelivered deed attached to the option agreement. In this respect it should be noted that the duration of Newton's power to exercise the option is coterminous with the contract restrictions. It seems clear that this arrangement was made so that Newton, when (and only when) it felt is was necessary, could acquire a dominant estate for the specific enforcement of the restrictions. Until such a contingency occurs, which apparently is regarded as unlikely by both Sylvania and Newton, the restrictions exist only by virtue of the collateral promises. [Footnotes are by Kirk, J. One has been omitted. — Ed.]

to impose them by contract is "beyond the authority conferred . . . [and] not in compliance with the terms and conditions governing its exercise" and therefore is invalid.

Moreover, c. 40A, § 6 (see also § 7), prescribes explicitly the procedural steps which must be taken prior to the adoption, amendment or repeal of ordinances or by-laws relating to land restrictions. Included among the steps is the requirement of public hearings before both the planning board and the city council after notice thereof has been given to the city's inhabitants so that "all interested persons shall be given an opportunity to be heard." There is no similar requirement for notice or hearing when restrictions are to be imposed by a city on a parcel of land, however large, by contract. What we have, then, is not only an invalid method for imposing restrictions but an invalid method which admits the added evil of circumvention of the declared legislative requirement that interested parties be fully informed of the particulars of proposed municipal land restriction and be given an opportunity to be heard on these particulars.

The majority, however, states that the restrictions here imposed are not "zoning restrictions" and equates them with contract restrictions negotiated by private landowners for the benefit of adjoining land. I submit that this characterization will not withstand analysis. In the first place, the benefit of these contract restrictions does not run to or with any land now owned by Newton. Secondly, and more significantly, these restrictions were negotiated and agreed to by Newton and Sylvania in conjunction with, and as an integral part of, the enactment of the amendment to the Newton zoning ordinance. The amendment subjected the land to restrictions uniformly imposed on limited manufacturing districts; the contract subjected the land to additional restrictions in order, as the opinion recognizes, "to ameliorate the effect of the pending drastic change of zoning classification."

To my mind, the conclusion seems inescapable that, in truth and substance, the action of Newton was not the mere rezoning of a parcel of land which was already subject to privately negotiated contract restrictions but was, rather, one double-barrelled attempt to exercise the zoning power delegated to it by the Legislature under c. 40A, § 2. If the phrases "zoning restrictions" and "exercise of the zoning power" have any meaning, they must include the restrictions here imposed by contract. To say, as the majority in effect says, that they are not "zoning restrictions" or do not constitute "an exercise of the zoning power" because the city imposes them by contract and not by ordinance seems to me to be a play on words and to beg the question. The purpose and effect of their imposition is the same whether they are accomplished by ordinance or contract. It is the method of imposition which is the critical issue.

Whatever the action of Newton may or may not be called, it (1) in fact results in the imposition of restrictions by a city (Newton is the party that can and would enforce these restrictions) (2) for the purposes set out in c. 40A, §§ 2, 3, (3) upon the use of land by the owner (4) by the contract method (5) which method is prohibited by the Legislature (6) which alone can prescribe the method, and (7) hence is illegal.

Although the burden of the foregoing discussion is the invalidity of the contract restrictions, it is my opinion that the amendment to the zoning ordinance is itself also invalid. Newton's use of two methods in close and complementary coordination to accomplish a single purpose, namely the regulation of use of Sylvania's land is, in fact and in substance, a single act. All indications are that, unless Newton had first obtained the additional contract restrictions, it would not have effected the "drastic change of zoning classification" by enacting the amendment. As the opinion states, the amendment and the contract were mutually induced.

The elimination of the invalid contract restrictions, here used in combination with the ordinance restrictions resulting from the amendment to accomplish a single purpose, defeats the single purpose. It also reveals the essential oneness or interdependence of the methods used. Thus viewed as one, it would seem inevitably to follow that such ordinance restrictions fall with the contract restrictions as being in excess of the power conferred in c. 40A, § 2.[154]

I would require compliance with the statute, and accordingly would reverse the decision.

Comments: 1. Was the City of Newton "contractually" bound to rezone from a single-family residence to a limited manufacturing use classification at any time prior to the council's adoption of the rezoning amendment on June 27, 1960? Was the council "contractually" bound not to repeal the rezoning amendment during the period from June 27 to July 7, 1960? Was the mayor "contractually" bound to approve the rezoning amendment on or before July 7, 1960? If the mayor had disapproved it, would the council have been "contractually" bound to override the mayor by a two thirds vote of its entire membership? Once the rezoning amendment was approved and the option agreement and attached deed were recorded, was the City of Newton "contractually" bound to keep the zoning classification placed on Sylvania's land by the rezoning amendment in effect so long as Sylvania or

----

[154] Whether Newton could accomplish by a lawful exercise of its delegated power completely and precisely what it has attempted to accomplish by an unlawful exercise of power is, in my mind, an open question.

its successors in interest should use the land for an electronics manufacturing plan? If you think that the answer to all these questions is "no," why should the procedure used in the principal case be called "contract" zoning? Was the court correct in stating that the council's zoning decision was *not* conditioned upon the validity of the option agreement and that it "made an appropriate zoning decision when it determined that the locus, subject to *whatever* limitations on its use the option effectively placed thereon, be put in the limited manufacturing district"?

2. When did Sylvania become "contractually" bound to observe the restrictions in the deed attached to the option agreement? On June 27, July 7, or July 8, 1960? What was the consideration for Sylvania's agreement to these restrictions? What would be the consideration for its observance of these restrictions during the 30-year option period? Suppose Sylvania, instead of developing the land in question should sell it to a manufacturing concern that sought to use the land in a way that would violate the deed restrictions; could the City of Newton enjoin such violation? If so, on what legal or equitable theory? Do you think the city would have been on safer ground if it had required Sylvania to convey the entire tract to the city and had then reconveyed to Sylvania by deed containing an express condition that Sylvania and its successors in interest should observe the restrictions, with an express right of entry reserved to the city in the event of a breach of the condition?

3. When the plaintiffs decided to challenge the Sylvania tract rezoning in the principal case, did they run a substantial risk that the court might hold the additional land use restrictions contained in the recorded deed invalid but sustain the change from a single-family residential use classification to a limited manufacturing use classification? Compare *Church v. Islip,* cited in the principal case, where the New York Court of Appeals said, "the Town Board could have, presumably, zoned this . . . corner for business without any [additional] restrictions." See also *Cross v. Hall County,* 235 S.E.2d 379, 383 (Ga. 1977):

> Where the conditional zoning is otherwise valid, the conditions imposed for the protection or benefit of neighbors cannot be attacked successfully by those neighbors. When the zoning change itself is valid as to the neighbors . . ., the conditions attached thereto in favor of the neighbors do not invalidate either the zoning change or the conditions.

4. Suppose that there had been no challenge by third parties to the "conditional" rezoning procedure in the principal case, and that Sylvania had later refused to observe the additional land use restrictions contained in the recorded deed on the ground that they violate the statutory mandate that all zoning regulations "shall be uniform for each class or kind of buildings throughout each district." If the court should accept this argument, would it be likely simply to hold that the added restrictions were invalid, or that the entire rezoning transaction was void so that the land would revert to its prior zoning classification? See Comment, Contract and Conditional Zoning: A Tool for Zoning Flexibility, 23 Hastings L.J. 825, 836 (1972), observing that, where a municipality seeks to enforce the added restrictions and the landowner resists, the courts generally either sustain the added restrictions or hold them invalid without deciding the validity of the rezoning amendment itself, although a court clearly has the discretion to invalidate both the amendment and the added restrictions.

In *Cross, supra* Comment 3, the court said: "The owner of the rezoned land may be estopped from objecting to the conditions by having proposed or consented to them. And the conditions may be upheld against the unestopped landowner as being sustainable under the police power." 235 S.E.2d at 383 n. 2.

5. In addition to the cases cited in *Sylvania, supra,* as holding that "contract" or "conditional" rezoning is invalid, see *Cederberg v. City of Rockford,* 291 N.E.2d 249 (Ill. App. 1973), holding void an amendment rezoning land from residential to local business use because the amendment was adopted only because of the owner's executing a restrictive covenant limiting the otherwise permissible uses under the local business classification to "offices." The court emphasized that there was "no indication in the record that the rezoning was necessary or that it was granted only after a consideration of the appropriate use of the land within the total zoning scheme of the community," and that the restrictive covenant was therefore invalid. The court also stated that the record disclosed "that the City gave no consideration to the statutory standards of public health, safety, comfort, morals, and welfare," and that the rezoning amendment, standing alone, was not valid.

In addition to *Sylvania, Scrutton,* and *Church v. Islip* (cited and discussed in *Sylvania, supra*), cases upholding "contract" or "conditional" rezoning include *Cross v. Hall County,* 235 S.E.2d 379 (Ga. 1977); *Funger v. Mayor & Council,* 233 A.2d 168 (Md. 1966); *Town of Somerset v. County Council,* 181 A.2d 671 (Md. 1962); *State v. City of Spokane,* 422 P.2d 790 (Wash. 1967); *State ex rel. Zupancic v. Schimenz,* 174 N.W.2d 533 (Wis. 1970).

6. Does the "conditional" rezoning technique adopted by Newton in the *Sylvania* case have any advantage, from the city's viewpoint over the "special exception" or the "floating zone" technique? What are the real differences between these three "flexible" zoning techniques?

SCRUTTON v. COUNTY OF SACRAMENTO

California Court of Appeal
275 Cal.App.2d 412, 79 Cal.Rptr. 872 (1969)

FRIEDMAN, Acting P.J. — Mrs. Bessie Scrutton, the plaintiff, brought a declaratory relief action against the County of Sacramento and appeals from a summary judgment favoring the county. . . .

. . . In May 1964 Mrs. Scrutton filed an application with the County Planning Commission seeking to have the property rezoned from agricultural to multiple family residential to permit its development for residential apartment units.

The planning commission recommended that the application be approved subject to conditions. Section 23(H) of the county's basic zoning ordinance provides: "The Board of Supervisors may impose conditions to the zoning reclassification of property where it finds that said conditions must be imposed so as not to create problems inimical to the public health, safety and general welfare of the County of Sacramento."

Among the requirements proposed by the planning commission were that Mrs. Scrutton dedicate a 10-foot right of way for widening Whitney Avenue and improve it with pavement, sidewalk, curbs and gutters; that on the east edge of her property she dedicate a 27-foot strip to form the west half of Foster Way; that she join an assessment district which would improve the west half of Foster Way with paving, sidewalk, curbs and gutters.

The board of supervisors then held a hearing to consider the application. The board expressed agreement with the conditions recommended by the planning commission, except that it imposed the additional requirement that Mrs. Scrutton pave Foster Way at her own expense instead of financing the work through a neighborhood assessment district. Before adopting the rezoning ordinance sought by Mrs. Scrutton, the board of supervisors tendered a deed and contract for her signature. According to the board's usual procedures, it would not formally adopt the rezoning ordinance until the applicant returned the executed deed and contract. Under the contract proffered Mrs. Scrutton, she would commit herself to comply with all the conditions imposed by the county, and any failure on her part would cause the property's reversion to agricultural zoning.

Mrs. Scrutton . . . refused to sign the proposed contract, then filed this declaratory relief action to test the validity of the supervisors' demands for dedicating the Foster Way frontage and paving it at her own expense.

Mrs. Scrutton's complaint alleges that Whitney Avenue on the north will provide the sole vehicular access to her planned apartment development; that she does not plan on access to and from Foster Way; that the property across the street on Foster Way is owned by a school district which has dedicated and paved a 27-foot longitudinal strip forming the eastern half of Foster Way; that her action in dedicating and paving a 27-foot strip as the western half of Foster Way will not benefit her own property or her proposed apartment development. Her complaint also pointed to two development-ripe parcels owned by others to the south of her property, which were without northward access to Whitney Avenue but would, if the county's demands are met, be supplied with such access.

Although somewhat indirectly, Mrs. Scrutton's complaint charges that the Foster Way improvement project is unreasonably aimed at accommodating public needs unconnected with her own apartment development. The county filed an answer denying her claim of lack of benefit from the Foster Way widening project. The county's answer extolled the Foster Way project as a benefit to Mrs. Scrutton's property, but was silent as to the project's utility for public uses unrelated to her apartments. The county moved for a summary judgment, supporting its motion by affidavits averring that the Foster Way project would provide on-street parking for Mrs. Scrutton's tenants and assist in fire protection. Like the county's answer, its affidavits were reticent on the project's utility for unrelated public services, conceding that "this benefit inures to all property generally, including the Plaintiff's property." The trial court granted the summary judgment motion.

. . . .

Chapter 4 of Title 7 of the Government Code (§§ 65800-65907) establishes standards for the adoption and administration of zoning regulations by counties and noncharterd cities. Among such standards is that of uniformity within land use zones. "All such regulations shall be uniform for each class or kind of building or use of land throughout each zone. . . ." (Gov.Code, § 65852.) Another provision of the state law recognizes that variances may be granted subject to individualized conditions. (Gov.Code, § 65906.) There is no statute specifically authorizing the imposition of conditions upon rezoning individual parcels.

"Conditional zoning" is an appropriate phrase to describe a zoning change which permits use of a particular property subject to conditions not generally applicable to land similarly zoned. . . . Plaintiff contends that the conditional rezoning attempted here exceeds Sacramento County's authority under state law and violates that law's uniformity demand.

County zoning regulations are a manifestation of the local police power conferred by article XI, section 11, of the State Constitution, not an exercise of authority delegated by statute.[155] . . . In their intrinsic character and by express declaration the state laws on county and city zoning are designed as standardizing limitations over local zoning practices, not as specific grants of authority to legislate.[156] The state statutes' silence on conditional rezoning is not

---

[155] Article XI, section 11, of the California Constitution: "Any county, city, town, or township may make and enforce within its limits all such local, police, sanitary, and other regulations as are not in conflict with general laws." [This is the constitutional home rule provision.—Eds.]

[156] Government Code, section 65800, declares: "It is the purpose of this chapter to provide for the adoption and administration of zoning laws, ordinances, rules and regulations by counties and cities, as well as to implement such general plan as may be in effect in any such county or city. The Legislature declares that in enacting this chapter it is its intention to provide only a minimum of limitation in order that counties and cities may exercise the maximum degree of control over local zoning matters."

a denial of power to pursue that practice. The practice must find its own justification as an appropriate exercise of the local police power.

So-called "Euclidean" zoning divides the community into homogeneous land use zones. Individual parcels may often be allowed a justified escape from this rigid grouping without detriment to zoning objectives. Rezoning an individual parcel is simply one of a variety of techniques for achieving flexibility in land use. ... California elucidations of the local police power recognize that other kinds of application for change in regulated land use may be granted subject to the landowner's compliance with reasonable conditions. The power to impose such conditions has been upheld in connection with the approval of subdivisions ... with the grant of building permits ... and with the grant of zoning variances. ... The power to impose conditions on rezoning furthers the well-being of landowners generally, promotes community development and serves the general welfare.

Like other changes in land use, the rezoning of an individual parcel may benefit the landowner but generate augmented demands for public services or create deleterious effects in the neighborhood. Reasonably conceived conditions harmonize the landowner's need with the public's interest. In New York, the authority to reclassify subject to reasonable conditions has been upheld as a manifestation of the general authority to reclassify without conditions. ... The same police power which supports the imposition of reasonable conditions upon other kinds of change in land use sustains the power of California counties to engage in "conditional rezoning."

Government Code section 65852, supra, aims at the general objective of uniform land use within each land zone. Conceivably, a condition evolved under section 23(H) of the county ordinance might illegally broaden or narrow permissible land uses in violation of the state law's uniformity standard. ... Alternatively, section 23(H) may be utilized to impose conditions in no way affecting the property's availability for uses identical with those of other property in the same zoning classification. Conditional zoning which does not affect the property's use does not violate the uniformity objective. The latter alternative characterizes the present case. The conditions imposed by the county would not prevent Mrs. Scrutton from using her property for all purposes within the multiple residential classification. We conclude that section 23(H) is a valid expression of Sacramento County's zoning power.

Quite aside from the validity of section 23(H), plaintiff attacks the county's action as "contract zoning" by which the county, in exchange for the landowner's covenants, would bargain away a portion of its future power over zoning. The police power to zone and rezone may not be restricted by contract. ... The phrase "contract zoning" has no legal significance and simply refers to a reclassification of land use in which the landowner agrees to perform conditions not imposed on other land in the same classification. No reported California decision deals with it. It has been criticized and defended, nullified in some states, sustained in others. . . .

. . . Here the county itself does not become party to an express contract. Yet, when the zoning agency exacts a concomitant contract from the landowner, it holds out an implied or moral assurance that it will not quickly reverse or alter its decision. In a sense this assurance tends to freeze the property's status. The suspension of continuing police power is theoretical rather than real. . . . The contract zoning procedure pursued here entails neither a formal nor a practical surrender of the police power.

Plaintiff has a valid objection to the reversion feature of the proposed rezoning. In effect, the proposed contract declares that the landowner's breach of covenant will be met by automatic reversion from the multiple residential to the original agricultural classification or by reversion through action of the board of supervisors. The reversion would amount to a second rezoning. Automatic reversion would violate the procedural directions of state law, which demands that rezoning be accomplished through notice, hearings and planning commission inquiry. . . . Even if procedural directions were followed, the reversion would violate substantive limitations upon the supervisors' legislative power. . . . Although the courts do not ordinarily inquire into legislative motivation, the proceedings on their face would characterize the reversion ordinance as a forfeiture rather than a legislative decision on land use. . . .

The county, nevertheless, has alternative remedies . . . based upon such theories as breach of contract, breach of restrictive covenant and breach of equitable servitude. . . .

Lastly the inquiry focuses on validity of the specific demands attacked by Mrs. Scrutton's suit — that she dedicate a 27 by 650-foot strip as the western half of Foster Way and install pavement, gutter, curb and sidewalk at her own expense.

As noted earlier, the police power permits the imposition of reasonable conditions upon the landowner's proposal. Not all conditions are valid. A grant of public privilege may not be conditioned upon the deprivation of constitutional protections. . . . The police power "cannot extend beyond the necessities of the case and be made a cloak to destroy constitutional rights as to the inviolateness of private property." . . . An arbitrarily conceived exaction will be nullified as a disguised attempt to take private property for public use without resort to eminent domain or as a mask for discriminatory taxation. . . .

Although "reasonableness" has been postulated as the hallmark of validity, a more precise standard is available. . . . Conditions imposed on the grant of land use applications are valid if reasonably conceived to fulfill public needs emanating from the landowner's proposed use.

The California decisions illustrate two kinds of need: the community's protection against potentially deleterious effects of the landowner's proposal . . . and the community's need for facilities to meet public service demands created by the proposal. . . . While decisions invalidating the exaction rely upon theories of constitutional invasion, their springboard is the lack of relationship between the exaction and the proposed use. . . .

The relationship between the condition exacted by the public authority and the use proposed by the landowner presents a factual inquiry for the trial court. In order to show a lack of relationship, the landowner must present evidence. . . . The court can seldom if ever resolve this inquiry without taking evidence. Mrs. Scrutton's claim of arbitrary imposition required that kind of inquiry by the trial court.

The county's supporting affidavits, on the other hand, fell short of the target. In essence they sought to demonstrate that the landowner's dedication of a 27 by 650-foot strip and her expenditure for paving it would benefit her proposed apartments. They contained no showing that Mrs. Scrutton's apartment project would generate traffic or other conditions on Foster Way which would reasonably necessitate widening and improving the street at her sole expense.

It is true that some of the courts have justified the exaction not only for its fulfillment of public needs caused by the proposed development, but also because it would benefit the landowner financially. . . . Standing alone, the landowner's economic benefit supplies inadequate underpinning for the exaction. The police power forms the exaction's constitutional foundation. That power is aimed at public need, not private profit. The landowner should be free to reject the paternalism which forces him into an exaction conceived for his personal benefit. The decisions seem to utilize the "private benefit" notion as judicial gloss after the prime essential, a public burden emanating from the development, has been discerned. . . . The fulfillment of public needs emanating from the proposed land use is the *sine qua non* of the exaction's reasonableness.

The county's affidavits did not entitle it to judgment in the action and the trial court thus erred in granting the summary judgment motion. . . .

The judgment is reversed and the cause remanded to the trial court for proceedings compatible with the views expressed in this opinion.

Comments: 1. In the principal case, on remand, if the county fails to establish the requisite "relationship between the condition exacted by the public authority and the use proposed by the landowner," what kind of decree should the trial court enter? Should it declare that the landowner is entitled to the rezoning she seeks, without the conditions imposed by the county, or that the existing agricultural use zoning will remain in effect?

2. Although there have been many attempts to distinguish "contract" from "conditional" rezoning, it is clearly unprofitable, if not totally impossible, to do so. Meshenberg asserts that "contract" rezoning involves an agreement by the municipality "to limit, at least for a period, its power to reclassify the land," while "conditional" rezoning does not; but he admits that "the distinction is somewhat artificial." M. Meshenberg, *supra* p. 716 at 36. Moreover, a municipal governing body would rarely, if ever, enter into any such agreement, since it would clearly be held invalid. In *Cross v. Hall County,* 235 S.E.2d 379 (Ga. 1977), the court said that "contract zoning is invalid and . . . conditional zoning is valid," explaining further that "conditional zoning" is valid when the conditions are "imposed pursuant to the police power for the protection or benefit of neighbors to ameliorate the effects of the zoning change," but that "conditions imposed on rezoning are generally invalid, particularly where the zoning board is motivated to allow the change by the conditions . . . proposed by the rezoning applicant, so that the rezoning is granted as a consequence of the conditions rather than as an exercise of legislative discretion." *Id.* at 382. Do you understand this distinction?

3. A more useful set of distinctions is elaborated in Comment, Contract and Conditional Zoning: A Tool for Zoning Flexibility, 23 Hastings L.J. 825 (1972), where the following forms of "contract" or "conditional" rezoning are distinguished and discussed:

(a) A bilateral contract between a municipality and a landowner or developer which includes a promise by the city to rezone the land in accordance with the terms of the contract and a promise by the owner or developer to observe restrictions on the use of the land in addition to those imposed by the new zoning classification. This, of course, "amounts to an illegal abrogation of the city's police power," in the view of most courts, and is generally held invalid for that reason. *Id.* at 838.

(b) A unilateral contract which provides that in consideration of the municipality's rezoning of the land the landowner or developer will observe restrictions on the use of the land in addition to those imposed by the new zoning classification. This is said to have the following advantages:

> The city has made no binding promise and thus there is no abrogation of the police power. The legislature may enforce the contract on the basis of specific performance, and if the contract also provides for covenants running with the land, it is enforceable by the city as against subsequent takers of the rezoned property. Since the promise is not binding until the rezoning legislation is passed, the landowner is also protected.

Id. at 837.

(c) Passage of a rezoning amendment conditioned either (i) upon completion of specified work on the land in question before the rezoning amendment is passed, or (ii) conditioned upon subsequent completion of specified work or imposition on the land of added restrictions specified in the amendment. However, method (i) is said to place "an undue burden on the landowner since he may expend funds in performing the required acts . . . only to find the rezoning ordinance rejected and his alterations in violation of the present ordinances"; and method (ii) "has been unfavorably received by both the courts and the legal writers. A New York court held such an ordinance invalid because it was not immediately effective and instead purported to change zoning in the future after the conditions were met." *Id.* at 839.

(d) Passage of a rezoning amendment conditioned upon the prior dedication and/or improvement of other land.

> Although there is danger that the landowner may dedicate the land and the city then refuse to pass the rezoning ordinance, he may protect himself by a condition precedent in the grant that the dedication is not to be effective until the zoning legislation is enacted. The enforcement procedure is a simple refusal to pass the zoning amendment until the land is dedicated.

Id. at 840. But, as the *Scrutton* case shows, the dedication requirement may be held invalid if not reasonably related to the land use proposed by the landowner or developer.

(e) Passage of a zoning amendment conditioned upon the prior execution and recordation of a restrictive covenant limiting the use of the subject land. This is essentially what occurred in the *Sylvania* case, although the rezoning amendment did not expressly recite that it was so conditioned. The Comment, *supra,* asserts that "several problems concerning the enforceability of the covenant arise when this method is used," *id.* at 841, but it seems clear that the problems are no different than in cases where method (b), *supra,* is used.

4. Despite the trend toward judicial acceptance of "contract" or "conditional" rezoning, a recent study suggests that use of this technique to implement inclusionary zoning programs should be eschewed in states where its legal validity has been denied or even questioned, although "either device could be theoretically promising" for that purpose. *See* H. Franklin, D. Falk, and A. Levin, In-Zoning: A Guide for Policy-Makers on Inclusionary Land Use Programs 119 (1975).

5. Compare the "conditional" rezoning authorization in the Sacramento County zoning ordinance, sustained in *Scrutton,* with Article XXVIII, § 6 of the Fulton County, Georgia, 1966 zoning resolution:

> 1. Each category for zoning shall have a subhead thereunder to be known as "Conditional" for that category.
> 2. Whenever any application for a change in the District Maps is accompanied or supported by specific plans and design for a particular development and use, and the Commissioners of Roads and Revenue, after public hearing . . . , approve such specific plans and design and such particular development and use and also approve such change in the District Maps, then the property may be rezoned for the proper category as set forth in the Zoning

Resolution . . . as "CONDITIONAL" under that category and the building inspector shall issue a building permit for the development of such property only in strict compliance with the plans submitted.

3. . . . .

4. If for any reason development and use of property approved in accordance with the procedure outlined in 1, 2, and 3 above cannot be accomplished, such plans shall not be altered, changed, or varied, except after approval by the Commissioners of Roads and Revenue.

5. Nevertheless, when conditional zoning has been granted, but no affirmative action to perform said conditions, or to obtain a building permit subject to such conditions, and such status shall continue for 12 months from date of such conditional zoning, the property shall revert to its original status prior to such conditional zoning.

The Fulton County "conditional" rezoning provision, *supra,* apparently requires each applicant to submit a site plan for the proposed development, but it is not clear how the site plan relates to the "conditions" mentioned in paragraph 5. Perhaps the "conditions" are, in substance, modifications of the site plan as originally submitted, after negotiations between the developer and the Commissioners. Site plan approval procedures are treated in more detail *infra* p. 738.

6. "Conditional" rezoning sometimes incorporates a "tentative zone change" procedure. For example, Los Angeles Land Use Development Code § 1-511.03 (1971) provides as follows:

When the [Planning] Commission or Council finds that an application for a zone change is consistent with the objectives of this Code, provided certain dedications of land, waivers of access, or installations of improvements in a public right-of-way or on private property are completed or security for improvements is offered and accepted within a specified time period, it shall recommend or adopt the zone change subject to compliance with specified conditions.

In such cases, the ordinance changing the zone of the property concerned shall, instead of immediately and finally rezoning the property, place it in the (T) Tentative Zone Change classification. The property shall remain in said temporary classification until such time as the rezoning proceedings either terminate or are completed in accordance with the provisions of Article 1-72 (Temporary Classification (T) Tentative Zone Change).

Completion of the rezoning proceedings "in accordance with the provisions of Article 1-72" means approval by the Planning Commission of the zone change and removal of the "(T) classification. Meshenberg has observed that "this provision can permit establishing a large number of zones, each with individual specifications and characteristics, although it is intended to be used only infrequently and only under special circumstances." (M. Meshenberg, *supra* at 41.) It is not clear, however, whether § 1-511.03 is intended to authorize the imposition of additional use restrictions in connection with rezoning, or whether it is intended to authorize only the imposition of requirements for "dedications of land, waivers of access, or installations of improvements."

7. R.I. Gen. Laws § 45-24-4.1 (1970) provides as follows:

> . . . [T]he town or city council may, in approving a zone change limit such change to one (1) of the permitted uses in the zone to which the subject land is rezoned, and impose such conditions upon the use of land as it deems necessary. The responsible city or town official shall cause the limitations so imposed to be clearly noted on the zoning map.

In *Sweetman v. Town of Cumberland,* 364 A.2d 1277 (R.I. 1976), the court held that the provision set out above authorizes the local governing body to limit the application of the conditions imposed to those parcels which are rezoned, and that identical conditions need not be imposed on land in the same use classification but not covered by the rezoning amendment. As the court pointed out, if a local governing body wished to limit all lots in the same classification equally, it need only enact a more detailed general ordinance. The court also held that there was no conflict between the provision set out above and the zoning "uniformity" requirement, since the authorization for "conditional" rezoning was granted "notwithstanding the uniformity provision in the zoning enabling act." As thus interpreted, the court held that the provision set out above was not violative of equal protection as permitting imposition of different conditions upon parcels of land bearing the same use classifications, nor violative of due process as permitting municipal councils to propose conditions in an arbitrary and capricious manner.

Do you think the Rhode Island statutory provision set out above is one that other states ought to adopt? Does it make "floating zones" and "special exceptions" unnecessary? How well does it fulfill the following suggested criteria for "conditional" rezoning enabling legislation?

> (1) That contract zoning and conditional zoning be provided for, both as pertains to agreements between landowners and between a landowner and a municipal authority, subject to rather stringent requirements restricting its applicability to bona fide transitional zones, i.e., where two or more competing and incompatible uses each have valid claims.
>
> (2) That there be established specified limits as to the time period subsequent to contractual rezoning during which the municipality would be estopped to rescind the decision or to upzone, the time period to be of sufficient length to justify the owner's expenditures yet short enough that the municipality's capacity to control its own growth and development would not be seriously compromised.
>
> (3) That specified consequences attend a breach of conditions by the owner of the subject property:
>
> (a) where the conditions involve ongoing performance and breach occurs after completion of construction, specific performance would be available by injunction;
>
> (b) where the performance of conditions must necessarily precede completion and either they are breached or there appears the strong likelihood that they will be breached, injunction would

be available to halt construction until compliance is established; and

    (c) if the conditions are of such character that their breach, once accomplished, seems likely to preclude their subsequent performance, such as would be involved in any substantial structural violations, the use's cessation should be provided for within a time period that gives a reasonable credit, not to exceed a specified time limit, say, two years, for the length of time during which the owner did comply; and

    (d) that provisions be included for the cessation of municipal supervision and of the conditions themselves if a substantial amount of surrounding land is also downzoned.

Comment, Toward a Strategy for Utilization of Contract and Conditional Zoning, 51 J. Urb. L. 94, 110-11 (1973).

c. Site Plan Review Requirements

Many modern zoning ordinances require the land developer to obtain approval of a "site plan" for his proposed development from the planning commission. The "site plan" provision of the zoning ordinance generally requires the plan to show the proposed layout of buildings and open space, including parking areas, and the provisions for access to and from the public street system. Site plan review requirements are often included in zoning ordinance provisions authorizing "special exceptions," "special use permits," "conditional use permits" and "floating zone" amendments. They also often imposed in connection with applications for straight or "conditional" rezoning, for subdivision plat approval, and for permits to build on unsubdivided land. Indeed, many zoning ordinances require site plan reviews as a prerequisite to most forms of new land development except the construction of one- or two-family houses on single lots. Site plan review requirements are, of course, an almost invariable feature of planned unit development (PUD) ordinance provisions. PUD's are discussed in detail *infra* p. 854.

In the early 1950's, local governing bodies began putting site plan review requirements into their zoning ordinances without any express statutory authorization. In New Jersey, such requirements were sustained as valid under a planning enabling act provision authorizing the governing body to refer any matter or class of matters to the planning board before final action thereon by the municipal body or officer having final authority, "with or without the provision that final action thereon shall not be taken until the planning board has submitted its report thereon or has had a reasonable time [fixed by the ordinance] to submit its report." *Kozesnik v. Montgomery Township,* 131 A.2d 9 (N.J. 1957); *Newark Milk & Cream Co. v. Parsippany-Troy Hills Township,* 135 A.2d 682 (N.J. Super. 1957); *Wilson v. Borough of Mountainside,* 201 A.2d 540 (N.J. 1964). In the *Newark Milk* case, Hall, J., said that in reviewing site plans the planning board "may only consider those [matters] having a relation to the public interest, and not those which are merely matters of private concern in the use of property, having no connection with or effect upon adjoining owners, adjoining areas outside the district or the community and public interest at large," and that "intrusion of aesthetic considerations on a basis beyond that of conservation of the value of property" was unwarranted. In *Wilson* and several other cases, the New Jersey courts have made it clear that, under the guise of site plan review, the planning board may not take over or interfere with the statutory power of the zoning board of adjustment to pass on applications for special exceptions and variances. *See Saddle River Country Day School v. Saddle River,* 144 A.2d 425 (N.J. App. Div. 1958), *aff'd,* 150 A.2d 34 (N.J. 1959); *Hill Homeowners Ass'n v. Zoning Bd. of Adjustment,* 322 A.2d 501 (N.J. Super. 1974); *Bederson v. Ocean Township,* 338 A.2d 39 (N.J. Super. 1975).

Site plan review requirements were sustained in Pennsylvania in the 1960's without express statutory authorization. *Sun Oil Co. v. Pittsburgh,* 169 A.2d 294 (Pa. 1961); *Kern v. Board of Adjustment,* 192 A.2d 345 (Pa. 1963); *Commercial Properties, Inc. v. Peternel,* 211 A.2d 514 (Pa. 1965).

Although the Massachusetts court held that site plan review requirements were *ultra vires* in *Coolidge v. Planning Bd.,* 151 N.E.2d 51 (Mass. 1958), it later approved site plan review by the planning board as a step in approval of "special exceptions" by the zoning board of adjustment in *Y.D. Dugout, Inc. v. Board of Appeals,* 255 N.E.2d 732 (Mass. 1970). (The Canton ordinance required applications for site plan approval to be submitted to the board of adjustment, which then referred the applications to the planning board for report, with the final decision reserved to the board of adjustment).

In Connecticut and Maryland, site plan review requirements also appear to be valid. *See McCrann v. Town Plan & Zoning Comm'n,* 282 A.2d 900 (Conn. 1971); *Colwell v. Howard County,* 354 A.2d 210 (Md. 1976). In *Colwell,* the court sustained a provision requiring site plan approval whenever the zoning map was amended with a further proviso that building permits must be applied for within one year of site plan approval for construction of 25 percent of the building floor area of the site plan, otherwise the amendment shall be void and the property shall "revert to the prior classification."

In New Hampshire, the Supreme Court appears to have confused "site plans" with "subdivision plats." See *Gosselin v. City of Nashua,* 321 A.2d 593 (N.H. 1974), stating that N.H. Rev. Stat. Ann. § 36:23 (Supp. 1975) provides for approval of site plans, although in fact the statute deals only with approval of subdivision plats by the planning board.

Several current state planning or land use control enabling acts expressly authorize site plan review requirements. *E.g.,* N.Y. Gen. City Law § 30-a (Supp. 1978):

1. a. Planning board approval of site plans. The body creating such planning board may, as part of a zoning ordinance ... or by local law adopted pursuant to other enabling law, authorize the planning board to review and approve, approve with modifications or disapprove site plans, prepared to specifications set forth in the said zoning ordinance or local law and/or in regulations of the planning board, showing the arrangement, layout and design of the proposed use of the land shown on such plan. Such ordinance or local law shall specify the uses for which such approval shall be required and the elements to be included in such plans submitted for approval; such elements may include, ... those relating to parking, means of access, screening, signs, landscaping, architectural features, location and dimensions of buildings, impact of the proposed use on adjacent land uses and such other elements as may reasonably be related to the health, safety and general welfare of the community. When an authorization to approve site plans is granted to a planning board ..., the terms thereof may condition the issuance of a building permit upon such approval by the planning board. When so authorized, a planning board may adopt such rules and regulations as it deems necessary ... to exercise the powers so granted. Plats showing lots, blocks or sites which are subject to review pursuant to ... [subdivision control regulations] shall continue to be subject to such review and shall not be subject to review under this paragraph.

b. Planning board approval of certain uses.... [The planning board may be authorized to approve conditional uses upon determining compliance with the conditions set out in the zoning ordinance.] ... Such conditions may include, ... the approval of plans for the site layout and design of the specified uses containing elements described in paragraph (a) of this subdivision.... [The second and third last sentences in paragraph (a) are repeated here. — Eds.]

N.Y. Town Law § 274-a (Supp. 1978) is identical to the statute set out above.

Compare N.J. Stat. Ann. § 40:55D-37 (Supp. 1978) which expressly authorizes the local governing body, by ordinance, to require "approval of site plans by resolution of the planning board as a condition for the issuance of a permit for any development, except that subdivision or individual lot applications for detached one or two dwelling-unit buildings shall be exempt from such site plan review." Approval by the planning board is unnecessary when the zoning board of adjustment reviews an application for a variance, in which case it has the power to grant site plan approval "subject to the same restrictions as the planning board. *Id.* § 40:55D-76 (Supp. 1978). An ordinance requiring site plan review "shall include and be limited to ... standards and requirements relating to: a. Preservation of existing natural resources on the site; b. Safe and efficient vehicular and pedestrian circulation, parking and loading; c. Screening, landscaping and location of structures; and d. Exterior lighting needed for safety reasons in addition to any requirements for street lighting" where there is no zoning ordinance and no PUD ordinance. *Id.* § 40:55D-41 (Supp. 1978). When a municipal zoning ordinance is in effect, or there are PUD provisions in the subdivision ordinance, site plan standards and requirements may be much more elaborate. *Id.* §§ 40:55D-38, 40:55D-39 (Supp. 1978). The review by the planning board of any conditional use application "shall include any required site plan review." *Id.* § 40:55D-67 (Supp. 1978).

3. The Role of the Comprehensive Plan in the Zoning Process

As we have seen, judicial decisions considering the zoning process for the most part have ignored the "comprehensive plan" requirement, even though local comprehensive planning is widespread and legislation authorizing the planning process has been widely available for over 50 years. When the courts have been forced to consider the "comprehensive plan" requirement, they have generally concluded that the "comprehensive plan" may be found in the zoning ordinance itself. The *Fasano* case, *supra* p. 693, was one of the first major court decisions to give prominent recognition to the role of the separate "comprehensive plan" in the zoning process, and it appears to have ushered in a new era. Other courts are giving increased recognition to the role of the "comprehensive plan" in the zoning process; several state legislatures have made local planning mandatory; and in some instances this legislation explicitly requires that zoning be consistent with a locally adopted "comprehensive plan."

SABO v. TOWNSHIP OF MONROE

Supreme Court of Michigan
394 Mich. 531, 232 N.W.2d 584 (1975)

[At the time of this case, only five members of a seven-man court were sitting. The facts were that plaintiffs sought to build a mobile home park on their land, and sought a rezoning to commercial to permit this use. When the township refused plaintiffs brought this action to have the ordinance invalidated as applied to their land. One issue in the case was whether or not a separately adopted master plan was essential to the validity of the zoning ordinance; the trial court held that it was not.

[While voting to affirm the Court of Appeals, which had reversed the trial court, Justice Levin for the majority held that no independently adopted master plan was necessary in Michigan. "The 'plan' limitation in the zoning enabling act requires that the community zone in a pre-established and comprehensive manner rather than on an ad hoc basis. The 'plan' required for zoning purposes is not dependent on the adoption of a master plan and may properly emanate from the zoning ordinance or map itself." *Id.* at 586. Justice Williams filed a separate opinion, in which he disagreed on the need for a plan under Michigan statutes. His opinion reviews the interpretation of the Standard Act's "in accordance" requirement in other states. — Eds.]

WILLIAMS, Justice, dissenting (to reverse the trial court).

. . . .

II — IS THE TOWNSHIP ZONING ORDINANCE VOID AS NOT BASED ON A MASTER PLAN

Plaintiffs contend that the township ordinance is not entitled to a presumption of reasonableness because a master plan had not been adopted and the township had never retained the services of a professional planner.

Defendant township does not dispute these facts but maintains, on the other hand, that while cities may be required to adopt a master plan, townships need only consider a basic plan. It argues that a basic plan may be the zoning ordinance itself, and therefore failure to adopt a master plan has no bearing on the presumed validity and reasonableness of a township zoning ordinance.

This is not the law.

[Justice Williams then reviews the applicable Michigan statutes, and concludes: — Eds.]

Michigan requires that a zoning ordinance be based on a plan, and that the plan is something different from the ordinance. From this foundation, certain consequences follow, namely, if the ordinance is not based on a plan, the statute has not been followed, and the zoning is invalid.

Precedent from other states is not persuasive, because the Michigan statute is unique.

III — MICHIGAN STATUTE COMPARED WITH OTHER STATES

. . . .

B. Other State Statutes

Although there appears to be general understanding that there is a difference between planning and zoning, courts have often misconstrued the relationship between the two when interpreting statutes based upon the language of the model zoning enabling act.

The Standard State Zoning Enabling Act requires zoning regulations to "be made in accordance with a comprehensive plan." . . . The enabling legislation of most states also includes some variation of this requirement. . . . Most court decisions in other states have relied on construing the precise language of their state statutes. These statutes are all different from the compulsory planning-zoning language of the Michigan Act, and, to that extent, are not valid precedent for interpreting our own.

The leading case cited as holding that ordinance and plan are one and the same is *Kozesnik v. Montgomery Twp.,* 24 N.J. 154 131 A.2d 1 (1957). . . .

Whatever the wisdom of this statutory interpretation, the language it analyzes is not the language of the Michigan statute. Its validity is further reduced by the grudging acceptance of the approach by some courts,[157] and by the even narrower contortions taken by other courts cited by my brother Levin which have derived their reasoning from *Kozesnik* and their statutory language from the Enabling Act. There is still another line of cases which has attempted to resolve the problem more properly by analyzing the basic relationship between planning and zoning with results different from those in *Kozesnik* and its progeny.

Thus, the judicial construction of individual state zoning and planning statutes is not quite as homologous as one might suppose from a reading of some commentators. The concern expressed in the opinions is both to protect the landowner from arbitrary restrictions on the use of his or her property, as well as to ensure that local

---

157 The Washington Supreme Court cited *Kozesnik* and interpreted permissive statutory language as approving the *Kozesnik* approach, at the same time noting that "administrative wisdom, good planning practices, and the prospect of greater local zoning consistency may suggest the desirability of some definitive written articulation of a 'master' or 'comprehensive' plan." *Shelton v. Bellevue,* 73 Wash.2d 28, 36, 435 P.2d 949, 954 (1968). . . .

authorities act for the benefit of the community as a whole following a deliberate consideration of alternatives.

To this end, our Legislature has required that township zoning ordinances "be based upon a plan." Such language and such intent militates against our analyzing whether the zoning ordinance is a comprehensive plan. To do so is to ignore a carefully-thought-out statutory scheme requiring a plan, and then a zoning ordinance to implement the plan.

It is obvious that Monroe Township did not fulfill the plan requirement.

Comments: 1. In some of the states that originally followed the prevailing view the comprehensive plan has now been given an independent effect by legislation requiring zoning to be consistent with an adopted plan. This is partially true of New Jersey. In New Jersey, zoning must be consistent with the plan unless a zoning ordinance, amendment or revision is adopted by a majority of the governing body "with the reasons" for not complying with this requirement. N.J. Stat. Ann. § 40:55D-62(a) (West Supp. 1978).

2. The remainder of this section considers the growing trend in court decisions and legislative enactments, both to require a mandatory local planning process and to require that zoning be consistent with a locally adopted land use plan. *See generally* Mandelker, The Role of the Local Comprehensive Plan in Land Use Regulation, 74 Mich. L. Rev. 899 (1976). Note should first be taken of court decisions which, while not moving to a full-blown consistency requirement, have nevertheless extended the majority view that no plan is required. Foremost among these cases is *Udell v. Haas,* 235 N.E.2d 897 (N.Y. 1968). That case has been described as follows:

> In *Udell,* a small village on Long Island had rezoned a parcel of land, located on its periphery and abutting a major highway, from commercial to residential uses. The court found the downzoning invalid, relying in part on the principle that it had not been "in accordance with a comprehensive plan" as required by the New York state zoning enabling statute. The New York court has never interpreted this statute, which follows the Standard State Zoning Enabling Act, to require the adoption of an independent comprehensive plan. It is, however, willing to find that the land use policies of a community are expressed in a comprehensive plan, if one exists, as well as in the zoning ordinance and map. In this case, the village had continuously zoned the area in which the landowner's parcel was located for commercial uses, at least since the mid-1930s. In 1968 it adopted a "developmental policy" as an amendment to its zoning ordinance that appeared to confirm this zoning. This policy called for a suburban, low-density community. Most of the small portion of the village area that was zoned for commercial use was, like the parcel in *Udell,* located on the periphery of the community and adjacent to nonresidential uses in other neighboring communities.

The downzoning had been accomplished very quickly, after it became apparent that the owner of the parcel intended to build commercially as permitted by the existing zoning classification. There was testimony that the downzoning was accomplished in part to accommodate the "feeling of the Village" that no extensive commercial use should be permitted in that area. These circumstances led the court to hold that the downzoning was not "in accordance" with a comprehensive plan. As the court pointed out, zoning could easily degenerate into "arbitrary infringements on the property rights of the landowner. To assure that this does not happen, our courts must require local zoning authorities to pay more than mock obeisance to the statutory mandate that zoning be 'in accordance with a comprehensive plan.' There must be some showing that the change does not conflict with the community's basic scheme for land use." The problem is no less serious when an upzoning is made at the behest of a single landowner, a circumstance that led the Pennsylvania court in Eves to call for comprehensive planning as the basis for a zoning change. *Id.* at 937-38. A few courts have also held that in the absence of a comprehensive plan the presumption of validity usually accorded zoning ordinances is shifted or weakened. *See, e.g., Forestview Homeowners Ass'n v. County of Cook,* 309 N.E.2d 763 (Ill. App. 1974) (rezoning for apartments held invalid).

Some courts which refuse to require zoning consistency with a comprehensive plan will also invalidate zoning amendments even though the amendment is consistent with the plan. A leading example is *Chapman v. Montgomery County,* 271 A.2d 156 (Md. 1970). Here the court invalidated a rezoning from rural residential to commercial of a 5.8 acre tract in a fast-growing area of the county. The rezoning was consistent with the county plan and was carried out to avoid an alternative not favored by the plan, the expansion of another nearby shopping center. Noting that the plan is not to be equated in legal significance with the zoning ordinance, the court added that proof of a substantial growth in population which had occurred in the neighborhood might justify a rezoning to higher residential densities but not a rezoning for shopping center development. Note the difficulties created for the planning and zoning process if projections of population growth may not be used as the basis for rezoning to intensive commercial uses needed to serve expected demand. The *Chapman* case is influenced, of course, by the unique Maryland rule that zoning amendments must be justified by a change in neighborhood land uses or a mistake in the original zoning ordinance. *See supra* p. 690.

4. By far the major judicial developments in the area of mandatory planning and zoning consistency with the comprehensive plan have occurred in cases decided by the Oregon Supreme Court and Court of Appeals. The first case to consider the comprehensive plan requirement in Oregon was *Fasano v. Board of County Comm'rs,* 507 P.2d 23 (Or. 1973), reproduced *supra* p. 693. In summing up the comprehensive plan requirement in that state the court held: We believe that the state legislature has conditioned the county's power to zone upon the prerequisite that the zoning attempt to further the general welfare of the community through consciousness, in a prospective sense, of the factors mentioned above. In other words, except as noted later in this opinion, it must be proved that the change is in conformance with the comprehensive plan.

In proving that the change is in conformance with the comprehensive plan in this case, the proof, at a minimum, should show (1) there is a public need for a change of the kind in question, and (2) that need will be best served by changing the classification of the particular piece of property in question as compared with other available property.

Id. at 28.

The next case in which the Oregon Supreme Court considered the effect of comprehensive planning on zoning arose outside the zoning amendment context and approached the problem from a different tangent.

BAKER v. CITY OF MILWAUKIE

Supreme Court of Oregon
271 Ore. 500, 533 P.2d 772 (1975)

Before O'CONNELL, C. J., and McALLISTER, HOLMAN, TONGUE, HOWELL, SLOPER and LEAVY, Justices.

HOWELL, Justice.

This is an appeal from the dismissal of a writ of mandamus. The plaintiff sought to compel the City of Milwaukie to conform a zoning ordinance to its comprehensive plan, to cancel a variance approved by the Milwaukie Planning Commission, and to suspend the issuance of building permits in areas of the city where the zoning ordinance allows a more intensive use than that set forth in the comprehensive plan. The trial court sustained the City's demurrer to the alternative writ. The plaintiff refused to plead further and the court dismissed the writ. The Court of Appeals reversed the action of the trial court but on grounds not substantially in favor of the plaintiff, and plaintiff's petition for review to this court was allowed.

Basically, the petition for the alternative writ states that plaintiff is a landowner in the City of Milwaukie. On October 17, 1968, the City of Milwaukie adopted a zoning ordinance which designated plaintiff's land and the surrounding area "A 1 B" (residential apartment-business office). This category allowed 39 units per acre. On November 11, 1969, a comprehensive plan for the City of Milwaukie was adopted by the Planning Commission. This comprehensive plan designated plaintiff's land the surrounding area as high density residential, allowing 17 units per acre. On January 12, 1970, the Milwaukie City Council passed a resolution adopting the above plan as the comprehensive plan for the City of Milwaukie.

On February 27, 1973, without public hearing and against staff recommendation, the Milwaukie City Planning Commission granted a variance authorizing a proposed 95-unit apartment complex near plaintiff's property with one and one-half parking spaces per unit rather than the required two.

Subsequent to the granting of the variance, an application was made for a building permit for the construction of a 102-unit apartment on property immediately adjacent to plaintiff's property. This 102-unit complex would result in 26 units per acre—less than the 39 units allowed by the zoning ordinance but substantially more than the 17 units allowed by the comprehensive plan.

After demand was made on the City Council and the Building Inspector to conform the zoning ordinance to the comprehensive plan, to cancel the variance previously granted, and to suspend the issuance of building permits where the zoning in the city did not conform to the comprehensive plan, the plaintiff brought this proceeding. Her petition alleged, in relevant part:

VIII

"Even though obligated to do so and even though more than three years have expired between approval of the comprehensive plan and the present, Defendants City Councilmen have not even though they have a duty to do so, taken steps to modify the zoning in the area of concern to conform to the comprehensive plan for such area. Defendant inspector has failed or refused to indicate that he will suspend issuance of a building permit for the area of concern until such time as the zoning of the City of Milwaukie conforms to the comprehensive plan for such city."

The defendants filed a return to the alternative writ in which they state:

> The defendants have not done as they were herein commanded, and the cause of their omission is that there is no obligation that the zoning ordinance of the city of Milwaukie be conformed to the comprehensive plan subsequently adopted by resolution.

At the same time the defendants demurred to the petition on the grounds that several causes of action were improperly united and that the petition did not state facts sufficient to constitute a cause of action. The trial court sustained the demurrer on the grounds that the "facts set forth in the petition are insufficient to sustain the relief prayed for in the petition." The trial court did not rule on defendants' demurrer that several causes of action were improperly united.

The Court of Appeals reversed solely on the ground that the plaintiff had alleged sufficient facts to support her claim with regard to the improper granting of the variance. In all other respects the Court of Appeals held that the facts stated in the petition were insufficient. *Baker v. City of Milwaukie,* 17 Or.App. 89, 520 P.2d 479 (1974). We granted review to consider the effect of the adoption, by a municipality, of a comprehensive plan on pre-existing and conflicting zoning ordinances.

The Comprehensive Plan is the Controlling Land Use Planning Instrument for the City of Milwaukie

The defendants argue that "the zoning ordinance would govern land use with a definite and precise requirement, and would control over the comprehensive plan." Thus the defendants contend that although the City has passed a comprehensive plan, there is no duty to effectuate it through the enactment of conforming zoning ordinances. They further argue that the present conflicting zoning ordinances remain in effect until the City decides to replace them with ordinances which are in accord with the comprehensive plan.

We agree with the plaintiff and the amici curiae (Northwest Environmental Defense Center, Oregon Environmental Council, and Oregon Chapter of the American Institute of Planners) that the position of defendants evidences a fundamental misunderstanding of the relationship between planning and zoning.

In order to answer the question of whether a city, once it has adopted a comprehensive plan, has a duty to zone in accord with that plan, it is first necessary to discuss the relationship between planning and zoning.

This court has recently recognized the controlling effect of the comprehensive plan on land use planning in a community:

> The basic instrument for county or municipal land use planning is the 'comprehensive plan.' . . . The plan has been described as a general plan to control and direct the use and development of property in a municipality. . . . *Fasano v. Washington Co. Comm.,* 64 Or. 574, 582, 507 P.2d 23, 27 (1973) (citations omitted).

Zoning, on the other hand, is the means by which the comprehensive plan is effectuated.

This servient relationship of zoning to planning was acknowledged in Oregon in 1919 with the passage of the requirement that municipal zoning be "in accord with a well considered plan." [158] *See* Or. Laws 1919, ch. 300; ORS 227.240(1). " 'Instead of being the city plan, for which it is so often mistaken, . . . zoning is but one of the devices for giving effect to it.' " Haar, The Master Plan: An Impermanent Constitution, 20 Law & Contemp. Prob. 353, 362 (1955).[159] *See also Udell v. Haas,* 21 N.Y.2d 463, 288 N.Y.S.2d 888, 235 N.E.2d 897 (1968).

---

[158] In this context there appears to be no functional distinction between the terms "comprehensive plan," "master plan," "general plan," and "well considered plan." *See* 1 Rathkopf. The Law of Zoning and Planning 9-1 (1959); Haar, The Master Plan: An Impermanent Constitution, 20 Law & Contemp. Prob. 353, 354 (1955).

[159] As noted by the Attorney General of Oregon:

" . . . The comprehensive plan is not *merely* a guideline which may be

Some writers have likened the comprehensive plan to a constitution. Thus it has been said that a comprehensive plan is a "constitution for all future development within the city." *O'Loane v. O'Rourke,* 231 Cal.App.2d 774, 782, 42 Cal.Rptr. 283, 288 (1965).

> . . . If the plan is regarded not as vest-pocket tool of the planning commission, but as a broad statement to be adopted by the most representative municipal body — the local legislature — then the plan becomes a law through such adoption. A unique type of law, it should be noted, in that it purports to bind future legislatures when they enact implementary materials. So far as impact is concerned, the law purports to control the enactment of other laws (the so-called implementary legislation) solely. It thus has the cardinal characteristic of a constitution. . . . Haar, supra at 375.

While this analogy between a comprehensive plan and a constitution may be helpful in determining the relationship between planning and zoning, it must be remembered that the comprehensive plan is flexible and subject to change when the needs of the community demand. "[U]nlike [a constitution] it is subject to amendatory procedures not significantly different from the course followed in enacting ordinary legislation." Haar, supra at 375.

In the instant case, as noted above, the zoning ordinance was passed in October, 1968. The comprehensive plan was adopted by the Planning Commission in November, 1969, and adopted by the City Council in January, 1970. The plan recites:

> The City of Milwaukie has adopted a new zoning ordinance [apparently referring to the ordinance enacted in October, 1968] that was developed in conjunction with the Comprehensive Plan. Basic features of the new ordinance as adopted are consistent with the Plan described in this report.

Plaintiff alleges that an examination of the ordinance and the plan shows that a conflict exists, at least in the area in question in this case.[160]

---

followed or disregarded at will; although the zoning ordinances establish the detail they must do so within the policies established by the comprehensive plan. The comprehensive plan is thus analogous to legislation granting rule-making power but establishing the purpose for which and the limits within which that power may be exercised." (Emphasis in original) 36 Op.Or. AG 1044, 1046 (1974).

[160] The fact that the zoning ordinance was "developed in conjunction with the Comprehensive Plan" and yet conflicts with that very plan is itself strong evidence that proper planning did not go into the development of the zoning ordinance and that that ordinance is not "in accord with a well considered plan." ORS 227.240(1).

The defendants argue, and the Court of Appeals held, that there is no duty[161] to adopt a written comprehensive plan such as that adopted by the City of Milwaukie. However, this begs the question. The fact is that the City of Milwaukie *has* adopted a comprehensive plan. And that plan is "the basic instrument for county or municipal land use planning." *Fasano v. Washington Co. Comm.,* supra, 264 Or. at 582, 507 P.2d at 27. If that plan is to have any efficacy as the basic planning tool for the City of Milwaukie, it must be given preference over conflicting prior zoning ordinances. To hold otherwise would allow a city to go through the motions and expense of formulating a comprehensive plan and then relegating that document to oblivion through continued reliance on the older zoning ordinances.

We agree with the Supreme Court of Pennsylvania, which held in *Eves v. Zoning Bd. of Adjustment of Lower Wynedd Twp.,* 401 Pa. 211, 164 A.2d 7, 10 (1960):

> The role of the township supervisors in the field of zoning, as contemplated by the enabling legislation,

---

[161] Prior to 1973 there was some disagreement as to whether municipalities were required to adopt a comprehensive plan. Or.Laws 1969, ch. 324 (ORS 215.505 et seq.) at least express a state policy in favor of comprehensive planning at all levels of government. Any ambiguity in this area has been cleared up through the passage of Or.Laws 1973, ch. 80 (ORS ch. 197). ORS 197.175(2) provides:

> (2) Pursuant to ORS 197.005 to 197.430, 215.055, 215.510, 215.515, 215.535 and 453.345, each city and county in this state shall:

> (a) Prepare and adopt comprehensive plans consistent with state-wide planning goals and guidelines approved by the commission; and

> (b) Enact zoning, subdivision and other ordinances or regulations to implement their comprehensive plans.

ORS 197.015(4) provides:

> (4) "Comprehensive plan" means a generalized, coordinated land use map and policy statement of the governing body of a state agency, city, county or special district that interrelates all functional and natural systems and activities relating to the use of lands, including but not limited to sewer and water systems, transportation systems, educational systems, recreational facilities, and natural resources and air and water quality management programs. "Comprehensive" means all-inclusive, both in terms of the geographic area covered and functional and natural activities and systems occurring in the area covered by the plan. "General nature" means a summary of policies and proposals in broad categories and does not necessarily indicate specific locations of any area, activity or use. A plan is "coordinated" when the needs of all levels of governments, semi-public and private agencies and the citizens of Oregon have been considered and accommodated as much as possible. "Land" includes water, both surface and subsurface, and the air.

See Macpherson and Paulus, Senate Bill 100: The Oregon Land Conservation and Development Act, 10 Will.L.J. 414 (1974); 36 Op. Or. AG 960, 972 (1974).

emerges quite clearly upon consideration of the power granted the supervisors and the duties they are bound to perform. *Their duty is to implement the comprehensive plan by enacting zoning regulations in accordance therewith. . . .* (Emphasis added.)[162]

Likewise, the City of Milwaukie, upon adopting a comprehensive plan, had a duty to implement that plan through the enactment of zoning ordinances in accordance therewith.[163]

A Properly Enacted Comprehensive Plan, Although Denominated a "Resolution," Controls Zoning Decisions in the City of Milwaukie

The Court of Appeals, in holding that "the zoning ordinance is the controlling document in the city of Milwaukie zoning scheme" (520 P.2d at 483), relied in part on the fact that the comprehensive plan was adopted by resolution rather than by ordinance:

> . . . . First, it should be noted that a resolution is not law but merely a form in which the legislative body expresses an opinion. *Rowley v. City of Medford,* 132 Or. 405, 414, 285 P. 1111 (1930). . . . *Baker v. City of Milwaukie,* supra, 520 P.2d at 482.

The above holding is a correct statement of the law. However, it does not settle the question of whether the comprehensive plan of Milwaukie controls zoning decisions.

To determine the true character of a legislative enactment it is necessary to look beyond the title. 5 McQuillin on Municipal Corporations § 15.02 (1969) states:

> . . . .
>
> Generally, whether what is done by a municipal legislative body is an ordinance or a resolution depends not on what the action is called but on the reality. . . . [W]here a resolution is in substance and effect an ordinance or permanent regulation, the name given to it is immaterial. If it is passed with all the formalities of an ordinance it thereby becomes a legislative act, and it is not important whether it be called ordinance or resolution. McQuillin, supra at 46. (Footnotes omitted.)

---

[162] [The holding of the *Eves* case has now been substantially qualified in Pennsylvania. *See Russell v. Pennsylvania Township Planning Comm'n,* 348 A.2d 499 (Pa. Commw. Ct. 1975) (noting that subsequent cases have eliminated the *Eves* planning mandate). — Eds.]

[163] This opinion deals only with the question of the effect of the enactment of a comprehensive plan on conflicting zoning ordinances. Of course, where the plan adopts general parameters of long term growth with a provision that the intensity of use or the density of living units shall not exceed a certain amount, a more restrictive zoning ordinance may be in accord with that plan. However, between the time of the enactment of the comprehensive plan and the implementing zoning ordinances, no land use may occur which would exceed the limits set by the plan.

The approach of looking to the substance of the action rather than the mere title has been followed in Oregon. . . .

Thus it is necessary for this court to determine whether a comprehensive plan is legislative and permanent in nature or administrative and temporary.

In an exhaustive opinion, the California Court of Appeals dealt with the question of whether a comprehensive plan, adopted as a resolution, was a legislative or administrative act. *O'Loane v. O'Rourke,* 231 Cal.App.2d 774, 42 Cal.Rptr. 283 (1965). In that case, as in the instant case, the argument was made that "the general plan is not a zoning ordinance, that it has no legislative effect, that the adoption of such a plan is an administrative and executive act and not a legislative act." 231 Cal.App.2d at 779, 42 Cal.Rptr. at 286. With regard to the nature of the general plan, the court said:

> It is apparent that the plan is, in short, a constitution for all future development within the city. No mechanical reading of the plan itself is sufficient. To argue that property rights are not affected by the general plan (as the city so asserts) as adopted ignores that which is obvious. Any zoning ordinance adopted in the future would surely be interpreted in part by its fidelity to the general plan as well as by the standards of due process. Frequently it has occurred that where a general plan was adopted, and later a zoning change was made which appeared to be in accord with the plan, that fact in and of itself was some evidentiary weight in the determination as to whether the zoning ordinance was proper or otherwise. If the general plan is anything at all, it is a meaningful enactment and definitely affects the community and, among other things, changes land market values. The general plan is legislatively adopted by the council. True, it is couched in part in general terms, but there are many specifics, and once adopted it becomes very effective. Many facets of activities between other public agencies and the city are effectively determined by the plan. Any subdivision or other development would necessarily be considered in its relation to the general plan, and such consideration practically by itself would be a sufficient legislative guide to the exercise of such discretions. 231 Cal.App.2d at 782-83, 42 Cal.Rptr. at 288.

Finally, the court held:

> The adoption of the general plan is, in effect, the adoption of a policy, and in many respects, entirely new policy. The plan is of permanent and general character, it is a declaration of public purpose and, as such, supposedly sets forth what kind of a city the community wants and, supposedly, represents the judgment of the electors of the

city with reference to the physical form and character the city is to assume. 231 Cal.App.2d at 785, 42 Cal.Rptr. at 289.

See also Haar, In Accordance with a Comprehensive Plan, 68 Harv.L.Rev. 1154, 1175 (1955).

The Attorney General of Oregon has also reached the conclusion that the comprehensive plan is legislative in nature. "The comprehensive plan thus has all the characteristics of legislation. . . ." 36 Op.Or.AG 1044, 1046 (1974).

If this court is to give the comprehensive plan the meaningful and dominant role anticipated by the 1919 Oregon Legislature (ORS 227.240(1)) and reaffirmed by the 1973 Legislature (ORS ch. 197, it must view the plan as legislative and permanent in nature. To hold otherwise would relegate the comprehensive plan to the role of "a vest-pocket tool of the planning commission." Haar, The Master Plan: An Impermanent Constitution, supra at 375. And our conclusion is the same although the comprehensive plan in the instant case was designated a "resolution."

Conclusion

In summary, we conclude that a comprehensive plan is the controlling land use planning instrument for a city. Upon passage of a comprehensive plan a city assumes a responsibility to effectuate that plan and conform prior conflicting zoning ordinances to it. We further hold that the zoning decisions of a city must be in accord with that plan and a zoning ordinance which allows a more intensive use than that prescribed in the plan must fail.

In the instant case, we agree with the Court of Appeals that the plaintiff has stated a cause of action with regard to the granting of the variance. We further hold that the plaintiff has stated a cause of action in seeking to compel the City of Milwaukie to conform its zoning ordinances to the comprehensive plan and to suspend the issuance of building permits in violation of the plan. This case must go beyond the pleading stages to determine whether, in fact, the zoning ordinance is in accord with the comprehensive plan, whether the comprehensive plan was validly enacted, and whether the variance was properly granted.

Defendants' demurrer should have been overruled.

Affirmed as modified.

LEAVY, Justice Pro Tem. (dissenting). [Omitted.]

Comments: 1. As footnote 144 of the *Baker* case indicates, mandatory planning in Oregon is now required by statute. (The Oregon statute providing for state administrative review of local planning is discussed in Chapter 9). However, the requirement that zoning be consistent with the comprehensive plan remains judicially imposed, so that the limits of this requirement must be worked out through judicial decision. Contrast the handling of the consistency requirement in those states which have imposed it through legislation, discussed *infra* p. 757. Since the consistency requirement is a matter of judicial innovation in Oregon, it becomes important to determine just what the Oregon courts have required in mandating this responsibility.

The key to an understanding of *Fasano and Baker* is the context in which they were handed down. Both considered zoning changes to more intensive uses, and in both cases these changes were attacked by third party challengers. The effect of these two cases is to provide additional weight to third parties who wish to challenge local zoning changes to more intensive uses. From this perspective, the *Fasano-Baker* approach stabilizes existing zoning patterns unless changes are justified by planning policy.

This position was taken by the Oregon Court of Appeals in a post- *Baker* case, *Pohrman v. Klamath County Comm'rs,* 550 P.2d 1236 (Ore. App. 1976). In that case the county had amended the plan to provide a more intensive use than what was allowed by the zoning ordinance. Relying on footnote 163 of the *Baker* case, the court held that "there is no obligation imposed upon local governments to immediately make more restrictive zoning ordinances consistent with less restrictive comprehensive plans." *Id.* at 1239.

Note also that a variety of qualifications on the plan consistency rule were adopted by the *Fasano* opinion, but not repeated in *Baker.* Assuming that these qualifications remain the law, their impact is unclear.

For example, the *Fasano* opinion appears to hold that the rezoning at the rezoned site cannot be supported if an alternative site for the proposed use in available. An important case applying this limitation is *Duddles v. City Council,* 535 P.2d 583 (Ore. App. 1975). A tract was rezoned for commercial use, although another tract immediately across from it had previously been zoned commercial. The court concluded that commercial development at both sites was inconsistent with the plan. It indicated that the city's alternatives were to indicate clearly in its plan that commercial development at both sites was consistent with the plan, or to downzone the previously zoned commercial tract if it appeared that the tract rezoned in this case was more appropriate for commercial development.

See also Marracci v. City of Scappoose, 552 P.2d 552 (Ore. App. 1976). The court held that the future designation of a more intensive use does not compel an immediate zoning change to the more intensive use. If there is no timing provision in the plan indicating when the rezoning to the more intensive use should take place, that decision is to be made by the legislative governing body subject only to "limited judicial review for patent arbitrariness." *Id.* at 553. On the *Fasano-Baker* cases *see generally* Bross, Circling the Squares of Euclidean Zoning: Zoning Predestination and Planning Free Will, 6 Envt'l Law 97 (1975).

2. Another question raised by the *Fasano-Baker* cases is whether they apply to all types of zoning changes or only to the zoning changes considered in those decisions. An earlier pre-*Fasano* Oregon Supreme Court case, *Archdiocese of Portland v. County of Washington,* 458 P.2d 682 (Ore. 1969), held that, since the conditional use is expressly provided for in the zoning ordinance, and since it "reveals the legislative plan," the decision on whether or not to grant the conditional use should be accorded the usual presumption of legislative regularity. Consistency with the local comprehensive plan was not required.

The question to be asked next is whether the *Archdiocese* view of the conditional use survives the *Fasano-Baker* holdings. This question was considered in *Kristensen v. City of Eugene Planning Comm'n*, 544 P.2d 591 (Ore. App. 1976). In this case, adjacent neighbors appealed a grant of a conditional use permit for a mobile home park. Noting that it had held the procedural requirements of *Fasano* applicable to a conditional use permit, the court then considered whether the substantive requirements of *Fasano* also applied. The court first noted that no specific evidence had been introduced to indicate that the conditional use was inconsistent with the comprehensive plan. Neither was it possible to determine whether other property was available for mobile home use, as mobile homes were not a permitted use in any zone in the city but required approval as a conditional use in all zones.

The court then turned to the public need test of *Fasano* and held it inapplicable to conditional uses. It commented:

> . . . *Fasano* involved a zone change, i.e., a deviation from the prior legislative judgment of public need for the various uses of property. By contrast, a conditional use is a permitted use, albeit not outright permitted; "the granting of an application for a conditional use does not constitute a deviation from the [zoning] ordinance but is in compliance with it." . . . [Citing *Archdiocese.* — Eds.] Because of this fundamental difference between changing zoning and approving a conditional use, we conclude that the designation of a use as conditional in a zoning ordinance is sufficient proof of public need for such a use.

Id. at 593. However, the court adapted the "spirit" of *Fasano* to add that the applicant for the conditional use must "bear the burden" of proving that the conditional use "reasonably" meets the need recognized by the zoning ordinance. *Id.* Does this statement mean that the burden to prove compliance with the conditional use provisions of the ordinance shifts to the landowner receiving the conditional use in cases such as this, in which the conditional use is attacked by a third party? *See also Hawkins v. County of Marin*, 126 Cal.Rptr. 754 (Cal. App. 1976) (conditional use need not comply with comprehensive plan).

Are there policy reasons for exempting conditional uses from compliance with the comprehensive plan? For example, is it not true that most conditional uses are similar to and marginal to the uses allowed in the zones in which they are permitted? And since "floating zone" and "planned unit development" provisions in zoning ordinances normally include "standards" to govern the decision of the local governing body in deciding whether to "tie-down" a "floating zone" classification to a particular parcel or to rezone a tract for "planned unit development," is it not arguable that the local governing body's action should be presumed valid when it finds that the ordinance standards have been satisfied? (A rather detailed treatment of planned unit developments will be found *infra* in Chapter 6, Part A.)

The independent vitality of the public need test has now been questioned by the Oregon Supreme Court.

When we held that a single-tract zone change must be shown to
meet a public need, and to be the best way of meeting that need,
we were requiring only what was implicit in the legislation
governing planning and zoning that land use decisions made at
the instance of a private party be made only for reasons having
to do with the needs and welfare of the community at large rather
than for the accommodation of individual landowners or private
developers.

South of Sunnyside Neighborhood League v. Board of Comm'rs, 569 P.2d
1063, 1073 (Ore. 1977).

3. The earlier discussion of comprehensive plans noted the difference
between more precise, mapped plans, and the more open-ended policy
plans which have become increasingly attractive to plan-makers. *See supra*
chapter 2. Obviously, the extent to which a comprehensive plan can provide
guidance in land use decision-making will vary with the degree of
preciseness it provides, a point made explicitly in a footnote to the *Fasano*
case. This increasing attractiveness of policy plans creates problems for
courts imposing plan consistency requirements, for "[t]he degree of
specificity provided by the plan to guide land use control administration has
thus often declined at the same time that a substantial expansion in the
range of policies covered by the plan has complicated decision-making."
Mandelker, *supra* at 919.

How a policy plan might function as a guide to zoning decisions has now
been faced by the Oregon Supreme Court in *Green v. Hayward,* 552 P.2d
815 (Ore. 1976). In this case a lumber mill received a zoning amendment
to expand its site to provide increased space for log storage and improved
sewage disposal capacity, and to construct a bark-processing plant which
could convert bark, a waste product of its mill operations, into salable
products. The county in which the mill was located had adopted a plan
which called generally for a policy of urban containment, and which
designated the area in which the mill site was located for agricultural uses.
There were findings that the plant expansion served some but not all of the
policies of the comprehensive plan which were not directed to land use
allocations.

First commenting on the role of the comprehensive plan in zoning
administration, the court noted "that a local government's zoning map . . .
[need not] coincide in detail with the map portion of the comprehensive
plan." *Id.* at 818. The legislature had left the form the plan was to take to
its draftsmen, and the plan in question "was intended to illustrate what the
text calls the 'broad allocation' of land within the area shown, but not to
put a limit on the permissible uses of each and every tract within that area."
Id. at 819. "We are reluctant to hold that one or a few . . . general
statements may be severed from the Plan as a whole and used in isolation
as justification for a rezoning decision." *Id.* at 821.

Next the court turned to a set of "minimum location standards" for
industrial development in "areas not otherwise shown for industrial
development" in the plan. *Id.* at 821. These were the only plan standards
applicable to this development, but the findings of the county board were
"far from clear" on whether these location standards had been met. *Id.* at

822. Although concerned about the adequacy of these findings, the court nonetheless upheld the rezoning:

> . . . There is evidence in the record before the Board which would support findings that: (1) the proposed facility, by enabling Bohemia to utilize a waste product on the site, would reduce traffic problems rather than generate additional traffic; (2) the "intent to rezone" procedure, together with permit requirements of other agencies, will insure compatibility of Bohemia's expansion with adjacent areas; (3) no additional utilities and services will have to be provided; and (4) because of its association with an existing industrial facility, the new plant would not disrupt the continuity of a neighborhood or community. Although much of this evidence was controverted, a determination by the Board that the minimum location standards were met would not be arbitrary.

Id. at 823. The court then considered but dismissed an argument that the rezoning should not have been granted as other land previously zoned for heavy industry was available. Ordinarily, the court said, this argument would be given considerable weight, as the integrity of comprehensive planning would be "seriously undermined" if a landowner could obtain a rezoning simply because he did not own land already zoned for his purposes, or if his development would be less profitable in an appropriately zoned area. *Id.* at 824. However, in this case the rezoning was in the "public interest" as without the rezoning no such plant would be built in the county, and the plant expansion was necessary to construct a facility to process the bark waste product.

Has the Oregon court in the *Green* case undermined the plan consistency requirement as it was stated in the *Baker* case? Could it be argued that the zoning change in the *Green* case was so marginal in scope that it should have been exempted from the plan consistency requirement? Note that the Oregon Court of Appeals has held that the consistency of zoning with a comprehensive plan may be attacked without first exhausting possible administrative remedies. *Fifth Ave. Corp. v. Washington County,* 560 P.2d 656 (Ore. App. 1977). The court reasoned that the consistency question raised matters of law.

A NOTE ON MANDATORY LOCAL PLANNING AND THE STATUTORY REQUIREMENT THAT LAND USE CONTROLS BE CONSISTENT WITH THE PLAN

Several states have now enacted legislation mandating planning by local governments and requiring zoning and, in some instances, land use controls generally be consistent with the mandatory plan. Two states which have pioneered in this legislation are California and Florida, and their legislation will be examined here.

California was one of the first states to enact a statutory requirement for mandatory local planning, Cal. Govt. Code § 65300 (West 1974). Both mandatory and optional plan elements are required by statute, but mandatory substantive planning policies are required only for the housing element. It "shall make adequate provision for the housing needs of all economic segments of the community," *id.* § 65302(c) (Deering Supp. 1977). The zoning enabling legislation requires local zoning to be consistent with the plan and defines "consistent" as follows: "[t]he various land uses authorized by the ordinance are [to be] compatible with the objectives, policies, general land uses and programs specified in [the] plan." *Id.* § 65860(a)(ii). There is a comparable requirement for subdivision controls, *id.* § 66473.5. Note that the consistency requirement only applies to land uses "authorized" by the ordinance. Would it apply to conditional uses approved under the ordinance? *See Hawkins v. County of Marin, supra* p. 755.

Compatibility is the key term linking zoning to the plan under the California law, and some insight on its meaning has been provided in advisory guidelines, California Council on Intergov'tl Relations, General Plan Guidelines II-11, II-13 (1973). The Council first notes that the plan is generalized and long-range while the zoning ordinance has "immediate force and effect on each parcel of land." It then adds that the zoning ordinance should be considered consistent with the plan when its "allowable uses and standards . . . tend to further the policies of the general plan and do not inhibit or obstruct the attainment of those articulated policies." Is this advice consistent with the interpretation of the plan consistency requirement as elaborated by the Oregon courts?

Compliance with the consistency requirement can be enforced in California through judicial action, *id.* § 65860(b). What if a California municipality adopted a plan containing a housing element which did not properly provide for community housing needs? Could a California court issue an order mandating the adoption by the locality of the policies necessary to carry out this statutory mandate? *See Youngblood v. Board of Supervisors,* 139 Cal. Rptr. 741 (Cal. App. 1977) (mandamus may issue to compel board to amend zoning ordinance to conform to amendments to comprehensive plan) (appeal pending).

The Florida mandatory planning and zoning consistency requirement has been described as follows:

Florida has recently adopted a consistency provision that is both more focused and more extensive in scope than that of California. The Florida Local Government Comprehensive Planning Act of 1975 mandates planning by counties, municipalites, and special districts. County plans are to govern within the limits of municipalities and special districts that fail to prepare plans, while the state planning agency may impose its own plan in any county that does not complete one by a fixed statutory deadline. Mandatory and optional elements are prescribed for all plans; these include a mandatory housing element that must provide for low- and moderate-income housing needs. There is some guidance for the preparation of growth control programs, and the statute lists the coordination of the various planning elements as a major goal of the planning process.

This statutory comprehensive planning framework provides the basis for an extensive consistency provision that is directed both to development by government agencies and to local land use regulations: "After a comprehensive plan ... has been adopted ... all development undertaken by, and all actions taken in regard to development orders by, [*sic*] governmental agencies in regard to land covered by such plan ... shall be consistent with such plan.... All land development regulations enacted or amended shall be consistent with the adopted comprehensive plan...." This provision is reinforced by one stating that it is the intent of the act that local land development regulations implement the comprehensive plan, and by another authorizing judicial review of the relationship between the comprehensive plan and implementing governmental actions or land development regulations, in any litigation challenging these actions or regulations. Land development regulations include zoning, subdivision controls, and all other measures "controlling the development of land."

Mandelker, *supra* at 960-61.

Note that the Florida statute extends the consistency requirement to land development regulations other than the zoning ordinance, and specifically includes amendments to these regulations. Note also the far-reaching extension of the consistency requirement to include "development orders" by governmental agencies. A development order is defined as "any order granting, denying, or granting with conditions an application for a development permit." Fla. Stat. Ann. § 163.3164(5) (Supp. 1978). This definition extends the consistency requirement to any governmental action authorizing land development. It apparently covers conditional uses as well as development permits issued under non-zoning ordinances. Does the Florida consistency requirement apply to development by governmental agencies?

Comments: 1. Recall that the plan consistency requirement was adopted by the Oregon Supreme Court out of a fear that local governments would not be able to resist pressures for land use changes from developers. Does mandatory planning and the requirement that zoning be consistent with the plan entirely foreclose this possibility? In *Mountain Defense League v. Board of Supervisors,* 135 Cal. Rptr. 588 (Cal. App. 1977), the court upheld as valid an amendment to the county general plan made simultaneously with the approval of a developer's private development plan. The private plan apparently serves as a specific plan and is authorized by the California legislation. California law now limits amendments to the general plan to three times a year, Cal. Govt. Code § 65361 (West 1975), and a similar procedure in Baltimore County, Maryland, has been judicially approved, *Coppolino v. County Bd. of Appeals,* 328 A.2d 55, 61 (1974). Compare *Marggi v. Druecker,* 533 P.2d 1372 (Ore. App. 1975), holding that a general plan amendment covering a 5.29 acre tract is quasi-judicial and requires a judicial-type hearing.

2. In *Youngblood v. Board of Supervisors,* 139 Cal. Rptr. 741 (Cal. App. 1977), a group of neighbors brought an action to enforce the statutory duty of the county governing body to rezone the area in which a large residential subdivision was proposed in order to conform the zoning to the applicable county general plan. Tentative subdivision approval was granted to the developer, under zoning consistent with the provisions of the general plan as it then existed, about two and one-half weeks before the general plan was amended to decrease the allowable density in the area where the proposed subdivision was located. Subsequently, the governing body gave final approval to the subdivision, although the planned density within the subdivision was greater than that specified in the amended general plan, after refusing to rezone the area to conform the density permitted under the zoning ordinance to that permitted by the amended general plan. The court rejected arguments of the subdivider based on the California statute granting a subdivider the right to have his final subdivision map approved if it is in substantial compliance with the tentative map and is filed within a specified time. It held that (1) the governing body disobeyed its statutory duty in accepting a final subdivision map not consistent with the general plan in effect at the time when approval of the final map was sought; and (2) the governing body was subject to a mandatory statutory duty to rezone the area covered by the amendment to the general plan, within a reasonable time, to make its zoning conform with the amended general plan. This case is on appeal.

3. A few courts have placed substantive requirements on plan amendments. In *Dalton v. City and County of Honolulu,* 462 P.2d 199 (Hawaii 1969), the court considered a plan and zoning amendment under a provision of the Honolulu charter that then required all zoning ordinances to implement and conform to the general plan. A general plan and zoning ordinance amendment for medium-density housing had been enacted by the council on the same day without referring the plan amendment to the plan director and plan commission for advice, as required by the charter. These amendments were invalidated, partly because the charter procedures were not followed. In addition, the court held that any plan amendment must be accompanied by new studies showing the need for additional housing, that the housing should be located at the proposed site, and that the proposed location is the "best site." *Id.* at 209. These substantive requirements echo the limitations placed on zoning amendments by the *Fasano* case, *supra* p. 693. Note that the *Dalton* case permits piece-meal amendment to the plan. Possibly the requirements imposed by that case could be manipulated by planning agencies willing to make sufficient studies and findings to justify plan amendments proposed by developers. See also *South of Sunnyside Neighborhood League v. Board of Comm'rs, supra,* holding that a single tract map amendment to a comprehensive plan must conform to the policies and goals of the plan.

4. Assuming that local planning is now to be made mandatory, and that local land use controls must be consistent with the plan, what kinds of policies should legislation require the plan to adopt? Consult the planning enabling legislation reproduced *supra* pp. 70-78, and especially the California statute mandating a housing element with substantive policies. What reason is there for mandating the substantive policies of the housing element, but not other elements? For an argument that planning legislation should at least mandate a plan that demonstrates the critical linkages among environmental protection, growth control, and low-income housing policies, and should indicate or provide clear guidance for planning issues of regional or state-wide significance see Mandelker, *supra* at 952.

5. There are not many cases in which the policies of the plan have been reviewed in litigation in which an attack has been launched on a zoning ordinance and the plan has been pleaded in defense. For one such case see *Norbeck Village Joint Venture v. Montgomery County Council,* 254 A.2d 700 (Md. 1969), in which the court relied on planning policies to support a massive downzoning to low density residential use. *Compare Christine Bldg. Co. v. City of Troy,* 116 N.W.2d 816 (Mich. 1962) (contra in large lot zoning case), *with Padover v. Township of Farmington,* 132 N.W.2d 687 (Mich. 1965) (concurring opinion would rely on plan to uphold large lot zoning). *See also Wilson v. Borough of Mountainside,* 201 A.2d 540 (N.J. 1964). The court affirmed an attack on residential zoning in the borough and noted:

> ... [I]t is elementary that every district use classification is not saved simply because it is part of a comprehensive community plan. The plan to be a valid and effective influence in support of zoning regulations must not be a capricious one and its existence will generally not *ipso facto* insulate from scrutiny or invalidity the use classification of a substantial area which is established to be realistically unreasonable.

Id. at 552.

6. For helpful literature on the mandatory planning and plan consistency requirement see Catalano & DiMento, Mandating Consistency Between General Plans and Zoning Ordinances: The California Experience, 8 Nat. Res. Law. 455 (1975); Sullivan & Kressel, Twenty Years After — Renewed Significance of the Comprehensive Plan Requirement, 8 Urb. L. Ann. 33 (1975); Tarlock, Kentucky Planning and Land Use Control Enabling Legislation: An Analysis of the 1966 Revision of K.R.S. Chapter 100, 56 Ky. L.J. 556 (1968) (discusses Kentucky plan consistency requirement); Note, Comprehensive Land Use Plans and the Consistency Requirement, 2 Fla. St. L. Rev. 766 (1974).

For a survey reviewing early experience under the California zoning consistency requirement see DiMento, Looking Back: Consistency in Interpretation of and Response to the Consistency Requirement, A.B. 1301,

2 Pepperdine L. Rev. S196 (1975). The author surveyed the response of California counties to the requirement and concluded:

> Most counties have taken a compromise position on the behavior required to realize consistency as it is presently understood (typically as "compatibility" in general terms — not direct one-to-one conformity). They have made some initial attempts to revise and develop their general plans; at the same time they have sought to effect some semblance of consistency in the short run by altering their existing general plans to reflect present zoning regulations.

Id. at S213.

4. Initiative and Referendum

Recent years have seen renewed interest in the initiative and referendum as part of the local zoning process. The reasons for this development, and the pros and cons of the initiative and referendum as it applies to zoning, have been summarized in a recent student note:

> This recent trend in the direction of increased public participation in land use decisionmaking is both understandable and desirable. Heightened community sensitivity to the quality of the environment and increasing voter skepticism of the judgment of public officials provide much of the impetus for referenda. Moreover, such popular decisionmaking is consistent with the cardinal principle of our democratic system that decisions be made with the consent of the governed.
>
> At the same time, however, the use of the referendum to override the rezoning decisions of public bodies carries with it certain disadvantages. An individual landowner who seeks a rezoning may not be able to rely upon the electorate to make a reasoned decision that takes into account all the relevant information concerning the proposal and its impact on the municipality. Moreover, communities recognize now more than ever before the importance of planning coordinated and rational land use decisions, a goal that may be inconsistent with the referendum process.

Note, The Proper Use of Referenda in Zoning, 29 Stan. L. Rev. 819 (1977).

While the procedures for direct voter participation in the zoning process can loosely be designated referenda, it is important to carefully distinguish the initiative from the referendum process because the two procedures have very different impacts on zoning procedures. One writer has made the following distinction:

> INITIATIVE A procedure permitting a specified number of voters to propose changes in a constitution, municipal charter, laws, or ordinances. These proposals are then

accepted or rejected by voters at the polls. The REFERENDUM permits voters to accept or reject at the polls changes in a constitution, municipal charter, laws, or ordinances which have been proposed by a legislative body. A referendum follows favorable action by a legislative body; the initiative is designed to operate independently of the legislature.

C. Adrian, State and Local Governments 85 (4th ed. 1976).

Beginning with the turn of the century, many states began to adopt constitutional and statutory provisions authorizing the initiative and referendum process at both state and local levels. This reform reflected the dominant populism of that period, which favored a variety of changes that would return the management of government to the people, as well as serious concern over the domination of state legislatures by interest groups and lobbyists. Today almost all of the states have constitutional provisions authorizing the referendum at the state level, most of which also authorize referendums at the local level, while about half of the states authorize the initiative process both for state and local government. The initiative and referendum are used more extensively in some states than others, and tend to be used rather more frequently in the west coast states. For a summary of these constitutional provisions see Council of State Governments, The Book of the States: 1976-77, at 216-18 (1976).

As applied to the zoning process, a referendum follows a zoning action by the legislative body and may either be mandatory or permissive. If the referendum is permissive a zoning ordinance will not be submitted to popular vote unless a voter petition for a referendum is filed. In some states, the legislative body may also propose that a referendum be held. Frequently the referendum is used to block zoning amendments that provide for a more intensive use of a single piece of property and in some communities has developed a distinctive anti-growth bias. Referenda have also been used to block subsidized, low- and moderate-income housing projects.

A zoning initiative is a voter-initiated zoning proposal which in some states is placed directly on the ballot following submission of a petition carrying the required number of voting signatures. Under a variant of this process, the legislative body is first given an opportunity to accept or reject the measure before the election is held. While it is unlikely that something as comprehensive as community-wide rezoning would be proposed through an initiative, this process has been used to propose specific zoning amendments such as height restrictions and growth moratoria. In many cases the initiative is also used as a substitute for the referendum. If the legislative body enacts a zoning amendment which the voters wish to challenge, an initiative proposal may be filed calling for the repeal of the amendment and reinstatement of the prior zoning. This approach may be used if the period of time for filing a referendum is limited, as it may not be possible to collect all the signatures necessary for a referendum in the time provided.

The kinds of zoning actions that are subject to the initiative and referendum are about as wide as the zoning process, with the limitation that only legislative and not administrative zoning actions may be subject to electoral review. This limitation will restrict the use of the initiative and referendum in states in which the zoning amendment has been characterized as a quasi-judicial and not a legislative action. *See supra* p. 700. In addition, even if a court does not go quite this far, the detailed notice and hearing procedures which the zoning enabling legislation requires prior to the enactment of any zoning measure may be viewed as a bar to the availability of the initiative and referendum.

These comments apply to the way in which state courts view the initiative and referendum. Constitutional objections to the initiative and referendum may also be raised in federal courts. They were given consideration in the following Supreme Court decision, which deals with a mandatory zoning referendum. When reading this decision remember that it does not preclude a different view of either the referendum or the initiative in a state court.

CITY OF EASTLAKE v. FOREST CITY ENTERPRISES, INC.

United States Supreme Court
426 U.S. 668, 96 S. Ct. 2358, 49 L. Ed. 2d 132 (1976)

Mr. CHIEF JUSTICE BURGER delivered the opinion of the Court.

The question in this case is whether a city charter provision requiring proposed land use changes to be ratified by 55% of the votes cast violates the due process rights of a landowner who applies for a zoning change.

The city of Eastlake, Ohio, a suburb of Cleveland, has a comprehensive zoning plan codified in a municipal ordinance. Respondent, a real estate developer, acquired an eight-acre parcel of real estate in Eastlake zoned for "light industrial" uses at the time of purchase.

In May 1971, respondent applied to the City Planning Commission for a zoning change to permit construction of a multifamily, high-rise apartment building. The Planning Commission recommended the proposed change to the City Council, which under Eastlake's procedures could either accept or reject the Planning Commission's recommendation. Meanwhile, by popular vote, the voters of Eastlake amended the city charter to require that any changes in land use agreed to by the Council be approved by a 55% vote in a referendum.[164] The City Council approved the Planning Commission's recommendation for reclassification of respondent's property to permit the proposed project. Respondent then applied to the Planning Commission for "parking and yard" approval for the proposed building. The Commission rejected the application, on the ground that the City Council's rezoning action had not yet been submitted to the voters for ratification.

Respondent then filed an action in state court, seeking a judgment declaring the charter provision invalid as an unconstitutional delegation of legislative power to the people. While the case was pending, the City Council's action was submitted to a referendum, but the proposed zoning change was not approved by the requisite 55% margin. Following the election, the Court of Common Pleas and the Ohio Court of Appeals sustained the charter provision.

The Ohio Supreme Court reversed. 41 Ohio St. 2d 187, 324 N. E. 2d 740 (1975). Concluding that enactment of zoning and rezoning provisions is a legislative function, the court held that a popular referendum requirement, lacking standards to guide the decision of the voters, permitted the police power to be exercised in a standardless, hence arbitrary and capricious manner. Relying on this Court's decisions in *Washington ex rel. Seattle Trust Co. v. Roberge,* 278 U. S. 116 (1928), *Thomas Cusack Co. v. Chicago,* 242 U. S. 526 (1917), and *Eubank v. Richmond,* 226 U. S. 137 (1912), but distinguishing *James v. Valtierra,* 402 U. S. 137 (1971), the court concluded that the referendum provision constituted an unlawful delegation of legislative power.

We reverse.

I

The conclusion that Eastlake's procedure violates federal constitutional guarantees rests upon the proposition that a zoning referendum involves a delegation of legislative power. A referendum cannot, however, be characterized as a delegation of power. Under

---

[164] As adopted by the voters, Art. VIII, § 3, of the Eastlake City Charter provides in pertinent part:

"That any change to the existing land uses or any change whatsoever to any ordinance . . . cannot be approved unless and until it shall have been submitted to the Planning Commission, for approval or disapproval. That in the event the city council should approve any of the preceding changes, or enactments, whether approved or disapproved by the Planning Commission it shall not be approved or passed by the declaration of an emergency, and it shall not be effective, but it shall be mandatory that the same be approved by a 55% favorable vote of all votes cast of the qualified electors of the City of Eastlake at the next regular municipal election, if one shall occur not less than sixty (60) or more than one hundred and twenty (120) days after its passage, otherwise at a special election falling on the generally established day of the primary election. . . ."

our constitutional assumptions, all power derives from the people, who can delegate it to representative instruments which they create. See, *e. g.,* Federalist Papers, No. 39 (Madison). In establishing legislative bodies, the people can reserve to themselves power to deal directly with matters which might otherwise be assigned to the legislature. *Hunter v. Erickson,* 393 U. S. 385, 392 (1969).

The reservation of such power is the basis for the town meeting, a tradition which continues to this day in some States as both a practical and symbolic part of our democratic processes. The referendum, similarly, is a means for direct political participation, allowing the people the final decision, amounting to a veto power, over enactments of representative bodies. The practice is designed to "give citizens a voice on questions of public policy." *James v. Valtierra, supra,* at 141.

In framing a state constitution, the people of Ohio specifically reserved the power of referendum to the people of each municipality within the State.

> The initiative and referendum powers are hereby reserved to the people of each municipality on all questions which such municipalities may now or hereafter be authorized by law to control by legislative action. . . . Ohio Const., Art. II, § 1f.

To be subject to Ohio's referendum procedure, the question must be one within the scope of legislative power. The Ohio Supreme Court expressly found that the City Council's action in rezoning respondent's eight acres from light industrial to high-density residential use was legislative in nature.[165] Distinguishing between administrative and legislative acts, the court separated the power to zone or rezone, by passage or amendment of a zoning ordinance, from the power to grant relief from unnecessary hardship. The former function was found to be legislative in nature.[166] . . .

---

[165] The land use change requested by respondent would likely entail the provision of additional city services, such as schools and police and fire protection. Cf. *James v. Valtierra,* 402 U. S. 137, 143 n. 4 (1971). The change would also diminish the land area available for industrial purposes, thereby affecting Eastlake's potential economic development.

[166] The power of initiative or referendum may be reserved or conferred "with respect to any matter, legislative or administrative, within the realm of local affairs . . . ." 5 E. McQuillan, Municipal Corporations § 16.54, p. 208 (3d ed., 1969). However, the Ohio Supreme Court concluded that only land use changes granted by the City Council when acting in a *legislative* capacity were subject to the referendum process. Under the court's binding interpretation of state law, a property owner seeking relief from unnecessary hardship occasioned by zoning restrictions would not be subject to Eastlake's referendum procedure. For example, if unforeseeable future changes give rise to hardship on the owner, the holding of

II

The Ohio Supreme Court further concluded that the amendment to the city charter constituted a "delegation" of power violative of federal constitutional guarantees because the voters were given no standards to guide their decision. Under Eastlake's procedure, the Ohio Supreme Court reasoned, no mechanism existed, nor indeed could exist, to assure that the voters would act rationally in passing upon a proposed zoning change. This meant that "appropriate legislative action [would] be made dependent upon the potentially arbitrary and unreasonable whims of the voting public." 41 Ohio St. 2d, at 195, 324 N. E. 2d, at 746. The potential for arbitrariness in the process, the court concluded, violated due process.

Courts have frequently held in other contexts that a congressional delegation of power to a regulatory entity must be accompanied by discernible standards, so that the delegatee's action can be measured for its fidelity to the legislative will. . . . Assuming, *arguendo,* their relevance to state governmental functions, these cases involved a delegation of power by the legislature to regulatory bodies, which are not directly responsible to the people; this doctrine is inapplicable where, as here, rather than dealing with a delegation of power, we deal with a power reserved by the people to themselves.[167]

In basing its claim on federal due process requirements, respondent also invokes *Euclid v. Ambler Realty Co.,* 272 U. S. 365 (1926), but it does not rely on the direct teaching of that case. Under *Euclid,* a property owner can challenge a zoning restriction if the measure is "clearly arbitrary and unreasonable, having no substantial relation to the public health, safety, morals, or general welfare." *Id.,* at 395. If the substantive result of the referendum is arbitrary and capricious, bearing no relation to the police power, then the fact that the voters of Eastlake wish it so would not save the restriction. As

---

the Ohio Supreme Court provides avenues of administrative relief not subject to the referendum process.

167 The Ohio Supreme Court's analysis of the requirements for standards flowing from the Fourteenth Amendment also sweeps too broadly. Except as a legislative history informs an analysis of legislative action, there is no more advance assurance that a legislative body will act by conscientiously applying consistent standards than there is with respect to voters. For example, there is no certainty that the City Council in this case would act on the basis of "standards" explicit or otherwise in Eastlake's comprehensive zoning ordinance. Nor is there any assurance that townspeople assembling in a town meeting, as the people of Eastlake could do, *Hunter v. Erickson,* 393 U. S. 385, 392 (1969), will act according to consistent standards. The critical constitutional inquiry, rather, is whether the zoning restriction produces arbitrary or capricious results.

this Court held in invalidating a charter amendment enacted by referendum:

> The sovereignty of the people is itself subject to those constitutional limitations which have been duly adopted and remained unrepealed. *Hunter v. Erickson,* 393 U. S., at 392.
> . . . .

But no challenge of the sort contemplated in *Euclid v. Ambler Realty* is before us. The Ohio Supreme Court did not hold, and respondent does not argue, that the present zoning classification under Eastlake's comprehensive ordinance violates the principles established in *Euclid v. Ambler Realty.* If respondent considers the referendum result itself to be unreasonable, the zoning restriction is open to challenge in state court, where the scope of the state remedy available to respondent would be determined as a matter of state law, as well as under Fourteenth Amendment standards. That being so, nothing more is required by the Constitution.

Nothing in our cases is inconsistent with this conclusion. Two decisions of this Court were relied on by the Ohio Supreme Court in invalidating Eastlake's procedure. The thread common to both decisions is the delegation of legislative power, originally given by the people to a legislative body, and in turn delegated by the legislature to a *narrow segment* of the community, not to the people at large. In *Eubank v. City of Richmond,* 226 U. S. 137 (1912), the Court invalidated a city ordinance which conferred the power to establish building setback lines upon the owners of two-thirds of the property abutting any street. Similarly, in *Washington ex rel. Seattle Title Trust Co. v. Roberge,* 278 U. S. 116 (1928), the Court struck down an ordinance which permitted the establishment of philanthropic homes for the aged in residential areas, but only upon the written consent of the owners of two-thirds of the property within 400 feet of the proposed facility.

Neither *Eubank* nor *Roberge* involved a referendum procedure such as we have in this case; the standardless delegation of power to a limited group of property owners condemned by the Court in *Eubank* and *Roberge* is not to be equated with decisionmaking by the people through the referendum process. The Court of Appeals for the Ninth Circuit put it this way:

> A referendum, however, is far more than an expression of ambiguously founded neighborhood preference. It is the city itself legislating through its voters — an exercise by the voters of their traditional right through direct legislation to override the views of their elected representatives as to what serves the public interest. *Southern Alameda Spanish Speaking Organization v. City of Union City, California,* 424 F. 2d 291, 294 (1970).

Our decision in *James v. Valtierra,* upholding California's mandatory referendum requirement, confirms this view. Mr. Justice Black, speaking for the Court in that case, said:

> This procedure ensures that *all the people* of a community will have a voice in a decision which may lead to large expenditures of local governmental funds for increased public services . . . . 402 U. S., at 143 (emphasis added).

Mr. Justice Black went on to say that a referendum procedure, such as the one at issue here, is a classic demonstration of "devotion to democracy . . . ." *Id.,* at 141. As a basic instrument of democratic government, the referendum process does not, in itself, violate the Due Process Clause of the Fourteenth Amendment when applied to a rezoning ordinance.[168] Since the rezoning decision in this case was properly reserved to the people of Eastlake under the Ohio Constitution, the Ohio Supreme Court erred in holding invalid, on federal constitutional grounds, the charter amendment permitting the voters to decide whether the zoned use of respondent's property could be altered.

The judgment of the Ohio Supreme Court is reversed, and the case is remanded for further proceedings not inconsistent with this opinion.

Reversed and remanded.

Mr. Justice Powell, dissenting.

There can be no doubt as to the propriety and legality of submitting generally applicable legislative questions, including zoning provisions, to a popular referendum. But here the only issue concerned the status of a single small parcel owned by a single

---

[168] The fears expressed in dissent rest on the proposition that the procedure at issue here is "fundamentally unfair" to landowners; this fails to take into account the mechanisms for relief potentially available to property owners whose desired land use changes are rejected by the voters. First, if hardship is occasioned by zoning restrictions, *administrative* relief is potentially available. Indeed, the very purpose of "variances" allowed by zoning officials is to avoid "practical difficulties and unnecessary hardship." 8 E. McQuillan, Municipal Corporations § 25.159, p. 511 (3d ed. 1965). As we noted, . . . remedies remain available under the Ohio Supreme Court's holding and provide a means to challenge unreasonable or arbitrary action. *Euclid v. Ambler Realty Co.,* 272 U. S. 365 (1926).

The situation presented in this case is not one of a zoning action denigrating the use or depreciating the value of land; instead, it involves an effort to *change* a reasonable zoning restriction. No existing rights are being impaired; new use rights are being sought from the City Council. Thus, this case involves an owner's seeking approval of a new use free from the restrictions attached to the land when it was acquired.

"person." This procedure, affording no realistic opportunity for the affected person to be heard, even by the electorate, is fundamentally unfair. The "spot" referendum technique appears to open disquieting opportunities for local government bodies to bypass normal protective procedures for resolving issues affecting individual rights.

MR. JUSTICE STEVENS, with whom MR. JUSTICE BRENNAN joins, dissenting.

The city's reliance on the town meeting process of decisionmaking tends to obfuscate the two critical issues in this case. These issues are (1) whether the procedure which a city employs in deciding to grant or to deny a property owner's request for a change in the zoning of his property must comply with the Due Process Clause of the Fourteenth Amendment; and (2) if so, whether the procedure employed by the city of Eastlake is fundamentally fair?

I

. . . .

Subject to limitations imposed by the common law of nuisance and zoning restrictions, the owner of real property has the right to develop his land to his own economic advantage. As land continues to become more scarce, and as land use planning constantly becomes more sophisticated, the needs and the opportunities for unforeseen uses of specific parcels of real estate continually increase. For that reason, no matter how comprehensive a zoning plan may be, it regularly contains some mechanism for granting variances, amendments, or exemptions for specific uses of specific pieces of property. No responsibly prepared plan could wholly deny the need for presently unforeseeable future change.

A zoning code is unlike other legislation affecting the use of property. The deprivation caused by a zoning code is customarily qualified by recognizing the property owner's right to apply for an amendment or variance to accommodate his individual needs. The expectancy that particular changes consistent with the basic zoning plan will be allowed frequently and on their merits is a normal incident of property ownership. When the governing body offers the owner the opportunity to seek such a change — whether that opportunity is denominated a privilege or a right — it is affording protection to the owner's interest in making legitimate use of his property.

The fact that an individual owner (like any other petitioner or plaintiff) may not have a legal right to the relief he seeks does not mean that he has no right to fair procedure in the consideration of the merits of his application. The fact that codes regularly provide a procedure for granting individual exceptions or changes, the fact that such changes are granted in individual cases with great frequency, and the fact that the particular code in the record before us contemplates that changes consistent with the basic plan will be allowed, all support my opinion that the opportunity to apply for an amendment is an aspect of property ownership protected by the Due Process Clause of the Fourteenth Amendment.

This conclusion is supported by the few cases in this Court which have decided zoning questions, and by many well-reasoned state-court decisions. . . .

[Stevens then discusses the *Eubank* and the *Roberge* cases. — Eds.] Implicitly, both cases hold that the process of making decisions affecting the use of particular pieces of property must meet constitutional standards.

Although this Court has decided only a handful of zoning cases, literally thousands of zoning disputes have been resolved by state courts. Those courts have repeatedly identified the obvious difference between the adoption of a comprehensive citywide plan by legislative action and the decision of particular issues involving specific uses of specific parcels. In the former situation there is generally great deference to the judgment of the legislature; in the latter situation state courts have not hesitated to correct manifest injustice. . . .

Specialists in the practice of zoning law are unhappily familiar with the potential for abuse which exists when inadequate procedural safeguards apply to the dispensation of special grants. The power to deny arbitrarily may give rise to the power to exact intolerable conditions. The insistence on fair procedure in this area of the law falls squarely within the purpose of the Due Process Clause of the Fourteenth Amendment.

II

When we examine a state procedure for the purpose of deciding whether it comports with the constitutional standard of due process, the fact that a State may give it a "legislative" label should not save an otherwise invalid procedure. We should, however, give some deference to the conclusion of the highest court of the State that the procedure represents an arbitrary and unreasonable way of handling a local problem.

In this case, the Ohio courts arrived at the conclusion that Art. VIII, § 3, of the charter of the city of Eastlake, as amended on November 2, 1971, is wholly invalid in three stages. At no stage of the case has there been any suggestion that respondent's proposed use of its property would be inconsistent with the city's basic zoning plan, or would have any impact on the municipal budget or adversely affect the city's potential economic development. . . .

As the Justices of the Ohio Supreme Court recognized, we are concerned with the fairness of a provision for determining the right to make a particular use of a particular parcel of land. In such cases, the state courts have frequently described the capricious character of a decision supported by majority sentiment rather than reference to articulable standards. Moreover, they have limited statutory referendum procedures to apply only to approvals of comprehensive zoning ordinances as opposed to amendments affecting specific parcels. This conclusion has been supported by characterizing particular amendments as "administrative" and revision of an entire plan as "legislative."

In this case the Ohio Supreme Court characterized the Council's approval of respondent's proposal as "legislative." I think many state courts would have characterized it as "administrative." The courts thus may well differ in their selection of the label to apply to this action, but I find substantial agreement among state tribunals on the proposition that requiring a citywide referendum for approval of a particular proposal like this is manifestly unreasonable. Surely that is my view.

The essence of fair procedure is that the interested parties be given a reasonable opportunity to have their dispute resolved on the merits by reference to articulable rules. If a dispute involves only the conflicting rights of private litigants, it is elementary that the decisionmaker must be impartial and qualified to understand and to apply the controlling rules.

I have no doubt about the validity of the initiative or the referendum as an appropriate method of deciding questions of community policy. I think it is equally clear that the popular vote is not an acceptable method of adjudicating the rights of individual litigants. The problem presented by this case is unique, because it may involve a three-sided controversy, in which there is at least potential conflict between the rights of the property owner and the rights of his neighbors, and also potential conflict with the public interest in preserving the city's basic zoning plan. If the latter aspect of the controversy were predominant, the referendum would be an acceptable procedure. On the other hand, when the record indicates without contradiction that there is no threat to the general public interest in preserving the city's plan — as it does in this case, since respondent's proposal was approved by both the Planning Commission and the City Council and there has been no allegation that the use of this eight-acre parcel for apartments rather than light industry would adversely affect the community or raise any policy issue of citywide concern — I think the case should be treated as one in which it is essential that the private property owner be given a fair opportunity to have his claim determined on the merits. . . .

Comments: 1. Does Chief Justice Burger's majority opinion implicitly adopt the assumption that zoning amendments occur infrequently in the zoning process and so do not involve a legislative action? Does Justice Stevens' different characterization of the zoning amendment compel a different result in *Eastlake* under the teaching of *Eubank* and *Roberge*? Is it an answer to an attack on the process through which zoning amendments are enacted that the landowner has a substantive opportunity to overturn a zoning restriction that is unconstitutionally applied to him? Could he do so in a variance proceeding, as Chief Justice Burger suggests? For discussion of the *Eastlake* decision see the student Note, *supra* p. 762, at 825-44.

The student Note makes a series of criticisms of the use of mandatory referenda in the zoning process. Voters are likely to be uninformed about the zoning proposal, and so incapable of making an informed choice. If the referendum result is judicially reviewed the court will not have a record of any kind on which it can base its decision. See *Ranjel v. City of Lansing*, 417 F.2d 321, 324 (6th Cir. 1969), in which the court refused to upset an unfavorable referendum on a zoning change which would have allowed a subsidized housing project. It suggested that judicial review of the referendum "would entail an intolerable invasion of the privacy that must protect an exercise of the franchise."

The student Note also suggests that developers forced to face a mandatory referendum will bypass the local legislative body entirely and seek an electoral zoning change directly through the initiative. If this occurs there will be no opportunity for the mutual bargaining between the municipality and the developer which is often necessary to adjust the developer's proposal. Mandatory referenda also delay the development process, interfere with comprehensive planning and frustrate attempts by the municipality to zone for regional needs. What is your evaluation of these criticisms? Would they be entirely eliminated if the referendum were made permissive and not mandatory, as the student Note also suggests?

2. A more detailed summary of two of the earlier referendum cases relied on by the Supreme Court may help provide a better perspective on the *Eastlake* opinion:

Hunter v. Erickson, 393 U.S. 385 (1969). The city of Akron, Ohio, enacted a fair housing ordinance that prohibited discrimination in the sale or rental of housing. After plaintiff filed a complaint under the ordinance the city charter was amended to require a referendum on any ordinance of this type. The city also had a long-standing referendum procedure under which a referendum could be had on almost any city ordinance following the filing of a petition by ten percent of the electors.

The charter provision mandating a referendum on fair housing ordinances was held unconstitutional, as it was "an explicitly racial classification treating racial housing matters differently from other racial and housing matters." *Id.* at 389. The court noted that while the law applied on its face to both majority and minority groups its "impact" fell on the minority. *Id.* at 391. Since the mandatory referendum was based on a racial classification it bore a heavier burden of justification than other classifications. It was not justified by "insisting that a State may distribute legislative power as it desires and that the people may retain for themselves the power over certain subjects . . . [as there is a violation of] the Fourteenth Amendment." *Id.* at 392. The concurring opinion noted that the optional referendum procedure was grounded upon "general democratic principle," and that procedures of this type "do not violate the Equal Protection clause simply because they occasionally operate to disadvantage Negro political interests." *Id.* at 394.

James v. Valtierra, 402 U.S. 137 (1971). The decision was written by Justice Black, who had dissented in *Hunter.* This case considered the validity of an amendment to the California state constitution that mandated a referendum on all local public housing projects. These projects are built by local agencies and governments and receive federal subsidies. The court upheld the California constitutional amendment in a brief opinion, distinguishing *Hunter* on the ground that the California procedure "requires referendum approval for any low-rent public housing project, not only for projects which will be occupied by a racial minority." There was no support in the record for "any claim that a law seemingly neutral on its face is in fact aimed at a racial minority." *Id.* at 141.

Justice Black chose not to examine the impact of the amendment, which arguably fell disproportionately on minority groups such as blacks who make up a large number of the tenants in low-income subsidized housing projects. However, he seemed to reject this line of analysis by commenting that "a lawmaking procedure that 'disadvantages' a particular group does not always deny equal protection." *Id.* at 142. Nor would the court analyze governmental structures to determine whether they disadvantaged "any of the shifting and diverse groups that make up the American people." *Id.* The dissent would have invalidated the California mandatory referendum as a suspect classification based on poverty status. The *Valtierra* case thus represents a refusal by the Supreme Court, acknowledged or not, to extend to the referendum issue its holdings that, in other areas of concern, a classification based on poverty is constitutionally suspect. *See, e.g., Harper v. Virginia Bd. of Elections,* 383 U.S. 663 (1966) (state and local governments may not discriminate against the poor in exercise of voting rights by requiring them to pay a poll tax).

Justice Black also relied in his decision on the fact that California had extensively provided for mandatory referenda on a variety of subjects, and that there was justification for mandating the referendum in this case because localities in which public housing projects are located might be subject to large expenditures for public services needed by these projects. In a footnote, Black noted that public housing projects were exempt by federal law from local property taxation and that in-lieu payments required as a substitute for local taxation were ordinarily less than the taxes that otherwise would have been levied. Chief Justice Burger used a similar municipal burden rationale in the *Eastlake* case. Was he justified in doing so in the *Eastlake* setting?

3. State courts must also deal with due process objections to the initiative and referendum. How they might deal with this issue is indicated by the decision that follows.

TOWNSHIP OF SPARTA v. SPILLANE

Superior Court of New Jersey, Appellate Division

125 N.J. Super. 519, 312 A.2d 154 (1973)

Petition for certification denied, 64 N.J. 493, 317 A.2d 706 (1974)

Before Judges CARTON, SEIDMAN and GOLDMANN.
The opinion of the court was delivered by
CARTON, P. J. A. D.

The issue to be resolved in these appeals is whether the referendum procedure provided for in the Faulkner Act applies to an amendment to the zoning ordinance of a municipality which has adopted the provisions of that act. The Township of Sparta and Township of Mount Olive cases involve this identical issue. Consequently they will be considered together, although they have not been formally consolidated.

Sparta has operated since 1960 under the Council-Manager Plan B of the Faulkner Act, N.J.S.A. 40:69A-99 et seq. On April 12, 1972 the township council adopted an amendment to its zoning ordinance authorizing a Planned Unit Development (P.U.D.) pursuant to N.J.S.A. 40:55-55 to 67. The plans for the P.U.D. were originally proposed by a subsidiary of a large corporation owning about 2,000 acres in Sparta.

The amendatory ordinance was referred to and acted upon favorably by the planning board after extended public hearings. Thereafter defendants in the Sparta action filed a petition with the municipal clerk seeking a referendum pursuant to N.J.S.A. 40:69A-185. The petition was found sufficient by the township clerk to comply with N.J.S.A. 40:69A-187, whereupon Sparta Township sought a declaratory judgment to determine whether the referendum provisions of the Faulkner Act were applicable to amendments of a zoning ordinance. The trial judge granted the township's motion for summary judgment, holding that such provisions were not applicable.

Mount Olive Township operated under the Mayor and Council Plan E of the Faulkner Act, N.J.S.A. 40:69A-68 to 73. On August 25, 1972 the township council, over strong opposition, adopted an ordinance amending the township zoning ordinance by establishing a new zone denominated C-R (Commercial-Recreational). Permissible uses in this zone included permanent year-round or seasonal amusement parks. Two of the defendants in the Mount

Olive case own about two-thirds of the land in the newly created C-R zone on which they intend to construct and operate a major amusement park. The lands in question are located near Interstate Route 80 and were originally zoned for industrial uses.

The amendment was approved by the mayor after its passage by the council. On September 18 the plaintiffs in the Mount Olive case filed a petition with the township clerk for a referendum on the amendatory ordinance. This petition was found to comply with the statutory requirement.

As in the Sparta action, a declaratory judgment was sought by the municipality as to the applicability of the referendum procedures to the ordinance. The trial judge ruled in this case, as did the trial judge in the Sparta litigation, that the referendum procedure was not applicable.

The issue raised here presents a queston not directly decided before in New Jersey. The Faulkner Act, in pertinent part, provides:

> The voters shall also have the power of referendum which is the power to approve or reject at the polls any ordinance submitted by the council to the voters or any ordinance passed by the council, against which a referendum petition has been filed as herein provided. No ordinance passed by the municipal council, except when otherwise required by general law or permitted by the provisions of section 17-32(b) of this act, shall take effect before twenty days from the time of its final passage and its approval by the mayor where such approval is required. . . . [N.J.S.A. 40:69A-185]

A companion section of the statute (N.J.S.A. 40:69A-184) provides a slightly different procedure for expressing public participation in municipal government through the initiative process:

> The voters of any municipality may propose any ordinance and may adopt or reject the same at the polls, such power being known as the initiative. . . .

The Faulkner Act was adopted in order to encourage public participation in municipal affairs in the face of normal apathy and lethargy in such matters. The act gave municipalities the option of choosing one form or another of local government best suited to its needs. It was a legislative demonstration of the democratic ideal of giving the people the right of choosing the form of government they preferred and the opportunity to exercise the powers under that form to the furthest limits. Some 76 of the 567 municipalities of this State have adopted one form or another of the forms of government authorized under the Faulkner Act.

The initiative and referendum processes authorized by the act comprise two useful instruments of plebiscite power and provide a means of arousing public interest. Ordinary rules of construction would, of course, dictate that such provisions should be liberally construed. See 5 McQuillin, Municipal Corporations, § 16.48 at 199-200 (1969), where the author advocates that these procedures should be respected and given wide use if possible. It should be noted, however, that he adds a caveat that any grant of the power of initiative and referendum and its exercise are subject to and must be construed with governing constitutional and statutory provisions. 5 McQuillin, *supra* at § 16.50. . . .

Undeniably, zoning issues often are of great public interest and some, as in the present case, may concern the entire population of the municipality involved. In both the cases before us it has been argued forcefully that the proposed ordinances change or alter the complexion of the municipalities. Thus, the ultimate question is whether major decisions should be made by the planning boards and governing bodies, with only voiced public approval or dissent as prescribed in the Zoning Act, or whether they should be open to a final decision by the vote of the entire population. This issue pits the philosophy of comprehensive zoning planned by a panel of experts and adopted by elected and appointed officials, against the philosophy of a wider public participation and choice in municipal affairs.

Other states faced with similar problems of referendum provisions have arrived at conflicting determinations. . . . However, the decisions of other states furnish little aid here since the laws of the states involved differ in substantial respects from the New Jersey statutes.

Our consideration of the applicability of the referendum provided for in the Faulkner Act to the zoning procedure logically should begin with an examination of the treatment accorded by our courts to the companion process of the initiative. *Smith v. Livingston Tp.,* 106 N.J.Super. 444, 256 A.2d 85 (Ch.Div.1969), aff'd o. b. 54 N.J. 525, 257 A.2d 698 (1969), held that the initiative was not applicable to amendatory zoning ordinances. In so holding, Judge Mintz found that the zoning statutes represented an exclusive grant of power by the Legislature to municipalities generally and was not impliedly superseded by the later adopted Faulkner Act. He noted that the Zoning Act is specific in detailing the manner in which zoning ordinances may be amended; that steps in the zoning procedure include consideration by the municipal planning board, the opportunity of property owners to object, and approval by the governing body. He also pointed out that in the event of objection by the property owners involved, a vote of two-thirds of the governing body is required to effect a change in the zoning ordinance (N.J.S.A. 40:55-34 to 35). He likewise observed that the initiative and referendum provisions in the Faulkner Act contain no specific reference to zoning. He concluded that if the initiative procedure were allowed to be applied to zoning matters, it would "disregard the valuable expertise of the planning board, and permit the electorate to defeat the beneficent purpose of the comprehensive zoning ordinance." 106 N.J. Super. at 457, 256 A.2d at 92.

Appellants argue that a referendum is sufficiently dissimilar to an initiative as to justify treating it differently. They stress the fact that a referendum merely adds an additional stage which follows the governing body's approval and does not, as in the case of the initiative, provide a substitute for legislative action by the governing body. Consequently, they reason, a proposed zoning change should no more than any other legislative act be immune from further public examination. They point also to the fact that the planning board would not be altogether by-passed as in the case of initiative since a referendum begun by a petitioner would not occur until after the adoption of the zoning amendment and such adoption could not occur until the planning board had reviewed the amendment and made its recommendation. N.J.S.A. 40:55-35 and N.J.S.A. 40:69A-185.

These arguments have some cogency. However, we conclude that essentially the same considerations which bar application of the initiative process to zoning ordinance amendments apply in the case of the referendum.

Zoning is intended to be accomplished in accordance with a comprehensive plan and should reflect both present and prospective needs of the community.... Among other things, the social, economic and physical characteristics of the community should be considered. The achievement of these goals might well be jeopardized by piecemeal attacks on the zoning ordinances if referenda were permissible for review of any amendment. Sporadic attacks on a municipality's comprehensive plan would tend to fragment zoning without any overriding concept. That concept should not be discarded because planning boards and governing bodies may not always have acted in the best interest of the public and may not, in every case, have demonstrated the expertise which they might be expected to develop.

The spirit and thrust of *Smith v. Livingston Tp., supra,* requires treatment of both processes in the same fashion in their relation to the zoning procedure. Such considerations stem from the exclusivity and uniqueness of the Zoning Act itself (and the related Planning Act) and the Legislature's evident intention of providing uniformity of procedure for all municipalities in the State in zoning matters.

Thus, the Legislature has authorized governing bodies of municipalities to establish administrative agencies to assist them in the performance of functions in this area and has laid down very specific and detailed procedure to be followed by all governmental bodies in carrying out such functions. Such comprehensive and precise treatment demonstrates the special concern of the Legislature in this important area of municipal regulation.

Moreover, certain aspects of the zoning statute seem inherently incompatible with the referendum process. N.J.S.A. 40:55-35 provides three avenues by which an amendment to a zoning ordinance may be effected; first, following approval by the planning board the governing body passes the amended ordinance; second, upon rejection by the planning board the amended ordinance may be approved by two-thirds of the governing body; third, should at least 20% of the landowners directly or contiguously affected by the proposed amendment object, the governing body must pass the amended ordinance by a two-thirds vote. A zoning ordinance amendment does not become operative unless the planning board and governing body have acted. . . . Whether the referendum stems from a submission of an ordinance by the governing body directly to the voters or by a referendum petition filed by the necessary number of voters, the so-called veto power of the planning board or protesting landowners would be rendered meaningless. A simple majority of the voters would be all that was necessary to approve or disapprove the ordinance.

We are not satisfied that the publicity which might accompany the referendum campaign and the exposure and discussion of the issues generated thereby justify disregarding these procedural requirements. . . . In this connection we note that the zoning statute requires public notice of proposed zoning changes (N.J.S.A. 40:55-34). Moreover, from common experience we know that zoning amendments of a controversial nature, especially those which may greatly affect the entire population of the community, are often widely discussed and vigorously debated at the public hearings prior to adoption.

. . . .

Both judgments appealed from are affirmed.

———————

Comments: 1. The principal case details most of the objections which state courts disallowing the use of the referendum in zoning have advanced. New Jersey, by statute, has now exempted zoning ordinances and amendments from both the initiative and referendum. N.J. Stat. Ann. § 40:55D-65(b) (Supp. 1978). Note that the New Jersey court did not consider possible due process objections to the referendum which might arise from the fact that the referendum, by definition, precludes observance of the notice and hearing requirements contained in zoning enabling legislation. Since the referendum occurs after the zoning amendment has been enacted by the legislative body following the statutory notice and hearing, most state courts have either not perceived or have not found a due process violation on this account. See *City of Fort Collins v. Dooney,*

496 P.2d 316 (Colo. 1972), upholding the application of a referendum to a zoning map amendment and noting that "[t]he fact that due process requirements may be met in one manner when the change is by council action does not preclude other procedures from meeting due process requirements. . . ." *Id.* at 319. Quoting from another case, the court then added that " '[t]he election campaign, the debate and airing of opposing opinions, supplant a public hearing prior to the adoption of an ordinance by the municipal governing body.' " *Id.* How realistic is this assumption?

The *Ft. Collins* case relied on the nature of the referendum as a "fundamental right" of the people in holding that a home rule charter provision allowing a referendum on "all" ordinances could not be construed to exempt zoning amendments. However, the court added that its holding was not intended to strip the property owner of his constitutional rights. "We can conceive of situations where the court might hold that the action of the electorate was arbitrary and capricious." *Id.*

For other cases upholding zoning referenda on zoning map amendments see *Queen Creek Land & Cattle Corp. v. Yavapi County Bd. of Supervisors,* 501 P.2d 391 (Ariz. 1972), noting that the referendum does not change the zoning as an initiative does and that the notice and hearing process is accomplished prior to the referendum; *Cook-Johnson Realty Co. v. Bertolini,* 239 N.E.2d 80 (Ohio 1968), upholding a permissive referendum and noting that the only effect of a successful referendum is to restore the zoning to what it was before the map amendment was requested; and *City of Coral Gables v. Carmichael,* 256 So.2d 404 (Fla. Ct. App.), *cert. denied,* 268 So.2d 1 (Fla. 1972), rejecting due process objections on the authority of *James v. Valtierra, supra.* For a case agreeing with the principal case on statutory conflict grounds and reviewing authorities in accord see *Elliott v. City of Clawson,* 175 N.W.2d 821 (Mich. App. 1970). *Compare State ex rel. Wahlmann v. Reim,* 445 S.W.2d 336 (Mo. 1969), rejecting the statutory conflict argument and upholding a referendum on a newly-enacted comprehensive zoning ordinance though noting that it might not be available for "isolated amendments." *Id.* at 338. The cases are collected in Annot., 72 A.L.R.3d 1030 (1976).

2. The suggestion by the Missouri court that the referendum may not be applicable to "isolated amendments" reflects the accepted limitation on the referendum process, that it is available only for legislative and not for administrative actions. Recall the *Fasano* case, *supra* p. 693, holding that zoning amendment is a quasi-judicial and not a legislative action and is thus not subject to the normal presumption of constitutionality. This issue has also arisen in the referendum context. *Compare Denney v. City of Duluth,* 202 N.W.2d 892 (Minn. 1973) (amendment legislative), and *Forman v. Eagle Thrifty Drugs and Markets, Inc.,* 516 P.2d 1234 (Nev. 1974) (same), *with West v. City of Portage,* 221 N.W.2d 303 (Mich. 1974) (*contra;* plurality opinion). *See State ex rel. Srovnal v. Linton,* 346 N.E.2d 764 (Ohio 1976), holding that a zoning exception is administrative.

O'Loane v. O'Rourke, 42 Cal. Rptr. 283 (Cal. App. 1965), is a case holding that the adoption of a comprehensive plan is a legislative act subject to referendum:

> It is apparent that the plan is, in short, a constitution for all future development within the city. . . . To argue that property

rights are not affected by the general plan (as the city so asserts) as adopted ignores that which is obvious. Any zoning ordinance adopted in the future would surely be interpreted in part by its fidelity to the general plan as well as by the standards of the process.

Id. at 288. Note that California now requires that zoning be consistent with the comprehensive plan, *supra* p. 758.

In home rule states, whether a zoning ordinance or comprehensive plan is subject to referendum may depend on whether it is considered a matter of statewide or local concern. *See Allison v. Washington County,* 548 P.2d 188 (Ore. App. 1976), noting that a comprehensive plan was a legislative act but adding that it would not be subject to referendum if it covered matters of statewide concern.

3. There are not many cases considering the use of the initiative in zoning, but most have held against it. Unlike the referendum, which follows legislative adoption of a zoning measure in which statutory notice and hearing requirements have been observed, a successful initiative will result in the enactment of a zoning measure without the statutory notice and hearing. For this reason, courts may find that the zoning initiative violates the statutory notice and hearing procedures, and some courts have found a denial of procedural due process as well. *See, e.g., City of Scottsdale v. Superior Court,* 439 P.2d 290 (Ariz. 1968); *Andover Dev. Corp. v. City of New Smyrna Beach,* 328 So.2d 231 (Fla. Ct. App.), *cert. denied,* 341 So.2d 290 (Fla. 1976); *Smith v. Township of Livingston,* 256 A.2d 85 (N.J. Super.), *aff'd,* 257 A.2d 698 (N.J. 1969); *Forman, supra; Hancock v. Rouse,* 437 S.W.2d 1 (Tex. Civ. App. 1969). These cases all considered the use of the initiative as a means of repealing a zoning amendment applicable to a single parcel of land, and this fact may have led these courts to emphasize the notice and hearing problem.

The California Supreme Court has now taken a different view of the initiative in zoning which to some extent is contrary to the cases just cited, some of which had relied on earlier California opinions holding the initiative unavailable. In *San Diego Bldg. Contractors Ass'n v. City Council,* 529 P.2d 570 (Cal. 1974), *appeal dismissed,* 427 U.S. 901 (1976), the voters by initiative enacted a thirty-foot height limit on buildings to be constructed within a prescribed coastal zone. Relying on long-standing Supreme Court precedent, *Bi-Metallic Co. v. State Bd. of Equalization,* 239 U.S. 441 (1915), the California court held that notice and hearing were not required for a general zoning ordinance, which was a legislative act. The court noted that it was "not faced in the instant case with any of the great number of more limited 'administrative' zoning decisions, such as the grant of a variance or the award of a conditional use permit, which are adjudicatory in nature and which thus involve entirely different constitutional considerations." *Id.* at 574. What about a zoning map amendment?

Then, in *Associated Homebuilders, Inc. v. City of Livermore,* 557 P.2d 473 (Cal. 1976), the California Supreme Court considered the validity of an initiative ordinance which enacted a growth moratorium for the city. It held that the initiative procedure did not conflict with the notice and hearing and other provisions of the zoning enabling act on the ground that no such conflict was intended. The court noted that the right to the initiative was reserved in the constitution and that if the zoning act were construed to bar the initiative it might be of doubtful constitutionality. *Id.* at 479-80. An earlier case holding to the contrary was overruled. There was a reference to the constitutional provision authorizing the initiative as "[d]rafted in light of the theory that all power of government ultimately resides in the people," *id.* at 477, an echo of the *Eastlake* case. While *Livermore* deals with a general zoning restriction, it may be significant that the earlier case which was overruled considered an initiative enacting a zoning change for a single parcel of land.

The dissenting opinion contains a strong statement of the reasons why the initiative should not be available in the zoning process. It noted in part that "[f]undamentally, the zoning statutes contemplate that to achieve orderly and wise land use regulation any change in zoning ordinances is not to be made until the experts in the field have had an opportunity to evaluate the effects of the change after notice hearing and report." *Id.* at 491. And what of the requirement, in California, that zoning must be consistent with an adopted comprehensive plan?

4. For a thorough analysis of the use of the initiative and referendum in zoning see Comment, The Initiative and Referendum's Use in Zoning, 64 Cal. L. Rev. 74, 93 (1976). This author concludes:

> The initiative process contains adequate safeguards against arbitrary decisionmaking; the open process of a political campaign is likely to reveal to the voters adequate information upon which to make an intelligent decision. Even if some prejudice may be suffered by individual property owners, courts should consider the unique educational and participatory values represented by the initiative. Moreover, the protection of property owners may be accomplished by means other than categorically prohibiting the initiative's use. Courts should consider the possibility of heightened judicial scrutiny of the substance of initiative measures which seem to focus on an individual parcel rather than on broad community objectives; this type of review would be in accord with the close judicial scrutiny of "spot-zoning" discussed above. Courts concerned about forcing property owners to wage both a political campaign and a subsequent legal challenge may wish to consider relaxing the traditional judicial reluctance to rule on the validity of an initiative measure prior to passage.

Chapter 5

SUBDIVISION CONTROLS

The focus to this point has largely been on zoning, the regulation of land development through the adoption of zoning ordinances specifying permitted and conditional uses of land. This chapter considers subdivision control, a related land use control technique which applies when land is first subdivided and made available for development. The importance of subdivision control in land use regulation arises from the fact that raw land which is farmed or otherwise used for nonurban purposes is usually held in relatively large tracts. If it is to be made available for urban development it must first be subdivided into blocks and lots which are suitable for building purposes. It is this need to make land available for building in small individual units that creates the opportunity for controls over the subdivision process.

Initially, subdivision controls were first adopted in rudimentary form as land platting legislation toward the close of the Nineteenth Century, and were directed toward an easing of land conveyance problems. Historically, land has been conveyed by boundary metes and bounds description. This method of conveyancing requires a reference to boundary markers, distances and directions which are often confusing and unreliable, leading to disputes over land ownership and titles. To avoid these problems, land developers prepared so-called plats of subdivisions on which the blocks and lots were shown. Once a plat was recorded, parcel conveyance could be by reference to blocks and lots within the plat, *e.g.,* "Lot 5 in Block 4 of Milligan's Addition to the City of Indian Falls." The early platting laws simply required the recording of these subdivision plats in the appropriate records office, after which the conveyance of lots within the plat could be made "with reference" to the plat in the manner just indicated. Many of these early laws mandated the recording of subdivision plats before conveyances "with reference" to the plat could be made.

It soon became apparent that the subdivision control process could accomplish substantive objectives as well. Many of the early subdivisions were cursed with poor design and layout and inadequate streets and facilities. Often the subdivider would leave his development with badly constructed streets which would soon crumble, leaving the homeowners to be assessed with the cost of street improvements which became necessary once the original streets wore out. Other problems arose when subdividers planned their subdivisions independently, with the result that streets did not connect properly from one subdivision to the next. This practice has not disappeared. A recent survey of new subdivisions in Jefferson County, Missouri, which then did not have subdivision control, found several hundred dead-end subdivision streets ending at hills, gullies and other unlikely places. This problem to some extent can be handled by official map laws, see *supra* p. 90, but this technique is not widespread.

Some states thus amended their subdivision platting legislation late in the Nineteenth Century to require subdivision streets to conform to the municipal street system plan. When the Standard State Planning Enabling Act was written in the 1920's, these early subdivision platting statutes were used as a model for subdivision control provisions that were included in the Act. The scope of public control over subdivisions contemplated at that time is indicated by the text of the Standard Act, which incorporated these early statutory requirements and added others requiring the provision of on-site facilities necessary to service the subdivision development:

> Section 13. Whenever a planning commission shall have adopted a major street plan . . . [which is on file in the office of the county recorder], then no plat of a subdivision of land . . . shall be filed or recorded until it shall have been approved by such planning commission. . . .
>
> Section 14. Before exercising . . . [subdivision control] powers . . . the planning commission shall adopt regulations governing the subdivision of land within its jurisdiction. Such regulations may provide for the proper arrangement of streets in relation to other existing or planned streets and to the master plan, for adequate and convenient open spaces for traffic, utilities, access of firefighting apparatus, recreation, light and air, and for the avoidance of congestion of population, including minimum width and areas of lots.
>
> Such regulations may include provisions as to the extent to which streets and other ways shall be graded and improved and to which water and sewer and other utility mains, piping, or other facilities shall be installed as a condition precedent to the approval of the plat. . . .

Standard City Planning Enabling Act (U.S. Dep't of Commerce, 1928). For general background on the control of subdivisions see Melli, Subdivision Control in Wisconsin, 1953 Wis. L. Rev. 389. In many states the subdivision control legislation is still based on the provisions of the Standard Act.

More modern subdivision control legislation has extended the substantive requirements applicable to new subdivisions in several directions, and has tended to view the act of subdividing as a triggering event which calls into play a range of controls which shape and give character to new development in the community. This shift in direction needs emphasis. Subdivision control has gradually evolved from a simple control over the recording of new subdivision plats to an extensive set of controls over new land development. Some of these more modern subdivision control enabling acts are reproduced below.

This newer legislation has added a variety of requirements to the provisions of the Standard Act. The number of on-site facilities required has been extended, new subdivisions have been restricted in floodplains and on environmentally sensitive land, and the phasing of new development has been controlled in connection with the provision of public facilities. Another common feature of the newer subdivision controls, though not generally authorized by legislation, is a requirement that land be dedicated without compensation or cash payments made for public facilities such as parks and schools. In the materials that follow, the structure of subdivision controls is examined; the substantive restrictions applicable to new developments is considered; land dedications and development charges are analyzed; and attention is given to the protection available to subdividers against changes in land development requirements as they move through the land development process.

A. THE STRUCTURE OF SUBDIVISION CONTROL

1. Enabling Legislation

This section contains examples of subdivision control enabling legislation that illustrate the modern approach to subdivision control. In reviewing this legislation, concentrate especially on the substantive controls that are required or authorized.

CONNECTICUT GENERAL STATUTES (1977)

Section 8-18. Definitions. As used in this chapter: "Commission" means a planning commission; . . . "subdivision" means the division of a tract or parcel of land into three or more parts or lots for the purpose, whether immediate or future, of sale or building development expressly excluding development for municipal, conservation or agricultural purposes, and includes resubdivision; "resubdivision" means a change in a map of an approved or recorded subdivision or resubdivision if such change (a) affects any street layout shown on such map, (b) affects any area reserved thereon for public use or (c) diminishes the size of any lot shown thereon and creates an additional building lot, if any of the lots shown thereon have been conveyed after the approval or recording of such map. . . .

Section 8-25. Subdivision of land. No subdivision of land shall be made until a plan for such subdivision has been approved by the commission. Any person, firm or corporation making any subdivision of land without the approval of the commission shall be fined not more than two hundred dollars for each lot sold or offered for sale

or so subdivided. . . . Such regulations shall provide that the land to
be subdivided shall be of such character that it can be used for
building purposes without danger to health or the public safety, that
proper provision shall be made for water, drainage and sewerage
and, in areas contiguous to brooks, rivers or other bodies of water
subject to flooding, including tidal flooding, that proper provision
shall be made for protective flood control measures and that the
proposed streets are in harmony with existing or proposed principal
thoroughfares shown in the plan of development . . .,especially in
regard to safe intersections with such thoroughfares, and so arranged
and of such width, as to provide an adequate and convenient system
for present and prospective traffic needs. Such regulations shall also
provide that the commission may provide open spaces for parks and
playgrounds when, and in places, deemed proper by the planning
commission, which open spaces for parks and playgrounds shall be
shown on the subdivision plan. The commission may also prescribe
the extent to which and the manner in which streets shall be graded
and improved and public utilities and services provided and, in lieu
of the completion of such work and installations previous to the final
approval of a plan, the commission may accept a bond in an amount
and with surety and conditions satisfactory to it securing to the
municipality the actual construction and installation of such
improvements and utilities within a period specified in the bond. . . .

Comments: 1. In what ways has the Connecticut statute expanded on the
subdivision requirements contained in the Standard Act? Note the provision
authorizing the exclusion of land subject to flooding. For a more extensive
provision see Ariz. Rev. Stat. Ann. § 9-463.01(C)(4) (Supp. 1975). This
provision authorizes municipalities to:

> Determine that certain lands may either not be subdivided, by
> reason of adverse topography, periodic inundation, adverse soils,
> subsidence of the earth's surface, high water table, lack of water
> or other natural or man-made hazard to life or property, or control
> the lot size, establish special grading and drainage requirements,
> and impose other regulations deemed reasonable and necessary
> for the public health, safety or general welfare on any lands to be
> subdivided affected by such characteristics.

Does this statute provide an alternative to prohibition of development on
these lands? What is it? *See also* Ariz. Rev. Stat. Ann. § 45-2342(C)(1)
(Supp. 1977) (state floodplain board shall establish floodplain regulations
for subdivisions). For discussion of environmental land use controls see
infra Chapter 7.

2. Many states also provide authority to state health and environmental
agencies to regulate on-site wells and on-site sewage disposal through septic
tanks and similar facilities. *E.g.,* Mich. Stat. Ann. § 26.430(105)(g) (1970),
requiring the approval of all subdivisions to be conditioned on compliance
with the rules of the state department of health "relating to suitability of

soils for subdivisions not served by public water and public sewers;" N.H. Rev. Stat. Ann. § 149-E:3 (Supp. 1977), authorizing the state water supply and pollution control commission to specify "standards, procedures and criteria" for sewage or waste disposal systems in subdivisions. Acceptability of on-site systems under these laws is usually based on the ability of the soil to handle waste disposal. Denial of a state permit will foreclose development of the site unless the developer ties in with public facilities. The importance of these state health laws in the development of new subdivisions is often neglected. Note also that the state permit law adds another approval stage to the subdivision control process.

3. The form in which the definition of subdivision is put in the Connecticut law is typical and has created problems of enforcement in subdivision control. Discussion of these problems can be found *infra* p. 801.

4. One of the most advanced subdivision control enabling statutes is found in California, no doubt as a response to the intensive land development activity which has characterized that state. Excerpts from the California law follow.

CALIFORNIA GOVERNMENT CODE (Deering Supp. 1977)

66411. Regulation and control of the design and improvement of subdivisions are vested in the legislative bodies of local agencies. Each local agency shall by ordinance regulate and control subdivisions for which this . . . [statute] requires a tentative and final or parcel map. Such ordinance shall specifically provide for proper grading and erosion control, including the prevention of sedimentation or damage to offsite property. . . .

66412. This . . . [statute] shall be inapplicable to:
(a) The financing or leasing of apartments, offices, stores or similar space within apartment buildings, industrial buildings, commercial buildings, mobilehome parks or trailer parks. . . .

66418. "Design" means: (1) street alignments, grades and widths; (2) drainage and sanitary facilities and utilities, including alignments and grades thereof; (3) location and size of all required easements and rights-of-way; (4) fire roads and firebreaks; (5) lot size and configuration; (6) traffic access; (7) grading; (8) land to be dedicated for park or recreational purposes; and (9) such other specific requirements in the plan and configuration of the entire subdivision as may be necessary or convenient to insure conformity to or implementation of the general plan. . . .

66419. (a) "Improvement" refers to such street work and utilities to be installed, or agreed to be installed, by the subdivider on the land to be used for public or private streets, highways, ways, and easements, as are necessary for the general use of the lot owners in the subdivision and local neighborhood traffic and drainage needs as a condition precedent to the approval and acceptance of the final map thereof.

(b) "Improvement" also refers to such other specific improvements or types of improvements, the installation of which, either by the subdivider, by public agencies, by private utilities, by any other entity approved by the local agency or by a combination thereof, is necessary or convenient to insure conformity to or implementation of the general plan. . . . or any specific plan. . . .

66474. A legislative body of a city or county shall deny approval of a final or tentative subdivision map if it makes any of the following findings:

(a) That the proposed map is not consistent with applicable general and specific plans.

(b) That the design or improvement of the proposed subdivision is not consistent with applicable general and specific plans.

(c) That the site is not physically suitable for the type of development.

(d) That the site is not physically suitable for the proposed density of development.

(e) That the design of the subdivision or the proposed improvements are likely to cause substantial environmental damage or substantially and avoidably injure fish or wildlife or their habitat.

(f) That the design of the subdivision or the type of improvements is likely to cause serious public health problems.

(g) That the design of the subdivision or the type of improvements will conflict with easements, acquired by the public at large, for access through or use of, property within the proposed subdivision. . . .

———

Comments: The key to the reach of subdivision regulations in California lies in the definitions of "design" and "improvement," as well as in the requirement that the ordinance contain provisions necessary to implement the community plan. For a discussion of planning enabling legislation see *supra* pp. 70-81. Since the California planning enabling legislation contains a comprehensive list of mandatory and optional planning elements, see *supra* p. 75, the scope of subdivision control regulation in California will be as wide as the policies contained in the local plan. For another statute containing a comprehensive list of subdivision control standards see N.J. Stat. Ann. §§ 40:55D-38 to 40:55D-42 (West Supp. 1977).

Note also the environmental review criteria built into the California statute. For another statute containing similar environmental criteria see Colo. Rev. Stat. § 30-28-133 (1973). These requirements are novel in subdivision control enabling legislation.

———

NEW HAMPSHIRE REVISED STATUTES ANNOTATED § 36:21 (Supp. 1977)

Before exercising . . . [subdivision control powers], the planning board shall adopt regulations governing the subdivision of land within its jurisdiction. Such regulations may provide against such scattered or premature subdivision of land as would involve danger or injury to health, safety or prosperity by reason of the lack of water supply, drainage, transportation, or other public services, or necessitate an excessive expenditure of public funds for the supply of such services. . . . [The remainder of this section generally follows the provisions of the Standard Act, *supra,* in its enabling authority for subdivision control. — Eds.]

Comments: 1. New Hampshire is one of the few states that has authorized the use of subdivision controls as a timing and growth management technique. Maryland legislation contains authority for what is known as an adequate public facilities ordinance. Md. Ann. Code art. 43, § 387C (Supp. 1977). The ordinance is based on mandated comprehensive plans "for the provision of adequate water supply systems and sewerage and solid waste disposal systems and solid waste acceptance facilities." *Id.* § 387C(a)(1). These plans must "[p]rovide for the orderly expansion and extension" of these facilities. *Id.* § 387C(b)(4)(i). The statute then provides:

> 3. No State or local authority empowered to grant building permits or to approve subdivision plans, maps, or plats, shall grant any such permit or record or approve any such plan, map, or plat which provides for individual or community water supply or sewerage systems, or for solid waste acceptance facilities, unless such systems or facilities are found to be in conformance with the county plan, amendments, or revisions thereof. This means that:
>
> (i) No building permit shall be approved (1) where existing facilities are inadequate to serve the proposed development, taking into consideration all other existing and approved developments in the service area, or (2) which will cause facilities for conveyance, pumping, storage or treatment of water, sewage or solid waste to be overloaded.
>
> (ii) No subdivision plat shall be approved in areas where, taking into account all existing and approved subdivision plats and building permits in the service area, facilities for conveyance, pumping, storage, or treatment of water, sewage, and solid waste to serve the proposed development would either (1) not be completed in time to serve the development, or (2) if completed, would not be adequate to serve the development without causing overloading of the facilities.

Id. § 387C(d)(3). There is authority in the State Department of Health to "[p]rovide for control, limitation or prohibition of installing or using individual or community water supply or sewerage systems," *id.* § 387C(c)(1)(i), and to require the installation of and connection to community water supply, sewerage or solid waste systems, *id.* § 387C(c)(1)(v).

Within this framework, the adequate public facilities ordinance can be used as a growth control and timing technique in a manner very similar to the points system approved in the *Ramapo* case, *infra* p. 1037. Whether the adoption and implementation of this technique in the subdivision rather than the zoning context raises different legal and constitutional issues should be considered once the materials that follow on the substantive reach of the subdivision control ordinance have been examined.

Finally, a broadly-phrased grant of subdivision control authority is contained in the Washington legislation. It provides that "[t]he city, town, or county legislative body shall inquire into the public use and interest proposed to be served by the establishment of the subdivision or dedication." Wash. Rev. Code Ann. § 58.17.110 (Supp. 1977). Conceivably, this broad grant of authority might include the authority to impose the timing and growth controls specifically authorized in the New Hampshire and Maryland legislation.

2. For early discussions of subdivision control legislation, which are still helpful, see Reps, Control of Land Subdivision by Municipal Planning Boards, 40 Cornell L.Q. 258 (1955); Note, Land Subdivision Control, 65 Harv. L. Rev. 1226 (1952); Note, Platting, Planning and Protection, A Summary of Subdivision Statutes, 36 N.Y.U.L. Rev. 1205 (1961).

---

2. The Subdivision Control Ordinance: Standards and Procedures

At this point, and before examining the content of a typical subdivision control ordinance, we might first summarize the major characteristics of subdivision control regulation. This land use control technique is based on platting or tract-splitting as its triggering legally consequential event. Major developments such as apartments, mobile home parks, industrial parks and shopping centers are outside the subdivision control process because they usually do not require the division and sale of individual lots. For this reason, subdivision control is usually applied primarily to single-family residential development.

The subdivision control process thus creates a fair amount of fragmentation in the local land use control system. Not only are many developments outside the reach of the subdivision control ordinance, but that ordinance overlaps in turn with the zoning ordinance, which often controls some of the same aspects of land development. This overlap with zoning also requires dual local approvals in many instances, as many developments will require both zoning and subdivision control approval. True, many subdivisions will be presented for approval for single family development in zoning districts in which the development is allowable. But the tendency of many jurisdictions to zone at density levels just below market demand may require a rezoning even for single family subdivisions. In this situation, dual approvals will be required, thereby lengthening and complicating the land use control system for the developer. Planned unit development controls, see *infra* p. 854, are one attempt at the local level to integrate this dual system of control.

This fragmentation in control technique has been overcome in the American Law Institute's Model Land Development Code, which has integrated conventional zoning and subdivision control into a unified land development control system. Special permits for development, which are authorized under that system, may be issued for what is commonly treated as a subdivision under the traditional subdivision control enabling legislation:

> If a development ordinance does not permit a division of land into parcels as general development, the [local] Land Development Agency shall grant a special development permit for the division of land into parcels if it finds that each parcel resulting from the division can reasonably be developed under the general or special development provisions of the development ordinance.

American Law Institute, A Model Land Development Code § 2-203 (1976). As commentary to the Code notes, "This control will not be exercised as part of the ordinary course of development regulation, not under any separate procedure for land subdivision." *Id.* at 46-47. The authority to impose substantive requirements on subdivisions must thus be found in other provisions of the Code authorizing land development regulation.

The ALI Code has generally provided, through the special permit system, for a method of administrative review of new development that extends beyond the subdivision control context. Under the traditional system, in which zoning and subdivision control administration are separated, it is only in the subdivision control ordinance that a purely administrative system of land use control is provided. It is to be distinguished from the as-of-right, predesignation of permitted land uses that characterizes the zoning ordinance.

In the subdivision control ordinance, which may be fairly complex, a series of substantive standards are provided for each of the facilities which are authorized to be regulated by the subdivision control statute. The following example, taken from a model subdivision control ordinance, illustrates typical design standards for streets:

4.18 *Street Design*
Proposed streets shall be in harmony and conformance with existing and proposed streets, as shown on the Town (City) Master Plan or Official Map. Street patterns shall give due consideration to contours and natural features. Where required by the Board, provision shall be made for the extension of the street pattern to abutting undeveloped property. Every proposed street in a subdivision shall be laid out and constructed as required by these regulations. Where a subdivision abuts an existing street with an inadequate alignment, or right-of-way width, the subdivision plat shall include in the street dedication all land needed to meet the standards established by these regulations, and as approved by the Board.

Permanent dead end streets shall not exceed 600 feet in length, and shall terminate in a turnaround 100 feet in diameter, with a paved area 80 feet in diameter.

Temporary dead end streets, where future extension to another outlet is approved by the Board, or where indicated on the plan, may exceed 600 feet in length. In such cases the full width of the right-of-way to the subdivision property line shall be dedicated to the municipality.

Except where it is impracticable, because of the character of the land, streets shall intersect so that within 75 feet of the intersection the street lines are at right angles, and the grade within 100 feet does not exceed one percent. No structure or planting shall impair corner visibility.

The plan of any proposed subdivision shall show all work required to connect and complete the improvements and utilities between the proposed street pattern and any connecting street in an existing subdivision.

All streets shall be constructed and paved, and all bridges, culverts, drainage structures, storm sewers, gutters, drainage ditches, and other improvements required by the subdivision plat and accompanying documents, shall be installed in conformance with the standards and specifications adopted by the governing body.

4.19 *Classification of Streets*

The classification of Town (City) streets shall be as defined in the Town (City) Master Plan or Official Map, and the classification of new streets and streets not shown on such plan shall be as determined by the Board. The following standards of design shall apply to streets maintained by the Town (City):

Classification	Minimum Pavement Width Feet	Minimum Right-of-Way Feet	Maximum Gradient Percent	Minimum Centerline Radius of Curve Feet
Arterial	44	100	5%	955
Major Collector	40	80	8	700
Minor Collector	30	60	10	400
Local Service	24	50	12	125

The minimum gradient shall be 0.5 percent.

The Board may modify the maximum and minimum gradient for short lengths of streets where, in its judgment, existing topographic conditions or the preservation of natural features indicate that such modification will result in the best subdivision of land.

The Board may require greater width of right-of-way where, in its judgment, the demands of present or future traffic make it desirable or where topographic conditions create a need for greater width for grading.

Office of State Planning, State of New Hampshire, Handbook of Subdivision Practice 107-08 (1972). Comparable requirements are provided for other facilities. For a comprehensive model subdivision control ordinance see R. Freilich & P. Levi, Model Subdivision Regulations: Text and Commentary (1975).

The subdivision control approval process usually consists of a fairly standardized procedure in which the subdivision plat is submitted for review, given tentative and then final approval, and then placed on record. These procedures permit a process of review and negotiation between the planning agency and the developer in which the requirements of the subdivision control ordinance are applied to the particular subdivision under review. How this review and approval procedure works is outlined in the following excerpt:

GREEN, LAND SUBDIVISION IN PRINCIPLES AND PRACTICE OF URBAN PLANNING 443, 449-54 (W. Goodman & E. Freund eds. 1968)

PROCEDURES

A fairly common set of procedures involves the following five steps prior to the time that the developer is permitted to make sales of his lots. . . .

Pre-Application Procedures. Many subdivision regulations suggest (without requiring) that the developer begin by submitting a "back-of-an-envelope" sketch of his proposed subdivision to the planning staff for its recommendations, along with a map of the general location, indicating the principal features. This gives him an opportunity to secure guidance as to what will probably be required of him before he has incurred great expense in making detailed plans and provides the planner with information in undertaking a review of the plat. . . .

Preliminary Plat. The first formal action normally required of the developer is submission of a "preliminary plat" for approval by the appropriate local agency. While the name suggests that the decision on this plat is rather tentative, nothing could be further from the truth. The decision made on the preliminary plat is the most important step in the entire approval process, because on the basis of this decision work will begin on opening and constructing streets, installing utilities systems, and so forth. After expenditures have been made on such permanent installations, it is extremely unlikely that any major changes will be required or made at a later stage in the approval process.

Because of this importance, regulations usually spell out in considerable detail the information to be shown on or to accompany the preliminary plat. In the absence of such information the chances of an unfortunate mistake by the approval agency are magnified, so the draftsman of the regulations must treat these provisions with some care. . . .

The plat must be submitted in sufficient time and with enough copies to permit consideration and recommendations by various interested agencies, such as the city engineer, the department of public works, the school board, the recreation commission, the health department, and so on. All these recommendations should be received by the approval agency prior to its hearing.

Under most ordinances the planning commission grants or denies approval of the preliminary plat. In a few instances the local governing board or any agency made up of representatives of various interested municipal departments may have this responsibility. Whatever the case, the approval agency customarily meets with the applicant after consideration of the recommendations by the interested departments and either approves, approves subject to stated conditions, or disapproves of the plat. Not infrequently there will be considerable negotiation and discussion between the developer and the approval agency, at which time agreement may be reached as to appropriate modifications in the plat or conditions on the approval. Some regulations provide for an appeal to the local governing board from the decision made at this time, although this is not usual.

Construction of Improvements. Most subdivision regulations prohibit the construction of any improvements in a subdivision until the preliminary plat has been approved. Once this approval has been granted, however, the prohibition reverses and becomes an affirmative requirement that improvements be made before the final plat is submitted for approval.

Frequently the developer is given three or four options; e.g., he may (1) actually complete construction of all required improvements, (2) post a performance bond guaranteeing such construction within a given period, (3) submit a petition that the municipality construct the improvements and levy the cost against lots in the subdivision under its usual special-assessment procedures, or (4) give the municipality a mortgage on the property in the subdivision, releasable in stages as improvements are completed.

The municipality's decision as to how wide a range of options to offer developers usually turns on the extent to which it wishes to restrain the rate of subdivision activity. If it is threatened by a wave of "premature subdivision," it may put on the brakes by simply requiring that developers incur the expense of completing installation of improvements before they can make any sales of lots.

Because of the growing practice of marketing houses and lots rather than undeveloped building sites in a new subdivision, provision is made in most current subdivision regulations for issuance of building permits for construction of houses concurrently with the construction of streets, utilities, and other improvements.

From an administrative standpoint, a great deal of the responsibility for enforcement of subdivision regulations shifts during this phase from the planning staff to the city engineer and other officials concerned that proper construction standards are met. Their certificates that improvements have been completed in accordance with the city's standards are a usual prerequisite to submission of the final plat to the municipality.

Final Plat. While subdivision regulations customarily require submission and approval of a "final plat," some cities report that it is preferable to require two rather different plats at this stage. The first is denominated an "engineering plat" which might be thought of as an "as-built" plat giving details of construction and location of the improvements which have been installed. The primary purpose of this plat is to provide the city engineer and other interested departments with a permanent record of the location, size, and design of underground utilities, for their use in the course of maintaining such installations. The second could be denominated either a "plat for record" or a "final plat," which shows primarily information relating to land titles (exact lot lines, street rights-of-way, utilities easements, deed restrictions, etc.). It is intended as the plat to be filed in the county registry of deeds (or county recorder's office). Where only a single "final plat" is required, it must show information of both types, frequently at the expense of clarity.

The final plat represents the final stage at which the plat approval agency can do anything about the subdivision. Usually the regulations provide for its submission in approximately the same manner as was required for the preliminary plat, with adequate time and number of copies for distribution to the interested departments who made recommendations earlier. At this time the intention is to assure that the recorded plat will be in accordance with the plans approved earlier and that construction has taken place in accordance with such plans. Under some regulations the local governing board approves the final plat, even though the planning commission was the approval agency for the preliminary plat.

Usually the final plat must be submitted within a stated period (such as a year) after the preliminary plat was approved, unless the developer wishes to start from the beginning once more. This is to prevent the developer from putting the municipal government to the trouble and expense of the approval process when he has no immediate intention of carrying out his plans. At the same time, the statutes of some states recognize that the developer should have some protection against a city's making major changes in its requirements between the time of preliminary plat approval and submission of the final plat. These statutes prevent changes in the zoning of the area for a reasonable period (perhaps two years) after preliminary approval.

Recording of Plat. The final step prior to sale of lots in the subdivision is the recording of the approved plat. The regulations should assure that the final plat is in a form and size which meets the requirements of the registry of deeds. It is not uncommon for other provisions of state law than the subdivision-regulation enabling act to regulate certain aspects of the recording process, such as the size of plats, required certificates of accuracy by the surveyor, certificates of ownership, or other details. In many cases it will be found wise to include such requirements in the subdivision regulations, either specifically or by reference, for the benefit of the property owner who might otherwise overlook them.

    . . . .

Fees. Because the expenses of checking both the plats submitted and the construction work which is done may be substantial, many subdivision regulations provide for payment to the city of fees to cover some of these administrative costs. The few court cases in which the legality of this requirement has been challenged have uniformly been decided in favor of the city. However, any fees imposed should bear a reasonable relationship to the actual costs incurred by the city and they should not be so great as to constitute an impediment to subdivision activity.

Fee bases vary widely. Some regulations provide for a flat fee for all subdivisions, regardless of their size. In other cases there may be a basic charge, plus an additional amount for each lot, each foot of street constructed, each foot of utilities installed, etc. Engineering inspections are particularly costly, and it would seem that a sliding scale to reflect the costs of inspecting varying amounts of improvements would be the most equitable approach.

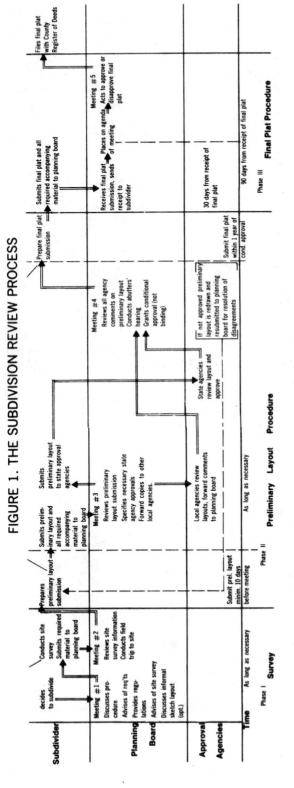

FIGURE 1. THE SUBDIVISION REVIEW PROCESS

Source: Office of State Planning, State of New Hampshire, Handbook of Subdivision Practice 18-19 (1972).

MAP 1. PRELIMINARY SUBDIVISION LAYOUT

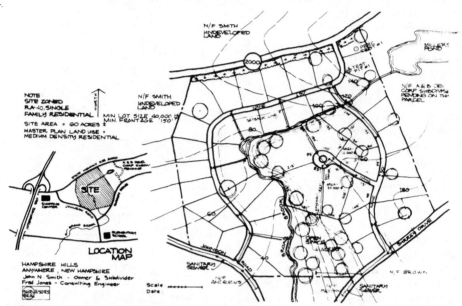

Source: Office of State Planning, State of New Hampshire, Handbook of Subdivision Practice 26 (1972).

MAP 2. FINAL SUBDIVISION PLAT

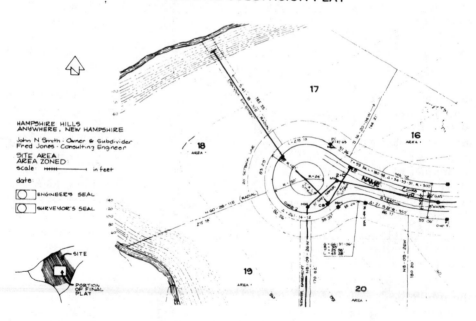

Source: Office of State Planning, State of New Hampshire, Handbook of Subdivision Practice 30 (1972).

Comments: 1. The process of review and negotiation afforded by the subdivision control ordinance creates an entirely different climate for the review of land development proposals than the zoning ordinance. In zoning administration, the outcome of the zoning process is a decision either permitting or not permitting the use of land proposed by the developer, an outcome which is clearly favorable or unfavorable to the developer's interests and which easily triggers a due process or equal protection claim when the development is disallowed. In subdivision control, the planning agency administers a large number of development standards, none of which is sufficiently significant on its own to have a drastic impact on development costs. This fact, the substantial amount of discretion usually built into the administration of the ordinance, and the opportunities for compromise and negotiation in the review process, usually allow for a working out of differences and forestall judicial attacks by developers unhappy with the outcome of a subdivision review.

For example, the model ordinance, § 4.18 *supra* p. 792, requires a minimum pavement width of 24 feet for local service streets and allows the planning board to require a greater width if "the demands of present or future traffic make it desirable." Assume that the board decides to require a greater width of 26 feet, but after negotiation with the developer reduces the requirement to 25 feet. The developer is unlikely to appeal. Because of the discretion accorded the board in imposing this added requirement, a court decision overturning the additional pavement width is not likely. In addition, the extra cost of the additional pavement is sufficiently marginal from the developer's perspective so that an appeal is not worthwhile. These characteristics of the subdivision control process help explain why litigation over subdivision control review is infrequent as compared to litigation over zoning restrictions.

Planners like the process of negotiation and compromise built into subdivision review because it allows them to review proposed subdivisions for assurances on what really interests them — who the developer is, whether it has a good track record in the community, whether it can be depended on to complete the project, and the like. Discretionary standards built into subdivision control ordinances also allow for considerable control in the planning agency over subdivision design, another issue of great interest to planners. In the discussion of planned unit developments, *infra* p. 854, we will examine an even more sophisticated development review technique, modeled on subdivision review, which combines the elements of the subdivision control process with the opportunity to modify elements of the zoning ordinance in order to create more attractive and better designed development projects.

Figure 1 is a schematic presentation of the elements of the subdivision review procedure. Maps 1 and 2 illustrate typical preliminary subdivision layouts and a final subdivision plat.

2. *Enforcement problems.* Problems of draftsmanship and coverage in the subdivision control enabling legislation have created difficult problems of enforcement and easy avenues of evasion which make it possible for subdividers to escape subdivision control review in many instances. One set of problems arises from the definition of subdivision which is contained in the enabling legislation. Most enabling acts now contain a subdivision definition; the definition in the Connecticut statute, *supra* p. 785, is typical. Note that the statute requires a division of land into three or more parcels, and that this division must be for the "purpose . . . of sale or building development." *See generally* R. Anderson, American Law of Zoning § 23.02 (2d ed. 1977).

A similar "purpose" clause led to difficulties in the application of a subdivision definition in the New York health law authorizing state department of health approval of subdivisions. *Slavin v. Ingraham,* 339 N.E.2d 157 (N.Y. 1975). At the time of the case, the health law defined subdivision as "any tract of land . . . divided into five or more parcels . . . for sale or rent as residential lots or residential building plots." The owners of a tract of land sold off a large number of lots of varying sizes, and without exception a residential dwelling was constructed on each of these parcels.

Nevertheless, the court found that no subdivision had taken place within the meaning of the statute. There were no covenants restricting the parcels to residential use, no zoning regulations were applicable, and "the record is barren of proof that petitioners sold the pieces of realty singly or collectively for residential purposes or held themselves out as subdividers of the land for said purposes." *Id.* at 159. The court was unwilling to attribute a residential use of these parcels after their sale to the sellers. There was a dissent, which noted that "[u]nder these circumstances, it would cast common sense to the winds to fail to infer that petitioners knew that the parcels of their property was being marketed for residential use. . . ." *Id.* at 160. *Cf. Herrick v. Ingraham,* 363 N.Y.S.2d 665 (N.Y. App. Div. 1975) (random sale of lots in rural area for recreational purposes not a subdivision). However, a void for vagueness objection to the statutory subdivision definition has been rejected. *State v. Rutkowski,* 380 N.E.2d 166 (N.Y. 1978).

There is a conflict of authority over whether municipalities may expand on the definition of subdivision which is contained in the enabling legislation. *Compare Peninsula Corp. v. Planning & Zoning Comm'n,* 199 A.2d 1 (Conn. 1964) (statutory definition controlling), *with Delaware Midland Corp. v. Incorporated Village of Westhampton Beach,* 359 N.Y.S.2d 944 (N.Y. Sup. Ct. 1974) (trial court; *contra*), *aff'd,* 369 N.Y.S.2d 378 (N.Y. App. Div. 1975), 355 N.E.2d 302 (N.Y. 1976).

There are limits to municipal imagination, however. Even when the definition of subdivision is expanded to include the "dedication of a road through a tract" an apartment developer who creates an access road may be clever enough to avoid the ordinance. *See Vinyard v. St. Louis County,* 399 S.W.2d 99 (Mo. 1966). *Cf. Gerber v. Town of Clarkstown,* 356 N.Y.S.2d 926 (N.Y. Sup. Ct. 1974) (trial court; condominium not a subdivision).

Note that the Connecticut statute prohibits the subdivision of land unless plat for the subdivision has been approved. Other statutes provide for more indirect sanctions. The Standard Planning Act, *supra* § 16, provided for a statutory monetary penalty whenever the owner of land sold land "by reference to or exhibition" of a plat before having the plat approved. Many state statutes contain this provision. For a liberal interpretation of this kind of provision of the facts see *Commonwealth v. Fisher,* 350 A.2d 428 (Pa. Commw. Ct. 1976) (penalty not void as restraint on alienation).

Nevertheless, evasion of the prohibition is easy under this kind of statute if the landowner simply conveys a parcel out of a larger tract through a conventional metes and bounds boundary description. Nothing in the statute prevents the records clerk from accepting this kind of a conveyance for recording. Several remedies have been suggested to meet this evasion problem. If they go too far, the statute may be held unconstitutional as a restraint on alienation. *Kass v. Lewin,* 104 So.2d 572 (Fla. 1958). The statute considered in the *Kass* case provided that "no lands shall be conveyed" until the subdivision plat had been "approved and recorded." There are a variety of other possibilities:

(1) Building permits can be refused in subdivisions which have not been approved under the subdivision control ordinance. The difficulty here is that this practice places the penalty for lack of compliance on the buyer of a lot in the unapproved subdivision. For cases refusing to sustain this practice when a building permit was withheld from an innocent purchaser see *Keizer v. Adams,* 471 P.2d 938 (Cal. 1970); *State ex rel. Craven v. City of Tacoma,* 385 P.2d 372 (Wash. 1963). The *Keizer* case did point out that a deed made contrary to the terms of the act in an unapproved subdivision was voidable at the option of the grantee. For a statute conferring this remedy see Wash. Rev. Code Ann. § 58.17.210 (Supp. 1977). *Compare Pratt v. Adams,* 40 Cal. Rptr. 505 (Cal. App. 1964) (permit may be refused to lot owner who participated in partition action intended to evade subdivision law).

(2) Some statutes forbid the issuing of a building permit except on a lot which abuts a street which is "suitably improved" to the satisfaction of the municipality. For a case upholding this requirement see *Brous v. Smith,* 106 N.E.2d 503 (N.Y. 1952). This requirement will at least prevent the building of homes on streets that have not been accepted by the municipality, and the municipality can use this leverage to compel compliance with the subdivision control ordinance. However, the New York law exempts construction on an existing highway. Since street improvement is one of the important keys to enforcement under subdivision control ordinances, strip development along existing highways is difficult to control. The problem is compounded by statutes which place a number of lots minimum in the subdivision definition, and exempt subdivisions with three or five lots. This exemption allows the small builder to construct two to three houses at a time along a highway without having to get approval. *See Jack Homes, Inc. v. Baldwin,* 241 N.Y.S.2d 487 (N.Y. Sup. Ct. 1963) (trial court).

(3) As noted earlier, some statutes, like the Connecticut law, require plan commission approval for all subdivisions, whether or not they are to be recorded. But this requirement must be accompanied by a tight definition of subdivision, *i.e.,* the division of any lot or parcel into two or more lots or parcels. This kind of law presents enforcement problems. It also arouses political resistance from small builders who must go through expensive and time-consuming procedures to get approval, and from farmers who must

secure plan commission approval before they can sell their sons a quarter-section on which to build a house.

Some statutes have tried to meet these objections by enacting exemptions or reduced approval requirements for small or so-called "minor" subdivisions. The California statute is one example:

> A tentative and final map shall be required for all subdivisions creating five or more parcels, five or more condominiums . . . or a community apartment project containing five or more parcels, except where:
>
> (a) The land before division contains less than five acres, each parcel created by the division abuts upon a maintained public street or highway and no dedications or improvements are required by the legislative body, or
>
> (b) Each parcel created by the division has a gross area of 20 acres or more and has an approved access to a maintained public street or highway, or
>
> (c) The land consists of a parcel or parcels of land having approved access to a public street or highway which comprises part of a tract of land zoned for industrial or commercial development, and which has the approval of the governing body as to street alignments and widths, or
>
> (d) Each parcel created by the division has a gross area of not less than 40 acres or is not less than a quarter of a quarter section; provided, however, that a local ordinance may specify tentative and final map approval for a subdivision in which one or more of the resultant parcels is between 40 acres and 60 acres in size.
> A parcel map shall be required for those subdivisions described in subdivisions (a), (b), (c), and (d).

Cal. Gov't Code § 66426 (Deering Supp. 1977). Distinguishing between large and small subdivisions for purposes of regulations has been approved. *Noble v. Chairman & Members of Township Comm'n,* 219 A.2d 335 (N.J. Super. 1966).

(4) A variety of other remedies are available. The sale of lots in an unapproved subdivision may be enjoined. *See, e.g.,* N.Y. Town Law § 268(2) (Supp. 1977). Purchasers may sue to set aside conveyances in a subdivision which has not been approved. An alternative Blue Sky approach has been suggested; the seller would be required to inform buyers that the lots offered for sale is in an unapproved subdivision. *See generally* Note, Prevention of Subdivision Control Evasion in Indiana, 40 Ind. L.J. 445 (1965).

(5) Sanctions may be applied by the federal mortgage insuring agency. If the agency refuses to insure a house built in an unapproved subdivision, the builder who contemplates using federally-insured mortgages may be required to comply with the subdivision ordinance.

B. SUBSTANTIVE CONTROLS AND REQUIREMENTS

GARIPAY v. TOWN OF HANOVER

Supreme Court of New Hampshire
116 N.H. 34, 351 A.2d 64 (1976)

GRIFFITH, Justice.

This is an appeal under RSA 36:34 (Supp. 1975) from a decision of the planning board to the town of Hanover denying plaintiffs' agents' requests for preliminary approval of a subdivision in that town. The issues were submitted to the trial court on an agreed statement of facts and transferred without ruling by *Johnson,* J. The planning board's denial of the request for approval of the subdivision was based on a finding that Hemlock Road, the access road connecting the proposed subdivision to the main network of town roads, would be inadequate to handle the increased traffic created by forty-nine new homes. The question presented to us in whether the planning board is authorized under RSA ch. 36 and the town ordinances to reject a subdivision proposal which intrinsically conforms to the requirements of the town zoning ordinance and regulations solely because of the inadequacy of an offsite, town-owned road.

The dangers posed by the inadequacy of Hemlock Road to accommodate increased traffic demands are discussed at length in the minutes of the planning board meetings of December 18, 1973, January 8, 1974, and January 15, 1975. The location of the proposed subdivision is on top of a hill to which Hemlock Road provides the only access. This road is described as "narrow, steep and winding, having a width of fourteen or sixteen feet, shoulders only two feet wide, a grade which at times exceeds 15%, and a course which results in "at least one horseshoe curve." Consequently, the planning board found that the road would pose "a serious danger to both pedestrian and vehicular traffic." The town police chief expressed "serious reservations about [his] department being able to respond to an emergency in this area, in the wintertime." There was evidence that in winter the steepness of the road often forces residents to leave their cars at the foot of the hill, and that while the limited available space can accommodate the present vehicles, congestion created by further abandoned cars from the subdivision could cause serious hazards.

The plaintiffs do not contest the accuracy of these findings. Their argument is that the planning board is precluded from considering offsite factors and must limit its investigation to whether the subdivision internally complies with state and town requirements. In our opinion both the state-enabling legislation and the Hanover subdivision regulations provide authority for the board's decision.

RSA 36:21 (Supp. 1975) provides that town planning boards may promulgate regulations which "provide against such scattered or premature subdivision of land as would involve danger or injury to health, safety, or prosperity by reason of the lack of ... transportation ... or other public services, or necessitate an excessive expenditure of public funds for the supply of such services." Pursuant to this statute, Hanover has enacted article III (B) of its subdivision regulations, which uses language identical to that quoted above. These provisions plainly empower the planning board to take offsite factors into its consideration, insofar as they render subdivisions "scattered or premature."

The plaintiffs argue that the proposed subdivision cannot be deemed "scattered or premature" because there are already some eighteen homes in the area. Plaintiffs further maintain that such a finding is precluded by language on a map contained in the Hanover master plan, which designates the site "to be developed after 1970." According to this argument once an area is found not to be premature for a particular degree of development, it must be found ripe for all levels of development. In other words, where there are presently some homes in the area, the planning board may not find that an addition of forty-nine homes would be premature, regardless of the amount of public services available.

We reject this interpretation as too narrow, for prematurity is a relative rather than an absolute concept. The statute, by defining a "scattered and premature" development as one which poses a danger to the public through insufficiency of services, sets up a guide for the planning board's determination. The board must ascertain what amount of development, in relation to what quantum of services available, will present the hazard described in the statute and regulations. At the point where such a hazard is created, further development becomes premature. Thus in the instant case, although the available services suffice to meet the need of the present eighteen homes, when an additional forty-nine homes will endanger the well-being of residents both within and contiguous to the development, the statute and regulations authorize the planning board to find the subdivision premature. Thus the action of the Hanover Planning Board was within its statutory mandate.

Case law in other jurisdictions recognizes that absent specific statutory authority a planning board is authorized to reject a proposed subdivision because of an inadequate offsite access road under a general statutory mandate such as that found in RSA 36:21 (Supp.1975): "[Planning board regulations] generally may include provisions which will tend to create conditions favorable to health, safety, convenience, or prosperity." *Mtr. of Pearson Kent Corp. v. Bear,* 28 N.Y.2d 396, 322 N.Y.S.2d 235, 271 N.E.2d 218 (1971);

Forest Constr. Co. v. Planning & Zoning Comm'n, 155 Conn. 669, 236 A.2d 917 (1967); *see Isabelle v. Newbury,* 114 N. H. 399, 402, 321 A.2d 570, 572 (1974). "Subdivision controls are imposed on the supportable premise that a new subdivision is not an island, but an integral part of the whole community which must mesh efficiently with the municipal pattern of streets, sewers, water lines and other installations which provide essential services and vehicular access.... [O]ffsite circumstances may be considered by the reviewing board, and may provide the basis for denying approval of a plat." 3 R. Anderson, American Law of Zoning § 19.36 (1968).

Appeal dismissed.

GRIMES, J., did not sit; the others concurred.

BAKER v. PLANNING BOARD OF FRAMINGHAM

Supreme Judicial Court of Massachusetts
353 Mass. 141, 228 N.E.2d 831 (1967)

KIRK, Justice. In the Superior Court the judge entered a decree that the planning board of Framingham (the board) had exceeded its authority in disapproving the definitive plan for the subdivision of approximately eleven acres of land owned by the plaintiff (Baker). The decree annulled the decision of the board and directed that it promptly take further proceedings under the subdivision control law consistent with the applicable statutes and the decree.... The board's appeal brings the case to us.

Baker's bill in equity was brought under G.L. c. 41, § 81BB. After the parties were at issue on the pleadings, the case was referred to a master whose report was confirmed by interlocutory decree, from which no appeal was taken. No report of the evidence was authorized; no summary of the evidence was requested. The only questions presented, therefore, are (1) whether the findings of the master are contradictory, mutually inconsistent or plainly wrong, and (2) whether the decree is within the scope of the pleadings and supported by the facts found. . . .

We summarize the admissions made in the pleadings and the facts found by the master which, in light of the standard of review and the arguments made, are pertinent to the issues to be resolved. In December, 1934, Baker and her husband granted to the town by recorded deed an easement (ten feet wide), through land owned by them, for the purpose of constructing and maintaining a pipe drain or excavating and maintaining a ditch of "sufficient depth to permit without interruption the flow of surface water and drainage" through the Baker land. The town excavated a ditch which received water accumulating on Brook Street and channeled the water across Baker's land to land of another where it entered a fifteen inch drain controlled by the town, and thence was carried to the Sudbury River. Because of the development of land in the area since the easement was granted, including the construction of a church with a large paved parking lot, the volume of water now accumulating on Brook Street during heavy rainstorms has greatly increased. The ditch cannot carry off the increased volume of water to the drain pipe on the adjoining land, and the drain pipe, in turn, cannot carry away the water which is collected in and over the ditch. The result is that the Baker land becomes flooded for a considerable area on both sides of the ditch, and the land consequently serves as a flood control or "retention area" for the town, to the extent of 16,200 cubic feet of water, during and after heavy rains and thaws.

Baker's definitive plan was submitted on February 26, 1965. A preliminary plan had been submitted earlier. The board of health approved the definitive plan. G.L. c. 41, §§ 81M, 81U. The planning board did not modify the definitive plan but, by majority vote, disapproved it and stated its reasons. G.L. c. 41, § 81U. In summary, the board's reasons for disapproval relate to the sewerage and water drainage systems proposed in the definitive plan. The sewerage system would require the construction and maintenance of a lift or pumping station to tie in with the town's sewerage system, whereas the board favored a gravity system which would not require a lift station. The proposed water drainage system, although adequate for the subdivision, would deprive the town of the retention area on Baker's land and, in consequence, would overtax the downstream drainage system outside the subdivision. The board stated that neither the preliminary nor the definitive plan, as submitted, delineated the town's drainage easement across the Baker land. The board disapproved on the additional ground that "[a]pproval . . . would not be in the best interest of the Town, since it would negate the PURPOSE section 81-M" with special reference to ". . . securing safety in cases of . . . flood, . . . securing adequate provision for water, sewerage, drainage and other requirements where necessary in a subdivision.'" [These citations are to the subdivision control enabling act. — Eds.]

Additional findings by the master were that the majority of the board believed that they were justified in disapproving the plan because of the additional expense which the town would incur by the enlargement of the town's drainage system to compensate for the loss of use of the Baker land as a water retention area, and by the construction and maintenance of the lift station for the sewerage system. The plan with respect to the sewerage and drainage systems for the subdivision met all of the requirements of the statutes and of the rules and regulations of the board. The town already operates several lift or pumping stations in its sewerage system. The omission from the plans of the town's easement across Baker's land did not deceive and was not intended to deceive the board, but was the result of an understanding between the town engineer and Baker's engineer that the town probably would reroute its drainage system through pipes on one of the streets shown on the plans.

The master's ultimate finding was that the board "had but a single reason for disapproving the . . . [definitive] plan, namely, the extra cost to the Town of handling the sewage and surface drainage produced by the subdivision." We think that the ultimate finding of the master cannot be aid to be plainly wrong and that his subsidiary findings are consistent with it.

The decree based on the master's report was right. Our decisions dealing with the powers of planning boards as clarified by G.L. c. 41 § 81M, hold that, having exercised due regard for insuring compliance with the applicable zoning by-law, approval under § 81U should be given to a plan if it complies with the recommendations of the board of health and the reasonable rules and regulations of the planning board. . . . The zoning by-law is not in issue; the board of health has given its approval; there is no violation of, or failure to comply with, existing rules and regulations. Obviously a planning board may not exercise its authority to disapprove a plan so that a town may continue to use the owner's land as a water storage area and thereby deprive the owner of reasonable use of it. The board's action appears to be based on the assumption that it may disapprove a plan when it considers that "the best interest of the Town" or "the public interest" would be served by the disapproval of installations which meet the established requirements. This is an erroneous assumption and was fully dealt with in *Daley Constr. Co., Inc. v. Planning Bd. of Randolph,* 340 Mass. 149, 163 N.E.2d 27, where the remedial purpose of § 81M was discussed. It was beyond the board's authority to disapprove the plan.

Decree affirmed.

Comments: 1. Both *Baker* and *Garipay* raise questions about the use of subdivision control to monitor growth within the community and the validity of denying subdivision approval on the basis of conditions not intrinsic to the subdivision itself. Would the planning commission in *Garipay* have been within the scope of its authority if the New Hampshire statute (*see supra* p. 788) had not specifically provided against the "scattered or premature subdivision of land" ? In *Pearson Kent Corp. v. Bear,* 271 N.E.2d 218 (N.Y. 1971), "[t]he [planning] commission denied petitioner's development approval, not because it regarded the plan itself as intrinsically not acceptable but because the project was so located as to create danger to nearby residents in the inadequate approaches to the development from the greatly increased demands to be exerted on the existing approaches." *Id.* at 219. In a brief opinion, the court noted that while the local charter and subdivision control law were "addressed to approval or disapproval internal to the subdivision" the commission was not prevented from considering "the impact of the proposed development on adjacent territory and property within its jurisdiction. . . . These matters are the routine functions of the commission." *Id.* Do these holdings improperly give control over new subdivisions to municipalities through the power to withold improvements to off-site public facilities? If the developer because of these decisions is forced to make off-site improvements is this a valid exercise of the subdivision control power? Was this the vice of the *Baker* case?

Baker was qualified in *Hamilton v. Planning Bd.,* 345 N.E.2d 906 (Mass. App. Ct. 1976), in which the planning board disapproved the subdivision because of the failure to meet flooding problems through adequate drainage on the subdivision site.

> The judge's finding that the board's decision was motivated by the need to protect proposed homes within the locus sufficiently distinguishes the present case from those in which a planning board had disapproved a plan adequate for the proposed subdivision solely because it would overtax existing municipal facilities or otherwise adversely affect the public interest.

Id. at 907, citing *Baker.*

2. Design and access considerations pose much less of a problem since they present a design question which relates directly to the subdivision. In fact, the adequacy of the subdivider's plans for streets and highways is an important factor in the review process. Planning commissions will often require, as a condition to subdivision approval, that internal streets be of sufficient width and satisfactory design, and that access be adequate.

In *Forest Constr. Co. v. Planning & Zoning Comm'n,* 236 A.2d 917 (Conn. 1967), a subdivision was denied approval because only one access was provided for 110 lots, thereby causing all traffic from the subdivision to be discharged at one intersection. The denial was found to be within the commission's authority to reject applications for development which would be hazardous to the health and welfare of the community. *See also Burke & McCaffrey v. City of Merriam,* 424 P.2d 483 (Kan. 1967) (upholding denial of subdivision because of plan's cul-de-sac design); *Isabelle v. Town of Newbury,* 321 A.2d 570 (N.H. 1974) (upholding denial of subdivision because lot ownership pattern jeopardized access in case of fire).

3. Some courts will reverse the denial of a subdivision when it is based on extrinsic factors considered to be beyond the authority conferred by the statute. In *Dosman v. Area Plan Comm'n,* 312 N.E.2d 880 (Ind. App. 1974), the plan commission denied an application for a proposed subdivision on the ground that low-rent public housing, to be built in the subdivision, would be "detrimental to the value of surrounding property." Apparently no standards in the subdivision control ordinance authorized denial for this reason. The denial was reversed on the ground that the commission exceeded its authority because it only had the power to determine whether the subdivision met the standards established by the ordinance. *See Owens v. Glenarm Land Co.,* 539 P.2d 544 (Ariz. App. 1975) (county board held to be without authority to require proof of the availability of domestic water as a condition to approval). *Cf. Robinson v. Lintz,* 420 P.2d 923 (Ariz. 1966) (county may not avoid time limits of subdivision control statute by purporting to act under related enabling legislation).

4. Lurking behind some of these cases is an attempt by municipalities to manipulate the subdivision control process by forcing developers to provide services and facilities not properly chargeable to the subdivision. Courts have held that the developer cannot be forced to resolve problems common to the community for which he is not responsible. In *Baltimore Plan Comm'n v. Victor Dev. Co.,* 275 A.2d 478 (Md. App. 1971), the court held that the commission could not reject the subdivision on the ground that the occupancy of apartments proposed for the subdivision would create an increase in the local population which would in turn cause the public schools to be overcrowded.

In *Florham Park Inv. Co. v. Planning Bd.,* 224 A.2d 352 (N.J.L. 1966), approval of a subdivision was denied because it was thought that construction of a planned highway across the subdivision would make lots in the subdivision substandard as required by local regulations. This denial was reversed, the court noting that "[t]o deprive plaintiff of the right to use and improve its property for an indefinite time, while awaiting the final action of a third party which may come in one year or ten or never, is arbitrary and unreasonable." *Id.* at 356. Some weight was placed by the court on the fact that the highway agency's plans for the highway were indefinite. What if the route were permanently fixed and known? Would this be a reason for denial? Consult the material on official maps, *supra* p. 90. *See also Divan Builders, Inc. v. Planning Bd.,* 300 A.2d 883 (N.J.L. 1973) (developer could not be made to contribute to construction cost of off-site municipal drainage system as condition to subdivision approval).

C. DEDICATIONS AND DEVELOPMENT CHARGES

In many of the cases discussed in the preceding section the subdivision had been disapproved because facilities intended to serve the subdivision were inadequate. In these cases, does the municipality have an alternative to disapproval which can assure that the required facility will be provided? For example, if a subdivision is submitted with inadequate internal streets and exits, could the municipality simply require the subdivider to dedicate additional land for streets and exits as needed, and then approve the subdivision once this condition has been met?

In addition to requiring the provision of necessary on-site facilities, such as streets and drainage facilities, municipalities may frequently require, as a condition to plat approval, that subdivision developers dedicate a certain portion of the land in the development to the municipality to be used for public purposes such as streets and highways, parks and schools. Construction of the improvement is usually required in the case of streets and other internal improvements actually serving the subdivision. Land dedications only are usually required for parks and schools; the facility is then improved or constructed by the municipality. When the subdivision is too small or topographical conditions such that a land dedication cannot reasonably be required for schools and parks, the municipality may require the subdivider to pay a fee in lieu of dedication which is equivalent to the amount of land that would otherwise have been dedicated by the developer. Usually the developer is required to contribute a fixed amount for each lot.

These land dedications and lot fees have presented a series of complex conceptual issues for resolution when developers have challenged them in court. Land dedications and lot fees are often challenged by developers on the ground that they constitute a taking without compensation. Land set aside for these improvements subtracts from the land available for development, while lot fees (unless they are passed on to homebuyers in the subdivision) are a charge against the developer's profits. Because these constitutional issues arise in the subdivision control rather than in the zoning setting, conventional zoning-police power justifications may not be available and municipalities have invoked numerous theories to uphold dedication and lot fee requirements. The simplest and superficially the easiest justification for these requirements arises from the supposed voluntary nature of the subdivision control process. Developers are not compelled to subdivide their land. If they do, this act is voluntary, a request for approval from the municipality which can be viewed as a privilege to be bestowed on the developer at the municipality's discretion. While the privilege rationale has seen its day in the United States Supreme Court and elsewhere, it occasionally reappears in the subdivision control context as a justification for dedications and lot fees. Thus in *Mid-Continent Builders, Inc. v. Midwest City*, 539 P.2d 1377 (Okla. 1975), the Oklahoma court invoked reasoning of this kind to justify subdivision improvement requirements:

> It is also to be remembered, in regard to Appellant's contention that the city "took" their property by forcing

them to dedicate the water mains to city use as a condition of approving their plat, that no one required Appellants to subdivide this property and devote it to the public enterprise of city building. They could have kept it unplatted and have devoted it to any use that did not require the filing of a plat and an invitation to people to come in, to buy tracts and to build homes. However, when they did embark upon these developmental activities, necessarily they must comply with the existing ordinances.

Id. at 1379. How realistic is the court's characterization of the voluntary nature of the subdivider's decision in view of the materials reviewed in the last section on subdivision recording requirements? For general discussion of the standards under which subdivision dedications and fees have been appraised see Johnston, Constitutionality of Subdivision Control Exactions: The Quest for a Rationale, 52 Cornell L.Q. 871 (1967); Note, Subdivision Land Dedication: Objectives and Objections, 27 Stan. L. Rev. 419 (1975).

A somewhat different rationale for internal subdivision improvement requirements is offered by the following case.

BLEVENS v. CITY OF MANCHESTER

Supreme Court of New Hampshire
103 N.H. 284, 170 A.2d 121 (1961)

Petition, for a declaratory judgment (RSA 491:22) seeking a decree of the court that the subdivision ordinance of the city of Manchester adopted October 7, 1958 pursuant to the enabling statute (RSA 36:19 — 36:29) does not apply to the plaintiffs' property acquired by a series of purchases between the years 1936 and 1956. The ordinance imposes a penalty on persons selling a lot within a subdivision unless the plan of said subdivision has been approved by the city planning board. The ordinance which incorporates the regulations of the planning board further provides that no plan showing a subdivision will be approved unless the subdivider pays for all street grading and surfacing, curbing, sidewalks, water mains, sewers and other improvements.

Prior to the enactment of the ordinance, all of the land owned by the plaintiffs was subdivided into numbered house lots and such subdivision was approved by the city surveyor or by the city engineer, and plans showing such subdivision were filed in the Hillsborough County Registry of Deeds. The plaintiffs "have been, since 1946 to 1958, actively engaged in developing their property into a single-family residential area. A substantial number of house lots were sold and a substantial number of private homes were built on this property. All sales were made by reference to the publicly recorded plot showing subdivision of the property. . . . The Court finds that in the development of the property petitioners have expended substantial sums of money and have devoted a great deal of their own labor."

The plaintiffs excepted to findings of the Court and to the following ruling: "The Court rules that the petitioners have not acquired any vested right to continue development sales without compliance with the ordinance and that they may not proceed with the development without compliance with the ordinance." The plaintiffs' exceptions were reserved and transferred by Griffith, J. Additional facts appear in the opinion.

. . . .

KENISON, Chief Justice.

The power of the State to pass enabling legislation permitting municipal ordinances to regulate the subdivision of land has been sustained generally as a proper exercise of the police power. . . . "Since the subdivision of a large tract of land into a number of small building lots and the development thereof, either for residential or industrial purposes increases the value of the land in the aggregate to the subdivider and at the same time imposes new burdens upon the municipality and, if uncontrolled, upon other elements in the community, the validity of imposing a duty upon the subdivider to comply with reasonable conditions relating to location, site plan, location of and width of roads and sidewalks, the installation of necessary storm drains and sewers, and to restrictions on lot sizes so that the subdivision will conform to the local requirements for the safety, health and general welfare of the subsequent owners of the individual lots therein and of the community has been generally recognized." 2 Rathkopf, The Law of Zoning and Planning, ch. 71, § 9 (1960).

Statutes, like RSA 36:19 — 36:29, regulating the subdivision of land seek to promote the orderly and planned growth of relatively undeveloped areas within a municipality. . . . Planless growth and haphazard development accentuate municipal problems in the demand for streets, water and sanitary services which have a direct relation to traffic safety and health. . . . The subdivision of land has a definite economic impact upon the municipality and hence the regulation of subdivision activities has been sustained as a means by which the interests of the public and the general taxpayer may be safeguarded and protected. Since the subdivider of land creates the need for local improvements which are of special benefit to the subdivision, it is considered reasonable that he should bear the cost rather than the municipality and the general taxpayer. . . .

The plaintiffs' contention that "the police power is not involved" in this litigation cannot be accepted. The fact that the lot areas may be satisfactory to the subdivider and prospective purchasers, or that the streets and drainage are also satisfactory to them does not bar the application of the subdivision statute and the ordinance enacted pursuant to it. . . . "One of the problems that has arisen is that of seeing to it that building lots are not laid out and sold and houses put thereon without some decent minimum of street paving and without some decent safety and health minimum of water and sanitary facilities. We all know that where subdivision of land is unregulated lots are sold without paving, water, drainage, or sanitary facilities, and then later the community feels forced to protect the residents and take over the streets and in some way or other provide for the facilities. One of the ways in which law and legislation are attempting to prevent just such situations is that of requiring paving, water, and drainage facilities to be installed, up to minimum public specifications, as a condition of approval of the plat. By means, therefore, of this city planning approach and technique and these developments in modes of subdivision regulation, and evils of the inharmonious street system, overcongestion of population, and deficiency in paving and sanitation and water facilities are coming to be reduced and prevented." Bettman, City and Regional Planning Papers 74 (1946).

. . . .

The subdivision ordinance is attacked on the ground it is arbitrary and discriminatory. At the corner of Fairfield Street and Blevens Drive as shown on the plaintiffs' map are four lots, Nos. 145, 219, 232 and 146. The first two are owned by individual owners, the third is admittedly not subject to the subdivision ordinance while the fourth owned by the plaintiffs is subject to the ordinance. These lots are beyond the portion of Fairfield Street which has been accepted by the city, and as shown by the plan, lot 146 is situated in an unimproved block of twelve lots wholly surrounded by unaccepted streets. If the plaintiffs must under the ordinance supply municipal services for that lot, it will in effect be beneficial to the other lots not subject to the subdivision regulation. This is the price of progress in any attempt to improve land development, subject however to any right to relief because of "practical difficulty or unnecessary hardship" as provided by RSA 36:26. It is no different from the effect of zoning generally where certain property may be zoned in one class and a continguous property in another. The city must have a starting point for any new law or ordinance and it is not discriminatory merely because every lot of land is not regulated in the same degree. . . . The Trial Court has found that there has been no discrimination against the plaintiffs and the record supports that finding.

It is contended that the subdivision law and ordinance is unreasonable and contrary to public policy. Planning for land use has "become an accepted part of municipal law." Savage, Land Planning and Democratic Purposes, 34 Notre Dame Law. 65, 66 (1958). . . . The ordinance contemplates that a plat may be submitted for approval which covers "only a part of the subdividers entire holding," in which case a sketch of prospective future streets "of the unsubmitted part shall be furnished." A subdivider may thus avoid the expense of improving more land than will be immediately required. Both the statute and the ordinance provide for the granting in proper cases of exceptions, or variances from the literal enforcement of the regulations, to avoid "undue hardship" or "practical difficulty or unnecessary hardship." RSA 36:26. . . . Thus flexibility in applying the regulations to partially developed subdivisions is provided for. Certain lots owned by the plaintiffs were acquired by them as individual lots from a previous subdivider. As to them, the statute appears to be inapplicable. RSA 36:1, subd. VIII.

We conclude that the subdivision law (RSA 36:19—36:29) and the Manchester ordinance which conforms to this law are valid and constitutional. What was said in 1954 by a unanimous court in *Berman v. Parker,* 348 U.S. 26, 33, 75 S.Ct. 98, 102, 99 L.Ed. 27, is pertinent to this case: "The concept of public welfare is broad and inclusive . . . . The values it represents are spiritual as well as physical, aesthetic as well as monetary. It is within the power of the legislature to determine that the community should be beautiful as well as healthy, spacious as well as clean, well-balanced as well as carefully patrolled."

Exceptions overruled.

All concurred.

Comments: 1. The police power rationale applied by the principal case is typical of the more modern approach to subdivision control dedications. Courts today will rarely invalidate municipal subdivision control ordinances providing for the dedication of internal streets and other internal facilities which are required by the subdivision. For an interesting case applying the nexus test to a proposed dedication for a through street in a small subdivision see *Brazer v. Borough of Mountainside,* 262 A.2d 857 (N.J. 1970).

2. The dedication of land for streets and highways becomes more troublesome when the land dedicated is not to be used for the improvement and extension of internal thoroughfares within the subdivision, but rather, is to be used for streets and highways adjacent to the subdivision. The California Supreme Court dealt with this issue in *Ayres v. City Council,* 207 P.2d 1 (Cal. 1947). In this case the city conditioned approval of the subdivision on the dedication of an 80-foot wide strip of land to be used for the extension of a nearby cross-street. While relying in part on the voluntary rationale, and on the fact that the dedication would result in a net reduction of development costs, the court also sustained the dedication as "reasonably related to potential traffic needs." *Id.* at 6. It added:

> In a growing metropolitan area each additional subdivision adds to the traffic burden. It is no defense to the conditions imposed in a subdivision map proceeding that their fulfillment will incidentally also benefit the city as a whole. Nor is it a valid objection to say that the conditions contemplate future as well as more immediate needs.

Id. at 7.

Compare *181 Inc. v. Salem County Planning Bd.,* 336 A.2d 501 (N.J.L. 1975), *modified on other grounds,* 356 A.2d 34 (N.J. Super. 1976). Here the court held that a compulsory dedication of a right-of-way along a county road by a landowner seeking site plan approval was unconstitutional. The planning board had felt that there was a sufficient nexus between the proposed subdivision and the widening of the road in the future to justify the compulsory dedication. The New Jersey court, however, stated that in order to require the dedication of a right-of-way by a property owner seeking approval of a subdivision plan "it must appear that the purpose and action by the developer will forthwith or in the immediate future so burden the abutting road through increased traffic" that the dedication is required. *Id.* at 506.

Compare *R.G. Dunbar, Inc. v. Toledo Plan Comm'n,* 367 N.E.2d 1193 (Ohio App. 1976). The city's street plan showed a major thoroughfare through a subdivision, although the precise right-of-way had not been approved and the city had no immediate plans for developing the thoroughfare. A required dedication for the thoroughfare was rejected as unconstitutional, the court holding that the city could not require a dedication for a major thoroughfare which was to serve community needs. The dedication would have taken up about one third of the subdivision. Neither could the dedication be upheld as a "freeze" on the property.

3. Municipal ordinances providing that the developer pay for linear facilities such as water main extensions and sewers are generally upheld by the courts, although they too may pose some nexus problems. For cases upholding requirements of this type see *Deerfied Estates v. Township of East Brunswick,* 286 A.2d 498 (N.J. 1972) (water mains); *Mid-Continent Builders, supra* (same); *Crownhill Homes, Inc. v. City of San Antonio,* 433 S.W.2d 448 (Tex. Civ. App. 1968) (same). These cases occasionally make references to special assessment procedures under which abutting landowners are assessed for improvements of this type on the ground that the increase in value accruing to the property confers a compensating benefit. *See* D. Mandelker & D. Netsch, State and Local Government in a Federal System 327-53 (1977). Municipal facilities not conferring a benefit on adjacent property have usually been excluded from special assessment on the ground that no proximate benefits are conferred on property assessed for these improvements. *See Heavens v. King County Rural Library Dist.,* 404 P.2d 453 (Wash. 1965). Parks and schools, which are usually financed from general public revenues, usually fall within this latter category. This historical background should be kept in mind when appraising the park and school fee cases, which follow.

Some courts have been led by the special assessment analogy to impose a benefit as well as a nexus requirement for subdivision dedications and exactions. That is, the dedication or exaction must be proportional to the needs created by and benefits conferred upon the subdivision. *See Land/Vest Properties, Inc. v. Town of Plainfield,* 379 A.2d 200 (N.H. 1977).

4. Land dedications have also been upheld outside the subdivision control context. In *Bringle v. Board of Supervisors,* 351 P.2d 765 (Cal. 1960), plaintiff was granted a variance upon the condition that he dedicate to the county an easement for a right-of-way in order to widen a street. The California court upheld the dedication, noting that reasonable conditions may be attached to the granting of a variance in order to preserve the general purpose and intent of the zoning ordinance. Later, in *Southern Pac. Co. v. City of Los Angeles,* 51 Cal. Rptr. 197 (Cal. App. 1966), the court upheld a zoning ordinance requiring a landowner to dedicate a portion of his property for street widening purposes as a condition precedent to obtaining a building permit. Citing *Ayres, supra,* the court sustained the dedication by reasoning that "if the ... [landowner] desires the benefits resulting from the improvement or change in the character of the land, [it] ... must meet any reasonable condition imposed by the municipality before the issuance of a building permit" is granted. *Id.* at 202. *Contra, City of Corpus Christi v. Unitarian Church,* 436 S.W.2d 923 (Tex. Civ. App. 1968); *Board of Supervisors v. Rowe,* 216 S.E.2d 199 (Va. 1975). California now requires dedications required for use or building permits or variances to be reasonably related to the use of the property. Cal. Gov't Code § 65909(1) (Deering 1974).

Compare *Transamerica Title Ins. Co. v. City of Tucson,* 533 P.2d 693 (Ariz. App. 1975), in which the court invalidated a dedication requirement imposed as a condition to rezoning plaintiff's land. The court stated that there was "no evidence that the rezoning of the land will cause any appreciable burden on the streets over and above that which would emanate from the land prior to rezoning." *Id.* at 698. *Accord,* on similar facts, *Mid-Way Cabinet Fixture Mfg. v. County of San Joaquin,* 65 Cal. Rptr. 37 (Cal. App. 1968). Some courts have been willing to allow municipalities to impose involuntary dedications as a condition to annexation. *Mayor & Council v. Brookeville Turnpike Constr. Co.,* 228 A.2d 263 (Md. 1967). It is not entirely clear in this instance that the municipality may only insist on dedications for facilities related to the subdivision.

5. The following case picks up the trail of our discussion of land dedications and lot fees in the subdivision control context. It has become a leading case on the requirement that the developer contribute to the cost of park and recreation facilities.

ASSOCIATED HOMEBUILDERS OF GREATER EAST BAY, INC. v. CITY OF WALNUT CREEK

Supreme Court of California
5 Cal. 3d 633, 484 P.2d 606 (1971), *appeal dismissed,* 404 U.S. 878 (1971)

Mosk, Justice.

Section 11546 of the Business and Professions Code authorizes the governing body of a city or county to require that a subdivider must, as a condition to the approval of a subdivision map, dedicate land or pay fees in lieu thereof for park or recreational purposes. In this class action for declaratory and injunctive relief, Associated Home Builders of the Greater East Bay, Incorporated (hereinafter called Associated) challenges the constitutionality of section 11546 as well as legislation passed by the City of Walnut Creek to implement the section. It is also asserted that the city's enactments do not comply with the requirements set forth in the section. The trial court found in favor of the city, and Associated appeals from the ensuing judgment.

Section 11546 of the Business and Professions Code provides:

"The governing body of a city or county may by ordinance require the dedication of land, the payment of fees in lieu thereof, or a combination of both, for park or recreational purposes as a condition to the approval of a final subdivision map, provided that:

"(a) The ordinance has been in effect for a period of 30 days prior to the filing of the tentative map of the subdivision.

"(b) The ordinance includes definite standards for determining the proportion of a subdivision to be dedicated and the amount of any fee to be paid in lieu thereof.

"(c) The land, fees, or combination thereof are to be used only for the purpose of providing park or recreational facilities to serve the subdivision.

"(d) The legislative body has adopted a general plan containing a recreational element, and the park and recreation facilities are in accordance with definite principles and standards contained therein.

"(e) The amount and location of land to be dedicated or the fees to be paid shall bear a reasonable relationship to the use of the park and recreational facilities by the future inhabitants of the subdivision.

"(f) The city or county must specify when development of the park or recreational facilities will begin.

"(g) Only the payment of fees may be required in subdivisions containing fifty (50) parcels or less.

"The provisions of this section do not apply to industrial subdivisions."

Section 10-1.516 of the Walnut Creek Municipal Code, which will be discussed *infra,* refers to a general park and recreational plan adopted by the city. It provides that if a park or recreational facility indicated on the general plan falls within a proposed subdivision the land must be dedicated for park use by the subdivider in a ratio (set forth in a resolution) determined by the type of residence built and the number of future occupants. Pursuant to the ratio, two and one-half acres of park or recreation land must be provided for each 1,000 new residents. If, however, no park is designated on the master plan and the subdivision is within three-fourths of a mile radius of a park or a proposed park, or the dedication of land is not feasible, the subdivider must pay a fee equal to the value of the land which he would have been required to dedicate under the formula.[1]

Section 11546 and the city's ordinance are designed to maintain and preserve open space for the recreational use of the residents of new subdivisions. The adoption of a general plan (subd. (d)) avoids the pitfall of compelling exactions from subdividers of land which may be inadequate in size or unsuitable in location or topography for the facilities necessary to serve the new residents. Under the legislative scheme, the park must be in sufficient proximity to the subdivision which contributes land to serve the future residents. Thus subdividers, providing land or its monetary equivalent, afford the means for the community to acquire a parcel of sufficient size and appropriate character, located near each subdivision which makes a contribution, to serve the general recreational needs of the new residents.

If a subdivision does not contain land designated on the master plan as a recreation area, the subdivider pays a fee which is to be used for providing park or recreational facilities to serve the subdivision. One purpose of requiring payment of a fee in lieu of dedication is to avoid penalizing the subdivider who owns land containing an area designated as park land on the master plan. It would, of course, be patently unfair and perhaps discriminatory to require such a property owner to dedicate land, while exacting no contribution from a subdivider in precisely the same position except for the fortuitous circumstance that his land does not contain an area which has been designated as park land on the plan.

Constitutionality of Section 11546

Associated's primary contention is that section 11546 violates the equal protection and due process clauses of the federal and state Constitutions in that it deprives a subdivider of his property without just compensation. It is asserted that the state is avoiding the obligation of compensation by the device of requiring the subdivider

---

[1] The requirement of dedication is qualified as to subdivisions containing 50 parcels or less. In order to comply with subdivision (g) of section 11546 only the payment of fees may be required in subdivisions of such size.

to dedicate land or pay a fee for park or recreational purposes, that such contributions are used to pay for public facilities enjoyed by all citizens of the city and only incidentally by subdivision residents, and that all taxpayers should share in the cost of these public facilities. Thus, it is asserted, the future residents of the subdivision, who will ultimately bear the burden imposed on the subdivider, will be required to pay for recreational facilities the need for which stems not from the development of any one subdivision but from the needs of the community as a whole.

In order to avoid these constitutional pitfalls, claims Associated, a dedication requirement is justified only if it can be shown that the need for additional park and recreational facilities is attributable to the increase in population stimulated by the new subdivision alone and the validity of the section may not be upheld upon the theory that all subdivisions to be built in the future will create the need for such facilities.

In *Ayres v. City Council of City of Los Angeles* (1949) 34 Cal.2d 31, 207 P.2d 1, we rejected similar arguments. In that case, a city imposed upon a subdivider certain conditions for the development of a residential tract, including a requirement that he dedicate a strip of land abutting a major thoroughfare bordering one side of the subdivision but from which there was no access into the subdivision. The subdivider insisted that he could be compelled to dedicate land only for streets within the subdivision to expedite the traffic flow therein and that no dedication could be required for additions to existing streets and highways. Moreover, he asserted, the city had been contemplating condemning the property for the purposes indicated in any event, the benefit to the lot owners in the tract would be relatively small compared to the benefit to the city at large, and the dedication requirement amounted, therefore, to the exercise of the power of eminent domain under the guise of subdivision map proceedings.

We held that the city was not acting in eminent domain but, rather, that a subdivider who was seeking to acquire the advantages of subdivision had the duty to comply with reasonable conditions for dedication so as to conform to the welfare of the lot owners and the general public. We held, further, that the conditions were not improper because their fulfillment would incidentally benefit the city as a whole or because future as well as immediate needs were taken into consideration and that potential as well as present population factors affecting the neighborhood could be considered in formulating the conditions imposed upon the subdivider. We do not find in *Ayres* support for the principle urged by Associated that a dedication requirement may be upheld only if the particular subdivision creates the need for dedication.

Even if it were not for the authority of *Ayres* we would have no doubt that section 11546 can be justified on the basis of a general public need for recreational facilities caused by present and future subdivisions. The elimination of open space in California is a melancholy aspect of the unprecedented population increase which has characterized our state in the last few decades. Manifestly governmental entities have the responsibility to provide park and recreation land to accommodate this human expansion despite the inexorable decrease of open space available to fulfill such need. These factors have been recognized by the recent adoption of art. XXVIII of the Constitution, which provides that it is in the best interests of the state to maintain and preserve open space lands to assure the enjoyment of natural resources and scenic beauty for the economic and social well-being of the state and its citizens. Statutes which further the underlying policy expressed in the constitutional section must be upheld whenever possible in order to effecuate its salutary purposes.

The legislative committee which recommended the enactment of section 11546 emphasized that land pressure due to increasing population has intensified the need for open space, that parks are essential for a full community life, and that local officials have been besieged by demands for more park space. . . . The urgency of the problem in California is vividly described in other portions of the report. . . .

These problem are not confined to contemporary California. It has been estimated that by the year 2000 the metropolitan population of the United States will increase by 110 to 145 million, that 57 to 75 million of the increase will occur in areas which are now unincorporated open land encircling metropolitan centers, and that the demand for outdoor recreation will increase tenfold over the 1956 requirement. . . . Walnut Creek is a typical growth community. Located minutes' distance by motor vehicle from the metropolitan environs of Oakland and East Bay communities, the city population rose from 9,903 in 1960 to 36,606 in 1970, an increase of more than 365 percent in a decade.

We see no persuasive reason in the face of these urgent needs caused by present and anticipated future population growth on the one hand and the disappearance of open land on the other to hold that a statute requiring the dedication of land by a subdivider may be justified only upon the ground that the particular subdivider upon whom an exaction has been imposed will, solely by the development of his subdivision, increase the need for recreational facilities to such an extent that additional land for such facilities will be required.

Associated next contends that even if it be conceded that no showing of a direct relationship between a particular subdivision and an increase in the community's recreational needs is required, nevertheless the subdivider cannot be compelled to dedicate land for such needs, or pay a fee, unless his contribution will necessarily and primarily benefit the particular subdivision. Whether or not such a direct connection is required by constitutional considerations, section 11546 provides the nexus which concerns Associated. The act requires that the land dedicated or the fees paid are to be used only for the purpose of providing park or recreational facilities to serve the subdivision (subd. (c))[2] and (subd. (e)) that the amount and location of land or fees shall bear a reasonable relationship to the use of the facilities by the future inhabitants of the subdivision.[3]

---

[2] We do not deem subdivision (c) to mean that the facilities purchased with a particular contribution may only be used by the residents of the subdivision which made the contribution; rather, that the fees may not be diverted to any purpose other than for park or recreational facilities which will be available for use by those residents. Clearly, the constitutionality of the exaction is not dependent upon exclusive use of the facilities by those who will occupy the subdivision. *Ayres* teaches that the fact the public will also benefit from the use made of the land dedicated is not a ground for holding an exaction invalid.

[3] Amicus curiae Sierra Club urges that the requirement of dedication or the payment of a fee may be justified under the state's police power even if the recreational facilities provided by the subdivider's contribution are not used for the specific benefit of the future residents of the subdivision but are employed for facilities used by the general public. Ordinarily if land within the subdivision is dedicated for a park it may be assumed that those who will reside in the subdivision will make primary use of the park. The problem of connecting the facilities with the use made of them by the subdivision residents arises when a fee in lieu of dedication is required. In view of the provisions of section 11546, we need not decide in the present case whether a subdivider may be compelled to make a contribution to a park which is, for example, not conveniently located to the subdivision. Parenthetically, however, we perceive merit in the position of amicus curiae. It is difficult to see why, in the light of the need for recreational facilities described above and the increasing mobility of our population, a subdivider's fee in lieu of dedication may not be used to purchase or develop land some distance from the subdivision but which would also be available for use by subdivision residents. If, for example, the governing body of a city has determined, as has the city in the present case, that a specific amount of park land is required for a stated number of inhabitants, if this determination is reasonable, and there is a park already developed close to the subdivision to meet the needs of its residents, it seems reasonable to employ the fee to purchase land in another area of the city for park purposes to maintain the proper balance between the number of persons in the community and the amount of park land available. The subdivider who deliberately or fortuitously develops land close to an already completed park diminishes the supply of open land and adds residents who require park space within the city as a whole. A similar rationale was employed in *Southern Pac. Co. v. City of Los Angeles* (1966) 242 Cal.App.2d 38, 51 Cal.Rptr. 197, to uphold an ordinance requiring dedication of property for street widening as a condition of obtaining a building permit. . . .

Another assertion by Associated is that the only exactions imposed upon subdividers which may be valid are those directly related to the health and safety of the subdivision residents and necessary to the use and habitation of the subdivision, such as sewers, streets and drainage facilities. While it is true that such improvements are categories directly required by the health and safety of subdivision residents, it cannot be said that recreational facilities are not also related to these salutary purposes. So far as we are aware, no case has held a dedication condition invalid on the ground that, unlike sewers or streets, recreational facilities are not sufficiently related to the health and welfare of subdivision residents to justify the requirement of dedication. As shall appear hereinafter, several other jurisdictions have upheld exactions similar to those imposed by section 11546 on the ground that the influx of new residents increases the need for park and recreational facilities.[4]

Associated next poses as an eventuality that, if the requirements of section 11546 are upheld as a valid exercise of the police power on the theory that new residents of the subdivision must pay the cost of park land needs engendered by their entry into the community, a city or county could also require contributions from a subdivider for such services as added costs of fire and police protection, the construction of a new city hall, or even a general contribution to defray the additional cost of all types of governmental services necessitated by the entry of the new residents.

This proposition overlooks the unique problem involved in utilization of raw land. Undeveloped land in a community is a limited resource which is difficult to conserve in a period of increased population pressure. The development of a new subdivision in and of itself has the counterproductive effect of consuming a substantial supply of this precious commodity, while at the same time increasing the need for park and recreational land. In terms of economics, subdivisions diminish supply and increase demand. Another answer to Associated's assertion is found in the provisions of section 11546 itself. As we have seen, the section requires that land dedicated or in-lieu fees are to be used for the recreational needs of the subdivision which renders the exaction. Since the increase in residents creates the need for additional park land and the land or fees are used for facilities for the new residents, although not to the

---

[4] The only case cited by Associated which declared a statute similar to section 11546 to be unconstitutional recognized the need for recreational facilities caused by the influx of new residents but held that the need for such facilities must be "specifically and uniquely attributable" to the subdivider's activities and that the record did not indicate that this requirement had been met. (*Pioneer Trust & Sav. Bank v. Village of Mount Prospect* (1961), 22 Ill. 2d 375, 176 N.E.2d 799, 802.) We have rejected this rationale in our previous discussion.

exclusion of others, the circumstances may be distinguished from a more general or diffuse need created for such areawide services as fire and police protection.[5]

Associated claims that section 11546 constitutes a special burden upon the future inhabitants of the subdivision since the amount the subdivider must contribute will ultimately be reflected in the increased cost of homes to the future residents. It is asserted that a double tax will be imposed on the new residents because they must not only pay for the initial cost of the park but will also be required to assume property taxes which will be used for its development and maintenance.[6] Double taxation occurs only when "two taxes of the same character are imposed on the same property, for the same purpose, by the same taxing authority within the same jurisdiction during the same taxing period." (Rhyne, Municipal Law, p. 673.) Obviously the dedication or fee required of the subdivider and the property taxes paid by the later residents of the subdivision do not meet this definition. If Associated's claim were valid the prior residents of a community could also claim double taxation since their tax dollars were utilized to purchase and maintain public facilities which will be used by the newcomers who did not contribute to their acquisition.

Another contention by Associated is that section 11546 arbitrarily imposes its requirements only upon subdividers whereas those who do not subdivide are free from its exactions. The example is suggested of an apartment house build [built] on land which is not subdivided. The future occupants may live the same distance from a public park and have the same right to use the recreational facilities

---

[5] We do not imply that only those exactions from a subdivider are valid which present the special considerations set forth with regard to section 11546 but hold only that the exactions required by the section are justified by special factors not applicable to such matters as the increased cost of governmental services. In this connection we note that the Attorney General has filed an amicus curiae brief expressing concern that our holding regarding the validity of section 11546 may reflect upon the constitutionality of two recently enacted statutes requiring subdividers to provide public access to coastlines and to inland waters owned by a public agency. (Bus. & Prof.Code, §§ 11610.5, 11610.7.) Those sections are not involved in this proceeding and nothing we have said here is intended to reflect upon their validity.

[6] If Associated does not actually pay the exaction but merely passes the cost on to the consumer, a question arises as to its standing in this proceeding since it suffers no detriment and is not authorized to represent the consumers who it asserts will be taxed. Rather than relying upon that proposition, however, we prefer to decide the matter on the merits.

as the residents of a nearby subdivision, yet the builder of the apartment house is not required to contribute to park facilities because he has constructed his apartment without subdividing. This point has some arguable merit in the sense that the apartment builder, by increasing the population of an area, may add to the need for public recreational facilities to the same extent as the subdivider. However, the apartment is generally vertical, while the subdivision is horizontal. The Legislature could reasonably have assumed that an apartment house is thus ordinarily constructed upon land considerably smaller in dimension than most subdivisons and the erection of the apartments is, therefore, not decreasing the limited supply of open space to the same extent as the formation of a subdivision. This significant distinction justifies legislatively treating the builder of an apartment house who does not subdivide differently than the creator of a subdivision.

. . . .

Many of the issues raised by Associated have been discussed in the cases and law reviews. The clear weight of authority upholds the constitutionality of statutes similar to section 11546. While Illinois has held an ordinance requiring a subdivider to dedicate land for park purposes to be unconstitutional (*Pioneer Trust & Savings Bank v. Village of Mount Prospect,* supra, 22 Ill.2d 375, 176 N.E.2d 799, 801-802), Montana has reached a contrary conclusion (*Billings Properties, Inc. v. Yellowstone County* (1964), 144 Mont. 25, 394 P.2d 182). New York and Wisconsin have affirmed the validity of statutes requiring either dedication or a fee in lieu thereof (*Jenad, Inc. v. Village of Scarsdale,* supra, 18 N.Y.2d 78, 271 N.Y.S.2d 955, 218 N.E.2d 673; *Jordan v. Village of Menomonee Falls* (Wis.1965), supra, 28 Wis.2d 608, 137 N.W.2d 442). . . .

The rationale of the cases affirming constitutionality indicate the dedication statutes are valid under the state's police power. They reason that the subdivider realizes a profit from governmental approval of a subdivision since his land is rendered more valuable by the fact of subdivision, and in return for his benefit the city may require him to dedicate a portion of his land for park purposes whenever the influx of new residents will increase the need for park and recreational facilities. (*Jordan v. Village of Menomonee Falls,* supra, 28 Wis.2d 608, 137 N.W.2d 442, 448; *Billings Properties, Inc. v. Yellowstone County,* supra, 144 Mont. 25, 394 P.2d 182, 187.) Such exactions have been compared to admittedly valid zoning regulations such as minimum lot size and setback requirements. (*Jenad, Inc. v. Village of Scarsdale,* supra, 18 N.Y.2d 78, 271 N.Y.S.2d 955, 958, 218 N.E.2d 673.

Constitutionality of Section 10-1.516 of the Walnut Creek Municipal Code

Turning from the state statute to the Municipal Code, Associated argues that the fees the subdivider must pay in lieu of dedicating land are, under the city's ordinance, determined arbitrarily and without a reasonable relationship to principles of equality. It is claimed, for example, that a subdivider who develops high-density land may be required to pay a higher fee in lieu of dedication than one who develops low-density land even though both builders may be responsible for bringing the same number of new residents into the community. This may be true because the higher-density land is frequently more valuable and the fee is measured by the amount of land required by the number of persons in the subdivision.[7]

While the owner of more valuable land which will support a greater number of living units may be required to pay a higher fee for each new resident than the owner of less valuable land with a lower density, it does not follow that there is no reasonable relationship between the use of the facilities by future residents and the fee charged the subdivider. It is a proper assumption that persons occupying housing in a high-density area will use the public recreational facilities more consistently than those residents in single family homes who have private yards and more open space readily at their individual disposal.

. . . .

It may come to pass, as Associated states, that subdividers will transfer the cost of the land dedicated or the in-lieu fee to the consumers who ultimately purchase homes in the subdivision, thereby to some extent increasing the price of houses to newcomers. While we recognize the ominous possibility that the contributions required by a city can be deliberately set unreasonably high in order to prevent the influx of economically depressed persons into the community, a circumstance which would present serious social and legal problems, there is nothing to indicate that the enactments of *Walnut Creek* in the present case raise such a spectre. The desirability of encouraging subdividers to build low-cost housing

---

[7] Associated poses as an example a subdivider who owns 25 acres of land valued at $20,000 an acre, who divides his land into 100 lots for single family residences and one who owns 50 acres worth $10,000 each, which he divides into 100 lots, two to an acre. The city assumes four occupants to each single family home. Each subdivider brings 400 persons into the community and each must contribute one acre or its cash equivalent for park purposes under the city's formula. Therefore, the first subdivider contributes $20,000 while the second is required to contribute only $10,000 although both increase the community's population by the same number of new residents.

cannot be denied and unreasonable exactions could defeat this object, but these considerations must be balanced against the phenomenon of the appallingly rapid disappearance of open areas in and around our cities. We believe section 11546 constitutes a valiant attempt to solve this urgent problem, and we cannot say that its provisions or the city's enactments pursuant to the section are constitutionally deficient.

The judgment is affirmed.

WRIGHT, C. J., and McCOMB, PETERS, TOBRINER, BURKE and SULLIVAN, JJ., concur.

Comments: 1. Within the past 20 years it has become typical for local governments to enact subdivision ordinances requiring exactions from the developer in the form of land dedications for schools, park and recreational facilities, or fees in lieu of dedication to be used by the municipality for the acquisition of such sites. As in the case of streets and highways, the locality's purpose in demanding these exactions is to place the cost of these facilities on the land developer on the argument that as the development generates the need for these facilities it should share in the expense of providing for them. Park and school exactions create problems not present in the case of road and highway exactions, however. Since parks and schools are a community facility enjoyed by users other than the residents of the subdivision charged for these facilities, it is more difficult to link their provision with the particular development charged with providing sites for them. The line between an acceptable and an unacceptable subdivision exaction for school and park sites is thus harder to draw. *See generally* M. Brooks, Mandatory Dedication of Land or Fees-In-Lieu of Land for Parks and Schools (American Soc'y of Planning Officials, Planning Advisory Service Rep. No. 266, 1971); Heyman & Gilhool, The Constitutionality of Imposing Increased Community Costs on New Subdivision Residents Through Subdivision Exactions, 73 Yale L.J. 1119 (1963).

Consider also the following comment in *West Park Ave. v. Ocean Township,* 224 A.2d 1 (N.J. 1966), finding no statutory authority to levy a lot fee charge for educational purposes:

> But as to services which traditionally have been supported by general taxation, other considerations are evident. The dollar burden would likely be unequal if new homes were subjected to a charge in addition to the general tax rate. As to education, for example, the vacant land has contributed for years to the cost of existing educational facilities, and that land and the dwellings to be erected will continue to contribute with all other real property to the payment of bonds issued for the existing facilities and to the cost of renovating or replacing those facilities. Hence there would be an imbalance if new construction alone were to bear the capital cost of new schools while being also charged with the capital costs of schools serving other portions of the school district.

Id. at 4-5. Can the same arguments be made in connection with land dedications for on-site roads and other facilities? For land dedications for widening adjacent roads? Why or why not?

2. Various theories have been developed to support the constitutionality of subdivision exactions for school and park sites. The New Jersey Supreme Court has applied its nexus test, see *supra* p. 814, to charges levied for the provision of off-site drainage facilities, and arguably would apply the same test to school and park exactions if authorized. *Divan Builders, Inc. v. Planning Bd.,* 334 A.2d 30 (N.J. 1975).

An even narrower test which has acquired some following was announced by the Illinois Supreme Court in *Pioneer Trust & Sav. Bank v. Village of Mount Prospect,* 176 N.E.2d 799 (Ill. 1961). This case was an attack on a local subdivision control ordinance requiring the dedication of at least one acre of land for park and school sites for each sixty building sites. This provision was held invalid, the court following a principle announced in an earlier case that the developer is required to assume only those costs "specifically and uniquely attributable" to his development. *Id.* at 801. The court noted that the need for the dedication had not been established on the record:

> The agreed statement of facts shows that the present school facilities of Mount Prospect are near capacity. This is the result of the total development of the community. If this whole community had not developed to such an extent or if the existing school facilities were greater, the purported need supposedly would not be present.

Id. at 802. For cases applying the *Pioneer* test see *Aunt Hack Ridge Estates, Inc. v. Planning Comm'n,* 273 A.2d 880 (Conn. 1970) (lot fee for parks upheld); *Schwing v. City of Baton Rouge,* 249 So.2d 304 (La. App. 1971) (road widening invalidated).

Meanwhile, a study of subdivision exactions in Illinois revealed a variety of techniques through which municipalities have evaded the *Pioneer* requirements. Platt & Maloney-Merkle, Municipal Improvisation: Open Space Exactions in the Land of Pioneer Trust, 5 Urb. Law 706 (1973) (*e.g.,* dedication imposed on rezoning). In *Board of Educ. v. Surety Developers, Inc.,* 347 N.E.2d 149 (Ill. 1975), the Illinois Supreme Court sustained a dedication and monetary contribution for schools negotiated in proceedings leading up to the grant of a special use permit. The court found that the dedication and contribution were properly attached as conditions to the permit, and distinguished *Pioneer.* The court noted:

> By contrast, the subdivision before us was not an addition to an existing municipality but the commencement of a new one. This case arose precisely because defendant chose to purchase and develop land in a sparsely settled rural area, so far from public sewer and water facilities that it had to construct community facilities. Defendant dramatically changed the character of the surrounding area.

Id. at 154. See also *Krughoff v. City of Naperville,* 354 N.E.2d 489 (Ill. App. 1976), upholding the Naperville school and park site exaction requirement, which was contained in its subdivision control and planned unit development ordinances, as within the *Pioneer* rule. The Naperville ordinance related the park exaction to ultimate population in the subdivision, and required "the dedication of land to be used as school sites pursuant to criteria for optimum capacity, location, and site size of elementary, junior high, and high schools to serve the population of the development." *Id.* at 493. The Naperville ordinance, discussed in Platt & Maloney-Merkle, *supra* at 716-19, appears to use more sophisticated criteria than the ordinance struck down in *Pioneer.* It this enough to make the *Pioneer* test of invalidation inapplicable? For a discussion of the criteria to be used for determing school and park exactions and a cost-accounting formula designed to accomplish this purpose see Heyman & Gilhool, *supra* at 1141-46.

The Illinois Supreme Court, in an opinion which barely touched on the constitutional issues, upheld the Naperville ordinance. 369 N.E.2d 892 (Ill. 1977). It did appear to reaffirm the *Pioneer Trust* rule by noting that "the circuit court found that the required contributions of land, or money in lieu of land, were 'uniquely attributable to' and fairly apportioned to the need for new school and park facilities created by the proposed developments." *Id.* at 895. Neither was there discrimination "against property owners in the low- and middle-income group because the land dedication requirement is based on population rather than property valuation." *Id.* at 896. What is the constitutional basis for this claim?

3. Since the statute upheld in *Walnut Creek* could be argued to fit the specifically and uniquely attributable rule of *Pioneer Trust,* the limits of the California court's dictum, which appeared to expand on that rule, are not clear. *Jordan v. Village of Menomonee Falls,* 137 N.W.2d 442 (Wis. 1965), *appeal dismissed,* 385 U.S. 4 (1966), offers a formulation which may satisfy the Califonia court:

[The Wisconsin court first quoted the *Pioneer* rule and continued:]

> We deem this to be an acceptable statement of the yardstick to be applied, provided the words "specifically and uniquely attributable to his activity" are not so restrictively applied as to cast an unreasonable burden of proof upon the municipality which has enacted the ordinance under attack. In most instances it would be impossible for the municipality to prove that the land required to be dedicated for a park or a school site was to meet a need solely attributable to the anticipated influx of people into the community to occupy this particular subdivision. On the other hand, the municipality might well be able to establish that a group of subdivisions approved over a period of several years had been responsible for bringing into the community a considerable number of people making it necessary that the land dedications required of the subdividers be utilized for school, park and recreational purposes for the benefit of such influx. In the absence of contravening evidence this would establish a reasonable basis for finding that the need for the acquisition was occasioned by the activity of the subdivider
>
> . . . .
>
> We conclude that a required dedication of land for school, park or recreational sites as a condition for approval of the subdivision plat should be upheld as a valid exercise of police power if the evidence reasonably establishes that the municipality will be

required to provide more land for schools, parks and playgrounds as a result of approval of the subdivision.

Id. at 447-48. *See also Home Builders Ass'n v. City of Kansas City,* 555 S.W.2d 832 (Mo. 1977) (mandatory dedication for recreational purposes valid if reasonably attributable to developer's activity).

The *Jenad* case, cited in *Walnut Creek,* purported to follow *Menomonee Falls* but was not troubled by a failure to prove actual need in the case of the subdivision under review. See *Collis v. City of Bloomington,* 246 N.W.2d 19 (Minn. 1976), upholding a statute requiring a "reasonable portion" of each subdivision to be dedicated for parks or playgrounds, or a cash payment made in lieu of the dedication, and interpreting the California, New York and Wisconsin cases to "hold that a reasonable relationship between the approval of the subdivision and the municipality's need for land is required." *Id.* at 26. For discussion of the earlier cases see Johnston, *supra* at 913-21. *Cf. Billings Properties, Inc. v. Yellowstone County,* 394 P.2d 182 (Mont. 1964) (deferentially upholding statute requiring dedication of land for park and playground purposes). With these cases compare the statement in *Walnut Creek* that a dedication "can be justified on the basis of a general public need for recreational facilities caused by present and future subdivisions." And see footnote 3 of that opinion. Does *Walnut Creek* modify the *Mid-Way Cabinet* case, *supra* p. 816?

4. Does footnote 3 of the *Walnut Creek* opinion perhaps give a clue to the criteria which dicta in that case suggest should be applied to subdivision exactions? The hypothetical contemplated by that footnote can apparently be stated as follows: A developer plans a new subdivision adjacent to a public park which is quite adequate to serve the needs of that subdivision. Nevertheless, based on the community's open space plan and open space-population ratio, park facilities available throughout the community after the subdivision is built will not meet the plan's standards. Under the net detriment theory, the subdivider will apparently be required to pay a sum of money to the community sufficient to remedy this deficit in community park space.

What problems are there with this approach? Note, for example, the passing suggestion in footnote 3 that the community's open space standard must be reasonable. What if the community adopts a reasonable standard but consistently underbudgets general funds for park acquisition, thus creating a net detriment in community open space which it then uses as the basis for exacting fees and dedications from developers for parks? While not considering the standards problem, Professor Ellickson has argued that the principal problem in these cases is an equity problem — fairness of treatment as among landowners — and not a due process problem. Ellickson, Suburban Growth Controls: An Economic and Legal Analysis, 86 Yale L.J. 385, 45-89 (1977). He thus argues that "if a municipality mixes special and general revenues in financing a service, the portion financed by general revenues should presumptively be distributed equally per dwelling unit." *Id.* at 460. Landowners assessed with park fees, for example, would be entitled to an offset equivalent to the benefits received by other landowners from parks financed by general revenues. Ellickson's formula apparently addresses the double taxation problem, *see West Park supra* p.

826. What basis does he have for demanding a temporal equal protection in the law of land use controls? *Compare Winney v. Board of Comm'rs,* 369 N.E.2d 661 (Ind. App. 1977) (sewer tap-in fees may vary over time). Could a state statute or municipal ordinance provide that the municipal contribution to facilities such as streets, parks and schools should in no case be excessive, and authorize an appropriate increase in developer contributions on a case-by-case basis to avoid excessive municipal contributions? Would such a provision violate Ellickson's principle? *See Land/Vest Properties, Inc., supra* at 205.

5. In footnote 6 of the *Walnut Creek* opinion, the court suggests that if the costs of the exaction are passed on to homebuyers in the subdivision the developer would not have standing to contest the charge. Several studies have suggested that development charges are, in fact, passed on, but these studies have been criticized as misleading:

> Some authors, of course, have recognized the possibility that development charges might be at least partly borne by landowners or others.... Several other efforts to apply formal economic analysis have oversimplified the problem and thus produced potentially misleading answers. One study assumed the supply of land for residences to be wholly inelastic in the relevant price range and therefore concluded that development charges are always entirely borne by landowners. Adelstein & Edelson, *Subdivision Exactions and Congestion Externalities,* 5 J. Legal Stud. 147, 160-61 & n.37 (1976). Another author also adopted the dubious assumption of a vertical supply curve but nevertheless concluded that developers can usually pass on the cost of park exactions because the availability of parks will shift up the demand curve. Note, *Subdivision Land Dedication: Objectives and Objections,* 27 Stan. L. Rev. 419, 421-30 (1975). No such shift would occur, however, if, for example, the municipality had a prior policy of providing free parks in all neighborhoods. The preexisting demand curve would then reflect consumers' expectations that they would receive park services.

Ellickson, *supra* at 399, n. 34. The Stanford article also contended that shifts in the demand curve due to the availability of park land within the subdivision would raise the price of lots sufficiently to allow the developer to recoup the cost of dedication or the fees, thus washing out the taking-due process objection. *Id.* at 423-24. For judicial recognition of this possibility see *Aunt Hack Ridge Estates v. Planning Comm'n,* 273 A.2d 880, 885 (Conn. 1970).

6. Since the Standard Act and many of the state subdivision control acts that followed it make no express provision for land dedications and lot fees, some courts have avoided constitutional problems raised by these exactions by finding a lack of statutory authority to demand them. *See, e.g., Admiral Dev. Corp. v. City of Maitland,* 267 So.2d 860 (Fla. Dist. Ct. App. 1972) (land dedication); *West Park Ave. v. Ocean Township,* 224 A.2d 1 (N.J. 1966) (lot fee). *Cf. Cimarron Corp. v. Board of County Comm'rs,* 563 P.2d 946 (Colo. 1977) (statute construed to authorize dedication or lot fees as alternatives). Compare cases like *Menomonee Falls* and *Jenad, supra,* which have been able to rely on generalized language in the statute to support dedication and fee requirements. Thus, the statute in *Jenad* required subdivisions submitted for approval to show suitably located parks.

Lot fees also fall under attack as taxes not authorized by state legislation. *See Haugen v. Gleeson,* 359 P.2d 108 (Ore. 1961) (unauthorized tax because fees not earmarked for benefit of subdivision). Compare *Jenad, supra,* in which the court stated that fees in lieu of dedication are not taxes but are "fees imposed on the transaction of obtaining plat approval." *Id.* at 676. In *Jenad* the fees were earmarked for park purposes but not for use within the contributing subdivision.

The American Law Institute's Model Land Development Code (1976) authorizes the land development agency to condition a special development permit on:

> (a) provision by the developer of streets, other rights-of-way, utilities, parks, and other open space, but the required provision must be of a quality and quantity no more than reasonably necessary for the proposed development; or
>
> (b) payment of an equivalent amount of money into a fund for the provision of streets, other rights-of-way, utilities, parks or other open space if the Land Development Agency finds that the provision thereof under paragraph (a) is not feasible;. . .

Id. § 2-103(3). Note that schools are not included and that land dedication is the preferred alternative.

In addition to the California statute construed in the principal case, other statutes have also authorized dedications and fees, *e.g.,* Ariz. Rev. Stat. § 9-463.01 (D)-(F) (Supp. 1975) (compensation to developer required); Colo. Rev. Stat. § 30-28-133(4)(a) (1973) (park and school sites or fees "reasonably necessary" to serve subdivision); Vt. Stat. Ann. tit. 24, § 4417(5) (1975) (dedication limited to 15 percent of plat; fees to be used to serve needs of area surrounding subdivision).

7. Recall the comment at the close of the *Walnut Creek* opinion that subdivision exactions may have an exclusionary impact. For a holding that comparable municipal exactions imposed within the planned unit development context have an exclusionary impact on developers seeking to build low- and moderate-income housing see *Oakwood at Madison, Inc. v. Township of Madison,* 371 A.2d 1192, 1211 (N.J. 1977).

8. Municipalities have found methods, outside the subdivision control context, to charge developers with the cost of expanding municipal facilities. These techniques, though not strictly a part of the subdivision control process, are important to consider here because they raise problems similar to those raised by the subdivision control exaction cases. The following opinion illustrates the problem.

CONTRACTORS & BUILDERS ASS'N OF PINELLAS COUNTY v. CITY OF DUNEDIN

Supreme Court of Florida
329 So.2d 314 (1976)

HATCHETT, Justice.

In an action for declaratory judgment, brought against the City of

Dunedin in Circuit Court, provisions of certain ordinances [8] were adjudged defective, as being an *ultra vires* attempt by the city to impose taxes; and the city was enjoined from collecting fees the ordinances required as a precondition for municipal water and sewerage service. In addition, the Circuit Court ordered the City to refund the fees, but only to persons who had paid under protest. On appeal to the District Court of Appeals, Second District, that court reversed the circuit court judgment, *City of Dunedin, Florida v. Contractors and Builders Association of Pinellas County, etc. et al.,* 312 So.2d 763; and, on June 10, 1975, certified that its decision passed upon a question of great public interest. As is customary in cases where such certificates have been entered, we exercise our discretion to review on its merits the decision below. . . .

---

[8] The ordinances setting water and sewerage connection charges or otherwise pertinent are the following:

Sec. 25-14. *Sewage connection required; notice.*

The owner of any house, building, or property used for human occupancy, employment, recreation, or other purpose, situated within the city and abutting on any street, alley or right-of-way in which there is now located or may in the future be located a public sanitary or combined sewer of the city, is hereby required at his expense to install suitable toilet facilities therein, and to connect such facilities directly with the proper public sewer in accordance with the provisions of this chapter, within ninety (90) days after date of official notice to do so, provided that said public sewer is within two hundred (200) feet of the house, building, or properties used for human occupancy. . . .

Sec. 25-31. *Same — Classes of permits; contents; inspection fees.*

There shall be two classes of building sewer permits: (1) for residential and commercial service; and (2) for service to establishments producing industrial waste. In either case, the owner or his agent shall make application on a special form furnished by the city. The permit application shall be supplemented by any plans, specifications, or other information considered pertinent in the judgment of the city sewer superintendent. No permit will be issued unless the assessment as set forth in section 25-71(c) and (d) has been paid. . . .

Sec. 25-32. *Same — Costs paid by owner.*

All costs and expense incident to the installation, connection and maintenance of the building and collector sewers shall be borne by the owners. The owners shall indemnify the city from any loss or damage that may directly or indirectly be occasioned by the installation of the building sewer.

Sec. 25-71. *Meters — Connection or installation charge.*

(a) The connection charge for the installation of a meter inside the city shall be as follows:

⅝" meter . . . . $ 95.00

1" meter 170.00

Plaintiffs in the trial court, petitioners here, are building contractors, an incorporated association of contractors, and owners of land situated within the city limits of Dunedin.[9] They do not complain of all the fees Dunedin requires to be collected upon issuance of building permits, but contend that monies which the city collects and earmarks for "capital improvements to the [water and sewerage] system as a whole" (R. 725) constitute taxes, which a municipality is forbidden to impose, in the absence of enabling legislation. It is agreed on all sides that "a municipality cannot impose a tax, other than ad valorem taxes, unless authorized by

1-½" meter	$ 265.00
2" meter	360.00

(b) The connection charge for the installation of a meter outside the city limits shall be as follows:

⅝" meter	$105.00
1" meter	180.00
1-½" meter	290.00
2" meter	390.00

(c) In addition to the meter installation charges described herein, there shall be paid an assessment to defray the cost of production, distribution, transmission and treatment facilities for water and sewer provided that the expense of the City of Dunedin, as follows:

Each dwelling unit; for water	$325.00
for sewer	475.00
Each transient unit; for water	150.00
for sewer	275.00
Each business unit; for water	325.00
for sewer	475.00

(d) The assessments as set forth herein shall be payable upon issuance of the building permit for said unit or units in the case of new construction, or in the case of a presently existing structure or structures, such assessments shall be payable when the permits for water or sewer connections are issued.

Petitioners challenge as unlawful the fees prescribed by Dunedin, Fla. Code § 25-71(c).

[9] Petitioners take the position that the ordinance is bad, if for no other reason, then because it denies equal protection of the laws to new residents of Dunedin. There is a substantial question whether petitioners here have standing to assert new residents' rights. *Construction Industry Association of Sonoma County v. City of Petaluma,* 522 F. 2d 897, 44 U.S.L.W. 2093 (9th Cir., 1975). Assuming standing *arguendo,* the ordinance easily meets the rational basis test, see *post, pp.* 319-320, and no right to travel interstate is affected, contrary to petitioners' assertion. *Cf.* Annot., 63 A.L.R.3d 1184 (1975). In *Shapiro v. Thompson,* 394 U.S. 618, 89 S.Ct. 1322, 22 L.Ed.2d 600 (1969), welfare recipients were disqualified as such for one year by moving into Connecticut. Under Dunedin's ordinance, a joint water and sewer connection costs approximately $800.00, regardless of whether the new user comes from Dunedin, elsewhere in Florida, or from another state or country.

general law," 312 So.2d at 766, and that no general law gives such authorization here. Respondent contends that these fees are not taxes, but user charges analogous to fees collected by privately owned utilities for services rendered. For the reasons stated in Judge Grimes' scholarly opinion, we accept this analogy, but we decline to uphold a revenue generating ordinance that omits provisions we deem crucial to its validity. We are unpersuaded, moreover, that the limitations, which the city has in fact placed on fees collected pursuant to Dunedin, Fla. Code §§ 25-31, 25-71(c) and (d), can suffice to make those fees "just and equitable", within the meaning of Fla.Stat. § 180.13(2) (1973). In principle, however, we see nothing wrong with transferring to the new user of a municipally owned water or sewer system a fair share of the costs new use of the system involves.

Petitioners contend that Dunedin has imposed a tax under the guise of setting charges for water and sewer connections, relying on *Broward County v. Janis Development Corp.*, 311 So.2d 371 (Fla. 4th Dist.1975) aff'g *Janis Development Corp. v. City of Sunrise*, 40 Fla.Supp. 41 (17th Cir. 1973); *Pizza Palace of Miami v. City of Hialeah*, 242 So.2d 203 (Fla. 3d Dist. 1972); and *Venditti-Siraro, Inc. v. City of Hollywood*, 39 Fla.Supp. 121 (17th Cir. 1973). The *Pizza Palace* case is wholly inapposite, and the others are readily distinguishable. Only if the moneys collected in *Venditti-Siraro* and *Janis Development* had been used to underwrite the administrative costs of issuing building permits, or other costs incurred in enforcing building codes, would those cases be analogous to the present one. Compare *State ex rel. Harkow v. McCarthy*, 126 Fla. 433, 171 So. 314 (1936) with *City of Panama City v. State*, 60 So.2d 658 (Fla.1952). The analogy would be very close if the fees had been earmarked for future capital outlay: for example, acquisition of automobiles for building inspectors to use in their work.

But the fees in *Janis Development* and *Venditti-Siraro* bore no relationship to (and were greatly in excess of) the costs of the regulation which was supposed to justify their collection. In each case, the fees were required to be paid as a condition for issuance of building permits. In the *Janis Development* case, $200.00 per dwelling unit built was put into a fund for road maintenance. In *Venditti-Siraro*, one percent of estimated construction costs went into a fund for parks. Because the surcharges were collected for purposes extraneous to the enforcement of the building code, the courts concluded that the surcharges amounted in law to taxes, which the municipalities had not been authorized to impose. In contrast, evidence was adduced here that the connection fees were less than costs Dunedin was destined to incur in accommodating new users of its water and sewer systems. We join many other courts in rejecting the contention that such connection fees are taxes.[10]

The avowed purpose of the ordinance in the present case is to raise money in order to expand the water and sewerage systems, so as to meet the increased demand which additional connections to the system create. *The municipality seeks to shift to the user expenses incurred on his account.* A private utility in the same circumstances would presumably do the same thing, in which event surely even petitioners would not suggest that the private corporation was attempting to levy a tax on its customers.

Under the constitution, Dunedin, as the corporate proprietor of its water and sewer systems, can exercise the powers of any other such proprietor (except as Fla.Stat. §§ 180.01 *et seq.,* or statutes enacted hereafter, may otherwise provide.) Municipal corporations have "governmental, corporate and proprietary powers" and "may exercise any power for municipal purposes, except as otherwise provided by law." Fla.Const. art. VIII, § 2(b); *City of Miami Beach v. Fleetwood Hotel, Inc.,* 261 So.2d 801 (Fla.1972). "Implicit in the power to provide municipal services is the power to construct, maintain and operate the necessary facilities." *Cooksey v. Utilities Commission,* 261 So.2d 129, 130 (Fla. 1972). There are no provisions in Chapter 180, Florida Statutes, expressly governing capital acquisition other than through deficit financing,[11] but it is provided that the "legislative body of the municipality . . . may establish just and equitable rates or charges" for water and sewerage. Fla.Stat. § 180.13(2) (1973). See generally Annot., 61 A.L.R.3d 1236, 1248-1259 (1975).

When a municipality sells debentures as a means of financing the extension or enlargement of a public utility, the indebtedness thus incurred is eventually made good with utility revenues; and anticipated revenues "may be pledged to secure moneys advanced for the . . . improvement." Fla.Stat. § 180.07(2) (1973). When money for capital outlay is borrowed, water and sewer rates are set

---

[10] The Supreme Court of Illinois, in *Hartman v. Aurora Sanitary District,* 23 Ill.2d 109, 177 N.E.2d 214 (1961), observed at 219:

> We have found that such reasonable charges have been uniformly sustained as a service charge rather than a tax. . . .

[11] Special assessments are another common means of financing sewer construction. Fla. Stat. § 170.01 (1973). The fees in controversy here are not special assessments. They are charges for use of water and sewer facilities; the property owner who does not use the facilities does not pay the fee. Under no circumstances would the fees constitute a lien on realty.

with a view towards raising the money necessary to repay the loan. . . . *State v. City of Miami,* 113 Fla. 280, 152 So. 6 (1933) (*reh. den.* 1934) ("certificates of indebtedness . . . are payable as to both principal and interest solely out of a special fund to be created . . . out of the net earnings." At 13).

Water and sewer rates and chages do not, therefore, cease to be "just and equitable" merely because they are set high enough to meet the system's capital requirements, as well as to defray operating expenses. . . . We see no reason to require that a municipality resort to deficit financing, in order to raise capital by means of utility rates and charges. On the contrary, sound public policy militates against any such inflexibility.[12] It may be a simpler technical task to amortize a known outlay, than to predict population trends and the other variables necessary to arrive at an accurate forecast of future capital needs. But raising capital for future use by means of rates and charges may permit a municipality to take advantage of favorable conditions, which would alter before money could be raised through issuance of debt securities; and the day may not be far distant when municipalities cannot compete successfully with other borrowers for needed capital. The weight of authority supports the view that raising capital for future outlay is a legitimate consideration in setting rates and charges. *Hayes v. City of Albany,* 7 Or.App. 277, 490 P.2d 1018 (1971); *Hartman v. Aurora Sanitary District,* 23 Ill.2d 109, 177 N.E.2d 214 (1961); *Home Builders Ass'n of Greater Salt Lake v. Provo City,* 28 Utah 2d 402, 503 P.2d 451 (1972).

It is also established that differential utility rates and charges may be "just and equitable". Fla.Stat. § 180.13(2) (1973); *Hayes v. City of Albany, supra,* notwithstanding the differential. In *Brandel v. Civil City of Lawrenceburg,* 249 Ind. 47, 230 N.E.2d 778 (1967), the court upheld an ordinance setting differential connection charges where two distinct sewerage systems had been engineered in the same political entity. The user connecting to the more expensive system paid a higher connection charge. Another common type of differential charge makes the character of the user determinative of utility rates:

---

[12] Petitioners cite *Norwick v. Village of Winfield,* 81 Ill.App.2d 197, 225 N.E.2d 30 (2d Dist.1967) in which it was held that an Illinois municipality was without authority to raise money for future capital requirements, by collecting connection fees in excess of actual connection costs. But the decision in that case turned on the construction of a statute granting the Village of Winfield municipal powers, and is of no relevance to the present case. The Illinois court remarked: "The Village directs our attention to foreign cases. These are of no assistance . . . . This is particularly true in states with so-called 'home rule' municipalities [like Florida]."

> In determining reasonable rate relationships, a municipality may sometimes take into account the purpose for which a customer receives the service. . . . Courts have recognized that differences in sewer use rates for residential customers and various other customers may be reasonable. Some customers may be subject to a flat rate while other customers are subject to rates based on water consumption or type and number of receptacles. *Rutherford v. City of Omaha*, 183 Neb. 398, 160 N.W.2d 223, 228 (1968) (authorities omitted)

Dunedin distinguishes between residential and commercial users, on one hand, and industrial users, on the other. . . . [P]etitioners do not question this distinction. Here the issue is whether differential connection charges are "just and equitable", when they vary depending on the time at which the connection to the utility system is made.

Raising expansion capital by setting connection charges, which do not exceed a *pro rata* share of reasonably anticipated costs of expansion, is permissible where expansion is reasonably required, *if use of the money collected is limited to meeting the costs of expansion.* Users "who benefit especially, not from the maintenance of the system, but by the extension of the system . . . should bear the cost of that extension." *Hartman v. Aurora Sanitary District, supra,* 177 N.E.2d at 218. On the other hand, it is not "just and equitable" for a municipally owned utility to impose the entire burden of capital expenditures, including replacement of existing plant, on persons connecting to a water and sewer system after an arbitrarily chosen time certain.

The cost of new facilities should be borne by new users to the extent new use requires new facilities, but only to that extent. When new facilities must be built in any event, looking only to new users for necessary capital gives old users a windfall at the expense of new users.

When certificates of indebtedness are outstanding, new users, like old users, pay rates which include the costs of retiring the certificates, which represent original capitalization. . . . New users thus share with old users the cost of original facilities. For purposes of allocating the cost of replacing original facilities, it is arbitrary and irrational to distinguish between old and new users, all of whom bear the expense of the old plant and all of whom will use the new plant.[13] The limitation on use of the funds, shown to exist *de facto* in the present

---

[13] There is authority to the contrary. *Hartman v. Aurora Sanitary District, supra; Home Builders Ass'n of Greater Salt Lake v. Provo City, supra.* In *Provo City,* an ordinance like Dunedin's was upheld even though the fees were used for "general operating expenses." 503 P.2d at 451. We reject the view these cases represent.

case, has the effect of placing the whole burden of supplementary capitalization, including replacement of fully depreciated assets, on a class chosen arbitrarily for that purpose.

In *Hayes v. City of Albany, supra,* the situation was very much like the situation here. An existing system faced the imminent prospect of expansion and, as of a date certain, residential connection fees climbed from $25 to $255. (An hypothetical industrial user's charges soared from $200 to a prohibitive $400,000.) These charges were to be deposited in a fund restricted as follows:

> All monies received from the Sewer Connection Charges plus interest, if any, shall be deposited in the Sanitary Sewer Capital Reserve Fund . . . and shall be expended from that fund only for the purpose of making major emergency repairs, extending or oversizing, separating, or constructing new additions to the treatment plant or collection and interceptor systems. 490 P.2d at 1020.

If the ordinance in the present case had so restricted use of the fees which it required to be collected, there would be little question as to its validity. We conclude that the ordinance in the present case cannot stand as it is written.

The same considerations which underlie statutes of frauds require that a revenue producing ordinance explicitly set forth restrictions on revenues it generates, where such restrictions are essential to its validity. As between private parties, a contract "that is not to be performed within the space of one year," Fla.Stat. § 725.01 (1973), or which is "for the sale of goods for the price of $500 or more," Fla. Stat. § 672.201 (1973), is unenforceable unless reduced to writing, with certain exceptions not pertinent here. Counsel for respondent has represented that the fees collected under the ordinance exceed $196,000.00. Brief for Respondent at 53. Nothing in the record indicates that capital outlay for expansion will be completed within a year's time.

The failure to include necessary restrictions on the use of the fund is bound to result in confusion, at best. City personnel may come and go before the fund is exhausted, yet there is nothing in writing to guide their use of these moneys, although certain uses, even within the water and sewer systems, would undercut the legal basis for the fund's existence. There is no justification for such casual handling of public moneys, and we therefore hold that the ordinance is defective for failure to spell out necessary restrictions on the use of fees it authorizes to be collected.[14]

---

[14] If subsection c were excised from Dunedin, Fla.Code § 25-71, the ordinance would be unobjectionable, because reasonable meter connection charges may permissibly furnish utility revenues for unrestricted use within the utility system. The validity of such charges does not depend on limitation of their use.

Nothing we decide, however, prevents Dunedin from adopting another sewer connection charge ordinance, incorporating appropriate restrictions on use of the revenues it produces. Dunedin is at liberty, moreover, to adopt an ordinance restricting the use of moneys already collected. We pretermit any discussion of refunds for that reason.

The decision of the District Court of Appeal is quashed and this case is remanded to the District Court with directions that the District Court dispose of the question of costs; and that the District Court thereafter remand for further proceedings in the trial court not inconsistent with this opinion. In the trial court's consideration *de novo* of the question of refunds the chancellor is at liberty to take into account all pertinent developments since entry of his original decree.

It is so ordered.

ADKINS, C. J., and ROBERTS, OVERTON and ENGLAND, JJ., concur.

Comments: 1. User fees and charges are yet another device used by municipalities to raise revenues for capital improvements to municipal facilities. Although the legal concepts are different, the application of these fees to fund off-site facilities such as municipal water and sewer systems accomplishes the same objective as subdivision exactions. Equity problems are more apparent in the user fee cases because the fee is part of a user charge system that applies both to old and new users of the utility service. Differentials in user charges are thus more visible to the courts; in the subdivision exaction cases there is no comparable charge on old residents which can be compared to the subdivision exaction levied on developers of new subdivisions. The principal case illustrates one approach to the handling of these equity problems in the impact fee situation. It is sensitive to the cross-owner equity problems raised by Ellickson, *supra* p. 829.

2. The salient issue in the impact fee cases is whether and to what extent municipalities can levy these charges. If the court finds that the municipality has the authority to levy the charge and that its proceeds may be used for capital expansion, and if it classifies the charge as a user fee and not a tax, it will not usually perceive the charge as raising insurmountable constitutional due process or equal protection problems. When authority to levy the user charge is found, the general trend has been for the courts to defer to the legislative decision to set the amount of the charge and to uphold it unless flagrantly unreasonable. See *Hartman v. Aurora Sanitary Dist.*, 177 N.E.2d 214 (Ill. 1961), discussed in the principal case, which upheld a 160 dollar charge for connection to the city's sewer line. As the principal case indicates, however, not all courts have been willing to find authority to levy the charge. *See, e.g., Clarke v. City of Bettendorf*, 158 N.W.2d 125 (Iowa 1968).

3. It is not entirely clear whether the user fee cases have handled the equity problems inherent in differential charges by adopting the benefit theories prevalent in some of the subdivision exaction cases. Some courts have at least insisted that funds collected through user fees be used for the improvement of the system to which the developer is connecting. *Compare Hayes v. City of Albany,* 490 P.2d 1018 (Ore. 1971) (upholding connection fee when proceeds used to develop and maintain city's sewer system), *with Weber Basin Home Builders Ass'n v. Roy City,* 487 P.2d 866 (Utah 1971) (*contra,* when proceeds of building permit fee went into city's general fund). Occasionally, a court will use a contract or voluntary connection theory to uphold the differential charge. *See Spalding v. Granite City,* 113 N.E.2d 567 (Ill. 1953). In the *Spalding* case there was no allegation that the property owner would be forced to connect with the system. Since most courts are willing to dismiss constitutional objections to a requirement that property owners be forced to give up on-site disposal systems and connect to public facilities, see *Bedford Township v. Bates,* 233 N.W.2d 706 (Mich. App. 1975), the contract rationale appears tenuous in this context.

4. The most difficult problems arise when impact fees are used to finance additions to or replacement of existing capital plant facilities. To what extent can a municipality differentiate between existing users and new users when levying fees to secure funds to maintain or extend an existing sewer or water system? Remember that the *Dunedin* court asserted that new residents should bear only the burden of financing the expansion of the existing system and should not have to assume responsibility for costs, such as the replacement of existing plant, which should be borne as well by existing users.

A somewhat different rationale for user fees and charges was adopted in *Airwick Indus., Inc. v. Carlstadt Sewerage Auth.,* 270 A.2d 18 (N.J. 1970), *cert. denied,* 402 U.S. 967 (1971). In this case the authority determined to build an extension of its sewer system to serve a previously undeveloped and unsewered part of the authority area. The extension was to be paid for out of a bond issue to be in turn funded by connection fees levied in the newly serviced area. Sewage facilities in the authority's area had previously been financed out of general taxation revenues.

In upholding the connection fees the court first considered an equal protection argument, based on the objection that users in the newly serviced area were to be taxed twice because general tax revenues from their properties would also help pay off the older system. This argument was rejected, the court noting that on-site disposal systems were objectionable on pollution grounds while the cost of individual systems was prohibitive. Land in the newly-serviced area would thus be unsalable unless the sewer extension was carried out. *Id.* at 21.

Next the court considered the validity of the connection charge schedule. This schedule was based on annual increments in connection fees which increased in amount each year after services became available, up to a maximum amount to be levied after the third year. This stepped sytem of charges was upheld. The court explained:

> ... Patently, part of the construction cost was necessitated by provision for adequate future service for unimproved properties as well as improved lands. It is conceivable that without the

availability of an adequate sewerage disposal system that land might have to remain unimproved. That the actual users of the facility receive a benefit for which they should pay, is self-evident. It does not follow, however, from the fact that unimproved properties do not make any present use of the facilities, that they receive no present benefit therefrom. To the contrary, upon completion of installation, the unimproved properties also receive an immediate benefit from the mere availability of the system for service. All properties within the section serviced are beneficiaries of the expenditure — the improved for immediate present use and the unimproved for potential future use. Both classes receive an immediate enhancement in value from the mere existence of the system. The only equitable manner to distribute the original cost, is for the unimproved properties to bear part of that cost in exchange for the increment in value received and for the potential standby service. It is certainly not equitable for the improved lands, during their use of the system, to pay the entire original installation and construction cost, thereby paying for the present and future benefit received and to be received by the unimproved properties as well. There are, therefore, two categories of properties which should be fairly called upon to pay for the original construction cost, *i.e.,* the improved and unimproved properties.

Id. at 25. What rationale for user charges has the New Jersey court adopted? Is it consistent with the theory of the principal case? *Airwick* was relied on in *Home Builders Ass'n v. Provo City,* 503 P.2d 451 (Utah 1972) to sustain a connection fee to be used for new collector lines as well as the replacement and enlargement of an existing sewerage plant, the retirement of bonded debt on the sewers and general operating expenses.

Compare these other approaches to the differential fee problem:

Brandel v. City of Lawrenceburg, 230 N.E.2d 178 (Ind. 1967). In this case the ordinance established a 200 dollar fee for those who connected to the new section of the sewerage system and a $62.50 fee for those who connected to the older part of the system. The court responded to the allegation that the ordinance was discriminatory by stating that "the original cost of the older system was less and therefore the charges for its use would be less than the costs of the new system." *Id.* at 781.

Hartman v. Aurora Sanitary Dist., supra. The area of the sanitary district was originally 10 square miles and annexations extended its area to 34 square miles. An ordinance of the district imposed an "inspection" fee on property owners in the original area and a connection and inspection fee on property owners in the annexed area. In upholding the differential charges the court reasoned that the property owners who benefited by the extension of the system into an entirely new area should bear the cost of that extension.

5. While the courts have been willing to accord considerable discretion to municipalities and special districts when setting connection fees for capital improvements, they are more likely to intervene when a charge ostensibly levied simply to cover the costs of connection does not appear reasonably related to these costs, *e.g., Strahan v. City of Aurora,* 311 N.E.2d 876 (Ohio 1973). *Cf. Merrelli v. City of St. Clair Shores,* 96 N.W.2d 144

(Mich. 1959) (building permit fee not reasonably related to cost of issuance).

What if the municipality simply levies a bedroom tax on new dwellings built by developers, the ordinance stating that its purpose is to raise funds to alleviate "the serious environmental and ecological problems created by new developments in the community"? The California courts have upheld these charges. See *Westfield-Palos Verdes Co. v. City of Rancho Palos Verdes,* 141 Cal. Rptr. 36 (Cal. App. 1977), holding that the charge was not regulatory because its true purpose was to halt development, and that the method to be chosen for raising funds to cope with environmental problems created by new developments was strictly a matter for legislative judgment.

Disproportionate burden or reasonableness problems also arise in the subdivision control context, as courts may invalidate an exaction because it is excessive as applied to a particular developer. In *East Neck Estates v. Luschinger,* 305 N.Y.S.2d 922 (N.Y. Sup. Ct.) (1969) (trial court), the planning board required plaintiff to dedicate a portion of his shore front property as a condition to plat approval. The court invalidated the dedication because the strip of land to be dedicated was worth one third of the total value of plaintiff's property. *See also Frank Ansuini v. City of Cranston,* 264 A.2d 910 (R.I. 1970). The municipal ordinance required developers to dedicate seven percent of their land for recreational purposes. This requirement was invalidated on the ground that the mandatory seven percent dedication was arbitrary and could be unreasonable as applied to a particular developer.

6. Differential charges of the kind considered here present some complex conceptual problems in the allocation of joint costs among different users. For discussion see J. Bonbright, Principles of Public Utility Rates 350-68 (1961); Littlechild & Thompson, Aircraft Landing Fees: A Game Theory Approach, 8 Bell J. Econ. 186 (1977).

7. Consider the following statute authorizing the levying of fees for drainage or sewerage facilities. Which of the theories presented in the cases considered here does it adopt?

> There may be imposed by local ordinance a requirement for the payment of fees for purposes of defraying the actual or estimated costs of constructing planned drainage facilities for the removal of surface and storm waters from local or neighborhood drainage areas and of constructing planned sanitary sewer facilities for local sanitary sewer areas, subject to the following conditions:
>
> (a) The ordinance has been in effect for a period of at least 30 days prior to the filing of the tentative map or parcel map if no tentative map is required.
>
> (b) The ordinance refers to a drainage or sanitary sewer plan adopted for a particular drainage or sanitary sewer area which contains an estimate of the total costs of constructing the local drainage or sanitary sewer facilities required by the plan, and a map of such area showing its boundaries and the location of such facilities.
>
> (c) [Drainage or sanitary sewer plan must be in conformity with county or special district general drainage or sanitary sewer plans, if any. — Eds.]

(d) The costs, whether actual or estimated, are based upon findings by the legislative body which has adopted the local plan, that subdivision and development of property within the planned local drainage area or local sanitary sewer area will require construction of the facilities described in the drainage or sewer plan, and that the fees are fairly apportioned within such areas either on the basis of benefits conferred on property proposed for subdivision or on the need for such facilities created by the proposed subdivision and development of other property within such areas.

(e) The fee as to any property proposed for subdivision within such a local area does not exceed the pro rata share of the amount of the total actual or estimated costs of all facilities within such area which would be assessable on such property if such costs were apportioned uniformly on a per-acre basis.

(f) The drainage or sanitary sewer facilities planned are in addition to existing facilities serving the area at the time of the adoption of such a plan for the area.

Such fees shall be paid to the local public agencies which provide drainage or sanitary sewer facilities, and shall be deposited by such agencies into a "planned local drainage facilities fund" and a "planned local sanitary sewer fund," respectively. Separate funds shall be established for each local drainage and sanitary sewer area. Moneys in such funds shall be expended solely for the construction or reimbursement for construction of local drainage or sanitary sewer facilities within the area from which the fees comprising the fund were collected, or to reimburse the local agency for the cost of engineering and administrative services to form the district and design and construct the facilities. The local ordinance may provide for the acceptance of considerations in lieu of the payment of fees.

. . . .

A local agency receiving fees pursuant to this section may incur an indebtedness for the construction of drainage or sanitary sewer facilities within a local drainage or sanitary sewer area; provided that the sole security for repayment of such indebtedness shall be moneys in the planned local drainage or sanitary sewer facilities fund.

Cal. Gov't Code § 66483 (Deering Supp. 1977).

D. PROTECTING THE DEVELOPER FROM CHANGE

As the introductory materials to this chapter indicate, subdivision developments go through a preliminary as well as a final plat stage before they are approved, and building in the subdivision in any event may not proceed until building permits are issued. This procedure can be time-consuming, and the subdivider is at the mercy of the municipality at least up to the time that building permits are obtained. In this interim period, political changes in the municipality or policy decisions leading to changes in the subdivision control or zoning ordinance may interfere with the subdivider's plans and force him to redesign his subdivision or abandon it altogether. These changes can be costly, and so the risk of change is a serious one.

Zoning map changes, which can lower the density in the subdivision, are especially troublesome.

Vested rights do not even attach immediately on issuance of a building permit, see *supra* p. 674, and the rule in subdivision control appears to be that the mere recording of an approved subdivision plat does not protect the subdivider against changes in the subdivision control ordinance. *Blevens v. City of Manchester, supra* p. 811. See also *Boutet v. Planning Bd.*, 253 A.2d 53 (Me. 1969), holding that preliminary approval of a plat "gave no rights whatsoever to the landowner to compel final approval. . . ." *Id.* at 56. The planning board in *Boutet* had insisted, when the subdivider applied for final approval, that he exclude from the subdivision a buffer strip which had earlier been included.

A few states have attempted to meet this problem through legislation providing some degree of assurance that local land use regulations applicable at the time of preliminary approval will not be changed. The extent of the protection given to the developer under this type of legislation is indicated in the following case:

LEVIN v. TOWNSHIP OF LIVINGSTON

Supreme Court of New Jersey
35 N.J. 500, 173 A.2d 391 (1961)

The opinion of the court was delivered by
HALL, J.

This case involves a narrow, but deeply rooted, aspect of land subdivision regulation by a municipality. Specifically the question is: When, in the course of the planning and construction of a development, do the municipality's specifications for street pavement which it requires the developer to install as an improvement become fixed so that it may not thereafter upgrade them?

Plaintiffs were engaged as landowners in residential subdivision development in the Township of Livingston. Their operations contemplated the laying out of lots and streets and the installation of utilities and other improvements on previously unimproved land, the construction of homes on the lots, and the ultimate sale thereof to individual purchasers. We are concerned with three sections of their developments which were in various stages of municipal approval and physical construction when the township, on March 21, 1960, amended its street ordinance to require thereafter pavement of bituminous concrete instead of the previously specified penetration macadam. The change expressly did not apply to streets in the course of construction if the curbs had been installed and the base course laid at the time of adoption of the amendment.

Plaintiffs then brought this action against the township seeking an adjudication that the amendment could not validly apply to the sections in question. An immutable right was claimed to install streets paved with penetration macadam by reason of prior municipal approval action under the Municipal Planning Act of 1953 (N.J.S.A. 40:55-1.1 et seq., L.1953, c. 433) and the local subdivision regulation ordinance adopted pursuant thereto on June 21, 1954. The factual situation concerning the status of approval is different as to each section and each was the subject of a separate count in the complaint. The first count related to those sections of the Cherry Hill development as to which only tentative approval had been granted, the second to Section 2 of the same development which had received final approval, and the third to Collins Estates, Section 1B, where the situation is unclear.

The Law Division held, 62 N.J.Super. 395, 163 A.2d 221 (1960), that the amendment to the street ordinance was properly applicable to each of the three sections and denied plaintiffs any relief. Their appeal was certified on our own motion while pending in the Appellate Division.

The precise problem must necessarily be considered in the light of the whole scheme of subdivision regulation prescribed in the state enabling act and its implementation in Livingston by local ordinance, at least to the extent that such a panoramic view has pertinence to the current issue.

Subdivision control, like zoning, is a tool of overall community planning. They are "closely related . . . in that both are preventive measures intended to avert community blight and deterioration by requiring that new development proceed in defined ways and according to prescribed standards. Zoning relates to the type of building development which can take place on the land; subdivision control relates to the way in which the land is divided and made ready for building development." Cunningham, "Control of Land Use in New Jersey Under The 1953 Planning Statutes," 15 Rutgers L.Rev. 1, 45-46, n. 175 (1960).

. . . . [The court then details the provisions for subdivision control as contained in the New Jersey enabling legislation. — Eds.]

The requirements for plat approval provide the means and character of regulation. Under the statute, these fall into two distinct categories, with different attributes. The first, which is mandatory, is broad and relates to layout, design and other basic general terms and conditions. The second, with which we are particularly concerned, is permissive, involving specific tangible "improvements," above and beyond the general terms and conditions, which the municipality may by ordinance compel the developer to install at his expense.

. . . .

The purposes behind and the scope of the required general terms and conditions are equally plain. At inception the planning board must pass upon basic matters of the highest significance to future community growth and well-being and the welfare of individuals who will ultimately become owners and occupants in the subdivision. . . . For instance, it is of essential importance to determine whether the whole tract proposed to be subdivided is fundamentally suitable for the projected development from the standpoint of area, topography, drainage, soil characteristics, accessibility, availability of utilities and the like, or, if not, in whole or in part, whether and to what extent special conditions can be imposed to make it so. . . . It must also decide upon the best layout of lots and streets and whether it conforms to the ordinance design and to the master plan and official map (if the municipality has adopted such). It must consider the impact upon adjacent areas and the effect of other pertinent ordinances of the municipality. Special drainage and sanitary sewage disposal problems may require particular remedies to be undertaken. In certain situations it may temporarily reserve portions of the tract for schools, parks and playgrounds. In short, at inception the board has the very great responsibility of doing everything possible to avoid future problems of vital importance to the community and subsequent individual property owners.

The Livingston ordinance implements these purposes by specifying standards in detail and prescribing the information which must be furnished on or with the preliminary plat with respect to the layout and characteristics of the entire development. With particular reference to streets, the design standards require that "[t]he arrangement, character, extent, width, grade and location of all streets shall conform to the Master Plan and Official Map, and shall be considered in relation to existing and planned streets, to topographical conditions, to public convenience and safety, and in relation to the proposed uses of the land to be served by such streets" and goes on to specify in greater detail provisions for the arrangement and related aspects of proposed streets not already shown on the master plan or official map. The "character" of the street, as used in the quoted portion of the ordinance, obviously refers to function and type, such as arterial, collector and so forth, and not, as plaintiffs suggest, to specifications of construction. The greater detail provisions mentioned similarly do not encompass matters of construction. These ordinance provisions are clearly within the scope and intent of the enabling act provisions relating to general "conditions to be required" and street design standards which must be included in the local legislation.

Early determination of the basic matters of which we have been speaking is likewise of great importance to the developer. He needs to know in the beginning whether his tract and development scheme can ultimately gain the final approval of the municipality and what will be required of him with respect to the most financially significant items of layout and the like, so that he may decide whether it is economically feasible to go ahead. And, in fairness, he should be enabled to make this decision before he has made or committed himself to large expenditures. So the general revision of the planning act in 1953 introduced for the first time a two-step approval procedure, permitting municipalities to provide for "tentative approval" of plats, N.J.S.A. 40:55-1.18, by which these basic matters may be settled. From what has been said, it is obvious that tentative approval is the most important phase of the subdivision regulation process. Most municipalities, including Livingston, have accepted the option thus given them and make this procedure compulsory. In order to give meaning to such preliminary approval and furnish the developer assurance upon which he may rely, the statutory section goes on to provide that tentative approval shall confer upon the applicant the following rights for a three-year period thereafter:

"(1) that the *general terms and conditions* upon which the tentative approval was granted will not be changed.

"(2) that the said applicant may submit on or before the expiration date the whole or part or parts of said plat for *final approval.*" (Emphasis added.)

. . . .

Final approval under the two-step procedure amounts to endorsement of the final form of the plat to be filed in the county recording office after board investigation and determination that the terms and conditions of tentative approval have been met and that required improvements, shortly to be mentioned more fully, have been installed or provided for, N.J.S.A. 40:55-1.21. Final approval, while perfunctory to a certain extent, is not only the key to the right and requirement to file the map, N.J.S.A. 40:55-1.17, but is also, as we view the legislative scheme, the prerequisite to the obtaining of any building permit, N.J.S.A. 40:55-1.39, and to the transfer, sale or agreement to sell any of the land in the subdivision, N.J.S.A. 40:55-1.23. It contemplates that a subdivider has decided to go ahead and that he is ready to proceed promptly with complete development and building construction at least in the section for which he seeks such approval.

This brings us to a consideration of the second category of requirements for plat approval — the matter of "improvements." Here it is evident the Legislature was thinking and talking about something above, beyond and distinct from requirements imposed as general terms and conditions of which we have been speaking. A distinct section of the 1953 planning act, N.J.S.A. 40:55-1.21, provides:

"Before the final approval of plats the governing body may require, in accordance with the standards adopted by ordinance, the installation, or the furnishing of a performance guarantee in lieu thereof, of any or all of the following improvements it may deem to be necessary or appropriate: street grading, pavement, gutters, curbs, sidewalks, street lighting, shade trees, surveyor's monuments, water mains, culverts, storm sewers, sanitary sewers or other means of sewage disposal, drainage structures, and such other subdivision improvements as the municipal governing body may find necessary in the public interest."

. . . .

From what we have said so far, it is apparent that we agree with the trial court that specifications for street pavement are not "general terms or conditions" and so are not guaranteed to the developer against change under the provisions of N.J.S.A. 40:55-1.18, at least until final approval. We think this is clear as a matter of statutory construction most favorable to the municipality. As has been pointed out, construction details are not intrinsically the kind of thing intended to be encompassed by the quoted phrase and the Legislature has prescribed distinct treatment for improvements, under different statutory sections, geared to final, and not temporary, approval. A municipality should not, in the public interest, be precluded from making desirable changes in construction specifications for improvements prior to final approval (and in fact should not have the power to contract away in advance the right to do so), unless the enabling legislation compels such a result. Here we think quite the opposite is true. Moreover, compared to the basic conditions of development layout, an upgrading of the type of street pavement is a relatively minor item to the developer which it is not unfair to change when balanced against the future public benefit to be derived from the enhanced requirements.

We do feel, however, contrary to the view of the trial judge, that there comes a point in the approval process where the developer is to be protected against further changes of this nature. We discern a legislative intent that the point is reached when a proper and valid final approval is granted in accordance with the statute and ordinance. This is not a matter of accrual of "vested rights" or some similarly labelled concept, but rather one of statutory construction. At the time of final approval either the improvements have been installed pursuant to the then requirements — and no one can validly contend that a municipal change after completion could force the developer to tear up the work and do it over according to later upgraded specifications — or the developer has posted security to guarantee that the improvements will be constructed. The amount of the guarantee is based upon the municipality's estimate of the cost of construction pursuant to the municipal standards at that time and the security given represents, either by the conditions of the surety bond or the terms of an escrow agreement, a contract that specified improvements will be completed according to the then specifications. In fact, in the case of streets, frequently, as here, the performance bond will specify the precise kind of pavement to be installed. The statute permits the security as a substitute for performance and we believe it is intended that the decisive point has then been reached.

. . . .

[The court then found that protection from changes in the paving requirement were to be extended only to that part of the development which had received final approval, and noted also that the record concerning the status of the Collins Estate development was confusing. A question was raised concerning the length of time during which final approval would be effective, but the court did not decide that question. It refused to find an equitable estoppel in favor of the developer simply because he had commenced land preparation, had entered into contracts for paving, and had advertised houses at a price based in part on the amount agreed to be paid under the paving contracts. However, the court noted that "there may be situations where equities of this kind are so strong that an estoppel against municipal action will arise. . . ." — Eds.]

The judgment of the Law Division is affirmed as to the first count of the complaint, reversed as to the second count and reversed and remanded for further proceedings consistent with this opinion as to the third count. No costs to either party.

For affirmance of first count, reversal on second count and reversal and remandment on third count: Chief Justice WEINTRAUB and Justices FRANCIS, HALL, SCHETTINO and HANEMAN — 5.

Opposed: None.

————————

Comments: 1. The New Jersey subdivision control legislation is better developed than most, but most local subdivision control ordinances follow the format of the New Jersey legislation, making a distinction between preliminary and final approval and often making similar distinctions in the nature of the improvements required. Might the New Jersey court have interpreted the protective provision differently if subdivision control procedures and the substantive requirements of the ordinance had been left to local discretion?

2. A real question arises concerning the scope of protection which should be offered the developer at the preliminary approval stage. While his need to be protected against unstabilizing change should be recognized, the municipality at the same time needs the opportunity to vary the substantive content of regulations when change is needed. Compare Conn. Gen. Stat. § 8-26a (1977), protecting the subdivider for a period of five years after final approval against changes in the subdivision regulations or zoning ordinance; Mass. Ann. Laws ch. 40A, § 7A (Supp. 1977), providing protection against changes in the zoning ordinance for a period of seven years from the final approval of the subdivision plat. *But see Island Properties, Inc. v. Martha's Vineyard Comm'n*, 361 N.E.2d 385 (Mass. 1977), holding that the Massachusetts statute did not protect the subdivider against the imposition of critical area controls adopted under a state statute enacted shortly after the approval of the subdivision. The Commission is a regional agency authorized to impose selective land use controls throughout the island which supersede local land use regulations. For a discussion of critical area controls see *infra* p. 1244.

Retsky v. Municipal Util. Auth., 219 A.2d 197 (N.J.L. 1966). The township subdivision control ordinance provided that preliminary subdivision approval was subject to the authority's approval of the plans and specifications for any sewage or water system in the subdivision. Preliminary approval was given by the township but the authority refused to approve the subdivider's water and sewage plans. Since preliminary approval had not been perfected under the ordinance, the court held that it did not have to reach the problem whether sewerage and drainage structures were "general terms and conditions" of an approval which fell within the protective provisions of the statute. To an argument that the township had improperly delegated approval powers to the utility authority, the court answered that the statutes authorized the municipality to "delegate the entire sewage and water supply problem to a municipal utilities authority; otherwise, there is little or no necessity for the existence of such an entity." *Id.* at 200.

The New Jersey statute was amended subsequent to the decision in the principal case to specify some of the "general terms and conditions" which may not be changed once preliminary approval is given, and the "layout and design standards for streets, curbs and sidewalks" were explicitly brought within this term. N.J. Stat. Ann. § 40:55D-49(a) (West Supp. 1977). This list of included terms and conditions is not exclusive, however, and the statute also provides, as amended, that "nothing herein shall be construed to prevent the municipality from modifying by ordinance such general terms and conditions of preliminary approval as relate to public health and welfare." *Id.* Lot sizes are also included within the list of protected terms and conditions. They had been brought under the provisions of the act as they appear in the principal case before amendment in *Hilton Acres v. Klein*, 165 A.2d 819 (N.J. Super. 1960).

3. Note that the statute in its original form gave the developer a three-year protection against changes after preliminary approval, but said nothing about the effect of a final approval or a building permit on the protection period. If a final approval was given six months after preliminary approval, would the subdivider have an additional two and one-half years in which to secure his building permit? In *Sandler v. Board of Adjustment*, 273 A.2d 775 (N.J. Super. 1971), the court indicated that while a major subdivider would have a reasonable time after final approval to secure a building permit, the three-year period merely indicated the outer reach of the law's protection. In that case, subdivision approval was obtained simply to allow a redivision of a lot, and no additional terms or conditions were imposed on the redivision. The court held that the subdivider was subject to a change in the zoning ordinance enacted three months after approval of the redivision and three weeks before the subdivider applied for a building permit. The amended New Jersey statute now handles this problem, generally, by providing for a two-year period of protection once final approval has been given. *Id.* § 40:55D-52(a). Is this a satisfactory solution? How would you handle this problem?

Chapter 6

THE CUTTING EDGE: INNOVATIVE LAND USE CONTROLS

We now turn to a series of innovative land use management strategies that have extended the conventional land use regulation system. A few of these strategies are relatively new and some have been with us for some time, at least in concept, but all provide new techniques for land management — thus, the cutting edge. Some of these strategies provide new forms of land use regulation. They either implement new substantive purposes or restructure the administrative process of land use regulation to make that process more sensitive to land use control problems. Planned unit development, for example, is both an innovative administrative technique for regulating large-scale development as well as a regulatory measure intended to improve project design. Aesthetic and historic preservation controls extend land use regulation beyond the control of use and density to recognize the importance of good design and the preservation of historic resources in our environment.

Other innovative strategies expand and in some fashion modify the conventional police power approach to land use regulation. Transfer of development rights attempts to ease the police power-eminent domain deadlock. It compensates landowners for the loss of development rights in regulatory programs, shifting those rights elsewhere to landowners who in turn reimburse the original owner for the loss of those rights. Historic preservation happens to be one control program in which transfer of development rights can be useful. Land banking attempts to overcome difficulties in plan implementation through the public ownership and disposition of land for development. This technique is also viewed as a method through which the public can recapture some of the increment in land value that occurs when development takes place. Unearned increment taxation to recapture the increment in land value from new development is another technique for accomplishing this purpose.

Land use management reforms offer no panaceas, and the innovative strategies discussed in this chapter may often create more problems than they solve. The discerning student will want to consider whether any or all of these innovative strategies have a permanent place in the land use management system.

A. PLANNED UNIT DEVELOPMENT (PUD)

COUNCIL TURNS DOWN PUD!

Cosconing, May 22nd. — Voting at two o'clock a.m. last night, the town council again turned down a proposed PUD to have been built by Fauna Realty Company. Zoning on the Company's tract stands at its original one-acre level. Spokesmen for the Company indicate that they will now build identical dwellings on the tract. "If cheesebox design is what they want, that's what they'll get," one company official said.

Fauna's proposal called for townhouses and apartments placed in an original design around a man-made lake. Densities would have gone up. The design would have preserved attractive features of the site, which is in the fashionable Upper Seatack neighborhood. Plans for the townhouses and apartments had been drawn by a nationally respected architectural firm.

None of this appeased residents in the area. Organized as the Save Our Seatack (SOS) association, they turned out by the hundreds at last night's meeting. George Pepone, President of SOS, spoke out against the higher densities. "We bought here because this was an aesthetic, suburban community," he told the council. "We want to keep it that way." Highlight of the meeting was a parade of neighborhood children carrying signs reading "STOP PUD." The council's unanimous vote denying the PUD was contrary to the recommendation of its planning commission and planning director.

———————

Exclusionary zoning? Racial discrimination in the suburbs? Hardly. The townhouses and apartments proposed by the developer in this fictitious but all too real account were priced in the upper income market. Then why all the fuss? The planned unit development in this story is an example of a new development concept which is increasily taking over a large segment of the market for new housing. The problems raised by planned unit developments, and the kinds of issues which led to the rejection of this PUD proposal will be the subject of this section.

Some background is needed on the growth of the planned unit development idea. Conventional zoning and subdivision control have proceeded on the basis of "crude categories." Zoning districts divide the community into zones which roughly separate uses according to compatibility criteria. Subdivision control ordinances divide land into lots and blocks. They tend to produce uniform developments in basic "cell" patterns, in which all of the land is used and all of the building lots are of the same size.

This approach to land development may have fit the building practices of the early Twentieth Century, when residential development proceeded slowly and houses were built one at a time. (It also met the judicial penchant for equal treatment.) With the coming of the post-war years, the pattern of residential development shifted. Large-scale developers, building hundreds of homes at a time on large tracts, became common. This kind of development prompted the need for a control system in which the entire development could be reviewed as an entity and advantage taken of the design and other opportunities which large-scale development creates. For examples see M. Huntoon, PUD: A Better Way for the Suburbs, (Urban Land Inst. 1971).

The process through which these unified large-scale developments are reviewed is known by different names but is referred to here as planned unit development (PUD) control. We begin an analysis of PUD's with a brief discussion of PUD controls, and the range of opportunities they present.

D. MANDELKER, CONTROLLING PLANNED RESIDENTIAL DEVELOPMENTS 3-8 (American Soc'y of Planning Officials, 1966)

NEW TECHNIQUES FOR OLD: THE BASIS OF CHANGE

Traditional zoning is geared to controlling the placement of a single structure on a single lot — the lot is the basic regulatory unit. This approach was fostered by the development techniques of the 1920's when the gridiron street pattern was king and when development occurred one lot at a time.

Traditional zoning — at least in its original form — was also noted for its rigid separation of different uses into different zones. Residential uses, reflecting the conventional market view, were segregated from commercial and industrial uses. Single-family and two-family houses were segregated from apartments, which were considered a different "use."

Planned development regulations mark a substantial departure from tradition. First, they apply to entire developments rather than to individual lots. The regulations provide for the calculation of densities on a project basis and permit other adjustments based on a unified plan, adjustments which are not possible under traditional zoning. The application of controls to entire developments, then, is a fundamental characteristic of planned development regulations.

Second, planned development regulations abandon or substantially modify the traditional self-executing form of zoning regulation. In theory at least (although numerous established practices deviate from this theory), traditional zoning regulations leave no place for the exercise of official discretion when development is proposed; a developer need only obtain a building permit from the building inspector. Planned developments, on the other hand, are governed by more general standards which are applied when development is proposed. Some discretion is inevitably involved in the application of the general standards.

Finally, planned development regulations may also represent a partial or total abandonment of traditional use districting. For example, some planned development regulations authorize the approval of plans that call for commercial as well as residential uses. Still more commonly, the regulations provide for "mixed" residential developments, thus abandoning (and high time!) the "use" distinction between apartments and single-family houses.

ADVANTAGES OF PLANNED DEVELOPMENT REGULATION

Planned development controls permit today's large-scale developer to take advantage of the opportunities offered by his scale of operation. In this way, these controls can help secure a better residential environment. Although the more specific objectives of planned development controls are harder to isolate, several have been suggested.

Improved Design

Some desirable design innovations are impossible under standard zoning bulk controls. . . . Other innovations, while legally possible under traditional zoning, are impractical unless the developer is willing to make financial sacrifices. Staggered front yards, for example, are permissible under most zoning ordinances so long as the shallowest yards meet the minimum, but in practice, market pressures cause developers to provide only the minimum required yard.

Perhaps the most important design advantage of planned development regulation is that it permits the unified treatment of site design — without the restrictions imposed by the application of fixed yard and height requirements to individual lots. Freedom from the lot pattern can allow a reallocation of project densities which can produce more interesting project design.

This design freedom is especially important in the development of rough terrain. Traditional zoning often appears to assume flat land, to which the lot and block pattern can be applied without sacrifice of building lots. In rough country, where this assumption does not apply, the developer must often resort to overgrading to create building sites. But planned development regulations, allowing reallocation of densities, can reduce or eliminate any financial sacrifice from leaving rough terrain in its natural state.

Since planned development zoning is not self-executing, it permits an opportunity for the review of site design in conjunction with the approval of the development plan. Although design review is not uncommon in connection with conventional zoning (particularly in California), many administrators view the opportunity for site plan review as one of the chief advantages of planned development regulations. And this review may prove to be of great value in the many communities where rezoning applicants present plans for one project but then — after the rezoning is granted — build something quite different.

Lower Costs

Planned development regulations often . contemplate the reallocation of project densities, with higher densities on part of the site offsetting common open areas. When residences are concentrated in part of the development, street and utility costs can often be substantially lowered because frontages are reduced. Not having to level and prepare rough terrain may also produce savings.

More Useful Open Space

The unusable side and front yards required by traditional zoning can be reduced or even eliminated under some planned development provisions, and less area need be devoted to individual lots. Land thus "saved" can be set aside as common open space for use by all project residents.

In addition, planned development provisions can help make up for deficiencies in the amount of public open space. Some subdivision control ordinances have tried to remedy these deficiencies by requiring developers to dedicate open space for public use, but the courts have generally not approved these compulsory exactions. By trading off lower lot sizes for common open space, planned development provisions come close to achieving by indirection the dedications that the courts have not permitted directly; the effect is often about the same whether the open space is publicly- or privately-owned. Of course, public open space dedications under planned development provisions, unlike those under conventional subdivision regulations, do not reduce the total number of dwelling units permitted in the development.

Mixing of Residential Building Types

Despite the amenities now associated with many apartment developments, zoning ordinances still generally separate apartments from single-family homes. Although this separation of building types is not inherent in traditional zoning, it is so well-established that it is extremely difficult to break down in practice. Some planned development provisions do eliminate distinctions among residential building types and thus permit more variety in development.

Increased Density

Planned development regulations usually permit a mixture of residential densities within a development, allowing higher densities on one part of the tract in return for common open space elsewhere. Some provisions go further, permitting net densities in a planned development to be greater than those otherwise allowed by the zoning ordinance (in fact, planned development controls may strike an observer as a technique for making higher residential densities more palatable to suburbanites). One theory for allowing density increases is that superior design makes greater densities possible with no reduction of amenities.

As this review has indicated, several of the objectives of planned development regulations coincide with goals long favored by many planners — mixed-use developments, more open space, more "flexibility," lower housing costs, and higher densities. A few provisions authorizing planned development regulation have been on the statute books for many years, but were very rarely used; the current interest in planned development regulation reflects increasing market acceptance of the planned development idea. The demand for unified site treatments in urban renewal projects, the trend toward apartments in the suburbs, and dissatisfaction with the monotony of conventionally built residential subdivisions are some of the factors that have prompted greater community interest in these regulations.

. . . .

CLASSIFICATION OF PLANNED DEVELOPMENTS

Several types of planned development regulations have been adopted, but they are not easy to classify. Four general types appear to predominate, and the character and effect of planned development regulations can be understood better if each of these categories is described.

Density Transfer Systems

The simplest and least controversial of the planned development techniques, the "density transfer," is best exemplified by cluster development. Under this system, minimum lot sizes (and usually yard requirements) are smaller than those normally required by the zoning ordinance. The permitted building types, however, are unaffected — a density transfer system will not allow apartments in a single-family zone. Nor does a density transfer system affect the over-all density of development — the area "saved" through lot-size reductions is merely retained within the development, most often being designated as common open space. [For an interesting case sustaining the transfer of development rights in the context of a PUD ordinance see *Dupont Circle Citizens Ass'n v. District of Columbia Zoning Comm'n,* 355 A.2d 550 (D.C. Ct. App. 1976). — Eds.]

Varying Residential Types; No Increase in Density

Some planned development ordinances allow multi-family or single-family structures (or both), but still prohibit any increase in density. The provision of common open space though not unusual, may not be required by such an ordinance.

Varying Residential Types; Density Increases Allowed

Some of the ordinances which allow a variety of residential types also authorize an increase in density. Ordinarily, these increases are subject to standards contained in the ordinance.

Mixed-Use Projects

To a variety of dwelling types the planned development ordinance may also add other uses, such as ancillary shopping or even a neighborhood or community shopping center. Industrial uses may also be allowed. Increases in residential density may or may not be permitted. If the scale of a mixed-use project is sufficiently extensive, it can take on the character of an entire planned community or "new town."

MAP 1. A RESIDENTIAL DENSITY TRANSFER PLANNED UNIT DEVELOPMENT

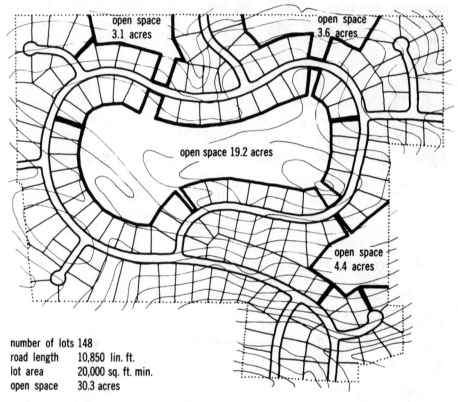

open space
3.1 acres

open space
3.6 acres

open space 19.2 acres

open space
4.4 acres

number of lots 148
road length   10,850 lin. ft.
lot area   20,000 sq. ft. min.
open space   30.3 acres

Source: Office of State Planning, State of New Hampshire, Handbook of Subdivision Practice 82 (1972).

Comments: 1. Map 1 illustrates a simple residential, density transfer planned unit development and illustrates the regulatory problems presented by this kind of project. What has happened is that open space areas have been provided throughout the development for common use. Lot sizes have been reduced for the individual lots, but this apparent increase in density is offset by the open space areas; there is no net density increase in the development. Under variants of the PUD approach, as discussed in the excerpt, densities could have been increased as well, and new building types such as townhouses and apartments added. If this were a larger PUD, a retail shopping area could also have been included.

An initial thought is that the project shown by Map 1 does not look all that bad. Then why all the fuss in our introductory problem? Richard Babcock, the well-known Chicage zoning lawyer, may have the answer:

> The initial response is one of enthusiasm for the novel plot plan. It does have a catchy design. The local commissioner is as intrigued as he would be by four-color copy in an ad in the *New Yorker* magazine. The emotional empathy rises. Then there is a pause. This proposal represents people, not tonic water. The emotional graph levels off. And down it zooms as some practical soul asks: "What kind of nut would move to Wedgewood and not want his own backyard?"
>
> Another client asks: "Well, if your costs are less, then, of course, you expect to reduce your prices?" With that the jig is up.

R. Babcock, The Zoning Game 31-32 (1966).

2. Various regulatory possibilities are available for the review and approval of this PUD. In this case, since densities are not increased and the development is entirely single-family, the approval of the PUD could be carried out as part of normal subdivision review procedure. If densities are increased or different building types or nonresidential uses added, zoning review will be essential if, as is usually the case, these new densities, building types, or uses are not permitted in the zoning district applicable to the development at the time it is proposed. In this situation, the PUD review and approval process will combine elements of both subdivision and zoning review.

An initial problem to be considered in evaluating PUD regulation is whether PUD controls can be included in local subdivision control or zoning ordinances authorized by zoning and subdivision control enabling acts, which still generally follow the form of the Standard Acts. PUD review procedures present one set of problems. Most PUD ordinances require a two-stage process contemplating the review of both a preliminary and a final PUD plan, a review procedure modeled on subdivision control, see *supra* p. 793. This procedure is easily assimilated into subdivision control ordinances, which authorize this kind of review system, but present more difficult problems when incorporated into zoning ordinances. One question is whether the zoning statute authorizes this kind of case-by-case review. Obvious candidates for adaptation to include this review system are the special exception and conditional use procedures, and the zoning amendment process.

How to adapt PUD procedures to the zoning district system presents other problems. There are several possibilities. Under one approach, a PUD district is included in the ordinance. This district usually contains use requirements, development standards, and procedures. It may be treated as a floating zone; the PUD district is incorporated into the zoning ordinance text but is not mapped until an application for a PUD is made. Approval of the PUD will then usually take the form of a zoning amendment. This method will probably be satisfactory in any jurisdiction which approves the floating zone concept. Under a second districting approach the PUD district is included in the text of the ordinance and is also mapped, usually as an overlay district. It then imposes a set of mandatory requirements in addition to those contained in the zoning ordinance. PUD regulations may also be administered as a special exception or conditional use.

A variety of problems arise from these zoning procedures. One set of issues revolves around the local zoning agency which is to administer the PUD regulations. If the PUD district is mapped, and the regulatory problem is the application of the PUD standards to individual PUD developments, an argument can be made that the planning commission can carry out this function. However, the Standard Act (and practically all the state legislation) does not explicitly confer this power on the commission. If some element of discretion is built into the PUD regulatory procedure, the delegation of the regulatory function to the planning commission is more difficult to uphold. In this instance, the local governing body may have to be part of the PUD approval process, especially if density increases are contemplated in the PUD.

Another problem is the uniformity issue. Recall that the Standard Zoning Act requires that all zoning regulations be uniform throughout each zoning district. "Because single-use districts are a fairly common feature of conventional zoning practice, many have inferred that the uniform regulation requirement when applied to use regulations means that only one kind of land use may be permitted within a given district. Thus the argument goes that the mixture of uses contemplated by the typical PUD ordinance is beyond the power of the local legislature." F. So, D. Mosena, & F. Bangs, Planned Unit Development Ordinances 48 (American Soc'y of Planning Officials, Planning Advisory Service Rep. No. 291, 1973). It was also thought that the courts might recoil against the flexible case-by-case approval that is inherent in the PUD process, and that the courts might object to "sensitive" zoning which would react specifically to the particularized development plans of an individual developer. *See* Krasnowiecki, Legal Aspects of Planned Unit Development in Theory and Practice in Frontiers of Planned Unit Development, 99, 101-02 (R. Burchell ed. 1973).

This section will first examine the treatment of planned unit development ordinances under the conventional standard enabling legislation, and will then consider some of the substantive and procedural problems in the PUD regulatory process. Attention will then be directed to model planned unit development legislation which has been enacted in some jurisdictions.

1. The PUD Process Under Conventional Land Use Control Legislation

TODD MART, INC. v. TOWN BOARD OF TOWN OF WEBSTER

New York Supreme Court, Appellate Division
(Intermediate Court)
49 App. Div. 2d 12, 370 N.Y.S.2d 683 (1975)

Before MARSH, P.J., and MOULE, MAHONEY, GOLDMAN and WITMER, JJ.

OPINION

COLEMAN, Justice.

Petitioner-respondent Todd Mart, Inc. (Todd), a developer of retail shopping centers, brought this Article 78 proceeding to annul a decision of the respondents-appellants, Town Board of the Town of Webster and Town of Webster (Town Board) denying petitioner's application to rezone 20 acres of land for the construction of a shopping center. Special Term reversed the Town Board's determination and remitted the matter to the Town Board "to make necessary findings of fact."

Under the Town of Webster Zoning Ordinance and Official Map which were adopted on June 26, 1969 in accordance with "the general intent of a comprehensive plan," the subject property, presently owned by petitioner, was placed in a C-S commercial shopping center district. The permitted uses in such a district are limited to single family dwellings, and various public, religious and agricultural uses (Webster Zoning Ordinance § 59-11A). The ordinance provides that "The Town Board may establish a PCS planned shopping center district in a C-S District in accordance with procedures set forth in Articles IV and V hereof" (Section 59-19).

In accordance with the ordinance petitioner submitted a sketch plan for the shopping center to the Webster Planning Board. The submitted plan indicated that the shopping center would be enclosed and include a theater, bank, supermarket, general department store, and numerous other shops. After several meetings and discussions of the sketch plan application the Planning Board submitted a favorable report to the Town Board. Thereafter, on July 12, 1973 the Town Board passed the following resolution at its regular meeting:

> that the proposed Monroe Mall-Todd Mart Incorporated PUD project on the corner of Five Mile Line Road and Ridge Road, appears to meet the objectives set forth in Section 59-23 of the Zoning Ordinance and would be in the public interest.
> Further, that the project be referred to the Planning Board for progression of preliminary plans under Section 59-26 of the Zoning Ordinance.

This favorable determination was made pursuant to subsection D of section 59-25 of the ordinance which provides in relevant part that:

> Such determination or recommendations by the Town Board shall be advisory only and shall not constitute approval or disapproval of the plans for the project, nor shall it constitute a commitment or agreement by the Town Board to take any further action whether in the nature of legislation or otherwise in connection with such proposal.

Under the PUD zoning procedure the next step provided for application for Planning Board approval of a preliminary development plan, followed by a public hearing by the Town Board and then reconsideration by that Board. Article IV, section 59-26 of the ordinance provides:

> If after the public hearing the Town Board shall determine that the proposed development conforms to applicable state, county and town laws, ordinances and regulations, and is in the public interest, it shall adopt a resolution declaring its intention to zone the applicant's property for the proposed planned unit development upon the applicant receiving approval of final plans therefor from the Planning Board and upon the developer meeting such additional conditions as the Town Board shall deem appropriate in each case and shall set forth in such resolution.

Eventually the Planning Board on December 20, 1973 gave preliminary approval of the plan subject to conditions relating to drainage, signs, construction of an access road and other matters, and it referred the application to the Town Board. After substantial opposition voiced by several residents at public hearings held on February 14th and May 9, 1974 the Town Board on May 23, 1974, by unanimous resolution, denied "the request for 'intent to re-zone'." The Town Board's refusal to declare its intention to rezone was supported by 18 specific findings included among which were incompatibility with the existing residential character of the area; increased automobile traffic, noise, and congestion on the highway, close to the busiest intersection in the Town; inadequate flood control plans as affecting soil erosion and pollutants; poor and unsuitable soil conditions for commercial development which would be a source of potential blight; material changes in the ultimate access from the original plan which had been approved by the Planning Board; petitions in opposition signed and submitted at the two public hearings by 587 residents; and no adequate provision for buffers. The Town Board in its findings concluded that petitioner had not proved that the proposed shopping center would create "a more desirable environment" and that approval of "this shopping center would not be in the public interest."

After this action by the Town Board, petitioner commenced the present Article 78 proceeding to annul the Town Board's determination and to secure an order requiring that its property be rezoned as requested. The petition also alleged that the zoning ordinance as applied by the Town Board was "unlawful and illegal and an unconstitutional deprivation of petitioner's due process and confiscatory." Special Term, noting that the constitutionality of the ordinance was not questioned, properly stated that the "question for determination is whether the action of the Town Board is legislative or administrative." The court answered the question by holding that the Town Board's denial of the application for a declaration of "intent to rezone" was administrative in nature and was not legislative. Special Term with particularity reviewed the factual findings of the Town Board and held that these findings were "conclusory statements" which are "arbitrary and unreasonable" and therefore required remand to the Town Board for further factual development.

This appeal presents a relatively new concept in New York zoning law — the planned unit development (PUD). Essentially, "The planned unit development technique is a legislative response to changing patterns of land development and the demonstrated shortcomings of orthodox zoning regulations." (1 Anderson, New York Zoning Law and Practice (2d ed.), § 8.28.) The "changing patterns" are the relatively recent prevalence of large scale developments, such as new towns and suburbs around urban communities; the related shortcomings of orthodox zoning are its inflexibility and inability to mix diverse land-uses within a localized district. The planned unit development concept has evolved to meet these specific land-use control problems. It made available to communities a maximum choice in types of environment. It creates a flexible floating zone which, as in the instant case, hovers without definite boundaries until subsequent action by the zoning authority affixes it to an identified area. It multiplies the community's options to provide for compatible and efficient uses of land.

The usual PUD technique, as in the Webster Zoning Ordinance, involves a two-stage process: 1 — description of the permissible type or types of PUD districts in the original zoning ordinance, and 2 — location and approval of particular PUD districts by supplemental action at a later time. This secondary stage usually involves regulation of the developer's land-use planning by public planning officials and then formal amendment of the zoning ordinance and map to locate an approved PUD district (1 Anderson, New York Zoning Law and Practice (2d ed.), §§ 8.28-8.34). The instant case raises the issue of whether this secondary determination approving or rejecting a PUD zoning change is a legislative or administrative determination. If the determination of the Webster Town Board is "administrative," then petitioner's proper procedural form is the Article 78 proceeding which it instituted. If, however, the determination is "legislative," then an Article 78 review is inappropriate; for in that event petitioner's proper procedural course would be a declaratory judgment action to test the validity or constitutionality of the legislative action. This procedural distinction is of limited significance in the case at bar because the courts under CPLR 103(c) may review challenged zoning determinations even though the improper procedural form has been employed. . . . More importantly, however, the "legislative-administrative" distinction determines the substantive standard for judicial review of the zoning determination. If the determination is characterized as administrative, a more exacting judicial inquiry is permitted, that is, whether the challenged determination is contrary to local standards, arbitrary, capricious, discriminatory, an abuse of discretion, or supported by substantial evidence (CPLR 7803). On the other hand, if the challenged determination is legislative, judicial review is more limited. Such a review may only ascertain whether the local legislative body had authority to act as it did under its zoning enabling statute (see Town Law, §§ 260-264) or whether the legislative action is an unconstitutional taking or deprivation of due process or equal protection under the Fifth and Fourteenth Amendments. Because such a due process challenge questions the reasonableness of the police power regulation (zoning), the substantive standard for review of legislative zoning determinations approaches the "arbitrary-capricious-discriminatory" standard used in reviewing purely administrative determinations. See, *Dauernheim, Inc. v. Town Bd. of Hempstead* (33 N.Y.2d 468, 471-472, 354 N.Y.S.2d 909, 912, 310 N.E.2d 516, 517-518) [an action seeking zoning ordinance amendment where the court analogized two standards for granting an administrative variance]; *Matter of Bernhard v. Caso* (19 N.Y.2d 192, 197, 278 N.Y.S.2d 818, 822, 225 N.E.2d 521, 524) [denial of permit upheld because Town Board's decision was based on the public interest]; *Rodgers v. Village of Tarrytown* (302 N.Y. 115, 121-123, 96 N.E.2d 731, 733-734) [constitutionality of floating zone].

Because of the paucity of appellate decisions in our State dealing with the distinction between "administrative" and "legislative" actions in connection with planned unit development zoning, we turn to other jurisdictions which have dealt with the problem. A majority of such jurisdictions hold that the secondary determination, whether to approve a particular planned unit development district, is a legislative function exercised by the local zoning authority. Last year the Supreme Court of Washington stated our position succinctly in the imposition of a PUD on a specific parcel of land. In commenting on the legal nature and effect of the statute it stated "[i]t is inescapable that application of the PUD to this tract constituted an act of rezoning." (*Lutz v. The City of Longview,* 83 Wash.2d 566, 569, 520 P.2d 1374, 1376.) Similar precedents holding the requirement of rezoning to be a legislative act are *Village 2 at New Hope, Inc.* (429 Pa. 626, 241 A.2d 81) [zoning ordinance establishing a PUD is presumed valid legislation]; *Moore v. City of Boulder* (29 Colo.App. 248, 484 P.2d 134) [rezoning a single parcel within single family residence district to PUD district is a legislative act]; *Orinda Homeowners Committee v. Board of Supervisors* (11 Cal.App.3d 768, 90 Cal.Rptr. 88) [ordinance rezoning for a residential PUD is legislative function].

Turning to the Town of Webster ordinance, section 59-19 provides the authority for the Town Board's action. It is couched in precatory language and provides that "[t]he Town Board *may establish* (emphasis added) a PCS Planned Shopping Center District in a C-S District in accordance with the procedures —." These procedures required three steps by the Board, the last of which, in order to give approval of final development plans, is that the Board (only after the public hearing) "*shall* then *enact* the *legislation* to create the appropriate planned unit development district" (emphasis added). There is no suggestion of delegation of final authority to the Planning Board. The standards established by the ordinance are certainly no less broad than the general standard applied to local legislatures when enacting or amending zoning ordinances (Town Law, §§ 261, 263). Surely, the "intent to rezone" is no less a legislative act than an amendment to zoning ordinances and must be performed by the Town Board.

Support for this conclusion is found in *Rodgers v. Village of Tarrytown* (302 N.Y. 115, 121, 96 N.E.2d 731, 733, supra). In *Rodgers* the Village legislative body enacted an ordinance authorizing 10 acres zoned for garden type apartments. These zones were "floating" until located on the zoning map by subsequent amendment of the zoning ordinance by the Trustees, the local legislative body. In affirming the dismissal of an action to declare the floating zone provision invalid the Court of Appeals treated this second-stage zoning determination as a "legislative" act and stated that "the power of a village to amend its basic zoning ordinance in such a way as reasonably to promote the general welfare cannot be questioned. Just as clearly, decision as to how a community shall be zoned or rezoned, as to how various properties should be classified or reclassified, rests with the local legislative body; its judgment and determination will be conclusive, beyond interference from the courts, unless shown to be arbitrary, and the burden of establishing such arbitrariness is imposed upon him who asserts it" (*Rodgers* at 121, 96 N.E.2d at 733). The Town of Webster's planned unit development concept involves an analogous two-stage legislative process and this standard of "reasonableness" required by *Rodgers* governs judicial review of the Town Board's decision.

Petitioner contends that there is a distinction between the "floating zone" in *Rodgers* and Webster's ordinance in that the Webster planned shopping center district can only be located in a single zone, the C-S district, whereas in *Rodgers* the floating apartment zone could be located in any of the previously established zones. Thus, argues petitioner, the Board completed the "legislative" zoning decision in 1969 when the C-S district was written into the ordinance and subsequent decisions on proposed shopping center districts required merely administrative standards. Although the Board did restrict its discretion to approve planned shopping centers to existing C-S districts, it does not follow that the Board's secondary decision to rezone or not to rezone was "administrative" rather than "legislative." The Zoning Ordinance and Master Plan did not limit the C-S district use to shopping centers only. Other residential and commercial uses were permitted, as well as public uses. Petitioner's position would deprive the PUD technique of its most important ingredient, its flexibility by ignoring the broad legislative discretion which the Town Board reserved to itself (Webster Zoning Ordinance § 59-26(D)).

Petitioner cites *Matter of North Shore Steak House, Inc. v. Bd. of Appeals of Inc. Vil. of Thomaston* (30 N.Y.2d 238, 331 N.Y.S.2d 645, 282 N.E.2d 606) and *Matter of Lemir Realty Corp. v. Larkin* (11 N.Y.2d 20, 226 N.Y.S.2d 374, 181 N.E.2d 407) in support of its contention that the Town's PUD procedures are analogous to an application for a special use permit, which involves only administrative action even though the local legislature reserves authority to make the determination. The distinguishing factor between special use permits and planned unit developments is the size and significance of the proposed development. Whereas special use permits usually seek approval for a specified single use on a small parcel, such as service stations and swimming pools, the PUD is by its very nature a multi-use proposal for large scale developments such as shopping centers, planned integrated communities (new towns), or similar multi-uses on large parcels of land. It is obvious that petitioner's proposed shopping center of many large and small stores, including a department store, a supermarket, a theater and a bank, constructed on 20 acres of land has a greater impact on the body politic and the community in which it is planned than application to convert a small parcel to a single use. A broad determination by the Town's legislative body is more appropriate for this task than an administrative determination made according to specified standards. The procedures set forth in the Town's zoning ordinance indicate that such a broad, legislative determination was intended (Webster Zoning Ordinance §§ 59-24 — 59-27).

Lastly, we turn to a brief consideration of the constitutionality of the Board's action as applied to petitioner's application. Petitioner does not urge that the Board's determination was in violation of the zoning enabling legislation (Town Law, §§ 261-284). Nor has petitioner presented any evidence of inability to make a reasonable financial return by employing other permissible C-S uses, in support of its allegations that the zoning ordinance as applied is confiscatory in violation of the Fifth and Fourteenth Amendments. . . . Therefore, the remaining issue is whether the Board's determination deprives petitioner of due process of law, that is, whether its determination is an unreasonable exercise of the zoning, police powers. *Rodgers v. Village of Tarrytown* (302 N.Y. 115, 121, 96 N.E.2d 731, 733, *supra*) imposes the burden of proving the legislative zoning decision unreasonable squarely upon petitioner. If the decision is "fairly debatable," the legislature's judgment is conclusive. . . . The arguments which were advanced for and against the proposed shopping center were indeed "fairly debatable." The Planning Board's role was purely advisory and the ultimate decision had to be made by the elected, legislative officials. No evidence was produced to support a judicial determination that the Board's action was arbitrary or discriminatory.

The judgment should be reversed and the petition dismissed.

Judgment unanimously reversed without costs and petition dismissed.

MARSH, P. J., and MOULE, MAHONEY and WITMER, JJ., concur.

Comments: 1. Although the PUD in the principal case is a bit unusual as it was for a commercial development only, the PUD ordinance in that case is an example of a "floating" PUD district which is first included in the zoning ordinance text and later applied to a particular piece of property. Courts receptive to the floating zone technique are likely to approve this form of PUD ordinance. A floating PUD district was also approved in *Town of North Hempstead v. Village of North Hills,* 342 N.E.2d 566 (N.Y. 1975), again on the authority of the *Rodgers* case. (This case is reproduced *supra* p. 706.) The court rejected a claim that the ordinance was "exclusionary unconstitutionally discriminatory" because it had a four-acre minimum requirement for PUD's. Quoting from *Rodgers,* the court noted that PUD's would blend more harmoniously with their surroundings and would place less of a burden on community facilities if placed on larger tracts of land rather than scattered around the community. Neither was the ordinance discriminatory because PUD's were allowed only in one residential zone. The court found that 80 percent of the land in the community was in this zone.

Other courts have had little difficulty rejecting challenges to PUD ordinances based on lack of uniformity. In *Orinda Homeowners Comm. v. Board of Supervisors,* 90 Cal. Rptr. 88 (Cal. App. 1970), the court had this to say on the uniformity requirement:

> . . . [The zoning enabling statute] provides that the *regulations* shall be uniform for each class or kind of building or use of land throughout the zone. It does not state that the units must be alike even as to their character, whether single family or multi-family. In conventional zoning, where apartment houses are permitted in a particular zone, single family dwellings, being regarded (whether rightly or wrongly) as a "higher" use, are also allowed. This causes no conflict with . . . [the statute].

Id. at 90-91. See also *Chrinko v. South Brunswick Township Planning Bd.,* 187 A.2d 221 (N.J.L. 1963), noting that the PUD ordinance "accomplishes uniformity because the option is open to all developers within a zoning district, and escapes the vice that it is compulsory." *Id.* at 225. The court also noted that the PUD ordinance was not invalid because it incidentally benefits the PUD developer. *Id.* at 227.

An argument related to the uniformity requirement may arise out of the bargaining and negotiation which usually precede a PUD approval. In *Rutland Environmental Protection Ass'n v. Kane County,* 334 N.E.2d 215 (Ill. App. 1975), the argument was made that this kind of negotiation was invalid as contract zoning, see *supra* p.718. The argument was rejected, the court noting that "[s]ince the overall aims of . . . [PUD] zoning cannot be accomplished without negotiations and because conferences are indeed mandated by the regulating ordinance, the conduct of the . . . [county] cannot be read as contributing to contract zoning." *Id.* at 219. Note that the PUD is usually conditioned in the sense that the PUD must be in compliance with specific development requirements contained in the approved PUD development plan. How is it that the legislative body can approve the PUD plan and yet avoid arguments that it has illegally conditioned the exercise of legislative power? Krasnowiecki, *supra* at 102, suggests that "zoning changes granted at the request of a particular applicant can be limited by ordinance to the proposal as described in the plans and oral testimony presented by the applicant in support of his request," citing *Albright v. Town of Manilus,* 268 N.E.2d 785 (N.Y. 1971).

2. Note the bind that the principal case places on those wishing to challenge PUD ordinances and approvals. (Usually the challengers are third parties owning residences near the proposed PUD.) If the ordinance provision authorizing the PUD is immune from attack, there will be no opportunity for challenge until the PUD is approved. *See Schwartz v. Town Plan & Zoning Comm'n,* 357 A.2d 495 (Conn. 1975). The preceding discussion has indicated that challenges to the ordinance may be limited. *But cf. Harnett v. Board of Zoning, Subdivision & Bldg. Appeals,* 350 F. Supp. 1159 (D. St. Croix 1972) (standards for PUD-like zone inadequate). And one New York court has held PUD's unauthorized by the zoning statute, *Marshall v. Village of Wappinger Falls,* 279 N.Y.S.2d 654 (N.Y. App. Div. 1967). See *contra,* on the delegation of power and statutory authority points, *Raum v. Board of Supervisors,* 342 A.2d 450 (Pa. Commw. Ct.1975).

In the *Raum* case the locality used the second variant of the PUD districting approach, and rezoned the land to five previously existing zoning districts to implement a PUD which had been shown on the local comprehensive plan. This approach presents even fewer opportunities for challenge than the floating zone technique employed in the principal case.

When specific legislative rezonings for PUD's have been attacked on spot zoning and other grounds the courts seem to have had little difficulty in sustaining the rezoning under conventional rezoning principles. *See, e.g., Loh v. Town Plan & Zoning Comm'n,* 282 A.2d 894 (Conn. 1971); *Moore v. City of Boulder,* 484 P.2d 134 (Colo. App. 1971).

3. *PUD's as conditional or special uses.* Is there an inference in the principal case that PUD's may not be handled as special or conditional uses under the zoning ordinance? Consider the following cases:

Appeal of Moreland, 497 P.2d 1287 (Okla. 1972). Acting under a local PUD ordinance, the board of adjustment approved a PUD for a mobile home park and retail shopping center. The ordinance was upheld as falling within the provisions of the state zoning act allowing the board to grant special exceptions. Since the board's function was to determine whether the PUD complied with the provisions of the ordinance, it was acting in a quasi-judicial and not a legislative capacity. No revision of the local comprehensive plan or zoning ordinance could be carried out by the board, and the ordinance required that any approved PUD's be devoted primarily to residential purposes and only secondarily to nonresidential uses. No improper delegation of power was found. The ordinance provided a series of design standards, and also required that approved PUD's conform to the "intent and purposes" of the local zoning ordinance and the local and regional comprehensive plans.

Chandler v. Kroiss, 190 N.W.2d 427 (Minn. 1972). The PUD ordinance authorized the legislative body to grant special permits for PUD's. Since the PUD contemplated multifamily development which was not a permitted use under the zoning ordinance, an argument was made that a variance should have been requested. This argument was rejected, the court noting that the PUD ordinance provided for a "hybrid" procedure combining the variance and special exception. "To the extent that the result of the proceeding for approval of a planned unit development thus alters the established, allowed land usages of the village, it has the same effect as would a succession of variances or rezonings." *Id.* at 476.

Lutz v. City of Longview, 520 P.2d 1374 (Wash. 1974). This case considered a floating zone PUD. The planning commission was authorized to approve PUD's as authorized by the PUD provision of the zoning ordinance, and in this case approved a PUD for multifamily use in a single-family area. Holding that such a change in use is a legislative function, the court held that PUD approval under the ordinance could not be delegated to the planning commission. Is this case consistent with the principal case?

The *Lutz* case distinguished *Cheney v. Village 2 at New Hope, Inc.,* 241 A.2d 81 (Pa. 1968). In *Cheney* the legislative body first rezoned a tract of land to the PUD district; approval of the PUD under the ordinance provisions was then left to the planning commission. This delegation of authority to the commission was held proper, although the court in *Cheney* noted that no specific provision authorizing this delegation was contained in the zoning legislation. *Cheney* has been considered the leading case authorizing the PUD technique under the provisions of the Standard Zoning Act. (Pennsylvania has since adopted the model PUD act, see *infra* p. 884.) However, the authority of *Cheney* is limited by the fact that the PUD ordinance adopted by the local council specified uses, densities and building spacing requirements; in addition, the council had specifically rezoned the tract in question to the PUD district. Thus, the only question was whether the planning commission was the proper agency to approve the PUD under the ordinance terms.

Although noting that under the PUD ordinance the planning commission was authorized to approve building uses as well as the PUD plan, and that this function was not a traditional commission responsibility, the court acquiesced in this new delegation of authority. It was not prohibited by the statute, the court noted, and delegation of PUD approval to the legislative body would be unworkable. The board of adjustment was not the proper body to carry out this responsibility given its specifically delineated statutory duties.

What is determinative of the results in these cases? The nature of the PUD approval decision, the extent of the change in use, the local agency given authority to approve the PUD, or a combination of these factors? Conn. Gen. Stat. § 8-2 (1977) provides that the local zoning ordinance "may provide that certain classes or kinds of buildings, structures or use of land are permitted only after obtaining a special permit or special exception from a . . . planning commission . . . subject to standards set forth in the [zoning] regulations." Which of the PUD procedures considered in the above cases would be judicially acceptable if power to approve the PUD were delegated to a planning commission under this statute?

4. In *Prince George's County v. M & B Constr. Co.*, 297 A.2d 683 (Md. 1972), a PUD ordinance was adopted which delegated approval of PUD's to the planning commission. PUD's were a permitted use in residential zones; single-family dwellings and townhouses were permitted in PUD's. Reductions in lot sizes were allowed subject to a minimum lot size requirement, but existing densities and building bulk in approved PUD's were to remain the same. Amendments were made both to the zoning and subdivision control ordinances to allow PUD's, and the court held that the approval of PUD's was properly delegated to the planning commission as part of its subdivision control powers. PUD's authorized by this ordinance appear to fall in the density transfer category, see *supra* p. 858. Does this fact help support the court's opinion?

A provision in one of the early model planning acts authorizing density transfer PUD's has been adopted in a few states. For discussion of the New York version of this provision see *Rouse v. O'Connell*, 353 N.Y.S.2d 124 (N.Y. Sup. Ct. 1974) (trial court). *See generally* on the problems raised in these Comments, Aloi, Legal Problems in Planned Unit Development: Uniformity, Comprehensive Planning, Conditions, and the Floating Zone, 1 Real Est. L.J. 5 (1972).

5. What is the role of the comprehensive plan in the PUD process? The *Lutz* case, *supra,* indicated that the lack of specific guidelines for PUD's in the comprehensive plan did not mean that an approval of a PUD would be invalid as spot zoning. In the *Chandler* case, *supra,* the court approved with little comment a provision in the PUD ordinance which stated that approval of a PUD not consistent with the comprehensive plan would be considered an amendment to the plan. No definitive cases considering PUD's have yet been handed down in states which have adopted a requirement that zoning be consistent with a comprehensive plan. *See supra* p. 757.

6. In view of these cases, how would you evaluate the observation of many commentators that an amendment of land use control legislation is not necessary in order to adopt and implement a PUD ordinance? Do the cases allow sufficient flexibility in the adoption of PUD ordinances to carry out all the objectives of PUD procedures? Is there sufficient flexibility in the selection of the local agency to review and approve a PUD?

2. The PUD Process: Standards, Procedures, and Amendments

It is now possible to look more closely at some of the details of the PUD review process, especially at the standards applicable to PUD projects and the nature of the PUD development process, including the all-important question of how that process works once approval has been given. The question of standards for approval can be considered first. Since the PUD will be reviewed and considered as an entire entity, traditional lot-by-lot standards found in zoning ordinances cannot be used, and standards must be independently constructed under which the entire PUD project can be evaluated.

Standards for PUD developments can be handled in one of two ways. Recall once more the discussion of Map 1, *supra* p. 860, and the comment made there that in many cases the approval of the PUD will require changes in the uses and densities permitted by the applicable zoning ordinance. One approach is to provide in the PUD ordinance for standards indicating how these changes are to be made. For example, the ordinance can provide for marginal increases in density, or for additional uses not permitted in the zoning district applicable to the PUD.

Another approach is to provide an independent set of standards for PUD's which are applicable independently of the existing zoning ordinance. Densities can be stated in terms of allowable dwelling units per acre, and a list of permitted and conditional uses can also be provided. Design and bulk standards are also usually provided, and can be handled in the same manner. The PUD ordinance can either allow modifications in lot size, setback, or other requirements, or can provide for an independent set of requirements to be applied to the PUD without reference to existing regulations.

Under many ordinances, PUD approval is based on compliance with this independent set of density, use, and design standards. Some PUD ordinances also provide an independent set of substantive criteria for reviewing the entire PUD as an entity. For example, the ordinance might provide that a PUD may be approved if:

(1) The final plan of the planned unit development is consistent with the community comprehensive plan; and

(2) The final plan of the planned unit development is an effective and unified treatment of the development possibilities on the project site; and

(3) The final plan of the planned unit development is harmonized with an existing or proposed development in the area surrounding the project site.

Generalized PUD approval standards of the kind just quoted inject a considerable amount of discretion in the PUD approval process. The question that next arises is whether a reviewing court can in any way limit that discretion, or whether it must accept as almost conclusively final the decision of the reviewing agency, whether it is to approve or deny. As the discussion and the *Todd Mart* case have indicated, when PUD's are approved as amendments to the zoning ordinance the courts may have little scope for review if the amendment is treated as a legislative action. There may be more scope for judicial review if a different view is taken, as the following case indicates.

RK DEVELOPMENT CORP. v. CITY OF NORWALK

Supreme Court of Connecticut
156 Conn. 369, 242 A.2d 781 (1968)

RYAN, Associate Justice. The plaintiff, the owner of a tract of land, 4.641 acres in area, located in a B residence zone in the city of Norwalk, filed with the planning commission of the city an application for approval of its plan for a planned residential development to be constructed on its land. The proposed development is a permitted use under the building zone regulations in a B residence zone. The planning commission reviewed the plan over a period of several months, held two public hearings, and, on December 22, 1965, approved the plan. It was then transmitted to the common council on January 6, 1966. On January 11, 1966, the common council referred the plan to its committee on public works. On February 24, 1966, the public works committee at a special meeting of the common council recommended to the council that the application be denied. The motion to deny the plaintiff's application was approved by the council. The plaintiff appealed to the Court of Common Pleas, alleging that Thomas G. Hannon, a member of the common council, was a participant in and an active leader among persons in the neighborhood opposing the plaintiff's plan, that he testified in opposition thereto before the planning commission, that the pertinent regulations did not require approval of the plan by the council and that, in any event, its action was unlawful, arbitrary, and in abuse of its discretion. The trial court in its memorandum of decision found that the council, in considering the plaintiff's application, was acting as a legislative body and for that reason its action could not be reversed unless it was manifestly and palpably incorrect, and that the procedures of the planning commission and that of the council were correct. The court, however, concluded that Hannon, an elected legislative official, had, through his wife, a financial interest in land adjoining that of the plaintiff and that his efforts before the planning commission to defeat the plaintiff's application conflicted with his duty as a councilman. The appeal was sustained for this reason. The defendant then appealed to this court, and the plaintiff filed a cross appeal. . . .

There is nothing in the record before us to indicate that Hannon exerted any improper influence on his associates in the council, and we impute no such influence to him by our decision in this case. The trial court, however, has expressly found that he put himself on record at the hearing before the planning commission with full knowledge that his stated opposition would later be transmitted by the commission to the council. . . . We must conclude, therefore, that the trial court was not in error in sustaining the plaintiff's appeal. . . .

The plaintiff also urges that the action of the council was groundless and arbitrary. It is fundamental that in passing on the plaintiff's application the council, acting in its administrative capacity, is to be controlled by the regulations for planned residential development and the regulations concerning subdivision adopted for its guidance. If the plan submitted conforms to these regulations, the council has no discretion or choice but to approve it. . . . The council gave the following reason for disapproval of the plaintiff's plan: "The safety for the sake of the children as well as the people living up there; the welfare of the community and also the health hazards." Section 3(A) (2) (b) of the regulations for planned residential developments provides as follows: " 'Review and approval' shall mean that the reviewing agency as hereinbefore provided shall review the site plans with particular reference to the following regulations: (a) The design of facilities, the use of which may cause nuisance to the adjacent properties, such as the provisions of Section 3,Subsections l to r herein, shall be reviewed for compliance. (b) Traffic Access — All proposed traffic access ways shall be adequate in number, width, grade, alignment and visibility from access points, and are located at the proper distance from street corners, entrances to schools and other places of assembly. (c) Circulation of traffic for parking — The interior circulation system shall be adequate and the required parking spaces shall be equally accessible. (d) Disposition of open space and recreational areas — Such spaces shall be dispersed in such a way as to insure the safety and welfare of resident children."

Additional regulations requiring consideration by the council are set forth in § 3(A) (3). These are detailed and specific in their requirements.

The reason given by the council for its disapproval was vague, uncertain in meaning and provided no information to the plaintiff to enable it to know wherein the plan submitted failed to satisfy the requirements of the regulations. Certainly if the plan had failed in any respect to conform to the regulations, it was the duty and obligation of the council to so indicate. This it failed to do. The council cannot, in utter disregard of the regulations, disapprove the plan for a reason it would not be required to apply to all applications for planned residential developments as to which the same reason obtained. It would amount to substitution of the pure discretion of the council for a discretion controlled by fixed standards applying to all cases of a like nature. It would deprive the plaintiff of its property without due process of law. . . . There was no regulation prohibiting the plaintiff's plan for a planned residential development in Norwalk for any reason assigned by the council, and its action in refusing approval was illegal.

There was error in the conclusions of the trail court so far as it held that the common council, in passing on plans for planned residential developments, acted in its legislative capacity; that in considering such applications it could act for reasons best known to itself; and that the reason given by the common council for its final decision was valid. The judgment of the trial court sustaining the plaintiff's appeal, however, was correct.

There is no error.

In this opinion ALCORN, HOUSE and THIM, JJ., concurred.

COVELLO, J., dissented.

Comments: 1. If quite specific use, design and similar standards are the only standards contained in the ordinance for the approval of PUD's, the approving agency may grope for other and sometimes spurious reasons to deny approval. In these cases, as the principal case indicates, the courts will often reverse. Thus in *Hall v. Korth,* 244 So.2d 766 (Fla. Dist. Ct. App. 1971), the court reversed a denial of a PUD by a county legislative body in a case in which the only evidence introduced against the PUD consisted of "bald" assertions by objectors. The trial court had noted that " '[t]he perimeter land in the proposed development would carry the exact zoning of the adjoining lands outside the development. This clearly protects the adjoining property owners.' " *Id.* at 767.

When the PUD has complied with all of the specific requirements of the ordinance a denial is that much harder to support. *See LaSalle Nat'l Bank v. County of Lake,* 325 N.E.2d 105 (Ill. App. 1975). In that case the county board of supervisors had denied a special use for a PUD, based on a recommendation that the " '. . . planned development at this location is premature at this time.' " *Id.* at 109. While noting that approval need not follow automatically from compliance with ordinance standards, the court added that "a legislative body must exercise its power in a reasonable way and adherence to these standards is a strong indication of reasonableness." *Id.* at 111. *Compare Coronet Homes, Inc. v. McKenzie,* 430 P.2d 219 (Nev. 1968). The court upheld the denial of a special use for a residential PUD in an opinion which was hostile to the use of the PUD process to increase residential densities above those in the area surrounding the PUD. See also *Ford Leasing Dev. Co. v. Board of County Comm'rs,* 528 P.2d 237 (Colo. 1974), upholding a denial of a rezoning for a PUD and noting that approval of PUD's is not mandatory under the ordinance. "Planned development is not a catch-all. It is not supposed to inject in a neighborhood a use which would otherwise not be allowed. It should not usurp the discretionary function of the Board." *Id.* at 240.

There is a dilemma in these cases. Decisions like *Coronet Homes* and *Ford Leasing* appear hostile to the PUD concept and will no doubt encourage local communities to find reason to turn down PUD projects. Yet court decisions restricting local discretion to disapprove PUD's may deny localities needed controls over PUD's and put PUD controls in disfavor. Drafting ordinance standards to take care of this problem is not easy, as the discussion that follows will show. *Cf.* the *LaSalle Nat'l Bank* case, *supra,* in which the court dismissed objections that a golf course to be provided in the PUD need only be operated for five years under the PUD plan. "Even if the open space were no longer used for a golf course, the land in its natural state is well suited for a variety of recreational uses." *Id.* at 112. What if the ordinance required recreational facilities to be operated in perpetuity by an association of PUD homeowners? If there was a default in this obligation would the municipality have an effective remedy?

2. Difficulties may also arise if the PUD ordinance attempts to give the municipality greater control over PUD projects. In *Soble Constr. Co. v. Zoning Hearing Bd.,* 329 A.2d 912 (Pa. Commw. Ct. 1974), the ordinance provided that "[t]he proposed developer shall demonstrate that a sufficient market exists for the type, size and character of the development proposed." The court noted that "we fail to see how a showing of the sufficiency of a market bears any reasonable relationship to the public health, safety, morals or general welfare. It is unlawful for a municipality to zone or refuse to zone land for the purpose of limiting competition with existing commercial facilities." *Id.* at 917. The PUD proposed in that case was for multifamily use. *See also DeMaria v. Enfield Planning & Zoning Comm'n,* 271 A.2d 105 (Conn. 1970). The zoning agency denied a PUD for apartments because of the "esthetic [*sic*] effect of the complex in relation to the existing neighborhood and the town in general," and because "the complex of apartments as submitted on the plans does not present a satisfactory image of what . . . apartments should convey to the Town." *Id.* at 108. Reversing the denial, the court noted that "vague and undefined aesthetic considerations" alone are not enough to support the police power, on which all zoning is based. *Id.*

Krasnowiecki, *supra* at 104-05, notes that municipalities are concerned about run-away PUD development. They do not want any more housing, they want to limit that housing to some minimal quota, especially if it is to be in the form of townhouses and apartments, and "[w]ith respect to most forms of intensive development, especially apartment and townhouse, municipalities want to retain the power to discriminate between developers." *Id.* at 105. He argues that courts should legitimate quota and timing controls in order to give communities more control over PUD developments. *Id.* at 108. Consult the materials on quota controls, *infra* p. 1034, to assess their applicability to the PUD context.

3. It is clear that the opportunities for negotiation built into the PUD approval process offer opportunities to practice exclusionary zoning. Especially is this so if the densities at which a community is zoned are so low that development is impracticable, forcing all developers to apply for PUD approval in order to build. Communities can then impose costly requirements on developers as part of the approval process, thus raising the cost of housing in PUD developments and accomplishing an exclusionary purpose.

Coscoming, the community in the story at the beginning of this section, might have restricted PUD development and increased PUD costs through a series of simple expedients. PUD developers could have been required to build schools for school pupils expected to reside in the PUD. (Is this a proper subdivision requirement? *See supra* p. 817.) PUD's could have been limited to a few zoning districts in the community and these zones could have been mapped in outlying areas where service connection costs are high. Connection to services would then have been required. The PUD approval process could have been lengthened by increasing the time required for reviews. As a final twist, off-site improvements benefiting the entire community could have been required.

This particular strategy was challenged and held unconstitutional as exclusionary in *Oakwood at Madison, Inc. v. Township of Madison,* 371 A.2d 1192, 1211-12 (N.J. 1977), reproduced *supra* p. 488. The court's remedy was to direct the township to remove all of the cost-generating features of the PUD ordinance. For additional cost-generating PUD requirements see *Southern Burlington NAACP v. Township of Mount Laurel,* 336 A.2d 713, 721-22 (N.J.), *cert. denied,* 423 U.S. 808 (1975), reproduced *supra* p. 454. PUD developers were required in their leases to provide that no school-age children be permitted to live in one-bedroom apartments, and that no more than two school-age children be allowed to reside in any two-bedroom unit.

Excesses such as these have led one leading commentator to condemn PUD's entirely:

> The existence of such a bargaining system [in PUD ordinances — Eds.] may prove to be a heaven-sent opportunity for a municipality to evade judicial strictures against exclusionary zoning, and to strike a cooperative pose, always ready to do something about critical needs — if only the perfect proposal would come along — but always in fact retaining a veto, and so always able to avoid any real action.

N. Williams, 2 American Land Planning Law 229 (1974). What do you think? At this point, can you strike a balance between the advantages and disadvantages of the PUD process? Review again the materials on inclusionary zoning, *supra* p. 606.

4. Project design including environmental design standards are extremely important in PUD administration. Unlike zoning and subdivision control, the review of planned unit developments usually incorporates a review of project design, including the preservation of environmental amenities and an evaluation of the relationship of buildings and structures to the site and to projected open space areas. Municipalities have seized on these opportunities to incorporate quite specific design standards in their PUD ordinances. Design review is implemented by having the developer submit detailed final plans of the project, including in some cases sketches and elevation drawings as well as plans for internal circulation systems and open spaces. Design review can then be authorized by the following type of provision:

> The council may approve the final development plan if it provides for safe, efficient, convenient and harmonious groupings of structures, uses and facilities; for appropriate relation of space inside and outside buildings to intended uses and natural and structural features; and for preservation of desirable natural and environmental features and minimum disturbance to the natural environment.

Would this provision be struck down as incorporating "vague" aesthetic standards? See the *DeMaria* case, *supra*.

A NOTE ON SOME DEVELOPMENTAL PROBLEMS IN PUD CONTROLS

Space does not permit consideration of all aspects of planned unit development controls. A few of the more important problems will be considered here.

Concept approval. Planned unit development provides some savings and advantages to developers, especially if densities are increased. Even if they are not, site improvement costs are reduced when lot sizes are decreased because lot frontages will be shorter and the cost of linear services will be less. Nevertheless, PUD controls also impose added costs on developers. PUD's require sensitive site planning, all of which takes time and costs money. Developers facing heavy front end costs are not likely to undertake them without some assurance of approval from the local approval agency.

For this reason, many PUD ordinances contain an additional first step in the approval process in which the developer presents an outline or concept plan containing the major features of the PUD. Zoning approval, if needed, is intended to be based on the concept plan. A study of PUD controls, Planned Unit Development Ordinances, *supra* at 15, found that many local agencies were fearful of concept plan approval. ". . . [M]any local governments are highly protective of their zone change powers, preferring to grant it later in the review process, often not until after approval of the final development plan." As an alternative, the study suggests an informal pre-application conference on the PUD in which the developer can get informal feedback from the community on what will be required. Is this an adequate substitute?

Density controls. Note that in density transfer PUD's, see Map 1, *supra* p. 860, lot sizes will be reduced in return for compensating open space, while overall densities remain the same. How this trade-off is calculated raises some ticklish problems. Possibilities are discussed in the PUD ordinance report, *supra* at 27;

> A combination of tools may be used to control micro densities within such projects. Minimum lot sizes may be reduced to allow clustering, retaining floor area and building height requirements. Some ordinances only establish maximum gross project densities at "x" number of dwelling units per acre, using a building spacing requirement to take over the minimum lot size function. [*I.e.,* no minimum lot sizes are required but the ordinance provides criteria for "adequate" spaces between buildings. — Eds.] Building heights and floor areas may also be used in combination with the above techniques to establish the upper limits of micro densities within a project.

How provisions of this kind might work is illustrated by the following problem:

PROBLEM

Your client is a developer who owns a 100-acre tract of undeveloped land. Thirty acres in the tract consist of slopes and gullies which are difficult to develop. The applicable zoning regulations allow two dwelling units to the acre, but the PUD provisions in the ordinance permit a reduction in lot sizes provided the aggregate density permitted by the zoning ordinance is not exceeded. You now argue to the local council that your developer should be allowed to place 200 dwelling units on the 70 usable acres provided that the other 30 acres are set aside as public open space. What about it?

(1) What if the local ordinance provides that in calculating PUD densities the council may exclude "any land which by reason of size, shape or location, or for other good cause, is not reasonably suitable for single-family residential development"? For a provision of this kind see *Gruver-Cooley Jade Corp. v. Perlis,* 251 A.2d 589 (Md. 1969). Compare *Board of Supervisors v. Centre Hills Country Club,* 333 A.2d 822 (Pa. Commw. Ct. 1975), holding that in determining allowable density within a PUD the developer may not count as part of the PUD an adjacent golf course not used exclusively by residents of the PUD.

(2) PUD ordinances may attempt to deal with the open space problem by providing qualitative criteria under which the approving

agency can evaluate the quality of open space areas to be included in the PUD. *See* Planned Unit Development Ordinances, *supra* at 30-34. A rudimentary provision of this type might provide that no open space areas may be provided in the PUD unless they "contribute to the quality, livability and amenity of the planned unit development." Is this enough? See *Mountcrest Estates, Inc. v. Mayor & Township Comm.*, 232 A.2d 674 (N.J. Super. 1967), invalidating a PUD ordinance open space provision because it did not specify the uses to which the open space could be put. See also the *LaSalle Nat'l Bank* case, *supra*.

The maintenance of open space areas in PUD's presents a series of difficult ordinance drafting and enforcement problems. Usually a homeowner's association is formed to hold and manage open space areas. Dedication to a public entity is another possibility. If title is placed in a homeowner's association it will have to be given the authority to enforce the protective covenants which are usually executed, and which restrict the use of the open space areas to their intended purpose. Problems may arise concerning the legal capacity of the association to enforce the covenants, if the view is adopted that the entity seeking to enforce must own property benefited by the covenants; ordinarily, the association will not own property in the development. However, there is authority that property ownership by the association is not required, *e.g., Merrionette Manor Homes Improvement Ass'n v. Heda,* 136 N.E.2d 556 (Ill. App. 1956); *Neponsit Property Owners' Ass'n v. Emigrant Indus. Sav. Bank,* 15 N.E.2d 793 (N.Y. 1938).

Providing for enforcement of the covenants by a public authority is another possibility. The English decision, *London County Council v. Allen,* [1914] 3 K.B. 642, disapproving this method of enforcement does not seem to be in favor in this country. In any event, the power of enforcement can be lodged in a public agency by statute, *e.g.,* Wis. Stat. Ann. § 236.293 (1975).

(3) Can the municipality get better leverage on the PUD in the Problem by first downzoning areas in which PUD's are allowed to lower densities and then offering to raise densities in PUD's in which compensating open space is provided? This procedure was upheld in the *Mountcrest* case, *supra.* Is there an argument here that the total effect of this process is to force from the developer an open space dedication which otherwise would be unconstitutional under normal subdivision control practices? *See supra* p. 817.

(4) What if the council argues that the PUD concentrates more dwellings on less land and thus will require less in the way of internal streets, so that this factor should be taken into account in determining density? How would you handle this problem? *See Peabody v. City of Phoenix,* 485 P.2d 565 (Ariz. App. 1971)

(ordinance allowed internal streets to be counted in "net development area" used to compute PUD density).

(5) Some PUD ordinances provide density bonuses to the developer in return for providing improved design and amenity features in the development. For examples of these provisions see Planned Unit Development Ordinances, *supra* at 27-28.

(6) So far, we have been calculating project density by starting with the densities allowable by the zoning ordinance, and then varying these requirements. It might be better to drop this technique and develop an independent method of calculating project density which does not depend on the existing ordinance. An imaginative system of this kind is described in [Baltimore] Regional Planning Council, Environmental Characteristic Planning: Physical Development Standards for Character Control (1969). The report suggests that density controls be developed by building on the following variables:

> Floor Area Ratio: Maximum square footage of building permitted for each square foot of land area
>
> Height-Distance Standards: The relationship between the height of a building and its distance from the site boundary or from another building
>
> Density Ratio: The maximum number of dwelling units or people permitted per acre
>
> Outdoor Space Ratio: The proportion of the site to remain open or uncovered by structures
>
> Parking Space Ratio: The minimum number of parking spaces required for each dwelling unit
>
> Landscaped Space Ratio: The minimum square footage of nonvehicular outdoor space required for each square foot of floor area.

A system based on variables like these has actually been developed by the federal mortgage-insuring agency and is in use in some PUD ordinances. For a description of this system see F. Bair, Intensity Zoning: Regulating Townhouses, Apartments, and Planned Developments (American Soc'y of Planning Officials, Planning Advisory Serv. Rep. No. 314, 1976).

Obviously, these variables are interrelated. Where do you start? For example, the number of dwelling units allowed will affect the number of off-street parking spaces required on the site. It may not be possible to provide entirely for outdoor parking spaces without violating the Landscaped Space Ratio. If this happens, either the number of dwelling units will have to be decreased or parking spaces will have to be provided inside the structures with an appropriate Floor Area Ratio allowance.

Height-distance standards appear particularly difficult because terrain varies. The Baltimore report suggests that this problem might be handled by a combination of distance and height standards as affected by "angle of planes leaning inward from the development boundary, or the mid point between two walls of two structures within the development." *Id.*, at 30. Are you ready to go back to simple side yards?

Note that high-intensity or nonresidential PUD's may also require a fairly deep buffer zone along the perimeter to protect adjoining residential uses. This requirement was approved in *Armstrong v. McInnis*, 142 S.E.2d 670 (N.C. 1965).

Phasing and development in stages. Especially in large planned unit developments, the developer will usually proceed by stages and build one phase of the development at a time. What if the PUD contains both high-density and low-density areas? If the developer is allowed to proceed with the high density areas first, there is a risk that marketing or financial difficulties may force him to postpone or even drop the development of the low-density sections. To prevent this contingency, PUD ordinances may attempt to regulate the pace of development by requiring that the residential density in each phase not exceed the average residential density in the entire PUD, or exceed it by no more than a stated maximum. There is another dilemma here; if the density averaging provisions are too stringent the developer may have to distort the design of the PUD in order to be able to comply with this requirement, thus defeating the better design objective of the PUD process.

Amendments and enforcement. It is common in PUD ordinances to provide that the PUD plan, once it is approved, becomes the development control document which governs the development of the PUD. Quite naturally, problems come up during the development of the PUD which require changes to be made in the originally approved plan. The courts have not unexpectedly required that major changes in the plan may not be made administratively and must be carried out through the same process by which the original plan was approved. *Millbrae Ass'n for Residential Survival v. City of Millbrae*, 69 Cal. Rptr. 251 (Cal. App. 1968) (rezoning). Uncertainties about the amendment process can be handled through appropriate provisions in the PUD ordinance, which can separate minor and major changes and provide that minor changes can be made administratively. *See* Planned Unit Development Ordinances, *supra* at 21-22.

When amendments for major changes are granted they are subject to the same criteria when judicially reviewed as any zoning change. In a puzzling opinion, the Ohio Supreme Court upset an amendment to a PUD plan which would have added a condominium development to a golf course project contained in the PUD. *Gray v. Trustees, Monclova Township*, 313 N.E.2d 366 (Ohio 1974). "Under the amendment, the site will no longer be used primarily for the benefit of the permanent residents of Brynwyck, but will instead be partially transformed into a site of 'corporate condominiums' to be temporarily inhabited by transitory businessmen." *Id.* at 370. Since the legislative body made the change, it is not clear why it could not make a change in the uses provided in the PUD project. *Compare Chandler v. Kroiss, supra* (special use for PUD may be amended to allow changes not affecting basic use of property).

PUD development plans usually contain detailed information which is more extensive than what is required on ordinary subdivision plats. Sketches and site elevation drawings may be included, especially if multifamily development is contemplated. What happens if the PUD as built deviates from the sketch plans submitted as part of the PUD application? For a fascinating case dealing with this problem see *Frankland v. City of Lake Oswego,* 517 P.2d 1042 (Ore. 1973). The court found that the plan had been violated, and remanded the case to determine whether damages or an injunction requiring the removal of the building should be awarded.

Enforcement problems also arise if, after the PUD has been approved, the developer fails to make a timely start on his development. A reverter clause is a possibility in this situation; PUD approval can be conditioned on the developer's beginning the project within a stated period of time. A similar condition can be attached to the filing of a final plan once the preliminary plan has been approved. For a case approving this procedure in the context of an ordinary zoning amendment see *Colwell v. Howard County,* 354 A.2d 210 (Md. App. 1976). See also the *Scrutton* case, reproduced *supra* p. 728.

On the basis of the materials in this section, can you draft a PUD ordinance which properly takes account of the need for community control of the development, the need to give the developer sufficient flexibility to achieve good project design, and the need to avoid exclusionary elements in the PUD process? Suggestions for the drafting of PUD ordinances are contained in F. Bair, *supra,* and in Planned Unit Development Ordinances, *supra.* For a case study of a PUD see R. Burchell, Planned Unit Development: New Communities American Style (1972).

3. Model Planned Unit Development Legislation

Perceived problems in the enactment of planned unit development ordinances under conventional enabling legislation led in 1964 to the drafting of a model planned unit development statute which would authorize the enactment of PUD ordinances at the local level. The statute is reproduced in Babcock, Krasnowiecki, & McBride, The Model State Statute, 114 U. Pa. L. Rev. 140 (1965). This statute attempted to overcome the limitations on PUD's inherent in the conventional zoning legislation by making a series of fundamental changes in the PUD approval process. A single approving agency was to be designated at the local level, with the authority to issue a unitary permit covering all aspects of PUD development. Case-by-case approval of PUD's was authorized. Detailed procedural requirements were placed on PUD approvals and the review process was treated as an adjudication and not as legislative action. A development plan was required and was to provide the basis for continuing control over the planned unit development. Assurances against changes in public requirements were provided once approval was given. (See the similar requirements in some subdivision control statutes, *supra* p. 843.) Finally, the statute provided assurances for the maintenance of common open spaces provided in PUD's. *See generally* Krasnowiecki, *supra* at 100-05. *See also* Sternlieb, Burchell, Hughes, & Listokin, Planned Unit Development Legislation: A Summary of Necessary Considerations, 7 Urb. L. Ann. 71 (1974).

The model act has not exactly burned its way through the state legislatures. Six states have passed legislation based on it, notably Connecticut, New Jersey, and Pennsylvania, although New Jersey has since repealed its statute and redistributed its provisions (with modifications) throughout its planning enabling legislation. Another six states have briefer versions of PUD enabling legislation which is not based on the model act. *See* Planned Unit Development Ordinances, *supra* at 45-47. For examples of statutes following the model act see Conn. Gen. Stat. ch. 124a (1977); Pa. Stat. Ann. tit. 53, § 10701 *et seq.* (1968).

There has been a tendency in the cases to construe the model act strictly, thus placing unexpected restraints on municipalities using its authority to enact PUD ordinances. For example, the model act authorizes the customary two-step preliminary and final plan procedure for the review of PUD's. In *Township of Middletown v. Abel*, 297 A.2d 525 (Pa. Commw. Ct. 1972), the township required approval of a preliminary concept plan as a condition to the consideration of later plans, and then argued that its power to approve or disapprove the concept plan was not subject to judicial review. The court held that the concept plan requirement was not authorized by the enabling act. *Compare Niccollai v. Planning Bd.,* 372 A.2d 352 (N.J. Super. 1977) (PUD ordinances may only be enacted in compliance with PUD enabling act) with the *Raum* case, *supra (contra).*

The model act contains a series of standards to be applied to PUD developments which are similar to and extend those quoted *supra* p. 874. In *Doran Inv. Co. v. Muhlenberg Township*, 309 A.2d 450 (Pa. Commw. Ct. 1973), noted, 9 Urb. L. Ann. 273 (1975), the developer's plan conformed to these standards but the township nevertheless refused to give tentative approval. The court reversed, though noting that in some cases a conforming plan need not be given approval if the circumstances are "so exceptional as to support the conclusion that the plan . . . would not be in the public interest." *Id.* at 458. Nevertheless, *Doran* (if followed elsewhere) would indicate that the provision of specific substantive review standards in the model act has significantly diminished local authority to reject PUD's conforming with the statutory criteria.

In some respects, the model act has freed up the administration of PUD ordinances. For example, the model act criteria require findings and conclusions on "[t]he extent to which the development plan departs from zoning and subdivision regulations otherwise applicable." In the *Doran* case, *supra,* the argument was made that the PUD could not be approved because the plan departed from certain requirements in the zoning ordinance. This argument was rejected, the court noting that "[i]t is the very essence of a planned residential development that it may diverge from zoning requirements." *Id.* at 456. The earlier New Jersey version of the model act was interpreted to allow the enactment of a PUD ordinance which did not require PUD districts. *Rudderow v. Township Comm.,* 297 A.2d 583 (N.J. Super. 1972). This interpretation is consistent with the intent of the draftsmen that PUD's be handled through an adjudicative approval procedure.

Additional adoptions of the model act are unlikely in view of the fact that the ALI's Model Land Development Code has provided authority for planned unit development procedures as part of its process for the approval of special development permits. The applicable Code section is quite brief and provides as follows:

Section 2-210. Planned Unit Development

(1) A development ordinance may authorize the Land Development Agency to grant special development permission for planned unit development by specifying the types or characteristics of development that may be permitted, which may differ from one part of the community to another.

(2) Special development permits may be granted for planned unit development, including combinations of land uses within the project area, and may be based on site planning criteria relating to the project as a whole rather than to individual parcels, if the Land Development Agency finds that the development:

(a) will be consistent with a currently effective Land Development Plan; and

(b) is likely to be compatible with development permitted under the general development provisions of the ordinance on substantially all land in the vicinity of the proposed development; and

(c) will not significantly interfere with the enjoyment
of other land in the vicinity.

Is the authority to control PUD's as conferred by this provision
sufficient to cover all of the objections raised to the enactment of
PUD ordinances under conventional planning and zoning
legislation? Why do you suppose the draftsmen decided to provide
criteria for PUD approval but not to deal with any of the other
problems raised by PUD projects? In light of the cases discussed
above, especially *Doran, supra,* and the cases discussed in the
material on special uses, how much discretion does this section leave
to municipalities in approving or denying PUD projects?

A NOTE ON NEW TOWNS

A variant and more ambitious example of large-scale development
based on the planned unit development principle is the new town.
First tried and successfully implemented in Great Britain, the new
town idea was soon heralded in the United States as an approach to
the development of entire new communities that could achieve
significant design and planning objectives that otherwise would not
be possible.

The new town was envisaged as an entire new community, built
from the ground up and complete with shopping and industrial areas
as well as residential neighborhoods. One advantage of the new
community was that it was to be planned, developed and managed
under a single or unified management pursuant to a comprehensive
development plan. The plan would incorporate the highest design
principles, and would provide opportunities for lower income
housing in its residential areas. Part of the new town promise was
the hope that employment opportunities within the new town would
be available for a large proportion of its residents, thus reducing
work-trip commuting. This hope has been partially realized in Great
Britain.

Development control problems in new towns have been handled
to some extent by expanded versions of planned unit development
ordinances. Reston, a new town in the suburban Virginia sector of
the Washington, D.C., metropolitan area was built under a
specially-tailored planned unit development provision. For
discussion see Christensen, Land Use Control for the New
Community, 6 Harv. J. Legis. 496 (1969). The regulatory problems
are similar to those raised under more limited PUD ordinances.

Federal financial assistance for new towns was made available by
Title VII of the Housing and Community Development Act of 1970,
42 U.S.C. §§ 4501-32 (1976). This Title provided federal assistance
in the form of guarantees on debt obligations of new town

developers, interest grants and loans, special planning grants and loans, public service grants, technical assistance and demonstration projects. While a substantial number of new town communities were funded under the federal program, most were initiated by private developers and federal assistance primarily took the form of debt guarantees. The heavy participation of private rather than public developers probably reflects the limited funding of the federal program, but the result was that the planning and development of the new towns was left in private hands.

While the federally-funded program had some initial successes, growing financial difficulties triggered a study by the federal General Accounting Office that revealed serious deficiencies in the program as administered. U.S. General Accounting Office, Getting the New Communities Program Started: Progress and Problems (1974). This report found that the financial difficulties in the program were the result of poor planning by developers and the acceptance of incomplete and inadequate feasibility studies by the federal Department of Housing and Urban Development (HUD), which was charged with the administration of the program.

The recession in the early 1970's aggravated these difficulties, and HUD has now decided to foreclose and sell off several of the federally-funded new town communities. The future of the federal program is in doubt, although some privately financed and developed new towns, such as the Irvine Ranch development in California, are still going forward. For a thorough discussion of the new town idea, the federal program, and state legislation enacted to implement the new town concept see Note, New Communities: In Search of Cibola — Some Legislative Trails, 12 Urb. L. Ann. 177 (1976).

B. AESTHETICS AND DESIGN

Whether aesthetic considerations are a proper basis for regulation of land use and development under the police power has been a controversial issue for three quarters of a century. The issue has repeatedly been litigated in the context of outdoor advertising controls. In recent years, the courts have also had to consider whether aesthetic considerations are a proper basis for the "taking" of property interests under the power of eminent domain. And the validity of aesthetic controls over the design of residential and commercial structures has been the focus of a substantial amount of litigation. Outdoor advertising and other land use controls with an aesthetic dimension will be considered in this section.

The business of outdoor advertising on a commercial basis dates from the 1880's. Under the common law, advertising posters that for any reason were regarded as offensive or dangerous were dealt with under the doctrine of nuisance. From the 1890's onward, however, large-scale commercial promotion of billboard advertising became so aggressive and its methods so crude as to provoke prohibitory legislation, usually in the form of municipal ordinances. In the early cases the courts were generally hostile to these prohibitory ordinances, and many of them were declared unconstitutional. The courts said that billboards were not nuisances in fact and could not be made so by legislative fiat. Aesthetic considerations were held insufficient to justify use of the police power to impose rather modest restrictions upon the location of billboards. Even ordinances with the limited purpose of protecting the appearance of public parks and boulevards by restricting the placing of billboards near such places were disapproved. The rationale of many of these early court decisions was stated by a conservative New Jersey court as follows: "[a]esthetic considerations are a matter of luxury and indulgence rather than of necessity, and it is necessity alone which justifies the exercise of the police power to take private property without compensation." *City of Passaic v. Paterson Bill Posting, Advertising & Sign Painting Co.,* 62 A. 267, 268 (N.J. Ct. Err. & App. 1905).

Even in the early 1900's, however, cases can be found upholding municipal billboard regulations on the dual grounds of safety and amenity. The decision generally credited with having the greatest influence in changing judicial attitudes toward billboard regulations is *St. Louis Gunning Advertising Co. v. City of St. Louis,* 137 S.W. 929 (Mo. 1911), *appeal dismissed,* 231 U.S. 761 (1913). In an opinion covering 124 pages, the Missouri court discussed the evolution of the law up to that time and sustained a municipal ordinance regulating the size, height, and location of billboards. In an oft-quoted passage, the court said:

> ... The signboards upon which this class of advertisements are displayed are constant menaces to the public safety and welfare of the city; they endanger the public health, promote immorality, constitute hiding places and retreats for criminals and all classes of miscreants. They are also inartistic and unsightly.
>
> In cases of fire they often cause their spread and constitute barriers against their extinction; and in cases of high wind, their temporary character, frail structure and broad surface, render them liable to be blown down and to fall upon and injure those who may happen to be in their vicinity. The evidence shows and common observation teaches us that the ground in the rear thereof is being constantly used as privies and the dumping ground for all kinds of waste and deleterious matters, and thereby creating public nuisances and jeopardizing public health; the evidence also shows that behind these obstructions the lowest form of prostitution and other acts of immorality are frequently carried on, almost under public gaze; they offer

shelter and concealment for the criminal while lying in wait for his victim; and last, but not least, they obstruct the light, sunshine and air, which are so conducive to health and comfort.

Id. at 942.

Although the Missouri court, in the passage set out above, expressly mentioned the fact that signboards are "inartistic and unsightly," it made clear at a later point in its opinion that, in its view, aesthetic considerations alone were insufficient to justify the regulatory ordinance. *Id.* at 961. Commentators have tended to deride the public safety arguments in the *Gunning* case, and certainly the modern billboard, placed high above the ground and made of sturdy and noncombustible materials, does not match the court's description. But this line of argument can be carried too far.[1]

A growing appreciation of the close relationship between the value of property and the amenity of its surroundings has had a significant practical effect on judicial views on the scope of the police power in the years since the *Gunning* case. This relationship was noted in the *Euclid* case, which provided a solid constitutional footing for comprehensive zoning and thus made available a convenient framework for inclusion of outdoor advertising regulations in municipal ordinances that regulate land use in other respects. Whether the issues are the same when outdoor advertising controls are cloaked in a municipal zoning ordinance is a useful question to ask. In view of the origin of American city planning in the "city beautiful" movement, the failure to resolve this and other issues in regard to aesthetic controls at this late date is also a matter for thought.

UNITED ADVERTISING CORP. v. METUCHEN [2]

Supreme Court of New Jersey
42 N.J. 1, 198 A.2d 447 (1964)

The opinion of the court was delivered.

PER CURIAM. This case involves the validity of a provision of a zoning ordinance prohibiting outdoor advertising signs other than those related to a business conducted on the premises. Off-premise signs are prohibited throughout the municipality. Plaintiff sought to erect one such sign in a business district and another in a

---

[1] The day after one of the editors suggested this to a class in planning law, a young telephone operator was raped and stabbed behind a billboard in the central area of the city in which the class was held.

[2] [Metuchen is a surburban community lying south of Newark. — Eds.]

manufacturing district. Defendant obtained summary judgment on motion. We reversed, holding that plaintiff was entitled to adduce facts in support of its constitutional challenges. *United Advertising Corp. v. Borough of Metuchen,* 35 N.J. 193, 172 A.2d 429 (1961). The case was thereafter tried and judgment again rendered in favor of defendant. We certified plaintiff's appeal before the Appellate Division heard it.

Plaintiff wishes to erect billboards 12 feet in height by 25 feet in width. These are standard dimensions for billboards throughout the country. Plaintiff concedes its billboards do not belong in residential or scenic areas, but its business being lawful, it claims it should be permitted to operate among other businesses and in industrial districts as well.

Plaintiff's position was rejected in *United Advertising Corp. v. Borough of Raritan,* 11 N.J. 144, 93 A.2d 362 (1952), where the Court refused to strike down an ordinance barring off-premise signs throughout the municipality. Plaintiff contends that case was wrongly decided because the evils once thought to abound in this setting were unreal or had been eliminated by the time of that decision and in truth no zoning purpose remaining to be furthered by the ban. Further, plaintiff urges the discrimination between off-premise and on-premise signs violates the mandate of N.J.S.A. 40:55-31 that "All such regulations shall be uniform for each class or kind of buildings or other structures or uses of land throughout each district. . . ."

As to the first proposition, plaintiff starts with an analysis of *Thomas Cusack Co. v. City of Chicago,* 242 U.S. 526, 37 S. Ct. 190, 61 L. Ed. 472 (1917), one of the cases cited in the *Raritan* opinion. Cusack did not involve a zoning ordinance. Rather the ordinance was addressed to the special evils then charged to billboards. They included the accumulation of offensive materials and rubbish, and the shield afforded for immoral practices and for loiterers and criminals. As to such matters, plaintiff says that today billboards are so constructed, positioned and maintained that these ills no longer exist. In other words, plaintiff says that proper regulation will suffice and enforcement is not so burdensome that prohibition is warranted.

With respect to whether billboards create traffic hazards, a topic which came to the scene after *Cusack,* plaintiff says that, as to obstruction of view, appropriate setbacks are sufficient; and as to distraction of the motorist, plaintiff claims the billboard, although designed to attract, presents no hazard because a driver's peripheral vision will embrace the roadway while he looks left or right to read the advertisement, and in fact such momentary diversions prevent road hypnosis and thus mean safer driving. Expert testimony was offered to maintain the last proposition, and the trial court was persuaded by it. We have some reservations as to whether billboards would not be a hazard in heavy traffic where a driver has quite enough to do to watch for sudden movements of men and machines. At any rate, for present purposes we accept the trial court's agreement with that testimony.

That the evils which prompted earlier legislation may be gone or be well in hand does not end the inquiry, for new circumstances generate new problems. Since the time *Cusack* was decided, it has been universally recognized that the growth in population, in commerce, in industry, and in land utilization call for order in land uses, to preserve human values and to conserve property values. Hence our zoning statute authorizes ordinances to achieve aims made necessary by the new scene and expressed in R.S. 40:55-32, N.J.S.A.:

> Such regulations shall be in accordance with a comprehensive plan and designed for one or more of the following purposes: to lessen congestion in the streets; secure safety from fire, panic and other dangers; *promote* health, morals or *the general welfare;* provide adequate light and air; prevent the overcrowding of land or buildings; avoid undue concentration of population. Such regulations shall be made with reasonable consideration, among other things, to the character of the district and its peculiar suitability for particular uses, *and with a view of conserving the value of property and encouraging the most appropriate use of land throughout such municipality.*

We have italicized the portion which we think here pertinent.

As we have said, plaintiff concedes a billboard does not belong in a residential area or in places of scenic beauty. The concession is put in terms that billboards are a business use and hence may be barred wherever business does not belong. We think the concession is correct, not merely because billboards are a business use, but because they would clash with those settings whether they solicited an interest in toothpaste or in some charitable cause.

Much is said about zoning for aesthetics. If what is meant thereby is zoning for aesthetics as an end in itself, the issue may be said to be unexplored in our State, but if the question is whether aesthetics may play a part in a zoning judgment, the subject is hardly new. There are areas in which aesthetics and economics coalesce, areas in which a discordant sight is as hard an economic fact as an annoying odor or sound. We refer not to some sensitive or exquisite preference but to concepts of congruity held so widely that they are inseparable from the enjoyment and hence the value of property. Even the basic separation of industrial from commercial from residential, although obviously related to so much of the quoted statute as speaks of health and hazard, rests also on the aesthetic impact of uses upon the value of properties. Surely no one would say today that an industrial structure must be permitted in a residential district upon a showing that the operation to be conducted therein involves no significant congestion in the streets, or danger of fire or panic, or impediment of light and air, or overcrowding of land, or undue concentration of population. So also the recognition of different residential districts, with varying lot sizes, setbacks, and the like, rests upon the proposition that aesthetics should not be ignored when one seeks to promote "the general welfare," as the statute says, "with a view of conserving the value of property and encouraging the most appropriate use of land throughout such municipality." Our cases deem aesthetics to be relevant when they bear in a substantial way upon land utilization. . . .

Accordingly we are not persuaded that *Raritan* should be discarded on the thesis that it relied upon evils no longer pervasive. The aesthetic impact of billboards is an economic fact which may bear heavily upon the enjoyment and value of property. It is a relevant zoning consideration. . . .

This brings us to the charge that the ordinance, in barring off-premise signs while permitting on-premise signs, violates N.J.S.A. 40:55-31, which provides in part that "All such regulations shall be uniform for each class or kind of buildings or other structures or uses of land throughout each district. . . ." This issue of classification is in substance the same issue projected by plaintiff in *Raritan* and there decided against it, notwithstanding that here the stress, is more upon the statute than upon constitutional provisions barring unequal treatment.

The zoning statute relates to the uses of structures as well as to their nature, and the section upon which plaintiff relies must be read in that light. N.J.S.A. 40:55-30 provides that zoning ordinances may regulate "buildings and structures according to their construction, and the nature and extent of their use. . . ." A structure or use may be permitted if it is merely ancillary or incidental to a permitted principal use and still be barred if it is a separate, independent use. Here, the on-premise sign is a mere adjunct to a permitted business or industrial use, whereas the off-premise sign would be a separate, independent business effort. Hence it proves nothing to say that a sign is a sign.

There are obvious differences between an on-premise sign and an off-premise sign. Even if the baleful effect of both be in fact the same, still in one case the sign may be found tolerable because of its contribution to the business or enterprise on the premises. The hurt is thus supported by a need or gain not present in the case of the off-premise sign. This difference, it seems to us, suffices to support the classification.

And the classification is not impaired by the fact that the ordinance before us, if exploited relentlessly according to its literal terms, would permit on-premise signs with a total square footage in excess of that of the standard billboard. It would still be true that the permitted signs advance the business or industry on hand while an off-premise sign does not. Moreover, the sensibilities of neighbors and customers may offer a restraint which the off-premise advertiser would not feel. Still further, if experience should show that the maximum limitations upon size were ill-conceived, there is probably power to revise the ordinance and to compel compliance by existing on-premise signs whereas an off-premise sign, as part of separate business activity, might be claimed to be a nonconforming use, as *Raritan* suggested, and for that reason impervious to corrective measures. Finally, if the total impact of on-premise signs should prove to be too much, surely too much is enough. For all of these reasons we adhere to *Raritan*. Cf. *Metromedia, Inc. v. City of Pasadena,* 30 Cal. Rptr. 731 (D. Ct. App. 1963), appeal dismissed for want of a substantial federal question, 84 S. Ct. 636 (1964).

We find *Raritan* is appropriate here. Metuchen is a small municipality, covering 2.9 square miles, with a population of 14,000. Its essential character is residential. Its business and industrial areas are relatively limited and the municipal aim is to achieve the maximum degree of compatibility with the residential areas. The most that can be said with respect to the proof is that reasonable men can disagree as to whether the addition of off-premise signs would disserve the general welfare. Such policy questions are committed to the judgment of the local legislative bodies. As we have said so many times with respect to zoning and other legislative or *quasi*-legislative decisions, a judge may not interfere merely because he would have made a different policy decision if the power to decide had been his. A court can concern itself only with an abuse of delegated legislative power, and may set aside the legislative judgment only if arbitrariness clearly appears. Plaintiff has not sustained its burden.

We think it unnecessary to discuss the other points raised.

The judgment is affirmed.

For affirmance: Chief Justice WEINTRAUB and Justices JACOBS, FRANCIS, PROCTOR, SCHETTINO and HANEMAN — 6.

For reversal: Justice HALL — 1.

HALL, J. (dissenting). The majority decides that a zoning ordinance prohibition of all "off-premises" advertising signs in a municipality with the characteristics and aspirations of Metuchen is valid even if "on-premises" signs should be allowed without restriction. While the controversy commenced over the right to erect two standard-size billboards against embankments on railroad property — one in a business district and the other in a manufacturing zone — for temporary leasing by the plaintiff to various advertisers, the challenge which the court ultimately was called upon to decide was much more abstract and broad. The two proposed locations and their surroundings became merely illustrative. Though confined to Metuchen and similar type communities, the ruling upholds an outright prohibition of all signs, no matter what their kind, size or setting, which do not refer to a business or activity conducted on the premises where located. I am concerned with the rationale upon which this result is reached, as well as with the intertwined problem of discrimination in relation to on-premises signs.

This is an unusual billboard case in certain fundamental respects not fully adverted to in the majority opinion which, when considered, seem to me to make the true rationale somewhat different from that expressed and in turn place the classification question in a different light. I refer to the fact that, by stipulation of the parties, all of the stereotyped reasons ordinarily utilized to support the use of the police power in billboard cases were removed from consideration. It was agreed that the erection of the proposed billboards would not prevent adequate light and air from reaching any surrounding buildings or dwellings, would not produce objectionable noise, vibration, odor, smoke or the like, would not conceal immoral acts and would not decrease the property value of land in the borough or change the character of the business and manufacturing districts. The only conventional factor not excluded was highway safety and the trial court's finding in plaintiff's favor on this aspect (the municipality offered no affirmative evidence to attack the opinion of plaintiff's experts) has not been challenged. While these stipulations specifically referred to the two proposed signs, the argument of both sides indicates they were considered to have general application beyond the particular sites.

Accordingly, the municipality's defense of the ordinance provisions, presented primarily through the opinion of its planning expert, offered an approach entirely different from that customarily used in these cases. It was, in essence, grounded on an "image," if you will, in the minds of its own citizens and the world at large of a high-class built-up residential community, with a quality local business district and a relatively small industrial district (with commercial business also permitted) on one border, which it desires and plans to maintain and even up-grade. The thesis is that off-premises advertising signs are a jarring visual note and do not belong anywhere in such a picture. It is basically very different and much more frank than the old, stereotyped police power shibboleths which led this court in *United Advertising Corp. v. Borough of Raritan*, 11 N.J. 144, 93 A.2d 362 (1952) to justify billboard prohibition by simply saying abruptly: "It has long been settled that the unique nature of outdoor advertising and the nuisances fostered by billboards and similar outdoor structures located by persons in the business of outdoor advertising, justify the separate classification of such structures for the purposes of governmental regulation and restriction." (11 N.J. at p. 150, 93 A.2d at p. 365) and "It is enough that outdoor advertising has characteristic features which have long been deemed sufficient to sustain regulations or prohibitions peculiarly applicable to it." (11 N.J. at p. 151, 93 A.2d at p. 366).

In reality, as Metuchen's counsel conceded at oral argument, the thesis rests upon exercise of the police power, here through the medium of a zoning ordinance, for purely aesthetic reasons and purposes. The majority recognizes this to some extent, but seems unwilling to give it the exclusive effect which I think it can and should have in this particular situation. My colleagues dilute the concept by leaning upon the well accepted basis of economics, related to an alleged effect of off-premises signs upon the value of property throughout the municipality. Cf. *People v. Stover,* 12 N.Y.2d 462, 240 N.Y.S.2d 734, 191 N.E.2d 272 (Ct. App. 1963), commented upon in "Zoning, aesthetics, and the First Amendment," 64 COLUM. L. REV. 81 (1964). I strongly doubt that the reliance is factually sound or a meaningful crutch in the situation before us. Effect upon property values in any zoning district seems negatived by the parties' stipulation. But even if it is not, I find it impossible to think that a billboard in the manufacturing district can have any dollar effect on the value of a dwelling in a residential zone.

It seems to me that courts ought to face up to realities squarely and begin to give frank recognition to aesthetics as an appropriate basis in some areas for exercise of the police power to attain proper community objectives. See Dukeminier, "Zoning for Aesthetic Objectives: A Reappraisal," 20 Law and Contemporary Problems 218 (1955). While this has actually been done for a considerable time, judicial opinions generally expound some other reason. Many police power regulations are upheld where the true but unexpressed basis is that the activity or condition is considered by practically everyone to be an eyesore or offensive to some other sense. Many zoning regulations actually rest on aesthetic considerations, such as those prescribing suburban residential setback and yard distances.

The concept is admittedly a most difficult one to put into fair practice. Beauty and taste are almost impossible to legislate affirmatively on any very broad scale because they are generally such subjective and individual things, not easily susceptible of objective, non-arbitrary standards. . . . But that does not mean that they cannot be judicially recognized in some situations as proper community objectives. It would seem that the approach could validly be made and legislation sustained squarely on this basis at least with respect to the prohibition or strict regulation of those activities or conditions which a court can find that practically everyone agrees are non-beautiful in their particular environment, so long as more important values are not overriden. Junkyards and automobile graveyards, except in a special setting, come to mind as instances. (They are prohibited by the Metuchen zoning ordinance.) . . . And I think a court can properly say that we have reached that point with respect to outdoor advertising signs in many settings. The saturation of so much of the landscape with signs, both those with changing faces which plaintiff erects and those of all sizes and kinds conveying a permanent message, has caused a very widespread public revulsion because of their ugliness and marring effect. Black, God's Own Junkyard 11-16 (1964). The situation has become one of the "concepts of congruity held so widely," as the majority puts it. Since zoning and other local police power exercise in this state is confined by municipal boundaries, the predominant character of *Metuchen* seems to me to justify the prohibition of off-premises advertising signs throughout the borough for aesthetic reasons, and we ought to frankly put the conclusion on that ground. Whether similar action would be justified in other types of communities, as for example, in a large city with many heavy industrial uses, must await another day.

This leads to my point of difference with the result reached by the majority. The true basis for prohibition being aesthetics, the concept must extend to all similar situations and should be reasonably applied to on-premises signs as well. If not, the municipality is guilty of unfair, unequal and unreasonable treatment which would invalidate the off-premises prohibition. And that is the difficulty I find with the *Metuchen* scheme.

Granted that an owner or operator of a business or factory, whether it be on Main Street or in an outlying highway area, is entitled to identify his enterprise and seek to attract customers or generate good-will and that the aesthetically minded municipality must accordingly put up with some non-aesthetic conditions, it seem to me that the local businessman cannot have an unlimited right to put up signs without commensurate limitation. I cannot find any such right simply because the sign relates to the business and, whatever the privilege should be called, it should not be denominated an accessory use or given nonconforming use protection (and indeed even off-premises signs do not seem to me a sufficient land use to be entitled to that protection). It is common knowledge that on-premises signs are frequently just as ugly and offensive as conventional billboards, if not even more garish. Photographs in evidence in this case illustrate that such conditions do exist to some degree in the business district of Metuchen. . . .

Courts elsewhere have gone both ways on the question. Some, like *Metromedia, Inc. v. City of Pasadena,* 30 Cal. Rptr. 731 (D. Ct. App. 1963), appeal dismissed for want of a substantial federal question, 84 S. Ct. 636 (1964), sanction practically unlimited distinct treatment simply because on-premises signs relate to the business conducted at the site. Others forbid, and I think soundly, unreasonable discrimination. An example is *Sunad, Inc. v. City of Sarasota,* 122 So. 2d 611 (Fla. Sup. Ct. 1960). There the court said:

> Bearing in mind that aesthetics is the criterion by which the merits of the ordinance should be judged, we find insurmountable difficulty to a decision that a wall sign 300 square feet in size at non-point [sic] of sale would not offend while a sign of the same size on one of petitioner's billboards would, or that an unrestricted wall sign, at point of sale, would be inoffensive but one of petitioner's signs would shock refined senses, or for that matter, that a roof, ground, or other sign could be only 180 square feet while a wall sign could be at least 300 square feet and, if at point of sale, unlimited. (122 So. 2d, at pp. 614-15.)

While the Metuchen ordinance purports to restrict on-premises signs, in my opinion the regulation is so illusory in fact that it goes beyond the bounds of reasonable differentiation when off-premises signs are prohibited on the basis of aesthetics. While the square foot *size of single signs* in the business district is confined to 100 square feet, the *number* of such signs on one property is limited only by the front footage of the lot. For example, in the B-2 district, an enterprise on a 100-foot lot can have 1000 square feet of advertising sign space, with any number of signs in any place thereon, so long as no single sign is larger than 100 square feet. In the manufacturing district, if the property (and it may be a commercial as well as an industrial use) has a 300-foot frontage, it may maintain 4500 square feet of advertising space made up of any number of signs. Any sign may be as large as plaintiff's 300-square-foot billboards and erected anywhere on the premises so long as the top does not project higher than the maximum permissible height of principal structures in the district. It is obvious that there is substantially no recognition of aesthetics in these regulations and I feel strongly that such recognition must be given where aesthetics is the basis to exclude billboards. . . . I cannot but conclude that there is consequently such unreasonable leniency as to on-premises signs in Metuchen that, as the ordinance provisions now stand, complete prohibition of off-premises signs cannot be justified. . . .

Comments: 1. The *Metuchen* decision has received increasing support in cases in other states which, while not quite reaching the analytic elegance of the New Jersey court, nevertheless uphold ordinances excluding billboards from all or a portion of the municipality. These cases generally emphasize that the exclusion must be justified by the regulatory setting of the community in which the restriction is applied. *John Donnelly & Sons, Inc. v. Outdoor Advertising Bd.,* 339 N.E.2d 709 (Mass. 1975); *Naegele Outdoor Advertising Co. v. Village of Minnetonka,* 162 N.W.2d 206 (Minn. 1968) (excluded from residential districts); *Cromwell v. Ferrier,* 225 N.E.2d 749 (N.Y. 1967) (total exclusion); *Suffolk Outdoor Advertising Co. v. Hulse,* 373 N.E.2d 263 (N.Y. 1977) (total exclusion of "off-premises" signs). But see *John Donnelly & Sons v. Mallar,* 453 F. Supp. 1272 (D. Me. 1978).

In the *Suffolk* case, the New York court said that, although once open to question, it is now clear that the regulation of outdoor advertising for aesthetic purposes alone constitutes a valid exercise of the police power; and that, once it is established that the regulation enacted has a valid basis it need only be shown that it is reasonably related to the objective for which it was enacted in order to sustain its constitutionality. In the instant case, it could not be seriously argued that the ordinance's ban on "off-premises" advertising signs was not reasonably related to improving the aesthetics of the community; nor could it be said to be oppressive, since the ordinance permitted "on-premise" signs and thus provided an operative means of advertising. The New York court also rejected the contention that the prohibition of "off-premises" signs constituted a violation of the constitutional right of free speech. Conceding that "commercial speech" now falls within the protection of the First Amendment, the court said that the legislature may nevertheless regulate the time, place, or manner of commercial speech—as opposed to its content—to effectuate a significant governmental interest. Since the ordinance made no attempt to regulate the content of the commercial speech appearing on advertising signs, but rather regulated only the place and manner in which signs may be maintained, and since "aesthetics" constitutes a significant governmental interest, the ordinance did not violate the First Amendment. Judge Fuchsberg dissented on the First Amendment issue.

See also Veterans of Foreign Wars, etc. v. Steamboat Springs, 575 P.2d 835 (Colo. 1978), sustaining a comprehensive sign code which prohibited (with limited exceptions) erection of signs prior to acquisition of a city permit, payment of a fee, and compliance with the code's detailed regulations. The court held that, although plaintiffs had standing to challenge the sign code on constitutional grounds as facially overbroad and vague, the sign code was not facially overbroad; that a code provision prohibiting "off-premise signs" unless "necessary" to promote the interests of the use to which the sign related was not unconstitutionally vague for lack of sufficient standards; that the sign code did not constitute an invalid prior restraint on the exercise of First Amendment rights because of its requirement that a permit be obtained and a fee paid before any new sign could be erected; that regulations as to the extent to which signs could extend into or over public property was a valid exercise of the city's police power; and that the sign code's provisions requiring discontinuance of existing signs extending more than three feet into or over public property, but allowing other existing signs to remain indefinitely so long as there was no abandonment, damage, destruction or obsolescence, did not violate the equal protection clause of the Fourteenth Amendment.

For additional discussion of the First Amendment in connection with architectural regulation, see *infra* p. 918.

2. As might be expected, the Pennsylvania Supreme Court has held that total exclusion of outdoor advertising signs is not within the police power. *See Norate Corp. v. Zoning Bd. of Adjustment,* 207 A.2d 890 (Pa. 1965), where the court struck down a total exclusion of billboards in a suburban and apparently rather undeveloped area near Philadelphia. The Colorado Supreme Court has taken the same view. In 1971, Denver enacted two ordinances which (1) prohibited the erection of new outdoor advertising signs and (2) required removal of existing outdoor advertising signs over a period of five years in accordance with an "amortization" schedule depending upon the replacement value of particular signs. In *Art Neon Co. v. City & County of Denver,* 488 F.2d 118 (10th Cir. 1974), the U.S. Court of Appeals held that the second ordinance was valid, as construed to permit the five-year maximum period for removal of all nonconforming signs, but that the provision for different periods of amortization was unreasonable. The plaintiff apparently did not challenge the first ordinance. But both ordinances were successfully challenged in *Combined Communications Corp. v. City & County of Denver,* 542 P.2d 79 (Colo. 1975), where the Colorado Supreme Court, by a split decision, held that Denver had no authority either under its general police power or under its delegated zoning power to provide for total exclusion of "an entire industry" throughout the entire area of a major city, at least where the prohibited industry "does not constitute a public nuisance." The majority did not give separate consideration to the second ordinance requiring elimination of nonconforming signs because it was "so intertwined with" the invalid ordinance prohibiting erection of new signs. A dissenting judge noted that "amortization has been approved by respectable courts as a valid method of satisfying the 'just compensation' requirements of the Fourteenth Amendment."

Compare *Oregon City v. Hartke,* 400 F.2d 255 (Ore. 1965), upholding total exclusion of automobile wrecking yards from the city.

3. How should the courts react to a total prohibition of moving or flashing signs throughout the municipality? It was held invalid in *In re Appeal of Ammon R. Smith Auto Co.,* 223 A.2d 683 (Pa. 1966), the court relying on *Norate, supra* Comment 2, and finding the prohibition too insensitive to the sign regulation problem. *Contra, Kenyon Peck, Inc. v. Kennedy,* 168 S.E.2d 117 (Va. 1969), in which only moving signs were prohibited; the court relied heavily on the usual presumption of constitutionality. *See also State v. Diamond Motors, Inc.,* 429 P.2d 825 (Hawaii 1967).

In *Tunis-Huntingdon Dodge, Inc. v. Horn,* 290 N.Y.S.2d 7 (N.Y. App. Div. 1968), the appellate court sustained the refusal of the zoning board of appeals to grant a special exception permit for erection of a free-standing automobile dealer's sign with a 4.6' by 4.6' "rotating pentastar" on top. The board found that the applicant had not satisfied two of the standards applicable in such cases: "(a) That such sign is necessary for proper identification of the business . . . ; (b) That such sign does not contribute to the devaluation of any property in the area." The court agreed with these findings, and also said: "[M]erely because Chrysler Motors Corporation is desirous of adopting some special policy in regard to signs for its agencies is no reason why a municipality's zoning board must set aside its own views and submit subordinately to such corporate policy. . . ." Several signs were already on the premises.

See also *Arcadia Dev. Corp. v. City of Bloomington,* 125 N.W.2d 846 (Minn. 1964), a case which may be wrongly decided but which is nevertheless interesting. Here the developer wished to erect an entrance sign for his mobile home park. Under the municipal ordinance he could only erect a rooftop sign on his main building, to which he objected as aesthetically offensive. He contended that the city's ordinance was neither appropriate nor flexible enough to serve the "necessities" of business. The court struck down the city ordinance as unreasonable under all the circumstances.

4. Total prohibitions may be easier for courts to handle than more sophisticated sign ordinances which attempt to legislate performance standards, especially for on-site advertising. Attempted distinctions between on-premise and off-premise advertising have been troublesome. In *Metromedia, Inc. v. City of Pasadena,* 30 Cal. Rptr. 731 (Cal. App. 1963), *appeal dismissed,* 376 U.S. 186 (1964), cited in the *Metuchen* case, the city ordinance prohibited all rooftop signs, "excepting those which (1) bear the name of the building whereon the sign is located; (2) bear the name of the person, firm or corporation occupying the building or portion thereof and the type of business conducted by said person, firm or corporation." The ordinance was sustained against an attack that it authorized a discriminatory classification. How are on-premise signs any more offensive than off-premise signs? Testimony for the sign company in the *Metromedia* case indicated that "sign-clutter" was more a result of on-premise rather than off-premise advertising, and the company argued from this evidence that the city's ordinance was not the best solution to the sign problem. While the court admitted that much could be said for the sign company's position, it refused on self-restraint grounds to upset the ordinance.

5. Judicial recognition that the highway advertiser is essentially "seizing for private benefit an opportunity created for a quite different purpose by the expenditure of public money in the construction of public ways" [3] and that "the regulation of billboards and their restriction is not so much a regulation of private property as it is a regulation of the use of the streets and other public thoroughfares" [4] led ultimately, in *Kelbro, Inc. v. Myrick,* 30 A.2d 527, 530 (Vt. 1943), to a holding that "the right of view [from the highway] of the owner or occupant of the abutting property is limited to such right as is appurtenant to that property and includes the right to display only goods or advertising matter pertaining to business conducted thereon." [5] Under this theory, of course, the distinction between "on-premises" and "off-premises" signs in the principal case and in *Metromedia, supra* Comment 4, is rational and not unconstitutionally

---

[3] *General Outdoor Advertising Co. v. Department of Pub. Works,* 193 N.E. 799, 808 (Mass. 1935), *appeal dismissed,* 297 U.S. 725 (1936).

[4] *Churchill & Tait v. Rafferty,* 32 Phillippines 580, 609 (1915), *appeal dismissed,* 248 U.S. 591 (1918).

[5] *Kelbro* was reaffirmed in *Micalite Sign Corp. v. State Highway Dep't,* 236 A.2d 680 (Vt. 1967).

discriminatory. For an exhaustive discussion of the Vermont "property rights" approach to outdoor advertising control, see Wilson, Billboards and the Right to Be Seen from the Highway, 30 Geo. L.J. 723, 745-47 (1942).

6. The following summary of on-premise sign controls is based on a survey of sign regulations for urban commercial areas in 19 moderately sized cities which were chosen at random:

> . . . [These ordinances] are of almost infinite variety and range from the absence of control to minutely detailed controls of size, number, lighting, animation, etc. . . . For most areas which have stricter controls, . . . total sign area is generally restricted either by an absolute upper figure, by relationship of sign mass to building frontage, or by a combination of the two. Absolute total-area restriction means that the combined area of all permitted signs must not exceed a stipulated square foot figure. The sliding scale for building size allows adequate identification for larger, single-owned or occupied stores.
>
> Another control device is to limit the area size of each particular sign. . . . This type of control can be used without reference to absolute total figures by such individual regulation as depth of wall projection, distance from sidewalk, and height above rooftop. Controlling the sidewalk overhang of projecting signs can be an effective means of allowing stores with greater setback a means of more clearly identifying themselves. . . .
>
> The one type of sign that is permitted within all areas is the flat sign, attached parallel to the building wall, which generally may project from twelve to eighteen inches. Where there is an absolute square-foot total, the flat sign generally must remain within the prescribed limits. Other limitations on this type of sign include total height, distance from grade, and maximum and/or sliding scale size.
>
> Ground signs or pole signs are more strictly controlled. . . . Generally, restrictions on ground signs include placement in yard area, minimum and maximum heights from ground level, and sign area limitations either stipulated independently or within the total sign area restriction.
>
> Illumination control generally prohibits flashing beacons and other light from commercial areas that spills over into residential property.

M. Bricker, Regulation of On-Site Business Signs 13-15 (1970) (thesis on file in Washington University School of Law library in St. Louis, Missouri).

This survey reflects the ad hoc character of most on-premise sign regulation; note the criticisms of Justice Hall in his dissenting opinion in *Metuchen, supra.* A more sensitive system for controlling on-premise signs has been suggested in W. Ewald & D. Mandelker, Street Graphics (1971) (includes model ordinance). The Street Graphics system contains a set of performance standards, provided in tabular form, that generally adopt a proportionality rule for on-premise signs. Free-standing signs are related to the width of adjacent streets and to traffic speed; signs can be larger as streets get wider and traffic moves more quickly. Wall signs are related to building mass; they may occupy only a stated percentage of wall area. There are also provisions to moderate signing in areas adjacent to residential neighborhoods.

Perhaps the most controversial feature of the Street Graphics approach is the item of information. To control the communications load from signs, but not their content, each land use is limited to ten items of information on all of the signs on its premises, although these items may be distributed as the owner wishes. An item of information is defined as any of the following: "an abbreviation; a number; a symbol; a geometric shape." One purpose of the item of information limitation is to encourage the use of symbols and logos on signs that will improve their aesthetic merit. Does the items of information limitation raise free speech problems? *See infra* p. 918. Is it otherwise constitutional? The Street Graphics ordinance has been adopted in several communities.

7. The aesthetic-economic rationale for advertising sign controls is probably most persuasive when it is used to sustain municipal land use regulations (usually zoning regulations) that apply to urban areas, or land use regulations designed to maintain scenic or historic attractions in areas (urban or nonurban) which attract large numbers of tourists. *Murphy v. Town of Westport*, 40 A.2d 177 (Conn. 1944) (billboards — property values); *Sunad, Inc. v. City of Sarasota*, 122 So.2d 611 (Fla. 1960) (advertising signs — tourism); *Miami Beach v. Ocean & Inland Co.*, 3 So.2d 364 (Fla. 1941) (exclusive hotel and apartment zone — aesthetic appeal — tourism); *State ex rel. Civello v. City of New Orleans*, 97 So.2d 440 (La. 1923) (architectural control — property values); *Opinion of the Justices to the Senate*, 128 N.E.2d 563 (Mass. 1955) (historic district — architectural control — tourism); *Opinion of the Justices to the Senate*, 128 N.E.2d 557 (Mass. 1955) (same); *United Advertising Corp. v. Metuchen, supra* (principal case); *People v. Stover*, 191 N.E.2d 272 (N.Y.), *appeal dismissed*, 375 U.S. 42 (1963) (front yard clothes line — property values).

Traffic considerations may help justify sign controls when sign regulation is related to thoroughfares. Thus, in *Village of Larchmont v. Levine*, 225 N.Y.S.2d 452 (N.Y. Sup. Ct. 1961), an ordinance was upheld which prohibited the placement of a sign on the wall of a building facing traffic, even though the sign advertised on-premise business. The court relied on the close proximity of the sign to the street, its visibility to traffic, and the fact that the street narrowed at a point near the building.

8. The aesthetic-economic rationale for advertising sign controls becomes less persuasive when controls are applied to rural areas with slight scenic value. But traffic safety considerations may support sign controls. And it is pretty clear that preservation of scenic beauty along nonurban highways, both to preserve the right of the traveling public to aesthetic enjoyment and to protect the tourist industry as an economic asset of the state, is a legitimate police power objective. Closely linked with this objective is the idea that travelers on a public highway constructed with public funds have a right to be free from the intrusion of unwelcome advertising signs which derive their value to the advertiser entirely from the public investment in the highway. *E.g., Moore v. Ward*, 377 S.W.2d 881 (Ky. 1964); *General Outdoor Advertising Co. v. Department of Pub. Works*, 193 N.E. 799 (Mass. 1935), *appeal dismissed*, 297 U.S. 725 (1936); *Opinion of*

the Justices, 169 A.2d 762 (N.H. 1961); *New York State Thruway Auth. v. Ashley Motor Court, Inc.,* 176 N.E.2d 566 (N.Y. 1961); *Ghaster Properties, Inc. v. Preston,* 200 N.E.2d 328 (Ohio 1964); *Markham Advertising Co. v. State,* 429 P.2d 248 (Wash. 1968), *appeal dismissed,* 393 U.S. 316 (1969). Most of these cases relied upon both a traffic safety and an aesthetic values rationale in sustaining the sign controls. *Opinion of the Justices* and *Ghaster Properties* also relied in part on the *Kelbro* "property rights" rationale in expressly upholding the distinction between "off-premises" and "on-premises" signs against attack on equal protection grounds. In *Ashley Motor Court,* the New York court said:

> [I]t was the very construction of the Thruway which created the element of value in the land abutting the road. Billboards and other advertising signs are obviously of no use unless there is a highway to bring the traveler within the view of them. What was taken by the regulation, therefore, was the value which the Thruway itself had added to the land and of this the defendant cannot be heard to complain.

Id. at 569.

9. *Moore, Opinion of the Justices, Ashley Motor Court, Ghaster Properties,* and *Markham, supra,* all sustained the prohibition of "off-premises" advertising signs along interstate and other limited-access highways by state statutes enacted in the early 1960's to take advantage of the bonus provision of the Federal-Aid Highway Act of 1958. Since all of these cases involved statutes which provided for removal of lawfully erected nonconforming advertising signs without compensation, they furnish very strong *a fortiori* support for use of the police power to prevent erection of new signs in controlled areas adjacent to interstate and primary highways. Only two of the statutes provided for any "amortization" period before nonconforming signs were required to be removed — Kentucky (five years) and Washington (three years). In *Markham,* the Washington court, concluding that three years was a reasonable amortization period, pointed out that it had previously said "that it is within the legislature's power to forbid a use altogether without making any provision for an amortization period," citing *State v. Thomasson,* 378 P.2d 441 (Wash. 1963), and *State ex rel. Miller v. Cain,* 242 P.2d 505 (Wash. 1952).

As we have previously seen, elimination of nonconforming signs without compensation after an "amortization" period, pursuant to municipal zoning ordinance provisions, has generally been upheld, although there are some cases to the contrary. *See supra* p. 296. As is there indicated, the amortization technique had probably been used most successfully in the elimination of nonconforming outdoor advertising signs. For detailed treatment of the problem, see Comment, Constitutionality of Sign Amortization Ordinances, 9 Urb. L. Ann. 303 (1975).

NOTE ON OUTDOOR ADVERTISING CONTROL UNDER THE FEDERAL HIGHWAY BEAUTIFICATION ACT OF 1965 [6]

The Federal-Aid Highway Act of 1958 [7] was designed to persuade the several states to adopt effective billboard controls by holding out the "carrot" of a one-half percent increase in the federal share payable on interstate highway projects. The 1958 act was generally not very effective, and was largely superseded by Title I of the Highway Beautification Act of 1965,[8] which used the "stick" of a threatened 10 percent reduction in all federal highway aid to any state which fails to provide for "effective control of the erection and maintenance along the Interstate System and the primary system of outdoor advertising signs, displays, and devices" within 660 feet of the right-of-way and visible from the main traveled way of the system. The language of the 1965 act is clearly permissive and does not require any state to allow off-premises advertising signs in zoned or unzoned commercial or industrial areas; any state may, but need not, provide a blanket exemption for such signs in commercial and industrial areas. If a state does wish to provide such an exemption, the Secretary of Transportation must accept the determination of the state or some duly authorized local authority in zoning an area "commercial" or "industrial," and must accept its determination of what constitutes "customary use" with respect to off-premises advertising in these areas. Although the 1965 act allows any state to grant a blanket exemption for "on-premises" advertising signs, it may, if it chooses, prohibit or limit the construction or maintenance of such signs; and it may also prohibit or limit advertising signs located more than 660 feet from the right-of-way.

Subject to the exemptions discussed above, "effective control of the erection and maintenance . . . of outdoor advertising signs" includes (1) prohibition of the erection of new signs in controlled areas, and (2) provision for removal of existing nonconforming signs located in controlled areas. All of the state statutes enacted to comply with the 1965 Act rely upon the police power to prevent the erection of new signs in controlled areas. But the 1965 Act provides that "just compensation" is to be paid upon removal of any lawfully erected nonconforming signs. In all cases where "just compensation" is paid for sign removal, the federal share is 75 percent and the state share is 25 percent. But, as the court held in *Markham Advertising Co. v. State*, 439 P.2d 248 (Wash. 1968), the 1965 Act was not intended to create for affected sign owners and landowners any absolute

---

[6] 23 U.S.C. §§ 131, 136, 319 (1976).

[7] Pub. L. No. 85-767 (1958).

[8] 23 U.S.C. § 131 (1976) (the billboard control section).

federal right to compensation, and any state (like Washington) need not provide for compensation if it is willing to assume the risk that it will incur the 10 percent penalty as a result of failing to provide compensation.

Since few states have been willing to risk the loss of 10 percent of the total federal-aid highway funds that would otherwise be available to them, most of the state highway advertising control acts adopted to comply with the 1965 federal act have provided for payment of "just compensation" to sign owners and to landowners (where signs have been erected under advertising "leases") upon removal of lawfully erected nonconforming signs. That the risk of suffering the 10 percent penalty is substantial was indicated by an opinion of the Acting Attorney General of the United States issued November 16, 1965. In that opinion, the Acting Attorney General concluded that Title I must be read as requiring each state to afford just compensation upon removal of lawful but nonconforming outdoor advertising signs in order to avoid the 10 percent penalty — even though the state might prefer to use its police power to compel removal — and that there is no basis for holding this requirement to be unconstitutional. The Acting Attorney General's conclusion was sustained in *State v. Brinegar,* 379 F.Supp. 606 (D. Vt. 1974). Even after *Brinegar,* however, it can still be argued that a state may provide the "just compensation" required by the 1965 Act through the allowance of an "amortization" period during which nonconforming signs may be kept in place, rather than by paying compensation in money. The *Brinegar* opinion did not address this argument.

Although the language of the 1965 Act is not entirely clear, it appeared to require removal of such nonconforming signs either (1) by July 1, 1970, or (2) by the end of the fifth year after they became nonconforming. A state could have required removal at an earlier date, but clearly no state would have been subject to the 10 percent penalty if it had simply met the above deadlines for removal. In fact, however, a new subsection, added by amendment in 1968, authorized a further indefinite delay in removal of nonconforming signs by providing that no advertising signs should be required to be removed if the federal share of the just compensation to be paid upon removal should not be available for payment. Congress provided no funds for the sign removal program until 1970, and appropriations since then have been meager. As a consequence, although the sign removal program has been in progress since 1971, it still has a long way to go at the time of this writing.

It is obvious that the 1965 Federal Highway Beautification Act inadvertently created problems of concurrent state-local jurisdiction over advertising sign control which were not clearly handled in the federal legislation. Suppose, *e.g.,* that a city is traversed by a federal interstate highway on which nonconforming signs are located. Assume that the city adopts outdoor advertising regulations generally applicable throughout the city providing for the removal of all nonconforming signs without compensation after a five-year period. This ordinance can apply to the interstate highway under state law. However, the state stands to suffer a 10 percent penalty if the city applies its ordinance to the interstate highway signs. Is there an equal protection problem if the city then amends its ordinance to exempt the interstate highway signs from the requirement that nonconforming signs be amortized and removed without compensation within five years? In *Metromedia, Inc. v. City of San Diego,* 136 Cal. Rptr. 453 (Cal. App. 1977), the court suggested, in holding unconstitutional a city ordinance requiring the removal of all billboards in the city without compensation, that the ordinance would subject the state to the 10 percent federal penalty if the ordinance were applied to billboards adjacent to federal interstate and primary highways. This case is on appeal. In *Suffolk Outdoor Advertising Co. v. Hulse,* 373 N.E.2d 263 (N.Y. 1977), the court said, without mentioning the 10 percent penalty problem, that it found "no merit to plaintiffs' claim that the Federal Highway Beautification Act of 1965 . . . and Section 88 of the [New York] Highway Law preclude the removal of nonconforming billboards without compensation."

For a much more detailed treatment of the advertising sign control provisions of the 1965 Federal Highway Beautification Act, see Cunningham, Billboard Control Under the Highway Beautification Act of 1965, 71 Mich. L. Rev. 1295 (1973). *See also* R. Cunningham, Control of Highway Advertising Signs: Some Legal Problems (NCHRP Rep. No. 119, 1971); D. Mandelker & D. Netsch, State and Local Government in a Federal System 555-88 (1977).

REID v. ARCHITECTURAL BOARD OF REVIEW

Court of Appeals of Ohio
119 Ohio App. 67, 192 N.E.2d 74 (1963)

KOVACHY, Presiding Judge. This is an appeal on questions of law from a judgment rendered by the Court of Common Pleas in favor of the defendant appellee, The Architectural Board of the City of Cleveland Heights, Ohio.

Donna S. Reid, plaintiff, appellant herein, hereinafter designated applicant, applied to the Building Commissioner of the City of Cleveland Heights for a permit to build a residence on a lot owned by her and her husband on North Park Boulevard in Cleveland Heights. As required by ordinance, the plans and specifications were referred to the Architectural Board of Review, which Board, after due consideration, made the following order:

"The plan is for a single-story building and is submitted for a site in a multi-story residential neighborhood. The Board disapproves this project for the reason that it does not maintain the high character of community development in that it does not conform to the character of the houses in the area."

Upon appeal to the Court of Common Pleas, that court rendered a judgment in favor of the Board, holding (1) that the Codified Ordinances were constitutional enactments under the police power of the City; (2) that the Board had the power and authority to render the decision appealed from; (3) that the Board did not abuse its discretion; and (4) that due process was accorded applicant.

The Board is composed of three architects registered and authorized to practice architecture under Ohio laws with ten years of general practice as such.

Section 137.05 of the Codified Ordinances of the City of Cleveland Heights, titled "Purpose," reads as follows:

"The purposes of the Architectural Board of Review are to protect property on which buildings are constructed or altered, to maintain the high character of community development, and to protect real estate within this City from impairment or destruction of value, by regulating according to proper architectural principles the design, use of materials, finished grade lines and orientation of all new buildings, hereafter erected, and the moving, alteration, improvement, repair, adding to or razing in whole or in part of all existing buildings, and said Board shall exercise its powers and perform its duties for the accomplishment of said purposes only."

This ordinance is intended to:

1. protect property,

2. maintain high character of community development,

3. protect real estate from impairment or destruction of value, and the Board's powers are restricted "for the accomplishment of said purposes only."

These objectives are sought to be accomplished by regulating:

1. design,

2. use of material,

3. finished grade lines,

4. orientation (new buildings).

The Supreme Court of Ohio in paragraph six of the syllabus in the case of *Benjamin v. City of Columbus,* 167 Ohio St. 103, 146 N.E.2d 854, states:

"Whether an exercise of the police power does bear a real and substantial relation to the public health, safety, morals or general welfare of the public and whether it is unreasonable or arbitrary are questions which are committed in the first instance to the judgment and discretion of the legislative body, and, unless the decisions of such legislative body on those questions appear to be clearly erroneous, the courts will not invalidate them."

The City of Cleveland Heights is a suburb of the City of Cleveland and was organized to provide suitable and comfortable home surroundings for residents employed in Cleveland and its environs. It has no industry or railroads within its confines and is a well-regulated and carefully groomed community, primarily residential in character. An ordinance designed to protect values and to maintain "a high character of community development" is in the public interest and contributes to the general welfare. Moreover, the employment of highly trained personages such as architects for the purpose of applying their knowledge and experience in helping maintain the high standards of the community is laudable and salutary and serves the public good.

We determine and hold that Ordinance 137.05 is a constitutional exercise of the police power by the City Council and is, therefore, valid. . . .

Section 137.05, as outlined above, sets out criteria and standards for the Board to follow in passing upon an application for the building of a new home, which are definite as to the objective to be attained — to protect property, to maintain high character of community development, to protect real estate from impairment and destruction of value; specific as to matters to be considered and regulated — design, use of material, finished grade lines, orientation; instructive as to the method by which the matters specified are to be adjudged — "proper architectural principles" and informative as to the bounds within which it is to exercise these powers — "for the accomplishment of said purposes only."

When borne in mind that the members of the Board are highly trained experts in the field of architecture, the instruction that they resolve these questions on "proper architectural principles" is profoundly reasonable since such expression has reference to the basic knowledge on which their profession is founded.

It is our view, therefore, that Section 137.05 contains all the criteria and standards reasonably necessary for the Board to carry on the duties conferred upon it. . . .

We have read the bill of exceptions filed in this case carefully. It discloses that North Park Boulevard is in a district zoned for Class 1A residences not to exceed thirty-five feet in height or two and one-half stories, whichever is lesser, and which are required to cover not less than fifteen thousand square feet of lot space. This district extends through a park area with buildings on the north side and trees, ravines, and bushes hundreds of feet wide on its south side. The buildings on this boulevard are, in the main, dignified, stately and conventional structures, two and one-half stories high.

The house designed for the applicant, as described by applicant, is a flat-roofed complex of twenty modules, each of which is ten feet high, twelve feet square and arranged in a loosely formed "U" which winds its way through a grove of trees. About sixty per cent of the wall area of the house is glass and opens on an enclosed garden; the rest of the walls are of cement panels. A garage of the same modular construction stands off from the house, and these two structures, with their associated garden walls, trellises and courts, form a series of interior and exterior spaces, all under a canopy of trees and baffled from the street by a garden wall.

A wall ten feet high is part of the front structure of the house and garage and extends all around the garden area. It has no windows. Since the wall is of the same height as the structure of the house, no part of the house can be seen from the street. From all appearances, it is just a high wall with no indication of what is behind it. Not only does the house fail to conform in any manner with the other buildings but presents no identification that it is a structure for people to live in.

The Board, as well as the architect for the applicant, concede that this structure would be a very interesting home placed in a different environment. It is obvious that placed on North Park Boulevard, it would not only be out of keeping with and a radical departure from the structures now standing but would be most detrimental to the further development of the area since there are two vacant lots immediately to the east and a third vacant lot on the street bordering the westernmost lot.

Esthetics was a consideration that played a part in the ruling of the Board, but there were many other factors that influenced its decision. The structure designed is a single-story home in a multi-story neighborhood; it does not conform to the general character of other houses; it would affect adjacent homes and three vacant lots; it is of such a radical concept that any design not conforming to the general character of the neighborhood would have to be thereafter approved; when viewed from the street, it could indicate a commercial building; it does not conform to standards of the neighborhood; it does not preserve high character of neighborhood; it does not preserve property values; it would be detrimental to neighborhood on the lot where proposed and it would be detrimental to the future development of the neighborhood.

16 C.J.S. Constitutional Law § 195, Esthetic Conditions, p. 939, states:

"The concept of the public welfare is broad and inclusive. The values it represents are spiritual as well as physical, esthetic as well as monetary. It is within the power of the legislature to determine that the community should be beautiful as well as healthy, spacious as well as clean, well-balanced as well as carefully patrolled. Nevertheless, it is held that esthetic conditions alone are insufficient to support the invocation of the police power, although if a regulation finds a reasonable justification in serving a generally recognized ground for the exercise of that power, the fact that esthetic considerations play a part in its adoption does not affect its validity." [The first part of this quotation appears to be from *Berman v. Parker, supra* page 653.]

It is our determination and we hold that the record in this case discloses ample evidence to support the judgment of the trial court that the Board did not abuse its discretion in its decision in this matter.

We conclude, therefore, that no error prejudicial to the substantial rights of the applicant intervened in the trial of this cause and, consequently, overrule applicant's assignments of error and affirm the judgment.

Judgment affirmed.

SILBERT, J., concurs.

CORRIGAN, Judge (dissenting). I regret that I am unable to agree with the decision of my esteemed colleagues in this appeal which is on questions of law from a judgment of the Court of Common Pleas of Cuyahoga County, affirming an order of the Architectural Board of Review of the City of Cleveland Heights which disapproved the issuance to appellant herein of a building permit for a single family residence. The proceedings in the Court of Common Pleas were in the nature of an appeal, under favor of the provisions of Chapter 2506, Revised Code, from the decision of the Board.

To briefly review the factual situation, it appears from the record that on December 18, 1961, appellant completed her application with the plans requesting a building permit for a single proposed family residence to be constructed on a vacant lot on the north side of North Park Boulevard. Pursuant to the applicable ordinances of the City of Cleveland Heights, these plans were presented to the Board for review and consideration. A hearing was had on the application and on February 6, 1962, the Board denied the permit for the reason that the proposed residence "does not maintain the high character of community development in that it does not conform to the character of the houses in the area."

In this dissent it is deemed necessary merely to consider appellant's first assignment of error, namely, that the Board's denial of a permit was contrary to law in that it was based exclusively on an aesthetic consideration. That the Board's determination was based entirely on such a consideration is, to this member of the court, conclusively established by the record before us. Take for example these questions and answers in connection with the interrogation of the witness, Russell Ralph Peck, a registered architect, who is a

member of the Board of Architectural Review, at the trial in the
Common Pleas Court. . . .

"Q. I take it from what you say that the Board's essential concern
was with the appearance of this house from the outside?

"A. Exactly.

"Q. The Board wasn't concerned with the architectural treatment
of the interior?

"A. No.

"Q. Its sole consideration was the exterior appearance; is that
right?

"A. Yes, sir. . . .

"A. We don't like the appearance of that house in this
neighborhood." [Additional testimony reprinted in the opinion has
been omitted]. . . .

One of the sixteen stipulations entered into between the parties
in the trial court was to the effect that neither the Zoning Code nor
the Building Code of the Codified Ordinances of the City of
Cleveland Heights establishes a minimum height in terms of stories
or of feet to which residences must conform.

Another stipulation between the parties was that Architect Kelly's
design for the appellant's proposed home satisfies the Cleveland
Heights Zoning and Building Code requirements as to size, height,
mass and setback.

Further, it was stipulated that most residences in the City of
Cleveland Heights were built prior to World War II.

Therefore, the question presented under this assignment of error
is: does the Board have the right to prohibit a citizen from building
a house that does not conform to the other houses in the
neighborhood, as Mr. Peck testified, supra, or in other words, on
aesthetic considerations alone, where the design and plans of such
house meet the zoning and building code requirements and will not
threaten, endanger or impair the public health, safety or welfare, and
will not impair property values in the neighborhood?

This member of the court is of the opinion that the answer is an
emphatic negative in the light of the law that is applicable to the
situation.

First, to take up the decision of the Board: what answers do the
evidence provide as to "the character of the houses in the area," as
stated in the Board's decision. North Park Boulevard is an important
motor vehicle thoroughfare running generally east and west. On the
south side of the boulevard, there is a park area. There are no
sidewalks on either side of the boulevard in the block, at least, where
appellant's site is located. The homes along North Park Boulevard
show examples of Tudor, flat-roofed contemporary or modern,
Spanish, Colonial, and other types. Some are two and one-half or
three storied homes. The plaintiff's lot abuts to the north on the

south end of lots on Colchester Road. This latter street on both sides presents a prosaic succession of two-family homes, some of brick construction, some of wood, and some of a combination of both, all of two and one-half stories in height. Two lots west of the plaintiff's property and clearly within view from her lot are the modest frame single homes of two stories on both sides of Woodmere Drive. So here in one small area in Cleveland Heights we find a melange of architectural styles and of obviously varying lot sizes and price values. Then the question occurs as to what is the "character of the houses in the area." A fair definition would appear to consider "character" as the sum of qualities or features by which the area is distinguished from others or a sum of traits conferring distinctiveness. But, is there any distinctiveness to this area? It seems to reflect the result observable in any American suburb of the age of Cleveland Heights with localities of residences constituted of a mixture of architectural designs and of varying price values, most of which were obviously constructed at least from twenty-five to forty years ago. This is not the new surburbia, the packaged villages that are becoming the barracks of the new generation.

The residence proposed to be constructed on her lot by appellant does have character, in the opinion of this member of the court, judging from the description of the plans given by the architect and the model of the proposed construction introduced as an exhibit. It does have attributes conferring distinctiveness. It is one story with a flat roof. But there are other one-story modern homes on North Park Boulevard with flat roofs. The plans include a wall to be built at the setback line, 106 feet from North Park Boulevard, approximately seven feet high, with walls describing irregular courses on the easterly and westerly sides and a wall on the north side. If appellant does not wish to be bothered with a view of the 'round the clock vehicular traffic swishing past on North Park Boulevard to and from the marts of trade, she should be permitted this peace. If she wishes to screen out the view of the neighboring mixture of architectural styles and enjoy her trees and garden and other beauties of nature and whatever decoration she introduces within her walls and her home, these should be permitted to her. She feels that the plan submitted calls for a residence of beauty and utility and so does her architect.

It should be borne in mind that there is an important principle of eclecticism in architecture which implies freedom on the part of the architect or client or both to choose among the styles of the past and present that which seems to them most appropriate.

Should the appellant be required to sacrifice her choice of architectural plan for her property under the official municipal juggernaut of conformity in this case? Should her aesthetic sensibilities in connection with her selection of design for her proposed home be stifled because of the apparent belief in this community of the group as a source of creativity? Is she to sublimate herself in this group and suffer the frustration of individual creative aspirations? Is her artistic spirit to be imprisoned by the apparent beneficence of community life in Cleveland Heights? This member of the court thinks not under the record in this case and the pertinent legal principles applicable thereto.

The proposition that the regulatory powers of a municipality cannot be exercised for purely aesthetic reasons unrelated to the requirements of public health, safety or welfare is well settled in Ohio. . . .

Accordingly, the Board's disapproval of the issuance of a permit for aesthetic reasons alone is contrary to law and the claim of error is well taken.

For these reasons, it is my view that the judgment of the Court of Common Pleas should be reversed and the cause remanded with instructions to return the cause to the Board of Architectural Review of Cleveland Heights directing that body to approve the issuance of a building permit to appellant.

Comments: 1. *Accord, State ex rel. Saveland Park Holding Corp. v. Wieland,* 69 N.W.2d 217 (Wis. 1955), upholding a village ordinance which provided as follows:

> No building permit for any structure for which a building permit is required shall be issued unless it has been found as a fact by the Building Board by at least a majority vote, after a view of the site of the proposed structure, and an examination of the application papers for a building permit, which shall include exterior elevations of the proposed structure, that the exterior architectural appeal and functional plan of the proposed structure will, when erected, not be so at variance with either the exterior architectural appeal and functional plan of the structures already constructed or in the course of construction in the immediate neighborhood or the character of the applicable district established by Ordinance No. 117 [the general zoning ordinance of the village], or any ordinance amendatory thereof or supplementary thereto, as to cause a substantial depreciation in the property values of said neighborhood within said applicable district.

Subsequent sections of the ordinance provided that the Building Board should consist of three residents of the village, two of whom were to be architects, and provided a method of appeal from the decisions of the Building Board to the zoning board of appeals. Plaintiff's application for a building permit disclosed compliance with all provisions of the general zoning ordinance of the village, and the sole reason for the building inspector's refusal to grant a building permit was the failure of the Building

Board to make the necessary findings under the ordinance provision set out above. The court said that protection of property values clearly fell within the police power, and that it was "immaterial whether the zoning ordinance is grounded solely upon such objective or that such purpose is but one of several legitimate objectives." The court also found the standards governing the functioning of the Building Board were not "so indefinite as to subject applicants for building permits to the arbitrary discretion of such board."

To the same effect is *State ex rel. Stoyanoff v. Berkeley,* 458 S.W.2d 305 (Mo. 1970). Acting under an architectural review ordinance adopted by what was admitted to be a "fashionable" suburb of St. Louis, the review board disapproved issuance of a building permit for a modernistic dwelling shaped as a pyramid, and with a flat top, in a neighborhood of what the court called "traditional" Colonial, French Provincial, and English Tudor styles. Home values in the neighborhood ranged from $60,000 to $85,000 at the time of the case. A refusal to issue a building permit followed, and the refusal was upheld.

While appearing to accept an aesthetic justification for the ordinance, the court also relied on those provisions of the standard zoning enabling act "relating to the character of the district, its suitability for particular uses, and the conservation of the values of buildings therein." It commented that "[t]hese considerations, sanctioned by statute, are directly related to the general welfare of the community." No statutory objection was found to the creation of the review board, and the court dismissed delegation of power objections to the ordinance.

As criteria, the ordinance directed attention to "(1) whether the proposed house meets the customary architectural requirements in appearance and design for a house of the particular type which is proposed. . ., (2) whether the proposed house is in general conformity with the style and design of surrounding structures, and (3) whether the proposed house lends itself to the proper architectural development of the City; and . . . whether the proposed house will have an adverse effect on the stability of values in the surrounding area." In addition, the statement of purpose indicated that "unsightly, grotesque and unsuitable structures" were to be avoided. See *Contra,* on the delegation of power point, *Pacesetter Homes, Inc. v. Village of Olympia Fields,* 244 N.E.2d 369 (Ill. App. 1968) (ordinance administered by an architectural advisory committee). *See also Hankins v. Borough of Rockleigh,* 150 A.2d 63 (N.J. Super. 1959). The borough had adopted an ordinance requiring that housing design be "of early American, or of other architectural style conforming with the existing residential structure and with the rural surroundings in the Borough." Flat roofs were prohibited. The borough was about one square mile in area, had fifty homes and about 150 people. Few houses had been constructed within its limits in the past few years, and approximately eighty percent of the homes were over fifty years old. Several flat-roofed buildings had been constructed in the vicinity of the proposed house, and many of the older houses had flat-roofed extensions added to them. On the basis of this evidence, the court did not reach the aesthetic question because it found the ordinance unreasonable "in light of the actual physical development of the municipality." *Id.* at 66.

City of West Palm Beach v. State ex rel. Duffey, 30 So.2d 491 (Fla. 1947), is another unfavorable opinion on architectural controls.

2. Would your view toward the applicability of compatibility tests in architectural control be altered if they were imposed in the context of "historic district" zoning? Is the case for architectural controls stronger where preservation of the character of an area is important to the local economy because that character constitutes an attraction for tourists? Architectural controls in "historic districts" have frequently been sustained against constitutional challenge. *E.g., Vieux Carre Property Owners & Assocs. v. New Orleans,* 167 So.2d 367 (La. 1964); *New Orleans v. Levy,* 64 So.2d 798 (La. 1953); *New Orleans v. Pergament,* 5 So.2d 129 (La. 1941); *Opinion of the Justices to the Senate,* 128 N.E.2d 557 (Mass. 1955) (Nantucket and Siasconset); *Opinion of the Justices to the Senate,* 128 N.E.2d 563 (Mass. 1955) (Beacon Hill, Boston); *Santa Fe v. Gamble-Skogmo, Inc.,* 389 P.2d 13 (N.M. 1964). *See also Town of Deering ex rel. Bittenbender v. Tibbets,* 202 A.2d 232 (N.H. 1964). The town had no zoning regulations but it adopted an ordinance authorizing the town board to pass on the construction of new buildings within the vicinity of the town common to determine if they would "impair the atmosphere" of the town. Evidence indicated that buildings in the vicinity of the common were typical of early New Hampshire architecture. Acting under the ordinance, the town board turned down an application to build a prebuilt home in the vicinity of the common. The court sustained the ordinance as furthering the purpose of historical preservation and of promoting the general welfare of the town and the value of privately-owned properties within it. It said that "more than aesthetics" was involved.

The topic of "historic preservation" is treated in more detail in the next section.

3. LAKE FOREST, ILLINOIS, ARCHITECTURAL CONTROL ORDINANCE

[Lake Forest is an older suburb in the Chicago metropolitan area. This ordinance has not been tested judicially. It typifies a more sophisticated method of control which governs both similarity and dissimilarity in design. — Eds.]

9-A *Architectural Design.* (a) The City Council hereby finds that excessive similarity, dissimilarity or inappropriateness in exterior design and appearance of buildings in relation to the prevailing appearance of property in the vicinity thereof adversely affects the desirability of immediate and neighboring areas and impairs the benefits of occupancy of existing property in such areas, impairs the stability and taxable value of land and buildings in such areas, prevents the most appropriate use of real estate and the most appropriate development of such areas, produces degeneration of property in such areas with attendant deterioration of conditions affecting the public health, safety, comfort, morals and welfare of the citizens thereof, deprives the city of tax revenue which it otherwise could receive and destroys a proper balance in relationship between the taxable value of real property in such areas and the cost of the municipal services provided therefor. . . .

[The ordinance is administered by a Building Review Board. Findings by the Board that a proposed building does or does not comply with the architectural standards imposed by the ordinance are binding on the city's

Director of Building and Zoning. However, the review board's denial of a building permit is appealable to the city council. — Eds.]

(c) No building permit shall be issued for any new building or for remodeling or alteration of an existing building which, if erected, remodeled or altered, would produce one or more of the harmful effects set forth in Paragraph (a) of this Section 9-A. . . .

(f) In considering whether the erection, remodeling or alteration of a building will produce one or more of the harmful effects set forth in Paragraph (a) of this Section 9-A, the Director of Building and Zoning and the Building Review Board shall consider whether there exists one or more of the following:

(i) Excessive similarity or dissimilarity of design in relation to any other structure existing or for which a permit has been issued within a distance of 1,000 feet of the proposed site, or in relation to the characteristics of building design generally prevailing in the area, in respect to one or more of the following features:

(1) Apparently identical facade;

(2) Substantially identical size and arrangement of either doors, windows, porticoes or other openings or breaks in the facade facing the street, including a reverse arrangement thereof;

(3) Cubical contents;

(4) Gross floor area;

(5) Other significant design features, such as, but not limited to, roof line, height of building, construction, material, or quality of architectural design; or

(6) Location and elevation of building upon the site in relation to the topography of the site in relation to contiguous properties.

(ii) Inappropriateness in relation to any other property in the same or any adjoining district of design, landscaping, building materials and use thereof, orientation to site, or placement of parking, storage or refuse areas.

[This kind of "harmony" ordinance is typical of one variety of architectural control. — Eds.]

DUKEMINIER, ZONING FOR AESTHETIC OBJECTIVES: A REAPPRAISAL, 20 Law & Contemp. Prob. 218, 226-27 (1955)

Words simply do not have the kind of meaning that judges (and philosophers) are seeking when they ask, "What is beauty?" Words are neither "things" nor "ideas" that can be precisely measured; they have only uses or functions. The word beauty *means* nothing by itself. *To know the meaning of beauty is to know how to use it in an intelligible way to describe phenomena within a given context.* One can meaningfully say, for instance, that Corot's "The Forest of Fontainebleau" is a beautiful painting or that the cathedral at Chartres is a beautiful building, but it is fruitless to ask if either is a correct use of beautiful. Philosophy has many revelations to offer but true meaning of word symbols is not among them.

That words have no single correct meaning points up that whether an object or a relation is beautiful (or "equitable" or "reasonable") hinges upon the perspective of the persons using the word. This semantic indefiniteness does not, however, force us to the very extreme position of Humpty Dumpty (as some judges assume it does in matters of beauty but not in matters of equity or reasonableness). Of course, if a word cannot be intelligibly used by persons in communication then Humpty Dumpty is right, but there are good psychological and cultural reasons why the usage of words remains fairly stable, why people can and do meaningfully use the word beautiful.

What this adds up to is this. The cry for precise criteria might well be abandoned because it does not make sense. Beauty cannot be any more precisely defined than wealth, property, malice, or a host of multiordinal words to which courts are accustomed. Planners can give *reasons* for saying a particular arrangement of objects in the environment is beautiful based upon perspectives common in high degree among the people in a community, but they cannot *prove* it, and proof which is strictly unattainable should not be demanded. What is needed to decide whether beautiful can be used in an intelligible manner by planners is not a foredoomed search for precise criteria for its correct employment, but rather a clarification of some of the operations indicating how the general public and planners use the word and an evaluation of these operations by reference to community goals. It will have to be admitted that a satisfactory set of operations describing what is beautiful in the varying contexts of land use is not easy to come by. The problem of contriving definitions that meet the operational test of meaning is a complicated, difficult business, for most of the relevant formal indices of beauty (such as symmetry, variety, uniformity, balance, rhythm, simplicity, intricacy, and quantity) will have to be further defined operationally. It is easy enough for planners to say, "Let beauty represent the ratio of formal indices to function," but it is hard to know what, if anything, they would be talking about.

A NOTE ON ARCHITECTURAL CONTROLS AND THE FIRST AMENDMENT GUARANTY OF FREE SPEECH

Although challenges to aesthetic regulation based on "due process" have only rarely been successful, challenges based on the First Amendment guaranty of free speech may be more successful, at least with regard to architectural controls. Architectural expression should clearly not be given the constitutional protection accorded "pure speech," [9] since it necessarily involves action as well as expression. Nor is the analogy between architectural expression and "symbolic speech" perfect.[10] But the interest of both the architect and the client in freedom of architectural expression may well be entitled to protection under the First Amendment. This would be so even if architectural expression is considered to be only a form of "commercial speech." [11]

A series of recent Supreme Court opinions [12] indicates that municipal regulations restricting freedom of expression will be valid, when challenged on First Amendment grounds, only if the regulations are intended to (1) "promote aesthetic values or any other value 'unrelated to the suppression of free expression' "; [13] or (2) "restrict a mode of communication that 'intrudes on the privacy of the home, . . . makes it impractical for the unwilling viewer or auditor to avoid exposure,' . . . or otherwise reaches a group the [municipality] . . . has a right to protect"; [14] or (3) control only the place and manner of expression. Although it is strongly arguable that these recent opinions support restrictions on commercial advertising signs like those in *Metuchen, supra,* based on a combination of

---

[9] *See Buckley v. Valeo,* 424 U.S. 1, 14 (1976); Note, First Amendment Protection for Commercial Advertising: The New Constitutional Doctrine, 44 U. Chi. L. Rev. 205, 255 (1976).

[10] *See United States v. O'Brien,* 391 U.S. 367, 376 (1968); *Buckley v. Valeo,* 424 U.S. 1, 16-17 (1976); Note, Architecture, Aesthetic Zoning and the First Amendment, 28 Stan. L. Rev. 179, 185 n. 30 (1975); Note, Symbolic Speech, 9 Ind. L. Rev. 1009, 1011, 1014 (1976).

[11] Note, First Amendment Protection for Commercial Advertising: The New Constitutional Doctrine, 44 U. Chi. L. Rev. 205 (1976); *Virginia State Bd. of Pharmacy v. Virginia Citizens Consumer Council, Inc.,* 425 U.S. 748, 761 (1976) ("In suggesting that the lower value of commercial advertising allows more rigorous regulation of commercial speech than other varieties of speech, the Court posited an inverse relationship between the value of speech and the permissible degree of regulation."). Of course, neither the architect's nor the client's interest in the design for a structure is entirely "commercial."

[12] *Erznoznik v. City of Jacksonville,* 422 U.S. 205 (1975) (ordinance prohibiting all films containing nudity from exhibition in drive-in theatres where the screen was visible from a public place was void under First Amendment); *Young v. American Mini Theatres, Inc.,* 96 S. Ct. 2440 (1976) (ordinance requiring locational dispersal of "adult" threatres held valid as against First Amendment challenge); *Linmark Assocs. v. Township of Willingboro,* 97 S. Ct. 1614 (1977) (ordinance banning display of "For Sale" and "Sold" signs on front lawns was void under First Amendment).

[13] *Linmark, supra* n. 12, at 1619, quoting *United States v. O'Brien, supra* n. 10, at 377.

[14] *Linmark, supra* n. 12, at 1619, quoting *Erznoznik, supra* n. 12, at 209.

aesthetic and economic (property value) grounds,[15] the validity of architectural controls is left in considerable doubt.

Prima facie, it might seem that architectural controls would be legitimate whenever imposed "in order to promote aesthetic values." But clearly the aesthetic values sought to be promoted by architectural controls are not "unrelated to the suppression of free expression." Indeed, their very purpose is to suppress free architectural expression at variance with the values of the local governing body or the architectural review board which administers the architectural controls. It is hard to imagine any architectural style so intrusive "on the privacy of the home[s]" of neighbors as to justify restriction of the freedom of architectural expression. Architectural control ordinances that completely ban certain types of architecture certainly do more than merely regulate the place or manner of expression. Moreover, the fact that an architect and his client might be able to build somewhere else in a municipality may not be enough to validate architectural controls, for "[o]ne is not to have the exercise of his liberty of expression in appropriate places abridged on the plea that it may be exercised in some other place." [16] Ultimately, the validity of architectural controls challenged on First Amendment grounds will probably depend on the weight given to the local governmental interests asserted as the basis for such controls. A purely aesthetic justification for architectural controls would seem to be less compelling than Detroit's interest in restricting the concentration of "adult" theatres in *American Mini Theatres;* [17] and it is arguable that freedom of architectural expression is entitled to greater protection than the freedom to exhibit pornographic movies asserted in *Erznoznik.*[18] However, to the extent that architectural control ordinances are based on the protection of property values rationale, the justification for governmental restriction of the freedom of architectural expression is strengthened.

How strong must the local governmental interest in architectural controls be in order to justify restrictions on the freedom of architectural expression? In noncommercial free speech cases, the Supreme Court has used a "strict scrutiny" approach requiring proof

---

[15] *See Suffolk Outdoor Advertising Co. v. Hulse,* 373 N.E.2d 263 (N.Y. 1977), sustaining a total prohibition of "off-premises" advertising signs against *(inter alia)* a First Amendment challenge. Fuchsberg, J., dissenting, thought that the ordinance was void under the First Amendment.

[16] *Southeastern Promotions, Ltd. v. Conrad,* 420 U.S. 556 (1975). *But see Linmark, supra* n. 12, at 1618 (ordinance must leave "open ample alternative channels for communication" of commercial speech).

[17] *Supra* n. 12.

[18] *Ibid.*

of a "sufficiently compelling" governmental interest and that the least intrusive means for effectuating that interest has been adopted, with the means being substantially related to the compelling governmental interest.[19] In commercial speech cases, the Court has adopted a "balancing" approach but, by placing a heavy burden on the government to justify the restriction of freedom of speech, the Court has come close to the "compelling" government interest requirement.[20] Thus the commercial-noncommercial distinction will probably not have a significant effect on First Amendment challenges to architectural control ordinances. And if architectural expression is considered more closely akin to "symbolic speech" than to artistic self-expression, the Court would require a "sufficiently important governmental interest in regulating the nonspeech elements" to be shown in order to justify "incidental limitations on First Amendment freedoms." [21]

In any event, when architectural control ordinances are challenged on First Amendment grounds, justification of the restriction of the freedom of architectural expression will surely require more substantial evidence that the proscribed architectural styles have adverse effects on property values than has hitherto been required when architectural controls have been challenged on due process grounds.[22] And ordinances which give local officials broad discretion to determine whether or not a particular design will adversely affect property values may constitute an invalid prior restraint on freedom of expression, even if the discretion is exercised by an architectural review board composed largely of architects.[23]

---

[19] *Wooley v. Maynard,* 97 S. Ct. 1428, 1436 (1977); *Buckley v. Valeo, supra* n. 9, at 64 (1976); *Elrod v. Burns,* 427 U.S. 347, 362-63 (1976); *Nixon v. Administrator of Gen. Servs.,* 433 U.S. 425 (1977). *See generally,* The Supreme Court, 1976 Term, 91 Harv. L. Rev. 72, 205 (1977).

[20] *See Virginia State Bd. of Pharmacy v. Virginia Citizens Consumer Council, Inc., supra* n. 13, at 789; The Supreme Court, 1976 Term, 91 Harv. L. Rev. 72, 205-06 (1977). But see Ohralik v. Ohio State Bar Ass'n, — U.S. — (1978).

[21] *United States v. O'Brien, supra* n. 10, at 376.

[22] *See generally Smith v. Gogven,* 415 U.S. 566, 594 (1974); Blasi, The Checking Value in First Amendment Theory, 1977 Am. B. Foundation Research J. 521, 545 (1977); Note, Architecture, Aesthetic Zoning and the First Amendment, 28 Stan. L. Rev. 179, 190 (1975); Note, Freedom of Expression in the Land Use Planning Context, 28 U. Fla. L. Rev. 954, 983 (1973); Comment, Zoning, Aesthetics and the First Amendment, 64 Colum. L. Rev. 81, 106 (1964).

[23] See Note, Beyond the Eye of the Beholder: Aesthetics and Objectivity, 71 Mich. L. Rev. 1438, 1455-56 (1973) (architectural control ordinances do not employ precise standards and determinations that property values will be adversely affected are usually made by architects rather than appraisers or tax assessors); Comment, Zoning Ordinance — Enhancement of Aesthetic Values Alone Not Sufficient Basis for Exercise of Police Power in Florida, 4 Fla. St. U.L. Rev. 163, 168 n. 29 (1976) (major problem for boards of architectural review is lack of definite and objective standards).

For a fuller treatment of the architectural control problem, see Note, Architectural Expression: Police Power and the First Amendment, 16 Urb. L. Ann. — (1978), on which this editorial note is largely based. For a discussion of the broader problem of aesthetic controls generally (including First Amendment problems), see Williams, Subjectivity, Expression, and Privacy: Problems of Aesthetic Regulation, 62 Minn. L. Rev. 1 (1977).

Comments: Professor Sager believes that large-lot zoning restrictions are most easily justified on "aesthetic" grounds:

> Strong arguments can be made that even very large minimums, say of 5 acres, contribute substantially to the beauty of an area and may serve to preserve its distinctive character, whether it be formed of large aging estates or is essentially rural. However, this last argument can be turned against exclusionary zoning as well. The special character or beauty of a neighborhood is a kind of resource, the denial of which raises to special prominence the *desirability* complaint of the excluded. The response on behalf of the municipality, of course, is that without lot-size zoning the resource will be destroyed and the discussion of its distribution rendered moot.
>
> This raises the question of the least onerous alternative. In this setting, application of that principle would take the form of looking for means by which some or all of the aesthetic interests of the affected area could be preserved or advanced, but at a substantially smaller cost in exclusion. There do seem to exist courses of action that would accomplish this dual purpose. One would involve checkerboard, cluster, or similar zoning variants in which standard lot-size requirements are replaced by general density standards or by carefully mixed uses of land in close proximity. The city could undertake this fairly complicated land use scheme itself, or at least require developers of land subdivisions to do so. . . . Another possible approach which could be employed independently or in conjunction with the first, is the use of eminent domain and subdivision controls to produce public "green belts" or open-space areas so located as to preserve to the maximum extent the qualities toward which lot-size zoning is directed.

Sager, Tight Little Islands: Exclusionary Zoning, Equal Protection, and the Indigent, 21 Stan. L. Rev. 767, 797-98 (1969).

The use of "cluster" zoning in connection with "planned unit developments" was treated in detail in the immediately preceding section of this chapter. The use of subdivision controls to preserve open-space areas was dealt with in the immediately preceding chapter of this book. The following Note deals with the use of the "scenic easement" device to preserve open space for "aesthetic" purposes.

A NOTE ON SCENIC EASEMENTS

In situations where police power restrictions on land development would run the risk of being held invalid as "takings" or would be politically infeasible, and where the cost of public acquisition of open-space land in fee simple would be too great, preservation of scenic values may sometimes be accomplished by public acquisition of "scenic easements." It is not clear whether such easements should be regarded as common law negative easements of "prospect" or "view," or as "equitable servitudes." The Appraisal and Terminology Handbook of the American Institute of Real Estate Appraisers defines a "scenic easement" as "a restriction imposed upon the use of the property of the grantor for the purpose of preserving the natural state of scenic and historical attractiveness of adjacent lands of the grantee, usually the city, county, state or federal government."

"Scenic easement" forms in common use generally include the following:

1. A restriction of new buildings and structures (or major alterations thereof) to farm and residential buildings and structures only, plus a specific prohibition of further nonresidential construction, with a saving clause permitting the continuance of existing nonconforming uses.

2. An authorization for necessary public utility lines and roads.

3. A prohibition against cutting mature trees and shrubs, coupled with a provision authorizing normal maintenance of trees and shrubs.

4. A prohibition against dumping of any kind.

5. A prohibition against outdoor advertising, except for advertising of activities conducted on the premises.

In addition to the above restrictions or "negative rights," a "scenic easement" may, of course, also include the grant of one or more affirmative use privileges — *e.g.*, a public right of entry to a limited area for a scenic overlook along a highway, or a public (*i.e.*, highway department) right of entry to remove structures or plantings which are in violation of the restrictions or to repair damage done to plantings or other vegetation in violation of the restrictions.

It is reasonably clear that use of public funds to purchase "scenic easements" and that use of the eminent domain power to acquire "scenic easements" in cases where a voluntary sale cannot be negotiated do not violate state constitutional prohibitions against expenditure of public funds and use of the eminent domain power for nonpublic purposes. *E.g., Kamrowski v. State,* 142 N.W.2d 793

(Wis. 1966), upholding the use of eminent domain and public funds to acquire "scenic easements" along the Great River Road on the Wisconsin shore of the Mississippi River. The court rejected the plaintiff's arguments that public enjoyment of scenic beauty is not a "public use" of the land restricted by a "scenic easement" and that the enabling act did not contain adequate standards. The court said:

> The learned trial judge succinctly answered plaintiffs' claim that occupancy by the public is essential in order to have public use by saying that in the instant case, "the 'occupancy' is visual." The enjoyment of the scenic beauty by the public which passes along the highway seems to us to be a direct use by the public of the rights in land which have been taken in the form of a scenic easement, and not a mere incidental benefit from the owner's private use of the land.
>
> Plaintiffs appear to contend that the decision, made by the legislature, to preserve scenic resources, and the decision, made by the commission, to take scenic easements, upon certain terms, from plaintiffs involve purely aesthetic considerations. They say that such considerations are "illusory," "whimsical," and "highly controversial," and seem to argue that the legislative decision is therefore meaningless in terms of public interest and that the commission has no standard to follow.
> . . . .
>
> Whatever may be the law with respect to zoning restrictions based upon aesthetic considerations, a stronger argument can be made in support of the power to take property, in return for just compensation, in order to fulfill aesthetic concepts, than for the imposition of police power restrictions for such purposes. More importantly, however, we consider that the concept of preserving a scenic corridor along a parkway, with its emphasis upon maintaining a rural scene and preventing unsightly uses is sufficiently definite so that the legislature may be said to have made a meaningful decision in terms of public purpose, and to have fixed a standard which sufficiently guides the commission in performing its task.

Id. at 797.

The "scenic easement" device has been used both by the federal government and by state governments. When the Blue Ridge Parkway in Virginia and North Carolina and the Natchez Trace Parkway in Tennessee, Alabama and Mississippi were planned, partly in order to keep costs down and partly because the primary "public use" land adjacent to the Parkway roads was to be the enjoyment of scenic beauty, it was decided that only a portion of the land needed for the Parkways would be purchased in fee simple and that "scenic easements" would be purchased in the remaining land. The actual formula was 100 acres in fee simple and 50 acres subject to "scenic easements" per mile of Parkway. The Parkways, now substantially complete, have been constructed entirely with federal funds on land acquired by the states and donated to the National Park Service. The proposed "scenic easements" were also acquired by the states and transferred to the National Park Service. Ultimately, the "scenic easements" acquired along the Blue Ridge Parkway covered about 1,500 acres and those acquired along the Natchez Trace Parkway covered more than 4,500 acres.

The experience of the National Park Service with "scenic easements" along the Blue Ridge and Natchez Trace Parkways was rather unhappy. Difficulties arose chiefly from two causes: either the landowner wanted to harvest standing timber or to subdivide and develop his land for resort or residential use. The National Park Service had particular difficulty in enforcing the usual scenic easement restriction against cutting "mature trees and shrubs." It was often difficult to obtain an injunction to prevent anticipated violations because of judicial reluctance to issue injunctions in advance of actual damage. After a violation occurred, however, it was often difficult to prove damages. In at least two cases, however, a United States District Court ultimately issued an injunction.

As a result of the friction with servient land owners, difficulty in "policing" scenic easements, and difficulty in getting local state courts and United States District Courts to grant complete injunctive enforcement, the National Park Service practically discontinued the purchase of scenic easements and turned to a full fee simple purchase program for both the Blue Ridge and Natchez Trace Parkways in the 1950's. As a result of this change in policy, the Department of Interior requested and obtained legislation in 1961 to authorize *(inter alia)* the exchange of scenic easements over certain lands along the Blue Ridge and Natchez Trace Parkways for smaller areas in fee simple.

Experience with the "scenic easement" device in connection with the Great River Road — a scenic highway along both sides of the Mississippi River from New Orleans to Lake-of-the-Woods — has been more favorable. Although planning began in the 1930's, no state actually acquired any property for the proposed highway until the post-World War II period. Prior to passage of the Federal Highway Beautification Act of 1965, only six of the ten Mississippi River states had adopted legislation to authorize acquisition of "scenic easements" and other action necessary for development of the scenic features of the Great River Road, and only Wisconsin had actually made any substantial "scenic easement" acquisitions along its part of the highway. But Title III of the 1965 Highway Beautification Act [24] inspired many states, including several of the

---

[24] 23 U.S.C. § 319 (1976).

Mississippi River states, to enact legislation authorizing *(inter alia)* the acquisition of "scenic easements" adjacent to all federal-aid highways.

Although the Service has continued to encourage the Mississippi River states in carrying out the Great River Road project, its disillusionment with the scenic easement led it to oppose the use of scenic easements in the Ozarks. This opposition was unsuccessful, and Congress adopted legislation in 1964 authorizing the Secretary of Interior to acquire scenic easements along the Ozark National Scenic Riverways.[25] Since 1964, the National Park Service has apparently grown more receptive to the use of scenic easements. It has made substantial use of scenic easements in recent years in special situations to which they are particularly well adapted. For example, the Park Service has obtained a 48-acre scenic easement at Cumberland Gap National Historical Park,[26] a 46-acre scenic easement at Harper's Ferry National Historical Park,[27] a 21-acre scenic easement at Manassas National Battlefield Park,[28] and scenic easements covering at least 325 acres in the Piscataway Park area on the Potomac River shoreline opposite Mount Vernon. The latter were acquired under a 1961 Congressional Joint Resolution [29] which authorized the Secretary of Interior to acquire scenic easements and other interests in land in a defined area along the Maryland shore opposite Mount Vernon by donation or other appropriate means, and also to enter into "agreements and covenants" with property owners for the purpose of preserving the scenic beauty of the area.

More dramatic and controversial was the recent action of the National Park Service in taking a scenic easement on 47 acres of the Merrywood Estate adjacent to the George Washington National Park in Virginia. This scenic easement was acquired by the Service to block the plans of a group of builders for high-rise apartments on the adjacent land. The builders had purchased the tract and had succeeded in getting the local zoning changed to permit high-rise apartments. The National Park Service then invoked a federal statute [30] to condemn a scenic easement which would preclude any development for other than single-family dwellings and thus protect the scenic quality of the Potomac River palisades which form the

---

[25] 16 U.S.C. §§ 460m through 460m-7 (1976).

[26] 16 U.S.C. §§ 261-267 (1976).

[27] 16 U.S.C. §§ 450bb through 450bb-6 (1976).

[28] 16 U.S.C. § 429b (1976).

[29] 75 Stat. 780 (1961). The Resolution was entitled "Land Preservation — Maryland," and did not expressly designate the area as Piscataway Park.

[30] 16 U.S.C.A. § 1b(7) (1974).

frontage of the tract. The purchase price to the builders had been $650,000 before the rezoning. As plaintiffs in a suit against the government, they claimed the easement had reduced the value of the land from $2,354,700 to $295,000. The United States contended that $500,000 was a fair price for the easement. The condemnation jury awarded the plaintiffs $744,500, which was in excess of the original cost before the zoning change but well below the difference between the original cost and the estimated value when zoned for high-rise apartments.

For a detailed treatment of the "scenic easement" generally and as a tool for highway beautification, see Sutte & Cunningham, Scenic Easements: Legal, Administrative, and Valuation Problems and Procedures (NCHRP Report 56, 1968); Cunningham, Scenic Easements in the Highway Beautification Program, 45 Den. L.J. 168 (1968). *See also* Whyte, Securing Open Space for Urban America: Conservation Easements (Tech. Bull. 36, Urb. Land Inst., 1959); Whyte, Open Space Action Report to the Outdoor Recreation Resources Review Commission (Study Rep. 15, ORRRC, 1962); Williams, Land Acquisition for Outdoor Recreation — Analysis of Selected Legal Problems (Study Rep. 16, ORRRC, 1962).

C. HISTORIC PRESERVATION

Local programs for the preservation of historic areas are not new in this country, but they have become more widespread in recent years and their scope and character have changed in significant ways. Initially, of course, the idea was to preserve through legal means those historic areas that were familiar to everyone and that either had a special place in American history or distinctive architectural associations. Places like the French Quarter in New Orleans and Beacon Hill in Boston come to mind. In other instances, important historic locations such as Williamsburg, Virginia, were brought under private ownership and restored and converted into standing museums. More recently, the historic preservation movement has moved in new directions. Norman Williams makes the point:

> Under the "new preservation" a quite different approach — or at least emphasis — is indicated. First, the interest here is in the entire historical context, i.e., usually in groups of buildings and related open spaces, rather than in individual buildings. Second, the emphasis has shifted somewhat away from association with important historical events, at least as a sole interest, and towards buildings (and groups of buildings) which reflect the lifestyle of a given period, or which are valuable for their artistic merit or as representative of a distinctive historical style. Third, the

interest is quite as much in buildings of local and regional significance, historically and architecturally, as in those known nationally. Fourth, there has been a definite movement away from the notion that all historic buildings should be converted to museums; after all, even a large city can only have a limited number of successful museums. Moreover, the movement now clearly appeals to much larger groups of people. Finally, in many instances historic preservation work is being fitted into the overall planning process in the city.

3 N. Williams, American Land Planning Law 84 (Supp. 1977). In some instances the area may have historic associations but the buildings may not have any particular historic or architectual merit. Chinatown, in Honolulu, is one such example.

Efforts to preserve isolated landmarks of historic interest are not as well advanced as historic area preservation. The alarming disappearance of these landmarks, highlighted by events like the demolition of the old Chicago stock exchange building, has now given greater impetus to the landmark preservation movement.

We will concentrate here on local regulatory programs for the preservation of both historic areas and landmarks, but will direct our attention first to the historic area problem. Obviously, the use of the police power to achieve historic preservation without compensation to owners of buildings within historic areas raises important constitutional and other legal questions. One problem is whether historic area preservation ordinances are authorized in the absence of specific enabling legislation, a question answered in the affirmative in *City of Santa Fe v. Gamble-Skogmo, Inc.,* 389 P.2d 13 (N.M. 1964) (held authorized under zoning enabling act). This problem has become less important as at least 39 states now have specific legislation authorizing historic preservation districts. *See* Beckwith, Developments in the Law of Historic Preservation and a Reflection on Liberty, 12 Wake Forest L. Rev. 93, App. I (1976).

Constitutional problems are more serious. One question is whether historic district regulations serve a proper police power purpose. This issue can and has been handled by a reliance on aesthetic justifications, but the aesthetic rationale becomes diluted as historic preservation is applied to areas that may have historic or architectural meaning but that may not be visually pleasing. Note, then, the following rationale for the adoption of a historic district for the Old Town area in San Diego, California:

> Preservation of the image of Old Town as it existed prior to 1871, as reflected in the historical buildings in the area, as a visual story of the beginning of San Diego and as an educational exhibit of the birth place of California, contributes to the general welfare; gives the general public

attendant educational and cultural advantages; and by its encouragement of tourism is of general economic value.

Bohannon v. City of San Diego, 106 Cal. Rptr. 333 (Cal. App. 1973). Does the California court require that the buildings in an historic preservation area actually have any architectural value?

Another major constitutional issue arising in historic preservation district programs is the familiar due process-taking problem. Are the historic district regulations as applied to a particular property within the district confiscatory and thus a taking of property without due process of law?

In spite of the growing popularity of historic district preservation, there have not been many cases considering the constitutionality of historic district regulations although there have been some famous ones. These have largely been "first generation" cases in which state courts have been asked to pass on the constitutionality of historic district regulation in areas such as the French Quarter in New Orleans or Beacon Hill in Boston. Naturally, no court in states with historic masterpieces such as these would find constitutional objections to their preservation. The issues sharpen when, as in the case that follows, the area preserved has historic and architectural merit but is neither singular nor unique. After all, there are many pleasant town and village greens throughout New England. The case is also important because it illustrates the use of historic district regulations explicitly authorized by state enabling legislation.

FIGARSKY v. HISTORIC DISTRICT COMMISSION OF THE CITY OF NORWICH

Supreme Court of Connecticut
171 Conn. 198, 368 A.2d 163 (1976)

BARBER, Associate Justice.

The plaintiffs, owners of a house and lot located within the Norwich historic district, appealed to the Court of Common Pleas from a decision of the defendant commission denying their application for a certificate of appropriateness which would permit them to demolish the house. The court rendered judgment dismissing the appeal and the plaintiffs, upon the granting of certification, have appealed to this court.

The undisputed facts of the case are as follows: The Norwich historic district, established by the city of Norwich in 1967, pursuant to §§ 7-147a through 7-147m of the General Statutes, consists of the Norwichtown Green, which dates back to colonial days, and about one hundred buildings and lots surrounding, or in close proximity to, the green. The plaintiffs' property, which they purchased in 1963, is a two-story building zoned for commercial uses and is located just inside the bounds of the district. The property faces the green but is bounded on two sides by a McDonald's hamburger stand and parking lot. The building is in need of some repairs, which the Norwich building inspector has ordered the plaintiffs to undertake. Rather than make the repairs, however, the plaintiffs would prefer to demolish the building. In August, 1972, the plaintiffs applied to the building inspector for a demolition permit. The building inspector informed the plaintiffs that before such a permit could be issued a certificate of appropriateness was required. The plaintiffs, therefore, applied to the defendant for a certificate, filing their application with the building inspector on November 29, 1972. The defendant held a public hearing on the application on January 25, 1973. The hearing was attended by more than 100 persons, none of whom, except for the plaintiffs and their attorney, spoke in favor of granting the application. On the following day, the commission voted unanimously to deny the plaintiffs' application.

The plaintiffs maintain that the costs of the repairs necessary for the building are prohibitive. The building inspector has ordered the plaintiffs to repair the foundation and replace a door sill and hall floor, and the health department has ordered the plaintiffs to tie in to a newly accessible public sewer. At the hearing before the commission, the plaintiffs offered the testimony of a local contractor to the effect that the cost of these repairs, together with the cost of reroofing the building, would amount to between $15,000 and $18,000. The plaintiffs offered no evidence of the value of the house without repairs, its value if repaired, or the value of the lot if the building were razed. Nor did the plaintiffs disclose to the commission the use which they intended to make of the lot if the building were razed.

The commission also received numerous opinions from the plaintiffs' neighbors and from the Connecticut historical commission, the southeastern Connecticut regional planning agency, and the Connecticut society of architects, as to the historic value of the premises. The consensus of these opinions was that although the building itself is of little historic value or interest, it does, by virtue of its location, perform an important screening function, separating the green from an encroaching commercial district, and its preservation is important in maintaining the character of the historic district.[31] The commission stated its reasons for denying the

---

[31] A communication from the state historical commission stated, in part: "Competent authority has placed the date of construction in or about 1760 and identified the owner at that period as keeping an inn where lawyers at the nearby Court of Norwich were accommodated. On the exterior at least, the structure has undergone considerable alteration over the years but still retains its essential form and proportions, wholly in keeping with the scale and appearance of numerous other

application as follows: "The Commission is of the opinion that the building in question significantly contributes to the importance of the Norwichtown Green as an historic landmark, and the Commission would have violated its responsibilities as defined in [§§ 7-147a — 7-147k] to have permitted its demolition. In weighing all the considerations concerning this Application, the Commission was cognizant of [§ 7-147g, pertaining to permissible variations], but concluded that the hardships presented by the Applicant were not of sufficient magnitude to warrant granting approval for demolition."

Procedure upon an appeal from any decision of a historic district commission is the same as that for appeals from zoning boards. General Statutes § 7-147i. The controlling question which the trial court had to decide was whether the historic district commission had acted, as alleged in the appeal, illegally, arbitrarily and in abuse of the discretion vested in it. . . . Since the trial court decided the appeal solely on the record returned by the commission and made only a limited finding of facts on the issue of aggrievement, review by this court must be based on the record of the proceedings before the commission to determine whether the commission's decision is reasonably supported by the record. . . .

In their appeal, the plaintiffs allege that they will be forced to undergo economic hardship and loss as a result of not being permitted to demolish their building, and that the historic district commission, in denying their application for a certificate of

---

old buildings that border the Green area. Aside from the house proper, its site is of historic interest as occupying the original home lot of the Reverend James Fitch, religious leader of the first settlers. It often happens that buildings forming a recognizable grouping, as around a green, may not individually be especially notable for architecture or historical association. But together as a unified whole they constitute a significant entity, no part of which can be removed without a definite and usually adverse effect upon the character and appearance of the entire area. This is the condition that obtains in Norwich town.

"The commercially zoned district south and southeast of the site under consideration exhibits the unattractive characteristics of so many such areas, with disparate structures of poor design uncoordinated with one another and obtrusive advertising signs. It stands close upon the boundaries of the local historic district. If the property at 86 Town Street were demolished, it would remove the most important screening element between these evidences of low-grade commercialism and the attractiveness of the largely unspoiled Green. State recognition of the importance of this land has recently been affirmed by the erection of a historical marker under auspices of this Commission, which details the history of early years in Norwich and the central role of the Green in that history. Nomination of the entire area has been made to the National Register of Historic Places maintained by the Office of Archeology and Historic Preservation, National Park Service, United States Department of the Interior, under the National Historic Preservation Act of 1966, Public Law 89-665."

appropriateness, acted illegally, arbitrarily and in abuse of its discretion. Several claims of law which were overruled by the trial court are assigned as error.

. . . .

The plaintiffs' principal claim is that the Norwich historic district ordinance, implementing the state enabling act, is unconstitutional as applied to them, and that the denial of their application for a certificate of appropriateness to demolish their building amounts to a taking of their property for public use without compensation. More specifically, they contend that the ordinance is "vague aesthetic legislation," incapable of application in accordance with mandates of due process, and that because of the denial of their application they will be forced to expend large sums in the maintenance of their property without being able to put it to any practical use.

Neither the constitution of the United States, amendments five and fourteen, nor the constitution of Connecticut, article first, § 11, deny the state the power to regulate the uses to which an owner may devote his property.

"All property is held subject to the right of government to regulate its use in the exercise of the police power, so that it shall not be injurious to the rights of the community, or so that it may promote its health, morals, safety and welfare. The power of regulation by government is not unlimited; it cannot, as we have stated, be imposed unless it bears a rational relation to the subjects which fall fairly within the police power and unless the means used are not within constitutional inhibitions. The means used will fall within these inhibitions whenever they are destructive, confiscatory, or so unreasonable as to be arbitrary. *Euclid v. Ambler Realty Co.,* 272 U.S. 365, 47 S.Ct. 114, 71 L.Ed. 303. Regulations may result to some extent, practically in the taking of property, or the restricting its uses, and yet not be deemed confiscatory or unreasonable. Courts will not substitute their judgment for the legislative judgment when these considerations are fairly debatable. They will regard their validity . . . from the standpoint of existing conditions and present times." *State v. Hillman,* 110 Conn. 92, 105, 147 A. 294, 299. When, as here, a legislative enactment is challenged in its application as beyond the scope or as an abuse of the state's police power, two issues are raised: first, whether the object of the legislation falls within the police power; and second, whether the means by which the legislation attempts to reach that object are reasonable. . . .

"To be constitutionally valid, a regulation made under the police power must have a reasonable relation to the public health, safety, morality and welfare." *State v. Gordon,* 143 Conn. 698, 703, 125 A.2d 477, 480; *DeMello v. Plainville,* 170 Conn. 675, 679, 368 A.2d 71. No contention is made that the historic district ordinance contributes to the health or safety of the public; our inquiry is limited to whether the preservation of historic areas in a static form serves the amorphous concept of "the public welfare." See *Opinion of the Justices,* 333 Mass. 773, 778, 128 N.E.2d 557. "The concept of the public welfare is broad and inclusive. . . . The values it represents are spiritual as well as physical, aesthetic as well as monetary. It is within the power of the legislature to determine that the community should be beautiful as well as healthy, spacious as well as clean, well-balanced as well as carefully patrolled." *Berman v. Parker,* 348 U.S. 26, 33, 75 S.Ct. 98, 102, 99 L.Ed. 27. It is apparent from the language of the enabling statute [32] that the General Assembly, in enacting those statutes, was cognizant not only of the intangible benefits to be derived from historic districts, such as an increase in the public's awareness of its New England heritage, but of the economic benefits to be reaped as well, by augmenting the value of properties located within the old sections of the state's cities and towns, and encouraging tourism within the state. In a number of recent cases, it has been held that the preservation of a historical area or landmark as it was in the past falls within the meaning of general welfare and, consequently, the police power. See, *e. g., Maher v. New Orleans,* 516 F.2d 1051, 1060 (5th Cir.); *Annapolis v. Anne Arundel County,* 271 Md. 265, 316 A.2d 807; *Lutheran Church in America v. City of New York,* 35 N.Y.2d 121, 359 N.Y.S.2d 7, 316 N.E.2d 305; *Rebman v. Springfield,* 111 Ill.App.2d 430, 250 N.E.2d 282; *Opinion of the Justices,* supra, 773, 128 N.E.2d 557; . . . We cannot deny that the preservation of an area or cluster of buildings with exceptional historical and architectural significance may serve the public welfare.

The plaintiffs argue that the Norwich ordinance constitutes "vague aesthetic legislation," and point to our statement in *DeMaria v. Planning & Zoning Commission,* 159 Conn. 534, 541, 271 A.2d 105, 108, that "vague and undefined aesthetic considerations alone are insufficient to support the invocation of the police power," and our dictum to the same effect. *Gionfriddo v. Windsor,* 137 Conn. 701, 704, 81 A.2d 266. The "aesthetic considerations" involved in the Norwich ordinance are not, however, "vague and undefined"; § 7-147f of the General Statutes, incorporated by reference into the ordinance, sets out with some specificity the factors to be considered by the commission in passing upon an application for a certificate

---

[32] "[General Statutes] § *7-147a. Historic districts authorized.* . . . to promote the educational, cultural, economic and general welfare of the public through the preservation and protection of buildings, places and districts of historic interest by the maintenance of such as landmarks in the history of architecture, of the municipality, of the state or of the nation, and through the development of appropriate settings for such buildings, places and districts. . . ."

of appropriateness.[33] Nor, as we pointed out in the preceding discussion, do "aesthetic considerations alone" provide the basis for the ordinance. Furthermore, as long ago as *Windsor v. Whitney,* 95 Conn. 357, 368, 111 A. 354, we commented that the question of the relationship between aesthetics and the police power was not a settled question. In *State v. Kievman,* 116 Conn. 458, 465, 165 A. 601, we stated that a land use regulation was not invalid simply because it was based in part on aesthetic considerations. And in *Murphy, Inc. v. Westport,* 131 Conn. 292, 302, 40 A.2d 177, we indicated that aesthetic considerations may have a definite relation to the public welfare. Although we need not directly decide the issue in the present case, we note that other jurisdictions have recognized that "aesthetic considerations alone may warrant an exercise of the police power." *People v. Stover,* 12 N.Y.2d 462, 467, 240 N.Y.S.2d 734, 737, 191 N.E.2d 272, 274, appeal dismissed, 375 U.S. 42, 84 S.Ct. 147, 11 L.Ed.2d 107; . . . .

Having determined that the ordinance creating the Norwich historic district constitutes a valid exercise of the state's police power, we are left with the question of whether the application of that ordinance to the plaintiffs' property amounts to an unconstitutional deprivation of their property without compensation. In this context, it has often been noted that the police power, which regulates for the public good the uses to which private property may be put and requires no compensation, must be distinguished from the power of eminent domain, which takes private property for a public use and requires compensation to the owner. . . . The difference is primarily one of degree, and the amount of the owner's loss is the basic criterion for determining whether a purported exercise of the police power is valid, or whether it amounts to a taking necessitating the use of the power of eminent domain. See Sax, "Takings and the Police Power," 74 Yale L.J. 36. "A regulation which otherwise

---

[33] "[General Statutes] § *7-147f. Considerations in determining appropriateness.* If the commission determines that the proposed erection, construction, restoration, alteration, razing or parking will be appropriate, it shall issue a certificate of appropriateness. In passing upon appropriateness as to exterior architectural features the commission shall consider, in addition to any other pertinent factors, the historical and architectural value and significance, architectural style, general design, arrangement, texture and material of the architectural features involved and the relationship thereof to the exterior architectural style and pertinent features of other structures in the immediate neighborhood. In passing upon appropriateness as to parking, the commission shall take into consideration the size of such parking area, the visibility of cars parked therein, the closeness of such area to adjacent buildings and other similar factors. A certificate of appropriateness may be refused for any building or structure, the erection, reconstruction, restoration, alteration or razing of which, or any parking which, in the opinion of the commission, would be detrimental to the interest of the historic district."

constitutes a valid exercise of the police power may, as applied to a particular parcel of property, be confiscatory in that no reasonable use may be made of the property and it becomes of little or no value to the owner. . . .

Whether the denial of the plaintiffs' application for a certificate of appropriateness to demolish their building has rendered the Norwich ordinance, as applied to them, confiscatory, must be determined in the light of their particular circumstances as they have been shown to exist. . . . In regulating the use of land under the police power, the maximum possible enrichment of a particular landowner is not a controlling purpose. . . . It is only when the regulation practically destroys or greatly decreases the value of a specific piece of property that relief may be granted, provided it promotes substantial justice. . . . "The extent of that deprivation must be considered in light of the evils which the regulation is designed to prevent." *Chevron Oil Co. v. Zoning Board of Appeals,* 170 Conn. 146, 152, 365 A.2d 387, 390; see General Statutes § 7-147f.

The plaintiffs had the burden of proving that the historic district commission acted illegally, arbitrarily, in a confiscatory manner or in abuse of discretion. . . . This the plaintiffs failed to do. See . . . *Maher v. New Orleans,* 516 F. 2d 1051, 1067 (5th Cir.). The plaintiffs went no further than to present evidence that their house was unoccupied and in need of extensive repairs. There was no evidence offered that the house, if repaired, would not be of some value, or that the proximity of the McDonald's hamburger stand rendered the property of practically no value as a part of the historic district.

The Norwich historic district commission, after a full hearing, lawfully, reasonably and honestly exercised its judgment. The trial court was correct in not substituting its own judgment for that of the commission. . . .

There is no error.

In this opinion the other Judges concurred.

Comments: 1. The development review procedures provided in the *Norwich* historic district are typical of these ordinances. Note that the ordinance provides only for the review of exterior architectural features, thus allowing the building owner a variety of options in interior renovation and use. Many of the leading historic district cases are also cited in the *Norwich* decision.

2. Does the *Norwich* decision really give us an acceptable basis for justifying the purposes of historic district regulation? Note that, as in *Norwich,* the uses in an historic district may be quite mixed and there is no incompatibility rationale that justifies the restrictions as there is under the

conventional zoning ordinance. On the other hand, note that demolition of the building in the *Norwich* case might have had an unraveling effect. That is, it might have provided a "point of entry" for new buildings architecturally dissimilar from those in the historic area that would destroy its historic and architectural integrity. By enacting the historic district regulation the municipality centralizes control over the area to maintain its integrity, thus conferring a "reciprocity of advantage" on property owners in that all benefit from restrictions that maintain the area's existing character. Would this rationale provide a basis for upholding the district on constitutional grounds? *See* Gold, The Welfare Economics of Historic Preservation, 8 Conn. L. Rev. 348 (1976).

See also M & N Enterprises, Inc. v. City of Springfield, 250 N.E.2d 289 (Ill. App. 1969). Acting pursuant to explicit legislative authority, the city placed a four-block area around Abraham Lincoln's Springfield home in an historic district. A majority of this area was devoted to residential uses and had previously been zoned residential. Plaintiffs sought a rezoning to construct a motel and this rezoning was denied prior to the adoption of the historic district. Subsequently, plaintiffs sought a conditional use and variance to build a commercial wax museum and gift shop. No action was taken on this request, even though it was represented that the intended structure would have architectural features appropriate to the district. Plaintiffs then brought an action challenging the constitutionality of the historic district and the court found it constitutional, offering the following rationale:

> From our review of this record, we must conclude that the enhanced value of the plaintiff's property is directly related to . . . [the creation of the historic district]. The proximity of the property to the Lincoln Home increases its value, and yet it is clear that use not in conformity with the existing zoning would be detrimental to the Lincoln Home Area and the total concept of the municipality relating to historical preservation. When property has an enhanced value by reason of planning and zoning for historical preservation, the zoning ordinances to implement the planning can hardly be said to be confiscatory or unreasonable or unconstitutional simply because the owners seek to use it for commercial purposes to exploit the visitors and tourists attracted, in part at least, by the creation of the Historical District.

Id. at 293. See also the *Rebman* case, cited in the principal opinion.

3. There are at least four situations in which due process-taking problems can arise in the application of historic district controls to individual properties. These are as follows:

(1) The property owner seeks to build or remodel a building but does not wish to conform with architectural restrictions imposed in the historic district. This problem arose in the *Gamble-Skogmo* case, *supra* p. 928. Gamble-Skogmo wished to remodel their building in the historic district of the city but did not want to comply with a requirment that window panes not exceed thirty inches square. It argued that "such a minute detail of construction is only an attempt by the city to impose its idea of an aesthetic detail of architecture." The court answered:

They ignore the fact that the window pane requirement is only one of very many details of the historical architectural style which it is said has evolved within the City of Santa Fe from about the year 1600 to the present, which the ordinance seeks to protect and preserve. So far as the record discloses, the window design is as much a part of the Santa Fe style as are flat roofs, projecting vigas, and wooden lintels.

Id. at 17. What kind of restriction on architectural detail is justified if styles in the historic district are mixed?

(2) The historic district ordinance contains a requirement that buildings in the district must be maintained to prevent deterioration. An objection to this kind of requirement was raised in *Maher v. City of New Orleans,* 516 F.2d 1051 (5th Cir. 1975). The court simply held that "[o]nce it has been determined that the purpose of the Vieux Carré legislation is a proper one, upkeep of buildings appears reasonably necessary to the accomplishment of the goals of the Ordinance. . . . It may be that, in some set of circumstances, the expense of maintenance under the Ordinance — were the city to exact compliance — would be so unreasonable as to constitute a taking." *Id.* at 1066-67.

(3) A property owner in an historic district is ordered to repair a building that is in a deteriorated condition. This issue arose in *Lafayette Park Baptist Church v. Scott,* 553 S.W.2d 856 (Mo. App. 1977). The church owned and sought to demolish a double-entry town house in an historic district which was in a deteriorated condition. Permission to demolish was denied by the board of adjustment, which noted that it was feasible to restore the building. This decision was reversed in a muddled opinion, the court noting that historic district regulations were akin to zoning and that "economic considerations cannot be wholly discounted." The ordinance "must be interpreted to authorize demolition when the condition of the structure is such that the economics of restoration preclude the landowner from making any reasonable use of the property." *Id.* at 862. The court also noted that the cost of rehabilitation would exceed $50,000 and "that this cost was economically unwarranted for the end product which would result." *Id.* at 863. On what basis does the court reach this conclusion? If all of the dwellings in the historic area are rehabilitated is it possible that their value after rehabilitation will be more than their existing value plus the cost of repair? For discussion of historic preservation in declining neighborhoods see Gold, *supra* at 357-61.

(4) The owner wants to demolish his building simply to put it to a more profitable use. This problem was considered in the principal case and in *Maher, supra.* In Maher the court held:

An ordinance forbidding the demolition of certain structures, if it serves a permissible goal in an otherwise reasonable fashion, does not seem on its face constitutionally distinguishable from ordinances regulating other aspects of land ownership, such as building height, set back or limitations on use. . . . Nor did Maher demonstrate . . . that a taking occurred because the ordinance so diminished the property value as to leave Maher, in effect, nothing. In particular, Maher did not show that the sale of the property was impracticable, that commercial rental could not provide a reasonable rate of return, or that other potential use of the property was foreclosed.

Id. at 1066. Would a court apply to same principles if demolition of a landmark building not located in an historic district were prohibited?

4. Delegation of power objections may also be brought against historic district ordinances, and these may especially be serious if the district does not have the unique and special historic characteristics of a French Quarter or a Beacon Hill. In *Maher* the court rejected delegation of power objections, noting that the expectations and values to be implemented in protecting the New Orleans French Quarter had been specified in a special state constitutional provision, the ordinance, and in interpretive state court opinions. In addition, procedural safeguards were built into the ordinance and the ordinance specified that persons with a knowledge of architecture and history would be appointed to the commission charged with administering the ordinance. *Id.* at 1061-63. Is the latter point valid? See also the *Gamble-Skogmo* case, *supra.*

See also the American Law Institute's Model Land Development Code's provision for special preservation districts, which states that the ordinance shall specify criteria to be used by the land development agency in determining whether to allow development. "These criteria may include matters such as height, shape, size, placement, use, color, style, texture of structures, landscaping and relationships to surroundings, and shall be consistent with the Land Development Plan." § 2-209(3). Compare the criteria adopted in the Savannah, Georgia, historic district. *See* Tondro, An Historic Preservation Approach to Municipal Rehabilitation of Older Neighborhoods, 8 Conn. L. Rev. 248, 264-74, 306-11 (1976). The case histories in P. Myers & G. Binder, Neighborhood Conservation: Lessons from Three Cities (1977) are also helpful. For an exhaustive bibliography see E. Kettler & B. Reams, Historic Preservation Law: An Annotated Bibliography (1976).

5. When an individual landmark is designated for preservation this action is not reinforced by comparable restrictions on surrounding buildings, as occurs in the case of an historic district. A different constitutional perspective may then be taken, as the following case indicates.

LUTHERAN CHURCH IN AMERICA v. CITY OF NEW YORK

Court of Appeals of New York (highest court)
35 N.Y.2d 121, 316 N.E.2d 305 (1974)

GABRIELLI, Judge.

The question, as we choose to frame it in this case, is whether that part of the New York City Landmarks Preservation Law which purports to give the Landmarks Preservation Commission the authority to infringe upon the free use of individual premises remaining in private ownership is a valid use of the city's police power in cases where an owner organized for charitable purposes demonstrates hardship, economic or otherwise. Present also are procedural issues involving the nature of this action and the scope of judicial review exercised by the courts below.

The statutory scheme can be outlined as follows: By amendment to the New York City Charter and Administrative Code (ch. 8-A) the Landmarks Preservation Commission was created and given the power to designate historic districts and also to designate individual properties as historic landmarks. We are here concerned with the latter aspect. Based on the statutory scheme, designations can be made after notice and a public hearing (Administrative Code of City of New York, ch. 8-A, § 207-2.0, subds. a, c; § 207-12.0), but in determining whether or not to make the contemplated designation "the commission . . . shall not be confined to consideration of the facts, views, testimony or evidence submitted at such hearing." (§ 207-12.0, subd. b.) Should the owner of a building which has been designated a landmark desire to alter or demolish it, application may be made to the commission for such permission (§ 207-5.0, subd. a) which quite probably would not be forthcoming in cases where demolition is sought. It is further provided that the owner is expected to realize at least a 6% return on his property (§ 207-1.0, subd. q) and if he proves economic hardship by the fact of a lesser return the commission is given discretion to ease the hardship by effectuating a real estate tax rebate (§ 207-8.0, subd. c), or the commission is afforded the additional right of producing a buyer or lessee who could profitably utilize the premises without the sought-for alteration or demolition (§ 207-8.0, subd. a, par. [2]; subd. i); and then, should these remedies prove unrealistic or unobtainable the city, if it desires the preservation of the property enough, is given the power to condemn (§ 207-8.0, subd. g, par. [2]).

Plaintiff, a religious corporation, not subject to the ameliorative provisions of § 207-8.0 just noted, alleged in its complaint that it is the owner of certain land at the corner of Madison Avenue and 37th Street in New York City, improved with a residential building which had been previously converted to use for offices for plaintiff's corporate-religious purposes. The property was purchased in 1942 by plaintiff's predecessor, The United Lutheran Church in America, it having been used since its construction in 1853 until that time as a residence. In November, 1965 the commission designated plaintiff's building a "landmark", the consequence of which is that by reason of the Landmarks Law plaintiff could not alter or destroy the structure without the commission's approval. The structure involved, not included as a part of any landmark district, is situated in midtown Manhattan surrounded by a variety of structures including modern multistory office, apartment and other commercial structures. It appears undisputed that plaintiff's office space requirements increased to such an extent that, even with the addition of a brick wing in 1958, the building became totally inadequate. In addition, prior to the enactment of the Landmarks Law plaintiff had engaged an architect who had prepared sketches of a new building to be erected upon demolition of the existing building and these sketches had been presented to plaintiff during the summer of 1965.

On the basis of these facts the complaint spells out five causes of action. The remedy sought on the basis of any or all of those causes of action is a judgment declaring the subject designation void either because the Landmarks Law is void on its face, or void as applied to plaintiff.

In response to these causes of action, the answer submitted by the city and the commission states generally a lack of knowledge or information sufficient to form a belief concerning most of plaintiff's factual allegations. Then, as a "defense", it is alleged that the subject property is zoned residential; that an exhaustive study was made of the subject building which had been the home of J. P. Morgan, Jr.; that a public hearing was held on the question in September, 1965 notice of which was received by plaintiff which, in fact, appeared through counsel who spoke against the designation; and that the commission, after considering all the evidence, found, that the property has importance "because it was the residence of J. P. Morgan, Jr. during the first half of the twentieth century, that the house is significant as an early example of [Anglo-Italianate] architecture, that it is one of the few free standing Brownstones remaining in the City, that it displays an impressive amount of fine architectural detail and that it is a handsome building of great dignity." It was finally alleged that plaintiff's complaint, rather than starting an action, really commenced a proceeding against a public body which was untimely by reason of the four-month time limitation in CPLR 217. Despite this allegation and without benefit of a counterclaim, defendants then sought judgment declaring the constitutionality of the Landmarks Law generally and this designation in particular.

. . . .

. . . [A] hearing was held at Trial Term at which both parties simply expanded on the themes set up in the pleadings. Plaintiff's evidence was confined to the nature of its work, its space requirements, the inadequacies of the existing space, its plans to rebuild, and the impact of the designation on all of this. The only inroad made upon plaintiff's position in these respects was that it was shown that the premises were not zoned for the contemplated office building; a point we deem irrelevant to the issues before us. At the outset of defendants' case counsel for defendants commenced proof on the question whether the designation was reasonable in light of the building's history and design. Plaintiff's counsel complained that the reasonableness of the designation was not in issue since this was an action to test the commission's power to make the designation. This objection was overruled whereupon the defense produced a quantity of evidence tending to support the reason why the Morgan house was designated a landmark, i.e., because of the illustriousness of the families who lived there (before Morgan, Jr., the Phelps-Dodges) and because the house provided the only remaining example of the free standing Brownstone typical of the era. None of defendants' witnesses, however, testified that this house was an architectural masterpiece, nor was there any evidence that any significant historical event ever took place therein.

. . . .

. . . Since this is not a case where the constitutional questions have not before been raised, we see no obstacle to our passing on them for the first time. We may surmise that defendants chose to attempt justification of the designation and perhaps denigrate plaintiff's argument that in light of its dire need to rebuild, the designation was unduly restrictive. Since plaintiff's proof of economic hardship is substantially unchallenged we perceive that we have only questions of law and that we should decide them.

Government interference with an owner's use of private property under the police power runs the gamut from outright condemnation for which compensation is expressly provided to the regulation of the general use of land remaining in private ownership so that the use might harmonize with other uses in the vicinity. No compensation is awarded in the latter situation since there is no taking. Also, of course, where property is being put to a noxious use such use can be enjoined under the common-law doctrine of nuisance and, again, no compensation would be due the injunction having been for the common good and there having been no specific taking. Such government interference as just described is based on one of two concepts — either the government is acting in its enterprise capacity, where it takes unto itself private resources in use for the common good, or in its arbitral capacity, where it intervenes to straighten out situations in which the citizenry is in conflict over land use or where one person's use of his land is injurious to others. (Sax, Taking and The Police Power, 74 Yale L.J. 36, 62, 63.) Where government acts in its enterprise capacity, as where it takes land to widen a road, there is a compensable taking. Where government acts in its arbitral capacity, as where it legislates zoning or provides the machinery to enjoin noxious use, there is simply noncompensable regulation.

What do we have in the case before us where title remains in private hands and where the government regulation which severely restricts the use to which the property may be put is neither in pursuance of a general zoning plan, nor invoked to curtail noxious use?

A zoning ordinance in order to be validly applied cannot, for one thing, serve to prohibit use to which the property is devoted at the time of the enactment of the ordinance.... Here, plaintiff has submitted ample proof not seriously contested, that the use to which the property has been put for over 20 years would have to cease because of the inability under the designation to replace the building. Also, and of chief importance, zoning is void if confiscatory. In *Vernon Park Realty v. City of Mount Vernon,* 307 N.Y. 493, 498, 499, 121 N.E.2d 517, 519, it is stated: "However compelling and acute the community traffic problem may be, its solution does not lie in placing an undue and uncompensated burden on the individual owner of a single parcel of land in the guise of regulation, even for a public purpose.... Under such circumstances, the 1927 zoning ordinance and zoning map and the 1952 amendment, as they pertain to the plaintiff's property, are so unreasonable and arbitrary as to constitute an invasion of property rights, contrary to constitutional due process and, as such, are invalid, illegal and void enactments (U.S.Const., 5th and 14th Amendts.; N.Y.Const., art. I, §§ 6, 7 [citations])".

Pertinent also is *Morris County Land Improvement Co. v. Township of Parsippany-Troy Hills,* 40 N.J. 539, 193 A.2d 232, where, by way of a series of zoning amendments, the township regulated plaintiff's vacant land to the extent it limited the use to which it could be put to public recreational, wildlife sanctuary and township sewage treatment plant uses. The net effect of the municipality's actions in that case was to make the subject property an adjunct of the town's park and utility systems and the land had to a great extent, been added to the municipality's resources in several of its enterprise capacities, despite the facade of mere regulation (Sax, Taking and The Police Power, 74 Yale L.J. 36).

In the instant case it could likewise be well argued that the commission has added the Morgan house to the resources of the city by the designation (it being argued, *inter alia,* that the house, as a tourist attraction because of its designation, aids the city generally), and that while such designations might not wreak confiscatory results in all situations (as where business might well be promoted by the designation) it does have that effect here where plaintiff is deprived of the reasonable use of its land.

This court has stated that "[i]t is not necessary, in order to render a statute obnoxious to the restraints of the constitution, that it must in terms or in effect authorize an actual physical taking of the property or the thing itself, so long as it affects its free use and enjoyment, or the power of disposition at the will of the owner" (*Forster v. Scott,* 136 N.Y. 577, 584, 32 N.E. 976, 977; see also, *Matter of Keystone Assoc. v. Moerdler,* 19 N.Y.2d 78, 88, 278 N.Y.S.2d 185, 189, 224 N.E.2d 700, 703.)

The similarity between *Matter of Keystone Assoc. v. Moerdler* and *Forster v. Scott* on the one hand and this case, on the other, is that in all of them title and use remained in the record owner. But free use was so severely restricted as to be confiscatory. The factor common to the *Matter of Keystone Assoc. v. Moerdler* and *Forster v. Scott* cases, not found in the instant case, is that in those cases the *de facto* taking was linked to an avowed taking statute. Here, the Landmarks Law is not such and would not necessarily work such results in all cases. Defendants put tremendous emphasis on the point that here we see a valid exercise of the police power, not the exercise of the power of eminent domain. However, the *Vernon Park Realty* case (307 N.Y., at p. 499, 121 N.E.2d at p. 519, *supra*), clearly tells us that when police power regulation becomes confiscatory it loses its validity. Sax pointed this out in his analysis of the kind of power being utilized. So also does Justice Holmes in *Pennsylvania Coal Co. v. Mahon,* 260 U.S. 393, 43 S.Ct. 158, 67 L.Ed. 322 . . . .

The decision in *Matter of Trustees of Sailors' Snug Harbor v. Platt,* 29 A.D. 2d 376, 288 N.Y.S.2d 314, . . . [1968] although inconclusive on the question of confiscation since further facts had to be developed, is correct in refusing to declare the entire law unconstitutional on its face. The question posed there was whether in that instance regulation went too far. The buildings there sought to be preserved had become inadequate for their charitable purpose and were to be replaced. The Appellate Division ruled that where designation would prevent or seriously interfere with the carrying out of the charitable purpose it would be invalid. That is a simple enough concept and ought to apply here.

The landmark preservation problem has received considerable comment the net effect of which is general agreement that attempts to designate individual landmarks in high economic development areas is fraught with trouble (see, especially, Costonis, The Chicago Plan: Incentive Zoning And The Preservation of Urban Landmarks, 85 Harv.L.Rev. 574; Wolf, The Landmark Problem in New York, 22 Intramural L.Rev. of N.Y.U. 99).

As noted in the dissent, the statutory scheme (virtually all of § 207-8.0), providing for alternate proposals and perhaps ultimate condemnations in cases where economic return is insufficient or where there is no wish by the owner to sell or lease the property, is not applicable here. Plaintiff is a charitable organization and not otherwise subject to the various administrative alternatives set up in section 207-8.0 which could result in condemnation of the property sought to be altered or demolished. We save for another day consideration of those provisions where sought to be applied. What has occurred here, however, where the commission is attempting to force plaintiff to retain its property as is, without any sort of relief or adequate compensation, is nothing short of a naked taking. As in the New Jersey *Parsippany* case (40 N.J. 539, 193 A.2d 232, *supra*), the commission, without any move toward invoking the power of eminent domain, is attempting to add this property to the public use by purely and simply invading the owner's right to own and manage. Legitimate zoning stops far short of this because it does not appropriate to public use. Where the owner can make a case for alteration or demolition the municipality would have to relinquish the designation, provide agreeable alternatives or condemn the premises.

Such a case has been alleged and proved here, contrary to assertions in the dissent, and stands substantially unrebutted by the defendants. It is uncontested that the existing building is totally inadequate for plaintiff's legitimate needs and must be replaced if plaintiff is to be able freely and economically to use the premises especially as it appears that adjoining structures have been integrated with plaintiff's operation. The power given the municipality to force termination of plaintiff's free use of the premises short of condemnation (which would provide compensation for plaintiff's complete loss) directly violates plaintiff's rights under the Fifth and Fourteenth Amendments to the United States Constitution, and sections 6 and 7 of article I of the New York Constitution. As in *Vernon Park Realty v. City of Mount Vernon,* 307 N.Y. 493, 121 N.E.2d 517, *supra,* we find a situation exceeding the permissible limits of the zoning power.

The order appealed from should be modified, with costs, to the extent that the landmark designation as here applied is declared to be confiscatory.

JASEN, Judge (dissenting). [Omitted].

Comments: 1. In the *Snug Harbor* case, cited in the principal opinion, a charitable organization owned five buildings designated as historic landmarks which it used as housing for the elderly. It wished to replace them with modern structures. The court noted that "as a group these buildings were one of the two best examples of Greek Revival architecture in the country." It held:

> The criterion for commercial property is where the continuance of the landmark prevents the owner from obtaining an adequate return. A comparable test for a charity would be where maintenance of the landmark either physically or financially prevents or seriously interferes with carrying out the charitable purpose.... [The court should determine] whether the preservation of these buildings would seriously interfere with the use of the property, whether the buildings are capable of conversion to a useful purpose without excessive cost, or whether the cost of maintaining them without use would entail serious

expenditure — all in the light of the purposes and resources of the . . . [owner].

Id. at 316. Are these criteria consistent with the holding of the *Lutheran Church* case?

In *Manhattan Club v. Landmarks Preservation Comm'n,* 273 N.Y.S.2d 848 (N.Y. Sup. Ct. 1966) (trial court), the court sustained the designation of an historic mansion owned by the club and which the club wanted to raze. A refusal to allow demolition was upheld. The club "is free to do as it pleases with the interior of the building. It is guaranteed a reasonable return on its investment. And if no plan can be devised to materialize this guarantee, it may make such changes as it wishes." *Id.* at 852. *See also Mayor & Alderman v. Anne Arundel County,* 316 A.2d 807 (Md. 1974) (court upheld refusal to permit demolition of historic church); *Texas Antiquities Comm. v. Dallas Community College Dist.,* 554 S.W.2d 924 (Tex. 1977) (allowing demolition of deteriorated historic building when cost of restoration economically prohibitive).

2. In an important landmark case that came before the United States Supreme Court, *Penn Cent. Transp. Co. v. City of New York,* — U.S. — (1978), the court considered the constitutionality of the landmark designation of Grand Central Terminal in New York City. Penn Central, as owner of the Terminal, sought to capitalize on its strategic location by leasing the air rights over the Terminal for construction of a 59-story office building, a proposal that was rejected by the landmarks commission.

The court held the designation constitutional. "[T]he submission that . . . [Penn Central] may establish a 'taking' simply by showing that they have been denied the ability to exploit a property interest that they heretofore had believed was available for development is quite simply untenable. . . . [The Terminal's] designation as a landmark not only permits but contemplates that . . . [Penn Central] may continue to use the property precisely as it has for the past 65 years: as a railroad terminal containing office space and concessions." *Id.* at —, —. Is this holding consistent with the holding in *Lutheran Church?* The *Penn Central* case is reproduced *supra* p. 149.

The court also addressed the question whether landmark designation is fundamentally different from zoning or from historic district legislation because landmark controls "apply only to individuals who own selected properties." This contention was rejected. New York City's landmarks law "embodies a comprehensive plan to preserve structures of historic or aesthetic interest wherever they may be found in the city," and Penn Central's contention that it has been "solely burdened" is inaccurate because the landmark designation ordinance applies to vast numbers of structures. Over 400 landmarks had been designated, many of them close to the terminal. *Id.* at —.

3. Should the courts in the historic landmark cases concentrate on whether reasonable use of the building is possible or on the possibility that the building when demolished can be put to a more intensive and profitable use? In many instances the designated historic building may be undersized for its site, and if it is located in a commercial area and surrounded by taller and larger structures there may be an argument that the owner of the historic building has been deprived of its development rights on the site. Does *Lutheran Church* consider this issue? See also the *Fred F. French* case, reproduced *infra* p. 955. Similar problems are raised in the wetland protection cases, such as the *Morris Land* case discussed in the *Lutheran Church* opinion. For more on this issue see *infra* p. 1106.

For an application of economic analysis to the landmark preservation problem see Gold, The Welfare Economics of Historic Preservation, 8 Conn. L. Rev. 348 (1976). Gold argues that historic preservation might be a public good, "a good which through its provision for one individual automatically gives rise to free provision for other persons." From this perspective, the landmark owner who is not allowed to demolish an historic building is required to bear the entire cost of a collective benefit and the restriction should be found unconstitutional. "On the other hand, one might adopt a nontraditional viewpoint and define the status quo as the presence of a public good (the landmark building) and its elimination a public bad; therefore, the police power can prevent its destruction." *Id.* at 366.

4. The ALI Model Land Development Code's landmark site section provides:

> § 2-208(3) The Land Development Agency shall grant special development permission on a landmark site only if it finds that
> (a) the development is consistent with the special significance of the landmark; and
> (b) the development complies with any criteria specified in the development ordinance for development on the landmark site.

Assume that the owner of an office building designated as an historic landmark applies for permission to demolish his building and erect a new and larger office building in its place. Can the application be turned down under the ALI Code provision? If a decision is made to deny the application can it be attacked as an unconstitutional taking? What criteria in the New York City landmarks law would apply to this application?

5. How firm are the police power foundations for landmark preservation? Would you recommend abandonment of police power techniques for landmark preservation and urge reliance on alternative measures, such as the transfer of development rights concept discussed in the next section? Costonis warns "against an overly facile reliance upon zoning and historic districting precedents to justify the regulation of individual landmarks on a non-compensatory basis." J. Costonis, Space Adrift 19 (1974). Is his warning justified? For additional discussion of the landmark preservation cases see Gerstell, Needed: A Landmark Decision, 8 Urb. L. 213 (1976); Note, Urban Landmarks: Preserving Our Cities' Aesthetic and Cultural Resources, 39 Alb. L. Rev. 521 (1974).

6. Note should be taken of the National Historic Preservation Act of 1966. This Act directs the Secretary of Interior to "maintain a national register of districts, sites, buildings, structures, and objects significant in American history, architecture, archeology, and culture." 16 U.S.C. § 470a(a)(1) (1976). The most significant part of this statute is a protective provision directed to federal agencies having jurisdiction over federal or federally-assisted undertakings or authority to license any undertaking. *Id.* § 470f. These federal agencies are directed to "take into account the effect of the undertaking on any district, site, building, structure, or object that is included in the National Register." *Id.*

An Advisory Council on Historic Preservation is created by the statute, and is to comment on any federal action affecting National Register sites and properties. While Advisory Council comments are advisory, and while the Council has no veto power over federal actions, one case has indicated that its recommendations must at least be carefully taken into account. *Ely v. Velde,* 451 F.2d 1130, 1138 (4th Cir. 1971). A variety of federal or federally-assisted actions have come under Council review, including the construction of a high-rise apartment in the Savannah Historic District and construction of an expressway that would have severed the French Quarter in New Orleans from the Mississippi River.

There are limits, of course, to federal involvement. In *Edwards v. First Bank of Dundee,* 534 F.2d 1242 (7th Cir. 1976), a federal district court enjoined the bank from demolishing a house in an historic district listed in the national register until an advisory opinion had been received from the Advisory Council. The Court of Appeals reversed, holding that the National Historic Preservation Act did not apply. There was no federal funding or assistance. A federal agency had to approve a change in location so that the bank could erect a new structure on the site where the historic dwelling stood, but this agency did not have jurisdiction over demolition of the dwelling.

For discussion of the National Historic Preservation Act see Fowler, Protection of the Cultural Environment in Federal Environmental Law 1466 (E. Dolgin & T. Guilbert eds. 1974).

D. TRANSFER OF DEVELOPMENT RIGHTS

Regulatory programs such as historic preservation illustrate some of the pressures placed on noncompensatory police power techniques as these techniques are extended to new and controversial settings. These pressures have called forth an innovative technique for land use regulation that avoids police power strategies but which does not fall back on land acquisition or compensation by public agencies as an alternative. This technique, known as the transfer of development rights, relies on a compensating mechanism in the land use market. The right to development can be restricted at one location, such as an historic landmark, and the development rights taken away from this location can then be transferred to another. The owner of land at the transfer site will simply pay the owner of the land at the restricted site for the transferred development rights, so that any due process taking objections to the restriction can be avoided.

Transfer of development rights (TDR) systems can be used for a variety of purposes other than the site-to-site transfer described above. As the following selection indicates, TDR has also been proposed as a general land management tool and as a method for preserving environmentally sensitive areas.

F. JAMES & D. GALE, ZONING FOR SALE: A CRITICAL ANALYSIS OF TRANSFERABLE DEVELOPMENT RIGHTS PROGRAMS 12-19 (Urban Institute, 1977)

The attention paid TDR is due more to its promise for the future than to its accomplishments to date. In its more ambitious forms, TDR is designed to provide an overall structure within which current land-use planning tools might be applied, rather than simply an additional tool. It is hoped that TDR will insulate landowners from the windfalls and wipeouts that accompany current planning restrictions, and permit planning that is both effective and equitable in its economic impact.

TDR Proposals for New Jersey. The TDR plans that have created the most excitement are aimed at general land-use management goals. A plan proposed in New Jersey illustrates the hopes of some TDR advocates. A law proposed in 1973 would have enabled municipalities to adopt limited TDR plans aimed at the preservation of open space, environmentally sensitive areas, or other community land resources. This legislation failed, but helped to spawn a more elaborate scheme in 1974, the Chavooshian-Neiswan-Norman proposal, in which the TDR concept played a central role. The authors of this program proposed that localities use TDR as part of a Growth Management Program (GMP) which would take into account the capacities of the ecosystem and of existing public services to safely "absorb" new urban development in a given area. Each community would establish growth management regulations, such as zoning, to set maximum levels of development intensity.

The TDR program would help localities achieve the objectives of the GMP. The first step in the plan is the allocation of development rights to property owners throughout the community. Rights are to be distributed to each property owner in proportion to the assessed value of the property. Rights would also be issued to owners of developed land. These latter rights could not be transferred unless their owners first demolished the buildings to which the rights were originally assigned.

The GMP would prohibit development in some areas and permit intensive development in others. The number of development rights issued in the community would be commensurate with the amount of development permitted by the plan. Under the TDR plan, owners of development rights would buy and sell the rights among themselves. As with all TDR proposals, it is hoped that property owners permitted to undertake developments will purchase development rights from owners who may not develop their own property, or from owners of properties that would be less profitable to develop. These development rights transactions would tend to channel development into areas of the community where the profit incentives for development were greatest, and at the same time, enable the community to design development plans to meet public goals. Thus, TDR should encourage development patterns that are efficient from both private and public points of view.

In this New Jersey proposal, once a parcel is developed, its development rights will merge with the property and be nonnegotiable until the development is demolished, redeveloped, or altered to a different intensity or type of use. In order to give some flexibility in planning for community growth, the plan provides a way of adjusting the total number of unused development rights if GMP development regulations change. For instance, if permissible total density were increased, more rights would be issued on a proportional basis to all eligible owners. Development rights would be taxed like real property until "consumed" by a building project.

A number of similar plans have been proposed. Two such plans are the Chicago Plan and the Puerto Rico Plan. These plans illustrate the two main systems for redistributing development rights: the Chicago Plan calls for a private market in development rights; the Puerto Rico Plan is publicly administered.

The Chicago Plan. The Chicago Plan was originally proposed as a way of preserving the architecturally significant buildings designed by members of the renowned Chicago School of Architecture, which included such pioneers as Louis Sullivan and Frank Lloyd Wright. The preservation of these landmarks has proved difficult, largely because of the great cost, which public officials often have been unwilling to pay out of tax dollars. A primary objective of the Chicago Plan is to impose the costs of preservation on developers of new buildings. The basis assumptions are that new development is a primary threat to these old buildings and that development is sufficiently profitable to pay much of the cost of preserving selected landmarks.

The Chicago Plan proposes the creation of development rights transfer districts. Each district would include both areas where landmarks are located as well as other parts of the city where new construction is also likely. The owners of landmark buildings, which are typically undersized in relation to their downtown site would be permitted to sell their unused development rights to owners of other lots within their district who are undertaking new construction. Upon the sale of development rights, landmark owners would receive a real estate tax reduction, since their tax would be based on existing use rather than "highest and best" use of their property. The owners of properties receiving the development rights would be permitted to erect larger buildings than would normally be allowed under applicable zoning.

In return for the proceeds from the sale of development rights and the decrease in real estate taxes, landmark owners would agree to maintain the landmark in accordance with sound building management practices. If landmark owners were to refuse to sell their unused development rights and try to raze the building, the plan would empower the city to acquire the unused development rights (though not the structure itself, except in unusual circumstances) through its power of eminent domain. The money for such acquisitions (as well as other expenses involved in operating the plan) would come from a "development rights bank" with assets consisting of development rights acquired through condemnation, donated by private owners of other landmarks, or transferred from publicly owned properties. The bank would periodically sell some of these rights to developers or investors in order to raise money.

The authors of the Chicago Plan undertook an analysis of the likely market for development rights unused by landmark structures in the city. The analysis showed that if office rents were sufficiently high, private developers would be willing to pay money for the right to build structures larger than were permitted under standard zoning. However, under present circumstances, standard zoning and bonus provisions permit such intensive development on large sites it is doubtful whether there would be a demand for additional development rights. For example, under the city's existing zoning laws, owners of square-block sites in certain parts of Chicago are permitted to build office structures up to 140 stories high, far higher than the market for office space makes sensible.

One possible solution to this problem would be to formally "downzone" properties in prestigious locations in order to expand the demand for development rights. This possibility was entertained by the authors of the Chicago Plan, and though it was rejected as politically unrealistic, it has become one of the more controversial aspects of the plan.

The Puerto Rico Plan. The Puerto Rico Plan seeks to preserve significant environmental resources by prohibiting development in unique or endangered areas of the island. As in the Chicago Plan, the costs of preservation would be met through the sale of development rights permitting more intensive development in other areas. Unlike the Chicago Plan, the Puerto Rico Plan prohibits transfers of development rights among private parties.

The plan would be operated by the Puerto Rico Planning Board. This board is unusually comprehensive in its jurisdiction by mainland American standards because it has islandwide authority over land use and can zone land in urban areas as well as determine land use in other areas on a parcel-by-parcel basis as development proposals emerge. Its responsibilities include sound land development, natural resource protection, and improvement in the general social welfare.

Under the proposed TDR plan, the board would have the authority to establish Protective Environmental Zones (PEZs) in areas of critical environmental sensitivity. The board would regulate the type and amount of land development to be permitted in the PEZs, and would prohibit development clearly injurious to any PEZ. The board would also delineate transfer districts, within which property owners could purchase development rights. The board would then sell a variety of planning and zoning premiums to private property owners in the transfer districts.

The Planning Board itself would be a party to all transactions in development rights, purchasing the development rights of property owners in PEZs and obtaining funds for purchases through the sale of development rights, supplemented if necessary by general appropriations from the Commonwealth of Puerto Rico, gifts, or federal government grants. The types of development rights offered for sale in transfer districts would range from permission for property owners to develop their land more intensively, to actual purchase by the board of land to be sold for major private land-development projects. In this plan, development rights have no single definition and are not transferred among property owners as they are in private-market TDR plans.

One of the most important features of the Puerto Rico Plan is that it defines precisely the situations requiring compensation and the amount of compensation required. Determination of whether a PEZ landowner has suffered a compensable loss will be made through a device called the "Spectrum of Land Use Intensity." This spectrum has five gradations, from Zero Intensity Use (no development) to Most Profitable Use. An intermediate intensity of development, Reasonable Beneficial Use, will serve as the benchmark by which compensation will be determined. It corresponds, roughly, to the land use that would have been allowed under regular zoning in the absence of the TDR plan. Under the Puerto Rico Plan, compensation will be offered only when the effect of land-use controls reduces land values below that which would prevail in the land's Reasonable Beneficial Use.

. . . .

TDR clearly embodies both a faith in the efficacy of private markets and private enterprise and the desire for more effective planning and equitable regulation of private land-use decisions. If TDR can lessen the degree to which public planning and regulation diminish private property rights, planning and regulation should become more generally acceptable. This acceptability would be reinforced by the fact that under TDR some of the economic benefits from land development are shared by all property owners and by the general population in the form of better environmental protection and preservation, an aspect of TDR that would probably tend to make communities more open to private land development.

. . . .

Private-market TDR programs appear to promise a way to preserve historic buildings, to keep open space in its original state, and to improve land planning and management, all at no cost to a community. This no-cost aspect of TDR would make possible certain land-use achievements that could not be paid for out of public funds. Actually, TDR does not reduce the real economic costs of land-use regulation, but by imposing the costs on the development process, TDR shifts the costs out of the government budget and in the process may obscure who bears them. (See Chapter 4 for a fuller discussion of TDR costs.) Public TDR plans, such as the Puerto Rico Plan, bring the fiscal realities of exchanges in development rights to public attention. In these plans, public agencies receive cash from private developers in exchange for permission to carry out certain land-use activities. This cash, used to buy development rights from other property owners, becomes an explicit form of public expenditure for land-use planning and management.

. . . .

Comments: 1. There have been scattered applications of the TDR concept. New York City has had a site-to-site TDR program in operation for some years. Note, Development Rights Transfer in New York City, 82 Yale L.J. 338 (1972). This program has been subject to litigation. See the *Fred F. French* case, *infra.* The rural community of Eden, near Buffalo, New York, has adopted a more ambitious TDR program based on the New Jersey plan. Emanuel, Rural Eden Uses TDR to Save Agricultural Land, Practicing Planner, March, 1977, at 15. See also the collection of essays in Transferable Development Rights (American Soc'y of Planning Officials, Planning Advisory Service Rep. No. 304, 1975).

2. We can now examine a series of constitutional problems raised by TDR programs, and look first at constitutional problems likely to arise at the transfer site, where developers must purchase development rights in order to build at greater densities.

(1) *Uniformity.* TDR imposes a dual standard on lots in the transfer district. Developers may build at existing zoning levels without purchasing development rights, but may build more intensively only if development rights are purchased. Is there a uniformity problem? Professor Costonis argues that the uniformity objection has no merit, and relies on cases sustaining the constitutionality of PUD ordinances against uniformity objections. *See supra* p. 870. "A development transfer district is, in effect, a special development district in which bulk is redistributed in accordance with the density zoning technique. It encompasses an area of the community that is unique because of the concentration there of many of the community's landmark buildings." Costonis, The Chicago Plan: Incentive Zoning and the Preservation of Landmarks, 85 Harv. L. Rev. 574, 623 (1971). Does this argument hold if TDR is used for purposes other than landmark preservation?

(2) *Due process; taking.* The requirement that lot owners at transfer sites purchase additional development rights in order to carry out more intensive development may raise due process taking problems:

> If the existing zoning is sound, it may be claimed, relaxing bulk restrictions on transferee sites will overload public services and distort the urban landscape. . . . If it is too stringent, the proper course is to raise prevailing bulk limitations within the area generally and, in the process, to remove unwarranted public restrictions on the rights or property owners there.

Costonis, *supra* at 628. Costonis argues against this conclusion, pointing out that "it invests the numbers in the zoning code with an aura of scientific exactitude that is largely without foundation in fact." *Id.* at 629. Therefore, "the bulk increments allotted to development rights purchasers fall within a range that is defensible in planning terms." *Id.* at 630. In other words, communities may set zoning densities within a higher and lower range. If densities are set at the lower range, so that purchase of development rights is required to build at the higher range, no due process taking results.

Due process taking problems at transfer sites may be more serious if the community must first downzone existing densities in order to make a market for the purchase of development rights at these sites. For a discussion of downzoning see *infra* p. 1021.

Assuming that the purchase of development rights at the transfer site is viewed as a levy or charge on the right to development, an argument can be made that this charge is justifiable under the principles applied to uphold subdivision exactions. *See* Costonis, Development Rights Transfer: An Exploratory Essay, 83 Yale L.J. 75, 112-17 (1973). Consult the subdivision exaction cases, *supra* Chapter 5, and consider whether these cases support this argument. *See also* Note, The Unconstitutionality of Transferable Development Rights, 84 Yale L.J. 1101, 1115-17 (1975).

3. Do TDR programs require developers at transfer sites to pay twice for the right to develop at higher densities? Assume an unrestricted market for land with no TDR program. A developer interested in a lot at any one site will pay a price representing the use value of the land under existing zoning. He may also pay a premium, assuming the land is zoned at a level precluding high density development, that represents the expectancy that the land will at some time be zoned to the higher level. If a TDR program is now imposed, the developer must buy development rights in order to build at a higher density. The price for these rights will include the premium previously paid in the expectation that the density would eventually have been raised by a zoning change. Has the developer, to this extent, been charged twice for the right to develop? If so, does he have a due process taking objection? Is this situation likely to occur once the TDR program has been adopted and has been in operation for some time?

What price developers will pay for development rights at the transfer site is analyzed in Field & Conrad, Economic Issues in Programs of Transferable Development Rights, 51 Land Econ. 331 (1975). The authors point out that the transfer price of development rights at the transfer site will depend on how the market for development rights is organized, and the extent to which the public agency intervenes to manage the development right price. In a poorly organized market, with little or no public intervention, purchasers of development rights may be able to seek out holders of rights with low reservation prices and contract for their rights at these prices. In this event, the double charge may be reduced or eliminated, but questions may then arise concerning the adequacy of compensation to the restricted owners.

If the development right charge raises the price of land in the transfer district will this excess charge be passed on to tenants and purchasers of buildings constructed on the transfer site? "This depends on the degree of competition in markets for comparable developments, both within the planning area and in adjacent areas. The lower the degree of competition, . . . the higher the likelihood that development rights costs can be passed on to future occupants." *Id.* at 338.

If the cost of development rights is passed on, can TDR be faulted on equity grounds?

> [TDR] costs are even more inequitably skewed when compared to the total proportion of a given population that is beneficiary to TDR's presumed preservation services. Theoretically, a protected resource such as scenic open space or a historic mansion is a public good. That is, it is a commodity which, "if available to anyone, is equally available to all others." To be sure, in practice TDR's preserved resources are not likely to be equally accessible to *all* income or age groups in a jurisdiction. But it is just as certain that those who do have access and can visually enjoy a verdant meadow or an Italianate Victorian townhouse compose a considerably larger population than the burdened groups identified under compensatory and redistributive TDR measures. Therefore, it would seem compellingly apparent that TDR schemes of whatever stripe are likely to fail a test of equitability based on the criterion of benefits derived.

Gale, The Transfer of Development Rights: Some Equity Considerations, 14 Urb. L. Ann. 81, 94 (1977).

4. Professor Costonis has made two other arguments for TDR to justify the cost of development rights to the transfer site owner. The first relates to the elimination of negative externalities (see *supra* p. 31):

> One function of the law is to return the cost of an externality to its creator when the harm is deemed sufficiently grave in its societal impact. Development rights transfer serves this end admirably because it "closes the externalities loop" by charging the land development process with costs that formerly, and improperly, fell upon the community in the form of environmental degradation — or of expensive remedial programs to overcome it.

Costonis, Development Rights Transfer: Description & Perspectives for a Critique, Urb. Land, Jan., 1975, at 5, 9. Professor Gale has responded to this defense of TDR:

> The myriad revenues accruing to the community in the form of taxes, fees and user charges, as well as new employment from high density development, render the identification of community benefits at least as difficult as the determination of community impacts or negative externalities. It is by no means apparent then,

that Professor Costonis' argument dispenses with legitimate concern over TDR's questionable equity implications.

Gale, *supra* at 94, n. 59.

Costonis would also justify the acquisition of development rights by transfer site owners under an unearned increment theory:

> By regarding the development potential of private property in part as a community resource, on the other hand, development rights transfer enables government to share in the gains occasioned by rising land values. . . . Proportioned to what land economists have long regarded as the "unearned increment" in the value of private property, these revisions respond directly to the concern reflected in J.S. Mill's aphorism that "landlords grow richer in their sleep."

Costonis, *supra* at 8. The unearned increment problem is considered in greater detail at *infra* p. 980.

5. Problems also arise in TDR system because a claim can be made that the value returned to the restricted owner for the transfer of its development rights does not afford sufficient just compensation. This issue is considered in the following case.

FRED F. FRENCH INVESTING COMPANY, INC. v. CITY OF NEW YORK

Court of Appeals of New York
39 N.Y.2d 587, 350 N.E.2d 381, *appeal dismissed,* 429 U.S. 990 (1976)

BREITEL, Chief Judge.

Plaintiff Fred F. French Investing Co., purchase money mortgagee of Tudor City, a Manhattan residential complex, brought this action to declare unconstitutional a 1972 amendment to the New York City Zoning Resolution and seeks compensation as for "inverse" taking by eminent domain. The amendment purported to create a "Special Park District", and rezoned two private parks in the Tudor City complex exclusively as parks open to the public. It further provided for the granting to the defendant property owners of transferable development (air) rights usable elsewhere. It created the transferable rights by severing the above-surface development rights from the surface development rights, a device of recent invention.

Special Term, in a studied and painstaking opinion, declared the amendment unconstitutional and restored the former zoning classification, R-10, permitting residential and office building development. The Appellate Division, 47 A.D.2d 715, 366 N.Y.S.2d 346 unanimously affirmed, without opinion. By its appeal, the city seeks review of the declaration of unconstitutionality and the denial of its summary judgment motion on the issue of damages. By their cross appeals, plaintiff mortgagee and defendants, owners and mortgage interest guarantor, seek review of the denial of their summary judgment motions for compensation based on an "inverse" taking.

The issue is whether the rezoning of buildable private parks exclusively as parks open to the public, thereby prohibiting all reasonable income productive or other private use of the property, constitutes a deprivation of property rights without due process of law in violation of constitutional limitations.

There should be an affirmance. While the police power of the State to regulate the use of private property by zoning is broad indeed, it is not unlimited. The State may not, under the guise of regulation by zoning, deprive the owner of the reasonable income productive or other private use of his property and thus destroy all but a bare residue of its economic value. Such an exercise of the police power would be void as violative of the due process clauses of the State and Federal Constitutions (N.Y. Const., art. I, § 6; U.S. Const., 14th Amdt., § 1). In the instant case, the city has, despite the severance of above-surface development rights, by rezoning private parks exclusively as parks open to the public, deprived the owners of the reasonable income productive or other private use of their property. The attempted severance of the development rights with uncertain and contingent market value did not adequately preserve those rights. Hence, the 1972 zoning amendment is violative of constitutional limitations.

Tudor City is a four-acre residential complex built on an elevated level above East 42nd Street, across First Avenue from the United Nations in mid-town Manhattan. Planned and developed as a residential community, Tudor City consists of 10 large apartment buildings housing approximately 8,000 people, a hotel, four brownstone buildings, and two 15,000 square-foot private parks. The parks, covering about 18½ % of the area of the complex, are elevated from grade and located on the north and south sides of East 42nd Street, with a connecting viaduct.

On September 30, 1970, plaintiff sold the Tudor City complex to defendant Ramsgate Properties for $36,000,000. In addition to cash, plaintiff took back eight purchase money mortgages, two of which covered in part the two parks. Payment of the mortgage interest for three years was personally guaranteed by defendant Helmsley. Ramsgate thereafter conveyed, subject to plaintiff's mortgages, properties including the north and south parks to defendants, North Assemblage Co. and South Assemblage Co. Each of the mortgages secured in part by the parks has been in default since December 7, 1972.

Soon after acquiring the Tudor City property, the new owner announced plans to erect a building, said to be a 50-story tower, over East 42nd Street between First and Second Avenues. This plan would have required New York City Planning Commission approval of a shifting of development rights from the parks to the proposed adjoining site and a corresponding zoning change. Alternatively, the owner proposed to erect on each of the Tudor City park sites a building of maximum size permitted by the existing zoning regulations.

There was immediately an adverse public reaction to the owner's proposals, especially from Tudor City residents. After public hearings, the City Planning Commission recommended, over the dissent of one commissioner, and on December 7, 1972 the Board of Estimate approved, an amendment to the zoning resolution establishing Special Park District "P". By contemporaneous amendment to the zoning map, the two Tudor City parks were included within Special Park District "P".

Under the zoning amendment, "only passive recreational uses are permitted" in the Special Park District and improvements are limited to "structures incidental to passive recreational use". When the Special Park District would be mapped, the parks are required to be open daily to the public between 6:00 a. m. and 10:00 p. m.

The zoning amendment permits the transfer of development rights from a privately owned lot zoned as a Special Park District, denominated a "granting lot", to other areas in midtown Manhattan, bounded by 60th Street, Third Avenue, 38th Street and Eighth Avenue, denominated "receiving lots". Lots eligible to be receiving lots are those with a minimum lot size of 30,000 square feet and zoned to permit development at the maximum commercial density. The owner of a granting lot would be permitted to transfer part of his development rights to any eligible receiving lot, thereby increasing its maximum floor area up to 10%. Further increase in the receiving lot's floor area, limited to 20% of the maximum commercial density, is contingent upon a public hearing and approval by the City Planning Commission and the Board of Estimate. Development rights may be transferred by the owner directly to a receiving lot or to an individual or organization for later disposition to a receiving lot. Before development rights may be transferred, however, the Chairman of the City Planning Commission must certify the suitability of a plan for the continuing maintenance, at the owner's expense, of the granting lot as a park open to the public.

It is notable that the private parks become open to the public upon mapping of the Special Park District, and the opening does not depend upon the relocation and effective utilization of the transferable development rights. Indeed, the mapping occurred on December 7, 1972, and the development rights have never been marketed or used.

Plaintiff contends that the rezoning of the parks constitutes a compensable "taking" within the meaning of constitutional limitations.

The power of the State over private property extends from the regulation of its use under the police power to the actual taking of an easement or all or part of the fee under the eminent domain power. The distinction, although definable, between a compensable taking and a noncompensable regulation is not always susceptible of precise demarcation. Generally, as the court stated in *Lutheran Church in Amer. v. City of New York,* 35 N.Y.2d 121, 128-129, 359 N.Y.S.2d 7, 14, 316 N.E.2d 305, 310: "[G]overnment interference [with the use of private property] is based on one of two concepts — either the government is acting in its enterprise capacity, where it takes unto itself private resources in use for the common good, or in its arbitral capacity, where it intervenes to straighten out situations in which the citizenry is in conflict over land use or where one person's use of his land is injurious to others. (Sax, Taking and the Police Power, 74 Yale L.J. 36, 62, 63.) Where government acts in its enterprise capacity, as where it takes land to widen a road, there is a compensable taking. Where government acts in its arbitral capacity, as where it legislates zoning or provides the machinery to enjoin noxious use, there is simply noncompensable regulation."

As noted above, when the State "takes", that is appropriates, private property for public use, just compensation must be paid. In contrast, when there is only regulation of the uses of private property, no compensation need be paid. Of course, and this is often the beginning of confusion, a purported "regulation" may impose so onerous a burden on the property regulated that it has, in effect, deprived the owner of the reasonable income productive or other private use of his property and thus has destroyed its economic value. In all but exceptional cases, nevertheless, such a regulation does not constitute a "taking", and is therefore not compensable, but amounts to a deprivation or frustration of property rights without due process of law and is therefore invalid.

True, many cases have equated an invalid exercise of the regulating zoning power, perhaps only metaphorically, with a "taking" or a "confiscation" of property, terminology appropriate to the eminent domain power and the concomitant right to compensation when it is exercised. Thus, for example, in *Arverne Bay Constr. Co. v. Thatcher,* 278 N.Y. 222, 232, 15 N.E.2d 587, 592, the court stated "An ordinance which *permanently* so restricts the use of property that it cannot be used for any reasonable purpose goes, it is plain, beyond regulation, and must be recognized as a taking of the property." Similarly, in *Pennsylvania Coal Co. v. Mahon,* 260 U.S. 393, 415, 43 S.Ct. 158, 160, 67 L.Ed. 322, a police power and not an eminent domain case, Mr. Justice Holmes stated: "while property may be regulated to a certain extent, if regulation goes too far it will be recognized as a taking". . . .

The metaphor should not be confused with the reality. Close examination of the cases reveals that in none of them, anymore than in the *Pennsylvania Coal* case (*supra*), was there an actual "taking" under the eminent domain power, despite the use of the terms "taking" or "confiscatory". Instead, in each the gravamen of the constitutional challenge to the regulatory measure was that it was an invalid exercise of the police power under the due process clause, and the cases were decided under that rubric.... As has been cogently pointed out by Professor Costonis: "the goal of [challenges to regulatory measures] in conventional land use disputes is to preclude application of the measure to the restricted parcel on the basis of constitutional infirmity. What is achieved, in short, is declaratory relief. The sole exception to this mild outcome occurs where the challenged measure is either intended to eventuate in actual public ownership of the land or has already caused government to encroach on the land with trespassory consequences that are largely irreversible." (Costonis, "Fair" Compensation and the Accommodation Power: Antidotes for the Taking Impasse in Land Use Controversies, 1975 Col. L. Rev. 1021, 1035; . . . .)

In the present case, while there was a significant diminution in the value of the property, there was no actual appropriation or taking of the parks by title or governmental occupation. The amendment was declared void at Special Term a little over a year after its adoption. There was no physical invasion of the owner's property; nor was there an assumption by the city of the control or management of the parks. Indeed, the parks served the same function as before the amendment, except that they were now also open to the public. Absent factors of governmental displacement of private ownership, occupation or management, there was no "taking" within the meaning of constitutional limitations.... There was, therefore, no right to compensation as for a taking in eminent domain.

Since there was no taking within the meaning of constitutional limitations, plaintiff's remedy, at this stage of the litigation, would be a declaration of the amendment's invalidity, if that be the case. Thus, it is necessary to determine whether the zoning amendment was a valid exercise of the police power under the due process clauses of the State and Federal Constitutions.

The broad police power of the State to regulate the use of private property is not unlimited. Every enactment under the police power must be reasonable.... An exercise of the police power to regulate private property by zoning which is unreasonable constitutes a deprivation of property without due process of law....

What is an "unreasonable" exercise of the police power depends upon the relevant converging factors. Hence, the facts of each case must be evaluated in order to determine the private and social balance of convenience before the exercise of the power may be condemned as unreasonable. . . .

A zoning ordinance is unreasonable, under traditional police power and due process analysis, if it encroaches on the exercise of private property rights without substantial relation to a legitimate governmental purpose. A legitimate governmental purpose is, of course, one which furthers the public health, safety, morals or general welfare. . . . Moreover, a zoning ordinance, on similar police power analysis, is unreasonable if it is arbitrary, that is, if there is no reasonable relation between the end sought to be achieved by the regulation and the means used to achieve that end. . . .

Finally, and it is at this point that the confusion between the police power and the exercise of eminent domain most often occurs, a zoning ordinance is unreasonable if it frustrates the owner in the use of his property, that is, if it renders the property unsuitable for any reasonable income productive or other private use for which it is adapted and thus destroys its economic value, or all but a bare residue of its value. . . .

The ultimate evil of a deprivation of property, or better, a frustration of property rights, under the guise of an exercise of the police power is that it forces the owner to assume the cost of providing a benefit to the public without recoupment. There is no attempt to share the cost of the benefit among those benefited, that is, society at large. Instead, the accident of ownership determines who shall bear the cost initially. Of course, as further consequence, the ultimate economic cost of providing the benefit is hidden from those who in a democratic society are given the power of deciding whether or not they wish to obtain the benefit despite the ultimate economic cost, however initially distributed (Dunham, Legal and Economic Basis for Planning, 58 Col. L. Rev. 650, 665). In other words, the removal from productive use of private property has an ultimate social cost more easily concealed by imposing the cost on the owner alone. When successfully concealed, the public is not likely to have any objection to the "cost-free" benefit.

In this case, the zoning amendment is unreasonable and, therefore, unconstitutional because, without due process of law, it deprives the owner of all his property rights, except the bare title and a dubious future reversion of full use. The amendment renders the park property unsuitable for any reasonable income productive or other private use for which it is adapted and thus destroys its economic value and deprives plaintiff of its security for its mortgages. Indeed, as Rathkopf has characterized it, the case is an "extreme example" of a deprivation (1 Rathkopf, . . . [Law of Zoning and Planning, 4th Ed.] at p. 6-55; contra Marcus, Mandatory Development Rights Transfer and the Taking Clause: The Case of Manhattan's Tudor City Parks, 24 Buffalo L. Rev. 77, 93-94, 105).

It is recognized that the "value" of property is not a concrete or tangible attribute but an abstraction derived from the economic uses to which the property may be put. Thus, the development rights are an essential component of the value of the underlying property because they constitute some of the economic uses to which the property may be put. As such, they are a potentially valuable and even a transferable commodity and may not be disregarded in determining whether the ordinance has destroyed the economic value of the underlying property. . . .

Of course, the development rights of the parks were not nullified by the city's action. In an attempt to preserve the rights they were severed from the real property and made transferable to another section of mid-Manhattan in the city, but not to any particular parcel or place. There was thus created floating development rights, utterly unusable until they could be attached to some accommodating real property, available by happenstance of prior ownership, or by grant, purchase, or devise, and subject to the contingent approvals of administrative agencies. In such case, the development rights, disembodied abstractions of man's ingenuity, float in a limbo until restored to reality by reattachment to tangible real property. Put another way, it is a tolerable abstraction to consider development rights apart from the solid land from which as a matter of zoning law they derive. But severed, the development rights are a double abstraction until they are actually attached to a receiving parcel, yet to be identified, acquired, and subject to the contingent future approvals of administrative agencies, events which may never happen because of the exigencies of the market and the contingencies and exigencies of administrative action. The acceptance of this contingency-ridden arrangement, however, was mandatory under the amendment.

The problem with this arrangement, as Mr. Justice Waltemade so wisely observed at Special Term, is that it fails to assure preservation of the very real economic value of the development rights as they existed when still attached to the underlying property (77 Misc.2d 199, 201, 352 N.Y.S.2d 762, 764). By compelling the owner to enter an unpredictable real estate market to find a suitable receiving lot for the rights, or a purchaser who would then share the same interest in using additional development rights, the amendment renders uncertain and thus severely impairs the value of the development rights before they were severed (see Note, The Unconstitutionality of Transferable Development Rights, 84 Yale L.J. 1101, 1110-1111). Hence, when viewed in relation to both the value of the private parks after the amendment, and the value of the development rights detached from the private parks, the amendment destroyed the economic value of the property. It thus constituted a deprivation of property without due process of law.

None of this discussion of the effort to accomplish the highly beneficial purposes of creating additional park land in the teeming city bears any relation to other schemes, variously described as a "development bank" or the "Chicago Plan" (see Costonis, The Chicago Plan: Incentive Zoning and the Preservation of Urban Landmarks, 85 Harv. L. Rev. 574; Costonis, Development Rights Transfer: An Exploratory Essay, 83 Yale L.J. 75, 86-87). For under such schemes or variations of them, the owner of the granting parcel may be allowed just compensation for his development rights, instantly and in money, and the acquired development rights are then placed in a "bank" from which enterprises may for a price purchase development rights to use on land owned by them. Insofar as the owner of the granting parcel is concerned, his development rights are taken by the State, straightforwardly, and he is paid just compensation for them in eminent domain. The appropriating governmental entity recoups its disbursements, when, as, and if it obtains a purchaser for those rights. In contrast, the 1972 zoning amendment short-circuits the double-tracked compensation scheme but to do this leaves the granting parcel's owner's development rights in limbo until the day of salvation, if ever it comes.

With respect to damages caused by the unlawful zoning amendment the issue is not properly before the court. The owner never made such an unequivocal claim and still does not. Instead, it claims compensation for value appropriated as for an "inverse" taking in eminent domain. The mortgagees and personal guarantor make parallel claims. That view of the invalid amendment is not adopted for the reasons discussed at length earlier. The city, on the other hand, seeks a declaration with respect to such damages, but in the absence of allegation or proof that such damages lie, are claimed, or how they have been incurred, there can be no abstract declaration, and therefore there is none.

It would be a misreading of the discussion above to conclude that the court is insensitive to the inescapable need for government to devise methods, other than by outright appropriation of the fee, to meet urgent environmental needs of a densely concentrated urban population. It would be equally simplistic to ignore modern recognition of the principle that no property has value except as the community contributes to that value. The obverse of this principle is, therefore, of first significance: no property is an economic island, free from contributing to the welfare of the whole of which it is but a dependent part. The limits are that unfair or disproportionate burdens may not, constitutionally, be placed on single properties or their owners. The possible solutions undoubtedly lie somewhere in the areas of general taxation, assessments for public benefit (but with an expansion of the traditional views with respect to what are assessable public benefits), horizontal eminent domain illustrated by a true "taking" of development rights with corresponding compensation, development banks, and other devices which will insure rudimentary fairness in the allocation of economic burdens.

Solutions must be reached for the problems of modern zoning, urban and rural conservation, and last but not least landmark preservations, whether by particular buildings or historical districts. Unfortunately, the land planners are now only at the beginning of the path to solution. In the process of traversing that path further, new ideas and new standards of constitutional tolerance must and will evolve. It is enough to say that the loose-ended transferable development rights in this case fall short of achieving a fair allocation of economic burden. Even though the development rights have not been nullified, their severance has rendered their value so uncertain and contingent, as to deprive the property owner of their practical usefulness, except under rare and perhaps coincidental circumstances.

The legislative and administrative efforts to solve the zoning and landmark problem in modern society demonstrate the presence of ingenuity. . . . That ingenuity further pursued will in all likelihood achieve the goals without placing an impossible or unsuitable burden on the individual property owner, the public fisc, or the general taxpayer. These efforts are entitled to and will undoubtedly receive every encouragement. The task is difficult but not beyond management. The end is essential but the means must nevertheless conform to constitutional standards.

Accordingly, the order of the Appellate Division should be affirmed, without costs, and the certified question answered in the affirmative.

JASEN, GABRIELLI, JONES, WACHTLER, FUCHSBERG and COOKE, JJ., concur.

Order affirmed, etc.

Comments: 1. The *French* case is discussed in Costonis, *Fred F. French Investing Co. v. City of New York:* Losing a Battle But Winning a War, 28 Land Use L. & Zoning Dig. no. 7, at 6 (1976). Costonis notes Judge Breitel's recognition that development rights in land have economic value and may be transferred to other parcels. He also notes Judge Breitel's comment that land use control devices such as TDR must achieve "rudimentary fairness in the allocation of economic burdens," and asks whether the *French* decision bars all mandatory TDR programs. Costonis concludes that "it is the market that will establish whether development rights are a marketable commodity, like land, or, instead, a 'double abstraction,' of interest to metaphysicians perhaps but not to hard headed realtors." *Id.* at 8.

The discussion of the taking issue in the *French* case should also be compared with the analysis of this question in the historic preservation cases, *supra*. Is *French* consistent with these cases? Does the *French* case suggest that the preservation of historic landmarks will never be acceptable under the police power? If historic preservation under the police power is acceptable, to what extent is TDR needed or necessary? Note that the New York court's view of the compensability of over-restrictive land use regulation is consistent with the California view. *See supra* p. 252.

2. A mandatory TDR plan was also part of the landmarks designation program considered in the *Penn Central* case, *supra* p. 149. In order to forestall claims that the landmark designation of Grand Central Terminal was unconstitutional, the city had authorized the transfer of development rights from the Terminal site to adjoining properties, some of them owned by Penn Central. The TDR program was extensively considered in the state court decision, 366 N.E.2d 1271 (N.Y. 1977).

The highest New York court, again in an opinion by Judge Breitel, upheld the TDR program in this case with the following comments:

> Development rights, once transferred, may not be equivalent in value to development rights on the original site. But that, alone, does not mean that the substitution of rights amounts to a deprivation of property without due process of law. Land use regulation often diminishes the value of the property to the landowner. Constitutional standards, however, are offended only when that diminution leaves the owner with no reasonable use of the property. The situation with transferable development rights is analogous. If the substitute rights received provide reasonable compensation for a landowner forced to relinquish development rights on a landmark site, there has been no deprivation of due process. The compensation need not be the "just" compensation required in eminent domain, for there has been no attempt to take property. . . .
>
> The case at bar, like the *French* case, . . . fits neatly into this analysis. In *French* the development rights on the original site were quite valuable. The regulations deprived the original site of any possibility of producing a reasonable return, since only park uses were permitted on the land. And, the transferable development rights were left in legal limbo, not readily attachable to any other property, due to a lack of common ownership of the rights and a suitable site for using them. Hence, plaintiffs were deprived of property without due process of law. The regulation of Grand Central Terminal, by contrast, permitted productive use of the terminal site as it had been used for more than half a century, as a railroad terminal. In addition, the development rights were made transferable to numerous sites in the vicinity of the terminal, several owned by Penn Central, and at least one or two suitable for construction of office buildings. Since this regulation and substitution was reasonable, no due process violation resulted.

Id. at 1278.

Little consideration was given to the TDR program in the United States Supreme Court because the court found that no taking had occurred. The court did note that the transferable development rights might not have constituted just compensation if a taking had occurred, but added that these rights mitigated whatever financial burdens the landmark designation imposed and were to be taken into account in considering the impact of this regulation. *Id.* at —.

3. What further light does the *Penn Central* case shed on the "fairness" that Judge Breitel requires in TDR programs? In a speech commenting on his *French* and *Penn Central* opinions, Judge Breitel noted that in TDR programs "it becomes fairly clear that, to the extent that they [the transferable development rights — Eds.] are necessary to compensate the owner of the original site, they must be either in cash, acceptable in kind, or be sufficiently translatable into cash." Breitel, A Judicial View of Transferable Development Rights, 30 Land Use L. & Zoning Dig., no. 2, at 5, 6 (1978). He then distinguishes the two cases as follows:

> In the *Fred F. French* case, the owner at one point had been offered a tremendous price for those development rights somewhere else in mid-Manhattan. But by the time the case was decided, mid-Manhattan was terribly overbuilt and the value of the TDRs had dropped. That really isn't an accidental circumstance. This is the nature of our economy. This is the reason why the TDR transfers were found insufficient in *Fred F. French* and why, on the other hand, we found them of some value in *Penn Central*.

Id. Judge Breitel also notes, apparently with reference to *Penn Central*, that the neighboring properties were so profitable in their present use that development rights transferred to those properties would have to be heavily discounted. Nevertheless, he adds that if TDR is going to be accepted "we have to abandon the fiction or pretense that we are going to give the owner of the original site full value of that part which we take away from him, let alone the full fee interest; and, . . . that the TDR is not even going to come anywhere close to the exploitative value of the air rights over his land." *Id.* at 5.

Professor Costonis does not believe that the two cases can be distinguished:

> Moreover, both programs were mandatory in effect, both authorized the splitting of development rights, and both offered transfer districts which contained numerous sites suitable for development of the type desired. Indeed, the transfer rights in. . .[the *French* case] were potentially more valuable than those in. . .[*Penn Central*] because the transfer district was much larger and enjoyed median land values twice those of the parks themselves. . . . The two situations differed only in that the Tudor Parks owner, although a leading New York realtor-developer, apparently did not itself own land within the transfer district. While this difference may have made sale or use of the rights somewhat more problematic, it hardly negated their value, as evidenced by the "substantial offer" that the developer received for them.

Costonis, The Disparity Issue: A Context For the Grand Control Terminal Division, 91 Harv. L. Rev. 402, 419-20 (1977).

4. Simulated market analysis of TDR plans casts additional light on the extent to which the value of TDR's will fully compensate owners who are restricted from the full development of their land in TDR programs. For one such analysis see Berry & Steiker, An Economic Analysis of Transfer of Development Rights, 17 Nat. Resources J. 55 (1977). The authors apply their analysis to a New Jersey-type TDR system, see *supra* p. 948, in which the entire jurisdiction is subject to a TDR program and no development may occur without the purchase of development rights from landowners in areas restricted from development. The authors are skeptical that the transfer value of development rights under this kind of system will provide adequate compensation to owners of restricted land. A number of factors will determine whether exchange values for these rights will fully compensate these restricted owners: "[T]he revenues generated and costs associated with development, the amount of land put in the no-growth zone, and the number of development rights created." *Id.* at 73. However, if applied on a limited scale, as in site-to-site transfer situations such as those contemplated in the *French* and *Penn Central* cases, the exchange value of development rights can be expected to approach full compensation so long as the local land market is relatively active. *Id.*

The authors also note that in order for the exchange value of development rights to yield sufficient compensation to restricted owners the supply of those rights must be carefully managed with reference to the market demand for those rights. This kind of management requires public intervention to withhold rights from the market:

> The withholding action may be by 1) public purchase of development rights at some "parity price," 2) refusing to give out (or create) all the development rights in the first place, or 3) only the agency selling development rights and limiting sales so as to gain a high rent; the monopolist would then distribute the rents to the landowners in the no-growth zone in proportion to their losses of exchange value. All three remedies require administrative costs and the first requires a large initial expenditure (or bond issue) before substantial revenue from sales can be obtained.

Id. at 64, n. 23. Note that management problems may be serious even in a site-to-site TDR program aimed at protecting historic landmarks. As the number of landmarks protected by the program increases, the impact of the sale of development rights from these landmarks on the land market will also increase and substantial public management may be necessary in order to guarantee full compensation to restricted landmark owners. *See also* Field & Conrad, *supra* p. 953.

5. Another problem arising in the transfer of development rights to preserve historic landmarks in inner city areas arises from the fact that many zoning ordinances presently allow bonus increases in density to developers in return for providing street-level amenities, such as open plazas. These bonus systems are discussed *supra* p. 415. TDR plans attempt to overcome this problem by allowing marginal increases in site coverage at the transfer site as well as height increases, which are often the compensating bonus under density bonus ordinances. *See* J. Costonis, Space Adrift 95 (1974). Some incentive of this type appears necessary if the acquisition of development rights is to be made attractive to owners at transfer sites, but it creates new design complications:

Although the increased density permitted might be offset by the open space and amenity provided by the landmark, it is difficult to justify the density increase [by the landmark amenity]. . . when the landmark and the transferee site are physically distant. Unless strict limitations on such increases in site coverage are included in the transfer plan, design abuses that will aggravate the congestion and aridity of urban core areas are certain to result.

Note, Development Rights Transfer and Landmarks Preservation — Providing a Sense of Orientation, 9 Urb. L. Ann. 131, 154 (1975).

6. The literature on TDR is massive and growing. For additional discussion of proposed TDR plans see *Space Adrift, supra,* which discusses the proposed Chicago plan for landmark preservation; J. Costonis & R. DeVoy, The Puerto Rico Plan: Environmental Protection Through Development Rights Transfer (1975); Merriam, Making TDR Work, 56 N.C.L. Rev. 77 (1978); Rose, A Proposal for the Separation and Marketability of Development Rights as a Technique to Preserve Open Space, 51 J. Urb. L. 461 (1974). *See also* The Transfer of Development Rights: A New Technique of Land Use Regulation (J. Rose ed. 1975); Transferable Development Rights, *supra.*

E. LAND BANKING AND VALUE RECAPTURE

1. Land Banking

Difficulties in implementing comprehensive planning policies through zoning and other land use regulations have long spurred suggestions that public agencies simply acquire land intended for development and make it available on the private market in accordance with planning policies when the time comes to develop it. An illustrative hypothetical will indicate the problem and the solution:

> A comprehensive plan for a developing suburban area has designated several hundred acres near a highway interchange for industrial development. Much of that acreage is owned by a "speculator" who is waiting for land values to rise and who refuses to sell to an industrial developer who is interested in the tract. In desperation, the industrial developer seeks a rezoning for industrial use on another tract in an area designated by the plan for agricultural use. The county council reluctantly agrees and this land is rezoned industrial. Later, the speculator who owns most of the land at the industrial site designated by the plan sells for a healthy profit.

This kind of land use tragedy highlights the problems with conventional planning and land use control that have led to proposals for land banking systems. Under the land banking approach, a public land banking agency would acquire the designated industrial site from the unwilling speculator and resell or lease it to a developer who would carry out the plan's intentions.

Speculative profits would be forestalled and the policies of the plan would be carried out.

Land banking can also serve more specialized functions. A local housing agency, for example, faced with ever increasing prices for land needed for low-income housing, could acquire land in advance of its actual need, bank it, and use it for low-income housing development at some future time.

Land banking is not without its critics, who claim that limitations inherent in land market processes and the administration of a land banking system make its goals difficult to achieve. The following selection outlines the nature of a land banking system, discusses some of its legal problems, and points out some of its difficulties.

H. FRANKLIN, D. FALK, & A. LEVIN, IN-ZONING: A GUIDE FOR POLICY-MAKERS ON INCLUSIONARY LAND USE PROGRAMS 180-81, 183-84, 187-94 (1974)

DEFINING LAND BANKING

One of the major problems involved in trying to deal with the practical issues involved in land banking is the lack of specificity in defining the term. Broadly speaking, it can be applied to every form of acquisition of rights in real property in contemplation of some future use. It has been applied to activity by private parties, quasi-public organizations, and public bodies; it has been used to refer to acquisition of a few parcels and to the acquisition of the bulk of the land in a metropolitan area; its described purposes have been many and varied.

For the purpose here, land banking is defined only as a direct *public* activity, leaving aside purposeful large-scale land acquisitions by the private sector, such as that involved in new town development or major subdivisions. It also leaves aside such quasi-public activity by some foundations that assist public acquisition of land for conservation purposes.

Second, land banking for this purpose is concerned only with *undeveloped* land, leaving aside urban renewal activities concerned with redevelopment of blighted but predominantly built-up areas. Although some activities in the urban renewal program are directly analogous to those proposed for land banking and provide excellent operational guidance, many problems associated with redevelopment differ considerably from those involved in new development.

Finally, for clarity it is necessary to make some simplifying assumptions about the many possible purposes of land banking and consider it in only two categories:

1. Special-purpose land banking. This would encompass those forms of advanced land acquisition where the objective is to acquire land at lower prices for a specific public purpose or to preempt development of such land by others. It may range from comparatively small-scale activities such as acquiring sites for future fire stations or schools in advance of actual need, to major acquisitions of open-space areas or airport sites. It might also include acquisition of sites for future housing construction. In general, special-purpose land banking involves public participation in the private land market for public purposes rather than an attempt to change the nature of that private market. In cases where the amount of land acquired is large, or where the facility to be developed will enhance nearby land values, special-purpose land banking may have unintended spillover effects on the values and uses of land in a fairly wide area surrounding it. It is a rare large-scale land acquisition program where commencement of purchasing activities does not drive up asking prices. But for the most part, special-purpose land banking, because it is done on a small scale in relation to the relevant land market, does not have this effect.

2. General land banking. This would encompass a program aimed at acquiring large areas of land in an urban area without regard to specific future use, with the intent of controlling the nature and pattern of development and/or the price of land. Such a program, in effect, seeks to influence significantly the land market. How much land would be needed to achieve this purpose is totally a matter of conjecture. In Sweden, with an ongoing land banking process and a rigid system of development controls, the land banks aim to maintain an inventory equal to the amount of land required for five years of development. In this country, it has been suggested that the amount of land needed for an effective general land bank might be as much as 60% of the developable land in an urban area. . . .

THE DUALITY OF GOALS IN GENERAL LAND BANKING

Almost without exception, proposals for *general* land banking have been justified as:
     —providing for a more orderly process of urban growth, and
     —controlling the inflation of urban land prices.
Inherent in any general land banking proposal concerned with more orderly development is an intent to withhold some portion of an area's developable land from the market while only the "appropriate" land is released. Land price is in some substantial but still poorly understood way a function of the interaction of the supply of building sites with the demand for them, and this discussion is intended to suggest where analysis is needed rather than to imply that answers are readily available.

The problem is dynamic rather than static and will vary from one urban area to another. In the early years of a general land banking operation, it would be necessary to acquire land to create a working inventory — an action with potential land price inflationary effects. At some later point, when an adequate working inventory is acquired, land would be released for development, presumably at a rate equal to full market demand — with reduced inflationary effects.

Some general land banking proposals have recognized this problem, at least from the point of view of the costs of starting a land banking operation. They suggest that the initial accumulation of land be done beyond the present edge of suburban development, where prices have not yet risen to reflect urban values. This is, of course, quite a long-term view, since prices tend to reflect urban values many years in advance of actual development.

Under a program aimed at land price reduction, the bank would presumably acquire land almost randomly, without regard to growth or public facility plans, but hopefully selecting those parcels that offered the best "bargain" in terms of the relationship of present price to future value. During the acquisition phase, some increased price inflation in the rest of the market might have to be accepted. But when the bank had acquired a sufficient inventory to influence the market, it could then dispose of some of its land inventory at its cost, or at least at a price somewhat below going market price. Presumably it could undercut the private market because of the lower holding costs to a public agency and the absence of need for a speculative markup. . . .

THE AMERICAN LEGAL BASIS FOR LAND BANKING

To carry out a program of land banking, the organization involved must be legally empowered to acquire land, hold it, dispose of it, or use it itself. In the case of organizations that are not general-purpose units of government, the question of whether they have these powers must be answered by looking at statutory charters or articles of incorporation. However, powers granted in a charter may still be subject to legal questioning. Thus, a special-purpose organization might be granted the power of condemnation, but the actual use of such power may be subject to court test of its relationship to the purpose in the statute or charter. . . .

For general-purpose units of government, the earliest doctrines of common law generally held such powers to be an inherent part of sovereignty. But beginning with the Magna Carta and continuing through the Fifth and Fourteenth Amendments to the United States Constitution, that right has been subject to the requirements of due process and just compensation. The Fifth Amendment discusses the taking of property for "public use," which under early court decisions was confined to functions common to nineteenth century governmental activities. However, since the turn of the twentieth century, and particularly since the enactment of state urban renewal statutes and the later U.S. Supreme Court decision in *Berman* v. *Parker,* [348 U.S. 26 (1954)] in which the constitutionality of the District of Columbia urban renewal program was upheld, the courts have shown an increasing tendency to change the concept of direct "public use" to one of "public purpose." In this formulation, public purpose is a far broader concept.

The critical legal question for large-scale land banking is the extent to which the courts would uphold the use of the power of condemnation in order to assemble large tracts of land where the acquisition was intended to influence growth extrinsic to the land acquired. Although it is possible to conceive of limited types of land banking activities being carried out without this type of authority, it is not at all likely that land banking could be carried out on a sufficient scale to control urban growth or affect land prices without eminent domain powers.

In reviewing the trend of judicial opinion as it moved from "public use" to "public purpose" it becomes clear that favorable rulings on the use of condemnation power contain one or more of the following three elements:

1. The elimination of some specific evil. In the early urban renewal cases, the elimination of existing slum conditions as a danger to public health and safety was the overriding public purpose. This was coupled with the premise that slum conditions had to be treated on an area basis rather than just individual structures. In some cases involving predominantly undeveloped areas, the elimination of blighting conditions (such as unsound platting, clouded titles, etc.) that inhibited the proper development of the area were found to be a valid public purpose to justify the use of condemnation.

2. The presence of a plan (itself meeting the test of valid public purpose) involving significant changes to the area. This element is present in cases involving the use of condemnation for the prevention of future slum conditions. In cases involving direct public use, the courts have raised questions about the degree of futurity of the use and the specificity of the public purpose. Thus, condemnations have been upheld when the public use would occur within the decade, but have been invalidated when the public use was not likely for 30 years. [See the discussion of advance acquisition of land, *supra* p. —. — Eds.] Equally, condemnation has been upheld where the public uses were general in nature (i.e., specific plans were not yet completed) as long as a distinction could be made with situations where the use was only probable and for some remote, indefinite, or future use.

3. The establishment of a compatible environment near other public projects. In these cases the courts have held that takings in excess of immediate needs may be justified where necessary to promote the efficient use of the public facility or where they are incidental to the principal purposes of the project. Under this doctrine, public purpose could be found in acquiring land surrounding a reservoir or an airport to protect that use.

Given these lines of judicial opinion, it would seem clear that the use of condemnation in connection with land banking would have to be dependent upon the existence of some publicly-approved development plan. Just how specific that plan would have to be as to use, timing, and feasibility is open to question; however, the very need for such a plan might have a profound effect on the strategies and methods employed. Thus, those strategies that suggest land banking acquisition beyond the urbanizing fringe might well be infeasible because of the difficulty of producing the kind of plan that might legally be required — needs and uses would lie too far into the future to be acceptable. . . .

But the foregoing analysis is essentially speculative since no case deals specifically with a public effort to use the powers of condemnation to acquire a reserve of land for indefinite future development. However, there does exist one case that is tantalizingly close, but with enough significant differences to make its value as a precedent questionable.

In establishing the Land Administration in Puerto Rico, it was given broad powers to acquire land, including the use of the powers of condemnation. The latter was subject to only one substantive limitation — any land acquired by condemnation must be put to its intended use within 15 years from the date of acquisition. When one such acquisition by condemnation was contested in *Commonwealth of Puerto Rico v. Rosso,* [95 P.R.R. 488 (1967), *appeal dismissed,* 393 U.S. 14 (1968) — Eds.] the Supreme Court of Puerto Rico found that the grant of such powers was legal and appropriate. However, in doing so the court relied heavily on the finding of fact of the legislative assembly which, in part, stated:

> (a) That the Commonwealth of Puerto Rico is one of the most densely populated areas in the world; that urban lands, or lands adapted to urban development, are monopolized and kept unused by their owners, which creates an artificial shortage of land and raises its price . . . that the relative speedy rise in the price of land increases differences in income, inasmuch as unused land in Puerto Rico, both urban and rural, is controlled, to a large extent, by a small number of persons; . . .

Since density, land holding practices, or other social and economic problems in many parts of the United States differ from those of Puerto Rico, legislative findings of fact to support the use of condemnation for general land banking purposes would require more comprehensive investigation of the facts in urban areas. . . .

LAND COSTS AND FINANCING OF LAND BANKS

Whatever its form or purpose, land banking may be an expensive operation. While the potential benefits may justify such outlays, it is important that they be identified and, in the case of any operational decision, be quantified as precisely as possible. Because there are so many variables, and because there is no empirical experience (other than that with urban renewal), only the most general description is possible. Other than administrative costs, the basic cost is land and its carrying cost.

Depending on location, demand, etc., land prices can range from 25 cents a square foot to $600 a square foot, and short of current appraisals of the specific parcels involved, there is little chance of making any reasonable advance estimates. Even with current appraisals, there is a long history in public land purchases in which actual costs exceeded estimates by large margins. In the early years of a land banking operation, this would clearly be the largest cost involved, although in later years the carrying costs may very well exceed purchases. To the extent that purchases are projected in the future, an inflation factor of about 10% a year, compounded, must be included. The price of the land should also include such transaction costs as fees, commissions, title search, etc.

During the period between the time a land bank pays for land acquired and the time it receives payment on disposition, there is an ongoing cost of interest on the capital involved. If it is borrowed capital, the interest cost is an out-of-pocket expense; if it is donated capital (such as a federal community development grant), the interest cost is just as real even though it is only imputed. The proper rate of interest to be considered is of course complex, depending on such variables as length of financing, whether interest payments to lenders are exempt from federal income tax, nature of security or guarantee on debt, etc. It is also highly variable with the conditions of the capital market, which in recent times has been unsettled.

Unless a land bank were specifically exempt, it would have to pay property taxes on all land it owned. If it were exempt, the governments in the areas in which it did own land would be subsidizing it to the extent of foregone taxes. In either case, the property tax is a real cost irrespective of who bears it. A number of observers have suggested that nationally undeveloped land is taxed at a rate of about 2% of value. In those rare cases where assessments on undeveloped land are close to real value, this figure could be much higher.

While not absolutely essential to the simplest concepts of land banking, in all probability a land bank would want to engage to some extent in making improvements on the land it held in inventory in order to enhance its value at disposition. Such costs should be considered.

Offsetting these costs [is] the possibility of some revenue generating operations; e.g., leasing land in the inventory for farming until it is needed for development. However, the range of such activities is fairly limited and it is not likely that there would be significant revenues.

The financial planning for a land bank must be considered in two phases — the buildup of operating inventory and actual operations. During the inventory acquisition phase, there will be a continuing need for additional new investment with little, if any, offsetting revenue from the sale of land. The duration of this period is problematical. In the Swedish experience, there was frequently a 30-year gap between the period when land was first purchased and when it was ultimately developed; in the American urban renewal experience with large projects, a 10-year gap between the beginning of acquisition and significant disposition is not unusual.

Whether or not advance land acquisition (either as general or special-purpose land banking) is financially justifiable may depend on the strategies and methods used and particularly on the relationship between "holding" costs (interest, taxes, and administrative overhead) and the time elapsing between original purchase and disposition or use. This financial justification is particularly important for special-purpose land banking since one of the main rationales for carrying out such a program is to acquire the land at lower cost through advance purchase. The calculation involved is essentially that of compound interest, or the readily available tables of compound interest. For example, using an estimate of 8% per year holding cost (a very low level in terms of current economic conditions) and a parcel of land costing $100,000, the true cost would be:

in five years	$146,932
in 10 years	215,892
in 15 years	317,216
in 20 years	466,094
in 25 years	684,844

Obviously, errors in forecasting when the land will actually be sold or used, or changes in general economic conditions, can have great consequences on financial justification.

Because the financial justification is so important to special-purpose land banking, it is worth presenting an example of the financial consequences. Suppose such an organization contemplated the purchase of a tract of land currently available at $100,000 which it did not anticipate using for five years. Using an estimated holding cost of 8% per year, it would have to determine that it could not procure the same tract or a comparable one for less than $146,932 when the land would actually be needed. If unforeseen delays put off use for one additional year, the estimated future value would have to be $158,687. If changes in economic conditions resulted in the holding cost rising to 9%, the five-year estimate for comparable land would have to be $153,862, and the six-year estimate would have to be $167,709. These are, of course, minimal variations in potential costs. If a 10-year lag between purchase and use and a 10 percent effective holding cost is assumed, then the estimated future value of the land would have to be $259,374 to justify current purchase for use a decade later.

For organizations contemplating special-purpose land banking, an additional calculation may be necessary that far overrides any estimate of profit or loss from advance land acquisition. Essentially, it must be assumed that any such organization is short of resources (or at least feels so) and must make its decisions in terms of comparatively short-term goals and objectives. Thus, an organization concerned with the development of housing for low-income families might find that by investing part of its resources in low-cost land now it could hope to be in a far better position to provide such housing five years from now. Leaving aside the question of whether the saving would be real or just conjectural, the question would be: (a) should it use its current resources to provide housing now, or (b) reduce its current activities to provide more and better housing in the future. Faced with this choice, most organizations could be expected to choose the short-term objective unless the savings were sure and large. This is the type of question rarely raised in the existing literature, but clearly one that will greatly influence operational decision-making.

Comments: 1. Two major legal problems associated with land banking are discussed by the *In-Zoning* analysis: legal authority to engage in land banking and the constitutionality of land banking programs. Legal authority should not be troublesome for special purpose land banking by public agencies; it can be implied from existing legislation conferring land acquisition powers or can easily be added to existing legislative grants of authority.

General land banking is another matter. As an entirely new governmental program, it would require comprehensive enabling legislation. For a general land banking legislative proposal see American Law Institute, A Model Land Development Code Art. 6 (1976). Under the ALI proposal, the general land banking authority is lodged with a state agency. A regional agency is another possibility, but conferring general land banking authority on a county or municipality may create implementation problems. Because the local government is limited in jurisdiction, its land banking operations will not be able to include a sufficient segment of the land market.

The constitutionality of general land banking is not as troublesome as the above analysis would suggest, nor does it appear that general land banking would be constitutional as serving a public purpose only if it implements a comprehensive plan. In *Vermont Home Mortgage Credit Agency v. Montpelier Nat'l Bank*, 262 A.2d 445 (Vt. 1970), the court considered the constitutionality of the agency's enabling legislation, which authorized it to stimulate housing development by purchasing home mortgages from banks and savings and loan associations. The statute was sustained, in part, because the court recognized that imperfections in the housing market justified state intervention. "[W]e recognize that rising costs of money, here and elsewhere, have placed capital funds for home construction in critically short supply." Similarly, imperfections in the land use market that impede the successful implementation of planning policies should justify a land banking program adopted to overcome these market problems.

2. Judicial receptiveness to the constitutionality of land banking legislation will also be assisted by a legislative declaration of purpose, which the courts tend to respect. See the ALI code, § 6-101. In addition, it would seem that the enabling legislation should sufficiently describe the purpose of the land banking program so that there will be some guarantee that appropriate public purposes will be served. The ALI code provides: "[T]he State Land Reserve Agency shall adopt by rule . . . a land reserve policy describing the general purposes for which it intends to acquire, hold and dispose of land under this Article." § 6-103(1). Note that this approach leaves the determination of land banking policies to the land banking agency, and does not resolve the possibly conflicting objectives of land banking described by the *In-Zoning* selection. The policy problem is dumped in the agency's lap. It is possible that a court faced with deciding the constitutionality of a land banking statute might require a more specific indication of the scope of the land banking program. How would you draft such a statute?

3. A court asked to decide the constitutionality of a land banking statute, and a legislature asked to enact one, may wish to inquire further about the advantages of a land banking program and possible obstacles to the program's success. This inquiry would better help determine whether there is a public interest in the land banking program that justifies enactment of the legislation and a favorable court decision on its constitutionality. After all, if the purpose of a land banking program is simply to substitute public for private speculation in the land market, both a court and a legislature might balk.

The advantages of a land banking program are outlined in some detail in Fitch & Mack, Land Banking in The Good Earth of America 134, 142-45 (L. Harriss ed. 1974). These advantages can be summarized as follows:

Better planned development is possible because land banking can secure more beneficial locations for development and reduce the price of land made available for development. Public services should be more efficient and should cost less because a public agency will control the availability of sites for new development. Better planned development should lead in turn to improvements in aesthetic and environmental quality. Finally, through a land banking system land can be set aside to meet the housing needs of lower income families.

4. There have been several critiques of land banking that are more skeptical. *See, e.g.,* S. Kamm, Land Banking: Public Policy Alternatives and Dilemmas (Urban Institute, 1970). These criticisms are summarized in Davis, Issues in Municipal Public Land Banking, Annals of Regional Sci., Nov. 1976, at 55. Davis first considers the theoretical advantages to the public sector in the land assembly process:

> It is frequently argued that the public sector possesses certain financial advantages over the private sector in the process of land assembly. . . . These. . .are: a) economies of scale. . ., b) expropriation power. . ., c) lower holding costs. . ., and d) lower risk. . . . In regard to the first of these arguments, it is difficult to imagine what economies of scale exist in the process of land assembly itself. Such economies undoubtedly exist in the servicing of raw land, but of course these economies can be captured by the public sector through large-scale servicing operations regardless of whether actual ownership of the land is in private or public hands.

Id. at 56. Davis also makes the point about holding costs that was made in the *In-Zoning* selection. Other critics have also made the point, well-known to those familiar with public land acquisition practices, that "governments are likely ultimately to offer a price at the upper end of an uncertain price range to avoid the inconvenience, cost and adverse publicity of an expropriation, and/or an expropriational appeal." Carr & Smith, Public Land Banking and the Price of Land, 51 Land Econ. 316, 317 (1975).

Davis next points out that sales of land for development by the land banking agency at below-market prices do not necessarily lead to a net aggregate gain:

> By selling lots for less than could be obtained in the market, the city foregoes increased revenues. Had it chosen otherwise, the city could have employed these additional funds to provide new or additional services or to finance existing services, thus permitting a decrease in taxes. In either case, the cost of the subsidy to the lot purchasers is borne principally by the urban citizenry as a whole, either as consumers of public services or as taxpayers.

Id. at 58. Davis might have added that if public funds are devoted to tax decreases as an alternative to land banking, the tax decrease would be capitalized in land values and lead to an increase in land prices. The land banking program may also increase land prices, however. Especially if the land banking agency begins its program by acquiring a large land inventory quickly, this competitive pressure on the land supply may cause the price of land not acquired by the agency to rise. Carr & Smith, *supra* at 328. In this event, the land banking program will not lead to price savings, especially since the land banking agency must later buy into the market at prices artificially inflated by its own market operations.

Davis also questions whether speculation in the land market is necessarily detrimental:

> Speculative activity can be beneficial to the process of efficient allocation of the land to its highest and best use by raising the price to a level at which improvements to the land for less valuable uses

to society are economically unfeasible. In the hands of the
speculator the land remains vacant or under agricultural use from
which it can be readily converted to urban uses at a point in the
future when demand for the land has increased.

Id. at 61.

Speculation can be detrimental in the land market if speculators exercise
oligopolistic control, holding land to realize maximum capital gains and not
selling when conversion to developmental uses is optimal. In this situation,
the intervention of the land bank can be beneficial. It will be difficult and
costly, however, to determine when market conditions justify land bank
intervention to control oligopolistic pressures. Carr & Smith, *supra,* also
make this point: "[t]he main rationale for public land banks is the
elimination of oligopolistic pricing. However, this reduces land prices only
if the price reduction from eliminating oligopolistic behavior exceeds the
increase in the competitive price arising from the introduction of the land
bank." *Id.* at 329.

Carr & Smith also question the assumption that the land banking agency
will always purchase land in the "right" places that are consistent with
planning policies and zoning regulations:

> First, in general, zoning and planning decisions involve
> uncertainty both for the public and the private developer. These
> decisions are *not* known at the time of land acquisition either to
> the public or private developer because at that time these decisions
> have not been made. . . . Second, there is really little reason to
> anticipate the government agency will be right more often than
> private developers since the planning and zoning authorities are
> usually independent and the government agency would have no
> more information than private developers. Third, if a planning or
> zoning authority were to make decisions based on the ownership
> of the land rather than its intrinsic merits, development would
> proceed in a disorderly and suboptimal fashion.

Id. at 317-18. (Emphasis in original.)

How would you now appraise the argument sometimes made that a land
banking system will eliminate the windfall and wipeout problem? Consider
that land banking activities at the beginning of the land banking cycle may
raise prices in the market, benefiting those who sell land in the private
sector. Is this a windfall? Later, when the land banking agency begins to
sell land there may be a depressant effect on prices in the private sector.
Is this a wipeout? Can these windfalls and wipeouts be avoided?

5. The criticisms levied at land banking would seem to create a set of
dilemmas for the land banking agency. If the agency undertakes a
small-scale and selective program of land acquisition any detrimental effects
on land prices may be mitigated, but the program may not be extensive
enough to affect the land market. If land acquisition is extensive, the land
market may be influenced by the land banking program but the effects on
land prices may be adverse. If the agency acquires land substantially ahead
of the time when development is expected, it may find that it has made the
wrong choice when the time for development is reached. If the agency
defers land acquisition to a time that is close to the time for development,
it will lose the opportunity to purchase land at a substantially lower price

and will have to forego any land price savings in its land acquisition process. Is there any way out of these dilemmas?

6. To assure that land sold or leased out of a governmental land bank will be developed in accordance with its planning policies, the governmental land banking agency may not wish to rely solely on conventional zoning and subdivision controls. Instead, the land may be sold or leased subject to restrictive covenants designed to implement the applicable planning policies. The enforcement of such restrictive covenants by injunction will present no difficulty if the land is leased, since there will be privity of estate between the lessor and the lessee or its successors in interest and the restrictions will clearly "run" with the leasehold estate. If the land is sold, enforcement of the restrictive covenants against the original purchaser will present no difficulty, but enforcement against subsequent transferees of the land may be more difficult. If the land banking agency owns other land (a "dominant estate") that will be benefited by enforcement of the restrictions — *e.g.,* public park land — enforcement against subsequent transferees of the restricted land will be possible either on the theory that the restriction is an equitable servitude or that it is a covenant "running with the land." But if the land banking agency owns no other land that will be benefited by enforcement of the restrictions (*i.e.,* owns no "dominant estate"), enforcement against successors in interest of the original purchaser may be impossible. Hence it may be necessary to provide by statute that the burden of all restrictions imposed upon the sale of land out of the land bank shall be enforcible against the original purchaser and all successors in interest, whether or not their enforcement will benefit any "dominant estate" owned by the land banking agency.

Another way to assure that restrictions imposed by the land banking agency upon sale of land out of the land bank will be binding is to provide in the deed of conveyance that compliance with these restrictions shall be a condition of the transfer, and that upon any breach of the condition the land banking agency may terminate the estate granted to the purchaser and repossess the land. Such a provision will result in the purchaser's obtaining only a fee simple on a condition subsequent, and the condition will "run with the land" so as to be enforcible against any successor in interest of the original purchaser. Exercise of a power of termination is a drastic method of enforcement, however, and prospective purchasers of land from the land banking agency may be unwilling to take the land subject to a power of termination. Hence it would seem desirable to assure, so far as possible, that land use restrictions imposed by the land banking agency upon sale should be enforcible by injunction.

7. For additional literature on land banking see L. Fitch & R. Mack, Land Banking (1974); H. Flechner, Land Banking in the Control of Urban Development (1974); The Government Land Developers (N. Roberts ed. 1977) (reviews experience in United States and other countries); Note, Public Land Banking: A New Praxis for Urban Growth, 23 Case W. Res. L. Rev. 897 (1972); Comment, Land Banking: New Solutions for Old Problems, 39 Alb. L. Rev. 771 (1975) (discusses ALI proposal). For a discussion of a modified land banking program enacted by recent English legislation see Duerksen, England's Community Land Act: A Yankee's View, 12 Urb. L. Ann. 49 (1976).

2. Value Recapture

One of the purposes of a land bank is to internalize for the public agency the appreciation in land values that occurs as land becomes ripe for urbanization; the objective is to buy cheap and sell dear. An alternative strategy to accomplish the same objective is a tax or charge on the increment in land value that occurs when land is first developed, usually following zoning and related approvals by the local planning and land use control agency. This strategy contemplates that land in urbanizing areas remains in private hands. Rather than recapture the increment in land value through public ownership, the public agency simply taxes it away.

Value recapture generally takes two forms. In a more limited form, the public agency seeks to recapture some or all of the value to land accruing as the result of a public improvement, such as a sewage system or a street improvement. Special assessments levied against the benefits received from the improvement are one form of limited value recapture. *See* D. Mandelker & D. Netsch, State and Local Government in a Federal System 327-53 (1977). Development charges levied under subdivision control ordinances, which shift some of the cost of public improvements on developers, are another limited form of value recapture. *See supra* p. 831.

Value recapture strategies that make use of a development charge on all development of undeveloped land have been tried most conspicuously in Great Britain, where a Labor Government adopted and a Conservative Government then repealed two successive attempts at development charge legislation enacted first in 1947 and then in 1967. A current statutory attempt at levying an across-the-board development charge, the Community Land Act of 1975, is described in Duerksen, England's Community Land Act: A Yankee's View, 12 Urb. L. Ann. 49 (1976).

While a development charge on newly developed land similar to that imposed under the English legislation has never been adopted in this country, the state of Vermont has enacted a capital gains tax on land speculation which, in many ways, approximates the English approach. The Vermont tax, and the rationale under which it is levied, are discussed in the following article:

RECENT DEVELOPMENT, STATE TAXATION — USE OF TAXING POWER TO ACHIEVE ENVIRONMENTAL GOALS, 49 Washington Law Review 1159, 1160-62, 1164-66, 1171-72 (1974)

The land gains tax [Vt. Stat. Ann. tit. 32, § 10001 *et seq.* (Supp. 1977)] applies to gains realized from the sale or exchange of Vermont land held by the seller for less than six years. All sales or exhanges of land are taxable, excepting the first acre or less necessary for the use of the seller's principal residence. Only gains on *land* are taxed. When realty composed of both land and structures is sold, the gains are apportioned between the land and structures on the basis of fair market value; that proportion attributable to structures is not taxed.

Gains are taxed on a sliding-rate scale, the rate increasing directly with percentage of profit and inversely with length of holding period. The maximum tax rate of 60 percent is applied to a gain of 200 percent or more on land held less than one year. The minimum rate, 5 percent, applies to gains of 0-99 percent on land held between 5 and 6 years. When no gain is realized on the sale of land, or the land has been held six years or more, no tax is imposed.

The following example illustrates the operation of the tax. Suppose that a person bought a farm with an old house on it in August 1971 for $100,000 — $90,000 of the purchase price is attributable to the land and $10,000 to the house. Suppose further that he holds it without using it for a residence and sells it in June 1974 for $200,000. His total gain realized from the sale is $100,000. If $15,000 of the sale price is attributable to the house, he realizes a gain of $5,000 on the house, which the land gains statute does not tax; the remaining $95,000 gain is attributable to the land and is subject to the tax. Since the cost basis of the land was $90,000, the seller has realized more than a 100 percent gain upon sale of the land; he also has held it for two years but less than three. Consequently, his land gain is taxed at a 30 percent rate, and he pays $28,500.

A. Regulatory Objectives of the Land Gains Tax

The tax serves both regulatory and revenue-gathering functions. As a regulatory measure it is designed to curb short-term land speculation by limiting the profits available from short-term land sales and hence discouraging rapid turnover of land. This objective is deemed desirable because of the problems resulting from uncontrolled short-term speculation: increased land prices and property taxes, accelerated and inefficient development, loss of community aesthetic wealth and windfall profits.

. . . .

[The article notes that short-term speculation drives up the price of land and thus property taxes, thus forcing local residents out of the land market. Some commentators claim, however, that speculative activity in the market will not necessarily increase land prices. *See, e.g.,* Smith, The Ontario Land Speculation Tax: An Analysis of an Unearned Increment Land Tax, 52 Land Econ. 1, 2-4 (1976). The article also claims that short-term speculative activity accelerates the conversion of agricultural and open space land to urban use because the speculator's use of borrowed money puts pressure on him to sell. Again, this result will not occur if the speculator is holding out for long-term gain. Finally, the article claims that there will be a loss of community aesthetic wealth if the effect of short-term speculation is to force the development of land in aesthetically important areas. As will be noted later, an evaluation of the effects of short-term speculation is essential to an appraisal of the constitutionality of the Vermont land gains tax, since the law turns on the assumption that short-term speculation in land is harmful. Finally, the article considers the windfall profit rationale for the land gains tax, a rationale that underlies all attempts to tax away unearned increment in land value.—Eds.]

The windfall profits problem

While the concept of windfall profits is difficult to define precisely, it is generally used to refer to a gain which exceeds what prevailing standards of economic morality suggest is a fair return from a particular investment or activity. Windfall gain is judged "excessive" by reference to two criteria: the amount of capital or labor expended in the investment or activity, and the amount of social benefit arising from that activity. By the first criterion, a gain is unjustified when it is unearned; by the second, it is unjustified when it is realized without corresponding public benefit, or perhaps at the public expense. This second criterion has been discussed; the first presents a further policy justification for subjecting speculative gains to regulation and recapture.

In a speculative land market, land profits often include an "unearned increment" — an increase in value not attributable to the seller's efforts but to events outside his control. These increases are often called socially created or governmentally created values; typical urban and suburban examples are property value increases due to nearby construction of transit stops or sewer lines. In a rural setting, an increase in value may be created by the existence of undeveloped land or a pastoral landscape at a time of increased demand for rural recreational land. A major goal of land value increment taxation, of which the Vermont tax is but one example, is to minimize this unearned increment or recapture it so that it may inure to the benefit of society generally rather than solely to individuals.

[One important question to be faced in unearned increment tax programs is to determine how the revenues collected by the tax are to be used. One possibility is to use these revenues to support related programs having land use objectives. As one example, they could be set aside for use in an open space purchase program. In Vermont the revenues are used to provide property tax relief to residents, as explained below. Revenues from the tax thus help offset one of the adverse effects thought to flow from short-term speculation — an increase in the property tax burden.—Eds.]

Though land market regulation is a primary purpose of the tax, an equally important objective is to generate revenue for implementation of other state programs. At present, revenue from the tax provides funding for the preparation of statewide property tax maps and partially supports a property tax relief program for landowners with limited income.

. . . .

The land gains tax in Vermont is coordinated with a tax relief plan which incorporates features of progressive taxation. Any resident landowner who pays more than a specified percent of his annual income for property taxes on his house and two acres of land becomes eligible for a refund of the excess paid. The relief scheme therefore represents a partial shift in state tax policy away from the assumption that ownership of land bears a direct relationship to an ability or obligation to pay. This shift has a major impact in a state such as Vermont whose residents include many economically marginal farmers, because it relieves this class of taxpayers of part of the burden of public finance.

. . . .

[Shortly after the Vermont land gains tax was enacted it was challenged on constitutional grounds and sustained in *Andrews v. Lathrop,* 315 A.2d 860 (Vt. 1974). In part, the tax was alleged to violate the equal protection clause. How the Vermont court handled this objection is indicated below.—Eds.]

The plaintiffs charged in *Andrews* that the tax violates the equal protection clause by discriminating arbitrarily between those land sellers who have held land for less than six years and those who have held land for six years or more. The usual equal protection test is whether statutory classification is reasonably related to a legitimate government purpose. A challenger normally may show a violation by demonstrating either that the legislative purpose is impermissible or that the statutory discrimination between classes of citizens is not rationally related to a concededly permissible purpose. However, the Supreme Court has developed a special approach to review of state tax classifications under the equal protection clause, giving special deference to such classifications because of the legislature's superior familiarity with local conditions and with the policy justifications for distinguishing between classes of taxpayers. In tax cases the Court hesitates to redraw lines established by state legislatures and will uphold a tax law unless the challenger is able to negate every conceivable basis on which it might be sustained.

The *Andrews* court began its equal protection analysis by identifying the purpose of the tax as "the deterrence of land speculation." It found this purpose permissible because of "the increasing concern within the State over the use and development of land as a natural resource," and noted that "[s]peculation falls within the ambit of such concern as a land use; indeed it has a bearing on many other uses to which the land might be put." The court then determined that this purpose was rationally related to the tax classification based on length of the holding period:

> The tax places a burden on short-term ownership and on high profits in the resale of lands, two attributes of property ownership closely linked to the holding of land for speculative purposes. The taxing of short-term ownership as opposed to long-term ownership and the taxing of short-term ownership at a higher rate, is integral to the deterrent effect. No other objective of property ownership is so directly affected as is land speculation.

In reality, the tax's purpose is a bit more complex than the Vermont court's analysis indicates. The land gains tax is intended to curb speculation, but it also serves a broad range of other objectives. . . .

Characterization of the tax's purpose as simply "the deterrence of speculation" is thus both overbroad and overnarrow. It is too broad because the tax does not seek to deter all speculation but only that based on short-term holdings. It is too narrow in that "deterrence of speculation" is not the ultimate purpose of the act; its real objective is to discourage the harmful impact of speculation on economic and land use problems within the state. "Deterrence of speculation" — or more precisely, deterrence of short-term speculation — is simply a *policy* which the state has adopted as a means of combatting several more narrowly defined problems;. . . .

———————

Comments: 1. In appraising the Vermont court's handling of the equal protection problem consider the following comment on the impact of a similar land gains tax enacted by the Province of Ontario, Canada, and which also falls more heavily on short-term speculators:

> Since the small short-term speculator is likely to be engaged in competitive speculation while the large speculator-developer may be engaged in monopolistic speculation, the tax discourages a beneficial form of speculation and encourages an undesirable form. The tax will thus reduce liquidity in many real estate markets, increase market fluctuations and contribute to the increased concentration of holdings by large-scale speculators and developers.

Smith, *supra* at 4-5.

2. Plaintiffs in the *Andrews* case also raised a due process objection to the land gains tax stemming from the alleged double taxation of their property. Their argument was that the cumulative effect of federal and state taxation of profits from the purchase and sale of their property was confiscatory. This argument was also rejected by the Vermont court, which noted that the United States Supreme Court has not invalidated cumulative taxation *per se*, citing *Fort Smith Lumber Co. v. Arkansas,* 251 U.S. 532 (1920). Neither has the Supreme Court found a due process objection to the excessive taxation of business profits, although it has left open the possibility that a due process violation might be found if the effect of business taxation is excessively punitive. *City of Pittsburgh v. Alco Parking Corp.,* 417 U.S. 369 (1974), noted, 26 Hastings L.J. 215 (1974).

3. There has been considerable controversy over the effect of an unearned increment tax such as the Vermont land gains tax on land prices. The conflicting viewpoints are summarized in Rose, The Development Land Tax, 10 Urb. Stud. 271 (1973), who indicates that whether or not the tax increases land prices depends on when it is levied and on the manner in which a rezoning to a more intensive use is obtained.

The effect on housing prices of the Ontario land speculation tax, which is levied on both land and improvements, was indeterminate. Smith, *supra.* Under the original English unearned increment tax the developmental increment to land was taxed in full, with the hope that land would sell at its existing use value and would not reflect the development value in the land that was taxed away. This hope did not materialize, and there was also some indication that the effect of the tax was to encourage landowners to hold land off the market. Turvey, 63 Econ. J. 22, 310, 313 (1953).

Unless the impact of the increment tax on land is neutral, the tax will have a distributive effect on land values and there will be windfall gainers and losers. For example, if the tax leads to higher prices on undeveloped land the price of housing on already developed land, which is exempt from the tax, will rise. Just the reverse will occur if the tax results in lower land prices on undeveloped land. Should these concerns be taken into account by a court asked to consider whether an unearned increment tax raises equal protection problems? For discussion of these problems in the context of the Vermont capital gains tax see Baker, Controlling Land Use and Prices by Using Special Gain Taxation to Intervene in the Land Market: The Vermont Experiment, 4 Envt'l Aff. 427 (1975). *See generally* D. Hagman & D. Misczynski, Windfall for Wipeouts (1978).

4. Attention has also been given to more limited value recapture strategies that attempt to recover for the public some of the added increment in land values that often occurs in the vicinity of newly constructed public facilities. Take the case of a new public transit station, for example. If the station is constructed in a previously undeveloped area, it can be expected that land values around the station will rise and that landowners will enjoy windfall gains as they sell out at higher prices to developers. Special assessments for public improvements, which were noted earlier, are one method of recapturing land value increases in this situation.

Another method for dealing with this problem is through a technique known as excess condemnation. The public agency charged with constructing the transit station simply acquires the excess land around the station. At the appropriate time it then sells or leases the land for development and secures the increment in land value for itself. The use of excess condemnation powers for this purpose has been chilled by an early federal case, *City of Cincinnati v. Vester,* 33 F.2d 242 (6th Cir. 1929), *aff'd on other grounds,* 281 U.S. 439 (1930). In that case the city had justified excess condemnation on a recoupment theory, under which it argued that excess property could be acquired and sold to help recoup the cost of the public improvement. This theory was rejected by the court.

If the *Vester* case is still good law, excess condemnation solely to recapture land value increases does not appear constitutional. However, other courts as well as the *Vester* case support more limited theories under which excess condemnation may be employed. One of these is the protective theory, under which excess land may be acquired and then sold or leased back subject to conditions that protect the public facility. For example, excess land acquired around a transit station could be sold and reconveyed subject to conditions that assure low density development on the property, thus avoiding congestion in the area surrounding the station. For discussion see Callies & Duerksen, Value Recapture as a Source of Funds to Finance Public Projects, 8 Urb. L. Ann. 73 (1974).

5. Is it true that the increment to land value that occurs when land is developed is always unearned, as the Washington Law Review article on the Vermont tax suggests? Consider this hypothetical situation: a city of modest size is so situated that it can grow in only two of four directions. No decision has presently been made by the planning agency indicating in which direction the city will grow. Until this decision is made, it can be expected that land lying in either direction will sell at a premium reflecting the expectancy that the land use plan will favor its location. To the extent that the price for land reflects the development expectancy, the increase in development value that will occur when the land is developed has been internalized. There is no unearned increment.

Assume that the planning agency subsequently decides that development will occur in only one direction. Land purchased in this area will now sell at a price in excess of the premium previously paid. This price excess can be considered an unearned increment, except that some of it will (or could) be taxed away by increases in property taxes or by subdivision development charges. If any excess remains to the developer, can it be justified as the spoils of a gamble? Is there any *a priori* reason for taxing away the gains from gambling in the marketplace? And what about those landowners in our example who paid a premium for their land in the hope that development would occur and who were disappointed? Have they suffered wipeout losses or are they simply the victims of a gambling mistake?

Chapter 7

GROWTH MANAGEMENT

A. INTRODUCTORY CONCEPTS AND STRATEGIES

Probably no innovation in planning and land use control strategies has caught the public imagination more than the growth management, or growth control, movement. While growth management programs are receiving increasing attention at state and regional levels (*see* Chapter 9), the growth management movement has so far largely been a local phenomenon. This chapter considers the problems and legal issues arising in local growth management programs.

An initial question to ask is why the growth management movement has suddenly taken on so much importance, and how growth management differs from the conventional planning and land use controls that have been available for so long. And what is it? Consider the following:

> It is important to begin by defining the problem of growth that affects the community. Is it a case of too many people? Too much congestion? Excessive smog and other pollutants? A desire to protect remaining open space? And, for what purpose must growth be managed? To allocate limited resources to serve an expanding population or to prevent inefficient development patterns? Spipel, Too Much Growth: Guidelines for Action, Public Management, Vol. 56, No. 5, at 10, 11 (1974) (author is city manager of Palo Alto, California).

A more comprehensive summary of the elements of growth management programs is provided in the following excerpt:

D. GODSCHALK, D. BROWER, L. McBENNETT, & B. VESTAL, CONSTITUTIONAL ISSUES OF GROWTH MANAGEMENT 8-10 (1977)

ELEMENTS OF GROWTH MANAGEMENT

. . . [L]ocal growth management is defined as a conscious government program intended to influence the rate, amount, type, location, and/or quality of future development within a local jurisdiction. Growth management programs may include a statement of growth policy, a development plan, and various traditional and innovative implementation tools — regulations, administrative devices, taxation schemes, public investment programs, and land acquisition techniques. Our survey of practitioners verified that the intent to influence certain characteristics of growth and the use of a variety of governmental policies, plans, regulations, and management techniques are the major components of local growth management as it is found in operation. It should be noted that this definition, which in fact focuses on actively guiding growth, differs from the popular notion of stopping growth completely.

As defined, the growth management process attempts to influence the "primary" characteristics of growth: rate, amount, type, location, and quality. These are the essential input features of urban growth — the major avenues through which the overall form and nature of development can be affected. It is also possible to distinguish a secondary set of growth features that could be called "impact" characteristics. These features, such as environmental impact, fiscal impact, or impact on regional parity, are outputs that result from the development process itself. Analyzing the impacts of development is one way to judge the effectiveness and equity of growth management. A local government may attempt to limit negative growth impacts by managing primary growth characteristics — by minimizing the fiscal impact of new growth, for example, by directing it to locations already served by water and sewer systems and limiting its rate to a level that can be accommodated by planned public facilities.

Communities have adopted growth management programs for many reasons, not all of them explicit. Among the announced objectives have been protection of the natural environment, coordination of the demand for public services with the government's capacity to supply them, preservation of fiscal stability, provision of housing opportunities near jobs — especially for low- and moderate-income workers — and protection of the existing life style of the community. Sometimes hidden behind a legitimate facade, however, are suspect attempts to exclude minorities or people lower on the socioeconomic scale, or to promote the interests of the local community at the expense of neighboring communities. Since growth management may result in exclusion or inclusion of lower-income or minority groups, protection or destruction of the environment, and enhancement or diminution of the regional welfare, each locality must be prepared to assume responsibility for the potential effects of the achievement of its goals.

Because growth policy can be framed to achieve various combinations of objectives, it is important to consider not only the individual objectives and the primary characteristics of growth to be affected, but also the trade-offs between objectives that will not always be compatible. There will be cases where a certain amount of fiscal efficiency may have to be sacrificed to achieve social equity or environmental quality, for example. Good policy should offer guidelines to managers faced with difficult trade-offs, providing them with the relative priorities for different objectives.

Growth management programs usually go beyond traditional planning, zoning, and subdivision controls in both the characteristics of development influenced and the scope of government powers used. Thus, their impact is greater than the more limited planning and zoning efforts of past years. Zoning, the most widely adopted form of traditional development regulation, basically attempts to influence the type and location of land uses. Subdivision regulations attempt to influence the arrangement of residential lots and the orderly provision of public facilities. Long-range comprehensive plans provide a goal for the pattern of land use 20 or so years into the future. Growth management programs often add to these concerns a focus on the annual rate, the total amount, and/or the design quality of development. In broadening their objectives, local governments are attempting to regulate various growth characteristics in accordance with the capacity of the community to accommodate new population and employment. As the term management implies, these programs are immediate and dynamic, deploying public resources to achieve specific, short-term objectives within the framework of an overall plan by influencing the outputs of the private land development system.

In seeking actively to guide growth rather than simply react to development proposals, local governments engaged in growth management have used a variety of techniques, many of them untested, at least locally. For example, to influence the rate of growth, some communities have established annual limits on the number of building permits to be issued. They have enacted ordinances requiring that construction of new subdivisions be scheduled to coincide with available public facilities. To slow the growth rate temporarily, communities have imposed moratoria on water and sewer hookups or building permits. To influence the total amount of growth, communities have tried to set population caps that specify the maximum population or the number of dwelling units to be allowed. They also have tried to fix the population level in accordance with the carrying capacity of the public service systems. To influence design quality, communities have turned to planned unit development, incentive zoning, or design competitions, which provide for the application of qualitative standards to proposed projects. In using these often unfamiliar tools in conjunction with traditional planning and zoning techniques, many communities have run into problems due to lack of experience, unanticipated consequences, opposition from interest groups, and legal suits.

Comments: There have been several helpful surveys of growth management techniques and problems in addition to the study from which this excerpt was taken. *See, e.g.,* M. Gleeson et al., Urban Growth Management Systems (American Soc'y of Planning Officials, Planning Advisory Service Rep. Nos. 309-10, 1975) [hereinafter cited as Urban Growth]. An extensive compilation of articles and studies on growth management, including surveys of local experiences, is contained in Management and Control of Growth (R. Scott ed. 1975) [hereinafter cited as Management and Control].

The following article, which describes the background of the well-known growth management program in Boulder, Colorado, provides some of the flavor of growth management efforts at the local level. The growth management scene in Boulder continues to change, and not all of the personalities discussed in the article are still on-stage, but the article does capture the essence of the Boulder program and the controversy surrounding its adoption and implementation.

PENNE, A CASE STUDY IN THE MANAGEMENT OF URBAN GROWTH, Nation's Cities, September 1976, at 9-15

[Not all of the elements of the Boulder growth management program are explained in Penne's article. The essence of the system is further captured in this capsule summary:

> Boulder's strategy is to reduce growth from in-migration by cutting back industrial search efforts, to restrain and contain growth by acquiring greenbelts and scenic easements where there should be no development, and to charge the full cost of providing services to development that is permitted. Boulder has no open land left so developers either have to negotiate extension of city utilities or get their acreage annexed to the city.

[Urban Growth at 11. There is hardly any industry in the city and no major industrial employer has located there since a major IBM facility was built recently. The cost of providing services is recouped by levying a development charge for sewer and water hookups against new developments. These charges are substantially in excess of $1,000, but are waived for low-income housing if the charge is a deterrent to development. For discussion of development charges see *supra* p. 831. The scenic easement acquisition program is operable but only a very small amount of land has been purchased under this program. After this article was written, voters in the city did pass an initiative measure imposing an annual quota on new housing units in the city. This measure took its cue from a similar quota adopted as part of the Petaluma growth management plan, see *infra* p. 1056. As in Petaluma, the annual quota of building permits is distributed under ranking criteria for residential developments.

Accounts from Boulder indicate that the quota has led to a substantial increase in the price of existing homes in the city. Obviously, the final word on Boulder's growth management program has not been written. — Eds.]

Boulder has been, wrote *Christian Science Monitor* editor Robert Cahn, "one of the leaders in antigrowth sentiment . . . and is doing something about it." A report from the American Society of Planning Officials says that Boulder is "probably the farthest along on any city in the country when it comes to a public consciousness that growth can be controlled or significantly affected as a matter of public policy." In 1971 Boulder voters defeated a charter amendment to set a population limit for the city. However, they approved a resolution directing the city to "take all steps necessary to hold the rate of growth in the Boulder Valley substantially below that of the 1960s."

But the recent word direct from Boulder is not as clear. Boulder's director of planning and community development, Nolan Rosall, wrote in the February 1976 issue of *Practicing Planner,* "Even in as sophisticated and advanced a community as Boulder, with a strong positive national reputation, sound land-use planning and growth management are much easier to talk about than to achieve. Unless one wishes to appeal to strong negative values, such as keeping out the blacks or the poor, remaining more exclusive, or keeping taxes down, it is difficult to retain political consensus for meaningful change. Almost everyone agrees in the abstract, but unless they really fear the alternatives, they tend to stop short of implementation."

A visit to Boulder confirms the ambiguity of the situation, reveals the mix of interests and motives, and emphasizes the conflicts of ends and means that must exist in any city attempting to manage growth.

"Of all of the locations in the United States, surely no city can claim a more spectacular natural setting than Boulder." Allowing for guidebook extravagance, this opinion says much about the city's growth-management attempts. Saving the foothills and the mesas from bulldozers captures wide and strong support.

"Environment" may be an abstraction in other places. In Boulder it is real and obvious. The city hugs the mesas and reaches into the foothills of the Rockies on the west and opens into the Boulder Valley on the east. Standing at North Broadway and Pearl downtown, you can still see Boulder, the nineteenth century mining town, and still feel the power and attraction of the mountains that pile up in the distance. But only blocks away the threat that growth brings to twentieth century Boulder is evident in the fast food and chain store strip that is "Anywhere, U.S.A." The agreement on the importance of saving natural Boulder undergirds a broad consensus in support of growth control. Councilman Bob Trenka, a planner now working for one of Denver's largest developers, suggests two propositions that get general agreement in Boulder: "You have to control to some degree what happens to the future of Boulder," and, "Whatever kind of growth occurs must be quality."

. . . .

This basis consensus did not develop accidentally. From 20,000 people in 1950, Boulder has grown to more than 80,000 today. In the process both the mountains and the valley were scarred by uncontrolled development. As a consequence Boulder took a series of growth control actions.

In 1959 a "blue line" was drawn preventing the extension of water service into the hills west of the city limits, thus preserving them from urban development. The same strategy of "urban shaping" was applied in the valley to the east in 1961 when the extension of city water and sewer service outside the city limits was tied to growth development aims. In the early sixties, development decisions began to be guided by the "spokes of the wheel concept," which was intended to direct the extension of services along major arteries radiating from the center of Boulder, with development occurring along the rim. Another, and perhaps the most successful, urban shaping tool, the Greenbelt Program, was instituted in 1967 when Boulder voters approved a municipal sales tax increase with four-tenths of a cent for that purpose. And two years later the enactment of flood plain zoning added another option for guiding growth in the valley.

Many of the pieces were pulled together in the Boulder Valley Comprehensive Plan, which was enacted in 1970 to provide a general physical plan and a set of policies to guide growth in an orderly manner. The following year a 55-foot building height limit was approved to preserve the character of the city. In the next three years there followed: land-use regulations to help implement the comprehensive plan; interim growth policies which provided guidelines for review of proposed development; and the Boulder Area Growth Study Commission, which produced a report containing elaborate and ambitious recommendations for the city, the county, and the state.

In 1975 a growth management system which included a detailed application of the general growth policy was proposed but not approved.

. . . .

City planner Rosall in a July 1975 memorandum to the city council wrote, "At this point in the city's history, I frankly believe there is no real question about the need, desirability, and the strong legal basis for a growth management system. The problem, in my opinion, is not whether a system is needed, but rather that a stopgap interim growth policy has been practiced by the city for the past five years or more with frequently vague, ambiguous, often inconsistent, and sometimes unwritten regulations." The growth management system presented in 1975 was not well received in all quarters. The realtors' Hunter says, "The growth management system at first was too dictatorial, basically all right, but too detailed. It was unacceptable. We, the chamber, the league, and PLAN Boulder County stopped it in its tracks. Now we are talking about a comprehensive plan."

. . . .

Obviously there is another side to the Boulder story of consensus, tradition, and effective action.

From a distance the Boulder tradition might look like the product of easy evolution. Up close, however, Boulder's 20 years of experience with growth control has been stormy. The no-population-growth proposal was defeated, but a population control resolution was adopted. A city council which had been strong on growth control had to dilute its efforts by devoting time to other social issues. The previous city manager was released, at least in part, for his advocacy of a strong growth control system. Today the city council majority of five has swung away from strong support for growth control.

According to the chamber's Rod Benson, "You need a balance. The pendulum swung too far toward the environment and away from the economic. You need a balance of political activity with each of the interest groups staying about even. There will be tilts, but it avoids the complete changeover which produces tremendous upheavals. You want the pendulum to swing around the middle."

One result of such a delicate balance is that action is difficult. "As long as a proposal stays general," says Johnson, "it gets support, but not when it gets specific. Everybody admits growth control is good, but when it comes down to it, you step on somebody's toes." Council Member Paul Danish, a growth control proponent, thinks it "incredible that Boulder has never passed a growth control ordinance."

. . . .

The central dispute is control versus guidance. Danish has prepared an ordinance that would put an annual numerical limit on new residential units. "If you leave it open-ended, they will find some way around it. If you are serious, you must talk numbers. Until you decide what the rate of growth will be, everything else is beside the point."

This is most certainly not the consensus in Boulder. "I don't think," Hutchins says, "that you can handle growth with numbers." "We are growing at only 2.8 percent now," says Benson. "In the sixties it was 8 percent, and everybody agreed that was too much. The majority of the council agrees that 3 percent can be handled." Danish is not in that majority. And there is no majority that is willing to endorse any number officicially. "It is not just a numbers game," said Rosall. "Four hundred or 800 units can give very different outcomes. A quota without a proper base could be damaging. We can handle 2 percent."

[An annual building quota of 450 dwelling units has since been adopted by popular initiative.—Eds.]

Boulder's experience, as the city moves toward decisions about what sort of life should be possible there, has a core of relevance for other cities. . . .

Although the foremost concern is preserving the natural beauty, and the second is the prevention of low-quality sprawl, there is a strong complementary interest in concentrating development and revitalizing downtown. For some, this is simply part of the overall growth control strategy, making the center attractive while holding the fringe. "The downtown," states the Draft Comprehensive Plan Policies for the Central Area, "shall remain in its historic role as the governmental, entertainment, financial, office, and specialty retail center of the Boulder Valley. This shall be accomplished through combining concerted and comprehensive public policies and investments with private development and rehabilitation efforts." The most notable of these is a mall which has just gotten under way.

Councilman Bob White is committed to the importance of developing an "urban" alternative. "If the only consideration is the market," he says, "then every place will be the same." In a *Town and Country Review* article, White wrote, "We need to encourage the investment of time and money and architectural talent in our urban core areas; and at the same time, strongly discourage further sprawling suburban development. Our core city is a resource that has been too long neglected. It now presents an opportunity to meet many of our needs for the twenty-first century. We have only to rediscover the attractions of urban life in a quality environment."

Even in Boulder, a new city, there is a concern about preserving past investments. "The spiraling cost of new construction and the dwindling of our natural resources," wrote Prissy Bowron, one of the founders of Historic Boulder, "are now giving preservationists an opportunity to 'sell' the recycling of old building."

. . . .

Whether Boulder's deciding on permanence, stability, and the preservation of a particular way of life will produce success cannot yet be determined. Many problems must be faced, including the following.

The Robinson *decision.* [*See infra* p. 1077. — Eds.] In March of this year the Colorado Supreme Court decided that "inasmuch as Boulder is the sole and exclusive provider of water and sewer services in the area surrounding the subject property, it is a public utility. As such, it holds itself out as ready and able to serve those in the territory who require the service. There is no utility-related reason, such as insufficient water, preventing it from extending these services to the landowners. Unless such reasons exist, Boulder cannot refuse to serve the people in the subject area." This decision, which eliminated one of Boulder's most important growth guidance tools, was also of importance for other cities using the same tactic. It appears that Boulder's growth management program will be damaged seriously.

Boulderites, however, don't think so; . . . Boulder County long-range planner Bill Trimm thinks that the *Robinson* decision takes away a crutch. "It is the best thing that could have happened. The policies needed more support. Now they will have to open up a dialog on the realities of planning." Councilwoman Roberts agrees that "the *Robinson* decision makes the future easier because there are not as many choices." If they are right, a replacement will still have to be found.

Intergovernmental relations. Outsiders are surprised to find that there are other towns in the Boulder Valley, and Boulderites tend to ignore the fact. They are not all on the same course. Louisville, southeast of Boulder, is pursuing an enthusiastic annexation and development program. Longmont to the northeast has developed a growth control plan which county planner Trimm, formerly with Longmont, thinks is superior to Boulder's. And, of course, Boulder County is the receptacle for all of this activity, with greater responsibility placed on it by the *Robinson* decision. Trimm looks to the development of a county plan which will identify the spheres of influence for the cities.

County Commissioner Toevs says, "Politically, the sentiment in Boulder County is for controlled growth. We would like to avoid being another Westchester or Marin County. The controls in the county now are inadequate. We would appreciate more statutory authority."

Boulder cannot go it alone. The success of its growth management will depend on the actions of the county, the other valley cities, the state, and the general shape of future development in the region. Most of this is outside of Boulder's control.

Social questions. Growth management can be — must be — exclusionary. It is criticized for closing off residential possibilities for minorities and the poor. Boulder is an affluent community with a small minority population, but the issue has arisen. To date there have been no explosions. Boulder has incorporated a low- and moderate-income housing program into its plans. But Toevs sees the two commitments, "keeping a diverse population and controlling growth," to be on a long-term collision course. To what extent a community can keep the good life to itself is still an open question.

This kind of an agenda makes it clear that at no time will it be possible to say Boulder has finally succeeded. The future will be like the past, a process of constant adjusting. And so, although there is no formally adopted growth control plan in Boulder, a remark made by Hutchins suggests that may not be critical. "Maybe the plan is in action now, and we just don't realize it — in the dialog." Supporters of growth control are prone to judge their success by whether a plan is adopted. Opponents think they have succeeded if they prevent it. But Boulder grew without a growth plan, simply because many individual actions prompted by implicit agreement carried the city in that direction. The shift in the agreement, redirecting individual actions, may carry the city in another direction without the benefit of an explicit, strong, detailed growth management plan.

. . . .

Comments: 1. The Boulder experience indicates that growth management systems can be implemented by a wide variety of techniques, although growth control quotas and management systems that include procedures for the timing and phasing of new development will largely be the focus of this chapter. Additional local growth management programs are summarized in Urban Growth, ch. 2. *See also* Deutsch, Land Use Growth Controls: A Case Study of San Jose and Livermore, California, 15 Santa Clara Law. 1 (1975). A survey of growth management concepts can also be found in Scott, Management and Control of Growth: An Introduction and Summary in I Management and Control 2.

2. The Boulder article looks at growth management from the point of view of local needs and problems. There are other perspectives. For example, a leading urban economist has noted tensions between local growth management and the national interest in urban growth:

> One comes to understand better the tension between national and local interests in economic and population growth when one comes to appreciate the neat counterpoint between the comprehensive (but static) locational pattern of all population and industry, and the dynamic (but parochial) time rate of change of a locality. At the national level — from on high — the economic planner or his counterpart, the universalist free market, is typically not just insensitive, but oblivious to the pervasive impact of

differential and changing rates of growth on local well being. Growth and decline is the means toward the larger end of economic efficiency. At the local level — to city planners and to the man in the street — "orderly" rates of growth are where it's at, and their reflection in national locational patterns is much too complex and remote to be real. (Although one of the not too distant relatives of inefficiency — inflation — is not so unreal.)

It would be easy and comfortable to conclude, blandly, that the resolution of these very different perspectives and conflicting interests lies in "shared power" — joint decision making by the national, state and local governments. But I am troubled by the fact that both national locational patterns and the web of individual local growth rates need to be balanced-out in general systemic solutions. I am not suggesting that difficult and far reaching decisions on the division of powers in a federal system should be made on economic grounds alone. But it is my tentative judgment — a holding position — that if national and state planners could come to understand and be sensitive to the many direct and indirect effects of radical changes in local growth rates on the well being of a community, then they would be in the best position to solve the two equations simultaneously: the "ideal" system of cities and the inter-lock-time-rates of change. But to be good trustees for the welfare of localities the national government and the states should be not only representative and trustworthy, but also competent in the execution of that which they are about.

Thompson, Planning as Urban Growth Management: Still More Answers Than Questions, AIP Newsletter, Vol. 9, No. 12 at 7, 8 (Dec. 1974).

3. Social questions arising out of growth management were also touched on in the Boulder article. Social critics of local growth management programs voice even more strident objections:

It is clear . . . that most of the instrumentalities used by localities for controlling growth are regressive — *they hurt the poor without substantially hurting others, and sometimes in fact make the rich better off.* Most of our examples were taken from suburban communities where the concerns rested with the fear of over-population and environmental decay. Across the nation this conflict between the inner city and the outer city is played and replayed. Common to most metropolitan regions is a polarity in incomes, races and growth rates between the suburbs and core city. This supports the thesis that the no-growth suburbs can afford to give up something in order to obtain the environmental purity and population stability they desire. In other words, they should be willing to make a trade-off so that the instrumentalities they use are not regressive. Following this hypothesis: (a) The rich should be willing to pay for saving their environment. (b) Priority should be given to cleaning up the central city while environmental concerns are also directed toward saving suburban open space. (c) Economic growth not desired by the suburbs should be directed to central cities. (d) Public housing bonds should be included in bonds for open space to compensate the poor for increased suburban rents and land costs.

Concern over pollution has blinded many outer city dwellers to equity concerns. That the environment is seen as mainly a suburban issue (anti-sprawl) has caused some to label environmentalists "green bigots," who desire a green ring a la Ebenezer Howard to separate the white cities from the black city. But cleaning up the environment should be more important to the central cities, where smog and congestion affect daily living more than the prospect of another subdivision down the road affects outer city residents. In addition, the poor — since they are less mobile — are unable to escape environmental disamenities.

Industries and economic activity not desired by the suburbs should be redirected to the central city. Suburbs, however, should not be able to pick and choose — accepting non-nuisance industry while sending polluters to the core. Residential construction previously slated for suburban tracts should now go into city renewal and redevelopment. Thus, the symbiotic relationship of earlier decades would be restored and the suburbs will again acknowledge their dependence on the central city and forfeit their newly-gained self-sufficiency, growing independence and arrogance. Of late, the central-city/suburb symbiotic relationship has broken down into a parasitic one. The suburbs benefit from *borrowing size* from the core — taking advantage of city culture, shopping and employment, while refusing its disamenities and negative externalities. . . .

Agelasto, No-Growth and the Poor: Equity Considerations in Controlled Growth Policies in I Management and Control 426, 432. Consider also the findings of a study of growth and no-growth counties in Colorado, which found that per capita personal income was greater in the growth counties and increased at a more rapid rate in these counties between 1960 and 1970. The gap in per capita personal income between these counties also widened during this period. T. Lucas, The Direct Costs of Growth 11 (Colorado Land Use Comm'n, 1974).

4. Agelasto notes that growth management programs are largely a suburban phenomenon, and may thus aggravate the conflict between inner and outer cities in metropolitan areas. This observation should be kept in mind when the legal materials on local growth management are surveyed in this chapter. In addition, distinctions can be drawn in the types of settings in which local growth management programs are likely to be adopted. Boulder represents the prime instance of a growth management program adopted by an expanding suburban community. Its objective is to control growth at the edges of the city in order to achieve local objectives in shaping and limiting community size. Since growth management programs in this context operate to control entry into the community, they present potentially serious legal problems and may have an exclusionary effect.

Growth management programs may also be adopted by urbanizing counties in metropolitan areas. These programs may also operate as a constraint on urban expansion in the county, but the growth management program may be better balanced because it is adopted from a countywide perspective and because the political constituency of the county is often more diverse. For an excellent discussion of the growth management program of Fairfax County, Virginia, in the Washington, D.C., metropolitan area, see G. Dawson, No Little Plans (1977). The two major legal challenges to local growth management programs have been brought against an expanding suburb (Petaluma) and against a sub-county unit of government in New York State that controls growth outside the incorporated municipalities in its area (Ramapo).

5. As the Boulder article also indicates, interim development control measures are often needed in growth management programs during the time the municipality takes stock of its existing planning and land use control system and prepares for the adoption of its growth management strategy. Interim controls are thus an important element in growth management programs. They are discussed in the next section.

B. MORATORIA AND INTERIM CONTROLS

RIVKIN, GROWTH CONTROL VIA SEWER MORATORIA, 33 Urban Land 10, 11, 15 (1974)

. . . [T]he sewer moratorium has emerged as an important technique for growth control. It is being used in heavily populated areas of the country by local, state, and federal governments to restrain new development in the face of inadequate sewer facilities and resulting environmental degradation. Although some central cities employ moratoria, the technique is used primarily in suburbs, the seat of most development.

A moratorium can be applied in response to a variety of circumstances including:

> Insufficient capacity, or leaks, in trunk transmission lines or interceptors causing overflow of effluent on its way to treatment. Overflows can occur as a normal course or during peak periods.

> Use of the same transmission system for both sanitary sewage and storm drainage, resulting in backups and overflows during wet weather.

> Insufficient lines or treatment facilities, combined with local permissiveness toward septic tank development, resulting in pollution of ground water and streams.

> Insufficient capacity in the waste treatment facilities themselves resulting in overflows and pollution of water bodies at the plant.

> Inadequate standards of treatment resulting in constant discharge of pollutants at the final outfalls.

Governmental bodies have levied moratoria in response to one or more of these conditions, and governmental action normally comes along with a commitment to relieve the conditions eventually or within a fixed period of time.

Moratoria are being applied to areas of all sizes, including entire regions and jurisdictions serviced by inadequate networks of treatment facilities and lines, as well as individual watersheds or even neighborhoods that represent only portions of jurisdictions.

Given the variety of causes and impact areas, the governmental action termed "moratorium" can take many forms and consist of combinations of the following:

A freeze on new sewer authorizations (extension of trunk lines into currently unserviced areas).

A freeze on new sewer connections (the actual hookup of buildings to an existing trunk or feeder line).

A freeze on the issuance of new building permits, or a freeze on a class of building permits, such as multi-family.

A freeze on the approval of subdivision requests.

A freeze on rezonings or zonings to higher than presently developed densities.

A slowing down or quota allocation for any or all of the above within an affected area (a situation that can occur when the particular problem is not yet critical, but monitoring demonstrates that limits may be required).

Each of these is a restraining action. Although there may be instances of a complete and sudden freeze on building under the rubric of a sewer moratorium, we know of none. In general, building is allowed to continue under one or more of the above constraints with the implied policy that the process will eventually stop (existing permits will run out) if the crisis situation has not been corrected. This restraining rather than terminating character of sewer moratoria has perhaps been the chief cause of sudden short-term acceleration of development in some moratorium areas — certainly a most unexpected consequence. Builders, worried that even more severe restrictions will follow, have often responded by trying to complete approved development, including reserve permits, as fast as possible, thereby contributing to greater system overloads.

It is difficult to depict an accurate quantitative picture of the situation: the causes are diverse, impact areas are many, and actions classed under the general heading of "sewer moratorium" differ widely. The very different conditions and widespread lack of clear policies for dealing with their implications have led to extreme confusion for governments, builders, and citizens alike.

. . . .

PRESENT PRIORITIES

Several factors contribute to the increased importance of sewage as a public issue.

Higher Density Suburban Growth

In the late 1960s and during the past three years, the proportion of apartment and townhouse development in suburban areas has been increasing. At the same time, higher densities require a more "fail safe" approach to waste disposal than single-family detached housing. And, despite lower unit costs for connections because of concentration, higher densities present greater environmental danger to an inadequate system. A number of moratoria are on apartment construction only.

Citizen and Builder Protest

Municipal and industrial pollution have been principal targets of the environmental movement. The campaign against pollution in metropolitan and suburban areas has been fused with no growth or slow growth ideas from groups who see wastewater disposal inadequacies as a rationale for retarding development. Regardless of motivation, pressure has been mounting on decision-makers who control building permits and sewer service in high growth areas. The pressure has been to hold back construction authorizations until new water quality standards and new growth policies can be established.

. . .

Federal and State Legislation

Passage of the Water Pollution Control Act of 1965, and especially its amended version in 1972, along with associated state enabling legislation, has authorized higher levels of government to set and enforce water quality standards. The new standards are intended to put an end to water pollution, much of it caused by inadequate waste disposal, by 1985. . . .

Costs

Sewage disposal and treatment at the new standards is now a major item of governmental costs. In keeping with its standing as a claimant for the tax dollar, waste disposal has recently emerged as a public issue. Advanced wastewater treatment represents a quantum jump in costs over even secondary processing. According to EPA, the 1972 value of existing municipal sewage treatment plants was about $8.5 billion; the estimate of additional investment needed by 1985 to meet presently adopted and approved water quality standards is $15 billion. The National Water Commission estimates that capital costs for collector systems by 1985 would be $40 billion. . . .

An Assessment

The sewer moratorium is an example of a regrettable characteristic within the American governmental process — ad hoc, piecemeal efforts to solve a complex problem rapidly by simplistic means. The problems which produce wastewater disposal and treatment deficiencies are far deeper than technical shortcomings in a physical system. They involve fundamental and long-term issues of urban growth and social equity; they involve the process of land speculation, the nature of the building industry, and the political currents being stirred by environmentalists and advocates of zero population growth. Most actions to initiate moratoria have responded to an immediate physical need. Evidence does not suggest that responsible governmental bodies have considered the bulk of the relevant issues — or indeed are taking steps to do so now that impacts are being felt.

Some moratoria may have relieved the physical problem. On the positive side, also, must be added the impetus given to in-filling of vacant land near sewer connections which has been skipped over by past development. There is also a chance that moratoria on suburban areas plus the energy crisis may contribute to reconcentration within central cities where sewers and other utilities are available and under-utilized, and where land prices may become competitive with escalating suburban costs.

On the negative side, however, moratoria can and do contribute to the following:

Short-term spurts of construction followed by sudden sharp drops in activity if facilities to relieve the moratoria are not forthcoming; the result is a dangerous imbalance in housing production.

Hardships and inequities for small builders who are economically vulnerable.

Discrimination against apartments and other cost efficient higher-density housing in some areas.

Serious roadblocks to production of low and moderate income housing such as escalating costs of land where sites are available, and discrimination against higher densities.

A distinct encouragement of urban sprawl to jurisdictions not covered by the controls but within commuting distance of major employment centers. There is concomitant encouragement of septic tank development in these areas and package treatment facilities which may or may not be at non-polluting standards.

A stimulus to complicated bureaucratic processes and capital works delays as the several levels of government inevitably involved struggle to resolve administrative, environmental, and financial issues.

WESTWOOD FOREST ESTATES, INC. v. VILLAGE OF SOUTH NYACK

Court of Appeals of New York
23 N.Y.2d 424, 244 N.E.2d 700 (1969)

BREITEL, Judge.

This appeal involves the constitutional invalidity of an amendment to a zoning ordinance of the Village of South Nyack. The offending amendment barred the new construction of multiple dwellings throughout the village. The reason for adopting the amendment was concededly to alleviate the burden on the village's sewage disposal plant, and not because of any requirement of or change in the comprehensive plan for the development of the village.

After a trial without a jury, the Supreme Court, in an opinion, the Appellate Division affirming, held the amendment invalid because it was not related to a proper zoning purpose and because it effectively deprived plaintiff of any reasonable use of its property. At the same time it was observed that the village was not barred from taking appropriate action to prevent indiscriminate construction of apartment houses or from making appropriate provision for adequate sewage facilities.

Because the amendment was not properly related to zoning purposes, and because it restricted plaintiff's property to a use for which it is not adaptable, there should be an affirmance. On the other hand, the village would not be prevented from taking appropriate steps under its other and general police powers to control the hazards arising from temporary or permanent shortcomings of existing provisions for the disposal of sewage.

In August, 1963 plaintiff purchased a portion of its land in the village for $7,500; the remainder was purchased in April, 1965 for $54,000. The property was originally zoned for high-rise apartments. In September, 1964 the area was rezoned to permit only garden apartments. In August, 1965 the zoning ordinance was again amended to prohibit future apartment house construction in the entire village. The Planning Board resolution recommending the latest amendment was based on inquiries made of sanitation experts concerning the effects on the village's sewage system of a 68-unit garden apartment development, for which plaintiff had submitted plans.

Plaintiff's witnesses testified on the trial that its property would be worth about $125,000 if used for apartment construction, and $10,000 to $15,000 if used for one and two-family residences. The witnesses for the village estimated the value of plaintiff's property, if used for one and two-family residences, at $42,500.

There is a distinction between the proper use of the zoning power to carry out the purposes of the enabling statutes ..., and the improper use of the zoning power to effect the general police powers of a municipality. . . .

The village concededly rezoned plaintiff's land from a multiple residence to a single-family district to prevent an increase in the amount of effluent discharged into its sewer system, pending the construction of improved sewer facilities. The sanitation problem that would be created by the construction of a 68-unit garden apartment development was not due to the inadequacy of the sewer lines and pumping station to handle an increased flow. On the contrary, only 75% of the hydraulic capacity of the system was being utilized, and any additional effluent generated by habitation of the garden apartments could be absorbed easily. Rather, the problem was the hazard of increased pollution of the Hudson River, after inadequate treatment of the sewage effluent. A pollution problem due to the village's inadequate sewage treatment facilities had existed for years prior to plaintiff's application for a construction permit and prior to amendment of the zoning ordinance. Indeed, for some time the village had been the subject of criticism and efforts by the State and county agencies concerned with pollution to correct the conditions for which it was responsible and which were adding pollutants to the Hudson River.

A municipality has, of course, the power to take appropriate steps to deal with sanitation problems, including those created by inadequate biological treatment of sewage. The instant sanitation problem is, however, general to the community and not caused by the nature of plaintiff's land. . . . It is, therefore, impermissible to single out this plaintiff to bear a heavy financial burden because of a general condition in the community. . . .

The village relies upon criticisms of other government agencies concerned with pollution to justify its action. Notably, however, the Rockland County Health Department, although stating its reluctance "to put its blessing on adding additional amounts of sewage to an already poorly functioning system", stated that such approval might be obtained if there were a definite program of improvement for the sewer system and the new sewer connections were conditioned on the provision of financial contributions towards rebuilding the sewage disposal plant.

The amendment was also improper because it was not adopted in furtherance of a comprehensive plan. . . . The village did not revise its comprehensive zoning plan in order to avoid constructing new or additional sewage facilities adequate to service the increased population which would result from the construction of garden apartments. The restriction was, confessedly, a temporary expedient, apparently intended to be lifted at a later time when an improved sewer facility was completed. Thus, it was stated that the amendment "[did] not reflect any final judgment on the part of the present members of the [Planning] Board on the desirability of including apartment zoning provisions for appropriate areas of the village."

Finally, the amendment, which is not limited to any period of time, effectively prevents plaintiff from using its land for any purpose to which it is reasonably adapted. This is demonstrated by the marked discrepancy between the value of the property, if limited as to use by the amendment, and its value for the use to which it is adapted and which was permitted under the ordinance before it was amended. Such a destruction of value constitutes a taking of property in violation of the zoning power and only permissible through the exercise of the power of eminent domain. . . .

This is not to say that the village may not, pursuant to its other and general police powers, impose other restrictions or conditions on the granting of a building permit to plaintiff, such as a general assessment for reconstruction of the sewage system, granting of building permits for the planned garden apartment complex in stages, or perhaps even a moratorium on the issuance of any building permits, reasonably limited as to time. But, whatever the right of a municipality to impose " 'a . . . temporary restraint of beneficial enjoyment . . . where the interference is necessary to promote the ultimate good either of the municipality as a whole or of the immediate neighborhood' ", such restraint must be kept " 'within the limits of necessity' " and may not prevent permanently the reasonable use of private property for the only purposes to which it is practically adapted. . . . [Quoting from *Arverne Bay Constr. Co. v. Thatcher,* 15 N.E.2d 587, 590, 591 (N.Y. 1938), *supra* p. 236. — Eds.]

Accordingly, the order of the Appellate Division should be affirmed, with costs.

FULD, C. J., and BURKE, SCILEPPI, BERGAN, KEATING and JASEN, JJ., concur.

Order affirmed.

BELLE HARBOR REALTY CORP. v. KERR

Court of Appeals of New York
35 N.Y.2d 507, 323 N.E.2d 697 (1974)

WACHTLER, Judge.

Early in 1972, the Belle Harbor Realty Corp. (Belle Harbor) submitted to the City of New York a new building application for the construction of a four-story nursing home. To secure a written permit from the Commissioner of Buildings as required by the Administrative Code (Administrative Code of City of New York, § C26-109.1) a builder must first obtain approval of his building plans from the appropriate departments (Administrative Code, § C26-108.8). This procedure is designed to insure compliance with the requirements of the Building Code and other applicable laws and regulations. Between July 6 and September 25, 1972 the requisite approvals were issued to Belle Harbor by the Department of Buildings, the Department of Water Resources and the State Board of Social Welfare.

Prior to the issuance of the written permit, citizens concerned with the inadequacy of existing sewerage facilities commenced an action against the city and Belle Harbor seeking to enjoin the city from issuing the permit (*Oetjen v. Sigman,* Index No. 1296 11/72). The city cross-moved for dismissal contending that the petitioners lacked standing and that the issuance of the work permits was a ministerial act in light of the approvals evidencing Belle Harbor's compliance with all the building and zoning requirements. This motion was granted and the complaint was dismissed.

Shortly thereafter in response to numerous complaints of sewer backups the city investigated the sewerage facilities at the proposed site. The city discovered that the municipal sanitary sewers which would serve the proposed home had been installed in 1889, had six inch rather than eight inch pipes, and required the repeated removal of sand indicative of open joints. The sum of this inquiry was that the sewers were "grossly inadequate" for present use and therefore new sewer connections were unadvisable.

On the basis of this information the city notified Belle Harbor that the prior approvals were revoked. The city also indicated that plans were being made to consider a new sewer system for the area.

Belle Harbor reacted by commencing this article 78 proceeding to annul the city's revocation of its approval of the new building application and to compel the city to reissue all approvals and to issue all permits necessary to complete the construction of the proposed nursing home. Belle Harbor contended that the city had succumbed to community pressure thereby abdicating its civic professional responsibility. Moreover, Belle Harbor asserted that the revocations by the city was a delaying tactic until such time as the city council could act on proposed zoning changes which would adversely affect the construction of a nursing home in that area. The city responded by denying that it had bowed to political pressure. The city contended that the original approval for the sewer connections was given at a time when it did not know about the deteriorated condition of the sewers; consequently such approval was a mistake susceptible of revocation in the proper exercise of its police power.

Special Term agreed finding that the revocation of approvals and refusal to issue the permits were occasioned through a reasonable exercise of police power and dismissed the petition.

The Appellate Division reversed and directed the city to issue the requisite approvals and permits. Relying on *Westwood Forest Estates v. Village of South Nyack* . . . the Appellate Division majority held that it was impermissible for the city to punish a single landowner because of its own failure to construct adequate sewerage facilities.

We disagree with the Appellate Division majority and find that *Westwood Forest Estates (supra)* is not dispositive of the case at bar. In *Westwood* we held that a village could not utilize its zoning power to prohibit the new construction of multiple dwellings in order to avoid complying with State and county antipollution efforts. The situation before us is distinguishable in that it involves the general police power rather than the zoning power, and the sanitation problem is one of immediate direct impact rather than a generalized one. In contrast to the sewer system in *Westwood* which was operating at only 75% of capacity and was indisputably adequate, the system in Belle Harbor is alleged to be "an already overloaded, overflowing, backing-up, antiquated sewer system."

While we have consistently recognized the right of a municipality pursuant to its police powers to prevent conditions dangerous to public health and welfare . . . we have also insisted that any such restrictions or limitations must be kept " 'within the limits of necessity' ". (*Arverne Bay Constr. Co. v. Thatcher,* 278 N.Y. 222, 230, 15 N.E.2d 587, 591; . . . .)

Consequently a municipality may not invoke its police powers solely as a pretext to assuage strident community opposition. To justify interference with the beneficial enjoyment of property the municipality must establish that it has acted in response to a dire necessity, that its action is reasonably calculated to alleviate or prevent the crisis condition, and that it is presently taking steps to rectify the problem. When the general police power is invoked under such circumstances it must be considered an emergency measure and is circumscribed by the exigencies of that emergency.

The order of the Appellate Division should be reversed without costs, and the petition dismissed without prejudice to the commencement of a proceeding within 30 days from the date hereof to determine whether the revocation of the necessary building approvals was warranted as necessary to prevent a condition dangerous to public health and welfare or whether such revocation was based solely on a pretext that the construction would create a condition dangerous to public health and welfare.

BREITEL, C. J., and JASEN, GABRIELLI, JONES and STEVENS, JJ., concur.

Samuel Rabin, J., taking no part.
Order reversed, etc.

Comments: 1. What distinguishes the *Belle Harbor* from the *Westwood* case? Is it a distinction that in *Westwood* the capacity of the plant was underutilized? That the plant was inadequate and that a real danger from pollution was present? Why is it a distinction that in *Belle Harbor* the "police power" rather than the zoning power was used? Compare these cases with the *Baker* case, *supra* p. 805, in which the Massachusetts court held that subdivision approval could not be denied because the development of the subdivision would destroy a ponding area which acted as a retention area for stormwaters. Is that decision relevant to *Belle Harbor* and to *Westwood*?

Consider the suggestion in *Westwood* that a "general assessment" could be levied to raise funds for the improvement of the plant. Cases considered in the subdivision control chapter, see *supra* p. 831, also suggest that a development charge could be levied against a developer to meet his pro rata share of improvements to a municipal waste treatment or similar system. The courts were divided on whether a development charge could be levied to pay for improvements to an existing system. Of what relevance are these cases to the problem raised in *Westwood* and in *Belle Harbor*? A New York court has disapproved the levy of charges for this purpose, *Torsoe Bros. Constr. v. Board of Trustees*, 375 N.Y.S.2d 612 (N.Y. App. Div. 1975).

As in the subdivision lot fee cases, see *supra* p. 817, is there an opportunity for municipal manipulation here? For example, what if the inadequacy of the drainage system in *Belle Harbor* were due to the consistent refusal of the municipality to budget sufficient funds for improvement of the system? Is the health danger in this event simply a "pretext" which would not allow the refusal of the building permit?

The larger question raised by these cases is the extent to which a municipality may use public service inadequacies as a basis for managing new urban growth. This issue is considered in the context of the *Ramapo* case, *infra* p. 1037, and in Section E. of this chapter.

2. The constitutionality of a major ban on sewer service hook-ups in the Washington, D.C., metropolitan area was litigated in *Smoke Rise, Inc. v. Washington Suburban Sanitary Comm'n*, 400 F. Supp. 1369 (D. Md. 1975). In this case, because of severe water pollution in Montgomery and Prince George's Counties on the Maryland side of the metropolitan area, the State of Maryland Department of Mental Health and Hygiene ordered an extensive ban on additional hook-ups to sewer facilities provided by the Commission. By statute, the Commission is authorized as the sole supplier of sanitary sewer services in much of this two-county area. At the time of this case the moratorium had been in effect for five years, during which time steps had been taken by the Commission and by the county governments to improve sewer service both on an interim and on a permanent basis. However, the completion of this program had been delayed by

intergovernmental conflicts, including a conflict over the construction of an interceptor sewer crossing the District of Columbia.

The court first considered a challenge to the constitutionality of the moratorium as a taking of property and rejected the challenge on the ground that the moratorium was necessary "to prevent a public harm to the natural character of the waters of the state." *Id.* at 1382. Next the court considered the constitutionality of the moratorium as a deprivation of property; its constitutionality had been challenged on this score on the ground that it amounted improperly to a tacit no-growth policy. *Id.* at 1384. This contention was also rejected, the court noting that "[i]n Maryland, the courts have expressly upheld the use of sewer service restrictions as a tool to accomplish staged development and to guide growth within the limits of the comprehensive plan." *Id.* Moreover, in this case the Commission had actively pursued plans for the improvement of sewer service, so that "it cannot be said that the moratorium on sewer service has been effected for the improper purpose of restricting from Prince George's and Montgomery Counties, Maryland's fair share of metropolitan Washington's regional growth." *Id.* at 1385. Finally, the court held that the moratorium had been reasonable in duration, stressing the fact that federal grants for the improvement of sewer service were not clearly available until 1975, and that intergovernmental difficulties in the completion of the system had impeded its progress.

To what extent does *Smoke Rise* benefit from the fact that the moratorium was imposed by a regional sanitary district under orders from a state agency? What warrant is there under due process to consider the vagaries of federal funding when considering the constitutionality of a moratorium? Can you distinguish the area-wide ban on sewer hook-ups in *Smoke Rise* from the refusal of the individual building permit in *Belle Harbor?* From the zoning ban in *Westwood?* Review again the various forms of sewer moratoria discussed in the Rivkin article, *supra.*

3. That an interim zoning ordinance may be tailored to the protection of environmentally threatened areas while improvements are made to public facilities is indicated by *Cappture Realty Corp. v. Board of Adjustment,* 313 A.2d 624 (N.J.L. 1973), *aff'd,* 336 A.2d 30 (N.J. Super. 1975). An interim zoning ordinance prohibited, unless allowed by a special exception permit, all new development in the flood-prone area of a brook located within the Borough. A permit could not issue under the ordinance if it authorized development that would create additional surface water run-off. In part for this reason, a permit for an industrial project proposed by the corporation was denied.

The purpose of the interim zoning ordinance was to give the Borough time to construct flood protection works, and the court held that the rationale for interim zoning ordinances pending comprehensive revision of the zoning code applied in this situation as well. The court also upheld the interim restriction even though it was not certain that the proposed flood control projects would fully alleviate the flooding problem, and even though the impact of the proposed development on the flooding problem would be marginal as much of the surrounding area was already developed. Plaintiff's property was zoned for industrial use, and was surrounded by tracts developed industrially.

URBAN GROWTH MANAGEMENT SYSTEMS, American Society of Planning Officials, Planning Advisory Service Report Nos. 309-10, at 46-47 (1975)

Planning moratoriums and interim development controls. Interim development controls are an old but little used device to accomplish managed growth. First, a temporary ordinance is enacted to prevent or restrict further development until planning has been completed and permanent controls to implement the plan have been developed. The ordinance is intended to preserve the status quo in a particular section of a municipality pending adoption of a permanent implementing regulation. This is accomplished by allowing only that development which is in accord with the contemplated plan.

Most so-called "stop growth" or "freeze growth" ordinances are nothing more than interim development controls in the guise of developmental moratoriums. In many cases, however, the necessary plans on which to base the controls have not been worked out.

The biggest dilemma in drafting an interim ordinance is deciding which development should be allowed or prohibited during the planning period. Although a complete moratorium may be desirable, the courts have rarely upheld total prohibitions. Where a partial control is contemplated, existing zoning districts and prevailing land-use patterns should be compared with future plans and ordinances. Development can proceed during the interim period only if proposed future development adheres to existing regulations. Interim development controls are designed to serve three important functions. First, they permit planning and ordinance writing to proceed relatively free of development pressures. (The interim development control also can be used to amend the existing zoning scheme.) As such, the entire planning mechanism should be conceived as a dynamic process requiring periodic review of goals and controls. Such review is essential if planning is to be viewed as evolutionary and responsive to the unpredictable elements of technological and social change.

The second purpose of interim development control is to prevent uses that will not conform to the adopted ordinances. Interim controls help assure that the effectiveness of the system will not be destroyed before it has been fully implemented. Frequently, when word of a new zoning ordinance or development regulation slips out, developers seek building permits or begin construction of buildings before the ordinance goes into effect. Interim controls help preclude this race against time. Also, the planning commission can afford to be less hasty in finalizing the new plan, thus taking time to make it effective.

The final objective of interim zoning is the promotion of public debate on the issues involved. By giving the planning commission sufficient time to involve the public, thoughtless implementation can be avoided.

Interim development controls have been adopted by several states to protect statewide or regional areas while a complete plan for preservation of critical areas is being formulated. In California, bills have been proposed to create the California Tahoe Conservation Agency and the Bay Area Regional Planning Agency. Both agencies will make use of iterim ordinances during the formative period of the plan. The same is true in New York, where state commissioners are formulating proposals to protect such key areas as the Hudson River Valley and Adirondack Park. In New Jersey, iterim zoning regulation lasting two years is being used to protect the Hackensack Meadowlands while a master plan is prepared. Interim controls are used primarily by counties and municipalities that want to develop growth control systems.

The validity of interim zoning has been firmly established constitutionally and under the Standard Zoning Enabling Act. Courts generally have upheld the validity of interim controls for "reasonable" periods of time, reasonableness being determined on a case-by-case basis, usually with the complexity of the ordinance and its preceding planning requirements as a primary determinant.

BOARD OF SUPERVISORS OF FAIRFAX COUNTY v. HORNE

Supreme Court of Virginia
216 Va. 113, 215 S.E.2d 453 (1975)

Before I'ANSON, C. J., and HARRISON, COCHRAN, HARMAN, POFF and COMPTON, JJ.

COCHRAN, Justice.

In this appeal we consider the validity of county ordinances prohibiting for a specified period of time the filing of applications for approval of site plans and preliminary subdivision plats.

On January 7, 1974, the Board of Supervisors of Fairfax County, pursuant to a resolution stating that "emergency conditions" existed within the county because of "unprecedented and rapid growth," adopted an Interim Development Ordinance (IDO), on an emergency basis, by amending the County Zoning Ordinance to include the following:

"§ 30-19 Interim Development Ordinance

"30-19.1 This Article shall be in full force and effect from the date of its enactment until June 30, 1975, the date established for the adoption of the complete official zoning map of the entire county.

"30-19.2 During the period while this Article is in full force and effect for all real property in Fairfax County:

"(A) No application shall be accepted for, nor any approval granted for, a special permit, a special exception, a site plan under the Fairfax County Zoning Ordinance of 1959 as amended and revised, or a preliminary subdivision plat, except as provided in Section (C) of this Article.

"(B) Nothing contained in this Article shall be deemed to abrogate or annul any prior approval lawfully issued and in effect as of the date of enactment of this Article . . . .

"(C) . . .

2. No proposal for a public facility shall be subject to the provisions of Section (A) above.

"(D) No application for an amendment to the Zoning Ordinance of 1959 as amended and revised on the date of adoption of this Article shall be accepted or considered by the Planning Commission or the Board of Supervisors during the period while this Article is in effect."

The emergency ordinance was adopted without compliance with the statutory requirements for the enactment of either zoning ordinances or subdivision ordinances.

The purpose of the Ordinance was stated therein as follows:

". . . to protect the comprehensive plan and the new Zoning Ordinance and Official Zoning Map thereof and to insure their implementation by hereby adopting, pursuant to the authority vested in the Board of Supervisors, reasonable interim legislation for a reasonable time during consideration of the aforesaid proposed comprehensive plan, zoning ordinance and official zoning map thereof, to protect the public interest and welfare and prevent a race of diligence between property owners and the County during consideration of the proposed comprehensive plan, zoning ordinance and official zoning map thereof, which would in many instances result in the establishment of a pattern of land use and development which would be inconsistent with the comprehensive plan and violate its basic intent and purpose and fail to protect the community and its general welfare."

After complying with all statutory requirements for the enactment of a zoning ordinance the Board reenacted the IDO on March 4, 1974, the reenacted ordinance differing in no material respect from the emergency ordinance and confirming the effective period of the moratorium from January 7, 1974, through June 30, 1975.

After January 7, 1974, the appellees (Landowners) sought to develop their lands in accordance with existing zoning classifications. They submitted either site plans or preliminary subdivision plats which were rejected by the appropriate county official solely because of the IDO moratorium. The Landowners then initiated in the trial court against the Board and designated county officials (collectively, the Board) separate proceedings, subsequently consolidated, to have the ordinances declared invalid.

During the pendency of the litigation the Board amended IDO on June 24, 1974, to include the following provision:

> "All areas of the County which are not specifically designated as critical to the current comprehensive replanning of the County, based on planning and environmental criteria, shall be exempted from the restrictions of Section (A) of this Article upon formal adoption of a land release map or maps, and criteria."

The Board also adopted a land release map, effective July 1, 1974, which showed the areas of the county that were released, or could be released, from the IDO restrictions.

In the trial court the Landowners not only challenged the Board's authority to enact the IDO, but also adduced evidence for the purpose of showing that, even if such an ordinance could legally be enacted, there was no factual justification for the legislation. The Board introduced evidence of its approval of a Planned Land Use System under which, among other things, a comprehensive plan and a comprehensive new zoning ordinance would be recommended, and evidence of the Board's concern that uses not conforming with the projected zoning classifications might become vested pending the preparation, consideration and enactment of the new legislation.

The uncontradicted evidence showed that at least 70 site plans and preliminary subdivision plats filed on or before January 7, 1974, were processed after that date; that 45 submitted after that date were rejected because of the IDO; and that 107 submitted after that date were accepted because of certain administrative guidelines adopted by the County staff from time to time to eliminate inequities. The evidence also showed that the possibility of enactment of the IDO became publicly known on February 5, 1973, upon approval of the Planned Land Use System, and that there was no significant increase in the filing of site plans and preliminary subdivision plats between that date and January 7, 1974, the effective date of the IDO. There was no evidence that the proposed new zoning ordinance would affect the Landowners or that any of them had submitted plans or plats in order to evade the provisions of the proposed new ordinance.

The trial court heard the evidence *ore tenus* over a period of five days, beginning July 10, 1974. Near the close of the trial the trial court refused to permit the Board to raise as a defense, for the first time, the Landowners' failure to exhaust their administrative remedies, and the Board assigned no error to this ruling.

The trial court, by memorandum opinion filed August 12, 1974, concluded that the presumption of validity which attached to the emergency ordinance was rebutted by the evidence and that passage of that ordinance was arbitrary and capricious; that the Board had no express or implied authority to enact either the emergency ordinance or the March 4, 1974, ordinance, and the evidence did not disclose a necessity therefor; and that the legislation failed to comply with the uniformity requirement of zoning under Code § 15.1-488 (Repl.Vol.1973). The Board appeals the final decree entered August 16, 1974, in which the trial court, after ruling that the emergency ordinance was null and void and that the regularly enacted ordinance was "void insofar as it purports to prevent the acceptance and approval of preliminary subdivision plats and site plans," ordered the Board to "accept for filing preliminary plats of subdivision, final plats of subdivision and final site plans, and to process the same in a prompt manner. . . ."

The Board argues that enactment of the IDO was authorized either as a valid exercise of its police power or by express grant or necessary implication of the enabling statutes.

In Virginia the powers of boards of supervisors are fixed by statute and are limited to those conferred expressly or by necessary implication. . . . This rule is a corollary to Dillon's Rule that municipal corporations have only those powers expressly granted, those necessarily or fairly implied therefrom, and those that are essential and indispensable. . . .[1]

We have long upheld, as a valid exercise of delegated police power, local zoning regulations enacted under state enabling legislation. . . . We have acknowledged the presumption of validity that attaches to zoning ordinances, as legislative enactments of the local governing body, . . . a presumption, however, which we have held to be rebuttable. . . . But in the present case we are considering an ordinance which, though designated and adopted as a zoning ordinance, is, at least as to the parts in issue, a subdivision ordinance. It does not purport to change zoning classifications. It has certain characteristics of a zoning ordinance in that it proscribes for the specified period applications for rezoning, special building permits and, in the emergency ordinance, special exceptions to the zoning ordinance. We will assume, without deciding, that those provisions, which are not in issue, were validly enacted. We are concerned only with the provisions that prohibit the filing of subdivision plats and site plans.

The General Assembly has enacted detailed enabling legislation, codified under Title 15.1 "Counties, Cities and Towns" as Chapter

---

[1] [For discussion of Dillon's Rule see D. Mandelker & D. Netsch, State and Local Government in a Federal System 148-51 (1977). —Eds.]

11, entitled "Planning, Subdivision of Land and Zoning." Code §§ 15.1-427 et seq. (Repl.Vol.1973). Various provisions authorize the appointment of local planning commissions, § 15.1-427, and prescribe the duties of such commissions. § 15.1-444. Under § 151.-446 et seq., the local planning commission is required to prepare and recommend a comprehensive plan for the development of the area, and the procedures are specified for having the plan put into effect. The commission is empowered, but not required, by § 15.1-458 et seq. to have made, for approval by the governing body, an official map showing existing and proposed public streets, waterways and public areas. Section 15.1-464 provides for preparation by the commission of five year capital outlay programs for the political subdivision based on the comprehensive plan. Article 7 (§§ 15.1-465-485) sets forth with great specificity the powers and duties of local governing bodies to provide for the subdivision and development of land. Article 8 (§§ 15.1-486-498) prescribes with like specificity the purpose, permitted provisions, and procedures for adoption and revision of local zoning ordinances, requiring submission to the planning commission and public hearings before final approval by the governing body.

We have made a significant distinction between local regulations governing subdivisions, enacted pursuant to the enabling provisions of Article 7, and those governing zoning, enacted pursuant to the provisions of Article 8. We have held that approval of a site plan and issuance of a building permit are ministerial, rather than discretionary, acts, the performance of which may be enforced by mandamus when an applicant has complied with or is ready, willing and able to comply with the local requirements. . . . On the contrary, local zoning ordinances are legislative acts which, so long as their reasonableness is fairly debatable, will not be invalidated by us. . . .

The enabling subdivision legislation requires prompt action on subdivision plats and site plans by local officials. Although § 15.1-475 authorizes local governing bodies to provide for submission of preliminary plats for tentative approval under appropriate "rules of preparation and procedure," there is no statutory authority for the enactment of an interim development ordinance which suspends the submission of plats and site plans for a specified period of time. Section 15.1-466 enumerates various permissible provisions that, "among other things," may be included in local subdivision ordinances. In *Nat. Realty Corp. v. Virginia Beach,* 209 Va. 172, 163 S.E.2d 154 (1968), in construing § 15.1-466, we held that the municipality could not impose a fee for examination and approval of final subdivision plats in the absence of express statutory authority therefor. Such authority was thereafter expressly granted by amendment to the statute. Acts 1970, c. 436 at 653-54.

The enabling zoning legislation enumerates in § 15.1-491 various permissible provisions that may be included in local zoning ordinances. We deem it significant that this statute which, in paragraph (b) expressly permits the temporary application of a local zoning ordinance to newly annexed lands, and in paragraph (h) authorizes the requirement of site plan approval, makes no provision for temporarily suspending, under exigent circumstances, the filing of site plans.

Citing various scholarly dissertations on the subject, the Board has suggested various reasons to justify implied authorization for localities to enact interim development ordinances. *E. g.,* Freilich, Interim Development Controls: Essential Tools for Implementing Flexible Planning and Zoning, 49 J. Urban L. 65 (1971); Comment, Stopgap and Interim Legislation, a Device to Maintain the Status Quo of an Area Pending the Adoption of a Comprehensive Ordinance or Amendment Thereto, 18 Syracuse L.Rev. 837 (1967); Note, Stopgap Measures to Preserve the Status Quo Pending Comprehensive Zoning or Urban Redevelopment Legislation, 14 W.Res.L.Rev. 135 (1962). However, the General Assembly of Virginia has undertaken to achieve in the enabling legislation a delicate balance between the individual property rights of its citizens and the health, safety and general welfare of the public as promoted by reasonable restrictions on those property rights. We believe that it is peculiarly a function of the General Assembly to determine, subject to constitutional restraints, what revisions in the statutes may be required to maintain the appropriate balance between these important but frequently conflicting interests.

A review of cases from other jurisdictions reveals that courts have reached different conclusions, depending upon their construction of the local police power, as to the implied authority of a local governing body to enact interim development ordinances or similar legislation. *See* Annot., 30 A.L.R.3d 1196 (1970).

In *Phillips Petroleum Company v. City of Park Ridge,* 16 Ill.App.2d 555, 149 N.E.2d 344 (1958), the court held that, as there was no provision therefor in the enabling statutes, the city council could not by ordinance or resolution suspend a valid zoning ordinance. To the same effect are *Downey v. Sioux City,* 208 Iowa 1273, 227 N.W. 125 (1929), and *Alexander v. City of Minneapolis,* 267 Minn. 155, 125 N.W.2d 583 (1963).

The Board has cited numerous cases in support of its contention that it had necessarily implied authority to enact the IDO. Most of the cases on which the Board relies are distinguishable from the present case. In four of the cases, the local governing body had express statutory authorization or a broad constitutional grant of power, both lacking in Virginia, to enact interim development controls. In four other cases, the ordinance under consideration involved interim or temporary rezoning which did not have the effect of a development "freeze". In three of the cited cases, the interim ordinance was utilized in the contest of newly annexed territory. Another involved an emergency ordinance which restricted the power of the board of zoning adjustment to grant a variance. In three cases, the iterim development ordinances were struck down because of the governing bodies' failure to observe statutorily prescribed procedures in enacting them. Another was decided without adjudicating the validity of the "interim" ordinances. In another the court held that a county may adopt a zoning ordinance without first adopting a master plan and may thereafter deny a rezoning application filed by a landowner.

Two cases did involve ordinances which prohibited the issuance of building permits. In *Willdel Realty, Inc. v. New Castle County,* 270 A.2d 174 (Del.Ch.1970), the council suspended the issuance of building permits for a period of ninety days for land as to which a rezoning ordinance was pending. Although the court's holding as to the validity of that ordinance is unclear, it did indicate "doubt that [it] could be validly applied to [the] plaintiffs." *Id.* at 177. In *Cappture Realty Corp. v. Board of Adjustment,* 126 N.J.Super. 200, 313 A.2d 624 (1973), the issue was whether a municipality could temporarily delay construction in a flood plain pending completion of flood control projects.

In *Downham v. City Council of Alexandria,* 58 F.2d 784 (E.D.Va.1932), the only cited case arising in Virginia, the interim ordinance involved did not prohibit construction. It merely provided that applications for building permits had to be referred to the zoning and planning commission for consideration and recommendation to the city council. The landowner, who attempted to enjoin enforcement of the ordinance as applied to his property, as a denial of due process, failed to apply for a permit, and thus failed to exhaust his administrative remedies.

We conclude that there was no express or implied authority for the enactment by the Board of ordinances imposing a moratorium on the filing of site plans and preliminary subdivision plats, and to that extent, the ordinances adopted on January 7, 1974, and March 4, 1974, are invalid. Accordingly, the final decree entered by the trial court on August 16, 1974, is

Affirmed.

Comments: 1. Since the excerpt included just before the principal case stated that "[t]he validity of interim zoning has been firmly established constitutionally and under the Standard Zoning Enabling Act," how do you explain the principal opinion? Supposedly, the Virginia enabling legislation could be amended to permit the kind of development freeze that was enacted by the Fairfax County IDO. Does the court suggest, nevertheless, that such a freeze might be unconstitutional even if authorized by statute?

The IDO order and the *Horne* case formed an important episode in the attempt to prepare a growth management plan for the county. *Horne* was only one of several cases that challenged various regulatory aspects of the plan. The story of this litigation is told in Hazel, Growth Management Through Litigation, Urb. Land, November 1976, at 6. (Hazel was one of the attorneys for the developers in the *Horne* case.) Hazel's account of the circumstances leading up to the IDO is as follows:

> In November and December 1973, the [county] board recognized that several zoning applications deemed by the board to be of far-reaching significance would come to public hearing under existing land use plans before the ... [growth management planning] process could be concluded. Their concern and frustration over the continued erosion of county control gave way to panic on January 7, 1974. Through an Interim Development Ordinance (IDO), adopted on an emergency basis without benefit of public hearing, all zoning, planning, and building permit activity — the entire development process — was suspended for a period of 18 months. The emergency alleged was the anticipated surge in land use applications of all types, supposedly for the purpose of avoiding the ultimate impact of ... [the growth management plan]. Residents perceived the need to protect the value of their property. IDO is generally conceded by objective observers to have been a major strategic error by the county.

Id. at 12.

In her account of the Fairfax County growth management plan, Grace Dawson also notes the difficulties the county had in defending the IDO in the *Horne* case:

> In debating the question of the "race of diligence" that might have occurred had the ordinance not been enacted on an emergency basis, the county was hard pressed to come up with supporting data. Ruck [the planning director—Eds.] could not show, either from previous experiences with the imposition of moratoria in the county, or from data for the period between the time of ... [a county board resolution authorizing the growth management program, adopted on February 6, 1973 — Eds.] and the actual imposition of the ... [IDO] almost a year later, that such a "race" would have taken place.

G. Dawson, Make No Little Plans 60 (1977). If the county really pushed the "panic button" when it adopted the IDO, why did the court not place its decision on this ground?

The IDO experience indicates the difficulties of adopting interim controls when major changes in the comprehensive plan and zoning allocations are contemplated by the growth management program. Often the interim zoning ordinance will simply freeze in place the existing zoning in the community until the planned changes in the zoning ordinance can be made. It is this kind of interim zoning which has often been upheld in court. *See, e.g., Walworth County v. City of Elkhorn,* 133 N.W.2d 257 (Wis. 1965). The trouble in Fairfax County was that existing zoning was not consistent with the objectives of the growth management plan, so that this form of interim control would not have been sufficient.

2. There is not much authority on the validity of a total suspension of the development control process pending a revision in the comprehensive plan or zoning ordinance. With the principal case compare *Collura v. Town of Arlington,* 329 N.E.2d 733 (Mass. 1975). In *Collura* the town adopted a two-year moratorium on the construction of apartment buildings in certain areas of the town, pending a revision in its comprehensive plan. The Massachusetts court held that the adoption of the interim ordinance was authorized by the zoning enabling legislation, and stressed the fact that the town had complied with the statutory procedures for amending zoning ordinances. In addition, the purposes of the ordinance were found to be permissible. The court noted that the moratorium was only partial, that the length of the moratorium was reasonable, and that 68 percent of all new dwellings in the town in the last decade had been apartment units as compared to 17 percent in the previous decade, so that "the restriction was aimed at an interim solution to a matter of genuine planning significance." *Id.* at 738. See also *Hunter v. Adams,* 4 Cal. Rptr. 776 (Cal. App. 1960), upholding a freeze on building permits pending the development of an urban renewal plan. *Contra, State ex rel. Mumma v. Stansberry,* 214 N.E.2d 684 (Ohio App. 1964).

What do you think of this comment: "[w]e suggest, however, that . . . [interim zoning] ordinances would be acceptable to most courts if they were adopted in compliance with statutory notice and hearing requirements and were used to further legitimate governmental objectives." D. Heeter, Interim Zoning Ordinances 3 (American Soc'y of Planning Officials, Planning Advisory Service Rep. No. 242, 1969). See *Morales v. Haines,* 349 F. Supp. 684 (N.D. Ill. 1972) (one-year suspension of building permits for subsidized housing held to violate equal protection).

In *Matthews v. Board of Zoning Appeals,* 237 S.E.2d 128 (Va. 1977), a county placed its entire unincorporated area in an interim single-use residential district in which dwelling units on two-acre lots were permitted. The ordinance was to be in effect for one year while a comprehensive plan and zoning ordinance were being prepared. The court held that *Horne* was not controlling because "[i]n the present case, the Ordinance did not temporarily prohibit all new subdivision development in the county by suspending the operation of applicable ordinances; it merely purported to zone Greene County for a period not exceeding one year." *Id.* at 133. While the property in question was held not subject to the permanent zoning ordinance, the court looked to the permanent ordinance as the basis for its conclusion that the interim zoning ordinance was invalid. Eight zoning districts were provided by the permanent ordinance, including a nonresidential district, indicating to the court that the more restrictive interim ordinance was unreasonable.

Compare Meadowland Regional Dev. Agency v. Hackensack Meadowlands Dev. Comm'n, 293 A.2d 192 (N.J. Super.), *cert. denied,* 299 A.2d 69 (N.J. 1972). Legislation enacted in 1968 authorized the Commission to prepare a comprehensive plan for the redevelopment of the extensive Meadowlands area, adjacent to New York City. Pending adoption of a final plan, the Commission enacted an interim ordinance that put a freeze on construction in 10,000 acres of the planning area. Underscoring the need for comprehensive study of the total planning of the Meadowlands area, the court upheld the freeze ordinance. See also *New Jersey Shore Builders Ass'n v. Township of Ocean,* 319 A.2d 255 (N.J. Super.), *cert. denied,* 321 A.2d 253 (N.J. 1974), upholding a six-month moratorium on major subdivisions and industrial developments pending preparation of a comprehensive zoning revision. The court urged the legislature to take action to provide the "standards applicable to such enactments."

3. An interim development control ordinance enacted through the initiative process to afford time to prepare a growth management study was upheld in *Builders Ass'n v. Superior Court,* 529 P.2d 582 (Cal. 1974), *appeal dismissed,* 427 U.S. 901 (1976). The ordinance was a reaction to the overcrowding of schools in the city of San Jose, and applied to those areas of the city in which the school problem was serious. In these areas, additional rezoning of land for residential development was restricted unless the affected school district certified that the party seeking the rezoning had agreed to provide a satisfactory alternative to permanent school construction.

Since interim zoning is generally upheld in California, see *Miller v. Board of Pub. Works,* 23 P. 381 (Cal. 1925), plaintiffs apparently decided not to attack the validity of the interim zoning concept. They alleged, in part, that the ordinance had unlawfully delegated zoning power to the school districts, an objection the court answered by noting that the ordinance had not conferred rezoning power on these districts and that the city could "condition approval of the zoning application upon certification by the school district that adequate facilities can be provided." *Id.* at 587. Answering a contention that the ordinance unconstitutionally discriminated between property lacking residential zoning and property already zoned residentially, the court held that "[c]ertainly there is nothing irrational in the voters' determination to permit residential construction, pending completion of a thorough study of problems of residential development, only by those owners whose property has already been found suitable for such construction." *Id.* A right to travel objection was also dismissed, see *infra* p. 1071. For discussion of the use of initiative and referendum in zoning see *supra* p. 762.

4. Both the principal case and the San Jose case were conceptual attacks on the interim control; that is, they challenged the general validity of the interim control ordinance and not its application to a particular developer or parcel of land. When owners of land who have been frustrated by the interim control have brought attacks on the interim regulations as applied to their property, the impact of the interim controls on the developer's expectations have often led the courts to invalidate the control as applied. The cases pro and con are collected in Annot., 30 A.L.R.3d 1235-50 (1970), and the results obviously vary with the circumstances. There is ordinarily no zoning estoppel in these situations, but the courts may hold the interim controls inapplicable if they are impressed by the equities of the landowner's case. The problem is complicated by the fact that a downzoning of the property may also occur during the interim period, a subject shortly to be discussed.

A good case illustrating these problems is *Ogo Assoc. v. City of Torrance,* 112 Cal. Rptr. 761 (Cal. App. 1974). Plaintiff applied for a building permit to build a federally subsidized housing project in a mixed use area in which the plaintiff's property had been zoned to permit this use for eight years. The city next enacted an ordinance placing a moratorium on all new construction in the area and a permanent ordinance in the interim period changing the zoning on plaintiff's tract to a use not allowing the proposed project. It then refused to issue plaintiff a building permit. Although plaintiff had not satisfied all of the conditions for the building permit prior to the adoption of the moratorium ordinance, the court remanded the case to allow plaintiff to prove its claim of racial and economic discrimination in the adoption of the moratorium ordinance and permanent zoning change. For discussion see Mandelker, Downzoning to Control Growth Draws a Close Look by the Courts, 3 Real Est. L.J. 402 (1975). For seemingly contrary opinions by the Minnesota Supreme Court in fact situations roughly comparable to the *Ogo* case compare *Almquist v. Town of Marshan,* 245 N.W.2d 819 (Minn. 1976) (interim moratorium may be applied to pending development), with *Alexander v. City of Minneapolis,* 125 N.W.2d 583 (Minn. 1963) (*contra*).

5. Some states have adopted statutes authorizing interim zoning ordinances. These vary in scope, and most contain time limitations on the authorized interim controls. *See, e.g.,* Cal. Gov't Code § 65858 (Deering 1974) (interim ordinance prohibiting uses in conflict with contemplated zoning proposal; four-month limit); Minn. Stat. Ann. § 394.34 (1968) (counties; interim ordinance limited to one year authorized when revision in plan or land use controls pending); Utah Code Ann. § 10-9-18(g) (1973) (interim ordinance prohibiting commercial and residential uses and establishing site requirements for residential buildings; six-month limit). For a significant case construing a statute authorizing "broad protective controls" in areas that cannot be precisely mapped to permit a five-year holding zone see *State v. Snohomish County,* 488 P.2d 511 (Wash. 1971). Washington also authorizes, with no time limit, an interim zoning ordinance classifying and regulating uses pending adopting of a zoning revision. Wash. Rev. Code Ann. § 36.70.790 (1964).

C. DOWNZONING

A consideration of downzoning problems belongs in a chapter on growth management because piecemeal and sometimes massive downzonings often accompany the adoption of a growth management strategy. The reason why downzoing is often necessary in a growth management program is indicated in the following selection.

ASSOCIATION OF BAY AREA GOVERNMENTS, ZONING AND GROWTH IN THE SAN FRANCISCO BAY AREA 4, 5, (1973).

[The study first compared the zoning holding capacity of counties in the Bay Area with projected population growth and found that the zoned holding capacity of these counties was in most cases twice the population projections. In one county the zoning exceeded the population projection by 700 percent! The study does not indicate the densities at which the existing zoning would allow new development to take place. — Eds.]

What's Wrong with Zoning?

The basic problem shown by these comparisons is that in many places zoning and planning have not been used together to fulfill general plan growth and land use policies. Local, regional, and state growth targets or expectations for the foreseeable future are far exceeded by current zoning capacities. There is little relationship between present growth planning and the implicit growth potential of zoning. Based on past growth, present trends, and reasonable future expectations, the likelihood of achieving the maximum zoned population is small. But because zoning is the primary method by which local governments manage use of the land, the way zoning operates to channel population growth and physical development is of great importance. Using land use regulation as part of a comprehensive planning process is the best method by which local general purpose governments can participate — constrained by the powers delegated to special districts, the private sector, regional agencies, and the State and Federal governments — in the management of growth within their own jurisdictions.

There are three basic factors that should be considered in planning for managed growth through zoning: (1) how much — what will be the growth level at a given time for which services will be needed; (2) where — how will the growth be distributed spatially so that such services can be provided in the right locations; and (3) how fast — at what rate will the growth occur in relation to growth targets so that services can be provided at the proper time. Zoning as currently practiced is more directly concerned with managing where growth occurs and qualitative factors, less directly concerned with how much and least concerned with how fast.

In most cases, a given area of land is designated in a certain use zone at a given density of development. Theoretically the use area can be developed to the maximum allowed density with the timing and placement of development left to the operation of economic and other forces. Zoning now exercises little control over distribution or timing of land use within the zoning district. Scattered development may occur; some areas may be quickly developed to their maximum density, while others may lie completely idle. Zoning now acts mostly to segregate different land uses, rather than to manage expansion in an orderly and timely process to fulfill a comprehensive plan.

Traditional zoning has led almost inevitably to overzoning. Zoning was originally intended to segregate various land uses and to abate nuisances, thereby protecting existing property values and insuring marketability. In this purpose it succeeded. Zoning more recently has additionally become the main tool by which local governments attempt to control land use to protect community benefits. This aim has met with less success, because zoning does not reflect the general plan and does not contain provisions to order and time development to achieve the community's overall objectives, as articulated in the general plan. . . .

Inconsistency of zoning with general plan policies at best lessens and at worst negates rational attempts at orderly and timely growth, resulting in the weakening of zoning as a land use management tool. It seems reasonable that a county whose general plan targets a total population of one-half million people at some given time in the future should be zoned for no more than one-half million people. If that were the case, new development could be guided into portions of the community or county which were planned to accommodate it. If the same county, however, is overzoned by one million people, the distributive and timing process automatically becomes less certain and less controllable, resulting in overuse of some facilities, underuse of others, and urban sprawl. If half a million new people are allowed to settle anywhere within an area designated for one million people, patterns of expansion are likely to be less compact, less ordered, and less economical in terms of utilities, services, and access than in better controlled situations. . . .

NORBECK VILLAGE JOINT VENTURE v. MONTGOMERY COUNTY COUNCIL

Court of Appeals of Maryland
254 Md. 59, 254 A.2d 700 (1969)

HAMMOND, Chief Judge. The appeal is from the action of Judge Pugh in affirming the reclassification of the appellants' land under a sectional map amendment of the Olney area (a comprehensive rezoning of almost 50 square miles), adopted by the Montgomery County Council, sitting as a district council, on the proposal of the Maryland-National Capital Park and Planning Commission (MNCPPC).

In 1966 all the members of the Montgomery County Council save one were denied reelection by the voters of the County. By its actions taken on November 9, 10 and 11 the lame-duck Council granted a great number of rezonings. The new Council moved to reconsider some 75 of these and appointed an ad hoc committee of County legal officers, other lawyers and zoning experts to recommend further procedures and proceedings. . . .

Included in the specified midnight rezonings moved to be reconsidered by the new Council was application E-928, a proposal by MNCPPC for sectional map amendment of the Olney region, filed on July 28, 1966, to implement a General Plan for the Maryland-Washington Regional District which the MNCPPC had adopted in early 1964, and a Master Plan approved by the District Council on August 31, 1966, both envisioning Olney as a satellite low density community ultimately to have 19,000 people at the core and 10,000 on the fringe. The Plans contemplated a green belt of open spaces and parks to shield the Olney area from the ever-lengthening and overcrowding suburban sprawl coming out of Washington, and changed the zoning designation of appellants' land, some 183 acres in the southeast quadrant along the east side of Georgia Avenue, from R-R (half acre lots) to R-A (two acre lots), as it did some 12,000 other acres. A public hearing was held on October 17, 1966 on E-928. Officials of MNCPPC and of the County Citizens Planning Association offered extensive testimony in support of the application and it also was supported by the technical staff of the planning Commission and the Commission. The appellants presented several experts to refute the concepts of the Master Plan urging in essence that the prior policy of allowing all the small houses that the ever-increasing population of the County would buy or rent be allowed in the Olney area, which would lead to a population of some 200,000 despite the conceded inadequacy of sewerage and roads. The old Council rejected the Master Plan it had approved a few months earlier by denying application E-928.

The new Council, on December 6, 1966, extended until March 7, 1967, some three weeks after it had resolved to reconsider the various cases, the time for final action on its reconsideration of E-928. On December 29, 1966, the Planning Commission filed a comprehensive rezoning plan, application E-998, encompassing 49.5 square miles — some 30,000 acres, including those of appellants — to implement the Olney and vicinity Master Plan. By Resolution No. 6-221 of February 21, 1967, the Council allowed the withdrawal of E-928 without prejudice, having taken no action whatever on the merits of E-928. The appellants who had prevailed on E-928 before the old Council did not appeal from the action of the new Council in permitting its withdrawal.

The Planning Commission adopted the recommendation of its technical staff to the District Council that E-998 be approved. A public hearing was held on E-998 on April 21, 1967. MNCPPC's director, Hewins, testified in favor of the application as an implementation of the joint purposes of the Master Plan: the preservation of open spaces and the protection of the watershed area. He described the background of the Olney community plan as a result of the General Plan — Year 2000 Plan — which provided for the development of wedges and corridors throughout the county. Satellite corridors included plans for corridor cities such as

Gaithersburg and Germantown with planned population in excess of 100,000. Olney as a self-identifiable community with its own hospital, schools, commercial area, and theater was qualified and selected as a satellite community. The Olney area was selected above other possible locations in the County for this development because of its geographical setting and natural amenities which encouraged the planned growth concept. No other area was found to possess the assets of the Olney community. Hewins further testified that this plan was in accordance with sound planning principles. According to Hewins, the plan promoted a land use pattern within which an integrated cultural-social-community service complex can develop around a 75-acre shopping district. Also, he said that the Plan's highway network provides convenient access to residents of the community and fits into the broader transportation needs of the region.

A purpose of the Plan was described as promoting the physical isolation of Olney from suburban sprawl. Low density residential zoning was recommended to break the development pattern from the suburbs. The proposed zoning in the plan is in accordance with existing development. It was stated that a serious deficiency of public services would exist if the Master Plan was not adopted. The plan was to accomplish a staged development using the tools of zoning and sewer access to avoid the excess costs of public services. A critical element of the Plan was to encourage earlier growth along the 70S corridor rather than on the Patuxent River Watershed thereby protecting the basin from pollution. Hewins did point out that cluster development of the R-A zone could be served by sewers, but the District Council reserved the power to approve these applications separately as a tool to guide growth within the desired limits.

Appellants presented several experts to challenge the credibility of the Master Plan. The appellants pointed to the need for R-R development of middle income housing and the natural development of the "Georgia Avenue corridor."

Appellants make three arguments: . . . 2 — the granting of E-998 resulted in an unconstitutional taking of appellants' property by substituting zoning for eminent domain and depriving appellants of all reasonable use of their property; 3 — the decision in E-998 was not in accordance with the public health, safety, security, morals and general welfare and therefore was arbitrary, unreasonable, discriminatory and otherwise illegal. . . .

The appellants argue that for the County to decrease the permissible density of their land and that of other similarly zoned land and to refuse to furnish sewerage to their land in order to control the growth of population and to continue the present open space in the Olney region was to use zoning and planning impermissibly as a substitute for eminent domain and to reduce so substantitally the value of their land as to amount to confiscation.

If these contentions are sound, no zoning would ever have been allowed or sustained and all comprehensive rezoning would have to continue or increase permissible density, not reduce it. All original zoning decreases the right to use property as the owner pleases. Zoning places restrictions on property that was free of any restriction and the value of some if not most of that property necessarily is going to be lessened. None of this as such invalidates. comprehensive zoning; original or subsequent. . . . The broad test of the validity of a comprehensive rezoning is whether it bears a substantial relationship to the public health, comfort, order, safety, convenience, morals and general welfare, and such zoning enjoys a strong presumption of validity and correctness. . . . A property owner has no vested right to the continuance of the zoning status of his or neighboring property, merely the right to rely on the rule that a change will not be made unless it is required for the public good. . . . In *County Com'rs Queen Anne's County v. Miles,* 246 Md. 355, 368, 228 A.2d 450, 457, a minimum area zoning that limited residential use to five acres was upheld. Judge Oppenheimer for the Court said:

> [I]f the [comprehensive zoning] has a substantial relationship to the general welfare of the community in that it can fairly be taken as reasonable effort to plan for the future within the framework of the County's economic and social life, it is not unconsitutional because under it some persons may suffer loss and others be benefited.

. . . On these grounds piecemeal zoning changes from commercial to residential use have been upheld. . . . For an individual property owner to escape the binding impact of a comprehensive rezoning he must show that the plan lacks the necessary relationship to the general public interest and welfare that is presumed or that the effect of the plan is to deprive him of any reasonable use of his property.

The record clearly supports, if indeed it does not require, the finding Judge Pugh made that the challenged rezoning was not arbitrary, discriminatory or illegal. The Olney plan, in conformity with the General Plan, was a carefully thought out, carefully implemented policy of preserving a portion of Montgomery County, presently suitable (by reason of its geographical setting and natural amenities which encouraged the planned growth concept) for preservation as a self-identifiable community with its own hospital, schools, commercial area and theater, as a relatively low residential area which would break and hold back the spreading urban intrusion into the country. The plan sought to encourage earlier growth along the interstate 70S corridor rather than on the Patuxent River Watershed, thereby protecting the basin from pollution. Appellants dispute the validity of the concept underlying the plan and of the legality of the plan but do not suggest that it was not conceived and adopted in the utmost good faith, and they did not overcome the strong presumption that the plan was valid legislative action, a presumption buttressed in this case by reason of the fact that the plan implemented the General Plan and the Master Plan. . . .

The Olney area roads, sewers, schools and fire and police protection will not according to the record presently support urban or intense development, and to install the additional facilities that would be necessary to support a changed pattern would place a burden on the taxpayers that the County legislative body thinks is unwarranted and beyond its present reasonable capabilities.

The appellants did not, by an Olney plan country mile, meet their heavy burden of showing that the rezoning they dispute confiscates their property. The governing rule is that he who claims confiscatory action must show that the protested zoning precludes use of his property for any purpose for which it is reasonably adapted. It is not enough for the owner to show that the exercise of the police power, an essential attribute of sovereignty, by a rezoning or a failure to rezone results in substantial loss or hardship. . . .

Under § 111-5 a number of uses are permitted as of right in an R-A zone and under the succeeding paragraph b any of a further list of special exception uses may be availed of, many of which would be practicable under the Olney regional plan. There was no effort to show that appellants' land could not be utilized for any of the permitted uses.

Futhermore, the testimony was that the appellants could not do more with the land as R-R (as it was when they bought it prior to 1965) than they could under its rezoned status of R-A. They had attempted to have the County extend sewerage to the property when it was rezoned R-R and had been turned down. They did show that land in that area zoned R-A was worth $2,000 to $3,500 an acre and that land zoned R-R was worth $3,500 to $8,000 an acre. The present paper worth of their holdings say appellants, was cut by two-thirds by the rezoning, a substantial loss, but it can hardly be argued reasonably that land that is worth $2,000 to $3,500 an acre has been confiscated. Indeed, after the rezoning they voluntarily sold 65 of their 183 acres to the County for park use at an apparently satisfactory price. In *Marino v. City of Baltimore,* 215 Md. 206, 137 A.2d 198, the property was worth $14,000 under its existing residential zoning and was worth $140,000 if rezoned commercial as the owner asked unsuccessfully that it be. We held that this loss to the owner was not controlling.

What we have already said disposes, in our view, of appellants' third contention, a general and abstract statement that the decision in E-998 was not in accordance with the public health, safety, security, morals and general welfare and was therefore arbitrary, unreasonable, discriminatory or otherwise illegal.

Order affirmed, with costs.

BOARD OF SUPERVISORS v. SNELL
CONSTRUCTION CORPORATION

Supreme Court of Virginia
214 Va. 655, 202 S.E.2d 889 (1974)

Before Snead, C.J., and I'Anson, Carrico, Harrison, Cochran, Harman and Poff, JJ.

Poff, Justice. This appeal presents our first opportunity to consider the standard to be applied in judicial review of the validity of a zoning ordinance, enacted on motion of the zoning authority, which effects a piecemeal reduction of permissible residential density (downzoning).

Under the 1964 Annandale Comprehensive Master Plan, a 26-acre tract of land lying south of State Route 236 between Backlick Road on the east and Ravensworth Road on the west in Annandale, now owned by Snell Construction Corporation and Preston Construction Corporation (landowners), was zoned for low residential density. On May 16, 1969, landowners filed an application for increased density on a 16-acre portion of the tract. At that time, the 1964 plan was being considered for revision. On February 25, 1970, the Board of Supervisors of Fairfax County (the Board) adopted a new Annandale Master Plan. That plan, comprehending the entire Annandale complex, included two zoning districts affecting the 26-acre tract, one permitting high density and the other medium density.

Representing the southern boundary of the high density district, the dividing line between the two districts is shown on maps of the 1970 plan as a "collector" road running approximately parallel to Route 236 across landowners' property and connecting Backlick and Ravensworth. A dispute arose whether the eastern terminus of the dividing line was intended to be at Jayhawk Street 1300 feet south of Route 236 or at Falcon Street 1500 feet south. It was fixed in an undated errata sheet prepared by staff (never formally approved by the Board) at Falcon Street.

On December 28, 1970, at the express urging of the county land use staff, landowners filed an amended application requesting high density zoning in the northern portion of the 26-acre tract and medium density in the southern portion in accordance with the new Master Plan. Their application showed the eastern terminus of the dividing line at Falcon Street. The Planning Commission disapproved the amended application but recommended that the entire 26 acres be zoned to the density requested in the original application. On May 26, 1971 the Board declined the recommendation and adopted an ordinance granting landowners' amended application.

On April 17, 1972 a newly-elected Board of Supervisors, proceeding on its own motion, adopted an ordinance reducing the high density authorized by the old Board in the May 26, 1971 ordinance to medium density and fixing the eastern terminus of the southern boundary of the high density district at Jayhawk Street.

Landowners filed a motion for declaratory judgment praying that the trial court declare the April 17, 1972 ordinance void and the May 26, 1971 ordinance valid. By letter opinion dated November 14, 1972 and final decree entered November 24, 1972 the trial court granted landowners' prayer, ruling that "the defendants can change the zoning, provided there is a substantial change in circumstances or a mistake", finding that "the evidence does not support a finding of substantial change in circumstances or mistake as to merit the downzoning on April 17, 1972", and holding that "the action of Defendants . . . in downzoning the Complainant's property . . . [was] arbitrary, capricious and unreasonable and, therefore, illegal, invalid and void".

We look first to the policy and purposes of the zoning statutes adopted by the General Assembly, Code Title 15.1, Chapter 11. Read as a whole, the statutes strike a deliberate balance between private property rights and public interests.

> This chapter is intended to encourage local governments to improve public health, safety, convenience or welfare and to plan for the future development of communities to the end that transportation systems be carefully planned; that new community centers be developed with adequate highway, utility, health, educational, and recreational facilities; that the needs of agriculture, industry and business be recognized in future growth; that residential areas be provided with healthy surrounding for family life; and that the growth of the community be consonant with the efficient and economical use of public funds. Code § 15.1-427 (Repl.Vol.1973).

The statutes recognize that public power over private property rights should be exercised judiciously and equitably. That policy springs not only from public respect for personal rights and individual integrity but also from enlightened public self-interest. The General Assembly has recognized that it is in the public interest that private land not required for public use be put to its optimum use to fulfill societal needs. One purpose of zoning ordinances is "to encourage economic development activities that provide desirable employment and enlarge the tax base", Code § 15.1-489 (Repl.Vol.1973), and "[z]oning ordinances . . . shall be drawn with reasonable consideration for . . . the conservation of properties and their values. . . ." Code § 15.1-490 (Repl.Vol.1973).

Under the private enterprise system, land use is influenced by the profit motive. Profit flows from investments of time, talent, and capital. Landowners venture investments only when the prospects of profit are reasonable. Prospects are reasonable only when permissible land use is reasonably predictable. The Virginia landowner always confronts the possibility that permissible land use may be changed by a comprehensive zoning ordinance reducing profit prospects; yet, the Virginia statutes assure him that such a change will not be made suddenly, arbitrarily, or capriciously but only after a period of investigation and community planning.

We look next to general principles governing judicial review of zoning ordinances.

> The legislative branch of a local government in the exercise of its police power has wide discretion in the enactment and amendment of zoning ordinances. Its action is presumed to be valid so long as it is not unreasonable and arbitrary. The burden of proof is on him who assails it to prove that it is clearly unreasonable, arbitrary or capricious, and that it bears no reasonable or substantial relation to the safety, morals, or general welfare. The court will not substitute its judgment for that of a legislative body, and if the reasonableness of a zoning ordinance is fairly debatable it must be sustained. [Citations omitted]. *Board of Supervisors v. Carper,* 200 Va. 653, 660, 107 S.E.2d 390, 395 (1959).

These principles were articulated in a case involving a comprehensive amendment to a comprehensive zoning ordinance. All are sound. Insofar as apposite, we apply them here. But here, the April 17, 1972 ordinance is not a comprehensive zoning ordinance. Rather, it is a piecemeal zoning ordinance; one initiated by the zoning authority on its own motion; one selectively addressed to landowners' single parcel and an adjacent parcel; and one that reduces the permissible residential density *below* that recommended by a duly-adopted Master Plan.

Inherent in the presumption of legislative validity stated in *Carper* is a presumption of reasonableness. But, as Carper makes plain, the presumption of reasonableness is not absolute. Where presumptive reasonableness is challenged by probative evidence of unreasonableness, the challenge must be met by some evidence of reasonableness. If evidence of reasonableness is sufficient to make the question fairly debatable, the ordinance "must be sustained". If not, the evidence of unreasonableness defeats the presumption of reasonableness and the ordinance cannot be sustained.

With respect to the validity of a piecemeal downzoning ordinance such as that here involved, we are of opinion that when an aggrieved landowner makes a *prima facie* showing that since enactment of the prior ordinance there has been no change in circumstances substantially affecting the public health, safety, or welfare, the burden of going forward with evidence of such mistake, fraud, or changed circumstances shifts to the governing body. If the governing body produces evidence sufficient to make reasonableness fairly debatable, the ordinance must be sustained. If not, the ordinance is unreasonable and void.[2]

The rule we have stated promotes the policy and purposes of the zoning statutes. While the landowner is always faced with the possibility of comprehensive rezoning, the rule we have stated assures him that, barring mistake or fraud in the prior zoning ordinance, his legitimate profit prospects will not be reduced by a piecemeal zoning ordinance reducing permissible use of his land until circumstances substantially affecting the public interest have changed. Such stability and predictability in the law serve the interest of both the landowner and the public.

The rule applied by the trial court is not inconsistent with the rule we have adopted. But the Board argues that the trial court should have found that the evidence satisfied the rule. It says that the action of the old Board in enacting the May 26, 1971 ordinance locating the collector road as shown in landowners' amended application at Falcon Street was a mistake within the meaning of the rule because the 1970 comprehensive plan intended it to be located at Jayhawk Street. We do not agree. Even if we assume that the 1970 plan intended the location to be at Jayhawk Street rather than Falcon Street (and the record does not resolve the dispute), it does not follow that the location fixed in the May 26, 1971 ordinance was a mistake. The statutes do not make the comprehensive plan a zoning ordinance but only a comprehensive guideline for zoning ordinances. The precise location of boundaries between zoning

---

[2] The rule we adopt is similar to the rule applied in Maryland. "[T]o sustain a piecemeal change [from the prior zoning], there must be *strong* evidence of mistake in the original zoning, or else of a substantial change in conditions." *Board of County Commissioners for Prince George's County v. Edmonds*, 240 Md. 680, 687, 215 A.2d 209, 213 (1965). (Emphasis supplied). The Virginia rule differs from the Maryland rule in two important respects: (1) The Virginia rule is limited in application to piecemeal downzoning such as that here involved; and (2) The Virginia rule does not require the governing body to produce *strong* evidence, but evidence sufficient to render the issue of reasonableness "fairly debatable."

districts is a function of the zoning process, and in making a zoning judgement the governing body must consider not only the general boundary guidelines of the plan but also location of property lines, physical characteristics of the land, and other factors affecting optimum geographical alignment.

The trial court ruled that the evidence did not support a finding of substantial change in circumstances in the 11 month interval between adoption of the May 26, 1971 ordinance (which complied with the guidelines of the new Master Plan) and adoption of the April 17, 1972 piecemeal downzoning ordinance. In its brief the Board conceded that "[t]he testimony from all witnesses on the issues of both sewer and traffic consistently supported the conclusion that there had been no change in circumstances in the area". Indeed, with respect to sewer capacity and facilities for removing pollutants, two witnesses testified that circumstances had improved, and the fire chief testified that in addition to increased departmental manpower, two new fire stations serving the community were in the design stage.

The Board urges us to hold as a matter of law that a changed Board of Supervisors constitutes a "changed circumstance" within the meaning of the rule applied by the trial court. We must decline. As indicated above, the "changed circumstance" which justifies piecemeal downzoning is one substantially affecting the public health, safety, or welfare. Such a change should be objectively verifiable from evidence. A newly elected governing body is not such a change. While a new Board is not bound by the legislative acts of an old Board, in amending them the new Board is bound by rules of law.

Next, the Board argues in its brief that "a zoning action . . . is reasonably related to the health, safety and welfare . . . if the evidence renders the existence of such a relationship fairly debatable". But that principle must be read in context with the rule applied by the trial court. Proceeding consciously under that rule, the Board produced no probative evidence of mistake or fraud in the prior ordinance or of changed circumstances substantially affecting the public health, safety, or welfare. Reasonableness was, therefore, not fairly debatable, and the trial court's holding that "the action of the defendants on April 17, 1972 . . . was arbitrary, capricious and unreasonable and, therefore, illegal, invalid and void" was not plainly erroneous.

Finally, the Board contends that admission of testimony of legislative motive was prejudicial error. Since reasonableness was not fairly debatable and the ordinance was void, we need not consider whether testimony concerning legislative motive was prejudicial.

Finding no prejudicial error, we affirm the decree.

Affirmed.

Comments: 1. Since the Virginia court applied the Maryland change-mistake rule (which otherwise has little following) to a piecemeal downzoning, the issue in both cases is whether this rule applies to a comprehensive rezoning and whether a comprehensive zoning has occurred. The Maryland court has since followed *Norbeck* and has made it clear that the change-mistake rule does not apply when the downzoning is comprehensive. *County Council for Montgomery County v. District Land Corp.,* 337 A.2d 712 (Md. 1975).

What distinguishes these two cases, and what distinguishes them in turn from *Ogo Assoc., supra* p. 1021? Do shades of vested rights-zoning estoppel doctrine inhabit the *Snell* opinion? Will the fact that a comprehensive downzoning implements the comprehensive plan always save the day? Note that the Maryland court has not always accepted the policies of the comprehensive plan as binding on zoning decisions. *See Board of County Comm'rs v. Kay,* 215 A.2d 206 (Md. 1965). See also the discussion of the role of the comprehensive plan in the zoning process, *supra* p. 741. *Snell* was decided before the growth management plan in Fairfax County was undertaken, but that decision convinced local planners that a new comprehensive plan was necessary as the basis for needed zoning and other measures to implement the county's growth management policy.

2. Even in states that do not give the comprehensive plan binding force in zoning decisions, a piecemeal downzoning inconsistent with long-established zoning policy may find judicial disfavor. *See, e.g., Udell v. Haas,* 235 N.E.2d 897 (N.Y. 1968). Compare *Grimpel Assocs. v. Cohalan,* 361 N.E.2d 1025 (N.Y. 1977), which invalidated a downzoning from business to residential use of a parcel surrounded by business uses and by major thoroughfares. The court noted that the rezoning reduced the value of the property by 92 percent, and that this proof, though not dispositive, "tends to establish that the property is not reasonably suited for the uses prescribed." *Id.* at 1027. If *Grimpel* indicates that downzoning to uses inconsistent with surrounding uses will be disfavored, why is this so? See also the *Westwood* case, *supra* p. 1003.

In *Mountcrest Estates v. Mayor & Township Comm.,* 232 A.2d 674 (N.J. Super.), *cert. denied,* 234 A.2d 402 (N.J. 1967), the township passed a downzoning ordinance increasing lot sizes in its "B" residential district. Mountcrest argued that the downzoning was invalid because 85 percent of the lots in the "B" district were built upon or platted at the previous higher density. This argument did not impress the court, which upheld the downzoning. Existing uses were a factor to consider, but the plan evidenced by the zoning ordinance was mutable and a presumption of validity attached to the amended ordinance. "The municipality's problems with respect to congestion, overcrowding and inability to provide public facilities due to the population explosion will be lessened because between 180 and 250 fewer homes can be built in the 'B' district under the amended ordinance than could have been built before the amendments — a possible difference in population of from 500 to 1,000 persons." *Id.* at 677.

In *Monmouth Junction Mobile Home Park v. South Brunswick Township,* 256 A.2d 721 (N.J.Super.), *cert. denied,* 259 A.2d 4 (N.J. 1969), the township increased the space requirement in mobile home parks, with the result that the number of spaces allowed in the parks was reduced. It was argued that the ordinance was unconstitutionally retroactive and deprived the park owners of vested rights. This argument was rejected by the court, which noted that mobile home parks were subject to regulation under the police power even though the use of private property is restricted. "Plaintiffs acquire no immunity from the exercise of the police power because prior to the adoption of the ordinance their parks may have been in conformity with the then applicable ordinance." *Id.* at 724. Why is this case distinguishable from the zoning cases discussed *supra*?

3. The two principal cases suggest that the purpose to be achieved by a downzoning may be an important factor bearing on its constitutionality. Thus in *Chucta v. Planning & Zoning Comm'n,* 225 A.2d 822 (Conn. 1967), the court upheld a downzoning which increased the minimum lot size and lot frontage requirements in the rural area of a township. It noted that "the upgrading of the zone in question was desirable, in view of existing schools and other public facilities, and to provide adequately for a safe water supply and proper disposition of sewage." *Id.* at 825.

Compare *Kavanewsky v. Zoning Bd. of Appeals,* 279 A.2d 567 (Conn. 1971), in which a town doubled the density requirements in one of the two zoning districts into which it was divided. The court noted that the downzoning was " 'made in demand of the people to keep Warren a rural community with open spaces and keep undesirable businesses out.' We agree, ... that the reason given ... is not in accordance with the requirements of" the purposes provision of the state zoning enabling act, which followed the Standard Act. *Id.* at 571.

See also *Steel Hill Dev. Co. v. Town of Sanbornton,* 469 F.2d 956 (1st Cir. 1972), upholding as an interim measure a downzoning in residential density in a sparsely populated town in order to prevent an influx of urban dwellers seeking vacation homes. It was undisputed that a sudden spurt in growth would activate potentially hazardous and harmful enviromental conditions. The Sanbornton ordinance placed about 70 percent of the developer's land in a "Forest Conservation District" in which the minimum lot size was six acres and 30 percent in an "Agricultural District" in which the minimum lot size was three acres. The effect of this downzoning was to block a proposed development of 500 to 515 family units on a 510-acre tract, a development that would have doubled the town's population.

D. TIMING, PHASING AND QUOTA PROBLEMS

Service problems resulting from accelerated growth often lie at the heart of interim zoning and downzoning strategies. They may also provide the basis for more explicit and permanent growth management programs that control service extension problems through timing, phasing and quota systems. These systems respond to a serious growth management problem. The provision of public facilities and services in this country has historically been lodged in governmental entities, such as special districts, which are divorced from planning and land use control agencies. Consequently, the timing of new development in relation to the provision of necessary services and facilities has been difficult to achieve. The result has been not only environmental pollution but undesirable, scattered, low-density development patterns brought about in part by the necessity for large residential lots sufficient in size to provide on-site water supply and sewage disposal. To what extent should local communities be allowed to deal with these problems, and should there be any restraints on local growth control plans? What do studies of public service efficiencies tell us about the viability of growth control programs? How should public service timing properly be linked with land use controls?

This section examines these questions in more detail, concentrating on the linkages between urban development and the provision of necessary facilities and services that an adequate growth policy demands. We look first at a selection which provides perspective on economies of size and scale in providing needed utility services, an issue which is of some importance in development growth management programs that take service needs into account.

D. A. DOWNING, THE ROLE OF WATER AND SEWER EXTENSION FINANCING IN GUIDING URBAN RESIDENTIAL GROWTH 23-7 (Report No. 19, Water Resources Research Center, University of Tennessee, 1973)

Water and Sewer Costs

Possibly the most important elements affecting cost are the economies of scale, particularly for treatment facilities. Of spatial significance are economies of density and distance which influence the cost of water and sewer system extensions. The costs of serving individual developments demonstrate both scale and spatial economies.

Economies and public services. In the economic analysis of the business firm, the concept of economies of scale is very important. Utilities, such as sewer and water systems, can achieve lower costs as the scale of operations increases due to a more efficient utilization of inputs. Graphically, economies of scale are usually represented by a curve showing declining costs per unit of output as the total output increases up to a point where diseconomies of scale cause an increase in costs per unit of output.

The attainment of greater efficiency through economies of scale is often posed as a justification for governmental consolidation. Yet numerous studies of economic efficiency in the provision of public services "suggest that there are no significant scale economies in public services, though the validity of this generalization varies from service to service." Water and sewage services seem to be among the few public services which do exhibit economies of scale. . . .

Treatment economies. Various studies have shown that there are very clear unit cost savings from constructing and operating water and sewer treatment facilities at increased scale. For example, a report . . . indicates that the per capita cost for sewage treatment facilities declines as the population served increases. . . .

Similar economies are demonstrated . . . for water treatment. A California study indicates that as flow capacity of a water treatment plant increases, the unit operation and maintenance costs decrease.

Utility line economies. Water distribution and sewage collection lines also exhibit cost economies. Such economies are not only a function of size, as with treatment facilities, but also relate to population density and distance to or from a treatment plant. These elements will be explored in more depth in the following survey of research concerning sewer line economies by Paul B. Downing in *The Economics of Urban Sewage Disposal* [1969].

Downing's analysis involves a hypothetical city of 100,000 which is as yet unsewered. His cost figures relate to providing service to a 160-acre subdivision at varying distances from the treatment plant and at varying population densities. He assumes relatively flat terrain resulting in the need for a pumping station every two miles. Sewer size is assumed to decrease in size as distance from the plant increases starting as large as 48 inches and decreasing to as small as 12 inches. Marginal cost estimates . . . include both capital and operating costs. These estimates reflect the proportion of transmission costs attributable to the subdivision, assuming that the transmission lines are constructed to also serve the city of 100,000 people.

The marginal cost [analysis] reveals several cost relations of significance to this study:

First: Per capita transmission costs, which involve the transport of sewage from the subdivision collection point to the treatment plant, generally decrease as population density increases. (For example, if the subdivision is located 15 miles from the treatment plant, per capita transmission costs will decrease from $11.50 at a density of 1 person per acre to $4.60 at a density of 64 persons per acre.)

Second: Per capita transmission costs also increase as distance from the subdivision to the treatment plant increases. (For example, if the density is 16 persons per acre per capita, transmission costs will increase from $.50 at 5 miles from the treatment plant to $10.90 at 25 miles from the treatment plant.)

Third: Per capita collection costs, within the subdivision, decrease as population density increases. (For example, collection costs within a subdivision will decrease from $14.59 at a density of 1 person per acre to $1.22 at a density of 64 persons per acre.)

In sum, transmission costs are inversely related to population density and directly related to distance from a treatment plant and collection costs are also inversely related to population density. . . .

Comments: This study suggests that land use densities are directly related to the efficient provision of some public services, a point to remember when evaluating growth management programs that use utility extension policy as a key element in growth control. For a collection of essays discussing the land use aspects of service delivery see Local Service Pricing Policies and Their Effect on Urban Spatial Structure (P. Downing ed. 1977).

Related to the question of service efficiencies is the issue of optimum city size. Planners have been enchanted for years with the possibility of finding an optimum city size at which the provision of services will be most efficient, but the literature on size optima remains inconclusive. For discussion of this problem see E. Finkler, Nongrowth as a Planning Alternative 18-22 (American Soc'y of Planning Officials, Planning Advisory Service Rep. No. 283, 1972); H. Richardson, The Economics of Urban Size (1973).

One of the best known of the growth management systems was implemented in the town of Ramapo, New York, and contains timing elements linked to service delivery which implicitly placed limits on the amount of growth to be allowed. The decision of the highest New York court, upholding the Ramapo plan, follows.

GOLDEN v. PLANNING BOARD OF THE TOWN OF RAMAPO

Court of Appeals of New York

30 N.Y.2d 359, 285 N.E.2d 291, *appeal dismissed,* 409 U.S. 1003, 93 S. Ct. 436, 34 L. Ed. 2d 294 (1972)

[*Note:* The opinion has been edited in part by omitting the extensive primary and secondary citations provided by the court.—Eds.]

SCILEPPI, Judge. Both cases arise out of the 1969 amendments to the Town of Ramapo's Zoning Ordinance. In *Golden,* petitioners, the owner of record and contract vendee, by way of a proceeding pursuant to CPLR article 78 sought an order reviewing and annulling a decision and determination of the Planning Board of the Town of Ramapo which denied their application for preliminary approval of a residential subdivision plat because of an admitted failure to secure a special permit as required by section 46-13.1 of the Town zoning ordinance prohibiting subdivision approval except where the residential developer has secured, prior to the application for plat approval, a special permit or a variance pursuant to section F of the ordinance. Special Term sustained the amendments and granted summary judgment. On appeal, the Appellate Division elected, since all necessary parties were before the court, to treat the proceeding as an action for declaratory judgment and reversed, 37 A.D.2d 236, 324 N.Y.S.2d 178.

The plaintiffs in *Rockland County Builders Association,* on the other hand, sought, in an action for declaratory judgment, to set aside the ordinance as unconstitutional and commenced the present action after the Planning Board had denied plaintiff Mildred Rhodes preliminary plat approval for her parcel of property because of a conceded failure on her part to obtain a special permit as required under the challenged ordinance. The remaining plaintiffs, Rockland County Builders Association, a membership corporation composed of builders engaged in the purchase of land and construction of residences of all types through the Town, as well as the Eldorado Developing Corporation, possessed of some 12 acres situate within the Town, apparently have never made application for approval of a plat and have never sought a special permit, as a prerequisite to such approval. Special Term, concluding that the constitutional attack was premature because of the asserted failure to exhaust administrative remedies (cf. *Old Farm Road v. Town of New Castle,* 26 N.Y.2d 462, 311 N.Y.S.2d 500, 259 N.E.2d 920), denied their motion for summary judgment and granted defendants' cross motion to dismiss. On appeal, the Appellate Division, 37 A.D.2d 783, 324 N.Y.S.2d 190, held that the parties were presently aggrieved and relying on *Golden,* reversed and granted plaintiffs' motion for summary judgment.

Among the complaining parties, Rockland County Builders in not a property owner and Eldorado has never sought preliminary approval of a subdivision plat. Petitioner Golden and plaintiff Rhodes have both sought plat approval and have been denied the same for failure to apply for a special permit. Though the builders are obviously not aggrieved by the recent amendments, landowners prior to gaining approval for subdivision, of necessity, would be required to apply for a special permit, which, absent certain enumerated improvements would invariably be denied. The prescription is mandatory and, were we to conclude that the standards established for the permit's issuance were unconstitutional, quite unlike the situation obtaining in *Old Farm Road v. Town of New Castle,* 26 N.Y.2d 462, 311 N.Y.S.2d 500, 259 N.E.2d 920, *supra,* the ordinance itself could admit of no constitutionally permissible construction so as to require initial administrative relief to determine whether injury has occurred (*id.,* at p. 464, 311 N.Y.S.2d at p. 501, 259 N.E.2d at p. 920). The attack by the subdividing landowner is directed against the ordinance in its entirety, and the thrust of the petition and complaint, respectively, is that the ordinance of itself operates to destroy the value and marketability of the subject premises for residential use and thus constitutes a present invasion of the property rights of the complaining landholders. The alleged harm is thus immediate and is sufficient to raise a justiciable issue as to the validity of the subject ordinance. . . .

Experiencing the pressures of an increase in population and the ancillary problem of providing municipal facilities and services,[3] the Town of Ramapo, as early as 1964, made application for grant under section 801 of the Housing Act of 1964 (78 U.S.Stat. 769) to develop a master plan. The plan's preparation included a four-volume study of the existing land uses, public facilities, transportation, industry and commerce, housing needs and projected population trends. The proposals appearing in the studies were subsequently adopted pursuant to section 272-a of the Town Law, Consol.Laws, c. 62, in July, 1966 and implemented by way of a master plan. The master plan was followed by the adoption of a comprehensive zoning ordinance. Additional sewage district and drainage studies were undertaken which culminated in the adoption of a capital budget, providing for the development of the improvements specified in the master plan within the next six years. Pursuant to section 271 of the Town Law, authorizing comprehensive planning, and as a supplement to the

---

[3] The Town's allegations that present facilities are inadequate to service increasing demands goes uncontested. We must assume, therefore, that the proposed improvements, both as to their nature and extent, reflect legitimate community needs and are not veiled efforts at exclusion (see *National Land & Inv. Co. v. Easttown Twp. Bd. of Adj.,* 419 Pa. 504, 215 A.2d 597). In the period 1940-1968 population in the unincorporated areas of the Town increased 285.9%. Between the years of 1950-1960 the increase, again in unincorporated areas, was 130.8%; from 1960-1966 some 78.5%; and from the years 1966-1969 20.4%. In terms of real numbers, population figures compare at 58,626 as of 1966 with the largest increment of growth since the decennial census occurring in the undeveloped areas. Projected figures, assuming current land use and zoning trends, approximate a total Town population of 120,000 by 1985. Growth is expected to be heaviest in the currently undeveloped western and northern tiers of the Town, predominantly in the form of submission development with some apartment construction. A growth rate of some 1,000 residential units per annum has been experienced in the unincorporated areas of the Town.

capital budget, the Town Board adopted a capital program which provides for the location and sequence of additional capital improvements for the 12 years following the life of the capital budget. The two plans, covering a period of 18 years, detail the capital improvements projected for maximum development and conform to the specifications set forth in the master plan, the official map and drainage plan.

Based upon these criteria, the Town subsequently adopted the subject amendments for the alleged purpose of eliminating premature subdivision and urban sprawl. Residential development is to proceed according to the provision of adequate municipal facilities and services, with the assurance that any concomitant restraint upon property use is to be of a "temporary" nature and that other private uses, including the construction of individual housing, are authorized.

The amendments did not rezone or reclassify any land into different residential or use districts,[4] but, for the purposes of implementing the proposals appearing in the comprehensive plan, consist, in the main, of additions to the definitional sections of the ordinance, section 46-3, and the adoption of a new class of "Special Permit Uses", designated "Residential Development Use." "Residential Development Use" is defined as "The erection or construction of dwellings or any vacant plots, lots or parcels of land" (§ 46-3, as amd.); and, any person who acts so as to come within that definition, "shall be deemed to be engaged in residential development which shall be a separate use classification under this ordinance and subject to the requirement of obtaining a special permit from the Town Board" (§ 46-3, as amd.).

---

[4] As of July, 1966, the only available figures, six residential zoning districts with varying lot size and density requirements accounted for in excess of nine tenths of the Town's unincorporated land area. Of these the RR classification (80,000 square feet minimum lot area) plus R-35 zone (35,000 square feet minimum lot area) comprise over one half of all zoned areas. The subject sites are presently zoned RR-50 (50,000 square feet minimum lot area). The reasonableness of these minimum lot requirements is not presently controverted, though we are referred to no compelling need in their behalf. . . . Under present zoning regulations, the population of the unincorporated areas could be increased by about 14,600 families (3.5 people) when all suitable vacant land is occupied. Housing values as of 1960 in the unincorporated areas range from a modest $15,000 (approx. 30%) to higher than $25,000 (25%), with the undeveloped western tier of Town showing the highest percentage of values in excess of $25,000 (41%). Significantly, for the same year only about one half of one per cent of all housing units were occupied by nonwhite families. Efforts at adjusting this disparity are reflected in the creation of a public housing authority and the authority's proposal to construct biracial low-income family housing. . . .

The standards for the issuance of special permits are framed in terms of the availability to the proposed subdivision plat of five essential facilities of services; specifically (1) public sanitary sewers or approved substitutes; (2) drainage facilities; (3) improved public parks or recreation facilities, including public schools; (4) State, county or town roads — major, secondary or collector; and, (5) firehouses. No special permit shall issue unless the proposed residential development has accumulated 15 development points, to be computed on a sliding scale of values assigned to the specified improvements under the statute. Subdivision is thus a function of immediate availability to the proposed plat of certain municipal improvements; the avowed purpose of the amendments being to phase residential development to the Town's ability to provide the above facilities or services.

Certain savings and remedial provisions are designed to relieve of potentially unreasonable restrictions. Thus, the board may issue special permits vesting a present right to proceed with residential development in such year as the development meets the required point minimum, but in no event later than the final year of the 18-year capital plan. The approved special use permit is fully assignable, and improvements scheduled for completion within one year from the date of an application are to be credited as though existing on the date of the application. A prospective developer may advance the date of subdivision approval by agreeing to provide those improvements which will bring the proposed plat within the number of development points required by the amendments. And applications are authorized to the "Development Easement Acquisition Commission" for a reduction of the assessed valuation. Finally, upon application to the Town Board, the development point requirements may be varied should the board determine that such a variance or modification is consistent with the on-going development plan.

The undisputed effect of these integrated efforts in land use planning and development is to provide an over-all program of orderly growth and adequate facilities through a sequential development policy commensurate with progressing availability and capacity of public facilities. While its goals are clear and its purposes undisputably laudatory, serious questions are raised as to the manner in which these ends are to be effected, not the least of which relates to their legal viability under present zoning enabling legislation, particularly sections 261 and 263 of the Town Law. The owners of the subject premises argue, and the Appellate Division has sustained the proposition, that the primary purpose of the amending ordinance is to control or regulate population growth within the Town and as such is not within the authorized objectives of the zoning enabling legislation. We disagree.

In enacting the challenged amendments, the Town Board has sought to control subdivision in all residential districts, pending the provision (public or private) at some future date of various services and facilities. A reading of the relevant statutory provisions reveals that there is no specific authorization for the "sequential" and "timing" controls adopted here. That, of course, cannot be said to end the matter, for the additional inquiry remains as to whether the challenged amendments find their basis within the perimeters of the devices authorized and purposes sanctioned under current enabling legislation. Our concern is, as it should be, with the effects of the statutory scheme taken as a whole and its role in the propagation of a viable policy of land use and planning. . . .

[The court then analyzed the provisions of the New York Town Law authorizing zoning ordinances. These provisions are based on the Standard Zoning Enabling Act, and the court found that the power "to restrict and regulate" conferred by the Town Law includes "by way of necessary implication, the authority to direct the growth of population for the purposes indicated, within the confines of the township. It is the matrix of land use restrictions, common to each of the enumerated powers and sanctioned goals, a necessary concomitant to the municipalities' recognized authority to determine the lines along which local development shall proceed, though it may divert it from its natural course." The court then turned to the alleged prohibitory effect of the Ramapo controls. — Eds.]

It is argued, nevertheless, that the timing controls currently in issue are not legislatively authorized since their effect is to prohibit subdivision absent precedent or concurrent action of the Town, and hence constitutes an unauthorized blanket interdiction against subdivision.

It is, indeed, true that the Planning Board is not in an absolute sense statutorily authorized to deny the right to subdivide. That is not, however, what is sought to be accomplished here. The Planning Board has the right to refuse approval of subdivision plats in the absence of those improvements specified in section 277, and the fact that it is the Town and not the subdividing owner or land developer who is required to make those improvements before the plat will be approved cannot be said to transform the scheme into an absolute prohibition any more than it would be so where it was the developer who refused to provide the facilities required for plat approval.[5]

---

[5] The difference between the ordinary situation and the situation said to subsist here resides in the fact that where plat approval is denied for want of various improvements, the developer is free to provide those improvements at his own expense. In the ordinary case where the proposed improvements will not be completed before the plat is filed the developer's obligation is secured by a performance bond. . . . On the other hand, in the present case, plat approval is

Denial of subdivision plat approval, invariably amounts to a prohibition against subdivision, albeit a conditional one . . . and to say that the Planning Board lacks the authority to deny subdivision rights is to mistake the nature of our inquiry which is essentially whether development may be conditioned pending the provision by the municipality of specified services and facilities. Whether it is the municipality or the developer who is to provide the improvements, the objective is the same — to provide adequate facilities, off-site and on-site; and in either case subdivision rights are conditioned, not denied. . . .

Experience, over the last quarter century, however with greater technological integration and drastic shifts in population distribution has pointed up serious defects and community autonomy in land use controls has come under increasing attack by legal commentators, and students of urban problems alike, because of its pronounced insularism and its correlative role in producing distortions in metropolitan growth patterns, and perhaps more importantly, in crippling efforts toward regional and State-wide problem solving, be it pollution, decent housing, or public transportation. . . .

Recognition of communal and regional interdependence, in turn, has resulted in proposals for schemes of regional and State-wide planning, in the hope that decisions would then correspond roughly to their level of impact. . . . Yet, as salutary as such proposals may be, the power to zone under current law is vested in local municipalities, and we are constrained to resolve the issues

---

conditioned upon the Town's obligation to undertake improvements in roads, sewers and recreational facilities. As the Town may not be held to its program, practices do vary from year to year "and fiscal needs cannot be frozen beyond review and recall" (concurring opn. Hopkins, J., 37 A.D.2d 244, 324 N.Y.S.2d 187), the "patient owner" who relied on the capital program for qualification then is said to face the prospect that the improvements will be delayed and the impediments established by the ordinance further extended by the Town's failure to adhere to its own schedule.

The reasoning, as far as it goes, cannot be challenged. Yet, in passing on the validity of the ordinance on its face, we must assume not only the Town's good faith, but its assiduous adherence to the program's scheduled implementation. We cannot, it is true, adjudicate in a vacuum and we would be remiss not to consider the substantial risk that the Town may eventually default in its obligations. Yet, those are future events, the staple of a clairvoyant, not of a court in its deliberations. The threat of default is not so imminent or likely that it would warrant our prognosticating and striking down these amendments as invalid on their face. When and if the danger should materialize, the aggrieved landowner can seek relief by way of an article 78 proceeding, declaring the ordinance unconstitutional as applied to his property. Alternatively, should it arise at some future point in time that the Town must fail in its enterprise, an action for a declaratory judgment will indeed prove the most effective vehicle for relieving property owners of what would constitute absolute prohibitions.

accordingly. What does become more apparent in treating with the problem, however, is that though the issues are framed in terms of the developer's due process rights, those rights cannot, realistically speaking, be viewed separately and apart from the rights of others " 'in search of a [more] comfortable place to live.' " . . .

There is, then, something inherently suspect in a scheme which, apart from its professed purposes, effects a restriction upon the free mobility of a people until sometime in the future when projected facilities are available to meet increased demands. Although zoning must include schemes designed to allow municipalities to more effectively contend with the increased demands of evolving and growing communities, under its guise, townships have been wont to try their hand at an array of exclusionary devices in the hope of avoiding the very burden which growth must inevitably bring. . . . Though the conflict engendered by such tactics is certainly real, and its implications vast, accumulated evidence, scientific and social, points circumspectly at the hazards of undirected growth and the naive, somewhat nostalgic imperative that egalitarianism is a function of growth. . . .

Of course, these problems cannot be solved by Ramapo or any single municipality, but depend upon the accommodation of widely disparate interests for their ultimate resolution. To that end, State-wide or regional control of planning would insure that interests broader than that of the municipality underlie various land use policies. Nevertheless, that should not be the only context in which growth devices such as these, aimed at population assimilation, not exclusion, will be sustained; especially where, as here, we would have no alternative but to strike the provision down in the wistful hope that the efforts of the State Office of Planning Coordination and the American Law Institute will soon bear fruit. [The reference is to legislation proposed by the Institute and the state office calling for state review of local land use control decisions. — Eds.]

Hence, unless we are to ignore the plain meaning of the statutory delegation, this much is clear: phased growth is well within the ambit of existing enabling legislation. And, of course, it is no answer to point to emergent problems to buttress the conclusion that such innovative schemes are beyond the perimeters of statutory authorization. These considerations, admittedly real, to the extent which they are relevant, bear solely upon the continued viability of "localism" in land use regulation; obviously, they can neither add nor detract from the initial grant of authority, obsolescent though it may be. The answer which Ramapo has posed can by no means be termed definitive; it is, however, a first practical step toward controlled growth achieved without forsaking broader social purposes.

The evolution of more sophisticated efforts to contend with the increasing complexities of urban and suburban growth has been met by a corresponding reluctance upon the part of the judiciary to substitute its judgment as to the plan's over-all effectiveness for the considered deliberations of its progenitors. . . . Implicit in such a philosophy of judicial self-restraint is the growing awareness that matters of land use and development are peculiarly within the expertise of students of city and suburban planning, and thus well within the legislative prerogative, not lightly to be impeded. . . . To this same end, we have afforded such regulations, the usual presumption of validity attending the exercise of the police power, and have cast the burden of proving their invalidity upon the party challenging their enactment. . . . Deference in the matter of the regulations' over-all effectiveness, however, is not to be viewed as an abdication of judicial responsibility, and ours remains the function of defining the metes and bounds beyond which local regulations may not venture, regardless of their professedly beneficent purposes.

The subject ordinance is said to advance legitimate zoning purposes as it assures that each new home built in the township will have at least a minimum of public services in the categories regulated by the ordinance. The Town argues that various public facilities are presently being constructed but that for want of time and money it has been unable to provide such services and facilities at a pace commensurate with increased public need. It is urged that although the zoning power includes reasonable restrictions upon the private use of property, exacted in the hope of development according to well-laid plans, calculated to advance the public welfare of the community in the future . . . , the subject regulations go further and seek to avoid the increased responsibilities and economic burdens which time and growth must ultimately bring. . . .

It is the nature of all land use and development regulations to circumscribe the course of growth within a particular town or district and to that extent such restrictions invariably impede the forces of natural growth. . . . Where those restrictions upon the beneficial use and enjoyment of land are necessary to promote the ultimate good of the community and are within the bounds of reason, they have been sustained. "Zoning [, however,] is a means by which a governmental body can plan for the future — it may not be used as a means to deny the future" *National Land & Inv. Co. v. Easttown Twp. Bd. of Adj.,* 419 Pa. 504, 528, 215 A.2d 597, 610, *supra*). Its exercise assumes that development shall not stop at the community's threshold, but only that whatever growth there may be shall proceed along a predetermined course. . . . It is inextricably bound to the dynamics of community life and its function is to guide, not to isolate or facilitate efforts at avoiding the ordinary incidents of growth. What segregates permissible from impermissible restrictions, depends in the final analysis upon the purpose of the restrictions and their impact in terms of both the community and general public interest. . . . The line of delineation between the two is not a constant, but will be found to vary with prevailing circumstances and conditions. . . .

What we will not countenance, then, under any guise, is community efforts at immunization or exclusion. But, far from being exclusionary, the present amendments merely seek, by the implementation of sequential development and timed growth, to provide a balanced cohesive community dedicated to the efficient utilization of land. The restrictions conform to the community's considered land use policies as expressed in its comprehensive plan and represent a bona fide effort to maximize population density consistent with orderly growth. True other alternatives, such as requiring off-site improvements as a prerequisite to subdivision, may be available, but the choice as how best to proceed, in view of the difficulties attending such exactions . . . , cannot be faulted.

Perhaps even more importantly, timed growth, unlike the minimum lot requirements recently struck down by the Pennsylvania Supreme Court as exclusionary, does not impose permanent restrictions upon land use. . . . Its obvious purpose is to prevent premature subdivision absent essential municipal facilities and to insure continuous development commensurate with the Town's obligation to provide such facilities. They seek, not to freeze population at present levels but to maximize growth by the efficient use of land, and in so doing testify to this community's continuing role in population assimilation. In sum, Ramapo asks not that it be left alone, but only that it be allowed to prevent the kind of deterioration that has transformed well-ordered and thriving residential communities into blighted ghettos with attendant hazards to health, security and social stability — a danger not without substantial basis in fact.

We only require that communities confront the challenge of population growth with open doors. Where in grappling with that problem, the community undertakes, by imposing temporary restrictions upon development, to provide required municipal services in a rational manner, courts are rightfully reluctant to strike down such schemes. The timing controls challenged here parallel recent proposals put forth by various study groups and have their genesis in certain of the pronouncements of this and the courts of sister States. . . . While these controls are typically proposed as an adjunct of regional planning . . . , the preeminent protection against their abuse resides in the mandatory on-going planning and development requirement, present here, which attends their implementation and use. . . .

We may assume, therefore, that the present amendments are the product of foresighted planning calculated to promote the welfare of the township. The Town has imposed temporary restrictions upon land use in residential areas while committing itself to a program of development. It has utilized its comprehensive plan to implement its timing controls and has coupled with these restrictions provisions for low and moderate income housing on a large scale. Considered as a whole, it represents both in its inception and implementation a reasonable attempt to provide for the sequential, orderly development of land in conjunction with the needs of the community, as well as individual parcels of land, while simultaneously obviating the blighted aftermath which the initial failure to provide needed facilities so often brings.

The proposed amendments have the effect of restricting development for onwards to 18 years in certain areas. Whether the subject parcels will be so restricted for the full term is not clear, for it is equally probable that the proposed facilities will be brought into these areas well before that time. Assuming, however, that the restrictions will remain outstanding for the life of the program, they still fall short of a confiscation within the meaning of the Constitution.

An ordinance which seeks to permanently restrict the use of property so that it may not be used for any reasonable purpose must be recognized as a taking: The only difference between the restriction and an outright taking in such a case "is that the restriction leaves the owner subject to the burden of payment of taxation, while outright confiscation would relieve him of that burden" (*Arverne Bay Constr. Co. v. Thatcher,* . . .). An appreciably different situation obtains where the restriction constitutes a *temporary* restriction, promising that the property may be put to a profitable use within a reasonable time. The hardship of holding unproductive property for some time might be compensated for by the ultimate benefit inuring to the individual owner in the form of a substantial increase in valuation; or, for that matter, the landowner might be compelled to chafe under the temporary restriction, without the benefit of such compensation, when that burden serves to promote the public good. . . .

We are reminded, however, that these restrictions threaten to burden individual parcels for as long as a full generation and that such a restriction cannot, in any context, be viewed as a temporary expedient. The Town, on the other hand, contends that the landowner is not deprived of either the best use of his land or of numerous other appropriate uses, still permitted within various residential districts, including the construction of a single-family residence, and consequently, it cannot be deemed confiscatory. Although no proof has been submitted on reduction of value, the landowners point to obvious disparity between the value of the property, if limited in use by the subject amendments and its value for residential development purposes, and argue that the diminution is so considerable that for all intents and purposes the land cannot presently or in the near future be put to profitable or beneficial use, without violation of the restrictions.

Every restriction on the use of property entails hardships for some individual owners. Those difficulties are invariably the product of police regulation and the pecuniary profits of the individual must in the long run be subordinated to the needs of the community. . . . The fact that the ordinance limits the use of, and may depreciate the value of the property will not render it unconstitutional, however, unless it can be shown that the measure is either unreasonable in terms of necessity or the diminution in value is such as to be tantamount to a confiscation. . . . Diminution, in turn, is a relative factor and though its magnitude is an indicia of a taking, it does not of itself establish a confiscation. . . .

Without a doubt restrictions upon the property in the present case are substantial in nature and duration. They are not, however, absolute. The amendments contemplate a definite term, as the development points are designed to operate for a maximum period of 18 years and during that period, the Town is committed to the construction and installation of capital improvements. The net result of the on-going development provision is that individual parcels may be committed to a residential development use prior to the expiration of the maximum period. Similarly, property owners under the terms of the amendments may elect to accelerate the date of development by installing, at their own expense, the necessary public services to bring the parcel within the required number of development points. While even the best of plans may not always be realized, in the absence of proof to the contrary, we must assume the Town will put its best effort forward in implementing the physical and fiscal timetable outlined under the plan. Should subsequent events prove this assumption unwarranted, or should the Town because of some unforeseen event fail in its primary obligation to these landowners, there will be ample opportunity to undo the restrictions upon default. For the present, at least, we are constrained to proceed upon the assumption that the program will be fully and timely implemented. . . .

Thus, unlike the situation presented in *Arverne Bay Constr. Co. v. Thatcher,* 278 N.Y. 222, 15 N.E.2d 587, *supra,* the present amendments propose restrictions of a certain duration and founded upon estimate determined by fact. Prognostication on our part in upholding the ordinance proceeds upon the presently permissible inference that within a reasonable time the subject property will be put to the desired use at an appreciated value. In the interim assessed valuations for real estate tax purposes reflect the impact of the proposed restrictions. . . . The proposed restraints, mitigated by the prospect of appreciated value and interim reductions in assessed value, and measured in terms of the nature and magnitude of the project undertaken, are within the limits of necessity.

In sum, where it is clear that the existing physical and financial resources of the community are inadequate to furnish the essential services and facilities which a substantial increase in population requires, there is a rational basis for "phased growth" and hence, the challenged ordinance is not violative of the Federal and State Constitutions. Accordingly, the order appealed from should be reversed and the actions remitted to Special Term for entry of a judgment declaring section 46-13.1 of the Town Ordinance constitutional.

BREITEL, Judge (dissenting).

[The dissenting opinion is devoted primarily to a discussion of the enabling legislation, and a holding that the Ramapo plan is not authorized under the existing enabling acts. However, while putting aside the constitutional questions for future decision, Judge Breitel adds the following: — Eds.]

A glance at history suggests that Ramapo's plan to have public services installed in advance of development is unrealistic. Richard Babcock, the distinguished practitioner in land development law, some years ago addressed himself to the natural desire of communities to stay development while they caught up with the inexorable thrust of population growth and movement. He observed eloquently that this country was built and is still being built by people who moved about, innovated, pioneered, and created industry and employment, and thereby provided both the need and the means for the public services and facilities that followed (Babcock, The Zoning Game, at pp. 149-150). Thus, the movement has not been in the other direction, first the provision of public and utility services and then the building of homes, farms, and businesses. This court has said as much, in effect, in *Westwood Forest Estates v. Village of South Nyack,* 23 N.Y.2d 424, 297 N.Y.S.2d 129, 244 N.E.2d 700, *supra*) unanimously and in reliance on commonplace authority and precedent.

As said earlier, when the problem arose outside the State the judicial response has been the same, frustrating communities, intent on walling themselves from the mainstream of development, namely, that the effort was invalid under existing enabling acts or unconstitutional. . . . The response may not be charged to judicial conservatism or self-restraint. In short, it has not been illiberal. It has indeed reflected the larger understanding that American society is at a critical crossroads in the accommodation of urbanization and suburban living, with effects that are no longer confined, bad as they are, to ethnic exclusion or "snob" zoning. . . . Ramapo would preserve its nature, delightful as that may be, but the supervening question is whether it alone may decide this or whether it must be decided by the larger community represented by the Legislature. Legally, politically, economically, and sociologically, the base for determination must be larger than that provided by the town fathers.

Accordingly, I dissent and vote to affirm the orders in both cases.

FULD, C.J., and BURKE, BERGAN and GIBSON, JJ., concur with SCILEPPI, J.

BREITEL, J., dissents and votes to affirm in a separate opinion in which JASEN, J., concurs.

H. FRANKLIN, CONTROLLING URBAN GROWTH—BUT FOR WHOM? 13-15 (Potomac Institute, 1973)

[Franklin first notes that the Town of Ramapo, like midwestern townships, is a general function unit of government covering rural and urbanizing areas. It surrounds several incorporated villages, which exclusively control land use within their boundaries. The largest of these, Spring Valley, is discussed in the following excerpt. It should also be noted that annexation by villages is very difficult in New York. The Town of Ramapo is located 35 miles from Columbus Circle in New York City, bordering the Hudson River on the New Jersey state line. Very close to Ramapo in New Jersey is the Mahwah assembly plant of the Ford Motor Company, which employs thousands of workers. — Eds.]

. . . .

Only the *un*incorporated area of the town is subject to the controlled growth ordinance. Statistics from the 1970 census for that area and the incorporated villages shed light on the residential separation of the races in the area. Ramapo Township, including the incorporated villages, has 71,739 white residents and 4,563 black residents. Of the black residents, however, 4,147 live in the incorporated Village of Spring Valley. Indeed, the Village of Spring Valley in relation to the unincorporated Township of Ramapo is a microcosm of metropolitan America. In 1960, blacks comprised nine percent of the population of Spring Valley. By 1970, that proportion grew to 20 percent. If the population of the major incorporated villages, particularly Spring Valley, is considered separately, it is apparent that very few black people live in Ramapo's unincorporated area, in which the controlled growth ordinance applies. As indicated by the court's opinion, in 1960 less than one-half of one percent of the households in the unincorporated portions of the town were black. In 1970, after a decade of rapid development, which evoked the controlled growth ordinance, this figure rose slightly to little more than one percent.

The court's formal but curiously insubstantial concern over this racial disparity is expressed in its acceptance of Ramapo's public housing program as a sufficient response (see footnote [4] of the opinion), notwithstanding the fact that very few black families reside in Ramapo's public housing. Public schools in the area are operated by two special districts which have busing plans in effect to avoid racial concentrations in the schools.

The basic *spatial* zoning pattern determines the volume of the town's population growth; the controlled growth ordinance determines the timing of this volume over an 18-year span. The existing spatial zoning pattern therefore remains not only as important as before the timing ordinance; it is strengthened against changes over time which ordinarily occur in the absence of timing controls. Ramapo's spatial regulations establish six residential districts with various lot size restrictions. These districts range from one requiring at least 80,000 square feet (one acre is 43,560 square feet) to a district permitting 7,500 square-foot minimum lots. This last district covers only *one percent* of the vacant land suitable for development. Of all vacant land set aside for residential use, fully 65 percent is limited to what may fairly be described as "large lot" zoning — with minimum required lot areas of 25,000 to 80,000 square feet. The lawsuit arose in connection with the proposed development of 50,000 square-foot lots. The plaintiffs did not contest the legality of this minimum lot requirement since they were content to develop under this standard, although the court suggested that it doubted the "compelling need" for such a minimum (see footnote [4] of the court's opinion).

Employment within the town has concentrated in the two largest incorporated villages of Spring Valley and Suffern. Ramapo's development plan explicitly spells out that the highest permitted residential densities (these are, however, only 2-4 families per gross acre) "surround the villages of Spring Valley and Suffern."

There is no district in the Town of Ramapo that is set aside for multifamily housing. Prior to 1966, however, Ramapo's zoning did provide for low-density, 8-10 unit per acre dwellings. The Ramapo Development Plan explains this decision in these terms:

> ". . . [T]he provision of opportunities for extensive multi-family development would be inconsistent with one of the prime objectives of the Plan, to keep future population growth at a moderate level so as to preserve the general character of the Town and to avoid overburdening public facilities."

As a result, multifamily housing is now limited to the incorporated areas, such as Suffern and Spring Valley, which already contain most of such housing. Thus, all residential zones in Ramapo are limited to single family housing, with the minor exception that housing for the elderly is permitted only in "laboratory-office" districts planned for nonresidential use. These districts are intended as "buffer zones" between single family and commercial uses.

No further public housing is planned in Ramapo, and no FHA-subsidized housing is under way or contemplated in the town. It is thought, however, that additional privately sponsored housing for the elderly may be developed with federal interest subsidies in the nonresidential districts that permit housing for the elderly. The capital program does not schedule the investment of any public resources to stimulate or assist state or federally-subsidized housing. These facts indicate that the statement . . . in the court's opinion that Ramapo "has utilized its comprehensive plan to implement its timing controls and has coupled with these restrictions provisions for low and moderate income housing on a large scale" is unfounded.

It further appears that the capital plan contemplates housing densities that cannot support anything other than single family housing even if the zoning permitted higher densities, which it does not. This means that FHA-subsidized, single family houses could be the only form of subsidized housing possible in residential areas. [In addition, federal subsidies for privately built housing have now been terminated. — Eds.]

It is also important to note that the town's controlled growth ordinance is not applicable to commercial and industrial development, which the town has made a concerted effort to attract, although thus far without marked success. . . .

[Franklin also notes that development will be postponed until 1986 on fully 48 percent of the vacant lots available under the zoning ordinance just prior to the adoption of the Ramapo plan. *Id.* at 16. With reference to the capital facilities included in the town's capital improvement program, he notes that the county is responsible for the construction of interceptor sewers, while the township is only responsible for the installation of lateral sewers. *Id.* at 17. In addition, firehouses are not provided by the Town of Ramapo but are the responsibility of special service districts that must be formed by local residents. Scott, Comments on Ramapo, 24 Zoning Dig. 75, 77 (1972). For additional analysis of the *Ramapo* case, see Bosselman, Can the Town of Ramapo Pass a Law to Bind the Whole World?, 1 Fla. St. U.L. Rev. 234 (1973). — Eds.]

Comments: 1. In the *Westwood* case, reproduced *supra* p. 1003 and decided by Judge Breitel, the New York court had invalidated a village ordinance lowering the density for apartment zoning in order to reduce the amount of effluent discharged into its sewer system. The court held that the village could not impose the financial burden of the downzoning on apartment uses solely because of a "general condition in the community."

Arverne Bay, reproduced *supra* p. 236, was a downzoning from "unrestricted" to residential which was part of a comprehensive rezoning amendment along a boulevard in Brooklyn. The area was still semi-rural and in transition, and thus the zoning for residential development was premature. As the court pointed out, the justification for the rezoning was "in the control over future development which will result from such restrictions". Taking note of the uncertainties surrounding the eventual residential development of the area and the permanent nature of the restriction, the court held it unconstitutional. To what extent are these cases qualified by the *Ramapo* decision?

2. Is *Ramapo* qualified by *Charles v. Diamond,* 360 N.E.2d 1295 (N.Y. 1977)? In that case a village had provided sewer service, and a local ordinance required developers to connect with the village sewer system. While the village had issued a building permit to a developer who sought connection with the village system, the state environmental agency informed the developer that it could not connect to the village system until deficiencies in the system had been corrected, and likewise instructed the county health department to refuse a system connection. The developer then brought an action against the state and county agencies and the village contending that their actions amounted to an unconstitutional appropriation of its property.

While remanding the case for trial because the record had not been sufficiently developed to decide the constitutional issues, the New York highest court noted that temporary restrictions on development because of service difficulties were justified, but that permanent restrictions were not. A series of factors were identified to determine how long a restriction on development for this reason could last, including the extent of the sewer problem, the ability of the community to raise the necessary capital, and the role of the state and federal governments. An extensive delay would be justified "only if the remedial steps are of sufficient magnitude to require extensive preparations, including preliminary studies, applications for assistance to other governmental entities, the raising of large amounts of capital, and the letting of work contracts." *Id.* at 1301.

Noting that it had accepted development delays of up to 18 years in the *Ramapo* decision, the court then noted that "the crucial factor, perhaps even the decisive one, is whether the ultimate cost of the benefit is being shared by the members of the community at large, or, rather, is being hidden from the public by the placement of the entire burden upon particular property owners." *Id.* at 1300. Is this statement a further extension of the court's dictum in footnote [5] of the *Ramapo* decision? Recall that *Ramapo* did not consider the growth management plan as applied to a particular property owner. The court also commented in *Charles,* again citing *Ramapo,* that the municipality "must be committed firmly to the construction and installation of the necessary improvements." *Id.* at 1301. Do *Ramapo* and *Charles* create a Catch-22 situation for a municipality attempting a growth management plan of this type? The municipality must be firmly committed to a reasonable time schedule in providing necessary public improvements, but making this commitment may be difficult if not undesirable because it locks the municipality into a fixed, long-range planning program. Note that the court in *Charles* ordered the municipality to comply with the state consent orders and indicated, obliquely, that it did not believe that this command infringed improperly on the municipality's authority. *Id.* at 1303.

In view of *Charles,* the subsequent history of the Ramapo plan may be of interest. The history of the Ramapo plan up to 1974 was reviewed in Emanuel, Ramapo's Managed Growth Program, [AIP] Planners' Notebook, vol. 4, no. 5, at 1 (1974). Emanuel notes that "[a]lthough there have been necessary fluctuations in the budgeting process, the Town has maintained a financial commitment to the execution of capital improvements." *Id.* at 8. However, unexpected flooding resulting from hurricanes in 1971 and 1972 caused the town to appropriate 1.5 million dollars to cope with storm damage, and much of the work scheduled for the capital budget in those years had to be deferred. In addition,

> [T]he completion of the sewer program is dependent upon the receipt of federal and state aid funds; since 1969, such funds have been extremely limited and no significant allocations have been · made with respect to the proposed extension of the Rockland County sewer systems, which are related to the continued implementation of the Town's sewer network.

Id. Would these circumstances permit a delay in the provision of public services under the guidelines laid down in *Charles v. Diamond*?

With these cases compare *Petersen v. City of Decorah,* 259 N.W.2d 553 (Iowa App. 1977). Plaintiff's land was placed in an agricultural use district defined by the ordinance as "intended to reserve areas suitable for nonagricultural use until the land is needed for development in accordance with a future land use plan." A rezoning to allow plaintiff to build a shopping center was denied because the city indicated that it was holding the land for future industrial development. The court struck down the agricultural zoning, noting that no industry had been attracted to the city since 1964 and that the city had admitted that the plaintiff's property was adaptable to use as a shopping center. It was also clear that the land was not suitable for agricultural purposes.

Some communities may also avoid adopting an explicit growth management policy and simply plan informally for the extension of municipal services so that growth is phased and timed in accordance with an unofficial growth management plan. *See, e.g.,* the description of the Prince George's County, Maryland, growth management plan in Urban Growth at 21-22. Are there dangers in this approach in view of *Charles v. Diamond, supra*? See also the *Robinson* case, *infra* p. —.

3. Note that no downzoning was required in the Ramapo plan. Existing zoning was already at low densities, and Franklin has noted that the points and permit system simply reinforced this low density strategy. Subsequent to *Ramapo,* however, in a case arising in nearby Westchester County, *Berenson v. Town of New Castle,* 341 N.E.2d 236 (N.Y. 1975), a developer attacked the town zoning ordinance which provided for one-acre and two-acre minimum lot sizes in two of its residential districts and which

excluded multifamily dwellings altogether. *Berenson* is discussed *supra* p. —. While noting that in *Ramapo* it had "ruled that a town may permissibly adopt a program providing for phased growth," the court also noted that in that case "we were careful to note that 'community efforts at immunization or exclusion' would not be countenanced." *Id.* at 241. The court then proceeded to hold that the multifamily exclusion in *Berenson* would be held unconstitutional if it prevented the town from meeting its share of regional housing needs. To what extent does *Berenson* qualify *Ramapo*?

4. What the opinion in the *Ramapo* case neglects to point out is that the point system utilized by the ordinance is to some extent based on the distance of the required facilities from "each separate lot or plot capable of being improved with a residential dwelling". Thus:

(5) Fire house:

Within 1 mile	3 points
Within 2 miles	1 point
Further than 2 miles	0 points

Compare Department of Planning and Community Development, A Report on Population Growth in the City of Aurora [Colorado] 41 (1973), noting that "[t]he safety zone within which a fire station can adequately serve an area can be viewed as a diamond, with the station at the center". Fire protection, according to this report, is measured by distance from the station in time, with five minutes being the outer limit for safety purposes. Obviously, the time it takes for a fire truck to reach a fire depends on the nature of the road network and topography. What then about the fairness of the distance formula used in the *Ramapo* plan? Note that fire protection is not provided by the town but by special districts that must be specially created for this purpose.

The entire Ramapo ordinance is reproduced in 24 Zoning Dig. 68 (1972). Points for drainage are based on "Percentage of Required Drainage Capacity Available". Scott, *id.* at 77, notes that

> This rating is based on the capacity of drainage systems, at points along the system, to handle peak drainage, based not on the incremental change of the builder's development, but on the rating given for projected complete development of all the land in the . . . area. . . . Thus, the first developer to come into the area must make an improvement (if he wants the maximum number of points) which will relieve the burden on future development in that area.

Any problems with this method of assessment?

In explaining how the point system was developed, Emanual makes the following observations:

> In attempting to arrive at a reasonable point spread within each category and at the total eligible point score of 15 which was finally incorporated into the zoning regulations, a series of extensive trial and error analyses were performed. First of all, all existing undeveloped land areas in the unincorporated portion of the Town were mapped and the potential development capacity for each area then computed based upon existing zoning. Then a

series of different overall scoring systems were tested to determine the number of lots or building units which would become eligible for approval each year, based upon the projected capital budget and capital plan. These calculations also gave the Town a measure of the probable annual rate of land consumption measured against its ultimate capacity.

In this intricate process, certain variables were fortunately held generally constant. One was the capital budget in combination with the capital plan, producing an 18 year spread for projected public improvements. The other was the concept that the Town should reach virtual development saturation at the end of the life of the capital plan, based upon the recommendation of the Town master plan.

Id. at 5. What do these comments indicate about the validity of Ramapo's point system approach? On the other hand, could the point system be justified on the ground that the amount of development it permits is reasonable in relationship to the town's capacity, and that the system is simple to administer and thus reduces burdens on the administering staff and on developers? Note that schools were not included in the point system even though school overload was a major concern of Ramapo planners. Schools were omitted because they are a special district function and the town does not control them. It was hoped that school costs could be indirectly controlled through a growth management system based on other public facilities.

There is some indication that the Ramapo plan is fairly consistent with developmental objectives proposed for the area by applicable state and regional plans. Would the decision made in the Ramapo plan to concentrate development in the villages be subject to criticism if the villages were unincorporated and were simply areas of urban concentration within the township? In other words, are the developmental strategy problems raised by the Ramapo plan a planning problem or a governmental problem? For additional commentary on the Ramapo plan see II Management and Control 1-119.

5. The Ramapo plan thus emerges as a preset development control system whose remedial provisions and linkages with a comprehensive planning policy helped save the day in court. It does not contain an explicit quota on growth within the town, but the full impact of the plan's provisions is to impose a growth quota indirectly. In the next case a federal Court of Appeals considered a growth control program that explicitly contained a growth quota, at least on a temporary basis.

CONSTRUCTION INDUSTRY ASS'N OF SONOMA COUNTY v. CITY OF PETALUMA

United States Court of Appeals
522 F.2d 897 (9th Cir. 1975), *cert. denied,* 424 U.S. 934 (1976)

OPINION

Before BARNES and CHOY, Circuit Judges and EAST, District Judge.

CHOY, Circuit Judge:

The City of Petaluma (the City) appeals from a district court decision voiding as unconstitutional certain aspects of its five-year housing and zoning plan. We reverse.

Statement of Facts

The City is located in southern Sonoma County, about 40 miles north of San Francisco. In the 1950's and 1960's, Petaluma was a relatively self-sufficient town. It experienced a steady population growth from 10,315 in 1950 to 24,870 in 1970. Eventually, the City was drawn into the Bay Area metropolitan housing market as people working in San Francisco and San Rafael became willing to commute longer distances to secure relatively inexpensive housing available there. By November 1972, according to unofficial figures, Petaluma's population was at 30,500, a dramatic increase of almost 25 per cent in little over two years.

The increase in the City's population, not surprisingly, is reflected in the increase in the number of its housing units. From 1964 to 1971, the following number of residential housing units were completed:

1964	270	1968	379
1965	440	1969	358
1966	321	1970	591
1967	234	1971	891

In 1970 and 1971, the years of the most rapid growth, demand for housing in the City was even greater than above indicated. Taking 1970 and 1971 together, builders won approval of a total of 2000 permits although only 1482 were actually completed by the end of 1971.

Alarmed by the accelerated rate of growth in 1970 and 1971, the demand for even more housing, and the sprawl of the City eastward, the City adopted a temporary freeze on development in early 1971. The construction and zoning change moratorium was intended to give the City Council and the City planners an opportunity to study the housing and zoning situation and to develop short and long range plans. The Council made specific findings with respect to housing patterns and availability in Petaluma, including the following: That from 1960-1970 housing had been in almost unvarying 6000 square-foot lots laid out in regular grid patterns; that there was a density of approximately 4.5 housing units per acre in the single-family home areas; that during 1960-1970, 88 per cent of housing permits issued were for single-family detached homes; that in 1970, 83 per cent of Petaluma's housing was single-family dwellings; that the bulk of recent development (largely single-family homes) occurred in the eastern portion of the City, causing a large deficiency in moderately priced multi-family and apartment units on the east side.

To correct the imbalance between single-family and multi-family dwellings, curb the sprawl of the City on the east, and retard the accelerating growth of the City, the Council in 1972 adopted several resolutions, which collectively are called the "Petaluma Plan" (the Plan).

The Plan, on its face limited to a five-year period (1972-1977),[6] fixes a housing development growth rate not to exceed 500 dwelling units per year.[7] Each dwelling unit represents approximately three people. The 500-unit figure is somewhat misleading, however, because it applies only to housing units (hereinafter referred to as "development-units") that are part of projects involving five units or more. Thus, the 500-unit figure does not reflect any housing and population growth due to construction of single-family homes or even four-unit apartment buildings not part of any larger project.

The Plan also positions a 200 foot wide "greenbelt" around the City,[8] to serve as a boundary for urban expansion for at least five years, and with respect to the east and north sides of the City, for perhaps ten to fifteen years. One of the most innovative features of the Plan is the Residential Development Control System which provides procedures and criteria for the award of the annual 500 development-unit permits. At the heart of the allocation procedure is an intricate point system, whereby a builder accumulates points for conformity by his projects with the City's general plan and environmental design plans, for good architectural design, and for providing low and moderate income dwelling units and various recreational facilities. The Plan further directs that allocations of building permits are to be divided as evenly as feasible between the

---

[6] The district court found that although the Plan is ostensibly limited to a five-year period, official attempts have been made to perpetuate the Plan beyond 1977. Such attempts include the urban extension line (*see* text *infra*) and the agreement to purchase from the Sonoma County Water Agency only 9.8 million gallons of water per day through the year 1990. This flow is sufficient to support a population of 55,000. If the City were to grow at a rate of about 500 housing units per year (approximately three persons per unit), the City would reach a population of 55,000 about the year 1990. The 55,000 figure was mentioned by City officials as the projected optimal (and maximum) size of Petaluma. *See, e. g.,* R.T. at 135-43, 145-46.

[7] The allotment for each year is not an inflexible limitation. The Plan does provide for a 10 percent variance (50 units) below or above the 500 unit annual figure, but the expectation of the Council is that not more than 2500 units will be constructed during the five-year period.

[8] At some points this urban extension line is about one-quarter of a mile beyond the present City limits.

west and east sections of the City and between single-family dwellings and multiple residential units (including rental units),[9] that the sections of the City closest to the center are to be developed first in order to cause "infilling" of vacant area, and that 8 to 12 per cent of the housing units approved be for low and moderate income persons.

In a provision of the Plan, intended to maintain the close-in rural space outside and surrounding Petaluma, the City solicited Sonoma County to establish stringent subdivision and appropriate acreage parcel controls for the areas outside the urban extension line of the City and to limit severely further residential infilling.

Purpose of the Plan

The purpose of the Plan is much disputed in this case. According to general statements in the Plan itself, the Plan was devised to ensure that "development in the next five years, will take place in a reasonable, orderly, attractive manner, rather than in a completely haphazard and unattractive manner." The controversial 500-unit limitation on residential development-units was adopted by the City "[i]n order to protect its small town character and surrounding open space." [10] The other features of the Plan were designed to encourage an east-west balance in development, to provide for variety in densities and building types and wide ranges in prices and rents, to ensure infilling of close-in vacant areas, and to prevent the sprawl of the City to the east and north. The Construction Industry Association of Sonoma County (the Association) argues and the district court found, however, that the Plan was primarily enacted "to limit Petaluma's demographic and market growth rate in housing and in the immigration of new residents." *Construction Industry Assn. v. City of Petaluma,* 375 F.Supp. 574, 576 (N.D.Cal. 1974).

---

[9] By providing for the increase of multi-family dwellings (including townhouses as well as rental apartments), the Plan allows increased density. Whereas, during the years just preceding the Plan, housing density was about 4.5 units per acre, under the Plan single-family housing will consist of not only low (4.5 units per acre) but also medium density (4.5 to 10 units per acre). And multi-family housing, to comprise about half of the housing under the Plan, will be built at a density of 10 or more units per acre.

[10] After the appellees initiated this suit, the City attempted to show that the Plan was implemented to prevent the over-taxing of available water and sewage facilities. We find it unnecessary, however, to consider the claim that sewage and water problems justified implementation of the Plan.

Market Demand and Effect of the Plan

In 1970 and 1971, housing permits were allotted at the rate of 1000 annually, and there was no indication that without some governmental control on growth consumer demand would subside or even remain at the 1000-unit per year level. Thus, if Petaluma had imposed a flat 500-unit limitation on *all* residential housing, the effect of the Plan would clearly be to retard to a substantial degree the natural growth rate of the City. Petaluma, however, did not apply the 500-unit limitation across the board, but instead exempted all projects of four units or less. Because appellees failed to introduce any evidence whatsoever as to the number of exempt units expected to be built during the five-year period, the effect of the 500 *development-unit* limitation on the natural growth in housing is uncertain. For purposes of this decision, however, we will assume that the 500 development-unit growth rate is in fact below the reasonably anticipated market demand for such units and that absent the Petaluma Plan, the City would grow at a faster rate.

According to undisputed expert testimony at trial, if the Plan (limiting housing starts to approximately 6 per cent of existing housing stock each year) were to be adopted by municipalities throughout the region, the impact on the housing market would be substantial. For the decade 1970 to 1980, the shortfall in needed housing in the region would be about 105,000 units (or 25 per cent of the units needed). Further, the aggregate effect of a proliferation of the Plan throughout the San Francisco region would be a decline in regional housing stock quality, a loss of the mobility of current and prospective residents and a deterioration in the quality and choice of housing available to income earners with real incomes of $14,000 per year or less. If, however, the Plan were considered by itself and with respect to Petaluma only, there is no evidence to suggest that there would be a deterioration in the quality and choice of housing available there to persons in the lower and middle income brackets. Actually, the Plan increases the availability of multi-family units (owner-occupied and rental units) and low-income units which were rarely constructed in the pre-Plan days.

Court Proceedings

Two landowners (the Landowners) and the Association instituted this suit under 28 U.S.C. §§ 1331, 1343 and 42 U.S.C. § 1983 against the City and its officers and council members, claiming that the Petaluma Plan was unconstitutional. The district court ruled that certain aspects of the Plan unconstitutionally denied the right to travel insofar as they tended "to limit the natural population growth of the area." 375 F.Supp., at 588. The court enjoined the City and its agents from implementing the unconstitutional elements of the Plan, but the order was stayed by Justice Douglas pending this appeal.

. . . .

Standing

The City also challenges the standing of the Association and the Landowners to maintain the suit. The standing requirement raises the threshold question in every federal case whether plaintiff has made out a "case or controversy" between himself and the defendant within the meaning of Article III of the Constitution. In order to satisfy the constitutional requirement that courts decide only cases or controversies and to ensure the requisite concreteness of facts and adverseness of parties, plaintiff must show that he has a "personal stake in the outcome of the controversy," *Baker v. Carr,* 369 U.S. 186, 204, 82 S.Ct. 691, 703, 7 L.Ed.2d 663 (1962), or that he has suffered "some threatened or actual injury resulting from the putatively illegal action." *S. v. D.,* 410 U.S. 614, 617, 93 S.Ct. 1146, 1148, 35 L.Ed.2d 536 (1973). Further, the plaintiff must satisfy the additional court-imposed standing requirement that the "interest sought to be protected by the complainant is arguably within the zone of interests to be protected or regulated by the statute or constitutional guarantee in question." *Association of Data Processing Service Organizations, Inc. v. Camp,* 397 U.S. 150, 153, 90 S.Ct. 827, 830, 25 L.Ed.2d 184 (1970). A corollary to the "zone of interest" requirement is the well-recognized general rule that "even when the plaintiff has alleged injury sufficient to meet the 'case or controversy' requirement, . . . the plaintiff generally must assert his own legal rights and interests, and cannot rest his claim to relief on the legal rights or interests of third parties." *Warth v. Seldin,* 422 U.S. 490, 499, 95 S.Ct. 2197, 2205, 45 L.Ed.2d 343 (1975); . . . .

Appellees easily satisfy the "injury in fact" standing requirement. The Association alleges it has suffered in its own right monetary damages due to lost revenues. Sonoma County builders contribute dues to the Association in a sum proportionate to the amount of business the builders do in the area. Thus, in a very real sense a restriction on building in Petaluma causes economic injury to the Association.

The two Landowners also have already suffered or are threatened with a direct injury. It is their position that the Petaluma Plan operated, of itself, to adversely affect the value and marketability of their land for residential uses, and such an allegation is sufficient to show that they have a personal stake in the outcome of the controversy. . . .

Although appellees have suffered or are threatened with direct personal injury, the "zone of interest" requirement poses a huge stumbling block to their attempt to show standing. The primary federal claim upon which this suit is based — the right to travel or migrate — is a claim asserted not on the appellees' own behalf, but on behalf of a group of unknown third parties allegedly excluded from living in Petaluma. Although individual builders, the Association, and the Landowners are admittedly adversely affected by the Petaluma Plan, their economic interests are undisputedly outside the zone of interest to be protected by any purported constitutional right to travel. Accordingly, appellees' right to travel claim "falls squarely within the prudential standing rule that normally bars litigants from asserting the rights or legal interests of others in order to obtain relief from injury to themselves." *Warth v. Seldin,* 422 U.S. at 509, 95 S.Ct. at 2210.

There are several exceptions to this general rule, but plaintiffs do not fall within any of them. Congress may grant standing by statute to persons who might otherwise lack standing, *id.,* but here no statute expressly or by clear implication grants to persons in appellees' position a right of action based on third parties' right to travel. On several occasions, the Supreme Court has granted standing to persons whom a criminal statute directly affected to challenge the statute on the ground that if enforced it would infringe the rights of third parties. . . . No comparison, however, may be fairly drawn between appellees and the doctors facing criminal sanctions in *Bolton* and *Griswold.* [*Doe v. Bolton,* 410 U.S. 179 (1973), and *Griswold v. Connecticut,* 381 U.S. 479 (1965). — Eds.] Nor do appellees allege that the Petaluma Plan preclude[s] or otherwise adversely affects a relationship existing between them and the persons whose rights allegedly have been violated. . . . The only connection between any of the appellees and any of the persons who purportedly are excluded from Petaluma is the possibility that but for the Plan they would be parties to a purchase-sale agreement. There exists no special, on-going relationship between appellees and those whose rights allegedly are violated which militates in favor of granting standing. . . . Nor have the Association and the Landowners shown that their prosecution of the suit is necessary to ensure protection of the rights asserted. . . . Assuming *arguendo* that the constitutional right to travel applies to this case, those individuals whose mobility is impaired may bring suit on their own behalf and on behalf of those similarly situated. Although *Warth v. Seldin* denied standing to a group of low-income and minority-group plaintiffs challenging exclusionary zoning practices, the case is no bar to a suit against the City brought by a proper group of plaintiffs. The Court in *Warth v. Seldin* left open the federal court doors for plaintiffs who have some interest in a particular housing project and who, but for the restrictive zoning ordinances, would be able to reside in the community.

Although we conclude that appellees lack standing to assert the rights of third parties, they nonetheless [have] standing to maintain claims based on violations of rights personal to them. Accordingly, appellees have standing to challenge the Petaluma Plan on the grounds asserted in their complaint that the Plan is arbitrary and thus violative of their due process rights guaranteed by the Fourteenth Amendment and that the Plan poses an unreasonable burden on interstate commerce. . . . The fact that one of the Landowner's property lies wholly outside the present City boundaries and that the other's property lies mostly outside the boundaries is no bar to their challenging the City's Plan which has a direct, intended and immediate effect on the property. . . .

Other Challenges to the Plan

Although the district court rested its decision solely on the right to travel claim, all the facts and legal conclusions necessary to resolve appellees' other claims are part of the record. Thus, in order to promote judicial economy, we now dispose of the other challenges to the Plan. . . .

Substantive Due Process

Appellees claim that the Plan is arbitrary and unreasonable and, thus, violative of the due process clause of the Fourteenth Amendment. According to appellees, the Plan is nothing more than an exclusionary zoning device,[11] designed solely to insulate Petaluma from the urban complex in which it finds itself. The Association and the Landowners reject, as falling outside the scope of any legitimate governmental interest, the City's avowed purposes in implementing the Plan — the preservation of Petaluma's small town character and

---

[11] "Exclusionary zoning" is a phrase popularly used to describe suburban zoning regulations which have the effect, if not also the purpose, of preventing the migration of low and middle-income persons. Since a large percentage of racial minorities fall within the low and middle income brackets, exclusionary zoning regulations may also effectively wall out racial minorities. . . .

Most court challenges to and comment upon so-called exclusionary zoning focus on such traditional zoning devices as height limitations, minimum square footage and minimum lot size requirements, and the prohibition of multi-family dwellings or mobile homes. The Petaluma Plan is unique in that although it assertedly slows the growth rate it replaces the past pattern of single-family detached homes with an assortment of housing units, varying in price and design.

the avoidance of the social and environmental problems caused by an uncontrolled growth rate.

In attacking the validity of the Plan, appellees rely heavily on the district court's finding that the express purpose and the actual effect of the Plan is to exclude substantial numbers of people who would otherwise elect to move to the City. 375 F.Supp. at 581. The existence of an exclusionary purpose and effect reflects, however, only *one* side of the zoning regulation. Practically all zoning restrictions have as a purpose and effect the *exclusion* of some activity or type of structure or a certain density of inhabitants. And in reviewing the reasonableness of a zoning ordinance, our inquiry does not terminate with a finding that it is for an exclusionary purpose.[12] We must determine further whether the *exclusion* bears any rational relationship to a *legitimate state interest.* If it does not, then the zoning regulation is invalid. If, on the other hand, a legitimate state interest is furthered by the zoning regulation, we must defer to the legislative act. Being neither a super legislature nor a zoning board of appeal, a federal court is without authority to weigh and reappraise the factors considered or ignored by the legislative body in passing the challenged zoning regulation.[13] The reasonableness, not the wisdom, of the Petaluma Plan is at issue in this suit.

It is well settled that zoning regulations "must find their justification in some aspect of the police power, asserted for the public welfare." *Village of Euclid v. Ambler Realty Co.,* 272 U.S. 365, 387, 47 S.Ct. 114, 118, 71 L.Ed. 303 (1926). The concept of the public welfare, however, is not limited to the regulation of noxious activities or dangerous structures. As the Court stated in *Berman v. Parker,* 348 U.S. 26, 33, 75 S.Ct. 98, 102, 99 L.Ed. 27 (1954):

> The concept of the public welfare is broad and inclusive. The values it represents are spiritual as well as physical, aesthetic as well

---

[12] Our inquiry here is not unlike that involved in a case alleging denial of equal protection of the laws. The mere showing of some discrimination by the state is not sufficient to prove an invasion of one's constitutional rights. Most legislation to some extent discriminates between various classes of persons, business enterprises, or other entities. However, absent a suspect classification or invasion of fundamental rights, equal protection rights are violated only where the classification does not bear a rational relationship to a legitimate state interest. *See Ybarra v. City of Town of Los Altos Hills,* 503 F.2d 250, 254 (9th Cir. 1974).

[13] Appellees' brief is unnecessarily oversize (125 pages) mainly because it is rife with quotations from writers on regional planning, economic regulation and sociological policies and themes. These types of considerations are more appropriate for legislative bodies than for courts.

as monetary. It is within the power of the legislature to determine that the community should be beautiful as well as healthy, spacious as well as clean, well-balanced as well as carefully patrolled.

(citations omitted). *Accord, Village of Belle Terre v. Boraas,* 416 U.S. 1, 6, 9, 94 S.Ct. 1536, 39 L.Ed.2d 797 (1974).

In determining whether the City's interest in preserving its small town character and in avoiding uncontrolled and rapid growth falls within the broad concept of "public welfare," we are considerably assisted by two recent cases. *Belle Terre, supra,* and *Ybarra v. City of Town of Los Altos Hills,* 503 F.2d 250 (9th Cir. 1974), each of which upheld as not unreasonable a zoning regulation much more restrictive than the Petaluma Plan, are dispositive of the due process issue in this case.

In *Belle Terre* the Supreme Court rejected numerous challenges [14] to a village's restricting land use to one-family dwellings excluding lodging houses, boarding houses, fraternity houses or multiple-dwelling houses. By absolutely prohibiting the construction of or conversion of a building to other than single-family dwelling, the village ensured that it would never grow, if at all, much larger than its population of 700 living in 220 residences. Nonetheless, the Court found that the prohibition of boarding houses and other multi-family dwellings was reasonable and within the public welfare because such dwellings present urban problems, such as the occupation of a given space by more people, the increase in traffic and parked cars and the noise that comes with increased crowds. According to the Court,

A quiet place where yards are wide, people few, and motor vehicles restricted are legitimate guidelines in a land-use project addressed to family needs. This goal is a permissible one within *Berman v. Parker, supra.* The police power is not confined to elimination of filth, stench, and unhealthy places. It is ample to lay out zones where family values, youth values, and the blessings of quiet seclusion, and clean air make the area a sanctuary for people.

416 U.S. at 9, 94 S.Ct. at 1541. While dissenting from the majority opinion in *Belle Terre* on the ground that the regulation unreasonably burdened the exercise of First Amendment

---

[14] The plaintiffs in *Belle Terre* claimed *inter alia* that the ordinance interfered with a person's right to travel and right to migrate to and settle within a state.

The Supreme Court held that since the ordinance was not aimed at transients, there was no infringement of anyone's right to travel. 416 U.S. at 7, 94 S.Ct. 1536. Although due to appellees' lack of standing we do not reach today the right to travel issue, we note that the Petaluma Plan is not aimed at transients, nor does it penalize those who have recently exercised their right to travel. . . .

associational rights, Mr. Justice Marshall concurred in the Court's express holding that a local entity's zoning power is extremely broad:

> [L]ocal zoning authorities may properly act in furtherance of the objectives asserted to be served by the ordinance at issue here: *restricting uncontrolled growth,* solving traffic problems, keeping rental costs at a reasonable level, and making the community attractive to families. The police power which provides the justification for zoning is not narrowly confined. And, it is appropriate that we afford zoning authorities *considerable latitude in choosing the means by which to implement such purposes.*

416 U.S. at 13-14, 94 S.Ct. at 1543 (Marshall, J., dissenting) (emphasis added) (citations omitted).

Following the *Belle Terre* decision, this court in *Los Altos Hills* had an opportunity to review a zoning ordinance providing that a housing lot shall . . . contain not less than one acre and that no lot shall be occupied by more than one primary dwelling unit. The ordinance as a practical matter prevented poor people from living in Los Altos Hills and restricted the density, and thus the population, of the town. This court, nonetheless, found that the ordinance was rationally related to a legitimate governmental interest — *the preservation of the town's rural environment* — and, thus, did not violate the equal protection clause of the Fourteenth Amendment. 503 F.2d at 254.

Both the Belle Terre ordinance and the Los Altos Hills regulation had the purpose and effect of permanently restricting growth; nonetheless, the court in each case upheld the particular law before it on the ground that the regulation served a legitimate governmental interest falling within the concept of the public welfare: the preservation of quiet family neighborhoods (Belle Terre) and the preservation of a rural environment (Los Altos Hills). Even less restrictive or exclusionary than the above zoning ordinances is the Petaluma Plan which, unlike those ordinances, does not freeze the population at present or near-present levels.[15] Further, unlike the Los Altos Hills ordinance and the various zoning regulations struck down by state courts in recent years, the Petaluma Plan does not have the undesirable effect of walling out any particular income class nor any racial minority group.[16]

---

[15] Under the Petaluma Plan, the population is expected to increase at the rate of about 1500 persons annually. This rate approximates the rate of growth in the 1960's and represents about a 6 per cent increase per year over the present population.

[16] Although appellees have attempted to align their business interests in attacking the Plan with legitimate housing needs of the urban poor and racial minorities, the

Although we assume that some persons desirous of living in Petaluma will be excluded under the housing permit limitation and that, thus, the Plan may frustrate some legitimate regional housing needs, the Plan is not arbitrary or unreasonable. We agree with appellees that unlike the situation in the past most municipalities today are neither isolated nor wholly independent from neighboring municipalities and that, consequently, unilateral land use decisions by one local entity affect the needs and resources of an entire region. . . . It does not necessarily follow, however, that the *due process* rights of builders and landowners are violated merely because a local entity exercises in its own self-interest the police power lawfully delegated to it by the state. . . . If the present system of delegated zoning power does not effectively serve the state interest in furthering the general welfare of the region or entire state, it is the state legislature's and not the federal courts' role to intervene and adjust the system. As stated *supra,* the federal court is not a super zoning board and should not be called on to mark the point at which legitimate local interests in promoting the welfare of the community are outweighed by legitimate regional interests. . . .

We conclude therefore that under *Belle Terre* and *Los Altos Hills* the concept of the public welfare is sufficiently broad to uphold Petaluma's desire to preserve its small town character, its open spaces and low density of population, and to grow at an orderly and deliberate pace.[17]

Association has not alleged nor can it allege, based on the record in this case, that the Plan has the purpose and effect of excluding poor persons and racial minorities. . . . Contrary to the picture painted by appellees, the Petaluma Plan is "inclusionary" to the extent that it offers new opportunities, previously unavailable, to minorities and low and moderate-income persons. Under the pre-Plan system single-family, middle-income housing dominated the Petaluma market, and as a result low and moderate income persons were unable to secure housing in the area. The Plan radically changes the previous building pattern and requires that housing permits be evenly divided between single-family and multi-family units and that approximately eight to twelve per cent of the units be constructed specifically for low and moderate income persons.

In stark contrast, each of the exclusionary zoning regulations invalidated by state courts in recent years impeded the ability of low and moderate income persons to purchase or rent housing in the locality. . . .

[17] Our decision upholding the Plan as not in violation of the appellees' due process rights should not be read as a permanent endorsement of the Plan. In a few years the City itself for good reason may abandon the Plan or the state may decide to alter its laws delegating its zoning power to the local authorities; or to meet legitimate regional needs, regional zoning authorities may be established. . . . To be sure, housing needs in metropolitan areas like the San Francisco Bay Area are pressing and the needs are not being met by present methods of supplying housing. However, the federal court is not the proper forum for resolving these problems.

Commerce Clause

The district court found that housing in Petaluma and the surrounding areas is produced substantially through goods and services in interstate commerce and that curtailment of residential growth in Petaluma will cause serious dislocation to commerce. 375 F.Supp. at 577, 579. Our ruling today, however, that the Petaluma Plan represents a reasonable and legitimate exercise of the police power obviates the necessity of remanding the case for consideration of appellees' claim that the Plan unreasonably burdens interstate commerce.

It is well settled that a state regulation validly based on the police power does not impermissibly burden interstate commerce where the regulation neither discriminates against interstate commerce nor operates to disrupt its required uniformity. . . .

Consequently, since the local regulation here is rationally related to the social and environmental welfare of the community and does not discriminate against interstate commerce or operate to disrupt its required uniformity, appellees' claim that the Plan unreasonably burdens commerce must fail.

Reversed.

Comments: 1. Some additional aspects of the Petaluma Plan are not covered by the court's opinion. McGivern, Putting a Speed Limit on Growth, 38 Plan. 263 (1972) (author is planning director of Petaluma). McGivern notes that the city was divided by a freeway into an older western section and a newer eastern section where most of the recent growth had occurred. Part of the purpose of the plan was to redistribute future growth more equally between these two sections. The quotas are "to be established on a geographic basis (east, central, and west) [and] are based on the actual number of single-family and multifamily units proposed in the housing element of the Petaluma General Plan. . . . The council may also require that between 8 and 12 percent of each year's total quota shall be low- to moderate-income housing as defined by the housing element of the plan." *Id.* at 265.

The Residential Development Evaluation System is utilized to determine which developers will receive the annual quota of allowable dwelling units, and is based on a point system similar to Ramapo's. From zero to five points are awarded for each of the following public facilities factors:

The controversy stirred up by the present litigation, as indicated by the number and variety of *amici* on each side, and the complex economic, political and social factors involved in this case are compelling evidence that resolution of the important housing and environmental issues raised here is exclusively the domain of the legislature.

1. the capacity of the water system to provide for the needs of the proposed development without system extensions beyond those normally installed by the developer;

2. the capacity of the sanitary sewers to dispose of the wastes of the proposed development without system extensions beyond those normally installed by the developer;

3. the capacity of the drainage facilities to adequately dispose of the surface runoff of the proposed development without system extensions beyond those normally installed by the developer;

4. the ability of the Fire Department of the city to provide fire protection according to the established response standards of the city without the necessity of establishing a new station or requiring addition of major equipment to an existing station;

5. the capacity of the appropriate school to absorb the children expected to inhabit a proposed development without necessitating adding double sessions or other unusual scheduling or classroom overcrowding;

6. the capacity of major street linkage to provide for the needs of the proposed development without substantially altering existing traffic patterns or overloading the existing street system, and the availability of other public facilities (such as parks and playgrounds) to meet the additional demands for vital public services without extension of services beyond those provided by the developer.

It is reported that the evaluation system was utilized to require substantial contributions from developers for citywide facilities such as water, sewer, drainage, and fire protection.

The second review category is based on quality of design and contribution to public welfare and amenity. Developers are assigned from zero to 10 points on each of the following:

1. site and architectural design quality which may be indicated by the harmony of the proposed buildings in terms of size, height, color, and location with respect to existing neighboring development;

2. site and architectural design quality which may be indicated by the amount and character of landscaping and screening;

3. site and architectural design quality which may be indicated by the arrangement of the site for efficiency of circulation, on- and off-site traffic safety, privacy, etc.;

4. the provision of public and/or private usable open space and/or pathways along the Petaluma River or any creek;

5. contributions to and extensions of existing systems of foot or bicycle paths, equestrian trails, and the greenbelt provided for in the Environmental Design Plan;

6. the provision of needed public facilities such as critical linkages in the major street system, school rooms, or other vital public facilities;

7. the extent to which the proposed development accomplishes an orderly and contiguous extension of existing development as against "leap frog" development;

8. the provision of units to meet the city's policy goal of 8 per cent to 12 per cent low- and moderate-income dwelling units annually.

The city's development policy also contains the following interesting statements:

> — redress a deficiency in multi-family units in Petaluma and insure "a variety of densities and building types and, thus wide ranges of rents". [An attempt was also made to lower housing prices by zoning for compact housing types, such as townhouses. — Eds.]
>
> — "Strengthen and rehabilitate the Central Business District to continue as the principal commercial center in Southern Sonoma County" by severely limiting thoroughfare commercial zoning on the fringe.

2. The federal District Court opinion in *Petaluma*, 375 F. Supp. 574 (N.D. Cal. 1974), had adopted a "growth center" theory which in part supported its holding that the Petaluma Plan was unconstitutional. This theory had been developed by economic consultants to the plaintiffs, see Gruen, The Economics of Petaluma: Unconstitutional Regional Socio-Economic Impacts in II Management and Control 173. The District Court expressed the growth center theory as follows:

> (g) Growth throughout a metropolitan region takes place unevenly in certain "growth centers," areas having unused capacity which can be tapped or the ability to augment capacity to serve new residents.
>
> (1) Petaluma is such a growth center for the San Francisco metropolitan region.
>
> (2) Such centers serve, among other things, as residential centers for people who work elsewhere in the center cities complex, in other suburbs or in other job centers.
>
> (3) Residential growth in such centers, though larger than in some other cities in the region, is not disproportionately larger in the sense that market, economic, demographic and other forces within the region dictate that growth shall occur in substantial part in growth centers.
>
> (h) If such growth centers curtail residential growth to less than demographic and market rates, as has been attempted in the present case, serious and damaging dislocation will occur in the housing market, the commerce it represents, and in the travel and settlement of people in need and in search of housing. Even in cities in the region that do not qualify as "growth centers," the same exclusion of residential growth would lead to substantially the same adverse consequences, if the exclusion were region-wide.

Id. at 579. The court then noted that the growth that should occur in growth centers could not occur elsewhere. Front-end public facilities costs would be too high in new towns, facilities were not available in rural areas and would have to be provided later at great cost, and growth in older inner cities presented massive redevelopment problems that had not yet been solved. *Id.* at 579-80. To what extent does the growth center theory resemble the "developing municipality" theory of *Mount Laurel, supra* p. 454? Is it valid? Does a federal court have a constitutional basis for applying such a theory in considering local growth management programs? A state court? For additional discussion of the Petaluma Plan see II Management and Control 121-210.

3. In explaining the right to travel ground of its decision, the District Court noted that if the Petaluma quota plan were to proliferate throughout the region there would be a serious shortfall in needed housing. As a result, "[i]nterstate, intrastate and foreign travel would be seriously inhibited, as people trying to move into the region found housing either economically unavailable or simply nonexistent in reasonable quality." *Id.* at 580-81.

Recent decisions have not been kind to the right to travel doctrine as it has been applied in the land use controls context. Thus the *CEEED* case, cited in a footnote in the Court of Appeals *Petaluma* decision, had this to say about the right to travel doctrine as it affected the permit program of the interim California coastal act:

> It does not follow, however, that all regulations affecting travel, however indirect or inconsequential, constitute invasions of the fundamental right. The right may be invoked if the regulations "unreasonably burden or restrict" the freedom of movement. . . . In a particular case the question is whether the travel inhibited is of sufficient importance to individual liberty to give rise to a constitutional violation. . . . Thus far the United States Supreme Court has invoked the right to travel only in cases involving invidious discrimination, durational residence requirements or direct restrictions on interstate or foreign travel. . . . Our Supreme Court found no infringement of the right in a city charter provision requiring all officers and employees of the city to be or become residents of the city within six months after their appointment or employment. . . .
>
> We fail to see how the Coastal Initiative interferes with fundamental right to travel. It is not discriminatory; it imposes no durational residence requirement; it exacts no penalty for exercising the right to travel or to select one's place of residence. In short, it has no chilling effect on an individual's freedom of movement. To paraphrase the language of our Supreme Court . . . plaintiffs are stretching their case mightily to bring it within the scope of the fundamental right to travel.

CEEED v. California Coastal Zone Conservation Comm'n, 118 Cal. Rptr. 315, 333 (Cal. App. 1974). For additional discussion of the right to travel doctrine as it affects land use controls see *supra* p. 343 . For an analysis of growth controls that takes into account the competitive position of suburban units imposing growth management programs in the housing market see Ellickson, Suburban Growth Controls: An Economic and Legal Analysis, 86 Yale L.J. 385, 425-35 (1977).

4. Both the Ramapo and Petaluma growth management plans were adopted by municipalities that were part of a larger regional area, thus raising the exclusionary and right to travel problems discussed in connection with these plans. In a few metropolitan areas in this country regional agencies have adopted growth management programs on a regional basis which presumably can better balance growth opportunities throughout the region. The following hypothetical example of such a regional program is based on the growth management program adopted in the Twin Cities area in Minnesota, where the regional planning agency is unique in also having regulatory land use control powers as well as control over major capital improvement programs in the region.

D. GODSCHALK, D. BROWER, L. MCBENNETT, & B. VESTAL,
CONSTITUTIONAL ISSUES OF GROWTH MANAGEMENT 149-53

The metropolitan area of Freewheel is located in the heart of the corn belt. Entirely within a single state, it consists of a core composed of one central city and three other major cities, surrounded by suburbs spreading out into five counties. Although there are variations within counties, on the average the suburbs only consume about one-eighth of the land area in each. The rest of the land is dedicated primarily to agricultural use, although there are also some scattered forests, about 60 small towns, and five freestanding cities with more than 10,000 people in the nonsuburban area. In all, the Freewheel region is governed by 280 units of government (counties, townships, municipalities, school districts, and special districts), with 120 of these being incorporated municipalities. The local governments in the five counties have joined together in a Council of Governments (COG).

In the early 1960s, a general study done by the state planning office showed that urban development was taking place throughout a large area, following no discernible pattern, appearing to respond only to the availability of land and the whims of developers. Bedroom communities were being developed at increasing distances from the central core, often jumping over contiguous undeveloped areas to take advantage of less expensive land. Other people who worked in the central core were bypassing the new suburbs and instead moving to the existing small farm towns that were scattered throughout the counties. The study predicted that, within a few years, these new residents would fill all of the small towns within 45 minutes of the central core to the capacity of their local water and sewer systems. In addition, some suburban municipalities were beginning to compete with the central city for new industrial and commercial development. The study predicted that the central core would begin losing this competition to the suburbs, which would draw new employers with available open land, the proximity of a white-collar labor force, more relaxed land-use controls, and in some cases, subsidized sites and buildings. It concluded that water pollution, solid waste disposal, and transportation would become more obvious problems as the existing systems began to strain under increasing loads.

In 1965, a Council of Governments was organized under existing enabling legislation and was given the authority to "plan at the regional level" and "to encourage local planning." It was designated as the regional agency to review certain proposals by local governments to the federal government, and was given a mandate to obtain whatever federal and state funding it could.

. . . .

In the early 1970s, a taxpayers' organization made its own study of the growth in the area and reviewed the experience of the COG in its efforts to deal with development. The citizens found that conditions had worsened, and that most of the predictions made by the state study of a decade earlier had come true. . . .

The taxpayers' assessment found that the COG had been successful in raising money for local and regional plans, but that the regional plans dealt only with single functions of government, such as transportation, open space, law enforcement, and the like, with little effort being made to coordinate them. . . . However, since there was no comprehensive regional development plan, some places encouraged growth, some sought to slow it, and some were highly selective about the sort of growth that would be accepted, all without regard to the regional impact. . . .

The report of the taxpayers' organization was released during the state legislative campaign and was seized upon by several Young Turks who made growth management a campaign issue. They were elected, and in the ensuing legislative session introduced a series of bills that would, according to their detractors, add another "level of obstacles" and would drive free enterprise out of Freewheel. But by diligent negotiation and a few key compromises, several parts of the new legislative program were enacted.

The first part of the enacted program required the regional planning agency, the COG, to prepare a general development framework that would establish a long-range comprehensive regional growth policy, provide a means for coordinating public investments, and give guidance to government agencies and the private sector. The act further required all local units of government within the five-county region to prepare their own more detailed local comprehensive plans which were to be consistent with the general framework established by the regional plan.

The newly elected legislators were also instrumental in the passage of a water pollution act that required the state to promulgate and enforce water pollution standards. The act had the effect of precluding development in certain areas in which septic tanks were not feasible until public sewage treatment was available.

. . . .

GROWTH POLICIES

The COG developed its general development framework as required by statute. It established the long-range regional plan with which the local plans were to be consistent. The basic aims of the COG policy were to maintain a high quality of life, to accommodate projected growth rationally and economically, to ensure adequate housing at a reasonable cost, to protect the environment, and to promote economic growth. The primary assumption was that no numerical limits would be placed on growth; the COG believed that the Freewheel region had to be willing to take its share of national growth. This meant that a growth management system was needed that would provide for the accommodation of 750,000 new people, 450,000 new jobs, and 380,000 new housing units by the year 2000.

The COG planners decided that, on a regional level, their major efforts should be directed at influencing the location and type of development. While quality development was important to them, they felt this could be best handled on a local level. The major impacts they considered while formulating the development framework were environmental impact and regional parity.

Their resolve to concentrate on controlling the location of future growth was strengthened by the results of a study of the major cost differences that would be incurred if they followed a "guided growth alternative" as opposed to a "continuing trends alternative." The guided growth alternative consisted of locating new development on already serviced but undeveloped land wherever possible. Looking at the public service costs of major roads, storm drainage, sanitary sewer interceptors and trunks, and water mains, they found that the continuing trends alternative would cost $2.75 billion more than the guided growth alternative. The study concluded that there was enough serviced but undeveloped land within the Freewheel metropolitan area to accommodate 75 per cent of the projected new development from 1975 to 2000. It recommended that the other 25 per cent be located in areas contiguous to the existing serviced areas.

In order to implement a compact growth policy which would ensure that most development would locate in areas accessible to services, the COG adopted a staged urban service area concept. This combined a land classification system with a coordinated capital improvements program. It classified all of the land within the region into one of five categories: (1) metro centers, the central areas of the major cities; (2) fully developed areas, the remaining areas of the major cities plus the older suburban areas; (3) areas of planned urbanization, those newer suburban areas that already had or were scheduled to receive urban services; (4) freestanding growth centers, smaller towns with existing or planned full urban services, geographically removed from the center-city conglomeration; and (5) rural areas. Urban developments were to be allowed only in the Urban Service Area, which consisted of land that fell under one of the first four categories. The remainder of the metropolitan area, classified as the Rural Service Area, was to be used primarily for agriculture. The COG established the criteria for the designation of the urban and rural service area boundaries for the next 25 years at five-year intervals, but left actual mapping to the individual units of government.

The other part of the staged urban service area concept consisted of capital improvements programing, primarily for transportation, water, and sewer. The COG, as part of its general development framework, evolved regional functional plans for these elements. The local governments, by statute, then had to devise their own local comprehensive plans which were to be consistent with the general framework established by the COG. The COG was empowered to require modification of a local plan if it proved to be a substantial departure from the metropolitan system plan. The COG established the criteria for staging the provision of services in the urban service area at five year intervals, consistent with the boundaries drawn by the local units of government according to the COG's specifications.

The planners were concerned that the compact growth policy might have the undesirable effect of raising housing costs and continuing the concentration of lower-cost housing in the central cities. In order to guard against this possibility, the COG adopted the following goals: increasing the supply of housing, promoting housing choice, improving living environments, and encouraging the dispersal of low- and moderate-cost housing throughout the region. It identified housing needs in each local governmental unit by size, cost, and type — and it formulated a short-term allocation plan for subsidized housing. . . .

The last major policy of the COG was to try to reduce the incentives for fiscal zoning in order to make what would be best for the local welfare coincide more closely with what would be best for the region. To do this, the COG was able to get an act passed by the state legislature which allowed it to implement a form of tax base sharing. The act provided for the tax revenue from 50 per cent of the commercial-industrial growth in the five county Freewheel region since 1972 to be shared by all the property taxing units within the region. The effect of the system was to pool part of the area-wide tax base and reallocate it to municipalities in direct relation to their need as measured by population and in inverse relation to their fiscal capacity as measured by market value of taxable property per capita.

Comments: 1. Staged growth plans employing the growth centers concept and growth staging areas are gaining popularity at the regional and also at the municipal level as a balanced method of growth control which will minimize service costs while achieving development parity. For discussion of a similar plan developed for the City of San Diego see City of San Diego Planning Dep't, A Residential Growth Management Program for San Diego (1977). The Twin Cities area plan is discussed in Freilich & Ragsdale, Timing and Sequential Controls — The Essential Basis for Effective Regional Planning: An Analysis of the New Directions for Land Use Control in the Minneapolis-St. Paul Metropolitan Region, 58 Minn. L. Rev. 1009 (1974).

In a variant of the Twin Cities growth management system, a freestanding city may establish an urban limits or urban growth line and so manage its capital facilities and land development policy that all growth occurs within this line. See the discussion of the Sacramento, California, and Salem, Oregon, growth management systems in Urban Growth at 23-27. An urban limits policy will require a complementary land use control policy in the area beyond the urban limits line that will help prevent development in this area. *See, e.g.,* the *Norbeck* case, *supra* p. 1023. The English green belt program is an example of this kind of growth-preventive policy. *See* D. Mandelker, Green Belts and Urban Growth (1962).

Growth staging programs have also been developed by urbanizing counties. The following excerpt describes the staging program adopted for Prince George's County, one of the urbanizing counties on the Maryland side of the Washington, D.C., metropolitan area:

> The proposed staging policy, though not officially adopted, divides the county into four classes or areas for development purposes. These include preferred development areas, where services are available or readily extended; economic potential areas, which help balance the tax base and job-home mix; limited development areas, minor additions to existing development; and deferred development areas, about 55 per cent of the county, used only to correct health or environmental problems. The policy also sets forth population targets by sewer service area. The annual targets of 14,000 people and 8,000 jobs may be adjusted if two countywide threshhold [*sic*] ratios are not met: 26 jobs per 100 residents or $4,250 assessed value per capita. The targets may be exceeded for projects responding to the economic development policy or for incentives allowed in the comprehensive design policy. The designated areas and targets provide guidelines for capital improvement programs and for all requests for rezonings, subdivision, sewage authorizations, and building permits.
>
> The system relies primarily on two processes: first, capital programming to provide facilities, coordinated through the County Executive's office; and second, subdivision review by the Planning Board, a division of the two-county Maryland-National Capital Park and Planning Commission. The term staging is unpopular now in the county, so the process is referred to as "land-use management."
>
> The general plan, subsequent master plans, and the 10-year water and sewer plan are key factors in the county's linkages among growth control elements. The county zoning ordinance also summarizes several elements.

Urban Growth at 21. Note the extent to which these plans use the availability of sewer and similar services as a long-term control on development. Compare the Ramapo plan, in which sewer service is one of the services on which the point system is based, although the general availability and improvement of sewer services throughout the town has not made sewer availability one of the principal factors in determining where new growth will occur.

2. Regional growth management plans such as those described in the hypothetical excerpt above based on the Twin Cities model may raise constitutional issues similar to those considered in the *Norbeck* case, *supra.* Consider the following challenge to that hypothetical regional growth management plan which is posed by the authors:

... As a developer, M. Wrench was extremely upset with the Freewheel COG plan and with the county of Crankshaft for implementing local restrictions consistent with it. He owned 360 acres of land in Crankshaft County, just outside the boundaries of Gear, a freestanding growth center. Wrench had expectations of developing his land as Gear expanded. However, with the implementation of the development framework and Crankshaft's coordinated comprehensive plan, he found his land in the Rural Service Area, which was slated exclusively for agricultural uses for the next 25 years. Although it was very probable, but not certain, that the Urban Service Area would be expanded to include Wrench's property after 25 years since his property was adjacent to the area slated eventually to acquire services, it was definite, however, that he could not develop his land for residential, industrial, or commercial use at least until the year 2000.

Wrench thought this restriction placed an unfair burden on him and decided to challenge on taking grounds. He brought suit in state court against the COG and Crankshaft County to have the court invalidate the designation of the urban and rural service areas via the land classification and capital improvements program.

Constitutional Issues of Growth Management, *supra* at 153-54. How would you decide this case?

E. SERVICING PROBLEMS

In *Charles v. Diamond supra* p. 1053, the highest New York court considered the question of how long a municipality may delay the provision of public services and then use that delay as the basis for refusing approval to new development dependent on those services. The court in that case discussed but did not reach the question of whether, and to what extent, municipality is under a duty to provide public services to developers who ask for them. This issue is important in growth management programs. Consult again the discussion of the Boulder, Colorado, growth management program, *supra* p. 990, in which limitations on the provision of public services are an instrumental feature of the growth management system. Service limitations also figure, of course, in regional growth management programs such as those adopted in the Twin Cities area, and which has been described above. In the following case, which is mentioned in the Boulder article, the Colorado Supreme Court indicated its view of when municipalities were under a duty to provide public services to developers who were in need of them.

ROBINSON v. CITY OF BOULDER

Supreme Court of Colorado
__Colo. __, 547 P.2d 228 (1976)

DAY, Justice.

This is an appeal brought by appellant, City of Boulder (Boulder), seeking reversal of a trial court order mandating its extension of water and sewer service to appellees. We affirm.

Appellees (landowners) sought to subdivide approximately 79 acres of land in the Gunbarrel Hill area northeast of Boulder and outside of its city limits. The landowners proposed a residential development in conformity with its county rural residential (RR) zoning.

As a condition precedent to considering the question of development, the county required the landowners to secure water and sewer services; they were referred to the city for that purpose.

Boulder operates a water and sewer utility system. In the mid 1960's it defined an area beyond its corporate limits, including the subject property, for which it intended to be the only water and sewer servicing agency. The record reflects that this was accomplished in order to gain indirect control over the development of property located within the service area. Boulder contracted with and provided water and sewer service to the Boulder Valley Water and Sanitation District (the district), which is located within the service area. The subject property is immediately adjacent to the district. The contract between Boulder and the district vests in the former almost total control over water and sewer service within district boundaries. The latter functions in merely a nominal administrative capacity. For example, Boulder retains control over all engineering and construction aspects of the service as well as decision-making power over the district's authority to expand its boundaries. Pursuant to a city ordinance, the district cannot increase its service area without the approval of city council.

The landowners applied to the district for inclusion, and the application was accepted; however, Boulder disapproved the action on the grounds that the landowners' proposal was inconsistent with the Boulder Valley Comprehensive Plan and various aspects of the city's interim growth policy. The trial court found that:

> ... The City seeks to effect its growth rate regulation goals in the Gunbarrel Hill area by using its water and sewer utility as the means to accomplish its goals. ...

The decision was *not* based on Boulder's incapacity to supply the service or the property's remote location from existing facilities or any economic considerations.

The landowners then filed suit for declaratory relief, and the district court concluded that Boulder is operating in the capacity of a public utility in the Gunbarrel area. In terms of supplying water and sewer services, it must treat all members of the public within its franchise area alike — including these landowners. The court held that Boulder had unjustly discriminated against appellees by denying them service, while having previously approved service extensions to neighboring residential and industrial developments. The court concluded that Boulder can only refuse to extend its service to landowners for utility-related reasons. Growth control and land use planning considerations do not suffice. We agree.

I.

On appeal Boulder argues that its service program in Gunbarrel is not a public utility under the test which we enunciated in *City of Englewood v. Denver,* 123 Colo. 290, 229 P.2d 667 (1951):

> . . . to fall into the class of public utility, a business or enterprise must be impressed with a public interest and that those engaged in the conduct thereof must hold themselves out as serving or ready to serve all members of the public, who may require it, to the extent of their capacity. The nature of the service must be such that all members of the public have an enforceable right to demand it. . . .

Boulder contends that it has never held itself out as being ready to serve all members of the public to the extent of its capacity. The trial court made findings to the contrary and the record amply supports them. We summarize them:

(1) Boulder's extension of services to the Gunbarrel area created a new and major urban service area substantially distant from the city's corporate limits.

(2) Boulder entered into agreements with other local water and sanitation districts and municipalities which had the effect of precluding these entities from servicing Gunbarrel residents.

(3) Boulder opposed a water company's application before the Public Utilities Commission which would have provided water in a part of the city's delineated service area.

(4) Boulder's total control and dominance as the exclusive water and sewer servicing agency in the Gunbarrel area is demonstrated by the fact that Boulder County planning authorities, routinely and in compliance with the city's agreement, refer area landowners in need of such services to Boulder.

(5) The course of conduct followed by Boulder in providing water and sewer services to this area indicates that *it has held itself out to be the one and only such servicing agency* in the Gunbarrel area.

In light of such findings, the trial court's determination that Boulder had by its actions acceded to the status of a public utility in the Gunbarrel area was correct.

Boulder relies on *City of Englewood, supra,* to support its position that it is not operating as a public utility within the area in question; that reliance is misplaced. The determination that Denver did not operate as a public utility in supplying Englewood with water was premised on an entirely different factual background. Denver's supplying of water to Englewood users was wholly incidental to the operation of its water system which was established for the purpose of supplying Denver inhabitants. Denver did not "stake out" a territory in Englewood and seek to become the sole supplier of water in the territory. Here, by agreements with other suppliers to the effect that the latter would not service the Gunbarrel area and by opposing other methods or sources of supply, Boulder has secured a monopoly over area water and sewer utilities. Further, as the trial court pointed out:

> ... The City of Boulder had dedicated its water and sewer service to public use to benefit both the inhabitants of Boulder and the residents of the Gunbarrel Hill area in the interest of controlling the growth of the area and to provide living qualities which the City deems desirable. ...

II.

Boulder argues that even if its program satisfies the tests of a public utility in the Gunbarrel area that it may use public policy considerations in administering its service program. It contends that the rules which apply to private utilities should not apply to a governmental utility authorized to implement governmental objectives, one of which is the adoption of a master plan of development.

Section 31-23-106(1), C.R.S.1973, in relevant part, states:

... [This section enacts the language of the Standard Planning Act which authorizes the preparation of a comprehensive plan. — Eds.]

To this end, the city of Boulder and Boulder County jointly developed and adopted the Boulder Valley Comprehensive Plan, one of the purposes of which is to provide a basis for the discretionary land use decisions which it must make. Boulder also cites section 31-23-109, C.R.S.1973, which states in relevant part:

... [This section enacts the language of the Standard Planning Act which requires planning commission approval of any public facilities or utilities. — Eds.]

Boulder argues that its decision to deny the extension of services to the landowners in this case was based on the proposed development's noncompliance with growth projections outlined in the comprehensive plan. In the event of an alleged conflict between Boulder's public utility and land use planning duties we are asked to rule that the latter are paramount.

A municipality is without jurisdiction over territory outside its municipal limits in the absence of legislation. ... We find nothing in the above-cited statutes which indicates a legislative intent to broaden a city's authority in a case such as the one before us. In our view, sections 31-23-106(1) and 31-23-109 place ultimate governmental authority in matters pertaining to land use in unincorporated areas in the county. In effect, a city is given only an advisory role.

The record reflects that the proposed development would comply with county zoning regulations; and the county planning staff has indicated that it conforms with their interpretation of the comprehensive plan, though final consideration was put off pending a determination of whether the area would have adequate water and sewer facilities.

In view of the fact that it is the board of county commissioners — not Boulder — which must make the ultimate decision as to the approval or disapproval of the proposed development, we do not need to address the question of whether the Boulder Valley Comprehensive Plan relieves the City of Boulder of its duty to the public in its proprietary role as a public utility.

In conclusion, we hold that inasmuch as Boulder is the sole and exclusive provider of water and sewer services in the area surrounding the subject property, it is a public utility. As such, it holds itself out as ready and able to serve those in the territory who require the service. There is no utility related reason, such as insufficient water, preventing it from extending these services to the landowners. Unless such reasons exist, Boulder cannot refuse to serve the people in the subject area. . . .

Judgment affirmed.

Comments: 1. The utility extension problem considered in the *Robinson* case bears directly on the viability of plans, like the Ramapo plan, which link the growth management system to the provision of public services. Could a developer denied a residential permit under the Ramapo plan successfully argue under facts similar to those considered in *Robinson* that public services have been held out to developers in the area in which he is located so that a refusal to extend services to him could be overturned in court?

The first problem to consider is whether the holding out theory as adopted by the Colorado court would be adopted in the same form elsewhere. Utility extension problems in the growth management setting are discussed in Note, Control of the Timing and Location of Government and Utility Extensions, 26 Stan. L. Rev. 945 (1974). That Note indicates that the power to control utility extensions which is given to local governments is discretionary in most jurisdictions. *Id.* at 949. It also indicates that courts have accepted as a reason for allowing this discretion the scarce financial resources available to local governments and the desirability of allowing local officials to allocate these resources; a hostility to allowing local governments to assist land developers in speculation; and the difficulty in judicially enforcing an extension duty. *Id.* at 950-51.

A distinction may have to be made between refusals to extend municipal services within municipal limits and refusals to extend municipal services to extraterritorial areas. In *Corcoran v. Village of Bennington,* 266 A.2d 457 (Vt. 1970), the village was required to extend water and sewer services to a mobile home park. There was evidence that service had been arbitrarily withheld in order to implement a village policy against these parks. Later, in *Okemo Trailside Condominiums v. Blais,* 380 A.2d 84 (Vt. 1977), the same court held that a village could exercise discretion to determine whether it had excess capacity to service condominium units lying outside the village territorial limits. The court also seemed to affirm a planning reason for the denial, noting that "[o]vercommitment outside the municipal limits might . . . increase the impact of necessary additional construction on the local zoning law." *Id.* at 86. *Accord, Denby v. Brown,* 199 S.E.2d 214 (Ga. 1973).

These issues had also been litigated by the New Jersey courts in the *Reid* cases, in which the area requesting service was inside rather than outside the municipal territorial limits. In *Reid I, Reid Dev. Corp. v. Parsippany-Troy Hills Township,* 89 A.2d 667 (N.J. 1952), the township refused a water extension which would have enabled a developer to build on his lots. The court ordered the municipality to extend the service, and rejected a condition precedent to this extension that the developer increase its lot sizes to conform to municipal planning objectives.

While the case thus appears to have rejected an attempt to condition a service extension on compliance with land use objectives, the case was complicated by the fact that the township had not adopted the state's enabling act, a peculiar requirement then imposed by New Jersey law, and therefore could not adopt land use regulations. However, the lot size requirement was the only reason given for rejecting the developer's request. Neither did the court allow the municipality to refuse the request on economic grounds. Need was not denied, and the cost was not prohibitive.

In *Reid II,* 107 A.2d 20 (N.J. Super. 1954), a request for an additional water service extension in this area was again denied, and the court upheld the denial. The court distinguished *Reid I* as a case of "the municipality's withholding of the grant of the extension as a means of coercing the landowner into accepting a suggested change in the minimum lot size, which action was held to be an abuse of discretion." *Id.* at 20. In *Reid II* the reason for the refusal was found to be utility-related, because the municipality had limited funds and there were competing requests for service. Additionally, the court found that there was no immediate need for the extension, noting that the previous extension had not attracted a single customer. *Id.* at 22-23. For discussion of the *Reid* cases see the Note, *supra* at 953-58. Compare *Clark v. Board of Water & Sewer Comm'rs,* 234 N.E.2d 893 (Mass. 1968), ordering an extension of sewer service within the municipality when there was reasonable capacity to serve a proposed apartment complex.

In cases in which an extraterritorial extension of service has been requested, other courts have adopted the holding out theory of the *Robinson* case. An extension of services may be required when other landowners have been serviced in the immediate extraterritorial area, *Mayor & Council v. Goldberg,* 264 A.2d 113 (Md. 1970), or when the landowner is located in a buffer zone in which the municipal authorities had agreed to extend services, *Delmarva Enterprises, Inc. v. Mayor & Council,* 282 A.2d 601 (Del. 1971).

3. The Colorado court in the *Robinson* case ignored a freestanding Local Government Land Use Control Enabling Act enacted in 1974 and which provides land use regulatory powers in addition to those conferred by other legislation. Among the powers conferred by the 1974 act are the following:

> (f) Providing for phased development of services and facilities; . . .
> (h) Otherwise planning for and regulating the use of land so as to provide planned and orderly use of land and protection of the environment in a manner consistent with constitutional rights.

Colo. Rev. Stat. § 29-20-104 (Supp. 1976). Does this legislation authorize the denial of service that was at issue in the *Robinson* case? What constitutional rights might be infringed by a service denial? For example, could a developer denied service in circumstances similar to those in the *Robinson* case successfully claim a denial of equal protection? For additional discussion of extraterritorial utility service see D. Mandelker & D. Netsch, State and Local Government in a Federal System 429-39 (1977).

Chapter 8

ENVIRONMENTAL CONTROLS

A. INTRODUCTORY CONCEPTS AND STRATEGIES

Great Salt Meadow in Stratford, Connecticut

Approximately 600 acres remain of the Great Salt Meadow in Stratford, Connecticut. This expanse of yellow marsh grasses, salt hay, and numerous other plants is bordered by Lewis Gut, a tidal estuary winding from the edge of Bridgeport airport southwest to Long Island Sound. For much of its length, the Gut is bounded by a popular public beach. Important portions of the remaining meadow are in private ownership, and one owner, Rykar Industrial Corporation, is currently proposing an industrial facility and related upland construction for a 277-acre parcel of marshland adjoining the Gut.

The meadow is one of the few remaining undeveloped sites that might be suitable for such a facility in the industrial corridor between Boston and New York City. Local zoning regulations have permitted industrial development in the area since 1927. Rykar, which has held this land and adjoining parcels for over twenty years, has made substantial improvements in anticipation of development, including construction of a new railroad spur.

But recent Connecticut legislation to protect coastal wetlands has stymied Rykar's proposal to dredge and fill their marsh. In September 1970, the property was designated a protected "ecological unit," making a state permit mandatory for virtually all development. Rykar's application for a permit was ultimately denied on several grounds — that the property is in fact a tidal wetland subject to flooding, hurricane, and other natural disasters; that it benefits marine fisheries; and that the dredging would destroy shellfish grounds and endanger the adjoining beach. Rykar has alleged that the ruling results in an unconstitutional taking of its property, and the issue is now before the Superior Court of Hartford County, Connecticut.

From The Use of Land: A Citizens' Policy Guide to Urban Growth 148-49 (W. Reilly ed. 1973).

Environmental crises such as the crisis described in this excerpt have stimulated the enactment of a wide variety of national and state environmental protection legislation, much of which contains land use control features. This chapter reviews this legislation, and the land use control programs they contain, emphasizing statutes ranging from the National Environmental Policy Act and the national air and water quality acts to state legislation for wetlands and shorelands. Attention will also be paid to the impact on energy conservation of alternative patterns of land development.

One study has noted the following impacts of land development on environmental quality:

1) The environmental impact of land use development is pervasive in that almost all forms of economic activities — residential, industrial, transportation, recreation, etc. — have contributed to some instances of environmental degradation.

2) The environmental impact of present economic developmental decisions will be of a prolonged nature and may be irreversible.

3) The environmental problems posed by past land use or developmental processes are not always susceptible to solutions involving the application of a control technology.

4) The environmental consequences of land development decisions are not fully perceived when these decisions are made.

E. Croke, K. Croke, A. Kennedy, & L. Hoover, The Relationship Between Land Use and Environmental Protection 15 (1972).

Do land use controls have a role to play in protecting the quality of the environment? This issue is addressed in the following selection.

CROKE, AN EVALUATION OF THE IMPACT OF LAND USE ON ENVIRONMENTAL QUALITY IN ENVIRONMENT: A NEW FOCUS FOR LAND-USE PLANNING 217, 226-28 (1973)

LAND GUIDANCE AS A MECHANISM FOR ENVIRONMENTAL PROTECTION

... [T]here is a fairly close relationship between the types and quantity of environmental pollutants produced by a given parcel of land and the use and level of intensity to which that land has been developed. The impact on ambient air and water quality of the spatial distribution of pollution-producing activities has also been demonstrated through the use of atmospheric and hydrologic transport and dispersion models. It follows, in principle at least, that controls imposed on the distribution and intensity of land use should be at least as effective, and substantially more flexible, than source-oriented technology controls (because land-use-based restrictions on pollutant emissions need not be linked explicitly to any specific process or emission control schemes). The Cook County, Ill., emission density zoning controls, which restricted the allowable rate of emission of certain air pollutants per occupied acre of land, represent an early, albeit ineffective, attempt to take advantage of this concept. . . . In a similar vein, the State of Illinois has recently explored the feasibility of establishing buffer zones between agricultural areas saturated with pesticides and fertilizers and adjacent natural receiving waters that could be contaminated by polluted runoff.

Despite this history, comprehensive emission density limitations and environmental buffer zoning are at present little more than conceptually attractive devices for regulating the pollution potential of alternative land-use patterns. There are a number of other approaches that appear to be equally promising. In fact, the system of land guidance techniques normally applied by comprehensive planning agencies includes a wide variety of schemes which can be categorized under the general heading of advice, controls, inducements, development, and acquisition. . . .

. . . .

Although the utilization of such schemes to control pollution is not common as yet, environmental objectives have been introduced into many land-use guidance activities. For instance, airport, flood-plain, agricultural, conservation, and performance standards zoning all reflect environmental quality concerns. Moreover, hillside grading regulations and the purchase of easements or development rights have frequently been employed to reduce erosion or preserve scenic areas.

While land-use-oriented pollution controls are normally considered in a negative or restrictive context, it is important to note that there is a positive side to the tendency of pollution-producing activities to be densely concentrated. The dispersal of residential communities and suburban industrial operations can inhibit the deployment of large, efficient, centralized wastewater treatment and solid-waste-disposal facilities. The clustering of related activities can reduce significantly the cost of pollution control as demonstrated by a complex of metal plating plants in Cleveland that take advantage of joint waste treatment and reclamation systems. . . .

. . . [P]roviding or withholding public utilities such as transportation systems, water supply and wastewater treatment facilities, energy distribution systems, etc., is a potentially significant means of inducing environmentally desirable land development. In principle, economic incentives, such as spatially sensitive property taxes and pricing policies that internalize the societal cost of pollution, could also be employed to achieve preferred development patterns. To design such economic incentives, more quantified information is needed on the environmental costs and benefits associated with land development.

Comments: At this point, and to highlight the direction which land use controls in environmental legislation have taken, a few words are in order on the concepts and strategies which this legislation has adopted. There are two major characteristics of these concepts and strategies; one is institutional and one is substantive. Institutionally, the tendency in environmental land use control legislation has been to bypass existing land use control systems, both in the governmental agencies chosen to implement this legislation and in the types of control that have been adopted. Most apparent is an innate distrust of local government, local government decision-makers, and their willingness and capacity to take environmental factors into account in their decisions. Most environmental land use control legislation has placed implementation powers with national and state agencies.

This distrust may have some empirical support. One survey of environmental awareness among local planning agencies reached the following conclusion:

> While there is definitely a growing concern about environmental quality among local agencies, it is a recent phenomenon, tending to follow, not to lead, the general national environmental consciousness. Agencies tend to approach the issue by incorporating environmental quality goals into an already broad range of concerns — concerns which have the traditional bias toward urban values, comprehensiveness, and balance among multiple objectives — rather than by focusing on individual environmental problems.

E. Kaiser et al., Promoting Environmental Quality Through Urban Planning and Controls 430 (1973). This tendency to place environmental land use control legislation under the direction of national and state agencies has both advantages and disadvantages. The specific focus of this legislation and its relatively autonomous status in the hierarchy of controls over land use have allowed for an emphasis on environmental protection which otherwise might not be present. At the same time, the tendency to isolate environmental land use control programs from the mainstream of planning and land use control concerns has created duplication and overlap in regulatory systems and in some instances has been counterproductive.

The statement just quoted reveals a substantive bias in environmental controls which also distinguishes them from the conventional planning and land use control system. By inference, the statement suggests that environmental planning and control is biased toward nonurban values, is not comprehensive, and seeks to maximize specific environmental values at the expense of other competing values which impinge on the regulatory process. This absolutist tendency in environmental controls needs emphasis, as it tends to color the content of environmental planning and regulation. Nowhere is this ethically-laden and normative approach to land use allocation questions more apparent than in the ongoing controversy over the nondegradation of existing environmental resources, a controversy which has erupted most critically in the implementation of the national Clean Air Act but which underlies other environmental legislation as well.

The nondegradation requirement raises another aspect of environmental controls that does not always get attention — the potential bias against lower income groups. One effect of a nondegradation policy, for example, is to force air polluting industries into older cities, where lower income groups tend to live. An even sharper conflict between environmentalists and lower income groups arises in controversies over lower income housing:

> Under the guise of environmental protection, individuals and organizations have taken strong positions against low and moderate income housing developments. These run the full gamut from expressions that poor people pollute and would adversely affect the environment, to alleged inadequate sewage systems, to surface drainage and the protection of a recharge area. . . .
>
> One spokesman states directly that "[i]ncreasingly, housing programs are being challenged by ecologically oriented groups in concert with old style racial bigots." . . .
>
> But the housing rights advocates' most serious and far reaching concern with environmental protection programs center on the controls over future development and what kind of assurances will be represented within that development.

M. Brooks, Housing Equity and Environmental Protection: The Needless Conflict 9-10 (1976). *See also* Environmental Quality and Social Justice in Urban America (J. Smith ed. 1974). Is there another side to this argument?

One final comment is in order on the conceptual assumptions that underlie environmental controls legislation. This legislation falls into two major categories, a point forcefully put in an article coauthored by Senator Edward Muskie:

> With few exceptions, most federal laws for protecting the environment fall into one of two major categories, distinguished by different regulatory approaches and different intended and actual results. On the one hand, laws which we will term "standards-setting" statutes authorize an administrative agency (usually the Environmental Protection Agency (EPA)) to set and enforce environmental quality standards and regulations on the basis of detailed policy decisions made by the Congress. These statutes provide clear, substantive regulation of the quality of specific environmental resources such as air and water. On the other hand, a different set of laws which we will term federal "policy" statutes require federal agencies to conform to certain minimal procedural standards of conduct when their activities will have significant environmental effects. In other words, these statutes require that environmental considerations be taken into account as the federal government conducts its business, although the statutes themselves set no substantive environmental policies and require no particular substantive results.

Muskie & Cutler, A National Environmental Policy: Now You See It, Now You Don't, 25 Me. L. Rev. 163, 164 (1973). Similar differences appear in state environmental legislation.

This chapter begins with a major example of process-oriented environmental legislation — the National Environmental Policy Act and its state counterparts. The major contribution of this legislation is the requirement that an Environmental Impact Statement (EIS) be prepared for a wide variety of governmental and private projects. When an EIS must be prepared for land development and land use projects the EIS assumes important land use control dimensions.

B. NEPA, STATE EIS LAWS AND LAND USE

1. The National Environmental Policy Act

THE NATIONAL ENVIRONMENTAL POLICY ACT

Sec. 101. (a) The Congress, recognizing the profound impact of man's activity on the interrelations of all components of the natural environment, particularly the profound influences of population growth, high-density urbanization, industrial expansion, resource exploitation, and new and expanding technological advances and recognizing further the critical importance of restoring and maintaining environmental quality to the overall welfare and development of man, declares that it is the continuing policy of the Federal Government, in cooperation with State and local governments, and other concerned public and private organizations, to use all practicable means and measures, including financial and technical assistance, in a manner calculated to foster and promote the general welfare, to create and maintain conditions under which man and nature can exist in productive harmony, and fulfill the social, economic, and other requirements of present and future generations of Americans.

(b) In order to carry out the policy set forth in this Act, it is the continuing responsibility of the Federal Government to use all practicable means, consistent with other essential considerations of national policy, to improve and coordinate Federal plans, functions, programs, and resources to the end that the Nation may—

(1) fulfill the responsibilities of each generation as trustee of the environment for succeeding generations;

(2) assure for all Americans safe, healthful, productive, and esthetically and culturally pleasing surroundings;

(3) attain the widest range of beneficial uses of the environment without degradation, risk to health or safety, or other undesirable and unintended consequences;

(4) preserve important historic, cultural, and natural aspects of our national heritage, and maintain, wherever possible, an environment which supports diversity and variety of individual choice;

(5) achieve a balance between population and resource use which will permit high standards of living and a wide sharing of life's amenities; and

(6) enhance the quality of renewable resources and approach the maximum attainable recycling of depletable resources.

(c) The Congress recognizes that each person should enjoy a healthful environment and that each person has a responsibility to contribute to the preservation and enhancement of the environment.

Sec. 102. The Congress authorizes and directs that, to the fullest extent possible: (1) the policies, regulations, and public laws of the United States shall be interpreted and administered in accordance with the policies set forth in this Act, and (2) all agencies of the Federal Government shall —

(A) utilize a systematic, interdisciplinary approach which will insure the integrated use of the natural and social sciences and the environmental design arts in planning and in decisionmaking which may have an impact on man's environment;

(B) identify and develop methods and procedures, in consultation with the Council on Environmental Quality established by title II of this Act, which will insure that presently unquantified environmental amenities and values may be given appropriate consideration in decisionmaking along with economic and technical considerations;

(C) include in every recommendation or report on proposals for legislation and other major Federal actions significantly affecting the quality of the human environment, a detailed statement by the responsible official on —

(i) the environmental impact of the proposed action,

(ii) any adverse environmental effects which cannot be avoided should the proposal be implemented,

(iii) alternatives to the proposed action,

(iv) the relationship between local short-term uses of man's environment and the maintenance and enhancement of long-term productivity, and

(v) any irreversible and irretrievable commitments of resources which would be involved in the proposed action should it be implemented.

. . . .

(D) study, develop, and describe appropriate alternatives to recommend courses of action in any proposal which involves unresolved conflicts concerning alternative uses of available resources;

. . . .

Comments: 1. An initial question under NEPA is whether an EIS need be prepared at all. The statute calls for the preparation of an impact statement for every major federal *action* significantly affecting the *environment.* Our focus here is on the two words appearing in italics. With reference to possible land use control implications of NEPA, we want to know what kinds of actions fall under the statute and what kinds of environment are included.

Assistance in interpreting the statute is afforded by interpretations adopted by the Council on Environmental Quality (CEQ), created by Title II of NEPA and authorized by Executive Order to issue what first were called guidelines and what are now regulations interpreting the statute. *See* 40 C.F.R. § 1500.1 *et seq.* (1977). With reference to those actions which come within the statute, the CEQ has brought federally-built projects within that term — this interpretation would seem clear — and has extended the statute as well to include private projects such as housing projects which either are subsidized by federal funds or insured by the federal mortgage insuring agency. It is this latter extension of the statute, in particular, which has opened up opportunities for the EIS in the land development area.

Next to be considered is the type of environment covered by impact statements. While many believed the statute to be applicable only to natural environments, references in the statute to the influences of "high-density urbanization," see § 101(a), and the failure to limit the statute to natural environments have led some courts to the conclusion that urban as well as natural environments are included within the statute. Thus in *Hanly v. Mitchell,* 460 F.2d 640 (2d Cir.), *cert. denied,* 409 U.S. 990 (1972), the court considered whether an environmental impact statement was needed for an office building and detention center for persons awaiting trial to be built by the federal General Services Administration in downtown Manhattan. The court held that an EIS was required and that NEPA includes the "protection of the quality of life for city residents" within its scope. *Id.* at 647. Noise, traffic, overburdened mass transportation systems, crime, congestion and the availability of drugs were some of the impacts from the project mentioned as possibly affecting the quality of urban life.

With these interpretations of NEPA before us, we can turn to the following analysis of the statute as it applied to a housing project to be built by the Navy. Although the case considers a federally-built project, the issues raised would clearly be of concern in any review of a housing development falling under NEPA because of federal subsidies or federal mortgage insurance.

TOWN OF GROTON v. LAIRD

United States District Court
353 F. Supp. 344 (D. Conn. 1972)

BLUMENFELD, Chief Judge. Plaintiffs are the Town of Groton, Connecticut, and nine individual residents and taxpayers of the town. Alleging that defendants, officers in charge of the Naval Submarine Base located in Groton and their superiors in the Department of Defense, have failed to comply with the requirements of Section 102(2)(C) of the National Environmental Policy Act (NEPA), 42 U.S.C. § 4332(2)(C), they seek to enjoin all construction now being undertaken by the Navy on certain sites within the town.

I.

The relevant facts may be briefly stated. The Naval Submarine Base is a large complex located in Groton, and there is little doubt that the Navy's plans to improve the efficient operation of the Base presented for consideration here will shortly result in an increase in the resident population in the town. The Navy has long been concerned about the scarcity of housing in the area available at a cost which does not exceed the housing allowance granted its employees at the Base. In 1965, it began an initial exploration of possible sites in the general area and, out of ten surveyed, selected a lightly wooded and otherwise vacant plot known as Bailey Hill for the location of a 300-unit project. In 1967, some of the sites were resurveyed, and the selection of Bailey Hill was reaffirmed. Consultation with Groton officials about specifics of the project has occurred intermittently since that time with attendant publicity in various local newspapers. Controversy about the Bailey Hill housing began to bubble in April of this year, when townspeople living on nearby property began complaining that the project conflicted with the town's zoning provisions for the neighborhood and would change its character. In July, several members of the Town Planning Commission, who were attempting to prepare a new plan of land use development for Groton, met with officers from the Base, who discussed their own preliminary plans for future utilization of Navy property in the Groton area. At this meeting, several particular projects were pointed out, but the Commission did not receive a copy of the proposed plan, which the Navy apparently felt was too inchoate to be released. A month later, on August 23, 1972, Captain Hawkins, Commander of the Base, along with Lt. Comm. Thomas of the Northeast Regional Facilities Command, met with the same officials and disclosed the so-called Master Plan for all Navy activity in the area. This was a $120,000,000 proposal involving construction of various housing facilities, commercial buildings, a chapel — projects that would obviously have considerable impact on the town and its residents. Up to this point, no formal public statement as to environmental effect had been issued.

Several town officials, distressed by the Navy's plans, met with Secretary of the Navy Charles Ill in Washington. An agreement emerged from that meeting: the Navy would cease all construction except on the Bailey Hill project and would file within six months an environmental impact statement, as required by NEPA, covering everything included in the Master Plan. In return, the town would forbear bringing suit to stop the Bailey Hill construction, for which an impact statement would not be required. Several weeks later, in early October, town officials discovered that construction proceeding on a site located on Gungywump Road was not, as they had thought, a Navy building but a credit union building for the use of Navy personnel owned by a civilian corporation. Claiming that continued work on this one building violated the agreement and rendered it void, plaintiffs sought a temporary restraining order in this court and requested that *all* construction be enjoined until an environmental impact statement on the Bailey Hill housing was filed.

The plaintiffs' request for a temporary restraining order was denied, but a hearing on the application for a preliminary injunction was consolidated with a trial on the merits. See Fed.R.Civ.P. 65(a)(2). Since I find that defendants' actions have complied with the directives of the statute, the prayer for injunctive relief must be denied. . . .

III.

Section 102(2)(C) mandates that every federal agency undertaking any "major Federal actions significantly affecting the quality of the human environment" must file a detailed report examining, inter alia, the environmental impact of the action, unavoidable adverse environmental effects resulting from its implementation, and alternatives to the proposed action. This analysis has become known as the "environmental impact statement." More than a score of cases have established beyond question that failure to file the statement when one is required should result in an injunction against all further activity on the project until the agency has complied with the statute. But an environmental impact statement is not required every time a federal agency does anything. Before an environmental impact statement is required, two threshold factors must exist: the proposed action must be "major," and its effect on the human environment must be "significant." Both parties agreed that the Bailey Hill project, whether considered separately or together with the credit union building, constitutes a "major" action. The issue presented here is whether the environmental effect of the project will be "significant." The Navy, following both NEPA and its own regulations, OPNAV 6240.2A (defendants' Exhibit C), analyzed the environmental effects of the project and determined that they would not be significant. It, therefore, did not issue an impact statement but retained for its own planning purposes its "Assessment" of the project's expected environmental effect, which it continually updates.

This "threshold" determination of significance is a decision properly made in the first instance by the agency undertaking the action, but is reviewable by the courts. *Hanly v. Mitchell*, 460 F.2d 640, 644, 648 (2d Cir. 1972) (*Hanly I*). While the standard of review of such a decision had been expressly left open in this circuit, it was sub judice at the time of the hearing on this matter, and *Hanly II*, supra, 471 F.2d at 829, just recently decided, has now settled this issue. The proper standard is that set forth in Section 10(e) of the Administrative Procedure Act, 5 U.S.C. § 706(2)(A), which permits a reviewing court to set aside agency action only if it finds the action "arbitrary, capricious, an abuse of discretion or otherwise not in accordance with law." Under this test, the Navy's determination that the project did not fall within the legislative purpose is clearly correct.

It is incontrovertible that NEPA requires administrative consideration of factors affecting "the quality of life for city residents," [1] *Hanly I, supra,* 460 F.2d at 647, before decision is made that the proposed agency action will "significantly (affect) the quality of the human environment." In its determination of nonsignificance, the Navy's Assessment took into account the following factors: health, safety, local socio-economic factors, transportation systems, vehicular and air traffic patterns, utility systems, public services, and aesthetics. It concluded that "(n)o adverse effect on humans is anticipated." (Plaintiffs' Exhibit 6, "Environmental Assessment" § B(1)(a)). *Hanly II* holds that in making such determination

> "the agency in charge, although vested with broad discretion, should normally be required to review the purposed action in the light of at least two relevant factors: (1) the extent to which the action will cause adverse environmental effects in excess of those created by existing uses in the area affected by it, and (2) the absolute quantitative adverse environmental effects of the action itself, including the cumulative harm that results from its contribution to existing adverse conditions or uses in the affected area." *Id.,* 471 F.2d at 830.

While the second factor and the emphasis throughout *Hanly II* on the importance of measurement, see e.g., *id.,* 471 F.2d at 833, suggests that it would have been preferable for the defendants to have spelled out the projected effects in greater detail, with an attempt at quantification to afford added assurance that the interests for which Congress expressed its solicitude were indeed being safeguarded, it is apparent that their decision was guided by the strictures of the Act. The purpose of NEPA is to insure that all federal agencies inform every stage of their decision-making process with consideration of environmental factors, broadly understood. The Navy's process of decision which was followed in this case is fairly designed to comply with this purpose. Its Assessment tracts section 102(2)(C) in its discussion of environmental effects: § B(1) corresponds to section 102(2)(C)(i) of the Act, § B(2) corresponds to subsection (ii), etc. What Senator Jackson, the statute's principal author, described as the "action-forcing procedures" embodied in the statute, 115 Cong.Rec. 19009 (July 10, 1969), have been honored here.

Any lack of fuller explanation of the grounds for their determination is readily understandable in view of the particular nature of the project under dispute. The construction of new

---

[1] Anything that influences urban dwellers' quality of life is relevant when weighing significance. Crime, noise, stench, congestion, and even existence of drug traffic, are all to be considered as environmental factors.

dwellings to house additions to the town's population is contemplated by everyone. The Bailey Hill area is zoned for housing. The only difference between the Navy project and what the Town Zoning Commission has provided for the area's future is the number of units that the Navy will build on the tract. Testimony established that the land is zoned RS-12, whereas the Navy's project more closely approximates the standards of RMF (Residential Multi-Family). The difference between the two classifications is primarily that RS-12 imposes greater minimum set-back and dwelling area requirements. (Transcript at 31-34). Unlike *Goose Hollow Foothills League v. Romney,* 334 F.Supp. 877 (D.Or.1971), where a massive high-rise project was planned for an area containing no other high-rise buildings, the Navy project involves essentially the same use of Bailey Hill as that envisaged by the town.[2] The buildings will all be low-rise townhouses, with no more than six families occupying a single structure. (Transcript at 142). In designating the area for residential development, the Zoning Commission obviously foresaw the additional strain on roads, sewage, schools and other municipal services, which would inevitably result. The Navy also considered these factors in its Assessment (plaintiffs' Exhibit 6, § B(1)(g)), and the testimony of Lt. Comm. Thomas reveals that the Navy and the town have discussed thoroughly the problem of inadequate water facilities, and that the Navy has agreed to pay its fair share of the cost of constructing a new and fully adequate water delivery system. (Transcript at 146-48). The Navy cannot be faulted for failure to record in minute detail matters which had plainly been considered and approved by town authorities.

Plaintiffs spent considerable energy at the hearing attempting to demonstrate that the Navy project fails to conform to zoning requirements. See, e.g., direct examination of Lt. Comm. Thomas, Transcript at 149-51. Quite apart from the fact that the Navy is exempt from local zoning ordinances, NEPA is not a sort of meta-zoning law. It is not designed to enshrine existing zoning regulations on the theory that their violation presents a threat to environmental values. NEPA may not be used by communities to shore up large lot and other exclusionary zoning devices that price out low and even middle income families. Cf. Note, Snob Zoning: Must a Man's Home be a Castle?, 69 Mich.L.Rev. 339 (1970); Note, Large Lot Zoning, 78 Yale L.J. 1418, 1420-21, 1427-28 (1969). It is

---

[2] The nearly-identical character of the Navy project and the town's plans for the area is of prime importance in assessing significance. For "(w)here conduct conforms to existing uses, its adverse consequences will usually be less significant than when it represents a radical change." *Hanley II, supra,* 471 F.2d at 831. Thus, the "two relevant factors" set forth in Hanly II and quoted earlier in this opinion, at 349 *supra,* lead almost by definition to a conclusion of non-significance.

evident that the Navy's decision to undertake the Bailey Hill project was strongly influenced by its desire to upgrade the "quality of the human environment" enjoyed by its employees. Its Assessment reported:

"II. ENVIRONMENTAL ASSESSMENT.

"A. *Proposed Action*

. . .

"6. Existing Navy housing units are fully occupied and have a long waiting list of applicants. The Naval Base is located in a summer resort area which places the purchase or rental of private accommodations beyond the financial capability of most military personnel. Vacancies can be found, however, in luxury type apartment houses at rentals ranging from $195.00 per month for a one-bedroom apartment to $287.00 for a two-bedroom apartment.
"7. The site proposed for condemnation is zoned residential."

In addition, in evaluating alternatives, the Assessment states: "At the present time military personnel are cautioned not to move their families to the area until government or private accommodations are assured." Assessment § D(3).

In enacting NEPA, Congress has accorded so high a place to environmental values that administrators must consider abandoning the proposed action entirely if their investigation of environmental impact shows avoidable adverse effects. . . . While this consideration may turn out to have great force with regard to the remaining components of the Master Plan for which the Navy has agreed to file an impact statement in February 1973, it has no relevance to the Bailey Hill project. People have to have somewhere to live. There is no question that Groton has a serious housing shortage.

Plaintiffs' counsel suggested that consideration should have been given to putting the project in Ledyard, an adjoining town which abuts on the north end of the Base. (Transcript at 144-45). Aside from the fact that this suggestion smacks of trying to dump the problem into someone else's backyard — residents of Ledyard might well voice many of the same objections plaintiffs have offered here — such a decision would very possibly have had adverse environmental consequences. The Bailey Hill project is less than one mile from where its residents will work. Relocating the site to a more sparsely populated area in another town would have increased the distance between home and work for several hundred employees of the Base. The result would have been increased necessity for use of automobiles, and thus increased consumption of fuel resources, as well as greater air pollution, traffic congestion, and psychic irritation due to longer commuting under unpleasant conditions. While the Navy has not reviewed site selection alternatives since 1967 (Transcript at 154-55), absent any evidence whatever that any other site became available or feasible after NEPA's effective date of January 1, 1970, there was more than substantial evidence to support the conclusion in the Assessment that "(t)he proposed action is the only alternative known." Assessment § D(4). . . .

Comments: 1. Technically, the *Groton* case arose as a challenge to the Navy's decision not to file an EIS, but the court's analysis of environmental impact would also apply to judicial review of a prepared EIS. Several issues are raised by the case as they relate to the relevance of land use factors in the application of the statutory EIS requirement:

(1) *Relevance of local zoning.* In the *Groton* case, the near-compatibility of the project with local zoning restrictions was relied on by the court as a reason for not requiring an impact statement. This approach to the case reinforces the usual exemption of federal projects from local zoning restrictions, a problem to be faced whenever the project alleged to be subject to the EIS is federally owned.

A slightly different view of this problem was adopted in *Maryland-National Capital Park & Planning Comm'n v. United States Postal Serv.,* 487 F.2d 1029 (D.C. Cir. 1973). The postal service proposed to build a bulk mail facility in one of the Maryland suburban counties of Washington, D.C. While qualifying as one of the permitted uses in the applicable zoning ordinance, the facility was not one of the uses that had been contemplated in the applicable zone. In addition, there was no site review as required by the zoning ordinance.

The court noted that "there may even be a presumption" of no significant environmental impact under NEPA when a proposed facility complies with a local zoning ordinance, since the environmental effects "will be no greater than demanded by the residents acting through their elected representatives." *Id.* at 1036.

> When, on the other hand, the Federal Government exercises its sovereignty so as to override local zoning protections, NEPA requires more careful scrutiny. NEPA has full vitality, and its policies cannot be taken as effectuated by local land use control, where the proposal of the Federal Government reflects a distinctive difference in kind from the types of land use, proposed by private and local government sponsors, that can fairly be taken as within the scope of local controls.

Id. at 1037.

(2) *Compatibility with existing uses.* While there is no explicit discussion of surrounding uses in *Groton,* the fact that the surrounding area was also zoned residential and references by the court to existing development patterns suggest that the project would also have been compatible with existing development. When this is so, the federal courts have apparently

been willing to find no adverse environmental impact. Thus in *Hanly II,* discussed in the *Groton* opinion, the court laid down as one test of significant environmental impact "the extent to which the action will cause adverse environmental effects in excess of those created by existing uses in the area affected. . . ." *See Dalsis v. Hills,* 424 F. Supp. 784 (W.D.N.Y. 1976) (shopping center in urban renewal project not significantly different from surrounding commercial uses).

Goose Hollow Foothills League v. Romney, 334 F. Supp. 877 (D. Ore. 1971), also discussed in the *Groton* case, illustrates a case in which the uses proposed in the project were significantly different from those in the surrounding area. In *Goose Hollow* the developers received a loan from the federal Department of Housing and Urban Development to build a 221-unit, high-rise student apartment building in Portland. The court held that the failure to file an EIS was incorrect.

> Because the area presently has no high-rise buildings, the new building will undoubtedly change the character of the neighborhood. By housing a significant number of students, it will concentrate population in the area and serve to draw a greater concentration in the future.
>
> The defendants gave virtually no weight to these factors, or to the incidental increase in automobile traffic. Neither did the defendants indicate that any weight was given to the loss of the existing view from certain neighboring properties.

Id. at 879.

(3) *Socioeconomic impacts as environmental impacts.* Another important question raised by cases like *Groton* is whether social and economic impacts are among the environmental impacts which NEPA requires to be considered in impact statements. This question has not yet received a definitive answer. In *Hanly II, supra,* the court expressed doubts whether psychological and sociological impacts on neighbors counted as environmental impacts. In the *Postal Serv.* case, *supra,* the court rejected the notion that the influx of low-income workers at the facility, who to some extent would want to live in the immediate area, would rank as an environmental impact under the law.

This problem was raised in the context of low-income public housing in *Nucleus of Chicago Homeowners Ass'n v. Lynn,* 372 F. Supp. 147 (N.D. Ill. 1973), *aff'd,* 524 F.2d 225 (7th Cir. 1975). Plaintiffs in this case challenged the failure to prepare an EIS for an infill, scattered site public housing project that the Chicago Housing Authority had proposed for a middle-class neighborhood. This project was a response to a federal court decree ordering the dispersal of public housing sites in Chicago in order to achieve racial integration. Plaintiffs nevertheless argued that the social characteristics of the project tenants would have an adverse impact on the quality of the neighborhood environment. They relied on statistical findings and census data indicating that, as compared to residents in the neighborhood, public housing tenants were more disposed to criminal behavior and less disposed to hard work and the maintenance of their property.

These arguments were rejected in the federal district court, the trial judge making a careful distinction between the social and economic characteristics of the project tenants and any acts or actions resulting from these characteristics. He noted that a "class of persons per se" cannot be an environmental impact. On appeal, the Seventh Circuit Court of Appeals indicated its agreement with the district court, but did not resolve this issue as it found that the low density design of the project, coupled with the fact that it would be built on vacant, scattered lots in accordance with local zoning, indicated that the project was not likely to produce adverse environmental impacts. Generally, on this topic, see Ackerman, Impact Statements and Low-Cost Housing, 46 S. Cal. L. Rev. 754 (1973); Daffron, Using NEPA to Exclude the Poor, 4 Envt'l Aff. 81 (1975).

With these cases compare *Cedar-Riverside Environmental Defense Fund v. Hills,* 422 F. Supp. 294 (D. Minn. 1976), *dismissed as moot,* 560 F.2d 377 (8th Cir. 1977), in which the court considered and found inadequate an environmental impact statement prepared for an extensive in-town new town project planned for an inner city area in Minneapolis. One basis for the challenge to the impact statement was its failure to consider design alternatives to the high-rise residential housing which had been planned for the project. As the court noted, "[l]ow-rise, high-density cluster housing is a reasonable and feasible alternative which combines the positive effects of urban systems of high density with the avoidance of the negative social effects of high-rises and poorly planned high density which the EIS identifies. . . ." *Id.* at 301. The court considered the effect of high-rise living on children, noting that low-rise housing is clearly superior, and also noted that city and regional needs for low-income housing could not adequately be provided by the high-rise, high-density housing that had been planned for the project. For discussion see Pascal & Parliament, NEPA and the Human Environment: The Case of Cedar-Riverside, Land Use L. & Zoning Dig., vol. 29, no. 5, at 5 (1977).

A series of recent cases have considered arguments that an EIS is needed when the closing of a defense installation creates economic impacts, such as job losses in the area in which the base is located. Most of these cases have rejected these arguments. *See, e.g., National Ass'n of Gov't Employees v. Rumsfeld,* 413 F. Supp. 1224 (E.D. Pa. 1976), interpreting cases like the *Hanly* cases and *Postal Serv.* to mean that social and economic effects may be considered only when other, clearly environmental, effects are also present.

(4) *NEPA and exclusionary zoning.* By rejecting the argument that alternative sites to the Navy housing project should have been considered, the *Groton* case by inference refused to give weight under NEPA to an exclusionary argument which would have forced the location of the project elsewhere. To be considered with this case is *Trinity Episcopal School v. Romney,* 523 F.2d 88 (2d Cir. 1975). That case reviewed a decision by the City of New York to increase the number of low-income housing units in an urban renewal project on the upper Manhattan West Side. While holding that no significant environmental effects were created by the change, the court turned to the requirement in NEPA that requires federal agencies to consider "appropriate alternatives to recommended courses of action in any proposal which involves unresolved conflicts concerning alternative uses of available resources." While not all federal courts agree, the *Trinity* decision held that a study of alternatives was required even though no EIS was required.

Concerned about the overconcentration of low-income housing brought about the change in plans, the court called on the federal housing agency to study a wide range of alternatives to the plan revision. These alternatives included such possibilities as not building the low-income housing, shifting that housing to different locations, and scattering the low-income units to several locations rather than one. While influenced by the increase in low-income housing units that altered the original and more balanced housing mix, the *Trinity* case nevertheless adds a new dimension in the consideration of land use projects under NEPA because it invoked that part of NEPA requiring the consideration of alternatives. In the context of *Groton*, for example, an application of the *Trinity* rule might have required consideration of alternative sites for the housing project. To that extent, Trinity might support an attempt to use NEPA as an exclusionary device. Can *Trinity* be read outside its context as supporting exclusionary local zoning on the argument that the case requires consideration of alternatives for project sites which might lie outside the excluding community? *See* Jordan, Alternatives Under NEPA: Toward an Accommodation, 3 Ecology L.Q. 705 (1973). Generally, on the cases discussed in this section, see D. Mandelker, Environmental and Land Controls Legislation 139-45 (1976).

2. Is an EIS required on federally-funded regional plans? That question came up in a case in which the court considered the need for an EIS on the regional transportation plan to be prepared by the Atlanta regional planning agency, *Atlanta Coalition on the Transp. Crisis v. Atlanta Regional Comm'n,* 8 Env. Rep. Cases 1116 (N.D. Ga. 1975). The court found that no EIS was required because there was no sufficient federal control over the planning process to make that process a federal action. Federal funding was not enough to constitute federal control, and the planning process was not federalized for purposes of NEPA merely because the federal agency was required by federal statute to certify that the planning process met federal statutory requirements.

3. For a helpful but early review of NEPA litigation see F. Anderson, NEPA in the Courts (1973). The periodical literature is massive. Helpful articles include D'Amato & Baxter, The Impact of Impact Statements Upon Agency Responsibility: A Prescriptive Analysis, 59 Iowa L. Rev. 195 (1973); Leventhal, Environmental Decisionmaking and the Role of the Courts, 122 U. Pa. L. Rev. 509 (1974); Comment, Socioeconomic Impacts and the National Environmental Policy Act of 1969, 64 Geo. L.J. 1121 (1976).

2. State Environmental Policy Acts

Application to Land Use Controls

As of this writing, at least 15 states have followed the federal lead and have adopted state equivalents of NEPA which require the filing of environmental impact statements either by state or local governments or both. A few of these state acts apply to local approvals of private land development projects, and so extend the EIS requirement to local zoning and related actions affecting land use. California, Massachusetts, and Washington are in this group, and model state EIS legislation prepared by the Council of Governments also provides for the extension of the EIS requirement to the local land use control function. These adopted and proposed extensions of the EIS requirement to the land use control setting prompt an examination of the way in which the EIS requirement operates as a supplementary review of land use control decisions.

Most of the state environmental policy acts are exact replicas or attenuated versions of the federal statute. This imitation of the federal requirement has created problems in the application of the EIS requirement to land use controls, arising primarily from the borrowing of the key federal term "action" to describe the activities and projects which are brought under the state EIS laws. The amorphous nature of this term and the wide range of governmental and private activities to which it is potentially applicable create difficult interpretive problems when it is applied to the local land use control process.

The first case applying the state NEPA's to the land use control process arose under the California Environmental Quality Act (CEQA). That statute, enacted in 1970, is that state's counterpart to NEPA, but differs in some particulars from the federal legislation. The California statute requires an Environmental Impact Report (EIR) as its counterpart EIS requirement, and also differs from the federal statute by using the terms "action," "project," and "proposal" to describe the class of activities falling within the statute. Cal. Pub. Res. Code § 21100 (Derring Supp. 1977). Initially, that part of the statute applying to local governments also required an EIR on "projects" which local governments "intend to carry out." This latter phrase provided the basis for the California Supreme Court decision, *Friends of Mammoth v. Board of Supervisors,* 500 P.2d 1360, *modified, on denial of rehearing,* 502 P.2d 1049 (Cal. 1972), which applied the statutory EIR requirement to a conditional use and building permit for a private residential development project. For a discussion of *Mammoth* and the evolution of the California legislation see Hagman, NEPA's Progeny Inhabit the States — Were the Genes Defective? 7 Urb. L. Ann. 3 (1974).

The California court based its interpretation of CEQA on federal Council on Environmental Quality guidelines, which had interpreted NEPA to apply to any "entitlements for use." 40 C.F.R. § 1500.5(a)(3) (1977). This interpretation was relied on to buttress a conclusion that the term "project" in the California law likewise applied to land use controls which "entitled" developers to the "use" of land. The phrase authorizing a California EIR for "projects" which local governments "intend to carry out" was construed to mean only that the local government must have some minimal link with the land development in question. This link was interpreted to include the regulatory activities of local governments leading to the approval of a private development project.

California's legislation has since been amended to codify the result in *Mammoth,* so that many of the problems in applying state EIS requirements to land use controls have been resolved in that state. Elsewhere, the applicability of the state EIS laws to local approvals of private land development projects remains an open question, and the reach of the California law is still by no means settled. *See* Comment, Environmental Decision Making Under CEQA: A Quest for Uniformity, 24 U.C.L.A.L. Rev. 838 (1977).

One major problem arising under the state NEPA acts arises from the fact that land development projects proceed in stages through the land use control process, beginning with a comprehensive plan amendment and proceeding through zoning and often subdivision approvals to the issuance of a final building permit. An initial question is to determine at which of these stages the state EIS requirement applies, if at all. The problem is tied in with the fact that some local land use approvals require the exercise of discretion and some do not. An argument can be made that nondiscretionary approvals should be exempted from the EIS requirement because no exercise of judgment is required through which environmental impacts can be considered. California's statute expressly exempts nondiscretionary (called "ministerial") decisions from its EIR requirement. Elsewhere, absent legislative direction, the issue is more clouded. For example, the Washington Supreme Court has held that an EIS is required on a non-duplicative renewal of a building permit, and has suggested that an EIS is necessary only for discretionary governmental actions. *Eastlake Community Council v. Roanoke Assoc.,* 513 P.2d 36 (Wash. 1973). *Compare Plan for Arcadia, Inc. v. Arcadia City Council,* 117 Cal. Rptr. 96 (Cal. App. 1974) (final approval of subdivision plat not discretionary; no EIS required).

Problems in Applying the Environmental Impact Statement to Land Use Controls

Does the *Eastlake* case mean that an EIS must be prepared at each discretionary approval stage in the land use control process? If a comprehensive EIS is prepared at an early stage of the project will an EIS have to be prepared during later stages? In *Loveless v. Yantis,* 513 P.2d 1023 (Wash. 1973), the Washington court held that an environmental impact statement had to be filed in connection with a preliminary subdivision approval for a multifamily condominium to be located in an environmentally attractive area near Puget Sound. In dictum, the court noted that no additional impact statements would be required if environmental issues have previously been considered and if no "new information or developments have intervened since." *Id.* at 1029. Note, however, that most developments proceed from generalized to increasingly more detailed plans, which are likely to reveal "new" information requiring an additional impact statement. The *Loveless* holding is codified in Cal. Pub. Res. Code § 21166 (Deering 1976).

Is there any other way of handling this problem? See the California regulations interpreting CEQA, Cal. Admin. Code tit. 14, § 15068.5 (1976): "[t]he EIR on a general plan may be used as the foundation document for EIRs subsequently prepared for specific projects within the geographic area covered by the general plan."

Consider the following additional problems in the application of state EIS requirements to the land use control system:

1) *Stempel v. Department of Water Resources,* 508 P.2d 166 (Wash. 1973), adopted the position of the federal courts construing NEPA and held that the requirements of the state EIS act were to be read into and made a part of the substantive provisions of other state statutes. In *Stempel,* the state water resources department had approved an application to take water from a lake to service adjacent residential development, but did not prepare an EIS. The department argued that as its statute only required consideration of the "public welfare" in a water appropriation approval, there was no legislative mandate to consider environmental impacts. Rejecting this contention, the court held that the department was obligated under the state EIS law "to consider the total environment and ecological factors to the fullest extent in deciding major matters." *Id.* at 171.

Does this holding mean that a court reviewing an impact statement on a land development project may set aside an approval of that project if the criteria established by the state EIS law are not met? In *Polygon Corp. v. Seattle,* 578 P.2d 1309 (Wash. 1978), the court held that the state's EIS law confers discretion to deny a building permit application on the basis of adverse environmental effects disclosed in the EIS. See Cal. Pub. Code § 21002.1(c) (Deering Supp. 1977):

> In the event that economic, social, or other conditions make it infeasible to mitigate one or more significant effects of a project on the environment, such project may nonetheless be approved or carried out at the discretion of a public agency, provided that the project is otherwise permissible under applicable laws and regulations.

Nevertheless, a project approval might be set aside if the agency has improperly considered and balanced the environmental factors required to be evaluated by the EIS. *See Burger v. County of Mendocino,* 119 Cal. Rptr. 568 (Cal. App. 1975). What distinction is the court making? For a comparable interpretation of the federal law see *Kleppe v. Sierra Club,* 427 U.S. 390, n. 21 (1976).

2) What elements of the planning and land use control process are within the scope of state NEPA's? *Loveless, supra,* brought subdivision approvals within the Washington statute. Zoning ordinances, amendments, variances and conditional uses have been brought explicitly within the California act, Cal. Pub. Res. Code § 21080(a) (Deering Supp. 1977), and interim zoning ordinances have been included within the Washington statute as "proposals for

legislation." *Byers v. Board of Clallam County Comm'rs,* 529 P.2d 823 (Wash. 1974). What about comprehensive plans? Will state courts adopt the position of the *Atlanta* case, *supra,* that plans are so premature that they do not constitute actions or projects under the state laws? See *Edina Valley Ass'n v. San Luis Obispo County & Cities Area Planning Coordinating Council,* 136 Cal. Rptr. 665 (Cal. App. 1977), accepting the statutory interpretation of the California administrative guidelines and holding that a regional transportation plan requires an EIR under the California law. "It cannot be disputed that the Regional Transportation Plan at issue, when implemented, may have a significant effect upon the environment." *Id.* at 667.

In all of these cases the local ordinance or approval was in reaction to or authorized a specific development project. What about a zoning ordinance amendment which is not adopted with reference to a proposed project? Is the ordinance amendment automatically within the statute? For example, if a city council adopts a planned unit development provision as an amendment to its zoning ordinance must it file an EIS on the amendment prior to the approval of any projects under the ordinance? For a case suggesting that an EIS must be filed on the ordinance in this situation see *Rosenthal v. Board of Supervisors,* 119 Cal. Rptr. 282 (Cal. App. 1975). Could an argument be made that the enactment of an ordinance in cases such as this requires an EIS only if it independently may have an environmental impact?

3) As yet, the basis for judicial review of environmental impact statements on zoning and other land use control actions has not been extensively elaborated in the state cases. But see *Narrowsview Preservation Ass'n v. City of Tacoma,* 526 P.2d 897 (Wash. 1974), applying the test of the *Hanly,* case, *supra* p. 1099, in approving an EIS filed on a zoning change from single-family to planned unit development. Since the *Hanly* test requires consideration of environmental effects in excess of those created by existing uses in the area, the chances for disapproval of the EIS appear to increase as the departure of the proposed development from existing use patterns widens. Is this good planning? Or zoning? For discussion of the judicial review of EIR's in California see Environmental Decision Making Under CEQA, *supra* at 866-73, suggesting that the California courts have strengthened judicial review under CEQA by cutting back on the presumptive validity usually accorded agency decisions.

The scope of judicial review under the California statute may have been widened by an extension of the requirements for environmental statements to include the "growth-inducing impact of the proposed project," Cal. Pub. Res. Code § 21100(g) (Deering Supp. 1977), and "[m]itigation measures proposed to minimize the significant environmental effects," *id.* § 21100(c). Similar provisions are found in other state EIS laws.

Helpful reviews of state environmental impact statement requirements can be found in D. Mandelker, Environmental and Land Controls Legislation 147-62 (1976); T. Trzyna, Environmental Impact Requirements in the States (Center for California Public Affairs, 1974); Pearlman, State Environmental Policy Acts: Local Decision Making and Land Use Planning, 43 J. Am. Inst. Planners 42 (1977); Note, State Environmental Impact Statements, 15 Washburn L.J. 64 (1976).

Does the environmental impact statement provide a necessary corrective to a planning and land use control process which has been insensitive to environmental concerns, or is it a wasteful and counterproductive impediment to that process? Consider the following critique by Professor Hagman:

> Just as NEPA and NEPA-like state laws might be regarded as productive when applied to federal and state government development activities, a case might be made for throwing some new NEPA-like legislation at local and special districts engaged in development. They, also, have never been well-disciplined by local planning — special districts could generally override any objections of the general plan-making governments, and the plan-making governments typically ignored their own plans when that suited their purposes.
>
> But a better alternative would also have been simpler — amend traditional planning and control legislation to require more environmental consciousness and to strengthen provisions making general purpose and special district governments subject to the then-environmentally stronger traditional planning and land-use controls. That route was seemingly part of the thinking behind CEQA as originally enacted, which required EIR's only when the general purpose government had no conservation element. When they did have a conservation element (thus strengthening environmental consciousness) their projects had to accord with that element (thus subjecting local government projects to general planning constraints).

Hagman, *supra* at 46-47.

C. PROTECTION OF RESOURCE AREAS

State and national environmental policy acts require environmental impact statements so that potential damage to environmental resources can be more fully considered in governmental decision-making processes. This legislation is process-oriented. It does not impose substantive criteria for the review of land development.

This section considers a group of environmental control statutes that proceed on an entirely different assumption. Enacted increasingly at the state level, these statutes adopt substantive criteria under which land development in environmental resource areas is explicitly reviewed for approval or disapproval. The resource areas included here have related though somewhat different attributes, but the statutory programs identified for attention have in common a functional yet focused statutory purpose which has as its principal objective the protection of resource areas which would be damaged by new development.

This section is divided into two parts. The first considers wetlands and shorelands. Wetlands are transitional areas situated between land and bodies of water; they help protect water quality and have other environmental values. Shorelands are areas, including wetlands, that are adjacent to bodies of water. Environmentally-oriented land use controls applied in wetland and shoreland areas are distinguished by the fact that they are not always prohibitory, but attempt to shape and limit development so that the environmental function of the affected area is not disturbed.

The second part of this section deals with floodplains — areas that are regularly flooded by streams and rivers. Land use controls affecting floodplains are more likely to be prohibitory. Their purpose is to keep the floodplain area open so that it can serve its purpose of carying off excess flood water. A complementary purpose is to avoid placing development in areas in which periodic flooding may create dangers to life and safety. We turn first to land use controls applicable to wetlands and shorelands.

1. Wetlands and Shorelands

The special characteristics of wetland areas provide a forceful set of environmental justifications for wetland regulation. What role wetlands play in the natural environment is indicated in the following selection.

C. THUROW, W. TONER, & D. ERLEY, PERFORMANCE CONTROLS FOR SENSITIVE LANDS: A PRACTICAL GUIDE FOR LOCAL ADMINISTRATORS 171-90 (U.S.-EPA, 1975)

The Public Purpose and Wetland Ecology

Wetlands are defined as a transitional [area] between dry land and open water. They are areas of low topography, poor drainage, and standing water. Though we know when we are knee deep in water and when we are on dry land, the area in between is more difficult to recognize. This difficulty is primarily due to seasonal and yearly variations in the borders of wetlands. Waterlogged land in the spring may be dry through most of the summer and fall, and wetlands during years of extensive rainfall may be more extensive than during years of drought.

Though it is difficult to produce a universally accepted definition of exactly where wetlands end and other lands begin, wetlands are generally classified by their predominate water depth, the vegetation they support, and whether their waters are fresh or saline. Wetlands also vary according to climate, with marked differences in vegetation from north to south. . . .

Whatever their specific local values, wetlands do have a set of common natural functions that make valuable resources for society. The resource values of wetlands can be summarized as follows:

1. Wetlands affect the quality of water. Aquatic plants change inorganic nutrients into organic material, storing it in their leaves or in the peat, which is composed of their remains. The stems, leaves, and roots of these plants also slow the flow of water through a wetland, allowing the silt to settle out, as well as catching some of it themselves. Thus the removal of wetlands causes faster runoff of dirtier water. Consequently wetlands protect the downstream or offshore water resources of the community from siltation and pollution.

2. Wetlands also influence the quantity of water. They act to retain water during dry periods and hold it back during floods, thus keeping the water table high and relatively stable. One acre of marsh is capable of absorbing or holding 300,000 gallons of water, and thus helps protect the community against flooding and drought. Coastal wetlands also absorb storm impact.

3. Wetlands are important resources for overall environmental health and diversity. They provide essential breeding, nesting, resting, and feeding grounds and predator-escape cover for myriad forms of fish and wildlife. The presence of water is also attractive to many upland birds and animals. Since it is here that the food webs of land and water are most intimately connected, wetlands are important for supporting a wide variety of plants and animals. These factors have the social value of providing general environmental health; creating recreational, research, and educational sites; maintaining the economic functions of trapping and fishing; and adding to the aesthetics of the community.

In many ways wetlands present the classic case for public regulation. Most of their assets are public goods; if they are provided for one member of society they are provided for all of them. Consequently, the use values of wetlands are not considered through the regular system of the land market. An individual cannot sell his marsh filtering function on the market, nor can he price his groundwater protection system and sell it to others. Such values may play some role in land-use decisions, but they will generally be overweighed by the development potential of the land. . . .

Wetlands Protect Water Quality

Wetlands affect water quality by trapping and storing in plant tissue the nutrients from upland runoff and serving as a settling basin for silt from upland erosion. This natural filtering function of wetlands can be seriously damaged, however, by poor land-use practices. Since every wetland has a unique tolerance for filtering runoff from the uplands around it, development in the upland can create more nutrient and sediment inflow than the marsh is able to absorb. Moreover, development in and around the fringe of the marsh itself can destroy its ecological health and thus its filtering ability. . . .

. . .[T]he removal of wetlands by dredging or filling will have an immediate impact on the water quality of streams and lakes below them in the watershed system. . . .

Our public policy protecting wetlands must remember our ability to accelerate the eutrophication and siltation of wetlands. If the goal is clean water, we must do more than prevent the dredging and filling of wetlands because they filter nutrients and sediments. We cannot treat them as bottomless settling basins or nutrient traps. We must minimize nutrient inputs so that wetlands will continue to act as filters as long as possible, and we must control the amount of upland erosion so that wetlands will continue to trap sediments from runoff. And by regulating nutrient and sediment flow, we can maintain healthy marshes with diverse plant and animal communities.

Marshes and the Stability of Water Supply

Wetlands have value to a community because they moderate extremes in water supply. They retain water during dry periods and hold it back during floods, thus keeping the water table high and relatively stable. . . . Peat, the organic material deposited at the bottom of a wetland as plants die, can hold and maintain large quantities of water. By adding this organic material to window box soil, it can better withstand the drying effects of the sun and wind, and thus provide the necessary moisture for the plants. This absorptive property of the peat makes wetlands natural sponges which reduce the risks of flooding and drought.

. . . .

Wetlands and General Environmental Health and Diversity

Wetlands provide essential breeding, nesting, resting, and feeding grounds and predator escape cover for many kinds of fish and wildlife. Since the food webs of land and water are most intimately connected in wetlands, they are thus important for supporting a wide variety of both land and water animals. Likewise, wetlands provide habitats for a wide range of vegetative communities which could not exist without them. In these ways wetlands provide the benefits of healthy environment. They are sites for recreation, research, and education; they support wildlife and game for hunting, fishing and trapping, and they add to the aesthetics of the community. . . .

Comments: For a point of view suggesting that the benefits of wetlands are more uncertain than this report indicates see Walker, Wetlands Preservation and Management on Chesapeake Bay: The Role of Science in Natural Resource Policy, 1 Coastal Zone Manag. J. 75, 90 (1973):

> Thus far I have shown that the scientific justifications for coastal wetlands preservation are not quite as clear cut as they appear at first blush. The primary productivity of marshes is evident, but little can be said about the dependence of important species on marshes, nor the response of the estuarine ecosystem to marsh destruction. Similarly, water quality seems to be improved by wetlands, but the dynamics of nutrient cycling is too poorly understood to predict the impact of wetlands on overall estuarine water quality. The erosion, sediment, and flood control capacities of wetlands may only be modest, and are rather unpredictable. Finally, coastal wetlands are a part of a dynamic system in which some change is neither extraordinary nor necessarily irreversible.

In a reply to the Walker article, Odum & Skjei, The Issue of Wetlands Preservation and Management: A Second View, 1 Coastal Zone Manag. J. 151 (1973), the authors dispute Walker's findings and urge that uncertainties about the value of wetlands to the natural environment should not deter regulatory programs aimed at protecting these areas. They see the issue as one of making the necessary political tradeoffs inherent in any regulatory program requiring choices among competing values: "[w]hether or not wetlands are public goods or examples of market failure, the question is which of them, and to what extent, should be preserved and which should be sacrificed to achieve other social goals. . . ." *Id.* at 158. The statutes and cases that follow will indicate the extent to which the environmental and social benefits of wetlands have been considered deserving of regulatory protection.

STATUTORY PROGRAMS FOR WETLANDS PROTECTION

In some states, statutory programs for wetlands protection form part of more extensive regulatory programs for shoreland management, see *infra* p. 1121, or for coastal zone management, see *infra* p. 1141. We focus here on a more specialized group of statutes enacted solely to protect wetlands areas. They apply both to coastal and to inland wetlands. As of 1976, 14 states were reported to have wetlands legislation, and additional states are expected to join this list. N. Rosenbaum, Land Use and the Legislatures 69 (1976). This legislation usually establishes a set of criteria, a planning process, or both to identify and protect ecologically significant private wetlands.

These criteria are usually enforced through a state-administered permit system aimed principally at preventing the dredging and filling of wetland areas, but which may contain broader regulatory objectives. Typical of these statutes is the Georgia Coastal Marshlands Protection Act of 1970, parts of which are reproduced below.

GEORGIA COASTAL MARSHLANDS PROTECTION ACT OF 1970, GEORGIA CODE ANNOTATED (1974)

. . . .

§ 45-137 [Definitions]

. . . .

(a) "Coastal marshlands" hereinafter referred to as "marshlands" means any marshlands or salt marsh in the State of Georgia, within the estuarine area of the State, whether or not the tide waters reach the littoral areas through natural or artificial water courses. Marshlands shall include those areas upon which grow one, but not necessarily all, of the following: saltmarsh grass (Spartina alterniflora), black grass (Juncus gerardi), high-tide bush (Iva frutescens var. oraria). The occurrence and extent of salt marsh peat at the undisturbed surface shall be deemed to be conclusive evidence of the extent of a salt marsh or a part thereof.

(b) "Estuarine area" means all tidally-influenced waters, marshes and marshlands lying within a tide-elevation range from five and six-tenths feet above mean tide level and below.

. . . .

(e) "Political Subdivision" means the governing authority of a county or municipality in which the marshlands to be affected or any part thereof are located.

(f) "Agency" means the Coastal Marshlands Protection Agency.

§ 45-138 [Creation of agency]

[This section creates the agency and indicates how it shall be composed.]

§ 45-139 [Powers and duties of agency]

[This section states the powers and duties of the agency, including the power to promulgate rules and regulations and to "examine and pass upon applications to alter marshlands."]

§ 45-140 [Applications and procedures]

(a) No person shall remove, fill, dredge or drain or otherwise alter any marshlands in this State within the estuarine area thereof without first obtaining a permit from the Coastal Marshlands Protection Agency.

(b) Each application for such permit. . . shall include:

. . . .

(6) A certificate from the local governing authority(s) of the political subdivision(s) in which the property is located stating that

the applicant's proposal is not violative of any zoning law, ordinance or other local [restriction] which may be applicable thereto. If in the judgment of the agency a zoning permit is not needed prior to considering an application, it may waive this requirement and issue a conditional permit based upon the condition that the applicant acquire and forward a permit from the local political subdivision prior to commencement of work. No work shall commence until this requirement is fulfilled.

[Note that the Georgia law apparently provides for a local veto on a state wetlands permit, assuming that the law allows localities to set requirements more stringent than those contained in the state law. Most state wetlands laws are silent on the local role, and the courts are divided on whether in the absence of such a provision the state statute preempts local regulations. *Compare Lauricella v. Planning & Zoning Bd. of Appeals,* 342 A.2d 374 (Conn. Supp. 1974) (state law preempts), *with Golden v. Board of Selectmen,* 265 N.E.2d 573 (Mass. 1970) (*contra*). — Eds.]

. . . .

(e) In passing upon the application for permit, the agency shall consider the public interest which, for purposes of this law, shall be deemed to be the following considerations:

(1) Whether or not any unreasonably harmful obstruction to or alteration of the natural flow of navigational water within such area will arise as a result of the proposal

(2) Whether or not unreasonably harmful or increased erosion, shoaling of channels or stagnant areas of water will be created to such extent as to be contrary to the public interest

(3) Whether or not the granting of a permit and the completion of the applicant's proposal will unreasonably interfere with the conservation of fish, shrimp, oysters, crabs and clams or any marine life or wildlife or other natural resources, including but not limited to water and oxygen supply to such an extent as to be contrary to the public interest.

(f) If the agency finds that the application is not contrary to the public interest as heretofore specified, it shall issue to the applicant a permit. Such permit may be conditioned upon the applicant's amending the proposal to take whatever measures are necessary to protect the public interest. The agency shall act upon an application for permit within 90 days after the application is filed.

. . . .

(j) [Provides for administrative hearing and judicial review for persons aggrieved or adversely affected by orders issued under the act.]

Comments: 1. Note that the Georgia statute does not contain an absolute prohibition against the alteration of marshlands. Does the excerpt from Sensitive Lands, *supra,* provide any clues to when an "unreasonable" interference, obstruction, and the like can be found to have occurred under the Georgia statute?

2. A few wetlands statutes do not use the permit system, but authorize regulatory techniques akin to zoning. Thus, the Massachusetts statute authorizes the state agency to adopt protective orders "regulating, restricting or prohibiting dredging, filling, removing or otherwise altering, or polluting, coastal wetlands." Mass. Gen. Laws Ann. ch. 130, § 105 (Supp. 1977). While the statute does not specify how the protective order is to be implemented, it does provide that a "plan" of the lands affected as well as the order shall be recorded in the local land title registry. In practice, orders filed under the act specify uses allowed without qualification, such as hunting and fishing; uses allowed subject to conditions, such as roadways and utilities; and uses for which a permit must be obtained, such as excavations for boat channels and beaches. For discussion of the administration of the Massachusetts statute see F. Bosselman & D. Callies, The Quiet Revolution in Land Use Control 205-34 (1971). Under a variant of the Massachusetts law, the New York wetlands act authorizes the state agency to adopt land use regulations for protected wetlands, which then serve as one set of standards to be applied in passing on permit applications for dredge and fill and related activities. N.Y. Envir. Conserv. Law §§ 25-0302(1), 25-0403(1) (McKinney Supp. 1977).

The following case indicates one judicial reaction to the constitutionality of wetlands legislation.

STATE v. JOHNSON

Supreme Judicial Court of Maine
265 A.2d 711 (1970)

Before WILLIAMSON, C. J., and MARDEN, DUFRESNE, WEATHERBEE and POMEROY, JJ.

MARDEN, Justice.

On appeal from an injunction granted under the provisions of 12 M.R.S.A. §§ 4701-4709, inclusive, the Wetlands Act (Act),[3]

---

[3] Pertinent portions are quoted.

"§ 4701. *Procedure; hearing.*

"No person, agency or municipality shall remove, fill, dredge or drain sanitary sewage into, or otherwise alter any coastal wetland, as defined herein, without filing written notice of his intention to do so, including such plans as may be necessary to describe the proposed activity, with the municipal officers in the municipality affected and with the Wetlands Control Board. . . .

"For purposes of this chapter, coastal wetland is defined as any swamp, marsh, bog, beach, flat or other contiguous lowland above extreme low water which is subject to tidal action or normal storm flowage at any time excepting periods of maximum story activity."

. . . .

"§ 4702. *Permits.*

"Permit to undertake the proposed alteration shall be issued by the municipal

originating in Chapter 348 P.L. 1967, which places restrictions upon the alteration and use of wetlands, as therein defined, without permission from the municipal officers concerned and the State Wetlands Control Board (Board). The Act is a conservation measure under the police power of the State to protect the ecology of areas bordering coastal waters. The 1967 Act has been amended in no way pertinent to the present issue except by Section 8 of Chapter 379 of the Public Laws of 1969, which authorized alternatively a mandatory injunction for the restoration of any wetlands previously altered in violation of the Act.

The appellants own a tract of land about 220 feet wide and 700 feet long extending across salt water marshes between Atlantic Avenue on the east and the Webhannet River on the west in the Town of Wells. Westerly of the lots fronting on Atlantic Avenue the strip has been subdivided into lots for sale. The easterly 260 feet approximately of the strip has been filled and bears seasonal dwellings. Westerly of this 260 foot development is marsh-land flooded at high tide and drained, upon receding tide, into the River by a network of what our Maine historical novelist Kenneth E. Roberts called "eel runs," but referred to in the record as creeks. Similar marsh-land, undeveloped, lies to the north and south of appellants' strip, and westerly of the River, all of which makes up a substantial acreage (the extent not given in testimony, but of which we take judicial notice) of marsh-land known as the Wells Marshes. Appellants' land, by raising the grade above high water by the addition of fill, is adaptable to development for building purposes.

Following the effective date of the Act, an application to the municipal officers, with notice to the Wetlands Control Board, for

---

officers within 7 days of such hearing providing the Wetlands Control Board approves. Such permit may be conditioned upon the applicant amending his proposal to take whatever measures are deemed necessary by either the municipality or the Wetlands Control Board to protect the public interest. Approval may be withheld by either the municipal officers or the board when in the opinion of either body the proposal would threaten the public safety, health or welfare, would adversely affect the value or enjoyment of the property of abutting owners, or would be damaging to the conservation of public or private water supplies or of wildlife or freshwater, estuarine or marine fisheries."

. . . .

"*§ 4704. Appeal*

"Appeal may be taken to the Superior Court within 30 days after the denial of a permit or the issuance of a conditional permit for the purpose of determining whether the action appealed from so restricts the use of the property as to deprive the owner of the reasonable use thereof, and is therefore an unreasonable exercise of police power, or which constitutes the equivalent of a taking without compensation. The court upon such a finding may set aside the action appealed from."

permission to fill a portion of this land was denied by the Board, an administrative appeal was taken and the case reported to this Court, which appears sub nom. *Johnson v. Maine Wetlands Control Board, Me.,* 250 A.2d 825 (Case No. 1) and in which the constitutionality of the Act was challenged. We held, by decision filed March 11, 1969 that absent a record of evidence as to the nature of the land involved and the benefits or harm to be expected from the denial of the permit, the case would have to be remanded.

Subsequent to March 11, 1969 fill was deposited on the land in question, as the result of which the State sought an injunction, the granting of which brings this case before us on appeal (Case No. 2). It is stipulated that the evidence in this case should be accepted as the evidence lacking in (Case No. 1) and that the two cases be consolidated for final determination of both.

The record establishes that the land which the appellants propose to build up by fill and build upon for sale, or to be offered for sale to be built upon, are coastal wetlands within the definition of the Act and that the refusal by the Board to permit the deposit of such fill prevents the development as proposed. The single Justice found that the property is a portion of a salt marsh area, a valuable natural resource of the State, that the highest and best use for the land, so filled, is for housing, and that unfilled it has no commercial value.

The issue is the same in both, namely, whether the denial of permit (Case No. 1) and the injunction (Case No. 2) so limit the use to plaintiffs of their land that such deprivation of use amounts to a taking of their property without constitutional due process and just compensation.[4]

Due Process

Due process of law has a dual aspect, procedural and substantive. . . .

. . . .

Substantively, "the terms 'law of the land' and 'due process of law'. . . are identical in meaning." *Michaud v. City of Bangor,* 159 Me. 491, 493, 196 A.2d 106, 108.

It is "the constitutional guaranty that no person shall be deprived of . . . property for arbitrary reasons, such a deprivation being constitutionally supportable only if the conduct from which the deprivation flows is proscribed by reasonable legislation (that is, legislation the enactment of which is within the scope of legislative authority) reasonably applied (that is, for a purpose consonant with the purpose of the legislation itself)." 16 Am.Jur.2d, Constitutional Law § 550.

---

[4] Maine Constitution, Article I, § 6. "He shall not be. . .deprived of his. . . property . . . but by . . . the law of the land."

"Section 21. Private property shall not be taken for public uses without just compensation, ..."

It is this substantive due process which is challenged in the Act. In this connection it must be noted that § 4704 (Footnote 1) by its terms equates a deprivation "of the reasonable use" of an owner's property with "an unreasonable exercise of police power."

The constitutional aspect of the current problem is to be determined by consideration of the extent to which appellants are deprived of their usual incidents of ownership, — for the conduct of the public authorities with relation to appellants' land is not a "taking" in the traditional sense. Our State has applied a strict construction of the constitutional provisions as to land. . . .

We find no constitutional definition of the word "deprive," *Munn v. Illinois,* 94 U.S. 113, 123, 24 L.Ed. 77, since the constitutionally protected right of property is not unlimited. It is subject to reasonable restraints and regulations in the public interest by means of the legitimate exercise of police power. . . . The exercise of this police power may properly regulate the use of property and if the owner suffers injury "it is either damnum absque injuria, or, in the theory of the law, he is compensated for it by sharing in the general benefits which the regulations are intended . . . to secure." *State v. Robb,* 100 Me. 180, 186, 60 A. 874, 876. The determination of unconstitutional deprivation is difficult and judicial decisions are diverse. Broadly speaking, deprivation of property contrary to constitutional guaranty occurs "if it deprives an owner of one of its essential attributes, destroys its value, restricts or interrupts its common necessary, or profitable use, hampers the owner in the application of it to the purposes of trade, or imposes conditions upon the right to hold or use it and thereby seriously impairs its value." 16 Am.Jur.2d, Constitutional Law § 367. . . .

Conditions so burdensome may be imposed that they are equivalent to an outright taking, although the title to the property and some vestiges of its uses remain in the owner. . . .

A guiding principle appears in the frequently cited case of *Pennsylvania Coal Company v. Mahon et al.,* 260 U.S. 393, 413, 43 S.Ct. 158, 159-160, 67 L.Ed. 322 (1922) where Mr. Justice Holmes declared:

> "Government hardly could go on if to some extent values incident to property could not be diminished without paying for every such change in the general law. As long recognized some values are enjoyed under an implied limitation and must yield to the police power. But obviously the implied limitation must have its limits or the contract and due process clauses are gone. One fact for consideration in determining such limits is the extent of the diminution. When it reaches a certain magnitude, in most if not in all cases there must be an exercise of eminent domain and compensation to sustain the act. So the question depends upon the particular facts."

> . . . .

"We are in danger of forgetting that a strong public desire to improve the public condition is not enough to warrant achieving the desire by a shorter cut than the constitutional way of paying for the change. As we already have said this is a question of degree — and therefore cannot be disposed of by general propositions." At page 416.

. . . .

Confrontation between public interests and private interests is common in the application of zoning laws, with which the Wetlands Act may be analogized, and the great majority of which, upon their facts, are held to be reasonable exercise of the police power. There are, however, zoning restrictions which have been recognized as equivalent to a taking of the property restricted. . . .

The same result has been reached as to zoning laws which identify their purposes as ones of conservation. See . . . the rationale expressed in *Commissioner of Natural Resources et al. v. S. Volpe & Co., Inc.,* 349 Mass. 104, 206 N.E.2d 666 (1965) (involving "dredge and fill" Act); and *MacGibbon et al. v. Board of Appeals of Duxbury,* 347 Mass. 690, 200 N.E.2d 254 (1964) and 255 N.E.2d 347 (Mass. 1970).

There has, as well, been restrictive conservation legislation which has been held not equivalent to taking. . . .

Of the above, the Massachusetts cases are of particular significance inasmuch as the "dredge and fill" Act discussed in *Volpe* is expressed in terms closely parallel to our Wetlands Act and the zoning ordinance in *MacGibbon* deals with facts closely akin to those before us.

Between the public interest in braking and eventually stopping the insidious despoliation of our natural resources which have for so long been taken for granted, on the one hand, and the protection of appellants' property rights on the other, the issue is cast.

Here the single Justice has found that the area of which appellants' land is a part "is a valuable natural resource of the State of Maine and plays an important role in the conservation and development of aquatic and marine life, game birds and waterfowl," which bespeaks the public interest involved and the protection of which is sought by Section 4702 of the Act. With relation to appellants' interest the single Justice found that appellants' land absent the addition of fill "has no commercial value whatever." These findings are supported by the evidence and are conclusive. . . .

As distinguished from conventional zoning for town protection, the area of Wetlands representing a "valuable natural resource of the State," of which appellants' holdings are but a minute part, is of statewide concern. The benefits from its preservation extend beyond town limits and are state-wide. The cost of its preservation should be publicly borne. To leave appellants with commercially valueless land in upholding the restriction presently imposed, is to charge them with more than their just share of the cost of this state-wide conservation program, granting fully its commendable purpose. . . . [T]heir compensation by sharing in the benefits which this restriction is intended to secure is so disproportionate to their deprivation of reasonable use that such exercise of the State's police power is unreasonable.

The application of the Wetlands restriction in the terms of the denial of appellants' proposal to fill, and enjoining them from so doing deprives them of the reasonable use of their property and within Section 4704 is both an unreasonable exercise of police power and equivalent to taking within constitutional considerations.

    . . . .

Holding, as we do, that the prohibition against the filling of appellants' land, upon the facts peculiar to the case, is an unreasonable exercise of police power, it does not follow that the restriction as to draining sanitary sewage into coastal wetland is subject to the same infirmity. Additional considerations of health and pollution which are "separable from and independent of" the "fill" restriction may well support validity of the Act in those areas of concern. . . .

Within the provisions of Section 4704, the denial of the permit to fill (Case No. 1) and the injunction (Case No. 2) are "set aside."

Appeal sustained in both cases.

WEBBER, J., did not sit.

Comments: 1. Did the Maine court hold its wetlands statute unconstitutional because the landowner was left after the permit denial with no "reasonable use" of his land, or because the burden of maintaining the wetlands in its natural conditions in order to confer a public benefit fell too heavily on the affected landowner? For another view of the burden-benefit issue in a wetlands regulation context see the *Just* case, *infra* p. 1121.

Shortly after the decision in the principal case the Massachusetts court held, without discussion, that a local ordinance regulating wetlands and similar to the Georgia statute excerpted above was a "permissible exercise of municipal zoning power." *Golden v. Board of Selectmen,* 265 N.E.2d 573, 575 (Mass. 1970). The court stated that the local board "had the power to deny the permit as long as its decision was not 'based on a legally untenable ground, or . . . [was not] unreasonable, whimsical, capricious or arbitrary,'" *Id.* at 576, quoting from the *MacGibbon* case, which was discussed in the principal opinion. Should we distinguish between (1) a decision to deny a wetlands permit on the ground that it "unreasonably" alters the natural condition of the wetland, and (2) the result of that decision, which is to foreclose all development of the land on which the permit is denied? .

In the *Volpe* case, cited in the principal opinion, suit was brought to enjoin a landowner from filling 49.4 acres owned by it in a 78-acre marsh, in violation of a condition imposed by the state resources commissioner. The court remanded the case for additional evidence and defined the issues in the case as follows:

> In summary, our views are that the finding that Broad Marsh is a "saltmarsh" necessary to preserve and protect marine fisheries is not plainly wrong; that, considered apart from the taking issue, the rulings that the prohibition of filing the marsh is a condition authorized by . . . [the statute], are correct as upholding a valid public purpose; and that whether the defendant is the uncompensated victim of a taking invalid without compensation depends upon further findings as to what uses the marshland may still be put and possibly upon other issues which have not been argued and which are enumerated below.
>
> The final decree is reversed. The case is remanded for the following purposes:
>
> First, for the taking of further evidence and for further findings on the following matters:
>
> 1. The portions, if any, of the 49.4 acres (the locus) which the owner desires to improve below the line of mean high water (see *Commonwealth v. City of Roxbury*, 9 Gray, 451, 483).
>
> 2. The uses which can be made of the locus in its natural state (a) independently of other land of the owner in the area; (b) in conjunction with other land of the owner.
>
> 3. The assessed value of the locus for each of the five years, 1960 to 1964, inclusive.
>
> 4. The cost of the locus to the defendant.
>
> 5. The present fair market value of the locus (a) subject to the limitations imposed by the Commissioner; (b) free of such limitations.
>
> 6. The estimated cost of the improvements proposed by the defendant.
>
> 7. Any relevant rules and regulations prescribed by the Director of Marine Fisheries.
>
> 8. Any relevant by-laws (including zoning provisions) or regulations of the town of Wareham.
>
> Second, for further hearings to develop any relevant evidence on each of the following issues, none of which has been argued and as to which we express no opinion. Briefs and oral arguments should be directed at least to such issues upon any subsequent appeal to this court.
>
> A. Would the Commonwealth, by the imposition of the proposed restriction, take property without just compensation, if there is no substantial possible use of the locus while subject to the proposed restriction which will yield to the owner of the locus a fair return (1) upon the amount of his investment in the locus, or (2) upon what would be the fair market value of the locus free of the restriction?
>
> B. If it is contended that the land, if subject to the proposed restriction, may be profitably used in connection with other land, is this relevant, and, if so, to what extent?
>
> C. Is it relevant to questions A or B that the locus is not suitable in its present state for residential or commercial use?
>
> D. Is it relevant to questions A and B that the proposed filling, at least in part, will change coastal marshland, subject at times to tidal flow into upland?

Id. at 671-72.

2. Another earlier case holding wetlands regulation unconstitutional is *Morris County Land Improvement Co. v. Township of Parsippany-Troy Hills,* 193 A.2d 232 (N.J. 1963). In this case the plaintiff wished to expand its sand and gravel business, but to do so had to fill part of an inland wetlands area. This activity was prohibited under a local zoning ordinance which forbade any major developmental use in the wetland area. This ordinance was held unconstitutional. After noting that the purpose of the ordinance was to retain the land in its natural state, the court, in language reminiscent of *State v. Johnson,* commented:

> It is equally obvious from the proofs, and legally of the highest significance, that the main purpose of enacting regulations with the practical effect of retaining the meadows in their natural state was for a public benefit. This benefit is twofold, with somewhat interrelated aspects: first, use of the area as a water detention basin in aid of flood control in the lower reaches of the Passaic Valley far beyond this municipality; and second, preservation of the land as open space for the benefits which would accrue to the local public from an undeveloped use such as that of a nature refuge. . . .

Id. at 240 (opinion by Justice Hall).

That the New Jersey Supreme Court has had second thoughts on this issue is indicated in *AMG Assocs. v. Township of Springfield,* 319 A.2d 705 (N.J. 1974) (opinion by Justice Hall). In a footnote the court noted:

> The approach to the taking problem, and the result, may be different where vital ecological and environmental considerations of recent cognizance have brought about rather drastic land use restriction in furtherance of a policy designed to protect important public interests wide in scope and territory, as for example, the coastal wetlands act, . . . and various kinds of flood plain use regulation. Cases arising in such a context may properly call for a reexamination of some of the statements 10 years ago in the largely locally limited *Morris County Land* case. . . .

Id. at 711, n. 4. The New Jersey courts, at least, do not appear inclined to extend *Morris Land. See, e.g., Toms River Affiliates v. Department of Environmental Protection,* 355 A.2d 679 (N.J. Super.), *cert. denied,* 364 A.2d 1077 (N.J. 1976), holding that the denial of a permit for condominium housing under the coastal facilities review act was not unconstitutional on the ground that alternative uses were available, and citing *AMG.*

3. It was left to the Wisconsin Supreme Court to take the most aggressive stance on the taking issue question as it arose in the wetlands context. Since that case in fact arose in the context of a shorelands protection program not limited to wetlands protection, we should first examine the general outlines of shoreland regulation.

Recall the observation in Sensitive Lands, *supra* p. 1107, that regulations for areas upland from wetlands must also be adopted if damage to wetlands is to be prevented from erosion carrying nutrients into wetlands areas, excessive water runoff, and the like. Some states have enacted statutes more comprehensive than the wetlands acts and which provide for specialized regulation in all shoreland areas adjacent to lakes, coasts, and streams, including wetlands that may lie within these shoreland areas. The *Just* case, which follows, construes a local shorelands ordinance which is the product of one of these comprehensive shoreland protection regulatory statutes.

The Wisconsin statute considered in *Just* required all counties in the state to adopt shorelands ordinances approved by the state resources agency or to submit to direct regulation by this agency. The statute was applicable to all lands in the unincorporated areas of counties within a strip 1,000 feet deep along lakes and 300 feet deep along streams, or to the landward side of the floodplain along streams, whichever was greater. The resources agency was directed to prepare a model shorelands ordinance based on a series of statutory criteria. These criteria favored domestic uses; uses and locations tending to minimize or avoid pollution; and the dispersal of uses throughout a shorelands area rather than their concentration or undue proximity. These criteria also provided that "[a]reas in which the existing or potential economic value of public, recreational or similar uses exceeds the existing or potential economic value of any other use shall be classified primarily on the basis of the higher economic use value." Wis. Stat. Ann. § 144.26 (Supp. 1977).

The model ordinance incorporates zoning, subdivision control and sanitary regulations; only the zoning regulations were at issue in the *Just* case. Three zoning districts were established: (1) conservancy; (2) recreational-residential; and (3) general purpose. Further details on the ordinance regulations are contained in the *Just* opinion.

JUST v. MARINETTE COUNTY

Supreme Court of Wisconsin
56 Wis. 2d 7, 201 N.W.2d 761 (1972)
Noted, 86 HARV. L. REV. 1582 (1973)

These two cases were consolidated for trial and argued together on appeal. In case number 106, Ronald Just and Kathryn L. Just, his wife (Justs), sought a declaratory judgment stating: (1) The shoreland zoning ordinance of the respondent Marinette County (Marinette) was unconstitutional, (2) their property was not "wetlands" as defined in the ordinance, and (3) the prohibition against the filling of wetlands was unconstitutional. In case number 107, Marinette county sought a mandatory injunction to restrain the Justs from placing fill material on their property without first obtaining a conditional-use permit as required by the ordinance and also a forfeiture for their violation of the ordinance in having placed fill on their lands without a permit. The trial court held the ordinance was valid, the Justs' property was "wetlands," the Justs had violated the ordinance and they were subject to a forfeiture of $100. From the judgments, the Justs appeal.

On this appeal the state of Wisconsin has intervened as a party-respondent pursuant to sec. 274.12(6), Stats., because of the issue of constitutionality. The state considers the appeal to be a challenge to the underlying secs. 59.971 and 144.26, Stats., and a challenge to the state's comprehensive program to protect navigable waters through shoreland regulation. . . .

HALLOWS, Chief Justice. Marinette county's Shoreland Zoning Ordinance Number 24 was adopted September 19, 1967, became effective October 9, 1967, and follows a model ordinance published by the Wisconsin Department of Resource Development in July of 1967. *See* Kusler, Water Quality Protection For Inland Lakes in Wisconsin: A Comprehensive Approach to Water Pollution, 1970 Wis.L.Rev. 35, 62-63. The ordinance was designed to meet standards and criteria for shoreland regulation which the legislature required to be promulgated by the department of natural resources under sec. 144.26, Stats. These standards are found in 6 Wis.Adm.Code, sec. NR 115.03, May, 1971, Register No. 185. The legislation, secs. 59.971 and 144.26, Stats., authorizing the ordinance was enacted as a part of the Water Quality Act of 1965 by ch. 614, Laws of 1965.

Shorelands for the purpose of ordinances are defined in sec. 59.971(1), Stats., as lands within 1,000 feet of the normal highwater elevation of navigable lakes, ponds, or flowages and 300 feet from a navigable river or stream or to the landward side of the flood plain, whichever distance is greater. The state shoreland program is unique. All county shoreland zoning ordinances must be approved by the department of natural resources prior to their becoming effective. 6 Wis.Adm.Code, sec. NR 115.04, May, 1971, Register No. 185. If a county does not enact a shoreland zoning ordinance which complies with the state's standards, the department of natural resources may enact such an ordinance for the county. Sec. 59.971(6), Stats.

There can be no disagreement over the public purpose sought to be obtained by the ordinance. Its basic purpose is to protect navigable waters and the public rights therein from the degradation and deterioration which results from uncontrolled use and development of shorelands. In the Navigable Waters Protection Act, sec. 144.26, the purpose of the state's shoreland regulation program is stated as being to "aid in the fulfillment of the state's role as trustee of its navigable waters and to promote public health, safety, convenience and general welfare." In sec. 59.971(1), which grants authority for shoreland zoning to counties, the same purposes are reaffirmed. The Marinette county shoreland zoning ordinance in secs. 1.2 and 1.3 states the uncontrolled use of shorelands and pollution of navigable waters of Marinette county adversely affect public health, safety, convenience, and general welfare and impair the tax base.

The shoreland zoning ordinance divides the shorelands of Marinette county into general purpose districts, general recreation districts, and conservancy districts. A "conservancy" district is required by the statutory minimum standards and is defined in sec. 3.4 of the ordinance to include "all shorelands designated as swamps or marshes on the United States Geological Survey maps which have been designated as the Shoreland Zoning Map of Marinette County, Wisconsin or on the detailed Insert Shoreland Zoning Maps." The ordinance provides for permitted uses [5] and conditional uses.[6] One of the conditional uses requiring a permit under sec. 3.42(4) is the filling, drainage or dredging of wetlands according to the provisions of sec. 5 of the ordinance. "Wetlands" are defined in sec. 2.29 as "(a)reas where ground water is at or near the surface much of the year or where any segment of plant cover is deemed an aquatic according to N.C. Fassett's "Manual of Aquatic Plants." Section 5.42(2) of the ordinance requires a conditional-use permit for any filling or grading "Of any area which is within three hundred feet horizontal distance of a navigable water and which has surface drainage toward the water and on which there is: (a) Filling of more than five hundred square feet of any wetland which is contiguous to the water. . . (d) Filling or grading of more than 2,000 square feet on slopes of twelve per cent or less."

In April of 1961, several years prior to the passage of this ordinance, the Justs purchased 36.4 acres of land in the town of Lake along the south shore of Lake Noquebay, a navigable lake in Marinette county. This land had a frontage of 1,266.7 feet on the lake and was purchased partially for personal use and partially for resale. During the years 1964, 1966, and 1967, the Justs made five sales of parcels having frontage and extending back from the lake some 600

---

[5] "3.41 Permitted Uses.

(1) Harvesting of any wild crop such as marsh hay, ferns, moss, wild rice, berries, tree fruits and tree seeds.

(2) Sustained yield forestry subject to the provisions of Section 5.0 relating to removal of shore cover.

(3) Utilities such as, but not restricted to, telephone, telegraph and power transmission lines.

(4) Hunting, fishing, preservation of scenic, historic and scientific areas and wildlife preserves.

(5) Non-resident buildings used solely in conjunction with raising water fowl, minnows, and other similar lowland animals, fowl or fish.

(6) Hiking trails and bridle paths.

(7) Accessory uses.

(8) Signs, subject to the restriction of Section 2.0."

[6] "3.42 Conditional Uses. The following uses are permitted upon issuance of a Conditional Use Permit as provided in Section 9.0 and issuance of a Department of Resource Development permit where required by Section 30.11, 30.12, 30.19, 30.195 and 31.05 of the Wisconsin Statutes.

(1) General farming provided farm animals shall be kept one hundred feet from any non-farm residence.

(2) Dams, power plants, flowages and ponds.

(3) Relocation of any water course.

(4) Filling, drainage or dredging of wetlands according to the provisions of Section 5.0 of this ordinance.

(5) Removal of top soil or peat.

(6) Cranberry bogs.

(7) Piers, Docks, boathouses."

feet, leaving the property involved in these suits. This property has a frontage of 366.7 feet and the south one half contains a stand of cedar, pine, various hard woods, birch and red maple. The north one half, closer to the lake, is barren of trees except immediately along the shore. The south three fourths of this north one half is populated with various plant grasses and vegetation including some plants which N. C. Fassett in his manual of aquatic plants has classified as "aquatic." There are also non-aquatic plants which grow upon the land. Along the shoreline there is a belt of trees. The shoreline is from one foot to 3.2 feet higher than the lake level and there is a narrow belt of higher land along the shore known as a "pressure ridge" or "ice heave," varying in width from one to three feet. South of this point, the natural level of the land ranges one to two feet above lake level. The land slopes generally toward the lake but has a slope less than twelve per cent. No water flows onto the land from the lake, but there is some surface water which collects on land and stands in pools.

The land owned by the Justs is designated as swamps or marshes on the United States Geological Survey Map and is located within 1,000 feet of the normal high-water elevation of the lake. Thus, the property is included in a conservancy district and, by sec. 2.29 of the ordinance, classified as "wetlands." Consequently, in order to place more than 500 square feet of fill on this property, the Justs were required to obtain a conditional-use permit from the zoning administrator of the county and pay a fee of $20 or incur a forfeiture of $10 to $200 for each day of violation.

In February and March of 1968, six months after the ordinance became effective, Ronald Just, without securing a conditional-use permit, hauled 1,040 square yards of sand onto this property and filled an area approximately 20-feet wide commencing at the southwest corner and extending almost 600 feet north to the northwest corner near the shoreline, then easterly along the shoreline almost to the lot line. He stayed back from the pressure ridge about 20 feet. More than 500 square feet of this fill was upon wetlands located contiguous to the water and which had surface drainage toward the lake. The fill within 300 feet of the lake also was more than 2,000 square feet on a slope less than 12 percent. It is not seriously contended that the Justs did not violate the ordinance and the trial court correctly found a violation.

The real issue is whether the conservancy district provisions and the wetlands-filling restrictions are unconstitutional because they amount to a constructive taking of the Justs' land without compensation. Marinette county and the state of Wisconsin argue the restrictions of the conservancy district and wetlands provisions constitute a proper exercise of the police power of the state and do not so severely limit the use or depreciate the value of the land as to constitute a taking without compensation.

To state the issue in more meaningful terms, it is a conflict between the public interest in stopping the [despoliation] of natural resources, which our citizens until recently have taken as inevitable and for granted, and an owner's asserted right to use his property as he wishes. The protection of public rights may be accomplished by the exercise of the police power unless the damage to the property owner is too great and amounts to a confiscation. The securing or taking of a benefit not presently enjoyed by the public for its use is obtained by the government through its power of eminent domain. The distinction between the exercise of the police power and condemnation has been said to be a matter of degree of damage to the property owner. In the valid exercise of the police power reasonably restricting the use of property, the damage suffered by the owner is said to be incidental. However, where the restriction is so great the landowner ought not to bear such a burden for the public good, the restriction has been held to be a constructive taking even though the actual use or forbidden use has not been transferred to the government so as to be a taking in the traditional sense. *Stefan Auto Body v. State Highway Comm.* (1963), 21 Wis.2d 363, 124 N.W.2d 319. . . . Whether a taking has occurred depends upon whether "the restriction practically or substantially renders the land useless for all reasonable purposes." *Buhler v. Racine County, supra.* The loss caused the individual must be weighed to determine if it is more than he should bear. As this court stated in *Stefan,* at pp. 369-370, 124 N.W.2d 319, p. 323, ". . . if the damage is such as to be suffered by many similarly situated and is in the nature of a restriction on the use to which land may be put and ought to be borne by the individual as a member of society for the good of the public safety, health or general welfare, it is said to be a reasonable exercise of the police power, but if the damage is so great to the individual that he ought not to bear it under contemporary standards, then courts are inclined to treat it as a 'taking' of the property or an unreasonable exercise of the police power."

Many years ago, Professor Freund stated in his work on The Police Power, sec. 511, at 546-547, "It may be said that the state takes property by eminent domain because it is useful to the public, and under the police power because it is harmful. . . . From this results the difference between the power of eminent domain and the police power, that the former recognises a right to compensation, while the latter on principle does not." Thus the necessity for monetary compensation for loss suffered to an owner by police power restriction arises when restrictions are placed on property in order to create a public benefit rather than to prevent a public harm. Rathkopf, The Law of Zoning and Planning, Vol. 1, ch. 6, pp. 6-7.

This case causes us to reexamine the concepts of public benefit in contrast to public harm and the scope of an owner's right to use of his property. In the instant case we have a restriction on the use of a citizens' property, not to secure a benefit for the public, but to prevent a harm from the change in the natural character of the citizens' property. We start with the premise that lakes and rivers in their natural state are unpolluted and the pollution which now exists is man made. The state of Wisconsin under the trust doctrine has a duty to eradicate the present pollution and to prevent further pollution in its navigable waters. This is not, in a legal sense, a gain or a securing of a benefit by the maintaining of the natural *status quo* of the environment. What makes this case different from most condemnation or police power zoning cases is the interrelationship of the wetlands, the swamps and the natural environment of shorelands to the purity of the water and to such natural resources as navigation, fishing, and scenic beauty. Swamps and wetlands were once considered wasteland, undesirable, and not picturesque. But as the people became more sophisticated, an appreciation was acquired that swamps and wetlands serve a vital role in nature, are part of the balance of nature and are essential to the purity of the water in our lakes and streams. Swamps and wetlands are a necessary part of the ecological creation and now, even to the uninitiated, possess their own beauty in nature.

Is the ownership of a parcel of land so absolute that man can change its nature to suit any of his purposes? The great forests of our state were stripped on the theory man's ownership was unlimited. But in forestry, the land at least was used naturally, only the natural fruit of the land (the trees) were taken. The [despoliage] was in the failure to look to the future and provide for the reforestation of the land. An owner of land has no absolute and unlimited right to change the essential natural character of his land so as to use it for a purpose for which it was unsuited in its natural state and which injures the rights of others. The exercise of the police power in zoning must be reasonable and we think it is not an unreasonable exercise of that power to prevent harm to public rights by limiting the use of private property to its natural uses.

This is not a case where an owner is prevented from using his land for natural and indigenous uses. The uses consistent with the nature of the land are allowed and other uses recognized and still others permitted by special permit. The shoreland zoning ordinance prevents to some extent the changing of the natural character of the land within 1,000 feet of a navigable lake and 300 feet of a navigable river because of such land's interrelation to the contiguous water. The changing of wetlands and swamps to the damage of the general public by upsetting the natural environment and the natural relationship is not a reasonable use of that land which is protected from police power regulation. Changes and filling to some extent are permitted because the extent of such changes and fillings does not cause harm. We realize no case in Wisconsin has yet dealt with shoreland regulations and there are several cases in other states which seem to hold such regulations unconstitutional; but nothing this court has said or held in prior cases indicate[s] that destroying the natural character of a swamp or a wetland so as to make that location available for human habitation is a reasonable use of that land when the new use, although of a more economical value to the owner, causes a harm to the general public.

Wisconsin has long held that laws and regulations to prevent pollution and to protect the waters of this state from degradation are valid police-power enactments. . . . The active public trust duty of the state of Wisconsin in respect to navigable waters requires the state not only to promote navigation but also to protect and preserve those waters for fishing, recreation, and scenic beauty. . . . To further this duty, the legislature may delegate authority to local units of the government, which the state did by requiring counties to pass shoreland zoning ordinances. . . .

This is not a case of an isolated swamp unrelated to a navigable lake or stream, the change of which would cause no harm to public rights. Lands adjacent to or near navigable waters exist in a special relationship to the state. They have been held subject to special taxation, *Soens v. City of Racine* (1860), 10 Wis. 271, and are subject to state public trust powers, *Wisconsin P. & L. Co. v. Public Service Comm.* (1958), 5 Wis.2d 167, 92 N.W.2d 241; and since the Laws of 1935, ch. 303, counties have been authorized to create special zoning districts along waterways and zone them for restrictive conservancy purposes. The restrictions in the Marinette county ordinance upon wetlands within 1,000 feet of Lake Noquebay which prevent the placing of excess fill upon such land without a permit [are] not confiscatory or unreasonable.

Cases wherein a confiscation was found cannot be relied upon by the Justs. In *State v. Herwig* (1962), 17 Wis.2d 442, 117 N.W.2d 335, a "taking" was found where a regulation which prohibited hunting on farmland had the effect of establishing a game refuge and resulted in an unnatural, concentrated foraging of the owner's land by waterfowl. In *State v. Becker,* supra, the court held void a law which established a wildlife refuge (and prohibited hunting) on private property. In *Benka v. Consolidated Water Power Co.* (1929), 198 Wis. 472, 224 N.W. 718, the court held if damages to plaintiff's property were in fact caused by flooding from a dam constructed by a public utility, those damages constituted a "taking" within the meaning of the condemnation statutes. In *Bino v. Hurley* (1955), 273 Wis. 10, 76 N.W.2d 571, the court held unconstitutional as a "taking" without compensation an ordinance which, in attempting to prevent pollution, prohibited the owners of land surrounding a lake from bathing, boating, or swimming in the lake. In *Piper v. Ekern* (1923), 180 Wis. 586, 593, 194 N.W. 159, 162, the court held a statute which limited the height of buildings surrounding the state capitol to be unnecessary for the public health, safety, or welfare and, thus, to constitute an unreasonable exercise of the police power. In all these cases the unreasonableness of the exercise of the police power lay in excessive restriction of the natural use of the land or rights in relation thereto.

Cases holding the exercise of police power to be reasonable likewise provide no assistance to Marinette county in their argument. In *More-Way North Corp. v. State Highway Comm.* (1969), 44 Wis.2d 165, 175 N.W.2d 749, the court held that no "taking" occurred as a result of the state's lowering the grade of a highway, which necessitated plaintiff's reconstruction of its parking lot and loss of 42 parking spaces. In *Wisconsin Power & Light Co. v. Columbia County* (1958), 3 Wis.2d 1, 87 N.W.2d 279, no "taking" was found where the county, in relocating a highway, deposited gravel close to plaintiff's tower, causing it to tilt. In *Nick v. State Highway Comm.*, supra, the court held where property itself is not physically taken by the state, a restriction of access to a highway, while it may decrease the value of the land, does not entitle the owner to compensation. In *Buhler* the court held the mere depreciation of value was not sufficient ground to enjoin the county from enforcing the ordinance. In *Hasslinger v. Hartland* (1940), 234 Wis. 201, 290 N.W. 647, the court noted that "(a)ssuming an actionable nuisance by the creation of odors which make occupation of plaintiffs' farm inconvenient . . . and impair its value, it cannot be said that defendant has dispossessed plaintiffs or taken their property."

The Justs rely on several cases from other jurisdictions which have held zoning regulations involving flood plain districts, flood basins and wetlands to be so confiscatory as to amount to a taking because the owners of the land were prevented from improving such property for residential or commercial purposes. While some of these cases may be distinguished on their facts, it is doubtful whether these differences go to the basic rationale which permeates the decision that an owner has a right to use his property in any way and for any purpose he sees fit. In *Dooley v. Town Plan & Zon. Com. of Town of Fairfield* (1964), 151 Conn. 304, 197 A.2d 770, the court held the restriction on land located in a flood plain district prevented its being used for residential or business purposes and thus the restriction destroyed the economic value to the owner. The court recognized the land was needed for a public purpose as it was part of the area in which the tidal stream overflowed when abnormally high tides existed, but the property was half a mile from the ocean and therefore could not be used for marina or boathouse purposes. In *Morris County Land I. Co. v. Parsippany-Troy Hills Tp.* (1963), 40 N.J. 539,

193 A.2d 232, a flood basin zoning ordinance was involved which required the controversial land to be retained in its natural state. The plaintiff owned 66 acres of a 1,500-acre swamp which was part of a river basin and acted as a natural detention basin for flood waters in times of very heavy rainfall. There was an extraneous issue that the freezing regulations were intended as a stop-gap until such time as the government would buy the property under a flood-control project. However, the court took the view the zoning had an effect of preserving the land as an open space as a water-detention basin and only the government or the public would be benefited, to the complete damage of the owner.

In *State v. Johnson* (1970), Me., 265 A.2d 711, the Wetlands Act restricted the alteration and use of certain wetlands without permission. The act was a conservation measure enacted under the police power to protect the ecology of areas bordering the coastal waters. The plaintiff owned a small tract of a salt-water marsh which was flooded at high tide. By filling, the land would be adapted for building purposes. The court held the restrictions against filling constituted a deprivation of a reasonable use of the owner's property and, thus, an unreasonable exercise of the police power. In *MacGibbon v. Board of Appeals of Duxbury* (1970), 356 Mass. 635, 255 N.E.2d 347, the plaintiff owned seven acres of land which were under water about twice a month in a shoreland area. He was denied a permit to excavate and fill part of his property. The purpose of the ordinance was to preserve from despoilage natural features and resources such as salt marshes, wetlands, and ponds. The court took the view the preservation of privately owned land in its natural, unspoiled state for the enjoyment and benefit of the public by preventing the owner from using it for any practical purpose was not within the limit and scope of the police power and the ordinance was not saved by the use of special permits.

It seems to us that filling a swamp not otherwise commercially usable is not in and of itself an existing use, which is prevented, but rather is the preparation for some future use which is not indigenous to a swamp. Too much stress is laid on the right of an owner to change commercially valueless land when that change does damage to the rights of the public. It is observed that a use of special permits is a means of control and accomplishing the purpose of the zoning ordinance as distinguished from the old concept of providing for variances. The special permit technique is now common practice and has met with judicial approval, and we think it is of some significance in considering whether or not a particular zoning ordinance is reasonable.

A recent case sustaining the validity of a zoning ordinance establishing a flood plain district is *Turnpike Realty Company v. Town of Dedham* (June, 1972), 72 Mass. 1303, 284 N.E.2d 891. The court held the validity of the ordinance was supported by valid considerations of public welfare, the conservation of "natural conditions, wildlife and open spaces." The ordinance provided that lands which were subject to seasonal or periodic flooding could not be used for residences or other purposes in such a manner as to endanger the health, safety or occupancy thereof and prohibited the erection of structures or buildings which required land to be filled. This case is analogous to the instant facts. The ordinance had a public purpose to preserve the natural condition of the area. No change was allowed which would injure the purposes sought to be preserved and through the special-permit technique, particular land within the zoning district could be excepted from the restrictions.

The Justs argue their property has been severely depreciated in value. But this depreciation of value is not based on the use of the land in its natural state but on what the land would be worth if it could be filled and used for the location of a dwelling. While loss of value is to be considered in determining whether a restriction is a constructive taking, value based upon changing the character of the land at the expense of harm to public rights is not an essential factor or controlling.

We are not unmindful of the warning in *Pennsylvania Coal Co. v. Mahon* (1922), 260 U.S. 393, 416, 43 S.Ct. 158, 160, 67 L.Ed. 322:

> ... We are in danger of forgetting that a strong public desire to improve the public condition is not enough to warrant achieving the desire by a shorter cut than the constitutional way of paying for the change.

This observation refers to the improvement of the public condition, the securing of a benefit not presently enjoyed and to which the public is not entitled. The shoreland zoning ordinance preserves nature, the environment, and natural resources as they were created and to which the people have a present right. The ordinance does not create or improve the public condition but only preserves nature from the despoilage and harm resulting from the unrestricted activities of humans. . . .

Comments: 1. Another view of the resource protection problem was adopted in *Potomac Sand & Gravel Co. v. Governor of Maryland,* 293 A.2d 241 (Md.), *cert. denied,* 409 U.S. 1040 (1972). While it is another wetlands case, *Potomac* should be examined here as providing another dimension on the rationale of *Just.*

Potomac considered the constitutionality of a statute absolutely prohibiting dredging and filling in tidal wetlands. Its constitutionality was upheld in an opinion that has strong nuisance overtones, no doubt prompted by the absolute prohibition of the statute, which resembles a nuisance-type judicial remedy. Thus, the court cited several passages from *Commonwealth v. Tewksbury*, 11 Met. 55 (Mass. 1846), an early case upholding a statute prohibiting the taking of sand, stones or gravel from beaches. The *Potomac* case quoted the following conventional nuisance maxims from *Tewksbury*:

> All property is acquired and held under the tacit condition that it shall not be so used as to injure the equal rights of others, or to destroy or greatly impair the public rights and interests of the community; under the maxim of the common law, *sic utere tuo ut alienum non laedas*. . . . In such cases, we think, it is competent for the legislature to interpose, and by positive enactment to prohibit a use of property which would be injurious to the public, ...

Id. at 247. The *Potomac* case also distinguished *State v. Johnson* because that case dealt with a statute authorizing a permit procedure while the Maryland statute enacted an absolute prohibition.

Under what conceptual theory might nuisance-like concepts be applicable to wetlands and shoreland regulation? An answer to this question is provided in the analysis of police power-taking problems provided in Sax, Takings, Private Property and Public Rights, 81 Yale L.J. 149 (1971). At this point it is helpful to review his arguments for supporting police power regulation as it applies in the wetlands context:

> The view here would recognize diffusely-held claims as public rights, entitled to equal consideration in legislative or judicial resolution of conflicting claims to the common resource base, without regard to the manner in which they are held. . . . The wetlands owner thus does not use only his own tract, but demands, as a condition of developing his property, that the ocean users tolerate a change in their use of the ocean. Similarly, the ocean users demand that the wetlands owner restrict his use. . . . The question raised here is why, if he wishes to impose a restriction on the use of the ocean to promote his activities on his own land, the wetlands owner ought not be compelled to buy *that* right?
>
> . . . .
>
> The purpose of the analysis stated above is not to permit a redistribution of land to achieve the most socially beneficial use, but only to put competing resource-owners in a position of equality when each of them seeks to make a use that involves some imposition (spillover) on his neighbors, and those demands are in conflict.

Id. at 159-60, 161. To what extent does the Sax analysis support the rationale in *Just?* In *Potomac?* For cases upholding wetlands regulations which contain echoes of the Sax view see *Brecciaroli v. Connecticut Comm'r of Envt'l Protection*, 362 A.2d 948 (Conn. 1975) (also noting that the landowner was not deprived of all reasonable use of his land); *Candlestick Properties, Inc. v. San Francisco Bay Conservation & Dev. Comm'n*, 89 Cal. Rptr. 897 (Cal. App. 1970). Distinguishing *Morris Land, supra. Candlestick* noted that "[t]he purpose of the regulations and restrictions imposed in the instant case is not merely to provide open spaces. Rather, they are designed to preserve the existing character of the bay while it is determined how the bay should be developed in the future." *Id.* at 906.

Sibson v. State, 336 A.2d 239 (N.H. 1975), is another case upholding wetlands regulation which appears to stretch even beyond the Sax formulation. After noting that it had been urged to reject the traditional formula of *Pennsylvania Coal, supra* p. 141, the court noted that a "different approach" had been suggested.

> Under the proposed rule, if the action of the State is a valid exercise of the police power proscribing activities that could harm the public, then there is no taking under the eminent domain clause. It is only when the state action appropriates property for the public use at the expense of the property owner that compensation is due,

citing several articles including Sax, *supra. Id.* at 241. Next the court cited with approval *Mugler v. Kansas,* 123 U.S. 623 (1887), upholding the Kansas prohibition law shutting down a brewery without compensation. Language from the *Just* case stating the rule that an owner of land has no absolute right to change the "natural character" of his land was then quoted, and the court concluded: "[w]e hold that the denial of the permit to fill the saltmarsh of the plaintiffs was a valid exercise of the police power proscribing future activities that would be harmful to the public and that, therefore, there was no taking under the eminent domain clause," *id.* at 243, again citing *Mugler.* What has *Sibson* held? *See* Stever, Sibson: Some Unanswered Questions, Land Use L. & Zoning Dig., vol. 27, no. 8, at 15 (1975).

2. For discussion of the wetlands and shorelands legislation see F. Bosselman & D. Callies, The Quiet Revolution in Land Use Control 108-35, 205-61 (discussing operation of San Francisco Bay, Massachusetts, and Wisconsin programs); D. Mandelker, Environmental and Land Controls Legislation 248-54 (1976) (wetlands permit legislation); Kusler, Water Quality Protection for Inland Lakes in Wisconsin: A Comprehensive Approach to Water Pollution, 1970 Wis. L. Rev. 35; Note, Assimilating Human Activity into the Shoreland Environment: The Michigan Shoreland Protection and Management Act of 1970, 62 Iowa L. Rev. 149 (1976); Note, State Land Use Regulation — A Survey of Recent Legislative Approaches, 56 Minn. L. Rev. 869, 889-901 (1972).

3. The dredge and fill permit program of the U.S. Army Corps of Engineers, which historically has been limited to navigable waters, was extended by judicial interpretation to include wetland areas. For discussion see Ablard & O'Neill, Wetland Protection and Section 404 of the Federal Water Pollution Control Act Amendments of 1972: A Corps of Engineers Renaissance, 1 Vt. L. Rev. 51 (1976).

4. The *Just* case upheld the land use restriction in that case through an unusal extension of the public trust doctrine to wetland areas, and other cases upholding wetland regulation appear influenced by public trust concepts, which are usually confined to navigable waters. For discussion see Sax, The Public Trust Doctrine in Natural Resources Law: Effective Judicial Intervention, 68 Mich. L. Rev. 471 (1968); Note, The Public Trust in Public Waterways, 7 Urb. L. Ann. 219 (1974).

2. Floodplains

Continuing loss of life and astronomical property losses from floods have prompted regulatory techniques aimed at restricting and preventing development in floodplain areas. Indeed, the enactment of floodplain regulatory programs has been extensively stimulated by a national program of flood insurance, which is conditioned on the enactment of floodplain regulations at the local level. While the regulatory techniques used in floodplain regulation are similar to those used in wetland and shoreland control, there are some differences, which are explored in the following article.

PLATER, THE TAKINGS ISSUE IN A NATURAL SETTING: FLOODLINES AND THE POLICE POWER, 52 Texas Law Review 201, 203-06, 218-20 (1974)

I. Policy Decisions

A. *Resource Confrontation: Rivers, Humans, and Law*

Flood levels are perfectly natural occurrences in the life of a river. When circumstances combine to load a river with large volumes of water, it responds according to the laws of physics, expanding to take all space necessary to carry its burden. Since watersheds have differing contours, rainfall patterns, soil permeability, and human interference, every river is unique. But in the course of time every natural river system inevitably produces floods. In its natural state the floodplain acts as the river's self-regulator, responding like a farflung reservoir to retard and hold waters until downstream levels subside sufficiently to receive them. Even in the flood current area, where the water force is greatest, floods usually do not destroy the floodplain environment. Nature mitigates potential damages by discouraging fragile and intolerant floodplain development, and the environmental disruptions that do occur heal naturally and quickly. The disasters occur when humans, refusing to follow nature's example, push out onto the river's territory and risk destruction to themselves and others.

Human settlement on floodplains does not occur for lack of capacity to identify the danger. By correlating various data from watershed areas, hydrologists can compute the probable frequency of future flood levels with surprising accuracy. Even where floodplains are not immediately discernible to the eye, they can be accurately defined, mapped, and avoided. The technical ability to delineate floods, however, has not prevented man from challenging rivers in head-on confrontation by developing floodplains. Approximately five percent of the United States population now lives on floodplains, and the amount of that development continually increases. The final result is that floods, when they inevitably strike, take rising tolls in lives and property.

Ironically, the flood hazard is increasing not only because of the mere presence of increased investment and occupancy on the floodplain, but also because human interference with natural conditions over the years causes flood levels to rise. Human encroachment on the floodplain's carrying capacity and modification of runoff characteristics have increased the percentage chance that a given flood elevation will be reached or exceeded each year. By far the most common and significant encroachment is the inexpensive dumped or diked fill operation that raises property up from the floodplain. Those encroachments fairly effectively diminish dangers to the buildings on them, but they have very serious consequences elsewhere in the resource network. Encroachments anywhere in the floodplain displace the floodplain's natural storage capacity; the degree of displacement depends upon the nature of the encroachment.

At first glance the effect may seem minimal; the total storage loss from an individual encroachment in the 100-year flood may amount to less than a hundred cubic yards of water. Measured against the value of an individual investment, the potential harm due to this floodflow increment may be small, and it may be infinitesimal compared to total downstream flood stages. Moreover, until recently hydrologists apparently doubted the importance of floodplain storage, assuming that the floodway currents were the only significant floodflow element. For these reasons some legal observers concluded that the encroachment-displacement effect was an insufficient justification for regulations excluding development from the floodplain. Using the same assumptions, several courts and legislatures have implied the same conclusion. While individual encroachments may have minimal local displacement effects, however, their cumulative consequences throughout a watershed seriously increase the frequently of floods and aggravate downstream damages. . . .

The probability that a flood will reach a given elevation in a particular year thus increases with additional floodplain development. Parcels that were threatened only by 250-year floods a generation ago may now fall within the 100-year floodlines. Since today's marginal location may be in the path of the next major flood, these rising levels emphasize the urgency of preventing all unnecessary human development in the floodplain. As a constitutional matter, this aspect of flood causation is important for the defense of regulatory measures that attempt to keep people off the floodplains. Regulating potential flood victims may not seem so harsh if they are viewed as contributing causes as well as potential victims of future floods.

. . . .

D. The Police Power: Floodplain Regulations

Floodplain regulations are analogous to standard land use districting schemes, controlling all uses of land within the hydrologically defined areas subject to floods of a designated frequency. Administered by a permit or zone procedure, they essentially establish a flood set-back rule for most development. Schedules of permitted and prohibited uses usually establish a gradient of restrictions within the floodplain area, decreasing in severity at the floodplain's fringes. Flexibility can be built into regulations through criteria for permits that authorize uses that do not increase flood levels or cause or sustain significant damage. Regulations may condition permits on structural modifications or other changes. When a proposed installation would cause increases in flood levels, but its net benefits would outweigh damages, it can be subject to special exception procedures.

. . . .

The similarity of floodplain regulations to other established land use regulations makes them relatively easy to initiate and administer. Several adequate model ordinances exist, backed by a fairly extensive legal commentary. Authority to issue regulations at the local level usually is present in general zoning and police power enabling acts, if not, the notoriety of recent floods should reduce the difficulty of obtaining specific legislative authorization. In practice, zoning authorities can incorporate floodplain districts as overlays on existing zone maps, or they can administer them separately. In either event, the graphic nature of the basic floodplain maps makes them easy to comprehend and apply, facilitating public notice, incorporation in title records, administrative handling, and judicial review. Conscientiously administered regulations, of course, impose costs upon government treasuries; base data, mapping, drafting, and enforcement procedures require substantial public expenditures. The costs of administering a floodplain management system, however, are infinitesimal compared to the cost of a single dam or a major flood. If conscientiously and comprehensively administered throughout a watershed, floodplain regulations can exclude all uses that pose dangers to floodplain inhabitants, but allow special uses in which the necessity for particular developments outweighs the disutility of their placement.

In practice, however, the regulatory approach has had its failings. Most of the more than 500 units of government that have promulgated floodplain management legislation are low-level governmental entities that rarely attempt to coordinate their efforts within watershed systems. Without coordinated basin-wide management policies, the fragmented administration of floodplain regulations severely limits their effectiveness. State level regulation is probably the most practical method to bring entire watersheds up to minimum regulatory levels. Though states are generally chary of invading the political domain of local governments, a firmly established trend points in that direction. Raising the level of governmental control has other benefits. Technical information, which currently represents substantial opportunity costs to small towns, can be generated more easily at the state level. Communication with relevant federal agencies may be easier. Removal of administration from the local level may alleviate heavy local pressures for modification, and state level regulation may possess enhanced standing in the court.

Comments: 1. The Figure which follows illustrates schematically the regulatory approach taken by a typical floodplain district. (The floodway is the unobstructed part of the floodplain consisting of the stream channel and overbank areas capable of carrying a selected flood discharge and is intended to carry the deep and fast-moving water. The adjacent flood fringe is intended to carry the shallow and slow-moving water.) Note that while developmental uses are prohibited in the floodway, they may be allowed in the flood fringe if protective steps are taken (*e.g.,* dwellings elevated above flood level). This distinction is important, as the following pair of cases indicates:

Vartelas v. Water Resources Comm'n, 153 A.2d 822 (Conn. 1959). Acting under the authority of a state statute, the commission established an encroachment line along a river, within which no structure could be placed unless authorized by the commission. The encroachment line left only sixty square feet of plaintiff's property for the erection of a structure, unless the commission gives its permission. Plaintiff challenged the constitutionality of the law and the court upheld it as a reasonable regulation designed to reduce hazard to life and property under the police power. The court also held that the plaintiff had not been finally deprived of the reasonable use of his property because the commission might authorize a structure beyond the encroachment line which did not impair the capacity of the river channel in time of flood. For example, it might authorize construction of a building on piers or cantilevers.

Dooley v. Town Plan & Zoning Comm'n, 197 A.2d 770 (Conn. 1964). The Town of Fairfield enacted a floodplain zoning district restricting the use of land within the district to parks and recreational facilities, governmental wildlife sanctuaries, farming and accessory motor vehicle parking. This ordinance was held unconstitutional, as the use of plaintiff's land had, for all practical purposes, been rendered impossible. The court noted that farming had long since been ruled out in the area. In addition, the court hinted that the ordinance had been passed to lower future acquisition costs. Is this case undercut by *Brecciaroli, supra* p. 1131?

FLOODPLAIN DISTRICT REGULATION

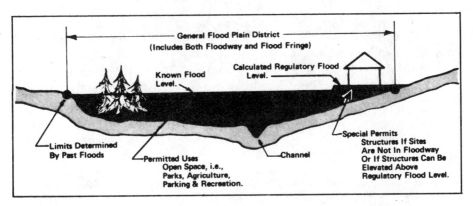

Source: American Soc'y of Planning Officials, Regulations for Flood Plains, Fig. 17, p. 45 (Planning Advisory Service Rep. No. 277 (1972).

To date there has been no aggressive floodplain regulation case which, like the *Just* case, marks out the permissible limits of floodplain regulation under the police power. The cases appear evenly divided, the adverse decisions no doubt prompted by what Plater calls the "novel police power objectives and dramatic erosions of market value" which the floodplain cases present. *Id.* at 222. The following additional cases are typical:

Maple Leaf Investors, Inc. v. State, 565 P.2d 1162 (Wash. 1977). The court held constitutional a floodplain regulation imposed by a state agency. It noted that "[t]he question essentially is one of social policy which requires the balancing of the public interest in regulating the use of private property against the interests of private landowners not to be encumbered by restrictions on the use of their property," *id.* at 1164, citing *Pennsylvania Coal.* In addition, the court noted that there was no question of a taking because the police power was being exercised to protect public health and safety; there was a rational relationship between the floodplain regulation and the objective of the legislation. Thirty percent of the restricted property was in the flood fringe, and there was no finding that the restrictions prevented the landowner from making a profitable use of its property. "Nature has placed it where it is and, if [the state] . . . had done nothing with respect to flood-plain zoning the property would still be subject to physical realities." *Id.* at 1166. *Compare Sturdy Homes, Inc. v. Township of Redford,* 186 N.W.2d 43 (Mich. App. 1971) (floodplain ordinance found confiscatory where no danger of flooding).

Compare Rains v. Washington Dep't of Fisheries, 575 P.2d 1057 (Wash. 1978). Plaintiff applied for and was refused a permit to rechannel a creek flowing on his land to avoid flooding and damage to his property. The permit was denied because of the probable damage to fish life. Later the creek overflowed and plaintiff brought an action in tort and inverse condemnation for the damages. Recovery was denied, the court noting that "[t]he most that can be said here is that, in the exercise of its police power to protect fish life for the benefit of all its citizens, the state restricted the extent to which . . . [plaintiff] could change the bed of Morse Creek." *Id.* at 1060.

Turnpike Realty Co. v. Town of Dedham, 284 N.E.2d 891 (Mass. 1972), *cert. denied,* 409 U.S. 1108 (1973). The court upheld a floodplain ordinance prohibiting all developmental uses of the restricted land, even though the value of the Turnpike property was allegedly reduced from $431,000 to $53,000. Applying the residual value test, the court held that though there was "substantial diminution" in the value of the land there was no unconstitutional "deprivation of property." *Id.* at 900. Earlier the court had also noted that restrictions in the use of the land "must be balanced against the potential harm to the community from overdevelopment of a flood plain area." *Id.*

Turner v. County of Del Norte, 101 Cal. Rptr. 93 (Cal. App. 1972). Plaintiff's property was located in a floodplain that had been flooded several times over the past 40 years. He brought an action in inverse condemnation claiming that restrictions imposed by a county floodplain ordinance took his property without just compensation having been paid. These restrictions prohibited the construction of permanent buildings but did permit public parks and recreation developments, boating facilities, campgrounds, agricultural uses and trailer parks operated on a seasonal basis. The ordinance was held constitutional. The court noted: "[t]he zoning ordinance in question imposes no restrictions more stringent than the existing danger demands. Respondents may use their lands in a number of ways which may be of economic benefit to them." *Id.* at 96.

2. Most land use control enabling acts now contain provisions authorizing the local adoption of floodplain regulations, and a large number of states have enacted programs calling for a state role in floodplain regulation. Some of these statutes call for direct state regulation in floodplains, see the *Vartelas* case, *supra.* Others provide for a cooperative state-local relationship in which the statute provides standards for local floodplain ordinances which localities within the state are required to adopt. The second group of statutes may or may not combine direct state regulation with state-mandated local regulation, and may or may not require state approval of local floodplain ordinances. *See, e.g.,* Iowa Code Ann. § 455A.35 (West 1971), authorizing both direct state regulation and state approval of local regulations; Wis. Stat. Ann. § 87.30 (West Supp. 1977), authorizing state adoption of floodplain regulations if a locality fails to do so. The following Arizona statute mandates the adoption of local floodplain ordinances consistent with statutory standards but does not provide for state review:

> **A.** Within sixty days after the effective date of this section, the Arizona water commission shall develop and adopt criteria for establishing the one hundred-year flood for the state of Arizona.
> **B.** The floodplain board, within its area of jurisdiction shall delineate or may require, by ordinance, developers of subdivisions to delineate for areas where development is ongoing or imminent, and thereafter as development becomes imminent, floodplains consistent with the criteria developed by the Arizona water commission. The floodplains so designated shall be submitted to the water commission.

C. The floodplain board shall adopt floodplain regulations which shall include the following:

1. Regulations for all subdivision of land, construction of dwelling units or commercial or industrial structures or uses which may divert, retard or obstruct flood water and threaten public health, safety or the general welfare.

2. Regulations which establish minimum flood protection elevations and flood damage prevention requirements for uses, structures and facilities which are vulnerable to flood damage. Regulations adopted under this section are to be in accordance with state and local land use plans and ordinances, if any.

3. Regulations which provide for coordination by the floodplain board with all other interested and affected political subdivisions and state agencies.

4. Regulations which require that any dwelling built within a floodplain shall be constructed so as to place the minimum floor elevation of the dwelling unit above the high water line of the one hundred-year flood except that the floodplain board may adopt a variance procedure for floodplains within its jurisdiction.

Ariz. Rev. Stat. § 45-2342 (Supp. 1977). "Floodplain board" is defined to mean "the governing body of an incorporated town or city, charter city or county." *Id.* § 45-2341(8). Which of the regulations mandated by the Arizona statute will be useful in the floodway and which in the flood fringe?

For discussion of floodplain ordinances and statutes see American Soc'y of Planning Officials, Regulations for Flood Plains (Planning Advisory Service Rep. No. 277, 1972); Note, Flood Plain Zoning for Flood Loss Control, 50 Iowa L. Rev. 552 (1965); Note, State Land Use Regulation — A Survey of Recent Legislative Approaches, 56 Minn. L. Rev. 869, 917-21 (1972); Note, Minnesota's Flood Plain Management Act — State Guidance of Land Use Controls, 55 Minn. L. Rev. 1163 (1971). For an earlier and comprehensive review of the legal issues see Dunham, Flood Control Via the Police Power, 107 U. Pa. L. Rev. 1098 (1959).

3. The enactment of floodplain regulations at the state and local level has been stimulated by the National Flood Insurance Program. The federal statute authorizing this program provides that no flood insurance will be provided under the program "unless an appropriate public body shall have adopted adequate land use and control measures (with effective enforcement provisions) which the Secretary [of Housing and Urban Development] finds are consistent with the comprehensive criteria for land management and use under section 4102 of this title." 42 U.S.C. § 4022 (1976). Section 4102 provides:

> ... [T]he Secretary shall from time to time develop comprehensive criteria designed to encourage, where necessary, the adoption of adequate State and local measures which, to the maximum extent feasible, will —
> (1) constrict the development of land which is exposed to flood damage where appropriate,
> (2) guide the development of proposed construction away from locations which are threatened by flood hazards,
> (3) assist in reducing damage caused by floods, and

> (4) otherwise improve the long-range land management and
> use of flood-prone areas,

and he shall work closely with and provide any necessary technical
assistance to State, interstate, and local governmental agencies, to
encourage the application of such criteria and the adoption and
enforcement of such measures.

The federal regulations on land use regulations for floodplains are
presently found at 24 C.F.R. pt. 1910 (1977). Some states have enacted
comprehensive statutes to authorize their localities to take advantage of the
federal flood insurance program, *e.g.,* Tex. Rev. Civ. Stat. Ann. art. 8830-13
(Vernon Supp. 1971). The Texas statute authorizes local governments to
take all actions necessary to comply with the requirements of the national
flood insurance program, including "[m]aking appropriate land use
adjustments to constrict the development of land which is exposed to flood
damage and minimize damage caused by flood hazards." *Id.* § 5(1). For
discussion of the federal flood insurance program see Comptroller General
of the United States, Formidable Administrative Problems Challenge
Achieving National Flood Insurance Program Objectives (1976); Tierney,
The National Flood Insurance Program: Explanation and Legal
Implications, 8 Urb. Law 279 (1976).

   4. As part of its revision of state enabling legislation for land use controls,
the American Law Institute's Model Land Development Code included
statutory authority at the state level for the designation and regulation of
what the Code calls critical areas. While an important application of the
Code's critical area provisions is contemplated in natural resource areas
threatened by new and unregulated development, the critical area concept
is important primarily as part of the ongoing transfer of land use control
authority to the state level. Consideration of this regulatory concept has
therefore been deferred to Chapter 9, *infra* p. 1244.

   5. *Agricultural zoning.* It is but a short step from wetlands and floodplain
control to agricultural zoning, the regulation of rural land use to keep land
in agricultural production. Often agricultural zoning is carried out through
large lot zoning that requires very large lot sizes but which still allows
single-family residences on each lot. A bolder approach to agricultural
zoning utilizes the minimum tract size approach, requiring minimum tract
sizes of ten acres and up in agricultural areas, but prohibits any residences
on the tract except as accessory to the dominant agricultural use.

   It has been argued that exclusive agricultural zoning is constitutionally
suspect because it prevents any developmental use of land. But see the
Consolidated Rock Prods. Co. case, *supra* p. 245, upholding a prohibition
on rock and gravel operations in an agricultural-residential zone. There is
support for exclusive agricultural zoning in California. *See, e.g., Gisler v.
County of Madera,* 112 Cal. Rptr. 919 (Cal. App. 1974), upholding an
exclusive 18-acre agricultural zone. The court noted that "the property
always has been and still is used for agricultural purposes, as is all the
property in the surrounding area."

   Compare *Smeja v. County of Boone,* 339 N.E.2d 452 (Ill. App. 1975).
Plaintiff sought to have a 50-acre tract rezoned from agricultural to
residential use. The court noted that "the issue on appeal . . . requires no
different analysis than any other proposed rezoning." It then held the

agricultural zoning unconstitutional, finding that the surrounding area had been substantially committed to nonagricultural uses. In addition, the tract consisted of 15 acres of submarginal agricultural land and 35 acres of woods, leading the court to doubt its suitability for agricultural use. *See also Kmiec v. Town of Spider Lake,* 211 N.W.2d 471 (Wis. 1973) (agricultural zoning invalid as applied to land having "negative" value for farming).

D. COASTAL ZONE MANAGEMENT

One important environmental resource area, the coastal zones of our coastal and Great Lakes states, has been the subject of national legislation aimed at improving regulatory systems for these coastal areas. Some states had moved to protect coastal areas prior to the enactment of the National Coastal Zone Management Act in 1972; one example is the Georgia Coastal Marshlands Protection Act, reproduced *supra* p. 1111. Congress, nevertheless, believed that regulatory programs in coastal areas were generally inadequate, that local governments along the coasts were inattentive to coastal protection problems, and that national legislation which would stimulate an expanded state role in coastal zone management was needed. These were the major concerns that prompted enactment of the national legislation.

The national coastal legislation is voluntary. State participation is not mandated, but is encouraged through the availability of federal grants for the planning and administration of state coastal zone programs. No substantive policies for coastal management are adopted by the national legislation. It requires a process for the consideration of coastal management issues at the state level, but leaves the determination of coastal zone management policies to the states. A substantive direction for state coastal programs is indicated to some extent by the Congressional findings and declaration of policy. They should be scrutinized to determine whether the state coastal programs encouraged by the statute are to be directed entirely to environmental concerns.

The first section of this chapter reviews the major features of the national coastal zone management legislation. State coastal programs are reviewed in the second section.

1. The National Coastal Zone Management Act of 1972

The major provisions of the national legislation follow. Only those provisions are included that specify the contents of state and state-directed coastal zone programs. The coastal energy impact program, which provides for grants and loans to states impacted by coastal energy facilities, is omitted. The Act is found at 16 U.S.C. § 1451 *et seq.* (1976). References below are to the section numbers as they appeared in the bill as enacted. The program authorized by this legislation is presently administered by the Office of Coastal Zone Management of the National Oceanic and Atmospheric Administration (NOAA), which presently is located in the Department of Commerce.

Short Title

Sec. 301. This title may be cited as the "Coastal Zone Management Act of 1972".

Congressional Findings

Sec. 302. The Congress finds that —

(a) There is a national interest in the effective management, beneficial use, protection, and development of the coastal zone;

(b) The coastal zone is rich in a variety of natural commercial, recreational, ecological, industrial, and esthetic resources of immediate and potential value to the present and future well-being of the Nation;

(c) The increasing and competing demands upon the lands and waters of our coastal zone occasioned by population growth and economic development, including requirements for industry, commerce, residential development, recreation, extraction of mineral resources and fossil fuels, transportation and navigation, waste disposal, and harvesting of fish, shellfish, and other living marine resources, have resulted in the loss of living marine resources, wildlife, nutrient-rich areas, permanent and adverse changes to ecological systems, decreasing open space for public use, and shoreline erosion;

(d) The coastal zone, and the fish, shellfish, other living marine resources, and wildlife therein, are ecologically fragile and consequently extremely vulnerable to destruction by man's alterations;

(e) Important ecological, cultural, historic, and esthetic values in the coastal zone which are essential to the well-being of all citizens are being irretrievably damaged or lost;

(f) Special natural and scenic characteristics are being damaged by ill-planned development that threatens these values;

(g) In light of competing demands and the urgent need to protect and to give high priority to natural systems in the coastal zone, present state and local institutional arrangements for planning and regulating land and water uses in such areas are inadequate; and

(h) The key to more effective protection and use of the land and water resources of the coastal zone is to encourage the states to exercise their full authority over the lands and waters in the coastal zone by assisting the states, in cooperation with Federal and local governments and other vitally affected interests, in developing land and water use programs for the coastal zone, including unified policies, criteria, standards, methods, and processes for dealing with land and water use decisions of more than local significance. . . .

DECLARATION OF POLICY

SEC. 303. The Congress finds and declares that it is the national policy (a) to preserve, protect, develop, and where possible, to restore or enhance, the resources of the Nation's coastal zone for this and succeeding generations, (b) to encourage and assist the states to exercise effectively their responsibilities in the coastal zone through the development and implementation of management programs to achieve wise use of land and water resources of the coastal zone giving full consideration to ecological, cultural, historic, and esthetic values as well as to needs for economic development, (c) for all Federal agencies engaged in programs affecting the coastal zone to cooperate and participate with state and local governments and regional agencies in effectuating the purposes of this title, and (d) to encourage the participation of the public, of Federal, state, and local governments and of regional agencies in the development of coastal zone management programs. With respect to implementation of such management programs, it is the national policy to encourage cooperation among the various state and regional agencies including establishment of interstate and regional agreements, cooperative procedures, and joint action particularly regarding environmental problems.

DEFINITIONS

SEC. 304. . . .

(1) The term "coastal zone" means the coastal waters (including the lands therein and thereunder) and the adjacent shorelands (including the waters therein and thereunder), strongly influenced by each other and in proximity to the shorelines of the several coastal states, and includes islands, transitional and intertidal areas, salt marshes, wetlands, and beaches. The zone extends, in Great Lakes waters to the international boundary between the United States and Canada and, in other areas, seaward to the outer limit of the United States territorial sea. The zone extends inland from the shorelines only to the extent necessary to control shorelands, the uses of which have a direct and significant impact on the coastal waters. Excluded from the coastal zone are lands the use of which is by law subject

solely to the discretion of or which is held in trust by the Federal Government, its officers or agents. . . .

(9) The term "land use" means activities which are conducted in, or on the shorelands within, the coastal zone, subject to the requirements outlined in section 307(g) of this title. . . .

(11) The term "management program" includes, but is not limited to, a comprehensive statement in words, maps, illustrations, or other media of communication, prepared and adopted by the state in accordance with the provisions of this chapter, setting forth objectives, policies, and standards to guide public and private uses of lands and waters in the coastal zone. . . .

MANAGEMENT PROGRAM DEVELOPMENT GRANTS — AUTHORIZATION

SEC. 305.

(a) The Secretary may make grants to any coastal state —

(1) under subsection (c) of this section for the purpose of assisting such state in the development of a management program for the land and water resources of its coastal zone; . . .

(b) The management program for each coastal state shall include each of the following requirements:

(1) An identification of the boundaries of the coastal zone subject to the management program.

(2) A definition of what shall constitute permissible land uses and water uses within the coastal zone which have a direct and significant impact on the coastal waters.

(3) An inventory and designation of areas of particular concern within the coastal zone.

(4) An identification of the means by which the state proposes to exert control over the land uses and water uses referred to in paragraph (2), including a listing of relevant constitutional provisions, laws, regulations, and judicial decisions.

(5) Broad guidelines on priorities of uses in particular areas, including specifically those uses of lowest priority.

(6) A description of the organizational structure proposed to implement such management program, including the responsibilities and interrelationships of local, areawide, state, regional, and interstate agencies in the management process. . . .

[Subsection (c) sets the federal grant at 80 percent of total state costs in any one year. Subsection (h) requires any state that has completed its development of its management program to submit the program to the Secretary of Commerce for review and approval. After a management program has been approved the state will be eligible for grants under Section 306. — Eds.]

ADMINISTRATIVE GRANTS — AUTHORIZATION

SEC. 306.

[This section first provides for 80 percent federal grants to the states of the cost of administering a state coastal program. Paragraph (c) contains approval requirements for state programs. Section 306(c)(1) provides that the Commerce Secretary may approve a state program developed in accordance with federal rules and regulations. Section 306(c)(2) requires coordination of the state program with local, areawide and interstate agencies. It also provides in Section 306(c)(2)(B) that the state coastal agency must notify any local government if a management program by the state agency would conflict with "any local zoning ordinance, decision, or other action." The local government is given a 30-day period to comment on the program decision, but the Act provides that the state agency is only required to "consider" these local comments. Section 306(c)(4) requires that the state coastal program be approved by the governor. Section 306(c)(5) requires the governor to designate "a single state agency to receive and administer the grants for implementing" the state coastal program. Additional requirements contained in Section 306 follow. — Eds.]

Prior to granting approval of a management program submitted by a coastal state, the Secretary shall find that: . . .

(8) The management program provides for adequate consideration of the national interest involved in planning for, and in the siting of, facilities (including energy facilities in, or which significantly affect, such state's coastal zone) which are necessary to meet requirements which are other than local in nature. In the case of such energy facilities, the Secretary shall find that the state has given consideration to any applicable interstate energy plan or program.

(9) The management program makes provision for procedures whereby specific areas may be designated for the purpose of preserving or restoring them for their conservation, recreational, ecological, or esthetic values.

(d) Prior to granting approval of the management program, the Secretary shall find that the state, acting through its chosen agency or agencies, including local governments, areawide agencies . . ., regional agencies, or interstate agencies, has authority for the management of the coastal zone in accordance with the management program. Such authority shall include power —

(1) to administer land and water use regulations, control development in order to ensure compliance with the management program, and to resolve conflicts among competing uses; and

(2) to acquire fee simple and less than fee simple interests in lands, waters, and other property through condemnation or other means when necessary to achieve conformance with the management program.

(e) Prior to granting approval, the Secretary shall also find that the program provides:

(1) for any one or a combination of the following general techniques for control of land and water uses within the coastal zone;

(A) State establishment of criteria and standards for local implementation subject to administrative review and enforcement of compliance;

(B) Direct state land and water use planning and regulation; or

(C) State administrative review for consistency with the management program of all development plans, projects, or land and water use regulations, including exceptions and variances thereto, proposed by any state or local authority or private developer, with power to approve or disapprove after public notice and an opportunity for hearings.

(2) for a method of assuring that local land and water use regulations within the coastal zone do not unreasonably restrict or exclude land and water uses of regional benefit.

. . . .

SEC. 307.

[This section provides, generally, that federal programs, permits and activities affecting the coastal zone of any coastal state must be consistent with that state's management program. This section provides the means for integrating federal activities in the coastal zone with state coastal programs, and is the counterpart to those provisions of the statute requiring state supervision of local regulatory actions affecting the coastal zone. — Eds.]

———

Comments: 1. Ambiguities in the structure of the National Coastal Zone Management Act create difficulties for coastal states as they attempt to comply with the statutory mandate for state supervision of local regulatory programs in the coastal zone. The statute, like most federal grant-in-aid legislation, requires designation of a single state agency to receive and disburse grants made under the program, but the Act does not state that it is this agency which is to be charged with actually administering the regulatory aspects of the state coastal program. Note also that the regulatory powers required by Section 306(d) may be exercised by local governments. Section 306(e)(1) specifies the three basic means of state control that are apparently to be the heart of the state coastal program. Generally, either direct state control or state administrative review of local actions is required. These means of state control are further qualified by other requirements contained in the statute. One is the requirement in § 306(e)(2) that the state coastal program assure "that local land and water use regulations ... do not unreasonably restrict or exclude land and water uses of regional benefit." A second is implied by the requirement in Section 304(b)(3) that the state inventory and designate areas of "particular concern." These last two state means of regulation apparently contemplate the methods of state review of local land use control actions proposed by the American Law Institute's Model Land Development Code discussed in Chapter 9, *infra.* For discussion of the land use regulation provisions of the national legislation see Mandelker & Sherry, The National Coastal Zone Management Act of 1972, 7 Urb. L. Ann. 119 (1974).

2. These ambiguities in the national legislation permit a wide variety of responses at the state level to the statutory program requirements, especially since the national legislation nowhere requires that new state coastal zone legislation be enacted to comply with the national law. Note also the statutory definition of a coastal zone, which apparently contemplates a relatively narrow coastal strip and says nothing about urban areas, which in some states have been entirely excluded.

Consider, in view of the requirements of the national legislation, whether the following state responses to the national statutory requirements would be accepted by the federal Office of Coastal Zone Management:

1) A coastal state enacts new coastal zone legislation providing that all local permits for major developments in the coastal zone must be reviewed at the state level by a new state coastal agency. That agency may designate "particular" areas in which local land use controls are displaced and all development requires a state permit.

2) Georgia decides that its Coastal Marshlands Protection Act, *supra* p. 1111, satisfies the requirements of the national legislation.

3) Wisconsin decides that its shorelands zoning act, amended to apply to shorelands along the Great Lakes but excluding incorporated municipalities, satisfies the requirements of the national legislation. See the *Just* case, *supra* p. 1121.

4) A state legislature adopts a series of coastal zone policies. The Governor issues an executive order requiring all state agencies to adhere to these policies. The policies are enforceable against local governments under an environmental standing act allowing private citizens to bring suit to enforce the coastal policies and other environmental legislation. See *American Petroleum Institute v. Knecht,* 456 F. Supp. 889 (D. Cal. 1978), holding that a state coastal management program need not contain a "zoning map" inflexibly indicating permitted uses in the coastal zone. The case is on appeal.

3. A series of policies adopted by the federal Office of Coastal Zone Management have further specified the content of state programs that will be approved under the statute. Stress is placed on the adoption of explicit and enforceable state coastal zone policies. These policies may be enforced through court rather than state administrative action. New legislation is not necessarily required and the states may satisfy the federal requirements through the "networking" of existing coastal and environmental legislation to make up the state coastal zone program. Finally, states may adopt a "two-tiered" approach to its coastal zone program, providing for intensive regulation through a permit system or otherwise along a narrow coastal strip and a weaker regulatory program in a second tier inland of the coastal strip. It is in the second tier that the networking concept may be implemented. Do these policies shed any further light on whether the state coastal programs described in Comment 2 would be acceptable under the national legislation?

4. See a critical report on the coastal zone program by the General Accounting Office, see Comptroller General of the United States, The Coastal Zone Management Program: An Uncertain Future (1976). The Office was critical of federal guidance in the program and noted difficulties in program implementation due primarily to a stiffening political climate. As the report noted;

> . . . In our opinion, resistance exists because (1) local governments may regard coastal zone management as an example of Federal-State interference in planning decisions traditionally made by localities and (2) the public, especially coastal landowners, contend that State management programs infringe on their private property rights and affect property values by restricting the uses to which their land can be put.

Id. at 27. The report also noted state complaints that federal assistance "lacked systematic and comprehensive guidance in interpreting . . . [federal] regulations." *Id.* at 43.

2. State Coastal Zone Programs

Three varieties of state coastal zone programs that were emerging to meet the requirements of the national act were described in the Comptroller General's report, *supra:* comprehensive legislation like the national act; special purpose legislation such as wetlands and other natural resource protection legislation; and legislation that does not address coastal resources or issues specifically but which is applied in coastal areas. Some of this legislation is modeled on comprehensive state land use control legislation of the type described in Chapter 9. Indeed, Oregon is using its comprehensive state land use control legislation as the means for implementing its state coastal program. *See infra* p. 1238.

We will focus here on a variety of state coastal programs that have been adopted specifically to address coastal concerns. One of the best known of these is the statutory program enacted in California in 1976, and which replaced an earlier coastal zone regulatory program which relied on a permit system to control development in coastal areas. The interim program is described in R. Healy, Land Use and the States 64-102 (1976).

THE CALIFORNIA COASTAL ACT OF 1976

This statute enacts a state coastal program for a coastal zone which generally extends 1,000 yards inland from the mean high tideline of the sea. Cal. Pub. Res. Code § 30103 (Deering Supp. 1977). For this area the statute enacts a detailed set of coastal policies, which were based on a massive, 442-page state coastal plan. These policies provide the basis for the preparation of local coastal elements of local comprehensive plans, which in California are mandated by state legislation. *See supra* p. 75. These plans, along with all local zoning ordinances and other controls implementing the plan, are to be approved by the regional commissions subject to an appeal to the state commission. Once the local coastal plans have been approved, any development in the coastal area must receive a coastal development permit from the local government having jurisdiction. These permits must be consistent with the policies of the local plan, and are appealable to the state commission on a limited basis. Interim controls are also provided for the period prior to the approval of the local coastal plans.

We will concentrate here on the statutory coastal policies. These policies are the heart of the legislation; they provide the basis for local preparation and state approval of the local coastal plans, which in turn provide the basis for the coastal permit program. In reviewing these policies consider whether they are consistent with the findings and policy of the national law; whether and to what extent they differ from the policies implicit in legislation such as the Georgia Marshland Protection Act and the Wisconsin shoreland zoning act; and whether they provide an adequate basis for balancing competing claims to the use of coastal resources.

The statutory coastal policies are first qualified by a statement of basic goals:

> The Legislature further finds and declares that the basic goals of the state for the coastal zone are to:
> (a) Protect, maintain, and, where feasible, enhance and restore the overall quality of the coastal zone environment and its natural and manmade resources.
> (b) Assure orderly, balanced utilization and conservation of coastal zone resources taking into account the social and economic needs of the people of the state.
> (c) Maximize public access to and along the coast and maximize public recreational opportunities in the coastal zone consistent with sound resources conservation principles and constitutionally protected rights of private property owners.
> (d) Assure priority for coastal-dependent development over other development on the coast.
> (e) Encourage state and local initiatives and cooperation in

preparing procedures to implement coordinated planning and development for mutually beneficial uses, including educational uses, in the coastal zone.

§ 3001.5.

From the array of statutory coastal policies it is instructive to select the policy applying generally to new development in the coastal zone:

New development, except as otherwise provided in this division, shall be located within, contiguous with, or in close proximity to, existing developed areas able to accommodate it or, where such areas are not able to accommodate it, in other areas with adequate public services and where it will not have significant adverse effects, either individually or cumulatively, on coastal resources.

§ 30250. Note that this policy does not necessarily require local governments in the coastal zone to provide additional areas for growth and development. One commentator on the plan therefore argues that it is anti-growth. Ellickson, Ticket to Thermidor: A Commentary on the Proposed California Coastal Plan, 46 S. Cal. L. Rev. 715, 724-32 (1976). Ellickson bases his argument, in part, on the point that the state commission actually does not have the power to override restrictive local planning policies. This assertion should be evaluated in light of the permit and plan review and approval procedure provided by the statute. See also the following statutory policy for housing:

Lower cost visitor and recreational facilities and housing opportunities for persons of low and moderate income shall be protected, encouraged, and, where feasible, provided. Developments providing public recreational opportunities are preferred. New housing in the coastal zone shall be developed in conformity with the standards, policies, and goals of [the mandatory local housing elements which must be part of local comprehensive plans].

§ 30213. Additional statutory policies are provided for public access to the coast, recreation, marine environment, land resources and industrial development. Among the policies on land resources are the following:

(a) Environmentally sensitive habitat areas shall be protected against any significant disruption of habitat values, and only uses dependent on such resources shall be allowed in such areas.
(b) Development in areas adjacent to environmentally sensitive habitat areas and parks and recreation areas shall be sited and designed to prevent impacts which would significantly degrade such areas, and shall be compatible with the continuance of such habitat areas.

§ 30240. Wetland areas would apparently be brought within these policies.

The statute then provides:

> Consistent with the basic goals set forth in Section 30001.5, [see *supra*] and except as may be otherwise specifically provided . . ., the policies of this chapter shall constitute the standards by which the adequacy of local coastal programs, . . . and, the permissibility of proposed developments . . . are determined. All public agencies carrying out or supporting activities outside the coastal zone that could have a direct impact on resources within the coastal zone shall consider the effect of such actions on coastal zone resources in order to assure that these policies are achieved.

§ 30200.

Comments: 1. As an example of regulatory legislation with a definite environmental focus, the California coastal law stands in direct contrast to the wetlands and shorelands legislation discussed *supra.* That legislation is directed to the protection of a specific environmental resource, prohibits a circumscribed list of developmental activities, and confers direct regulatory permit authority on a state agency. The California coastal law attempts a comprehensive regulatory program covering the coastal area as an identified coastal resource. It enacts a regulatory program with shared state and local responsibilities based on a local planning effort subject to an extensive list of enumerated statutory coastal policies. The California law thus depends heavily on up-front statutory and local planning policies to govern its development permit process, the plans in turn being subject to review at the regional and state level for compliance with the statutory policies. The effectiveness of this program will depend on how effectively local governments are able to translate the generally stated statutory policies into local coastal plans that provide sufficient direction for the administration of the development permit process.

Of some interest here is the fact that over 90 percent of the applications for development permits were approved under the interim statute which preceded the 1976 law. R. Healy, *supra* at 75. See also Douglas & Petrillo, California's Coast: The Struggle Today — A Plan For Tomorrow (I), 4 Fla. St. L. Rev. 177 (1976). Some fear, as well, that the extensive delegation of power to local governments under the 1976 law will weaken the coastal program. Note, for example, the following provision in the 1976 law dealing with conflicts among statutory coastal policies:

> The legislature . . . declares that in carrying out the provisions of this . . . [law these policy] conflicts be resolved in a manner which on balance is the most protective of significant coastal resources. In this context, the Legislature declares that broader policies which, for example, serve to concentrate development in close

proximity to urban and employment centers may be more protective, overall, than specific wildlife habitat and other similar resource policies.

§ 30007.5. How is this legislative direction to be translated into local coastal plans? If this legislative direction is simply copied verbatim into local plans, how should it be applied? For a series of articles on the California plan see 49 S. Cal. L. Rev. 710-83 (1976).

2. The Comptroller General's report, *supra,* described several other approaches states were taking to meet the requirements of the national CZMA. Examples from Washington and Michigan follow.

Washington

Washington's coastal zone management program is . . . primarily procedural. It is based on existing special-purpose legislation and is a cooperative effort between local governments and the State department of ecology. Local governments, including all counties and incorporated cities bordering the Pacific Ocean or Puget Sound, must develop "master programs" — comprehensive plans that establish goals, policies, regulations, and standards for coastal resource use control. Within its jurisdiction, each local master plan specifies permissible "environments," ranging from urban areas to shorelands to be preserved in their natural state. Each plan also regulates resource use within these designated environments. Criteria for regulating resource uses stem from existing legislation, natural resource inventories, and guidelines developed by the department of ecology. On the basis of consistency with the State act and State guidelines, the department approves local master plans and, on the basis of these plans, it develops an overall State management program.

Under Washington law, coastal zone land and water uses are controlled through a permit system which deals with coastal issues as they arise. This system, administered by local governments subject to the department of ecology's appellate review, requires a permit for developments valued at $1,000 or more on marine water areas, associated wetlands, and land within 200 feet of the ordinary high water mark. It provides a 30-day review period in which any aggrieved party can appeal a local action. Although subject to continued refinement, Washington's permit system has been in effect since June 1, 1971.

. . . .

Michigan

Michigan's approach to coastal zone management planning is . . . procedural, based on existing special-purpose legislation. It is concerned with developing standards to measure proposed coastal resource uses on a case-by-case basis. Michigan also stresses identifying areas of particular concern. Like Washington, regulatory machinery already exists in Michigan, especially for high-risk erosion areas, flood risk areas, and environmental areas important to preserving and maintaining fish and wildlife. Michigan intends to coordinate with other existing authorities to meet CZMA's requirements.

. . . Although the State department of natural resources is responsible for managing coastal zone planning, 10 regional planning councils assist by

— formulating local and regional goals and objectives,
— developing information on local government regulatory
— practices and development programs,
— coordinating shoreland planning and other ongoing planning programs.
— assisting in public information and local government participation,
— providing a review and advisory function, and
— participating in final program formulation.

Id. at 16-18. For discussion of the Washington legislation see Crooks, The Washington Shoreline Management Act of 1971, 49 Wash. L. Rev. 423 (1974). On the national and state coastal zone programs *see generally* D. Mandelker, Environmental and Land Controls Legislation, ch. VI (1976).

3. Most courts have so far had little difficulty with the constitutionality of state coastal zone legislation. When the California Supreme Court was asked to pass on the constitutionality of the interim coastal law they upheld it with little difficulty as an interim control measure. *State v. Superior Court,* 524 P.2d 1281 (Cal. 1974). See also *Toms River Affiliates v. Department of Environmental Protection,* 355 A.2d 679 (N.J. Super.), *cert. denied,* 364 A.2d 1077 (N.J. 1976), summarily dismissing a claim that a denial of a permit for a condominium was an unconstitutional taking under the New Jersey coastal law. The court noted that alternative uses for the land were available.

In *State v. Pacesetter Constr. Co.,* 571 P.2d 196 (Wash. 1977), the Washington Supreme Court considered the constitutionality of a development restriction imposed by the Shoreline Management Act. In this case a challenge was brought to a provision of the Act imposing a 35-foot height restriction on building improvements in shoreline areas. The court upheld the restriction, interpreting its *Maple Leaf* case, *supra,* which upheld a state-imposed floodplain regulation, as having adopted a balancing approach to police power taking problems. The court also added:

> The 35 foot maximum height limitations on building improvements in wetland areas . . . are restrictions not only for the benefit of Pacesetter's neighbors but also for the benefit of Pacesetter itself and its potential grantees, serving to protect the view from Pacesetter's property. For all the record shows, the reciprocal protection afforded Pacesetter may substantially diminish or completely offset whatever diminution in value Pacesetter might otherwise sustain by being compelled to comply. . . .

Id. at 200.

E. AIR AND WATER QUALITY PROGRAMS

In addition to the National Environmental Policy Act and the National Coastal Zone Management Act, Congress has enacted two major statutory programs for the control of air and water pollution.

Unlike NEPA, which requires the preparation of an environmental impact statement in which environmental impacts are considered and evaluated by the decision-making agency, the air and water quality acts contain or authorize standards which determine the level of pollution permissible in the air and water. These statutes rely primarily on the control of air pollution emissions and water effluent discharges to achieve and maintain the national air and water quality standards. But land use controls and air and water quality control measures with land use implications form an important part of the air and water quality programs. It is these land use control elements that are the focus of this section.

Structure of the Air and Water Quality Programs

Understanding the role of land use controls in the air and water quality programs first requires an understanding of their basic structure at the national level. Both the air and water quality programs have as their main statutory objective the attainment of statutory air and water quality standards, and these standards must be met within time periods prescribed by the legislation. The National Ambient Air Quality Standards (NAAQS) are the focus of the air quality legislation, which requires that these standards both be attained and maintained. These standards are set nationally by the Environmental Protection Agency (EPA), the federal agency charged with the administration of the air and water quality legislation. For each pollutant covered by the act, the air quality standards limit the amount of pollution allowable in the air over specified periods of time. There are two sets of standards. Primary standards are established to protect the public health while secondary standards are established to protect the public welfare. The primary standards are the more stringent. These standards must be achieved in air quality control regions designated throughout the country. Each major city or metropolitan area is generally included in a single region.

The NAAQS apply to stationary sources of pollution, such as industrial plants and power plants, but are not directly enforced against these sources. For new stationary sources of pollution the act authorizes EPA to set uniform national performance standards that limit the amount of pollution emitted by each source during the production process. Compliance with these performance standards is enforced at the state level. Emissions from existing stationary sources of pollution are regulated by the states through a state implementation plan (SIP), which sets forth the state's air pollution control strategy. A related but separate set of statutory performance requirements is applicable to air pollution generated by motor vehicles, and requires a gradual reduction in the amount of pollution they generate.

Water quality standards are also imposed in the water quality program mandated by the Federal Water Pollution Control Act, and this legislation also provides controls over effluent discharges from water pollution sources. These controls, along with other components of the program, are intended to achieve a national clean water goal, initially specified to be attained in 1983. Controls over effluent discharges from water pollution sources, such as industrial plants and public wastewater treatment plants, are enforced through a permit system. This system is initially to be administered at the federal level but will gradually be transferred to the states. Another important component of the water quality legislation is the massive program of federal matching grants for the construction of public wastewater treatment works, which is intended to expand and upgrade treatment facilities.

The air and water quality programs are thus based on very different regulatory principles than conventional land use controls, which implement community-wide land use policies intended to produce optimal land development patterns. Air and water quality controls are directed solely to the reduction of emissions from pollution sources, and the achievement of national air and water quality standards and goals.

A final distinction between the air and water quality programs and more conventional land use controls lies in the role accorded the planning function. A state implementation plan is required in the air quality program, but it is a plan only in the sense that it plans for the implementation and enforcement of air quality standards at the state level. A similar state program is required in the federal water quality legislation. These plans and programs are not traditional land use plans. Major planning efforts that include land use planning have also been required in the air and water quality programs, but the linkages between these planning efforts and the state implementation and enforcement programs are not yet fully developed.

Land Use Controls in Air and Water Quality Programs

The air and water quality programs have certain distinctive impacts on land use and development that must be kept in mind when the potential for land use controls in these programs is evaluated. These programs have important short-run consequences for land use. As an example, emission and effluent controls imposed on polluters may often influence the location of stationary pollution sources and will have an immediate and short-run impact on land use patterns. In addition, both programs but especially the water quality program have long-range planning and control elements that affect land development and are intended to achieve and maintain air and water quality over an extended period of time. The most important example is the regional water quality planning and control program contained in the water quality act.

These programs also have both direct and indirect impacts on land use. The extensive permit controls placed on new sources of pollution are an example of a control with a direct effect on land use. Land use and development are also affected indirectly. Decisions on major sources of pollution, such as power plants, will have an indirect effect on the location of new and related development, such as residential development, which is not directly controlled under the air and water quality programs.

It is also necessary to distinguish the geographic levels at which land use controls in these programs can be imposed. One possibility is to adjust the growth and development patterns of urban regions so that pollution will be minimized. For clues on how this might be done see Chapter 1, *supra* p. 724. Next, controls may be placed both on polluters and receptors. Sources that emit and which are sensitive to pollution can be located so that pollution impacts are minimized. An example would be the location of industrial sources of pollution downwind rather than upwind in metropolitan areas. Finally, adjustments can be made in site planning to take account of pollution problems. An example is the construction of retention ponds in residential developments to hold back stormwater during storms. We will focus here on regional and source control strategies that have been adopted under this legislation.

Comments: The national air pollution legislation is known as the Clean Air Act and may be found at 42 U.S.C. § 7401 *et seq.* (Supp. 1977). For discussion see W. Rodgers, Environmental Law, ch. III (1977). The national water pollution legislation is known as the Federal Water Pollution Control Act and may be found at 33 U.S.C. § 1251 *et seq.* (1976), as amended. For discussion see W. Rodgers, *supra* ch. IV. Statutory references will be made to the section numbers of each act as they appeared in the original legislation, as amended. The water quality legislation may also be referred to as the Clean Water Act.

1. Air Quality

Two major components of the air quality program affect the nature of the land use controls employed in that program. One is the Air Quality Control Region (AQCR), see § 107, which is the geographic area within which the air quality standards must be met within each state. The regional strategies in the air quality program are tied to a great extent to these regions. The other is the State Implementation Plan (SIP), see § 110. This plan is the heart of the implementation program required under the air quality legislation, and contains the statute's land use controls.

At first, the air quality statute contained a provision in the section requiring state implementation plans that authorized "land-use . . . controls" in these plans "as may be necessary" to attain and maintain the air quality standards. See Mandelker & Rothschild, The Role of Land-Use Controls in Combating Air Pollution Under the Clean Air Act of 1970, 3 Ecology L.Q. 235 (1973). This broad mandate has now been withdrawn by Congress. The statute now authorizes "such other measures as may be necessary to insure attainment and maintenance of . . . [the air quality standards], including, but not limited to, transportation controls, air quality maintenance plans, and preconstruction review of direct sources of air pollution. . . ." § 110(a)(2)(B). The conference report on the legislation indicates that no other land use controls may be included in state implementation plans. H.R. Rep. No. 564, 95th Cong., 1st Sess. 127 (1977).

This statutory listing is incomplete. Other controls, such as specifically authorized controls to prevent the degradation of air quality when it is better than national standards require, can also be classified as land use controls. The land use controls authorized by the Clean Air Act can conveniently be divided into three categories: controls applicable on a regional basis; controls applicable to sources of pollution; and controls imposed in transportation control plans. Each will be discussed in turn.

a. *Area Controls*

While initially the Clean Air Act did not differentiate among Air Quality Control Regions, it soon became apparent that different strategies would have to be developed for these regions depending on their progress in meeting air quality standards. Roughly, the regions can be divided into those in which the standards have not been met, the nonattainment areas, and those in which the standards have been or will be met but which require additional measures to maintain air quality, the maintenance areas. In addition, there are areas, usually outside the metropolitan Air Quality Control Regions, in which the air is better than what the national standards require — the nondegradation areas. Controls either explicitly or implicitly containing land use strategies have now been adopted for each of these areas.

Nonattainment areas. Understanding the statutory controls applicable in these areas requires that a distinction be made between the emission controls applied to existing and to new stationary sources. Existing source controls are generally contained in the state implementation plans, while new source emissions are controlled by national performance standards adopted by EPA, § 111. However, no new source may be approved if, after June 30, 1979:

> the emissions from such facility will cause or contribute to concentrations of any pollutant for which a national ambient air quality standard is exceeded in such [nonattainment] area, unless, as of the time of application for a permit . . ., such [state implementation] plan meets the requirements [of the statute relating to nonattainment area plans.]

§ 110(a)(2)(I).

This requirement presents a problem. Since air quality standards for most pollutants will usually be exceeded in nonattainment areas, how can any new sources of pollution locate in these areas? If new sources will not be allowed, how can any new growth occur in these areas? The Act now contains an emission offset policy which attempts to handle this problem. The Act first provides that the plan for a nonattainment area shall: "expressly identify and quantify the emissions, if any, of any such pollutant which will be allowed to result from the construction and operation of major new or modified stationary sources for each such [nonattainment] area." § 172(b)(5). The statute then requires a permit program:

> The permit program . . . shall provide that permits to construct and operate may be issued if —
> (1) the permitting agency determines that —
> (A) by the time the facility is to commence operation, total allowable emissions from existing sources in the [air quality control] region, from new sources which are not major emitting facilities, and from the proposed facility will be sufficiently less than total emissions from existing sources allowed under the implementation plan prior to the application for such permit to construct or modify so as . . . [generally, to attain the air quality standards by 1982.]
> (B) that emissions of such pollutant resulting from the proposed new or modified major stationary source will not cause or contribute to emissions levels which exceed the allowance permitted for such pollutant for such area from new or modified major stationary sources under section 172 (b);
> (2) the proposed source is required to comply with the lowest achievable emission rate; . . .

§ 173.

Now assume that a major industrial facility wishes to locate in a nonattainment area. What must it show in order to secure a permit under the statute? Does the statute contemplate an agreement between this source and existing sources under which emission reductions by existing sources may be credited to the new source, so that the new source may locate in the nonattainment area if these reductions are sufficient to meet the statutory requirements? How would this offset be negotiated? Is a transfer of emission rights contemplated?

Air quality maintenance areas. Plans for these areas are explicitly contemplated by the land use controls section of the statute, *supra.* Grants are also authorized for air quality maintenance plans, § 175. The air quality maintenance planning process thus appears to be left for implementation to regulations adopted by EPA, and first published after a federal Court of Appeals held the initial maintenance strategies inadequate, *NRDC v. EPA*, 475 F.2d 968 (D.C. Cir. 1973). The following excerpt contains a brief description of EPA air quality maintenance planning policy.

D. MANDELKER, ENVIRONMENTAL AND LAND CONTROLS LEGISLATION 187-88 (1976)

Since air quality maintenance problems arise primarily from the impact that new growth and development can be expected to have on pollution levels, the air quality maintenance regulations adopted by EPA rely on an area-wide air quality maintenance planning effort as the principal tool for assuring the maintenance of air quality standards once they are achieved. Regulations for air quality maintenance area planning require the states to identify and EPA to confirm those areas within any state which, "due to current air quality and/or projected growth rate" may have some potential for exceeding any national air quality standard within the succeeding 10-year period. States are then to conduct the necessary analysis to determine whether or not future growth and development will lead to a violation of the national standards. They must then submit an air quality maintenance plan that contains the necessary revisions to the state's control strategy and such other measures as are necessary to maintain the national standards over a period of time to be specified by EPA.

While conceptually simple in its design, air quality maintenance planning raises a host of institutional and legal issues that must be resolved if it is to be fully effective, expecially as EPA permits though it does not require the use of local and other land development control powers to implement the air quality maintenance plan. Critical here are the relationships between air quality maintenance planning and other planning programs that affect the air quality maintenance problem, such as the related land use, transportation, and coastal zone planning that is carried out with federal financial assistance. Of equal importance is the role of local governments and other sub-state agencies in the administration of the implementation phase of the air quality maintenance plan.

EPA has decided not to use the leverage implicit in the Clean Air Act to rationalize all local and regional planning and plan implementation programs within the framework of the air quality maintenance planning process. It has relied instead on the ability of the state air pollution control agencies to secure the necessary accommodation between air quality maintenance planning and related planning programs through the voluntary coordination of air quality maintenance planning with other planning programs. Furthermore, not all of the legal measures required to implement the air quality maintenance plan need be adopted and enforced by the air pollution control agencies, but may be carried out by local governments within the air quality maintenance area. Nevertheless, the state air pollution control agency necessarily remains responsible for the implementation of the plan should other agencies default in their responsibilities. EPA has therefore avoided a direct confrontation on the difficult and necessary decisions that will have to be made in the restructuring of land development controls, and institutional arrangements for their implementation, that air quality maintenance planning requires.

Prevention of significant deterioration (nondegradation). In contrast with air quality maintenance planning, an explicit state permit program is provided for the regulation of major new and modified stationary sources in so-called nondegradation areas — those areas of the state in which the air is cleaner than the national air quality standards require. Like many other land use strategies in the Clean Air Act, the nondegradation policy was a response to a court decree. In a brief and cryptic opinion, a federal district court interpreted one of the purposes of the Act — "to protect and enhance the quality of the Nation's air resources," § 101(b)(1) — to require a policy of nondegradation. *Sierra Club v. Ruckelshaus,* 344 F. Supp. 253 (D.D.C.), *aff'd per curiam,* 4. ERC 1815 (D.C. Cir. 1972), *aff'd by an equally divided Court, sub. nom. Fri v. Sierra Club,* 412 U.S. 541 (1973). The absence of written opinions in the decisions affirming the district court decision left EPA short of guidance for a nondegradation policy, except for a statement in the final decree of the district court. That decree enjoined EPA to review state implementation plans "to insure that ... [they do] not permit significant deterioration of existing air quality in any portion of any state where the existing air quality is better than one or more of the secondary [air quality] standards promulgated by the Administrator [of EPA]." *Sierra Club v. Ruckelshaus,* No. 1031-72 (D.D.C., filed May 30, 1972).

It was this mandate to prevent "significant" deterioration of air quality that guided EPA in the preparation of regulations implementing the court order. The structure of these regulations, and a brief description of the policy behind them, is indicated in an excerpt from the following case, which approved the regulations.

SIERRA CLUB v. ENVIRONMENTAL PROTECTION AGENCY

District of Columbia Court of Appeals
540 F.2d 1114 (1976), *cert. denied,* 430 U.S. 959 (1977)

... [T]he Administrator reviewed and disapproved all state plans insofar as they failed to provide for prevention of significant deterioration.... Four alternative sets of regulations were proposed for public comment, in an effort to determine what meaning to give the concept of "significant deterioration." [7] Final regulations were [then] published....

---

[7] 38 Fed.Reg. 18986 (July 16, 1973). In proposing alternative solutions, EPA posed for public debate the problem of how significant deterioration was to be defined:

> The basis for preventing significant deterioration ... lies in a desire to protect aesthetic, scenic, and recreational values, particularly in rural areas, and in concern that some air pollutants may have adverse effects that have not been documented in such a way as to permit their consideration in the formulation of national ambient air quality scientific data on the kind and extent of adverse effect of air pollution levels below the secondary standards, significant deterioration must necessarily be defined without a direct quantitative relationship to specific adverse effects on public health and welfare.
>
> ....
>
> The relative significance of air quality versus economic growth may be a variable dependent upon regional conditions. For example, relatively minor deterioration of the aesthetic quality of the air may be very significant in a recreational area in which great pride (and economic development) is derived from the "clean air." Conversely, in areas with severe unemployment and little recreational value, the same level of deterioration might very well be considered "insignificant" in comparison to the favorable impact of new industrial growth with resultant employment and other economic opportunities. Accordingly, the definition of what constitutes significant deterioration must be accomplished in a manner to minimize the imposition of inequitable regulations on different segments of the Nation.

Id. at 18987, 18988.

III. THE REGULATIONS

In promulgating final regulations EPA was concerned primarily with the meaning of "significant deterioration." As it stated in the discussion preceding the new regulations:

> Most of the comments implicitly recognized that there is a need to develop resources in presently clean areas of the country, and that significant deterioration regulations should not preclude all growth, but should ensure that growth occurs in an environmentally acceptable manner. However, there are some areas, such as national parks, where any deterioration would probably be viewed as significant. A single nationwide deterioration increment would not be able to accommodate these two situations.

39 Fed.Reg. at 42520. The solution was to prescribe, for those areas with air cleaner than the national standards, three classes of allowable total increments above the levels of particulate matter and sulfur dioxide pollution as of January 1, 1975, with the intention that each area could determine which class would prevent significant deterioration of its air in light of the area's air quality and social and economic needs and objectives:

> Class I applie[s] to areas in which practically any change in air quality would be considered significant; Class II applie[s] to areas in which deterioration normally accompanying moderate well-controlled growth would be considered insignificant; and Class III applie[s] to those areas in which deterioration up to the national standards would be considered insignificant.
>
>   . . . .
>
> Since the consideration of "air quality factors" alone essentially leads to an arbitrary definition of what is "significant," this term only has meaning when the economic and social implications are analyzed and considered. Therefore, the Administrator believes that it is most important to recognize and consider these implications, since the consideration of air quality factors alone provides no basis for selecting one deterioration increment over another.

Comments: 1. The 1977 amendments to the Clean Air Act generally codified the EPA nondegradation policy, although the air quality increments allowable in the three classes were reduced and the lowest of either the national primary or secondary standard adopted as a maximum on the allowable increment. § 163. However, the air quality standard may not be reached if the allowable statutory increment is lower. Enforcement of the nondegradation policy is implemented through preconstruction review of major stationary pollution sources including 28 categories of major stationary sources designated in the act. § 165. Other pollutants in addition to the two mentioned in the *Sierra Club* opinion will also eventually be brought within the program. § 166.

The key to the implementation of the nondegradation requirement as a land use control strategy is the procedure for the redesignation of nondegradation areas. Under the statute, all nondegradation areas identified in a state, see § 107(d)(1)(D)(E), are initially classified as Class II areas except for major national parks and wilderness areas, which are classified as Class I. § 162. The statute then provides the following procedure for the redesignation of areas (except for federal lands) and which cover a redesignation to Class III (this class provides the maximum allowable pollution increment and serves as the growth and development area under the nondegradation policy):

> § 164(b)(1)(A). Prior to redesignation of any area under this part, notice shall be afforded and public hearings shall be conducted.... Prior to any such public hearing a satisfactory description and analysis of the health, environmental, economic, social, and energy effects of the proposed redesignation shall be prepared and made available for public inspection....
>
> . . . .
>
> (2) The Administrator [of EPA] may disapprove the redesignation of any area only if he finds, after notice and opportunity for public hearing, that such redesignation does not meet the procedural requirements of this section....

The underlying policy behind this approach, insofar as it affects the federal role in a nondegradation policy, is indicated by the following comment from the House of Representatives committee report:

> The committee purposely chose not to dictate a Federal response to balancing sometimes conflicting goals. It purposely chose not to dictate what State and local decisions on air quality deterioration must be. Maximum flexibility and State discretion are the bases of the committee's approach. The committee carefully balanced State and national interests by providing for a fair and open process in which State and local governments and the people they represent will be free to carry out the reasoned weighing of environmental and economic goals and needs.

H.R. Rep. No. 294, 95th Cong., 1st Sess. 146 (1977).

2. Is the nondegradation policy a land use control? Consider the following comments by the Senate committee report on the 1976 version of the nondegradation requirement, which was generally similar to the requirement as enacted in 1977:

> Some critics have charged that some proposals for preventing significant deterioration would constitute a Federal land use policy based entirely on the provisions of the Clean Air Act. The Committee believes the Clean Air Act must not become a Federal land use control program. For this reason, the Committee's proposal assures that the States have sole air quality classification authority.... (In addition all pre-construction review and permit requirements are to be carried out through State programs.)

Therefore, there can be no doubt whatsoever that the Committee's proposal does not constitute Federal land use control. . . . Since the Committee bill allows each State to control air quality over *all* State and private lands, and over *nearly all* Federal lands, it clearly corrects this shortcoming in the existing regulations.

Moreover, the bill in question only regulates air quality and emissions, not land use, although the Committee encourages the States to husband carefully their limited clean air resources — one of the purposes of this section. Thus, EPA may not require States to meet requirements of this section by imposing land use controls. Nor may funds be withheld from States to induce them to adopt and implement land use controls. This does not differ from existing laws. Of course, air quality is not the only, let alone the decisive, factor in influencing a State's growth decisions. And though air quality and emission requirements must be met, they are merely one of many sets of factors the State may wish to consider. In determining whether to reclassify an area, States are directed by the bill to prepare analyses not only of health and environmental impacts, but also of economic, energy, and social impacts. These analyses are to be available to the public so that the hearings can be a forum for consideration of economic, energy, and environmental factors.

S. Rep. No. 1175, 94th Cong., 2d Sess. 129 (1976).

3. The nondegradation policy does not really prevent degradation at all. As structured by Congress, and aptly named "Prevention of Significant Deterioration of Air Quality," the classification system as modified by the redesignation process, is a national growth policy applied through the Clean Air Act, the Senate committee report notwithstanding.

Consider the following problem: a major new industrial plant wishes to locate in the State of Metro. It has several options. It can locate in one of the big cities, which are all in nonattainment areas, but only if it can negotiate emission offsets with existing polluters. This route is troublesome, especially as the industrial plant may have to make payments for emission control improvements to existing polluters in order to get them to agree to emission reductions. It could locate in an air quality maintenence area, except that the allowable growth increments in the one maintenance area located in the state are not sufficient to allow it.

That leaves the nondegradation areas. In the Class I and Class II areas in the state the allowable pollution increments are not sufficient. There is one Class III area in which the pollution increment is sufficient but it is not conveniently located. That means that the industrial plant must seek the redesignation of an existing Class II area to a Class III area. If it is successful in so doing, its construction will have significant growth impacts since new roads and other public facilities will have to be provided, as well as housing and related commercial uses. In short, the application of the nondegradation requirement can have substantial growth implications for the state.

4. In the above example, how big or how small may a redesignated Class III area be? Note the following comment from H.R. Rep. No. 294, *supra* at 147:

> For instance, if a State wished to designate its entire area as class III, and the area contains no Federal lands . . . the State could do

so. Conversely, if it wished to designate some parts class I and retain some class II areas, it may draw classification boundaries in any way it chooses — by entire air quality control regions, along county lines, or even along smaller subcounty lines.

5. How will the nondegradation policy relate to a state coastal zone management program such as the program required by the California act, *supra* p. 1149? Under that act, a state coastal permit is required if the plant locates in a coastal zone. However, since the National Coastal Zone Management Act, *supra* p. 1141, makes requirements imposed under the Clean Air Act binding on state coastal zone programs, the plant cannot be built unless a permit is approved under the state's nondegradation policy. If a nondegradation permit is issued, is a coastal permit still required? Note that the substantive decision on the nondegradation permit is in the hands of the state. How can a state coordinate these two programs?

6. The constitutionality of the nondegradation regulations adopted by EPA was upheld in *Sierra Club v. EPA, supra* p. 1161, in the following language:

> We find the arguments challenging the constitutionality of the nondeterioration regulations to be insubstantial. Regulation of air pollution clearly is within the power of the federal government under the commerce clause, and we can see no basis on which to distinguish deterioration of air cleaner than national standards from pollution in other contexts. Nor do we agree that the regulations bear no rational relationship to protection of public health and welfare and therefore violate the due process clause of the Fifth Amendment. There is a rational relationship between air quality deterioration and the public health and welfare, and there is a proper legislative purpose in prevention of significant deterioration of air quality. Neither can the regulations be construed as an unconstitutional "taking" under the Fifth Amendment, any more than existing emission control regulations represent such a "taking." The use of private land certainly is limited, but the limitation is not so extreme as to represent an appropriation of the land.

Id. at 1139-40.

b. Source Controls

Preconstruction review. As noted earlier, the Clean Air Act contains a provision for the preconstruction review of new stationary sources of pollution subject to the national emission limitation standards imposed under § 111 of the Act. This preconstruction review process must:

> provide for adequate authority to prevent the construction or modification of any new [stationary] source to which a standard of performance under section 111 will apply at any location which the State determines will prevent the attainment or maintenance within any air quality control region (or portion

thereof) within such State of a national ambient air quality primary or secondary standard. . . .

§ 110(a)(4).

This requirement clearly is a land use control. It sweeps more widely than nondegradation because it applies to all new stationary sources, and it is applicable whenever a national air quality standard is threatened. Few court decisions have so far considered state preconstruction review procedures, and they have upheld these procedures in state plans even though not stated with the greatest clarity. *E.g., NRDC v. EPA,* 507 F.2d 905, 918 (9th Cir. 1974). There is evidence, however, that the states seldom use their preconstruction review procedures to deny approval of a new source at the location at which it is to be built. Review appears to be confined to the controls to be used to reduce emissions.

Indirect sources. One of the most revolutionary EPA land use control strategies was its indirect source review procedures. These procedures were adopted by EPA as part of the settlement arising out of the decision requiring better initiatives for air quality maintenance. They were an attempt to influence pollution levels from motor vehicles by controlling the location of new developments that attract vehicle traffic, and in this way indirectly contribute to air pollution from this source.

As applied to private developments, this land use control strategy was simple. First, practically all private developments for commercial, industrial and residential use were brought under the review procedures including shopping centers, industrial parks, and apartment buildings but excluding single-family residential subdivisions. Next, a threshold criterion was applied, and for administrative convenience this criterion was based on the size of parking facilities associated with the development. If the development included associated parking facilities over a certain size it was included for review. Because the minimum size threshold was set fairly high, many small developments were excluded and so the indirect source review procedure emerged as a land use control measure applicable to major developments.

Finally, as in many of Clean Air Act land use control measures, the test for the review of an indirect source was whether it would cause or exacerbate the violation of a national air quality standard. In the case of private developments qualifying as indirect sources the applicable standard was the standard for carbon monoxide, which is one of the principal pollutants emitted by motor vehicles. The limitation of indirect source review to the control of carbon monoxide emissions by motor vehicles attracted to major private developments underscores its limited objectives. This pollutant appears in concentration whenever motor vehicle traffic is heavily congested, producing carbon monoxide build-up because of slower speeds and increased idling time, but dissipates easily over the surrounding area to a level at which no harmful health effects occur. The expectation was that design or modest location changes of indirect sources subject to review would avoid impermissible carbon monoxide concentrations without requiring disapproval of the development.

Major highways and airport projects were also made subject to the indirect source review procedures, and this review covered other pollutants that are emitted by motor vehicles besides carbon monoxide. The cutoff point was high, so that only a relatively few major projects would have been reviewed. That concession did not prevent outcries from the Federal Highway Agency, which is charged with responsibility for the highway program and which objected to EPA's intrusion into its domain. The problem of coordination was complicated because the federal highway act contains a provision requiring all federally funded highways to be consistent with state air quality implementation plans. 23 U.S.C. § 109(j) (1976). Presently, federal highway regulations place the determination of consistency under this provision with the Federal Highway Agency. 23 C.F.R. § 770.205(b)(7) (1977). For discussion of the EPA indirect source review regulations see Comment, The Control of Complex Emissions Sources — A Step Toward Land Use Planning, 4 Ecology L.Q. 693 (1975).

Opposition to the indirect source review procedures, and Congressional prohibition of related parking management regulations, finally led to EPA suspension of the indirect source regulations in 1974. Their fate was reviewed during subsequent consideration of amendments to the Clean Air Act, and Congress finally resolved their place in the air quality programs in the following manner:

> § 110(a)(5)(A)(i) Any State may include in a State implementation plan, but the Administrator may not require as a condition of approval such plan under this section, any indirect source review program. The Administrator may approve and enforce, as part of an applicable implementation plan, an indirect source review program which the State chooses to adopt and submit as part of its plan.
>
> (B) The Administrator shall have the authority to promulgate, implement and enforce regulations ... respecting indirect source review programs which apply only to federally assisted highways, airports, and other major federally assisted indirect sources and federally owned or operated indirect sources.
>
> (C) For purposes of this paragraph, the term "indirect source" means a facility, building, structure, installation, real property,

road, or highway which attracts, or may attract, mobile sources of pollution. Such term includes parking lots, parking garages, and other facilities subject to any measure for management of parking supply . . . including regulation of existing off-street parking but such term does not include new or existing on-street parking. Direct emissions sources or facilities at, within, or associated with, any indirect source shall not be deemed indirect sources for the purpose of the paragraph.

(D) For purposes of this section the term "indirect source review program" means the facility-by-facility preconstruction or premodification review of indirect sources of air pollution, including such measures as are necessary to assure, or assist in assuring, that a new or modified indirect source will not attract mobile sources of air pollution, the emissions from which would cause or contribute to air pollution concentrations —

(i) exceeding any national primary ambient air quality standard for a mobile source-related air pollutant after the primary standard attainment date, or

(ii) preventing maintenance of any such standard after such date.

The effect of the amendment is to retain EPA's authority to adopt indirect source regulations for federal highways and airports and other federal sources, but to delegate to the states, this time entirely within their discretion, the authority to adopt indirect source review programs as they choose. Does the statute confer any authority on EPA to review the content of state indirect source control programs? Note the definition of an "indirect source review program" in paragraph (D). Does it authorize a program broader than the program earlier adopted in the EPA regulations? Since the decision to adopt the program rests with the states, why is this definition necessary?

The indirect source review program authorized by this section should be compared with the comparable state program for the review of developments of regional impact as authorized by the American Law Institute's Model Land Development Code, see *infra* p. 1244. The criteria for developments of regional impact are to some extent similar to the criteria for designating indirect sources. How would a state coordinate these two programs consistent with a provision in a Clean Air Act preempting any less stringent state pollution controls?

Note also that the definition of indirect source excludes on-street parking. Regulation of on-street parking is one of the strategies contemplated in the transportation control programs authorized by the Clean Air Act, which are considered next.

c. Transportation Control Plans

We have so far been considering Title I of the Clean Air Act, which provides a program for the control of stationary sources of pollution.

Title II of the Act contains a complementary program for the control of pollutants from motor vehicles. Essentially, this program requires improvements in the emission control capability of motor vehicle engines to achieve stated reductions in the amount of pollutants emitted by these engines over a stated period of time.

Alternatively, a reduction in emissions from motor vehicles can be achieved indirectly, through controls over motor vehicle use aimed at reducing Vehicle Miles Traveled (VMT). The indirect source review strategy discussed earlier is one such form of indirect control. Another is the Transportation Control Plan (TCP), a strategy explicitly authorized by the statute for state implementation plans, and which contains a variety of transportation controls aimed at reducing motor vehicle use. The following article indicates the nature of the strategies adopted in Transportation Control Plans.

SCHOFER, TRANSPORTATION POLICY AND AIR QUALITY MANAGEMENT: SOME CURRENT PERSPECTIVES IN PROCEEDINGS OF THE NATIONAL CONFERENCE ON LAND USE PLANNING, TRANSPORTATION PLANNING, AND AIR QUALITY MANAGEMENT 27-30 (1975)

Perhaps there is no easier way to begin to understand the dimensions of the problem at hand than to examine the transportation control strategies proposed for meeting air quality implementation requirements in the nearly 40 urban areas which recently faced the Federally-established mandate to respond to their own critical air quality problems. A review of these implementation plans shows that three classes of strategies are typically considered: reductions in vehicle emissions through such mechanisms as technological change, improved maintenance standards, and vehicle inspections; improvements in traffic flow characteristics; and reduction in the vehicle miles of travel in the urban areas. The first class of strategies can make — and is making — significant contributions to relieving the problem at hand. Traffic-flow improvements can also have great promise, and tend to be welcomed even by trip-makers who care little about air quality. It is apparent, however, that what sets these problem regions apart from the rest of the nation is the need to reduce vehicle miles of travel in order to meet ambient air quality standards.

. . . .

A more promising, but still long-term approach to reducing the demand for travel is to restructure urban land use. Simulation studies have shown that the clustering of land uses — particularly employment — can achieve reductions in travel on the order of 25 percent or more, with concomitant reductions in air pollution and energy consumption. These reductions promise to be larger than those obtainable through limitations in the use of the auto. Yet, historically we have approached land use development in the United States through free-market processes, with some application of directed investments in urban infrastructure to guide spatial trends. This leaves us with a weak set of control strategies producing impacts which have a high degree of uncertainty, and which require long time periods to obtain. On this note, it is interesting to observe that many of the critical region implementation plans discuss the merits of land use control, but none seem to adopt this approach to solving the air quality problem. This is perhaps the most realistic component of such plans.

The preferred strategy, as reflected in the implementation plans, is to bring about modal shifts, primarily from the low-level-of-occupancy automobile to various forms of public transit, as well as to carpooling, which for all practical purposes is a different mode from one driver in one car. . . .

Transit improvement strategies being considered in the implementation plans focus primarily on perturbation of existing bus operations, although some promise is held in the long term for new fixed-guideway rapid transit. Short-term changes considered include expanded bus service, express service, express services on exclusive lanes, improved connectivity of existing transit services, provision of fringe parking, and price reductions. Auto disincentives considered include reduced parking availability in CBD's, increased parking prices, auto-free zones and streets which reduce capacity, vehicle use and fuel taxes, and, in the extreme, gasoline rationing.

What are the ramifications of such changes? Perhaps the principal need for concern derives from the simple fact that no one really knows. In the narrowest sense, we cannot develop a definitive information base for deciding, with a reasonable level of confidence, what effect any one of these component strategies will have on urban travel and the desired modal shift. More broadly, the techniques of demand analysis which are available, and the smaller set which has been applied in the development of implementation plans, do not permit us to understand the travel behavior implications of collections of strategies applied together. We have relied on partial equilibrium approaches to determining the aggregate effects of groups of control methods, all the while stating that, of course, we cannot really add up the expected individual effects.

Perhaps most important, we have not yet faced the more serious, long-term problem: what will these proposed changes in the allocation of transportation services within a region, in terms of service levels and price by mode and area, do to accessibility, mobility, land values, land use, and the quality of urban life? While the specific answers to these questions for a particular area are not known and may not be knowable, it seems relatively likely that these control strategies threaten — or promise — to bring about major shifts in the social and economic balance of power. If this is the case, legislation alone will not solve the problem.

Comments: A fragmented set of provisions for transportation control plans emerged in the 1977 amendments to the Clean Air Act, derived from a more explicit provision contained in the Senate-passed bill. The Act, though indirectly, requires the preparation of a transportation control plan "for each [air quality control] region in which the national primary standard for carbon monoxide or photochemical oxidants [8] will not be attained by July 1, 1979." § 174(a). These are two of the pollutants emitted by motor vehicles. Because these pollutants are controlled principally by the motor vehicle emission control program, the inference is that transportation control plans are required in regions in which that program cannot achieve the emission reductions necessary to meet national air quality standards. At the time the 1977 amendments were passed, transportation control plans were required in 31 major metropolitan areas and more were expected to be added.

The striking feature of the transportation control provisions is the requirement that transportation control planning be carried out by a regional planning agency. There is a strong preference for the regional agency designated to carry out the regional transportation planning process under the federal highway act, the regional agency responsible for air quality maintenance planning, or the agency with both such responsibilities. § 174(a). The Senate committee report also noted that coordination with areawide water quality plans required under the Federal Water Pollution Control Act was expected, S. Rep. No. 127, 95th Cong., 1st Sess. 38 (1977), and coordination with transportation and air quality maintenance planning is required. § 174(b).

Another section of the Act, § 108(e), authorizes EPA to provide information on 28 listed transportation control strategies to guide the states in the preparation of transportation control plans. These strategies include those discussed in the Schofer article, *supra,* but some strategies have been omitted. Parking surcharges were prohibited by an earlier amendment to the Act, gasoline rationing is not included on the list, and controls on new parking facilities are omitted because they are covered under the indirect source review provisions.

A major case considering transportation control plans arose when a federal Court of Appeals was asked to review a plan promulgated by EPA for the metropolitan Boston, Massachusetts, area. This decision follows. The plan contained controls on new parking facilities, a strategy no longer authorized for transportation control plans but explicitly allowed to be included in indirect source review programs. The case thus serves as judicial guidance on both of these strategies.

---

[8] Photochemical oxidants are formed by a chemical reaction between hydrocarbons and oxides of nitrogen in the air, and are a contributor to smog. Hydrocarbons and oxides of nitrogen are both produced by the combustion process in motor vehicle engines.

SOUTH TERMINAL CORP. v. ENVIRONMENTAL PROTECTION AGENCY

United States Court of Appeals
504 F.2d 646 (1st Cir. 1974)

Before COFFIN, Chief Judge, McENTEE and CAMPBELL, Circuit Judges.

LEVIN H. CAMPBELL, Circuit Judge.

[The court noted that "[a]t the heart of the plan is a strategy of cutting down emissions by discouraging the use of vehicles. Off-street and on-street parking spaces are to be 'frozen' or cut back, and the construction of new parking facilities is regulated." *Id.* at 655. Among the facilities affected was the parking facility at the area's major commercial airport; the constitutional implications of this restriction are discussed in the opinion.

[The court first considered whether the plan was arbitrary and capricious, a standard of review that had been adopted by several federal Courts of Appeal and that is codified in the 1977 amendments. *See* § 307(b)(9). Only those portions of the decisions considering the alleged arbitrary nature of the plan and the constitutional issues are reproduced here. — Eds.]

V

WHETHER TRANSPORTATION CONTROLS ARE
ABRITRARY AND CAPRICIOUS

1. The "freeze" boils down to the requirement that no new parking spaces be created after October 15, 1973, in the more congested portions of Boston, Cambridge, and some other outlying areas. There are important exceptions: residential spaces (parking adjacent to homes, apartments, condominiums, etc.), employee parking outside the Boston core (so long as it complies with the separate employee parking restrictions), and free customer parking. Our role, of course, is not to decide whether the freeze device is an ideal solution; Congress delegated to EPA the authority (assuming the state did not exercise it) to select the preferred means. We cannot say that such a freeze is arbitrary and capricious assuming EPA is able to support by credible data its position as to the magnitude of the need for carbon monoxide emission reductions in relevant segments of the region. Indeed, the enlargement of parking facilities in areas where the public health requires curtailing the flow of traffic would itself seem irrational. The exemption for residents, customers and, in parts of the area, employees, would seem a reasonable attempt to ameliorate the hardship upon individuals and businesses.

. . . .

The contention that the Agency did not consider alternatives is belied by the record. EPA paid attention to and rejected a wide range of strategies, including mechanical emission control devices, episodic based vehicle prohibition, gasoline rationing, staggering work hours, shortening the work week, gaseous fuel conversion, and the sticker system.

The Second Circuit has stated:

> There is no reason to make a distinction between explanations for negative exclusions and the affirmative choice. In circumstances of this kind, the petitioners must carry the burden of going forward with a reasonable claim of something important overlooked instead of placing on the Administrator the burden of knocking down all possible objections in advance. If nothing can be done until everything is explained, the mandate of the statute will never be translated into accomplishment.

Natural Resources Defense Council, Inc. v. EPA, 494 F.2d 519, 525 (2d Cir. 1974). . . . We think it clear that petitioners have not met this burden.

5. Petitioners contend that all the transportation controls are arbitrary because the Administrator has paid too little attention to the plan's economic and social impact. The material portions of the Clean Air Act itself do not mention economic or social impact, and it seems plain that Congress intended the Administrator to enforce compliance with air quality standards even if the costs were great. Particularly in the case of primary standards — those set as "requisite to public health" — Congress' position is not extreme or unprecedented. Minimum public health requirements are often, perhaps usually, set without consideration of other economic impact. Thus, insofar as petitioners claim that either EPA or ourselves would be empowered to reject measures necessary to ensure compliance with primary air quality standards simply because after weighing the advantages of safe air against the economic detriment, we thought the latter consideration took priority, petitioners would be incorrect. Congress has already made a judgment the other way, and EPA and the courts are bound. . . .

Economic considerations may play some role, however, in EPA's selection among alternative means to achieve its mandated clean air goal. EPA guidelines encourage states to identify the "costs and benefits" of alternative control strategies. Although we do not read the Act as requiring EPA to engage in exhaustive cost benefit studies or to initiate elaborate planning exercises, it could be abitrary and capricious for the Agency to reject obviously less burdensome but equally effective controls in favor of more expensive or onerous ones. But we think a considerable part of the burden of suggesting attractive alternative strategies is upon those, like the petitioners, who dislike the present ones. The record discloses that the Administrator has chosen rationally among the viable alternatives presented. We conclude that he did not abuse his discretion or go beyond his statutory authority with respect to the economic and social aspects of the plan.

VI

CONSTITUTIONAL OBJECTIONS

. . . .

D. *Taking Without Just Compensation*

The airport petitioners and all parking operators in the Boston core area seek to convince us that the regulations constitute a taking without just compensation. The regulations as applied to Logan exterminate some 1,100 planned-upon spaces and arguably confiscate the revenues that otherwise would have accrued from them. The 40 percent vacancy rate rule in the Boston core area compels building space to stand idle; the situation is arguably most disadvantageous to garage owners, for their space is least likely to have a reasonable alternative use. The garage owners may argue that it is as if the Government had taken title to 40 percent of their spaces; it would matter little if thereafter the Government kept the space idle, devoted it to some other nonremunerative end, or found some other use for it.

However, the Government has not taken title to the spaces, and the decision about alternative uses of the space has been left to the owner. The takings clause is ordinarily not offended by regulation of uses, even though the regulation may severely or even drastically affect the value of the land or real property. If the highest-valued use of the property is forbidden by regulations of general applicability, no taking has occurred so long as other lower-valued, reasonable uses are left to the property's owner. *Goldblatt v. Town of Hempstead,* 369 U.S. 590, 592, 82 S.Ct. 987, 8 L.Ed.2d 130 (1962); *Turnpike Realty Co. v. Town of Dedham,* 1972 Mass.Adv. Sh. 1303, 284 N.E.2d 891, cert. denied, 409 U.S. 1108, 93 S.Ct. 908, 34 L.Ed.2d 689 (1973).

Three situations must be distinguished. First, a particular use of a parcel of property may be regulated or forbidden. Second, all uses of a parcel may be forbidden. Third, a right to use or burden property in a particular and permitted way may be transferred from the original owner to another person, or to a governmental body. Only the second and third situations are thought of as takings today. Thus in *Pennsylvania Coal Co. v. Mahon,* 260 U.S. 393, 43 S. Ct. 158, 67 L.Ed. 322 (1922), the transfer from mineral owners to surface owners of the right to control subsidence in the land was held to be a compensable taking. At the same time the Court recognized the first situation, stating:

Government hardly could go on if to some extent values incident to property could not be diminished without paying for every such change in the general law. *Id.* at 413, 43 S.Ct. at 159.

Our situation fits within the boundaries of the first type. EPA's rule is of general applicability, regulating one use of those available. The right to use is not extinguished entirely; nor is it transferred to anyone else. Indeed, the ingenuity of operators may result in fewer disadvantages than urged. For example, some operators may be able to "buy" from others the right to use spaces, leaving the seller of spaces free to use the land under his parking lot for other purposes while the buyer enjoys a higher occupancy rate.

In any event, even a diminution of profits or a requirement that some loss be suffered is not enough, when all other accoutrements of ownership remain, to be a "taking".

Finally, the Government reminds us that the restriction on parking availability in the Boston core area will allow entrepreneurs to increase their prices, as is the natural consequence when supply is reduced and demand is unchanged. The Government has effectively created a parking cartel that, depending on the elasticity of demand for parking, may increase rather than decrease profits. What will happen to profits cannot be predicted, but in view of the possibility of their increase we are not impressed by the claim that the regulation is so serious, and so forecloses alternatives, that a compensable taking has occurred.

. . . .

Comments: 1. Contrast the court's handling of these issues under the Clean Air Act with the way in which a state court might approach the same problem had these controls been imposed under a conventional zoning ordinance. Are you impressed with the way in which the court handled the taking issue? The analysis of this issue in *South Terminal* was relied on by the court in *Sierra Club, supra* p. 1161. Was this reliance misplaced?

2. The role of social and economic factors in the adoption and administration of land use and transportation controls under the Clean Air Act has not yet been definitively resolved. See Mandelker & Rothschild, *supra* at 252-53. In *Union Elec. Co. v. EPA,* 427 U.S. 246 (1976), the Supreme Court held that a stationary source of pollution could not raise compliance claims of economic and technological infeasibility in an action brought to challenge emission limitations in a state implementation plan. The case does not resolve the issue as it might arise in the land use and transportation controls context. See Bleicher, Economic and Technical Feasibility in Clean Air Act Enforcement Against Stationary Sources, 89 Harv. L. Rev. 316 (1975).

3. On the question of state authority to adopt land use-oriented controls in air quality programs see *Public Serv. Co. v. New Mexico Environmental Improvement Bd.,* 549 P.2d 638 (N.M. 1976). The court held that the state agency was without authority to set emission levels more stringent than the federal standards to allow a margin for industrial growth in the Four Corners area of New Mexico. For additional discussion of land use and transportation controls under the Clean Air Act see Bolbach, Land Use Controls Under the Clean Air Act, 6 Seton Hall L. Rev. 413 (1975); Comment, Transportation Control Plans: Secondary Measures to Control Automobile Pollution, 8 Tex. Tech. L. Rev. 361 (1976). For discussion of the controversial Los Angeles TCP see Chernow, Implementing the Clean Air Act in Los Angeles: The Duty to Achieve the Impossible, 4 Ecology L.Q. 537 (1975).

4. The transportation control plans provoked intense controversy, arising from gasoline rationing proposals for Los Angeles and like stringent measures in other cities, and EPA was then forced to bring actions in federal courts in which it attempted to compel the states to enforce the plans. With one exception, the federal Courts of Appeals held, generally, that EPA had no statutory authority to enforce the plans and that, if it did, serious constitutional questions would be raised under the Tenth Amendment to the federal constitution. *See, e.g., Maryland v. EPA,* 530 F.2d 215 (4th Cir. 1975); *District of Columbia v. Train,* 521 F.2d 971 (D.C. Cir. 1975); *Brown v. EPA,* 521 F.2d 827 (9th Cir. 1975). The Supreme Court granted certiorari but then vacated the judgments below and remanded the cases when EPA admitted in oral argument that it had retreated from its position that the plans were enforceable against the states in federal court. *EPA v. Brown,* 431 U.S. 99 (1977). EPA also withdrew many of the objectionable features of the TCP's. For example, in Boston all but the parking freeze and commuter vehicle incentives of the plan were withdrawn. *See* 41 Fed. Reg. 10223 (1976); 40 Fed. Reg. 25151 (1975). The 1977 amendments appear to leave to the states the initial decision concerning what transportation controls to apply.

2. Water Quality

The extensive program for cleaning up the nation's waters legislated by the Federal Water Pollution Control Act has two major components. Controls are placed over effluent discharges by sources of water pollution under a National Permit Discharge Elimination System (NPDES), initially administered by EPA but whose administration may be delegated to the states under federal standards. In addition, the statute has provided for a massive program of federal grants for the improvement and construction of wastewater treatment and collection facilities. The statute also provides a national clean water "zero discharge" goal as the statute's objective, and then provides for the adoption of state water quality standards for waters within the state. Both the national goal and the quality standards serve as the basis for strengthening controls over sources of pollution when effluent limitations are not sufficient to achieve the goal or the quality standards.

Unlike the Clean Air Act, the FWPCA also contains explicit water quality planning requirements of the conventional variety. That is, the states and regions within states are required to prepare and adopt water quality plans which control both the location of new treatment facilities and the location of new development so that the objectives of the statute can be achieved. These planning provisions contain important regulatory requirements which apply to area (nonpoint) sources of pollution, such as urban stormwater runoff, as well as to the specific (point) sources of pollution such as industrial plants. Water quality levels are affected as much by pollution from nonpoint sources as they are from the point sources; in some areas, the nonpoint sources are the more serious problem.

Clearly, a program with controls as extensive as this over wastewater treatment plants and industrial polluters has important land use consequences. We focus here on two of the major land use dimensions of the water pollution control program — the role that treatment plants play in influencing development patterns and the land use control implications of the water quality planning programs. The article that follows traces some of the developmental impacts of the federal grant program for treatment works.

NOTE, SEWERS, CLEAN WATER, AND PLANNED GROWTH: RESTRUCTURING THE FEDERAL POLLUTION ABATEMENT EFFORT, 86 Yale Law Journal 733, 739-44 (1977)

[The FWPCA authorized 18 billion dollars in federal grants to assist municipalities in upgrading existing waste treatment systems and constructing new sewage treatment plants (STP's) and interceptor sewers, thus promising a remarkable improvement in community waste treatment facilities. In the selection that follows the author deals with the growth impacts of STP's, focusing on the federal statute's reserve capacity requirement and on decisions influencing the location of new plants. The reserve capacity requirement arises from a requirement of the Act, § 204(a)(5), that "the size and capacity of such [STP] works relate directly to the needs to be served by such works, including sufficient reserve capacity." — Eds.]

1. *Extent*

On review of a construction grant application, the EPA's determination of the reserve STP capacity to be funded influences the extent or amount of development that can occur in a municipality. The EPA requires that sewer facilities be designed in light of expected population increases in the area to be served. In the past, STPs were often designed to provide for approximately 20 years of population growth; more recent projects have sometimes had shorter design periods. Municipal population projections may be further adjusted to take into account the extra growth induced by the availability of reserve treatment capacity. For example, the EPA concluded that the population of Scarborough, Maine, ultimately would be 25% larger as a result of the proposed sewer project.

Construction of facilities able to treat substantially more wastewater than is presently generated by a locality will have two effects on the extent of growth. First, growth in excess of an STP's capacity may be impractical because of the relative cost to private developers of providing their own waste disposal systems, or because there are local restrictions on the use of waste treatment alternatives. Hence, the determination of reserve treatment capacity may effectively place a ceiling on a municipality's size.

Second, the limit set by existing reserve capacity is likely to constitute a self-fulfilling prophecy. This is due to the Act's financing scheme. Although the federal share of construction costs is 75%, a project still requires some local investment in construction, as well as local financing of all maintenance and operating costs. The Act requires that the latter be raised through the assessment of "user charges" that may run in excess of $200 per user per year. Accordingly, it is likely that localities will encourage growth in order to fill STP capacity and thereby lower charges for present users. Growth will occur to exhaust the STP's reserve capacity.

2. *Pace*

The availability of reserve STP capacity may cause the pace of growth, or the extent of new development in each year, to accelerate. This acceleration may consist initially of a "spurt" in development activity immediately upon completion of a sewer project. If growth has been slowed by the inability of a locality to accommodate the waste treatment needs of new homes, the immediate availability of reserve capacity may release built-up development pressures. Localities in fact may encourage the spurt in growth in order to raise funds to pay for reserve capacity. In addition, a locality's annual growth rate may increase due to development induced by available reserve capacity.

A New Jersey example reflects the impact of a new STP on both immediate and sustained growth rates. In 1965 the unsewered township of East Windsor, New Jersey, formed a municipal utilities authority and decided to build substantial waste treatment capacity, while its neighbor, West Windsor, hesitated to undertake sewer construction. Although the number of residential building permits authorized annually in West Windsor dropped significantly, the number authorized in East Windsor increased twelvefold in anticipation of STP construction and remained substantially higher than that for West Windsor over the next decade.

3. *Location*

Perhaps the most important impact is the influence of Title

II-funded sewers on the location of development. This impact results from the placement of STPs and of the interceptor sewers that transport wastes from pollution sources to STPs. Treatment works projects receiving construction grants are likely to be located in polluted areas; localities that cannot demonstrate a need for pollution abatement may not be funded. Furthermore, before the EPA Administrator can approve a construction grant, the 1972 FWPCA requires him to determine that the proposed project has been given priority over other treatment works projects by the state water pollution control agency. The state agencies are instructed by the 1972 FWPCA to "rank, in order of priority," projects needed to achieve the Act's pollution abatement deadlines. Hence, waste treatment systems with reserve capacity are likely to be built, and to stimulate growth, in or adjacent to polluted areas. This general tendency is illustrated in New Hampshire's Winnipesaukee Lakes Region, where the EPA recommended a regional STP to sewer the region's more polluted areas first.

An additional impact on the location of development may result from the EPA's policy of regionalization: construction grant applicants are instructed by EPA guidelines to consider regional waste treatment alternatives. Regional solutions may result in the construction of one or more central STPs that require laying interceptor sewers through open or restricted-growth lands to connect treatment plants with polluted areas. In Chester County, Pennsylvania, for example, connection of one settled area to an area in which a central STP was to be located necessitated routing an interceptor sewer through "a very rural setting." One study concluded that half of the land sewered by 52 interceptor sewer projects was vacant. Typically such sewers have been built with sufficient reserve capacity to serve 50 years of growth. Given local pressures to add users in order to spread the operation, maintenance, and construction costs of the sewer, it is likely that localities will face pressures to permit development of the vacant land.

Comments: 1. The federal statute has now been amended to require the EPA Administrator to determine reserve capacity by taking into account population growth and "associated commercial and industrial establishments" within the jurisdiction served by the treatment plant. This determination may be based on an areawide water quality plan or "an applicable municipal master plan of development." Does this amendment remedy any of the problems discussed in the article? For additional discussion of the growth impacts of the construction grant program see Urban Systems Research & Engineering, Inc., Interceptor Sewers and Suburban Sprawl (1974).

Section 316 of the Clean Air Act authorizes the EPA Administrator to withhold a grant for sewage treatment works if new treatment capacity will be created that can be anticipated to cause an increase in air pollution over what is allowed in a state implementation plan for a nonattainment area. In addition, a grant may be withheld if it is not in conformity with an applicable state implementation plan. How does this section affect the impact of sewage treatment plant construction on growth and development patterns?

2. The impact of sewer extensions on growth and development was considered in *Community College v. Fox,* 342 A.2d 468 (Pa. Commw. Ct. 1975). In that case the state Department of Environmental Resources (DER) granted a permit for an interceptor sewer extension which was vacated by the state Environmental Hearing Board (EHB). The extension crossed a largely undeveloped area to serve the college and had a 90 percent reserve capacity. It was vacated by the Board, in part, because it would stimulate development in the area and would destroy the option to preserve all or a part of the area as public open space.

In a complex opinion, based in part on a special environmental protection provision in the Pennsylvania constitution, the Commonwealth Court reversed the Board. It held that the state water quality act, under which the Board acted, was intended to control and eliminate water pollution. *Id.* at 479. While the Board could consider the secondary consequences of pollution in its decisions, the court disagreed with the Board's conclusion that it could consider

> the question "of possibly preserving open space, and recreational uses of particular waters, to be considered as balanced against potential [or accelerated] development of a particular watershed." Here we believe that the EHB has reached a much broader interpretation of the law than was intended by the General Assembly in its enactment. . . . We cannot say, as did the EHB, that the DER should evaluate local planning decisions or decide for itself what the best present and future uses of a watershed might be.

Id. at 480.

3. The water quality planning provisions of the FWPCA are an attempt to provide a planning framework for decisions on treatment plants and sewer extensions, as well as for the regulation of point and nonpoint sources of pollution that affect water quality. These provisions appear primarily at two places in the Act. Section 303(e) provides for a statewide continuing water quality planning process whose content is only vaguely provided by the statute. A more detailed regional water quality planning process is provided by Section 208. This latter provision also refers ambiguously to a state role in planning. Following a court decision interpreting Section 208 also to require a statewide planning effort, the EPA effectively combined the 303(e) and 208 planning functions by regulation. *Natural Resources Defense Council v. Train,* 396 F. Supp. 1386 (D.D.C. 1975), *aff'd,* 564 F.2d 573 (D.C. Cir. 1977). The article that follows describes the major elements of the Section 208 planning program.

COMMENT, AREAWIDE PLANNING UNDER THE FEDERAL WATER POLLUTION CONTROL ACT AMENDMENTS OF 1972: INTER-GOVERNMENTAL AND LAND USE IMPLICATIONS, 54 Texas Law Review 1047, 1052-58 (1976)

The Section 208 Implementation Process

Section 208 integrates the Act's various pollution abatement and prevention programs into a multistep process involving state, local, and federal officials. The first step deals with the intrastate allocation of planning authority between state and areawide planning agencies. The Governor of each state, subject to EPA approval and in consultation with local officials, must designate areas having "substantial water quality control problems" resulting from "urban-industrial concentrations or other factors." For each area designated, the Governor must select a regional planning agency controlled by local governments in the area. The state acts as the planning agency for nondesignated areas. The second step concerns plan development. Both state and areawide planning agencies must prepare long-range plans that provide for adequate waste treatment facilities and a regulatory program for the control of all point and nonpoint sources of pollution. Each plan must also include a financial and managerial program for carrying out other elements of the plan. The third step concerns approval of the plans and designation of agencies to implement them. The Governor must submit completed plans to the EPA for approval and designate one or more state, regional, or local "management agencies" to carry out the plans. The EPA must disapprove any plan that does not satisfy the statutory requirements, and it may also disapprove the proposed designation of any management agency that does not possess the implementative authority specified by section 208. The final step requires management agencies to implement the plans under EPA supervision. To encourage the enforcement of section 208 plans, the Act prohibits the EPA from making any construction grants or issuing any discharge permits that conflict with an approved plan. In addition, the Act vests ultimate authority for enforcement with the courts by authorizing citizen suits against the EPA to force compliance.

Implications for Land Use and Growth Management

Environmental quality is intimately related to patterns of land use and growth. Without the land use and growth management provisions of section 208, the other programs established by the Act might prove ineffective: a community relying solely on the construction grant and discharge permit programs might substantially eliminate the discharge from point sources such as municipal sewage and industrial wastes, only to discover that the rivers and streams remain polluted from nonpoint sources. The runoff from nearby farmlands, for example, might contain chemical fertilizers, pesticides, and animal wastes deleterious to water quality. In addition, a new, expensive, and efficient sewage treatment plan can actually stimulate creation of new pollution sources if extensive new sewer lines extending into undeveloped territory on the urban fringe accompany the expanded treatment capacity. Residential and commercial development attracted by the new facilities might soon outstrip the added treatment capacity and generate new nonpoint source pollution as well. Land use planning and growth management policies are needed both to control nonpoint source pollution and to protect waste treatment plants from overload.

In addition to enhancing the effectiveness of the construction grant and discharge permit programs, land use and growth measures may help to avoid inequities inherent in a water quality program that previously relied solely on treating wastes. A program discriminates unfairly if it requires a chemical plant to treat its wastes before discharge into a public body of water without also requiring an agricultural or silvicultural producer to control the pesticides and other runoff emanating from its fields or forests. Land use and growth management techniques may also reduce the cost of meeting the 1983 goal of water that would support fishing and swimming. The public expense in developing and implementing regulatory programs will rarely approach the cost of constructing and operating waste treatment facilities, and a motivated community can minimize its need for new treatment capacity through growth management. The cost-effectiveness factor assumes particular significance because the Act contemplates the expenditure of many billions of dollars for the construction of waste treatment facilities.

Provisions of Section 208 Related to Land Use and Growth

Section 208 mandates the development of plans that include land use and growth management techniques as part of an overall strategy for improving water quality. First, each areawide waste treatment management plan approved by the EPA must include procedures to identify and to control specified nonpoint sources of pollution, particularly urban stormwater runoff, agricultural runoff, and runoff from construction activity. Control of nonpoint sources can entail regulating either the manner of pollution or the location of the pollution-generating activities. For example, a city might reduce pollution from a riverbank garbage dump either by utilizing sanitary landfill techniques or by relocating the dump. Similarly, a county could minimize pollution from agricultural runoff by prohibiting the use of harmful fertilizers and pesticides on croplands adjacent to sensitive waters or by zoning adjacent lands unsuitable for agricultural activity. A city might require construction companies to adopt erosion and sediment control techniques as a prerequisite to receiving a building permit or might simply prohibit construction activity in sensitive areas.

Second, each plan must identify all waste treatment works necessary to meet municipal and industrial needs over a twenty-year period, any related land acquisition requirements, and the necessary wastewater collection systems. Furthermore, each plan must establish priorities for the construction of treatment works and a time schedule for their initiation and completion. The availability of public sewage treatment facilities comprises a key determinant of the pattern and pace of urban growth. As a result, in determining when and where to construct treatment plants and sewer lines, the 208 planning agency must make major decisions about community growth patterns.

Third, each plan must include a program to regulate "the location, modification, and construction of any facilities" that may result in point source discharge of pollutants. The scope and purpose of this provision has not clearly emerged. In the Senate debate on the Act, Senator Edmund S. Muskie suggested a distinction between the NPDES program, which concerns permits controlling the quantity and quality of point source discharges, and the 208 regulatory program, which deals with the location of facilities resulting in such discharges. Muskie stated that the permit program is "control oriented," while section 208 is "prevention oriented." If Muskie's distinction is correct, section 208 contemplates the utilization of land use and growth management measures to prevent an accumulation of facilities that would overload existing or planned waste treatment plants. In this sense, the term "facilities" would encompass houses, factories, stores, and offices, as well as treatment plants — any building in which wastewater is collected and transported for treatment. A broad range of techniques apply in this context, including zoning, subdivision regulations, building codes, and development permits. For example, a city could protect its treatment plants by coordinating the issuance of construction and development permits with the availability of treatment capacity.

Several section 208 provisions concerning the implementation authority of management agencies have implications for land use and growth. Each designated management agency must have the authority to withhold waste treatment services from any municipality or subdivision that does not comply with the 208 plan. The agency might exercise this power by imposing temporary sewer connection moratoria to hamper development in selected areas. A moratorium can prove useful both in protecting treatment facilities from overload and in discouraging activities that generate nonpoint source pollution. Management agencies must also have the authority to contract with industries to treat industrial wastes and to assess the appropriate fees. The management agency could exercise influence over the rate of industrial development in the planning area by limiting the treatment capacity available for industrial use. Of course, a company unable to hook up to the public waste treatment system may construct its own treatment facilities if the cost does not become prohibitive and the facilities satisfy the requirements for a discharge permit.

Comments: Opinions differ on the effectiveness of Section 208 planning as a growth control. The author of the Yale Law Journal student Note, *supra* at 753, observes:

> Although § 208 clearly encompasses land-use or growth-planning considerations, the EPA interprets the provision simply to authorize the utilization of land-use requirements as a non-sewer means of achieving water quality objectives. The agency's outlook is therefore functional: Congress intended only that a comprehensive approach to waste treatment management planning be developed; § 208 was not enacted to provide a means of designing treatment works projects to implement planned growth objectives.

Consider these comments in light of the following case.

COMMONWEALTH v. TRAUTNER

Commonwealth Court of Pennsylvania
19 Pa. Commw. Ct. 116, 338 A.2d 718 (1975)

Before CRUMLISH, Jr., KRAMER and ROGERS, JJ.

OPINION

KRAMER, Judge.

This is an appeal by the Department of Environmental Resources (DER) from an order of the Environmental Hearing Board (Board), dated August 1, 1974, in which the Board sustained an appeal by David A. Trautner (Trautner). Trautner had appealed from DER's denial of a permit for an individual on-lot sewage treatment system.

Trautner owns a parcel of land in Hepburn Township (Township), a rural municipality located near Williamsport. Recently the Township has experienced growth and development, which has resulted in construction activity in previously unpopulated areas of the municipality.

Like all Pennsylvania municipalities, the Township is required to file with DER an acceptable comprehensive plan for the disposal of sewage, pursuant to the Sewage Facilities Act (Act), Act of January 24, 1966, P.L. (1965) 1535, as amended, 35 P. S. § 750.1 et seq.

(Supp. 1974-1975). Sections 3 and 5 of the Act, 35 P.S. §§ 750.3 and 750.5 (Supp. 1974-1975) provide, *inter alia,* for the promulgation of regulations governing review and acceptance of official plans, and for periodic revisions (by the municipality) of such plans. From the record it appears that there is no question that the Township has filed an acceptable initial comprehensive plan, and the only real controversy in the instant case involves the Township's attempt to amend its plan to accommodate the construction of a home in a hitherto undeveloped (and consequently unplanned) area.

The comprehensive plan filed by the Township did not envisage the construction of a home on Trautner's lot, and, in support of *his* application for a permit, the Township filed with DER a brief amendment to its plan which read, in its substantive portion, as follows:

"Now, therefore, be and it is hereby resolved, that the Township of Hepburn does hereby revise said Township's official plan in order to provide for the individual residential sewage treatment facility for the David A. Trautner property."

DER rejected Trautner's permit on alternative grounds, specifying that (1) the above-quoted resolution was an inadequate revision under DER regulation 71.16(b), 25 Pa.Code § 71.16(b); and (2) the project was not located in an "isolated area", as required by regulation 91.32, 25 Pa.Code § 91.32.

Our scope of review is governed by section 44 of the Administrative Agency Law, Act of June 4, 1945, P.L. 1388, as amended, 71 P.S. § 1710.44, which provides, *inter alia,* for review for errors of law, violations of constitutional rights, and the determination of whether the findings of the Board are supported by substantial evidence.

DER raises two basic questions, one of which may be disposed of quickly. Regulation 91.32, 25 Pa.Code § 91.32, reads as follows:

"(a) The Department will look with disfavor upon applications for sewerage permits for private sewerage projects *to be located within the built-up parts of cities, boroughs, and first and second class townships.*

"(b) Generally, issuance of such sewerage permits will be limited to proper private sewerage projects *located in the rural parts of first and second class townships,* and for which areas there appears to be *no present necessity* for public sewerage." (Emphasis added.)

... After reviewing the record, we have no difficulty concluding that the Board's finding, that Trautner's lot is isolated and rural, is supported by the record. ...

The regulations which underlie the second issue in this case are complex, but the essence of the controversy may be succinctly described. Regulations 91.31(a) and (b), 25 Pa.Code § 91.31(a) and (b), require that a private project (such as Trautner's) be in conformity with a "comprehensive program of water quality management" before departmental approval (i.e., the issuance of a permit) will be granted. Regulation 71.16, dealing with revision of municipal plans (for comprehensive water quality management), specifies that an effective revision must include certain data which was not provided in the instant case. DER reasons that since the Township's plan was not revised in accordance with the regulations, the Trautner sewage proposal was not in conformity with a "comprehensive program of water quality management" and, hence, Trautner's application should have been denied.

The problem with DER's position is that, under the regulations currently in effect, a property owner can be effectively denied his right to use his property until such time as *the municipality* has satisfied DER that sewage disposal on the property is in conformity "with a comprehensive program of water quality management". The burden is placed upon the property owner to motivate his municipality to (1) comply with the regulations relevant to amending municipal plans; and (2) satisfy DER that the property owner's plan for sewage disposal is otherwise acceptable. If the municipality fails to act to amend its plan, or cannot or will not fully satisfy DER, for whatever reasons, the property owner is left with no sewage permit and no opportunity to use his land in what is otherwise a completely lawful manner. This situation is confiscatory and tantamount to a taking without due process of law.

DER argues that the property owner has a remedy for municipal inaction in regulation 71.17, 25 Pa.Code § 71.17, which reads as follows:

"(a) Any person who is a resident or property owner in a municipality may request the Department to order the municipality to revise its official plan where said person can show that the official plan is inadequate to meet the resident's or property owner's sewage disposal needs. The request to the Department shall contain a description of the area of the municipality in question and an enumeration of all reasons advanced by said person to show the official plan's inadequacy.

"(b) If the Department refuses to order a revision requested under subsection (a) of this section, it will notify the person in writing of the reasons for such refusal. Any person aggrieved by the action of the Department may appeal to the Environmental Hearing Board pursuant to Chapter 21 of this Title (relating to rules of practice and procedure)."

It is certainly true that this regulation provides the property owner with a course of action to follow. It does not, however, necessarily provide an adequate means of protecting the owner's property rights. The landowner is still not free to use his land until such time as another party, over whom he has absolutely no control, acts in a manner satisfactory to DER. There is no guarantee that such action will occur within a reasonable time, or for that matter, ever occur.

Even if municipal officials failed to comply with an order directing them to revise their official plan and were fined or eventually found in contempt, the property owner would still not have DER approval for his project. Likewise, a municipality may *refuse* to revise its plan to include an on-lot system because of plans for a community sewage system to be constructed some time in the distant future. The property owner can be effectively denied the use of his land while a plan, which is to be implemented at some indefinite time, if at all, is managed by local officials. Such community-wide planning can involve action by the officials of several municipalities, a local authority, and DER, and can involve complicated and time-consuming financing and negotiations. The use of the "isolated area" requirement of regulation 91.32 as a basis for denying Trautner's permit in the instant case is evidence of the position DER might take if the municipality itself [were] of the opinion that community-wide sewage facilities would be desirable in the foreseeable future. While we realize that DER and local officials are obligated to make adequate plans for the disposal of sewage, under the present regulatory scheme, a property owner, such as Trautner, can be denied the reasonable use of his property while all of the various parties involved pursue agreement among themselves regarding what precisely is to be done with an area in transition from "isolated" to non-isolated status.

We have carefully examined the record and the regulatory scheme involved in this case and we conclude that, as applied to Trautner's circumstances, the regulations noted above constitute an unreasonable restriction on the use of his land and are, in effect, a confiscation without due process of law. By sustaining DER's appeal we would be enforcing these regulations in derogation of Trautner's constitutional rights, and this we cannot do. Accordingly, we

ORDER

And now, this 19th day of May, 1975, it is hereby ordered that the order of the Environmental Hearing Board, dated August 1, 1974, requiring that the Department of Environmental Resources issue a permit to David A. Trautner for the construction and operation of an individual on-lot sewage treatment system, is affirmed.

Comments: 1. Would the court have reached a different result in this case if the state agency had denied the permit because of perceived health hazards that would be created by an on-lot system? What if the state agency had articulated a policy that on-lot systems were not to be allowed in areas in which substantial growth was expected in the near future? How would the Pennsylvania Commonwealth Court react if a landowner had been denied a residential permit under the Ramapo plan, see *supra* p. 1037, in part because of lack of availability of sewer services?

2. For additional discussion of Section 208 planning see Goldfarb, Water Quality Management Planning: The Fate of 208, 8 Tol. L. Rev. 105 (1976); Phillips, Developments in Water Quality and Land Use Planning: Problems in the Application of the Federal Water Pollution Control Act Amendments of 1972, 10 Urb. L. Ann. 43 (1975). State authority to comply with the substantive requirements imposed by Section 208 is reviewed extensively in School of Public and Environmental Affairs, Indiana Univ., Problems and Approaches to Areawide Water Quality Management: Appendix B (1973).

3. Another water quality-related federal program contains an interesting section with important land use implications. Section 1424(e) of the Safe Drinking Water Act of 1974, 42 U.S.C. § 300h-3(e) (1976), contains an important limitation on new development affecting aquifers. This section grew out of litigation over a federally insured new town to be located near San Antonio, Texas, and which was to be located in part over the Edwards Aquifer. Litigation challenging the new town under NEPA and the FWPCA was lost in part because water quality standards had not been issued for the aquifer by EPA. *Sierra Club v. Lynn,* 364 F. Supp. 834 (W.D. Tex. 1973), *aff'd in part and rev'd in part,* 502 F.2d 43 (5th Cir. 1974). This decision hastened the enactment of the Safe Drinking Water Act, which establishes a scheme of national drinking water standards for public water supply systems.

Section 1424(e) was introduced on the floor of the House by the congressman representing the San Antonio district. Under this provision, EPA may determine "that an area has an aquifer which is the sole or principal drinking water source for the area and which, if contaminated, would create a significant hazard to public health." After such a determination has been published in the Federal Register, "no commitment for Federal financial assistance (through a grant, contract, loan guarantee, or otherwise) may be entered into for any project which the [EPA] Administrator determines may contaminate such aquifer through a recharge zone so as to create a signficant hazard to public health." This provision would foreclose any federal subsidies or mortgage insurance for housing and other developments in designated aquifer areas, and is clearly directed at the new town development near San Antonio.

The section raises a number of interpretive problems. For example, how "significant" must a health hazard be before an aquifer can be designated? May EPA in making a designation under this section consider possible contamination from future projects as well as those actually planned or contemplated when a designation is requested? EPA designated the Edwards Aquifer under this section, indicating that vulnerability of an aquifer to contamination raises a presumption of a significant health hazard. 40 Fed. Reg. 58344 (1975). However, EPA guidelines for reviewing land development projects proposed over designated aquifers do not provide for a review of the cumulative impact of isolated projects. 40 C.F.R. § 149.8 (1977). For discussion of Section 1424(e) see Wheatley & Castaneda, Protection of Underground Drinking Water Supplies: The Gonzalez Amendment to the Safe Drinking Water Act, 8 St. Mary's L.J. 40 (1976) (taking a limited view of the statute); Section 1424(e) of the Safe Drinking Water Act: An Effective Measure Against Groundwater Pollution, 6 Envt'l L. Rep. 50121 (1976).

4. Is it possible to sort out the series of environmental control programs that have been enacted at the national level in recent years and discover a consensus on common goals and objectives? Note that there may be conflicts even within the pollution control programs. One problem that has occurred is that federally-financed construction of sewage treatment plants and improvements has encouraged development in areas in which there are severe air pollution problems. Congress responded to this problem with § 316 of the Clean Air Act, added in the 1977 amendments. This section prohibits federal funding of sewage treatment plants which "may reasonably be anticipated to cause or contribute to. . .an increase in emissions of any air pollutant in excess of the increase provided for under" state nonattainment plans or the nondegradation provisions of the statute. What do you think of this provision? Do you agree with its priorities?

Are there any elements of the pollution control programs that can be expected to have a regressive impact on low-income groups? What about the nondegradation provisions of the Clean Air Act? Will these provisions tend to force new sources of air pollution into built-up areas? Is this regressive?

F. ENERGY AND LAND USE

The energy crisis — mounting demands for energy sources and dwindling supplies — has focused attention on the role that land use planning and control can play in energy conservation programs. This problem can be approached from a variety of perspectives, and program possibilities include such diverse strategies as improved home construction design to reduce heat loss, stepped-up programs to divert work and other trips to public transportation, and at the grander scale, the redesign of metropolitan regions to achieve more efficient energy use.

We concentrate here on the last strategy, which ties in well with some of the growth and development control approaches to environmental problems we have been considering in this chapter. Alternative perspectives on the relationship between growth and development patterns and energy use are provided in the following two selections. The first reviews a now famous study on development alternatives which, though entirely hypothetical, claimed to find distinct energy and environmental advantages in one form of urban development rather than another. The second reports an actual study of how projected development alternatives affect energy consumption in the Washington, D.C., metropolitan area. When reading these selections the reader may wish to consult again the materials on metropolitan development patterns included in Chapter 1.

A. ALTSHULER, BOOK REVIEW, REAL ESTATE RESEARCH CORPORATION, THE COSTS OF SPRAWL (1975), 43 Journal of the American Institute of Planners 207 (1977)

The Costs of Sprawl is certainly the most significant attack on urban sprawl that has appeared in the current decade. It bids fair to enter the planning pantheon as the authoritative and virtual last word on the subject, to be relied upon by large numbers of students and planning practitioners who have only read summary statements of its conclusions. . . .

The book is the final report of the most elaborate effort that has yet been made to isolate the variable of density from its usual correlates of structural age, obsolescent layout, and low income population, thereby to measure some of the most important consequences of urban form per se. Sponsored jointly by the U.S. Council on Environmental Quality, the Department of Housing and Urban Development, and the Environmental Protection Agency, the project was carried out by the Real Estate Research Corporation. Since its publication in 1974, *The Costs of Sprawl* has become one of the most widely—and uncritically—cited sources in the planning literature. Its central conclusion, that low density development is extremely costly on energy, environmental, and fiscal grounds, has been generally accepted as authoritative—even by those who doubt the feasibility of vigorous action to shape urban form in the American political context.

The basic study method was to make detailed estimates of the costs associated with six hypothetical new communities, each containing 10,000 dwelling units, each housing an "average" urban fringe population mix, and each constructed in a "typical" environmental setting. The six communities are described as follows:

1. A high density "planned" community consisting 40 percent of highrise apartments (thirty units per net residential acre), 30 percent of walkup apartments (fifteen units per acre), 20 percent of townhouse units (ten per acre), and 10 percent of clustered single family homes (five per acre)

2 and 3. Two low density communities, one representing typical current "sprawl" development and the other "planned" low density development, the former consisting 75 percent of detached single family homes (three per acre) and 25 percent of clustered single family homes (five per acre), the latter consisting of the same two housing types in the reverse ratio

4, 5, and 6. Three communities of intermediate density, each consisting in equal proportions of the five housing types represented in the study, but differing from one another in their postulated degree of planning (i.e., community design) for optimal energy conservation and environmental protection. . . .

For purposes of simplification we shall focus, as the report itself does, primarily on the two extremes (1 and 2). These represent, respectively, optimally planned high density development and "typical" low density sprawl. Their postulated average densities are 19.0 and 3.5 dwelling units per acre, respectively.

The main conclusions, sharply highlighted in the *Executive Summary* volume of the report, are as follows:

1. The high density planned community would be optimal with reference to all four key indicators examined: energy cost, environmental impact, capital cost, and operating cost; the low density sprawl community would be least desirable with reference to all four

2. The high density planned community would require 44 percent less energy than the low density sprawl community

3. It would also generate 45 percent less air pollution

4. The high density planned community would require a capital investment, public and private combined, 44 percent less than the low density sprawl community; the largest proportionate saving would be in road and utility construction (55 percent), but the largest absolute saving would be in the cost of residential construction itself

5. The operating cost of community services would be about 11 percent lower in the high density planned community than in the low density sprawl community.

These findings, needless to say, add up to a very powerful indictment of the American penchant for low density living. Before voting for conviction, though, it would seem prudent to ask at least three questions: (a) have the results of the prototype analysis been calibrated against the experience of actual communities? (b) does the report itself fully support these summary conclusions? and (c) are the reported advantages of the high density planned community over the low density sprawl community primarily due to the density factor or the planning (i.e., optimal community design) factor? The answers seem to be as follows.

(1) To date, the results of the prototype analysis have *not* been calibrated against the experience of real communities. Previous research and analysis based on the experience of actual communities, moreover, point predominantly in the opposite direction from *The Costs of Sprawl*. The key question, it appears, is whether density per se affects the demand level for community services. The authors of *The Costs of Sprawl* explicitly assumed that it did not. Numerous other analysts, however, have judged that the residents of high density communities do seem to require and/or demand more expensive packages of community services than those who live at low densities.

The main explanations hypothesized for the correlation found in previous studies between high density and high expenditure levels, aside from community age and population mix, have been as follows. The residents of low density communities frequently get along contentedly without sidewalks, with utility lines above rather than below ground, and with street lights only on main streets. They may be satisfied with less professional fire protection, because fires are less prone to spread where structural densities are low. With less shared community space, there is likely to be less demand for paid police and maintenance services. With a clear commitment to the automobile, there will generally be less demand for transit expenditures. With people less dependent on community services generally, service employee unions tend to be less powerful and thus unit costs tend to be lower.

Even within the framework of its own assumptions, moreover, the analysis of community service operating costs in *The Costs of Sprawl* contains some surprising omissions. For example:

1. Although the report assumes that residents of high density communities will make substantially greater use of public transit than residents of the lower density communities, it does not include any estimates of mass transit expenditures
2. Although the high density community would have two and-a-half times as much vacant land (exclusive of recreational open space) as the low density sprawl community—65 percent of total land area versus 24 percent—no extra expenditures are estimated for policing and maintaining the additional acreage
3. Although high-rise apartment buildings normally require paid staffs to tend their "shared" spaces, no estimates are made of the likely cost of such staff.

Despite these and several other apparent sources of undercounting with reference to the operating costs of the high density community, the authors of *The Costs of Sprawl* find a saving per household of only $238 a year in this cost category as a result of density increasing from 3.5 to 19.0 units per acre and of careful planning replacing haphazard development. (Four-fifths of the saving, they judge, would be attributable to the density factor alone.) Considering the omissions alone, it seems highly doubtful that the claimed saving would hold in practice.

(2) The energy, pollution, and capital cost comparisons in *The Costs of Sprawl* all require correction for the fact that the authors assumed different space standards for the several types of dwelling units. At the extremes, they assumed that single family households would require 1,600 square feet whereas households occupying high-rise apartments would require only 900 square feet. Overall, the high density community was assumed to consist of dwelling units 34 percent smaller on average than those in the two low density communities.

(3) The energy savings attributed in the report to high density appear grossly overstated. The main sources of exaggeration are four. First, the report examines only three aspects of total urban energy consumption: residential space heating, residential air conditioning, and automobile travel within the local community itself. Together (though the report neglects to say so), these elements account for only about one-fifth of urban energy consumption. Second, the report shows a 41 percent saving in heating and air conditioning costs attributable to high density. The 34 percent differential in average dwelling unit size, however, accounts for five-sixths of this saving. Third, the report shows a 49 percent reduction in energy consumption for travel as one moves from the low density sprawl community to the high density planned community. There is a clear error in the calculation, however. The text of the report states unambiguously (and correctly) that the opportunities for travel savings are confined to convenience shopping, school, and other trips of a very local nature. In the calculations, however, credit is taken for a reduction in all types of travel. Thus, the report estimates that the average household in the high density planned community would travel only 9,891 miles per year, whereas the average household in the low density sprawl community would travel 19,673 miles per year. . . . Precise data are unavailable, but it seems reasonable to assume that, at most, 20 percent of annual household auto mileage is for intraneighborhood travel. If one utilizes the 20 percent assumption, four-fifths of the claimed saving in auto energy consumption for the high density pattern evaporates. Fourth, the report states, as noted previously, that the high density patterns would facilitate the substitution of mass transit for some automobile travel. The auto travel reduction is apparently reflected in the fuel consumption estimate; but no offsetting estimate is made of mass transit fuel consumption. We cannot estimate the precise impact of this factor, because the report does not include any specific estimate of modal shift or transit vehicle mileage.

If one holds dwelling unit size constant and allows only 20 percent of the claimed auto travel saving (but still levies no charge, due to inadequate data, for mass transit energy usage), the energy demand differential between the high density planned community and the low density sprawl community shrinks from 44 percent to 14 percent. If one compares the high density planned community with the low density *planned* community, moreover, the differential falls to 6 percent. These percentages, of course, are relative to the share of total energy consumption accounted for by the uses under consideration, roughly one-fifth. In short, the saving in *total* urban energy consumption attributable to the shift from low density residential sprawl to planned high density is about 3 percent, and that attributable to the density factor alone is about 1 percent.

The obvious next question, of course, is whether increased residential density would be likely to cause a more general increase in urban area density. The answer, most probably, is that in most cases the "multiplier" effect would be very minor. There are, doubtless, threshold effects. If density varies within the range that still entails extreme auto dominance, for example, it seems reasonable to assume that commercial activities will still be arranged in the suburban pattern—along major roads, with ample parking space, in low rise buildings. Only if people can be induced to live at densities similar to those in the older central cities (10,000 per square mile and up) does this seem likely to change significantly. Even if such a shift were achieved, moreover, the technical and economic forces that determine industrial energy demand (by far the largest single category of total urban energy demand) and that have made for industrial diffusion in the postwar period would be unaffected. Finally, it bears note that residential uses generally account for only about 30 percent of urban land use. Thus, a doubling of average urban residential densities would, by itself, entail a reduction of only 15 percent in the total land area of any urban region.

ROBERTS, ENERGY AND LAND USE: ANALYSIS OF ALTERNATIVE DEVELOPMENT PATTERNS, Environmental Comment, September 1975, at 2, 4-9

[This is a study of the effect of alternative development and growth patterns on energy use in the Washington, D.C., metropolitan area. The study first determined the present balance between energy supply and energy demand, an essential step if the leverage points at which energy use can be diminished are to be identified. Energy use was divided between Automobile (21.0%), Residential (47.2%) and Commercial, Industrial, Institutional (31.4%). The last category includes multifamily uses. Energy sources were as follows: Electricity (including wasted electricity), 35.0%; Oil, 14.1%; Natural Gas, 19.0%; Gasoline, 21.5%; and Other, 10.4%. The study notes that "[i]n terms of sources of energy, the transportation sector is almost entirely dependent on gasoline, while the residential and commercial/industrial/institutional sectors require substantial amounts of natural gas, oil, and electricity." *Id.* at 2-3. The study continues by estimating the impact of alternative development patterns on energy conservation. — Eds.]

ALTERNATIVE DEVELOPMENT SCENARIOS

The basic approach use in developing the scenarios for analysis of energy consumption according to alternative development patterns was to take the same increments of growth from the present base and arrange the land uses, economic activities, and levels of transportation in various useful ways. The following assumptions were required:

- Total population, total number of households, and total employment do not vary by scenario.
- Existing development, in the base year, is assumed not to change, so that only the increment of development will vary: the location, densities, and dwelling unit mixes for the increment of development will vary; the mix of total employment by type of job is assumed not to change, however.
- It is assumed that the present network of highways will not change, with no significant addition of freeways or arterials; the question of adequate capacity in the transportation system for future levels of use is not addressed.
- It is also assumed that the full 98-mile METRO system, now partially constructed, is completed, and that planned levels of rail, feeder bus, and route-oriented bus service will be available for all scenarios.
- The base year refers to present levels and locations of activities; the forecast year represents a 15 to 20 year period of time, so that land use changes might be implemented and so that the increment of population is large enough to allow significant changes.

. . . .

A. Dense Center

This scenario assumes that all added households and employment will be concentrated in the metropolitan center, with somewhat higher density residential development.

B. Transit-Oriented

The emphasis in this scenario is on the planned METRO system, with all new households and employment located in areas where planned stops on the rapid rail system are located. Densities are moderately higher.

C. Wedges and Corridors

The prevailing plan for development in the metropolitan Washington area calls for emphasis on radial transportation routes from the metropolitan center, and development in those corridors; wedges of open land without development would be reserved between corridors. This alternative reflects that plan.

D. Beltway-Oriented

Since much of the recent growth in the metropolitan Washington has been focused on the Capital Beltway, a circumurban expressway that rings the metropolitan center, this alternative extrapolates that trend. All added households and employment are concentrated in vacant areas adjacent to the Beltway.

E. Sprawl

In this scenario, the increment of households is assumed to locate beyond the Beltway in low density, largely single-family units; employment on the other hand is concentrated in the metropolitan center (office uses) or around the Beltway (retail uses).

. . . .

ALTERNATIVE CONSUMPTION PATTERNS

. . . [Energy consumption was estimated for the residential sector on a per dwelling basis and for the commercial/industrial/institutional section on a per employee basis because of difficulties in using any other measure. Transportation use was estimated according to the allocation of residences and jobs. The METRO or public transit sector was held constant. — Eds.]

. . . In the residential sector, the largest consuming alternative is "Sprawl" and the least consuming is "Dense Center"; the degree of variation between them is 35 percent, for the increment of development. This means that for the households added to the housing stock of the metropolitan area between now and the forecast year, about one-third of the energy consumed in the "sprawl" alternative could be saved by building at higher densities. Another way of stating this is that energy consumption in the "Sprawl" alternative increases by 46 percent from the base year, while the "Dense Center" alternative increases by 34 percent.

In the transportatation sector, the amount of variation is much greater. The number of vehicle miles traveled differs according to scenario, and therefore the amount of energy consumed. The largest amount of variation is between "Sprawl" and "Transit-Oriented" development, with a difference of 113 percent for the increment of development. Total development by the forecast year varies by 25 percent. If the forecast year is compared to the base year, energy consumption by automobile increased by 60 percent with "Sprawl," but only 28 percent with the "Transit-Oriented" development. The "Dense Center" alternative is close to "Transit-Oriented," with an increase over the base year of 30 percent. The potential for energy savings, then, is about one-half by the forecast year. This difference is attributable to three factors: shorter trip lengths, fewer trips, and a higher level of ridership on public transit. This latter factor is discussed in more detail below.

In terms of differences in total energy consumed, the amount of variation is reduced when the sectors that were held constant — employment (commercial/industrial/institutional) and public transit (METRO) — are added. The least consuming alternative is "Dense

Center," closely followed by "Transit-Oriented." The most consuming alternative is "Sprawl." Between these two extremes are found "Wedges and Corridors" and "Beltway-Oriented." The degree of variation among the alternatives — highest and lowest — for the increment of development to the forecast year is 31 percent; for total development, the difference amounts to 9 percent. This means that if the most-conserving scenario — "Dense Center" — is implemented, there is a potential for 9 percent total energy reduction over that required for the most consuming scenario — "Sprawl." This, then, is the measure of the potential for energy reduction by alternative land use patterns.

The differences in mass transit ridership are of particular importance. . . . [C]onsiderable variation is found among the alternatives. In the case of the journey-to-work, all alternatives improve over the base year, although "Beltway-Oriented" development is only slightly better. The largest improvement in mass transit use is found in the "Dense Center" alternative. The relatively lower use in "Beltway-Oriented" is explained by the improved access and orientation to freeway travel in that alternative; such a situation increases the dependency on the automobile. In the case of the journey-to-work, where employment is located in the urban core, all alternatives improve in mass transit ridership. The differences are smaller, with "Dense Center" development having the highest level of use.

ENERGY AND LAND USE

Energy relates to land use in several ways, as follows:
• There are possibilities for savings in energy consumption by land use means in construction projects or where capital investment is required. If more compact development occurs, there are potential savings in materials, in installation, and in construction.
• Similarly, with more compact and contiguous development, there are potential savings in operating and maintenance requirements for energy. With shorter distances and more efficient coverage of an area, for instance, police and fire patrols, school bus routes, and other urban services can be provided with less energy. The provision of private goods and services, such as service or delivery calls, can be less consuming, as well.
• These areas for potential savings assume two features of future development — use of clustering techniques with somewhat higher densities for shorter distances, and elimination of leapfrog development in order to limit the amount of extraneous travel as well.

• Further savings will result if land uses are organized in such a manner that fewer trips are required and if a number of land uses are related, so that multi-purpose trips are possible. If major centers of activity — for employment, shopping, and education — are located at the junction of public transit systems, then more efficient use of both land and transportation is possible.

• Another way in which land use relates to energy use, particularly at higher densities, is that some technologies become available that would not be possible if land uses were not organized in a certain manner. Obviously, without certain threshold densities public transportation would not be feasible — whether bus or fixed-rail systems. In addition, the use of total energy systems, where the waste heat from combustion for heating is captured and used, is limited to certain sizes and groupings of structures. If the capability to use solid waste materials as a fuel source in the total energy system is added, then requisite densities become even more important.

In summary, the attributes of an energy-efficient land use pattern seem to include the following: development at somewhat higher densities, with clustering techniques as well as use of natural amenities on the site to reduce heating, cooling, and lighting loads; contiguous development with no leapfrogging; orientation to public transportation and reduced, more efficient use of the automobile; use of certain technical options that require some reorganization of present land use patterns in order to be implemented; and general relationships among land uses that will result in less travel, less material requirements, and less land and structural area per dwelling unit.

STATEMENT OF ISSUES

The magnitude of energy conservation by land use arrangements has been estimated, but the costs of conservation have not been fully considered. Energy efficiency is important, but it may not prove the overriding factor. Some of the issues that are involved with relating energy and land use include the following:

Changes in density and mobility. The prevailing dream of a single-family home and use of the private automobile are well-ingrained in the consumer's mind; these features of present lifestyles will only reluctantly be sacrificed. Since analysis of future scenarios seems to indicate that these areas show the potential for conservation, either preferences are changed or preferred lifestyles are altered. In either case, adjustments to higher densities and to limited mobility will be required.

Equity considerations. If changes occur in order to conserve energy, and if present trends in growth and development are altered by whatever means, then the question arises as to who bears the cost. Land use changes mean that private rights might be sacrificed for the wider public interest. Or the impacts of energy conservation might fall more heavily on lower-income families, who may have less capability to change consuming habits to adjust to energy conservation and land use changes.

Pricing effects. Since land use changes should have some market connection, so that plans are not totally devoid of an economic reality, most of the changes will be implemented through market mechanisms. The question then arises as to the potential leverage on energy consumption that can be exerted by means of price adjustments. In the near term, consumers are limited by the choices available to them, so that higher prices for energy will have relatively little effect on reducing consumption. In the longer-run, adjustments to price are more possible — by purchasing a smaller automobile, or a more energy-efficient residence.

Governmental effects. Although many of the incentives or disincentives for energy conservation may operate through economic markets, the framework for such actions is set by governmental activity. If governments seek to conserve energy by land use means, such changes will have to be reflected in comprehensive plans, zoning decisions, and capital improvements. The question then is where public authorities may most effectively exert leverage for energy conservation, not only in relation to land use but in other areas as well.

Optimality and conflicting objectives. As was stated previously, perhaps the most fundamental issue relating energy and land use is the number of objectives that might be possible in growth and development. It is possible to suggest land use measures that would result in some optimal level of energy conservation, but when the objective of energy conservation is compared with other objectives, a sub-optimal level of conservation may prove more desirable. If the need for economic growth, employment opportunity, community balance, or maintenance of the quality of life is more important, then the relationship between land use and energy conservation is less important, and possible reductions of energy use more remote.

––––––––

Comments: 1. Both of these selections indicate that the modification of land use and growth patterns to achieve economies in the use of energy present difficult policy problems. These have been described by one commentator, who discusses the problem of government intervention in the economy in what she calls the third stage of governmental intervention, a stage that includes land use controls to achieve energy conservation as well as other environmentally-oriented land use regulations:

> [T]he country is confronting a third generation of issues involving Government intervention. These issues have several common characteristics: they are highly technical and highly complicated; they are not subject to resolution by spending; they cut across the interests of a wide variety of interest groups; and they concern economic resources that are seen to be shrinking rather than expanding. They cannot be settled by the traditional method of buying off — doing a little something for — the various competing interests. There is not much room for maneuver, not much that can be traded off. The solutions involve not giving things to people but asking them to give things up — something the Government has usually achieved only in time of war.

Drew, A Reporter at Large: The Energy Bazaar, The New Yorker, July 21, 1975, at 35. For additional discussion of land use and energy issues see C. Harwood, Using Land to Save Energy (1977). The Harwood study discusses the legal aspects of a variety of land use control techniques to conserve energy, including techniques encouraging high density development. Which of the regulatory techniques reviewed in this book would be useful in achieving high density residential development intended to reduce energy consumption?

2. Does the methodology used in the Washington, D.C., study have the same shortcomings that Professor Altshuler saw in the Costs of Sprawl study? Are the conclusions of the two studies similar?

A NOTE ON ELECTRIC POWER PLANT SITING LEGISLATION

Difficult environmental and land use problems have arisen in controversies over the siting of new power plant generating facilities. These problems are expected to become even more serious as some estimates project as many as 490 new power plants to be built by 1980. Conflicts have arisen over whether municipalities have the power to regulate power plant location under their zoning or related ordinances. Many courts have held that decision-making power over the location of power plants is a matter of statewide interest that falls within the exclusive jurisdiction of the state utility commission, *e.g., In re Public Serv. Elec. & Gas Co.,* 173 A.2d 233 (N.J. 1961). *See* Note, Application of Local Zoning Ordinances to State-Controlled Public Utilities and Licenses: A Study in Preemption, 1965 Wash. U.L.Q. 195. Some state utility commission laws also give the commission exclusive authority over site location and preempt local zoning. In reviewing commission decisions under these statutes, the courts have tended to emphasize the state's interest in efficient utility service at the expense of local concerns over the adverse impact the plant might have in the community. *See, e.g., Town of Wenham v. Department of Pub. Util.,* 127 N.E.2d 291 (Mass. 1955).

Several states have now responded to the site location problem by enacting power plant siting acts, which may also cover transmission line locations as well, and which place the authority for making these decisions with the governor, the state utilities agency, or a special state siting agency. *See* N. Rosenbaum, Land Use and the Legislatures 43-46 (1976). This legislation often contains provisions that require the incorporation of environmental considerations in the site location decision-making process. The Vermont legislation, though quite brief, indicates the kinds of factors which this legislation requires to be taken into account. Approval of an electric generating facility or high voltage electric line must receive the approval of the state Public Service Board, which must find that the construction:

(1) will not unduly interfere with the orderly development of the region with due consideration being given to the recommendations of the municipal and regional planning commissions and the municipal legislative bodies;

(2) is required to meet the need for present and future demand for service;

(3) will not adversely affect system stability and reliability and economic factors; and

(4) will not have an undue adverse effect on aesthetics, historic sites, air and water purity, the natural environment and the public health and safety.

Vt. Stat. Ann. tit. 30, § 248 (1970).

The Vermont Supreme Court has upheld Public Service Board determinations authorizing electric transmission lines. See *Petition of Vt. Elec. Power Co.,* 306 A.2d 687 (Vt. 1973) (municipality "not insisting on high standards of development" could not object because impairment of local unique views); *Vermont Elec. Power Co. v. Bandel,* 375 A.2d 975 (Vt. 1977) (Board entitled to weigh effect of alternative locations on scenic preservation).

Some critics have argued that simply to require the state utility commission to consider the environmental impacts of siting decisions is not a sufficient solution since the commission will tend to give a higher priority to service needs than to environmental concerns. Tarlock, Tippy, and Francis, Environmental Regulation of Power Plant Siting: Existing and Proposed Institutions, 45 S. Cal. L. Rev. 502, 546-53 (1972). They urge that if the plant "will have an adverse environmental impact and . . . [if] feasible alternatives exist, the burden of proving the necessity of the plan[t] should shift to the utility." *Id.* at 55-51. They also urge that the commission be required to undertake environmental studies of the impact of the plant. *Id.* at 551-52. Some of the power plant siting acts have at least required the utilities to submit a wide range of information and studies on proposed sites, including a discussion of environmental impacts. *See* N.Y. Pub. Serv. Law § 142(1)(a) (McKinney Supp. 1977).

The more fundamental problem may be that the power plant siting laws are not well related to state and regional planning processes, so that the plant location decision is taken outside the state and regional planning process. Note that the Vermont statute, *supra,* attempts to give some consideration to municipal and regional planning recommendations. Some states have responded to this problem by providing for a statewide planning process to identify sites for power plants and transmission lines, and by limiting sites for these facilities to locations designated in the plan. *See, e.g.,* Minn. Stat. Ann. §§ 116C.5.-116C.69 (West 1977). For a model power plant siting act containing a planning requirement see Lippek, Power and the Environment: A Statutory Approach to Electric Facility Siting, 47 Wash. L. Rev. 35 (1971).

On the local preemption issue, some courts have held that the state siting law preempts local ordinances even in the absence of an express preemption provision, *e.g., City of South Burlington v. Vermont Elec. Power Co.,* 344 A.2d 19 (Vt. 1975), and some of the power plant siting acts contain explicit provisions preempting local ordinances, *e.g.,* Minn. Stat. Ann. § 116C.61(1) (1977). Federal legislation which would provide a federal regulatory program for approval of power plant sites and transmission lines has been pending for some time, but has not yet been enacted. For discussion of early versions of this legislation see Journey, Power Plant Siting — A Road Map of the Problem, 48 Notre Dame Law. 273 (1972). For a helpful study of electric energy and siting problems see Association of the Bar of the City of New York, Electricity and the Environment (1972).

A NOTE ON IMPACT ZONING AND ON INTEGRATING ENVIRONMENTAL CONCERNS IN THE LAND USE PLANNING AND REGULATION PROCESS

We noted at the beginning of this chapter that land use planning had not historically been sensitive to environmental concerns. It is now time to ask whether the traditional land use planning and regulation process can be restructured to integrate these concerns more successfully, and whether this approach to dealing with the land use dimension of environmental problems is preferable to the various regulatory techniques that have been considered in this chapter.

One method of incorporating environmental concerns in the zoning process is the technique known as building block zoning, and which is described *supra* p. 419. This technique attempts to relate zoning regulations to environmental conditions, and is close kin to another innovative technique, impact zoning, which has the same purpose. Impact zoning, which incorporates impacts other than the environmental, has been described as "a process accompanying development that measures the consequences of changes in a community in terms of *demands* related to the *capacities* of the natural, physical, market, and fiscal systems." Rahenkamp, Ditmer, & Ruggles, Impact Zoning: A Technique for Responsible Land Use Management, Plan Canada, vol. 17, no. 1, at 48, 50 (1977). A more complete description follows:

PERFORMANCE ZONING OR IMPACT ZONING

Another use to which these predictive models have been put is in performance zoning or impact zoning. This work was begun in the 1950s with industrial performance zoning, but it has been extended considerably in the last decade to include natural resource protection. A number of communities already have designed and adopted regulations controlling runoff and erosion. Naperville, Illinois, for example, requires all new developments to maintain the same rate of runoff as the site had prior to development. The developer is allowed to design any system that will meet this objective for storm-water drainage. Other communities have developed similar standards for other resources such as aquifer recharge areas, shorelands, and steep slopes.

The intent of performance zoning is to replace the tranditional use specifications with a broad set of numerical standards. If a proposed development met these standards, it would be permitted on a given site, irrespective of the particular kind of use it was — single-family homes, apartments, industrial development, and so forth. However, performance standards at present are too limited to allow the use of a "pure" performance approach. They can predict some of the variables in development, but not all. Their most successful application has been industrial performance zoning. The standards for noise, glare, vibration, smoke, traffic generation, and so forth have allowed communities to define individual industrial zones by the standards alone. They no longer need a list of permitted industries for each industrial zone. Most commonly, performance standards are used within a traditional districting situation. In these situations the zoning districts continue to specify a set of permitted and prohibited uses, but other uses are allowed through special permit provisions if they meet particular standards. This technique is particularly useful for resource conservation districts where the list of permitted uses is necessarily limited or restrictive. For example, the typical wetland district will allow only nonintensive uses, such as grazing, recreation, or gardening; and no activity that requires dredging or filling is permitted. However, additional uses can be permitted through a special permit provision if the development meets the standards necessary to allow the wetland to continue to function. In this way, the performance standards (although not sophisticated enough to allow all uses to be defined by them) can allow for some flexibility within what would otherwise be a highly restrictive district.

There have been some attempts in recent years to move performance zoning closer to the pure model by combining individual performance standards into a more comprehensive list of development standards. This work has been loosely characterized as impact zoning. These systems build on what is good in environmental performance zoning and industrial performance zoning, but they also have attempted to include other factors. The most important of these are the fiscal impacts of development — particularly as they relate to public facilities such as sewers, water supply, and roads. IBM has been working on such a system for Broward County, Florida.

A community that has information on the expected increase in public service demands from new development balanced with the expected revenues from that development could then set policies dealing with the economic consequences of development by including fiscal analysis in its controls (e.g., it could require that "all development must pay its own way"). With such a control, the developer would meet this standard by varying his location decisions, his development timing, or the particular combination or mix of units he is designing, or provide the public facilities himself. These controls would have some of the same goals as the development tax or subdivision exactions in that they would shift some of the community's costs from the development back onto the development itself. But techniques for internalizing development costs continue to rely on estimated costs using land or money exactions based on, say, size or density, or impact taxes based on the number of bedrooms. Proponents of impact zoning devices contend that actual impacts can be determined and charges assessed to new development accordingly. These controls and costs would be individualized for each development, and a developer might be able to lower the requirements by adjusting the style or location of his development.

M. Meshenberg, The Administration of Flexible Zoning Techniques 57-58 (American Soc'y of Planning Officials, Planning Advisory Service Rep. No. 318, 1976).

Impact zoning has its limitations. Predictive instruments — called models — that enable decision makers to predict the impact of new development on the environment are not fully developed, are expensive to formulate, and so far have not been easily moved from one community to another because a separate data base must be developed for each community setting. Impact zoning also relies on another controversial planning technique, carrying capacity analysis, which starts with the assumption that the environment has a finite capacity for absorbing new development that should not be exceeded. For a helpful set of articles on the carrying capacity concept see the symposium issue, Carrying Capacity as a Planning Tool, Environmental Comment, Dec., 1977 (includes bibliography). Impact analysis can also be carried out as part of the comprehensive planning process, and some planning enabling legislation now contains specific requirements for the preparation of environmental or natural resource elements as part of the comprehensive plan. *See, e.g.*, the California statute, *supra* p. 75.

Whether environmental concerns should be integrated into the land use planning and regulation process or treated in distinct, environmentally focused regulatory programs raises a host of difficult questions. Planners may argue that environmentally-oriented land use controls are single-minded in their approach and prevent the trade-offs necessary to a full accommodation of competing interests in the land development control process. Environmentalists may argue that environmental values may be ignored in the planning and zoning process, and are important enough to demand protection in programs explicitly directed to environmental control problems. Note also that the proliferation of control techniques leads to a certain amount of redundancy. Should an environmental impact statement be filed on a comprehensive plan in California that includes an adequate environmental element? [9]

---

[9] An important regulatory control over the environmental impact of surface mining for coal is provided by the national Surface Mining Control and Reclamation Act of 1977, 30 U.S.C. § 1201 *et seq.* (Supp. 1977). The basic aim of this statute is to assure the restoration of coal-mined land to a "condition capable of supporting the uses of which it was capable of supporting prior to any mining, or higher or better uses." § 1265(b)(2). To achieve this goal the statute provides for a state-administered permit program requiring the submission and approval of reclamation plans prior to the beginning of mining operations. State programs must be approved by the federal Department of the Interior.

There is a land use control in this statute, which authorizes the states to "designate an area as unsuitable for . . . surface coal mining operations if the State regulatory authority determines that reclamation . . . is not technologically and economically feasible." § 1272. For discussion of the statute see Comment, 8 Envt'l L. Rep. 10004 (1978). *See also* Note, Strip Mining: Methods of Control by the Three Levels of Government, 8 Urb. L. Ann. 143 (1974).

Chapter 9

STATE AND REGIONAL PLANNING AND DEVELOPMENT CONTROL

A. INTRODUCTORY CONCEPTS AND STRATEGIES

The focus to this point has been on land use controls adopted and exercised at the local government level. Recent years have seen a new development in land use control legislation that has shifted responsiblity for the planning and control of development to the state and to regional levels. This change, termed by Fred Bosselman and Dave Callies the "Quiet Revolution" in land use controls, has altered traditional governmental relationships in dealing with land use issues, and has profoundly influenced the manner in which we deal with land use issues.

Much of the impetus for a state and regional role in land use regulation derives from a growing concern about the environment. Indeed, as Chapter 8 has indicated, national programs for the control of air and water pollution rely extensively on state and regional enforcement and also have important land use control components. The National Coastal Zone Management Act has also stimulated important new regulatory measures shifting the control of land use to the state level, as in the California Coastal Act of 1976. There is another set of state and regional planning and land development controls that also shifts responsibility to state and regional agencies but which is not as clearly focused as the environmental legislation:

> [This new legislation] ... presents a number of thorny issues — economic, social, political, and legal. Unlike pollution controls, land use controls have no ideal of "pure" land to which they can refer. The potential impacts of controls on land values are immense. The most efficient division of responsibility between local, state, and national governments is unclear. Land use regulations offer potential areas of conflict with both national energy and housing policies. There is no shortage of proposed land use policies, but there is little knowledge of how well particular policies work or what economic, political, or social forces they face.

R. Healy, Land Use and the States 1-2 (1976).

Healy gives four reasons for an augmented state interest in land use control problems; these apply as well at the regional level. First, many land use problems spill across the boundaries of political jurisdictions. There are some 3,000 county governments in the United States, together with 18,000 municipalities and 17,000 townships. "The effects of land use changes can spill over these jurisdictional boundaries in ways as obvious as a smokestack's plume or as subtle as a flow of retail dollars." *Id.* at 7.

Next, often there is a conflict between the interests of the local jurisdiction regulating land use and the interests of a larger and broader jurisdiction.

> [C]onflicts in land use preferences may occur within metropolitan areas. Often they involve local rejection of developments that impose costs locally but benefit a larger area. Sanitary landfills and public housing projects are frequently shunned by those places where they would be best sited from a regional standpoint. Often it is the city with the least affluent, least articulate electorate that winds up with the facilities rejected by the other jurisdictions in the region.

Id. at 10.

Third, many local governments in undeveloped areas of a state or region lack effective land use controls. Often the decision to avoid land use regulation is intentional; outlying areas need new employment centers, for example, and may be oblivious to the public service costs that these developments often bring. An absence of local land use controls was one of the factors that prompted the enactment of Vermont's state land use regulation act.

Finally, state investment in public facilities such as highways, state licensing of power plant facilities, and state health laws that determine the acceptability of septic tanks and on-site water systems have an important influence on local and regional land development. This interest has been recognized at the national level in the areawide water quality planning requirements of the Federal Water Pollution Control Act. *See supra* p. 1181.

This shift in planning and regulatory powers is not often willingly accepted at the local level. As Healy notes:

> Deciding permitted land uses is one of the major discretionary powers of local goverment. It can be used to reward political friends, penalize enemies, or simply to put into practice a local official's ideal vision of his community. In a more sinister sense, such power can be a marketable commodity. One state legislator, a supporter of a state land use control bill, said of the local officials who opposed it, "These guys want to keep this their own ball game. There are a lot of political contributions available from people in the development business. The local officials don't want it all going to [the governor]."

Id. at 163.

These pressures for the enactment of state and regional planning and land development control legislation, and the political restraints on state and regional programs, should be carefully noted in the pages that follow. There is also an important difference in the basis for state as compared to regional programs. State legislation is often long on development control powers but may be short on the necessary planning framework. Regional planning is relatively well advanced, but regional powers of land use regulation are rarely conferred. Does the previous discussion indicate any reason for these differences?

B. REGIONAL PLANNING AND DEVELOPMENT CONTROL

Regional planning in the post World War II years has been heavily influenced by the requirements in federal legislation. This legislation is of two types. Federal legislation not tied to specific program requirements offers assistance for comprehensive planning at the regional level under Section 701 of the federal housing act, see *supra* p. 81, a program which has been subject to increasing criticism for lack of results. Federal legislation such as the areawide water quality planning program of the Federal Water Pollution Control Act is tied to federally funded public improvement projects, in this case wastewater treatment plants.

Federal legislation has also influenced the governmental structure under which regional planning is carried out. The institutional structure favored by the federal government is the Council of Governments, a voluntary association of local governments in the region which has increasingly been given regional planning responsibilities under federal legislation. Section 208 of the Federal Water Pollution Control Act, for example, designates the Councils of Government as the appropriate regional planning agency, and they have also been designated as the regional planning agency for transportation planning required under the federal aid highway act and the Urban Mass Transportation Act. These are two of the major federal regional planning efforts that have a direct impact on land development and growth patterns.

The following selection discusses the evolution of the federal interest in regional planning, the role of the Councils of Government (COG's), and the strengths and failings of the regional planning process. It appears as part of the commentary to the American Law Institute's Model Land Development Code, which rejects the notion of separately constituted regional planning agencies. Instead, regional planning is to be carried out by regional departments of the state planning agency, a decision motivated by the Code's preference for the state rather than the region as the proper location for planning and land use controls above the local government level.

Since regional planning agencies are seldom given implementation or review powers by state legislation, the federal government has provided some bite to regional planning through the so-called

Project Notification and Review System (PNRS). Under this system regional agencies are required to review any federally assisted projects for which funds are requested by governmental units in the region. As the ALI Code commentary notes, the regional agencies designated to carry out this review process are known as Clearinghouses. At the metropolitan level, the Clearinghouses must also be regional planning agencies. There has been considerable controversy over the exercise of the Clearinghouse function. Many observers claim that the voluntary nature of local government association with the regional planning agency leads it to an exercise of caution when reviewing applications for federal aid by member governmental units.

AMERICAN LAW INSTITUTE, A MODEL LAND DEVELOPMENT CODE 308-13 (1976)

The idea of regional planning is not new. Many early state enabling acts authorized local governments to band together for the purpose of creating and financing a regional planning agency. The makeup of these early regional planning agencies generally followed the pattern of local planning agencies of the period — they were controlled by boards of citizens interested in planning.

These acts also enabled the participating local governments to agree to submit development proposals and proposed zoning legislation to the regional agency for comment. Submission was voluntary, however, and the comments did not affect directly the validity of any local action taken either without comment or after receipt of adverse comments. Thus the commissions were given the function of preparing regional plans but no power to make them effective. . . .

When the federal government began to develop the interstate highway program in the late 1950's, it became apparent that the absence of effective regional planning would seriously hamper the highway network. All too often the federal and state highway agencies could find no one who could even predict, much less control, the location where future development would take place. In response, Congress attached to the Federal Aid Highway Act of 1962 a requirement that regional transportation planning be undertaken for metropolitan areas. 23 U.S.C. § 134 (1970).

At about the same time the Senate Subcommittee on Intergovernmental Relations instituted a series of studies of metropolitan planning in the United States which concluded that the existing system of metropolitan planning was largely ineffective. . . .

The subcommittee concluded that the real power needed for effective planning was in the hands of local elected officials. These officials had little respect for the regional planning commissioners who were viewed as ivory tower types who never had to carry a precinct.

The federal response was to propose that the metropolitan planning agency should be a Council of Governments made up of elected public officials from the local goverments in the metropolitan area.

. . . .

Beginning in the mid-60's the Department of Housing and Urban Development began urging the creation of regional councils consisting of representatives from each of the local governments in the area. . . . In the late 1960's the federal government was increasingly interested in relating its own developmental activities and grants-in-aid programs to comprehensive state, metropolitan, or regional planning. While for some years many types of developmental projects financed in part by the federal government required a showing that the project was in accordance with an overall plan for the local area in which the project was located, a requirement of consistency with or comment by an agency having a broader view of the total situation was added in the 1960's.

Section 204(a) of the Demonstration Cities and Metropolitan Development Act of 1966 requires that all applications from metropolitan areas for federal loans or grants for open-space land projects or for the planning or construction of various facilities be submitted for review to an areawide agency designated to perform regional planning for the area. The Act further provides that "to the greatest practicable extent" the area agency should be composed of, or be responsible to, the elected officials of local governments.

The Intergovernmental Cooperation Act of 1968 extended the statutory requirements for areawide review and evaluation. Section 401(a) requires that rules and regulations be established governing the "formulation, evaluation, and review of federal programs and projects having a significant impact on area and community development." Section 403 initially authorized the Bureau of the Budget to develop the appropriate regulations.

The product of that mandate was Circular A-95 now administered by the U.S. Office of Management and Budget. Part I of the Circular requires any applicant for federal assistance under any of the programs listed in Attachment D to the Circular to notify designated state and areawide planning and development clearinghouses of an intent to apply for assistance. The clearinghouses are then given an opportunity to comment on the applications in relation to state, areawide, and local plans and programs. The comments from state and areawide clearinghouses are strictly advisory. The federal agency is free to fund the request in the face of negative recommendations; however, A-95 has been revised to require that where a clearinghouse has recommended against approval of an application, the funding agency must explain in writing to the commenting agency its decision to approve the application. Because the results

of A-95 review procedures are strictly advisory, the principal function
of the process is to encourage intergovernmental cooperation and
communication. . . .

. . . .

Councils of Governments have often been created by contract
between cooperating governments to coordinate areawide planning
on a voluntary basis. The legal basis for COG formation has varied.
In some cases state legislation has been enacted authorizing
interlocal confederations. For example, the Association of Bay Area
Governments was organized in 1961 under the California Joint
Exercise of Powers Act of 1921. CALIF. GOV'T CODE §§ 6500-6513.
Other regional agencies such as the Atlanta Regional Commission
(GA. LAWS 1971, Act No. 5) are organized under specific enabling
acts. Still other areawide planning organizations are established
without formal express or implied state action. ADVISORY
COMMISSION ON INTERGOVERNMENTAL RELATIONS, REGIONAL
DECISION MAKING: NEW STRATEGIES FOR SUBSTATE DISTRICTS 50
(1973).

. . . .

Insofar as planning is concerned, some of the most highly praised
efforts at regional planning have been accomplished by agencies that
did not fit the HUD-OMB mold, such as the San Francisco Bay
Conservation and Development Commission, the Adirondack Park
Agency, the Twin Cities Regional Council, the Hackensack
Meadowlands Development Commission and the Tahoe Regional
Planning Agency. . . . Despite the success of such specialized
planning agencies the Federal Office of Management and Budget
would like to see them eliminated. In an attempt to reduce the
confusion surrounding numerous and conflicting regional
boundaries OMB through Part IV of A-95 (originally Circular A-80)
is encouraging the states to establish uniform substate boundaries
for regional planning and all other functions. Federal agencies are
encouraged but not required to use these substate districts for their
own regional planning programs.

Approximately 45 states now have some type of substate districting
programs, although the extent to which those regional boundaries
are actually used for federal and state programs varies greatly. The
federally-proposed system involves uniform substate districts in
which regional planning is undertaken by a Council of Governments
which also reviews and comments on applications for federal grants.
Although federal officials defend the system's usefulness, students
and observers of the system have been quite critical of its
effectiveness.

First, the review and coordination procedures established by A-95
have been called inadequate because the procedure is only advisory,
and because there are significant gaps in the federal programs
covered. . . .

Second, many commentators have observed that local officials view the regional planning agency as strictly a mechanism for gaining federal funding. In that context attempts at regional planning are minimal. As Melvin Mogulof has pointed out:

> [The COG] receives its legitimacy from its member governments — but those governments do not seem to want the COG to emerge as a force different and distinct from the sum of its governmental parts. Member governments do not generally see the COG as an independent source of regional influence but rather as a service giver, a coordinator, a communications forum, and an insurance device for the continued flow of federal funds to local governments. Mogulof, *Regional Planning, Clearance, and Evaluation: A Look at the A-95 Process,* 37 J. AMER. INST. OF PLANNERS 419 (1971).

The more that metropolitan agencies have been asked to review functions that bring them into potential conflict with local governments, the more the structural weaknesses of most such organizations have become apparent. The late Dennis O'Harrow pointed out that they seemed "to be plagued by political Golden Rulism: I'll vote for whatever you want in your county because I expect you to vote for whatever I want in my county." 33 ASPO NEWSLETTER 14 (1967).

Third, it is argued that a basic flaw in the regional confederal arrangement is that it is usually voluntary. . . . The member governments are free to join the regional agency, and to withdraw; free to give financial support, or to refrain; free to make genuine efforts at regional coordination, free not to. . . .

All of these political factors encourage Councils of Governments to engage in passive, consensus planning, giving each local government whatever it wants regardless of the effect on the region. This has led to the fourth category of criticism of the system — the absence of regional planning that really faces tough issues:

> A-95 procedures are designed as a screen to ensure comprehensive planning. However, the project-by-project review and comment process of A-95 precludes a broad initiating role in comprehensive planning for A-95 reviewers. Furthermore, because of its frequent poor quality and small quantity, local comprehensive planning is an inadequate yardstick for measuring applications for federal or federally assisted projects. The absence of good comprehensive planning to serve as a basis for judging applications under A-95 procedures has lessened the need to make harsh decisions. This may well account for the uncontroversial nature of A-95's

widespread implementation. NAT'L ACADEMY OF SCIENCES & NAT'L ACADEMY OF ENGINEERING, REVENUE SHARING AND THE PLANNING PROCESS 26 (1974).

Even among the regional councils which are engaged in comprehensive and functional planning, the results are not encouraging because the agencies "lack the power to implement [the plans] directly or to compel or coerce constituent general purpose jurisdictions or special districts to carry out or abide by them." ADVISORY COMMISSION ON INTERGOVERNMENTAL RELATIONS, REGIONAL DECISION MAKING: NEW STRATEGIES FOR SUBSTATE DISTRICTS 109 (1973). These independent, regional councils of government are essentially then in governmental limbo. They have governmental powers from neither the local governments, the state, nor the federal government. Planning in this context is isolated from the political process; the 701-funded planning capability of these regional agencies is not being fully utilized within local decision-making structures. NAT'L ACADEMY, *op. cit.,* at 23-24. Essentially, then, "the planning process is not effectively integrated with the political stages of decision and implementation." *Id.* at 8.

> The creation of councils of local governments has changed the actors in substate regionalism from appointed planning commissioners to elected local officials, and it has broadened regional interests to some extent. But these organizations have not shifted the power to implement plans from the local to the regional levels, and they have not had any widespread or visible success in modifying the actions which local governments take toward greater conformance with areawide goals or plans. TASK FORCE ON NATURAL RESOURCES AND LAND USE INFORMATION AND TECHNOLOGY, INTERGOVERNMENTAL RELATIONS 25 (1974).

A number of commentators have therefore accounted for the popularity, if not the "success," of the existing federally-sponsored system by apointing to its blandness. Essentially the clearinghouse function serves to "clear" and not to evaluate proposals of member governments. As Mogulof has emphasized, the COG's have failed to make essential distinctions between good and bad applications from a regional point of view. "On a de facto basis almost everything is good — because the system finds that almost nothing is bad." Mogulof, *Regional Planning, Clearance, and Evaluation: A Look at the A-95 Process,* 37 J. AMER. INST. PLANNERS 420 (1971). The facade of regional planning is backed by very little substance.

Comments: While the federally-stimulated structure for regional planning should in theory provide some integration of regional planning efforts, the proliferation of federal programs with regional planning requirements with little coordination has instead led to a fragmentation of regional planning efforts. This problem is documented in the following excerpt from a review of regional planning problems.

COMPTROLLER GENERAL OF THE UNITED STATES, FEDERALLY ASSISTED AREAWIDE PLANNING: NEED TO SIMPLIFY POLICIES AND PRACTICES 19-20 (1977)

FEDERAL PLANNING PROGRAMS ARE NOT FULLY COORDINATED

The Intergovernmental Cooperation Act of 1968 and OMB Circular A-95, part IV, call for coordinated planning at the local and areawide levels. Our review shows that because of the establishment of separate Federal planning programs and Federal agencies' and State governments' use of single-purpose organizations instead of the designated areawide comprehensive planning agencies, a myriad of organizations, planning on an areawide basis in similar functional areas, has been created. Typically, in a given geographic area no one organization is responsible for overseeing all planning. As a result, coordinated areawide planning is difficult, if not impossible, to achieve and is not fully taking place.

Several studies documenting the difficulties involved in achieving the coordination goals of the act and Circular A-95 call attention to problems resulting from the growth of Federal programs and planning organizations, differing geographic boundaries for planning, and differing administrative requirements. Two studies have especially highlighted fundamental issues at the Federal, State, and local levels.

The 1969 Federal Interagency Task Force on Planning Assistance study of 36 Federal planning programs stated:

"... This analysis clearly revealed that these programs evolved outside of any consistent policy or administrative framework. In short, the combined package of programs did not represent an interrelated system or process. These programs were established in piecemeal fashion at various times to satisfy particular needs or demands. Only one Congress has failed to establish at least one new program since 1946. Most of these programs are directly linked with a particular functional concern or interest. To a considerable extent, each separate program encourages its own consistency at the State, area-wide, and local levels. This fosters duplication, conflict in goals, and wasteful expenditure of public monies. This heritage makes it difficult, if not impossible, to direct these programs toward the solution of related problems or to even piece them together to provide effective mutual support for broad National, State, and local objectives. ..."

In 1973, the Advisory Commission on Intergovernmental Relations completed a massive 2-year study which concluded that the structure of local government was approaching "wild chaos." The Commission reported:

"... A major cause is the mad-paced proliferation of areawide governmental units. In less than a decade and a half, thousands of new structures that are larger than cities but smaller than States have been established by Federal, State, local governments. Most of them are single purpose, although some are multipurpose. The majority have boundaries that do not match the borders of cities and counties.

"These new bodies were formed because of a mismatch between the jurisdictional reach of existing local governments and mounting areawide problems. But no coherent regional strategy has existed. Whenever the need was felt for an areawide structure, one was set up in a vacuum with little heed to other units. Thus, the resultant chaos.

"The question no longer is whether there will be systems of regional governance. These structures exist and more are being created every year. The real questions before Federal, State, and local government now are: What can be done to reduce the fragmentation at this crucial level of government? How should these areawide structures relate to existing general purpose local governments and special districts?"

Comments: 1. We shall turn later in this section to planning and implementation efforts at the regional level which do attempt to provide some integration of the regional planning effort, at least as it affects land use and development problems. Before doing so we should first take a look at what regional planning is all about. Is it simply local planning writ large at the regional level or are there special attributes of regional planning which set it off from the local planning effort? How regional planning differs from local planning is indicated in the following brief summary of regional planning problems:

Setting for Metropolitan Planning
. . . .

1. *Multiple sectors.* Metropolitan planning deals with multiple sectors of activity, where "sector" is defined as a specific sub-system, for example, transportation, water supply, housing, elementary and secondary education, that is customarily planned and managed as a unit. Depending upon the particular way that problems and tasks are assigned, there may be as many as 10 to 15 individual "sectors" in a typical metropolitan planning activity. . . .

2. *Multiple jurisdictions.* Metropolitan areas typically contain multiple political jurisdictions, often a mixture of cities, towns,

counties, with general governmental powers, and special purpose districts of metropolitan or sub-metropolitan scope, with planning and development powers over specific sectors, such as water-supply and sewage disposal, transit, and parks. Any one or combination of these political jurisdictions may make investment decisions of metropolitan significance. . . .

3. *Variable time scales.* The time scale used in metropolitan planning is highly variable, ranging from short-range — one or two years — to very long-range — 40 to 50 years. This is a consequence of the many different sectors and political jurisdictions involved in metropolitan planning and decision-making. . . .

4. *Diversity of programs.* Metropolitan planning includes many important program sectors, as education, health and welfare, that are primarily operational, management and regulatory in nature. . . .

5. *Numerous and complex objectives.* Because of the complex institutional pattern of metropolitan areas, fundamental and operational objectives for metropolitan planning are numerous and take on very complex forms.

M. Hufschmidt, The Metropolitan Planning Process: An Exploratory Study 65-66 (1970).

2. To provide examples of the varying frameworks in which regional planning can be carried out we will look first at an aspect of regional planning related to a functional problem, the provision of lower cost housing, and then at a regional plan that provides a comprehensive developmental framework for the growth of a region. Regional housing and fair share plans are a response to local exclusionary zoning policies, and attempt to provide a regional basis under which local responsibilities for lower income housing can be determined. Review the *Mount Laurel* and *Oakwood* cases, *supra* p. 454 and p. 488, which called for a fair share regional approach to lower income housing programs as a basis for local zoning which would overcome judicial objections to local zoning exclusions. The following excerpt describes the conceptual basis for fair share regional housing plans and indicates their basic components.

H. FRANKLIN, D. FALK, & A. LEVIN, IN-ZONING: A GUIDE FOR POLICY-MAKERS ON INCLUSIONARY LAND USE PROGRAMS 145-51 (1974)

The Regional Housing Allocation Plan

Most officially approved plans start from the premise that suburban areas do not want lower income housing development because it represents a political, fiscal, social and aesthetic burden. In order to make such a distribution plan palatable to these areas, however, plans have been promoted as distribution of a "fair share" of this unwanted burden. Each constituent area within the jurisdiction receives no more than its "fair share." Moreover, it does so under the plan with knowledge that all other areas within the regional planning jurisdiction will also take their "fair share." As long as each area understood it was to be asked to receive no more than it "deserved," and that other areas would do likewise, the plan seemed a better option than the possibility of being forced to receive some unlimited or unknown amount of unwanted housing. In other words, the fair share concept responded in some degree to the fear of "inundation."

Advocates of equal opportunities for all citizens regardless of race or income view housing distribution policies, on the other hand, as a mechanism for "opening up" or redistributing opportunities for better housing, employment, and education. The "open suburbs" movement and the organizations promoting these social policies are the clearest advocates of this view.

Essentially, they hold that all citizens have the right to choose to live wherever they wish and that public policy should provide maximum opportunities for them to do so. This "civil rights" approach also emphasizes that access to housing opportunities represents access to many other economic and social opportunities. To proponents of this view, a housing allocation policy that permits or mandates *any* limit to such opportunities recognizes unacceptable limits on the right to such opportunities, particularly when the limit is set at what is regarded as token levels. In this view, the allocation plan should be a means of correcting past injustices, a way to assist in identifying goals to be pursued, and an indication of each community's initial obligation to relieve housing inequities throughout a region.

Both theories or approaches adopt the view ... that the amelioration of urban problems of poor housing, crime, pollution, congestion, and unemployment are dependent, in part, on the resources of suburban areas in the metropolitan area. With diminishing federal subsidies for lower income housing and rising housing costs, it is possible that regional housing allocation plans will become regarded in some areas as a way to handle the competition for scarce resources rather than the distribution of unwanted burdens.

A. THE ORIGIN OF THE HOUSING ALLOCATION PLAN

In 1968, the "housing element" was required by federal legislation to become part of the overall work program of any agency receiving federal urban planning assistance funds. HUD recommended that the housing element focus on the coordination of housing plans with other regional plans, to identify user needs and define strategies for meeting them, and to promote equal housing opportunities through, among other means, responsive zoning and subdivision legislation prepared with federal planning assistance funds.

With the need for dispersal of federal housing becoming increasingly recognized, with regional agencies looking for ways to be effective planning organizations, and with the housing element becoming HUD's new regional planning focus, the unique initiatives of the Miami Valley Regional Planning Commission in Dayton, Ohio, became the catalyst for numerous attempts to allocate low- and moderate-income housing throughout a region. . . .

HUD gave special consideration to the Miami Valley Regional Planning Commission in continued support of its housing allocation plan, and made promises to other agencies preparing similar plans to encourage the approach as an appropriate mechanism for regional housing planning efforts.

Federal involvement in issues of housing opportunities reached a peak in the early 1970s. Using President Nixon's June 11, 1971 statement on federal policies relative to equal housing opportunity as the clarification of existing policy on racial discrimination, HUD prepared "project selection criteria" and "affirmative marketing requirements." They became effective February 1972. . . .

These criteria set forth several factors for rating applications for federal housing subsidy projects as either superior, adequate, or poor. Many of the criteria placed emphasis on the location of the proposed project; other criteria focused on the need for housing, environmental factors, minority opportunities, sponsor performance, and management. The location criteria emphasized, among other factors, increased opportunities for housing locations, avoidance of concentrating subsidized housing, and the formulation of areawide plans that included a housing element relative to needs and goals for low- and moderate-income housing as well as balanced production throughout a metropolitan area.

[The project selection criteria are undergoing revision as of this writing, and no doubt will be revised again, but the major policy thrust toward the dispersal of subsidized housing units is confirmed by the federal Housing and Community Development Act of 1974, and so will continue to be reflected in the project selection criteria.—Eds.]

Federal encouragement therefore has exerted the major influence, direct and indirect, on the preparation of housing allocation plans. Some agencies relied on federal requirements to support or explain their housing recommendations. One such plan, for example, states:

"The Department of Housing and Urban Development has indicated that all jurisdictions that participate in housing programs should develop some method for distributing these units in an equitable manner."

. . . .

B. DEFINING THE HOUSING ALLOCATION PLAN

Housing allocation plans have grown so rapidly in number that definitions of them are quite general and varied. Probably the earliest definition came from a report published by the American Society of Planning Officials: "The allocation plan outlines the dispersal

policies for the future development of lower income housing units."
Later definitions have stated:

> "Fair-share housing plans typically determine where housing
> — especially low- and moderate-income units — should be built
> within a region, according to such criteria as broadening the
> economic mix in communities and the placement of housing in
> environmentally suitable locations."

. . . .

Housing allocation plans have three principal dimensions. First,
of course, is a numerical dimension — a designated number of lower
income housing units to be allocated by the plan. This number can
be based on the need for housing, the units allocated to a region
through some funding source, or some other base. . . .

Second, a housing allocation plan has a time element — a period
over which the plan is to operate. Some plans allocate housing units
needed over the next five years; others will apportion a percentage
of the subsidized units to be allocated over the next year. . . .

The third dimension is spatial — the allocation of housing units
to geographic subareas or political jurisdictions in a region. This
allocation in theory can be static or dynamic. A static allocation would
recognize a subarea's present need in relation to overall regional
need and allocate units in relative proportion; such an allocation
would give great weight to the needs of localities with the greatest
concentrations of lower income people and the poorest housing. . . .
A dynamic allocation would recognize the opportunity for mobility
to be afforded to those in need to live throughout the region and
would give relatively more weight to providing lower income housing
in localities that have relatively few lower income residents in
recognition that more should be accommodated. . . .

Given these three elements, housing plans that merely identify
current unmet housing needs, or that only establish suitable site
location criteria for housing, or that only determine what land should
be zoned residentially, or that merely project the housing needs for
the future within the region, cannot be termed housing allocation
plans.

To be relevant to inclusionary land use objectives, then, a housing
allocation plan must be a plan that distributes a specific number or
proportion of housing units throughout a jurisdiction by means of
a dispersal formula that attempts both to increase the existing supply
of that housing in certain areas and to increase the locational
opportunities of the households to be served by such units.

Comments: 1. The influence of federal requirements on the development
of housing allocation plans is clear. Although they are not required by
federal legislation, except to the extent that the housing element required
by federal planning assistance legislation encourages them, housing

allocation plans can be tied by the federal government to housing subsidy and community development programs. As of this writing, for example, areas with housing allocation plans stand to benefit under federal regulations in the distribution of federal housing subsidies. At the same time, housing allocation planning may not always be consistent with other regional planning efforts. What if communities to which a large share of lower income housing is allocated are not scheduled for upgrading in wastewater treatment facilities under Section 208 planning? Or is the lower income housing increment so minimal that this problem is largely academic?

How the housing allocation plan might be implemented is indicated by the experience in the Minneapolis-St. Paul Twin Cities area in Minnesota. There the regional Clearinghouse agency, the Metropolitan Council, includes a review of housing performance under the housing allocation plan as part of its review of a local governmental unit's application for funding under other federal assistance programs, such as the sewer and water program. The Council's comments on the locality's performance in providing lower income housing are then reported to the appropriate federal agency as part of the Council's recommendations on whether the project applied for, such as a sewer or water project, should be funded. In addition, compliance with the housing allocation plan is one of the criteria considered when the Council as Clearinghouse agency reviews housing developments submitted for federal funding. In-Zoning, *supra* at 162-63. For additional discussion of housing allocation plans see D. Listokin, Fair Share Housing Allocation (1976).

2. Probably the most successful of the regional planning agencies nationally is the Metropolitan Council for the Twin Cities area in Minnesota, whose policies for the implementation of housing allocation plans have just been described. This agency is not a COG. Under the authorizing legislation, the members of the Council are appointed by the governor, and so the Council does not technically qualify as a voluntary associaton of governments.

The Metropolitan Council has been given planning and implementation powers far in excess of those possessed by comparable agencies elsewhere. Central to the Council's planning program is the Development Guide, which "shall" consist of a compilation of policy statements, goals, standards, programs, and maps prescribing guides for an orderly and economic development, public and private, of the metropolitan area." Minn. Stat. Ann. § 473.145 (Supp. 1977). It is also to adopt policy plans for metropolitan commissions, such as the waste control and transit commission, as well as an open space and solid waste plan. Council review for approval of all metropolitan commission development programs and budgets is also provided. It may also review and suspend if inconsistent with the development guide any comprehensive plan of an independent commission, board or agency within the area if the plan will have a metropolitan effect. *Id.* §§ 473.161-165. Highway projects must also be approved by the Council. *Id.* § 473.167. Finally, the Council reviews all applications by local government units within its area for federal or state aid, thus establishing its Clearinghouse review function. *Id.* § 473.171.

Two other important powers of the Metropolitan Council should be noted. The Council may review any privately or publicly proposed "matters of metropolitan significance" for consistency, among other criteria, with the development guide, and may suspend action on the matter of metropolitan significance for 12 months. *Id.* § 473.173. Finally, the Council is to review the comprehensive plans of local government units and the capital improvement programs of school districts to determine their consistency with the metropolitan system plans. *Id.* § 473.175. If a local government unit fails to adopt a local comprehensive plan consistent with the system plans the Metropolitan Council may take appropriate action in court. *Id.* The system plans cover airports, metropolitan waste control, transportation, and regional recreation open space. *Id.* § 473.852(8).

As the Council's powers of review operate in practice, the plans and projects submitted for review are generally evaluated for consistency with its Development Guide, which contains the various system plans required by the statute. In addition, it contains a Development Framework which specifies a Metropolitan Urban Service Area within which urban services will be made available, and which determines where new growth is to occur. The Development Guide and Framework are thus examples of a comprehensive regional growth and development policy which, in the Twin Cities area, is integrated through the control exercised by the Council over the provision of basic metropolitan services.

The following selection describes in detail how the Urban Service Areas, the key to the metropolitan growth policy, were selected, and explains how the regional plans are implemented to achieve the objectives of regional planning policy. For more discussion of the Twin Cities system see Freilich & Ragsdale, Timing and Sequential Controls — The Essential Basis for Effective Regional Planning: An Analysis of the New Directions for Land Use Control in the Minneapolis-St. Paul Metropolitan Region, 58 Minn. L. Rev. 1009 (1974).

P. REICHERT, GROWTH MANAGEMENT IN THE TWIN CITIES METROPOLITAN AREA: THE DEVELOPMENT FRAMEWORK PLANNING PROCESS 25-26, 39, 43-44 (1976)

Developing Criteria For the Metropolitan Urban Service Area

The next step in the process was to establish the criteria that would define a proper balance between urban land demand and supply. In translating the interim policies into a Development Framework Plan map, the concept of an Urban Service Area distinct from a Rural Service Area and expanded over time as necessary to accommodate urbanization needs was developed. In terms of developing a staging process — or a process by which the urban land supply would be maintained in balance with the urban land demand — the Framework policies were synthesized into a conceptual objective: maximize the choice of lifestyle in the Metropolitan Area subject to the constraints of 1) orderly and economic development, and 2) protection of both the natural and man-made environment.

Two factors provided for choices of lifestyle. First, directional choice for living and working opportunities was provided by forecasting household unit and employment demand as described above by sectors rather than by proposing a single metropolitan-wide growth allocation determined simply by filling in development where the greatest availability of urban services existed. Second, choice was further enhanced by providing staged urban-land area commitments for each sector which are proportionate to, but significantly greater than, the actual land needs. An oversupply of land equal to at least five years' additional demand was to be maintained at all times with respect to the land served by metropolitan services. The five-year overage factor was based primarily on judgment.

The concept was to provide enough urban land within each sector of the Metropolitan Urban Service Area to encourage realistic (in terms of scale) public zoning and service investment and to allow for reasonable private planning. Both of these are necessary to prevent land prices from artificially increasing. To provide more than a five-year oversupply of serviced land would undermine the economic benefits of the staging plan. In addition, adequate land was provided within each sector of the Urban Service Area to accommodate the total sector population demand even though a percentage of the population would locate outside the Area in Freestanding Growth Centers, Rural Town Centers and on large parcels at very low densities in the general rural use regions. Since the overage factor was based on judgment, a housing and land price monitoring system was called for.

Orderly and economic development was defined as maximizing the use of public dollar investments in services; i.e., sewers, roads, water systems, schools, transit, police, fire protection, parks, etc. Development should occur first in areas provided with the greatest combined complement of costly metropolitan and local public services. New land should be staged for urbanization in a contiguous manner minimizing additional public expenditures. Since metropolitan-wide investments are involved, such staging must focus on the orderly and economic provision of metro scale services.

Protection of the natural and man-made enviornment meant that development should occur without degradation to the environment, both to preserve the natural ecological system and to avoid the unnecessary expenditures and potential hardships associated with improperly located man-made development. Preserving the natural hydrologic system and locating development where compatible with the soil characteristics and the physical terrain is a basic concept of the Development Framework.

In summary, the following criteria were developed and used for defining the Urban Service Area:

1. The Urban Service Area in each sector must have enough developable land to accommodate the total forecasted sector demand for urban land.

2. The Urban Service Area in each sector must at all times include enough developable land to meet the demand for urban land for an additional five years. This oversupply of land is needed to

allow locational choice within sectors, accommodate variations in the projected growth rates, provide adequate lead time for planning and construction, and prevent increased land prices caused by a shortage of developable land.

3. The Urban Service Area must permit reasonable economy in the provision of metropolitan services. It should maximize the use of existing investments in sewers, highways, parks, transit, and other metropolitan and local services. It should also minimize the cost of providing additional services.

4. The Urban Service Area should reflect prior service commitments and restrictions made by the Metropolitan Council.

5. The Urban Service Area should be defined in terms of time, and the boundaries should be expanded periodically to 1990 to meet forecasted need.

6. Areas with soils that present severe constraints to urban development should not be considered part of the potential supply of land for urban development.

7. Agriculture should be recognized as an important land use which is particularly vulnerable to urban pressures. Land well-suited for commercial agriculture should not be considered part of the potential supply of land for urban development.

. . . .

METROPOLITAN DEVELOPMENT GUIDE, TWIN CITIES, MINNESOTA

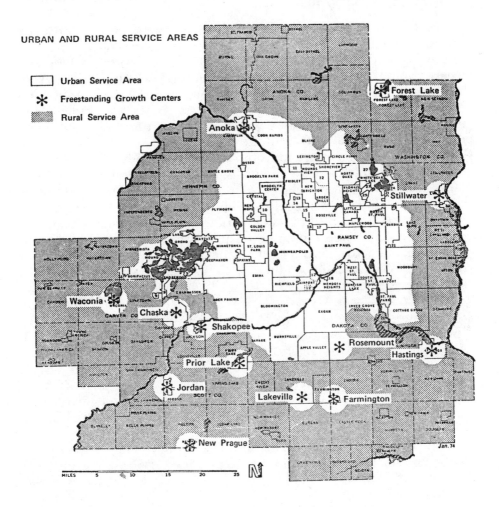

THE METROPOLITAN DEVELOPMENT FRAMEWORK APPLIED

The concept of a Development Framework evolved from the necessity of having some basis for coordinating and resolving conflicts among a wide variety of functional plans, capital programs, local municipal plans and A-95 reviews. . . .

Metropolitan Policy Plans

The Framework has provided three major premises to coordinate the metropolitan functional policy plans for sewers, transportation, and parks. First, the Framework identified the general urban area where capital investments in these functions should be concentrated during the next 15 years. Second, population, household, and employment forecasts were provided at both a regional and municipal level for functional planning. While these forecasts were extended to the year 2000 and the design life of some facilities, such as an interceptor sewer, may be as long as 40 or 50 years, the forecasts provide a base line for timing capital investments. Moreover, the Framework forecasts emphasize the need to place sub-area forecasting for facility design in a regional context. A third major contribution of the Framework to functional facility planning has been its renewed emphasis on programming maintenance and replacement of the existing infrastructure of sewers and roads, as opposed to continually adding to the serviced area through new facility construction.

The Council's newly adopted Waste Management Policy Plan directs the metropolitan Waste Control Commission to provide a coordinated metropolitan sewer system within the Urban Service Area only. New sewer facilities are planned and timed to serve those areas indicated in the Framework as future additions to the Urban Service Area. The restriction of metropolitan sewer service to the Urban Service Area has resulted in a smaller geographic jurisdiction for the Waste Control Commission than previously assigned by the Council in the 1970 sewer plan.

The Council's new Transportation Policy Plan directs the Metropolitan Transit Commission to provide service only within the Urban Service Area. Similarly, the Federal-Aid Urban Highway geographic boundary has been defined to correspond to the Urban Service Area. The 1976 Capital Budgets of the Metropolitan Waste Control and Transit Commissions were reviewed by the Council for consistency with the Framework resulting in some amendments before they were approved by the Council.

The Council's Recreation Open Space Policy Plan is being reassessed for consistency with the Development Framework. The Framework emphasizes high priority for acquisition of regional park sites within the Urban Service Area and discourages parks within the prime agricultural areas.

In addition to these three major physical plans, the Council's housing allocation plan, which is used to evaluate requests for federal Community Development Act Section 8 housing subsidy grants, has been revised to comply with the Development Framework.

Local Plans

The mandatory planning bill was heatedly debated during the 1975 legislative session but was referred back to committee by a narrow margin in the Senate and thus was not introduced in the House. Opponents of the bill hoped that its defeat would mean defeat of the Development Framework itself.

The bill was again debated in the 1976 session and was finally passed after going through a conference committee of both houses. The bill establishes an *integrated planning system* for local governments, school districts and the Metropolitan Council in the seven-county Metropolitan Area.

The Metropolitan Council, which is presently required to prepare and adopt plans for metropolitan systems (sewers, highways and transit, airports, regional parks), will assist local governments and school districts by preparing and submitting to each a metropolitan systems statement by July, 1977. Each statement will identify currently projected capacities, locations and timing for metropolitan public facilities that are expected to serve the local government's jurisdiction.

In turn, each *city* will prepare by January 1, 1980 a comprehensive plan which must contain at least: 1) a land use plan including a housing element indicating the city's plans to accommodate its fair share of low- and moderate-cost housing; 2) a public facilities plan to address transportation, sewer, and park and open space needs; and 3) a local implementation program. The implementation program will describe measures including zoning and subdivision regulations and capital improvements program to be undertaken to implement the comprehensive plan. If urban development is anticipated by the city, then its plan would also identify areas anticipated to be urbanized at five-year increments.

Each *town* with planning powers will prepare a comprehensive plan with the same elements as in the city comprehensive plan. Towns may elect to have the county prepare their plan.

Each *county* will prepare a public facilities plan to address transportation, parks and open space, and solid waste disposal needs, and an implementation program. Counties other than Hennepin and Ramsey must also prepare a land use plan for their unincorporated areas.

Each *school district* will prepare a capital improvements program for new school sites and buildings.

The Metropolitan Council will *review* and *comment* on all local government plans and programs on the basis of their compatibility with one another and their consistency with the Metropolitan Development Guide. The Council may *require* the modification of a local government plan if it represents "substantial impact on or departure from" the metropolitan system plans for sewers, transportation, airports and parks. The Council will *review* and *comment* on school district capital programs.

In addition, the bill calls for the Council to establish a modest cost private housing advisory committee to study potential means of reducing housing costs through modifications in zoning, subdivision, and building codes. The Council must make recommendations to the Legislature by January 1, 1977.

The Framework policies and plan are also proving to be effective for infusing a regional perspective into local municipal planning efforts by indicating whether a community should consider itself as urban or rural. After making this initial identification, the community can begin to relate its planning to the appropriate Framework policies. In addition, population and household growth forecasts based on and contained in the Framework provide a sound estimate to each municipality of what share of the region's growth it may expect to receive over the next 15-25 years.

Comments: 1. Is the Metropolitan Council's development plan simply a growth control plan or does it implement other developmental objectives at the regional level? How does it compare with a growth control plan like the Ramapo plan, *supra* p. 1037? Note how the housing allocation plan for the region is integrated with the overall comprehensive policies of the Development Framework. For additional discussion of the history of the Metropolitan Council see Advisory Commission on Intergovernmental Relations, Substate Regionalism and the Federal System II: Regional Governance — Promise and Performance, ch. IV (1973).

2. To what extent does the Metropolitan Council's Development Framework reflect the various facets of regional planning as outlined in the excerpt from Professor Hufschmidt's study, *supra* p. 1216? Is the Development Framework a "good" or a "bad" regional plan? What criteria would you use to make this judgment? Consider the following prescription for preparing a regional development framework:

Regional Development Framework. The regional framework should be a statement of activity location, arrangement, and interaction in sufficient detail to provide a basis for testing the facility-service system plans. This plan ought to reflect the development objectives of the region in terms of detailed performance standards and criteria. The plan should be regarded as a resolution of these standards and criteria, existing conditions, activity interrelationships and the growth predicted for the entire region. Activity interrelationships, preferably stated in the form of urban development models, should be used to allocate regional growth to small districts in conformance with the standards and criteria specified. A cyclic process should be employed to test plan sensitivity to variations in standards and criteria within the context of the agreed upon objectives and in conjunction with testing of the facility-service system plans. The framework should be fully revised every five years.

D. Boyce, N. Day, & C. McDonald, Metropolitan Plan Making 107 (1970). To what extent do the criteria for selecting the urban service areas in the Metropolitan Council's plan meet these criteria? How would you classify the criteria specified in the excerpt just quoted? For example, are they efficiency criteria? *See supra* p. 31.

3. The Metropolitan Council experience indicates the importance of regional institutions of governance to the success of regional planning efforts. The Council's governmental system is integrated in the sense that this agency has been given strategic governmental controls over both metropolitan public facility systems and land use regulation. As Robert Einsweiler, AIP, and former executive director of the Council, has pointed out, the Council stands alone among regional agencies in having created an integrated system. Elsewhere, integration is partial. A few regional agencies have acquired regulatory powers over land use, and are thus able to exercise control in the area of land use regulation. Examples are the Tahoe Regional Planning Agency, established by interstate compact, which exercises regulatory jurisdiction in the bi-state Lake Tahoe area of California and Nevada. Another is the Adirondack Park Agency created by statute in New York State, which exercises regulatory land use authority in the Adirondack Park area. To be compared with these agencies are other metropolitan entities, such as the Municipality of Metropolitan Seattle, or Metro, which in fact is an areawide metropolitan special district with authority over a wide range of metropolitan public facility programs but no authority over land use matters. These examples of partial metropolitan integration are more typical of the national scene than the Twin Cities Metropolitan Council and its integrated system. Partially integrated metropolitan service and land use delivery systems quite clearly complicate the role of regional planning.

For discussion of the Adirondack Park Act see Booth, The Adirondack Park Act: A Challenge in Regional Land Use Planning, 43 Geo. Wash. L. Rev. 612 (1975); Note, Preserving Scenic Areas: The Adirondack Land Use Program, 84 Yale L.J. 1705 (1975). *See also* J. Kusler, Public/Private Parks and Management of Private Lands for Park Protection (Institute for Envt'l Studies, Univ. of Wisconsin, 1974). The Adirondack Park Act was sustained against home rule objections in *Wambat Realty Corp. v. State of New York,* 362 N.E.2d 581 (N.Y. 1977).

Another regional land use control program which has received national attention is the permit program administered by the San Francisco Bay Conservation and Development Commission, and which is intended to limit the further filling of the Bay for developmental purposes. For discussion see F. Bosselman & D. Callies, The Quiet Revolution in Land Use Control 108-35 (1971); Schoop & Hirten, The San Francisco Bay Plan: Combining Policy with Police Power, 37 J. Am. Inst. Planners 2 (1971); Note, Saving

San Francisco Bay: A Case Study on Environmental Legislation, 23 Stan. L. Rev. 349 (1971). *See also* Marks & Taber, Prospects for Regional Planning in California, 4 Pac. L.J. 117 (1973). The constitutionality of the San Francisco Bay Act was upheld in *Candlestick Properties, Inc v. San Francisco Bay Conserv. & Dev. Comm'n,* 89 Cal. Rptr. 897 (Cal. App. 1970).

C. STATE PLANNING AND DEVELOPMENT CONTROL

1. State Planning

State planning has a long history in this country, although it has seldom produced (and probably should not produce) land use plans of the conventional variety. State land use controls are of more recent origin, and are often administered independently of the state plan. In this section we will look at some of the paramount issues in state planning, and then examine state land use control programs.

More than its local counterpart, state planning has reflected the policy priorities of the federal government. It was financial stimulus from the federal level that first prompted state planning in the financial depression of the 1930's, and state planning at that time largely reflected the city planning process. This early effort disappeared with the Second World War, only to emerge at its close with its focus largely shifted to the encouragement of state economic development. By the 1950's and 1960's, the emergence of a series of federally funded planning programs for federally aided facilities such as highways led to an emphasis on program coordination.

This evolution in the state planning process, more fully described in American Law Institute, A Model Land Development Code 291-99 (1976) led to some soul-searching as the 1960's drew to a close. Notably, in a report on state planning prepared in 1967, and quoted in the ALI Code commentary, *id.* at 296-97, the National Governors' Conference had this to say on the state planning function as it related to conventional city planning:

> A state plan . . . is not a city plan written larger. The 1961 state planner did not distinguish between the physically oriented . . . [local] government with its sewers, streets and schools, and the regionally oriented state government, with its health, education and employment services. While the physical facilities plan of a local government can be implemented through the zoning ordinance, no such simple device is available to state government. The physical facilities of state government are widely scattered individual hospitals, parks, office buildings, jails or university buildings. The state planning process must concern itself with the executive-legislative process of setting goals, adopting budgets, and choosing programs.

Committee on State Planning, A Strategy for Planning: A Report to the National Governors' Conference 5 (1967).

As the 1970's approached, states began to reassert their interest in physical land use planning, in environmental protection and in growth management. The following report summarizes the contemporary focus of planning by state governments.

COUNCIL OF STATE GOVERNMENTS, STATE COMMUNITY DEVELOPMENT POLICY 54-57 (1976)

A State Planning Process

Planning by various state agencies is an important tool for the efficient and effective provision of community infrastructure and services. Yet such focused planning limits the State's ability to relate various policies and programs for maximum effectiveness. Many functional plans in housing, transportation, and wastewater treatment, written under federal sponsorship to guide program development and investment, tend to embrace narrowly conceived objectives. State officials must develop an overall policy framework as the basis for evaluating myriad plans and programs of the separate agencies and units of state and local governments. . . . [S]tate planning is assuming a new content — it is more than the preparation and aggregation of functional program plans.

State planning is a process designed to enhance the State's capability to plan for and manage growth within its boundaries, and not solely a device to produce concrete plans of a substantive nature. In the United States political and economic system, state officials cannot hope to completely control the growth forces within the State, but they must know how state activities can be most effective. A state plan, as a comprehensive policy framework, enables them to define the role, limitations, and priorities of state government in growth management. Each agency within state government contributes to its management capability with internal policies and programs to achieve defined objectives. Comprehensive state planning is needed to link state, local, and federal activities so that they interact in a complementary manner. If conflict between policies and programs is to be minimized, there must be coordination among all units and levels of government.

A state planning process must provide a central decision-making entity with the ability to synthesize state programs and the various activities affecting them and to provide direction to state government activities. It must assist state officials in efforts to coordinate functional policies and programs at all levels of government and to identify the needs and objectives of state government which do not fall within any single agency's domain. State planning is, in short, a comprehensive, integrated process of goal definition, problem analyses, policy development, program design, resource allocation, and performance evalution — from the viewpoint of the State as a whole.

Planning in the State

Few States currently use planning as a broad management tool in spite of the increase in central state planning. There is frequent uncertainty among participants in state planning activities of the function of planning. In the development of state policy, the major activity of state planning ranges among States from document preparation, to development of legislation, to coordinative responsibility, or to stimulation of citizen involvement. In some States, state planning activities are closely tied to the budget. In others, long-term public investment is the main link between state planning and budgeting.

In most States, state planning efforts are still confined to physical development, economic development planning, or inter-governmental relations and local assistance; but new concerns and perspectives on state planning are emerging in response to the intergovernmental, environmental, and economic conditions of the 1970s. State planning is emerging from a specific "task" perspective to a concept of growth policy planning and management. Land use and economic development concerns remain in the forefront of state planning. The focus is changing from land use control or economic expansion to use of land and economic development activities as tools for growth management. . . .

. . . The most serious planning deficiency in most States is the lack of overall state policy guidelines against which to evaluate their own and federal activities. Since the effectiveness of coordination rests on the development and continuous evaluation and revision of a state policy framework, this mission becomes the central function of a state planning process. . . .

Goals and Policies

A state planning process does not determine the content of a State's goals and objectives. The specific policy framework emerges from a process which permits state officials to examine the various objectives of state agencies, and the needs and problems of the State as a whole. Many States have official growth plans or policy guidelines, or have established a state-level growth commission or process as part of the process of identifying state goals. Relatively few of these statements or studies have moved beyond recognition of needs and the identification of some key growth-related activities over which the State may exercise some initiative. . . .

The goals which evolve from a planning process vary among the States in both content and formality. The goal may be economic diversification to prevent erosion of an economic base, as in the case of Michigan's automobile-based economy, or to build up an initial industrial economic base, as in many of the southern States. Most of the northeastern States have diverse economies, and the major objective of state policies is to maintain the competitive position of these States as national economic conditions change. In other States, purely economic considerations are less paramount. The goals which set the policy framework are balanced between economic development and environmental protection. Hawaii's sophisticated Growth Policies Plan sets forth a current policy of a development program which achieves economic progress while preserving the unique environmental character of the Islands. Many States where market forces are contributing to significant growth adopt similar goals of balanced growth. In a few cases, growth commissions and state planning processes have resulted in formally adopted plans which provide the policy framework for coordination.

Coordination can and does occur in many States without an articulated policy base. The Governor and members of his cabinet or state planning office mediate between agencies to resolve conflicts in the interests of a coherent policy. However, the policy which emerges from mediation is likely to be only the common denominator of agency objectives and to lack the integrative ability of a policy which is developed to guide state agencies' activities. . . .

There are other, less formal means by which state officials can develop a policy framework for programs in the State. A study and compilation of existing state policies is a first step to bringing coherency into state policies and programs. The Governor, through annual messages, budgets, and separate policy statements or executive orders, can set a policy framework for legislative and agency programs.

Comments: The Council of State Governments report suggests some of the distinctive features of state planning — the greater difficulties of program coordination at the state level, the often selective nature of the state planning process, and the importance of finding a proper political setting. Lawyers might well now ask how the statutory mandate for the state planning function should be incorporated in state enabling legislation. This legislation is reviewed in D. Mandelker, Environmental and Land Controls Legislation 42-55 (1976), along with model acts for state planning contained in the ALI Code and in an earlier proposal put forth by the Advisory Commission on Intergovernmental Relations. Most of the existing state legislation is rudimentary; often the state is simply authorized to do a plan. The ALI Code model act provisions for state planning tend to echo the Code provisions for local planning, see *supra* p. 79, and call for studies on a list of "matters found by the [state planning] Agency to be important to future development," including population, land use, capital facilities, environmental and natural resource areas, and the like. Code § 8-402(1). The Code then provides for a state Land Development Plan which is to "define in general terms state land-use policies and objectives." Code § 8-403(1). Objectives, policies and standards contained in the plan are to cover the list of matters studied. The plan is to coordinate these objectives, policies and standards and analyze their "probable social, environmental and economic consequences." To what extent do the ALI Code proposals authorize the exercise of the state planning function along the lines indicated in the Council of State Governments report?

An alternative statutory model for state planning has now been provided by the Advisory Commission on Intergovernmental Relations in an updated version of its original model legislation. The revised model act follows. For discussion see also Council of State Governments, State Growth Management, ch. III (1976).

ADVISORY COMMISSION ON INTERGOVERNMENTAL RELATIONS, 5 STATE LEGISLATIVE PROGRAM: ENVIRONMENT, LAND USE AND GROWTH POLICY 19-22 (1975)

SECTION 8. *State Development Plan.*

(a) The [state planning] agency shall prepare or cause to be prepared and, . . . shall publish the state development plan. Preparation and revision of the plan shall be a continuing process. Such process, to the extent feasible, shall consider studies, reports, and plans of the various departments of state and local government, regional planning agencies, and the Federal government, and shall consider existing and prospective resources, capabilities, and needs of state, regional, and local levels of government. The most current version of each state substantive, regional, and local plan shall be submitted to the agency not later than [*date*] of each year, and shall be incorporated into the state development plan without change, except in those cases where a change is necessary to resolve explicitly identified conflicts and those necessary to assure conformance with statewide, regional, or areawide policies established within the framework of legislative action.

(b) The initial state development plan shall be submitted to the governor not later than [*date*]. Thereafter the plan shall be updated annually.

(c) The state development plan shall be based on the best available data and shall provide guidance to state, local, and regional agencies for the coordinated and orderly social, economic, and physical development of the state in accordance with the policies, objectives, and standards, established and approved by the [*legislature*] relating to the:

(1) management and prudent use of the state's resources, including land, water, air, and energy;

(2) efficient and productive utilization of water resources, including watershed management, maintenance of water quality, and flood damage protection;

(3) preservation of areas, structures, and sites of historical, archeological, architectural, recreational, scenic, or environmental significance;

(4) location and utilization of parks and recreation and wilderness areas;

(5) location and balanced utilization of airport, highway, and public transportation facilities;

(6) location and operation of refineries and sewage, waste water treatment, solid waste disposal, and electric generating facilities;

(7) development and location of commerce and industry;

(8) location of public office buildings, colleges and universities, and health, welfare, and correctional institutions;

(9) development and location of housing, including low and moderate income housing, urban and community development, and open spaces related thereto;

(10) provision of health services, manpower development, employment opportunity, educational services, elimination of poverty, crime control, and social and rehabilitative services; and

(11) preservation and efficient utilization of prime agricultural lands.

(d) The state development plan shall describe programs whereby the objectives and policies set forth therein may be implemented. Alternative programs with appropriate analyses may be provided.

(e) The agency shall to the extent possible and appropriate consider Federal agency plans.

(f) All state departments, local governments, substate district organizations, and regional planning districts shall assist the agency to the maximum possible extent in carrying out the purposes of this act.

(g) Prior to submitting the plan to the governor, the agency shall hold a public hearing on the proposed plan in each of the [substate or regional planning districts]. Notice and procedures for these hearings shall comply with the [*state administrative practices act*].

. . . .

[Section 9 provides for submission of the plan to the state legislature. There are two alternatives for legislative adoption. Under one, the plan is considered adopted unless expressly disapproved by the legislature. Under the second, express approval by the legislature is required.—Eds.]

SECTION 10. *State Land Management Plan.*

(a) As an element of the state development plan, the agency shall prepare or cause to be prepared the state land management plan. This plan, which may consist of policy objectives and guidelines, maps or other appropriate material, shall guide decisions relating to public and private development within the state. The plan shall include, without limitation, principles for designating various types of public and private land use within particular areas; a comprehensive analysis of existing and proposed facilities, including transportation, parks, schools, public building and institutions, electrical generation facilities, refineries, and waste disposal areas;

proposals for protecting the state's natural resources and agricultural lands; designation of areas appropriate for urban growth and new community sites, and procedures for identifying and protecting critical areas.

(b) To the maximum possible extent, local and regional land management plans and implementation of such plans shall be consistent with, and further the policies contained in, the state land management plan. The agency shall furnish to local governments and regional agencies, upon request, assistance in developing plans and regulatory programs and by rule shall establish specific procedures for agency review of proposed local and regional land management plans and programs prior to adoption; however, such review shall be accomplished by the agency at the request of a local or regional government agency. The agency review shall identify specific inconsistencies between the state land management plan and a proposed local or regional plan or program and shall clearly set forth agency objections based on such inconsistencies. The agency, ... may institute appropriate judicial proceedings to insure maximum compliance with the state land management plan and policies contained therein, including declaratory actions to invalidate provisions of local or regional plans, programs, or development orders that conflict with state policies.

(c) To further implementation of this section, the agency shall continuously consider and analyze land resource management and regulation and shall recommend appropriate new legislation, draft model ordinances to assist local governments, and examine techniques for encouraging well planned development and growth, including, without limitation, [new communities, land banks, urban development authorities, and development rights transfer].

Comments: 1. The Advisory Commission states that its model act is based on the ALI Code, on the Florida state comprehensive planning act, and on the Oregon comprehensive planning legislation, which is discussed below. *Id.* at 14. To what extent does the ACIR model differ from the ALI model? Note that the ACIR draftsmen also state that their act is intended to authorize "a continuous policy planning process, with plans oriented to carrying out legislative policies, objectives, and standards." *Id.* at 15. The continuing process approach reflects the ALI Code's preferences for the organization of the planning function, see *supra* p. 79. Presumably, legislative adoption of policies, objectives and standards is intended to provide political sanction for the plan. To what extent does the ACIR model act authorize the selective state planning that is described in the Council of State Governments report, *supra*?

One problem with the ACIR model state planning act as well as with most state planning legislation is that it calls for coordination but fails to provide the mechanism for coordination. For example, how is the state planning policy for highways and transportation to be applied effectively to the state department of transportation, usually a large and potent bureaucracy with important ties both to federal agencies and to a vocal state constituency? The problem is aggravated in states in which the governor has no effective control over this agency, which may be subject to administrative direction by an independent board or commission. Legislative adoption of the state plan may not alter this situation. Political interests sympathetic to the state transportation department will simply exert their influence in the legislature to alter the state plan in a manner acceptable to the transportation agency. Or else the state plan will be watered down to objectives, standards and policies which are so general that they are not capable of effective enforcement.

2. Note the intergovernmental implications of the state land management plan. Section 10 provides for state review of local plans and regulatory programs to determine their consistency with the state plan. Judicial action is authorized by the state agency to enforce compliance with the state plan by local and regional agencies, but not by state agencies. Does Comment 1, *supra,* give some inkling of the possible reason for this omission?

3. Most state planning legislation has not contained authority for land use control regulations that implement the policies of the plan. The ACIR model state planning act does contain provisions for the regulation of Development of Regional Impact, a technique borrowed from the ALI Code, see *infra* p. 1244. Under one alternative provided by the model act, these developments are to be regulated according to the policies contained in the state plan.

Recent years have seen the adoption of state legislation that provides explicitly for the exercise of regulatory functions at the state level, sometimes tied to the state plan and sometimes not. An examination of these recent state regulatory programs follows, beginning with an analysis of the Oregon planning legislation, which provides for a stronger method of state review of local plans than the ACIR model act.

2. State Regulation of Land Development

As in state planning, federal initiatives have also been largely responsible for the adoption of state land development control legislation. The National Coastal Zone Management Act, discussed in Chapter 8, is an example of national, environmentally-based legislation, that requires a state regulatory as well as a state planning process. No such national legislation has been enacted that would provide a stimulus to state land development controls that are comprehensive in nature and that are not environmentally oriented. Legislation of this kind was considered in Congress in the early 1970's but was not adopted. See N. Lyday, The Law of the Land: Debating National Land Use Legislation 1970-75 (1976). Like the national coastal legislation, this act would also have required a state planning process with policies to be developed and implemented through designated state land use controls. These controls were modeled on the selective state land use control system of the American Law Institute's Model Land Development Code.

The absence of a federal stimulus for state land development control legislation has left the states to determine what kind of state regulation system they want, if any. Most influential here is the state land development control system proposed by the Article 7 of the American Law Institute's Model Land Development Code, which has been entirely adopted in Florida and has influenced other states. The Florida legislation is considered *infra* p. 1244.

A framework for examining the state land development control systems now to be considered may be helpful. These systems exhibit a variety of characteristics, but two seem paramount in any analysis of this legislation:

(1) *Planning component.* Is the state land use control system based on and related to a state land use plan, or does it operate independently of state planning policies? Consult again the materials on state planning, *supra.* The uncertainties of state planning, and the ALI Code's preference for land use control systems not fastened on a plan or planning process, has led many states to adopt land use control systems not dependent on a plan. Elsewhere, as in Vermont, the legislation contemplated a state plan but political difficulties prevented its enactment.

(2) *Integration with local land use controls.* Some state land use control systems are integrated with local controls, and simply provide a method for reviewing local planning policies and regulatory decisions. The ALI Code system is in this category. Other states have enacted what are called double veto systems, in which approval must be obtained from the state as well as the local land use controls agency. Vermont is in this category.

We begin this section with the Oregon state land use law, a statute which has provided for comprehensive review of local planning as well as a selective form of land use regulation at the state level.

a. Oregon: State Guidance for Mandatory Planning

Recall that Oregon is a state in which comprehensive planning is now mandatory at the local level. *See supra* p. 746. That state has now enacted legislation providing for state level review of local plans to determine their compliance with statewide planning goals. The legislation in many ways is similar to the California coastal legislation except that it is applicable throughout the state and the planning goals are adopted by a state administrative agency rather than enacted by legislation. In addition, the Oregon legislation provides for a limited state regulation of development projects. This part of the legislation reflects the ALI Code. *See infra* p. 1244. The Oregon system of state review has also been adapted as its method for implementing its state coastal management program.

The administrative structure of the Oregon program is simple. Administrative responsibility is lodged in a state Land Conservation and Development Commission (LCDC), which is served by staff in a state Land Conservation and Development Department. Both are subject to advice from a Joint Legislative Committee on Land Use. The Oregon law has survived an effort at repeal; a public referendum to repeal the law failed, 3-2, in the fall 1976, election.

The following discussion reviews the major provisions of the Oregon law through the 1977 legislative session. Citations are from the Oregon Revised Statutes.

(1) *Goals and guidelines.* At the heart of the law are the goals and guidelines to be adopted by the commission. These are defined as follows:

> "Goals" mean the mandatory state-wide planning standards adopted by the commission. . . .
> "Guidelines" mean suggested approaches designed to aid cities and counties in preparation, adoption and implementation of comprehensive plans in compliance with goals and to aid state agencies and special districts in the preparation, adoption and implementation of plans, programs and regulations in compliance with goals. Guidelines shall be advisory and shall not limit state agencies, cities, counties and special districts to a single approach.

§ 197.015(7)(8).

The statute further provides that the commission, in adopting and revising statewide planning goals, shall:

> (a) Consider the existing comprehensive plans of cities and counties and the plans and programs affecting land use of state agencies and special districts in order to preserve functional and local aspects of land conservation and development.
> (b) Give priority consideration to the following areas and activities:
> (A) Those activities listed in ORS 197.400 [see below—Eds.];
> (B) Lands adjacent to freeway interchanges;
> (C) Estuarine areas;
> (D) Tide, marsh and wetland areas;
> (E) Lakes and lakeshore areas;
> (F) Wilderness, recreational and outstanding scenic areas;
> (G) Beaches, dunes, coastal headlands and related areas;
> (H) Wild and scenic rivers and related lands;
> (I) Flood plains and areas of geologic hazard;
> (J) Unique wildlife habitats; and

    (K) Agricultural land.
    (c) Make a finding of state-wide need for the adoption of any new goal or the revision of any existing goal.
    (d) Design goals to allow a reasonable degree of flexibility in the application of goals by state agencies, cities, counties and special districts.

§ 197.230(1).

Statewide goals are implemented by cities and counties through their planning and land use control powers. They are required to adopt plans and to implement these plans through land use controls, and their planning and "zoning" responsibilities, including the annexation of unincorporated territory, must be exercised in accordance with the statewide goals. § 197.175. The commission may review any comprehensive plan or land use control ordinance considered to be inconsistent with the statewide goals. § 197.300. This review is triggered by a petition from a city, county, special district or state agency. *Id.* In addition, the statute provides, § 197.275:

    (2) After the commission acknowledges a city or county comprehensive plan and implementing ordinances to be in compliance with the goals. . . , the goals shall apply to land conservation and development actions and annexations only through the acknowledged comprehensive plan and implementing ordinances unless:

        (a) The acknowledged comprehensive plan and implementing ordinances do not control the action or annexation under consideration; or

        (b) Substantial changes in conditions have occurred which render the comprehensive plan and implementing ordinances inapplicable to the action or annexation.

Compare this provision with the state legislation mandating consistency of local land use controls with local comprehensive plans, *supra* p. 757. Similar provisions requiring compliance with the statewide goals are applicable to special districts and state agencies, §§ 197.185, 197.190, and the actions and plans of these districts and agencies are also subject to review under § 197.300.

The Oregon statute also provides for the regulation at the state level of activities of statewide significance, which are defined in § 197.400(1) as follows:

    (a) The planning and siting of public transportation facilities.

    (b) The planning and siting of public sewerage systems, water supply systems and solid waste disposal sites and facilities.

    (c) The planning and siting of public schools.

These activities may not be initiated without a permit from the commission. § 197.415. In general concept, these provisions for the control of activities of statewide significance parallel the provisions of the American Law Institute's Model Land Development Code for Development of Regional Impact, *infra* p. 1244, except that the Code provides for state review of local decisions on these developments and does not provide for a state permit.

Like the ALI Code, the Oregon law also provides for the designation, in this case by the legislature, of areas of critical state concern. § 197.405(2)(5). The Oregon law provides that the commission may make the following provisions for land use regulation in critical areas. The commission:

> (c) May include a management plan for the area indicating the programs and regulations of state and local agencies, if any, unaffected by the proposed state regulations for the area;
>
> (d) May establish permissible use limitations for all or part of the area; . . .
>
> (f) May designate permissible use standards for all or part of the lands within the area or establish standards for issuance or denial of designated state or local permits regulating specified uses of lands in the area, or both.

§ 197.405(2). These provisions for land use regulation in critical areas should be compared with the comparable provisions in the ALI Code, as reflected in Florida's version of the Code, *infra* p. 1246.

Enforcement provisions are also included in the Oregon law. The commission is authorized to issue "compliance acknowledgements" and planning extensions, and "shall issue" orders requiring cities, counties, special districts and state agencies to bring their plans, ordinances and programs into compliance with the statewide goals.

Comments: 1. The commission has now adopted a series of goals covering a variety of topics such as the protection of environmental resources, the provision of public facilities, transportation needs and urbanization policy. Guidelines have also been adopted which further specify the manner in which the goals are to be achieved. (Recall that only the goals are mandatory.) Are the goals and guidelines a state plan? If not, how would you classify them?

The urbanization goals and guidelines are of particular importance because they contain the elements of a state urban growth policy to be implemented at the local level through the local planning process. Excerpts from the urbanization goals and guidelines follow.

OREGON LAND CONSERVATION AND DEVELOPMENT COMMISSION, STATE-WIDE PLANNING GOALS AND GUIDELINES 38-40 (1975)

14—URBANIZATION

GOAL:

To provide for an orderly and efficient transition from rural to urban land use.

Urban growth boundaries shall be established to identify and separate urbanizable land from rural land.

Establishment and change of the boundaries shall be based upon consideration of the following factors:

(1) Demonstrated need to accommodate long-range urban population growth requirements consistent with LCDC goals;

(2) Need for housing, employment opportunities, and livability;

(3) Orderly and economic provision for public facilities and services;

(4) Maximum efficiency of land uses within and on the fringe of the existing urban area;

(5) Environmental, energy, economic and social consequences;

(6) Retention of agricultural land as defined, with Class I being the highest priority for retention and Class VI the lowest priority; and,

(7) Compatibility of the proposed urban uses with nearby agricultural activities.

The results of the above considerations shall be included in the comprehensive plan. . . .

. . . .

Land within the boundaries separating urbanizable land from rural land shall be considered available over time for urban uses. Conversion of urbanizable land to urban uses shall be based on consideration of:

(1) Orderly, economic provision for public facilities and services;

(2) Availability of sufficient land for the various uses to insure choices in the market place;

(3) LCDC goals; and,

(4) Encouragement of development within urban areas before conversion of urbanizable areas.

GUIDELINES:

A. PLANNING:

1. Plans should designate sufficient amounts of urbanizable land to accommodate the need for further urban expansion, taking into account (1) the growth policy of the area, (2) population needs (by the year 2000), (3) the carrying capacity of the planning area, and (4) open space and recreational needs.

2. The size of the parcels of urbanizable land that are converted to urban land should be of adequate dimension so as to maximize the utility of the land resource and enable the logical and efficient extension of services to such parcels.

3. Plans providing for the transition from rural to urban land use should take into consideration as a major determinant the carrying capacity of the air, land and water resources of the planning area. The land conservation and development actions provided for by such plans should not exceed the carrying capacity of such resources.

B. IMPLEMENTATION RELATED:

1. The type, location and phasing of public facilities and services are factors which should be utilized to direct urban expansion.

2. The type, design, phasing and location of major public transportation facilities (i.e., all modes: air, marine, rail, mass transit, highways, bicycle and pedestrian) and improvements thereto are factors which should be utilized to support urban expansion into urbanizable areas and restrict it from rural areas.

3. Financial incentives should be provided to assist in maintaining the use and character of lands adjacent to urbanizable areas.

4. Local land use controls and ordinances should be mutually supporting, adopted and enforced to integrate the type, timing and location of public facilities and services in a manner to accommodate increased public demands as urbanizable lands become more urbanized.

5. Additional methods and devices for guiding urban land use should include but not be limited to the following: (1) tax incentives and disincentives; (2) multiple use and joint development practices; (3) fee and less-than-fee acquisition techniques; and (4) capital improvement programming.

6. Plans should provide for a detailed management program to assign respective implementation roles and responsibilities to those governmental bodies operating in the planning area and having interests in carrying out the goal.

Compare the growth management policy contemplated by the urbanization goals and guidelines with the various local growth management programs considered in Chapter 7. Do these goals and guidelines permit a local growth management program similar to the program adopted in Ramapo? In Petulama? How would the growth management programs adopted in those municipalities be affected by the application of the urbanization goals and guidelines to their programs?

2. Is the state land use control system contained in the Oregon law a double veto system as described above, a system integrated with local planning and controls, or a system containing elements of both? Why and to what extent? How much control may the commission exercise over the programs and planning policies of other state agencies? Where does the commission get its review powers if no petition for review is filed under the statute? See ORS § 197.040(2)(e), authorizing the commission to "[r]eview comprehensive plans for conformance with state-wide planning goals". For discussion see Macpherson & Paulus, Senate Bill 100: The Oregon Land Conservation and Development Act, 10 Willamette L.J. 414 (1974). For the history of the Oregon legislation see C. Little, The New Oregon Trail (Conservation Foundation, 1974).

3. To what extent do the statewide goals bind the local planning process? In *South of Sunnyside Neighborhood League v. Board of Comm'rs,* 569 P.2d 1063 (Ore. 1977), a challenge was taken to a change in a county comprehensive plan that changed a designation of a 65-acre parcel on the plan map from medium density planned residential to planned commercial. The court applied the *Fasano* test, *supra* p. 693, and held that the change in the plan map must conform to the policies of the plan. The court then held that the statewide goals were also applicable to the plan map change and announced the following rule for compliance with those goals:

> Since the overall compliance of the plan with the applicable goals is required by statute, an amendment to the plan map which complies with the plan's goals and policies can be assumed to comply with the applicable statewide goals insofar as they speak to the formulation of an overall plan. Insofar as the relevant goals contain no specific directives or prohibitions intended to govern the decision under consideration, we see no need to test the entire plan for compliance with all of them each time the plan map is amended to change the permissible use of a single parcel. It will be enough to show that such a change is consistent with the overall design of the plan itself.

Id. at 1073-74. Has the court held that an amendment to the plan map need never be reviewed for compliance with the state goals once LCDC has approved the plan as consistent with those goals?

b. Florida and the ALI: The DRI and Critical Area Process

Oregon's state land use legislation relies heavily on a mandatory planning requirement and on state level review of planning policies to provide a basis for the exercise of local land use planning and control powers. Article 7 of the American Law Institute's Model Land Development Code, which has been enacted with modifications in Florida, is based on very different premises. There is no mandatory local planning requirement in the Code, and while state planning agency review of local plans is provided in Article 8 this review is not linked with the independent state level control powers in Article 7. Neither are the state land use control powers authorized by the Code generally linked with a state land use plan.

The ALI Code's state land use controls are also integrated with and highly deferential to the exercise of local land use control powers. For example, one component of the ALI Code system is the review at the state level of development of regional impact (DRI) or benefit which is disapproved by a local land use controls agency. DRI is defined as development likely to have spillover effects beyond the jurisdiction in which it is located, while development of regional benefit is development that serves regional as compared with local needs. An appellate review of these developments is provided at the state level; the Code does not enact a state permit system.

In addition, the Code provides for the designation at the state level of areas of critical state concern, the adoption by the state planning agency of development policies for these areas, and the review of local land use regulations within these areas for consistency with these policies. Development within critical areas may only be approved if consistent with local land use regulations, as amended to comply with the adopted state agency policies for the critical area. A variety of areas are eligible for designation as critical areas, including resource areas such as wetlands and areas adjacent to major public facilities, such as highway interchanges. While only

Florida has adopted both the DRI and critical area process, the critical area provisions have been adopted by several other states. N. Rosenbaum, Land Use and the Legislatures 73-75 (1976). Florida did not adopt the development of regional benefit provisions. Do you see any consistent rationale behind the ALI Code state land use control system? Review Healy's analysis of the reasons for state land use legislation, *supra* p. 1207.

Florida's version of Article 7 of the ALI Code, known as Florida Environmental Land and Water Management Act of 1972, was the product of a gubernatorial Task Force on Resource Management. The Task Force was formed to provide a legislative response to Florida's land and water management problems, including a severe drought which had imperiled the state's water supply. The following article explains the basic features of the Act. It was written by Professor Gilbert Finnell who along with Fred Bosselman, a leading Chicago land use lawyer, was its chief legal draftsman. The text of relevant provisions of the Act has been inserted where appropriate.

Note that administrative responsibility under the Act has been lodged primarily with the state's Administration Commission, which is defined as the governor and the cabinet. Fla. Stat. Ann. § 380.031(1) (West Supp. 1977). The cabinet is elected in Florida. This is a change from the ALI Code, which placed administrative responsibility with the state planning agency and provided for an independent state adjudicatory appeal board. Why do you suppose this change was made?

Like the Code, the Florida Act applies to the control of "development." "Development" is defined as "the carrying out of any building or mining operation or the making of any material change in the use or appearance of any structure or land and the dividing of land into three or more parcels." § 380.04(1). A "land development regulation" is defined to "include local zoning, subdivision, building, and other regulations controlling the development of land." § 380.031(7).

FINNELL, SAVING PARADISE: THE FLORIDA ENVIRONMENTAL LAND AND WATER MANAGEMENT ACT OF 1972, 1973 Urban Law Annual 103, 118-19, 124-27, 129-34

AREAS OF CRITICAL STATE CONCERN

Designation of Areas of Critical State Concern (Critical Areas) is Florida's geographical technique for state participation in land development regulation. The basic concept can be visualized on the simplified chart below.

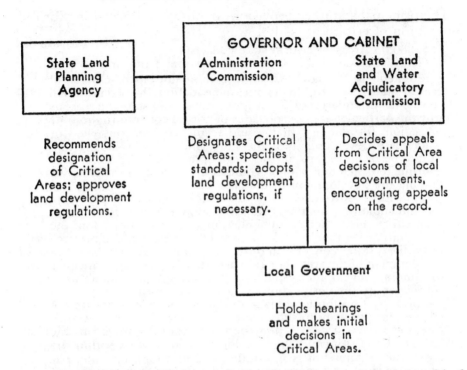

The Administration Commission designates a discrete geographical area as a Critical Area, specifies standards with which each affected local government's land development regulations must comply, and adopts, if local government fails to submit adequate regulations, suitable land development regulations to be administered by local government. A developer proposing development within the Critical Area applies for a development permit to the relevant local government, and the local government conducts an initial hearing on the application and issues its development order, granting or denying the permit. The order of local government is final, subject to judicial review, unless appealed to the Florida Land and Water Adjudicatory Commission, or unless some other requirement of the Act remains unfulfilled. . . .

If a proposed development is located within a Critical Area, the developer applies to local government for a development permit. Local government then proceeds exactly as it would have prior to enactment of the Environmental Land Act except for some changes designed to protect the state or regional interest. The principal changes relate to improved procedures and to the parties to the hearing with standing to appeal.

The development order of local government is final, subject to judicial review, unless a party with standing stays the effectiveness of the order by a timely and effective appeal or unless some other requirement of the Act remains unfulfilled.

[The principal statutory provisions defining and providing for the designation of critical areas follow:

§ 380.05 Areas of critical state concern.—

(1)(a) The state land planning agency may from time to time recommend to the administration commission specific areas of critical state concern. In its recommendation the agency shall specify the boundaries of the proposed areas and state the reasons why the particular area proposed is of critical concern to the state or region, the dangers that would result from uncontrolled or inadequate development of the area, and the advantages that would be achieved from the development of the area in a coordinated manner and recommend specific principles for guiding the development of the area. . . .

(b) Within forty-five (45) days following receipt of a recommendation from the agency, the administration commission shall either reject the recommendation as tendered or adopt the same with or without modification and by rule designate the area of critical state concern and the principles for guiding the development of the area. The rule may specify that such principles for guiding development shall apply to development undertaken subsequent to the designation of the area of critical state concern but prior to the adoption of land development regulations for the critical area pursuant to subsections (6) and (8). In adopting such rule, the administration commission shall consider the economic impact of the principles on development in process within the area. The commission is not authorized to adopt any rule that would provide for a moratorium on development in any area of critical state concern.

(2) An area of critical state concern may be designated only for:

(a) An area containing, or having a significant impact upon, environmental, historical, natural, or archaeological resources of regional or statewide importance.

(b) An area significantly affected by, or having a significant effect upon, an existing or proposed major public facility or other area of major public investment.

(c) A proposed area of major development potential, which may include a proposed site of a new community, designated in a state land development plan.

(3) [Regional planning agencies may recommend critical areas and local governments may do so where there is no regional agency.]

(4) [Regional planning agency to give notice to local governments affected before recommending critical area to administration commission. — Eds.]

DEVELOPMENT OF REGIONAL IMPACT

Defining certain development activities as "Development of Regional Impact" (DRI) is Florida's functional technique for state participation in land development regulation. The simplified chart below should help to visualize this process.

If a developer proposes to undertake DRI, *i.e.,* ". . . any development which, because of its character, magnitude or location, would have a substantial effect upon the health, safety or welfare of citizens of more than one county . . . ," the developer applies for a development permit to the relevant local government, if any, but when the local government hears the application, it must consider, in addition to its usual findings: (1) the regional impact of the proposed development as reported by the Regional Planning Agency and (2) the consistency of the proposed development with any applicable state land development plan. The local government's development order is final, subject to judicial review, unless the order is appealed to the State Land and Water Adjudicatory Commission.

A. *The Administrative Regulations Defining Development of Regional Impact*

Unlike the Critical Areas technique, which is applicable only in a specific geographic area, the DRI section may be applicable anywhere within the State if the proposed development constitutes DRI. . . .

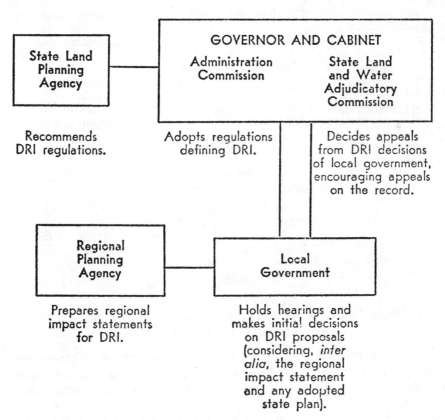

1. Procedure for Administrative Designation of DRI

The Legislature has empowered the Administration Commission, by rule, to adopt regulations "to be used in determining whether particular developments shall be presumed to be of regional impact." In addition to the procedural safeguards of the Florida APA, the standards which the Administration Commission must consider and be guided by are: . . . .

[These standards are provided by § 380.06(2):

> The state land planning agency shall recommend to the Administration Commission specific guidelines and standards for adoption pursuant to this subsection. The Administration Commission shall by rule adopt guidelines and standards to be used in determining whether particular developments shall be presumed to be of regional impact. Such guidelines and standards shall be subject to legislative review. . . . In adopting its guidelines and standards, the Administration Commission shall consider and be guided by:
>
> (a) The extent to which the development would create or alleviate environmental problems such as air or water pollution or noise.
>
> (b) The amount of pedestrian or vehicular traffic likely to be generated.
>
> (c) The number of persons likely to be residents, employees, or otherwise present.
>
> (d) The size of the site to be occupied.
>
> (e) The likelihood that additional or subsidiary development will be generated.
>
> (f) The extent to which the development would create an additional demand for, or additional use of, energy, including the energy requirements of subsidiary developments.
>
> (g) The unique qualities of particular areas of the state.

[The ALI Code does not provide a definition of development of regional impact. The comparable Code provision provides:

> § 7-301(1). The State Land Planning Agency shall by rule define categories of Development of Regional Impact that, because of the nature or magnitude of the development or the nature and magnitude of its effect on the surrounding environment, are likely in the judgment of the Agency to present issues of state or regional significance.—Eds.]

2. Balanced Implementation through Balanced Designation of DRI—or Saving Paradise for Whom?

The words of the Act, the placement of the administrative responsibility for implementation, and the pronouncements and floor debate of the Bill's sponsors all stress that the Act is not "preservationist," but rather "attempts to establish processes and administrative structures within which all factors can be balanced." The Act is concerned with extraterritorial decisions of substantial impact upon the region and State which, if left entirely to local government, might be decided only upon consideration of local impact. The regional impact might be environmental, *e.g.,* a proposed development of desirable impact upon the local community—one that would raise the tax base, but one with a substantial adverse impact on the region's water supply. But the impact might also be socio-economic, *e.g.,* "snob zoning," which, by unduly exclusive residential restrictions, might shift a disproportionate housing burden to other adjacent communities. Thus, if the DRI purposes are to be achieved, there should be an array of DRI regulations that implement the total environmental, economic and social purposes of the Act. . . .

B. *The Decision-Making Process for Development of Regional Impact*

1. Jurisdictional and Procedural Requirements

If a proposed development is DRI, the developer must comply with requirements, in addition to the usual ones, that are designed to assure that the State and regional impact of the development will be considered by the local government. The jurisdiction of the development will depend upon whether the development is located within a completely unregulated area, within an Area of Critical State Concern or within an area of a local government that has zoning regulations in effect but has not been designated an Area of Critical State Concern.

a. If the land is located in an unregulated area, the developer will give written notice to the State Land Planning Agency and to any local government having jurisdiction to adopt zoning or subdivision regulations for the area in which the development is proposed. Then, after 90 days from such notice, if no zoning or subdivision regulations have been adopted nor designation of Critical Area rule issued, the developer may undertake development.

b. If the land is located in an Area of Critical State Concern, the developer may undertake development after it has been approved under the requirements of the Critical Area section. A request for development permission within an Area of Critical State Concern is subject to the Critical Area requirements whether or not the requested development is DRI.

c. If the land is located within the area of a local government that has zoning regulations in effect or if after receiving notice, the local government adopts regulations (but is not within a Critical Area), the developer may undertake development (1) after receiving final approval from the appropriate local government, which order has not been appealed within 30 days after the order, or (2) upon completion of the appeal process, if the effectiveness of the order of local government has been stayed by filing an effective timely notice of appeal to the Florida Land and Water Adjudicatory Commission.

2. Role of the Regional Planning Agency

If the State Land Planning Agency has designated a Regional Planning Agency for the area in which a DRI permit is requested, the Regional Planning Agency, within . . . [50] days after receipt of notice of a proposed DRI, must prepare a report and make recommendations—a type of regional impact statement—to the local government having jurisdiction of the DRI application. . . .

[There is no comparable procedure in the ALI Code. The Florida statute provides the following guidance for the regional agency report, § 360.08(8):

In preparing its report and recommendations the regional planning agency shall consider whether, and the extent to which:
  (a) The development will have a favorable or unfavorable impact on the environment and natural resources of the region.
  (b) The development will have a favorable or unfavorable impact on the economy of the region.
  (c) The development will efficiently use or unduly burden water, sewer, solid waste disposal, or other necessary public facilities.
  (d) The development will efficiently use or unduly burden public transportation facilities.
  (e) The development will favorably or adversely affect the ability of people to find adequate housing reasonably accessible to their places of employment.
  (f) The development complies with such other criteria for determining regional impact as the regional planning agency shall deem appropriate, including, but not limited to, the extent to which the development would create an additional demand for, or additional use of, energy. — Eds.]

A major deficiency of the land development regulatory process prior to the Environmental Land Act was the inherent inability of the process to provide suitable decision-makers and adequate findings that would assure consideration of extraterritorial impact—whether beneficial or detrimental. The process was undemocratic; it presumably considered local cost and benefit, but likely ignored cost and benefit to the total citizenry affected by the decision. Furthermore, the incentive structure within which local decision-makers operated tipped the scales in favor of economic considerations to the probable disregard of environmental and social considerations. The regional impact statement, then, is designed to remedy in part these two major weaknesses of the prior system.

But note the limitations of the increased regional role. First, the regional agency's role is clearly a planning and advisory role, not a regulatory one. The Environmental Land Act does not establish a system of regional general-purpose governments; it does not add a regional layer to the decision-making process. Second, the 30-day period within which the regional impact statement must be completed may be inadequate, particularly in the early periods of administration of the Act, to develop fully the environmental, economic and social impact. . . .

3. Role of the Local Government

When a developer applies for a DRI permit to a local government which is not in a Critical Area, the local government proceeds as it would have prior to enactment of the Environmental Land Act except for some important changes designed to protect the state or regional interest. The principal changes relate to improved procedures, applicable standards, required findings and parties to the hearing with standing to appeal. . . .

[The standards provided by the Act are as follows, § 380.06(11):

If the development is not located in an area of critical state concern, in considering whether the development shall be approved, denied, or approved subject to conditions, restrictions, or limitations, the local government shall consider whether, and the extent in which:

(a) The development unreasonably interferes with the achievement of the objectives of an adopted state land development plan applicable to the area;

(b) The development is consistent with the local land development regulations; and

(c) The development is consistent with the report and recommendations of the regional planning agency submitted pursuant to subsection (8) of this section.—Eds.]

Although Florida's DRI section is modeled after part of the ALI tentative code, the ALI model requires a cost-benefit analysis in which local government "shall grant" a permit if certain requirements are met, including a finding that "the probable net balance exceeds the probable net detriment." Florida's act utilizes essentially the same criteria as ALI, but requires only that local government "shall consider" the criteria.

THE ADJUDICATORY PROCESS

In order to assure that local governments comply with the state specified standards, the Act creates the Florida Land and Water Adjudicatory Commission, consisting of the Governor and Cabinet, to hear appeals from local governments' development orders in Areas of Critical State Concern or in regard to Development of Regional Impact. A development order of local government is final, subject to judicial review, unless a party with standing stays the effectiveness of the order by a timely and effective appeal or unless some other requirement of the Act remains unfulfilled.

Those with standing to appeal include only the owner of the property affected by the order, the developer, the appropriate Regional Planning Agency and the State Land Planning Agency. The Adjudicatory Commission may permit "materially affected parties" to intervene in the appeal, however, upon motion and good cause shown.

Considering the potential number of appeals that may be generated under the Act, most appeals to the State may likely begin with a hearing before a hearing officer, which the Adjudicatory Commission is empowered to designate. But whether or not the initial appeal is assigned to a hearing officer, the Adjudicatory Commission's final order must be based upon a hearing before the Commission pursuant to the provisions of the Florida [Administrative Procedure Act].

[The Act provides that the Adjudicatory Commission "shall issue a decision granting or denying permission to develop pursuant to the standards of this chapter." Is there any ambiguity in this provision?—Eds.]

Comments: 1. The ALI Code provides a slightly different set of standards for the review of Development of Regional Impact. These are as follows:

Section 7-304. Standards Applicable to Permits for Development of Regional Impact

(1) If the development of regional impact is authorized by the ordinance of the local government the Land Development Agency shall deny the permit only if it finds that the probable net detriment from the development exceeds the probable net benefit. . . .

(2) If the development of regional impact is not authorized by the development ordinance it shall grant the permit only if it finds that

(a) the probable net benefit from the development exceeds the probable net detriment . . . ; and

(b) the development does not substantially or unreasonably interfere with the ability to achieve the objectives of an applicable local or state Land Development Plan; and

(c) the development departs from the ordinance no more than is reasonably necessary to enable a substantial segment of the population of the state to obtain reasonable access to housing, employment, educational or recreational opportunities.
. . . .

Section 7-402. Areas and Factors to be Considered

In reaching its decision the Agency shall not restrict its consideration to benefit and detriment within the local jurisdiction, but shall consider all relevant and material evidence offered to show the impact of the development on surrounding areas. Detriments or benefits shall not be denied consideration on the ground that they are indirect, intangible or not readily quantifiable. In evaluating detriments and benefits . . . the Agency may consider, with other relevant factors, whether or not the absence of such development denies adequate facilities to the surrounding areas in respect to employment opportunities, housing, utility services, charitable facilities or other amenities related to the general welfare, and whether or not

(1) development at the proposed location is or is not essential or especially appropriate in view of the available alternatives within or without the jurisdiction;

(2) development in the manner proposed will have a favorable or unfavorable impact on the environment in comparison to alternative methods;

(3) the development will favorably or adversely affect other persons or property and, if so, whether because of circumstances peculiar to the location the effect is likely to be greater than is ordinarily associated with the development of the type proposed;

(4) if development of the type proposed imposes immediate cost burdens on the local government, whether the amount of development of that type which has taken place in the territory of the local government is more or less than an equitable share of the development of that type needed in the general area or region;

(5) the development will favorably or adversely affect the ability of people to find adequate housing reasonably accessible to their place of employment;

(6) the development will favorably or adversely affect the provision of municipal services and the burden of taxpayers in making provision therefor;

(7) the development will efficiently use or unduly burden public or public-aided transportation or other facilities which have been developed or are to be developed within the next [5] years;

(8) the development will further, or will adversely affect, the objectives of development built or aided by governmental agencies within the past [5] years or to be developed in the next [5] years;

(9) the development is in furtherance of or contradictory to objectives and policies set forth in a State Land Development Plan for the area. [; and]

[(10) the development will aid or interfere with the ability of the local government to achieve the objectives set forth in any Land Development Plan and current short-term program.]

The category of development of regional benefit which is included as development of regional impact in the ALI Code but omitted in the Florida law is defined as follows, § 7-301(4):

Any development of regional benefit, as defined in this subsection, which is not otherwise included within the category of development of regional impact in the rule adopted under this subsection (1), shall nevertheless be treated as development of regional impact if the developer notifies the Land Development Agency at the time of his application for a development permit that he elects to proceed under this Part. "Development of regional benefit" means:

(a) development by a governmental agency other than the local government that created the Land Development Agency or another agency created solely by that local government;

(b) development which will be used for charitable purposes, including religious or educational facilities, and which serves or is intended to serve a substantial number of persons who do not reside within the boundaries of the local government creating the Land Development Agency;

(c) development by a public utility which is or will be employed to a substantial degree to provide services in an area beyond the territorial jurisdiction of the local government creating the Land Development Agency; and

(d) development of housing for persons of low and moderate income.

Why do you suppose the development of regional benefit category was omitted in the Florida legislation?

2. Are the ALI Code and the Florida law clear in indicating the function to be served by the designation of critical areas? Reread the definition of areas subject to designation under the Florida law as critical, *supra* p. 1248. With the exception of the area of "major development potential," the Florida law tracks the ALI Code. A Florida (intermediate) District Court of Appeal has now held paragraphs (a) and (b) of the Florida law unconstitutional as an invalid delegation of power. *Cross Key Waterways v. Askew,* 351 So.2d 1062 (Fla. 1977). The court found no fault with the terms used to define a critical area, but held that the statute "does not establish or provide for establishing priorities or other means for identifying and choosing among the resources the Act is intended to preserve." *Id.* at 1069. In addition, "[t]he Act also lacks suitable standards for identification of local governments whose stewardship of valued resources is to be deemed inadequate to protect state and regional interests." *Id.* at 1069-70. Paragraph (c), authorizing the delegation of an area of major development potential, was indicated in dictum to be a constitutionally permissible delegation because the state plan must meet independent statutory standards and be approved by the legislature. The *Cross Key* case was affirmed, — So.2d — (Fla. 1978).

3. Where are the policies for the designation of critical areas and the adoption of land use controls for these areas to come from? Note that the criteria for the designation of critical areas are not generally linked to the state plan, and that the state agency's power to adopt policies for critical areas is open-ended. These policies must correspond to the reasons for designating the critical area, but there is no constraint on what reasons for designation may be selected by the state agency. The ALI Code, at 259-60, does state that studies leading up to the state plan can form the basis for the designation of a critical area.

How is the designation of a critical area, and the policies adopted for that area, to be reviewed? The critical area is designated by rule, and the ALI Code provides that rules adopted by state planning agencies are subject to judicial review, § 9-101. However, commentary to the critical area provisions of the Code states that designations of critical areas are not reviewable. *See* the ALI Code at 263. Apparently, a review of a designation is only to be available when a developer files an application for development and then appeals a specific refusal to approve that development. What do you think of this interpretation? Why would it be important to seek review of a critical area designation at an earlier date?

The administration of land use controls within critical areas presents another problem. One restriction is that the state agency may only adopt controls which the local government is authorized to adopt, see § 380.05(b)(8) of the Florida law. Is this restriction necessary? Problems may also arise because the state agency may only modify local land use controls and has no control under the critical area process over the administration of these controls. This limitation may present problems under ordinances containing planned unit development provisions, which are generalized in content and which rise or fall on their manner of implementation. Without control over specific planned unit development decisions, the state agency may be without effective power over the planned unit development control process. Does a development located within a critical area nevertheless fall within the procedures and requirements for the review of developments of regional impact? The ALI Code makes the DRI process inapplicable, § 7-207(4). How is this problem handled under the Florida law?

Note that the state agency in the critical area process reviews local land use control regulations and not the local plan. This approach, again, is consistent with the ALI Code's avoidance of a mandatory local planning requirement. The Code does state that any local control over development that is exercised according to a local plan must be consistent with the "principles for guiding development" within a designated critical area. § 7-203(2). Nevertheless, there is no direct review of local plans under the critical area process. This review can occur under the state planning article of the Code but the Code, unlike the Oregon state land use law, does not authorize the state planning agency to disapprove and modify an element of the local plan. Tension may then arise if a local planning agency designates a critical area restricted from development as an area of development potential, and goes so far as to plan for the extension of public facilities in this area. This local planning decision remains essentially beyond the reach of the critical area process. For discussion see D. Mandelker, Environmental and Land Controls Legislation 66-86 (1976).

Florida has now adopted mandatory planning legislation, and this legislation requires that local land use controls be consistent with the adopted local plan. See Fla. Stat. Ann. § 163.3161 et seq. (West Supp. 1978). Consistency with the plan is judicially reviewable. Is there a potential conflict between this statute and the statutory critical area process?

4. Both the Florida legislation and the ALI Code provide a set of factors to be considered in reviewing development of regional impact. Compare the approach of comparable legislation enacted in Colorado. Colo. Rev. Stat. § 24-65.1-101 et seq. (Supp. 1976). This statute provides for control over areas and activities of state interest, but delegates all substantive review power to local governments subject to substantive development guidelines spelled out in the statute. Activities of state interest are generally the selection of sites for public facilities. The statute then provides the following criteria for review of sewer and water extensions:

Section 24-65.1-204(b): "Major extensions of domestic water and sewage treatment systems shall be permitted in those areas in which the anticipated growth and development that may occur as a result of such extension can be accommodated within the financial and environmental capacity of the area to sustain such growth and development." How would the Ramapo plan fare under this statutory test? Similar statutory guidelines are provided for other public facilities in the Colorado law. For discussion of the Colorado legislation see Bermingham, 1974 Land Use Legislation in Colorado, 51 Den. L.J. 467 (1974).

The reach of the DRI process in Florida has also been affected by the definition of DRI adopted by the Administration Commission. The Commission has responded to the statutory definition, *supra* p. 1250, by listing a series of developments which are presumed to be developments of regional impact. Rules and Regulations of the State of Florida, ch. 22F-2. These regulations generally adopt a threshold approach to defining DRI. Thus the test for bringing attraction and amusement facilities under the DRI definition is based on the number of parking spaces provided. § 22F-2.02. The test for residential developments is based on the number of residential units provided and is staggered by the size of the county in which they are located; the smaller the county the fewer dwelling units it takes to bring the project under the statute. § 22F-2.10. Is this approach to the definition of DRI the only reasonable way to interpret the statute? Apparently the threshold limits are so high that much development escapes the DRI review process, leading some counties such as Dade County (Miami) to adopt their own DRI review ordinances. *But see General Dev. Corp. v. Division of State Planning,* 353 So.2d 1199 (Fla. 1977) (administrative definition of DRI only presumptive indication of coverage under the Act). *See also Pinellas County v. Lake Padgett Pines,* 333 So.2d 472 (Fla. 1976) (development of well water supply by regional water management district).

To what extent can the Florida DRI procedure correct abuses arising in exclusionary local zoning regulations? The ALI Code DRI procedure? This problem is somewhat alleviated in Florida because the Florida mandatory comprehensive planning act contains a provision requiring the adoption of a housing element in the local plan which must make provision for lower income housing needs. Fla. Stat. Ann. § 163.3177(6)(f) (West Supp. 1978). What bearing will compliance with a locally prepared housing plan have on the DRI review process? Is there any way to reconcile the two statutes?

The effectiveness of the DRI process will also depend on the willingness of developers refused permission at the local level to appeal to the state agency, and on the willingness of neighbors and other potential third parties having standing to take an appeal of local approvals alleged to be inconsistent with the statutory criteria. The Code also provides that the state planning agency may appeal if it has intervened in the local proceedings in which the development application is heard. § 7-402. Does this generally passive and reactive review function weaken the effectiveness of the DRI process?

c. Other States

We will look briefly at state land use control systems in two other states, Hawaii and Vermont. Each state has adopted powerful state land use controls unique to its setting and circumstances, and that employ a double veto system to achieve control over land use at the state level.

(1) Hawaii: State Districting

The geologic origins of the Hawaiian islands — volcanic peaks rising from the ocean floor — dictate the special characteristics of the Hawaii state land use law. Ninety percent of the state's population lives in urban clusters along the coasts, there is no heavy industry, agriculture is the main commercial pursuit, confined largely to valley floors between the mountain peaks, and the remaining land is either highly mountainous or otherwise off limits for urbanization. Politically, the governmental structure of the state is also simple. There are only four county governments at the sub-state level. No island contains more than one county although some counties cover more than one island. There are no organized municipal governments within the counties. Eighty percent of the state's population lives on Oahu, where the urban cluster of Honolulu is located. Land use plans have been adopted in all the counties.

This simple governmental and land use structure led the Hawaiian legislature in 1961 to enact a state land use law which took the expedient of dividing the state into three self-explanatory state land use districts — Agriculture, Conservation and Urban. (A transitional Rural District was created later, but it is not significant and is not found on Oahu). To administer the state districting system a State Land Use Commission was created with powers to designate and later to amend state district boundaries.

County zoning powers are retained within the agricultural districts but permitted uses must be compatible with uses permitted by Land Use Commission regulations, which do not allow any urban development. Uses within the conservation districts are regulated by the state Department of Land and Natural Resources. Uses within the urban districts are determined by the counties, creating a two-way veto that has been troublesome. The state Commission may designate land for urban development but there is no requirement that county zoning respond to this designation. Likewise, the Commission need not recognize urban development designations contained in county plans.

The most important charge of the Commission is its responsibility for shifting land from agricultural or conservation into urban use. Since urban development in Hawaii clusters along the coasts, and since the most valuable agricultural land is inland, especially on Oahu, the Land Use Law effectively establishes an inland urban growth boundary. This boundary has been under considerable pressure. There has been an ongoing controversy over the basis for shifting land into urban use and the amount of vacant land that should be available for urban development at any one point in time.

The criteria for land use district boundary changes, including changes in the urban district classification, were not originally linked to the state's general plan, which was also adopted in 1961. Instead, the Commission when designating urban districts was directed by the statute to set aside a "sufficient reserve area for foreseeable urban growth." Every five years the Commission was to conduct a statewide boundary review which would, of course, include a review of urban district areas. This five-year boundary review requirement was dropped from the legislation in 1975. Otherwise, boundary changes occur when petitions for amendments to district boundaries are presented by property owners who wish to develop their land. Originally, the test to be applied to boundary amendments stressed the need for the boundary change as indicated by "conditions and trends in development." The developmental bias in this test and ambiguities in Commission regulations governing boundary changes led to charges that the Commission was releasing too much land for urban development. The legislature responded with procedural and substantive changes in the Land Use Law that have placed restraints on its decision-making authority:

(1) *Adjudicatory procedures.* While the state has a state administrative procedures act, the application of this act to Commission procedures was never clear and the Commission at first operated under the equivalent of rule-making procedures. This procedure set the stage for irregularities including claimed ex parte contacts with petitioners for boundary changes, which were much criticized. In 1974, in a decision which did not reference similar developments on the mainland, the state supreme court held that the Commission was bound by the contested case procedures for adjudicatory proceedings contained in the administrative procedure act. *Town v. Land Use Comm'n,* 524 P.2d 84 (Hawaii 1974). This requirement was codified in amendments to the Land Use Law adopted in 1975. Hawaii Rev. Stat. § 205-4 (1977). These changes substantially dilute the policy-making function of the Commission, since the Commission as an adjudicating body is required to follow criteria for boundary changes written into the law and not make policy changes on its own. These criteria were also supplied in the 1975 revisions.

(2) *Planning and land use guidance policies.* Hawaiians have long seen a state plan as the most effective way of providing a binding policy for the development of the state's land and natural resources. *See* Catanese, Hawaii: Plan? or Process? Plan., *supra* p. 66. The early 1961 state general plan had been in conventional mapped form, but when the plan was redone in 1967 the state planning department simply prepared a series of reports and avoided any land use policy commitments. The 1975 legislation revised the state planning act, called for a new state plan to address a variety of land use and related

policies, and included a direction to include in the plan a land use guidance policy (not defined) to guide the Commission in making its decisions on boundary changes. At the same time, the Land Use Law was revised and the test for boundary amendments to land use districts made to read as follows:

> No amendment of a land use district boundary shall be approved unless the commission finds upon the clear preponderance of the evidence that the proposed boundary is reasonable and not violative ... [of the statutory definition of the uses and activities allowed in land use districts] and consistent with the interim policies and criteria established ... [by the legislature] or any State plan enacted by the legislature which plan shall supersede any interim guidance policies.

Hawaii Rev. Stat. § 205-4(g) (Supp. 1977). An extensive state policy plan containing many pages of policies and guidelines was adopted by the state legislature in 1978. This plan incorporates in modified form an Interim Land Use Guidance Policy adopted by the legislature in 1975 to guide the Land Use Commission, although the interim statutory guidance policy is continued for a brief period until the state plan takes effect.

The legislative interim policies and criteria applicable to the Land Use Commission are as follows. They are effective until 1979, when they will be replaced by similar policies in a state plan adopted by the legislature in 1978.

INTERIM STATEWIDE LAND USE GUIDANCE POLICY

The interim policies are:

(1) Land use amendments shall be approved only as reasonably necessary to accommodate growth and development, provided there are no significant adverse effects upon agricultural, natural, environmental, recreational, scenic, historic, or other resources of the area.

(2) Lands to be reclassified as an urban district shall have adequate public services and facilities or as can be so provided at reasonable costs to the petitioner.

(3) Maximum use shall be made of existing services and facilities, and scattered urban development shall be avoided.

(4) Urban districts shall be contiguous to an existing urban district or shall constitute all or a part of a self-contained urban center.

(5) Preference shall be given to amendment petitions which will provide permanent employment, or needed housing accessible to existing or proposed employment centers, or assist in providing a balanced housing supply for all economic and social groups.

(6) In establishing the boundaries of the districts in each county, the commission shall give consideration to the general plan of the county.

(7) Insofar as practicable conservation lands shall not be reclassified as urban lands.

(8) The commission is encouraged to reclassify urban lands which are incompatible with the interim statewide land use guidance policy or are not developed in a timely manner.

Hawaii Rev. Stat. § 205-16.1 (1977). Compare these policies with the urbanization policy adopted by the Oregon Land Conservation and Development Commission. How do they differ?

The land use control program in Hawaii has been further complicated by two additional legislative enactments. An environmental impact statement law enacted in 1974 applies to private development in four areas, including conservation districts and shoreline areas, and also applies to developer-initiated county plan amendments. Hawaii Rev. Stat. § 343-4(a)(2) (1977). In addition, a shoreline protection act adopted in 1975 requires a county permit for major development in the coastal area. Hawaii Rev. Stat. ch. 205A, pt. II (1977). The shoreline protection act has been selected as the keystone of Hawaii's coastal zone management program, although permits issued under that act are now subject to a set of legislatively adopted coastal management policies. The Hawaii coastal zone management program was approved by the federal agency in 1978.

For additional discussion of the Hawaii Land Use Law see F. Bosselman & D. Callies, The Quiet Revolution in Land Use Control 5-53 (1971); D. Mandelker, Environmental and Land Controls Legislation, ch. VII (1976); P. Myers, Zoning Hawaii (Conservation Foundation, 1976).

(2) Vermont: State Permits

The Vermont state land use legislation takes yet another approach to the control of land development. Adopted in 1970, this legislation creates a state permit system for major developments throughout the state. Applications for state permits are reviewed under statutory criteria, not related generally to planning and zoning policies, which require an evaluation of the impacts of the development at its site. As local zoning approval is still required, the Vermont law can be classified as a double veto system. The legislation also called for the legislative adoption of a state plan which was to guide the permit approval process, but political difficulties interfered and the state plan was not adopted.

Development subject to review under the Vermont law is defined as follows:

(1) developments involving the construction of housing projects and the construction or maintenance of mobile homes or trailer parks of ten or more units;
(2) developments involving the construction of improvements for commercial or industrial purposes on a tract of more than one acre in towns without permanent zoning and subdivision by-laws and

on a tract of more than ten acres in towns with such controls;
(3) developments involving the construction of improvements for state or municipal purposes of a size of more than ten acres; and
(4) all developments above an elevation of 2,500 feet.

Vt. Stat. Ann. tit. 10, § 6001(3) (Supp. 1977).

The original ten statutory criteria to be considered when reviewing developments under the statute were as follows:

(1) would not result in undue water or air pollution;
(2) would have sufficient water available to meet its foreseeable needs;
(3) would not cause an unreasonable burden on an existing water supply if one was to be utilized;
(4) would not cause unreasonable soil erosion or reduce the capacity of the land to hold water so that a dangerous or unhealthy condition might result;
(5) would not cause unreasonable highway congestion or unsafe conditions with respect to the use of existing or proposed highways;
(6) would not impose an unreasonable burden on the ability of a city or town to provide educational services;
(7) would not impose an unreasonable burden on the ability of a city or town to provide municipal or governmental services;
(8) would not have an undue adverse impact upon the area's scenic or natural beauty, aesthetics, historic sites, or rare and irreplaceable natural assets;
(9) would be in conformance with any of the state plans adopted upon Act 250; and
(10) would be in conformance with any duly adopted local or regional plan or capital program.

Vt. Stat. Ann. tit. 10, § 6086(a)(1)-(10) (Supp. 1977). The burden is on the applicant to show compliance with criteria (1) through (4) as well as (9) and (10). Opposing parties must show failure to comply with criteria (5) through (8). No permit may be denied solely because criteria (5) through (7) have not been met.

While the land use plan contemplated by the legislature was not adopted, the statute also called for two other plans to precede the land use plan. These plans were prepared. First came an Interim Land Capability and Development Plan generally consisting of maps showing resource and other restraints on land development. It was succeeded by a Land Capability and Development Plan which superseded the interim plan and was adopted in the 1973 legislature. This plan included a series of policies which were to provide the basis for the state land use plan, and which were to guide the efforts of local and regional planning commissions and other state agencies. These policies covered planning for land use and development, the conservation and use of natural resources, and the linkages between governmental services and growth rates.

While these policies are not applied in the administration of the act, the plan as adopted by the legislature also added to the ten basic permit criteria initially contained in the legislation. These additions are explained by David Heeter:

> . . . Originally, it was intended that there would be one or more criteria to implement each of the [plan's] policies. This relationship became confused during the drafting and legislative processes, and the resulting criteria attempted to accomplish four basic purposes. First, some criteria sought to minimize the adverse impact of development upon lands with significant resource values, such as agricultural and forestry soils, shorelines, wildlife habitats, public water supplies, etc. Second, other criteria attempted to protect the public from having to assume unreasonable or unscheduled burdens by directing development away from hazardous areas, such as floodplains, and floodways, or by balancing the impact of development against the ability of the public to support it. Third, several criteria sought to protect the investment that had already been made in governmental and quasi-public facilities and services by closely scrutinizing development on adjacent lands. Finally, one criterion anticipated the energy crisis by some six months and provided that development should reflect principles of energy conservation and incorporate the best available technology for the efficient use and recovery of energy. The new criteria applied to all major subdivisions and developments as did the original ones.

Heeter, Almost Getting it Together in Vermont in D. Mandelker, Environmental and Land Controls Legislation 323, 352 (1976).

One of the criteria added by the 1973 amendments deals with growth management. It provides:

> **Impact of growth.** In considering an application, the district commission or the board shall take into consideration the growth in population experienced by the town and region in question and whether or not the proposed development would significantly affect their existing and potential financial capacity to reasonably accommodate both the total growth and the rate of growth otherwise expected for the town and region and the total growth and rate of growth which would result from the development if approved. After considering anticipated costs for education, highway access and maintenance, sewage disposal, water supply, police and fire services and other factors relating to the public health, safety and welfare, the district commission or the board shall impose conditions which prevent undue burden upon the town and region in accommodating growth caused by the proposed development or subdivision. . . . [T]he burden of proof that proposed development will significantly affect existing or potential financial capacity of the town and region to accommodate such growth is upon any party opposing an application, excepting however, where the town has a duly adopted capital improvement program the burden shall be on the applicant.

Vt. Stat. Ann. tit. 10, § 6086(a)(9)(A) (Supp. 1977). Compare this growth policy with the interim land use guidance policy enacted by the Hawaii legislature for the state Land Use Commission and with the urbanization policy of the Oregon Land Conservation and Development Commission.

Several other changes relating to Act 250 were also enacted by the 1973 legislature. In one of the more important, "a provision was added which required that 'full account and consideration' be given to duly adopted regional plans and town plans, capital improvements programs, and by-laws [ordinances — Eds.] unless the policies in the capability and development plan provided otherwise, but the language it used came dangerously close to requiring that the state plan conform to town and regional plans." Heeter, *supra* at 355.

According to information supplied by the Vermont Natural Resources Council, 2,449 applications for development permits had been filed as of September 1, 1976. Of these, 89 percent had been approved, three percent had been denied, five percent had been withdrawn, and another three percent were awaiting action. Most permits were issued with conditions, which usually require measures to mitigate any adverse environmental impacts created by the development. How does the control system authorized by the Vermont law compare with the Hawaii land use law? With the Florida DRI process? With a state environmental impact statement requirement for private development?

For additional discussion of the Vermont law see Bosselman & Callies, *supra* at 54-107; P. Myers, So Goes Vermont (1974). In a major case construing the Vermont law, the Vermont Supreme Court upheld a denial of a permit for a wild animal farm. *In re Wildlife Wonderland, Inc.,* 346 A.2d 645 (Vt. 1975). The court refused to consider objections to statutory criteria requiring consideration of aesthetic and scenic values.

D. COORDINATED HEARINGS AND ONE-STOP SYSTEMS

The enactment of state land use control systems, including coastal, wetlands and other environmentally protective legislation, has led to a proliferation of development permits at the state level. As many as 30 to 40 permits must be obtained at the state level in some states, including permits required under the national air and water quality legislation.

In response to this problem, several states have experimented with a variety of procedures to simplify the permit process at the state level, and in some instances this legislation extends to the local level as well. The most radical proposal calls for a one-stop permit procedure under which a single permit would be issued for each development after consideration of all statutory requirements imposed under any applicable permit legislation. A less radical proposal has been advanced by the American Law Institute's Model Land Development Code, which provides for a joint hearing when multiple permits are required, see Art. 2, pt. 4. Coordinated hearing procedures have been adopted in several states, including Maryland, whose legislation is discussed in the following article. The Maryland legislation can be found at Md. Ann. Code art. 78A, §§ 57-67 (Supp. 1977).

MINER, COORDINATION OF DEVELOPMENT REGULATION: UNTANGLING THE MAZE, ENVIRONMENTAL COMMENT, May 1976, at 1, 5-6

Current Programs

The major testing ground for the coordination techniques has been at the state level, where the majority of environmental regulations are enforced. The problem of coordination at the state level is complicated by the fact that agencies are large and geographically dispersed and have competing objectives (conservation vs. economic development) and separate constituencies.

The problems associated with coordination at the state level do not apply for the most part to local government, where the development approval process is somewhat more centralized and where problems are more resolvable by informal means. Nevertheless, many city councils, planning commissions, and zoning boards of appeals are increasingly inclined to exercise considerable discretionary power, and this can lengthen the development process. Also, conflicts between local departments and their respective regulations pose serious coordination problems. Consequently, there is a growing interest in formalizing coordination procedures at the local level.

. . . .

Maryland

The Development and Construction Permits Administrative Procedure (S.B. 810) was signed into law in May 1975. The purpose of the law is:

> • To eliminate unnecessary delay, unreasonable expense, and duplication of effort in obtaining necessary permits. . . .
> • To remove impediments to the effective expression of public comment on these projects.

The law creates the position of a coordinator who is appointed by the Board of Public Works. (In Maryland the Board is headed by the governor and exercises budgetary control over state agencies.) The coordinator is responsible for developing a master permit application form, must advise "persons proposing projects of the various permits that may be required, and shall furnish relevant information to the applicants concerning the required procedures for obtaining these permits." The master application contains information regarding permits that are required by state agencies. The procedure also includes provisions for joint hearings among state agencies and local governments.

S.B. 810's permit coordination procedure is started at the request of the applicant. Upon filing a master application with the coordinator, the applicant may request a joint hearing either between the local government and state agencies or among the state agencies alone. The applicant must forward copies of all required local and state permit applications to the coordinator, who then distributes them to the relevant state agencies. The local government must approve or deny the request for a joint hearing with all or any one of the state agencies within 10 days of receipt of notice from the coordinator. If the local government opts for a joint hearing and if only one state agency is involved, the state agency must participate. A joint hearing must be held within 90 days after the state agencies decide to participate. The hearing is held in the county in which the development is proposed.

A consolidated hearing of only state agencies may be requested if no local permit is required, if all local permits have been issued, or if a local permit cannot be issued until one or more state permits are issued. A hearing must be held within 90 days after the coordinator has received a completed master application. An agency need not attend a consolidated hearing if a hearing is not normally required for a permit it issues.

S.B. 810 imposes time limits on the issuance of state permits. Local government permits are issued in accordance with local regulations. State agencies that participate in a joint hearing with a local government or in a consolidated hearing with other state agencies must act before notice of decision by the local government or conclusion of a consolidated hearing. If the local government denies a permit, a state agency may deny its permit for that reason. Those state agencies that do not participate in a joint or consolidated hearing must act within 60 days of receipt of a permit application. If a state agency does not act within the prescribed time limits, the permit is deemed automatically approved. Specific guidelines are included for granting an extension of time. The applicant may appeal any request for an extension of time based on the need for more information to the particular agency's board of review or, if there is no board, to the Board of Public Works.

S.B. 810 does not contain a provision for consolidating appeals. Administrative and judicial review of local government and state agency actions are in accordance with existing procedures governing the issuance of permits. The State Permit Coordinator has been very pleased with the extent of cooperation among agencies in developing the Master Application Form. The Coordinator believes that state agencies will not coordinate their activities on their own, thus making necessary an independent Permit Coordinator. Both the Coordinator and the law itself make it clear that S.B. 810 is not an attempt to interfere with the decision-making process of individual agencies.

According to the Permit Coordinator, the location of his office is an important factor in the procedure. "We have no authority, we only keep records and set up consolidated hearings, however, we are an arm of the Board of Public Works, which exercises budgetary control over all state agencies." ...

Comments: 1. Coordinated hearing legislation has also been enacted in several other states, including Alaska, Minnesota, Oregon, and Washington. The statutes vary in coverage and in the extent to which local government participation is mandated. The Washington law provides an option to local governments to process local rezonings, variances and conditional uses through the state's coordinated hearings procedure. Wash. Rev. Code Ann. § 90.62.100(2)(a) (Supp. 1978). If local governments choose not to participate their zoning approvals will be processed separately. Difficulties may arise in coordinating state and local government approvals. State permits are issued by administrative agencies or departments while many local approvals, such as rezonings, go through the local legislative body. Differences in hearing and approval procedures may make a joint or coordinated hearing difficult if not impossible.

2. A series of problems have arisen under coordinated hearing legislation. Delay is one. Although this legislation can place time limits on agency decisions, this kind of limitation on the decision-making process is often resisted politically. In Washington, the Department of Ecology as the responsible agency has the authority to impose time limits, but they have been difficult to set administratively. California has now passed legislation mandating decisions on development projects within time periods ranging from six to 18 months. Cal. Gov't Code §§ 65950-65954 (Deering Supp. 1977).

Delays also occur under coordinated hearing procedures when approvals must be secured from local governments before the coordinated hearing can be held. For example, if local governments in Washington elect not to participate in the coordinated hearing procedure, a certification that local zoning has been obtained must be filed before the coordinated hearing procedure can begin. Similar problems arise in states with environmental impact statement requirements. A coordinated hearing may not be held under the Minnesota law unless a certification has been received that an environmental impact statement has been completed if one is required. Minn. Stat. Ann. § 116C.26(1) (Supp. 1977). An alternative procedure could provide for the filing and consideration of a draft environmental impact statement at the time the coordinated hearing is held.

Problems also arise because the coordinated hearing laws generally provide that the record developed at the coordinated hearing process is to be informational only; it does not serve as the record on which the final agency decisions are made. See the Washington law, § 90.62.030(3). It would be better if the record developed at the coordinated hearing provided the basis for agency decisions. The Minnesota statute, § 116C.28 provides that coordinated hearings shall be held under the contested case procedures of the state administrative procedures act, which requires that a record be developed.

3. An assessment of coordinated hearing legislation is provided in F. Bosselman, D. Feurer, & C. Siemon, The Permit Explosion, ch. 3 (1976). They note, *id.* at 29, that even though conflicts and inconsistencies in the standards and requirements of different agencies may become apparent during the coordinated hearing process, "[p]resent coordinated permitting processes authorize individual agencies to make their own decisions without being bound by the decisions of the other participating agencies (except when otherwise required by state law.) " In this situation, the permit will be denied if only one of the participating agencies concludes that its standards and criteria require a denial of the permit. Is there any way out of this dilemma short of wholesale statutory revision of the permit programs? When conflicts in policy and the interpretation of policy arise in the coordinating hearing process, an opportunity should be presented to resolve these conflicts. But how is this to be done? If the state coastal agency stoutly maintains that to grant the permit would mean a violation of state coastal policy, how can this policy objection be resolved without diluting (at least in the coastal agency's eyes) the effectiveness of the state coastal program?

For discussion of the Washington law see Corker & Elliott, The Environmental Coordination Procedures Act of 1973, 49 Wash. L. Rev. 463 (1974). For the Alaska law see Alaska Stat. §§ 46.35.010 *et seq.* (Supp. 1977). For the Oregon law see Ore. Rev. Stat. §§ 447.800 *et seq.*

4. Permit and development approval requirements also overlap at the local level. The Permit Explosion, *id.* at 31-36, discusses a variety of experiments at the local level that have attempted to provide coordinated approval procedures. The Fairfax County, Virginia, experience is typical. (The county is in the Washington, D.C., metropolitan area):

> Fairfax County has developed a form of "one-stop shopping" for securing building approval. Among the county offices which may act on a building permit application are the building department, office of land design, zoning administrator, sanitation department, health department, fire marshall, tax assessor, housing and license department, and, in some cases, the county environmental protection agency. Beginning in September 1974, a procedure was established under which an applicant can file an initial application with the building department. The department ascertains whether all data required by other agencies is included and, if so, sends the application on to each permitting agency. The building department then keeps track of the application as it is processed by these agencies; it does not, however, play the role of mediator like the Los Angeles CICED. The process is mandatory for most projects; some minor projects, requiring only a few permits, can still be processed by filing individual applications with separate agencies and walking them through.
>
> A number of persons interviewed in Fairfax County suggested

that the process has had the effect of improving the quality of work of the various agencies. Because an applicant files a single application with the building department, there are fewer interruptions in the work of each agency. Initially, there were problems of missing data in applications accepted by the building department, and individual agencies had to contact applicants to secure information. This problem is lessening as the building department becomes more familiar with the needs of the individual agencies. Respondents differed on whether the process has speeded up the processing of applications; some felt that, as bugs are worked out, the process will operate more efficiently.

Id. at 35.

Chapter 10

PROPERTY TAXATION AND LAND DEVELOP-MENT

These materials have been devoted almost entirely to the official system of land use controls, the zoning ordinance and related regulatory measures that guide the use of land. In the words of Norman Williams, there is another, unofficial system of land use control: "[t]he second system is not normally thought of as a land use control system at all; yet it is now really more powerful and tends to dominate the official system." Williams, The Three Systems of Land Use Control, 25 Rutgers L. Rev. 80, 82 (1970). Williams is referring here to the local real property tax. While not all would agree with his conclusion, real property taxes do have significant impacts on land development and must be considered in any discussion of public measures that affect land use.

Space does not permit a full exploration of the interaction between the real property tax and land use. This chapter will focus instead on two reforms of the property tax that have significant land use impacts — the preferential assessment of agricultural land and site value taxation. A word is first in order on the nature of the real property tax and how it is administered.

The real property tax is levied by general purpose local governments, such as cities and counties, and by special districts such as school districts. In many parts of the country the property tax is the mainstay of local government revenues. It is levied on the total assessed value of both land and improvements, although assessed values in many areas are substantially below market value. Each jurisdiction levying the tax applies a local tax rate to assessed land and improvement values. While the tax rate varies around the country, and while it is higher in some regions (particularly in the northeast) than in others, an effective tax rate of two percent of market value is typical.

Both of the property tax reforms considered here affect the conversion of undeveloped land to urban use. It is thus important to note that assessment differentials within the property tax structure will affect the land conversion process because outlying residential and agricultural property tends to be underassessed relative to inner-city residential and nonresidential property. This comparative assessment advantage cuts two ways on the land conversion process. Lower assessments are capitalized into land values and raise the price of outlying land relative to land closer to urban centers. At the same time, the holding cost of undeveloped land tends to be lower because it is assessed at a comparatively lower level. Lower annual taxes may make it easier for traders in undeveloped land to hold that land off the market until it is ready for development. Additional helpful background on the local real property tax is provided by H. Aaron, Who Pays the Property Tax? (1975).

The two property tax reforms considered in this chapter have been proposed for contrary reasons. Preferential assessment of agricultural land lowers property taxes in order to keep that land in agricultural use and prevent its premature development. Site value taxation increases the property tax on undeveloped land to force development on land that is either vacant or that is being put to an underintensive use. Preferential assessment of agricultural land has been widely adopted, while site value taxation remains largely an academic idea. In evaluating the materials that follow, it should be instructive to ask why one of these reforms has been widely adopted and the other not; whether either should be adopted or continued; and whether both strategies could be pursued simultaneously consistent with community land use and development goals.

A. PREFERENTIAL ASSESSMENT OF AGRICULTURAL LAND

Rapid and low density urbanization in our metropolitan areas has focused attention on agricultural land as a disappearing natural resource. While agricultural zoning and related growth management techniques can be effective in protecting agricultural land from urban development, they are subject to political pressure and have not usually been sufficient to prevent the conversion of agricultural land to urban use. To provide a financial incentive for the retention of agricultural land, practically all states have enacted some form of tax relief which accords that land preferential treatment. Tax relief under this legislation usually provides for the assessment of agricultural land at its value for agricultural purposes rather than at its value for urban development, thus providing an abatement of property taxes to agricultural landowners.

Preferential assessment of agricultural land can be expected to raise constitutional problems under constitutional provisions in most states that require uniformity of taxation within taxing jurisdictions. Preferential assessment can be attacked as a classification for property tax purposes that violates the uniformity requirement. While the judicial response to preferential assessment programs challenged under uniformity provisions was mixed, most states have now adopted constitutional provisions explicitly authorizing preferential assessment programs. The following study describes the nature of these programs and assesses their problems and effectiveness.

R. BARLOWE & T. ALTER, USE-VALUE ASSESSMENT OF FARM AND OPEN SPACE LANDS 3-7, 9-10, 12-13, 15-16, 30-31 (Research Report 308, Agricultural Experiment Station, Michigan State University, 1976)

Almost 24 million acres shifted from rural to urban uses between the end of World War II and 1975. This urbanization movement affected some areas and communities to a far greater extent than others. Overall, it has provided capital gains for some owners and speculators and land development opportunities for promoters, builders and potential residents. At the same time, it has led to higher taxes for many owners, shifting of large areas of open space to more congested uses, and numerous premature and poorly planned developments.

PREFERENTIAL USE-VALUE ASSESSMENT

Several states have adopted a simple form of preferential use-value assessment. Iowa's law, for example, contains the brief provision that the assessed value of agricultural land shall be "based only on its current use." . . .

Maryland's original use-value assessment law of 1956 further provided that lands "actively devoted to farm or agricultural use will be assessed on the basis of such use, and shall not be assessed as if subdivided or on any other basis." . . . Longer statements are found in most laws. But this simple provision for the preferential tax treatment of farmlands is accepted in the laws of 10 states. . . . With this approach, owners of qualifying farm and open space lands can realize the full benefits of preferential use-value assessment and withdraw lands from classification without penalty at any time.

Simple preferential use-value assessment has been advanced as an appropriate means for providing a tax break for an overburdened and deserving group of taxpayers. It has been criticized, however, as a measure that permits some landowners to "have their cake and eat it too." Owners benefit from lower property taxes as long as they retain their lands in the tax programs. But there is no requirement that they keep their lands in their present use. They are free to reap possible significant capital gains by shifting their lands to other uses. Speculators can use this approach to benefit from the taxation of their lands at its value for agriculture and easily afford to forego the temptation to sell out to prospective buyers while they wait for higher bidders to come along.

Recognition of this prospect of windfall profits has caused most legislatures to take the position that obligations must be associated with the benefits to be derived from use-value assessment. With deferred tax arrangements, landowners are expected to keep their classified lands in agricultural and open space uses or pay penalties

in the form of rollback or land use conversion taxes when they shift
their lands to other uses.

Deferred Taxes

Most states with use-value assessment programs use some version
of the deferred tax or penalty-for-withdrawal principle. New Jersey's
Farmland Assessment Act of 1964 is an excellent example of this
approach. This law authorizes owners of eligible agricultural and
horticultural lands to apply each year for a special tax assessment
classification. Classified lands are assessed at their agricultural or
horticultural use values. When lands are withdrawn from
classification or the land use changes, the assessor determines the
full assessed value of the property under the standards applied to
nonclassified lands. Then a rollback tax equal to the difference
between the taxes paid and those that would have been paid during
the current year and the two preceding years is levied. . . .
. . . .

A different version of deferred taxation has been adopted in
Connecticut. . . . Connecticut's law of 1963 accepted the preferential
use-value assessment approach. An additional provision calling for
a conveyance tax on lands sold to others or shifted to unauthorized
uses was added in 1972.

This tax, designed to encourage continued ownership of farm,
forest, and open space lands, levies a tax penalty equal to 10% of
the property value if it is sold or its use changes within the first year
after acquisition of ownership or first year of classification. The tax
is then scaled down 1% each year so that a 1% conveyance tax applies
in the 10th year and no tax thereafter. This conveyance tax is not
to be confused with the real estate transfer tax applied to all real
estate sales in Connecticut. . . . [Currently, about 23 states have
deferred taxation provisions. *See Hoffman v. Clark,* 372 N.E.2d 74
(Ill. 1977) (does not violate equal protection). — Eds.]

Requirements for Planning or Zoning

Several states use deferred taxing arrangements in combination
with additional policy features. Some of these have requirements for
zoning or planning board approval. Oregon . . . distinguishes
between farmland zoned for agriculture and nonzoned farmland.
Use-value assessment applies automatically to lands zoned for
agriculture but owners of farmland not zoned as such can apply for
tax classification.

Classification is terminated if the zoning status of the zoned lands
is changed, in which case there is no penalty if the owner did not
request the change, or if lands are shifted to nonagricultural use. Tax
benefits are rolled back for the period of classification or for a

maximum of 10 yr when zoned lands are shifted to other uses. Owners of declassified nonzoned lands pay the rollback tax plus interest and an additional 20% penalty if they fail to give their assessors prior notice of changes in land use. . . .

Nebraska . . . uses a less complicated formula requiring that farmlands be zoned agricultural if they are to qualify for use-value assessment. Declassification calls for payment of a 5-yr rollback of taxes (or for the period of classification if shorter) plus interest. . . .

Virginia . . . authorizes local governments to adopt deferred tax ordinances containing a 5-yr rollback feature. Before adopting these ordinances, however, the cities, counties or towns must first adopt land use plans that delineate the areas that may be classified as agricultural, horticultural, forest or open space. . . .

Florida employs preferential use-value assessment in combination with agricultural land zoning in its law applying to farmlands. Lands zoned for agriculture are supposedly assessed at their value for this use. Other owners can apply to their county assessors for tax classification. Modifications of zoning classifications to permit nonagricultural uses, however, are interpreted as cause for declassification. . . .

Connecticut requires that applications for the tax classification of open space lands be submitted to local planning commissions. Comparable provisions calling for zoning compliance or for local planning board approval are found in the laws of California, Hawaii, Maryland, Vermont and Washington.

RESTRICTIVE AGREEMENTS

Eleven states employ varying versions of the approaches discussed above in combination with restrictive agreements. These agreements are described in the laws and literature as conservation easements, covenants, dedications, development right easements, discretionary easements, and as contracts for agricultural preserves or for open space and scenic easements. These arrangements call for agreements between landowners and authorized public agencies in which the owners agree to keep given lands in their current use for specified time periods in return for assurance that the lands will be assessed for property tax purposes at no more than their current use values.

California pioneered this approach by adopting the Land Conservation Act (Williamson Act) in 1965. . . . This frequently amended act authorizes cities and counties to designate lands as agricultural preserves to be used for agricultural, recreational, open space and other compatible uses. Rural land owners may enter into contracts with the cities and counties to have their lands classified as parts of these preserves. The contracts vest the local governments with conservation easements and provide that owners are to keep their lands in agricultural or other open space uses for 10 or more years. In return, the lands are taxed at their capitalized-income value for the permitted uses.

Contracts are automatically renewed for another year at the end of each year unless either the owner or the cities or counties serve notice of termination. Nine years notice is required for termination but contracts can be cancelled in advance of the termination date with public approval. Public hearings are required for cancellation proceedings. When contracts are cancelled, landowners must pay a cancellation fee equal to 12½% of the full cash value of the property at time of cancellation. This fee can be waived under appropriate circumstances by the local governing body with state approval. . . .

Another California law authorizes use-value assessments for rural open space preserves when the owners grant open space easements to cities or counties for 20 or more years. . . . A third law provides for comparable treatment of rural land areas on which the cities or counties hold scenic easements under contracts that run for at least 10 yr. . . . Arrangements also are made under California law for payment of subventions by the state to cities, counties and school districts to compensate in part for their loss of property tax revenues under the conservation easement program.

California's contract-for-easement approach has attracted considerable attention largely because of the emphasis given to preserving open space as a policy goal. Similar contractual arrangements are used in 10 other states — Florida (recreation and park lands), Hawaii, Maine (scenic easements), Maryland (country club holdings), Michigan, New Hampshire (open space preserves), New York (agricultural districts), Pennsylvania, Vermont and Washington. Some of these states require contracts on all lands classified for special tax treatment. Others use mixed arrangements that involve restrictive agreements with some classes of land but not others. The variety of approaches used is best illustrated by brief descriptions of the programs now in operation.

. . . [Only the description of the New York law is included. For a table summarizing the characteristics of state preferential taxation laws see Keene, Differential Assessment and the Preservation of Open Space, 14 Urb. L. Ann. 11, 18-19 (1977). Statutory citations are provided in *id.* n. 5, at 13. — Eds.]

New York enacted an Agricultural Districts Act in 1971. The act authorizes an owner or owners with 500 acres or 10% of the area of a proposed district to request the creation of an agricultural district. Beginning in 1975 the state commissioner of environmental conservation is also authorized to initiate action for creating new districts of 2,000 or more acres where not already created.

The agricultural districts are created through formal county governing board action after public hearings and consideration of factors such as extent of farming use and "county developmental patterns and needs." Once created, the county governing boards must review the districts every 8 yr and either extend or terminate them.

Owners of farmlands within agricultural districts are expected to share a long-term commitment for the continued use of their lands in agriculture. Lands within the districts are subject to use-value assessment. Local governmental controls may be modified to recognize the agricultural character of the district lands and forestall developments (such as limitations on farming practices or construction of water and sewer systems) that might undermine their long-time commitment and value for agricultural use. When district lands are converted to other uses, a rollback tax equal to the tax benefits received for the affected area during the preceding 5 yr is levied on the owners.

New York also authorizes agricultural use-value assessments with farmlands not included in formally organized agricultural districts. Landowners qualifying for this type of treatment must sign 8-yr agreements to keep lands in agricultural use. These agreements can be terminated without penalty with 7 years notice if an owner chooses not to renew his agreement at the end of any year. Owners who break their agreements by converting lands to unauthorized uses are charged a tax penalty equal to twice the property tax due in the year following declassification on all the land they had covered by agreement. . . .

DETERMINATIONS OF USE-VALUE

A critical problem in the administration of use-value assessment programs involves determination of use-value. With properties located at some distance from expanding cities and away from the pressures of competing land uses, one should find *de facto* use-value assessment. Current market value should provide *prima facie* evidence of the present use-value of land if the land has no alternate higher or better market use.

A different situation exists in areas where land values are influenced by competing demands and pressures. With these lands, it is usually difficult to say how much of the current market value is attributable to the current land use as compared with the expected values potential buyers associate with alternative uses.

Tax assessors traditionally place heavy emphasis on market comparisons when appraising the value of farm and open space lands. If three nearby farm properties with similar attributes have recently sold at prices of around $400 an acre, one can logically assume that a similar property should have a comparable value.

This value determination process becomes more complicated

when competing uses and investor speculation cause the going market price of farmland to rise to $800 an acre in a rural-urban fringe community and when some owners start to sell off residential building lots for $2,500 an acre. Market comparisons provide a workable means for determining highest and best market values at this point, but are poor indicators of current use-value.

Numerous approaches are used by the various states to determine use-value. Several states provide that farm and open space lands be assessed at no more than their current use-values and leave the problem of determination to the local assessors. Others go a step farther to list factors assessors should consider. Emphasis with these instructions is usually given to need for assessing land at its value for the authorized current use and not for subdivision of some other alternative use.

Maine, Montana and Nebraska specify that guidelines for use-value assessment will be prepared by a state taxation office. Michigan, New York and New Mexico (with grazing lands) require assessment of the classified lands by representatives of the state taxation office rather than by local assessors.

Four states — California, Colorado, Maine (with forest lands), and Washington — provide that assessors use a net income capitalization approach rather than sales comparisons in determining use-values. Colorado provides for use of an 11½% capitalization rate and Maine for a 10% rate. Washington specifies that the capitalization rate shall correspond with the long-term mortgage interest rate on farm real estate loans. California's assessors use a rate that reflects the yield on long-term government bonds plus components for risk, property taxes and amortization of investment.

Some states (e.g. Delaware, Massachusetts, New Hampshire, New Jersey, Virginia and Washington) provide for the designation of official land valuation committees. These committees advise state and local officials concerning the techniques and value benchmarks they should adopt in use-value determinations.

. . . .

EFFECTIVENESS OF USE-VALUE ASSESSMENT

. . . .

JUSTIFICATION AND OBJECTIVES

. . . .

Most of the initial support for use-value assessment in the 1950s came from farm groups. Farmers generally had enjoyed a "golden age" of property taxation during the war years when their property taxes were low relative to their rising incomes. This situation changed markedly after the war as taxes began to rise on a per acre basis, as a percentage of property value, and as a percentage of net farm income. . . . With this trend, rural land owners in most areas became tax-conscious. But the problem was most acute near the growing cities where rural owners were often caught in a tax squeeze of rising assessment levels and increasing millage rates.

Tax levies rose 10-, 20-, and 50-fold within a few years in many cases. With this prospect, owners were often happy to sell their lands, particularly when offered good prices. Many owners, however, wanted to continue farming. Use-value assessment was recommended both near the cities and farther away as a reasonable means for protecting the interests and securing tax justice for these owners.

Initial support for use-value assessment favored adoption of a simple system of preferential assessment. . . . This approach was soon criticized because it promised unwarranted tax savings to those owners including prospective land speculators. It was argued that responsibilities for keeping land in agriculture or penalties for removing it from this use should be associated with the differential taxing program.

Deferred taxing arrangements were devised to meet this objection. With this approach, rollback taxes are employed to discourage owners from applying for use-value assessment if they anticipate an early shifting of lands to other uses and to recoup some of the tax savings received by participants at their time of withdrawal.

With hundreds of investors seeking speculative profits and with no controls on development, the typical result is a more scattered pattern of development with some investors and developers extending operations farther out into a large transitional development zone. And with each additional mile that these investors move out to secure prospective development sites, larger and larger acreages shift to the transitional zone. Adding one mile on all sides of a city already 12 mi across, for example, adds 26,138 acres of transitional lands as compared with 4,021 acres when a mile is added to a city that is only 1 mi across.

Investors with choice sites and financial backing can often proceed with the development of lands in the transitional zone. Their activities have a ripple effect on the market and assessment values of all surrounding lands. Unfortunately, the limited need for new urban developments often makes much of this increase in land values illusory. Only a small portion of the transitional zone is needed for early development, and a real market for the development of much of the remaining area cannot realistically be expected for years to come.

This not uncommon situation leaves many speculative investors with holdings that have far higher ripening costs than they had initially expected. And more important, it has a blighting effect on the value of the remaining transitional lands for continued agricultural use simply because: 1) the land is assessed at an expected higher than normal agricultural value; 2) the scattered urban-oriented residents who have moved into the area demand new public services that earlier residents got along without and that require higher tax levies; 3) many of the remaining farm owners shift to patterns of management and thinking that contemplate the early sale of their properties; and 4) suburban developments in the midst of agricultural areas often leads to negative externalities such as undesirable odors, fly problems or spray drift for the suburbanites and disruption of soil drainage and farm machinery travel patterns and vandalism for the farmers.

Acceptance of the rollback tax feature has effectively moderated the potential use-value assessment has for favoring land speculation. But it has not eliminated the problem. As Wagenseil notes, the rollback approach can aid speculators who plan to hold land several years by: 1) reducing current land holding costs; 2) making much of their tax come due when they are best able to pay — after they sell the land; 3) allowing an interest free loan, if interest is not charged, on the value of the tax rollback; and 4) allowing them to evade the extra tax they otherwise would pay in the years before the rollback period begins. [*See* Wagenseil, Property Taxation of Agricultural and Open Space Land, 8 Harv. J. Legis. 165, 169 (1970). — Eds.]

A third phase of the use-value assessment movement emerged when proponents of land use planning and better land management accepted this approach as a policy tool that could contribute to the attainment of their goals. These groups supported the coupling of use-value assessment with provisions, calling for planning commission approval, agricultural zoning, or the designation of agricultural preserves. These additions made use-value assessment a more meaningful measure for implementing land use plans and policies.

. . . .

PROTECTING AGRICULTURAL AND OPEN SPACE LANDS

Use-value assessment has received considerable support from environmentalists and others who have seen it as a promising means of protecting agricultural and open space lands. Whether or not it has operated effectively for this purpose is still a matter of opinion. Observers in some states report that use-value assessment has slowed down the rate of land conversion to other uses while critics have sometimes denounced the programs of their states as failures. More time must elapse with most programs before one can definitely say that the special tax programs have had more than a temporary effect in slowing down the rate of land conversion.

How far use-value assessment programs can go in protecting agricultural and open space lands depends largely on the emphasis given to the current use-protection objective. Landowners have a natural economic incentive for favoring taxing arrangements that provide them with benefits and still leave them with the option of developing or selling their lands. A protection policy, in contrast, calls for tight declassification procedures that discourage or prevent withdrawals once lands have been accepted for classification.

These two objectives are in conflict. Programs that emphasize the first objective provide little protection for existing land uses while those that emphasize the protection goal offer little incentive for owner participation. Considerable emphasis has been given to protectionist goals in several laws enacted in the past decade, but even the most restrictive of these involves elements of compromise between the two objectives.

All of the lands covered by restrictive agreements or with rollback and penalty tax arrangements are now receiving some protection. Not as much land is listed under these programs as some might wish, and many areas enrolled receive only temporary protection since their owners can easily withdraw them from classification. All things considered, however, the various programs are operating reasonably well in providing the types of protection permitted by existing legislation.

A common criticism of present programs is that large tracts of agricultural and open space land located near expanding cities have not been classified under the tax programs and that urban developments often spread onto these lands rather than to areas of lower agricultural or scenic open space potential. This criticism ignores three important facts: 1) areas located near growing cities often involve lands that planners and city officials would classify as areas needed for urban expansion and thus are lands that these officials are authorized to exclude from eligibility in some states; 2) owners of land with development potential near cities often have little interest in special tax programs that may interfere with their abilities to sell their lands at a hoped-for profit within a few months or years; and 3) while use-value assessment can make it more difficult for developers to acquire some land areas, it has no built-in mechanism for telling developers where they should or must locate developments.

Use-value assessment programs can be a boon to owners who want to retain lands in rural uses. For them, it provides a safeguard against unwelcome tax pressures. This situation does not apply, however, when owners have no commitment for keeping land in its present use or when they are anxious to sell their holdings for a profit. As long as viable opportunities exist for shifting lands to more profitable uses, these owners are apt to view their lands as a ripening investment — a savings fund they should cash in at an appropriate time to secure funds for retirement or other purposes.

Tax concessions have little prospect for turning these plans around if the owners expect to sell or shift lands in the near future. They can help reduce land holding and ripening costs when the expected sales dates are some years off, but in the owners' expectations they can never be more than a temporary restraining measure.

The real hope with use-value assessment as a means for protecting agricultural and open-space lands over a considerable time span lies with the possible inducements it offers landowners located some distance from the current suburban land market. These owners still think in terms of the continued and long term operation of their land as agricultural and natural areas. If they can be encouraged to participate in tax classification, restrictive agreement, and special district programs before pressures arise for shifts to other uses, it may be possible to protect large blocks of land as agricultural and open space domains. Hopefully, group pressures will cause these owners to reenroll, while owner solidarity will discourage diversions of land for other uses.

Special provisions such as those found in the New York law that protect owners in agricultural districts from special assessments for sewers, water systems and other urban development-oriented improvements can provide a major tool for protecting existing land uses in these areas. Agricultural or open space zoning or formal designation as a preservation district also can aid this protection process.

All three of these steps — blocking of holdings, protection from special assessments, and zoning or district status — are needed to deter development. These measures can effectively discourage new land developments as long as the owners of lands around the fringes hold. Their ultimate success in preserving open space, however, depends on the attitudes and decisions of those operators located at the fringe.

For use-value assessment to enjoy long run success in protecting agricultural and open space lands, it must: 1) offer a realistic tax saving incentive to owners to remain under the program; 2) encourage participants to keep land in its present use; 3) have the cooperation of local assessors and officials in administering the program; and 4) be supplemented with other land use programs that permit coordinated public and private efforts in the direction of land use.

Comments: 1. Statistics indicating a massive conversion of agricultural land to urban use would suggest an agricultural holocaust justifying preferential assessment of agricultural land. These figures must be further examined, however, to determine whether the best agricultural land actually lies near metropolitan areas and whether that land is threatened by additional urban development. One careful study of this problem indicates that the 43 percent of our land area that is in metropolitan areas and counties adjacent to these areas contains 52 percent of our prime farmland. D. Vining, K. Bieri, & A. Strauss, Urbanization of Prime Agricultural Land in the United States: A Statistical Analysis 32 (Regional Science Research Inst., 1977). But this study disagreed with findings of another study that these prime farmlands were threatened with further urbanization. Their findings indicate that as urban development is becoming more dispersed it is moving away from areas containing prime farmlands. What implication does this finding have, if true, on the policy and content of preferential assessment legislation?

2. Preferential assessment laws are intended to have a uniform effect in their area of operation on incentives to hold agricultural land. The property tax savings to be expected from these laws will nonetheless vary considerably depending upon the setting in which they are applied. Keene, *supra* at 28, discusses this problem:

> There are three factors relating to the land market and the real property tax system in a particular landowner's taxing jurisdiction which influence the magnitude of the tax benefits he might receive from differential assessment.
>
> The first factor is difference between the assessed value of the land based on fair market value and its assessed value based on current-use or farm value. Obviously, farmers at the rural-urban fringe would, in principle, enjoy the largest reduction, although the fact that *de facto* preferential assessment of farmland is widespread in these areas may, in practice, reduce the magnitude of the benefit. In these areas, differential assessment would protect the farmer against future increases in tax burden resulting from rising land value and reassessment.
>
> The second factor is the percentage which the assessed value of farm land and associated real estate improvements, such as barns, throughout the taxing jurisdiction, is of the total assessed value tax base before the establishment of differential assessment. If all realty in the jurisdiction is in eligible agricultural use, there would be no benefit to an individual farmer. The assessed value of his land would be reduced, but, since the tax revenue needs of the municipality would remain the same, his tax rate would go up by an amount sufficient to produce the same tax revenue, and his tax bill would remain unchanged. At the other extreme, if there is a very small amount of eligible land in a jurisdiction, the tax saving for its owner would be proportional to the reduction in assessment. . . .
>
> The third factor is the percentage which the assessed value of the improvements on a particular farm is of its total assessed value before differential assessment. The tax benefit usually involves only taxes on land, and improvements continue to be assessed at fair market value. In general, if an individual owner is to be better

off after the institution of a differential assessment program, the percentage of his farm's value which is in eligible land must be at least as large as the percent of the entire tax base which is in eligible land. Thus, not all farmers will enjoy a net benefit from a differential assessment program. Those with a high proportion of improvement value to land value may see their tax bills rise, even though their land is assessed at a lower rate.

Does this analysis suggest that revisions should be made in preferential assessment laws to take these factors into account? How would these factors affect the implementation of existing preferential assessment laws, which are not sensitive to these considerations?

3. As the discussion of preferential assessment laws has indicated, see *supra* p. 1273, very few of these laws link preferential assessment with zoning or with the comprehensive plan. One exception is Hawaii. Recall that this state is divided by a state Land Use Commission into four land use districts, one of which is an agricultural district. *See supra* p. 1259. The Hawaii preferential assessment law tracks this state land use districting to some extent. Property tax assessment in that state is carried out statewide by the state tax department. By statute, it is to divide the state for purposes of assessment into six classes, including an agricultural class, and "[i]n assigning land to one of the general classes . . . shall give major consideration to the districting established by the land use commission." Haw. Rev. Stat. § 256-10(d)(2) (1977). For discussion of the Hawaii tax, see the extensive review of preferential farm tax legislation prepared by the Council on Environmental Quality, Untaxing Open Space 164-201 (1976).

Consider the way in which other states have handled this problem:

Nebraska: "Any land which is within an agricultural use zone and which is used exclusively for agricultural use shall be assessed at its actual value for agricultural use." Neb. Rev. Stat. § 77-1344(1) (Supp. 1974). "Agricultural use zone shall mean any land designated for agricultural use by any political subdivision pursuant to" the state zoning enabling legislation. *Id.* § 77-1343(2).

How is a political subdivision to designate land for agricultural use? Under its zoning ordinance? What kind of zoning district does this requirement imply? Would a large lot zoning district allowing dwelling units for residential purposes be sufficient? Nebraska also has a mandatory planning requirement for counties and a further requirement that county zoning ordinances be consistent with the county plan. How does this requirement affect the agricultural zoning provision in the preferential taxation law?

Pennsylvania: Under one of the Pennsylvania preferential assessment laws the preference is available if the county and the landowner enter into a restrictive agreement. The legislation provides: "[n]o land shall be subject to the provisions of this act unless designated as farm, forest, water supply or open space land in a plan adopted following a public hearing by the planning commission of the municipality, county or region in which the land is located." Pa. Stat. Ann. tit. 16, § 11942 (Supp. 1978).

Note that these statutes shift the initiative both for agricultural zoning and for preferential assessment to the planning and zoning agency. Is this desirable? Generally, a preferential assessment under this legislation is withdrawn when the farm land covered by the assessment is shifted to urban use. Compare the statewide planning goals adopted under the Oregon state land use legislation, *supra* p. 1242, which contains a policy both for agricultural zoning and for the conversion of land from agricultural to urban use. *See* Untaxing Open Space, *supra* at 217-19.

Recall also the experience under the California law, which indicated that land close to metropolitan areas was not generally brought under the preferential assessment legislation. It is possible to link preferential assessment with a policy for urban expansion. The Florida law contains a land use dimension because it authorizes counties in that state to classify land within their areas as agricultural and nonagricultural for purposes of applying preferential assessment. The law then provides:

> The board of county commissioners may also reclassify lands classified as agricultural to nonagricultural when there is contiguous urban or metropolitan development and the board of county commissioners finds that the continued use of such lands for agricultural purposes will act as a deterrent to the timely and orderly expansion of the community.

Fla. Stat. Ann. § 193.461 (West Supp. 1978). Preferential assessment is not available on lands not classified as agricultural.

4. Can preferential assessment of farmland in areas restricted from development under growth management plans help sustain the constitutionality of this restriction? Note that preferential assessment will reduce property taxes and thus holding costs on the land that is restricted. Professor Costonis argues that the tax reductions on land restricted from immediate development under the Ramapo plan, see *supra* p. 1037, helped save that plan from constitutional attack. Costonis, "Fair" Compensation and the Accommodation Power: Antidotes for the Taking Impasse in Land Use Controversies, 75 Colum. L. Rev. 1021, 1056-58 (1975). The Costonis article should be consulted for an argument that cases like *Ramapo* have recognized an "accommodation power" in land use controls midway between full noncompensatory police power regulation and compensated taking. The accommodation power describes "a class of regulatory measures ... that escapes the confiscation objection only by affording burdened landowners fair compensation in the form of economic trade-offs." *Id.* at 1058 (emphasis omitted).

5. Whether or not preferential assessment of farmland will achieve its objectives depends on whether and to what extent it will influence the farmer's decision to hold on to agricultural land. Most commentators have been pessimistic on this point:

> Except for a few specific situations, which account for a small fraction of potential sales of farmland, differential assessment is not likely to be effective in achieving land use objectives. Whether or not a particular farm is sold and converted to a non-open use depends on three sets of considerations: supply factors, demand factors, and governmental approval of the proposed development. Differential assessment operates primarily on one of the supply factors, by reducing the income squeeze which farmers in rural-urban fringe areas experience as a result of rising real property taxes. It has a secondary impact on the demand side

because it permits farmer-buyers, speculators and developers either to offer somewhat more for the land or to buy more land at the same price because their carrying costs are reduced. This latter effect is difficult to appraise, but is likely to be marginal because the buyer will normally be simply exchanging tax costs on the land for interest costs on the money he has to borrow either to pay the higher price or to buy additional land.

It is clear, however, that all forms of differential assessment help to insulate the farmer from market pressures to sell which come to bear on him in the form of higher property taxes based on rising property values. They make it easier for him to schedule the sale of his land at a time, such as retirement, which fits into his estate planning.

Untaxing Open Space, *supra* at 77-78. *See also* T. Plaut, The Real Property Tax, Differential Assessment, and the Loss of Farmland on the Urban Fringe 4 (Regional Science Research Institute, 1977) (main cost of holding appreciating land is not real property taxes but foregone interest on alternative investment). In appraising these conclusions, keep in mind that the average national annual property tax as a percentage of property value is around two percent; it may be slightly less for agricultural property, which is often underassessed even in the absence of preferential taxation legislation. There have been some studies on the influence of preferential assessment on the farmer's decision to sell, but they have been inconclusive. These studies are discussed in Keene, *supra* at 42-44.

Note also that the impact of preferential assessment programs may depend on whether participation is voluntary or mandatory. See Hansen & Schwartz, Landowner Behavior at the Rural-Urban Fringe in Response to Preferential Property Taxation, 51 Land Econ. 341, 351 (1975) (participation in Califormia restricted agreement program reduced because of unrealistic expectations about land development potential). Compare the Hawaii program, *supra* Comment 3, in which the state department of taxation determines which land is to be classified agricultural.

6. Some states have enacted statutes providing that the effect of zoning regulations is to be taken into account when assessing land for property tax purposes. The California legislation is one such example:

> In the assessment of land, the assessor shall consider the effect upon value of any enforceable restrictions to which the use of land may be subjected. Such restrictions shall include, but are not limited to: (a) zoning; .... There shall be a rebuttable presumption that restrictions will not be removed or substantially modified in the predictable future and that they will substantially equate the value of the land to the value attributable to the legally permissible use or uses.

Cal. Rev. & Tax. Code § 402.1 (Deering Supp. 1977). Grounds for rebutting the presumption include "the past history of like use restrictions in the jurisdiction in question." *Id.* Does this ground for rebuttal undercut the effectiveness of this provision?

Does this California legislation achieve the same results as a preferential assessment law? For example, assume that a county in California zones a large area devoted to agricultural production for agricultural use. Does this section require that this agriculturally zoned land must then be assessed at its agricultural value?

7. To what extent has preferential farm taxation been justified on efficiency grounds and to what extent on equity grounds? Note that preferential taxation will serve an equity goal to the extent that it protects small farmers who otherwise might be forced out of production. Efficiency goals will also be advanced to the extent that preferential taxation prevents semi-monopoly conditions in agriculture that may result if the property tax load forces small farmers to sell out to larger operators who can better bear the tax burden.

B. THE SITE VALUE TAX

Quite simply, the site value tax is a tax only on the land itself; improvements are not taxed. The following Note discusses the economics of the site value tax and legal and practical problems in its implementation.

NOTE, SITE VALUE TAXATION: ECONOMIC INCENTIVES AND LAND USE PLANNING, 9 Harvard Journal on Legislation 115, 124-27, 130-31, 136-38 (1971)

ECONOMICS OF THE SITE VALUE TAX

Contemporary supporters of site value taxation as a substitute for the present property tax make their case by stressing the theoretical neutrality of the former scheme. Unlike a levy on both land and buildings, a tax based solely upon unimproved land value should be invariant with development decisions. "What was optimal development in the absence of the [site value] tax will remain optimal in its presence." When compared to the present tax system, however, the practical neutrality of the site value scheme seems questionable. As the following pages explain, land value taxation provides four incentives for increased economic development: (a) the unburdening of improvements; (b) emphasis on holding-costs; (c) fixed cost effects; and (d) capitalization of property taxes. This section also considers two further aspects of site value taxation. These are the transferability and the equity of the tax.

A. *The Unburdening of Improvements*

By assessing land only, site value taxation eliminates the tax burden on buildings and other improvements. Because the levy is thus constant for all levels of operating outlay and replacement, neither construction nor remodeling is penalized. Because the tax is assessed equally on occupied and unoccupied structures, no artificial burden affects building resource allocation. Land development corresponds more directly to market developments. Although the tax doubtless increases the burden on land values, the corresponding removal of that burden from improvements should result in a net tax reduction to owners of "efficiently utilized" parcels, *i.e.* where property improvements outvalue land.

B. *Emphasis on Holding-Costs*

By escalating the relative cost of holding unimproved property, site value taxation (demand permitting) encourages more intensive land uses and discourages speculation. This holding-cost effect has two aspects: a maximizing insistence impact and a time-persistence or accumulation factor. The first follows because the strongest pressures for economic development are induced on sites with the largest increase in taxes. Land value assessment is based upon the potential earning value of the property; thus, these sites are also those offering the largest development capacity.

The time-persistence factor is derived from the annually-recurring liability that the American property tax places upon the property owner, regardless of whether his property is used or not. As the tax rate on land is increased (or correspondingly, the differential rate between land and improvements is escalated) the time-accumulation burden becomes more acute for owners of undeveloped land.

Thus, under a site value scheme, the holder of vacant property is confronted with three choices: (a) leaving the land vacant and bearing the tax; (b) offsetting the tax burden by achieving more efficient site utilization; or (c) selling the land to escape the time-persistence of the tax. As the tax rate increases, the first choice becomes financially untenable and the owner is induced either to develop the property or sell it to someone who will. The owner is thereby introduced to the fixed cost factor of land value taxation.

C. *Fixed Cost Effects of Site Value Taxation*

A fixed cost effect results because the amount of a land value tax bears no relation to the extent of development of any given site. Rather, since the levy is derived solely from unimproved land value, its amount depends upon the advantages of property location. Because any increase in the tax will be determined only by an increase in land value, the particular land use will not alter total property tax costs; the tax is neutral with reference to development expenses. Average tax costs per unit of improvement will decline as the investment in improvements (presumably spread over more units) increases, thus leading any investor to develop his property to its maximum efficient capacity.

D. *Capitalization of Property Taxes*

Site value taxation affects the capitalization of property taxes in several ways. To facilitate discussion of these effects two assumptions must be made: (a) the parcel involved is unique, so that the buyers have no alternative opportunities; and (b) the rate of the site tax is expected to remain constant. Under these conditions, a purchaser of property will deduct the capitalized value of the tax from the sale price of the land. Considered alone, this effect should lower the sale price of the property, regardless of the type of property tax imposed. However, by removing the tax on improvements, site valuation precludes capitalization of future building taxes. This result, coupled with the fixed tax effect noted above, increases the value of sites suitable for the construction of improvements. The potential increase in sale price is proportional to the degree to which a given parcel will support intensive improvements. Even under a site value scheme, however, capitalization may reduce parcel value if the rate of tax is expected to increase. . . . But as Professor Arthur Becker asserts, " [t]he fixed cost and unburdening effects . . . will win out over the capitalization and holding cost effects on land that is strategically located or in great demand for nonlocational reasons."

E. *Nontransferable Aspect of Site Value Taxation*

[Because the supply of land is fixed and because each site is unique, it is argued that the site value tax cannot be passed on by the seller. In central cities and elsewhere, however, where tenants of substandard housing and other property users are not mobile, there is a possibility that the site value tax will be passed on to buyers and renters. This was the experience when the site value tax was adopted in rural India. — Eds.]

. . . .

F. *Tax Equity*

The equity argument in favor of site value taxation is based upon the belief that land value is not derived from the labor and actions of property owners. Rather, the value of a site is largely a consequence of collective investment, community development, and population growth. As Henry George explained, "[l]and . . . was not produced. It was created." Thus, through the natural processes of development, land owners are able to realize substantial "unearned increments." Proponents of the site value system observe that community taxation to recapture these "windfall" amounts is entirely appropriate. The community, rather than individual owners, should reap the benefits of increases in land value which stem from collective action.

. . . .

The equity attributes of a land value system must be balanced, however, by at least one complication. In their purchase prices, most landowners have already paid for at least part of the unearned increment in land value. Limiting taxation to site value *increments* would avoid expropriation of past increases in property worth which may have been previously paid for by new owners. But any improvement in fairness resulting from an increment-only system might be insignificant in relation to the overall increase in equity offered by a total site value scheme. The "economic advantages of land value increment taxation are likely to be marginal ones." "By and large," the site value equity argument "makes sense."

[These equity arguments reflect similar comments levied against the taxation of unearned increment in land value, see *supra* p. —. Consider also that the site value tax will generate a one-time levy on land value increment at the time the tax is first imposed. Landowners who at that time hold vacant or underutilized land will, in effect, pay a one-time tax on unearned increment at the time the levy on their land is increased to reflect the shift to site value taxation. At the same time, some owners of developed and fully utilized land may experience a one-time windfall. —Eds.]

III. PRACTICAL ATTRIBUTES AND DETRIMENTS OF SITE VALUE TAXATION

[The Note discusses several problems, including public acceptance and difficulties in valuation and administration. Some jurisdictions that have tried the site value tax have abandoned it because of popular disapproval. Problems arise in factoring out site from improved values for purposes of taxation. Opinion is divided on how difficult or how easy this task can be. —Eds.]

. . . .

C. *Revenue Sufficiency*

Even if site value can be calculated with reasonable accuracy, the elimination of a tax on improvements would lead to an appreciable reduction in the total tax base. If the total government spending supported by the tax base remains constant or increases, the rate of taxation would have to be escalated. The difficult question is whether such an increase could raise the required public revenue without becoming confiscatory.

Several factors resulting from the untaxing of buildings should justify an increase in the tax rate under a site value system. In many areas, land is presently underassessed, thus warranting taxation at full worth under a site value scheme. Moreover, removing the tax on improvements would increase economic ground rents by an amount equalling the loss of building taxes. Use of a site value tax stimulates growth and development expectations, thereby adding to the portion of the tax base attributable to land value increments. The equity of any increase in taxes must also be considered. Because a site value tax is generally not passed on to tenants, it falls wholly upon property owners. Further, because land ownership is largely concentrated in wealthier classes, the tax is progressive. Thus, less reason exists for limiting any increase in tax rates.

Mason Gaffney notes that the sufficiency of land as a revenue base depends upon the factors which enter into the calculation of site value. In arid regions, water rights may be worth more than land surface. Utility privileges, easements, rights to emit pollutants, and shipping routes all affect land value and should therefore be taxed and assessed. The use of certain economic indicators to calculate the expected revenue loss from site value taxation may also lead to misleading results. The book value of corporate investment properties seldom reflects true economic-rental value. Similarly, the contract rent reflected in national income accounts is defined differently than the economic rent used to measure the impact of a site value levy.

Perhaps most important, land value taxation has provided adequate revenues in operation. Sydney, Australia, and Johannesburg, South Africa, both use the system. Each city has been able to finance municipal needs without instituting a confiscatory tax. In both cities, land values remain high. In Pittsburgh, the graded tax system led to a rate in the late 1960's of only 1.6 percent. . . .

Other analysts contest the suggestion that a site value system would provide an adequate revenue base. Dick Netzer notes that some calculations suggest that the present yield of property taxes on nonfarm property appreciably exceeds the total rental value of privately owned nonfarm land. Thus, he concludes that "even a 100 percent site value tax might not yield enough to fully replace the existing property tax [on real property]." Plunkett asserts that by eliminating improvements from taxation, the land value tax would remove 75 percent of the tax base and cause a tremendous increase in rates. The Rawson study of Burnaby, British Columbia, also suggests that a site value system would result in a substantial rate escalation.

. . . .

On balance, the questionable adequacy of land as a tax base seems to be the most serious obstacle to the implementation of site value taxation in this country. Neither adequacy nor inadequacy of yield has been definitely shown. Opponents of the site value scheme offer strong practical evidence to suggest that elimination of improvement taxation will destroy the tax base and escalate rates. Proponents contest these figures and suggest that the equity of a land value tax mitigates the impact of rate increases. In addition, they observe that for tax purposes land is presently undervalued, due to low assessment percentages and the failure to consider complex external variables.

. . . [The Note then discusses possible legal obstacles to site value taxation. Practically all states have consitutional provisions requiring property taxation to be uniform. Provisions in some of these states would bar a differential taxation system that exempted buildings. Problems would also arise under constitutional debt limitation provisions which in some cases fix local debt as a percentage of assessed property values. If site value taxation reduces assessed values in a community the amount of debt constitutionally allowable will also fall. —Eds.]

Comments: 1. Whether or not site value taxation will have the desired effect on investment in real estate depends on how the market will respond to a tax that shifts the tax burden from improvements to land. One way of looking at this problem is to consider the marginal net return that can be expected to accrue to improvements on vacant property. Since improvements are not taxed under the site value tax, investment in improvements should increase if a sufficient marginal net return can be expected on these improvements. While some studies have indicated that the land development market would not be sensitive to a shift in the property tax to land, other studies indicate the contrary. *See, e.g.,* Pollock & Shoup, The Effect of Shifting the Property Tax Base from Improvement Value to Land Value: An Empirical Estimate, 53 Land Econ. 67 (1977). Using data on the Waikiki resort area in Honolulu, the authors estimated that the long-run equilibrium investment in improvements would increase by a maximum of 25 percent. (Studies reaching contrary results are cited in this article.)

The holding costs of higher taxes on vacant land under the site value approach are also expected to encourage development on vacant land, but there are qualifications:

> Whether or not vacant land located within areas of high density development will be put into production also depends on demand conditions. Tax theory would claim that an increase in the cost of holding vacant land forces the owner to place the land into use. . . . While the total supply of land is considered to be fixed and, therefore, inelastic, one must also recognize that the urban real estate market is composed of many sub-markets which are structured according to land use zoning. Governmental policy decisions may adjust the supply within these submarkets; and, therefore, the disposition of an undeveloped parcel of urban real estate becomes a function of the traditional supply and demand conditions within a particular market. . . . Given the supply and demand conditions, the decision whether or not to develop the

property will also depend upon the return expected by the owner and the holding costs.

Smith, Land Value Versus Real Property Taxation, A Case Study Comparison, 46 Land Econ. 305, 311-12 (1970). The author's simulated study of the impact of a site value tax in the city of San Bernardino, California, did indicate that taxes would have increased on vacant land in suburban areas.

2. Assuming that the site value tax encourages the improvement of undeveloped land in outer metropolitan areas, and the redevelopment of underutilized land in urban areas, it is not clear that the impact of the tax on land development patterns will necessarily be favorable. One problem is that the switch to the site value tax may not necessarily make inner developed areas competitive in tax load with suburban areas.

> The relevant question is whether or not the switch to the site value tax would reduce the tax load in the central city to a level below that imposed in the suburbs where tax rates are allegedly lower. The issue is complicated by the fact that improvements erected in the suburbs are likely to spread over a larger land area than those in the central city, thus precluding any off-the-cuff comparison.

Legler, Alternative Forms of Property Taxation as a Stimulus to Urban Redevelopment: Some Critical Comments, 1971 Land Use Cont. Ann. 157, 161. Indeed, Smith, *supra* at 310, found that property taxes on low density single-family residential development in his study were reduced under the site value approach because of the high proportion of land relative to the dwelling unit.

Other problems arise with the site value tax because of its tendency to encourage high density development no matter what the nature of the present land use and no matter whether high density development is desirable. For example, a simulated study of the impact of a site value tax in two North Carolina cities indicated that tax increases would occur on low-income residential property. Chester, The Site Value Tax: Its Potential Effect on Urban and County Land Values in North Carolina, 2 Carolina Plan. 43, 46 (1976). The tax in this situation could not be passed on to low-income tenants of these dwellings, or absorbed by low-income homeowners, and the owners of these dwellings would not necessarily have the financial means to redevelop their properties. Abandonment may result. And where would low-income families go? To the fringe, where land values are less? To high-rise apartments built to capitalize on site value tax opportunities?

Development on vacant land in suburban areas would no doubt occur at greater densities under the site value tax. These densities might possibly lead to lower community public facility costs, but could create other problems by adding to congestion. Neither is there any guarantee that the site value tax in undeveloped areas would lead to greater densities in the right places. A site value tax could also make the holding costs of open space land unbearable. Legler, *supra* at 163, finds evidence of this in his study of Waikiki, where a partial shift by the state to site value taxation compelled hotel owners to convert street-level gardens and open spaces to commercial uses. Hawaii's partial site value tax has now been repealed. Haw. Rev. Stat. § 248-2 (1977). For a description of the tax see the Harvard Journal on Legislation Note, *supra* at 151-54.

3. For a variety of reasons, the impact of the site value tax in jurisdictions where it has been tried is inconclusive. Thus, in Pittsburgh, Pennsylvania, the impact of the site value tax was muted because only half of the tax was shifted to the land and because school district and county taxes were excluded. Harrison, Housing Rehabilitation and the Pittsburgh Graded Property Tax, 2 Duq. L. Rev. 213 (1964). In Australian cities where the site value tax is used the tax rates are low and there are numerous exemptions from the tax. Harvard Journal on Legislation Note, *supra* at 148-50. See also the studies summarized in Hagman, The Single Tax and Land-Use Planning: Henry George Updated, 12 U.C.L.A. L. Rev. 762, 784-87 (1965). For a collection of essays evaluating the site value tax see The Assessment of Land Value (D. Holland ed. 1970).

4. What does this discussion of the site value tax indicate about the relationship between this tax and land use planning and zoning? Some commentators have argued that the site value tax will be optimal only if used in conjunction with land use controls. Under this variant of the site value tax, the tax would be limited to areas in which the effects of the tax would be favorable. The zoning ordinance would also put a limit on permitted densities so that some of the worst excesses of site value taxation could be avoided. Hawaii's partial site value tax used this approach, and confined the tax to urban areas. There are problems with this approach, which may require land use zoning to be more precise than it is or should be.

Are there alternatives to the site value tax? Consider the land banking possibility, discussed *supra* p. 967. Like land banking, the site value tax is an attempt to bridge the gap between land use regulation and land development. Public agencies regulate land use, but private entrepreneurs build. As long as we have a pluralist society, this gap is likely to remain. Any attempt to bridge it is likely to be imperfect.

Table of Cases

Principal cases and the pages on which they
appear are in italics. Quoted and cited
cases and their page references are
in roman.

E

F

H

I

J

Index

A

B

C

D

E

F

Date Due

NOV 5 1984			
NOV 4 '85			
APR 12 '91			
APR 26 '91			
SEP 30 '93			
OCT 14 '93			
OCT 29 '93			
NOV 16 '94			